Anonymus

The Indian Mirror

January 9. 1876

Anonymus

The Indian Mirror
January 9. 1876

ISBN/EAN: 9783742822093

Manufactured in Europe, USA, Canada, Australia, Japa

Cover: Foto ©Thomas Meinert / pixelio.de

Manufactured and distributed by brebook publishing software
(www.brebook.com)

Anonymus

The Indian Mirror

The Indian Mirror.

SUNDAY EDITION.

VOL. XV] CALCUTTA, SUNDAY, JANUARY 9, 1876 { REGISTERED AT THE GENERAL POST OFFICE. } [NO. 7

CONTENTS.

NOTICE.

Letters and all other communications relating to the literary department of the Paper should be addressed to "The Editor."

All letters on the business of the Press should be addressed, and all remittance made payable to the Manager of this Paper. Particular attention is solicited to this notice.

Subscribers will be good enough to give prompt notice of any delay, or irregularity in delivery of the Paper.

Editorial Notes.

OWING to the annual holiday we take on New Year's Day, the last number of the Sunday *Mirror* was not issued. The announcement made to this effect in the daily edition of the paper, did not reach those who subscribe for the Sunday edition only.

WE have received a copy of the New Year's Brahmo Diary. It is neatly got up and contains a much greater variety of useful information than the Diary of the past year. There is also considerable improvement in the size and appearance. We recommend it to all those who wish to have a complete and handy Native diary.

THE Forty-sixth Anniversary of the Brahmo Somaj will take place on Monday, the 24th instant. The Utsab will take place the day before, Sunday, and Babu Keshub Chunder Sen's anniversary address on Saturday, the 22nd. Already friends are coming in for the festival from the mofussil.

AT an evening party at Government House, held on the 29th ultimo, the leader of the progressive Brahmos was among other gentlemen, kindly introduced to the Prince of Wales by the Viceroy, at the special request of His Royal Highness. The Prince received the Babu most cordially, referred to his visit to England, and conversed with him for some minutes with the utmost kindness and affability. His Royal Highness assured him that he had been greatly interested with his visit to this country.

WE find in the *Spectator* a number of passages given from the different writings of Professor Tyndal, expressive of his idea about the Deity. Evidently with Mr. Herbert Spencer, for whom he has such intense admiration, Tyndal thinks the Great Power whose existence he repeatedly admits, to be "inscrutable to the intellect of man. As little in our day, as in the days of Job can man by searching find this Power out, the Power whose garment is seen in the visible universe." To the intellect he is certainly "inscrutable," but is He so to faith and love?

A BOMBAY contemporary discovers a startling error in the following passage in the address presented to the Prince of Wales by the missionaries and Native Cristians of Tinnevelly, and rebukes their ignorance:—"Native Christianity has not yet unlearnt all the evil conversation received by tradition from a hundred generations, perhaps a thousand, of preceeding heathenism." Our contemporary thereupon remarks:—"Surely this must be slip of the pen. A thousand generations, even as short-lived as ours, would require more than 33,000 years. The heathenism of India is not much more than 3,000 years old."

WE think Dr. Mohendra Lall Sircar has every right to expect that the leaders of the new movement for the teaching of the Practical Sciences should pay to his advice the deference which he fully deserves, not only as a scientific man, but as one who has desired the dissemination of scientific knowledge long before any body else made a stir in that direction. If a large sum of money has been collected by the influence of the higher officials, that ought not to blind the leaders of the Indian League to the principle of co-operation without which there can be no real progress in any country, far less in our own.

THE reason why we approve so heartily of Professor Monier Williams' project of founding an Indian Institute at Oxford, is that we have long felt the want of good sound moral education for those of our young men who proceed to England for the prosecution of their studies. They return most of them clever and competent, but whether they gain or lose morally, we do not like to say. Our impression is that a great many do not gain. And the fact is sufficiently well-accounted for by the temptations to which they are exposed in London lodgings. If the Oxford University can furnish the moral control that it so much needed, it will have done a great work. Nor is that all. The society of learned men and students to be obtainable here will be of very great value, the advantages of which can be matched by nothing which the young men now have in London or elsewhere.

WITH the sincere pleasure one feels for the reward of real merit, we congratulate Sir Stuart Hogg on his recent acquirement of knighthood. He has fully deserved the honor that has been conferred on him, and his worst opponents must admit that in genuine talent and energy, Calcutta never possessed a chief who can for a moment be compared with him. He is wanting in tact, his trenchant high-handedness has often and most naturally provoked great irritation and hostility, and with those who have rigorously opposed him here, we have taken part. The annoyance however has been more than compensated for by the admirable conduct of the difficult arrangements that had to be made during the late festivities. And everything that has been entrusted, to Sir Stuart Hogg has been carried out with a fullness, neatness, energy, and effect beyond all praise. Sir Stuart Hogg we know, is destined for higher positions than he now occupies. May he fill them all with the credit which his talents amply promise.

WE ask the Impartial public whether the scene that took place at Belgachia after the departure of the royal party, did or did not confirm our views on such matters. The excesses of drinking, and the after effects, as pourtrayed by a contemporary, from whom we quoted the other day, are painful enough. And when in addition it is borne in mind that the dancing girls, who formed a principal item of amusement in the earlier part of the evening, might still have been present at the place (we shall be glad to be assured they were not), the blessings of Nautches, and their claims upon public encouragement will be at once understood. We must however absolve the Committee of the Native Entertainment at Belgachia from all responsibility in this matter. The refreshments were intended solely for the European guests present, and it was far from the Committee's intention and plans that any Hindu gentlemen should go and partake of the "forbidden food."

THE statement made by Professor Monier Williams and reported in our columns sometime back by a correspondent in Bombay, that Englishmen in India have "caught the contagion of caste from the Hindus," has called forth the following remarks in the *Bombay Guardian*:—"Is there no help for it, and is lamentation of the evil all that good men can do? This, indeed, would be a sad state of matters. But the spirit that dictates this conclusion is itself the spirit of caste. It is this devotion to custom, this idolising of existing things, that has kept the land so long enslaved in the bondage of the caste system. A good man will not bow down to this golden image. It is not necessary that the existing state of society in this country should be conserved in things that violate the laws of God and preclude true progress. We must abandon that definition of a good man which makes him to be one that never offends anybody. No man can possibly be a good man who is not willing to be stigmatized as bad. This is the great want of India—men that find their life in the favor of God, and follow the divine will unflinchingly, whithersoever it leads them."

MR TAWNEY, Professor of the Presidency College, writes an interesting and really learned article on the "*Bhagavat Gita* and Christianity" in the last number of the *Calcutta Review*. He writes to controvert the theory, of which Dr. Lorinzer is the most eminent representative, that this celebrated Sanskrit poem is borrowed from the New Testament which even in those early times made its way into India. Professor Tawney first points out a satisfactory number of parallels between the speculations of Greek and Hindu philosophers, and then says "there is absolutely no satisfactory evidence that any of the early Greek philosophers had any intercourse with the sages of India. It follows that in this case the theory of borrowing is not applicable ** If then these numerous resemblances between European and Indian civilization are not considered to imply the mutual interdependence of the two systems, ** we can not help coming to the conclusion that Dr. Lorinzer's theory cannot be yet considered to be established on any solid basis, and that his treatise, however interesting, forms but one more addition to the mass of plausible conjecture which Sanskrit scholars have in this century presented to the world."

OUR readers may have noticed the absence of street-beggars in Calcutta during the stay of His Royal Highness the Prince of Wales in our midst. Now that his august presence has been removed to a distance, the beggars have reappeared, and their cries screams, and importunities fill the air. It is said that the Police ordered them to disperse, and ply their trade out of the limits of the city. We believe the story. The Prince, or any of his Staff must not know that there is beggary in the metropolis of India. Now this concealment of the real state of things, which we must say we regret, has characterized most of the arrangements in welcome of the Prince. Why should not His Royal Highness know that India is poor, very poor! That though there is wealth enough among the wealthy classes, and a portion of that wealth may be wrung out by the pressure of circumstances, among which we of course include official influence, the masses and the middle classes in Bengal, at least, live in indigence. Let us give the heartiest welcome to ours future Emperor everywhere, but let us not meanly conceal our poverty from him. Who know that if the Prince had known the extent of pauperism in Calcutta, he would not have contributed a handsome amount of money in aid of the poor as he did in Bombay!

THE DESIRE OF HAPPINESS.

THE pursuit of pleasure defeats its own object. Those who make it a point to search for pleasure, never find it. The expense of time, and energy, and anxiety necessary for such a search becomes so great that desire is exhausted very often by the time the object is attained, or even if strong desire still remains, the pleasure reaped seldom answers expectation. Then there is the inevitable admixture of pain with every form of earthly pleasure when anxiously sought—pain both before and after—the pain of fear, the fear of loss and disappointment, the pain of satiety, the pain of the conscious worthlessness of the pleasure when enjoyed, and when too late. Philosophers therefore who think a great deal of worldly happiness, nay who think it to be the *summum bonum* of existence and deny any other object to human life, say that pleasure ought never to be the subject of pursuit, because like the rain-bow at the horizon, it eludes all attempts to reach it. The object of pursuit in life ought to be usefulness, the improvement and happiness of others, (these utilitarian philosophers say), and then pleasure will come of itself unsought, and will be the more enjoyable for coming in that way. As examples of this it is said that those who laboriously provide for good food and good clothing, ultimately lose all pleasure in the same, but are morbidly conscious of the least deficiency in the articles of their luxurious ease.

Let us ask ourselves how far these observations are applicable to the religious world. There are many who seek religion, because they seek joy. They would say perhaps that they do not seek the happiness of this world, but that of the next. There are not a few who seek happiness in this life, as well as in the next. They do not want, they say, the pleasures of the senses, they want the pleasures of the soul. But be it the pleasure of the senses, or of the soul, it is subject to the same rule. Those who live for pleasure never attain it. Pleasure comes as often from realties, as from imagination. When a man imagines he is joyful, wants to acquire happiness by the exercise of his fancy, he does get a sort of pleasure. Only as in the case of bodily pleasures, this imagined happiness of the soul does not last. And that happiness which does not last, is a disguised name of unhappiness. When it goes away it leaves a double pain behind it. Joy ought to be the effect, never the object of religious life. The happiness that comes by seeking is seldom the gift of God. It may be the reward of man, the reward of thoughtfulness, of inward exercise, or outward service. So long as the exercise remains, so long the joy remains. When action fails, the happiness goes with it, though the desire remains unsatisfied. Leave the therefore desire of happiness from the begining, serve God, and serve man for the sake of service, for the discharge of the vow of lifelong servitude, and peace and joy will attend you. God is joy. He whose attainment of joy means the attainment of God, is crowned with undying happiness. He who follows religion with the object of happiness is guilty of a modified and refined form of worldliness. True happiness flies from his grasp.

Devotional.

IN disease, and in the feebleness of my heart, I call upon thee, my God. When I enjoyed the priceless gift of health, I trifled with it. I did not make the right use of the powers of my body. Now that I am stretched on the bed of pain and feebleness, I remember my shortcomings, and filled with vain regret. Lord, if I ever recover my health and spirits again, teach me to consecrate them to thee, and thy work. If I rise never more to enjoy the physical gifts thou didst once bless me with, enable me to look up to thee with resignation and faith. But whether I shall be well again or not, give unto me in the midst of my sufferings and feebleness thy grace, the blessed consciousness of thy nearness, that even in pain and weakness I may find my repose in thee.

TEACH us O Lord, to purify, and exalt the domestic relations of our life. The affection that binds us to our own is sacred, it is but the recast of thy loving care for thy family. As thy living relation with us all is pure, ever-ennobling, ever-productive of goodness and happiness, so may our affection for each other be. We pray to thee that we may never lack in doing what is our share towards the lasting wisdom and peace of those who naturally related to us, love, and are loved with genuine tenderness. May we be able to make them, and they to make us holier and heavenlier day by day, make our family the seat of every virtue, and grace, where thou mayst dwell with us evermore.

WE beseech thee O God, feed, clothe, and take care of all those who have taken the vow of thy missionary service. Friends in this World they have but few, none to think of them, and keep their family from sufferings of body and mind. Even good men look down upon them, heed not their cries because they are poor missionaries. They have no claim upon any one but upon thee, O Lord, whose servants they are. Cast upon them thy pitying glance, Protect them, and their dear ones from suffering and sorrow, train up their uncared for children in virtue and in truth, give cheerfulness and good consolation to their dejected wives, that in all things they may all be worthy of that love which thou undoubtedly bearest for them.

Correspondence.

CHRISTIAN ESTIMATE OF THE BRAHMO LEADER.

To the Editor of the *Indian Mirror*.

SIR,—There seems to be a general nation prevalent among the Bengali Native Christians that Babu Keshub Chunder Sen, the leader of the Progressive Brahmos, is a proud man, fond of dress and show, and the opinions expressed of him at various times in the leading Christian periodicals lead me to think that some of the European ministers, too, entertain the same idea. This, I believe, is a mistake which should be corrected.

I am a Christian, and have observed this gentleman very carefully and critically, with the object of learning if he carries out in practice the humility and self-denial he advocates in theory. I have also visited him and have had a good opportunity of forming a tolerably correct estimate of his true character, and am sorry I have to say that of the many hundred Christian ministers I know I can think of a very few who comes up to him in real Christian spirit, while I can remember none who surpasses him in gentleness of disposition, in tenderness of feeling or in godly piety. I do not certainly agree with Keshub Babu in his understanding of what true religion is, but it does not follow that because one has different views from me I should consider him a hypocrite or offer him inimical remarks. But then this is an error most Christians fall into. I do not mean to condemn the Christians wholesale, but I may say it would do well if the many that look down upon such really good men like Keshub Babu would first see they are worthy followers of their all-praised master, and learn that charity which forms almost the basis of Christianity and which would teach them to observe every improvement for the better, not with malice and hatred, but with admiration and joy. It requires no recommendation of mine to confirm the high character which Keshub Babu has established for himself among truly great people, but I write this letter merely to remind our Christian friends that their conduct shows the absence of that charity without which our Lord says, all is nothing.

Yours truly,
CHRISTIAN CHARITY.

The Brahmo Somaj.

THE following report of the Chittagong Brahmo Somaj has been forwarded to us by a correspondent :—

Divine Service was conducted almost throughout the year by our Local minister Babu Rajeswar Gupta. Babu Peary Mohun Chowdry one of the Missionaries of the Brahmo Somaj of India did the work of one minister nearly for 15 or 16 Sundays, during his stay in Chittagong. Babus Kasi Chunder Gupta and Ram Kumar Bhuttacherji conducted the Service for three Sundays only. The subjects of sermons preached were as follows :—1. Private religious exercises. 2. *Shakti.* 3. *Joga.* (*i.e.* directly to see, to hear, and to touch God) 4. Communion with true devotees. 5. Spirit of true asceticism.

From the 25th July 1875 Divine Service was begun to be held in the evening instead of in the morning.

CONGREGATIONAL MEETING (*Friday*).

The object of this meeting which is held every Friday in the Mandir was clearly defined last year. It is to extend the spirit of Brahmoism in this district. Some students of the neighbouring schools attend this meeting.

SANGAT SHAVA (*Thursday*).

This institution was organized more than 4 years ago for mutual conversation on spiritual matters among the Brahmos. But as all the Brahmos were not found to attend its meetings, it was converted last year into *Sadhak Somaj* (*i. e.* a number of men, who are determined to carry out the resolutions made in their meetings in their lives.)

One of the rules of this Somaj is, that all the members should repair to some neighbouring hill for solitary communion with their Heavenly Father every Saturday, when practicable."

We extract the following remarks about the Brahmo Somaj from Mr. Routledge's *Indian Notes* published in *Macmillan's Magazine* :—"Education in India would be very imperfectly dealt with even in outline, without reference to the Brahmists, but it will only be possible now in this paper to glance at them. It is a year or so more than a century since Rammohun Roy, the great founder of Brahmoism, was born of a high and wealthy Brahminical family, in Burdwan. He was instructed in all the learning of his caste, but at an early age he doubted, and eventually after years of study, travel, and communion with men of different races and creeds, he began to teach, both to classes of his countrymen and through the press. I do not purpose to tell anything of the history of the two bodies into which the followers of Rammohun Roy are now divided. It may be useful, however, to say that the elder body, the Adi Somaj, is known for its wish to remain Hindu, while the younger body, the Progressive Somaj, does not affect to claim any part in Hinduism as a creed. Both Churches contain some pure and gentle spirit. Each has a literature with maxims and sentiments in which holiness of life is the central theme.

I may add that the elder body of the Brahmists is now scarcely at all divided from orthodox Hindus in anything but faith. There is no social antagonism between them; and, in this certainly lies as much hopefulness for India as in the impulse of the younger body, which is working very hopefully. I never met Mr. Sen where talk was possible, but a younger brother of his I met under very favorable circumstances, and I had some pleasant conversation with him. I thought I never had met any where a gentler spirit or one that was more likely in the future to help to infuse kind and generous sentiments into the minds of his countrymen."

Literary.

PROPOSAL FOR THE FOUNDING OF AN INDIAN INSTITUTE AT OXFORD.

IT is hoped that, if the present system of educating the Civil Service of India be maintained, Oxford will become an effective and attractive training-ground for this purpose.

Under any circumstances the oldest and most central University in England may well become a place where all workers in the field of Indian knowledge should receive aid and encouragement. In that case a building and appliances will certainly be needed that shall be wholly dedicated to the promotion of Indian studies and to the diffusion throughout England of correct information on every subject bearing on the welfare of the Queen's Indian Empire.

The principal aim of such an Institution would be to form a centre of union, intercourse, inquiry, and instruction for all engaged in Indian studies.

It would contain Lecture rooms suited to the use of Professors of the classical languages of India and of teachers of the Indian vernaculars, and of Indian law and history—to be hereafter attached to it, the teachers being paid either by the University, or by separate endowments like that of the Boden Professorship. It would also contain a Library and Museum, and might combine appliances for other Oriental studies, so as to furnish the selected candidates for the Indian Civil Service with the means of preparing themselves for examinations and for obtaining degrees in an Indian school, should such a school be hereafter established at Oxford.

Another great object of the Institution would be to encourage and facilitate the residence of young Indians at Oxford. Indeed, an increasing number of the Natives of India already frequent our University. It is thought, therefore, that a scheme which will tend especially to their advantage is sure to meet with support in India.

It is believed that a sum of about £20,000 would suffice for the erection of an Institute, and the endowment of a Curator, and application might be made to the University for a suitable site.

It may be assumed that when an Indian Institute with a Library and Museum is once established at Oxford, contributions of books, MSS. and objects of interest, illustrating the ethnology, archaeology, religious systems, domestic and social life of the Natives of India will rapidly come in from India itself, from old University men resident there, and from all interested in making Oxford a centre of Oriental studies.

Communications with offers of assistance may be addressed to the Boden Professor of Sanskrit, Oxford, or to Professor Monier Williams, care of Messrs. King, Hamilton & Co., Calcutta, or care of Messrs. King, King & Co., Bombay; or to any members of the Calcutta, Bombay and Madras Committees.

No pecuniary aid will be asked for until the project is more fully matured. Any sums of money that may voluntarily offered will be invested in the names of Lord Lawrence, Sir Edward Colebrooke and other trustees. It as proposed that a subscription of £1 per annum and upwards shall entitle to membership, and a donation of £25 to life-membership.

PATRON.

His Royal Highness the Prince of Wales, K.G.

VICE-PATRONS.

His Royal Highness Prince Leopold, K.G.
His Excellency Lord Northbrook, Viceroy of India.
His Hon. Sir Richard Temple, K.C.S.I., Lieutenant-Governor of Bengal.
The Right Hon. Lord Lawrence, G.C.B., G.C.S.I.
The Righ Hon. Sir Bartle Frere, Bart, G.C.S.I., K.C.B.
Hon. D. C. L. Oxon.
The Right Hon. Earl of Carnarvon, D.C.L., High Stewart of the University of Oxford, Secretary of State for the Colonies.
The Right Hon. Sir Stafford Northcote, Bart, M.P., Chancellor of the Exchequer.
The Right Hon. W. E. Gladstone, M.P.
The Right Hon. Sir William Henry Gregory, K.C.M.G., Governor of Ceylon.
His Grace the Archbishop of Canterbury.
His Grace the Archbishop of York.
Sir Edward Colebrooke, M.P.
The Hon. Sir John Strachey, K.C.S.I., Lieutenant-Governor, N. W. P.
The Hon. Sir Alexander Arbuthnot, K.C.S.I.
Sir Douglas Forsyth, K.C.S.I.
The Hon. E. C. Bayley.
The Hon. T. C. Hope.
The Hon. Ashley Eden.
His Highness the Maharajah of Jeypore.
His Highness the Maharajah of Travancore.
His Highness the Maharajah of Punnah.

MESSRS. TRUBNER & Co. have published a Narrative by Dr. Bellew of the Mission to Kashgar in 1873-74, under the title of "Kashmir and Kashgar." The author, according to the advertisement of the book, gives a vivid sketch of the Amir's household and character.

MESSRS. H. SOTHERAN and Co., of Piccadilly, London, have, it is stated, received an order to forward twenty more copies of Rousselet's "India and its Native Princes" to Calcutta, for presents to be given by the Prince of Wales to the *Princes* and Chiefs of India.

The Week

IT is said that Lord Northbrook approves of the choice of Lord Lytton as his successor.

IT is stated that Sir T. Madhava Rao intends shortly to open an Arts College at Baroda.

HIS HIGHNESS the Maharajah Holkar is bringing out a large Durbar Room made of iron from England, at a cost of rupees forty thousand for the reception of H. R. H. the Prince of Wales at Indore.

THE following minor Chiefs of Central India will be present at the Agra Durbar to be held by H. R. H. the Prince of Wales:—The Rajahs of Tehri, Duttiah, Sumpthur, Punnah, Chirkari, Bijawar, Ajaigurth, Nagode, Myhere, and Baronda, the Nawab of Baoni, the Raises of Sahawul and Sutaitha, the Maharajah of Urcha, and the Dewas Rajah.

URJUN PAL of Harowti has succeeded to the vacant *guddi* of Kerowli in Rajputana.

IN consequence of the Prince's visit to this country, having attracted so much attention to it, a grand diorama of India is to be started in London.

THE second Annual Rajputana Exhibition of Indigenous Arts and Sciences will be opened shortly and be assisted with a grant of Rs. 2,000 from Government.

"ENLIGHTENMENT" will be cheaper in Calcutta from the 1st March next. A reduction of one rupee in the price of gas per 1,000 cubic feet has been announced by the Oriental Gas Company.

WE have received the first number of the *Benares Journal*, a weekly English newspaper.

MR. EASTWICK, ex-M. P., is now at Calcutta.

LATEST NEWS.

SIR RICHARD MEADE was to have left Bangalore on Monday last for Hyderabad.

THE Share Bazar and the Cotton Market at Bombay were closed on Tuesday last out of respect for the memory of the late Rao of Cutch.

THE Hon'ble D. Arbuthnot, member of the Madras Board of Revenue, will probably retire from the service in March next, and will be succeeded by Mr. Wederburn, Collector of Coimbatore.

SURGEON MAJOR G. S. Sutherland, M. D., Sanitary Commissioner for Oudh, will officiate as Statistical Officer to the Sanitary Commissioner with the Government of India during the absence of Surgeon-Major J. L. Bryden.

MIR SHAHAMUT ALI KHAN BAHADUR, C. S. I., Superintendent of Ruttam, is brought on the classified list as an Additional Political Agent of the 2nd Class.

MR. D. M. BARBOUR has received charge of the office of Under-Secretary to the Government of India in the Financial Department from Mr. J. A. Bourdillon. The services of Mr. Bourdillon are replaced at the disposal of the Government of Bengal.

THE Hon'ble Ashly Eden will shortly proceed to England on furlough.

THE Prince of Wales, we hear, has received a large live-stock by way of presents from the Chiefs and Zemindars assembled at Bankipore.

HIS ROYAL HIGHNESS the Prince of Wales left Lucknow yesterday for Unao (Oudh.) where after breakfast he had pigsticking. He was to have returned to Lucknow in the evening. To-day H. R. H. attends Divine Service in the morning at Lucknow after which he visits some of the places of interest in and adjoining Lucknow.

THE following special telegram has been received by the *Englishman* from Allahabad:—

ALLAHABAD, JANUARY 7.

Probably Lord Northbrook will come to Allahabad to meet the Prince on his return and take leave of him.

Mr. Aitchison leaves for Europe by the Steamer of the 10th February on one year's leave. Doctor Thornton will join the Foreign Office and relieve him about the 28th instant.

The Maharajah of Patiala will entertain the Prince at a grand banquet at Rajpur Railway Station on his way to Lahore.

The Lieutenant-Governor of the North-Western Provinces returned from Benares this evening.

THE India Office being desirous of pushing forward the Indian marine survey, it is under consideration to add another vessel to the number already on this service. An additional supply of surveying officers will also probably be obtained from the half-pay lists of the Royal navy.

SIR GEORGE CAMPBELL, delivered an address on Dec. 10, to the Indian Association at Manchester on the subject of Indian finance. He regretted that Lord Northbrook, by the remission of taxation, had reversed the policy of his predecessor who managed to have a yearly surplus, which was devoted to carrying out important public works. This policy, in his opinion, was necessary in order to develop the resources of the country. He did not taken a sanguine view of the growth of Indian revenue, and, on the other hand retrenchment had been carried as far, or nearly as far, as possible by a succession of economical Administrations. He denounced the salt-tax, which, he thought, should be remitted; but if that and the Customs duties were removed it would be necessary, in order to attain certain objects, "some" taxation must be resorted to.

The Prince's Visit.

THE following address from the missionaries and Native pastors of Benares has been sent to His Royal Highness.

May it please your Royal Highness,

The missionaries, Native pastors, and Native Christians of the Church of England, London and Baptist Missions of Benares, have assembled together to give a hearty welcome to your Royal Highness on your visit to this city. To all of us it is a source of intense pleasure and satisfaction, that your Royal Highness has graciously condescended to meet us here. We earnestly pray that the blessing of God may ever rest upon your Royal Highness, and upon your Royal mother, our Beloved Sovereign.

Signed by the missionaries and Native pastors, Benares, January 5th, 1876.

THE Special Correspondent of the *Indian Daily News* telegraphs from Lucknow that at the grand *fete* to-night [7th January] by the Oudh Talukdars the Prince was presented with a magnificent Jewelled crown, Garland, worth 7000, *Utter* boxes and artical of gold and silver. The Fireworks and illumination splendid. To-morrow, the pigsticking party is strictly private, Sunday rest, Monday probably Cawnpore, Prince drove through Native city to-day, with Sir George Couper and suite. The Natives were quite enthusiastic.

THE Maharajah of Benares has presented the Prince with an address in Sanskrit, together with an English translation, on behalf of himself, the Rajahs, Nawabs, and Native gentlemen of the city and province of Benares. The address is as follows:—

I.

"Glorious is our great and gracious Queen, exalted by high virtues, whose commands Princes love to bear like crowns on their heads.

II.

Whilst that mighty Empress rules over the earth with justice, the people, in the enjoyment of perpetual happiness, scarcely know what pain is.

III.

Fostering all her subjects with wisdom, justice, and charity, under her benign rule the arts and sciences flourish with unprecedented vigor, and cast into the shade the fame of bygone monarchs.

IV. & V.

That ancient Sanskrit language, free from faults, and ennobled with many excellences, which loved of yore to dwell in our sacred city, and which paralysed by the evil times had almost died away; that language as if sprinkled every moment with the water of life (amrit), under the benign influence of Her Majesty's rule, has now revived, and charming the ear of the learned like the sweet-voiced Vina, has crossed even the ocean and extended over all the earth.

VI

There has indeed risen this day a new sun in Kasi; for the flower of our desires is blooming; all the land around, along with our hopes, is brightening; and like lotuses our hearts are expanded.

VII.

Happy indeed we deem our fortune, as we in Benares see your Royal Highness to-day—we whose hearts have long yearned in anxiety, never having seen Her Gracious Majesty, or her beloved son, your Royal Self.

VIII.

And now, O Royal Prince, that the reign of our most gracious Queen may long extend, and that your Royal Highness may continue to enjoy the affections of Her devoted subjects, is our most fervent prayer."

Calcutta.

THE Maharajah of Punnah left Calcutta last Friday evening. His Highness visited the Calcutta Mint before his departure from here.

SOME Bengali youths have established a Bachelors' Association in Calcutta with the view of preventing early marriage.

THE Bank of Bengal has raised its rates of interest and discount one per cent. all round.

THE Commissioner of Police, Calcutta, has been knighted by the Prince of Wales. But his Deputy, Mr. Lambert, has received from H. R. H., a letter of thanks and the present of a ring. Lady and Sir Stuart Hogg have also received lithographic portraits of their Royal Highnesses the Prince and Princess of Wales.

SIR WILLIAM MUIR having, it is rumoured, resigned the Financial Membership of the Governor-General's Council, either Sir Lewis Malet or Mr. E. F. Harrison is likely to succeed him.

MR. A. T. T. PETERSON has arrived at Calcutta, not for the purpose of practising at the Bar again but in connection with the affairs of the Bengal Coal Company. His stay here will be very short.

MR. J. PITT-KENNEDY, Standing Counsel for the Presidency of Fort William in Bengal, resumed charge of his duties on the 16th ulimo.

LIEUTENANT-COLONEL I. F. Tenant, the new Mint Master of Calcutta, has arrived here.

THE Maharajah of Putiala remains for a short time at Calcutta.

THE P. & O. Co.'s s. s. *Deccan*, Commander G. D. Gaby, arrived in Bombay Harbour on Tuesday last, morning, with the English Mails of the 17th December on board. The following is the list of passengers:—

From Southampton.—Mr. E. P. Brown, Mr. and Miss Duell, Miss Smyth, Lieut. Bayle, Mrs. Lucas, Mr. Buchanan, Mr. Unsworth, Mr. Dusden, Captain Carden, Mr. and Mrs. Grice and infant, Major and Mrs. Travers, Mr. and Mrs. Young, Mr. Duerdin, for Melbourne.

From Malta, for Melbourne.—Mr. and Mrs. Ettershank and infant, Mrs. and Miss Patterson.

From Venice.—Dr. Lewis, Mr. Douglas, Mr. Clarke, Mr. Schenck.

From Brindisi.—Mr. and Mrs. Hay, Mr. Runelberg, Mr. Mar otti, Major Hasted, Mr. H. Millet, Mr. R. Millet, Mr. and Mrs. Purcell, Mr. Davis, Rev. Mr. McGrew, Mr. Kobler, Mr. Bany, Mr. Courter, Mr. McCall, Dr. Treille.

From Suez.—Mr. T. Masson, Mr. M. Ode, Mr. Winterhalter.

From Aden.—Lieut. Howard and servant, Mr. R. Sorabji and daughter, Mr. S. Pestonji, 17 Native Deck Passengers.

THE Town Hall witnessed the organization of two important institutions yesterday afternoon. The Committee appointed to consider Professor Monier Williams' project of an Indian Institute at Oxford resolved upon co-operating with the authorities of the Oxford University for the establishment of an Institute for the special benefit of Indian students. Another meeting was subsequently held at which resolutions were passed and speeches made inaugurating a Branch of Miss Carpenter's National Indian Association at Bristol. Both these meetings, coming so soon after the Prince's visit, go far to confirm the hope already inspired by that visit that England and India will day after day be more closely knit in the bonds of mutual regard and intercourse.

Public Engagement.

THIS evening, 6 P. M. Evangelistic service in the Free Church Institution Hall, Nimtollah Street. Address by the Rev. John Hector, M. A. Bengali Hymns to Hindu Music.

Law

POLICE—8TH JANUARY, 1876

[*Before F. J. Marsden, Esq.*]

The Rev. E. C. Johnson, of Kenderdine's Lane, applied for a summons against his wet-nurse for having deserted his service, thus endangering the life of his infant. The Magistrate granted the application.

A LASKAR was charged by his Captain with the theft of a piece of rope valued at four annas. The defendant was, on conviction, sentenced to a whipping of seven stripes.

(*Before P. D. Dickens, Esq.*)

AN East Indian, named Edward D'Morrah, a compositor in the Bengal Secretariat Press, charged a Portuguese, named Maximo Ventura, with having assaulted him on the 17th ultimo at Blackburn's Lane.

Messrs. Fink and Cranenburgh appeared for the prosecution, and Babu Gopal Lal Seal for the defence.

From the evidence for the prosecution it appeared that the complainant and his family have, at the request of his niece's husband, who had that same evening returned from a voyage after an absence of two years, gone with him to point out her house to him, and that, shortly after all of them had entered, the defendant suddenly sprang upon the complainant, and assaulted him most severely. The cause of the assault was this. The family with whom the complainant's niece was then living did not wish that she should go back with her husband to the house of the complainant, whose family had brought her up from the infancy, but wished her to live with another man; and as the complainant pointed out her house to her husband, the defendant was employed to assault him.

BABU Gopal Lal Seal endeavoured to prove that the complainant had been assaulted by sombody else, but failed.

The Magistrate, after ascertaining that the defendant had not previously been convicted of a similar offence, fined him Rs. 8.

Selection.

PROFESSOR CLIFFORD ON RIGHT AND WRONG.

(*Spectator.*)

PROFESSOR CLIFFORD has contributed a remarkably lucid paper to the new number of the *Fortnightly Review* on "Right and Wrong," and the Scientific Ground of their Distinction, which states with admirable force and definiteness of outline, his view of the true conditions and the foundation of morality. That view appears to us as far removed as it is well possible to be from the true one; and were it not that Mr. Clifford evidently regards his paper as a vigorous blow struck at his opponents, those who regard the freedom of the will as a condition of moral action, and who believe in a moral law which promote, indeed, but is not adapted merely to promote, the temporal well-being of the society it governs, would be tempted to think that there could no better recipe against the errors of Mr. Clifford's creed than a careful study of Mr. Clifford's essay. False as it is that the perfect clearness of an idea is a guarantee of its truth, it certainly is very frequently either a guarantee of its truth or a guarantee of its falsehood, and perhaps the latter is the next best thing to the former, considering the great attraction of the human mind for the ambiguous,—an attraction which leads it to hesitate between truth and error.

Mr. Clifford could not be clearer than he is. In discussing responsibility, he makes it evident that he regards circumstances as being "responsible" for that which they determine, in just the sense in which he regards human choice as responsible for what it determines. He does not, indeed, call circumstances *morally* responsible for what they determine. He would not say that the paper on which he writes, is morally responsible for the whiteness of the effect on the eye of the writer, for he prudently limits moral responsibility to responsibility accompanied by consciousness. But he explicitly maintains that the word 'responsible' is rightly used of mere circumstances, though, it then expresses only part of the sense which belongs to it when applied to a conscious agent. "Suppose," he says, "I have a number of punches of various shapes, some square, some oblong, some oval, some round, and that I am going to punch a hole in a piece of paper. *Where* I may punch the hole may be fixed by any kind of circumstances, but the shape of the hole depends on the punch I take. May we say that the punch is responsible for the shape of the hole, but not for the position of it? It may be said that this is not the whole of the meaning of the word 'responsible', even in its lowest sense: that it ought never to be used except of a conscious agent. Still, this is part of its meaning; if we regard an event as determined by a variety of circumstances, a man's choice being among them, we say that he is responsible for just that choice which *is* left him by the other circumstances." And Professor Clifford goes on to make it perfectly evident that even when he adds the adjective "morally" and speaks of a man as morally responsible for such actions only as he does consciously, and his tendency to do or refrain from which might be altered by human praise or blame, he is still using the word 'responsible' in the same sense. He does not at all mean that the man, being what he was, and the circumstances being what they were, the action could have been different, but only that the action was due to the man's character and consciousness in just the same way as the shape of the hole was due to the shape of the punch. If you want to make the action the same or different on some future occasion, you must, by the proper and judicious use of praise or blame, and reward or punishment, give an additional constancy or a new modification to the character; just as if we want the shape of the hole to be the same or different, you must take care to secure uniformity or difference in the shape of the punch you use to make it. And it is clear that Mr. Clifford would dispense 'praise' and 'blame' from the non-natural motive which has always been adopted, and indeed has necessarily been adopted by his school of thought as the only legitimate one,—that is, *not* from any regard to the past, which, having been absolutely determinate, is not really the proper object of any thing but like or dislike,—totally different things from 'praise' and 'blame,'—but solely with relation to the future, which praise or blame may be expected to modify. For he says of moral actions, as understood by the free-willists, "I find myself unable to conceive any distinct sense in which responsibility" [Professor Clifford uses responsibility, of course, as already explained] "could apply in this case; nor do I see at all how it could be reasonable to use praise or blame. If the action does not depend on the character, what is the use of trying to alter the character?" The reply is, of course, that praise and blame are not primarily moral *medicines* used to produce a better condition of moral health, but involuntary moral judgments on past actions *which might have been otherwise*; and that praise and blame are as inapplicable, therefore, to actions considered as absolutely determinate, as they are to the shape of the punch, or the circumstances of space and time. How untrue to psychological fact that Mr. Clifford is in this test for the applicability of praise and blame, we may see by this, that praise and blame are often withheld by true moral insight where they would very powerfully affect the future formation of the character, and alter it in the right direction, solely on the ground that they are inapplicable to the past, and not therefore *deserved*. You do not praise a child who in your opinion had no struggle to do right, even though praise, if given, would be likely to make it do right again; and you withhold the praise for a very simple reason, that you do not believe it to have deserved praise. And nothing can show more clearly than this does, that praise and blame are not applicable at all to actions regarded as determinate before they were done, but only to actions for which, at the moment they were done, might have been substituted other worse or better actions. The whole use of praise and blame, in Mr. Mill's and Mr. Clifford's school of morality, is an unreal and indeed insincere use; these judgments being necessarily used in that school with a view to determining the drift of action in the future, whereas their natural use, the only use which the common usage of moral qualification of actions which might have been otherwise than they are.

But Professor Clifford not only puts a thoroughly superior meaning on moral responsibility as the condition of all right and wrong actions and the words 'praise' and 'blame,'—but he lays down in this paper the basis of a scientific foundation of right and wrong, entirely in keeping no doubt, with his conception of moral responsibility, and, therefore also presenting a curious parody on the inner meaning of right and wrong, as it is understood, we venture to say, by ninety-nine people in every hundred. Right and wrong actions mean, to Professor Clifford the sort of actions which tend to increase or diminish the true prosperity of the *community* in which an individual lives, as distinguished from his own individual prosperity. And the way in which this loyalty to the community has elaborated a conscience, has been by the ordinary path of 'natural selection',—no community having succeeded in enduring, without having also succeeded in inspiring its individual members with this deep inherited loyalty to the interests of that community. In all cases of conflicting interests between the individual and the community, we understand Professor Clifford to hold that the 'the conscience' simply represents the voice of the community speaking in the individual and protesting against his preference of his own welfare to the welfare of the whole community. Where, however, various lesser and greater circles of social life, like the family and nation put forward conflicting claims which fight against each other in the mind, Mr. Clifford holds that there can be no general rule of right and wrong. "We have to choose the less of two evils; but this is not right altogether in the same sense in which it is right to speak the truth. There is something wrong in the circumstances that we should have to choose an evil at all. The actual course to be pursued will vary with the progress of society; that evil which at first was greater will become less, and in a perfect society the conflict will be resolved into harmony. But meanwhile these cases of exception must be carefully kept distinct from the straightforward cases of right and wrong, and they always imply an obligation to mend the circumstances, if we can." No more candid confession, as it seems to us, of the utter inadequacy of the asserted distinction to cover the meaning of right and wrong, could be found than this sentence. In the first place, if only an imperfect obligation can be produced wherever the desire for the well-being of a smaller community of which the individual is a member, comes into collision with that for the well-being of a wider community, of which he is also a member, why is there not the same imperfectness of obligation where the desire for the well-being of the individual himself comes into collision with that for the well-being of the community? A capacity for promoting individual self-interest must have been "naturally selected," even prior to the development of the feeling for the interest of the community, and the earlier has at least as good a claim as the latter. The truth is that there is not, in Professor Clifford's scientific foundation of ethics, even the glimmering of the rule of obligation at all. He shows that a certain class of sympathies identified with family, or clan, or nation actually does grow up, and that unless it did, the family or the clan or the nation would not prosper. But he does not give us the ghost of a reason why the wider sympathy *ought* to be preferred to the narrower, unless it happens to be strong enough to assert its own imperious authority over the narrower; and he even admits that in case of a true collision of interests, no ethical rule can be laid down, and that all that can be done is to try to reduce as much as possible the conflict between the two, and that in the meantime, "that evil which at first was greater will become less"—which means, we suppose, that if it were in one stage of society better, on the whole, to stick to the family and sacrifice the clan, and in another to stick to the clan and sacrifice the family, we might yet hope for a time in which the interests of family [illegible] clan would become identical. Very probably; in the meantime, what is the conscience to be guided by? And why is the individual to ignore his own claims in the moral *melee*? If the family feeling rightly triumph over clannish feeling at one stage of social development, and the clannish feeling over the family feeling at another, and there is no clue to tell which is the triumph of the right, why not admit the same as to the conflicts between the individual interests and the interests of either family or clan? Clearly it is not the greater *extent* of the community which determines the obligation in Mr. Clifford's view, as he thinks the interests of the smaller community may sometimes be legitimately preferred. Why, then, may not the interests of the individual be legitimately preferred to that of the family in certain stages of family development? Mr. Clifford suggests to us no shadow even of an answer, for the very simple reason that he suggests no ground of moral obligation throughout his theory at all, but only states the sorts of conflicts of motives which demand a moral judgement,—a demand which he does not attempt to supply. Indeed, it is clearly false to say that it is the interest of the community, struggling against the interest of the individual which produces the respect for veracity, expect towards the particular and often very limited community directly implicated. If the true origin of the conscience is the identification of the individual with the community in which he is brought up, the feeling of the ancient civilized world that all outside it was barbarous, and ought to be sacrificed to the good of the inner pale of an intellectual nationality, was as right as the sacrifice of the individual to the same inner circle of national life was right. And if so, veracity towards the outer world, veracity towards the slave and barbarians, is not a duty at all, except so far as the formation of a habit of veracity might have been expedient to foster the impulse to be truthful with the higher-souled of a special race. In this way it is not veracity at all which is a duty, but only such veracity as helps on the development of a special race. If that be an account of the moral obligation of veracity it is equally an account of the moral obligation of feudalism, while feudalism favored the development of society; and veracity, only differs from feudalism in this,—that it is applicable in a growing degree to each successive stage of society, while feudalism was applicable only to one. The truth is, that Mr. Clifford does not give the least account of the origin of obligation, but only of the historical origin of a particular propensity to which sooner or later, obligation somehow attaches. A theory of moral obligation is not to be found in his essay. He expressly refrains from saying that it is always our duty to aid either the smaller social group against the larger, or the larger against the smaller; indeed he leaves the whole moral problem to be solved after his account of the origin of that problem has been admitted. Has he really once asked himself why a particular action or motive is right or wrong? Has he not been content to ask himself why a particular action or motive comes to be regarded with favor by one or more generations of thinking men?

REGISTERED NO. 8

THACKER SPINK AND CO.

CALCUTTA.

Illustrated and Fine Art Volumes for Presents, &c.

SPAIN. By the Baron Charles Davillier illustrated by Gustave Dore, translated by J. Thomson, F. R. G. S. 112 full-page illustrations, and 124 illustrations in the text. Impl. 4to. Rs. 40.

LEAVES from a SKETCH-BOOK: Pencilings of Travel at home and abroad. By Samuel Read, with descriptive and historical Notices by R. Acton, large 4to. Rs. 18-4.

THE WORKS of WILLIAM HOGARTH, reproduced from the Original Engravings on the Genius and Character of Hogarth. By Charles Lamb 2 vols, Rs. 60.

VIE MILITAIRE et RELIGIEUSE au MOYEN AGE. By Paul Lacroix, illustrate, Rs. 21-6.

THOSE HOLY FIELDS—PALESTINE, illustrated by Pen and Pencil, by the Rev. Samuel Manning. L.L.D., Rs. 5-6.

PICTURES of LIFE and CHARACTER By John Leech. 4 vols., in two half bound Rs. 40.

CARTOONS from Punch, by John Tenniel, 2nd series Rs. 23-8.

COURT BEAUTIES in the Reign of CHARLES 2nd; from the Originals in the Royal Gallery at Windsor, by Sir Peter Lely, and others, Rs. 13-8.

HISTORY of CARICATURE and of GROTESQUE in Art and Literature. By Thomas Wright, Esq., M.A., F.S.A., with illustrations, Rs. 15.

A JOURNEY ACROSS SOUTH AMERICA, from the Pacific Ocean to the Atlantic Ocean, By Paul Marcoy illustrated with 600 Engravings on Wood, drawn by Riou, and Eleven Maps printed in colors, from Drawings by the Author. In four Volumes folio, Rs. 54.

THE WINDOW, or the SONGS of the WRENS, words written for Music by Alfred Tennyson, the Music by Arthur Sullivan. Rs. 15.

THE FABLES of ÆSOP, with Illustrations by H. L. Stephens, Rs. 36-8.

LINDE DES RAJAHS, voyage dans l'Inde centrale et dans les Presidencies de Bombay et du Bengale, par Louis Rousselet, ouvrage contenant 317 gravures sur bois dessiens par nos plus celebres artistes, et six cartes, 4to Rs. 45-8.

DESCRIPTIVE ETHNOLOGY of BENGAL. By Colonel Edward Tinte Dalton, C. S. I. Illustrated by Lithograph Portraits copied from Photographs, 4to, half bound in morocco, Rs. 45.

PICTURES BY WILLIAM ETTY RA. With Descriptions and a Biographical Sketch of the Painter. By W. Cosmo Monkhouse, large 4to. Rs. 20.

LA FONTAIN'S FABLES. With Eighty-six full page and numerous smaller engravings, by Gustave Dore, Royal 4to, cloth gilt, Rs. 19-8.

ADVANTURES OF BARON MUNCHAUSEN. With Thirty-one full-page Engravings, by Gustave Dore, 4to, cloth, Rs. 6-12.

THE DORE GALLERY. Containing 250 of the finest Drawings of Gustave Dore selected from the "Dore Bible," "Milton's Paradise Lost," "Dante's Inferno," and "Purgatorio and Paradiso," &c. With Descriptive Letterpress and Memoir by Edmund Ollivier. Folio, cloth gilt, One Vol., complete, Rs. 67-8.

DANTE'S INFERNO. With Seventy-six full page Engravings, by Gustave Dore. Translated by Rev. H. F. Cary M.A., Crown Folio cloth, Rs. 34, elegantly bound in full morocco, Rs. 67-8.

DANTE'S PURGATORIO AND PARADISO. With Sixty full page Engravings, by Gustave Dore. Uniform with the Inferno and same price.

CASSELL'S ILLUSTRATD GOLDSMITH. With 108 Engravings. Imperial 8vo., cloth, Rs. 5.

CASSELL'S GULLIVER'S TRAVELS. With Eighty-eight Engravings by Morten. Imperial 8vo. 400 pp., cloth. Rs. 5.

TERMS CASH, WHICH SHOULD ACCOMPANY ORDERS.

A FASHIONABLE high wheeled C-spring Buggy by Dyces and Co., with silver plated mountings, quite new. Apply 12 Bentick Street. 9334.

!!! হুকা !!!

!!! HOOKAHS !!!

English made Hookahs of various choice designs, colours and sizes ranging in price from Rs. 2 to 5 each, 60 designs to choose from. Apply to

RADANAUTH CHOWDRY,
373, Jorasanko.

FOR SALE.

AT THE BRAHMO SOMAJ OF INDIA MISSION OFFICE.
No 13, Mirzapore Street.

		Rs.	As.	P.
Sacred Anthology	...	2	0	0
Last Days of Rajah Ram Mohun Roy	...	1	0	0
Essays, Theological and Ethical	...	1	0	0
Historical Sketch of the Brahmo Somaj	...	0	6	0
Jesus Christ, Europe and Asia	...	0	2	0
Future Church	...	0	2	0
Lecture at the Brahmo School	...	0	1	0
True Faith	...	0	2	0
Appeals to Young India	...	0	0	6
Brahmo Somaj Vindicated	...	0	2	0
Popular Tracts, No. 1 to 4	...	0	2	0
Destiny of Human Life	...	0	2	0
Reconstruction of Native Socie	...	0	1	0
Welcome Soiree in England	...	0	1	0
Lecture on Inspiration	.	0	4	0
Essential Principles of Brahma Dharma		0	1	0
Proceedings of the Marriage Law meeting at the Town Hall	...	0	2	6
Theistic Annual 1872	...	0	8	0
Ditto Ditto 1873	...	0	8	0
Ditto Ditto 1874	...	1	0	0
Ditto Ditto 1875	...	1	0	0
Lecture on Progress of Theism	...	0	2	0
Ditto Age of Enlightenment	...	0	3	0
Life of Educated Native	...	0	2	0
Lecture on Marriage Law	...	0	2	0
Ditto on the Jainas	...	0	2	0
Man the Son of God	...	0	1	0
Order of Service	...	0	1	0
Prayers for Different Occasions of Life		0	2	6
Divine Service in Hindee	...	0	1	0
Theistic Devotions	...	0	5	0
Behold the Light of Heaven in India		0	5	6
Epistles to the Theists in India		0	0	6
Lecture on Prayer		0	1	0
Ditto Alcohol	...	0	2	0
JUST RECEIVED FROM ENGLAND.				
Practical Sermons	Rs.	0	12	0
Memoir of Rev. Dr Carpenter	...	0	12	0
Morning and Evening Meditations	...	0	12	0
Channing's Perfect Life	...	1	0	0

JUST PUBLISHED

A COURSE OF ENGLISH READING,

CONSISTING OF

Selections from Modern English Authors for the use of

Candidates for the Entrance Examinations

OF THE INDIAN UNIVERSITIES,

Illustrated and annotated by

The Revd. K. S. MACDONALD, M.A.,
Free Church College.

To be had at the Bible and Tract Societies' House,
23, Chowringhee Road, Calcutta.
Part, I.—Price 12 Annas.

NOTICE.

THE ORIENTAL GAS COMPANY beg to announce that the price of Gas in Calcutta and Howrah will be reduced to Five Rupees per 1,000 feet from the 1st March next.

J. BLACKBURN,
Engineer and Manager.

January 1st, 1876.

M. Z. MARTIN & CO.,

THE CHINA AND JAPAN WAREHOUSE MERCHANTS AND COMMISSION AGENTS.

No. 4 Dalhousie Square, East.

SMITH STANISTREET & CO

Pharmaceutical Chemists & Druggists

BY APPOINTMENT

To His Excellency the Right Hon'ble

LORD NORTHBROOK, G.M.S.I.,

Governor-General of India,

&c., &c.

Syrup of Lactate of Iron. Prepared from the original recipe. Lactate of Iron, in various forms of preparation, has been in use in France, and generally through the Continent of Europe, for some years past, and is highly esteemed as one of the most valuable Chalybeate Tonic Remedies yet introduced. The Syrup being the most agreeable as well as convenient form of administration, is in most general use.

It is a most valuable remedy in the following diseases:—Chlorosis or Green Sickness, Leucorrhœa, Neuralgia, Enlargement of the Spleen, &c. In combination with quinine it has also been very successfully used in the cure of Fever, while to persons of delicate constitution, or enfeebled by disease, it is invaluable. In bottles, Rs. 2 each.

Syrup of the Phosphate of Iron, Rs. 2 per bottle.

Syrup of Phosphate of Iron and Strychnine, Rs. 2 per bottle.

Syrup of Phosphate of Iron and Quinine, Price Rs. 2-8 per bottle.

Syrup of Phosphate of Iron, Quinine and Strychnine, (Dr. Aitkin's Triple Tonic Syrup) Rs. 2-8 per bottle.

Smith, Stanistreet & Co.

Invite special attention to the following rates, the quality guaranteed as the best procurable:—

Pure Ærated Waters.

Made from Pure Water, obtained by the new process through the Patent Charcoal Filters.

				Rs.	As.
Ærated plain (Treble Ærated), per doz.			...	0	12
Soda Water	ditto	"	...	0	12
Gingerade	ditto	"	...	1	4
Lemonade	ditto	"	...	1	4
Tonic (Quinine)	ditto	"	...	1	4

The *Cash* must be sent with the order to obtain advantage of the above rates.

TO CLEAR OFF STOCK

J. DAVIS & Co.

Are selling their Wool Wrappers

HALF PRICE

No. 6 Government Place, Calcutta.

Ulcerations of all kinds.

There is no medicinal preparation which may be so thoroughly relied upon in the treatment of the above ailments as Holloways Ointment. Nothing can be more simple and safe than the manner in which it is applied, nothing more salutary than its action on the body, both locally and constitutionally. The Ointment rubbed round the part affected enters the pores as salt permeates meat. It quickly penetrates to the course of the evil and drive it from the system

Printed and Published by M. M. Bukhit, at the "Indian Mirror" Press, No 15, College Square, for the Proprietor.

The Indian Mirror.

SUNDAY EDITION.

VOL. XV] CALCUTTA, SUNDAY, JANUARY 16, 1876 {Registered at the General Post Office.} [No. 13

CONTENTS.

NOTICE.

Letters and all other communications relating to the literary department of the Paper should be addressed to "The Editor."

All letters on the business of the Press should be addressed, and all remittances made payable to the Manager of this Paper. Particular attention is solicited to this notice.

Subscribers will be good enough to give prompt notice of any delay, or irregularity in delivery of the Paper.

Editorial Notes.

The next number of the Theistic Annual s expected to be out or next Saturday. The contents are to be of the same kind as in other years, only the reports of missionary and other operations are to be more extensive this time. All Brahmos, and those who take interest in the affairs, of the Brahmos, should write in time to the Mission Office for copies.

The children of Brahmos who have left all connection with idolatry should be able to partake of the joy and excitement of the coming anniversary. Why should not a children's *fete* be organized in some Garden in connection with the anniversary where the little ones may enjoy themselves for a day to their heart's content?

Here is something which shows the "material" side of spiritualism, and must be provoking to its advocates. "At a spiritualistic *seance* in Liverpool the accredited medium—a young man—entered a cabinet, was tied up, and shortly afterwards was seen floating about as a beautiful female, covered with a gauze veil. A sceptic, however, seized hold of the apparition and called for a light; whereupon it was found that the materialised spirit face was a beautifully modelled gutta-percha mask, covered with a long cloth, which the medium waved about over his head, and "the spirit light" which surrounded the form was caused by phosphoric matches."

There was a pretty large meeting at the Town Hall on Saturday, the 8th instant, to hear Miss Carpenter's address on the National Indian Association. She pointed out the necessity of establishing a branch in Calcutta and a branch was accordingly founded with Sir Richard Temple as its President. The name proposed, "The Bengal National Indian Association," implies a geographical confusion and may not prove quite acceptable. As regards the work to be done, the Committee should submit a clear and definite programme before the public.

It is a pleasure to watch the progress of Hindu society. A decade back no Native could go to England without being cut off from kith and kin on his return, and subject to dire social penalties. But the case is different now. A young man of a wealthy and influential Hindu family in Calcutta, who has lately returned from England as a Barrister, has been readmitted into the society of his caste-fellows. Such toleration on the part of Hinduism is an encouraging proof of its growing elasticity and its tendency to adapt itself to the advanced spirit of the age, altough it may induce a little insincerity and duplicity in Native youths.

Dr. Mohendro Loll Sircar and his zealous co-adjutors must congratulate themselves on the successful accomplishment of their project. The meeting yesterday at the Senate House was a success, in spite of the controversy which was carried on between Dr. Sircar's friends and the leaders of the Indian League and the inevitable but pardonable display of "feelings" on either side. Those who believe that progress is the result of a conflict of ideas cannot regret the mild antagonism which characterized the proceedings of the meeting. It is desirable, however, that the two movements, should unite, and form a really powerful instrument for the promotion of science. The League's offer of co-operation was received with cheers, and Sir Richard Temple counselled amalgamation. Union is most desirable here, and we would hail it with pleasure.

Miss Carpenter has left Calcutta for the N. W. Provinces. She has delivered some very good lectures, replete with facts and experiences but with her usual clearness. She has established branches of the National Indian Association in Calcutta and Dacca, and she has visited many institutions, educational and otherwise, both in and outside of Calcutta. With Miss Carpenter's philanthropic objects, we have often said, we have real sympathy, though we cannot say that her efforts in India are at all suitable to the needs and circumstances of people here. Miss Carpenter is generally careful in the statements she makes, but now and then she says very odd things. For instance she said in a lecture which she delivered at Madras that it was the National Indian Association first established at Bristol that had taken up Babu Keshub Chunder Sen, and first offered him help when he was wandering about without any work in England. In the first place it is bad taste to such things, and in the second place the statement is unfounded. Is not Miss Carpenter aware that our friend went to Bristol after he had finished his great work in London, and after his English reputation had been made? It was Babu Keshub Chunder who opened the association by the request of Miss Carpenter, which gained influence by his name and connection. We have at hand all the facts of the case, and wonder how Miss Carpenter could have been led into such an incorrect statement.

We publish below the programme of our anniversary festival, for the information of our Brahmo readers :—

Thursday, 20 January.—English Service and sermon by Babu Protap Chunder Mozoomdar, in the Brahmo Mandir, at 8 P. M.

Friday, 21 January.—Conference of the Brahmo Somaj of India, in the Mandir, at 4-30 P. M.

Saturday, 22 January.—Morning Service at the minister's house, at 8 A. M. Anniversary Lecture by Babu Keshub Chunder Sen, at the Town Hall, at 4-30 P.M.

Sunday, 23 January.—Utsab from 7 A. M. to 9 P. M., in the Mandir.

Monday, 24 January.—Anniversary service in the morning and evening, in the Mandir, and Procession in the afternoon, to start from the minister's house at 5 P.M.

Tuesday, 25 January.—Meeting of Brahmo ladies for Divine service at 9 A. M., at the Bharat Asram.

Wednesday, 26 January.—Service, communion and collation in the Belgharia Villa.

OUR MUTUAL RELATIONS.

IT seems after all that it is more difficult to adjust our mutual relations with each other than to adjust our individual relations with God. Reverence and love, gratitude and devotion flow naturally and spontaneously to the Merciful Father, and know no obstruction save such as our own perverseness may occasion. Nothing is, nothing can be unfavorable on the Divine side to the growth and development of these sentiments. The Lord is "true, good and beautiful." To look at Him is to love Him. The Lovable is easily loved. The Adorable Fountain of Holiness is easily adored. There can be nothing in One so good and pure that can hinder our attachment or homage. If we cannot worship and serve Him as we should it is because of imperfections and iniquities in our own hearts which blind our sight and cripple our faculties and energies. Let us only set ourselves right, and our relations to the Supreme Being would be at once adjusted. All the disorder lies on one side. It is we that have erred. We have gone astray from the line of our natural relation to Father and Master He is true to that relation; we have proved false. The relation would be righted and adjusted if only our position were rectified. But in dealing with men we encounter two-fold difficulties and reverses. Those which result from our own antagonism, and those which are caused by the unwillingness and antagonism of others and the temptations to which they expose us. It is this double difficulty that has always obstructed the adjustment of our social relations and prevented the realization of true brotherhood on earth. In spite of isolated believers and devotees here and there the kingdom of heaven is not forthcoming. There are hundreds who believe in God and even love him, but they cannot lovingly unite. Each may enjoy individual and solitary communion with the Living Father, but they do not enjoy mutual communion as children of the same God. And why? Because of the two-fold difficulty we have mentioned above. If we fail to establish brotherly relations with others it is because we ourselves are antagonistic to such union, owing to our jealousy, anger, pride, selfishness, apathy, and peculiar tastes and habits, and secondly because these same causes acting in others conspire to prevent the desired union. Friendship is not possible if only one party makes advances. Both parties must regulate their individual and mutual relations before they can unite. How often does it happen that in spite of our anxiety to serve and please others we meet with repulses, because the hostile passions come in the way. How often too is it the case that while others are kind and forbearing we mar the prospects of friendly alliance by our own antagonistic temper or tastes. Love may go forth from a willing heart, but it is repelled by the stumbling block in the way. The gushing stream of affection beats on a hard rock and is thrown back. To bear and forbear is a stupendous difficulty, so says the world's experience. We are weak and unforgiving, and then the brother we wish to love is angry and provoking, selfish and cruel, and plants a thousand crosses in our path. To the weaknesses of the lover add the weakness of the loved, and we despair of brotherhood. Yet we must not shrink back in despair. We, who are God's servants, have no right to look for any earthly return for our services. Let us go on loving and serving notwithstanding all obstacles and hinderances. We love God knowing Him to be holy. We must love man knowing he may prove our greatest enemy.

MORAL TEACHING IN SCHOOLS.

THE subject of moral teaching seems to have awakened considerable attention in England. An interesting paper on the subject was read by Miss Manning, whose name is well known to all Hindu gentlemen who have been to England, at the Social Science Congress, Brighton, in last October. Moral training in schools, we have always held, is of infinitely greater importance in this country than in Europe. There the custom of imparting religious instructions in public seminaries answers that purpose very well. Every religion includes some morality, and Christianity teaches moral lessons perhaps the highest of all. We are aware that certain forms of the Christian religion pervert the simple moral teachings of the founder, but still even that perversion is better than the utter absence of all moral instruction that characterizes our Government schools here. The great dejection on the part of our educational authorities is that the difference of opinion on moral subjects among different classes of the community is so great that no positive principles could be taught without hurting the religious prejudices of some. Strange to say this is exactly the difficulty which the advocates of moral training have to meet in England also. The great aim of moral lessons, according to Miss Manning, ought to be to acquaint young people with the existence of a moral world, which is as true as the physical world. The relations of the moral world ought to be clearly described, and kept within their mental sight. Every child ought to be told what his relations with his parents are, or with his brothers and sisters, or with the lower animals by whom he is surrounded; how there are certain duties which these relationships imply, duties that must be discharged. There can not be much difference of opinion here, we submit, between different classes, and sects of our population. We agree in the main as to what our duties are in these particular relations of life, which if explained, and cultivated early would surely lay a solid substratum of character. Then says Miss Manning, "we ought to cultivate children's observing powers as to the invisible claims and possessions of others." This refers, we believe to the beauty of character, intellectual acquirements, social distinctions, age, wisdom, and circumstance. These are "the walls and fences which exist around them not less actual than those formed of bricks and stakes." Again we are told children should be impressed with "the supremacy of conscience," to whose dictates in early life, (and these dictates are heard in boyhood as much as in old age,) they should yield immediate and cheerful obediance. The elements of a noble character are to be traced in clear and prominent colours, and their opposites marked out with unmistakable precision. These virtues and vices instead of being put in a vague and abstract form, should be illustrated by such examples from history and from every day life as may make the most lasting impression on the child's mind and imagination. Different kinds of temper, responsibility, and work ought to be explained to them, with practical illustrations from their own lives, as those of others situated like themselves. The simplest lessons on manners and goodbreeding should be imparted, and enforced in their conduct towards each other. Questions of right conduct under difficulty and temptation, such as they are likely to meet, should be placed before them to answer. And their powers of moral criticism should be cultivated by laying before them instances of actions in which the mixture of good and evil, may exercise their minds as well as their hearts. Difficulties in carrying out this plan will inevitably arise, but, says Miss Manning, "we should no more on this account give up dealing with the many parts of the subject that are clear and defined, than we would move away out of a highly convenient house because it contained one or two imperfectly lighted corners. Mr. Gladstone's words on this matter are quoted: 'I submit,' he says, 'that duty is a power which rises with us in the morning, and goes to rest with us in the night. It is co-extensive with every action of our intelligence. It is a shadow that cleaves to us go where we will, and which only leaves us when we leave the light of life.

Devotional.

OUR anniversary festival draws near, Lord. Do thou prepare our hearts, and so increase our faith, earnestness and devotion that the season may be profitable unto us. How many such devotional festivals have we enjoyed by thy grace! But their fruits have not proved lasting. The festival that abides in the heart give thou unto us, that we may rejoice not for a day or week only, but everlastingly

THERE is nothing so precious, O God, as a pure heart, and it is this which I lack. I have sought it for years, and prayed for it, but I have not found it yet. Wilt thou not by the miraculous interposition of thy redeeming grace crush my sins completely, and give me the treasure of a clean heart, without which religion is a mockery, and my daily prayers the supplications of a hypocrite? Do give me that, O merciful Father, and whether I am rich or poor I shall be happy.

IN endeavouring to realize great objects and high principles I have failed in little things. Perhaps I was ambitious, O God, and my ambition has ruined me. I went about in quest of the kingdom of heaven, taught others how to live as a holy family, and always talked eloquently of regeneration, heavenly life and such things. But my pride, O Lord, thou hast confounded. For I feel that even the smaller virtues, such as veracity, honesty, kindness to the poor, are far from me. Teach me not to neglect these simple duties and keep me, Kind God, from the baser forms of iniquity.

ALMIGHTY God, my forefathers believed in the unreality of the material universe, and took care not to fasten their affections on earthly things. Though I do not regard what I see around me as altogether unreal teach me, Lord, to look upon the fascinating objects of the senses as hollow and transitory, and grant that I may never set my heart upon them, but upon the realities of the spirit-world. May I love thee, Spirit Eternal, above all things, and turn away from the baubles of the world.

The Bahmo Somaj.

INSTEAD of sermons we have now in the Brahma Mandir short discourses expounding the meaning and spirit of scriptural texts from the Srimathbhagabat and other Hindu books. Whether this change will prove acceptable and advantageous to the congregation remains to be seen. The majority will perhaps like it.

THE plan of dividing our annual procession into groups was a success last year, and will, we hope, be adopted this year. The new song may be taken up by the foremost group only, while the others may select some of the more popular tunes from our hymn book.

MORNING service has been held every day during the past week, and will continue to be held till the anniversary festival comes on, at the house of the minister.

THE vow which some of our Brahmo friends took some months ago to cook their own meals is no longer observed. The practice was brought to an end on Thursday last. A few, however, we understand, still hold on.

WE have often been asked who is responsible, for what appears in the daily and Sunday *Mirror*. The editors are responsible, and none else. Being honorary workers they have absolute authority in the conduct of the paper, and are not expected to give up their valued privilege of independence of opinion.

Provincial

MONGHYR.

[FROM OUR OWN CORRESPONDENT.]

The 23rd December 1875.

The ninth anniversary of the Behar Brahmo Somaj at Monghyr was celebrated on Sunday last the 19th instant with great *eclat*. The members seemed full of joy and enthusiasm upon entering into the *Mandir*, which was neatly and *tastefully* decorated on all sides with leaves flowers and fruits of various descriptions and colors. No sooner were the word *Satyam Gnyanamanantam* uttered from the pulpit than the whole congregation was wrapt in devotion, as, if, by a certain mysterious process, a new light was poured into them, to enliven their hearts and souls, which must have vividly perceived the presence of God that encompassed them.

Really my heart elates when I picture to myself the scene then presented, which was in truth one of devotion and enthusiasm, and there was perhaps not one among the congregation who did not feel himself happy at the sight, and the impressions wrought on their minds in consequence cannot be too soon obliterated.

The sermon, preached by the Minister Babo Dino Nath Mozoomdar after the first part of the proceedings was over, was a very eloquent and pathetic one. I never heard Babu Dino Nath speak with so much enthusiasm and vehemence as he did on this occasion, and every word that he uttered served to wring a response from the hearts of the audience, many of whose eyes were seen teeming with water, occasionally running down through the cheeks of their loving faces. With a short prayer by the minister and a few chosen hymns, which were chanted in chorus, terminated the proceeding of the morning service.

At 1 in the after-noon distribution of cloth, rice and pice to the poor and helpless (of whom about five hundred were assembled) took place, and the care and attention with which this charity was administered to them indicated a feeling which was I presume inherent in some and quite worthy of the Brahmos and others, who took part in the distribution, and could not but be highly admired. Some of the beggars presented themselves in complete nudity to the public gaze and they were really objects of pity and commiseration.

A little before 3 o'clock the Secretary read his annual report, shewing the transaction of the past twelve months, but there was nothing in it that could interest the public, except the eulogy offered to Mrs. Dear for her munificent donation of Rs 50 in aid of the building fund of the Somaj, which is yet incomplete without the surrounding walls, and the thanks to the Brahmo missionaries who visited the Somaj from time to time.

An hour and a half, from 3 to 4½ P. M., was set apart for Hindi Service, which was commenced precisely at the time stated by Baboo Nobacoomar Roy, whose address to the Beharies (about 30 of whom were present) was a very appropriate one inasmuch as he deplored their present condition with a sorrow, the tidings which touched the cord of the hearts of every one present, and the Beharies by themselves seemed to have heard him with the utmost alacrity.

The evening service, which also was conducted by Babu Dino Nath Mozumdar, commenced precisely at 5½ P. M. and within the course of a few minutes, after the minister ascended the pulpit, the *Mandir*, which was brilliantly illuminated, was filled and the audience seemed to have been highly delighted with what transpired at this time.

Among the audience I noticed two Brahmos from Lucknow, one from Gya, three from Bhaugulpoor and five from Jamalpoor, who joined their Monghyr brethern in the participation of the blessings that were showered upon them by their heavenly Father. Thus ended the commemoration ceremony of the most auspicious day on which the Behar Brahmo Somaj was established.

May the God of mercy grant the congregation peace and everlasting happiness and crown the endeavors of those Brahmos, who have devoted their lives and souls to the most sacred duty of propagating religion and disseminating its truths among men of all denominations, creeds and colors.

Correspondence.

DR. SIRCAR'S SCIENCE ASSOCIATION.

To the Editor of the *Indian Mirror*.

SIR,—An humble devotee of Science, I have for the last six years watched with deep anxiety and attention the progress of the movement inaugurated by Dr. Sircar to found a National association for the promotion of Science. No one can be a sincerer well-wisher of Dr. Sircar's patriotic schemes than I am and yet no one has more devoutly wished than your humble servant that some one had taken the trouble to acquaint Dr. Sircar with the shortcomings of his plan. It is now six years since the scheme has been in agitation, and is there not one man in Calcutta to point out that in the shape in which it has been presented, it is as vague and unintelligible as anything could be? You are the only one, Sir, who has said so, and you may rest assured that you carried the feelings and sentiments of all sensible men with you. There are times for all things—a time for the expression of public sympathy and a time when it ought to be seen whether the particular shape upon which the Sympathy is about to be expressed, is the proper and correct one. Dr. Sircar has obtained enough of public sympathy. This is the time for us to criticise and analyse what he has to give us. And strange to say that during the whole of this period, he has given us nothing in the shape of plan or idea. He has delivered lectures, collected subscriptions, persuaded people; but he has never except very recently told us what he wants to do. The public ought to have challenged Dr. Sircar long ago to come forward and explain to us his idea. The friction of opinions that would undoubtedly have taken place, would by this time have generated sufficient enthusiasm and heat to mould a better plan. As it is, I am the first to do this disagreeable duty, and I beg to tell him that the scheme which he has submitted to the public in the pamphlet which he has recently published is absurd and extremely unsatisfactory. I hope to be pardoned for this plain expression of opinion; but I shall explain myself. Dr. Sircar has collected Rs. 80,000 as subscriptions. Of this sum he wants to devote Rs. 50,000 to the erection of a building, and Rs. 30,000 towards the opening of three sections namely for Physics, Chemistry and Physiology. "For each of these sections" (I quote his own words; *vide* Page 61 of his pamphlet) he "would have a head worker selected from among the graduates of our colleges, of the Calcutta Medical College in particular, who should take charge of the section, devote himself entirely to the prosecution of the experimental study of the science assigned to it, by the aid of books and instruments placed at his disposal, and under the guidance of men who have made the subject their speciality. * * If we are happy in the selection of our workers, it is my firm belief they will succeed, in the course of a year, so to master their respective subjects that they will be able to deliver systematic lectures in them. * * When our workers become competent to teach in their respective subjects, which, I have assumed, is possible within a year, then we shall be able to institute two series of lectures on each subject, one general for the general public, and the other special for the instruction of a few who would like to form themselves into a class to learn the subjects. In this way we shall have in each section under the head-workers, a few Sub-workers as it were, who, by virtue of the training they will receive, will soon become workers in science themselves. * * In this way a taste for science will soon be disseminated among the several community, and science will then count her votaries by thousands and hundreds of thousand, instead of scarcely, as now by units."

I appeal to Dr. Sircar himself to say, whether the experiment, as above explained, is worth the cost. In the first place, I object to the name. The institution is not an "association," as it is frequently called, but a school. Nor ought there to be any association when there are no scientific men in Bengal, if it is a school, who are to be its students? Dr. Sircar says three graduates of our colleges, at first. So far good. But, query—will they be able to exhaust science within the incredibly short space of twelve months, and, secondly, if they are, will the community of students have any respect for them? I was myself a student once, and I well remember the feeling which was aroused in my mind whenever I saw our Professor (a European) fail in an experiment or stumble over a difficulty that feeling was one of utter contempt for his pretensions, or attainment. Conceive then the plight of a poor Bengali graduate who expected to satisfy the disagreable curiosity of inquisitive students after a year's study of the most difficult sciences. I for one will refuse to bow my heaud before such a quack, as he unmistakably promises to be, in case Dr. Sircar's idea is carried out to the letter. Dr. Sircar may rest assured that the gentlemen who will join his so-called association will be mostly students, and students will most certainly refuse to study under people who are only advanced by few years above them in knowledge. Have they not their own colleges where they may prosecute their studies? Why not apply the money to the improvement of those colleges, so that there may he additional facilities to their prosecuting the study of science? Dr. Sircar has to answer this question before the public. It is scarcely credible that the numerous gentlemen who have subscribed to his project will consent to their money being spent upon the creation of three quacks in the first year. It is to be remembered that this money will not suffice. Rs. 500 more will be required every month to keep the Association alive. Is all this money to be wasted upon absurd idea like this? Why not make over the money the Presidency College or the Medical College where special laboratories may be opened for students where they will conduct experiments themselves? In the Presidency College such a laboratory is already in existence, and it would be better if it were improved. Such a scheme would be intelligible and practicable. But to speak of a science Association where there are no scientific men, or of a school where there are no Professors is as absurd as to speak of sunbeams in cucumbers. We shall have a veritable Laputa in the projected Association; but the public are in want of a more prosaic place, and this the learned doctor fails to give us.

I have written the above with the best of intentions and hope it will be received and answered equally cordially.

Your's obediently,
ALPHA.

Scientific

A PHYSICIAN of Vienna named Kenegg, has proved that by making a small puncture in the skin and injecting "fatty liquid, or a solution of sugar, milk and yolk of egg, with a syringe, people may be comfortably "fed."

PROFESSOR TYNDALL, who has so long been trying to invent a noise horrible enough to warn mariners off dangerous rocks, has at last found what he wanted. With the aid of Mr. Douglas, of Trinity House, he has invented a trumpet, whose blast is strong enough to carry a man's head away if he got too near its mouth, and whose sound is warranted to be heard through fog and against wind at the distance of six miles over the sea. The trumpet contains within it a revolving cylinder, perforated with slits, and intended to make 24,000 revolutions per minute. These slits in the cylinder divide the sound into pulsations, thus adding to its power. It is intended that a high note shall be blown by ships and a low note from dangerous rocks in time of fog.

Literary.

IN examining the papers of the late George Grote, his widow has discovered a remarkable essay exhibiting the historian's opinions of Aristotle as a moral teacher. This precious paper, so interesting to the philosophical world, is printed among a group of posthumous papers, which will be published in a few days.

THE *Athenæum* says that ex-Colonel Valentine Baker, who was sent to the Perso-Turkoman frontier in the spring of 1873, and of whose map we made mention some time ago, has a volume in the press, under the title of 'Coming Events' in the East: Travels on the Perso-Turkoman Frontier.' Its publishers are Messrs. Chatto and Windus.

THE 4th December last was the eightieth birthday of Mr. Thomas Carlyle. May we venture to send our congratulations from this distance!

A BLACK marble slab in memory of Bishop Thirlwall has just been laid down in Westminister Abbey. The inscription is as follows:—"Connop Thirlwall, Scholar Historian, Theologian, for thirty-four years Bishop of St. David's. Born February 11 1797. Died July 27, 1875. 'Cor sapeins et intelligens ad discernendum judicium.' 'Gwyn ei fyd.'" The Latin text is from 1 Kings iii 11, 12—"A wise and understanding heart to discern judgment." It is enclosed in a fillet of brass. The three words in Welsh, engraved on a riband scroll of brass, are literally, "White is his world," meaning "Blessed is his state."

HER MAJESTY has conferred the Companionship of the Civil Order of the Bath upon Dr. W. B. Carpenter, F. R. S., Registrar of the University of London.

THE *Contemporary Review* for December publishes a rhymed Latin version, by the Right Hon. W. E. Gladstone, of the hymnus responsorius. The translation is made from the hymn by Dr. John Mason Neale (No. 254, "Hymns, Ancient and Modern," Revised and Enlarged), taken from the Greek of St Stephen the Sabaite.

WE deeply regret to announce the death of Mr. J. W. O'Sullivan, who was for a long time connected with the Indian Press. The deceased was for many years the sole editor of the *Phœnix*, a Calcutta daily journal, which was in existence some years back and which he conducted with great vigor and ability. He also edited for sometime the *Mofussilite* and the *Indian Statesman*. He was besides a large contributor to several Indian journals. His writings were generally characterised by the good humour which pervaded them, and by a natural, flowing style. He was a most ready writer, and a man of broad and liberal views. As an Irishman he was always felt of sparkling wit and we always left the greatest pleasure in his company. He originally belonged to the Indian Army, and acted for sometime as a Professor of Literature, we believe, in the late Hindu Metropolitan College. His remains were interred the day before yesterday in the Military Burial Ground, Bhowanipore.

*** This should have appeared in yesterday's *Mirror*, but, for some mistake on the part of the Printer, was not inserted.

MISS GORDON CUMMING, the lion hunter, is a member of a venturesome family. Her sister, Miss Constance Gordon Cumming, has written under the little of "From the Hebrides to the Himalayas,' a record of her wanderings, with many illustrations from her own drawings.

AT the meeting of the Orientalists, to be held at St. Petersburgh in September next, Oriental manuscripts, coins, arms, implements and other objects, illustrative of the history and industry of the East will be exhibited. The meeting is to be under the direction of an Imperial Commission, presided over by Professor Gregorieff, the well-known Geographer of Central Asia.

MESSRS. Cones' Directory has hitherto been the cheapest Directory in Calcutta. But it does not seem to have made its appearance this year. Messrs. Wyman & Co., however, have issued No. I of a new cheap Directory, called "The A.B.C Directory for Calcutta: containing also an Alphabetical List of the Civil Service, and much General Information useful to Mofussil Residents." The next number which will contain an alphabetical list of the Army, will be published on or about the 15th of April next. The third and last number which will complete the series, will be issued in July next. The Directory bears a rather curious name, but we believe A. B. C not only represent that the arrangement of the Directory is upon the alphabetical system, but also indicate the three numbers in which the Directory is to be issued. Directories, as a rule, are and can hardly be perfect. A great deal, however, of the accuracy of the work depends upon the efforts made by the publishers to obtain correct information. Messrs. Wyman & Co. seem not to be wanting in these efforts, and we daresay, when the series is completed, their Directory will be as useful a publication as could be desired for its price. So far as the present number goes, much pains seem to have been taken to make the Directory as accurate as possible, and, above all,—what is most wanted in a work of the kind,—to serve the purposes of a manual of easy reference. We believe Messrs. Wyman & Co. have at least been successful in attaining this last object.

THE *Fortnightly Review* of this month contains an article on the "Native Journals of India."

Gleanings.

WHY LIVE

Why live, when life is sad,
Death only sweet?
Why fight, when closest fight
Ends in defeat?
Why pray, when purest prayer
Dark thoughts assail?
Why strive, and strive again,
Only to fail?
Why hope, when life has proved
Our best hopes vain?
Why love, when love is fraught
With so much pain?
Why not cool heart and brain
In the deep wave?

Why not lie down and rest,
  In the still grave!
Live: there are many round
  Needing thy care.
Pray: there is One at hand
  Helping thy prayer.
Fight: for the love of God,
  Not for renown.
Strive: but in His great strength
  Not in thine own.
Hope: there is heaven's joy
  Laid up for thee.
Love: for true love outlives
  Its agony.
Fight, pray, and wrestle on,
  Loving God best;
Then, when thy work is done,
  Lie down and rest.

—*The quiver.*

The Week

MISS CARPENTER left Calcutta for the N. W. Provinces on Friday last.

AN English daily paper has been started at Lucknow, called the *Oudh Daily Reporter*.

HIS HIGHNESS the Maharajah of Putiala has subscribed two thousand and five hundred rupees to the Albert Hall Fund.

THE Punjab Native community have raised rupees thirty-thousand to give entertainment to the Prince of Wales at Lahore.

MR. GRIFFITHS of Bombay, an artist, has been commissioned by His Royal Highness the Prince of Wales to execute a large number of water-color sketches of Indian scenes.

IT is stated that the house which is being prepared by the Maharajah of Cashmere, at Jammu for the Prince of Wales has been considerably injured by an earthquake.

THE Native Chiefs who have arrived at Delhi to witness the manœuvres at the Camp of Exercise are Maharajahs of Gwalior, Bhurtpore and Ulwar, the Nawab of Jowrah and the Thakur of Bhowanaggur.

BAPUBHAI the eldest son of the late Rao of Cutch was installed on the *guddi* on the 3rd instant. He is 11 years of age.

THE Hon'ble Mr. justice Holloway of Madras will return to India from furlough early next month.

LORD LYTTON will, says the London correspondent of the *Bombay Gazette*, come out to succeed Lord Northbrook in April next.

MYSORE is threatened with a famine.

THE Prince paid a visit to the Maharajah of Vizianagram at Benares, previous to opening the new Town Hall.

THE chief Persian Munshi of H. H. the Nizam was stabbed on Wednesday last while engaged in evening prayer at a musjid.

THE Officiating President of the Madras Municipality has received from the Duke of Buckingham the sum of Rs. 10,000, presented by the Prince of Wales for distribution among the various charitable institutions at Madras.

COLONEL GOURLEY, one of the M. P.'s for Sunderland, landed at Madras on Monday last on his way back to England.

MR. COURTENAY, leader writer of the *Times* who was a guest of the Hon. Mr. Hobhouse during his stay in Calcutta, has proceeded to Madras.

IT appears that some Mussulmans in Candia having prevented Christians from entering a church, a contest arose, in the course of which about 20 persons are said to have fallen on both sides.

A RUSSIAN paper states that belief in the approaching end of the world has seized on the Cossacks of the Don. Many are giving up worldly affairs, wearing a shroud, and ordering their coffins, while numbers of men are repairing to Moscow to be consecrated priests.

LATEST NEWS.

THE Governor of Madras will return from his tour in the Godavery District on the 20th instant. His Excellency will inspect the irrigation works at Dowlaisheram and Coconada.

THE Governor of Bombay will return from his visit to the Southern Marhatha Country on the 13th February. His Excellency will stop at Kolhapore for four days, and, among other places, visit Sattara, Sholapore and Bijapore.

REUTER telegraphs to say that the Queen has announced her intention to visit Coburg on the 10th of April. Her Majesty afterwards proceeds to Baden.

THE *Englishman* hears that, when the Hon'ble A. Eden goes on leave, he will be succeeded in the Viceregal Council by Mr. F. Cockerell, Commissioner of Rajshahye, and that Mr. Mangles, from the Bengal Secretariat, will succeed Mr. Cockerell.

ONE consequence of the visit of so many Native Princes to Calcutta, has been the purchase of a large number of horses by them. The E. I. Railway Company, we know have for sometime been pressed for accommodation for the conveyance of these horses. The day before yesterday a telegram was received in town to the effect "that a horse box had broken loose from the Gidhour Station on the Chord Line last Thursday evening and ran down the incline towards Jamui after dark, and was run into by the down mail train. The engine and five carriages went off the line. The Native fireman and a fakir were killed and also three horses. Mail and passengers were sent on by special train."

THE following telegram from Bombay has been received by the *Pioneer*:—

BOMBAY, *13th January*.

INTIMATION has been received by local Post Offices by to-day's mail that, owing to enormous pressure of business in London on the 24th ultimo, many letters for India were left behind.

A PLOT, says the *Indian Public Opinion*, was recently discovered by the Amir of Cabul, in which Yahyah Khan, father-in-law to Yakub Khan, Mohamed Ibrahim Khan, the present Hakim of Cabul, and one of the sons of the Amir of Cabul and others are said to have been implicated. The object was digging an underground passage, to effect the escape of Yakub Khan. Yahyah Khan was expelled from the city, two friends of Mohamed Ibrahim Khan put to the sword, and the rest imprisoned.

THE cold is so extreme in Cabul that people are unable to move out of their houses.

A NEW and startling version of Mr. Margary's death has been brought to Peking by a French Priest resident at Yunnan. It states that he was decapitated while at a friendly dinner with a mandarin.

LADY HOBART has just sent out from England a wreath of "immortelles," which has been placed over the grave of the late Lord Hobart, in St. Mary's Church, Madras.

"NECKTIE parties" are a novelty being introduced into the Baptist Churches of Chicago. Each lady, married or single, is expected to wear an apron of some kind, and to bring a necktie made of the same material. These neckties are disposed of at the rate of ten cents each to the gentlemen present, and the proceeds are "devoted to the use of the Church."

A PRIVATE letter from Malacca to the *Straits Times* says, that the Chinese disturbances still continued, and in the country districts houses and shops were still being plundered and in some cases set fire to. About 200 Portuguese had been sworn in as special constables, and the heads of departments had been sent out in the country in various directions with small parties of troops. Mr. Magalhaens, with 12 European soldiers, had been despatched to the Durian Tungal district, where he arrested and sent to town 50 Chinese rioters, and subsequently returned with 22 more prisoners.

MR. C. D. C. WINTER, of the Bengal Civil Service, having obtained a certificate of high proficiency in Bengali, has been presented with the authorized donation of Rs1,000.

ACCORDING to the last official reports, "no rain has fallen in Madras except a slight sprinkling in Tanjore: rain is wanted in parts, but prospects are reported generally fair. No rain is reported from Bombay, Sind, the Central Provinces, Berar, Rajputana or Central India: the prospects of the rabi continue good in all these provinces. In Bengal no rain has fallen during the week except a trifling shower at Darjeeling: the showers of last week in the districts immediately south of the hills have been of considerable benefit: rain is wanted in the central and eastern districts and Chota Nagpore; prospects are however good, and the aman rice, the harvest of which is almost complete, has yielded a fair outturn generally. From the North-Western Provinces and Oudh no rain is reported: prospects are good, want of rain being felt seriously only in Bareilly. In the Punjab rain has fallen at Peshawur and Rawal Pindi, none elsewhere: reports are favorable. No rain has fallen in Assam, Burmah, or Mysore; in the last province the condition of the crops continues unimproved."

A CONTEMPORARY tells us that the chief delight of the Sultan of Turkey is cock-fighting. He invariably confers upon the feathered champions the name of some European sovereign, and modestly calls the strongest and most plucky after himself.

THE Native gentleman who determined upon getting a statue in memory of Mr. Powell, late of the Educational Department, at the new Presidency College or Senate House, Madras, have remitted £1,000 to England, and Mr. Acton, a well-know sculptor, will carry out the work. The statue will be made of Sicilian marble.

IT is stated that Mr. George Taylor, of the Bombay Bar, is busily engaged in conducting cases before the Baroda Durbar; and that should the result of them be successful it is not unlikely he would have a harvest of cases there.

The Prince's Visit.

THE following telegram from Delhi appear in the *Englishman* of yesterday:—

HEAD-QUARTERS CAMP, DELHI, JAN. 14.

The Prince visited the Kutub yesterday, dining afterwards with the Rifle Brigade. To-day the Force, under General Hardinge, attempts to capture the Ridge North of Delhi, with a view to further operations against the City Force under General Reid, who defends. The operations will last two days. At the review the appearance of the Native troops was much admired, the Native Officers and Havildars displaying great intelligence. There is a marked improvement in the drill and discipline of all the Native regiments and soldiers. There will be sports on the 17th. The Prince gives prize for the tent-pegging. The illuminations last night were rather poor.

Calcutta.

THE following is the list of Business to be brought forward at the Meeting of the Council of the Governor-General of India for the purpose of making Laws and Regulations, to be held on Tuesday, the 18th January 1876:—

1. The Hon'ble Mr. Eden to move that the Report of the Select Committee on the Bill to declare the law relating to interests in land, and to regulate the assessment and collection of land-revenue, capitation-tax, and other taxes in British Burmah, be taken into consideration.

2. Also to move that the Bill as amended be passed.

3. The Hon'ble Mr. Hobhouse to present the final Report of the Select Committee on the Bill to consolidate and amend the law relating to Native Passengers Ships and Coasting steamers.

4. Also to present the final Report of the Select Committee on the Bill to regulate the transport of Native labourers to British Burmah and their employment therein.

5. His Honor the Lieutenant Governor to move for leave to introduce a Bill to relieve from incumbrances certain estates in Chota Nagpore.

The object is stated in the title.

HIS EXCELLENCY the Viceroy, accompanied by the Hon'ble Miss Baring and Miss Paul has paid a visit on Thursday afternoon to the Zoological Gardens at Alipore, and were satisfied with the rapid progress made by the Committee.

SIR DOUGLAS FORSYTH has addressed the following letter to the *Englishman* :—

To the Editor of the *Englishman.*

SIR,—I have just seen in your paper the report of a lecture on the Prince of Wales, delivered by Babu Gosto Behary Mallik. The lecturer read portions only of his paper, and there are some passages in it now printed, regarding the action of the Government of India in the Baroda case, which I do not recollect to have heard read.

Had I heard them, I certainly should not have allowed them to pass unchallenged on uncontradicted. I should not have consented to take the chair on the occasion had I known that any such political sentiments would be expressed, and I take the earliest opportunity of expressing my disapproval of them.

T. D. FORSYTH.

14, London Street, January 13, 1876.

THE P. and O. Co.'s s. s. *Pera*, Captain R. Methven, sailed from Bombay on Monday last for Aden and Suez, with the English Mails and the following additional passengers :—

For Brindisi.—Mr. A. Steward, and Mr. A. Smallwood.

For Suez.—Mr. J. E. Adshead.

ACKNOWLEDGMENT.

The Times of India Bombay Calendar and Directory for 1876.

Public Engagements.

THIS Evening, 6 P. M. Musical Evangilistic Service in the Free Church Institution, Nimtollah. Address in Bengali by the Rev. S. C. Bannerjea, on "*Jesus, the Light of the World.*" Hymns sung to Hindu Music.

Advertisements

POSTAL NOTICES.

Mails for the Straits at Hongkong for transmission per Steamers *in [illegible]* and *Argyll* will be closed at the General Post Office on Tuesday the 18th Instant at 7 P.M.

Mails for Rangoon, Moulmein and Straits for transmission per Steamer *Ava* will be closed at the General Post Office on Sunday the 16th Instant at 7 P. M.

Mails for Persian Gulf for transmission per Steamer from Bombay will be closed at the General Post Office on Tuesday the 18th Instant at 7 P. M.

The next Overland Mail via Bombay will close at the General Post Office on Friday the 14th instant 1876, by which mails for Mauritius, St. Denis, Reunion, Zanzibar, Mozambique, Delagoa Bay Natal, Cape of Good Hope, the Comoro Islands and Madagascar can be forwarded.

2. Book post and pattern packets must be posted on the 13th idem.

N. B.—The Letter Box will close at 7 P. M. precisely, after which hour Overland letters, fully prepaid and bearing extra postages stamp of two (2) annas on each cover, will be received up to 7-30 P. M., or bearing an extra postage stamp of four (4) annas on each cover, up to 8 P. M.

Indian General Steam Navigation Company, Limited.

SCHOENE, KILBURN & Co.—*Managing Agent.*

ASSAM LINE.

NOTICE.

Steamers now leave Calcutta for Assam every Tuesday, Goalundo every Thursday and Debrooghur downward every Tuesday.

THE Str. "PROGRESS" will leave Calcutta for Assam, on Tuesday, the 18th instant.

Cargo will be received at the Company's Godowns, Nimtollah Ghat, until noon of Monday, the 17th.

THE Str. "CHUNAR" will leave Goalundo for Assam on Thursday, the 20th instant.

Cargo will be received at the Company's Godowns, No. 4. Fairlie Palace, up till noon of Tuesday, the 18th.

Goods forwarded to Goalundo for this vessel will be chargeable with Railway Freight from Calcutta to Goalundo in addition to the regular Freight of this Company.

Passengers should leave for Goalundo by Train of Wednesday, the 19 h.

CACHAR LINE NOTICE

REGULAR WEEKLY SERVICE.

Steamers now leave Calcutta for Cachar and Intermediate Stations every Tuesday and Chattuck downward every Monday.

A Steamer and "FLAT" will leave Calcutta for Cachar on Tuesday, the 18th instant.

Cargo will be received at the Company's Godowns, Nimtollah Ghat, up till noon of Monday, the 17th.

For further information regarding rates of Freight or passage money, apply to,

4 Fairlie Palace, *Calcutta, 12th Jan* 1876. G. J. SCOTT, *Secretary.*

"ROYAL TOURIST."

As the Proprietors of the Royal Journal cannot, after this, register subscribers for the illustrated edition of the paper, they are printing a SECOND EDITION, consisting of letter-press only, at the rate of Rs. 18-8 inclusive of postage, payable strictly in advance.

This edition of the "ROYAL TOURIST" will contain every letter from the special correspondents now following the Prince of Wales, and all the news and telegraphic matter relating to the tour.

HOMŒOPATHIC

MEDICINES.—From 4 annas per dram to—
BOXES.—Of various sizes, from 8 annas to—
BOXES.—Including Medicines, from 3 Rs. to—
Books; Pamphlets; Cholera-spirit Camphor; Absolute Alcohol; Family Guide in Bengalee and all requisites, &c. &c.

To be had at

DATTA'S HOMŒOPATHIC LABORATORY.

No. 312, CHITPORE ROAD, BUTTOLAH, CALCUTTA.

TERMS—CASH.

BABU BASANTA KUMARA DATTA,

HOMŒOPATHIC PRACTITIONER IN CHARGE.

M. Z. MARTIN & CO.,

THE CHINA AND JAPAN WAREHOUSE MERCHANTS AND COMMISSION AGENTS.

No. 4 Dalhousie Square, East.

ICE! ICE! ICE!

MADE IN FOUR MINUTES

THE PNEUMATIC ICE MACHINE

THIS IMPORTANT INVENTION IS CONSIDERED A BOON TO THOSE LIVING IN TROPICAL CLIMATES.

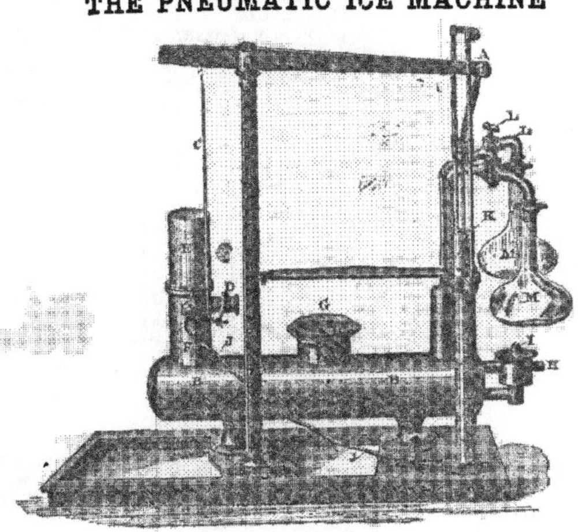

CAN BE WORKED BY THE MOST INEXPERIENCED HAND AND IS NOT LIABLE TO GET OUT OF ORDER.

From Rs. 175, each Machine complete.

MESSRS. ARLINGTON & CO,

AGENTS.

JUST PUBLISHED
THE BRAHMO POCKET DIARY
AND
ALMANAC
FOR
1876.
To be had at the Mission Office,
No. 13, Mirzapore Street.
Price 8 Annas.

ALBERT HALL.

PATRON.
His Honor the Lieutenant Governor of Bengal.
COUNCIL.
Hon'ble Sir William Muir, K. C. S. I.—*President.*
Rajah Roma Nath Tagore Bahadur, C. S. I.—*Vice-President.*
Hon'ble Ashley Eden, C. S. I.
Archdeacon Baly.
Colonel H. E. L. Thuiller, C. S. I.
Maharajah Kumar of Bettiah.
Rajah Komul Krishna Bahadur.
Rajah Joteendro Mohun Tagore Bahadur.
Babu Digumber Mitter C. S. I.
Hon'ble Nawab Ashgar Ali Bahadur, C. S. I.
Nawab Amir Ali Bahadur.
Moulvi Abdul Latif Khan Bahadur.
Manockji Rustomji Esq.
Babu Keshub Chunder Sen.
SUBSCRIPTIONS.

His Highness Maharajah Holkar ...	Rs.	8,000
His Highness Maharajah of Jeypore	"	5,000
Maharajah Kumar of Bettiah ...	"	2,000
Rajah of Bhinga ...	"	1,000
Maharajah of Hutwa ...	"	500
Rajah Komul Krisna Bahadur ...	"	500
Rajah Roma Nath Tagore Bahadur	"	200
Rajah Joteendro Mohun Tagore ...	"	500

NATIONAL COMPANY.

HOMŒOPATHIC CHEMISTS AND PUBLISHERS
SUPPLY ALL KINDS OF
HOMŒOPATHIC MEDICINES, BOOKS
CASES AND OTHER REQUISITES.
12 COLLEGE SQUARE,
Calcutta.

NOTICE.
THE ORIENTAL GAS COMPANY beg to announce that the price of Gas in Calcutta and Howrah will be reduced to Five Rupees per 1,000 feet from the 1st March next.

J. BLACKBURN,
Engineer and Manager.

January 1st, 1876.

THE CALCUTTA SCHOOL.

SESSION opened on the 10th of January, 1876. The following are the rates of fees :—

		Schooling fee.	Admission fee.
English Department.	Rs.	2 0 0	2 0 0
Vernacular "	...	1 0 0	1 0 0
Juvenile Class	...	0 8 0	0 8 0

Three Scholarships of Rupees Five each are available next year, to be held by the three most distinguished students of the School who successfully pass the Entrance Examination of December, 1876. There are besides six free studentships in the Entrance class open to competition, applications for which are to be made to the undersigned before the 1st of February next.

KRISHNA BIHARI SEN, M. A.

!!! हुक्का !!!
!!! HOOKAHS !!!
ENGLISH made Hookahs of various choice designs, colours and sizes ranging in price from Rs. 2 to 5 each, 60 designs to choose from. Apply to

BADANAUTH CHOWDRY,
373, Jorasanko

THE INDIAN MIRROR

THE CHEAPEST DAILY PAPER
IN
INDIA
AND
HAVING AN EXTENSIVE CIRCULATION

SUBSCRIPTIONS.

	Town.	Mofussil. Including Postage
Yearly	...Rs. 12 0 0	Rs. 23 0 0
Half-yearly	... " 6 8 0	" 11 8 0
Quarterly	... " 3 8 0	" 6 0 0
Monthly	... " 1 4 0	2 5 0

Cash sales, One Anna per copy.

Sunday Edition.
STRICTLY IN ADVANCE.
Per Annum ... ... Rs. 5
MOFUSSIL SUBSCRIBERS.
Per Annum ... ... Rs. 6 10 6

VIA SOUTHAMPTON. £ S. D.	VIA BRINDISI. £ S. D.
Per Annum 0 18 9	Per Annum 1 7 0

Cash sales, Two Annas per copy.

RATE OF ADVERTISING.
First Insertion, 8 lines and under, 1 Rupee.
Second and succeeding insertions, 2 Annas per line.
For Advertisements which are to be inserted for a considerable time special contracts may be made on application to the manager.

Domestic Occurrences	Non-Subscriber	... 1 Re.
	Subscriber	... 8 Ans
Public Engagement each insertion		... 1 Re.

FOR SALE.

AT THE BRAHMO SOMAJ OF INDIA
MISSION OFFICE.
No 13, Mirzapore Street.

		Rs.	As.	P
Sacred Anthology	...	2	0	0
Last Days of Rajah Ram Mohun Roy	...	1	0	0
Essays, Theological and Ethical	...	1	0	0
Historical Sketch of the Brahmo Somaj		0	6	0
Jesus Christ, Europe and Asia	...	0	3	0
Future Church	...	0	3	0
Lecture at the Brahmo School	...	0	1	0
True Faith	...	0	2	0
Appeals to Young India	...	0	0	6
Brahmo Somaj Vindicated	...	0	2	0
Popular Tracts, Nos. 1 to 4	...	0	2	0
Destiny of Human Life	...	0	2	0
Reconstruction of Native Socie	...	0	1	0
Welcome Soiree in England	...	0	1	0
Lecture on Inspiration	...	0	4	0
Essential Principles of Brahma Dharma		0	1	0
Proceedings of the Marriage Law meeting at the Town Hall	...	0	2	0
Theistic Annual 1872	...	0	8	0
Ditto Ditto 1873	...	0	8	0
Ditto Ditto 1874	...	1	0	0
Ditto Ditto 1875	...	1	0	0
Lecture on Progress of Theism	...	0	2	0
Ditto Age of Enlightenment	...	0	2	0
Life of Educated Native	...	0	2	0
Lecture on Marriage Law	...	0	2	0
Ditto on the Jainas	...	0	2	0
Man the Son of God	...	0	1	0
Order of Service	...	0	1	0
Prayers for Different Occasions of Life		0	3	0
Divine Service in Hindee	...	0	1	0
Theistic Devotions	...	0	6	0
Behold the Light of Heaven in India	...	0	8	0
Epistles to the Theists in India	...	0	0	6
Lecture on Prayer	...	0	1	6
Ditto Medical	...	0	2	0
JUST RECEIVED FROM ENGLAND.				
Practical Sermons	Rs.	0	12	0
Memoir of Rev. Dr Carpenter	...	0	12	0
Morning and Evening Meditations	...	0	12	0
Channing's Perfect Life	...	1	0	0

A FASHIONABLE high wheeled C spring Buggy by Dykes and Co., with silver plated mountings, quite new. Apply 12 Bentick Street.

9334.

SMITH STANISTREET & CO.

Pharmaceutical Chemists & Druggists
BY APPOINTMENT
To His Excellency the Right Hon'ble
LORD NORTHBROOK, G.M.S.I.,
Governor-General of India.
&c. &c.

SYRUP of Lactate of Iron Prepared from the original recipe. Lactate of Iron, in various forms of preparation, has been in use in France, and generally through the Continent of Europe, for some years past, and is highly esteemed as one of the most valuable Chalybeate Tonic Remedies yet introduced. The Syrup, being the most agreeable as well as convenient form of administration is in most general use.

It is a most valuable remedy in the following diseases :—Chlorosis or Green Sickness, Leucorrhœa, Neuralgia, Enlargement of the Spleen, &c. In combination with Quinine it has also been very successfully used in the cure of Fever, while to persons of delicate constitution, or enfeebled by disease, it is invaluable. In bottles, Rs. 2 each.

Syrup of the Phosphate of Iron, Rs. 2 per bottle.

Syrup of Phosphate of Iron and Strychnine, Rs. 2 per bottle.

Syrup of Phosphate of Iron and Quinine, Price Rs. 2-8 per bottle.

Syrup of Phosphate of Iron, Quinine and Strychnine, (Dr. Aitkin's Triple Tonic Syrup) Rs. 2-8 per bottle.

Smith, Stanistreet & Co.
Invite special attention to the following rates, the quality guaranteed as the best procurable :—

Pure Ærated Waters.
Made from Pure Water, obtained by the new process through the Patent Charcoal Filters.

				Rs.	As.
Ærated plain (Trible Ærated), per doz.			...	0	12
Soda Water	ditto		...	0	12
Gingerade	ditto	"	...	1	4
Lemonade	ditto	"	...	1	4
Tonic (Quinine)	ditto	"	...	1	4

The Cash must be sent with the order to obtain advantage of the above rates.

TO CLEAR OFF STOCK
J. DAVIS & Co.
Are selling their Wool Wrappers
HALF PRICE
No. 6 Government Place, Calcutta.

HOLLOWAY'S OINTMENT

Ulcerations of all kinds.

There is no medicinal preparation which may be so thoroughly relied upon in the treatment of the above ailments as Holloways Ointment. Nothing can be more simple and safe than the manner in which it is applied, nothing more salutary than its action on the body, both locally and constitutionally. The Ointment rubbed round the part affected enters the pores as salt permeates meat. It quickly penetrates to the core of the evil and drives it from the system

Printed and published by M. M. RUKHIT, at the "INDIAN MIRROR" PRESS, No 15, College Square, for the Proprietor.

The Indian Mirror.

SUNDAY EDITION.

VOL. XV] CALCUTTA, SUNDAY, JANUARY 23 1876 { REGISTERED AT THE GENERAL POST OFFICE } [NO. 19

CONTENTS.

NOTICE.

Letters and all other communications relating to the literary department of the Paper should be addressed to "The Editor."

All letters on the business of the Press should be addressed, and all remittance made payable to the Manager of this Paper. Particular attention is solicited to this notice.

Subscribers will be good enough to give prompt notice of any delay, or irregularity in delivery of the Paper.

Editorial Not s.

To-morrow being the Anniversary of the Brahmo Somaj, we claim our usual holiday. There will be no *Mirror*, therefore, on Tuesday next. We shall appear again on Wednesday morning.

THE following is the programme of the Utsab to be held to-morrow :—

Hymns	... 7 A. M.
Morning Service	... 7-30 ,,
Midday Service	... 1 P. M.
Readings	... 1-30 P. M.
Discourses	... 2 P. M.
Prayers and hymns	... 4 P. M.
Meditation	... 4-30 P. M.
Kirtan	... 5 P. M.
Evening Service	... 6-30 P. M.

THERE is one passage in Sir Richard Temple's minute on the Administration of Bengal referred to below, which is open to criticism. Sir Richard says :—"They (the Brahmos) preserve caste as a social and secular order without any religious sanction." This is not correct. Brahmoism is for all people, and it would be wrong to say that it tolerates caste distinctions of any kind, spiritual or secular. An iconoclast's creed is easily understood, and we hope to be intelligible when we say that our work is to pull down barriers and walls of all kinds, and that we tolerate no images or idols, be they in the shape of gods, or Brahmins or rich people.

THE Theistic Annual for 1876 was issued yesterday, pursuant to previous announcement. Several copies were sold at our Anniversary meeting last evening at the Town Hall. We have had time only to take a rapid glance through its pages, and like all the previous numbers it appears to us to be full of interest. Even to the general reader it cannot fail to be interesting, for it purports to be a year's record of the social and religious progress in India. The "Report of Missionary Operations" gives at one view the progress that Brahmoism is making in various parts of this country, such as East Bengal, Assam, Orissa, Lower Bengal, the N. W. Provinces, Sind, Bombay, and Guzerat. Much information can be obtained from this report in respect of the different Brahmo Somajes scattered over India. "Incidents and Anecdotes" are as instructive as they are entertaining. The article on the "Social Reforms in the Brahmo Somaj" which is from the editor's pen, ought to have a wide circulation, and, we dare say, will repay perusal. These Annuals supply us with a most valuable collection of information regarding the Brahmo Somaj, and throw a great deal of light over the work that is being done by the Somaj.

THE following is a translation of the Nagar Kirtan which is to be sung by the Brahmos to-day on the streets of Calcutta :

Mind, make the feet of the Lord thy everything. Gloomy to me would be this unreal world without that treasure.

Say, what temptation induces thee to remain forgetful? Worship Him, the Balm of life—ever-joyful, and your life will be blessed. Collect virtue so long as you live and call upon Him. Think of it—what you shall do on that last day!

Eschew then all worldly desires; O Soul, delay it not. Thy days are numbered. Be loving yourself, and be an ascetic in love, and in this spirit exercise love. In the garb of true beggars let us approach him and prostrate ourselves at His feet. There is no redemption except in the tears of a sinner. Oh! This burden of a sinful life I can no longer sustain. Let us resign our entire lives to Him and cry in an earnestly sorrowful spirit; and our sorrows shall disappear.

We shall hopefully serve Him with the tribute of our love and devotion. He shall give us the nectar of virtue, love, and reverence to His heart's content. Why should we be anxious? The ties of the world shall then be unloosed, and we will proclaim His name in the company of devout men. Into a loving communion with Him we shall enter intoxicated with the nectar of His Name. At the sight of these our desires shall be fulfilled, and we shall see heaven's mansion in our hearts.

Blessed be thy glory, Oh Merciful, Friend of the poor.

THE Anniversary lecture, delivered by Babu Keshub Chunder Sen yesterday at the Town Hall, on "Our Faith and our Experiences" was perhaps more successful than any previous ones which we had the pleasure of hearing. At least this is our opinion of the lecture, and many who were present on the occasion will probably agree with us in this respect. The lecture was marked not only by greater fervour of eloquence and of spirit, but was more practical in character as detailing the result of the experiences of the past religious life of the Brahmos. The past year was one full of trials and struggles, as every Brahmo will be able to testify; but the year has been fruitful of results as regards our spiritual advancement, and this was evident from the lecture itself. Another distinguishing feature of the lecture was that it was most catholic in spirit and most heart-stirring. In fact, the lecture was quite worthy of the great occasion of our Anniversary. So much for the lecture itself. As to the success of the meeting we have as much cause to rejoice. No less than two thousand people, we believe, were present in the Hall representing all classes of the community. The large Hall was filled to overflowing from one end of it to the other. The meeting was not only numerously but also most respectably attended. There was a larger number of European ladies and gentlemen present than on the last occasion. His Honor the Lieutenant-Governor of Bengal did us the honor of attending the meeting. There were also the Lord Bishop of Calcutta, the Hon'ble Mr. Inglis, the Hon'ble Mrs. Hobhouse, Mr. Fergusson, Mr. Lowe, Mr. James Wilson, the Rev. Mr. Thoburn, the Rev. Mr. Rossi Professor Parry, the Rev. Mr. Dall, Dr. Mohendralal Sircar, Mr. Mahomed Ally Zamindar of Furridpore, Mr. Rustomji and others. The lecture commenced with the singing of the following hymn :—

"I am easily reconciled with the sinner, if he cries unto me with a truly sorrowful heart.

I am awake day and night to see who calls upon me. And when I hear a cry, I can no longer rest.

Living in the heart, I know who wants me and in what spirit, and I am not deceived by false sorrow and repentance.

The proud sinners find me not; I am the Friend of the poor, I live in the broken heart; every one knows this."

The hymn was beautifully sung by Babu Troylucko Nath Sanyal.

BY far the most interesting portion in Sir Richard Temple's review of the Administration of Bengal is that which relates to social and moral progress. We publish elsewhere extracts from this able document. But that which is of real interest to the Brahmo community is His Honor's estimate of Brahmoism. It is encouraging to us to think that Government has taken so hopeful a view of our cause, and this view is all the more refreshing because it comes from an administrator who has closely studied Native society for many years and who has had, therefore, unexceptionable opportunities of coming to a correct judgment on the subject. As we wish to direct the special attention of our Brahmo readers to this passage in the Resolution, we extract it below :—

"Among the results of education, there are certain religious movements going on among the Hindus in these provinces, the precise extent of which I have found it impossible to measure by any trustworthy statistics, and the full purposes of which I have not been able to ascertain from any authority acknowledged by all the sections of the movement. But as I understand the case (subject to correction), there is one sect who adopt the Vedic religion of the ancient Hindus, which appears to be a sort of theism with a simple and primitive morality, without the superstructure known as Brahmanical Hinduism—that is, the Hinduism of later times. Whether they acknowledge caste as an institution with a religious sanction, is not certain; apparently they do in some degree. This sect is named "Adhi Brahmo," it comprises many persons of high character and social respectability; its members are not very numerous. There is another sect named "Brahmo;" by way of contradistinction, its members are often styled "the Progressive Brahmos." Their religion seems to be a pure abstract theism with an elevated standard of morality; they profess much respect for the Christian scriptures; they have hymns and prayer-books of their own, but no order of priesthood; they have places of worship; they preserve caste as a social and secular order without any religious sanction. Their leaders are earnest men of excellent repute; the doctrines of the sect appear to produce a good effect upon the lives and conduct of its members. The number of strict professing Brahmos is apparently not great; but the number of those who are Brahmos in mind and heart is said to be very considerable. Whether that be so or not, it appears that opinions and sentiments identical with, or similar to, those of the progressive Brahmos, are spreading among the educated classes of Hindus in these provinces; and this is a very important circumstance.

The societies which undertake to be orthodox Hindu, that is, to maintain the Hinduism of later times—the 'Dharma Sobha' and the 'Dharma Somaj'—are sustained in vitality, but whether they are making progress I am unable to say."

THE SURE AND THE UNSURE GROUND OF THEISM.*

EVERYTHING is passing away. "The eternal surge of time and tide rolls on." The short-lived beauty and brightness of human life fills the mind with gloom. Add to this the ever changeful scenes of the world, the wheel of happiness and sorrow moving round and round endlessly. There is no certainty anywhere. Every stroke of the pendulum carries the message of death to a thousand homes. "Vanity of vanities, all is vanity." The unreality of all things which appeal to the senses, is distressing enough. What shall we say when higher things also pass away. Knowledge and feeling, thought and philosophy, are equally subject to change. Nay even religion passes away. How many systems of faith have risen and fallen, ceremonies, sacraments, principles, doctrines, churches and communions, once full of the depth of life and meaning, lie spread before us now like dried leaves, like bleached bones on the sea-shore of time. Their vitality has long since passed away. Amidst this dreadful scene of uncertainty, what can we do, but seek rest in our inner consciousness of the Divine Reality. It is in the spontaneous sense of religion, apart from all theologies, that the man of doubt aspires to attain certainty, the man of despair finds hope again, the sorrow-worn, sin-worn wayfarer seeks light and consolation. Here then is the ground of the highest and best in human life, all else is fleeting. If this be really the ground of the highest and best, it is necessary that it should be sure. For if in our light there be darkness wherewith shall we be enlightened; if the very support of our life be unsure, whereupon shall we stand? Let us see therefore upon what Theism stands. You say it stands upon man's religious instincts, his intuitions about the existence and attributes of God, about the immortality of the soul. These are supplemented by the teachings of nature, you say—the facts and laws of the world. You will also perhaps insist upon the doctrine of prayer. I know you set great value upon the morality and purity of life, the supremacy of conscience. Nor is this all. You hold the brotherhood of man as a cardinal doctrine of Theism. These principles are so simple and universal that there is a general agreement about them among all nations of the earth. They form the basis of rationanl religion, of natural religion, of Theism. Even thinkers of the very extreme school of unbelief are not loathe to admit that the facts and laws of matter and of mind predominate to establish the existence of some sort of religion. God, according to them, may be imperfect, may be unknowable, but still there is a God. To men whose judgment is less worped by the hard and merciless demands of philosophical systems, these facts and laws are much more eloquent. It may be said that the whole foundation and superstructure of Natural Religion are built thereupon, added to the experiences, and exercises of religious life. What have all thesegiven us? Much progress, truth, and consolation. We stand here to-day, the objects of sympathy and congratulation from a great many, because we have acted according to the simple principles in our religious consciousness developed by the grace of God, and matured into deep spiritual experiences which find their echo everywhere. We are outside every creed, yet we are in every creed. But the question is what have we done after all? Have we done anything more than what other religions did before us? What is the use and mission of Theism in the world? What are the demands of humanity upon the Religion of the Future, about which we hear ever so much? These demands may be summarizd into two words :—(1.) The Reconciliation of Man with God. (2.) The Reconciliation of Man with Man. This phraseology is old. But see what its meaning is. In the first place such reconciliation means the harmony of science and religion. Why should we be compelled to believe without the justification of philosophy, and why should reason "lead us into the grey twilight of unbelief?" If both teach truth, why should there not be harmony between truth and truth, when all truth is God's? The best student of nature too frequently misreads her teachings. Even the faithful follower of God in the human soul cannot solve the problem of His providence. Doubt "that sees every thing double," and distrust the mother of despair, often reign where perfect faith should beget complete assurance. Within the deep belief of such men as we, there is "an innermost core of scepticism." How are such doubts and misgivings to be ultimately removed? Humanity demands a perfect solution of all questionings about the being, attributes, and providence of God. Can Natural Religion give this? In the second place the reconciliation of the sinner with the Saviour is demanded. Man's soul must feel rest in purity. The conscience must cease from troubling. The thorn in the flesh must be extracted. We cannot always live in the midst of miserable, humiliating struggles with positive sin. The poor soldier of God must have peace, at last, and repose,—the repose that comes from righteousness. Has humanity obtained it? Search all coun-

* The substance of a Sermon delivered by Babu Protap Chunder Mozumdar in the Brahma Mandir on Thursday, the 20th January, 1876.

tries, search all hearts, and say how many have found healing for their wounds, adequate remedy for the temptation that surrounds them, and conquered the evil that is raging within their hearts. Humanity demands deliverance from evil, and the ultimate reconciliation of the impure soul with the pure Spirit of God. Individual souls there may be, I am ready to acknoledge, who have found this rest and righteousness, the harmony of the purity above with the abiding indwelling purity within. But for humanity at large salvation is yet to come. Can Natural Religion, as it is now found, give us this? In the third place, man wants to be reconciled with man. One may say after reviewing the spiritual growth of the world, that in loving, worshipping and serving God, every nation and every religion has furnished us some examples. The main precepts of every religion, however much we may differ from it, if faithfully carried out, will produce good, and God-fearing men. But who has been able to make humanity a real brotherhood? "By this shall men know ye to be my disciples that ye love one another." That was the parting injunction. By this have men known ye to be my disciples, that ye have quarrelled and disagreed with one another! That is the present experience. We love each other very well, and call each other brethren and friends, so long as we live apart. But try the experience of living together, working together, independently on the ground of freedom and equality, and see how the angularities and difficulties of character and disposition, of habit and training, of want and desire collide, and there comes out of the conflict fire and storm, quarrel and heart-burning, meannesses and jealousies without number. Man, therefore, may be said to have made some progress towards his reconciliation with his God, but in reconciliation with his fellow-beings he has hardly made any progress at all. How often have we spoken of warring sects and of bloodshed in the sweet name of religion? Even amidst old and dear friends, co-religionists, co-worshippers there has been no reconciliation. Humanity therefore demands that from the future religion of the world. If Theism can satisfy these demands, there is a mission for it, there is real work for it, the whole world will want it, adopt it. If none of these demands can be met, if we cannot satisfy these crying wants of the religious world, we have no vocation in life, and our religion, in spite of our big words and evident zeal, is destined to pass away. Everything for which there is no occasion and use, shall fall. Systems have fallen. Empires have fallen, the tongues of prophets have been hushed, the dove of inspiration has flown back to its native heaven, and we too, if we have no real work in building the future of our race, must go when our time comes. Now consult your experiences and the history of your church, and say if such religious life as we have manifested, can satisfy the demands to which allusion has been made. If your resources and principles, exercises and offerings can give the world what it lacks, well and good; if not, we must either advance further, or die in stagnation. Our ground has been good enough for the position we now occupy, our progress has gone on so far as it can on that ground. Further it cannot go. If we want farther and surer progress, we must seek higher and surer ground for our religion. Human nature can go only a certain height, and then it must fall. That is the inevitable destiny of Natural Religion. If we want in our progress to go beyond nature, our religion must come from a source beyond nature. Supernatural progress in godliness and brotherliness can come from a supernatural religion. Religion to deserve its name, must be revealed. Do not be startled, I do not mean book revelations, I do not mean a religion of physical miracles. Mark me here.

(To be continued.)

Correspondence.

THE ALFRED HALL AT BENARES.

To the Editor of the *Indian Mirror*.

DEAR SIR,—The "Alfred Hall," opened by H. R. H. the Prince of Wales, is so called, because it was built by H. H. the Maharajah of Vizianagram, K. C. S. I., in commemoration of the visit of H. R. H. the Duke of Edinburgh to India and to Benares in particular. H. R. H. the Prince of Wales was much pleased when informed of the reason of the name "Alfred Hall."

Yours truly,
A. J. UNDERWOOD,
Secretary and Tutor to H. H. the Maharajah of Vizianagram, K. C. S. I.

BENARES,
The 20th January.

Devotional.

PRAYER.

(Communicated.)

OH Friend Unseen;—daily, hourly, Helper, Teacher, Comforter, Consoler, Father;—Help me to make some return to Thee, or thine, for these accumulating heaps of good, and piled up blessings. Do not crush me with the thought that—to whom much is given of him much will be required; and that according as I receive so must I give. Oh these blessed opportunities! these multiplying trusts! these ever-recurring invitations to be good and do good as Thou art, and as Thou doest;—and to be perfect even as our Father in heaven is perfect! What can I do but say that I love Thee,—and more and more try to make it true. Say that I love Thy children, my fellow-men, the poor and the poorest, the weak and the weakest, the vile and the vilest:—the evil and the good, the just and the unjust, and seek continually better ways of making them wise and true; of aiding them to see Thee even as I see Thee, shining through my darkest, saddest hours and most sinful gloom, with unwearied love and overpowering beneficence. If I have wronged any man, Oh Father, may I go and be just to my brother, my sister, thy children, before I dare offer my gift to Thee. May we all increasingly resemble thee, as sons and daughters follow the example and live the life of a good father and mother. Oh Spirit of Life and Love and Wisdom and Strength and Truth and Goodness, and Justice and Mercy and Holiness, show me thy way, in all thy works and in man thy best work; in thy holy children and the holiest that have trod the earth, honoring Thee the Father, in spite of scorn and hatred. So win me to be thine forever.

The Brahmo Somaj.

ALLUDING to the anniversary lecture of Babu Keshub Chunder Sen at the Town Hall, the *Indian Daily News* observes:—"These annual discourses generally give rise to some smart hitting afterwards. No great harm has been done to the Babu by these metaphorical cudgellings, and doubtless he will survive the next." We hope he will.

THE FORTY-SIXTH ANNIVERSARY OF THE BRAHMO SOMAJ

FIRST DAY.

OUR anniversary week commenced on Thursday last. Days before that Brahmos were observed pouring in large numbers into the metropolis and convincing by their very appearance the casual observer that something was going to happen. It is true that the Prince's visit somewhat interfered with the presence of many whom we should otherwise have expected at this season. The liberal manner in which Government allowed its servants to come to Calcutta to have a sight of the Prince, persuaded many theists residing in the Mofussil to avail themselves of the privilege, and as the Anniversary has closely followed the royal visit, they were prevented from paying a second visit to the metropolis. Nevertheless the number present in Calcutta is not small. We have representatives from twenty-six Brahmo Somajes in India, and of the places that have sent them we may mention Shillong in Assam, Kurrachee in Sind, Lahore in the Punjab, Ahmedabad in Bombay, Lucknow in Oudh, and Cuttack in Orissa. Though the Anniversary began on Thursday last, properly speaking its commencement may be dated about a week back. Prayer meetings have regularly been held in the house of the Minister, and conversations and communions have done much to prepare our brethren for the spiritual services of these days. The first regular and congregational service was held on Thursday, when Babu Protap Chunder Mozumdar delivered a practical and thoughtful sermon on the present needs of our religion. There were more than 500 persons, we believe, present in the Mandir, of whom Mr. Dall was the only European, we should be right in saying American. It was a matter of great regret that no tickets (we speak under correction) were given to our European friends in Calcutta. The service was in English and it would have been really good if they had come in large numbers to attend it. It is a pity that we so seldom endeavour to draw to our movement the intelligent sympathy and co-operation of liberal foreigners. When

Englishmen attend our meetings they do so out of a purely patronising spirit; it is hardly that we get a real worker among us. We allude to the fact simply with the view of drawing the attention of the community to a matter so important and so much essential to the progress of our cause. Let that go. When the service was gone through—it was an ordinary Bengali service in an English address, but none the less attractive and interesting for it—a series of texts from Christian, Mahomedan, Buddhist, Chinese and Hindu sacred books were read from Mr. Conway's Anthology. By the way we may say that a new edition of our own Texts from the Scriptures of various nations or the "Sloka Sangraha' has been printed and will be placed in the hands of our Brahmo readers to day. It has been considerably enlarged and improved. The larger the number of such books, the better for the cause of eclectic religion. The reading of texts was followed by a sermon by Babu Protap Chunder Mozumdar.

We reproduce a portion of this admirable sermon elsewhere.

The sermon was heard with deep attention. A Bengali hymn was sung after which the congregation dispersed.

SECOND DAY.

THE GENERAL CONFERENCE OF THE BRAHMOS.

PURSUANT to notice a General Conference of the Brahmo Somaj of India was held on Friday last at 4·30 P. M. About two hundred gentlemen were present. Babu Keshub Chunder Sen, Secretary, in the chair.

The Brahmo Somajes of the following places were represented at the meeting:—Lahore, Bhaugulpore, Allahabad, Gya, Lucknow Gournagur, Hurinabhi, Mymensing, Kishorgunj, Jaugulbari, Dacca, Bagachra, Hydrabad, Kurrachee, Kaligatcha, Gourifa, Balasore, Rampore Haut, Cuttack, Monghyr, Akan, Bhowanipore, Chandernagore, Barripore, Shillong, and Ahmedabad.

The Assistant Secretary, Babu Protap Chunder Mozumdar, then read the report of the last year. We regret that want of space compels us to withhold its publication to-day.

The following resolutions were then passed:—

Proposed by Babu Pisso Nath Roy and seconded by Mr. Naval Row:

"That the Report just read be adopted."

Proposed by Babu Keshub Chunder Sen and seconded by Babu Ananda Chunder Bose, M.A.

"That the Brahmo Somaj of India sends its fraternal greetings and cordial thanks to all fellow-Theists, liberal thinkers, reformers and philanthropists who are working alone or unitedly in distant lands for the benefit of mankind and the extension of God's kingdom."

Proposed by Babu Protap Chunder Mozumdar and seconded by Babu Durga Mohon Dass:

"That this meeting thanks God for the progress of enlightenment and the advancement of His true church not only in this land but in all parts of the civilized world."

Proposed by Babu Gunga Gobindo Nundy and seconded by Babu Gopal Chunder Ghose:

"That this meeting accords its best thanks to those who generously contributed to the mission fund and by pecuniary and other gifts provided for the maintenance of Brahmo missionaries and their families during the past year."

Proposed by Babu Shiva Nath Shastri and seconded by Babu Joy Gopal Sen: "That the thanks of the meeting be recorded for the following presentations:—

100 Copies of "Last Days of Rajah Ram Mohan Roy."
100 Copies of "Practical Sermons."
100 „ of "Memoirs."
25 „ of "Meditations,"

presented by Miss Carpenter to Babu Keshub Chunder Sen and presented by the latter to the Brahmo Somaj of India 240 copies of "Sacred Anthology" presented by Mr. Walter Thompson of Beheea.

It was also resolved at the suggestion of the Chairman that the Committee of Management appointed last year do continue to work and at the end of two months submit a report of its work to the Brahmo Somaj. At the conclusion of the meeting the Chairman invited all those that had any differences with him or with each other to meet him any day when the best efforts will be made to arrive at a reconciliation. Liberty, he said, was the birthright of every Brahmo. The Somaj would be abusing its name if it tried to suppress that gift. Differences must exist, and it ought to be expected that they will spring up in abundance. But they should see that such differences did not embitter their hearts. They believed in the same God, and so long as they did so, they should remain in perfect friendliness and harmony of feelings with each other. He invited them to come to him and hoped that all enmity should be forgotten and forgiven. The meeting then dispersed.

Literary.

THE English papers in Burmah are hardly well disposed towards the King. So it is his object to buy some of them up. A Rangoon paper says that the Agent of the King of Burmah has lately purchased all the types, papers, &c., of the *Friend of Burma*, for Rs. 1,510, at an execution sale.

THE *Indian Daily News* is our authority for stating that "the *Delhi Gazette* is in the market, and that a gentleman in Calcutta is negotiating with the vendors with the view of publishing the paper at Allahabad as an independent organ, in opposition to the *Pioneer*." We do not know how far the report is true. But an independent organ in the capital of the N. W. Provinces has become a necessity. The *Pioneer* by its cringing policy is doing a great deal of mischief to the country, and we are not far wrong in stating, to our rulers themselves. He may pretend to be a friend of Lord Northbrook, but, if all truth be told, he has much to answer for His Excellency's resignation.

THE *Indian Church Gazette* comes out in black borders in consequence of the death of Bishop Douglas of Bombay.

The Week

MR. GIRDLESTONE, Resident at Khatmandu, has arrived at Lucknow.

THE Bombay Temperance League held its second meeting on Tuesday last. General Gell took the chair.

MR. ALBERT GREY, Private Secretary to Sir Bartle Frere, has visited Lucknow, *en route* to the Punjab.

SIR RICHARD MEADE, the newly-appointed resident of Hyderabad, is coming to Calcutta in a few days to meet His Excellency the Viceroy.

THE *Bombay Gazette* hears on the most reliable authority that all the papers in connection with the Nizam's proposed visit to Bombay, and the circumstances which finally led to the Resident's resignation, will be called for in the House of Commons shortly after Parliament meets.

SIR LOUIS MALLET, who has been for some time the guest of the Viceroy in Calcutta, is suffering from slight fever. He goes to the Sandheads for change in the *Celerity*, accompanied by a doctor.

THE *Pioneer*, we are afraid, is wrong in stating that Mr. Justice Phear goes home next spring. We believe he does not leave India before July or or August next.

THOUGH the Maharajah of Cashmere did not give anything to the Dharma Rakhshini Sabha in Calcutta, His Highness, it appears, made a donation of Rs. 500 to the Sabha of the same name at Lucknow.

LORD LYTTON left Lisbon for London on the 13th instant.

AMONG the notabilities now at Delhi, are Mr. Ashburry, M. P. for Brighton, Lord Kerra, the three American officers and an Austrian Hussar.

MR. DIGBY, the editor of the *Ceylon Observer*, is the author of the article on the "Native Journals in India" in the January number of the *Fortnightly Review*.

PUNDIT Dyanund Saraswati is still clinging to the Bombay Presidency. He is now the "lion" at Baroda, where he intends stopping for a fortnight to deliver lectures on the Vedic religion.

SCARCITY of water is being felt in several parts of India. Complaints reach us from Kattywar as well as from Mysore.

THE Prince is said to have been delighted with the manœuvres of the Native troops at the Delhi Camp of Exercise.

FEMALE ticket-collectors for Native women who travel by the Railway, are to be met with now at Moradabad.

IN Madras a battle has just begun to rage between the Attorneys and Vakils with the same fury as was witnessed not long ago in Calcutta, when a fight between the same classes occurred here.

LATEST NEWS.

MR. FRANKS, late of the 51st Regiment, has been appointed tutor to the son and heir-apparent of Maharajah Holkar. Why is not a Rajkumar College established in Central India like that in Rajputana?

REUTER announces the appointment of Lord Napier of Magdala to the Governorship of Gibraltar.

MAJOR MUNRO, Commissioner of Derajat, has gone to Khelat, as Commissioner.

MR. GLADSTONE completed his sixty-sixth year on Dec. 29, having been born on Dec. 29, 1809. Mr. Disraeli was seventy years of age on Dec. 21.

MR. GASPER GREGORY, Barrister-at-law, Reporter to the High Court at Calcutta for the authorized Indian Law Reports, is granted six months' leave of absence, commencing from the 1st February next. Mr. J. G. Apcar, Barrister-at-law, is appointed to act in the room of Mr. Gregory.

AN exprienced Tobacco Curer practically acquainted with the Manufacture is wanted by the Secretary, Board of Revenue, Lower Provinces.

HYDERABAD, the present chief seat of Mussulmans in India, has of late been the scene of religious disturbances. The *Sunis* and *Shias* have fallen out, as they always do, and a venerable Moulvie has fallen a victim to fanaticism. He has been ruthlessly murdered. On the return of Sir Salar Jung from Calcutta the city has become somewhat quiet, however,

Sir Salar has ordered people not to carry arms when they leave the city.

THE following appears in the *Gazette of India*:—"THE Viceroy and Governor-General in Council has received with deep regret the intelligence of the death, on the 7th January 1876, of Captain J. Butler, Political Agent of the Naga Hills, from the effects of a spear wound which he received on Christmas Day, while accompanying a survey party into the Naga Hills. Captain Butler had only recently rendered very efficient service while attached to the Expedition which was organized for the punishment of the Naga villages concerned in the treacherous attack on Lieutenant Holcombe and his party, and on that occasion had fully sustained his previous reputation as an active Political Officer. In him the Government of India has lost an able servant, whose career, thus prematurely cut short, was full of promise."

The Prince' Visit.

THE following is the programme of the Prince of Wales' movements to-day and to-morrow;—

SUNDAY, 24TH JANUARY.

11 A. M.—Attends Divine Service either at Lahore or at Mian Mir, and in the evening if His Royal Highness pleases may drive on to Shadera, and back to Lahore.

MONDAY, 24TH JANUARY.

Leave Lahore. Arrive at Amritsar. Drive through the city to Rambagh and the Town Hall. Receive an address, and return to the Commissioner's house. Luncheon to be given by the Chiefs and Native gentlemen of Amritsar, followed by the presentation of Native gentlemen. At dark, view the illumination of the Sacred Tank and Durbar Sahib. Fireworks. Leave Amritsar.

Calcutta.

THE *Indo-European Correspondence* says that "Dr. C. Fabre-Tonnerre, late Health Officer of the town, has been paid by the Justices for Calcutta the amount of compensation, Rs35,000, voted by them at a previous meeting. The Doctor vacated his appointment from the 1st of this month, and intends, we hear, to retire to Europe." We hope the Doctor will now enjoy his *otium cum dignitate* in Europe on the 35,000Rs, pocketed by him, and bless the Calcutta Municipality for ever.

A BUILDING for the office of the Surveyor General has been designed. The Bengal Secretariat will be located in the old Writers' Buildings with certain adaptations for the purpose.

THE Government of Bengal is endeavouring to establish an Art Gallery in connection with the Calcutta School of Art, to be filled will copies of good pictures in Europe.

THE Judges of the Calcutta Court of Small Causes, though four in number, do not seem to be at all good hands at writing reports. We never read anything more stale and uninteresting than their report of the Court of 1874-75. Its brevity is almost most singular, and much of what they should have dwelt upon in their report is done by His Honor the Lieutenant Governor, who somewhat complains of the brevity. His Honor observes:—"Sir Richard Temple would, however, have been glad had they reviewed more minutely the figured statements submitted by them and had they brought into prominent relief those results which would seem to point to anything defective in the working of the Court, or to amendments which might be made with advantage in the existing Small Cause Court Acts." But perhaps the learned Judges think their Court to be perfect, and see no defect in its working, however much the public may view it. The punctuality with which the Report is submitted, draws the admiration of His Honor. But when punctuality is put against the brevity, the compliment goes for nothing. But probably the Judges thought that brevity was consistent with their dignity, for all Judges, whether high or low, are more or less tenacious of their dignity, if not for anything else. The learned Judges of the Calcutta Small Cause Court are no exception to the rule. The only leading facts that we have been able to gather from the too meagre reports are that the number of cases instituted in the Court during the year was 24,993, showing an increase of 400 over the number instituted during the year ending 31st March 1874. The amount in litigation was Rs. 15,70,142-10-7. From the resolution of Sir Richard Temple on the report it appears that it is likely that the work of recasting the several Acts relating to the Small Cause Court is to be shortly undertaken by the Legislature. Sir Richard Temple has recently sanctioned a redistribution of the authorized holidays of the Court with a view to meet the wishes of the Mahomedan community, whereby, in future, seven days will be deducted from the 30 days allowed for the Durga Pujah vacation, in return for the eight Mahomedan holidays on which the Court will now be closed. As regards law-brokers which infest the Court and which has so often been made the subject of public complaint, the Judges of the Court have intimated their willingness to admit, as "an approved agent," any mookhtear authorized to act in the High Court, or any Court subordinate to it. The financial result of the year has been that, against a net amount credited to Government in the cash account of Rs. 2,04,575, there was a total expenditure of Rs. 1,71,254, leaving a balance of Rs. 33,321 to be credited to the general revenues. In future years there will be a further annual saving of nearly Rs. 15,000, representing the rent paid for the old Court house.

THE following is the list of business to be brought forward at the Meeting of the Council of the Governor-General of India for the purpose of making laws and regulations, to be held on Tuesday, the 25th of January, 1876:—

1. The Hon'ble Mr. Hobhouse to move that the final Report of the Select Committee on the Bill to consolidate and amend the law relating to Native Passenger Ships and Coasting Steamers, be taken into consideration.

2. Also to move that the Bill as amended be passed.

3. Also to move that the final Report of the Select Committee on the Bill to regulate the transport of Native Laborers of British Burmah and their employment therein, be taken into consideration.

4. Also to move that the Bill as amended be passed.

5. Also to present the Report of the Select Committee on the Bill to consolidate and amend the law relating to Pleaders, Mukhtears and Revenue Agents in Northern India.

6. His Honor the Lieutenant-Governor to introduce the Bill to relieve from incumbrances certain estates in Chota Nagpore, and to move that it be referred to a Select Committee with instructions to report in a month.

MR. ALLEN, Barrister-at-Law, will likely act for Mr. MacEwen, Third Judge of the Calcutta Small Cause Court, who proceeds on leave in March next.

Selection

SOCIAL AND MORAL PROGRESS OF BENGAL.

[FROM SIR RICHARD TEMPLE'S MINUTE ON THE ADMINISTRATION OF BENGAL FOR 1874-75.]

FEMALE EDUCATION.

So far as indication can be afforded by the returns, female education does not appear to be making such progress as might be desired or expected. Efforts have been made from time to time in this direction by benevolent individuals or societies, with only a moderate degree of success, and this too obtained after many disappointments. The zenana missions have endeavoured to introduce the light of knowledge into the inner domestic life of the Natives; but it is as yet impossible to say whether these efforts have been fruitful in results. The arrangements hitherto made to establish normal shools for female teachers have scarcely succeeded.

Notwithstanding these unfavorable points, however, I believe that instruction, in reading and writing at least, is making rapid progress among the Bengali ladies of the families of the educated classes. This is a matter on which a judgment can only be formed upon statements received from those who are in a position to know. Now I am assured by almost every one of the many educated Native gentlemen consulted in different parts of the country that the ladies in their own families can read and write, and that they believe such to be the case in other families in their circle of acquaintance; they say that such was not the case, or much less the case, with the ladies of the preceding generation. Instruction of this sort is conducted quite privately. Whether it goes beyond reading and writing may be doubted; but even this much may be regarded as a step in advance.

Moreover, there is some hope that the rudimentary instruction of the very young girls in the poorer classes may form a part of the primary education which is being diffused over the country. In some places there will, we trust, be mixed schools for boys and girls of tender age, in other places schools for the girls alone. If once female education shall take hold of the lower classes, it will probably soon spread to the classes higher in the social scale.

In the present initiatory stage of female education in all classes of the people, the provision of competent female teachers is indispensable if any really good progress is to be speedily made. Under this view, then, the establishment of normal schools of various grades for female teachers becomes essentially important. The attention of all those interested in the cause will be drawn to this point.

CHRISTIAN MISSIONS.

The efforts of the various Christian missions for the education of the Natives, though perhaps, not materially increasing, are yet fully sustained. Several important schools and colleges for the education of the Natives belong to missionary societies, and are very largely attended, such as the Free Church of Scotland institution, St. Xavier's Roman Catholic college, the Baptist college, the Cathedral Mission college, the London Mission college, and others. The Church of England mission in the interior of Central Bengal, especially in Kishnagurh; the Baptist mission in parts of eastern Bengal and in Orissa; the Roman Catholic missionaries in various places; are still doing much in the way of education, of practical charity, and of general benevolence among the Natives; the missionaries are much respected by the villagers in whose neighbourhood they dwell, and are gratefully known as the never-failing friends of the poorer classes in all trials and emergencies. It is unquestionable that the presence in the interior of the country of Europeans like the missionaries, who exemplify in their character and conduct so many of the best consequences of our civilization, must have a beneficial effect on the public mind, and must raise our national repute in the eyes of the Natives. In Senthalia, and in those parts of the Chota Nagpore province which are inhabited by the Kol tribe, the popularity of the missionaries, their influence upon education, and their general power for good, are very marked.

After this review of our educational system, there still remain some few remarks to be made on some of the results of education.

SANSKRIT LEARNING.

It is generally believed that Sanskrit learning tends towards decline in Bengal, especially at such literary centres as Nuvadeepa or Nuddea, near Kishnagurh. This is perhaps unavoidable under the altered circumstances of the times. It is remarkable, however, that a proper interest in the historical associations of the ancient Hindus is kept alive among the Bengalis of present generation, as is evidenced by the frequent reproductions in Bengali of passages extracted from classic Sanskrit literature. In 1872 there was fear lest the excessive introduction of Sanskrit phraseology should render the new Bengali and Hindi literature pedantic; and steps were taken to prevent this occurring. Arrangements, however, are maintained for ensuring in our scholastic courses that element of Sanskrit learning which is essential to the due culture of the Bengali language.

BENGALI LITERATURE.

As will have been seen from the account just given of vernacular education, the formation of a Bengali literature is of high importance. There are and will continue to be, many translations made in Bengali of standard and useful English works, also of classical Sanskrit books both in poetry and prose. But the chief interest pertains to original works in Bengali of the present day. The best perhaps of these belong to the domain of fiction and imagination—dramas, novels, and poetical pieces of the lesser kinds. Several historical books have been prepared, not very elaborate, but sound and good so far as they go; and doubtless history is a field in which Bengalis are likely to excel. There are also ethical and didactic works of an elementary sort perhaps, but of some merit. Various rudimentary books on the several branches of science are beginning to be written derived from European sources, though many more are still required; and as the power of exact apprehension and clear exposition is inherent in the Bengali mind, it is probable that many capital works in this category will be forthcoming in the future.

Some doubts have been expressed as to whether the English language is quite so thoroughly studied and mastered by the present generation of Bengalis as it was by the past generation. Certainly the utmost watchfulness should be exercised to preserve among the Bengali youth, amidst the distractions of a complex and multiform education, the best standard of proficiency in English, for the cultivation of which language (after allowance has been made for all defects) they display an extraordinary aptitude which few foreign nations can equal. There have indeed in past times been Bengalis with an admirable knowledge of English both written and spoken, to whom the present generation may well look back as examplers. Still, besides those Bengalis who reside in England during the best years of their youth, and so become for a time naturalized in that country, there are at the present many Bengalis who have never left the shores of India, and yet have acquired a remarkably complete command of the English language, in proof of which may be cited such works or publications as the novel *Govinda Samanta*, the *Antiquities of Orissa*, the *Hindoo Patriot* newspaper, the *Travels of a Hindu*, and the *Calcutta Medical Journal*. And at public meetings where the proceedings are in English, the Bengalis generally display a readiness of speech, and sometimes a sort of eloquence, which redounds to their credit.

SOCIETIES AND ASSOCIATIONS.

Another result of education has been the formation of societies and associations, greater and lesser, in all parts of the country; they are about 60 in number, and they have about 2,000 members in all. Their objects are somewhat undefined perhaps, but pertain chiefly to educational and social matters, relating to political affairs only to the extent of representing to British authorities the wishes and interests of the people; so far they are harmless and in many respects actually laudable; they indicate a stir of thought and a movement in the national mind. The British Indian Association is one of the oldest and best known among these socities; it comprises many great landowners and others of wealth and station. The Social Science Association at Calcutta is largely supported by the Natives. The society for the reduction of marriage expenses has a specific object of the most useful character: its operations are chiefly in Behar.

VERNACULAR PRESS.

The growth within the last twenty years of the Bengali newspaper press, that is the newspapers published in the vernacular, is a remarkable and important circumstance. There are now about twenty prirciple newspapers and about thirty-six of lesser degree, or fifty-six in all, though the number is constantly changing. The circulation of the twenty principal papers cannot of course be accurately known, but is believed to be represented by about 20,000 copies; that of the lesser papers is much less, and probably does not exceed 5,000 copies; perhaps the total may amount to 30,000 copies. This circulation may not be thought considerable as compared with the size of all these provinces; but the number of readers must greatly exceed, and may be double or treble the number of copies. And though it is well to avoid even an approach to exaggeration in a matter of this sort, still we should not overlook the significance of these facts.

It is on the other hand to be remembered that a large portion of the educated Bengalis read the English newspapers, or those Native newspapers which are published in English.

Provided that we were sure that the vernacular press really expresses public opinion, we should thereby learn that which, as foreign rulers, we are so much concerned to know, and which is yet so hard to be known, namely, the feelings and wishes of the Natives. If the line followed by the vernacular press were generally that of praise of British persons and things, there might be suspicion of flattery; but as the line actually taken is often much the reverse, we may be confident that the comments are perfectly free and without reserve. I have accordingly paid due attention to this subject, and my general conclusion is decidedly favorable in respect to the loyalty and good-will of the Bengali press towards the Birish crown and nation, and towards British rule in the main. Occasionally, political observations are made of an evil tendency, and these whenever they occur must be condemned. But besides these, there is very much matter of a highly controversial character. Blame is constantly attributed to the British Government and administration; impracticable suggestions are frequently made; a disposition to find fault with everything that is done, or omitted to be done, and to be pleased with nothing, is sometimes manifested; an increasing jealousy is evinced regarding the bearing and demeanour of British people towards the Natives; there is a tendency to form inflated notions and aspirations out of visionary ideas, without due regard to the sobering influences of deep knowledge and practical thought. All this need not, in my opinion, excite surprise; it may sometimes indeed have some foundation in justice; and though it may be often mistaken, still it is very different from any spirit of general disloyalty. On the other hand, there frequently occur passages of signal loyalty the sincerity of which may claim acceptance, in the face of the adverse criticism upon other matters with which this press abounds. It frequently happens that in fundamental matters, relating to the attachment of the thinking section of the people to British rule; the acknowledgment of the superior advantages of British rule on the whole as compared with any other; the public confidence in the good intentions of the British crown, government, and nation towards the Natives; the gratitude of the Natives for external security, religious freedom, material prosperity, and English education;—the case on behalf of the British is put by the Bengali press with a wormth and an impressiveness hardly ever surpassed, and seldom equalled, by zealous advocates among ourselves.

A very natural desire is gaining ground among the Natives of Bengal to assert their rights according to the declared principles of British rule, and to urge their just claims to a full share in all the best things which the public service and the Government organization can afford. There is a healthy ambition among them to raise themselves by self-culture both individually and collectively, which culture seems likely to take its groove from the arts and sciences of the west. An increasing pride finds expression among them in respect to the achievements of the Hindu mind, which, though it may be carried too far, is yet a sure concomitant of national improvement. Ins hort, there is a short of intellectual restlessness and mental fermentation going on, of which the end is hard to be foreseen, but which we may with considerateness and thoughtfulness guide into a good direction.

The number of young men from Bengal, more probably than from any province in India, who visit England to complete their education, or to study for some profession, is gradually increasing. There has for some time past been a benevolent association in England for the purpose of affording information and friendly welcome to young Bengalis thus situated. There are projects afoot for affording educational centres around which these young men may congregate in connection with the universities at London and at Oxford. These projects deserve every encouragement for the sake not only of the youth of the rising generation, but also of confirming our own hold upon the regard of the people; for those Bengalis, who return to Bengal after an education in England, evince a vivid appreciation of the kindness and sympathy experienced by them there, and of the illimitable resources of Western civilization.

The loyalty which prevails in these provinces, was strikingly manifested during the recent visit of His Royal Highness the Prince of Wales. Besides the passing displays which are usual on occasions of national rejoicing, and which on this great occasion were distinguished by the highest degree of cordiality and enthusiasm, the wealthier Natives of all classes both in Bengal and in Behar are raising large subscriptions to commemorate the event by founding educational institutions, and by promoting other works of public usefulness, so that the visit of His Royal Highness will leave its mark of permanent beneficence on the country for all time comming.

Public Engagements.

MUSICAL EVANGELISTIC SERVICE.

THE Rev. John Fordyce (of Simla) will deliver an address in the Free Church Institution. Nimtollah Street, on Sunday Evening, 23rd instant, at 6 o'clock.

Hymns in Bengali, set to Hindu Music, will be sung.

Advertisements

PROGRAMME
OF THE
Forty-sixth Anniversary of the Brahmo Somaj.

Sunday, 23 January.—Service in the morning and evening, in the Mandir, and Procession in the afternoon, to start from the minister's house at 5 P. M.

Monday, 24 January.—Utsab from 7 A. M. to 9 P. M., in the Mandir.

Tuesday, 25 January.—Meeting of Brahmo ladies for Divine service at 9 A. M., at the Bharat Asram.

Wednesday, 26 January.—Service, communion and collation in the Belghoria Villa.

Indian General Steam Navigation Company, Limited.

SCHOENE, KILBURN & Co.—*Managing Agent.*

ASSAM LINE.

NOTICE.

Steamers now leave Calcutta for Assam every Tuesday, Goalundo every Thursday and Debrooghur downward every Tuesday.

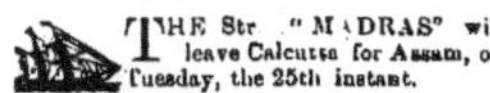

THE Str. "MADRAS" will leave Calcutta for Assam, on Tuesday, the 25th instant.

Cargo will be received at the Company's Godowns, Nimtollah Ghat, until noon of Monday, the 24th.

THE Str. "PROGRESS" single-handed will leave Goalundo for Assam on Thursday, the 27th instant.

Cargo will be received at the Company Godowns, No. 4, Fairlie Palace, up till noon of Tuesday, the 25th.

Goods forwarded to Goalundo for this vessel will be chargeable with Railway Freight from Calcutta to Goalundo in addition to the regular Freight of this Company.

Passengers should leave for Goalundo by Train of Wednesday the 26th.

CACHAR LINE NOTICE

REGULAR WEEKLY SERVICE.

Steamers now leave Calcutta for Cachar and Intermediate Stations every Tuesday and Chuttuck downward every Monday.

A Steamer and "FLAT" will leave Calcutta for Cachar on Tuesday, the 25th instant.

Cargo will be received at the Company's Godowns, Nimtollah Ghat, up till noon of Monday, the 24th.

For further information regarding rates of Freight or passage money, apply to.

4 Fairlie Palace, G. J. SCOTT,
Calcutta, 19th Jan 1876. *Secretary.*

THE CALCUTTA SCHOOL.

SESSION opened on the 10th of January, 1876 The following are the rates of fees :—

		Schooling fee.	Admission. fee.
English Department.	Rs.	2 0 0	2 0 0
Vernacular ,,	...	1 0 0	1 0 0
Juvenile Class	...	0 8 0	0 8 0

Three Scholarships of Rupees Five each are available next year, to be held by the three most distinguished students of the School who successfully pass the Entrance Examination of December, 1876. There are besides six free studentships in the Entrance class open to competition, applications for which are to be made to the undersigned before the 1st of February next.

KRISHNA BIHARI SEN, M. A.

HOMŒOPATHIC

MEDICINES.—From 4 annas per dram to—

BOXES.—Of various sizes, from 8 annas to—

BOXES.—Including Medicines, from 3 Rs. to—

Books ; Pamphlets ; Cholera-spirit Camphor ; Absolute Alcohol ; Family Guide in Bengalee and all requisites, &c. &c.

To be had at

DATTA'S HOMŒOPATHIC LABOPATORY.

No. 312, CHITPORE ROAD, BUTTOLAH, CALCUTTA.

TERMS—CASH.

BABU BASANTA KUMARA DATTA.

HOMŒOPATHIC PRACTITIONER IN CHARGE.

Printing Materials.

MILIER AND RICHARD'S PRESSE TYPES and all requisites always in Stock.

T. B. CASH
WING & CO.

ICE! ICE! ICE!

MADE IN FOUR MINUTES

THE PNEUMATIC ICE MACHINE

THIS IMPORTANT INVENTION IS CONSIDERED A BOON TO THOSE LIVING IN TROPICAL CLIMATES.

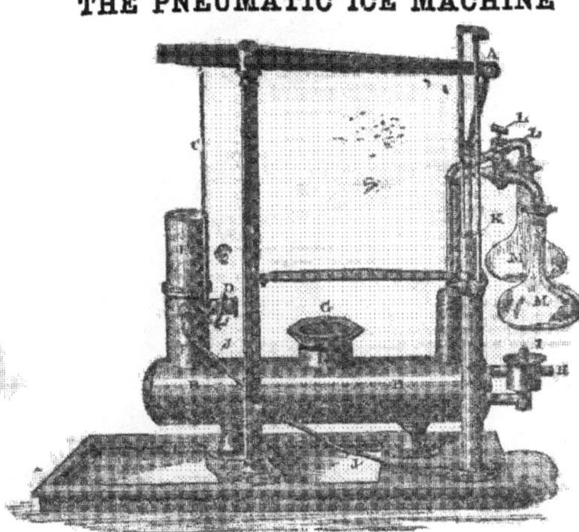

CAN BE WORKED BY THE MOST INEXPERIENCED HAND AND IS NOT LIABLE TO GET OUT OF ORDER.

From Rs. 175, each Machine complete.

MESSRS. ARLINGTON & CO.
AGENTS.

THACKER, SPINK AND CO.

BOOKSELLERS, PUBLISHERS, &c.,

No. 5, GOVERNMENT PLACE,

CALCUTTA.

THE INDIAN LAW REPORTS.

PUBLISHED UNDER AUTHORITY.

Terms of subscription, payable annually in advance:

	Without Postage.	with Postage.
From the Calcutta Series	Rs. 35	Rs. 40
" Madras Series ...	" 8	" 9
" Bombay Series ...	" 8	" 9
" Allahabad Series...	" 8	" 9
Complete set	" 45	" 50

JUST PUBLISHED.

The Regulations of the Bengal Code.

AN INDEX. By C. D. Field, Esq., M. A., LL.D., of the Inner Temple Barrister-at-Law. Extra large 8vo. cloth, price, Rs. 21.

THE FIFTH EDITION.

The Code of Criminal Procedure,

And other Laws and Rules of Practice relating to Procedure in the Criminal Courts of British India. With Notes containing the Opinions delivered by all the Superior Local Courts. By H. T. Prinsep, Esq., Bengal Civil Service, in Super Royal Octavo, Price, Rs. 16 cash, Rs. 18 credit; packing and postage, Rs. 1-8.

Manual of Surveying for India

Detailing the mode of Operations on the Trigonometrical, Topographical, and Revenue Surveys of India, compiled by Col. H. L. Thuillier and Lieut.-Col. R. Smyth. Third Edition, Revised and Enlarged. Rs. 16, or including Postage, Rs. 17-4. Credit, Rs. 18.

The Arian Witness:

OR THE TESTIMONY OF ARYAN SCRIPTURES,

In confirmation of Sacred History and Christian Doctrine, with dissertations on the primitive seat and early adventures of INDO-ARYANS. By REV. K. M. BANERJEA. *One volume 8vo., in paper covers, Rs. 3-4, in cloth lettered, Rs. 4.*

The Companion Reader

TO MESSRS. ROWE & WEBB'S

Hints on Study of English

WITH NOTES.—Price Rs. 3-8-0.

A FEW COPIES ONLY LEFT.

HOG HUNTING in LOWER BENGAL, Eight Chromolithograph Illustration. By **Percy Carpenter,** large folio, reduced price, Rs. 12.

FOR SALE.

Law Journal Reports

ANALYTICAL DIGEST Law Journal of Cases reported in all the Courts and the Law Journal Reports, old and new series, from the year 1822 to 1868, in 75 Volumes, 58 of which are bound in full Law calf, Rs. 750.

NOW READY

A Guide to the

SUBORDINATE CIVIL SERVICE EXAMINATIONS.

INCLUDING a Selection from Questions set in previous Examinations, and the orders of Government on the subject; together with a list of the names of Successful candidates in former years and the appointments which they now hold under Government. Compiled by W. H. Grimley, B. A. (CAMB.), B C S Superintendent of Subordinate Civil Service Examinations; and Secretary to the Central Examination Committee. Price, Rs. 4 Packing and Postage, As. 6. Calcutta:—Thacker, Spink and Co.

!!! हुक्का !!!

!!! HOOKAHS !!!

ENGLISH made Hookahs of various choice designs, colours and sizes ranging in price from Rs. 2 to 5 each, 60 designs to choose from. Apply to

RADANAUTH CHOWDRY,
878, Jorasanko

THE INDIAN MIRROR

THE CHEAPEST DAILY PAPER

IN

INDIA

AND

HAVING AN EXTENSIVE CIRCULATION

SUBSCRIPTIONS.

	TOWN.	MOFUSSIL. Including Postage
Yearly ...	Rs. 15 0 0	Rs. 26 [illegible]
Half yearly ...	" 8 8 0	" 11 8 0
Quarterly ...	" 2 8 0	" 6 0 0
Monthly ...	" 1 1 0	" 2 5 0

Cash sales, One Anna per copy.

Sunday Edition.

STRICTLY IN ADVANCE.

Per Annum ... ... Rs. 5

MOFUSSIL SUBSCRIBERS.

Per Annum ... ... Rs. 5 10 0

VIA SOUTHAMPTON	£ S. D.	VIA BRINDISI.	£ S. D.
Per Annum	0 13 9	Per Annum	1 7 0

Cash sales, Two Annas per copy.

RATE OF ADVERTISING.

First insertion, 5 lines and under, 1 Rupee.

Second and succeeding insertions, 2 Annas per line.

For Advertisements which are to be inserted for a considerable time special contracts may be made on application to the Manager.

Domestic Occurrences	Non-Subscriber	... 1 Re.
	Subscriber	... 8 Ans.
Public Engagement each insertion		... 1 Re.

FOR SALE,

AT THE BRAHMO SOMAJ OF INDIA

MISSION OFFICE,

No 13, Mirzapore Street.

	Rs.	As.	P.
Sacred Anthology ...	2	0	0
Last Days of Rajah Ram Mohun Roy ...	1	0	0
Essays, Theological and Ethical ...	1	0	0
Historical Sketch of the Brahmo Somaj	0	6	0
Jesus Christ, Europe and Asia ...	0	3	4
Future Church ...	0	3	0
Lecture at the Brahmo School ...	0	1	0
True Faith ...	0	2	0
Appeals to Young India ...	0	0	6
Brahmo Somaj Vindicated ...	0	2	0
Popular Tracts, Nos. 1 to 4 ...	0	2	0
Destiny of Human Life ...	0	2	0
Reconstruction of Native Society ...	0	1	6
Welcome Soiree in England ...	0	1	6
Lecture on Inspiration ...	0	4	0
Essential Principles of Brahma Dharma	0	1	0
Proceedings of the Marriage Law meeting at the Town Hall ...	0	2	
Theistic Annual 1872 ...	0	8	0
Ditto Ditto 1873 ...	0	8	0
Ditto Ditto 1874 ...	1	0	6
Ditto Ditto 1875 ...	1	0	6
Lecture on Progress of Theism ...	0	2	0
Ditto Age of Enlightenment ...	0	3	0
Life of Educated Native ...	0	2	0
Lecture on Marriage Law ...	0	2	0
Ditto on the Jumna ...	0	2	0
Man the Son of God ...	0	1	0
Order of Service ...	0	1	0
Prayers for Different Occasions of Life	0	3	0
Divine Service for Hindus ...	0	1	0
Theistic Devotions ...	0	5	0
Behold the Light of Heaven in India ...	0	3	6
Epistles to the Theists in India ...	0	0	6
Lecture on Prayer ...	0	1	6
Ditto Alcohol ...	0	2	0
JUST RECEIVED FROM ENGLAND.			
Practical Sermons ... Rs.	0	12	0
Memoir of Rev. Dr Carpenter ...	0	12	0
Morning and Evening Meditations ...	0	12	6
Channing's Perfect Life ...	1	0	0

A FASHIONABLE high wheeled Cappin Buggy by Dykes and Co., with silver plated mountings, quite new. Apply 12 Bentinck Street. 9384.

SMITH STANISTREET & CO.

Pharmaceutical Chemists & Druggists

BY APPOINTMENT

To His Excellency the Right Hon'ble

LORD NORTHBROOK, G.M.S.I.,

Governor-General of India,

&c., &c.,

SYRUP of Lactate of Iron. Prepared from the original recipe, Lactate of Iron, in various forms of preparation, has been in use in France, and generally through the Continent of Europe, for some years past, and is highly esteemed as one of the most valuable Chalybeate Tonic Remedies yet introduced. The Syrup being the most agreeable as well as convenient form of administration, is in most general use.

It is a most valuable remedy in the following diseases:—Chlorosis or Green Sickness, Leucorrhœa, Neuralgia, Enlargement of the Spleen, &c. In combination with quinine, it has also been very successfully used in the cure of Fever, while to persons of delicate constitution, or enfeebled by disease, it is invaluable. In bottles, Rs. 2 each.

Syrup of the Phosphate of Iron, Rs. 2 per bottle.

Syrup of Phosphate of Iron and Strychnine, Rs. 2 per bottle.

Syrup of Phosphate of Iron and Quinine, Price Rs. 2-8 per bottle.

Syrup of Phosphate of Iron, Quinine and Strychnine, (Dr. Aitkin's Triple Tonic Syrup.) Rs. 2-8 per bottle.

Smith, Stanistreet & Co.

Invite special attention to the following rates, the quality guaranteed as the best procurable:—

Pure Ærated Waters.

Made from Pure Water, obtained by the new process through the Patent Charcoal Filters.

		Rs.	As.
Ærated plain (Treble Ærated), per doz. ...		0	12
Soda Water	ditto ...	0	12
Gingerade	ditto ...	1	4
Lemonade	ditto ...	1	4
Tonic (Quinine)	ditto ...	2	4

The Cash must be sent with the order to obtain advantage of the above rates.

TO CLEAR OFF STOCK

J. DAVIS & Co.

Are selling their Wool Wrappers

HALF PRICE

No. 6 Government Place, Calcutta.

Ulcerations of all kinds

There is no medicinal preparation which may be so thoroughly relied upon in the treatments of the above ailments as Hollways Ointment. Nothing can be more simple and safe than the manner in which it is applied, nothing more salutary than its action on the body, both locally and constitutionally. The Ointment rubbed round the part affected enters the pores as salt penetrates meat. It quickly penetrates to the core of the evil and drive it from the system

Printed and published by M. M. Rukhit, at the "Indian Mirror" Press, No 15, College Square, for the Proprietor.

The Indian Mirror.

SUNDAY EDITION.

VOL. XV] CALCUTTA, SUNDAY, JANUARY 30, 1876 {REGISTERED AT THE GENERAL POST OFFICE.} [NO. 24

CONTENTS.

NOTICE.

Letters and all other communications relating to the literary department of the Paper should be addressed to "The Editor."

All letters on the business of the Press should be addressed, and all remittance made payable to the Manager of this Paper. Particular attention is solicited to this notice.

Subscribers will be good enough to give prompt notice of any delay, or irregularity in delivery of the Paper.

Editorial Notes.

WE are glad to learn that the scheme of the Albert Hall, which has in view the sacred object of promoting good feelings among the various sections of the divided community of Calcutta, is steadily progressing. The subscriptions already aggregated Rs. 21,500, including Maharani Sarnamai's contribution amounting to Rs. 1,000.

Is it true that "ministers of the Church of England are not very scrupulous about the use of other sermons than their own?" This decidedly serious accusation we find in an American paper. The writer facetiously suggests that the Anglican minister who purloins the product of other people's brains ought for consistency's sake to be very careful that "what he steals is in the regular succession." "How careless," continues the writer, "was Rev. George H. Connor, Vicar of Newport, Isle of Wight, England, when he selected the discourse which he preached at the funeral of the celebrated Bishop of Winchester. July 27, 1873, Rev. W. H. H. Murray, of Boston, now reveals the fact that this identical sermon was preached by himself to his own Park Street congregation in 1871. The vicar probably obtained the sermon in the Apostolic market, and was not aware of its origin. What a shock will he now experience when he learns that on an occasion so solemn, where even the shadow of irregularity would be a desecration, he actually preached one of Mr. Murray's sermons! O! O! It was cruel in Mr. Murray to publish the fact."

WE are glad to find Christian missionaries are awaking to the necessity of handling the faith of other religionists with some delicacy. We met a well-known Methodist preacher the other day, who although he did not seem to like "the partiality," as he called it, which we showed to the "idolators" said, he himself was never very hard with "those idolators." This forbearance is indeed creditable, and is perhaps the beginning of better things. "The gospel to the heathen," according to the good old orthodox sense of Dr. Duff, meant the good news brought to our nation by philanthropic bodies of missionary gentlemen that we are every one of us doomed to damnation, that our forefathers, those grand old Aryans, have gone to hell whence they have no opportunity of making an escape, even if they be willing to enter the fold of the Free Church of Scotland. A writer in the last number of the *Calcutta Review* says that the proclamation of this preliminary message of damnation has done more to alienate the Hindu people from Christianity than anything else. Perhaps it has. But enthusiastic missionaries think that no effective appeal can be made to the susceptible feelings of the Hindu unless he is informed in good strong language that he is born and bred in corruption, that damnation is his natural inheritance. Fire, brimstone, sulphur, blood and all other adjuncts of orthodox Christianity are perhaps matters, in which Western imaginations take delight. Gunpowder mitrailleuse petroleum and other amiable objects producing extensive bloodshed in Christian countries constitute the earthly counterparts of unearthly realities. To our people the smell of burnt gunpowder is disagreeable, and Hindu requires altogether less savoury articles, we venture to affirm, to build up his faith in the truth, and beneficence of the Christian religion. We hope these will be forthcoming in time. And when charity is extended to the "heathen," the Brahmos too may enjoy the benefit of the act.

ATTEMPTS have been made from time to time with more or less success, to collect accurate statistics regarding the total number of Brahmo families in India, that are prepared to apply the highest principles of reform to social and domestic life. Desirable as such information is, we do not think it is yet within our reach or is likely to be for some time to come. We hope, however, persevering efforts will eventually achieve the object in view. The Secretary of the Prarthana Somaj in Bombay has sent round a circular on this subject to the various Brahmo Somajes, which we give below:—"Dear Sir,—I take the liberty of forwarding to you a few copies of the accompanying statement with a view to ascertain how many Brahma families there are belonging to your Somaj, which have adopted or are prepared to adopt reformed social rule consistent with the principles of Theism, and to obtain such particulars of them as may be of use to similar families located in other places. It is intended that when the statements sent to different places have been received back duly filled in, the information should be printed in the form of a pamphlet, a copy of which will be supplied to every one whose name is included therein at cost price on his applying for the same. I need hardly say that a pamphlet as the one indicated above is calculated to prove very useful to reformed Brahmas desirous of forming themselves into an organized body for social purposes and of rendering assistance to each other; and I trust you will be so good as to have the enclosed form filled in by all your progressive friends and return the same to me as early as practicable. It may be explained that by the expression "reformed social rules," used in the statement is meant the eschewing of all that is idolatrous, superstitious, or injurious in the social customs of our forefathers and supplying what is wanted—i.e., prayers and thanksgivings to God in connection with all the social rites and ceremonies that may be adopted by Brahmas."

THE following proclamation was lately issued by the President of the United States:—"In accordance with a practice at once wise and beautiful, we have been accustomed, as the year is drawing to a close, to devote an occasion to the humble expression of our thanks to Almighty God for the ceaseless and distinguished benefits bestowed upon us as a nation, and for His mercies and protection during the closing year.

Amid the rich and free enjoyment of all our advantages, we should not forget the source from whence they are derived, and the extent of our obligations to the Father of all mercies. We have full reason to renew our thanks to Almighty God for favors bestowed upon us during the past year.

By His continuing mercy civil and religious liberty have been maintained; peace has reigned within our borders; labor and enterprise have produced their merited rewards and to His watchful providence we are indebted for security from pestilence and other national calamity.

Apart from national blessing each individual among us has occasion to thoughtfully recall and devoutly recognize the favors and protection which he has enjoyed. Now, therefore,

I, Ulysses S. Grant, President of the United States, do recommend that on Thursday, the 25th day of November the people of the United States, abstaining from all secular pursuits, and from their accustomed avocations, do assemble in their respective places of worship, and in such form as may seem most appropriate in their own hearts, offer to Almighty God their acknowledgments and thanks for His mercies, and their humble prayers for a continuance of His Divine favor.

In witness whereof I have hereunto set my hand and caused the seal of the United States, to be affixed.

Done in the City of Washington, this 27th day of October, in the year of our Lord, one thousand eight hundred and seventy-five, and of the independence of the United States the one hundredth.

U. S. GRANT.

THE SURE AND UNSURE GROUND OF THEISM.

(Continued from last Sunday's Mirror.)

(Continued from last Sunday's Mirror.)

IF then it be true that Theism, as it is now grounded, cannot satisfy the deepest demands of humanity, and that it requires a surer foundation, the foundation of Revealed Truth, it is necessary now to ask what is that Revelation of which I speak? You have been warned already that it is not, and cannot be a book, or a miracle, or a man in the usual sense of these words. Books are good, as records of God's dealings with mankind, miracles have a purpose, often a very profound one, men are essential for the progress, and sanctification of our race. But neither book, nor miracle, nor man can bring about the universal reconciliation necessary in the religious world. One thing is all-important here, the one great thing needful. There must be a REVELATION OF GOD'S WILL. Nothing will explain the ultimate mysteries of creation except the secrets of the Divine will, revealed in the heart of the faithful prophet, God alone can solve the last doubts about himself. And the final solution is the final wisdom of faith. Faith is either the knowledge of belief, or the knowledge of sight. The knowledge that comes from belief, on account of man's weakness and imperfections, is seldom competent to remove all questionings. The knowledge that comes from sight is clear and conclusive like the light, and forms the maturity of wisdom. Blessed is he whose faith has become sight, the sight of the deep secrets of God. But such faith is not possible to all. It is possible to him only who has known and carried out the will of God. His will is his existence. Everything else passes away, only the Divine will never passes away. He who has known and felt God's will in all things which he has come across, has found all that is worth finding in the intricate pathways of life. That is the one thing fixed amidst the fluent phenomena of the world. Philosophy is cognizant of the latter, and finds but the faint indication of a Life of Mystery beyond. Faith is cognizant of that Life, but never grasps its full meaning till the Living Will comes, touches it, and unseals its secrets. There flies away all doubting, then the grey twilight of dawning belief blazes as the midday sun, God seeks out the erring soul, the soul meets its approaching God in the fulness of His own light. He to whom God's mind lies revealed is taught from sources beyond his own nature. His religion, in the only sense of that word, is *supernatural.* Thrice blessed is that man in whom this glorious susceptibility of faith is awakened, and to whom the wisdom of the Divine will is made known.

What is sin? Man's will as opposed to the Saviour's. What is salvation? The doing of the Father's will as it is done in heaven. Ten thousand penances and performances of good work will not save a man. But a single bowing of the head will save him. Bowing of the head to what? To the Father's will. The clinging stain, plague-spot of sin, will not be washed out by all the sacraments of all the religions, by all the blood that has been shed by saints and martyrs, by all the tears of repentance that have been or shall ever be shed. Be you well assured of that. Let the sinner in all his concerns of life know the supreme will of the Saviour first; let the Divine purpose reveal itself, and enlighten all the dark corners of his being, the seats of selfishness, of lustfulness, the crooked by-ways of habit and imagination, and then let him commence the accomplishment of that Purpose. Is it known to you that even your sins may hasten the day of your salvation? As doubt aids the maturity of faith, so sin aids the attainment of salvation. Only you must have a proper sense of your sins. But nothing can give you that stinging sense of your unrighteousness, but the revelation of the Holy Spirit. Before that Pure and Perfect Witness the guilty soul pales, and shrinks into miserable littleness. Before the magnitude and majesty of the Will, which conscience tremblingly lays down as the absolute law of obedience and salvation, the sinner takes the vow of eternal allegiance. And then there is reconciliation. In spite of a thousand weaknesses and errors there is reconciliation between the sinner and the Saviour. And His grace is sufficient for us. Every true step of progress in sanctity is beyond one's own self. Self-will, which means the law of sin, yields itself to be crucified on the Rock of Ages, the will of God that never passes away. May the will of the All-holy God be revealed unto us, in every walk, in every concern, in every imperfection of this our frail life, and may live-long and eternal obedience to that Will be the stronghold of our peace unto salvation.

And we come lastly to consider the point of true brotherhood. All organization is vanity which stands not on the revealed purposes of Heaven. Why should we unite, why should we form ourselves into a church, what is there to attract men to each other? Is not every man competent to worship, serve, and find his Maker? What need is there for men to love and serve each other? The need becomes apparent when it is viewed in the light of revelation. The Supreme Purpose is revealed in its completeness not in one man, but in a group of figures, each one of which stands in a peculiar point of light. Perhaps one single soul cannot throw itself in all the possible attitudes through which the voice of revelation can send forth its blessed notes. The secrets of God are suited to the peculiar constitution of each of those who are called. And the servants of God must bow to, and learn from one another. Honor and glory to the will of God as manifested in each, means honor and glory to Him who is glorified in his servants. This essential relationship between the different sides of the Divine will, represented in the characters of leading men, forms the fundamental necessity of brotherhood and church-organization. Till the true brotherhood, and the true church be formed, God's will in its completeness will not be known to the world. Sure brotherhood means nothing more than true priesthood, and priesthood means nothing more than the true sonship and servantship of God. The poet is called the priest of nature because he has a ready ear for the secret harmonies of creation, harmonies to which others are deaf the philosopher is called the priest of knowledge because he has penetrated the veil and discovered the secrets of the temple of science. I ask why should not that man be called the true priest of religion who has had accorded to him the rare privilege of uplifting the veil that covers things divine from the unhallowed gaze of ordinary mortals, and penetrated into the depths of the revelation of the awful will of God? Those men to whom these secrets of Heaven are known, fall into an unconscious and loving fraternity. Their brotherhood is the typical brotherhood of all men in ages to come, their mutual love is the love of the Kingdom of Heaven. Can the mere benevolence and good offices of the world's religion produce such love and brotherhood? Else the world would not be a hotbed of factions and heart-burnings. Men who will love each other and form the church and brotherhood of the future, seek ye first the revelation of the will of God in each other, and then obey and honor it. How this will is be revealed in the Brahmo Somaj at the present time, remains to be seen. From what has been said, it must not be inferred that the Divine will has not been revealed in this world in times gone by. In all the prominent religions of mankind it has been manifested more or less fully. But inasmuch as our God is a living and active Personality, this will never ceases, but advances with the advance of our race. Every upward stage of human progress brings man face to face with the continually ascending regions of God's eternal purpose, and we in our day can no longer rest satisfied with what our predecessors, great and holy as they were, achieved before us. Nor is the will of God the same as before. Unchanging in its end and aim, the will of our Father often changes in its manifestations. And they are wise who wait and watch for new light at each successive age. What shall be the ground, and light of revelation for Theism? Reverently and humbly shall we attempt to forecast the future. In other religions it was one man only who found the light of revelation and dispensed it unto his followers and friends. In Theism the growth of men in light and salvation shall be simultaneous and inter-dependent. Not that the innate differences of human nature are to be ignored, not that the necessary relationship of the superior and the inferior is to be violated,—the central and surrounding figures must be duly associated, the leaders and followers arranged, but the revelation of God's will must come to all alike, and salvation must mean common progress, common spirituality and mutual service. The world is to be delivered from the evils of hearsay revelation, borrowed spirituality, of partial grace. All mankind will, in the end, form one priesthood, one brotherhood, one church, and find in the all-embracing revelation of the Supreme Will, their doubts reconciled, their sins forgiven, and their differences harmonized for ever. Amen!

Provincial

SYLHET.

[FROM OUR OWN CORRESPONDENT.]

The 20th January 1876.

THE Sylhet Sky Races commenced on the 18th instant. The Races will continue for three days. Several Tea Planters from the Mofussil have come to the station to take part in them.

The cultivators here could not obtain a good harvest this time as the late inundation did considerable damage to the crops.

To call for explanations from his subordinates is a great hobby with our Deputy Commissioner. Where asking a verbal question may very well serve the purpose, the Deputy Commissioner will make his subordinates write same half a sheet of paper quite unnecessarily. Cannot our Deputy Commissioner, to some extent, leave off this irksome practice?

We are very sorry to notice the death of Babu Rash Bihari Dutta, a well-known Native gentleman of this place. He was laboring under a complicated disease from a long time. He distinguished himself greatly by establishing an English School which is called after his name. His school was converted last year into a higher class one, and out of six boys sent up for the last Entrance Examination, three passed in the third division; but for want of proper management owing to the protracted illness of Rash Bihari Babu, the school reverted to its former status (middle class) from the 1st of January. The name of the Babu was conspicuously mentioned among others by the late Lieutenant-Governor, Sir George Campbell, in his Educational Minute for the year 1872-73. He was an Honorary Magistrate as also a member of all the local Committees.

The result of the Zillah School at the last Entrance Examination is not so good as on previous years. Out of six candidates sent up, only three have been successful, one in the 2nd and two in the 3rd Division.

We are very glad to find in our midst Babu Krishna Kumar Sen, who has lately come here from Mymensingh as an Extra Assistant Commissioner. The Babu is an excellent man, and we understand is a staunch follower of Brahmoism. We beg to draw his attention to the wretchedness of the local Brahmo Somaj and hope he will adopt some means to arouse the members from their long lethargy.

Devotional.

LET my salvation, O Lord, and that of others like me, bear witness to the truth of my religion. The world is then only convinced when they behold sinners saved. Let my life be a sufficient testimony unto myself of thy grace. Lord, give unto me peace in the midst of my struggles, strength to overcome my feebleness, and purity of will to be obedient and faithful to thee. Let my salvation be a miracle unto me, and unto all others who know me. Save me in thy power, O good Lord.

VOUCHSAFE unto me perfect pure-mindedness, O Lord, in relation to the other sex. O let the chastity of thy sight, feeling, thought, and imagination be able to bear the utmost scrutiny of thy all-seeing eye. Purify to the utmost all my relations with my wife, my sisters, and all those who inherit the holy attribute of thy motherhood. Let all carnality be banished for ever from my heart, which do thou condescend to make thy pure habitation. I am unfit yet, O Lord, to associate with thy daughters, because I have not known the right attitude of mind towards them. When wilt thou make me fit to be a member of thy household, where thy children, both sons and daughters, all reside in perfect peace and purity! O thou Holy One, deliver me not only from the evil of temptation, but make all temptation impossible to me.

MY son, drink always of the fountain of my purity, let my holiness be as a crown unto thee, and rejoice in my righteousness without hesitation. In my holy household I will make a place for thee, where thou shalt abide for ever. Amen!

The Brahmo Somaj.

OUR book of theistic texts, called *Sloka Sangraha* has reached its second edition. It is considerably enlarged, though we must say we wish it was larger and still more comprehensive. Texts have been taken from the following departments of the Hindu Shastras:—Rigveda; Yajurveda; all the Upanishads; Manu; Yogavashishta; Mahabharata; Vishnu Puran; Brahmanda Puran; Bhagvat, and Mahanirvan Tantra. There are extracts also from the Jewish scriptures; Christian scriptures; the Koran; and the Zend Avesta. All these texts are accompanied by suitable translations.

ON the occasion of the last anniversary the following new books were published:—The Theistic Annual for 1876; the enlarged and complete edition of the Sangit Pustaka, or book of Brahmo Somaj hymns; the second and enlarged edition of the biographical sketch of Dhruba and Prahlada; and the account of Fakir Bayajid.

RETROSPECT.

(Theistic Annual.)

THE last year has passed away in practices of penance and self-sacrifice. The trials and troubles of the preceding twelvemonth left to the Brahmo community the legacy of a lawsuit which entailed as much expense of money as the time and energy, adding to all a weight of anxiety which those only can sympathize with who have been placed under similar circumstances.

What the result has been is known to the public. The libellers were compelled in open court to render an unqualified apology for the cruel wrong they did to our cause, and our object being nothing more than public clearance of our character, the apology was accepted.

The leaders and missionaries of the Brahmo Somaj identify themselves so closely with the body of their co-religionists that they have never refused to bear the burden of the faults which may be justly laid to the doors of the community they represent. After their trouble and persecution therefore they commenced among themselves a fresh course of self-examination, and devotional exercises, reflection, and mutual communion, such as might lead them to detect and remedy the inherent deficiencies of their sense and their character. Arduous devotion led to earnest self-discipline, and self-discipline led to the establishment of certain forms and practices in which the spirit naturally embodied itself. Thus grew first the beginnings of what was subsequently termed Asceticism in the Brahmo Somaj. A great deal has been said about it already. There has been misunderstanding which you have tried to remove, with what effect we cannot say. The whole subject of Asceticism in connection with our movement is identical with strict moral and spiritual self-discipline for the control of the lower passions, and the development of the highest purity of character. We have never separated it from the cultivation of the tenderest feelings for the happiness and good of others, and an enthusiastic discharge of the every-day duties of life.

Some of our missionaries have been active during the year. The following places have been visited: Bhaugulpore, Monghyr, Bankipore, Hazaribag, Ranchi, and Gya in Behar; Benares, Allahabad, Cawnpore, Lucknow, and Delhi in the N. W. Provinces; Lahore, Simla and some of the intermediate stations in the Punjab; Jubbulpore in Central India; and Bombay in Western India. In Orissa, Cuttack was visited, and also Puri, where there is the great shrine of Juggernath. In East Bengal, Dacca, Mymensing, Sylhet, and Chittagong have been visited, and our agents also went to Gowhati, Nowgong, Shillong, Tezpur, and Gowalpara in Assam. In West Bengal, Burdwan, Rampur Hat, Azimgunge, Murshidabad, and Berhampur have received our preachers. So on the whole a long tract of country, has been traversed by our missionaries, whose reports we publish elsewhere.

If we reflect upon our institutions we cannot say that the Bharat Asram has made any progress during the last year. Though there are daily services as before, and the missionaries reside there, the spirit of the institution may be said on the whole to have declined. The inmates have made a certain amount of progress, and seem disinclined to advance further. The number of inmates however holds steady, there being fifty-one persons still living in it without counting the servants. Some attempt has been made during the past year to impart elementary moral and religious instructions to the boys and girls here, and also to add to their number a few from the outside. What the results are to be, time only can show.

The Brahmo Nikatan, of which we could not give a very favorable report last year, has improved under the new management. The arrangements are good, and the superintendence strict and efficacious. The number of Brahmo students living in the Niketan is at present twenty-six.

As evidence of foreign synathy we must acknowledge the friendly greetings we have received at different times from such persons as Mr. Charles Voysey, Mr. Moncure D. Conway, Miss F. P. Cobbe, Miss Collet, and Mr. R. Spears, the Secretary to the British and Foreign Unitarian Association all of whom show unabated good will and friendship. Mr. Walter Thomson, an influential landowner in Behar, who had lately been on a visit to England, presented to the Brahmo Somaj, in consultation evidently with Mr. Conway, two hundered and fifty copies of the latter's able publication called Sacred Anthology, the proceeds of the sale of which are to be devoted to the spread of liberal ideas on theological subjects among the people of this country. The British and Foreign Unitarian Association also having presented to us a large number of their publications and so have the Swedenborgian Society. Our best thanks are due to all these bodies for the valuable and practical sympathy they have thus manifested. About the latter end of the year we were favored with the visit of Count D'Alvella, member of the Council of Brabant, who has rendered the cause of Theism great service in the Continent of Europe by a report of the present theistic operations in London in the *Revue des Deux Mondes*. It is to be expected we shall now have a report of theistic operations in India.

The Mission Fund shows signs of prosperity. The contributions received last year for the support of the families of the missionaries were liberal. Many of the Brahmo missionaries were confined to Calcutta for various reasons, and so the expense of providing for their necessaries fell upon the Mission Office, thus adding to the cost of supporting their families. But in spite of their increased expense the original debt of the Mission Office has suffered no increase. The plan of inviting contributions in the shape not of money, but of food and clothing, has answered very well. A considerable quantity of rice and clothing has thus been received. This method of assisting the missionaries with the necessary articles of life creates a close bond of union between the givers and receivers. And our best thanks are due to those from whom such help has been obtained. In the missionary families, whom we have now to support, there are 12 men, 10 women, 15 boys and girls, and 9 infants, averaging in all to 46 souls. There are besides these two Brahmo missionary families supported out of their own paternal property.

If, in the face of such encouragement, we have not been able to advance as well as we should have done, the fault belongs entirely to ourselves. We can but hope and trust that in future years we may make a more fitting use of the advantages placed in our way, and be more worthy of the abundant grace which a Merciful Providence has showered on us. Our leaders are not satisfied with the amount of work we have been able to do, and we ourselves humbly acknowledge our shortcomings. May God strengthen our hands, purify our hearts, and elevate our souls, may we serve Him better, and more faithfully, in the blessed new year into which we enter to-day.

Literary.

PROFESSOR MONIER WILLIAMS visited the *Tols* of the Pundits of Bhatparah and Nuddea in Bengal.

DR. NORMAN CHEVERS, the able and respected Principal of the Medical College, is going away soon from India. In his last report submitted to the Director of Public Instruction, he writes:—

"In 1861-62 the total strength of pupils was 409. When the Bengali class was removed in November 1873, it had augmented to 1,441. Last session the strength of the English class alone was 504. In 1861-62 the schooling fees amounted to Rs. 1,842-8, in 1873-74 they were Rs. 35,136-8-0, not including those of the Bengali classes for four months. Last session the fees received from the English class alone amounted to Rs. 24,695. In 1861-62 the number of paying students was 33, in 1873-74 it was 1,076. I submit these results with pleasure, but without any wish to claim more than my due share of credit for bringing them about. These results were to be foreseen. The college was made over to me by my predecessors, Drs. Eatwell and Partridge, in admirable working order. My colleagues have always been a body of the most eminent medical men of their time, any one of whom, standing alone, would have given importance and reputation to the school. They have worked with me like brothers up to this day. Nearly all my assistants have been the very persons whom I would select, if I had to perform this very laborious and responsible duty over again. All that I claim for myself is, that I have worked as hard as any one of the staff to the best of my ability." But we hope what Dr. Chevers has not been able to say out of pure modesty will be said in loud and prolonged chorus by his numerous students from every part of the country. It is enough to say that, than Dr. Norman Chevers there are few more admired by the educated classes or who have done more to make the English name respected in this country.

The Week

PROFESSOR MONIER WILLIAMS after having stopped for a day at Lucknow, left for Agra on Monday last.

A GREAT agitation is being made in Madras for the employment of East Indias as sailors.

AMONG other amusements provided by the Maharajah of Cashmere at Jammu for H. R. H. the Prince of Wales, was a dance by some Llamas.

THE report of the Civil Service Grievances' Committee has been submitted to Government, the only dissentient member being Mr. Hope.

LORD LYTTON is expected to arrive in Calcutta on the 2nd April next *via* Bombay.

SIR LOUIS MALLET is obliged by ill-health to leave India at once. By next Monday's Mail steamer he returns home from Bombay.

THE *Pioneer* says that Sh Richard Meade came to Calcutta to discuss Hyderabad affairs in general with the Viceroy.

LATEST NEWS.

THE Government of India has taken the conduct of Khelat affairs out of the hands of Sir William Merewether, Commissioner of Sind.

THE *East* reports that Lord Ulick Browne, Commissioner of the Presidency Division, will shortly go on leave, and that Mr. H. Cockerell, from Dacca, will officiate for him.

THERE were about fifty Chiefs and Sirdars from the Southern Maratha Country present to receive His Excellency the Governor of Bombay at Kolapore, Rao Saheb Bal Parushram Shastri, the Deputy Educational Inspector of the Southern Division, read the address of welcome.

IT is said that during the absence on leave to England of Baron De H. Larpent, the Judge and Sessions Judge of Poona, and Agent for the Sirdars in the Deccan, Mr. W. H. Newnham, Barrister-at-Law and Judge of Ahmedabad, will be appointed to officiate for him.

THE King of Siam has adopted a peculiar method to secure his personal safety. He puts not his trust in man but in woman. He has a woman sentinel.

MR. DINSHAW MANECKJI PETIT is going to contribute a large sum towards the erection of a Brokers' Hall at Bombay.

THE *Pioneer* understands that it is not in contemplation to fill up, immediately, the vacancy in the Legislative Council which will arise when the Hon'ble Asheley Eden leaves India.

WHEN Captain W. F. Prideaux proceeds to the Persian Gulf to officiate for Colonel Ross as Resident, Mr. F. C. Daukes, C. S., Senior Attache in the Foreign Office, will act as Assistant Secretary.

WE are very much polned to hear that Major General Margary, the father of the murdered Mr. Margary, of the Bhamo expedition, has died from the effects of the shock received by him by the intelligence of his son's assassination. Poor Major General Margary had appealed to the English community sometime ago, through the columns of the *Times*, for satisfaction of his son's blood; but in vain, and we are afraid this preyed upon his mind too much.

ENGLAND seems to be preparing herself for any threatened wars. An increase in the Army Estimates will be asked for, when the Parliament meets next month.

THE success of the Native entertainment at Lahore to H. R. H. the Prince of Wales was chiefly due to the Maharajah of Kuppurthalla who contributed mostly to it. Most of the Punjab Chiefs were present; the little Rajah of Chumba was seated on the knee of Sir Henry Davies and the son of the Rajah of Faridkote at H. R. H.'s feet on the dais. Those Native gentlemen who had not attended the Levee, were presented to H. R. H. here. After the ordinary presentations were over, certain selected Chiefs were called up by the Secretary to the Punjab Government and invested by his Royal Highness with a medal commemorative of his visit. Amongst the recipients of this honor were the distinguished architect of the noble building in which the entertainment took place, Rai Mul Sing, Mahommad Hyat Khan, C. S. I., Sahib Khan, Tiwana, C. S. I., Moti Lall, E. A. C. and Gholam Mahommad Khan, Khagwani, E. A. C., the brother of the British envoy at the Court of Cabul.

THE only Talukdar of Oudh who had the honor of receiving presents and a private interview from the Prince of Wales, at Lucknow, was the Maharajah of Bulrampore who was presented with a gold medal commemorative of His Royal Highness' visit to India, and also a diamond ring of great beauty. We hear that except the Maharajah of Bulrampore, Rajah Amir Hossain and the late Sir Rajah Maun Sing's heir, the other Talukdars were not admitted even to the *fete* given to the Prince at Lucknow. Sir George Couper's administration of Oudh is proving too galling to the Talukdars. The local journals are not very outspoken, and the Talukdars are always in fear and trembling. But we are assured that at heart they are far from satisfied with Sir George's administration. The Talukdars, under his *regime*, have been reduced almost to the position of serfs.

ON the 26th instant, after the presentation of the Municipal address to the Prince of Wales at Agra, there was a Levee. The English version of the address was read by the President, and the vernacular one by the Native Assistant Secretary. The Levee was followed by visits from the Native Princes. There was an Evening Party on the same day held by Sir John Strachey at the Fort.

The Hindu residents of the Murbar Taluka, in the Tanna District, have, according to a Tanna vernacular paper, condemned the practice of drinking, and they have also resolved to outcast those of their community who may offend in this respect.

The Viceroy and Governor-General has been pleased to confer the title of "Rajah" upon the Jaghiredar of Sundur, in the Madras Presidency, as a hereditary distinction.

The Viceroy and Governor-General has been pleased to confer the title of "Nawab" upon the Jaghiredar of Banganapalle, in the Madras Presidency, as a hereditary distinction.

The escort to be marched up to Bhamo to meet the Yunan Mission, will consist only of about 300 men, Europeans and Natives.

The battle between the Attorneys and Vakils of the Madras High Court has ended triumphantly in favor of the latter. The *Madras Standard* writes :—"The question as to whether the High Court had jurisdiction to grant the Vakils certain privileges which are denied to the Attorneys, was decided in the affirmative by the Judges of the Court. The Court held that, besides the perfect legality of the arrangement, it was for the interests of the public that Vakils should be allowed to practice on the Original Side of the Court, as the services of Vakils do not cost clients so much as when an Attorney and Counsel have to be engaged. No fault could be found with the Vakils as to the manner in which they had hitherto discharged their functions. The matter was thus settled. The Court's decision is not likely to allay the bad blood occasioned between these two sections of the bar, intensified as it appears to be by a spirit of race antagonism, one party being composed entirely of Natives and the other mostly of Europeans." This last circumstance is indeed most unfortunate, and must be regretted.

The present Governor of Madras is determined to turn over a new leaf in the administration of that Presidency. Already he appears to give promise of being a successful ruler. The great cause of unpopularity of the late Lord Hobart was that he spent the greater part of the year in the hills. The Duke of Buckingham, however, has resolved not to spend more than three months at Ootacamund, after which His Grace goes on a tour through some of the important districts to see things for himself. For now-a-days one of the cardinal principles of Government in India means moving about the country as much as possible.

A new Municipal Bill for Madras has just been introduced in the local Council, and, as all Municipal Bills usually do, it has evoked a great deal of opposition, especially from the Native community who are about to hold a monster meeting to protest against the Bill. Happily Madras has got no Sir Stuart Hogg for its Municipal Chairman or for a member of its Council.

The Government of India is determined to take a threatening attitude in regard to Burmah. Colonel Duncan, the Resident at Mandalay, has been ordered not to take his boots off, in the presence of the King, on any account.

There is a rumour that Sir Salar Jung intends visiting England this year, as the guest of the Duke of Sutherland. But we do not credit it. Sir Salar cannot leave Hyderabad in its present disturbed state.

The Princes' Visit.

The following telegram from Agra dated the 28th instant, appears in the *Englishman*:—

"The Prince last night visited the Taj which, together with the Gardens, was illuminated, the former by lime light, and the latter by small oil lamps and colored lanterns hung from trees. The scene was most charming and fairy-like as the lime light played on the snow-white Taj, with dark starless clouds as a background. All the fountains in the gardens were playing, and thousands of floating lights were set adrift down the river, and went off with the current. A large number of Europeans and Natives assembled. The Prince is shooting to-day in the direction of Futtehpur Sikri. A grand Ball in the Dewani-am Palace comes off to-night."

The Prince of Wales when paying a return visit to the Maharajah of Kappurthalla, presented him with two gold glasses, a signet ring, a whip, two revolvers studded with precious stones, a sword and two hydraulic machines. The Maharajah presented the Prince with five sets of armour, inlaid with gold, and a set of pure gold goblets, all manufactured at Kappurthalla.

His Royal Highness the Prince of Wales, before leaving Calcutta, transmitted to the Maharajah of Hill Tipperah a Medallion portrait of himself, which he requested the Maharajah to accept and wear as a souvenir of his visit to Bengal.

H. H. the Maharajah of Vizianagram, K.C.S.I. and the Kumar Maharajah, had the honor of an interview with, and of paying their respects to, H. R. H. the Prince of Wales, at Agra, after the conclusion of the Levee on the 26th.

Calcutta.

Mr. J. E. O'Conor has been appointed to be Assistant Secretary to the Government of India in the Statistical Branch of the Department of Revenue, Agriculture and Commerce.

The managers of the Bengal Civil Fund elected for the present year, are Messrs. Louis Jackson, C. T. Buckland, Macdonnell, O'Kinealy, and Soutiar.

Mr. C. C. Macrae has with great reluctance consented to be re-elected President of the Council of the Calcutta Public Library. Rajah Narendra Krishna Bahadur and Dr. Mahendra Lall Sarkar have been elected Vice-Presidents. The following gentlemen have been elected members of the Council for the present year :—Mr. J. C. MacGregor, Mr. G. C. Sconce, Mr. G. W. W. Barclay, Captain Waterhouse, Mr. C. T. Davis, Mr. W. H. Kirkpatrick, Mr. James Hechle, Captain W. Smith, Mr. J. K. Maclachlan, Babu Piarichand Mitra, Babu Jadunath Ghose (1), Babu Jodunath Ghose (2), and Babu Amarendranath Chattarji.

Colonel H. Hyde, R.E., Master of the Calcutta Mint, will leave for England by to-morrow's Mail steamer from Bombay.

The suggestion which the *Indo-European Correspondence* lately made "that it would be a becoming act on the part of the University authorities in Calcutta to confer a fellowship on the Rev. Fr. Lafont, has met with the general approval of the press." For ourselves, we would heartly approve of the step, if taken by the University authorities. But unobtrusive, though really deserving, men are always kept in the background.

The Coroner, with jury yesterday, viewed the body of a European, named Charles Mathewson late a discharged seaman of the *B. S. St. George*, who was stabbed with a knife by another European, named James Samuel on the 27th instant, opposite the Eden Gardens. The deceased was, after being stabbed, removed to the Presidency Jail Hospital for treatment, but he expired there yesterday morning and his body was also viewed there preliminary to the usual inquest. The delinquent will be placed before the Magistrate on Monday.

The Hon'ble Mr. Justice Phear's lecture at the last meeting of the Bethune Society, on "Property in Land in Europe and India," was a most able and interesting one. The learned lecturer treated his subject most popularly. At the conclusion of the lecture, Babu Rajendranath Mitter proposed a vote of thanks to the lecturer, and suggested the translation of the lecture into Bengali and its subsequent publication. The Rajah of Pakur who was present on the occasion, most gladly undertook to bear all the necessary expenses for the purpose.

ACKNOWLEDGMENT.

Ruttnakur, a Bengali Magazine. By Nibarun Chunder Gupta. Calcutta. 1282.

Public Engagements.

Musical Evangelistic Service.—General Litchfield (American Consul) will Deliver an address in the Free Church Institution, Nimtollah Street, this evening, 30th instant, at 8-30 o'clock. Hymns in Bengali, set to Hindu Music, will be sung.

DOMESTIC OCCURRENCE.

Birth.

Singha.—At Bharut Asrum on Tuesday the 25th January 1876 the wife of Babu Ram Chunder Singha, of a daughter.

Law

POLICE.—29th January 1876.

[*Before F. J. Marsden, Esq.*]

Constable Eastworth charged a driver of a *thika gari* with rash and negligent driving. The defendant was on conviction, sentenced to a month's rigorous imprisonment.

Messrs. Moran & Co., charged a Native with having yesterday stolen some indigo from their mart. It appeared that the defendant had attended an indigo-sale at the mart, and that while he was leaving he was challenged by the *durwan* on suspicion, and his person searched, when the indigo was found. A former conviction was proved against the defendant, and the Magistrate sentenced him to three months' rigorous imprisonment and a whipping of ten stripes.

A sailor charged two others, named Carey and Fergusson, ship mates of his, with the theft of a handkerchief containing two rupees and a cap. The complainant said that he was yesterday in their company and drank with them. While all three were returning to their vessel, Fergusson put his hand on the complainant's mouth, and Carey took out the property from the complainant's pocket. After doing this, both ran away, but the complainant lodged an information at the Thana, and the defendants were subsequently arrested on board, the handkerchief being found with Carey. Fergusson proved an alibi, which the Magistrate believed. Carey, besides being found in possession of the handkerchief, was proved by a constable to have run away when the complainant raised an alarm. His Worship discharged Fergusson, and sentenced Carey to four months' rigorous imprisonment.

The fourth officer of the *S. S. Madura* charged four Desad coolies with the theft of five bottles of brandy from a case containing twelve. It appeared that they were loading the vessel in the hold where the case of brandy was, and that two of them became insensibly drunk, and the other two half drunk. They were convicted on the evidence of Mr. M. S. Gasper, a preventive officer, and sentenced to a whipping of ten stripes each.

(*Before P. D. Dickens, Esq.*)

One Dabi Sonar charged one Gopal Sonar with the theft of a gold waist-chain, valued at Rs. 350. It appeared that the two carried on business under the same roof, and that, at 7 P. M. of the 15th, the complainant gave the defendant the chain for the purpose of cleaning it. At nine the complainant asked the other to return the chain, but the defendant, after looking for it in his box, said that somebody had stolen it. Upon this the complainant had the defendant arrested on a charge of theft. While in the custody of the police, the defendant confessed that he had himself stolen the chain, and that he had buried it in a spot opposite his shop. The spot being dug, the chain was found. The prisoner was committed to the Sessions.

Selection

A LITERARY CENTO.

[A LADY of San Francisco is said to have occupied several years in hunting up and fitting together the following thirty-eight lines, from thirty-eight English poets. The names of the authors are given against each line.]

LIFE.

Why all this toil for triumph of an hour? — *Young.*
Life's a short summer, man a flower; — *Dr. Johnson.*
By turns we catch the vital breath and die — *Pope.*
The cradle and the tomb, alas! so nigh. — *Prior.*
To be is far better than not to be, — *Sewell.*
Though all man's life may seem a tragedy; — *Spenser.*
But light cares speak when mighty griefs are dumb, — *Daniel.*
The bottom is but shallow whence they come; — *Raleigh.*
Your fate is but the common fate of all! — *Longfellow.*
Unmingled joys, here, no man befall. — *Southwell.*
Nature to each allots his proper sphere, — *Congreve.*
Fortune makes folly her peculiar care. — *Churchill.*
Custom does not often reason overrule, — *Rochester.*
And throw a cruel sunshine on a fool. — *Armstrong.*
Live well, how long or short permit to Heaven; — *Milton.*
They who forgive most shall be most forgiven. — *Bailey.*
Sin may be clasped so close we cannot see its face; — *Trench.*
Vile intercourse where virtue has not place; — *Somerville.*
Then keep each passion down, however dear, — *Thompson.*
Thou pendulum betwixt a smile and tear; — *Byron.*
Her sensual snares let faithless Pleasures lay, — *Smollett.*
With craft and skill to ruin and betray. — *Crabbe.*
Soar not too high to fall, but stoop to rise; — *Massinger.*
We masters grow of all that we despise. — *Cowley.*
Oh! then renounce that impious self-esteem; — *Beattie.*
Riches have wings and grandeur is a dream. — *Cooper.*
Think not ambition wise because 'tis brave; — *Davenant.*
The paths of glory lead but to the grave. — *Gray.*
What is ambition? 'Tis a glorious cheat; — *Willis.*
Only destruction to the brave and great. — *Addison.*
What's all the gaudy glitter of a crown? — *Dryden.*
The way to bliss lies not on beds of down. — *Quarles.*
How long we live, not years but actions tell; — *Watkins.*
That man lives twice who lives the first life well. — *Herrick.*
Make, then, while yet ye may, your God your friend, — *Mason.*
Whom Christians worship, yet not comprehend. — *Hill.*
The trust that's given guard, and to yourself be just; — *Dana.*
For, live how we can, yet die we must. — *Shakespeare.*

—*California Scrap-book.*

Advertisements

Indian General Steam Navigation Company, Limited.

SCHOENE, KILBURN & Co.—*Managing Agent.*

ASSAM LINE.

NOTICE.

Steamers now leave Calcutta for Assam every Tuesday, Goalundo every Thursday and Debrooghur downward every Tuesday.

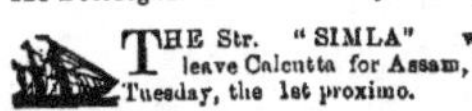

THE Str. "SIMLA" will leave Calcutta for Assam, on Tuesday, the 1st proximo.

Cargo will be received at the Company's Godowns, Nimtollah Ghat, until noon of Monday, the 31st instant.

THE Str. "MADRAS" will leave Goalundo for Assam on Thursday, the 3rd proximo.

Cargo will be received at the Company Godowns, No. 4, Fairlie Palace, up till noon of Monday, the 31st instant.

Goods forwarded to Goalundo for this vessel will be chargeable with Railway Freight from Calcutta to Goalundo in addition to the regular Freight of this Company.

Passengers should leave for Goalundo by Train of Wednesday, the 2nd proximo.

CACHAR LINE NOTICE

REGULAR WEEKLY SERVICE.

Steamers now leave Calcutta for Cachar and Intermediate Stations every Tuesday and Chuttuck downward every Monday.

A Steamer and "FLAT" will leave Calcutta for Cachar on Tuesday, the 1st proximo.

Cargo will be received at the Company's Godowns, Nimtollah Ghat, up till noon of Monday, the 31st.

For further information regarding rates of Freight or passage money, apply to

4 Fairlie Palace, G. J. SCOTT,
Calcutta, 26th Jan 1876. *Secretary.*

THE CALCUTTA SCHOOL.

SESSION opened on the 10th of January, 1876 The following are the rates of fees :—

		Schooling fee.	Admission. fee.
English Department.	Rs.	2 0 0	2 0 0
Vernacular „	...	1 0 0	1 0 0
Juvenile Class	...	0 8 0	0 8 0

Three Scholarships of Rupees Five each are available next year, to be held by the three most distinguished students of the School who successfully pass the Entrance Examination of December, 1876. There are besides six free studentships in the Entrance class open to competition, applications for which are to be made to the undersigned before the 1st of February next.

KRISHNA BIHARI SEN, M. A.

ALBERT HALL.

PATRON.

His Honor the Lieutenant Governor of Bengal.

COUNCIL.

Hon'ble Sir William Muir, K. C. S. I.—*President.*
Rajah Rama Nath Tagore Bahadur, C. S. I.—*Vice-President.*
Hon'ble Ashley Eden, C. S. I.
Archdeacon Baly.
Colonel H. E. L. Thuillier, C. S. I.
Maharajah Kumar of Bettiah.
Rajah Komul Krishna Bahadur.
Rajah Joteendro Mohun Tagore Bahadur.
Babu Digumber Mitter C. S. I.
Hon'ble Nawab Ashgar Ali Bahadur, C. S. I.
Nawab Amir Ali Bahadur.
Moulvi Abdul Latif Khan Bahadur.
Manockji Rustomji Esq.
Babu Keshub Chunder Sen.

SUBSCRIPTIONS.

His Highness Maharajah Holkar ...	Rs.	8,000
His Highness Maharajah of Jeypore	„	5,000
His Highness Maharajah of Putialah	„	2,500
Maharajah Kumar of Bettiah ...	„	2,000
Rajah of Bhinga ...	„	1,000
Maharajah of Hutwa ...	„	500
Rajah Komul Krisna Bahadur ...	„	500
Rajah Roma Nath Tagore Bahadur	„	200
Rajah Joteendro Mohun Tagore ...	„	500

M. Z. MARTIN & CO.,

THE CHINA AND JAPAN WAREHOUES MERCHANTS AND COMMISSION AGENTS.

No. 4 Dalhousie Square, East.

ICE! ICE! ICE!

MADE IN FOUR MINUTES

THE PNEUMATIC ICE MACHINE

THIS IMPORTANT INVENTION IS CONSIDERED A BOON TO THOSE LIVING IN TROPICAL CLIMATES.

CAN BE WORKED BY THE MOST INEXPERIENCED HAND AND IS NOT LIABLE TO GET OUT OF ORDER.

From Rs. 175, each Machine complete.

MESSRS. ARLINGTON & CO.

AGENTS.

REGISTERED NO 8

THACKER'S,PINK AND CO.

BOOKSELLERS, PUBLISHERS, &c.,

No. 5, GOVERNMENT PLACE.

CALCUTTA.

THE INDIAN LAW REPORTS.

PUBLISHED UNDER AUTHORITY.

Terms of subscription, payable annually in advance.

	Without Postage.	with Postage.
From the Calcutta Series	Rs. 35	Rs. 40
„ „ Madras Series ...	„ 8	„ 9
„ „ Bombay Series ...	„ 8	„ 9
„ „ Allahabad Series...	„ 8	„ 9
Complete set	„ 45	„ 50

JUST PUBLISHED.

The Regulations of the Bengal Code.

AN INDEX. By C. D. Field, Esq., M. A., LL.D., of the Inner Temple Barrister-at-Law, Extra large 8vo. cloth, price, Rs. 21.

THE FIFTH EDITION,

The Code of Criminal Procedure.

And other Laws and Rules of Practice relating to Procedure in the Criminal Courts of British India. With Notes containing the Opinions delivered by all the Superior Local Courts. By H. T. Prinsep, Esq., Bengal Civil Service, in Super Royal Octavo. Price, Rs. 16 cash, Rs. 18 credit; packing and postage, Rs. 1-8.

Manual of Surveying for India

Detailing the mode of Operations on the Trigonometrical, Topographical, and Revenue Surveys of India, compiled by Col. H. L. Thuillier and Lieut.-Col. R. Smyth. Third Edition. Revised and Enlarged. Rs. 16, or including Postage, Rs. 17-8. Credit, Rs. 18.

The Arian Witness;

OR THE TESTIMONY OF ARYAN

SCRIPTURES,

In confirmation of Sacred History and Christian Doctrine, with dissertations on the primitive seat and early adventures of INDO-ARYANS. By REV. K. M. BANERJEA. *One volume 8vo., in paper covers, Rs. 3-4, in cloth lettered, Rs. 4.*

The Companion Reader

TO MESSRS. ROWE & WEBBS

Hirts on Study of English

WITH NOTES —**Price Rs. 3-60.**

A FEW COPIES ONLY LEFT.

HOG HUNTING in LOWER BENGAL, Eight Chromolithograph Illustration. By Percy Carpenter, large folio, reduced price, Rs. 12.

FOR SALE.

Law Journal Reports

ANALYTICAL DIGEST Law Journal of Cases reported in all the Courts and the Law Journal Reports, old and new series, from the year 1822 to 1866, in 75 Volumes, 58 of which are bound in full Law calf, Rs. 750.

NOW READY

A Guide to the

SUBORDINATE CIVIL SERVICE EXAMINATIONS.

INCLUDING a Selection from Questions set in previous Examinations, and the orders of Government on the subject; together with a list of the names of Successful candidates in former years and the appointments which they now hold under Government. Compiled by W. H. Grimley, B. A., (CAMB.), B C S., Superintendent of Subordinate Civil Service Examinations; and Secretary to the Central Examination Committee. Price, Rs. 4 Packing and Postage, As. 6. Calcutta :—Thacker, Spink and C°.

!!! हुक्का !!!

!!! HOOKAHS !!!

ENGLISH made Hookahs of various choice designs, colours and sizes ranging in price from Rs. 2 to 5 each, 60 designs to choose from. Apply to

RADANAUTH CHOWDRY,
372, Jorasanko

THE INDIAN MIRROR

THE CHEAPEST DAILY PAPER

IN

INDIA

AND

HAVING AN EXTENSIVE CIRCULATION

SUBSCRIPTIONS.

	TOWN.	MOFUSSIL. Including Postage
Yearly	...Rs. 11 0 0	Rs. 24 0 0
Half yearly	... „ 6 3 0	„ 11 8 0
Quarterly	... „ 2 8 0	„ 6 0 0
Monthly	... „ 1 1 0	2 5 0

Cash sales, One Anna per copy.

Sunday Edition.

STRICTLY IN ADVANCE.

Per Annum ... ... Rs. 5

MOFUSSIL SUBSCRIBERS.

Per Annum ... ... Rs. 6 10 0

VIA SOUTHAMPTON.	£ S. D.	VIA BRINDISI.	£ S. D.
Per Annum	0 18 9	Per Annum	1 7 0

Cash sales, Two Annas per copy.

RATE OF ADVERTISING.

First insertion, 8 Lines and under, 1 Rupee.

Second and succeeding insertions, 2 Annas per line.

For Advertisements which are to be inserted for a considerable time special contracts may be made on application to the manager.

Domestic Occurrences	Non-Subscriber	... 1 Re.
	Subscriber	... 8 Ans.
Public Engagement each insertion		... 1 Re.

FOR SALE.

AT THE BRAHMO SOMAJ OF INDIA

MISSION OFFICE.

No 13, Mirzapore Street.

	Rs.	As.	P.
Sacred Anthology ...	2	0	0
Last Days of Rajah Ram Mohun Roy ...	1	0	0
Essays, Theological and Ethical ...	1	0	0
Historical Sketch of the Brahmo Somaj	0	6	0
Jesus Christ, Europe and Asia ...	0	3	6
Future Church ...	0	3	0
Lecture at the Brahmo School ...	0	1	0
True Faith ...	0	2	0
Appeals to Young India ...	0	0	6
Brahmo Somaj Vindicated ...	0	2	0
Popular Tracts, Nos. 1 to 4 ...	0	2	0
Destiny of Human Life ...	0	2	0
Reconstruction of Native Society ...	0	1	6
Welcome Soiree in England ...	0	1	6
Lecture on Inspiration ...	0	4	0
Essential Principles of Brahma Dharma	0	1	0
Proceedings of the Marriage Law meeting at the Town Hall ...	0	2	0
Theistic Annual 1872 ...	0	8	0
Ditto Ditto 1873 ...	0	8	0
Ditto Ditto 1874 ...	1	0	0
Ditto Ditto 1875 ...	1	0	0
Lecture on Progress of Theism ...	0	2	0
Little Age of Enlightenment ...	0	3	6
Life of Educated Native ...	0	2	0
Lecture on Marriage Law ...	0	2	0
Ditto on the Jains ...	0	2	0
Man the Son of God ...	0	1	0
Order of Service ...	0	1	0
Prayers for Different Occasions of Life	0	3	0
Divine Service in Hindee	0	1	0
Theistic Devotions	0	6	0
Behold the Light of Heaven in India ...	0	8	6(?)
Epistles to the Theists in India	0	0	6
Lecture on Prayer ...	0	1	0
Ditto Alcohol ...	0	2	0

JUST RECEIVED FROM ENGLAND.

	Rs.	As.	P.
Practical Sermons	0	12	0
Memoir of Rev. Dr Carpenter ...	0	12	0
Morning and Evening Meditations ...	0	12(?)	0
Channing's Perfect Life ...	1	0	0

A FASHIONABLE high wheeled C-spring Buggy by Dykes and Co., with silver plated mountings, quite **new.** Apply 12 Bentick Street,

9331.

SMITH STANISTREET & CO.

Pharmaceutical Chemists & Druggists

BY APPOINTMENT

To His Excellency the Right Hon'ble

LORD NORTHBROOK, G.M.S.I.,

Governor-General of India,

&c. &c.

Syrup of Lactate of Iron Prepared from the original recipe. Lactate of Iron, in various forms of preparation, has been in use in France, and generally through the Continent of Europe, for some years past, and is highly esteemed as one of the most valuable Chalybeate Tonic Remedies yet introduced. The Syrup, being the most agreeable as well as convenient form of administration is in most general use.

It is a most valuable remedy in the following diseases :—Chlorosis or Green Sickness, Leucorrhœa, Neuralgia, Enlargement of the Spleen, &c. In combination with quinine, it has also been very successfully used in the cure of Fever, while to persons of delicate constitution, or enfeebled by disease, it is invaluable. In bottles, Rs. 2 each.

Syrup of the Phosphate of Iron, Rs. 2 per bottle.

Syrup of Phosphate of Iron and Strychnine, Rs. 2 per bottle.

Syrup of Phosphate of Iron and Quinine, Price Rs. 2-8 per bottle

Syrup of Phosphate of Iron, Quinine and Strychnine. (Dr. Aitken's Triple Tonic Syrup.) Rs. 2-8 per bottle.

Smith, Stanistreet & Co.

Invite special attention to the following rates, the quality guaranteed as the best procurable :—

Pure Ærated Waters,

Made from Pure Water, obtained by the new process through the Patent Charcoal Filters.

			Rs.	As.
Ærated plain (Trible Ærated), per doz. ...			0	12
Soda Water	ditto	„ ...	0	12
Gingerade	ditto	„ ...	1	4
Lemonade	ditto	„ ...	1	4
Tonic (Quinine)	ditto	...	1	6

The Cash must be sent with **the order to obtain** advantage of the above **rates.**

TO CLEAR OFF STOCK

J. DAVIS & Co.

Are selling their Wool Wrappers

HALF PRICE

No. 6 Government Place, Calcutta.

HOLLOWAY'S PILLS

How to Enjoy Life

Is only known when the blood is pure, the circulation perfect, and the nerves in good order. The only safe and certain method of expelling all impurities is to take Holloway's Pills, which have the power of cleansing the blood from all noxious matters, expelling all humours which taint or impoverish it, thereby purify and invigorate and give general tone to the system. Young or old robust or delicate, may alike experience their beneficent effects. Myriads affirmed that these Pills possess marvellous power in securing those great secrets of health by purifying and regulating the fluids and strengthening the solids.

Printed and published by M. M. RUKHIT, at the "INDIAN MIRROR" PRESS, No 13, College Square, for the Proprietor.

The Indian Mirror.

SUNDAY EDITION.

VOL. XV.] CALCUTTA, SUNDAY, FEBRUARY 6, 1876 {Registered at the General Post Office.} [No. 30

CONTENTS.

NOTICE.

Letters and all other communications relating to the literary department of the Paper should be addressed to "The Editor."

All letters on the business of the Press should be addressed, and all remittances made payable to the Manager of this Paper. Particular attention is solicited to this notice.

Subscribers will be good enough to give prompt notice of any delay, or irregularity in delivery of the Paper.

Editorial Notes.

On Christmas-day, says the London *Inquirer*, "the day when the old legends tell us that the angels sang 'peace on earth, goodwill to men,' the Prince of Wales went to the service at the Cathedral at Calcutta. During the service the Athanasian Creed was said or sung, and H. R. H. had the pleasure of joining in the wholesale denunciation of nearly all his Indian entertainers to eternal damnation." It must be remembered that the Hindu Brahmins gave the Prince a real Hindu benediction in the old Vedic tune, in spite of such wholesale imprecation.

The series of Brahmo lectures we announced sometime back, and which were put off in consequence of the Prince's arrival and other circumstances, will most probably commence in the course of the next week. We are told that the minister of the Brahma Mandir intends to address the Brahmo community shortly on some important topics connected with the spiritual development and the general organization of the Brahmo Somaj. A few easy and popular lectures to the ladies of the Bharat Asram and Brahmo ladies generally are also said to be in contemplation. We should like to see a little more earnestness displayed in the matter of female education and discipline.

Each anniversary, as it refreshes our drooping spirits and reinvigorates our souls, opens to us a new career. A fresh path of duty, with fresh ideas, hopes and aspirations, is usually revealed to us about this time of the year, when we are roused by our great annual festival. What is the idea, then, which has struck us most as likely to be the guiding principle of our advanced classes in their onward march during the year just opened? Over and above the general elevation of our community there ought to be special progress in individual lives according to genius, disposition, tastes and opportunities. To us this seems to be the new principle of our movements. The time has come for *specific Theistic education*. Some of the more advanced and spiritually-minded men among our community ought to devote themselves, now that they have got a fair amount of general training, to specific forms of devotion and duty best suited to their capacities and habits. Such specific *sadhan* or culture is of the highest importance to the progress both of the individual and the community.

Nothing indeed can be broader or more liberal than the Christianity set forth in the following words, extracted from our Unitarian contemporary in London:—"Finally, whatever advance the human race can achieve, under whatever name or by whatever means, towards a larger charity, a profounder justice, a purer holiness, a more practical righteousness, and a universal brotherhood, is a triumph of Christianity itself, though its name may not be owned, or its direct influence not consciously realised. Even if progress seems wrought by the world rather than the Church, by science rather than theology, by philosophers rather than divines, by an enlightened public sentiment rather than by decrees of Councils and Synods; still the gain to Christianity in its essential moral being and influence is the same—Christ recognises the Good Samaritan of every religious profession, and by whatever name he may be called; for Christ is justice and truth, and freedom and righteousness, and whosoever worketh for these, in whatever cause is a fellow-worker of Christ."

The East is the land of mysticism. There is a strange pleasure in all transcendental feeling for us. The imagination is easily awakened, and set at rest with difficulty. Glowing pictures of unseen realities present themselves to the soaring mind, which is intoxicated with its own delight. The relations of life, the visions of immortality, and the sceneries of nature are easily blended and spiritualized, and suggest analogies, and affinities which men of grosser sentiments can not realise. Love, truth, wisdom, beauty embody themselves in transcendental forms, and are easily associated with the unseen nature of the Deity, who becomes the centre of these feelings and aspirations. The world gradually slackens its chains and its impressions become dull. Mental absorption becomes a habit, out of which escape becomes by degrees difficult. Metaphors, allegories, visions surround the man, he is always soaring in the midst of the clouds. Practical duty becomes distasteful. The pursuits of life altogether lose their charm. The man becomes a confirmed mystic. With certain phases of eastern mysticism we have deep sympathy. Hafiz, Sadi, Mowlana Roum, Nanak and others have great claims upon our admiration, but we aspire to join the highest mysticism of faith with the most practical duties of life. It is our object not to set aside the claims of any part of our nature.

It is necessary not to overlook the fact that superstition, or that which we call by this opprobrious name, because the word is purely relative and can be applied with greater or less accuracy to every system of religion, is, in the instance, of many nations, nothing more than religious faith. The conceptions of unseen realities with primitive mankind, have been always so deeply, nay obscurely figurative, that in examining the figures on the surface, we completely lose sight of the meaning that flows underneath. Max Muller beautifully illustrates this truth by the observation that the innermost thoughts of a people are always more profound than what their language can express. Objects, and not *words* are used to express the inexpressible. And in as much as objects are more tangible, at any rate often more permanent and attractive, than words, this plan answers very well so long as the persons who use them in illustration are present to explain their real meaning. But when these persons pass away, the objects which can always admit of many interpretations, conceal the original sense attached to them, and come to deceive, and frighten, and mistify, because so little is understood of them. This is the primary cause of all superstition. If the secret meaning of legends, traditions, and religious folk-lore is thus viewed, many of those savage nations among whom travellers are inclined to notice the absence of all religious belief, will be found possessed of strong faith, and traditional notions of heavenly things which commonly make up the best part of every known system of religion.

WE find Dr. Duff has come forward to question the propriety of the presence of H. R. H. the Prince of Wales at certain Hindu entertainments. Among other things he vigorously attacks the Nautches.

WE are quite at a loss to make out who "A Member of the Brahmo Somaj" is, that writes to the *Times* in defence of the civilization of India against the charge of barbarism, supposed to have been laid against us in connection with the Prince of Wales's visit. All that we can say is that a great many of our Rajahs and Chiefs have acted very barbarously in taxing their hard-pressed subjects to run into extravagant expense for the entertainment of His Royal Highness. Perhaps this species of barbarism is not without the sanction and sympathy, if it is not the direct result of moral pressure from more civilized agencies. But that is no excuse whatever.

HINDU sects are still in the process of formation. And the process is just at present perhaps more active among the Non-Aryan, than among the Aryan tribes. Mr. Lyall's article in one of the English Reviews not very long ago, in refutation to Professor Max Muller's statement that Brahminism is not a missionary religion, will be remembered by many of our readers. Mr. Lyall's argument was that inasmuch Non-Aryan tribes are admitted into the pale of orthodox Hindu communion by the profession of certain doctrines, the religion of the Brahmin is a missionary religion. In His general review of Rajputana, Mr. Lyall describes the rise of new religious movement among the Bheel of the Meywar-Guarat frontier. The leader of the movement is a man named Surji, himself a Bheel. His religion is essentially monotheistic. "He preaches the worship of one God, peace, and good will. His followers take an oath to abstain from all crimes and offences, spirituous liquors, and from causing death to any living thing. They bind themselves to live by the produce of the soil, and to bathe before eating. Surji has now a following of upwards of 1,000 Bhaguts, or believers, and three disciples, or apostles, ordained by himself to preach and convert." "All over India," says Mr. Lyall, "the appearance of teachers of this cast of mind among the Non-Aryan tribes may be noticed." Among the Sonthals, it is said, there is a fast growing religious movement of this kind. Among the Tributary Mehals of Orissa, so full of savage tribes, there is a strongly marked tendency towards a theistic reform. The Rajah Dhenkanal, the chief of one of the hill-tribes, and a man of considerable wealth and influence, has always shown great cordiality to our missionaries. If one of them ever thinks of making that part of the country his head-quarters, he may make many converts among the wild tribes of the Tributary Mehals.

IT will perhaps not be uninteresting to Brahmo Missionaries and others to learn some of the particulars of the training of young men who offer themselves to be Roman Catholic missionaries in foreign parts. As we take the account from a Protestant book on Missions, we may be sure of its impartiality. Attached to the Church of St. Francis Xavier in Paris is the "*Seminaire des Missions Estrangeres*, for training missionaries for foreign countries. The young men who join this seminary do not come from outside, but from the clerical colleges, selected by the tutors from the pupils at large. Those only are selected who show tendencies towards a missionary life. As these young men come mostly without the consent of their parents they come destitute of means and they have to be fed, clothed, and taught gratuitously. The highest age up to which admission into missionary life is possible is thirty, but they generally come at twenty. They have to be educated up to a standard before they are admitted. Their term of probation extends through a period of ten years during which they are kept under the strictest discipline. The principal duty they have to learn is the duty of obedience. The round of duties is wearisome, and the only recreation is to take a daily walk in double file. The meals must be silent, and any breach of discipline is punished with a bread and water diet. In a certain room the students have to spend daily a quarter of an hour for meditation. "On the walls are hung pictures which detail with extreme minuteness the tortures of those who have laid down their lives for the truth; beneath the pictures are the relics of the departed. At one place there are a few bones preserved under glass, at another a box with similar contents, but hermetically sealed and unopened since its arrival from China; the rope with which one was strangled, the clothes which another wore at the time of death, the discipline with which another tortured himself; these are the materials with which the future missionaries prepare themselves for the work which they have adopted as their own."

INSTINCTS.

WE are not opposed to habits of reflection. Such habits are undoubtedly of the highest importance to the success of all great enterprizes. No great work was ever undertaken or carried to a successful issue except after long, anxious and deep deliberation. Real progress, political, social and moral, is due to sound and sustained reflection. Admitting all this we must at the same time declare our conviction that there are times and occasions in life when men, instead of seeking light by long processes of reflection and reasoning, should act outright on the nobler impulses of the heart. Such occasions are not numerous; they do not come to us often. But when they come we must immediately lay aside our logic and philosophy, and follow without the least wavering or diffidence the guidance of our better instincts. At such times reflection is not only undesirable but sure to prove harmful. The more logical and reflective we are the greater will be the mischief. To act the part of a philosopher will be ruinous where mere common sense ought to be our guide. The value of philosophy we should be the last to ignore or underrate. All that we contend for is that what is good at one time may be positively injurious at another time, and that men should not always attempt to play the role of the philosopher. It seems to us that there are instincts in men which are appointed to subserve the highest purposes of life. They are not always respected, but rather despised by the educated classes. They are only the wild promptings of uncultured humanity, and cannot therefore fail to be treated with contempt by those who affect to prize only such things as are acquired by the highest cultivation of the intellectual powers. Whatever theorists may so, practical men, who have had abundant experience in the affairs of the world, must attach very great importance to natural instincts and moral impulses. We have been led to make these observations by the thrilling letter of Alfred Philip Stokes to the murderer of Harriet Lane recently published in the English papers. The circumstances, revealed therein, which led to the arrest of the murderer and his subsequent punishment, are indeed most remarkable, and cannot but convince even the most sceptical of the importance of following the true instincts of the soul. Were it not for these instincts the murderer would perhaps have mocked all investigations and inquiries and escaped punishment. What was it that roused Stokes' suspicions and curiosity to the highest pitch? What was it that led him, in the absence of any direct testimony, to pursue his "former friend" as the perpetrator of a most diabolical deed? It was not a "base and prying curiosity," as he himself assures us, but "a strange mysterious agency for which I can scarcely account." We, who believe in God's living Providence, do not regard this "agency" as an inexplicable mystery, but a clear fact of man's natural consciousness, to which both philosophy and theology bear testimony. According to popular notions it would be called *spiritual instinct*, or strong common sense. But all devout believers would prefer calling it by the only right name which belongs to it, we mean the *voice of God*. Some strange voice prompted Stokes to open the parcel and afterwards to follow the cab. Whose voice was it but God's? Let us hear what he himself says on this point. Addressing Wainwright, the murderer, he writes;—"The very instant your back was turned, I seemed to hear a supernatural voice say to me three times as distinctly as though it were a human voice somewhere near me, 'Open that parcel! Open that parcel! Open that parcel! Look in that parcel! Further on he says :—"I then seemed to hear the same supernatural voice address me again, and say "Murder; it is a murder. Will you conceal a murder?" Again,—" I immediately seemed to hear the same voice addressing me and saying, Follow that cab, follow that.'" Here we have most emphatic and repeated testimonies to a "Supernatural Voice." Verily, verily it was the Lord's voice, speaking like thunder in the depths of the soul that roused, electrified and moved the man, and following that voice he proved instrumental in bringing to light a most mysterious and shocking murder. Such are the ways in which God's over-ruling Providence carries out the high, beneficent and just purposes of His moral economy. He spoke to Stokes with a power, which he could not resist. And so He speaks to each one of us, daily and hourly, pointing out our duties, warning us against the dangers that beset our paths, and encouraging us in our onward career. But alas! few there are who listen to the solemn voice, fewer still who follow it with fidelity. May we learn to adore and obey the speaking God!

THE INSTINCT OF BROTHERHOOD VERIFIED.

CIRCUMSTANCES teach us more of religion than sermons. Human teachers often fail to appeal to the proper instincts in the proper way. But left to ourselves, when we have to fight with circumstances, the right chords in the heart are touched, the right feelings come out, and the right relations are established. Nowhere is this more strikingly proved than in the case of the instinct of brotherhood. Formal agencies have often failed here. Man will not recognize man as his brother. Defiance has come to be the normal attitude of one soul towards another. The teachableness of religious teachers has all but gone; and the consequence is their own disciples do not care to learn from them. Obedience to each other has not only become hard, but very nearly an impossible thing. Religiousness in one sense means independence, and independence means the setting at nought of all authority. This is the very soul of the religion of the day. Brotherhood under such circumstances is hopeless, because how is it to exist where no allegiance to a common principle of mutual subordination can be enforced. No one seems to have discovered the remedy to this evil. But see how the remedy comes of itself. Let a man be placed in imminent and fearful danger. Let a few of the real difficulties of life stare him in the face, difficulties out of which he does not see the way. We may at any time picture for ourselves a situation wherein our own means and intelligence become powerless to help us, and perhaps now and then every one falls into such situations. What then do we? Do we not run to the nearest friend upon whom we can rely? Often under such circumstances have men longed to throw themselves under the guidance and protection of others, that is such as they feel sure can be of service to them. The relation of one man with another becomes suddenly clear. Different orders of mind range themselves in the right position. The attitude of defiance is unconsciously changed. Obedience becomes a cheerful and natural duty, and brings with itself the ease and sense of security which they only know who have obeyed. The submission of the will follows as a matter of course. The superior man immediately recognizes the points of superiority in an inferior; and the inferior man yields the ready acquiescence to his superior so graceful in the right place. The dependence, the yielding cheerful obedience, the harmony of feeling, the deep trust and confidence, the love and gratitude born of mutual service and helpfulness in time of need, these spring out almost magically when in distress and terror we have fled to other's protection, and that protection has been cheerfully conferred upon us. We then feel that men are related, and are not altogether strangers to each other in this world. We feel a stinging regret that we did not recognize this truth before, and are humiliated because of our hard-heartedness, and pride. This is the verification of the instinct of brotherhood. Now the question is, are we not helpless, each one of us, in certain matters of our religious life? There is one perhaps who can not gain the mastery over his passions, there is another who cannot get the better of his temptations. There is a third whose dryness of heart is very great. A thousand wants afflict us, each one of which might any day prove to be our ruin. Thus placed, our weakness and resourcelessness repeatedly proved, is it not meet that we should begin to feel the pre-eminent necessity of help and protection from others. There are men around us to whom we would resort any moment if we felt ourselves in actual distress. Because we do not acknowledge our sinfulness to be a real danger, therefore we do not seek their aid. But there is this danger notwithstanding; let us beware that we awake not to it too late! Our instincts therefore should immediately lead us to seek anxiously the love and brotherly solicitude of men amongst whom Providence has placed us. Deference and obedience in certain matters to men ought to be our habitual attitude. The relationship which will make such attitude beneficial, morally, spiritually, even physically sometimes, ought to be at once found out. For that is the true ground of brotherhood.

The Interpreter

BECAUSE a man is once reclaimed and begins to lead a righteous life it does not necessarily follow that he will be always holy. If his heart is not sufficiently strong, he will fall again as soon as temptations overpower him. He will hold on in the path of purity only so long as his provisions last; he starves and sinks directly these are exhausted. There is a beautiful passage in the *Srimad bhagabat* (11-10-25) which translated runs thus:—So long as righteousness last man enjoys felicity in heaven, but as soon as his righteousness is spent he falls in the course of time even in spite of his reluctance. We must not rest satisfied with a little purity, but must continue to acquire more and more so that our spiritual provisions may never run short.

GITA 30, 1092 speaks of the "touch of Divinity." To many the expression is strange, and the idea of doctrine it embodies absurd. We hold that if there is any truth in the "perception of God's face" and the "hearing of God's word," there is deep meaning too in what believers regard as "touching the Pure Spirit." By analogy we could surely comprehend spiritual contiguity and nearness. In deep communion the soul touches the encircling and burning Presence of the Great Spirit, and is galvanized into devotional fervor by sacred touch. It is an overwhelming sense of extreme nearness and deep intercommunion.

Correspondence.

MORAL TRAINING OF THE YOUNG—A PASTORAL LETTER—HOW WE ARE BORN.

To the Editor of the *Indian Mirror.*

SIR,—I commenced the work of a pastor in America among the poor of the "Queen city of the West," St. Louis, in 1840. Just now, while destroying old letters, I chance upon one to which, if you think it will be of service, you are welcome. It treats of a subject that daily arises in domestic and pastoral experience; and of one hard to handle with discretion. This subject came up at Poona the other day, in our Social Conference on the moral training of the young. It will be of little use unless given as it came fresh from the pen. Here it is just as I sent it, years ago, to a Christian mother—"As Edie's mother, you have a right to know, and I am naturally anxious that you should know, what I recently told her. It was in reply to a remark of hers which showed no improper wish on the part of a child ten years old, to discover the Father's way of sending us from His own bosom, clothed and embodied, into this world. I should not, of my own accord, have called her attention to such a matter. Though, if the child were my own, I should care.

fully fore-warn and fore-arm my boy or girl against misguidance and mental defilement. I would do it indirectly and by parable or implication; as through the immaculate purity of flowers, and the vitalization of their seed. But when, as in Effie's case, an intelligent and pure questioning, self-moved, has already arisen in a young mind,—and one not my own, comes and asks to have this ever-present mystery explained,—I feel it a pastoral duty, in all simplicity, to reveal without equivocation so much of the truth as may be safely and wisely told. An observant child has probably mastered more of the problem than we wot of by using its eyes in the aviary or in the street. Let us tell truly, however reservedly, the little that we must tell. Yes; let dear Effie know the truth; for the truth alone can keep her free from the defilement that natural feeling, with ignorance and error are sure to bring. Effie's questioning arose in this wise. She heard her father say that a little one that died almost as soon as it was born 'was a seven month's child.' She sought to solve this problem; and confidingly came to me for help. Effie, said I, I remember asking some such question of my mother when I was a child, but her reply left me more puzzled than before I do not wish so to puzzle you. Nor do I see why you should not know God's way of bringing children into this world. We none of us can love a mother as we ought, till we learn that it was directly through that mother's bleeding heart that we entered into life. Every child is born out of its mother's heart. Why should you not know this? It can only make you wiser and better to know it. God first gives a child to a mother right into her heart. There for nine months it nestles within its mother's life, before, by wise hands, it is lifted out and breathes the common air. If, through weakness or accident, it should be ushered into the world too soon, as at seven months, it is usually too tender to live many days. Now, my dear Effie, you know what perhaps few children know. But this knowledge cannot hurt, it must help you, to love both God and your mother better than ever. Keep this thought deep in your own pure soul. Think of it in your prayers. And only tell it when the telling may save some friend from dangerous ignorance, and from speaking what is neither pure nor true. As the child thanked me and turned to go, I said, Effie, one word more. It was not from the heart itself but from a closet in our mother's side near the heart that you and I were born; You have now all I wish to say on this subject. We will not talk of it again. Tell mother all I have told you. Do not worry her with further questioning. Observe God's pure ways in all life, especially considering the lilies, how they are born and grow. And what you know not now God will teach you in good time. * * * This was what I told her; and Effie's mother, I trust you will be pleased with what I have done! * * * Such is an old Pastoral letter.

Yours &c.,
DALL.

BRAHMO HOLIDAYS.

To the Editor of the *Indian Mirror*.

SIR,—It would not be out of place, I hope, to draw the attention of the Brahmo public and especially those who are employed in public offices under Government to the desirability of sending up, in the name of the Brahmo Somaj, a memorial to Government to allow us, poor *Karanis* and subordinate officials, a holiday on the 11th Magh every year. Why should we not devote that day to religion and God under our beneficent Government when our Mahomedan and Hindu brethren enjoy certain privileges in that way during their festivals? The Board's rule has provided holidays for the Mahomedans during *Yeed*, *Bukreed* and other Mussulman festivals, and as to Hindu and Christian holidays in Government Offices, the list is too widely circulated to need any mention from me. Please allow this a little space in your Sunday Edition so that the question may be thoroughly ventilated, and oblige.

MOTIHARI,
The 23rd Jany. 1876.

Yours &c.,
PROKASH CHUNDER ROY.

The Brahmo Somaj.

THE procession on the occasion of the anniversary of the Intally Brahmo Somaj (Baniapuker) was a great success, and those who saw it speak very highly of the fervor and solemnity which characterized it. The morning service was conducted by Babu Protap Chunder Mozumdar in a pavilion erected for the purpose by the members of the Somaj and decorated with fowers, and the evening service was conducted by Babu Keshub Chunder Sen.

CERTAIN members of the congregation of the Brahma Mundir have been complaining for some time past that the language of the sermons is now and then too undignified and too metaphorical to be agreeable to cultivated ears, and needs therefore considerable improvement.

THE usual monthly service in the Mandir takes place this morning commencing at 7-30 A. M.

WE have received an account of the twenty-fifth Anniversary of the Chittagong Brahmo Somaj which took place on the 28th December last.

A CORRESPONDENT writes to say from Bankurah that the local prayer meeting has been accommodated by the head master of the Bankurah Zillah school in his own residence. But as the head master is about to retire on pension, the Brahmos are at a loss to know where they shall meet. The head master an elderly man of fifty five is pious and prayerful, and though he is a member of the conservative Somaj, "leads a life of reformation, and looks with esteem upon young men of the Progressive Brahmo Somaj." This is as it ought to be.

THERE are so many anniversaries of provincial Somajes taking place about this time of the year, that the hands of our missionary friends will be rather full.

WE do not approve of the reading of the declaration prescribed by law in the case of Brahmo marriages, in connection with the marriage service and rites that are performed before the pulpit. After the solemnity and sacredness of these proceeding the repitition by the married couple of the legal phraseology replete with allusion to fine, and imprisonment, sounds as incongruous as painful. This we noticed in the case of the Brahmo marriage that took place on last Wednesday. We recommend that the reading of the declaration should take place after service and the ceremonies in an adjoining room, apart from the assembly which is generally of a mixed character, and not likely to be edified by the provisions of the Act.

Literary.

IT will be remembered that before the Prince departed for India it was jocularly said that he would be worshipped by the Natives as a god, and even before he had fairly arrived in Bombay it was found that Hindu poets were apostrophizing him as an Avatar, or Incarnation of the Deity. But the force of Oriental folly could go, and has gone, further still. A document has been forwarded to London for publication and will soon be printed, which in its way is a curiosity. It is a poem in honor of the Prince's visit to India, written by a Canarese scholar. It would doubtless have been presented to the Prince by the author personally had his Royal Highness visited Mysore, as he at first intended. A short specimen of what this poem is like may perhaps startle the religious reader. We give a free translation of the opening verses:—

"Om! Invocation to the God, the Prince of Wales.
What is the use of the rain and the sun?
What is the need of the land and the sea, the air and food
Why should any other God be worshiped?
God is here among us, and in him only will I believe.
I have cast aside the *Trimurti*.
If I ask for rain, the Prince will give it;
If I ask for the sun, the Prince will smile.
Is he not omniscient, omnipresent, almighty, the essence of perfection?
I will breathe him, and he shall be my food.
O may I live in him, and be dissolved in his greatness, as the river is lost in the sea!
I have no need now to doubt in faith; my new religion is one of sight and knowledge.
I have seen the flower-face of my God!"

And so on, for a couple of hundred lines. Thus the Prince seems to have founded a new religion, without any desire or effort on his own part—the worship of himself! The best of it is that the writer of this production probably did *not* see the "flower-face of his God." As the demons of cholera prevented his deity from going to Bangalore and Mysore. However, the new convert may perhaps make a pilgrimage to London, to offer *pooja* to the Lord of the Three Plumes.—*Athenæum*.

THE Society for promoting Christian Knowledge have in preparation a work on Hygiene, by Dr. Parkes, of Netley; it is in the press, and will be entitled a "Manual on the personal Care of Health." The Society seems willing to assert the truth of the old proverb, that "cleanliness is next to godliness."

Scientific

CAPTAIN BURTON, the African explorer and Mrs. Burton are shortly expected at Bombay. They are passengers on board the Austro-Hungarian *S. S. Calypso*.

A MONSTER telescope, the largest, it is said, yet attempted, is now in course of construction at Mr. Grubb's new works, near Dublin. This instrument has been ordered by the Imperial and Royal Austro-Hungarian Government for the new observatory now in course of erection at Vienna. The object-glass will have an aperture of over twenty-six inches. The focal length will be about thirty-two feet, and the general form of mounting will be modified to suit the special requirements of such a monster instrument; the great base casting (weighing from seven to eight tons) will form a chamber (about 12 feet long, 4½ feet wide, and 8 feet high) for the clock, which will be massive in proportion to the other parts. The cube will be entirely of steel. It is expected that the whole instrument will be completed by the autumn of 1878.

Lieutenant Cameron's latest African letters were read on Jan. 10 at the meeting of the Royal Geographical Society. His zeal and his invaluable discoveries were not overpraised by Sir Henry Rawlinson. There is room in the field of scientific enterprise for a dozen Livingstones, Camerons, and Stanleys. Cameron has now proved his ability as an explorer. In a journey of over eighteen months the intrepid traveller has passed from Ujiji to Loanda, through the most inaccessible region of Africa. He has also apparently solved the old crux of geographers, and has established the disputed identity of the Lualaba and Congo Rivers. When Cameron returns to Europe he will be sure of a hearty welcome both in scientific and in commercial circles. To critics of the one kind he will be acceptable as a man whose combination of skill and manliness has enlarged the area of scientific knowledge, while by those of the second kind he will be admired as one who has opend up new possibilities of a splendid and lucrative trade.

Gleanings.

ALONE WITH GOD.

Have you tried it? If not, will you try it? If you have tried it, will you try it more? To be alone with God. The still hour, when no human voice or foot-fall diverts the mind from itself and Him who formed it,—what a wonderful time it is. What revelations are made. What experiences passed through, or commenced for more public development. Surely, then, the Holy Spirit comes to its creation to renew it in the likeness of God.

What wonderful praying has been known in secret. Read Daniel's prayer in the ninth chapter of his book. Read Paul's, in the first chapter of Ephesians, commencing at the sixteenth verse, and in the third chapter of the same letter commencing at the fourteenth verse. Read Jesus' prayer in the seventeenth chapter of the Gospel by the Apostle John. And when you have read one or all three, if you are not more thoroughly convinced of the mightiness and value of close communion between you and our Heavenly Father, by yourselves, we will be disappointed.

Cecil was right when he suggested: "I felt that all I know and that all I teach will be nothing for my soul, if I spend all my time, as some people do, in business or company. My soul starves to death in the best company, and God is often lost in prayers and ordinances. Enter into thy closet, said Jesus, and shut thy door. Some words in Scripture are very emphatical. Shut thy door, means much. It means, shut out only nonsense, but business; not only the company at home, it means, let the poor soul have a little rest and refreshment, and God have opportunity to speak to thee in a still, small voice, or He will speak to thee in thunder."

Consider Cecil's words, and create opportunity by retirement for God to speak to his listening servant or handmaid; lest God have to create His own opportunity by a sore trial or serious affliction or change or sorrow.—*Vt. Christian Messenger.*

A BRAVE SAILOR BOY.

One day a great ship out from New York was overtaken by a terrible storm, which lasted nearly a week.

One night, at the height of the tempest, the rigging at the mainmast head got tangled, and some one had to go up and change it. The mate called a boy belonging to the ship and ordered him aloft.

The lad touched his cap, but hesitated a moment, cast one frightened glance up and down at the swaying masts and furious sea, and then rushed across the deck and down into the forecastle. In about two minutes he appeared, and without a word seized the ratlins—the rope-ladders of the vessel—and flew up the rigging like a squirrel. With dizzy eyes the weather-beaten crew watched the boy at this fearful height.

"He will never come down alive," they said to each other.

But in twenty minutes the perilous job was done, and the boy safely descended, and straightening himself up, with a smile on his face, walked to the stern of the ship.

"What did you go below for when ordered aloft?" asked a passenger of the brave boy.

"I went—to pray," replied the boy with a blush and a quiver of the lip.

The Week

Lord Northbrook will proceed to England from Calcutta in the *Tenasserim*.

Mr. Courtney of the *Times* left Bombay for England by the last mail.

The Nizam of Hyderabad is after all to meet the Prince at the Caves of Ellora which His Royal Highness visits on his return journey to Bombay.

Eswunt Rao, the Jasud in the service of the ex-Guekwar, Mulhar Rao, who figured in the Baroda drama and was transported to Aden, has since died there.

Dr. Payne has been elected Health-Officer of Calcutta on a salary of Rs. 1,000 per month, and Mr. Alexander Pedler, Professor of Chemistry, Presidency College, has been appointed Analyst to the Justices on a salary of Rs. 300 per month.

Major Evan Smith, formerly of Zanzibar, and who has hitherto been acting as an *attaché* of the Foreign Office, is appointed First Assistant Resident, Hyderabad.

The India Office has publicly announced that Lord Northbrook expressed a desire to resign the Viceroyalty of India last summer.

Captain Clerk, the Nizam's tutor, left for England by the last Mail on leave.

The new College at Cuttack has been opened. The Principal appointed is Mr. Ager.

Mr. F. R. Hogg, Officiating Director-General of the Post Offices, has left Calcutta for Bombay and Madras on a month's tour of inspection.

The two vacancies in the Indian Council have been caused by the retirement of Sir Henry Montgomery and Sir George Clerk.

A telegram says that Her Royal Highness the Princess Beatrice is betrothed to Prince Louis of Battenberg who is now in India, travelling with His Royal Highness the Prince of Wales.

The Allahabad paper has it that Major Upperton of the 16th Bengal Cavalry, and not Colonel Bulwer, will be appointed the Military Secretary to Lord Lytton.

It is said that Sir Frederick Haines will come out as Commander-in Chief of India for one year only.

A terrible gunpowder explosion has taken place at Jeypore.

LATEST NEWS.

The announcement is made that the competitive examination of candidates for the Indian Civil Service will commence on April next.

Count Seckendorff, the Prussian officer, who has been travelling in India for some months, is now at Bombay, we hear, the guest of Brigadier-General Goll.

According to a vernacular contemporary, a feeling of uneasiness appears to prevail in Baroda, owing to its being rumoured that public tranquillity there is likely to be disturbed during the present Mohurrum festival.

It is in contemplation to appoint a public Prosecutor at Baroda.

Mr. Muniskot Josshot, Assistant to the Resident at Baroda, has been appointed to the post of Dewan at Kutch.

His Excellency Sir Philip Wodehouse, Governor of Bombay, was expected to reach Gunesh Khind, Poona, on Thursday last.

It is reported that a brother of Captain Trevor, Second Assistant Resident at Hyderabad, goes to Hyderabad under the auspices of Sir Salar Jung, to reform the Nizam's Law Courts.

The Missionaries of the London Mission at Bangalore have drawn up a scheme for establishing a fund for widows of all denominations.

The services of Mr. J Westland, c. s., are replaced at the disposal of the Financial Department, with effect from the 26th ultimo.

The *Times'* Paris correspondent concludes his very valuable picture of Lord Lytton, the new Viceroy, with the following account of a friend's remarks on the subject, which, he says, "perfectly sums up all I have said":—"Ever since the Prince of Wales' journey, and ever since I have read the marvellous descriptions which are like so many chapters of the 'Arabian Nights,' I have often thought I should like to see Lord Lytton appear in this frame—that type at once sumptuous and sober, strong and sympathetic who will carry to India the firm determination of making his will felt, will console himself for necessary privations by stealing from the extreme East the practical seat of its harmonies, and will bring us back a Lytton bronzed, with two volumes of new poems in his pocket and a whole new world in his head."

The Prince of Wales will leave Jeypore tomorrow evening for Moradabad, to shoot with Col. Ramsay in the Napal Terai where His Royal Highness stops till the 18th instant. From the 19th to the 2nd March His Royal Highness intends shooting with Sir Jung Bahadur.

Count Andrassy advises that a commission, composed of both Christians and Mahomedans, should be appointed to put the suggested reforms in Turkey in train.

An appeal signed by the Bishop and Archdeacon of Calcutta and headed "Anglo-Indian Educational Fund," is published, inviting aid for the education of the poor Whites and Eurasians. The appeal specifies four suggestions:—

1. Cheap Hills Schools.
2. Plains Schools in the larger stations with moderate charges.
3. A Normal School for training Teachers.
4. Nominations or Scholarships.

Major Lang, R. E., Principal of the Thomason Civil Engineering College, Rurki, will shortly proceed to Europe on furlough, and Captain Allan Cunningham, R. E., Mathematical Professor, will be appointed as his *locum tenens.*

The Duke of Sutherland has gone to Bombay *en route* to England.

There will be an Albert Hall at Jeypore like that in Calcutta. The Prince of Wales who is now at Jeypore has laid its foundation-stone there. It will be in commemoration of the Prince's visit and will cost the Maharajah two lacs of rupees.

The Government of India, have sanctioned the grant of jaghirs in Inam to two police officers in the Bombay Presidency for service done in connection with recent events at Baroda. The fortunate recipients of this mark of the Viceroy's favor are Gujanund Vithal and Khan Bahadur Akbar Ali. Gujanund receives grant of a village in any British taluka in the Bombay Presidency which he names, yielding an annual revenue of Rs. 1,200. It is to be held rent free by him during his life-time, but will be continued to his heirs and successors on payment of half the quit rent. Akbar Ali gets on similar terms a village in Inam yielding Rs. 500 a year.

THE proposed Chanda Valley Mineral Railway is in a very advanced state on paper, but the Indian Government are very anxious to construct it themselves, and on the broad gauge system.

HER MAJESTY Queen Victoria is expected at Coburg on a visit on the 10th of April, and will reside at the palace of the Duke of Edinburgh. Her Majesty intends proceeding to Baden-Baden,

HER MAJESTY the Queen proposes to open the approaching session of Parliament in person, and Her Majesty will be accompanied by Her Royal Highness the Princess of Wales.

HIS ROYAL HIGHNESS the Prince of Wales, as Most Worshipful the Grand Master of the English Grand Lodge of Freemasons, has appointed His Royal Highness Prince Leopold, who is Worshipful Master of a Craft Lodge, to be Right Worshipful Provincial Grand Master of Oxfordshire.

The Prince's Visit.

MAHARAJAH SCINDIA at the banquet at Gwalior made the following speech through General Daly:—

"May it please your Royal Highness and Gentlemen,—The Maharajah wishes me to tell you how profoundly grateful he is for the visit of His Royal Highness the Prince of Wales, and how thankful he is to Her Majesty for allowing her son to come to Gwalior. He wishes to express his unswerving loyalty to the English Crown, and calls upon you to drink the health of Her Majesty the Queen."

Calcutta.

A PUBLIC Meeting, in aid of the Additional Clergy Society, will be held at the Dalhousie Institute to-morrow, at 5. P. M. His Excellency the Viceroy will preside. His Honor the Lieutenant-Governor and other gentlemen will address the meeting.

DR. CANOZ, S. J., Bishop Vicar-Apostolic of Trichinopoly and Madura, has arrived in Calcutta.

LIEUTENANT LORD BERESFORD has been appointed an Aide-de-Camp to the Governor-General in the room of Captain E. Hartopp, who has been allowed to resign his appointment.

THIS seems to be the furlough-season in India, for there are many who are fast taking furloughs. It is said that Colonel Bacon, Deputy Secretary to the Government of India, in the Military Department, goes home immediately on a year's furlough.

THE *Indian Daily News* hears it rumoured that Mr. C. H. Wood, the Government Quinologist, who had once officiated in the post, is likely to be appointed as Professor of Chemistry at the Medical College at Calcutta and Chemical Examiner of Government *vice* Dr. F. N. Macnamara. There is also a rumour that Dr. W. J. Palmer will officiate for Dr. Partridge as First Surgeon in the Medical College Hospital and as Professor of Surgery at the College. Dr. Gayer is to officiate as Second Surgeon and Professor of Surgery *vice* Dr. Palmer.

WE regret to hear of the death by drowning of Captain E. J. Butler, the Deputy Master Attendant, Calcutta. Captain Butler, together with four officers of the *Serapis*, left Calcutta on Saturday morning in a famine steamer on a shooting excursion to Saugor. The steamer collided with the Steam Tug *Challenge* somewhere near Garden Reach.

THE Secretary of State for India, it appears, would as soon part with his blood as with his power of patronage; and he knows right well how to exercise it. It is said that the Hon'ble Mr. Paul, who has hitherto been officiating as Advocate General of Bengal, is not to be confirmed in that office, but that it has already been offered to, and accepted by, Mr. Cave, Q. C., of the Chancery Bar. This is dealing with Mr. Paul very shabbily, indeed.

THE British Indian Association will hold a public meeting on Saturday next at 3-30 P. M., for the purpose of taking into consideration the new Municipal Bill.

Public Engagements.

MUSICAL Evangelistic service.—The Rev. James Robertson, M. A., will deliver an address in the Free Church Institution, Nimtollah Street, this evening, 6th instant, at 6-30 o'clock. Hymns in Bengali, set to Hindu Music, will be sung.

DOMESTIC OCCURRENCES.

BIRTHS.

MAZUMDAR.—At 5-30. A. M. on Sunday, the 16th January 1876, at Dhubri in the District of Goalpara, the wife of Babu Koylash Chunder Mazumdar, of a son.

GUPTA.—At 9-50. A. M. on Sunday, the 14th February 1875, at Chittagong, the wife of Babu Golock Chundar Gupta, of a son.

Selection

THE REV DR. ALEXANDER DUFF ON THE PRESENCE OF THE PRINCE OF WALES AT SOME OF THE SPORTS AND AMUSEMENTS IN INDIA.

ON January 11 a meeting was held in Edinburgh of the Anglo-Indian Christian Union, for promoting the spiritual interests of our countrymen and other English-speaking people in India. The Rev. Dr. Duff, professor of evangelistic theology in the Free Church College, Edinburgh, for many years a well-known missionary in India, occupied the chair. In opening the proceedings, Dr. Duff said that the visit of the Prince of Wales to India related in an important degree to the object of that society. When that visit was undertaken it was understood that means were to be adopted to insure, if possible, that it should have an important bearing upon Christianity in India. They went forth to India with good resolutions on this subject. One of these they were led to believe was a determination to show a respect for the Sabbath of the Lord, which ought to be ever held holy and honorable. Another was that some attention should be paid to the labors of Christians in that land in connection with the spiritual enlightenment of the people of Indi . Now what were they to say about this? They had received some imperfect, fragmentary reports from India—a number of telegrams some of them obscure, and about things alleged to have been said in some quarters. On this account they must not prejudge the case, but calmly, dispassionately, as Christian men, wait and assertain all the real facts before they formed a final and deliberate judgment. Undoubtedly there were some things which had already excited unpleasant apprehensions. Idolatrous temples where visited; the Tooth of Buddha, the founder of the Budphist system, which prevailed so widely and tyrannically over the people, was inspected, and so on. The motives, the explanations, or the circumstances were not known, and therefore a deliberate judgment should not yet be formed. Then spectacles had been witnessed which had produced a feeling of painfulness on the part not only of Christian people in this land, but of respectable secular-minded people—exhibitions, for instance, of cruelty to animals; exhibitions which were prohibited within the British Isles by legislative enactment; exhibitions of a kind which were most odious and intolerable to myriads even of the Native population of India. Then again, spectacles such as the exhibitions of Native dancers—Nautch girls. He thought as Christians that if dancing was to be exhibited it ought to be left very much as an amusement to children, not to be made a recreation for grown-up men and women. In this respect the Hindu idolaters put us to shame. There was no respectable woman in India who would dance, certainly not dance in the presence of a mixed audience. They thought it a shameful thing to do it, and the honor of the family would be gone if they did. Those who had been in India knew that these Nautch girls were not respectable at all. They were either actually or by common repute bad women, low and degraded women. To his mind this was one of the most shocking things which he read among all the intelligence which had reached here—that the representative of a Court like the British Court, known all over the world for its purity, in comparison with all the other Courts in Europe or elsewhere—the Heir Apparent of the British Throne, should have had obtruded upon his eyes a dancing company of women who were in India known to be degraded, and low and vile. There was something incongruous in the thing. He did not blame the Prince; he blamed his advisers, who had not saved him from the dilemma of being constrained to witness such exhibitions. He could not help referring to this subject. He would be ashamed as a man and a Christian minister if he were silent. In a case like this they were bound to testify for truth, for righteousness, for pobity, for honor, for purity, for everything that was truly great. If the advisers of the Prince of Wales had only intimated to Native Princes that it was contrary to Brtish habits to witness brutalizing and cruel spectacles of animals tearing each other; that it was contrary to British usage to be introduced into a company of low and vile women and see them exhibiting themselves in low and vile dances—if this had been intimated, there was not a Chief in India, there was not a head Zemindar who would not have looked upon it as thing natural and congruous that they should have been told that this was not British, and, therefore, that they must not offend the Heir of the British Throne by asking him to witness any such exhibition. He believed the Prince would have been respected a thousand times more by the whole mass of the people in India if this had been done. The visit of the Prince, therefore, had an importantt bearing on this society, and he could not help alluding to it. At the same time, as he had already reminded them they must not prejudge the case. These things, perhaps, admitted of palliation or explanation and if so, let them as Christian people go, on the return of the Prince, and present an address of congratulation to him. But. if they were not satisfied, let them go forth, and in an honest plain, constitutional way, in simple plain, reverential language, humbly but fearlessly express their regrets, and add their prayers to God with regard to the future. In this way they would maintain their consistency and honor as British Christians.—*Home News.*

Advertisements

Indian General Steam Navigation Company, Limited.

SCHOENE, KILBURN & Co.—*Managing Agent.*

ASSAM LINE.

NOTICE.

Steamers now leave Calcutta for Assam every Tuesday, Goalundo every Thursday and Debrooghur downward every Tuesday.

THE Str. "ASSAM" will leave Calcutta for Assam, on Tuesday, the 8th instant.

Cargo will be received at the Company's Godowns, Nimtollah Ghat, until noon of Monday, the 7th instant.

THE Str. "SIMLA" will leave Goalundo for Assam on Thursday, the 10th instant.

Cargo will be received at the Company Godowns, No. 4, Fairlie Palace, up till noon of Monday, the 7th.

Goods forwarded to Goalundo for this vessel will be chargeable with Railway Freight from Calcutta to Goalundo in addition to the regular Freight of this Company.

Passengers should leave for Goalundo by Train of Wednesday, the 9th instant.

CACHAR LINE NOTICE

REGULAR WEEKLY SERVICE.

Steamers now leave Calcutta for Cachar and Intermediate Stations every Tuesday and Chattuck downward every Monday.

A Steamer and "FLAT" will leave Calcutta for Cachar on Tuesday, the 8th instant.

Cargo will be received at the Company's Godowns, Nimtollah Ghat, up till noon of Monday, the 7th.

For further information regarding rates of Freight or passage money, apply to.

4 Fairlie Palace, G. J. SCOTT,
Calcutta, 2nd Feb. 1876. *Secretary.*

THE CALCUTTA SCHOOL.

SESSION opened on the 10th of January, 1876. The following are the rates of fees :—

		Schooling fee.	Admission, fee.
English Department.	Rs.	2 0 0	2 0 0
Vernacular „	...	1 0 0	1 0 0
Juvenile Class	...	0 8 0	0 8 0

Three Scholarships of Rupees Five each are available next year, to be held by the three most distinguished students of the School who successfully pass the Entrance Examination of December, 1876. There are besides six free studentships in the Entrance class open to competition, applications for which are to be made to the undersigned before the 1st of February next.

KRISHNA BIHARI SEN, M. A.

ALBERT HALL.

PATRON.

His Honor the Lieutenant Governor of Bengal.

COUNCIL.

Hon'ble Sir William Muir, K. C. S. I.—*President.*
Rajah Rama Nath Tagore Bahadur, C. S. I.—*Vice-President.*
Hon'ble Ashley Eden, C. S. I.
Archdeacon Baly.
Colonel H. E. L. Thuiller, C. S. I.
Maharajah Kumar of Bettiah.
Rajah Komul Krishna Bahadur.
Rajah Joteendro Mohun Tagore Bahadur.
Babu Digumber Mitter C. S. I.
Hon'ble Nawab Ashgar Ali Bahadur, C. S. I.
Nawab Amir Ali Bahadur.
Moulvi Abdul Lutif Khan Bahadur.
Manockji Rustomji Esq.
Babu Keshub Chunder Sen.

SUBSCRIPTIONS.

His Highness Maharajah Holkar ...	Rs.	8,000
His Highness Maharajah of Jeypore	„	5,000
His Highness Maharajah of Putialah	„	2,500
Maharajah Kumar of Bettiah ...	„	2,000
Rajah of Bhinga ...	„	1,000
Maharajah of Hutwa ...	„	500
Rajah Komul Krisna Bahadur ...	„	500
Rajah Roma Nath Tagore Bahadur	„	200
Rajah Joteendro Mohun Tagore ...	„	500
Maharani Surnomoie, Cossim Bazar	„	1,000

M. Z. MARTIN & CO.,

THE CHINA AND JAPAN WAREHOUSE MERCHANTS AND COMMISSION AGENTS.

No. 4 Dalhousie Square, East.

ICE! ICE! ICE!

MADE IN FOUR MINUTES

THE PNEUMATIC ICE MACHINE

THIS IMPORTANT INVENTION IS CONSIDERED A BOON TO THOSE LIVING IN TROPICAL CLIMATES.

CAN BE WORKED BY THE MOST INEXPERIENCED HAND AND IS NOT LIABLE TO GET OUT OF ORDER.

From Rs. 175, each Machine complete.

MESSRS. ARLINGTON & CO.

AGENTS.

SIMILIA SIMILIBUS CURANTUR

HOMŒOPATHIC

MEDICINES.—From 4 annas per dram to—
BOXES.—Of various sizes, from 8 annas to—
BOOKS.—Including Medicines, from 3 Rs. to—
Books; Pamphlets; Cholera-spirit Camphor; Absolute Alcohol; Family Guide in Bengalee and all requisites, &c, &c,

To be had at

DATTA'S HOMŒOPATHIC LABORATORY.

No. 312, CHITPORE ROAD, BUTTOLAH, CALCUTTA.

TERMS—CASH.

BABU BASANTA KUMARA DUTTA,
HOMŒOPATHIC PRACTITIONER
IN CHARGE.

ESTABLISHED IN 1820.

C. LAZARUS & CO.

(INCORPORATED WEARWOOD & CO.)
CABINET MAKERS, UPHOLSTERERS
BILLIARD AND BAGATELLE TABLE
MANUFACTURERS.

BY APPOINTMENT
TO HIS EXCELLENCY
The Viceroy and Governor-General of India.
AND
TO HIS ROYAL HIGHNESS
THE
DUKE OF EDINBURGH

Billiard Tables.

C. LAZARUS & Co., as manufacturers, would invite particular attention to their large stock of fullsized Billiard Tables. One of the chief desiderata in a Billiard Table is to secure such an arrangement as will admit of a Ball being struck so as to attain the highest speed without its jumping. This, it need scarcely be said, depends entirely upon the arrangement of the cushions. C. L. & Co. mentioning this fact would state that the subject has largely occupied their attention and after repeated experiments and close consideration they have discovered a principle in the manufacture of cushions which answers admirably the end desired. Since the manufacture of their cushion on this new principle, C. L. & Co. have received testimonials from some of the first clubs in India speaking to the merits of the same. To secure *truth* with *speed*, that is to say, the maximum of speed compatible with preventing the Ball jumping, is the object which C. L. S. & Co. have had in view and which at length they have successfully attained. At the same time the cushions, it should be stated, are quite as durable or even more durable under the new principal of making up that under the old, With a view to the maintenance of the high character of their workmanship C. L. & Co. have secured for this branch of their business especially, the services of a gentleman who for many years was foreman to the eminent makers, Messrs. Burroughes and Watts, whose experience is a guarantee of the highest possible excellence in the manufacture of Billiard Tables and of everything connected with that department of their business.

Printing Materials.

MILLER AND RICHARD'S PRESS & TYPES and all requisites always in Stock.

TERMS CASH.

WING & CO.

!!! हुक्का !!!
!!! HOOKAHS !!!

ENGLISH made Hookahs of various choice designs, colours and sizes ranging in price from Rs. 2 to 5 each, 60 designs to choose from, Apply to

RADANAUTH CHOWDRY,
373, Jorasanko

THE INDIAN MIRROR

THE CHEAPEST DAILY PAPER
IN
INDIA
AND
HAVING AN EXTENSIVE CIRCULATION

SUBSCRIPTIONS.

	Town.	Mofussil, Including Postage.
Yearly	Rs. 12 0 0	Rs. 20 0 0
Half yearly	6 8 0	11 0 0
Quarterly	3 8 0	5 8 6
Monthly	1 8 0	2 8 0

Cash sales, One Anna per copy.

Sunday Edition,
STRICTLY IN ADVANCE.

Per Annum ... ... Rs. 5

MOFUSSIL SUBSCRIBERS.

Per Annum ... ... Rs. 6 10 0

VIA SOUTHAMPTON.		VIA BRINDISI.	
	£ S. D.		£ S. D.
Per Annum	0 15 6	Per Annum	1 7 6

Cash sales, Two Annas per copy.

RATE OF ADVERTISING.

First insertion, 8 lines and under, 1 Rupee.

Second and succeeding insertions, 2 Annas per line.

For Advertisements which are to be inserted for a considerable time special contracts may be **made on** application to the manager.

Domestic Occurrences	Non-Subscriber	1 Re.
	Subscriber	8 Ans
Public Engagement each insertion		1 Re.

FOR SALE.

AT THE BRAHMO SOMAJ OF INDIA
MISSION OFFICE.
No 13, Mirzapore Street.

	Rs.	As.	P.
Sacred Anthology ...	2	0	0
Last Days of Rajah Ram Mohun Roy ...	1	0	0
Essays, Theological and Ethical ...	1	0	0
Historical Sketch of the Brahmo Somaj	0	6	0
Jesus Christ, Europe and Asia ...	0	3	0
Future Church ...	0	3	0
Lecture at the Brahmo School ...	0	1	0
True Faith ...	0	2	0
Appeals to Young India ...	0	0	6
Brahmo Somaj Vindicated ...	0	2	0
Popular Tracts, No. 1 to 4 ...	0	2	0
Destiny of Human Life ...	0	2	0
Reconstruction of Native Society ...	0	1	0
Welcome Soiree in England ...	0	1	0
Lecture on Inspiration ...	0	4	0
Essential Principles of Brahma Dharma	0	1	0
Proceedings of the Marriage Law meeting at the Town Hall ...	0	2	0
Theistic Annual 1872 ...	0	8	0
Ditto Ditto 1873 ...	0	8	0
Ditto Ditto 1874 ...	1	0	0
Ditto Ditto 1875 ...	1	0	0
Lecture on Progress of Theism ...	0	2	0
Ditto Age of Enlightenment ...	0	2	0
Life of Educated Native ...	0	2	0
Lecture on Marriage Law ...	0	2	0
Ditto on the Jains ...	0	2	0
Man the Son of God ...	0	1	0
Order of Service ...	0	1	0
Prayers for Different Occasions of Life	0	3	0
Divine Service in Hindee ...	0	1	0
Theistic Devotions ...	0	5	0
Behold the Light of Heaven in India ...	0	3	0
Epistles to the Theists in India ...	0	0	6
Lecture on Prayer ...	0	1	0
Ditto Alcohol ...	0	2	0

JUST RECEIVED FROM ENGLAND.

	Rs.	As.	P.
Practical Sermons ...	0	12	0
Memoir of Rev. Dr Carpenter ...	0	12	0
Morning and Evening Meditations ...	0	12	0
Channing's Perfect Life ...	1	0	0

A FASHIONABLE high wheeled C-spring Buggy by Dykes and Co., with silver plated mountings, quite new. Apply 12 Bentinck Street.

SMITH STANISTREET & CO.

Pharmaceutical Chemists & Druggists
BY APPOINTMENT
To His Excellency the Right Hon'ble
LORD NORTHBROOK, G.M.S.I.,
Governor-General of India.
&c. &c.

SYRUP of Lactate of Iron Prepared from the original recipe. Lactate of Iron, in various forms of preparation, has been in use in France, and generally through the Continent of Europe, for some years past, and is highly esteemed as one of the most valuable Chalybeate Tonic Remedies yet introduced. The Syrup being the most agreeable as well as convenient form of administration is in most general use.

It is a most valuable remedy in the following diseases:—Chlorosis or Green Sickness, Leucorrhœa, Neuralgia, Enlargement of the Spleen, &c. In combination with quinine, it has also been very successfully used in the cure of Fever, while to persons of delicate constitution, or enfeebled by disease, it is invaluable. In bottles, Rs. 2 each.

Syrup of the Phosphate of Iron, Rs. 2 per bottle.

Syrup of Phosphate of Iron and Strychnine, Rs. 2 per bottle.

Syrup of Phosphate of Iron and Quinine, Price Rs. 2-8 per bottle.

Syrup of Phosphate of Iron, Quinine and Strychnine, (Dr. Aitkin's Triple Tonic Syrup) Rs. 2-8 per bottle.

Smith, Stanistreet & Co.

Invite special attention to the following rates, the quality guaranteed as the best procurable:—

Pure Ærated Waters.

Made from Pure Water, obtained by the new process through the Patent Charcoal Filters.

			Rs.	As.
Ærated plain (Triple Ærated), per doz. ...			0	12
Soda Water	ditto	" ...	0	12
Gingerade	ditto		1	4
Lemonade	ditto		1	4
Tonic (Quinine)	ditto	" ...	1	4

The *Cash* must be sent with the order to obtain advantage of the above rates.

TO CLEAR OFF STOCK

J. DAVIS & Co.

Are selling their Wool Wrappers

HALF PRICE.

No. 6 Government Place, Calcutta.

How to Enjoy Life

is only known when the blood is pure, its circulation perfect, and the nerves in good order. The only safe and certain method of expelling all impurities is to take Holloway's Pills, which have the power of cleansing the blood from all noxious matters, expelling all humours which taint or impoverish it, thereby purify and invigorate and give general tone to the system. Young or old robust or delicate, may alike experience their beneficent effects. Myriads affirmed that these Pills possess marvellous power in securing these great secrets of health by purifying and regulating the fluids and strengthening the whole.

Printed and published by M. M. RUKHIT, at the "INDIAN MIRROR" PRESS, No 15, College Square, for the Proprietor.

The Indian Mirror.

SUNDAY EDITION.

VOL. XVI] CALCUTTA, SUNDAY, FEBRUARY 13, 1876 {REGISTERED AT THE GENERAL POST OFFICE.} [NO. 36

CONTENTS.

NOTICE.

Letters and all other communications relating to the literary department of the Paper should be addressed to "The Editor."

All letters on the business of the Press should be addressed, and all remittance made payable to the Manager of this Paper. Particular attention is solicited to this notice.

Subscribers will be good enough to give prompt notice of any delay, or irregularity in delivery of the Paper.

Editorial Notes

WE have to remind our Brahmo readers that the minister's lecture comes off next Wednesday, in the hall of the Calcutta School, College Square, at 7-30 P. M. The subject is a most interesting one, and may be said to be the topic of the hour,—"The Lord called them and classified them."

BABU Srinath Dutt has been appointed Rector of the Calcutta School in succession to Babu Krishna Bihary Sen, who has been appointed Principal of the Jeypore College. We are glad that the Indian Reform Association have found so able and competent a successor, whose special qualification lies in the fact that he studied for three years in England, and was a distinguished student of the Presidency College. The students of the Calcutta School presented a farewell address to Babu Krishna Bihary Sen yesterday. Many were moved to tears.

THE current of religious thought among Brahmo devotees during the past week indicates a strong tendency towards the organization of a system of daily devotion and discipline, adapted to the higher wants and aspirations of the soul, and helpful to those who desire to settle for ever in the higher spheres of spirituality. The morning services held at the minister's house every day seem to have awakened a thirst for communion which demands more exalted and more systematic spiritual discipline than is now possible. Hence is it that all eyes are hopefully looking forward to the evolution of a plan of life adapted to true devotees.

IT is desirable that our prayers and devotional exercises should be strictly scientific and real. Every thing that is imaginary, sentimental, and shadowy ought to be eliminated, and every word that is uttered in adoration, prayer, or hymn must be thoroughly real. Religion is a science. It is the highest science. Nothing should therefore be cherished in our religious thoughts and sentiments except that which has been found to stand on a scientific basis. We must not pray for sentiment's sake, not even for enjoyment's sake. Let not devotion commend itself to us by its mere sweetness. Let us not indulge in rhetorical or poetical flights in the course of our prayers because it is a pleasure to do so. It is the glory of our faith that it shuns fancy and fiction, and accepts only what is real and scientific. We are glad to find the prayers of the Brahmo Somaj are gradually assuming a more scientific, and therefore a simpler form.

DO our fellow religionists know the value of sympathy? We suppose they do not. Ought there not be some among us who will deeply sympathise with the struggles and sorrows of others, and by their knowledge of, and conquest over evil, give that help which is the highest service man can do to man. There are many who are ready to give advice, many more who are ready to offer criticism. How few do we find, who are prepared to feel for our deficiencies, as a friend would feel, as a brother would feel, and labor to lead us out of our difficulties. It is one thing to pray *devotedly* and struggle for the good and for the salvation of a country, or a community, or the world at large; it is quite a different thing to feel personal interest in the hopes, aspiration, sorrows, and difficulties of individuals who wait with the burden of their trial, and look about in trust for some one. Can the Brahmos, may we us ask can the Brahmo Missionaries do this for each other? If they can, well and good, their organization will gain in firmness, solidity, and success. If they cannot, they must recommence their career as a church.

WE are ready to admit the difficulty which Christians of the orthodox school feel when they hear us making use of evangelical phraseology to express opinions and doctrines strange, and perhaps sacrilegious to them. But while writing and speaking in the English language on the subject of religion, we can not but adopt words familiar in Christian theology, to mean certain realities which we hold in common not perhaps with the rigorously evangelical, but with liberal Christian theologians of various types. Now such words as "the Kingdom of Heaven," "the Holy Spirit," "salvation" &c., can not be avoided in a discourse where the object of the speaker is to point out at once the error of certain popular conceptions which have received currency, and the truth which those conceptions, rightly interpreted, would convey to every unbiased mind. Christian expounders may state with their usual vehemence that the members of the Brahmo Somaj know nothing of the Holy Spirit, and claim the exclusive knowledge, enjoyment, and monopoly of that divine agency; we rest contented merely with putting before the public our sense of the matter, and completely ignoring what other people may think, or say about it. Any criticism of our views from a narrow and dogmatic point of view is simply useless. Let critics, if they want to controvert our position, meet us on our own ground.

WILLIAM KING THOMPSON was an American. He came from Brooklyn in New York, and had successfully run many a blockade, till he formed the terrible scheme which has made his name very nearly unparalleled in the history of crime. He wanted to ship a quantity of goods at Southampton, and insure them at the highest insurance rates as very valuable articles, being entitled to realize an exceedingly large sum of money in case of their loss at sea. Now with the goods he planned to put a case in which a number of torpedo shells were packed together with a clock-work machine which being wound up would go quietly for ten days, (the time the vessel will take to be in the high seas) and then put forth a hammer striking with the weight of 30 lbs. against any object nearest to it. In the present case the machine and the shells being put together, the shells would be struck, and in their explosion would destroy the ship, crew, passengers, freight, and everything. The machine was ordered in Germany and was put on board the *Mosel* one of the German Lloyd Steamers at Bremen. By some accident the ship was delayed, and the explosion took place before she had left that port, injuring the *Mosel* and a tug, killing about seventy men, and maiming scores of people who had been to the quay to bid farewell to their friends on board. "Great graves of blown off arms and legs were made," and Thompson in a fit of wild remorse cut his throat. Though not killed at first, he tore off the bandages, and died from the effects of the self-inflicted wound. To plot the massacre of hundreds of innocent men and women for the sake of a sum of money, the safe acquirement of which was after all problematical, and to meet with his doom so unexpectedly, shows a strange frustration of the ends of wickedness. Thompson's crime is incomparable.

APPROACH TO THE DEITY

THE philosophy of the Divine nature is simply beyond the power of understanding. If it had not been so, the greatest thinkers of the age would not have failed to attain the remotest knowledge of sacred things, in the denial of which their best reasonings have become a snare and a deception to mankind. If it had not been so, the highest and most elaborate efforts of religious men at theological speculation would have borne better fruit in convincing the sceptical of the truth of principles which to the simple and unsophisticated are self-evident. The Deity cannot be approached through the understanding. If the philosophy of the times proves anything, it proves this. When the understanding fails, men insist upon belief. Believe inspite of doubts, fasten your straying soul with the iron-hooks of belief, and you will be admitted into the kingdom of heaven. We are not in the least inclined to question the uses of such rigid belief; it is a great discipline, and has its reward. But we cannot say if the Deity can be approached through it either. Sentiment is next insisted upon. Combine belief with feeling. Try to feel, and move your heart with the things which you intellectually accept, and the intensity of your affections will quicken your whole nature. Your accustomed frigidity of spirit will relax, and you will be permitted to approach the presence of your God. We are very much indisposed to under-rate the advantages of good devout sentiment. There is no doubt that feelings move the soul very much, and often move it in the right direction. But still we must raise our warning voice to declare that emotion, satisfying and sanctifying as it often is, is no satisfactory passport to the blessed sight and enjoyment of the Divine Being and his attributes. It will be said next that the purity of character is the best recommendation and test on this subject. Blessed are the pure in heart for they shall see God. Doubtless this is true, quite as true as right sentiment, and right belief entitle a man to the ultimate attainment of God. But it is untrue also in one respect. A man may have the purest character, and still he may possess as little real wisdom about the presence and attributes of the great God, as another whose sinlessness of life is not worthy of comparison with his. From this we may conclude that no advantages of the intellect, no profusion of sentiment, no discipline of belief, and even no rectitude of life will enable a man to solve those profound problems of communion between the human spirit and the Divine soul, before which the philosophy and religion of the age stand dumb and awe-struck. No explanation, or exegesis, no conference, or commentary will bring in the final light. Though it must be admitted that everything is a help in that direction. The approach to the Deity is through Divine influence only. The powers of spiritual perception are awakened by the unmistakable reality of the Object before the soul. The Reality is the recommendation, the Reality is the test. The aptitudes and attitudes of the man to which the Divine nature addresses itself, we do not mean here to speak of, though it must be said there are such special aptitudes in some men more than in others. It is our purpose here only to insist upon the fact that when the soul perceives the approach of the Lord, it approaches him, and can approach him only on that condition. Men according to their temperaments, habits, and wants feel this approach in different ways, and their own approach to the Deity is regulated accordingly. It is impossible to count the inlets of human nature through which God makes his entrance thereinto. It is equally impossible to count the inlets and attractions in the Divine nature through which man is drawn to him. The Object is one, the entrances and approaches are different. The impressions and experiences must agree, though the processes must differ. Let us by all means make the right and impartial estimate of human gifts and faculties—of intellect, and emotion, of imagination and conscience; but let us not commit the painful mistake of circumscribing, or even defining the fields, and pastures, the streams, and hill-sides where God calls His children to unveil his awful face. Accuracy of sight, genuine perception of the Reality are no doubt desirable; but accuracy of definitions, and exactitude of processes must in the nature of the case be unattainable. Any straining of power, or speech, or feeling, or thought may end in great spiritual disorder. Let us by all means profit by the superior experiences of our teachers and elder brethren, let us compare our own humble experiences with theirs; let us go down into the deep places of the devotions and spiritual utterances of others because these things prepare the soul for its high destiny. But of one thing let us rest well assured. It is He alone who knows all the intricacies, bye-paths, and delicate surroundings of the soul, it is our God alone who can make our approach possible to him. It is he alone who can explain himself. He knows his times; his processes are known to himself only; he knows his children by name, their needs, weaknesses, their deep susceptibilities and disadvantages, he alone beholds as no one else can. Let him choose how he will call us to him. The foolishness of the uninstructed is counted wisdom before his eye; and the wisdom of the wise ends in confusion and overthrow. The stumblings of the lame and halt lead them into the right path, and the strength and the speed of the fast-goers pave their way to destruction. Let the Lord approach, and there is no one so dull and backward among us, who will not know how to approach him. Let the Lord speak, and there is no one so deaf or so dumb in our midst who will not hear, and answer in the right language of devotion. Let the Lord reveal himself, and we will all sing out the song of true adoration, and in the harmony of the united experiences of spiritual life.

UNNATURAL RELIGIOUS MEN.

THERE are some religious men who are so very "natural," that they can not be distinguished from the irreligious. They not only marry, multiply, live, and earn money like others, but even dance, drink, bet, and hunt foxes like their brethren. Their life is an effort to dress up the pleasantest things of this world in a gown and surplice. Such men set against themselves a strong tide of reaction, which brings on to the surface quite a different type of religious humanity. We call them unnatural religious men. Religion to great majority of men is an unnatural thing, and to them it is no wonder that its professors should push themselves several steps beyond the reach of ordinary flesh and blood. And not a few religious men there are who have the idea that to inspire a wholesome awe among the gentiles and sinners, they must always bear their caste-marks on their foreheads. To us religion being the most natural thing, it makes its followers much more natural than other men, in the best and highest sense of that word. But unnatural religious men take nature to be a term of reproach, and sink as far below it, or soar as far above it, as their dyspeptic imagination will allow. Unnatural religiousness may be bodily or mental. It finds vent in turning up the white of the eye at the shortest notice. The mouth is twitched and screwed into all fantastic shapes; the voice is dolorous, nasal and of the appointed pitch; the accents invariably keep "the regulation cut;" the eyebrows go up and down, backwards and forwards; and the whole face may look as unimpassioned and dry as a piece of canvas. Or this sort of religiousness may nestle in long uncombed beards, in bathless bodies, unshaven chins, uncut nails, unclean teeth, stiff shoulder-blades, straight backs, and clothes which seldom go to the wash. The mental manifestations are still more marked. The intellect is innocent of all culture. There is a pious and wholesome horror of philosophy. Books, especially thoughtful books, are discarded for the all-sufficient reason that they are not understood. Educated men are spoken of with the loftiest contempt, and the more rational and consequently more formidable they are, the greater is the scorn they get. There is constant and unremitting criticism of every system, of every man, of every event, of everything in the world in fact; only the pious critic never condescends to take the trouble of studying the facts and merits of the case, but always judges and condemns from the high pedestal of *a priori* convictions. There is much discussion, which sometimes waxes unnecessarily loud and hot, but the allowance of reason and logic therein is remarkably moderate. The principal ingredients are authoritative quotations, exclamations of "faith," threats about future destiny, and pungent personalities which seldom fail to silence the disputants either in shame and sorrow, or in speechless anger. If they are very hardy and determined controversialists, they still perhaps keep up the noise for a long while, and then become quiet from sheer exhaustion, to renew the fight and fly to each other's throat at the very next opportunity. The atmosphere rings with the ceaseless cries, quarrels, reasonings and contradictions of the unnatural religious men. Then as to feelings, they are always cut and dry. The right word, coined to express the right sentiment, is used to the right person, in the right place. The only trifling draw-back is the absence of the sentiment itself. The most over-flowing affection is lavished upon the world; the speech used for the purpose flows so fast that it sticks in the throat; deep, and oftentimes needlessly strong professions of humility are made; unsavoury comparisons are instituted between self and all manner of strange objects around us. But behind the stage there is a very reasonable amount of selfishness and self-esteem kept in reserve, lest the unappreciative should take the accomplished penitent at his word, and demand an equal measure of eloquence and life. The utmost anxiety for the salvation of the wicked world is expressed, and the lamentations against all hard-heartedness and sinfulness in the abstract are indeed touching. But friends and benefactors are heard to complain that the holy enthusiast is now and then very unfeeling himself, and ignores the ordinary friendships and obligations of life. Society finds its claims disregarded by him, and even the appeals of the domestic circle fail to make impression. The heart is like a piece of dry bone wrapped up, like Budha's tooth, in a glorious drapery of sentimental phrases. In moral and practical life the discrepancies are equally glaring. Self-indulgence under forms of asceticism is a frequent spectacle. Self-will under professions of obedience is by no means rare. Rags and tatters, fasts and vigils do not always show the right man. Only the deception concealed among the externals of righteousness, pains as well as disgusts. The voluptuary who carries his character on his face is almost harmless in his evident shame. The false devotee who covers his secret wickedness with sacred professions is a wolf in sheep's clothing, and deserves the very worst at the hands of outraged society. He condemns the innocent enjoyments of life, but festers and rots in the hidden ulcers and lusts of his soul. But what is the use of going on in this bitter strain? Let all religious men prove true to themselves, and show in their lives and teachings how beautiful, good, sweet, and sacred human nature can be. And then if by Divine Grace they ascend to regions of goodness and purity unattainable by their weaker brethren, their excellence will not reproach, but exalt the standard of humanity wherewith the actions and affections of common men are measured. True humanity is divinity in human shape, and the son of man is then only honored and glorified, when he has proved himself to be the son of God.

The Interpreter

HOW are we to find God? What is the way? To whom does He reveal Himself? To these questions the earlier scriptures of the Hindus return a simple reply. No elaborate machinery of redemption is there set forth, no complicated means are prescribed for the attainment of God and salvation. According to the Kathopanishad the 'way' is simple, extremely simple. It is faith in the truth "I am." "The Lord is not reached by words, by the mind or by the eye. He alone who says that God is, finds Him, who else can find him?" 6-12. Mark the words "He who says that *God is.*" The mere declaration of Divine existence, the mere assertion of the fact that the Lord *is*, is enough; nothing else is needed; that is the one thing needful. How awful is the import of these words, —"I am!" How few say with their hearts 'God is!'

HYPOCRISY means double dealing in plain language—wickedness within, semblance of righteousness outside. This is to be eschewed. But austerity within and pleasant countenance outside,—that is desirable, nay enjoined by Divine law. All attempts to *seem* righteous must be shunned and studiously avoided. The higher and more rigid exercises of the soul towards purity should be treated as secret matters between man and his Maker, and they ought, as far as is possible, to be concealed from men. Concealment here is a duty; putting on a mask is here an inviolable obligation. It may seem strange, but it is true. Hear what Jesus says—"When thou fastest, anoint thine head and wash thy face; that thou appear not unto men to fast, but unto thy Father which is in secret."

THOSE who have read carefully the sixth chapter of Matthew know, at least they ought to know, the true type of asceticism. Mere poverty or abstinence is not asceticism, nor should fasting nor idleness nor physical penances to be regarded as such. "Take *no thought* for your life, what ye shall eat or what ye shall drink,"—this is the essence of asceticism; in other words that self-possessed and tranquil resignation to Providence which abhors and banishes all anxiety for food and raiment as so much infidelity and scepticism. They who apprehend that God may desert them are men "of little faith." The motto of true asceticism is not "Starve," but "Let the Lord provide." Relying trustfully upon His providence "seek ye first the kingdom of heaven," and believe that the Lord will provide whatsoever is essential to your welfare.

Meditations

I HAVE seen a great many good men and women. There are some intensely anxious for their own improvement and peace. There are many who to this anxiety add anxiety for those who are nearest and dearest to them. The second set of people are better than the first. But how few are those who self-forgetful, and forgetful of all pertaining to self, are anxious for the good of others only!

How great how wonderful is the capacity of every soul to love and to obey.

THE joy of feeling that other men, those perhaps whom erewhile you thought to be your inferiors, are above you in the spiritual world, is humble, but exalting.

Brahmo Hymns

[*Translated from Bengali.*]

WHO art thou, always seated so near unto me? Thy nature, disposition and habits are very sweet; say what is thy name. Why lovest thou me so tenderly every day, and why intoxicated with love dost thou ceaselessly benefit me! Incomparable both in beauty and internal worth, thy like I have nowhere seen; with sweet attraction my heart is drawn to thee now and often. I know thee not and am not acquainted with thee, yet the heart is fascinated if it sees thee. I feel as if I knew thee. Oh! how strange! What relation dost thou bear to me, Father or Mother? Whoever thou mayst be, thou art mine and I am thine.

O MORAL Governor and Judge, who can violate thy decrees? Where is the man who has become happy by practising irreligion and vice! Thou vanquisher of pride, All-just, thy name is the chastiser of infidels; none can escape thy strict justice. Evil-minded men secretly do vicious deeds, and feel sorrow in the end, and reap the fruits of their own misdeeds. Thou art our Chastiser, Father, Merciful Dispenser, deliver this great sinner by dispensing punishment.

Devotional.

LEAD me, O thou God of prayer, to the place of communion which is wholly beyond the world, and where no earthly influence can any longer reach me. The house of worship built here is not unassailable, behold how the fatal noose of worldliness fastened round the soul, draws her away from thence very easily. I want to be at a place where the earth can not find me. Where is that place but in thee O Lord! Thou art thine own sanctuary, thine true alter is established in thee. Thou fillest thy own house, thou art all in all there. Lead thou me therefore within thee to worship, and to communion, to behold thee, and be with thee for ever.

TELL me O Lord, what is more valuable or more beautiful in life than the wealth of deep and genuine love? Nothing is more worthy of thee than that. Such love I have frittered away on the poor and passing objects of this world, reserving nothing for thee but vain hollow professions. My God, I feel that my affection has been wasted, and the waste has brought on me much humiliation and self-reproach. To thee, and to others who in thee are truly worthy, I have given nothing; to the unworthy, to those who insult, and trample upon my affection, I have given all. O, if I had loved thee with half the intensity which I have thrown away upon worthless pleasure and beauty, thou wouldst not have left me alone in my shame and sorrow. But human folly will never know thy value, the carnal man will never behold the beauty of thy Spirit. Descend, O thou fountain of all that is lovely and good, descend to fill my soul with thy grace, that in thee I may regain what I have lost, regive what I have hitherto withheld, and find the peace of devoting my whole heart to thee.

WHAT unbounded capacities of goodness and purity hast thou implanted in man's soul, my gracious God, and how poor is the use I have made of them. Return, and teach me to bless thee and enjoy the inheritance wherewith thou hast amply surrounded me. Enable me to make the fitting use of my opportunities and gifts, that I may find the power of calling myself thy servant, and thy son.

The Bramo Somaj.

DAILY morning service is held at the minister's house. Service commences generally at 6-30 A. M.

THE anniversary festival of the Harinavi Brahmo Somaj commenced yesterday. Babu Keshub Chunder Sen addressed the congregation in the afternoon.

SOME people might think it too bad of the Brahmos not to take the slightest notice of the invectives and insults which the lecture of their leader evoked from certain professing Christian writers and correspondents in the newspapers. Perhaps the mildest and most good-tempered review made, has been in the columns of the *Lucknow Witness*. As for the other productions perhaps the Brahmos can afford to pass over them in silence.

THE daughter of Babu Shib Chunder Sen of Delhi was married according to Brahmo rites on the 5th February last. The name of the bridegroom Babu.

A NUMBER of Brahmica ladies were invited by Mrs. Hobhouse at an afternoon party in her house on last Friday. About a dozen went. There was music, and as the evening deepened a magic lantern was brought into requisition, which displayed many interesting scenes and objects.

Gleanings.

Is a man never the better for having sinned? Is there in evil an educting power differing from any other, and to which the soul responds as it can to no other in the whole curriculum of discipline?

May it not be that the admission of the element of guilt, by one of God's great paradoxes, works upon the individual, as upon the universe, in what we call "the long run," an ultimate purity which cannot be evolved from any other element.

Is there not something distinctly rugged in the experience of remorse entering like iron tonic into the soul's blood? What other phase of spiritual life can by any law of spiritual substitution replace the humilities and the sweetnesses of repentance? What sinless character but would forever miss a charm in having missed the graces and joys of renewal? Is not the beauty of *acquired* holiness peculiar to itself alone?

Love feeleth no burden, considereth no pains, desireth above its strength, complaineth not of impossibility, for it thinketh all things possible. It is, therefore, able to undertake all things, and performeth and bringeth many things to pass; whereas he that loveth not, fainteth and sinketh under them. Love is sweet, sincere, pious, pleasant, and delightful, strong patient, prudent, long-suffering, and never seeking itself. For where one seeketh himself he falleth from love.

> Earth forges joy into a chain,
> Till fettered Love forgets its strength,
> Its purpose and its end; but Pain
> Restores its heritage at length,
> And bids Love rise again and be
> Eternal, mighty, pure, and free."

A. PROCTOR.

Literary.

MR. THOMAS CARLYSLE reached his eightieth year in last December. He received the congratulations of German and English savants, and a gold medal and a letter signed by Tennyson, Browning, Owen, Darwin, Harriet Martineau, Dean Stanly, Max Muller, Huxley, Caird, and Tulloch reached him at Chelsea on his birthday. The *Christian World* thus summarises the character of Carlysle:—With a volcanic genius, he has united the homely virtues with which he was made familiar in the cottage of his birth. He has himself declared, in one of his most impressive passages that there is no nobler spectacle than the peasant saint; but we confess that we have even a profounder veneration for the man who preserves the peasant's simplicity and purity of life while passing through the fires of speculation, and fighting as a man of letters in our modern world. May the best of blessings rest, during the remaining days of his earthly pilgrimage, on Thomas Carlysle!

WE observe with pleasure that English psychological science which has long had no adequate representative in periodical literature, is to acquire a quarterly organ in the year which is now just upon us. Professor Croom Robertson, of University College, London, whose philosophy indeed is not ours, but who is not proposing to limit his Review to any sect or school of thought, is to edit a Review of which the first number will appear in January under the title of "Mind." Mr. Herbet Spencer, Mr. Venn, the Rector of Lincoln College, Mr. Shadworth Hodgson, and last but not least, Mr. Henry Sidgwick, as well as the Editor, are to contribute to the first number.

The Week

SIR BARTLE FRERE and Canon Duckworth have left Lahore for Peshawar.

BABU Surendra Nath Banuerji joined the post of Head Master of the Metropolitan Institution, Calcutta, on the 11th.

MISS MARY CARPENTER delivered an address at the Prarthana Somaj Mandir, Bombay, on Wednesday last.

THE Hon'ble Louis Jackson of the High Court, will, it is stated, shortly visit Gya, in connection perhaps with Mr. Bignold's case.

THE Maharajah of Cashmere is said to have paid Messrs. Kellner and Co. the sum of Rs. 40,000 as table money during the Prince's visit to Cashmere.

LIKE Captain Burton, who is now at Bombay, Mr. Alfred H. Bowne, a European, has made a pilgrimage to Mecca, and just returned to Bombay.

THE investiture of the staff of his Royal Highness the Prince of Wales with the Order of the Star of India will take place at Allahabad.

THE Mohurrum has passed off quietly at Bombay.

MR. JOHN MARRIOTT, lately acting Judge of the Bombay High Court, succeeds Mr. Scoble as Advocate General, Bombay.

IT is said that Lieutenant-Colonel Wellesley, Lord Cowley's son, Military Attache at St. Petersburgh, is likely to come out in the suite of the new Viceroy.

AN English journal states (says the *Pioneer*) that the late Lord Lytton's unfinished romance of *Pausanias* is in the press. The work is edited by the coming Viceroy, who has written a long preface.

PROFESSOR MONIER WILLIAMS, who is the guest of Captain Nisbett, Deputy Commissioner, Lahore, attended a meeting of the Anjuman-i-Punjab, and was presented with an address in Sanskrit and Persian.

BABU NOBIN KRISHNA MUKERJI is appointed to be a Law Lecturer of the Hughly College.

REUTER telegraphs to say that Lord Lytton will embark from Brindisi in the steamer *Orontes*, which will leave Portsmouth on the 1st proximo.

MISS CARPENTER is now at Bombay, where she delivered an address and opened a branch of the National Indian Association, on Friday last.

THERE is a rumour at Jacobabad, that the Khan of Khelat has been murdered by the Sirdars of Beluchistan.

SMALL-POX is raging fearfully at Bombay just now.

AMONG the articles in the fourth volume of the forthcoming edition of the *Encyclopædia Britannica* will be—"Calcutta" by Dr. Hunter, the Biographer of Lord Mayo.

MR. J. TALBOYS WHEELER will shortly resume his appointment in Burmah of Secretary to the Local Government.

THE P. and O. Co.'s *S.S. Thibet* took away from Bombay, on Monday last, several nobilities, *viz.*, the Duke of Sutherland, Sir

Louis and Lady Mallet and Mr. Albert Grey Private Secretary to Sir Bartle Frere.

LATEST NEWS

The capital of Ceylon has followed the example of the capital of India by taking steps for the establishment of a Zoological Museum.

It is currently reported, says the *Sindian*, and the rumour has received confirmation from a private gentleman who has just arrived from Las Bayla, that Ebrahim Khan, the brother of the late Nurdin Mengel, has collected a force of about 18,000 men and intends attacking the Khan of Khelat at Mere, a fort at that place. Ebrahim Khan, who is in his own village, has cautioned the ex-Jam's son against moving about, or exposing himself to unnecessary risk, assuring him that he, Ebrahim Khan, is sufficient of himself to give a good account of the murderer of his brother.

There is a report current in Singapore that His Excellency Sir William Drummond Jervois has resigned.

The branch line from Ajmere to Nasirabad will be opened for public traffic on the 14th instant.

Mr. Ney Elias will sooner or later succeed Lieutenant C. B. Cooke as Officiating Political Agent at Bhamo.

Mr. Albert Grey, who came out as Private Secretary to Sir Bartle Frere, was obliged to resign his appointment through ill-health and left for England by last mail.

As nothing has been heard to the contrary, it may be inferred that the Mohurrum festival which ended at Hyderabad on Monday last, has passed off without street warfare or bloodshed.

The Bishop of Calcutta will shortly visit Peshawur.

His Excellency the Viceroy and Governor-General, as Grand Master, is pleased to appoint Mr. T. H. Thornton, c. s. i., to be the Secretary of the Most Exalted Order of the Star of India.

His Excellency the Viceroy and Governor-General is pleased to accept the resignation by the Hon'ble Ashley Eden, c. s. i., of his seat as an Additional Member of the Council of the Governor-General for making Laws and Regulations.

Mr. G. FitzGerald, Deputy Accountant General, Bengal, has been granted by Her Majesty's Secretary of State for India an extension of leave for six months on medical certificate.

Surgeon Major Alexander Garden, m. d., Civil Surgeon of Mussurie in the North-Western Provinces, is to officiate as Sanitary Commissioner of Oudh during the absence of Dr. G. S. Sutherland.

Lieutenant-Colonel R. Murray, Officiating Director General of Telegraphs in India, is granted subsidiary leave for a period not exceeding 30 days.

Sir William Gregory returned to Colombo from his visit to India, on the 30th of January.

His Excellency Sir Philip Wodehouse Governor of Bombay, left Poona for Sholapore on his way to Bijapore, on Monday last, by the evening train. His Excellency, after a stay of two days at Bijapore, will return to Poona, and then proceed to Bombay.

A lecture on the "Idea of the Infinite" was given, on Wednesday last, by the Right Rev. Bishop Meurin, in connection with the "Bombay Debating Society" in the St. Xavier's College Hall.

Notwithstanding the many precautions taken by the police to prohibit the sale of spirituous liquors and drugs, during the last five days of the Mohurrum at Bombay, several Mahomedans were placed, before Mr. Nana Moroji, at the Fort Police Court, charged with being drunk and disorderly the night previous; in some cases fines were inflicted, and in others the offenders were warned and discovered.

Sir Neville Chamberlain, the newly appointed Commander-in-Chief of Madras, held a Levee on Friday last, in the Banqueting Hall, Madras. The officers of the Head-Quarters Staff were first presented to His Excellency by Colonel Clarke, his Private Secretary.

The Prince's Visit.

The grand Nautch at Jeypore was danced by about fifty girls in the courtyard adjoining the reception room. The dancers were surrounded by men with torches.

Calcutta.

The *Statesman* says :—"There was a rumour again in town yesterday (Friday) that the Prince of Wales does really return to Calcutta, Dr. Fayrer having counselled his embarkation from this city, in consequence of the prevalence of small-pox in Bombay."

A meeting of orthodox Hindudom (says the *Englishman,*) has, we see, been convened by certain Hindu gentlemen, for Sunday next, at the house of the late Sir Rajah Radha Kanta Deb, to take measures for combating the growing subversion of orthodox Hindu manners and customs. The meeting might as well attempt to arrest the Ganges in its course.

The Directors of the Bank of Bengal, at their meeting on Thursday last, made no alteration in the rate of interest or discount.

In the case in which Haribol Chunder Ghosh and Keshab Chunder Mannah are charged with forgery and with uttering forged documents and which is now being enquired into by Mr. Dickens with a view to committal to the Sessions, the Magistrate has held that the confessions made by the defendants, and received by Moulvi Abdul Latif at his house at Toltallah, are not admissible. Under the circumstances it is feared that the prosecution will not succeed in bringing home the charges to the prisoners, for whom Mr. Lowe has been retained.

The meeting of the British Indian Association against the New Municipal Bill, held at the rooms of the Association last evening, was a most successful one. It was most respectably and influentially attended. Rajah Romanath Tagore was in the chair. No less than eight resolutions were passed. The first resolution was proposed by Babu Digumber Mitter, seconded by Rajah Norendra Krishna and supported by Mr. J. B. Knight. The second resolution was proposed by Mr. F. F. Wyman, seconded by Babu Seetul Doss Mullick and supported by Babu Chunder Nath Bose. The third resolution was passed by Mr. Jennings and seconded by Babu Norendronath Sen. The fourth resolution was proposed by Babu Debender Mullick and seconded by Dr. Mahendrolall Sircar. The fifth resolution was proposed by Babu Judulall Mullick and seconded by Mir Mahomed Hurmuz Shah. The sixth resolution was proposed by Mr. W. C. Bonnerji and seconded by Babu Dwarkanath Biswas. The seventh resolution was proposed by Mr. Manickji Rustomji and seconded by Mir Mahomed Ally. The eighth resolution was proposed by Mr. Vardon and seconded by Mir Vonlitzgy. A Memorial to His Honor the Lieutenant-Governor was adopted.

Public Engagements.

Wednesday, 16th February.—Babu Keshub Chunder Sen's Lecture, in the hall of the Calcutta School, at 7-30 p.m. Subject,—"The Lord called them and classified them."

Musical Evangelistic Service, the Rev. R. J. Ellis (Bengali Translator to Government) will deliver an address in Bengali in the Free Church Institution, Nimtollah Street, this Evening, 13th instant, at 6-30 o'clock. Hymns in Bengali, set to Hindu Music will be sung.

Law

POLICE.—12th February 1876.

[*Before F. J. Marsden, Esq.*]

A Ship-Captain charged one of his crew with absence without leave. The defendant pleaded guilty, and the Magistrate, taking into consideration the very good character given him by his Captain, sentenced him to a forfeiture of two days' wages.

A Mahomedan dresser in the Sealdah Hospital was charged with the theft of a bamboo from St. Paul's Cathedral, a glass window of which was under repairs. The defendant, who proved not guilty, and endeavoured to establish an alibi, was convicted on the evidence of the darwan and a Chowkidar, who arrested him with the bamboo in his possession in Circular Road. He was sentenced to a month's rigorous imprisonment.

A Khalasi charged another with the theft of a pair of silver anklets and an old watch. The defendant pleaded not guilty. It appeared that both the complainant and the defendant had gone to the former's house, and that shortly afterwards both the articles and the defendant were suddenly missing. The defendant who was arrested on suspicion, confessed to the arresting officer, but not after the usual denial at first, that he had pledged the articles, which were given to him for that purpose by the complainant's sister, to whom they belonged. The Magistrate, however, disbelieved the defence set up, and sentenced the defendant to four months' rigorous imprisonment.

Selection

METHOD OF MORAL TEACHING.

Supposing it to be allowed that sufficient material exists for special moral teaching, the important question arises, in what manner is this teaching to be conducted?—There is a faculty in children by means of which, I believe, the teacher can fix their attention on points of moral truth, and can enlist their sympathies and their will on the side of goodness. That faculty is the *Imagination*. It is always noticed that the imagination of the young is remarkably lively, agile, and playful. Everything that they see is a mirror through which they see numbers of other things; they invest the merest hints and outlines with substance, and the enjoyment of youth is greatly derived from this energy of fancy. Now ideas connected with moral science are particularly capable of being transferred into the mind through the medium of the imagination; indeed, I do not know how otherwise they can be introduced there at all. We realize what is invisible mainly through the visible. Every ethical word that we use shows this fact. 'Right' originally meant *straight*; 'independent,' *hanging on nothing*; 'steady,' *standing firm*, &c. In cases where we cannot trace a borrowed significance, we may be sure that the word has unfortunately been rubbed by age and use into its present characterless form. The whole language of morals consists of definitions of tangible objects and external relations, which we readily translate for ourselves into a system of higher meanings. And not only does the imagination thus supply us with pictures of moral ideas; through its influence also the emotions and the affections are drawn stimulated, and regulated. It re-vivifies for us the past, it enlarges the bounds of our present, it furnishes and peoples for us the future; consequently it exerts a strong qualifying power over our states of feeling: being one of the chief elements of sympathy, and the spring of elevating ideals, it becomes, what with truth it has been called, "the great formative agency by which character is moulded." As, then, this wonderful faculty is the necessary vehicle of moral science, and as children are largely endowed with it, and as its exercise gives them pleasure, we see that the teacher commands an instrument by means of which he may succeed in reaching and moving the minds and the wills of his pupils.

But granted that ethical truth flows readily through the channel of the Imagination, how practically can these lessons be rendered lively and impressive? I can only venture to offer a few suggestions on this point. The first thing to be aimed at is, I think, to call up a sharp definite idea of the subjects to be treated. Fortunately hazy notions are not acceptable to children's bright, acute, though hasty and untrained intellects. If we do not well explain what we mean, their thoughts will dart off to kites and kittens, or the equivalents which succeed these in interest, for no images but such as are real and appreciable do they care to contemplate. The teacher can therefore at once perceive whether he is arresting attention. To secure this necessary clearness and precision, it is often useful to begin by analyzing the word which conveys the subject, and next, the subject itself may be looked at in its material and its symbolic sense, the latter being shown to be in exact accordance with the former. The relations of the idea too to other allied ideas and its contrasts may be considered. Analogies will help to picture it, and various illustrations may be called for, through which its inherent qualities will be more fully recognized. If the subject allows, the teacher can recall past impressions in the children's lives, which will assist to arouse the desired state of feeling. In regard, for instance, to any of the relationships of life as that of companionship, he will represent and combine many of the occasions and possibilities of intercourse which conduce to a right view of that relationship. Out of time and space he will constantly collect as in a focus the truths of experience that bear upon his theme, and thus the sentiments of the pupils will be strengthened in a right direction. Of course in all this their own minds must be incited to action. It is not enough for them just to sit lazily gazing at stores of moral facts displayed by the teacher. Their intellects must accompany him in his researches, and must actually discover truth after truth, he only leading the way, for thus, and thus only, will the lessons produce a lasting impression. Then, too, the teacher will derive important help from the incidents out of history and biography which he and his class will contribute in illustration of the subject on hand. By means of these the children will be brought under the constraining force of example. For good deeds and high motives belonging to the past, though less strong in their influence than those which we can associate with persons living and present, yet often exert through the vivifying power of imagination, a most magnetizing effect. I am aware that this is no new suggestion. History has long been employed with effect in the service of morals, but usually, I think, in a somewhat desultory manner, while what I am urging is that fitting instances should be carefully sought out, and applied to the intensifying of the particular idea to which the children's attention is being directed. Again, the teacher need not confine himself to examples in the form of facts. Imaginary instances of conduct will also tell with much power on children's minds. They extremely enjoy to hear what they call 'suppose' stories out of the lives of boys and girls situated somewhat like themselves—how Edith and Susan made up their long quarrel—how Charles held to the truth in spite of self-interest and ridicule. Indeed the accounts of the efforts, temptations, merits, and demerits of improvised young persons may help to form the character even more surely than those of historical doings, partly because the surroundings in the former case can be more easily realized. The pupils may be encouraged to invent for themselves instances in point, and to give examples of the subject out of well-known works of fiction. It will be useful also to place before them practical problems to be solved, asking them how he would act in such a situation. A very wide field lies open to the teacher: poems, fables, proverbs, wise sayings, will pleasantly diversify the lesson; he can glean helpful material from philology, mental philosophy, and other sciences; he will continually appeal to the ethics of nature, and the symbolism of art. Certain that in some way or other he can gain admittance for his subject into the children's minds, if one road is blocked, he will try another, and though gate after gate prove closed, he will make fresh endeavours till he triumphs. Methods that answer with some pupils will fail with others, but each occasion will add to his experience, and will give him greater skill and facility. The essential points to remember is, that every element introduced into the lesson must tend to make more vivid and more welcome the ethical idea under consideration, because concentration of of aim is always important to success.

Indian General Steam Navigation Company, Limited.

SCHOENE, KILBURN & Co.—*Managing Agent.*

ASSAM LINE.

NOTICE.

Steamers now leave Calcutta for Assam every Tuesday, Goalundo every Thursday and Debrooghur downward every Tuesday.

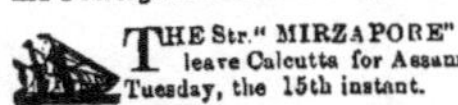

THE Str. " MIRZAPORE" will leave Calcutta for Assam, on Tuesday, the 15th instant.

Cargo will be received at the Company's Godowns, Nimtollah Ghat, until noon of Monday, the 14th instant.

THE Str. " ASSAM" will leave Goalundo for Assam on Thursday, the 17th instant.

Cargo will be received at the Company's Godowns, No. 4, Fairlie Palace, up till noon of Tuesday, the 15th.

Goods forwarded to Goalundo for this vessel will be chargeable with Railway Freight from Calcutta to Goalundo in addition to the regular Freight of this Company.

Passengers should leave for Goalundo by Train of Wednesday, the 16th instant.

CACHAR LINE NOTICE

REGULAR WEEKLY SERVICE.

Steamers now leave Calcutta for Cachar and Intermediate Stations every Tuesday and Chuttuck downward every Monday.

A Steamer and " FLAT" will leave Calcutta for Cachar on Tuesday, the 15th instant.

Cargo will be received at the Company's Godowns, Nimtollah Ghat, up till noon of Monday, the 14th.

For further information regarding rates of Freight or passage money, apply to.

4 Fairlie Palace, *Calcutta, 9th Feb.* 1876.

G. J. SCOTT, *Secretary.*

THE CALCUTTA SCHOOL.

SESSION opened on the 10th of January, 1876. The following are the rates of fees :—

		Schooling fee.	Admission. fee.
English Department.	Rs.	2 0 0	2 0 0
Vernacular	„ ...	1 0 0	1 0 0
Juvenile Class	...	0 8 0	0 8 0

Three Scholarships of Rupees Five each are available next year, to be held by the three most distinguished students of the School who successfully pass the Entrance Examination of December, 1876. There are besides five free studentships in the Entrance class open to competition, applications for which are to be made to the undersigned before the 15th of February next.

KRISHNA BIHARI SEN, M. A.

ALBERT HALL.

PATRON.

His Honor the Lieutenant Governor of Bengal.

COUNCIL.

Hon'ble Sir William Muir, K. C. S. I.—*President.*
Rajah Rama Nath Tagore Bahadur C. S. I.—*Vice-President.*
Hon'ble Ashley Eden, C. S. I.
Archdeacon Baly.
Colonel H. E. L. Thuiller, C. S. I.
Maharajah Kumar of Bettiah.
Rajah Komul Krishna Bahadur.
Rajah Joteendro Mohun Tagore Bahadur.
Babu Digumber Mitter C. S. I.
Hon'ble Nawab Ashgar Ali Bahadur, C. S. I.
Nawab Amir Ali Bahadur.
Moulvi Abdul Lutif Khan Bahadur.
Manockji Rustomji Esq.
Babu Keshub Chunder Sen.

SUBSCRIPTIONS.

His Highness Maharajah Holkar ...	Rs.	[illegible],000
His Highness Maharajah of Jeypore	„	[illegible]
His Highness Maharajah of Putialah	„	2,500
Maharajah Kumar of Bettiah	„	2,000
Rajah of Bhinga ...	„	1,000
Maharani Surnomoie, Cossim Bazar	„	1,000
Maharajah of Hutwa ...	„	500
Rajah Komul Krisna Bahadur ...	„	500
Rajah Roma Nath Tagore Bahadur	„	200
Rajah Joteendro Mohun Tagore ...	„	500

M. Z. MARTIN & CO.,

THE CHINA AND JAPAN WAREHOUES

MERCHANTS AND COMMISSION AGENTS.

No. 4 Dalhousie Square, East.

ICE! ICE! ICE!

MADE IN FOUR MINUTES

THE PNEUMATIC ICE MACHINE

THIS IMPORTANT INVENTION IS CONSIDERED A BOON TO THOSE LIVING IN TROPICAL CLIMATES.

CAN BE WORKED BY THE MOST INEXPERIENCED HAND AND IS NOT LIABLE TO GET OUT OF ORDER.

From Rs. 175, each Machine complete.

MESSRS. ARLINGTON & CO.

AGENTS.

BABU RADHAKANTA GHOSH
HOMŒOPATHIC PRACTITIONER,
12, College, Square.
Is practising here on moderate terms

BABU BASANTA KUMAR DUTTA,
Homœopathic Practitioner.
No. 20. Sucker Halder's Lane, Ahiritolah.

IN THE PRESS.

HOMŒOPATHIC

SERIES IN BENGALI—PICTORIAL.

১। সদৃশ-ভৈষজ্য-সার।

২। সদৃশ-চিকিৎসা-সার।

Will be published monthly.

Subscription for each copy 6 *ans*

ADVANCE SUBSCRIPTION FOR 12 COPIES 3 Rs.;
POSTAGE 8 ANS.

Letters should be addressed and all remittances made payable to the Manager at—

DATTA'S HOMŒOPATHIC LABORATORY.
No. 212, CHITPORE ROAD, [illegible], CALCUTTA.

যৌবনে যোগিনী।

NEW HISTORICAL TRAGEDY

BY

GOPAL CHUNDER MOOKERJEE.

Price, Re. 1, postage 2 ans.

To be had at 50, Grey Street, Shobabazar, and Sanskrit Press Depository.

"HOMŒPATHIC BOOKS FOR SALE."

Jahr's Symptomen Codex by Hempel 3 Vols.	... Rs.	75	0	0
Hahnemann's Chronic Diseases 5 Vols.	...	25	0	0

Enquire Manager *Indian Mirror.*

FOR SALE AT A VERY CHEAP PRICE!!
A handsome Mohogany Piano of Alexander Pers.
Apply to Babu Aditya Kumar Chattopadhyay, No. 3 Mirzapore Street.

NATIONAL COMPANY.
HOMŒOPATHIC CHMISTS AND PUBLISHERS
SUPPLY ALL KINDS OF
HOMŒOPATHIC MEDICINES, BOOKS
CASES AND OTHER REQUISITES,
12 COLLEGE SQUARE,
Calcutta.

A FASHIONABLE high wheeled C-spring Buggy by Dykes and Co, with silver plated mountings, quite new. Apply 12 Bentick Street.

THACKER, SPINK AND CO.
SCHOOL BOOKS.

SELECTIONS FROM MODERN ENGLISH LITERATURE. For the use of the Higher Classes of Indian Schools. By E. LETHBRIDGE Esq., M.A., 8 vo. Cloth. Rs. 2.

HISTORY OF INDIA. For Schools. Second Edition. By E. LETHBRIDGE, Esq., M.A., 18mo. Cloth. Rs. 2.

A SERIES OF SIX ENGLISH READING BOOKS. For Indian Children. By Peary Churn Sircar. Revised by E. LETHBRIDGE, Esq., M.A., FIRST BOOK, 3 Annas. SECOND BOOK, 4 Annas. THIRD BOOK, 5 Annas. FOURTH BOOK, 8 Annas. FIFTH BOOK, 9 Annas. SIXTH BOOK, 10 Annas.

*** *To purchasers of 20 copies of any single Book, a discount of 5 per cent. will be allowed.*

THE WORLD'S HISTORY. Compiled under the direction of E. LETHBRIDGE, Esq., M.A., As. 4.

THE WORLD'S HISTORY. Translated into Bengali. As. 8.

HISTORY AND GEOGRAPHY OF BENGAL: An Easy Introduction to. By E. LETHBRIDGE, Esq., M.A., As. 8.

A HISTORY OF ENGLAND. Compiled under the direction of E. LETHBRIDGE, Esq., M.A., As. 12.

AN EASY INTRODUCTION TO THE HISTORY OF INDIA. By E. LETHBRIDGE, Esq., M.A., As. 12.

EASY SELECTION'S. From English Literature for the use of middle classes in Indian Schools, with notes by E. LETHBRIDGE, Esq., M.A., As. 12.

HISTORY AND GEOGRAPHY OF BENGAL. Translated into Bengali. As. 8.

*** *New Edition Expected in a Few Days.*

ALGEBRAICAL EXERCISES. With Solutions for Student's preparing for the Entrance Examination of the Calcutta University. By SARAT CHANDRA MUKHOPADHYAY, M.A. Re. 1-4.

RUDIMENTS (THE) OF PHYSICAL GEOGRAPHY. For the use of Indian Schools. And a Glossary of the Technical Terms employed. Fourth Edition. By HENRY F. BLANFORD, F. G. S., Associate of the Royal School of Mines 16mo. Cloth. Re. 1-4.

ELEMENTARY TREATISE ON MECHANICS. Intended for use in Indian Colleges and Schools. By W. C. WILLSON, M.A., 16mo. Rs. 3.

ENGLISH PEOPLE (THE) AND THEIR LANGUAGE. Translated from the German of Loth by C. H. TAWNEY, M.A., Professor in the Presidency College, Calcutta. Stitched. As. 8.

NOTES ON SURVEYING. For the use of Schools. By J. M. Scott, M.A., C.E., Professor of Civil Engineering, Presidency College. Second Edition. Re. 1.

NOTICES ON PRACTICAL GEOMETRY AND THE CONSTRUCTION OF SCALES. Second Edition. Edited by J. M. SCOTT, M.A., C.E., Professor of Civil Engineering, Presidency College. Re. 1.

MILTON'S AREOPAGITICA. A Modern Version. With Notes, Appendix, &c. By SAMUEL LOBB, M.A. Rs. 3.

BENGALI ENTRANCE COURSE: Appointed by the Senate of the Calcutta University for the Examination of—

1876. R. 1-6.
Ditto 1877. Re. 1-6.

KUMARA SAMBHAVA OF KALIDASA. With Notes and Explanations in English. By the Rev. K. M. BANERJEA. Rs. 2-8.

RAGHU VANSA BY KALIDASA. With Notes and Grammatical Explanations. By the Rev. K. M. BANERJEA. Cantos 1 to 3, Rs. 2. Cantos 4 to 19, Rs. 3.

FIRST ARTS COURSE, 1877, Rs. 3. Scott's Talisman, which is read with the Course, As. 4.

B. A. COURSE, 1878. Rs. 3.

REID'S INQUIRY INTO THE HUMAN MIND. Rs. 1-4.

CALCUTTA UNIVERSITY CALENDAR 1875-76. Rs. 4.

UTTARACHARITA, a Sanscrit Drama by Bhavabhuti Edited with Notes by Iswarachandra Vidyasagar, Rs. 2.

SMITH STANISTREET & CO.

Pharmaceutical Chemists & Druggists

BY APPOINTMENT

To His Excellency the Right Hon'ble

LORD NORTHBROOK, G.M.S.I.,

Governor-General of India,

&c. &c.

Syrup of Lactate of Iron Prepared from the original recipe. Lactate of Iron, in various forms of preparation, has been in use in France and generally through the Continent of Europe, for some years past, and is highly esteemed as one of the most valuable Chalybeate Tonic Remedies yet introduced. The Syrup being the most agreeable as well as convenient form of administration is in most general use.

It is a most valuable remedy in the following diseases:—Chlorosis or Green Sickness, Leucorrhœa, Neuralgia, Enlargement of the Spleen, &c. In combination with quinine, it has also been very successfully used in the cure of Fever, while to persons of delicate constitution, or enfeebled by disease, it is invaluable. In bottles, Rs. 2 each.

Syrup of the Phosphate of Iron, Rs. 2 per bottle.

Syrup of Phosphate of Iron and Strychnine, Rs. 2 per bottle.

Syrup of Phosphate of Iron and Quinine, Price Rs. 2-8 per bottle.

Syrup of Phosphate of Iron, Quinine and Strychnine, (Dr. Aitken's Triple Tonic Syrup.) Rs. 2-8 per bottle.

Smith, Stanistreet & Co.

Invite special attention to the following rates, the quality guaranteed as the best procurable:—

Pure Ærated Waters.

Made from Pure Water, obtained by the new process through the Patent Charcoal Filters.

				Rs.	As.
Ærated plain (Triple Ærated), per doz.			...	0	12
Soda Water	ditto	"	...	0	12
Gingerade	ditto	"	...	1	4
Lemonade	ditto	"	...	1	4
Tonic (Quinine)	ditto	"	...	1	4

The *Cash* must be sent with the order to obtain advantage of the above rates.

TO CLEAR OFF STOCK

J. DAVIS & Co.

Are selling their Wool Wrappers

HALF PRICE

No. 6 Government Place, Calcutta.

HOLLOWAY'S PILLS

How to Enjoy Life

is only known when the blood is pure, its circulation perfect, and the nerves in good order. The only safe and certain method of expelling all impurities is to take Holloway's Pills, which have the power of cleansing the blood from all noxious matters, expelling all humours which taint or impoverish it, thereby purify and invigorate and give general tone to the system. Young or old robust or delicate, may alike experience their beneficent effects. Myriads affirmed that these Pills possess marvellous power in securing these great secrets of health by purifying and regulating the fluids and strengthening the solids.

Printed and published by M. M. RUKHIT, at the "INDIAN MIRROR" PRESS, No 15, College Square, for the Proprietor.

The Indian Mirror.

SUNDAY EDITION.

VOL. XV.] CALCUTTA, SUNDAY, FEBRUARY 20, 1876 {REGISTERED AT THE GENERAL POST OFFICE.} [NO. 42

CONTENTS.

NOTICE.

Letters and all other communications relating to the literary department of the Paper should be addressed to "The Editor."

All letters on the business of the Press should be addressed, and all remittance made payable to the Manager of this Paper. Particular attention is solicited to this notice.

Subscribers will be good enough to give prompt notice of any delay, or irregularity in delivery of the Paper.

Editorial Notes

UPWARDS of three hundred persons assembled on Wednesday last to hear the minister's lecture on "The Lord called them and classified them." The discourse, which lasted for an hour and half, purported to be a plea for the classification of Brahmo devotees. Whether it is expedient and feasible to organise distinct classes of Brahmo *Yogis* and *Bhaktas* is a question on which opinion is divided, and certainly there is much in India's past experiences which furnishes arguments against it. The subject, however, is one of vital importance, and demands careful consideration. The highest philosophy of spiritual development is involved in *Yoga*, and hence those among us who wish to cultivate it must learn to do so on a scientific basis and according to approved methods.

BLESSED are the peace-makers! To reconcile differences, to go about making friends of enemies is indeed a heavenly work. Society needs teachers, artisans, traders, merchants and doctors. It needs also a body of men whose special duty it will be to promote good will and love. How few, alas! are there even among Brahmos who follow this vocation! It is our co-religionists who more than any other people profess love, catholicity, and liberality, and the country may well expect their services in this good cause. The Brahmo's creed may be summed up in these words "UNIVERSAL LOVE,—*no enmity.*" Why should he not then, more than any other person, undertake the specific mission of the peace-maker? In his eye there is neither Jew nor Gentile, neither Hindu nor Mahomedan. To him all are friends, to whatever party, sect or nationality they may belong. Let him then go about loving and serving all.

THE question of dress is really an important question, for not in a few cases, peace of mind hangs upon it. The only symbol of respectability easily recognizable by society is a good dress. Of course it is most difficult to define one, especially in a country like India, where so many costumes are worn and so many different tastes indulged in. But still a general standard of dress appears needful. We Hindus can make out a Hindu gentleman at the very first look, whatever may be the kind of dress in which he is habited. With foreigners this is not possible. And numerous instances have been known in which Hindu gentlemen have been rudely treated by Europeans only because their dress gave rise to a deception as to their place in society. Cases also in which men who are not gentlemen have passed for such in virtue of the clothes worn by them, have not been very rare. Religious men in every country have a costume peculiar to them, and so have they here. But religiousness and mendicancy having gone hand in hand, a mendicant always puts on a religious garb, and a religious man gets no recognition for the clothes he puts on. As all men cannot be expected to wear trousers and *chapkans*, is it not necessary there should be an intermediate order of dress by which a Hindu gentleman, or a religious man may be recognized as such? The question is applicable with still greater force in the case of Hindu women, especially those who have begun to come out of the Zenana.

IT is a real problem with theologians as to whether the Jews, before the advent of Christ, believed in a future state of life. With orthodox Christian divines it is of course the rule to maintain that the Israelites were totally ignorant of this doctrine till Jesus preached it, and set upon it the seal of certainty by his resurrection. But liberal thinkers also find it exceedingly difficult to establish anything like a definite knowledge of immortality from the books of the Old Testament. The difficulty may be thus accounted for. The Israelites of old, though a monotheistic nation, were essentially, and almost absolutely worldly-minded. Worldly prosperity was their sole good and adversity in life their sole evil. Living in the Spirit of God, apart from and above the sensible world, was an experience as foreign as uninviting to them. They understood nothing of the Kingdom of Heaven that is "within," and ridiculed at it, and persecuted to death those who preached it. Death was to them the most terrible of all calamities. But all this does not in the least prove that they did not at times feel the flashes of immortality, or that they did not believe that the soul can live in a disembodied state. What is the meaning of Enoch's "walking with God during his appointed years; and then he was not, for God took him." What is the significance of the allegory of the ascension and disappearance of Elijah in a chariot of fire. That the idea of a material resurrection was current among the Jews is evident not only from the vision of Ezekiel, and other passages, but from the question asked about it to Jesus by the Sadducees who answered thus:—"But touching the resurrection of the dead, have ye not read that which was spoken unto you by God, saying, I am the God of Abraham, and the God of Isaac, and God of Jacob? God is not the God of the dead, but of the living." The Hebrew word *rephaim* means the manes of the dead, and the Hebrew notion of a *Sheol*, or an underground world, where the spirits of the departed lived a dark, ghostly, unquiet life, "feeble as a shade." Job describes it as "the land of darkness, like the blackness of death-shade, where there is no order and where the light is as darkness." These undeveloped notions of heaven and hell clearly indicate that the Israelites like all human beings believed in a life after death.

THE Lieutenant-Governor is now contemplating the erection of an Asylum for the blind and incurables of Calcutta. The project has so far taken the shape, that His Honor has applied to Government of India for land which is required for the site of the building, and the Secretary to the Public Works Department has addressed an official letter to Dr. Woodford inviting his assistance in ascertaining how far Native gentlemen of position are prepared to subscribe towards "the attainment of the beneficent and praiseworthy object." Now "Native gentlemen of position" by which expression we suppose His Honor means wealthy men, have had of late to subscribe to so many of Sir Richard

Temple's "beneficent and praiseworthy objects," that the new addition to the list will not all at once prepossess them in its favor. The blind and the incurables of Calcutta who infest our public streets, and present such scenes that during the visit of the Prince of Wales the charitable Sir Stuart Hogg had to enforce a temporary deportation of them, (an original method altogether of dealing with the pauper question) can be taken care of in the new Hospital, and real suffering relieved without encouragement given to fraud, and idleness, the experiment may be worth a trial. But even in that case we would demur as to the cost. A letter from the Public Works Secretary, speaking about land for a site and in so many words inviting public subscriptions, is ominous, and means before any relief to anybody is afforded, an outlay of two or three lacs of public money for a suitable building, of course with the maintenance of a competent working staff, European and Native, very likely with Dr. Woodford at its head. The Temple Asylum or the Northbrook Asylum, or whatever the name of the Asylum be, would then accommodate a handful of blind people without sufficient food, or clothing, or bedding, as is the case so often in our hospitals. For really charitable institutions, which give relief to the population, and help the distressed we have deep sympathy. Charity, through the Public Works Department, may cover a multitude of sins, but will fail in its one great end. Why should not Sir Richard strengthen the hands of the District Charitable Society, enlarging the operations of the Alms House, about which complaints are now and often heard, or adding to the wards of the Leper Asylum. At any rate the Lieutenant-Governor could explain the new scheme more fully, setting forth its objects, proving its necessity, and assuring the public against possible abuses, before His Honor can expect Native gentlemen of position to come forward with their money in their hands, which to do them justice, they have so often done of late, at his desire.

CLASSIFICATION OF DEVOTEES.

PURE Theism is the religion of nature. It is founded upon natural intuitions, and instincts. The light of nature is its scripture, and its salvation is nothing but obedience to the voice of nature. There is, it will probably be urged by those who think differently, such a thing as carnal nature in man. Of course there is. We do not deny it. By human nature we mean the higher nature, the human, not the bestial, the spiritual, not the carnal nature; and we believe we are right in saying that man's salvation means nothing more than the development of the principles and sentiments, imbedded in the very constitution of this higher nature. It is in this sense that we are to understand and interpret that deep maxim laid down, we believe, by Bishop Butler,—"To be true to nature is to be true to God." Let men only prove true to their own nature, and they are saved. Nature, as it comes fresh and pure from the hand of its Author, is our guide, and instructor, our revelation and inspiration, and all that we need is to follow it faithfully and strictly. No man became great in the moral world but by obeying the teachings and following the high impulses of nature. Our prophets and great men were they who were gifted with extraordinary natural powers and wisdom, and who soared with their spiritual instincts into the higher regions of heavenly life. Inspiration is supernatural, it is true but supernatural does not mean 'contrary to' but 'above nature.' In inspiration the soul enjoys flights of faith and devotion which are not vouchsafed to ordinary humanity, but only to extraordinary and gifted individuals. Men inspired with the genius of poetry or music or religion are not *un*natural, but only *super*natural. They are raised above ordinary humanity by their extraordinary genius. It is clear then that whether men require inspiration or salvation they need only be true and faithful to nature, and assiduously evolve all its higher instincts and impulses. This general principle applies fully to the doctrine of ordination. Constituted as human society is, ministers and missionaries are ordained by properly constituted societies and recognised authorities. In almost all churches men are ordained ministers by men. Natural Theism says men are ordained by nature, by the God of nature. They are not *made*, but they are *born* ministers. Ordination is a Divine call. Have we not all realized in some period of our lives the solemn fact of a Divine call? When we renounced idolatary and superstition and joined the true church of God, who called us but He? There was a stirring heavenly summons which stirred, roused and converted each of us, and called us to the Brahmo Somaj. It was a call to repentance, prayer, and conversion. That was the first call, the first invitation. The earliest chapter of our religious life began with it. But has there been no subsequent call, is there not likely to be another in future? Surely the first Divine call in man's life is not also the last. Once again is the believer called when he is required to settle in the spiritual world. After his admission into God's church he advances in knowledge, faith, and devotion, and then, if he is duly and specially qualified, he is called to enter a specific sphere of religious life. Spiritual progress may be compared to University education. The student who matriculates, and enters the University only begins his career. After going through the appointed course, he climbs to the highest degrees and distinctions, and then after completing his general education he enters into professional studies, and at last settles in a particular professional sphere of life, according to his natural inclinations and powers, as an engineer or doctor. So the Theist enters his church, and then as soon as he has acquired some sort of general training in devotion, faith, and piety, and in social virtues, he must naturally think of taking a particular line of progress, according to the peculiar bent of his own mind. There are three courses open to him, and he may take to one or other of these. His choice in the matter must be determined by nature, and not by the degrees of synods and councils. The three spheres of *Sadhan*, or spiritual training, and development, are *Yoga*, (communion) *Bhakti*, (love) and *Seba* (servitude). Some Theists may in after life settle down as *yogis*, some as *Bhaktas*, and some as *Sebaks*. What these classes of devotees respectively represent we hope to discuss hereafter.

THE ACTIVE GOD.

THE thought of the future is always distressing to those who have no faith in a living God. And let us rest well assured that it is not an easy thing to believe in a living God. The future is an object of uncertainty and fear to us because we do not know what it will produce. The joys and the hopes to-day when liable to be disturbed on the morrow, must necessarily beget pain and disquietude. But let us once remember that there is a living active God over-head, whose objects of solicitude we ever are, and our own anxiety ceases. When in addition to this fact it is borne in mind that our whole future entirely depends upon the will of God, who is always engaged in shaping our destiny, that all his dispensations concern us and our highest happiness in the future, we find no cause whatever to be distressed even when we come to think of the loss of what we enjoy as great pleasure in the present time. But religion loses nearly all its force and much of its consolation when it is understood to mean nothing more than an affair of the past, and a fact of history. Then however much as in it way instruct and improve us, and however great be the joy and consolation it may give on the reflection of God's merciful dealings with his children, it cannot allay all our fears about ourselves, nor can it meet all the demands of the future. The faith that we may summon up for this purpose will be dependent on a thousand difficulties which the past must accumulate, and keep it up as we may, it will at times slip away from our hands. When religion is a thing of the past, God is a thing of the past, a dead God, or at best one whose best and most fruitful season of activity was in times gone by. If he lives now, he lives in a semi-slumbering, abstract kind of life, and always makes references to what he did in the past, when we go to appeal to him for present needs. For some minds such a being may have great attractions, and practical value For us whose temptations and difficulties are so unprecedented, who live at a time, and in the midst of a society to which the old standards of religion are essentially inapplicable, a historical deity is not at all satisfying. If God's actions in the past are valuable and saving, they are so only in relation to, and in illustration of; his present actions and dealings. It is a present, and active God therefore whom we need for our wants and anxieties. All his dispensations are in the present and future. His highest purposes in relation to ourselves are yet concealed from us. Let us pray and watch that these may be revealed to us. Our deepest anxieties can be best thrown upon Him. His solicitude, and his activity will for us all that we need. We have but to serve and worship him with cheerful hearts and he will provide for us at all times.

The Interpeter

AN abstract deity, though philosophically acceptable, never pleases the heart. Hence is it that in all ages men have preferred to approach and adore the Great God as their Father. Even in the earliest scriptures of the Hindus, the Rig Veda, we find the Lord represented as the "Father of our father and mother." VI. 2.16.35. Again IV. 17.17. "He is a friend, a father, and the most fatherly of fathers." In another passage VIII. 87.11. He is spoken of as both "father and mother." The Deity is addressed also as *bhratah* or brother, and sometimes also as a kind friend "whose friendship is sweet and sweet thy guidance" VIII. 57.11.

ARE the Vedas the supreme scriptures of the Hindus, the highest and the purest record of Divine wisdom? Every Hindu will doubtless return an affirmative response. But we shall be agreeably surprised to find a different verdict in the Hindu Shastra itself. The following is a most striking passage in the Vedanta and the meaning is unmistakably clear:—"The Rig Veda, Yajur Veda, Sama Veda, Atharva Veda &c., are inferior knowledge. That which enables us to know the Eternal God is the highest scripture." It is quite clear then that even according to Hinduism there is something higer than the Vedas.

"O KING!" says the Mahabharat, (Santiparva 12.340) "he who becoming indifferent to happiness, looks above is a true ascetic and a vanquisher of the passion." This is just what we said the other day about the true nature of asceticism. Resignation is chief thing, not outward privation. Mere aversion to wealth and pomp is not *bairagya* (asceticism), nor is self-mortification. Faith in Providence, a trustful reliance upon the Father's loving kindness in matters of salvation as well as in temporal affairs, is the soul of asceticism, according to both Hindu and Christian scriptures.

HOW faith harmonizes irreconcilable facts! Mahabharat, Udyogaparba, 45, 343, tells a strange thing;—"His beauty is incomparable, none can see Him with the eye." This seems paradoxical. How can we speak of the Lord's "beauty" when we represent Him as invisible? If we cannot see Him, how can we realize His beauty? To the true believer, howevers there is nothing strange in this. Believing that God is Spirit and not visible matter, he yet sees the Divine Reality so vividly and so lovingly in the inmost soul, that he is led to exclaim.—"How incomparable thy beauty, O Lord!"

Provincial

KRISHNAGHUR BRAHMO SOMAJ.

[FROM OUR OWN CORRESPONDENT.]

IT is with feelings of great regret that I sit to write a few lines about the present state of the local Brahmo Somaj. I say regret, because the state of our beloved Somaj is very deplorable now. In my previous letters I carefully avoided mentioning anything about it, because I considered the subject too serious and sacred to be dealt with along with matters secular. The Krishnaghur Brahmo Somaj, if I am correctly informed, is the oldest Somaj next to the Calcutta Adi Somaj. It was founded by Babu Brajanath Mukerji and some of his friends with the substantial help of Babu Devendra Nath Tagore the venerable *Pradhan Acharya*. For some years after its foundation it made rapid progress and its success was brilliant. The touching and able sermons delivered by Babu Brajanath Mukerji attracted both young and old hearts and in a short time the numerical strength of the Somaj became such as could be wished under the circumstances. The attendance was always very great. The large hall sometimes used to be literally crowded with spectators, honest seekers of truth, and devout prayerful men. The external splendour of the Somaj was in keeping with its spiritual progress. In course of time a change came over the faith of the then members. As the old leader glided away, Babu Nugendro Nath Chatterji stepped in. Under the auspices of Nugendro Babu the Somaj showed unmistakeable signs of progress. Even reprobates, debauchees, and mammon worshippers were converted. Students without number sceptical and godless flocked in and many a gay Lothario steeped to the lips in the mire of iniquity, felt the worthlessness of the pleasures of the flesh and joined the Somaj and learnt to pray for mercy and peace. Ah! as I look back to the long forgotten past through the vista of memory what pleasing reminiscences surge up in my bosom. It was all sun-shine and joy then. The birds sang joy, the breeze blew joy, the moon shed joy, the sun shone joy and all earth was smiling and happy. Verily we thought the promised millenium had come and the Almighty Father had acknowledged us as his own children. We led a holy life, never forgot to say our prayers, always felt the presence of the Almighty Father. Yes, felt His divine presence even as I feel this pen, lived and moved in Him and never were we happier. Years rolled and circumstances compelled Nugendro Babu to leave Krishnaghur; just at that time many of his co-adjutors also went away to seek their own fortunes in distant places. Then came the reaction, for reaction it was and unhappily for Krishnaghur it still continues to be so. The stream of purity and holiness that flowed so freely has suddenly changed Covenanted Brahmos who were sworn to devote their lives to the cause of Brahmoism, do not come to the Brahmo Somaj; enthusiastic, earnest and prayerful hearts have grown callous. Here I am who had once the good fortune to taste the sweets of religion and who could really defy all worldly pleasures and aggrandizements for righteousness' sake, a fallen man, fallen so low as perhaps never to rise during life time! In the place of God I have substituted Mammon, in the place of holiness and purity I have substituted unrighteous things. But mine is not the only instance of conversion from God worship to Mammon worship. I am but one of the many of my species, and hence it is that I cite my own instance. Had there been a worthy leader among us, perhaps we would not have gone astray, perhaps we could still remain firm and steady to our faith. But the case was otherwise—we were left to shift for ourselves as best we could, and evil stole a march upon us. All the modern vices of the so-called civilization have since crept among us and we are spreading the contagion far and wide. Religion is but the fantasy of fools, and conscience a fiction, is our cry. Agreeably to the law of reaction we are as enthusiastic in decrying and condemning religion as we once were in extolling and cherishing it. Sad is our present condition and sadder is our future fate. What but real punishment can expiate our sins! In our own experience we learnt how sweet and delicious it was to worship God, and yet we have wilfully and persistently discarded that worship and slighted that God. Thou Merciful Father! have mercy upon us. Forgive us, and lead us once again to Thy holy House that we may be as happy as before.

Our Somaj is yet extent, but its existence is very precarious. The usual attendance is so small as scarcely to be taken into account. With the honorable exception of three or four gentlemen (perhaps I have exaggerated the number) others who occasionally attend the Somaj can hardly be counted as Brahmos. *Service* is conducted by two very good and sincere men, but, I am sure many will agree with me, they ought to be more enthusiastic and zealous. I am sorry to have been obliged to make this remark, about our ministers, but I trust they will excuse me inasmuch as I have done so from the best of motives. It is high time that some able missionary from the Brahmo Somaj of India should come to Krishnaghur, stop here for some time, and try to bring back the prodigals to the House of the Father or the cause of Brahmoism will be seriously affected—at least for sometime to come—at Krishnaghur. I hope the Brahmo Somaj of India will take this subject into proper consideration.

Meditation

—TAKE no man's words to guide you, nor guide you others by your own. Learn, however slowly, from the life of good man; and if you have anything like a life to show, preach by *that*. Words however wellspoken, and spoken by whomsoever they may be, are, though often attractive, invariably vague. They conceal the truth of life, which truth, unless it is lived out few can perceive. Words are nobody's property, and one may take credit to speak things which he does not understand. Words are then your own when they embody the facts of your life.

PERFECT yourself for private life, if you think that public life is reserved for you. Be assured you are mostly virtuous because no one, neither man nor woman cares to tempt you.

IF men knew you exactly as you are and as you know yourself, perhaps they would absolve you from blame for certain acts of yours which they misunderstood, but they would find you to be a greater monster than they ever imagined you to be.

IF you look at each of your friends separately perhaps you will have some cause to complain, but if you look at them all collectively the unmeritted unkindness of some, is more than to outweighed by the unmeritted kindness of others.

Brahmo Hymns

I AM readily reconciled to the sinner, if only once he calls upon me with a mournful heart. I am awake day and night to see who calls upon me, and I cannot stay if I hear the sinner's cries. Living in the midst of the heart I see who wants me and in what spirit. I am not deceived by insincere lamentations. Those who are arrogant sinners cannot see me. That I am the friend of the poor, and dwell in the broken heart, every one knows.

IN this kingdom of sin I will no longer remain; I will go to the Divine world, and live happily there under the shade of the Divine tree that gratifies all desires. I will sow the seed of love on the banks of the river of faith. I will fill the store-house of my heart with the resources of righteousness. With avidity I will drink nectar and become immortal, and always roll on the waves of love with the band of God's devotees. I will forget all hollow and base desires, and becoming a devout and loving ascetic I will unlock my heart and distribute the riches of love to all.

Devotional.

GOD of joy, thou art blissful because thou art ever pure. How can I pray for peace, without praying for purity? A reproachful conscience will not give man any rest. Therefore my supplication to thee will for ever be for the possession of a clean heart. Purge my soul from every vice, from every thing that takes away the freedom and cheerfulness of enjoying the light of thy holy face.

DELIVER me always from the terrible responsibility of judging my brothers. O Lord, and from the fatal ambition of being a teacher unto others set me free.

MAKE me dependent yet independent of human sympathy, dependent where I can by others' sympathy serve thee and find thee, independent where by courting the good feeling of others I fail to profit by the trials and difficulties of life. Whatever befalls, let me always be assured that thy arm supports me.

The Brahmo Somaj.

WE sincerely congratulate Babu Ram Sanker Sen, a member of the East Bengal Brahmo Somaj and for a long time a distinguished worker in Mymensing, on his appointment as a member of the Bengal Council.

WE give elsewhere the substance of the lecture delivered by the minister on Wednesday last.

THERE will be special service this morning at Akna, a village about two miles from Mugra. Babu Keshub Chunder Sen has proceeded there with a few other missionaries. The minister is expected back this evening, as he will have to conduct service in the Mandir.

DIVINE service commences at 7 P. M. in the Brahmo Mandir, instead of 6-30 as heretofore.

WE understand that the second lecture of the series will be given in the hall of the Calcutta School next Thursday. The subject is "Asceticism according to the Hindu scriptures."

RAMKRISHNA, a Hindu devotee, known as a *Paramhonsa*, now living at Dakhineshwar, is a remarkable man, and appears to have attained an extraordinary elevation of moral character and spirituality. Several Brahmo missionaries who have visited him from time to time speak highly of his devotion and purity and his deep insight into the realities of the inner world. Though a true Hindu he is said to sympathize heartily with the Brahmos of the advanced school. This is one of those striking facts, which go far to show that the devotional side of progressive Brahmoism is extremely popular among appreciative Hindus.

Gleanings.

LOVEST THOU ME.

I delivered thee when bound,
  And, when bleeding healed thy wound:
Sought thee wandering, set thee right,
  Turned thy darkness into light.
Can a woman's tender care
  Cease toward the child she bear?
Yes, she may forgetful be,
  Yet I will remember thee.
Mine is an unchanging love,
  Higher than the heights above;
Deeper than the depths beneath,
  Free and faithful, strong as death.
Thou shalt see my glory soon,
  When the work of grace is done;
Partner of my throne thou shalt be,—
  Say poor sinner Lovest thou Me?
Lord, it is my chief complaint,
  That my love is weak and faint;
Yet I love thee and adore,
  O for grace to love thee more.

Literary.

"THE Devil's Chain" is the title of a new book against intemperance by the author of "Ginx's Baby." It is dedicated to Sir Wilfred Lawson.

MOST Americans who read *the History the Civil War in America*, by the Comte de Paris (Joseph H. Coates & Co.), will be surprised by the grasp of the subject of our political system manifested by the author, as well as the clearness and force of his narrative of the great events which he participated in. Certainly it is a surprising circumstance that a young prince who had been educated in the belief that he was the legitimate heir to the throne of France, should not only have volunteered his services in our army to save the Republic from dismemberment, but should be able to give such excellent reasons for choosing the Union side in the great contest in which he was so eager to learn his first lessons in actual warfare. Professor Coppee pays him the very hig compliment of saying that in a large and philosophical view of American institutions he has rivalled de Tocqueville, and those who have read the *History*, carefully will not be inclined to deny it. But the merit of the Comte de Paris is in giving so clear and dispassionate a history of our civil war. Although he could not but feel more favorably disposed toward the men with whom he served and the cause which they supported, he seems to be perfectly impartial and just in his description of the Rebel leaders and their achievements; and he says in his note to Messrs. J. H. Coates & Co., the American publishers of his *History*, that he should be proud to have his share in raising the monument which is to perpetuate the memory of the heroism and the glory of the American soldier, without distinction of the blue and the gray coats. The translation of the *History* by Mr. L. F. Tasistro, who has been many years connected with the State Department, at Washington, is very well done, and to the editorship of the work by Professor Coppee may be attributed the absence of any errors in the military details, and purely technical descriptions.

THE Rev. R. R. SHIPPEN has edited and the American Unitarian Association has published a new devotional manual, entitled *Daily Praise and Prayer*. Each day in the year has a Scripture reading, a poetical selection and a prayer, the three taking up just a page. The book is very well prepared and deserves wide use. The Unitarians, if they believe less than other denominations, have a devotional spirit quite as deep, if the number of their manuals of prayer is any index.

The Week

SIR JOHN STRACHEY returned to Allahabad, on Wednesday last, after visiting Muttra, Agra and Delhi.

ARCHDEACON Baly has proceeded to Lahore, with reference to the Poor White question in which he is most interested.

THE Report on the Grievances of the Civil Service, as adopted by Government, goes to England by next mail, as also the new code of precedence.

HIS EXCELLENCY the Viceroy will leave Calcutta for Allahabad on the 4th March, to take part in the drawing room installation there.

SHOULD the Prince of Wales visit Lisbon on his return from India, a grand military review will be held in his honor.

SIR D. FORSYTH goes on leave this week, and he intends, we hear, to travel to England by way of China, Japan, and America. Captain

Trotter, R. E., will be Sir Douglas' travelling companion.

LATEST NEWS.

A SUIT has been brought by Her Highness the Begum of Bhopal against the G. I. P. Railway Company in the Bombay High Court to recover Rs64,655, for non-delivery of jewellery, gold and silver articles, and other property belonging to Her Highness and her followers, which were entrusted in November 1872 to the defendants as common carriers to be safely carried from Bombay to Hurda, and there delivered to the plaintiff. The suit is being heard by Mr. Justice Bayley. Mr. Latham and Mr. Lang, Barristers-at-law, appear for the plaintiff, and the Advocate General of Bombay and Mr. Hart for the defendant.

THERE was a very large gathering, chiefly of Parsi and Hindu gentlemen, in the Durbar Room, Town Hall, Bombay, on Monday last, to listen to Miss Mary Carpenter's address on the object and working of the "National Indian Association." Among those present were the Hon'ble Mr. Rogers, Mrs. and Miss Rogers, Lady Staveley, Messrs. Lynch, Grattan Geary, and Martin Wood, the Hon'ble Mahomed Ali Rogay, Mr. Pherozeshah Mehta, Mr. Dadabhoy Nowroji, Dr. Atmaram Pandurang and others interested in the objects of the Association.

MR. MOLESWORTH, Railway Consulting Engineer, has arrived at Rangoon.

MAJOR-GENERAL DONALD STEWART, Chief Commissioner of the Andamans, will succeed General Sir Charles Reid in command of the Lahore Division, Major-General Barwell, now officiating for Major General Stewart being confirmed as Chief Commissioner.

MR. GIRDLESTONE, Resident in Nepal, goes home for three months in the spring. Dr. Bellew will probably officiate for him.

THERE will be no *levee* during the Prince of Wales' stay in Allahabad.

THE great conspiracy case at Rangoon is over. The telegram from Rangoon to the *Indian Daily News* says:—Maung Bwah, the ringleader, has been sentenced to 21 years' imprisonment. Two others 14, five, six months, five others released, rest ten years. Great excitement prevails."

MR. TURTON SMITH is temporarily appointed to be Assistant Director General of the Post Office of India.

MR. F. DE H. LARPENT is appointed to be Accountant General, Bengal.

MR. TAUIA MADHADAVA RAO, Assistant Clerk to the Naib Dewan, has been appointed by the Baroda Durbar Private Secretary to Sir T. Madava Rao, in place of Mr. Raghonath Rao, who is now in Bombay *en route* to Madras.

SMALL-POX is now less virulent at Bombay.

THE Prince of Wales will arrive at Allahabad on the 4th of March in the morning, and leave on the evening of the 5th.

REUTER telegraphs to say that in the House of Commons, on Thursday last, a Bill enabling the Queen to adopt an additional title was read for the first time. The Prime Minister, in answering to several questions in the House, said that the choice of a new title was a prerogative of the Queen. Mr. Lowe and Mr. Forster both objected to the title "Empress" as despotic.

THE Tudor Ice Company in Bombay advertize that the price of ice is shortly to be reduced to three pice per pound. American apples are shortly expected by this Company.

MR. F. R. COCKERELL having been appointed a Member of the Governor-General's Legislative Council, the following changes will be made in the Bengal Commissionerships:—Lord Ulick Browne will go to the Rajshahye and Cooch Behar Division; Mr. C. T. Buckland will be Commissioner of the Presidency Division; Mr. H. A. Cockerell will take the Burdwan Division; and Mr. F. B Peacock will officiate again as Commissioner of Dacca.

Two of Mr. Birch's murderers at Perak are said to have been captured.

The Prince's Visit.

NOT only were several prisoners released from the Jail by the Maharajah of Cashmere in honor of the Prince's visit to Jammu, but also, according to the Lahore *Public Opinion*, Khilluts were liberally bestowed in all directions, the chiefs of Iskardo, Ladakh, Gilgit and Cashmere being specially honored, while even the coolies who were brought from Srinagar and other parts of Cashmere to work at the new palace were similarly rewarded. The travelling expenses of all the Chiefs who were summoned to Jammu and of the merchants who brought in goods from various parts of His Highness' territory were paid by the State and their goods exempted from the payment of the usual duty levied upon them, His Highness being determined that the occasion of the Prince's visit should be one of rejoicing and in future be looked upon by the people as a red letter day in their calendar. Khilluts were also, we understand, bestowed upon the traders above referred to.

Calcutta.

THACKER SPINK AND CO.'s Directory for 1876 is just out.

THE Hindu Mela commenced yesterday, and will continue till to-morrow at the garden of Rajah Budun Chand.

MR. W. ALFIN is appointed to officiate as Post Master of Calcutta during the absence of Mr. E. C. George, on furlough.

LEAVE on medical certificate for one year from 13th March next is granted to Mr. R. A. Sterndale, Assistant Commissioner of Paper Currency, Calcutta.

HIS HONOR the Lieutenant-Governor has, at the request of the Lord Bishop of Calcutta, been pleased to sanction a grant of Rs. 200 per mensem in aid of the funds of the Lady Canning Home for training Hospital Nurses, with effect from the 1st January 1876.

DR. H. CAYLEY, Officiating Ophthalmic Surgeon and Professor of Opthalmic Surgery, Medical College, Calcutta, is appointed to officiate also as Marine Surgeon, Calcutta.

DR. J. ELLIOT, Principal Medical Store-keeper, Bengal Presidency, has been appointed to officiate as Surgeon to the Presidency General Hospital, during the absence, on furlough, of Dr. J. Ewart.

THE *Englishman* understands that Mr. Fitzgerld, Barrister-at-Law, a nephew and pupil of Sir Henry Thring, the well-known Parliamentary draftsman (not Mr. Fitzpatrick, as stated by the *Indian Daily News*) has been offered the appointment of Secretary to the Bengal Legislative Council, with the promise of the reversion of the appointment of Secretary to the Government of India in the Legislative Department, should Mr. Whitley Stokes go on leave, or retire.

IT is rumoured that Sir William Merewether, Commissioner of Sind, is shortly expected to arrive in Calcutta.

THE *Indo-European Correspondence* says:—The Right Rev. Dr. Canoz, S. J., left Calcutta by the French Steamer *Tibre* on Tuesday last, returning to his Mission of Madura, *via* Madras.

THE *Pioneer's* Calcutta correspondent referring to the New Municipal Bill for Calcutta, thinks that "a concession of the kind," suggested by the Indian League, as to a *mandamus* obtained from the High Court, "might fairly meet the objections to the reservation of the arbitrary power in the hands of Government, and would go a great way to appease the almost universal outcry at present raised against the Bill." The writer may not be aware that Sir Richard Temple decidedly sets his face against such a concession. At least His Honor distinctly said so the other day to the Deputation from the British Indian Association.

REFERRING to the Deputation from the British Indian Association which waited on His Honor the Lieutenant-Governor at Belvedere, a correspondent of the *Statesman* sensibly writes:—The memorial had been in his hands for some considerable time, and he knew before it was read to him the gist of its contents. There was no reason, therefore, why a careful and courteous reply to it should not have been drawn up and read by His Honor to the Deputation instead of which His Honor receives a body of influential gentlemen and treats them almost as a lot of children, as though he were saying—"Now, then, what's all this fuss about? I'm afraid you don't know what you want, and if I won't give you what you are asking for, what will you do then? You really ought to know Government is very good to you, and gives all you ought to expect. My time is very valuable, and it's getting late, so good-bye,—charmed to have seen you, *au revoir*." Such, if stripped of its thought-concealing verbiage, was the sum of the Lieutenant-Governor's reply to the modest and moderate requirements of the memorial, and such his treatment of the Deputation. "We asked His Honor for an answer, and he propounds us a riddle," said one of the Deputation when descending the staircase at Belvedere after this little farce in one act had been played out.

WE have been requested to publish the following programme of the Hindu Mela:—

Sunday,—Arts' Exhibition, Athletic Sports, Games, Music, Songs, Agricultural and Horticultural Shows, Theatrical songs and other entertainments, Boat-race and Fire-works.

The Bowbazar Amateur concert party will be in attendance.

N. B.—The boat-race to take place, on Sunday morning, at 6½ on the River (which is close by the garden.) The race being over, a grand procession will be formed. Admission 1 Rupee.

Members of the National Society who are subscribers shall have free cards of admission; subscribers of rupees five and upwards will be provided with *reserved* seats in the Mela.

Ticket-holders will be entitled to see all kinds of entertainments and sports &c., free of charge.

Drunkards and disreputable women are strictly prohibited to enter the Mela compound.

Funds collected will go to the benefit of a place for the National Mela. The Maharajah of Benares will be present on the occasion.

ACKNOWLEDGMENT.

Bango Durpun for Aughran 1282.

Public Engagement.

MUSICAL Evangelistic Service. The Rev. Shib Chunder Bannerji will deliver an address in Bengali in the Free Church Institution, Nimtollah Street, this Evening, 20th instant, at 6-30 o'clock. Hymns in Bengali set to Hindu Music, will be sung.

Law

POLICE.—19TH FEBRUARY 1876.

[*Before P. D. Dickens, Esq.*]

MRS. J. Leigh, residing in the Muchoarrah section of the town, charged his Ayah with the theft of a silver watch and chain valued at Rs.48. Defendant pleaded guilty stating that she had committed the theft at the instigation of a servant boy. She was on her own admission of the charge, sentenced to 6 months' rigorous imprisonment.

THREE Natives were charged by a Mahomedan Merchant with the theft of 6 maunds worth of sugar. His Worship being of opinion on the evidence adduced, that the prisoners had conspired to rob the complainant convicted and sentenced them, the first defendant to 6 months' and 20 stripes, and the 2nd and 3rd to 3 months' rigorous imprisonment each.

Selection

THE ANNIVERSARY LECTURE OF BABU KESHUB CHUNDER SEN.

(Indian Daily News.)

In all the comments called forth by Babu Keshub Chunder Sen's last address at the Town Hall, there does not seem to be anything like a right appreciation of the position of surpassing importance which is there assumed. Even our correspondent Senior, whose letters evince great fairness of spirit, does not seem to us to have hit off the distinctive feature of the discourse. In the Babu's advocacy of what is called "the personality of the Holy Ghost," Senior sees "the article of a creed—a bi-une-God," and treats it as a sort of half-way house to the orthodox doctrine of a tri-une divinity. To view the lecture after this fashion is simply, we fear, to look at it under the categories of orthodoxy, and to clothe it in the forms of an understanding that has been narrowed by evangelical traditions; and there can scarcely be a surer way of missing its true significance. In a matter of this kind, the most judicious course is perhaps to fling away as much as possible of the prepossessions of a traditional training, and to look at the new Brahmic teaching in the light of its own naked truth, wherever that is possible. The earnestness of the Brahmo leader's utterances may perhaps be accepted as some kind of guarantee against the worse sorts of mental reservation, or in other words, as an evidence that his language expresses more or less closely his actual thoughts; and if this be the case, it is hardly unfair to say that the mere fact of his looking to the Universal Father for the gift of His Spirit cannot, by any logical process, yet discovered to other than theological schools, be tortured into implying that he has invented a "binity" of the Godhead. Doubtless Babu Keshub Chunder Sen has distinctly enough taught the doctrine of the personality of the Divine Being; but that will probably be found on reflection to differ materially from teaching, as the antiquated standards of an effete orthodoxy do, that the Spirit of God is actually a different person from that Father. Surely the analogy of human nature, which is understood even within the pale of orthodoxy to have been made in the image of the divine, may be said without exaggeration to conspire with all intelligent thinking in showing that the spirit of a being whether man or God, so far from being a different person from that being is under the changing conditions of phenomenal existence, the changeless essence of his identity. Indeed this seems to be the unequivocal teaching of the Great Apostle of the Gentiles, in the striking parallelism contained in the words, "What man knoweth the things of a man save the spirit of man which is in him? Even so the things of God knoweth no man, but the Spirit of God." In a word, if we transmute the old language into modern phrase, and for its technical and theological garb substitute a scientific form of thought, we shall call the doctrine of the spirit the doctrine of the Divine Essence, in other words, that God is a living person and not a mere abstraction.

What has been called above the distinctive feature in the lecture at the Town Hall, shows itself in the Brahmo's statement that Christ, when about to leave the world, made over the government of His Church to the Holy Spirit when there rang in the ears of a listening world the great fact of the succession of that Spirit as their Comforter, Light, Strength, and Salvation, whose work it should be to guide them into all truth. It would be difficult to alight upon a position more plain or more important. It marks, we will not say, the great central truth of Christianity as taught in the present age, but the central fact of the teaching of Christ Himself. It discloses, consciously or unconsciously, the source of the inspiration which pervaded the first disciples and teachers of Christianity and to which the books composing what is now called the "New Testament" are supposed to owe their origin. It was not the parchment roll or written covenant of any kind, that the Founder of Christianity seems to have been most anxious to leave behind Him as the sheet anchor of His followers, when departing from this earth; for the earliest of the gospels granting them the greatest antiquity which their most ardent advocates have ever claimed for them, was not written till many years after the death of Christ. What He did leave behind, the sole legacy bequeathed over and above the deathless heritage of truth which He had Himself taught, was the gift of the Spirit, the *fons et origo* of all His own matchless teaching. And in echoing this truth the Brahmo leader, it must candidly be acknowledged, must strike the unprepossessed mind as reproducing the religion of Christ rather more accurately than the most fervent worshipper of scripture can do, whose worship, as including the letter of the scriptures, it is a kind cruelty to designate as Bibliolatry.

To most true disciples of the Great Master who recognise Him as the real head of the human race—and in this recognition even the so called infidel philosopher, John Stuart Mill, would hardly differ from us: witness the remarkable utterances in his posthumous essays regarding Jesus of Nazareth—it ought surely to be a desirable thing that the same spirit which dwelt in the head should also dwell in the body, or, in other words, in our common humanity. And the man, call him Theist or Brahmo or Philosopher or Poet, who leads his fellow-men to the fountain-head of all true thought by opening their ears to the voice within, those inarticulate utterances which can be heard only by any one who is willing to carry out his convictions of duty at all risks, can alone, as it seems to us, be said to have fully struck the key-note of Christ's teaching.

It may not be known to some of our readers,—while we mention it not only for their sakes, but to illustrate the dangerous character of a too servile dependence upon the mere letter of scripture for our information as to what Christ taught,—that the most popular text of the prayer commonly known as the Lord's Prayer with which Christians are familiar from the nursery, is essentially defective. There are strong reasons for believing that the received version omits the vital petition in that prayer as originally taught by its author. Any one who examines the context in which it occurs in Luke's Gospel, will see that the burden of Christ's teaching as to what should be sought for in prayer, was that man should ask for the gift of the divine spirit; and yet, strange to say, the version which we possess of the prayer, as commonly taught, contains no reference to that "unspeakable gift." This of itself might make one suspicious of the integrity or genuineness of the text; but we are relieved of any danger which might be supposed to lurk in what is sometimes denounced as irresponsible speculation, by the reflection that there is satisfactory ground for believing that the original model of prayer furnished by Christ to His disciples actually did contain, as its opening petition, not the words "Hallowed be Thy name"; but the vital request "May Thy Holy Spirit come to us." This is the version actually given in the copy of the Gospel which was used by Marcion, and which he, with good reason, is believed to have obtained from the church at Sinope, and which, as Mr. Baring-Gould in his late erudite work upon the lost Gospels suggests, may have been Luke's original Gospel.

The fear of modern criticism and of its effects upon the letter of scripture, which has rather enslaved religious aspiration in the dark days of the past, may well be offered now up on the altar of the hope that, even though the earthen vessel of the letter were shivered to pieces, the treasure which it contains could never be lost. Manly trust of this sort would help mankind to welcome every attempt, whose object was to lead the living church of all good men and true, of every creed and race, to break away from the bondage of external law, into the freedom of the interior teaching, which was truly enough foreshadowed in the Jewish Holy of the Holies where alone the glory of the Unseen was ever burning brightly, and to which the high priest had to come from the outer courts of the tabernacle in order to reach the counsels of the Eternal.

Advertisements

Indian General Steam Navigation Company, Limited.

SCHOENE, KILBURN & Co.—*Managing Agent.*

ASSAM LINE.

NOTICE.

Steamers now leave Calcutta for Assam every Tuesday, Goalundo every Thursday and Debrooghur downward every Tuesday.

THE Str. "LAHORE" will leave Calcutta for Assam, on Tuesday, the 22nd instant.

Cargo will be received at the Company's Godowns, Nimtollah Ghat, until noon of Monday, the 21st instant.

THE Str. "MIRZAPORE" will leave Goalundo for Assam on Thursday, the 24th instant.

Cargo will be received at the Company's Godowns, No. 4, Fairlie Palace, up till noon of Tuesday, the 22nd.

Goods forwarded to Goalundo for this vessel will be chargeable with Railway Freight from Calcutta to Goalundo in addition to the regular Freight of this Company.

Passengers should leave for Goalundo by Train of Wednesday, the 23rd instant.

CACHAR LINE NOTICE

REGULAR WEEKLY SERVICE.

Steamers now leave Calcutta for Cachar and Intermediate Stations every Tuesday and Chuttuck downward every Monday.

A Steamer and "FLAT" will leave Calcutta for Cachar on Tuesday, the 22nd instant.

Cargo will be received at the Company's Godowns, Nimtollah Ghat, up till noon of Monday, the 21st.

For further information regarding rates of Freight or passage money, apply to

4 Fairlie Palace, G. J. SCOTT,
Calcutta, 16th Feb 1876. *Secretary.*

THE CALCUTTA SCHOOL.

SESSION opened on the 10th of January, 1876. The following are the rates of fees:—

		Schooling fee.	Admission fee.
English Department	Rs.	2 0 0	2 0 0
Vernacular	„	1 0 0	1 0 0
Juvenile Class	...	0 8 0	0 8 0

Three Scholarships of Rupees Five each are available next year, to be held by the three most distinguished students of the School who successfully pass the Entrance Examination of December, 1876. There are besides, five free studentships in the Entrance class open to competition, applications for which are to be made to the undersigned before the 15th of February next.

KRISHNA BIHARI SEN, M. A.

ALBERT HALL.

PATRON.

His Honor the Lieutenant Governor of Bengal.

COUNCIL.

Hon'ble Sir William Muir, K. C. S. I.—*President.*
Rajah Rama Nath Tagore Bahadur C. S. I.—*Vice-President.*
Hon'ble Ashley Eden, C. S. I.
Archdeacon Baly.
Colonel H. E. L. Thuiller, C. S. I.
Maharajah Kumar of Bettiah.
Rajah Komul Krishna Bahadur.
Rajah Joteendro Mohun Tagore Bahadur.
Babu Digumber Mitter C. S. I.
Hon'ble Nawab Ashgar Ali Bahadur, C. S. I.
Nawab Amir Ali Bahadur.
Moulvi Abdul Lutif Khan Bahadur.
Manockji Rustomji Esq.
Babu Keshub Chunder Sen.

SUBSCRIPTIONS.

His Highness Maharajah Holkar	...	Rs.	8,000
His Highness Maharajah of Jeypore		„	5,000
His Highness Maharajah of Putialah		„	2,500
Maharajah Kumar of Bettiah	...	„	2,000
Rajah of Bhinga	...	„	1,000
Maharani Surnomoie, Cossim Bazar		„	1,000
Maharajah of Hutwa	...	„	500
Rajah Komul Krishna Bahadur	...	„	500
Rajah Rama Nath Tagore Bahadur		„	200
Rajah Joteendro Mohun Tagore	...	„	500

M. Z. MARTIN & CO.,

THE CHINA AND JAPAN WAREHOUSES,
MERCHANTS AND COMMISSION AGENTS.
No. 4 Dalhousie Square, East.

ICE! ICE! ICE!

MADE IN FOUR MINUTES

THE PNEUMATIC ICE MACHINE

THIS IMPORTANT INVENTION IS CONSIDERED A BOON TO THOSE LIVING IN TROPICAL CLIMATES.

CAN BE WORKED BY THE MOST INEXPERIENCED HAND AND IS NOT LIABLE TO GET OUT OF ORDER.

From Rs. 175, each Machine complete.

MESSRS. ARLINGTON & CO.

AGENTS.

Printed and published by M. M. Rukhit, at the "Indian Mirror" Press, No 13, College Square, for the Proprietor.

The Indian Mirror.

SUNDAY EDITION.

VOL. XV] CALCUTTA, SUNDAY, FEBRUARY 27, 1876 {Registered at the General Post Office} [No. 48

CONTENTS.

NOTICE.

Letters and all other communications relating to the literary department of the Paper should be addressed to "The Editor."

All letters on the business of the Press should be addressed, and all remittances made payable to the Manager of this Paper. Particular attention is solicited to this notice.

Subscribers will be good enough to give prompt notice of any delay, or irregularity in delivery of the Paper.

Editorial Notes

THE lecture on Classification has been followed by action much sooner than was expected. Two of our missionary workers, whose spiritual character is of a more decided type, and whose future career is amply indicated by their past history, have been selected for systematic training under the minister, the one in *Yoga* or communion, and the other in *Bhakti* or love to God. Their initiation took place in due form on Thursday last. Their education will extend over a year for the present.

THE Hindu Pantheon, already terribly large, has received a new accession lately. The Prince of Wales, though himself a Christian, has been invested with divinity by a Canarese scholar, who thus apostrophises in verse :—

I have cast aside the Trimurti [the Trinity],
If I ask for rain, the Prince will give it ;
If I ask for the sun, the Prince will smile,
Is he not omniscient, omnipresent, almighty, the essence of perfection!
I will breathe him, and he shall be my food,
I have no need now to doubt in faith ; my new religion is one of sight and knowledge,
I have seen the flower-face of my God !

Query,—Will the Canarese votary venture to eat the *prasad* of his new *deota* ?

THAT most liberal and estimable body of men, the British and Foreign Unitarian Association, is, it seems, threatened with a schismatic division on vital principles. We are startled to read in their organ, the *Inquirer*, that Mr. Samuel Shaen was to have given notice, at the last quarterly meeting of the Association, of his intention to move,—"That the publication of the proposed works of Theodore Parker [the Discourse on Religion, Ten Sermons, and Prayers] is inconsistent with the object for which the Society is formed." We are anxious to know the results of the discussion.

LET a piece of open ground be selected in the Native town, and a temporary bamboo shed be erected over it, and let there be bi-weekly Sankirtan there, with popular lectures. This, we believe, is a national and effective method of preaching our simple faith to the lower classes of our countrymen. The shed may be removed from one part of the town to another, so that many thousand may be gradually reached. The idea is good, and a suitable place it will not be difficult to find. All that we require is a popular preacher and a band of popular singers; and the work of conquering the masses may begin at once. Is there none among our missionaries who can devote his life to such exalted work?—none who feels for the poor?

SATAN is busy in these days, establishing his claims to personality, and pushing himself even before the highest tribunal to assert his rights. An English paper records the following item of intelligence, too precious indeed in the nineteenth century:—"The suit brought by Mr. Jenkins, a parishioner of Clifton, against the Rev. Flavel Cook, the vicar of that parish, for having refused to administer the Sacrament because of Mr. Jenkins' views on the impersonality of Satan, came on for argument on Wednesday before the Judicial Committee of the Privy Council, on an appeal from a decision of Sir Robert Phillimore. Mr. Fitzjames Stephen, in support of the appeal, contended that by law established all parishioners should have the Sacrament administered by the clergyman after they gave due notice beforehand and presented themselves before him, unless they were notorious evil-livers. The arguments have not yet been brought to a conclusion." It is too bad to dispose of the ruler of the lower regions as an abstraction. Satan is not only a person, but an august personage.

IT is altogether a wrong opinion to hold that the spirit of asceticism was unknown to the Hindus of the pre-Budhistic era. Surely the Budhists have done more than any other community to introduce the forms of asceticism into Hindu society, their self-abnegation having been much more rigorous, complete, and disinterested than that of others. But in Manu, there are clear injunctions about the *Vanaprastha Ashram*, the *Panchatapa*, and other observances which demanded an extent of self-mortification at which even European ascetics would stand aghast. In some of the *Upanishads* also, such as the *Chandogya*, and *Brihataranyak* there is distinct mention of *Brahmacharya*, and other disciplines showing a clear and emphatic recognition of the spirit of asceticism. Budhism itself was essentially a Hindu movement though it set aside almost all the cardinal ideas of the Hindu creed of its time. It was a necessary reaction against the current of corruption, false theology, and worldliness which had crept into the constitution of the popular religion, and like all reactions it involved a mass of denials, protests, and sentimentalism that brought about its expulsion from the country.

NOW that the leaders of the Progressive Brahmo party have turned their attention very closely indeed, one might say almost exclusively, to the cultivation of the Hindu ideas of asceticism (*Byragya*,) of rapturous love (*Bhakti*), of communion (*Yoga*), of service (*Sheba*), should not Babu Debendra Nath Tagore, whose chief difference with the younger party seems to have been that he has always insisted upon preserving the Hindu spirit of the Brahmo Somaj movement, come forward with his valuable aid and experience to encourage, and lead his progressive brethren? This is exactly the time when co-operation of this kind is not only desirable, but eagerly sought, and if the venerable chief of the Brahmos has any profound lessons to teach, he may rest assured they will be listened to with the respect and submission to which he is fully entitled. There is another thing of which he ought to be told. The differences which the younger party had with him, some years ago, have lost their edge and significance with time, they are as eager as ever to learn from him, and tell him their difficulties if he is at all disposed to give them help. The differences need not intimidate him any longer.

MR. R. ROWE in his sprightly volume on Jack Afloat and Ashore, throws out a significant hint on slave-trade. Jack is made to say :—" Whaling I've been, sperming and Greenland, and I've been in the slave-trade. Well, what are coolies, but slaves? Ours mutinied twice. Put a hundred of them in irons. All died; 150 died together." When the people of England are considering, and are so unanimous in condemning the Fugitive Slave Circular, whereby all fugitive slaves seeking protection on board British warships, were to have been sent back to their owners in case the vessels happened to be in ports belonging to slave-owing States, they ought perhaps to pay some attention to the fact put forth above. Even now in our tea-plantations, inspite of so called Government vigilance, are not the coolies often most shamefully treated sometimes? But few care for such ill-treatment in India.

A MOST painful case, illustrating for what mercenary purposes marriages are sometimes contracted by certain people in the Hindu community, came before Mr. Justice Phear on the 2nd February last. A girl fifteen years old, evidently of the Sonar Bania caste, named Purnu Sundari, sues her husband Ghosto Behari Mullick for recovery of certain jewels fraudulently taken from her, for the nullification of a deed she was forced to sign, and for maintenance which she is entitled to as the lawful wife of the defendant. The girl was married in the hope that she should bring in a large quantity of gold and silver as is the custom in the Sonar Bania caste. The amount realized in the present case not being satisfactory, the husband wanted 1,000 Rs. more. Not getting this he began to ill-treat his wife, and when ill-treatment failed, he hit upon a new plan. He got a deed drawn up by which the poor wife was obliged to give up possession of her jewels, confess infidelity to her husband, repudiate all claim upon maintenance, and leave her husband's house for her father's. The young man thus pocketed gold and silver ornaments to the value of about Rs 2,500, be having the pleasure of stigmatizing his victim for life. Mr. Justice Phear was justly severe in his comments upon the conduct of the two attorneys who drew up the deed, Babus Tarabullub Chatterji, and Jogesh Chunder Chowdry, and most unhesitatingly gave a decree for the plaintiff. Our question is why should not the latter be prosecuted criminally? Such cases of brutality do happen now and then, only we never knew enterprising lawyers putting in their aid to sanction and perpetuate them, as the two Attorneys, according to Mr. Phear, have done in the present instance. Is there no public opinion among the attorneys of Calcutta?

"RELIGION is not two things, but one," so says Mr. Charles Beard, the ablest of English Unitarian preachers, we believe, next only to the venerable James Martineau himself. And in this sense he does not recognize any essential difference between Natural and Revealed religion. Babu Keshub Chunder Sen following very nearly the same line of thought in his recent lecture, argues that there is no difference between Natural, and Supernatural religion, the meaning of supernatural being only *above*, and not *against* nature. This of course is true. Now essentially considered there is not only no difference between Natural and Revealed and Natural and Supernatural religions, all being classifiable under the widest generalization of which the word Nature is capable, but hardly any difference between one religion and another, the spirit and essence of all being so closely analogous that Christian scholars contend for the common origin of two such heterogenous systems as those embodied in the *Bhagavat Gita* and the New Testament. The question to be dealt with is the question of existing distinctions. In the formation of the religious world certain modes of belief, and processes of mental operation have been stratified into a solid structure, intelligible only under distinctive names which men have consented to give them. We can appreciate the eclecticism which ignores distinctions, and views religion as a grand synthesis of the soul. But nevertheless the distinctions are real so far as they go. They indicate processes which may exclude each other, and sometimes act as contraries. For instance, the word Natural Religion, in generally accepted religious phraseology, means a system of belief which is the result of the exercise of human reason on the phenomena of nature. It is supposed to set its face against all higher light. Now inasmuch as natural phenomena are liable to various interpretations, and the laws of reason have yet to be ascertained, Natural Religion has no fixity and no status in the theological world. Revelation is just the opposite process. It is religion as given by the Supreme Spirit of Truth, often beyond the reach of reason, and sometimes in direct contradiction to reason. Ideal human nature is the perfection to which humanity aspires, but human nature, as we find it in daily experiences, is a poor affair. It has to be checked and contradicted. Theists, to avoid misunderstanding, should redefine and redistribute religious distinctions.

CLASSIFICATION OF DEVOTEES.

THERE are two Sanskrit words of deep significance which apply to the subject before us. These are *Sadhan* and *Sidha*. The former may be said to denote literally the process of accomplishing an object, and the latter the eventual fruition. A man takes a vow before God and then devotes his mind and body to its fulfilment. He goes through appointed means, and subjects himself to a systematic course of training and discipline and self-Government with a view to effect the object in view. This process of culture is *Sadhan*; he who is engaged in it is called a *Sadhak*; while he who has completed the work of cultivation, reaped the fruits of his labors, and fully accomplished his purpose is *Sidha*. Those who take up specific departments of life for culture may be easily classified according to their respective spheres of training. Some men may educate their souls and cultivate prayer, contemplation, and communion. Some may train and develop their feelings and sentiments, and learn to love their God with increasing fervor. Others may make the education of the will the chief object of their lives, and learn to obey Divine commandments in all their details. The three classes of devotees represent the soul, the heart, and the will, and may be characterized as *yogis*, *bhaktas*, and *shobaks*. The objects they have respectively in view are union with God, passionate attachment to God, and obedience to God. So long as they are engaged in learning and practising these particular principles of religon they are only *sadhaks*. When their objects are realized they are entitled to be honored and respected as *sidha yogi*, *sidha bhakta*, and *sidha shabak*. If we analyze the nature, temperament, tastes and habits of our fellow-devotees it will not be difficult to find out some among them whom nature has intended, as it were, for one or other of these classes. Those among us who are contemplative generally retire from society, love, solitude, see very little reality in matter, are self-possessed, and self-subdued, show the elements of *yoga*. They live in the spirit-world, and readily commune with spiritual realities. They welcome whatever is a help to the subjugation of the entire soul, and are always employed in conquering selfishness, carnality and worldliness. They are happy in prayer and meditation, and in the study of nature. The *bhaktas* on the other hand is most passionately fond of God, and delights in loving Him and loving all that pertains to Him. Nothing is welcome to him except what is sweet. The Lord's mercy is his food and raiment, his faith and salvation. Dryness of heart is to him a great sin, and he shuns it as a foe. The very utterance of the Divine name causes his heart to overflow and brings tears of joy to his eyes. The *shabak* delights in service and in the discharge of varied duties. He is most energetic and persevering. Activity is his life. Dullness is death to him. He is always doing good to others, and seeks heaven in obedience. Where these different elements of character manifest themselves in a peculiar degree they ought to be cultivated with care and constancy, so that nature's purposes may be fulfilled. In such culture exclusiveness and mutual antagonism should be avoided. All classes should respect and help each other.

TRAINING THE WILL.

It is a rare thing to find among the people of this country a man of really strong will. The automatic theory about human action is exemplified by our national character more perhaps than the character of any other nation. In the first place there is the strange influence of traditional customs. Men here seem to have lost the power of breaking through it. Then there is the influence of a religion which however mixed with impurities exercises a deep and really lasting influence upon the mind. Add to this the influence of climate, of surrounding circumstances, of example, and of various other things which cover the mind with a strong network of influences which few find the strength, or the courage, or even the wish to resist. Devotional feelings in the mind of the Hindu it is not very difficult to awaken. There have been mighty revivals of religious emotion all over the country, and in repeated succession. Among our own congregations we often witness excitement, and devotion really striking. Nor is it very difficult to stimulate the Hindu intellect to action. Profound reasoning, accuracy, thoughtfulness, and clear insight into things can be fostered among minds gifted with average powers. But it is a far more difficult thing to train the will. How far our people believe in the existence of the will as an element in the character, it is difficult to judge. Among educated people, that is those who have cultivated the study of philosophy, such a thing is known. But even they have been seldom taught to think of the will as a power in their possession which they can direct to obtain mastery over their circumstances. Not that therefore their will fails to take a direction. It is fashioned by the appetites, by the influences around, by the strongest motives excited in the heart by example, and interest. How this power so injuriously exercised can be shaken, is a problem deserving the attention of all religious teachers. It is a problem which has not yet been formally taken up by the Brahmo Somaj. But it will have to be taken up before long. It is high time that the powers of resolution, and action should be cultivated among the Brahmos. The training of the will is more or less difficult according to the nature of the person who undergoes the training. In supple and emotional natures the will may be easily reached through the medium of feelings, but the moral impression is most difficult to retain amidst the appeals which the world continually makes upon passions of the baser sort. The method of acting upon the will through impulses of the emotional nature, however efficacious in certain matters, and however well calculated to produce enthusiasm, is unreliable. Because in such training after all the passions retain the mastery. The will ought to be educated as such. The moral nature in itself is seldom a reality to those whose habits in life have been unconsciouly formed by society, or formed by the influence of the uppermost impulses for the time. In early life continued obstructions serve in a great measure to call out the forces of the will. Or when a man grows up, and has a great or absorbing purpose, if there be great difficulties towards the accomplishment of that purpose, the man either succumbs to the obstacles around him, or by supreme efforts of his moral nature triumphs, and appreciates the inestimable value of exercising his will. An absorbing purpose thus seems to be very groundwork on which the adequate action of the will is possible. Such a purpose may be good or bad. If it is good the will is trained to virtue and righteousness. If it is a vile purpose, the character of the man still gains in strength, but his will is trained to habits which ultimately prove to be his ruin, and not unfrequently of all around him. Brahmos then who want to train and cultivate their moral power, should first propose to themselves a great and all-engrossing purpose, and when that purpose is obstructed, the will should act to get over its obstacles, and acquire development and fulness. What other purpose can there be greater than possessing a sinless life, and entering into the depths of spirituality and wisdom?

The Interpreter

Do good to them that hate you; Love thine enemy, such are some of the precepts which abound in the Christian scriptures, enjoining the highest doctrine of forgiving love. Such precepts are not wanting in the Hindu scriptures. Take Mahabharat, Santiparva, 146,5528, "Even if thine enemy enter your house receive him with due hospitality. The tree does not deny him its shade who fells it." The precept of doing good to an enemy is perhaps nowhere so beautifully illustrated.

All honor to Menu for the subjoined test, in which he inculcates the highest and purest doctrine of toleration. The passage is really a remarkable one. "From poison extract nectar, hare words of wisdom even from the mouth of boys, imitate the good example even of an enemy, and accept gold even from an unholy place." 2,139.

The doctrine of "I am" is an ancient and Theistic truth. To every true believer the Lord vouchsafes the certain conviction of His own existence and reality, not through elaborate reasonings or *a posteriori* arguments, but in those thrilling words of direct self-assertion—"I am." These words are not new to our countrymen. In the Yoga Vashishtha 1826, we find the Hindu's God thus solemnly described:—"He who has neither head nor body and pervades all objects, He who repeatedly utters the words "I am," that Supreme Spirit is the God I worship.

Correspondence.

CHRISTIAN SYMPATHY.

To the Editor of the *Indian Mirror*.

My Dear Sir, or "my dear brother" if do not object. I am a Christian Missionary, and a somewhat regular reader of your Paper. I like its tone—its breadth of views—and above all its charity towards those who belong elsewhere than to the Brahmo Somaj fold. I was struck with a paragraph on your first page of the issue of January 30th in which you speak of the growing liberality on the part of Christian Missionaries towards non-Christians. So let it be! We hail with supreme delight every step in this direction. We believe, too, that in no other way can Christian Missionaries more successfully enlarge their sphere of usefulness, than by opening their eyes to the good which is found in Hinduism and Mahomedanism. As for despising such efforts as are being made by the Brahmo Somaj for the amelioration of the people of India, it appears to us folly born of bigotry. For one, I shall lend all possible encourgement to any of our Hindu friends who may be inclined to establish a Somaj in this town. Since we left our native land to labor for God in India, we have learned to look quite differently at some features of man's relation to God, and in our mind we feel well assured that if Jesus were now among men he would look much more kindly on the efforts of the Brahmo Somaj and similar institutions which have only the *holiness of life* for their object, than many of His followers are inclined to do. Wishing you God's blessing on every good word and work, I am yours in symathy,

A Christian Missionary.*

THE "GAJANANDA" FARCE.

To the Editor of the *Indian Mirror*.

Sir,—That objectionable farce "Gajanandi" was again brought on the stage of the Great National Theatre last night, but under a new name, and in a somewhat different garb. I must, however, candidly admit, that there was nothing obscene in it. The presence of the Police had no doubt something to do with it. The Director of the Theatre availed himself of a pause between the two Acts to harangue the audience in

* A good and sincere word spoken out of the heart as it has been by our correspondent is more encouraging than the writer can think of. Ed.—*I. M.*

eloquent language on behalf of his Company, and was quite successful too. This was a prostitution of talent and education, unprecedented, I believe, in the annals of dramatic representation.

Yours truly.
The 24th Feb. 1876. G. C. DEY.

Devotional.

How much of imaginary and unreal religion I shall have to leave to attain thy true knowledge, and enjoy the blessedness of thy presence, O Lord teach me. The sweetness of so-called devotion is not thy communion always, nor is the brightness of the mind to be always called the glory of thy presence. It is true these things come in thy name, they come and go, but never last. The seer knows they are not thy true sight. Seeing thee who can ever forget, and thy communion once enjoyed absorbs a man at all times. Suffer me to go down into the very depths of thy being, to know all that a soul like mine can, and should know for it is good to behold thee and know thee, and live in thee with heart, mind, and will.

O GOD, prosper those who set out to seek thee in right humility of spirit. Reveal thyself unto those who wait for thee. May thy blissfulness be their portion who have consented to bear the load of privation for thy sake. God, thou art the giver of all rewards, and deligence and painstaking patience are never lost sight of by thee. Let thy servants whom thou hast chosen, sow with the sweat of their brow, labor in rain and sunshine, suffer and sacrifice in thy name what they hold dear, and when thou thinkest fit thou shalt give them that abundance, which when a man reaps never sorrows suffers in this life again.

Meditations

THERE is a blessedness, past expression in feeling that God has been bountiful to me throughout. I have no complaint to make against his dispensations, his dealings have been full of mercy to me. Who knew before Lord, that thou didst love me so? Whenever a difficulty came, I asked myself as to who could deliver me? Would my God, could he safely get me out of this difficulty? Here is a trial for my faith, here is a trial for God's mercy.—So cried my unbelieving heart. When the difficulty came to a crisis, and just when my heart was palpitating with anxiety and fear, I was delivered, men say by accident, but I declare by the faithfulness of God's mercy! Many such difficulties have come and gone; many times have I faltered and fallen to the dust, but always in his grace have I found cause to be thankful. If it was in the power of difficulties and temptations to destroy me, I would have long ere this ceased to exist. But no, the Lord has spared me for his own purpose, spared me, poor worm that I am. Many are the miracles which have solved my moral difficulties—nay not moral only, but physical difficulties also. Shall I then hesitate to put my trust in God's promise? Men threatened me, they discouraged me, they laughed at my ambition, they trembled for my safety. They very well might. But I wonder to think how my God has carried me safely through. It is a blessed thought, it is a cheering strengthening thought. May such peaceful inward experiences be multiplied in the life of every theist.

My brother, let your relation with your God be hidden and deep. Have secrets in your mind which you can confide to Him alone. Have a real and unknown source of joy in him, unknown to all but yourself. Blessed is he who can fall back upon his God in secret. Blessed is he whose heart has a secret nobleness and dignity in his Father's assurances. Apart from the unsteady ground of human sympathy, apart from the deceiving comforts of the world, build your house of joy deep in your own being, where God shall visit you in the still hours of darkness and silence. True spirituality is unspoken; it is perceived, but seldom expressed, or if expressed, it runs underneath, and not over the surface of words.

The Brahmo Somaj.

BRAHMO MISSIONARIES RE-INITIATED.

BABUS AGHORE NATH GUPTA, and Bijoy Kissen Gossain stood up at the conclusion of the preliminary service in the minister's house on Thursday morning. Separate seats had been assigned to them, and on one side sat Pundit Gour Govind Upadhya with a heap of Sanskrit books arranged on a small stool set before him. All the missionaries of the Brahmo Somaj of India were called to stand up which they immediately did. The Upadhaya then read the Sanskrit translation of the sixteen rules of discipline drawn out by the minister for the guidance of the two applicants for initiation. The latter expressed their assent to follow the prescribed discipline, and begged help and light from above. Their missionary brethren who had remained standing all the while, blessed them with united voice. When all sat down again the minister gave his solemn charge to the two applicants. We have no space for a full report. But it was very much in the following strain :—A long while ago you two left the life of worldliness to enter into the life of religion. This day you leave the life of religion mixed with sin, worldliness, and unreality, for the pure and profound life of unmixed and genuine spirituality. Be initiated in deep *Sadhan* for this purpose. You have not yet beheld your God in due measure. To-day you set out on your way for that region where you will see the great mighty God giving his solemn dispensation with his own hand. From the first letter to the last of this dispensation everything is written by him. Nothing of it is by man. Where is the dispensation, where is your God? There, before you in the far distance. When you go there your hearts will be full of gladness. Bijoy you as a *Bhakta*, Aghore, you as a *Yogi go*, walk in that direction. I do not mean to give you honor to-day and admire you as great men; as very poor, and little creatures I throw your before you brethren and sisters. Your place is not over the heads of others, but at their feet. Whenever you see them, first look at their feet. First think of serving them, you take the vow of their service, and in all your lives show the example of humility. The conquest of the passions is a very difficult work But unless your tongue be pure, your hand be pure, and all your actions be pure, your religion is vain. Strong in the strength of the Lord cry out saying, Avaunt lustfulness; pride anger, covetousness, envy, avarice, ambition avaunt! Let these never come near your place of *tapasya*. The all-seeing God is your witness that you two resolve to conquer all vile passions, and devote yourselves to God entirely. How you are to keep your bodies and minds perfectly pure He will teach you. You do not know it, neither do I. What the Great Teacher teaches me, I will teach you. Keep good feeling with all. Wherever there is real obstruction, wherever there is real impurity, be it the company of man, of woman, or child, shun that company as you would shun poison. Whatever work disturbs your *Bhakti*, or your *Yoga*, leave it at once. Avoid all temptation like viper. The greatest of all sins is want of faith. Next to that sin is the desire of maintaining your old vices. Keep up your present discipline, breaking it will be a great transgression. If you have a commandment from God, and do not keep it, you will also be guilty of great sin. If others behave ill with you, you cannot on that account break the discipline to which you submit to-day. You Bijoy, who are initiated in *Bhakti*, bear in mind that inebriation in God is to be the great condition to which you aspire. And you Aghore who are initiated in *Yoga*, you should bear in mind that your aspiration ought to be to commune with your God always, in all places, and under all circumstances, with your eyes shut, as well as with your eyes open. Accept this discipline. There will be some difference between you, and those who sit around you. The message of light that comes through you, they will receive. I too do not accept this initiation, I too will learn from you. And may we all finally enter into the same blessedness.

BABU Dina Nath Mozumdar has proceeded to Bhaugulpore to celebrate the anniversary of the local Brahmo Somaj.

PUNDIT Gour Govind Upadhya delivered his lecture on Asceticism as inculcated by the Hindu Shasters on last Thursday. There was a good attendance. After the lecture questions were asked, and the President explained certain points.

OUR friend and brother, the Rev. C. H. A. Dall, has made a gift to the Mission Office of the Brahmo Somaj of India of his following pamphlets :—

Natural Foundation of all Religion ...	50 copies.
Theism No. I. ...	25 ditto.
Theism No. II. ...	50 ditto.
Brahmo Somaj of India ...	25 ditto.

We beg to acknowledge receipt of the above copies with many thanks.

Literary.

COLONEL NASSAU LEES, says the *Bombay Gazette*, who came out some months ago to India who has lately been prospecting the North-West, has now determined to settle down in Bombay and take editorial charge of the *Times of India*, of which journal he is the chief proprietor.

THE Copenhagen correspondent of the *Pall Mall Gazette*, writing on the 27th ult. says :—"The Swedish paper, the *Nyadagt Aleto*, has lately contained several leaders under the title 'Pictures of the Future,' which generally and no doubt correctly, have been ascribed to the King himself. These articles advocated a strong development of the Swedish Navy, and hinted indirectly at the establishment of a Scandinavian kingdom, including Denmark. A Stockholm correspondent writes to the well-informed *Snellposten* that it is the general talk in Stockholm that the King, during his recent visit to Berlin, made overtures for such a contingency, and the correspondent adds that it is very evident from expressions which have fallen from the King's own lips that these visits have left a very deep impression on his mind. The King and Queen will probably arrive at Christiania on Tuesday next. The preliminary steps are now being taken to hold a Scandinavian Exhibition at Christiania during the year 1880."

DR. MARTINEAU's answer to Professor Tyndall's recent article in the *Fortnightly Review*, will appear in the next number of the *Contemporary Review*. Mr. Matthew Arnold's recent lectures on Bishop Butler will be published in the February and March numbers of the same periodical.

WE learn that a new monthly magazine, likely to excite some attention, is about to be issued under the editorship of the

Reverent Charles Voysey, to be called the *Langman Magazine*. Its primary object, we are told, is to preserve the principles of true religion amid the decay of traditional beliefs; but this part of its work will be confined to one article in each number, while the bulk of the magazine will be composed of various essays on secular subjects, interspersed with entertaining literature. The first number is to appear in March.

Miss COBBE contributes to the current number of the *New Quarterly Magazine* a striking article entitled "Backward Ho!" the intent of which is to expose Spiritualism and Ritualism—which is done. But Miss Cobbe has a faith of her own, and believes, notwithstanding these "backward" waves, in another and greater reformation of religion.

ANOTHER new weekly paper is the *Secularist*, edited by Mr. G. J. Holyoake and Mr. G. W. Foote. It is the successor of the *Reasoner*, and its object is to show that the Secular is not necessarily Atheistic.

IT is proposed to publish on the 8th April next a new weekly paper, in Calcutta to be entitled the *Ten Journal and Planters' Chronicle*. Its Managing Agent is Mr. E. C. Kemp.

Scienti ic

SIR SAMUEL BAKER lectured at Plymouth lately on British influence in the advancement of Africa. He described his two expeditions, showed to how great an extent slave-hunting and slave-trading were carried on in the parts he had visited, and observed that the advance of Englishmen was always regarded by the chiefs with hostility; for in spite of any fugitive slave circular, it was well understood abroad that the presence of Englishmen meant sooner or later the suppression of slavery. He spoke in very high terms of the efforts of Lieutenant Cameron and Mr. Stanley, and expressed his conviction that the greatest achievement in African exploration was reserved for Colonel Gordon.

Gleanings

WHAT art Thou then, my God? What, but the Lord God? *For who is Lord but the Lord? or who is God save our God?* Most highest, most good, most potent, most omnipotent, most merciful, yet most just, most hidden, yet most present; most beautiful, yet most strong; stable, yet incomprehensive; unchangeable, yet all changing; never new, never old; all renewing, and *bringing age upon the proud and they know it not*, ever working, ever at rest, still gathering yet nothing lacking; supporting, filling, and over-spreading, creating, nourishing, and maturing; seeking, yet having all things. Thou lovest, without passion; art jealous, without anxiety; art angry, yet serene; changest Thy works, Thy purpose unchanged, receivest again what thou findest, yet didst never lose; never in need, yet rejoicing in gains; never covetous, yet exacting usury. Thou receivest over and above, that Thou mayest owe; and who hath aught that is not Thine? Thou payest debts, owing nothing; remittest debts losing nothing. And what have I now said, my God, my life, my holy joy? or what saith any man when he speaks of Thee? Yet woe to him that speaketh not, since mute are even the most eloquent. *Augustine's Confessions.*

The Week

IT is reported that Miss Carpenter will visit Madras again before she leaves India for England.

SIR BARTLE FRERE and the Revd. Canon R. Duckworth have left Lahore for Saharunpore *en route* for Mussoorie. They will next proceed to Nynee Tal and then join the camp of H. R. H. the Prince of Wales at Allahabad.

THE Duke of Buckingham, it appears, has come to Calcutta not on a pleasure trip, but to confer with His Excellency the Viceroy on several important questions.

IT is stated that Lieutenant-Colonel W. H. Beynon, Political Agent, Jeypore, is about to apply for leave.

LORD LYTTON may be expected to arrive in India on the 2nd April, if the new engines of the *Orontes* perform their functions properly. If not, his Lordship will be here on the 7th or thereabouts.

MADRAS is threatened with scarcity.

NOW that so much attention of the British Public is being drawn to India by the Prince's visit to this country, it is thought a fit opportunity to open an Indian loan in England.

THE Duke of Buckingham will leave Calcutta for Madras early next week.

THE Reverend Dr. Mylne, of Keble College, Oxford, has been nominated Bishop of Bombay in succession to the late Rev. Dr. Douglas deceased.

MR. H. G. PRITCHARD, the Government Solicitor, Madras, who had left that city in the steamer *Bokhara* sick the other day, died at Galle on board the above steamer.

COLONEL ALLEN JOHNSON, the First Assistant Deputy Secretary to the Government of India, Military Department, is appointed in the room of Colonel E. E. Bacon, as Deputy Secretary.

ALL the G vernment colleges and schools in Bengal—at least in Calcutta,—were closed on Wednesday last out of respect to the memory of the late Mr. Atkinson, the Director of Public Instruction.

LATEST NEWS.

MR. WILLIAM TAYLER, late of Patna, who left Bombay for England by last Monday's mail, took with him, a very large collection of sketches of Indian scenery and characteristic groups.

SIR WILLIAM ROBINSON has accepted the Vice-Patronship of the Madras Agricultural Society.

THE proprietor of the Elphinstone Hotel, Madras, has succeeded in obtaining Rs 1,500 from the Madras Government, being hotel expenses of H. E. the Governor of Pondicherry and suite during the Prince of Wales' stay in this city, though the latter stayed at the hotel only for two days.

SIXTY elephants for the use of the Nizam's Government were shipped at Rangoon for Coconada. The Burmese elephants are greatly prized by the Native Princes of India.

MR. MOLESWORTH, Consulting Engineer and Mr. Prince, the Superintending Railway Engineer, proceeded to Prome to inspect the proposed line of railway between that place and Thayetmyo.

AMONG other amusements to be provided for the Prince of Wales at Indore, there will be a Ball.

SIR BARTLE FRERE and Canon Duckworth were entertained at a pic-nic at Jamrud, Peshawur. They proceeded to the mouth of the Khyber, when some of the Khyberis exhibited their skill with their match locks.

THE proposed Industrial College in Behar in commemoration of the Prince's visit, will be established at Poosa, a place of two days' journey from Bankipore, because Mr. Metcalfe happens to be in love with the place. There is a great deal of public dissatisfaction on this account.

THE *Pioneer* is assured that the statement that Mr. George Sibley has been appointed Agent to the E. I. Railway Company in India, is premature at least.

THE six elephants presented to the Khedive by the British Government, which left Calcutta in the *Nizam* and *Mirzapore*, have all arrived safely, and have been landed at Suez.

KHAN BAHADUR YUSUF ALLI, Inspector of Police, Surat, left Bombay for the Punjab on Saturday last, in order to accompany the suite of His Royal Highness the Prince of Wales on His Royal Highness' return journey to Bombay, *en route* to England.

THE Hon'ble R. Cayley has been appointed Queen's Advocate in Ceylon, in the place of the late Sir Richard Morgan.

THE *Serapis* which is now at Bombay, has on board a menagerie which will be still further added to, before the Prince goes on board, by the presents made a few days ago by Sir Jung Bahadur. Young tigers, elephants, deer, dogs, birds, but apparently not reptiles, form the menagerie. His Royal Highness will thus have at home a beautiful collection of wild exotic animals and birds.

LORD LYTTON is working night and day, says the *World*, in order to be able to leave England early next month. Any spare time he can find he devotes to Mr. Millais, who is painting his portrait for and at the request of, his oldest and most valued friend.

THE hearing of the petition of Hirjebhoy Rustomji, a Parsi, commenced on Jan. 28, in the Court of Queen's Bench. It was a petition of right by a Parsi merchant at Hong Kong, who had been expelled from that place by the Chinese on the occasion of the first Chinese war, nearly forty years ago, complaining that the Crown had not indemnified him out of the money received for that purpose from the Emperor of China under the Treaty of Nankin. The Court dismissed the petition.

ACCORDING to a statement made by Sir Henry Peek in a public speech, the Princess Beatrice is engaged to be married to Prince Louise of Battenberg, of the Royal Navy, now with the Prince of Wales in India.

FROM the 1st of April next the rate of exchange for the ensuing year has been fixed by Her Majesty's Government at 1s. 9¾d. the rupee.

THE *Home News* believes that Lord Salisbury would be very loth to lose the services of Colonel Owen Burne, at Westminster, even if he had any wish to prolong his stay in India beyond such time as may be needful for initiating the new Viceroy into the working details of Indian official business.

MR. Hogg, the Director General of Post Offices, left Madras on Sunday last for Bombay.

HIS MAJESTY the Shah of Persia has sent a decoration of the Lion and Sun, set in brilliants, to his ambassador, Moin-el-Mulk, at Constantinople, for His Highness Ismael Pasha, the Khedive of Egypt, and His Excellency will shortly nominate one of the members of the embassy to convey the insignia to Egypt.

MR. KEMPSON, Director of Public Instruction, North-West Provinces, goes on leave immediately, and Mr. Griffith, Principal of the Benares College, officiates for him.

ON Thursday last, according to Reuter, "in replying to a deputation of merchants and others, whose interests lie in the cotton districts, the Marquis of Salisbury said that the Indian Government, for months past, had been instructed to prepare the way for the gradual abolition of the present import duties on manufactured cotton goods and yarns, and also to fix a period for their final entire abolition. If the finances of India were fortunate, he hoped the object which the deputation had in view would be speedily attained. The Marquis said he was not prepared to recommend a new tax for India."

THE small-pox epidemic is increasing a Bombay. Two temporary hospitals are being erected.

MR. L. A. GOODEVE, Barrister-at-Law, Chief Reporter in the High Court at Calcutta, for the Indian Law Reports, is granted a further extension of leave up to 15th November 1876, inclusive.

GENERAL Kauffman is about to resume the command of the Russian troops in Central Asia, which are to be considerably reinforced.

ISHAN Chodsha, a special envoy from the Emir of Bokhara, has arrived at Tashkend, to give explanations respecting the recent armaments in that country.

A MARRIAGE is arranged between Miss Louisa Charlotte Hamilton, eldest daughter of Lord and Lady Claud Hamilton, and Professor Tyndall.

IT is the intention of Her Majesty's Government, on the return of Mr. Cave, to send out to Egypt two gentlemen conversant with financial affairs, who will hold office under the Khedive, at whose request the step is taken.

Calcutta.

THE following is a further list of the donors to the Zoological Gardens, Calcutta :—

A. T. Maclean, Esq., C. S.	Rs.	100
Babu Hurri Prosad Chowdry	...	100
Prince Mahomed Rahimudin	...	200
Mrs. Voigt	...	100
The Maharajah of Benares	...	1,000
Col. J. Macdonald		150
Messrs. Robert & Charriol		250
W. Anderson, Esq.		100
Messrs. G. Henderson & Co.		250
Messrs. Mackinnon, Mackenzie & Co.	...	300
Messrs. Gisborne & Co.		250
The Hon'ble H. Bell, C. S.		100
Messrs. Shaw, Finlayson & Co.		100
Babu Chuckun Lall Roy	...	500
Sreemuti Bisheshuri Debia Chowdrani		250
Babu Tarinikant Johori		100
Babu Jogendra Kishore Roy		50
Rajah Bisseswur Mallah of Searsole		500
F. Clarke, Esq.		100

ACCORDING to the *Friend*, a rumour has for a day or two been current in Calcutta that Sir Richard Temple, offended at the peremptory tone of a communication from the Viceroy on Municipal matters, has resigned the Lieutenant-Governorship in a huff. We are not sure that there is any truth in the tale, but the scandal in question has now assumed such proportions that it certainly would not be strange if the Viceroy, amongst whose duties that of calling the minor Governments to order when needed, is one of the most important, should have thought it time to point out to his subordinate the unwisdom of needlessly outraging local public opinion.

THE Counsel who appeared yesterday before the Bengal Council on behalf of the Justices of Calcutta, were Messrs. Woodroffe, Lowe, and A. B. Miller.

THE *Indo-European Correspondence* is "half inclined to believe" that the distribution of the ten thousand rupees given by the Prince of Wales for the charities of Calcutta has not yet been made, for the simple reason that even Sir Stuart Hogg would hardly deal in so high-handed a manner with the Prince's gift as to ignore the existence of the many Catholic charities in Calcutta. We may inform our contemporary that Sir Stuart Hogg himself told a gentleman the other day that the distribution had been made.

LORD LYTTON'S Military Secretary, Colonel Colley, C.B., says the *Friend of India*, has seen service at the Cape, in China, and in the Ashantee war under Sir Garnet Wolseley. His talents are said to be of a high order for both military and civil employ. At the Staff College he passed one of the most brilliant examinations on record, and afterwards filled the Professorship of Military Administration there with distinguished success as an Instructor. On the Gold Coast, he had charge of the line of communication and the transport service, and discharged his duties in such a way as to call forth the highest encomiums from both his chief and his comrades. He accompanied Sir Garnet to Natal, and served that colony as Post-Master-General, Member of the Executive and Legislative Council, &c. He has lately held an important post in the Camp at Aldershot, which he relinquishes, at Lord Lytton's instance, to come to India. Our new Governor-General appears to be fortunate in his choice of Secretaries. Few Viceroys have landed in the country with two such good men to lean upon as Colonel Owen Burne and Colonel Colley.

THE Stewards elected for the next Calcutta Races are Lord Ulick Browne, C. S., Messrs. A. T. Maclean and J. A. Crawford, C. S., Lord William Beresford and Captain Roberts, R. A., with Captain Peacock as Honorary Secretary.

FROM the Health Officer's Report for the week ending 19th February 1876, we learn that there were altogether 280 deaths in the town against 211 in the previous week or 69 more. Classified the figures stand thus:—3 Europeans, 9 East Indian, 1 Native Christian, 194 Hindus, and 73 Mahomedans. Of these 96 died of fever, 41 of dysentery, 20 of diarrhoea, 34 of cholera, 1 of small-pox and 88 from other causes. The average mortality being 32·53 against 24·50, of the previous week.

ACKNOWLEDGMENTS.

Report on the Charitable Dispensaries under the Government of Bengal for the year 1874. By J. Fullarton Beatson Esq., M. D., Surgeon General, Indian Medical Department. Calcutta. 1875.

Report on the Administration of the Registration Department in Bengal for 1874-75. By P. Durley Esq., Officiating Inspector General of Registration. Calcutta. 1875.

Gyanankoor for Aughran, 1282.

Family Guide—Diseases of the Females—Datta's Series. Calcutta. 1876.

Public Engagement.

MUSICAL EVANGELISTIC SERVICE. Mr. I. Sherlock-Hubbard will deliver an address in the Free Church Institution, Nimtollah Street, on Sunday Evening, 27th instant, at 6-30 o'clock. Hymns in Bengali, set to Hindu Music, will be sung.

Law

POLICE.—26TH FEBRUARY 1876.

[*Before F. J. Marsden, Esq.*]

CAPTAIN Daniel Cavanagh, of the S. S. *Malta*, was charged by his cook with having criminally misappropriated a chest of clothes valued at Rs. 120, Mr. Moses, Pleader, appeared for the defendant, and denied the charge. From the evidence of the prosecutor it appeared that, on Wednesday last, he was discharged from the vessel, and paid up at the office. After receiving his wages, he went back on board for his chest of clothes, but the chief engineer told him, in the presence and hearing of the Captain, that the property would not be restored unless the defendant paid for [illegible] of tobacco, which he had used. One John Burke, who went with the prosecutor on board, corroborated the above statements, adding that the complainant had been abused when he asked for his property. To a question put by the Court, Mr. Moses replied that the Captain was willing to restore the property. Mr. Moses further undertook to see the property restored. Upon this the Magistrate dismissed the case.

Selection

MOODY AND SANKEY IN PHILADELPHIA.

THE incidents and accidents of the situation about the Moody and Sankey meetings are of interest. The Freight Depot is an immense edifice with large doors originally for wagons and drays at very short intervals on two sides of the building. It has a skylight running its entire length. It has been fitted up for its present uses at a cost of $10,000, the expense of the series of meetings being about as much more. The platform holds about six hundred people, and there are eleven hundred chairs in the audience room. It is a novel sight to witness the tides of people literally running in all possible directions, an hour before service time to secure good sittings, for though Mr. Moody and Mr. Sankey can both be readily heard all over the building, the distance from the remoter sittings is so great that they can scarcely be seen, so as to distinguish them at all, nor can one much more than tell whether they are sitting down or standing up. The great distances over the building render it impossible to give orders to ushers by ordinary methods, and hence a telegraphic communication is established with various portions of the room, which is operated from the platform immediately in the rear of the pulpit under the direction of Mr. Geo. H. Stuart, the President of the Young Men's Christian Association. Speaking tubes are also arranged throughout the building, so that all necessary communications between the various portions of the management can be conducted in the very midst of the services. When the order is given from the platform, all the doors are thrown open simultaneously, and in five minutes ten thousand people are upon the street.

The Inquiry Rooms are convenient, and the day we were in them, were crowded with persons apparently in great trouble on account of of their state. There was a lack of Christian workers on the occasion, and penitents had collected in groups for personal conversation. Mr. Moody has a handsomely furnished room under the platform, and he and Mr. Sankey reach the pulpit by a trap door immediately in the rear of the pulpit. Multitudes of people watch for their entrance, but few can divine how or when they so suddenly reach their place. One little girl asked her mother if they came down from heaven.

On Sunday morning last Mr. Moody preached to young men on 'Daniel.' I had heard that the most remarkable thing about Mr. Moody was, there was nothing remarkable; but this address was one amongst the most remarkable addresses I can now recall. I do not see why Mr. Moody might not command $500 a night for it as lecture, as well as Mr. Punshon for his, as in vigor of thought and a picture, modernizing and rendering real the incidents in Daniel's history, and the principles which are of universal application therein, combined with dramatic power and in everything else excepting rhetorical finish, it was fully equal to Mr. Punshon's lecture, and vastly more practical and better adapted to the American masses. I shall recollect it as amongst the great public addresses to which I have listned. In the afternoon the sermon was much more after the style so generally characterizing Mr. Moody's addresses, and the great manifestations of religious feeling on the part of the audience was entirely disproportionate to any sort of power discernible in the speaking or singing. The secret must be found in the closets and in the concerted prayer of Christians. Mr. Sankey's singing is well adapted for a mass meeting, but his voice is not equal to that of Mr. Fisher, in richness and pathos.

On Sunday afternoon a great number of dignitaries were in attendance on the services. One gentleman wearing a long robe of a coat with collar, and facing of fur, was shown to a conspicuous seat. "Who is that?" said one usher to another, "I don't know," said he, "some congressman, or some other poor man, I suppose." It proved to be Hon. Mr. Bancroft, the historian. In the evening General Grant and company attended the meeting.—*Northern Christian Advocate.*

Advertisements

Indian General Steam Navigation Company, Limited.

SCHOENE, KILBURN & Co.—*Managing Agent.*

ASSAM LINE.

NOTICE.

Steamers now leave Calcutta for Assam every Tuesday, Goalundo every Thursday and Debrooghur downward every Tuesday.

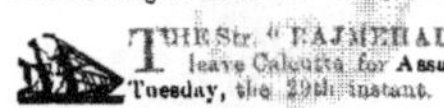

THE Str. "RAJMEHAL" will leave Calcutta for Assam, on Tuesday, the 29th instant.

Cargo will be received at the Company's Godowns, Nimtollah Ghat, until noon of Monday, the 28th instant.

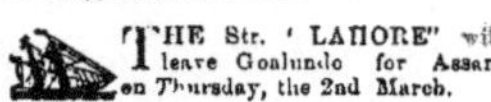

THE Str. "LAHORE" will leave Goalundo for Assam on Thursday, the 2nd March.

Cargo will be received at the Company's Godowns, No. 4, Fairlie Palace, up till noon of Tuesday, the 29th.

Goods forwarded to Goalundo for this vessel will be chargeable with Railway Freight from Calcutta to Goalundo in addition to the regular Freight of this Company.

Passengers should leave for Goalundo by Train of Wednesday, the 1st proximo

CACHAR LINE NOTICE

REGULAR WEEKLY SERVICE.

Steamers now leave Calcutta for Cachar and Intermediate Stations every Tuesday and Chuttuck downward every Monday.

A Steamer and "FLAT" will leave Calcutta for Cachar on Tuesday, the 29th instant.

Cargo will be received at the Company's Godowns, Nimtollah Ghat, up till noon of Monday, the 28th.

For further information regarding rates of Freight or passage money, apply to,

4 Fairlie Palace, Calcutta, 23rd *Feb.* 1876.

G. J. SCOTT, *Secretary.*

THE CALCUTTA SCHOOL.

SESSION opened on the 10th of January, 1876 The following are the rates of fees :—

		Schooling fee.	Admission. fee.
English Department	Rs.	2 0 0	2 0 0
Vernacular ,,	...	1 0 0	1 0 0
Juvenile Class	...	0 8 0	0 8 0

Three Scholarships of Rupees Five each are available next year, to be held by the three most distinguished students of the School who successfully pass the Entrance Examination of December, 1876. There are besides five free studentships in the Entrance class open to competition, applications for which are to be made to the undersigned before the 10th of February next.

KRISHNA BIHARI SEN

ALBERT HALL.

PATRON.

His Honor the Lieutenant Governor of Bengal.

COUNCIL.

Hon'ble Sir William Muir, K. C. S. I.—*President.*
Rajah Rama Nath Tagore Bahadur C. S. I.—*Vice-President.*
Hon'ble Ashley Eden, C. S. I.
Archdeacon Baly.
Colonel H. E. L. Thuiller, C. S. I.
Maharajah Kumar of Bettiah.
Rajah Komul Krishna Bahadur.
Rajah Joteendro Mohun Tagore Bahadur.
Babu Digumber Mitter C. S. I.
Hon'ble Nawab Ashgar Ali Bahadur, C. S. I.
Nawab Amir Ali Bahadur.
Moulvi Abdul Lutif Khan Bahadur.
Manockji Rustomji Esq.
Babu Keshub Chunder Sen.

SUBSCRIPTIONS.

His Highness Maharajah Holkar ...	Rs.	8,000
His Highness Maharajah of Jeypore	,,	5,000
His Highness Maharajah of Putialah	,,	2,500
Maharajah Kumar of Bettiah ...	,,	2,000
Rajah of Bhinga ...	,,	1,000
Maharani Surnomoie, Cossim Bazar	,,	1,000
Maharajah of Hutwa ...	,,	500
Rajah Komul Krisna Bahadur ...	,,	500
Rajah Rama Nath Tagore Bahadur	,,	200
Rajah Joteendro Mohun Tagore ...	,,	500

Printing Materials.

MILLER AND RICHARD'S PRESSE TYPES and all requisites always in Stock.

TERMS CASH

WING & CO

ICE! ICE! ICE!

MADE IN FOUR MINUTES

THE PNEUMATIC ICE MACHINE

THIS IMPORTANT INVENTION IS CONSIDERED A BOON TO THOSE LIVING IN TROPICAL CLIMATES.

CAN BE WORKED BY THE MOST INEXPERIENCED HAND AND IS NOT LIABLE TO GET OUT OF ORDER.

From Rs. 175, each Machine complete.

MESSRS. ARLINGTON & CO. *AGENTS.*

SMITH STANISTREET & CO.

Pharmaceutical Chemists & Druggists

BY APPOINTMENT

To His Excellency the Right Hon'ble

LORD NORTHBROOK, G.M.S.I.,

Governor-General of India,

&c. &c,

Syrup of Lactate of Iron Prepared from the original formula. Lactate of Iron, in various forms of preparation, has been in use in France, and generally through the Continent of Europe, for some years past, and is highly esteemed as one of the most valuable Chalybeate Tonic Remedies yet introduced. The Syrup, being the most agreeable as well as convenient form of administration is in most general use.

It is a most valuable remedy in the following diseases:—Chlorosis or Green Sickness, Leucorrhœa Neuralgia, Enlargement of the Spleen, &c. In combination with quinine, it has also been very successfully used in the cure of Fever, while in persons of delicate constitution, or enfeebled by disease, it is invaluable. In bottles, Rs. 1 each.

Syrup of the Phosphate of Iron, Rs. 2 per bottle.

Syrup of Phosphate of Iron and Strychnine, Rs. 2 per bottle.

Syrup of Phosphate of Iron and Quinine, Price Rs. 2-8 per bottle

Syrup of Phosphate of Iron, Quinine and Strychnine. (Dr. Aitkin's Triple Tonic Syrup.) Rs. 2-8 per bottle.

Smith, Stanistreet & Co.

Invite special attention to the following rates, the quality guaranteed as the best procurable :—

Pure Ærated Waters.

Made from Pure Water, obtained by the new process through the Patent Charcoal Filters,

				Rs.	As
Ærated plain (Trible Ærated), per doz.			...	0	12
Soda Water	ditto	"	...	0	12
Gingerade	ditto	"	...	1	4
Lemonade	ditto	"	...	1	[illegible]
Tonic (Quinine)	ditto		...	1	[illegible]

The Cask must be sent with the order to obtain advantage of the above rates.

!!! हुक्का !!!

!!! HOOKAHS !!!

ENGLISH made Hookahs of various choice designs, colours and sizes ranging in price from Rs. 2 to 5 each, 60 designs to choose from. Apply to

RADANAUTH CHOWDRY,
373, Jorasanko

BABU RADHAKANTA GHOSH

HOMŒOPATHIC PRACTITIONER,
12, College Square.

Is practising here on moderate terms.

NATIONAL COMPANY
HOMŒOPATHIC CHEMISTS AND PUBLISHERS
SUPPLY ALL KINDS OF
HOMŒOPATHIC MEDICINES BOOKS
CASES AND OTHER REQUISITES.
12 COLLEGE SQUARE,
Calcutta.

যৌবনে যোগিনী ।

NEW HISTORICAL TRAGEDY
BY
GOPAL CHUNDER MOOKERJEE,
Price, Re. 1, postage 2 ans,
To be had at 56, Grey Street, Shobabazar, and Sanskrit Press Depository.

HAROLD & CO.,

3, DALHOUSIE SQUARE, CALCUTTA.

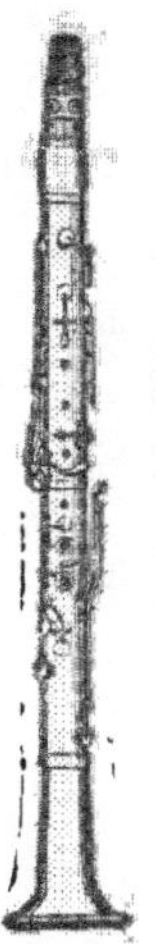

Superior Best made Clarionets Rs. 88

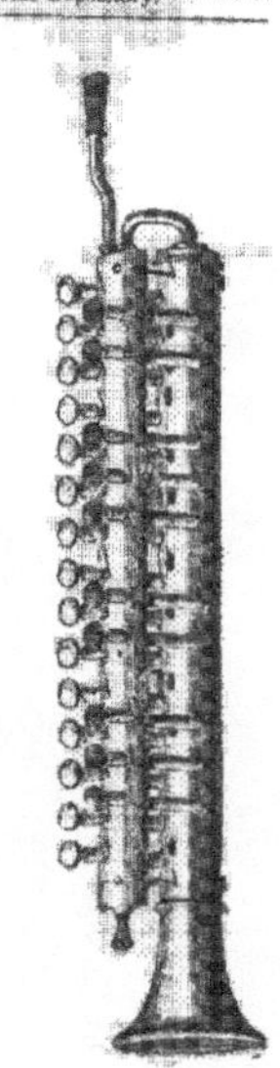

Pianetta Clarionetta Rs. 120

Sweet-toned Harmoni-flutes, from Rs. 60 each.

Warranted to be perfectly in tune.

SETAR MUSICAL BOXES AND HAND ORGANS,

Playing Bengalee and Hindustanee Tunes

Harold and Co., 3, Dalhousie Square, Calcutta.

Printed and published by M. M. Kubmit, at the "Indian Mirror" Press, No 15, College Square, for the Proprietor.

The Indian Mirror.

SUNDAY EDITION.

VOL. XV.] CALCUTTA, SUNDAY, MARCH 5, 1876. {REGISTERED AT THE GENERAL POST OFFICE.} [No. 54.

CONTENTS.

NOTICE.

Letters and all other communications relating to the literary department of the Paper should be addressed to "The Editor."

All letters on the business of the Press should be addressed, and all remittances made payable to the Manager of this Paper. Particular attention is solicited to this notice.

Subscribers will be good enough to give prompt notice of any delay, or irregularity in delivery of the Paper.

Editorial Notes

ALL those of our countrymen who have been to England, and who have had the good fortune to visit the Deanery of Westminister, must entertain the liveliest recollections of the grace and hospitality of Lady Augusta Stanley, the wife of the celebrated Dean of Westminister. This good lady's death is announced by Reuter's telegram. Lady Augusta's innate goodness of heart was held in as much regard and esteem as Dean Stanley's learning and manly piety. She was a friend to all the friends of the Dean, and her kindness to the people of this country was sincere and cordial. Peace be to her memory.

AUSTRALIA has sent out an unexpected but most cordial invitation to the Brahmo Somaj asking that a competent missionary may be deputed to visit the colonies and preach truth there for the benefit of those who are earnestly seeking the light of a purer Christianity. "There are thousands here," the message runs thus, "connected with the Churches, feeding on the husks of Christianity, but hungering for the corn, to whom the presentation of living Christianity would be a boon. The climate is salubrious and natural products are varied. Fruit is plentiful all the year round. We have several good stalls available for lectures or services, and a little band of earnest free-thinkers who would do all the work in arranging and conducting meetings. I could also obtain a guarantee of payment of passage money to and fro, and a Committee would so manage the services that they would at least pay all expenses here." There is a religious awakening on all sides, and Australia only echoes what the rest of the civilized world says. It is, however, a noteworthy fact that the Brahmo Somaj should be hailed by Christian nations as the best interpreter of Christ's religion. Will not the Somaj respond to the call? The time is coming when our missionary operations should be extended.

THERE is an outcry against vivisection because that leads to cruelty. But is it known to fashionable sentimental people, how much suffering and death their fondness for extravagant dress produces? An Inhabitant of this country who signed himself, "A Member of the Brahmo Somaj," wrote in the *Times* not long ago to expose the practice, so prevalent in Europe, of wearing the feathers of birds. Another gentleman, an Englishman, gives in the same paper, some startling statistics on this subject. The proceeds of a single sale of ornamental feathers show that, 97,000 herons must have been slaughtered for that only, and that all these feathers came from India. Mr. Newton observes that no country could supply 10,000 herons in a single breeding-season without nearly rooting out the stock. Moreover, 15,000 humming-birds and upwards were included in the sale, of which 740 were of a single kind. As far as we know, says the *Spectator*, none of these birds really diminished the stock of food available for man, so that in destroying them for mere show, we empty the world absolutely of a certain portion of its beauty and happiness,—while the beauty is certainly by no means made up in the ornamentation of feminine toilettes which is thus procured. In this age of fine morality, does no one really bestow a thought on the morality of such reckless spoliation of life as this?

IT is not against Brahmos only that Indian evangelicals direct their shafts of obloquy and contempt, eminent men among other Christian sects come in also for a proportionate amount of abuse. Our readers will remember the Indian visit of the Rev. William Taylor, the methodist preacher, who travelled in India for four years from 1871 to '75, and had ever so many successful "conflicts with Sin and Satan." The *Indian Evangelical Review*, the organ of the missionaries, makes a review of Mr. Taylor's Campaign in India, a book which that gentleman has published, and by a preliminary rejoicing over his good work, prepares the readers for "the criticisms" which are to follow. These criticisms are that Mr. Taylor has a wretchedly bad taste, that his self assertion and persistent assumption of superiority are great, that he is wanting in Christian courtesy and meekness, and is guilty of narrow-minded bigotry, ignorant prejudice, impudent effrontery, misrepresentation, and falsehood. Poor Mr. Taylor who is lectured upon "correct literary taste, and good manners," will perhaps be disposed to ask how far his reviewer has displayed these necessary virtues. Readers who want to know why these delicate compliments have been paid to the celebrated methodist preacher, should be told that he passes over the "old existing missions" in comparative silence, that it does not praise them as they want to be praised, and claims a *jus divinum* for his own labors. This the humble minded bearers of the gospel to the heathen can not bear. But they ought to bear in mind Mr. Taylor has written his book to report his own work, and not to advertise other people's transactions. Behold how these Christians love one another!

A STRICT follower of Budhism in India and Ceylon in these days is rare. He would be found to be exceedingly austere, and perhaps repulsive if he suddenly started up. This thought starts up in our mind while reading the review of the life of Arthur Schopenhaner written by Miss Zimmern. Schopenhaner as his name shows, was a German, and he was a Budhist, and a pessimist, as all Budhists ought to be. He held existence to be an unmitigated evil and firmly believed that desire lay at the root of all misery. He did not possess any faith in God, but found the world full of a blind impulse ever struggling to find manifestation in modes of life and suffering. Desire being the root of misery and evil, and all desire being reducible to the will to live, the suppression of desire meant the suppression of existence, and led to *Nirvana*. In all actions he upholds the doctrine of the most strict disinterestedness, and thinks that the principle of doing unto others as others would do unto you, has caught the taint of moral impurity His life was a strange commentary to these teachings. He was boastful and scornful, which are the last qualities to smooth a man's path through the world; and more than this, he was gloomy and suspicuous. "'It's safer trusting fear than faith,' was one of his favorite quotations," says Miss Zimmern. He kept pistols ready loaded near him at night; would never trust himself under the hand of a barber; was liable to the most wonderful panics on the outbreak of epidemics; carried a little leather drinking-cup about with him to the *table d'hote*, to guard against the danger of possible infection from drinking out of the cup used by any one who had had an infectious disease; and always wrote his accounts and notes on the investment of his property in some foreign language. He hid his valuables like a miser in out-of-the-way places, and labelled his bonds and cupons Arcana Medica, to divert suspicion. He cultivated, too, strange caprices, such as putting down a gold piece by his plate at the *table d'hote*, which he told inquirers was "to go to the poor, whenever he heard the officers [of the Army] discuss anything more serious than women, dogs, and horses." He shunned all men, and all men shunned him. Even with his mother he said to have quarrelled. His only friend was his dog."

THE body is a machine, is the mind a machine also? Is the whole man nothing but an automaton? It is needless to discuss this question in relation to the body, the immediate actions of which are produced by a series of processes over which we possess no conscious control. Philosophers describe those operations as molecular changes in the nervous system and in the brain according to fixed and inviolable laws. The important thing to know is how far the brain-mechanism is identified with the mechanism of thought in the mind. This question started up sometime ago in relation to Dr. Carpenter's lecture in the London Institution on the subject of unconscious mental work. Dr. Carpenter seems to lean to the doctrine of the automatic doctrine of the human mind in certain matters. This of course is vague. But it means we suppose that under certain influences, and within certain limits, the mind finds itself involved within the actions of laws, which deprive it of all conscious control over its own operations. The mind acts automatically under habits which grow so strong in the end, that the man hardly knows what he does. Human nature may be said to act automatically under the influence of Divine love, and piety becomes madness as in the case of Chaitanya. The bodily mechanism is strong in perfect harmony to the heavenly mechanism of the soul. But there is quite an opposite view to this. Materialists like Professor Clifford are found to maintain that the whole phenomenon of consciousness is nothing but the *inside view* of what by an outside observation is found to be only a number of molecular changes in the nervous system and the brain. To warn his hearers against their influence, Dr. Carpenter, who is as much an authority in psychology, as he is in physiology, speaks these pertinent words:—

"I ask you to take as your guiding star, as it were, in the conduct of your lives, these four words—I am, I ought, I can, I will.—'I am' is the expression of reflection or self-consciousness, the looking in upon our own trains of thought. If we do not feel *I am*, we do not think of ourselves and our own nature—we surrender ourselves. *I ought* expresses the sense of moral obligation. By steadily fixing our attention on *I ought*, the course of action is first directed right, and its continuance in that path becomes habitual. Then *I can*, the consciousness of power, is the foundation of all effort. And, lastly, it is not enough to say *I ought to do it*, and *I can do it*, but we must will to do it. The 'I AM,' 'I OUGHT,' 'I CAN,' 'I WILL' of the ego can train the mental, and bodily automaton, and make it do anything it is capable of executing."

THE FOUR VEDAS.

WE are not going to speak of the Rig, the Yajur, the Sam and the Atharva,—the four Vedas of the Hindus, which constitute the foundation and standard of their primitive faith. These are the Vedas of a particular religious sect only, of one among the hundred sects in the world. We propose to dwell on what we regard as the four Vedas of humanity, the four books of the universal scripture of mankind. Written by God's hand they are the natural and eternal Shastra, which is the heritage of all mankind and the wealth of all ages. Psychological analysis discovers and distinguishes four elements of humanity. These are mind, heart, soul and will; in other words cognition, emotion, devotion and concision. The human constitution is made up of these four departments, the intellectual, emotional, spiritual, and practical. To give the classification a more popular form, we may speak of thought, feeling, faith and action as constituting humanity. Now human nature, viewed in a philosophical sense and as coming fresh and unsophisticated from the Divine hand, is God's revelation to us. It is, to the Theist and to the philosopher both, the word of God. Both find in it wisdom and truth. All the elements of religion and morality are there. Out of them are formed, by reflection and arrangement, the sciences of true theology and ethics. On the tablet of the human constitution has the Divine hand engraven, in imperishable characters, the principles of truth and goodness, which when properly read, interpreted, developed and cultivated go to form true manhood. As this tablet of God's word is divided into four parts, students of divinity have to attend to and master the principles of each. Complete wisdom can then only be realized when all these four books are studied and comprehended. So likewise a true church is then only realised when all these are duly and fully realized in its creed and discipline. It must study and develop the four Vedas, that is, the Theology of the Mind, the Theology of the Heart, the Theology of the Soul and the Theology of the Will. These scriptures are vast. Each is vast, deep and unfathomable ocean of heavenly wisdom. Each is an inexhaustible mine of divine truth. Generation after generation passes away, centuries roll on, endless researches and investigations serve but to prove that only a drop of water has been taken out of the vast ocean. It seems therefore desirable and natural that some should study one Veda and others another *grantha*, according to constitutional aptitude and capacity, and develop these in their own lives by assiduous study and culture. They should certainly possess a general acquaintance with all the Vedas, and have wisdom, love, spirituality and obedience in a great measure. In a *greater* measure some of them, whom nature may have intended for the purpose, should cultivate particular branches of Theology, and realize in themselves and spread unto others the benefits of such special culture. Let all of us develop true Theistic manhood and be genuine Brahmos, but let those who are able and anxious cultivate special sciences in the spirit-world, and become *rishis*, *bhaktas*, *gnanis* or *sebaks*.

TRAINING THE WILL. II.

A GREAT and absorbing purpose in life cannot be the outgrowth of every type of human nature. Few things educate and exalt the will so much as deep real ambition. But of the profoundly ambitious you do not meet many in the world. We all make so much of little things that we strain all our energies to acquire them, and the really great aims of life escape us quite, or do but feebly draw out attention. There is no doubt that the vital forces of the moral nature are degraded and weakened by being directed to mean and small ends. After the degradation has once taken place, it is very difficult, if it is not actually impossible, to place the will once more in its rightful position. Yet men are surrounded by small ends everywhere, that smallness being in some cases concealed under the gloss of a false refinement, and in other cases under the excuse of necessity. The practical question is therefore how under ordinary circumstances such as meet us in everyday life, the training of the will is possible. It is hardly necessary to observe that abstractly speaking the training of the will means nothing. Its meaning then becomes intelligible when you speak of the formation of the habits of life. A man's habits show in what direction his will has been trained. Generally speaking a man's habits are formed for him not by himself consciously, but by the circumstances around him. The will acts passively so to say, and slowly loses that independence, and mastery over motives which ought to characterize its operations. This is very much our own condition. "What I would I do not, what I would not do that I do." This slavery to unworthy habits early formed, distinguishes human nature from the days when the great apostle of the gentiles preached his heart-stirring sermons. The knowledge of good is not wanting in us, even the motive presents itself among the ever-shifting wishes and aspirations of the heart. It is the strength to do the good that is wanting. Between the wish to live righteously, and the actual unrighteousness of life, there intervenes the terrible, the insuperable difficulty of formed habits. Ask the devoutest man you know, and if he speaks out of his heart, he will tell you that his practices are unworthy of his prayers. The self that communes with God, and beholds the glory of his face, is either destroyed, or hidden, or ignored, or forgotten; and it is quite a different self that acts and lives in the world. Yet it is the same man; a man that is a saint and a sinner at the same time, "an angel and a worm." The first shows the self of grace, that is what a man *should* be, what God can make him, and does make him from time to time. The latter shows the self of habits, what a man *is*, what he has made himself. How long is this sad, strange, perplexing contrast to continue in the good man's life? That which has been made, can it be unmade again? Can habits change? Can the higher self absorb the lower, can the lower self be sacrificed to the higher entirely? Upon an affirmative answer depends the whole future of humanity, upon the success or failure of a training for the will the whole answer depends. Be indifferent or unmindful to change the habits you have formed, and you will find perhaps when too late your religion has been little more than vanity, and a cloak for your sins. Be willing, be resolute, and take the vow to leave the habits which, by repeated experiences, you find stand in the way of your salvation, and your peace of mind, and you will soon find your religion is a power which can remove mountains. Few men know the power of their own faith. To effect a change then in the ordinary every habits of unrighteousness, nothing is so necessary as a resolute will to begin the change. Examine your habits carefully one by one, and deal with those which belong to the body first. Which of these mortify your conscience, disturb your devotions, make you ashamed of yourself in the presence of others? Take one, the simplest one, and strain your will to eschew it from the very next day. One effort makes the next effort easier, and brings with it a giant's strength. One success brings with it the light from heaven which makes the path to the next success clear. Thus try first of all to make your control over your body perfect. Make it clean, temperate, industrious, useful, entirely the servant of your highest will. The control of the will over the thoughts, feelings, desires, and imaginations of the mind is a much more difficult matter. But the man whose body has been made the veritable sanctuary of the Lord, has not to wait too long to find the best means to govern his inner nature. And thus in the end both the mind and the body serve the same purposes, and the training of a man's will becomes complete. But here commence other considerations. How can a vicious and enslaved will be its own legislator and reformer. Where is the feeble will to find the strength to carry out its own resolutions. Can strength come out of feebleness merely by wishing? And this point is so very important, interesting, and vital, that we reserve its consideration for our next.

Correspondence.

PRAYER.

To the Editor of the *Indian Mirror*.

SIR,—There is a great divergence of opinions among religionists of all denominations with regard to the necessity of prayer and its objects. The advocates of prayer say, prayer is the life of the soul—prayerlessness is therefore death. Whoever therefore has any thing to say on the subject is entitled to a hearing. What is prayer? Perhaps many will think it is useless to ask this question. Who knows it not? So common it is. I say, its very commonness makes it necessary to analyse it. Who does not know what man is? Plato defined man to be a featherless biped. Diogenes took a fowl, stripped it of all its feathers and sent it to the academicians, asking whether they would accept it as a man. The reason is that we generally neglect the analysis of ordinary things and consequently have very vague notions of them. To make it clear, let us take a single instance. A little child wants the moon, stretches its tiny hands and cannot reach it. Not succeeding, it insists upon the person in whose arms it is, to pluck out the moon from the sky. Analysing, we find two elements in it—(1) the feeling of a want, the will to obtain it; (2) a sense of inability and a craving for assistance. We may extend the number of elements in it to three. Without either of these there can be no prayer. It will not do simply to feel wants. Prometheus and Lucifer felt wants, but never prayed for the removal of those wants. The opponents of prayer say, God knows our wants and shall fulfil them. It is needless to pray. But we have seen above that there can be no prayer without Will. We are free beings, and God cannot compel us to have those things which we *will* not. As free beings we must actually pray if we wish to have our wants removed. Again, we cannot pray once for all. We cannot have a general notion of our wants, and a general Will is altogether unphilosophical, Will being a particular act of consciousness. It has been said "Thy will be done" is the best form of prayer. The identity of man's will with that of God is a condition which saints alone can attain. An ordinary sinner must attain that condition through incessant prayers. This is putting the cart before the horse. Again, if it be said that God would fulfil our wants without our prayers because He is good, as well we might hope He would keep us sinless because He is Holy. No, God requires that as free beings we must actually pray to Him whenever we feel a want. It has been said how do we know that what we get is really from God? Many a wicked man prays to his God and believes he has received strength from God; for instance the Thugs believe that they are assisted by the goddess Kali. Since there is no Kali, whence is this enthusiasm of the Thugs? I say it is from within, not from without. My opponent retorts: the strength you get by prayer is not from God but it results from the excitement of your mind. My answer is:—It is evident from the above consideration of what Prayer is that I do not pray for what I have already in me and it is not inconsistent that, He who has given me so much should give me more. Moreover, there is, I believe, a great difference between the effects of false and true prayers. Now it is indirectly admitted by my opponent that great enthusiasm and strength are the consequences of prayer. Thus, prayer being the condition of attaining such enthusiasm the necessity of prayer is established. And since those who pray, believe that they pray to the real God and their prayers are heard, the doctrine of prayer is by no means *inconsistent*. The opponents of prayer are inconsistent in appealing to latent powers which no philosopher of their school admits. It has been also said, the belief that we receive answer from God may be a deception of our mind. Many have been deceived by such beliefs. Pray, how do you distinguish deception from reality. Is it not through consciousness? Alas! if my consciousness cannot tell me what is mine and what is from God, I am helpless. Again, we may be deceived once or twice, but it does not follow that we must not believe ourselves at all. Your eye-sight may err, but it does not follow that you do not or should not trust your eyes. Should we pray for others? I ask, should a mother weep for the death of her child? No amount of reasoning can dissuade her from shedding tears, and why? because sympathy forms an essential part of her being. No philosopher of note has proved that sympathy is acquired. Should we pray for temporal things? Prayer implies confidence of success, and we cannot be confident that our prayers for temporal things are always right. It has been said to modify such prayers with such expressions as "if it pleaseth thee, Lord, &c." But this is inconsistent with the spirit of prayer, since it implies want of confidence in ourselves. Prayer implies that we earnestly want what we pray for. But praying in this manner we run the risk of not getting it if it does not agree with the will of God whereas we might get by our own exertion as we often get many wrong things. More consistently we may pray to God to prevent us from desiring such things.

Yours Obediently,
X. Y. Z.

THE WILL.

To the Editor of the *Indian Mirror*.

SIR,—One of the internal evidences of the truth of Brahmoism is the coincidence of conclusions arrived at by individual Brahmos thinking independently of each other. Your leader on the "Training the Will" which appeared in your Sunday issue of the 27th February 1876, is one of the many instances of such coincidence. During the two months before our last Magh Utsab it struck me again and again that the highest flights of devotional fervor which we (who are in the lower stage of the spiritual world) enjoy, are at best emotionand as such must necessarily be transcent, they are good in their way, but they cannot give us what we call life. We must look upon something other than emotions for a steady and tangible progressive religious life. But what that something was I knew not. I asked this question to myself often and often, but no satisfactory reply came until the Utsab, when the question was solved, a thought from within bearing the stamp of a higher source than myself struck me. What was this thought? It was that want of *nishta* which in intellectual language means strong will, was the source of all evil in me. This thought repeated itself several times since then becoming clearer and more definite. When I just decided upon giving out my experience to my brethren through your paper, your leader alluded to, came to my hands and agreeably surprised me and confirmed my faith.

I have something more to say. It is clear that the will must be trained, but what are the practical means, means that could be easily adopted by every Brahmo whatever may be his position in the spiritual world? The means or rather the principle which will guide the means appears to me clear enough. It is on the one hand giving up whatever of the world has hold on the mind, and on the other hand sticking to anything which one thinks it his duty to hold on, however disagreeable that thing may be. To express in other words it is controlling the wordly *Asakti* (love) on the one hand, and creating religious *Asakti* on the other hand by strengthening the sense of duty. To be practical we must begin with small things, *i.e.*, such *Asaktis* which are not very strong, and such duties which are not very disagreeable. For instance, imagine a man who has liking for one kind of reading and a dislike for another kind (both of the kinds are of course useful). Now let him make it a rule, say for three days, that he will not read what he likes and read only what he dislikes. Illustrations may be multiplied but they are needless.

One word more. Cultivation of the habits of seriousness is indispensibely necessary for all *sadhuks* (earnest religious men). Gossipping and what we call cheerful conversation and innocent pleasures, excepting in a few strong and formed minds, tell upon the spirit very much. We should as a body be very careful of them.

Yours faithfully.
R. M. B.

CALCUTTA.
The 27th February 1876.

Devotional.

I THANK thee, O blessed God, for the light with which thou dost renew and clothe the world every morning. I adore thee for the beauty and splendour which nature everywhere displays under that light. Teach me to seek the inner light which is far more renovating, and glorifying, and under its beneficient influence. Teach me to find the sweetness and sanctity of thy face.

SOUL of my soul, who but thou can understand the secrets of my heart? When wilt thou permit me to understand the secrets of thy purpose towards me? Essence of all beauty when wilt thou charm me with thy incomparable presence? Behold how my heart is anxious to enter the domain of thy righteousness. I am bruised with the thoughts of sin, give me O Lord the healing of thy embrace. I am smitten with the false fatal glare of youth and pleasure. The chaste holy handsomeness of thy face do thou reveal unto me.

The Brahmo Somaj.

THE monthly morning service in the Mandir will take place in the Mandir next Sunday at 7 A.M.

THE anniversary of the Bombay Prarthana Somaj will take place on the 26th proximo.

THE *Enquirer* reproduces our prayer on the occasion of the Prince of Wales' visit to Calcutta.

Brahmo Hymns

CAN I ever forsake him who loves me and seeks me with a sincere heart? As the cow goes after the calf and always keeps near, so I am always with my devotees. Resigning the charge of thy life into my hands be free from anxieties, there is no fear in the sea of the world. Who after worshipping me ever went back to the world, disappointed, not having seen me after crying unto me?

WHAT is the fear of anxiety, O my soul? He whose protection I have found, is almighty and infinite in mercy. If once with a sorrowful heart you address Him as the Merciful, that Friend of the poor and kind Protector of devotees will reveal Himself to you. What can the enemies do by dishonoring and persecuting me? I have heard the message of hope; I shall find life after death, that I may live in joy everlasting is his wish. Alone in the chambers of the heart I will spend my life in gladness and joy with that God of my life. Becoming pure in His company remain fearless and sitting in the citadel of faith shout forth Victory, Victory to the Merciful!

IT is not easy to be an ascetic. Renouncing the desire of pleasure and all worldly wishes the heart must be attached with love. Becoming tranquil, fearless and free from anxieties, a conqueror of passions, and being united with Divinity in communion, you must practise the highest communion, renounce self and become avaricious in godly avarice. Forgetting self the heart must be engaged in the good of others, and rejoicing in the happiness of the world must sacrifice self completely.

Gleanings

BREAK UP YOUR FALLOW GROUNDS

Break up your fallows, o'er matted with weeds,
Fit up the wild waste for righteousness' seeds;
Spare not a thistle, or nettle, or tare,
Leave not the root of a noxious weed there,
And plough the ground deep
Where the "devil-weeds" creep.
Throw out the stones and burn over the ground,
Let not the root of a bramble be found.
Fence the ground safely from pride and from sin,
Keep up the bars that they may not get in,
And put in good seed
That are free from all weeds.

Give the field culture and guard it about,
Lest your arch enemy root the wheat out.
Heaven will send you the rain and the sun,
And finish the work that it has begun.
Abundance of grain
Shalt thou reap for thy gain.

TO MY LITTLE SCHOLARS.

Guard your tongues 'gainst leaking;
To you, young, I'm speaking!
Put a bolt before the door;
Let no evil word get o'er!
Let no evil word get o'er!
Put a bolt before the door!
To you, young, I'm speaking,
Guard your tongues 'gainst leaking!

Guard your eyes moreover,
Free or under cover!
On the good reflecting aye,
Turn their glance from evil's way.
Turn their glance from evil's way
On the good reflecting aye,
Free or under cover,
Guard your eyes, moreover!

Guard your ears securely,
They will fool you surely,
If you evil words let in
It dishonors all within.
It dishonors all within
If you evil words let in,
They will fool you surely;
Guard your ears securely.

Guard the three forever,
'Gainst too free behavior,
Tongue, eyes, ears, are all inclined
To badness, and to evil blind.
To badness and to evil blind
Tongue, eyes, ears, are all inclined.
'Gainst too free behavior
Guard the three forever.

—*From the German.*

EXPERIMENTS may give us the accidents, not the essence of things, to reach that essence, science must maintain its connecting link with religion.

THE earth is a ladder towards heaven, and in order that we may be worthy to mount it, our whole life should be a hymn to God.

HOLD in honor your body, your faculties, and the material forces that surround you in nature. Instruments given to you by God for the discovery and fulfilment of your appointed aim, are good or evil according as they are used for other's benefit, or for your own, for egotism is the root of all evil, as sacrifice is the root of all virtue. *Jos. Mazzini.*

WHEN your toils and trouble are great, and you cannot attain peace, try to make some other troubled heart peaceful, and that will give you the peace which found no where. *W. M. Thackery.*

Scientific

THE new aeronautical invention, the para-kite, has been exhibited to the public at the Alexandra Park; but, as it was represented only by a small specimen, the results of the exhibition are not very tangible. The para-kite, which resembles an ordinary kite in many details, ascended to an altitude of 1,000 feet or thereabouts, remaining steady while held by the string; but its decent was too rapid to suggest an idea that it would be safe or comfortable for a human being to trust himself to it as a passenger.

MAGNETS prepared by compressing iron filings in tubes, have been exhibited to the

French Academy by M. Jamin. When soft iron filings are forcibly compressed by hydraulic pressure they acquire a coercive power equal to that of steel.

FOREL, a Swiss naturalist, has lately published an extensive work in quarto on the ants of his country. It is a worthy successor of the well-known book of Huber. It is very frequently quoted by Lubbock in his second paper on the habits of bees and ants, just received. Forel asserts that ants when they leave the pupal state, like bees, devote themselves to household duties and the care of the young not taking any part in the defense of the nest until a later periods of life. As regards the memory of ants, he convinced himself that they recognized their companions after a separation of four months; but he believes they would not do so for more than one season. The demonstrations made by ants that had been separated, that struck Huber as due to joy and satisfaction, Forel thinks are, in reality, signs of distrust and fear. Ants of different nests are generally hostile to each other; but it is not until three or four days after they quit the nest that they are able to distinguish friends from foes. Forel also bears testimony to the supposition that ants differ very considerably in mental activity and quickness.

LIEUTENANT CAMERON who has completed his journey across Africa, is expected home shortly. He started with three English companions, and of these Mr. Moffat died, Dr. Dillon shot himself, and Mr. Murphy returned to Zanziber with Dr. Livingstone's body.

Literary.

BY way of a reply perhaps to the "Black Pamphlet," the Bengal Government has just issued a volume on the Food Supply of Behar and Northern Bengal and the relief of the scarcity of 1874 in defence of Sir Richard Temple's famine policy. The author or compiler of the volume is Mr. Macdonnell B.C.S.

THE last number of the *Indian Charivari* contains a likeness of Sir Andrew Clarke, the Public Works Member of the Governor-General's Council. The following short account of him is given:—Sir A. Clarke entered the Royal Engineers in 1844, and we find him in 1848 taking part in the war in New Zealand, where he distinguished himself sufficiently to be mentioned in despatches. He was shortly after selected by Sir W. Denison, then Governor of Tasmania, and himself an Engineer Officer, as his Private Secretary, and after filling this Office to the satisfaction of every one, he was, some years after, appointed Surveyor-General in Victoria. In 1859, from political reasons, he resigned his appointment in Victoria, and returned to England, where he was shortly after appointed "Director of Admiralty Works" In this appointment he superintended many important public works, such as the construction of the Chatham Steam Mills and others, and his services were ultimately rewarded by the appointment of Governor of the Straits Settlements. Though his stay there was but short, he managed, ably assisted by Lady Clarke, to acquire great popularity, and his departure was much regretted. The Public Works Department in India is such a complicated piece of machinery that it must take any one some time to thoroughly master its details, and as yet we have seen no signs of Sir A. Clarke's reforming hand. But we live in hopes.

MRS. HARRIET BEECHER STOWE sends out a very pretty little book entitled, "Betty's Bright Idea," which contains three short stories.

A LONDON edition of the "Black Pamphlet," written against the famine policy of Sir Richard Temple, is just issued. It has a black cover. The author is said to be a Bengal Civilian. It has a prefatory letter to Mr. Fawcett; and if that gentleman does not make a stir on this subject in the Parliamentary Session just begun, the *Home News* says "our surprise will certainly be great."

THE *Contemporary Review* for February opens with a vigorous and closely-reasoned article by the Rev. James Martineau, entitled "Modern Materialism," in reply to one by Professor Tyndall, published in the November number.

Two hundred Indiana Editors with their wives have arrived at Philadelphia to witness the Centennial.

AN autotype fac-simile edition of Milton's Commonplace Book is going to be published in London from the manuscript recently discovered. It contains notes in Milton's handwriting from upward of eighty works read by him; and these notes are in general his deductions, and not mere extracts from the works read. There are other entries by four or five different hands, presumably made at Milton's dictation. The M.S. is quarto size and contains eighty written pages.

Original Literature.

THE YEAR 1876, NOW CURRENT.

WELCOME the baby year! Behold him crowned
With youth, and hope, and promise of the [spring.
The past is dead, his latest whisper drowned
In loyal shouts that hailed another king;
And he, to whom our canticles resound,
What does he bring?

NEW joys, new aims, our eager hearts reply,
Elate with hope, and glad with social mirth,
A thousand blessings,—aye and ere he die,
Fulness and plenty to the waiting earth;
With nobler fruit of aspirations high,
Born with his birth.

AH, fair new year, be kind to those we love,
And to us all more fraught with joy than [woe;
Thou comest pure and stainless from above,
Alas! Thou wilt not pure and stainless go,
Yet, welcome! Blest and happy thou canst [prove;
God grant it so.

LATEST NEWS.

MRS. SUBRAHMANYAM and her father, Rev. A. Venkataramiah (who went to England for a short visit on account of ill health), have left for Madras. Mr. Subrahmanyam will follow soon.

MIR ZULFIKAR ALI, grandson of the late Nawab of Surat, who was sent to England for education, has returned home.

THE Buffs do not return immediately from the Straits Settlements.

LORD NAPIER, after his visit to Allahabad, will probably return to Calcutta for a few days, and then start for Bombay.

23,360 MORMON women of Utah have petitioned against the abolition of polygamy.

AN association has been formed to develop the proposition that the Anglo-Saxon race is descended from the lost tribes of Israel.

FEMALE medical students are admitted to the Queen's Hospital, Birmingham.

IT would seem that the expenses attending the purchase of the Khedive's shares in the Suez Canal amount to £80,000, as the proposition which the Chancellor of the Exchequer intends to make to the House of Commons, on Monday next, is that the sum of £4,080,000 be granted to Her Majesty to enable her to acquire the property.

THE Sultan of Turkey has 800 wives and devotes to his own and their use £2,000,000 out of the £7,000,000 that constitutes the whole income of the Turkish Empire.

IT is stated that Her Majesty has been pleased to name March 25, as the date upon which she will probably leave England on her visit to the Continent.

THE services of Mr. H. B. Lawford of the Bengal Civil Service, are replaced at the disposal of the Government of Bengal with effect from the 12th October last.

THE Viceroy and Governor-General is pleased to confer upon the under-mentioned gentlemen, the title of "Khan Bahadur," as a personal distinction:—Mohammed Munawur, and Ghulam Mohummed Ghouse, Abdul Ali, grandsons of the late Prince Azim Jah Bahadur of Arcot, and Haji Zahur-ul-Din Ahmed, son-in-law of Nawab Ghausia Begum.

MR. A. J. L. CAPPEL, Officiating Deputy Director General, is appointed to officiate as Director General of Telegraphs in India as a temporary arrangement, *vice* Lieutenant-Colonel Murray, going on furlough.

LORD G. HAMILTON, in asking for leave in the House of Commons, to bring in a bill to amend the law relating to legislation in India, explained that it was substantially the bill which passed to the other House of Parliament last Session, and which consolidated the limitations upon the legislative powers of the Governor-General, with one exception, which it was proposed to omit, and provided that no court, save the High Court of one of the Presidencies, should have power to decide that any Act of the Governor-General was *ultra vires*. Leave was then given.

THERE is a rumour that Mr. Forster, just deceased, has bequeathed nearly the whole of his property to Lord Lytton, the son of his old friend, the late holder of that title, better known as Sir Edward Bulwer. The legacy is understood to be of much higher value than might have been expected.

THE *Times* is authorised to state that there is no foundation whatever for the recent statements which have been made with respect to the marriage of Princess Beatrice.

Calcutta.

THE Maharajah of Vizianagram has left Calcutta for Benares.

THE *Indian Daily News* says that Captain Jackson will shortly leave Calcutta for Simla to make the necessary arrangements for receiving Lady Lytton.

THE Hon'ble Mr. Justice Phear has obtained leave for three months from the 19th of April next.

MR. J. E. O'CONNOR, Assistant Secretary in the Statistical Branch of the Department of Revenue, Agriculture, and Commerce, is allowed privilege of absence for three months from the 6th March 1876.

THE bust of Babu Hurro Chunder Ghose, the late Third Judge of the Calcutta Small Cause Court, was unveiled by the Hon'ble Mr. Justice Macpherson yesterday evening, at the new Court premises. The Judges, Pleaders, and Officers of the Court, were present at the ceremony.

WE learn that a *Mudi* committed suicide at Ahiritollah on or about the 27th February last by strangulation. For 3 or 4 days previously he had locked himself up in his shop, and his death was only discovered on the 1st instant, putrid smell from his dead body having troubled the neighbourhood and the inmates of his house. Lately he had incurred some debts for the purpose of purchasing a house. But failing to satisfy these debts, he was much harassed by his creditors which was perhaps the cause of the rash act committed by him. He has left a poor old mother, an unfortunate widow and a number of children to lament his loss.

YESTERDAY before the Select Committee of the Bengal Council, consisting of Sir Stuart Hogg, Mr. Schalch, Mr. Reynolds, Mr. Dampier, Mr. Bell, Babu Kristo Dass Paul, the Advocate General, and Mr. Brookes appeared the Counsel, and delegates of the several public bodies in Calcutta, in connection with the New Municipal Bill. Mr. Branson, Mr. Jackson and Mr. Miller appeared for the Justices, Mr. Ingram for the British Indian Association; Messrs. Knight, Jennings and Wyman for the Trades' Association; and Babus Kally Mohun Doss, Rashbehary Ghosh, Sishir Coomar Ghosh and Jogesh Chunder Dutt for the Indian League. Mr. Ingram's speech on behalf of the British Indian Association was as able as it was outspoken. Mr. Branson was equally good. Babu Kallymohun Doss on behalf of the League spoke with a manliness which does him honor, as much against the Bill as almost the Counsel for the British Indian Association. Mr. Jennings also protested against the Bill. There was a rare unanimity in denouncing the Bill.

Public Engagements.

MUSICAL EVANGELISTIC SERVICE.—The Rev. K. S. Macdonald, M. A., will deliver an address in the Free Church Institution, Nimtollah Street, this evening, 5th inst., at 6-30 o'clock. Hymns in Bengali, set to Hindu Music, will be sung.

MUSICAL EVANGELISTIC SERVICE.—London Missionary Society's Institution, Bhowanipore, Rev. Dr. Jardine will conduct the first of a series on Sunday March 5 at ½ past 7 o'clock.

Law

POLICE.—4TH MARCH 1876.

[Before F. J. Marsden, Esq.]

IN the case in which the European, Macdonald, Sands charged with cheating Messrs. Redda and Co., and uttering as genuine a forged document, purporting to be an order on the Bank at Dacca for Rs. 400, Mr. Hume informed the Magistrate that the Agent of the Bank there had arrived, and applied that the case might be taken up on Tuesday. The Magistrate granted the application, and ordered that the accused should be informed of the alteration of the date of hearing.

[Before P. D. Dickens, Esq.]

THE case in which a Malay was charged with creating a disturbance, and assaulting a Chowkidar in the execution of his duty, and which Mr. Cranenburgh was instructed to defend on principle, as it was an entirely false one, was on the boards this day. Messrs. Fink and Cranenburgh appeared for the defendant. In consequence of the time of the Magistrate being otherwise taken up, the hearing of the case was adjourned to Monday.

Selection

THE DRUNKARD'S WIFE.

[FROM "JOHN DRAKE," A POEM.]

"JOHN lived and died without a mate,"
For so his tombstone verses state,
Leaving it to our wit to find
The reason why. Had John been blind,
And never seen the lovely faces,
The charms, the wiles, the smiles, the graces,
That lend such magic to the fair,
And weave the web of many a snare,
His tenderness towards the gentler sex
Would less bewilder and perplex.
Had John been deaf, and never heard
That voice which minstrels have preferr'd
To song of thrush or nightingale,
Or warblers of both hill and dale—
A woman's voice! so sweet and clear;
A woman's voice! divine and dear,
A woman's voice! that swells and trills,
That soothes and frets, inflames and chills.
That harms and charms, that melts and thrills,
That calls to life, and wounds and kills,
And all the tones of passion fills,
From eagle's scream to coo of dove,
The mystic melody of love;—
Had John not heard that voice, nor seen
That form, man's helpmate and man's queen,
The marvel is to zero 'minished,
The riddle read, the drama finished.
If woman's love he never knew,
Then woman's loss was unfelt too.
But say, ye prudent bachelors,
Whose pride the marriage tie abhors,
And plead, in self justification,
The henpecked husband's immolation,—
Say, did it never seem to you
That many a loving wife and true
To scolding vixen may be changed
By cold neglect, and faith estranged,
On part of him who once did vow
To love and cherish and endow?
Just picture to your mind such wife,
Living her worse than widowed life
At home!—if you can call *that* home
Where joys domestic never come;
With hungry infant at her breast,
That can't be sung or soothed to rest
(What song can that poor mother try,
Who but for love would wish to die?
Love for her children, and for him
Who makes heart sad, and eye grow dim);
With prattlers clamorous for bread,
And wondering that they are not fed;—
With empty cupboard, empty plate,
And no fire in the cheerless grate,
Nor light to temper the thick gloom
That mantles in that desolate room;
While howling tempests drive the rain
In torrents through the broken pane:
No fire, no food, no help, no hope!
Is there no poison, water, rope?
And then the thought that all this ruin
Is her degraded husband's doing;
Her husband drinking at "The Crown,"
In boisterous mirth, and gulping down
Her bread, her children's and his own.
Oh! say, ye patterns of mankind,
Of delicate ears and tastes refin'd,
Can woman bear all this and live?
Or living, bear it, and forgive?
Fired by intolerable wrong,
Has she no liberty of tongue?
But must ye blame the outraged wife,
And moralise on wedded life?
Call her heart-broken cries, with scorn,
Indignities which can't be borne!
Oh! rather blame the guilty cause,
That violates Heaven's wisest laws;
Neglects the gift which by caressing,
Would prove a treasure and a blessing.
O God! from Thy bright throne on high
Thou lookest down on misery!
On cruelty of man to man,
Thwarting Thine own benevolent plan;
On fields of carnage and of blood;
On fruitful lands made solitude;
On cities sacked, by flames devoured;
And fathers slain, and maids deflowered;
On stern oppression's galling chains,
And dungeons, racks, and throbbing pains;
On Negro's hopeless slavery,
Whom welcome death alone can free;
On superstition's stakes and fires,
Auto-de-fes and funeral pires;
On honest thrift to beggary brought
By machinations fraud hath wrought;
On virgin innocence betrayed,
And in the grave untimely laid;
On gaudy flaunting harlotry,
Hiding a life of agony.
These and ten thousand woes, O, God!
Thou viewest from thy pure abode.
Ambition, avarice, lust, and pride
Roll on the earth a fearful tide
Of grief and shame and misery,
Whose cry, O, God! goes up to Thee.
But, of all ills that curse our race,
The deepest fount of our disgrace,
Of other woes the concentration,
The essence, cause, and personation,
The chain of hardest, strongest link,
Is Satan's masterpiece—Strong Drink!
An engine framed with fiendish skill
To work his diabolic will;
The craftiest of all inventions,
It balketh not the fiend's intentions.
Child never fathered parent more—
His features more distinctly bore—
Than doth this paragon of evil,
The genuine offspring of the devil.
Its nature how can I declare,
Or with what figures it compare!
So many various names it bears,
So many hues and aspects wears,
Unlike, yet like, it seems to be
Of all bad things the epitome.—
A whip, that tickles while it scourges;
A spur, that lacerates while it urges;
An *ignis fatuus* of the gloom,
That lures its victim to his doom;
A meteoric flash and flicker,
That leaves the darkness tenfold thicker;
A thing inspiring mirth and gladness
That end in lasting grief and sadness;
A flush of hope to lighten care,
But hurrying on to blank despair;
Like Satan's self, 'tis all a cheat,
At once deceiver and deceit;
A snare, a mockery, and delusion,
Wrapping in tangle and confusion;
A signpost pointing the wrong way;
A knave that flatters to betray;
Throughout the world Strong Drink is known,
On hill, in dale, village and town;
Promising peace, it stirs up strife;
And health, it drains, the fount of life;
Of honest things the counterfeit,
Like worthless tares among the wheat;
Of God's good gifts a vile perversion;
On Nature's truth a gross aspersion.
Prompter and cause of much ill-doing,
Begun in fraud, it ends in ruin.
Not pestilence, whose fœtid breath
Is charged with poison and with death;—
Nor famine stalking through the land,
With visage gaunt and skinny hand;
Nor, war, whose fierce and fiery tread
Spreads desolation dire and dread;
Nor all the three fell fiends combined,
Bring half such woe to human kind
As that one demon, Alcohol!
O! why should mortal man extol
The flattering fiend? Why cultivate
A habit deadlier than fate?
Can none the needful wisdom give,
That man may reason, learn, and live?
Dash from his lips the poisonous bowl,
And rescue body, mind, and soul?
Pluck from the fire the half-burnt brand,
And stay his suicidal hand?
Oh! servants of the living God,
Ye heralds with salvation shod,
Lift your expostulating voice,
Denounce the curse that blights our joys,
The curse that makes your preaching vain,
And scatters half your garnered grain.
O! if ye wish your flocks to save
From a dishonored drunkard's grave,
Yourselves the tempting cup refuse,
And give no countenance to its use;
And nerve your people for the trial
By your own practice of denial,
And thus your true credentials prove
By works of sacrificing love.
O! did not the Good Shepherd give
His own life that the flock might live?
Then be it yours, in deed and word,
To emulate your loving Lord.
And you, ye framers of our laws,
Remove the evil in the cause;
O! for the honor of our nation,
Shut up the temples of temptation;
The temples where strong drink is sold,
And death and ruin bought for gold.
O! would ye that this realm should be
The home of freedom and the free?
Then strike the tyrant Strong Drink down,
And save our freedom and your own.
If it be beautiful to see
Our glorious tree of liberty,
Wise to secure its precious fruit,
Cut out the canker at its root.
So may it grow and flourish ever,
Like good tree planted by a river;
So may the people undismayed,
Repose beneath its healing shade.

Eastwood, Keighley. J. ROSS.

The Alliance News.

HAROLD & CO.,

3, DALHOUSIE SQUARE, CALCUTTA

HARMONIUMS.

Harold and Co., call attention to their unequalled stock of rich-toned Harmoniums made especially for India.

FROM RS. 90 TO RS. 900 EACH.

All kinds of Musical Instruments of the best description are always kept in Stock.

ICE! ICE! ICE!

MADE IN FOUR MINUTES

THE PNEUMATIC ICE MACHINE.

THIS IMPORTANT INVENTION IS CONSIDERED A BOON TO THOSE LIVING IN TROPICAL CLIMATES.

CAN BE WORKED BY THE MOST INEXPERIENCED HAND AND IS NOT LIABLE TO GET OUT OF ORDER.

From Rs. 175, each Machine complete.

MESSRS. ARLINGTON & CO.

AGENTS.

THACKER, SPINK AND CO.

SCHOOL BOOKS.

SELECTIONS FROM MODERN ENGLISH LITERATURE. For the use of the Higher Classes of Indian Schools. By E. LETHBRIDGE Esq., M.A., 8 vo. Cloth. Rs. 2.

HISTORY OF INDIA. For Schools. Second Edition. By E. LETHBRIDGE, Esq., M.A., Cloth. Rs. 2.

A SERIES OF SIX ENGLISH READING BOOKS. For Indian Children. By Peary Churn Sircar. Revised by E. LETHBRIDGE, Esq., M.A., FIRST BOOK, 3 Annas. SECOND BOOK, Annas. THIRD BOOK, 5 Annas. FOURTH BOOK, 8 Annas. FIFTH BOOK, Annas. SIXTH BOOK, 10 Annas.

*** To purchasers of 20 copies of any single Book, a discount of per cent. will be allowed.

THE WORLD'S HISTORY. Compiled under the direction of E. LETHBRIDGE, Esq., M.A.,

THE WORLD'S HISTORY. Translated into Bengali. As. 8.

HISTORY AND GEOGRAPHY OF BENGAL: An Easy Introduction to. By E. LETHBRIDGE, Esq., M.A., As. 8.

A HISTORY OF ENGLAND. Compiled under the direction of E. LETHBRIDGE, Esq., M.A., As. 12.

AN EASY INTRODUCTION TO THE HISTORY OF INDIA. By E. LETHBRIDGE, Esq., M.A., As. 12.

EASY SELECTIONS. From English Literature for the use of middle classes in Indian Schools, with notes by E. LETHBRIDGE, Esq., M.A., As. 12.

HISTORY AND GEOGRAPHY OF BENGAL. Translated into Bengali. As. 8.

*** New Edition Expected in a Few Days.

ALGEBRAICAL EXERCISES. With Solutions for Student's preparing for the Entrance Examination of the Calcutta University. By Sarat Chandra Mukhopadhyay, M.A. Re. 1-4.

RUDIMENTS (THE) OF PHYSICAL GEOGRAPHY. For the use of Indian Schools. And a Glossary of the Technical Terms employed. Fourth Edition. By HENRY F. BLANFORD, F. G. S., Associate of the Royal School of Mines 16mo. Cloth. Re. 1-4.

ELEMENTARY TREATISE ON MECHANICS. Intended for use in Indian Colleges and Schools. By W. G. WILLSON, M.A., 16mo. Rs. 3.

ENGLISH PEOPLE (THE) AND THEIR LANGUAGE. Translated from the German of Loth by C. H. TAWNEY, M.A., Professor in the Presidency College, Calcutta. Stitched. As. 8.

NOTES ON SURVEYING. For the use of Schools. By J. M. Scott, M. A., C. E., Professor of Civil Engineering, Presidency College. Second Edition. Re. 1.

NOTICES ON PRACTICAL GEOMETRY AND THE CONSTRUCTION OF SCALES. Second Edition. Edited by J. M. SCOTT, M. A., C. E., Professor of Civil Engineering, Presidency College. Re. 1.

MILTON'S AREOPAGITICA. A Modern Version. With Notes, Appendix, &c. By SAMUEL LOBB, M.A. Rs. 3.

BENGALI ENTRANCE COURSE. Appointed by the Senate of the Calcutta University for the Examination of—

1876. R. 1-6.
Ditto 1877. Re. 1-6.

KUMARA SAMBHAVA OF KALIDASA. With Notes and Explanations in English. By the Rev. K. M. BANERJEA. Rs. 2-8.

RAGHU VANSA BY KALIDASA. With Notes and Grammatical Explanations. By the Rev. K. M. BANERJEA. Cantos 1 to 3, Rs. 2. Cantos 4 to 10. Rs. 3.

FIRST ARTS COURSE, 1877, Rs. 3. Scott's Talisman, which is read with the Course, As. 4.

B. A. COURSE, 1878. Rs. 3.

REID'S INQUIRY INTO THE HUMAN MIND. Rs. 1-4.

CALCUTTA UNIVERSITY CALENDAR 1875-76. Rs. 4.

UTTARACHARITA, a Sanscrit Drama by Bhavabhuti Edited with Notes by Iswarachandra Vidyasagar, Rs. 2.

Indian General Steam Navigation Company, Limited.

SCHOENE, KILBURN & Co.—*Managing Agents.*

ASSAM LINE.

NOTICE.

Steamers now leave Calcutta for Assam every Tuesday, Goalundo every Thursday and Dobrooghur downward every Saturday.

THE Str. "PATNA" will leave Calcutta for Assam, on Tuesday, the 7th March.

Cargo will be received at the Company's Godowns, Nimtollah Ghat, until noon of Monday, the 6th proximo.

THE Str. "RAJMEHAL" will leave Goalundo for Assam on Thursday, the 9th instant.

Cargo will be received at the Company's Godowns, No. 4, Fairlie Palace, up till noon of Tuesday, the 7th.

Goods forwarded to Goalundo, for this vessel will be chargeable with Railway Freight from Calcutta to Goalundo in addition to the regular Freight of this Company.

Passengers should leave for Goalundo by Train of Wednesday, the 8th.

CACHAR LINE NOTICE

REGULAR WEEKLY SERVICE.

Steamers now leave Calcutta for Cachar and Intermediate Stations every Tuesday and Chattack downward every Tuesday.

A Steamer and "FLAT" will leave Calcutta for Cachar on Tuesday, the 7th March.

Cargo will be received at the Company's Godowns, Nimtollah Ghat, up till noon of Monday, the 6th proximo.

For further information regarding rates of Freight or passage money, apply to,

4 Fairlie Palace, G. J. SCOTT,
Calcutta, 1st March 1876. *Secretary.*

HOMŒOPATHIC

BABU BASANTA KUMAR DATTA,
Homœopathic Practitioner,
No. 20. Sucker Holder's Lane, Ahiritolah.

JUST ARRIVED
FROM ENGLAND

MEDICINES, AND ALL REQUISITES TOBE HAD AT

DATTA'S HOMŒOPATHIC LABORATORY.
No. 312, CHITPORE ROAD, BUTTOLAH, CALCUTTA.

BABU RADHAKANTA GHOSH
HOMŒOPATHIC PRACTITIONER,
12, College, Square,
Is practising here on moderate terms.

SMITH, STANISTREET & CO.

Pharmaceutical Chemists & Druggists

BY APPOINTMENT

To His Excellency the Right Hon'ble
LORD NORTHBROOK, G.M.S.I.,
Governor-General of India.

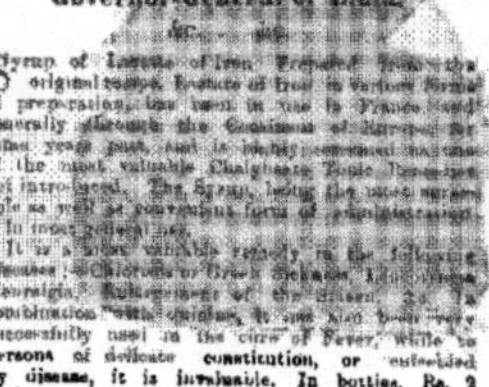

Syrup of Lactate of Iron. Prepared from the original recipe. Lactate of Iron in various forms of preparation, has been in use in France and generally throughout the Continent of Europe for some years past, and is highly esteemed as one of the most valuable Chalybeate Tonic Remedies yet introduced. The Syrup, being the most agreeable as well as convenient form of administration, is in most general use.

It is a most valuable remedy in the following diseases:—Chlorosis or Green Sickness, Neuralgia, Enlargement of the Spleen, &c. In combination with Quinine, it has also been very successfully used in the cure of Fever, while to persons of delicate constitution, or enfeebled by disease, it is invaluable. In bottles, Rs. 2 each.

Syrup of the Phosphate of Iron, Rs. 2 per bottle.

Syrup of Phosphate of Iron and Strychnine, Rs. 2 per bottle.

Syrup of Phosphate of Iron and Quinine, Price Rs. 2-8 per bottle

Syrup of Phosphate of Iron, Quinine and Strychnine, (Dr. Aitkin's Triple Tonic Syrup.) Rs. 2-8 per bottle.

Smith, Stanistreet & Co.

Invite special attention to the following rates, the quality guaranteed as the best procurable :—

Pure Ærated Waters.

Made from Pure Water, obtained by the new process through the Patent Charcoal Filters.

				Rs.	As.
Ærated plain (Trible Ærated), per doz.			...	0	12
Soda Water	ditto	"	...	0	12
Gingerade	ditto	"	...	1	4
Lemonade	ditto	"	...	1	
Tonic (Quinine)	ditto		...	1	

The *Cash* must be sent with the order to obtain advantage of the above rates

---

!!! হুঁকা!!!

!!! HOOKAHS !!!

ENGLISH made Hookahs of various choice designs, colours and sizes ranging in price from Rs. 2 to 5 each, 60 designs to choose from. Apply to

RADANAUTH CHOWDRY,
373, Jorasanko

হেমবনে যোগিণী।

NEW HISTORICAL TRAGEDY

BY

GOPAL CHUNDER MOOKERJEE,

Price, Re. 1, postage 2 ans.

To be had at 50, Grey Street, Shobabazar, and Sanskrit Press Depository.

NATIONAL COMPANY
HOMŒOPATHIC CHAMISTS AND PUBLISHERS
SUPPLY ALL KINDS OF
HOMŒOPATHIC MEDICINES, BOOKS
CASES AND OTHER REQUISITES.
12 COLLEGE SQUARE,
Calcutta.

Printed and published by M. M. RUKHIT, at the "INDIAN MIRROR" PRESS, No 15, College Square, for the Proprietor.

The Indian Mirror.

SUNDAY EDITION.

VOL XV] CALCUTTA, SUNDAY, MARCH, 12, 1876 {REGISTERED AT THE GENERAL POST OFFICE.} [No. 60

CONTENTS.

NOTICE.

Letters and all other communications relating to the literary department of the Paper should be addressed to "The Editor."

All letters on the business of the Press should be addressed, and all remittance made payable to the Manager of this Paper. Particular attention is solicited to this notice.

Subscribers will be good enough to give prompt notice of any delay, or irregularity in delivery of the Paper.

Editorial Not s

FOUR Pandits were sent to Benares, as the early history of the Brahmo Somaj informs us, to learn the four Vedas respectively, in that famous seat of learning. Now that the Vedas are no longer recognised as the infallible word of God, four persons have just been ordained to study the four Vedas of Theism,—the mind, the heart, the soul, and the will. The parallelism is striking; the more so as it is purely accidental. This we must say,—to study and cultivate the inner nature is far more difficult than the study of books. The Brahmo Somaj cannot fail to derive considerable and abiding benefits from these students of divinity. We shall watch their progress with deep interest.

DR. W. W. HUNTER'S recently published "Life of Lord Mayo" contains a brief communication from Mr. Fitz-James Stephen, the following extract from which will especially interest our Brahmo readers:—"Though Lord Mayo did me the honor to leave a very wide discretion in my hands, he kept a watchful eye on the proceedings of the Legislative Department, as on those of every other department of the Government. In every matter which he regarded as sufficiently important, he was sure to interpose with equal promptness and decision. The whole scheme and principle of the Marriage Act, for instance, was most carefully considered by him, and the result finally attained was due to a great extent to his careful consideration of the matter."

PERHAPS no crime fills the mind with more intense and involuntary horror than the one committed by the young man Denobundhu Bollel at Champatolla. He deliberately cut his mother's throat on a trivial suspicion, and not satisfied with that wanted to sever her head from her body, while the poor woman most violently resisted, and raised the whole neighbourhood by her screams. He was jealous of his wife, and had set his unfortunate mother to watch over her conduct, a duty which he thought, had not been performed by her with sufficient care. This miserable suspicion roused his anger, and in a fit of frenzy he fell upon the defenceless woman, and murdered her. One feels humiliated to call one's self a man while such atrocities surround us, and stare us in the face. Verily in brutality, man sometimes exceeds the brutes.

THE attitude assumed by the Brahmo Somaj in the systematic cultivation of different elements of devotion has, it seems, excited apprehensions in certain quarters, and led not a few to suppose that we are fast relapsing to the ancient order of things. Are we going to have *sannyasis, sadhus, paramhansas, bairagis* and *purahits* among us? Are we going to play the drama of Hindu asceticism and priesthood over again? No. The Brahmo *yogi* differs essentially from a Hindu *yogi*. The latter goes through pantheistic and respiratory processes of communion, and treats the world as a delusion and family duties as a sin. The Brahmo, if he is a true *yogi*, only subdues his passions, sacrifies worldliness, and delights in inward communion. That is all that the Brahmos mean by *yoga*.

A DECIDED change of religious tone, we are happy to notice, has come upon the able Bengali Magazine *Banga Darshan*. Our contemporary seemed but a little time ago a staunch follower of Mill, with a strange and irresistible bias for fatalism. Of late, however, specially in the last two numbers, there is an improvement in his views and spirit. A sound theistic element has entered into the faith of our contemporary, and his estimation of men, events, and principles, approaches very closely to what we ourselves entertain. This is a matter of deep and sincere pleasure to us, and we devoutly hope that the *Banga Darshan* will henceforth occupy a place worthy of itself, in the dissemination of views, and in the exercise of influence on the subjects of religion, and morality, comparable with what it has done towards improving the literature, and enlightening the tastes of educated Bengal.

IT is said, with truth we do not know, that a Shia Mahomedan is exceedingly lacks in his religious profession. This fact is brought forward to account for the rumoured change of Sir Salar Jung's creed from that of the Shia to that of the Sunni, as a compromise to the powerful Sunni agitators who embroil the present condition of Hyderabad. It is stated on the authority of Mr. Hughes that "the Shias admit a principle of religious compromise which is called *Takia*, whereby they can smoothe down or even deny the peculiarities of their religious belief inorder to save themselves from religious persecution. A Shia can therefore pass himself as a Sunni, or even curse the twelve Imams in order to avoid persecution." We repeat that we do not know how far this statement is correct, though we have little hesitation in declaring from our experience that Sunnis as a rule seem to be more strict in religious matters than Shias. We hope some of our Mahomedan readers will discuss this question.

THE *Friend of India* who is not an advocate of moral education in Government schools, draws attention to certain very objectionable passages contained in the selection from English authors for the use of the First Arts students. The passages complained of are from Crabbe's "Village," and Sir Walter Scott's "Woodstock." They are certainly immoral, and most unsuitable to young men whose imagination is so susceptible of taking in impressions as that of Bengali young men, and who are so ready to form opinions of English life from what they read in English books. An educational officer writes to the *Friend* bitterly complaining of "the gross carelessness" of the committee appointed for making selections in English for the Examinations of 1876-77. Surely such oversight is discreditable and only proves more clearly the necessity of keeping strict moral check over the studies and tastes of young men studying in our Universities.

THE *New York Evangelist* contains an article headed "A Chat with Keshub Chunder Sen, by Edward Warren Clark, (recently of the Imperial University of Japan.)" This gentleman called on our minister, during his visit to Calcutta, and embodies in this article the results of his searching observations. The writer thus speaks of the Babu:—"His statements were presented in very careful form, and he spoke with earnestness and dignity, though not always with that certainty of conviction which might characterize one who stood beyond the region of doubt, and felt himself in possession of truth at last. Personally, he is of commanding presence, genial in his manner, and evidently fitted to become a leader in a great movement. He is a Hindu of the nobler stamp; and is tall, well proportioned, and was dressed in a long white robe or sheet, the folds of which were thrown loosely over his shoulder in the usual style of his countrymen. He is of dark olive complexion, full round face, jet black hair, cut short; wears a small moustache, and an eye that looks straight at you, over his gold spectacle. We were struck with his youth, for he seems scarcely over thirty, and there was a freedom in his manner that made us feel at home at once in conversing with him."

EVEN in the midst of pressing political cares and engagements he found time to protect public morality and guard the youths of the country against corruption. This may be said of the noble-hearted Viceroy who now rules India. As soon as His Excellency saw that the Native theatres were vitiating public morals by indecent representations, he instantly wielded the legislative machinery to arrest the evil. The Executive were hardly less earnest and hastened to their duty with lightning speed. The offenders—gay young men who not content with exhibiting registered harlots on the stage, were contaminating themselves and others by enacting publicly most obscene pieces composed by themselves,—were at once brought before the Magistrate, and severely punished. We thank the Viceroy, and we thank the Police, and Mr. Dickens, the Magistrate, for such noble efforts to stem the tide of public immorality and corruption. We are glad to observe that Lord Northbrook's action in the matter has been duly appreciated by the Native community, as the following resolution unanimously passed at the last meeting of the Indian Reform Association will testify:—"This meeting rejoices that in the interests of public morality stringent and prompt measures have lately been adopted under the orders of the Viceroy for the suppression of obscene dramatic representations in Calcutta, and accords its warmest thanks to His Excellency the Viceroy."

HAPPILY the sharp controversy among the English Unitarians, which threatened to create a schism has been decided in the interests of liberal thought. Theism has prevailed over orthodoxy; the advanced Unitarians have triumphed over the conservative party. An equitable compromise was attempted in the shape of an amendment permitting the publication of all other works of Theodore Parker except the "Discourse," but even that amendment was lost. The original resolution moved by the Rev. Charles Clarke and seconded by the Rev. H. Enfield Dowson "That the Council repeats its instruction to the Committee to issue an edition of Theodore Parker's 'Sermons' and 'Prayers,' and an edition of his 'Discourse of Religion,' and desires that such publication be proceeded with without delay," was carried by a majority of 19 to 8. We heartily echo the hope expressed by the *Inquirer* that the decided majority in the vote on the publication of Parker's three works will now be generally accepted as the final settlement of this controversy; and that the members of this important Society will henceforth be even more closely united in the common aim of giving a fair representation in its publications and general proceedings to all varieties of Unitarian Christianity.

TRANSMIGRATION.

Is there no truth whatever in the Hindu doctrine of transmigration? Perhaps, there is. Let us reflect seriously, and try to evolve the true meaning of the doctrine. All over Hindustan, millions of men and women have for centuries believed that the soul migrates through successive stages of existence, comes back into this world again and again, and then rises gradually into higher worlds, till at last it reaches the Infinite Spirit. Is it possible that so ancient and widely prevalent a notion should be utterly devoid of a substratum of truth? We think not. The doctrine of transmigration admits of a rational explanation. We do not mean to justify the Hindu notion, nor are we prepared in the least measure to countenance its glaring absurdity and fallacy. We believe, however, that it is possible to take the doctrine in a purely spiritual sense, and reduce it into a real fact of life. Is it then true in any sense that man returns to the world after death? We say, Yes. By closely observing and analysing man's spiritual history we come to the conclusion that it indicates, not a continued and steady development, but a series of ups and downs, progression, and retrogression, rise and decline. These changes in the chequered history of man may not inappropriately be described as his *departure from* and *return to* the world. These are spiritual migrations. Where is the man among us who has been at once and completely saved from worldliness and sin? Have we seen any instance of absolute regeneration? Few are born again, in the sense of perfect renewal. Man is born again and again, now in the world, now in God; now born spiritually, now born carnally. This is not a mere metaphor. It is a reality, of which every man is a witness. Let us see what actually happens in life. By faith, repentance and prayer man leaves his vicious habits, subdues his worldly and carnal desires, and attains purity, in some measure, but not to perfection. His converted soul dead to the world may now be said to live in heaven with God. He is no longer in the world, and is not to be found in the walks of temporal life. After six months or a year perhaps he reappears on the platform of the world, and lives again as a worldly man, but his life is altogether more exalted and sanctified. A second time he takes the vow of asceticism and self-annihilation. Again he dies unto the world, and forsakes it. Again he returns to the world; he re-arranges his domestic life and social career upon a more elevated basis and a purer economy. Even this after a time pleases him not, and he renounces even this better world with ascetic disgust, and seeks a higher world. Thus man ascends gradually to higher forms of spirituality and devotion killing self and sin by degrees. This, we believe, is the true philosophy of transmigration.

THE HIGHER WILL.

CAN strength come out of weakness, purity out of what is impure, can freedom come out of bondage? Our will is sold in slavery to sinful habits, it has lost its strength and independence. Can it lay down the laws of its own reformation, and find out the best training for itself? Granted that under the directions of conscience our will can resist the approach of evil, can force itself to flee at times from certain courses of action. But is it not a fact that when a man's heart is corrupt, his judgment also becomes perverted; his conscience often remains inert; and he is left to drift away in the course of his own vicious inclinations. It is not an easy matter to decide when and how far to resist an inclination if it is present in the mind. Higher Will only can ordain laws for the guidance of our Will. We inherit its strength if we obey it in spirit. A man in disease, even though he be a medical man, cannot at times find the real causes of his suffering, far less prescribe any remedy for the same. He has to place himself under others' treatment, and to follow the directions given with accuracy and with faith. Let no one think meanly of mechanical compliance. Its effect on the mind is often marvellous. The show of discipline is bad, its substance is saving. Forms without spirit are killing, with spirit are indispensable. When self-imposed they may fail, when imposed through the agency of a Higher Will, they must always be successful. The discipline they involve, takes a man out of himself, and thus enables him to find out his true position, his real weakness. Everything that comes from the pure will of God, brings His purity along with it. It has nothing of human impurity in it, and nothing of human weakness. If it can be accepted in the faith somewhat commensurate with the love that sends it, it is the very highest training for the will possible. "Thy will be done," is the best education for our will. It has so much that crosses the cherished habits, and usual feelings of man, that to bear it cheerfully and resignedly when known, demands the highest exercises of the moral nature. We should not think that God's will is expressed, and has to be followed only in the highest, and most sacred spheres of life. On the contrary it should be realized and obeyed in the smallest and humblest trials to which we are likely to be subjected. If then out of our own hearts we can frame the laws to guide and train our will; if our own impure standard is too low for the elevation of our nature; inorder that the weekness and sluggishness of our moral nature may be removed, we must seek for discipline from outside, and the best and holiest souls in our midst may be able to lay it down for us. At all events let our wills be trained by following the Higher Will

Devotional.

My son, give me thy heart. Who knows or understands thy difficulties as I do, and who can remove them? The harmony which thou seekest is nowhere in the world; the wisdom, the peace, and the purity which thou wouldst have, no one can give but myself. Why followest thou the vain phantom of here below? There is no love in the world, it is all vexation and disappointment. I am worthy of thy love. Love thou me, and be still, and free from care.

My Father, take my heart. Thou knowest all my thoughts, and canst remove all the difficulties in my way. Everything is vain, false, and disappointing around me. Thou alone art true and abiding, as thou art holy, beautiful and good. Teach me to love thee, and be still in the depth of thy communion.

Brahmo Hymns

Renouncing worldly hopes I will cultivate communion. Bless me, Lord, that my heart's desire may be fulfilled. Surrendering body, mind and life and becoming a servant prostrate at thy feet, I will serve thy feet, Master, with singleness of heart. In meditation and contemplation, in repeating thy name, in self-mortification and in singing thy name I will spend my life with an easy and joyful heart. My days have been spent unprofitably, charmed with unreal pleasures. Now my wish is to live as a spiritually intoxicated ascetic.

He who knows the Supreme Intelligence and Light knows the truth; he who communes with Him in the heart finds shelter immovable. The one primeval Effulgence was He, countless rays emanate from Him; how much good, wisdom, virtue, love and beauty overspread the universe! The seven worlds sing Him, in the midst of that Light of the universe, no one finds a limit. The lotus-like feet I seek, give me mercy and joy. To whom else shall I repair? Thou art the destroyer of all men's sorrows.

The Brahmo Somaj.

Babu Debendra Nath Tagore has again gone up to the hills. He will probably stay for some time at Dalhousie, of which place he is immensely fond, there to enjoy the sweets of communion in solitude. How few there are among professed Brahmos who have learnt of that venerable devotee this phase of devotional life.

We are glad to learn Babu Shib Chunder Das of Connaghur, has recovered his health and has resumed his philanthropic work in the above town. It is owing to his exertions that Connaghur, with its boys' school, girls' school, dispensary and Brahmo Somaj, has become a model town, and it is to him that the local community, and especially the poor, the sick, the infirm, and the helpless, look as their guardian and friend. Here we see how much good work a single Brahmo may do.

We regret to record the death of Srimati Rajkumari Bannerji, the wife of Babu Sasipada Bannerji of Barahnagore. The melancholy event occurred on Wednesday last. Some of our missionary friends went over there, and the minister offered the funeral prayer at the residence of the Babu. The body was then carried to the burning ghat. After cremation the ashes were deposited in a corner of the compound of the house, where a suitable memorial is proposed to be erected. We have always been in favor of this Hindu custom *Samadhi*, prevalent among the Vaishnavas, and we should like to see it retained among the Brahmos. Some of our Dehra Doon friends, we believe, did something of the kind long ago. The promptings of natural affections demand a memorial of the departed.

On the 3rd instant, a widow lady in the Bharat Asram solemnly took the *brata* (vow) of *paricharica* for the period of a year. She will obediently serve her sisters as a servant.

The usual monthly service will commence to-day in the Mandir at 7-30 A.M.

We have to acknowledge with thanks the following Urdu publications kindly forwarded by the author, Sirdar Dyal Singh:—Nizam Kaumi or National Progress; Kasuf ol Ilham, or a translation of the Lecture on Inspiration, delivered by Babu Keshub Chunder Sen; Kholasa of Assol Brahma Dharma, or translation of Essential Principles of Brahmo Dharma; Rahat Hokiki or True Happiness.

A CHAPTER FROM REAL LIFE.

When I recall to mind the events of my past life and estimate the amount of obligations under which Brahmo Dharma has laid me, I am overpowered with emotions and my whole soul rises to bless that heavenly creed and Him who sent it to me for my salvation. My whole history bears striking testimony to the saving efficacy of the true creed. Born of rich parent and brought up in a most opulent family, amid the luxuries, pomp and splendour of an almost regal kind, I grew up without any idea of God. The world profusely showered its honors and felicities on me. If pleasure I sought, attendants unnumbered would rush forth to my service; if want troubled me, money would flow like the ceaseless tide of the sea to remove it; if luxury I required, thousand appliances and means which princely fortune could command or authority call foth, were instantaneously restored to for my benefit. Between the wish and the fruition I seldom saw any obstacle; I had but to issue an order, and express a wish and immediate satisfaction would follow. Affluence and ease brought temptations in their train and my heart unfortified fell a prey to them. The enjoyment of the present moment was all that I cared for, and little did I think of an hereafter. The world fascinated me with its charms, and as a slave I served it. I was sold to the senses, and I heeded not the holy monitor within. Conscience. I disposed from its high office, and instead thereof I set my capricious will. Religion and morality I wantonly defied, or heedlessly overlooked in the feverish excitement of my worldly career. Thus I went on for five years, from the sixteenth to the twentieth year of my life, intoxicated with the pleasures of the flesh, regardless of my spiritual interests and dead to conscience and God. It then pleased the Lord to reveal His loving kindness to me in a mysterious and unaccountable manner. Purely accidental was His providential interference for the salvation of my soul. Once on the occasion of a domestic calamity as I lay drooping and wailing in a retired spot, the God of glory suddenly revealed Himself in my heart, and so entirely charmed me and sweetened my heart and soul that for a time I continued ravished—quite immersed in a flood of divine light. The world outside and the world within both seemed bathed in a sweet and serene stream of celestial effulgence. What was it but the light of truth, the water of baptism, the message of salvation. Was it a vision that so charmed me? No. The living presence of the living God who could doubt! I saw it, I felt it, like a live coal it quickened me. It was an unmistaken revelation of God's mercy; I read it plain as golden letters in mid-day light. I clearly recognized His fingers in this saving dispensation. It is none other than my God, the Supreme Father and Mother, the friend of the sinners, the Protector of the helpless, detitute and cast away, who vouchsafed in His infinite mercy to appear in my corrupt heart, to heal me and to chasten me. His mercy so great and undeserved staggered me. The light of His countenance so pure, so holy, I dared not approach it; but His paternal love so sweet, so tender. I blessed Him, and my whole soul blessed Him. For a while in beatific ecstacy I lay, drinking largely the sweets of divine communion; no temporal care, no anxiety dared interrupt that sweet beatitude. But the joy was temporary. The heaving heart and the full soul gradually subsided. Once more I found myself in my lonely and dreary situation, and with vacant eyes I looked on the cheerless world around. The Divine image left, however, a dim and faint impression on my mind, and made me ever since anxious to behold it again. Thus did the great struggle for progress commence in my soul. I was persuaded that one thing alone could satisfy me and bring me peace—the sight of God's loving face. This became my life's highest and chiefest aim. All my aspiration and energies I concentrated in the pursuit of this great object. Days and weeks, months, and years,—rolled away,—my soul continued to be a scene of ceaseless struggle between the passions and conscience between darkness and light, between the world and God. I constantly prayed with all my heart and soul for strength and protection from the Lord in order effectually to purify my life and accomplish my cherished desire.

With singleness of vision and unity of purpose I followed His benevolent directions, and success daily crowned my efforts drawing me further and further away from my sins and failings. With His holy aid I went on victoriously through many a struggle and trial overcoming the temptations which had beset my paths and purging my soul of the accumulated iniquities of my past life. The inferior propensities were curbed, the wild fury of passions abated, conscience was reinstated in its exalted place, the world lost its attraction, and God became my only comfort and delight in this world of sorrow and sin. Brahmo Dharma like a kind mother filled my mind with saving truths, and my heart with the love of God, and helped me to discharge the manifold duties of life. She also brought me pious companions and friends, in whose company I found joy and strength, and with whom I joined in rapturous devotions to our common Father. Great was the change in my mind; greater still was my joy in having found the light of truth. But my progress did not stop here. The treasures I had gathered with the aid of Brahmo Dharma I naturally felt solicitous to offer to others, and for many years I have humbly labored for the propagation of the true religion. Brethren, contemplate the mighty efficacy of the faith that has gathered us together under the banner of the one True God. Truly it is the living faith. It not only illumines the mind with true knowledge, but it regenerates the whole man. It liberates us from the bondage of sin and makes us servants of the Lord. It chases away sorrow and suffering and gives us peace and happiness. It is the glory of Brahmo Dharma that it reforms the most desperate sinner, and exalts those who are hopelessly sunk in the abyss of wickedness. I repeat, therefore emphatically with overwhelming testimony of personal experience. Let him who seeketh salvation accept the true and saving creed of Brahmo Dharma.

Literary.

M. VANESSEN, a French writer, who lived some time in this country, has written a book about the English in India. He says the late mutiny was not a military mutiny, pure and simple, but the revolt of the people.

THE Lahore Guide, just issued, is the joint work of Messrs. Thornton and Kipling, the first of whom is now our Foreign Secretary, and the second, is the Principal of the Lahore School of Industry.

MISS COLENSO, daughter of the Bishop of Natal, is now publishing an interesting novel in the *Natal Colonist*.

THE following paragraph appears in the Bombay *Educational Record*: "The Gilchrist Scholarship of 100*l*. sterling for five years, with a free passage to and from England, attracted this year from the Bombay Presidency how many candidates do our readers think? Precisely two, both Christians. Not a single Hindu or Parsi was to be tempted to Europe by such a paltry bait. We cannot but regard this want of enterprise on the part of Natives of this country as somewhat discreditable. Scholarships of anything like equal value, immediate and prospective, offered in London and tenable in Bombay, would draw candidates by hundreds. It is this kind of apathy combined with claims habitually made which fairly lays Natives of this country open to the imputation of wanting all sorts of advantages, but without the trouble, self-denial, and discipline wherewith people of other nations are content to purchase them."

THE very laborious work on which Dr. A. C. Burnell, of the Madras Civil Service, has been engaged for the last five years, in drawing up a catalogue of the Tanjore Palace Library, is nearly completed, we are told. The catalogue will be published in England, and contains a list of the books and manuscripts systematically arranged, with an account of the authorship, antiquity, and contents of each. Nearly half of the MSS. are on *cadjan* leaves, and are as difficult to decipher as to understand. The library at Tanjore is about the largest in Southern India, and contains a vast collection of manuscripts; and the Maharajah Sivaji, who could both read and write English fairly, bestowed much care upon it. Many of the most valuable *cadjan* manuscripts are much injured, and transcribers have been employed to make copies of them. The library, known in the vernacular (Tamil) as the *Saraswati mahal* is in a large hall in the palace, and is under the care of a Native librarian, who has the assistance of Sanskrit Pundits in classifying and arranging the works. It might be well perhaps for the Royal Asiatic Society to undertake the restoration of the decaying MSS., for the value of such ancient documents cannot be rightly estimated.

PRACTICAL Ethics for Schools and Families; by Matilda Fletcher. A. S. Barnes, & Co., New York.

The peculiarity of this book is that it treats the various topics bearing upon the Practical Ethics, by questions and answers. Its division of topics is based upon the common designations of the virtues. It aims at simplicity, and is designed to be used in connection with a chart on which the virtues are represented in constellations. For sale at Wynkoop & Co's., Syracuse.—*The Independent.*

A GOOD many European celebrities are getting to be old men. Von Ranke, the historian, was 80 on the 28th of December, Carlyle was 80 a few days before him, and Disraeli was 70 last week. There has never been a time when there were so few young men of prominence in the world as at present. President Grant at 53 is about the only man of prominence now living who can be called young. There will soon be an open field for some of the youngsters of the present generation to show themselves in.

THE Secretary of State for India, it appears, has sent a despatch dated the 20th January 1876 on the subject of Babu Rajendralala Mittra's "Antiquities of Orissa." We received day before yesterday a letter from the Government of Bengal purporting to send us a copy of this despatch, but somehow or other it did not accompany the letter. We daresay it was a case of oversight.

Scientific

THIS year there will be two eclipses of the sun and two of the moon.

THE experiment made on the Oudh and Rohilkund Railway line with the punkahs, invented by Mr. Cooke, Locomotive Superintendent of that Railway, as a means of cooling railway carriages during the hot season in India, has been successful. Hitherto these punkahs have been applied to 1st class carriages only. The Government of India now directs that the experiment be continued, and that the application of the punkahs be extended to the carriages of the lower class. The Director of State Railways is also instructed to organize similar trials on State lines, and the attention of all Railway Managers is directed to the subject.

LEMONS can be preserved by varnishing them with a solution of shell-lac in alcohol. The skin of shell-lac formed is easily removed by rubbing the fruit in the hands.

THE French men make the best Engineers. We hear a French Engineer has projected a grand canal in the south of France, to unite the Mediterranean to the Bay of Biscay.

The Week

THE rumour that Sir Salar Jung has turned Sunni, is authoritatively contradicted.

DR. FAYRER, it is stated, went to see Cannon Duckworth at Lahore by special desire of Her Majesty the Queen, who had telegraphed from Osborne.

MR. H. B. MEDDLICOTT will take charge of the Geological Survey Department from Mr. Oldham, who is about to retire from the service.

MR. E. B. EASTWICK has gone towards Peshawur.

THE Bombay Revenue Jurisdiction Bill in spite of the great opposition it has met with, will probably be passed in the Governor-General's Council on Tuesday next.

THE head of the nobles of the Carnatic family, Azizul Mulke Bhahadur, is dead.

LORD NORTHBROOK will not be Earl Bearing but Earl of Michelldever, that being the name of the property which His Excellency owns in the country of Hampshire.

THE "Marriage Reformer" of Behar, Munshi Pearylcll, deserves well of his countrymen. As one of the rules for curtailment of marriage expenses among up-country *kaits* he has, at a public meeting of that caste at Arrah, got a resolution passed to the effect that Nautches on occasions of marriages should be discontinued.

THE amount offered by Sir Albert Sassoon for a bronze equestrian statue of the Prince of Wales at Bombay, is Rs 50,000.

AN Indian loan of twelve millions sterling has, it is stated, already been opened by the Secretary of State in London.

IT is likely that the work of proposed State Railway either from Bankipore or Futwa to Gya, is to be shortly commenced—probably by the beginning of next official year.

MR. ARCHIBALD FORBES of the London *Daily News*, Count G. d'Alviella of the *Independance Belge*, Mr. Julland Danvers, and Professor Monier Williams left Bombay for England by the last Mail.

SIR HENRY DAVIES, the Lieutenant-Governor of the Punjab, has been visiting all the Native States in that province. His Honor will afterwards proceed to Simla to meet the new Viceroy, Lord Lytton. His Honor, it is said, intends to stay with His Lordship for 10 or 15 days.

AT a Durbar held at Baroda, on Tuesday last, Mr. Melvill, the Agent, Governor-General was invested with the Insignia of the Companion of the Star of India, which was brought by a special messenger from the Foreign Office Calcutta.

THE Rajah of Durbhanga is expected in Darjiling shortly.

PLAGUE has appeared at Bagdad. Precautions have already been taken to prevent its spreading eastward.

LATEST NEWS.

THE young Rajah of Ulwar, Mangal Sing, seems to have still his enemies. Recently an attempt was made to upset the Train in which he travelled. An investigation is being made into this circumstance in a private way.

THE Lieutenant-Governor of the N. W. P. in his Administration Report, just issued, says that His Honor has taken steps with the view of securing to well-educated Natives of those Provinces a definite share in the higher posts under the Government.

IT is stated that for the past two months the pay of the Baroda troops under the Gaekwar was fallen into arrears, and the circumstance has caused much uneasiness among the soldiery.

THE return of the Buffs from the Straits has been delayed by the necessity of telegraphing to England for permission to use the *Himalaya*. The *Himalaya*, being a troopship belonging to the Home Government, cannot be used for Indian purposes without a reference to England.

It is stated that another young Native, noble, the Thakore of Sibhore, is to appear at the next Matriculation Examination of the Bombay University.

THE Administration Reports of the North-West Provinces and of Oudh for the year 1874-75, are just issued, but the *Pioneer* says they "are singularly destitute of interest, as far as the introductory summaries are concerned."

CANON DUCKWORTH remains much the same at Lahore.

MR. JUSTICE BOULNOIS has left Lahore for Delhi, where he goes to inspect the courts.

A YOUTH, bent on mischief, attempted to set fire to a Parsi fire-temple at Bombay. He has been taken into custody by the Police.

ANOTHER cargo of Alpine Ice has arrived at Bombay.

ARCHDEACON BALY was expected at Agra on Friday last.

ANGLO-INDIAN ladies must feel particularly thankful to the special Indian correspondent of the *Echo*, who is particularly complimentary to them. In one of his recent letters he says:—"Where our Anglo-Indian friends managed to get all the good looking wives, daughters, and sisters they have, or what they do with the old or the ugly ones, has been a puzzle to me ever since I landed in Bombay. Whether at this latter place, or in Madras, Calcutta, Benares, Lucknow, or Delhi, you really hardly ever see a plain, and never an ugly woman."

THE Madras Government seem really solicitous to promote the interests of the Mahomedans. Lately they enquired of the local Board of Revenue what effect had been given to the desire of Government that a larger share of public employment should be given to qualified Mahomedans. The Board in due course collected the reports of the several Collectors of the Districts on the subject. From these reports it a appears that "every opportunity is afforded to Mahomedans to enter the public service, and that if in some districts none were appointed since last report, was purely because no qualified men were available. The Board are of opinion that Mahomedans, as a rule, are aware that if qualified, their claims to enter the service will meet with favorable consideration." The Madras Government remark that "there is no reason to doubt that a great obstacle to the more general employment of Mahomedans in the public service is the absence of effort on their own part to qualify themselves educationally for other than the lowest posts." The Government "trust that the efforts now being made to promote their education will bear fruit in the near future." We hope it will. But the Mahomedans are a more conservative race than any other, perhaps, in India.

THE *Times of India* learns from a private telegram that Government four per cent. paper has been sold in London at 82.

IT appears that Sir Erskine Perry and Sir Robert Montgomery, Members of the India Council, dissent from the despatch of November last from the Secretary of State for India to the Viceroy, just presented to Parliament, on the Indian Tariff.

THE additional title that Her Majesty the Queen will take is that of Empress of India. Mr. Gladstone in the House of Commons, objected to the title on the ground that it might affect the status of the independent Princes of India.

THE ceremony of opening the Gas Works at Jeypore, was inaugurated by H. H. the Maharajah of that State, on Tuesday last.

HIS ROYAL HIGHNESS the Prince of Wales arrived at Bombay yesterday, and will embark for England day after to-morrow. The farewell address of the Bombay Municipal Corporation, prepared again by Mr. Maclean, will be presented to-morrow

MR. J. C. GEDDES, C. S. has been appointed for a period not exceeding three months, to revise the forms and accounts submitted to the Bengal High Court and to codify the rules and circulars issued by that Court.

MR. R. TAYLOR is appointed to officiate as Deputy Comptroller General.

DR. W. BELLEW, C.S.I., of the Bengal Medical Establishment, is to officiate as Residency Surgeon, Nipal.

IN recognition of the liberality and public spirit displayed by Lala Mela Ram, of Lahore, the Viceroy and Governor-General is pleased to confer upon him the title of "Rai," as a personal distinction.

ADMIRAL MACDONALD is ill at Poona.

THE Indian Staff Corps will not be abolished.

CAPTAIN WODEHOUSE, Sir Philip Wodehouse's nephew and A. D. C., has had a slight attack of small-pox, but is now convalescent.

The Prince's Visit.

IN commemoration of the Prince's visit to India, the Queen has been pleased to appoint H. R. H. to be Honorary Colonel of several Indian Regiments. A few other Regiments will be styled "Queen's Own" and the "Prince of Wales' Own."

THE Prince did not after all visit the Marble Rocks at Jabalpore. H. R. H. breakfasted in that station with Mr. Morris, the Chief Commissioner of the Central Provinces, and left immediately for Khundwah, lunching at Shohagpore. Ample preparation were made at the Marble Rocks, but all to no purpose.

Calcutta.

LORD NORTHBROOK with the Hon'ble Miss Baring and suite returned to Calcutta from Allahabad, on Friday last.

SIR RICHARD TEMPLE was expected back in Calcutta yesterday from Singbhum.

SRINATH CHUNDER BORELL who has been charged with matricide, is to be committed for trial at the ensuing Sessions of the High Court.

SEVERAL Marwaris and others were charged by the Police with singing obscene songs in the public streets, to the annoyance of respectable Native women and passers-by. Their defence was that, this being their Huli festival, they were under a mistaken notion of being privileged to sing obscene songs on the occasion. The Magistrate (Mr. Marsden) convicted, and fined them in sums varying from Rs. 3 to 5, observing that the sooner they drove this idea out of their heads the better. They had no right to make a noise in the public streets, much less to sing obscene songs, and thereby insult respectable women. It was excessively bad of them. If ever they were brought up again he would deal severely with them.

LORD NORTHBROOK has refused the petition in favor of the release of Amir Khan.

FURLOUGH for two years is granted to Mr. E. C. George, Post Master of Calcutta.

MR. A. C. LYALL, the Agent to the Governor-General in Rajputana, is now in Calcutta and will return to Rajputana on or about the 16th instant.

WE deeply regret to hear of the death of Babu Mohim Chunder Paul, the Deputy Magistrate of Barripore.

YESTERDAY the Convocation of the Calcutta University for conferring Degrees, was held at the Senate House. His Excellency was present.

Selection

MOTHER STEWART NIGHT.

ANOTHER American reformer has landed on our shores; this time in the shape of a lady, who, under the familiar name of Mother Stewart, has been privileged to head that whisky war in America of which at one time we heard so much, and which is as much needed here in London as in the cities of the United States. Mrs. Stewart, it seems, was born in Ohio, and was early led to devote herself to the cause of Christ. She will spend some weeks in London, and afterwards make her appearance in the provinces—not to lead a whisky war in the American fashion, for she believes that peculiar form of action has done its work and had its day, but to revive and stimulate temperance energies by the tale of her life and endeavours. As was to be expected, Mother Stewart has quite reached her prime. It is stated in print that she is nearly sixty years of age, and she looks it. She has been a church member forty-four years, and while her husband and sons were engaged in the service of their country during the Civil War, she was busily engaged in procuring and sending supplies to the sick and the wounded in camp and hospital. Her personal appearance calls for no particular comment; but for the benefit of the ladies let me remark, a contemporary states, that she has silvery hair arranged in soft, glossy ringlets, in the manner known to American ladies as the Martha Washington style.

In a quiet way Mother Stewart seems to have been forced into her present position. In some of the American States there is a law called the Adair law, by means of which the friends of a drunkard may prosecute the rum seller who has been the means of his destruction. On one occasion Mother Stewart was engaged in such a cause, which she personally conducted, and when she gained it she resolved to do more in the same line. As the ladies were on her side the movement grew and prospered. The clergy and the newspapers lent their aid. A great authority from Boston, Dr. Lewis, came to co-operate with her and to him it was due that the women went to work, and summoned up their energies to face the enemy in the streets. When Mother Stewart, with a hundred and fifty women behind, marched along, the whole country was thrilled. In one town sixteen drinking saloons were closed in one week. But nevertheless, in America the battle had not been won. The whole of the saloons had not been closed, nor had the men kept all their pledges. The liquor trade being wealthy, bought votes and controlled political parties—in Indiana the legislators had been bought for 40,000 dollars. But a great step had been taken: drunkards had been saved, and a great impulse had been given to the temperance reformation. The women had met in some large church or chapel, and then had gone forth in bands to do their noble work. All had joined in it—rich as well as poor. Those who could not go themselves, supplied those who did with coffee, and refreshment, and warm clothing, or went and did the household work of those who were engaged in the crusade. It was found that the most successful women at the work were plain, practical women of every-day life. In no case had home duties been neglected, or had husbands any reason to complain. One man, it is true, went away from home, as his wife would not give up her work, believing that she must obey God rather than man; but he thought better of it, and soon came back. Many of the women remained at their post as pickets from an early hour till late at night; and when they had gained the day and the drinking saloons were closed, how the poor drunkards' wives did rejoice, and what ringing there was of bells, and what burning of bonfires! Even the little children rejoiced, and it was found that they were greatly interested in the war, and on one occasion the friends had a separate service for children as early as nine in the morning. In no case had the devoted women been ill-treated, and while they were praying in the streets, no matter how wet and cold the weather was, the men stood by listening respectfully, and with uncovered heads. As to the reason why the women engaged in the work, the answer was not far to seek. It was a woman's question. There were no such suffering women in the world as drunkards' wives.

Thus much as to Mother Stewart's work, which lasted about two years, and which, she owns, has had its day. It was never intended to be of a permanent character. On Monday the lady made her first public appearance in England in Barnsbury Chapel, which was crowded in a way in which it was never been,

I should fancy, since it has had an independent existence. By half-past seven the place was full, but still the crowd kept pouring in, till all the aisles were blocked up, and there was scarce standing space in the school-room beyond. At eight the audience were gratified by sight of Mother Stewart, who at that hour seated herself in the pulpit, while below the pastor of the place, the Rev. John Morgan, gave out a hymn, offered up a short prayer, which excited many a hearty "Amen," and introduced Mother Stewart to the meeting. It was a trying time for the lady, but she was equal to the occasion. If her audience was large it was intensely sympathetic. The one great thought in her heart was the text which declares that no drunkard shall inherit the kingdom of heaven and after some time spent in detailing all her operations—at times, it seemed to me, with an unnecessary and truly feminine minuteness—she broke out in an impassioned appeal to her sisters to come to the rescue, first entreating them, if they were in the habit of using alcohol in any form, to abandon it altogether. She had come to help them to organise as she had been invited to come. There would soon be held in the metropolis a mass meeting of women on the all-important subject. She appealed to her sisters present to lend a helping hand. It was nearly to thousand years since Christ had come to preach the Gospel of glad tidings, and unless the women of England took up the temperance question, it would be ten thousand years before the world was ready for Him. The women would hold the fort, but the men were to bring up the rear—or, in other words, they would act in the sphere of polites, and get good legislation on the subject. It is to be feared Mother Stewart has too feeble a physique for any extended campaign in this country. Hers is the faith that can move mountains, but the body is weak, and the voice is thin. Be that as it may, she must have been quite satisfied on Monday night with her first appearance on the English stage.—*The Christian World.*

Printed and published by M. M. Rukhit, at the "Indian Mirror" Press, No. 15, College Square, for the Proprietor.

The Indian Mirror.

SUNDAY EDITION.

VOL. XV.] CALCUTTA, SUNDAY, MARCH, 26, 1876 {Registered at the General Post Office.} [No. 72

CONTENTS.

NOTICE.

Letters and all other communications relating to the literary department of the Paper should be addressed to "The Editor."

All letters on the business of the Press should be addressed, and all remittance made payable to the Manager of this Paper. Particular attention is solicited to this notice.

Subscribers will be good enough to give prompt notice of any delay, or irregularity in delivery of the Paper.

Editorial Notes

THE young ladies of the late Miss Akroyd's School did a very good thing on last Thursday evening. They presented a farewell address to Mrs. Phear, on the eve of her departure for Europe. Several Brahmicas were present, and one of the ladies who represented the Bharat Asram, gave thanks to Mrs. Phear on behalf of the ladies of that institution. We publish the address elsewhere.

CHAITANY'S leadership was most natural and beautiful. He not only loved his disciples and followers, but he also honored them. This is proved by the fact that he never scrupled to embrace even those who were men of low caste or were diseased. When such men thinking themselves unfit for his sacred touch shrank back and remonstrated, Chaitanya hugged them most lovingly, saying that he would be sanctified and saved by the touch of such devout and God-loving men. A master who so honored and respected his disciples was truly great.

TIME was when the Brahmos were unpopular among the Christian and popular among the Hindu community. There was also a time when they were esteemed by Christians, but hated by Hindus. The time, we hope, is coming when the better order of Christians and Hindus will both look upon us with favor while the narrow and ignorant classes will direct against us their fiercest spite and antagonism. Who can deny that if the true eclectic spirit of Theism be fully developed and organized in the Brahmo Somaj, the venerable Rishis of ancient India will regard it as their own Dharma, while Christ on the other hand will commend it as his own church. As years roll on may such eclecticism grow!

AMONG the signs of the times we may include the note-worthy event that the most orthodox Hindu family in Calcutta has just stood forth as an advocate of reform. Rajah Komul Krishna Bahadur, the venerable head of the Sobhabazar Raj family, if not a reformer, is at least a Broad Church Hindu, if we may say so. He seems to think that those who go to England do not cease to be Hindus, and ought not to be treated as outcasts by their relatives and kinsmen. He would go to the extent of conceding to them the privileges of marriage with members of their caste. The Low Church party have been alarmed, and countermeetings have been held but without any success. We should be glad to see the battle fought as it should be. In the mean time may we ask who is the Lord Shaftesbury of the Hindus?

To many of our countrymen the very word *Khrishtan* is repulsive and odious in the extreme. It calls to their minds most unpleasant and, in their opinion, unhallowed associations, and they hate Christ, Christianity and all things appertaining to them with intense hatred, and feel as if there can be nothing good in them and nothing good can come out of them. The word *Khrishtan* they hold to be synonymous with beef, brandy and onion, with tight trousers, garibaldi shirts and fashionable neck-tie, with contempt for parents and everything national, with flippancy, foppery and *hut mut* or overbearing manners. Why this prejudice against the Christian name let impartial critics try to ascertain. Both the calumniated and the calumniators have much to say to justify themselves. What we contend for is simply this that whatever prejudice there may be against the name 'Christian' there ought to be none against Christ. That name must be sweet to us all, to Christians as well as Hindus, to Europeans as well as Natives, for it represents nothing but meekness, love, purity, and asceticism. There is a moral beauty in that name which no thoughtful and devout heart can resist. It is a beauty that fascinates all, of whatever creed, who appreciates it. It is a pleasure even for a Hindu to recognise Christ as a Sweet Child of God.

THERE is a depth in real, and good music to which no religious souls can prove insensible. There is a profound harmony in real religion which is but half-expressible by the highest music of which human genius is capable. There is no Handel's Oratorio in India, there is no Halleleujah anthem chanted by a thousand voices rolling in the marble aisles of mighty cathedrals, and overpowering the mind in a wild trance of celestial delight. All this in our country we do not know. But the liquid notes of the Indian lute as they come floating at the still night hour, along the delicious breeze which steals accross the pure stream of the Ganges or Jumna, carry the mind far far beyond the earth on the wings of heavenward aspiration. The *Vina* of Narada, and the *Vanshi* of Krishna, and the sweet guitar the vibration of whose divine strings called forth the adoration of *Saraswati*, and caused her holy tears to flow as she sat in her bower of white lotuses, have become objects of the utmost sacredness. The deepest and best part of Hindu Music is strictly and exclusively religious. Yes even now as in former times the strokes of a master hand, and the notes of a master voice can cause the rain to descend, and the fire to flash. Why then, let us ask, are Brahmos so utterly indifferent to true music? What great religious movement has there been in India, or elsewhere whose development is not profoundly indebted to the magic of sweet sounds set to the magic of sweet sentiments? Nay the harmonies of song and the harmonies of the soul not only suggest each other strongly, but are frequently analogous, and interchangeable.

THE controversy between Professor Tyndall and Mr. Martineau is still going on. The former wrote an article in the *Contemporary Review* in reply to Mr. Martineau's criticisms on the Belfast address, and the latter has published a rejoinder in the same periodical,

The *Spectator* is of opinion that Mr. Martineau understands Professor Tyndall's philosophical position much better than that gentleman understands himself. The reason of this is this. "It has been one of Mr. Martineau's chief objects in life to discriminate accurately between the philosophical significance of various systems of thought, while it has been Professor Tyndall's duty chiefly to push forward science, rather than to analyze its logic, or to distinguish sharply its fundamental assumptions from the rationale of methods it pursues and the conclusions which it gathers." In the famous Belfast address, it will be remembered, Professor Tyndall reserved the whole field of knowledge and philosophy to materialistic science and quietly handed over religion to the emotions. To this Mr. Martineau replied that when emotion was found to be empty and unphilosophical, it should be stamped out. Professor Tyndall says that in stamping out emotion Mr. Martineau "kicked away the only philosophical foundation on which it is possible to build religion." Mr. Marteneau replies thus :—

> In thus refusing support from 'empty emotion,' I am said to 'kick away the only *philosophic foundation* on which it is possible to build religion.' Professor Tyndall is certainly unstinting from his builders about the solidity of his 'foundation;' and it can be only a very light and airy architecture, not to say an imaginary one, that can spring from such base; and perhaps it does not matter that it should be unable to face the winds. Nor is the inconsistency involved in this statement less surprising than its levity. Religion, it appears, has a 'philosophical foundation.' But 'philosophy' investigates the ultimate ground of cognition and the organic unity of what the several sciences assume. And a 'philosophical foundation' is a legitimated first principle for some one of these; it is a cognitive beginning—a *datum* of ulterior *quæsita*—and nothing but a science can have it. Religion, then, must be an organism of thought. Yet it is precisely in denial of this that my censor invents his new 'foundation.' Here, he tells us, we know nothing, we can think nothing; the intellectual life is dumb and blank; we do but blindly feel. How can a structure without truth repose on philosophy in its foundation?

A LIBERAL Christian theologian deservedly celebrated, who also enjoys the eminence of being one of the profoundest metaphysicians whom England has produced in the present century, writes a letter to us from which we make the following extract. We do not like to give out the writer's name at present, but the extract will show the strange difference that exists between every form of Christianity brought out into this country, and the beautiful spirit of that religion as it prevails among the pious and thoughtful souls at home. We wrote a paragraph in our last Sunday's issue about the right estimate of Christ. The extract we give below furnishes a most beautiful supplement to what we said :—Whilst I cling with warm affection to the Christian name, it is simply through reverence for that spirit of Christ, which is nothing else than the life of childlike surrender of the soul to God, and immediate communion with him. With the Christianity which interposes Christ as a "mediator" between us and the Heavenly Father I have no sympathy. It seems to me simply to contradict and undo the whole work of his life, which was to bring the human spirit and the Divine into living and immediate presence of each other, and leave us in possession for ever of that sublime and purifying consciousness. This life of God in the soul of man is no private property of any Sect or Church, but a universal fact seated in the reality of things: and whoever finds it and knows it from his own inner experience, has entered that brotherhood of the spirit which transcends the divisions of historical religions. Hence, the theism of India speaks to me, not simply as objectively interesting but with an appeal to my inmost sympathies. It is your happy lot to have a true and living faith unencumbered by a load of traditional theology. We are so heavily weighted with a complex theology that faith and love are half strangled by the burden, and have no stroke in their wings. But I will not complain or despond. The Providence of the world assigns to us our place and work and while I look with joy and hope on the mission opening before you in India, I am content, for my remaining days of service, to labor on the "stony ground" of an exhausted Christendom and try whether, here and there, the good seed can yet find some "deepness of earth."

IT is with intense anxiety that we watch the effects of the decision given by Mr. Justice Phear in the case of the Great National Theatre. Against the actors and managers of the Theatre individually we have not the remotest grudge, and we think we can honestly congratulate them on their release, though we must say that if they had not been acquitted, they should have quite deserved their punishment. These two sentiments, seemingly paradoxical, are not really inconsistent. Their personal escape is no doubt a matter of sincere joy to their friends, and in that sense a pleasure to us. But the cause of public morality would have been doubtlessly better preserved if the present misdemeanor which most inadequately represents the grossness of past offences, had not been so lightly passed over by the highest court in the country, whose decision cannot but exercise very great influence upon the judgment of the people. Nobody can be unaware of the utter looseness of speech, thought, and manners characteristic of a very large class among the rising generation who have added the treacherous sensualities of Europe to the flagrant voluptuousness of their own land. They draw away to their mischievous exhibitions on the stage and elsewhere all the pleasure-loving youth of Bengal who constitutionally imaginative and supple, most readily imbibe impressions, sentiments, and suggestions that prove to be their ruin in after life. There is no public opinion to check the evil; there is no authority either in society, or in individual men, either in the dead religion of the country, or in the secular education which Government can give, that can restrain the headlong career of the weak, and the carnally minded. The popular vernacular literature of the land overflows with filth. The obscenities are frequently open and as frequently covert, and more dangerous for that reason. Of course Government cannot, and should not step forward always to make the people moral by force. But when the limits of forbearance and noninterference have been fairly transcended, and the authorities feel it their duty to prevent the utter degradation of society by putting forth the arm of law, their object is defeated by the narrow-sighted perversity of a judicial decision that cannot detect gross and glaring immorality because it lies below the merest surface of things. What wonder that under such circumstances the licentious should take courage, and the land should be overrun by what they say and do?

GOING OUT AND COMING IN.

ONCE at least in life's drama the player must depart from the stage of the world. After this 'exit' there must be a re-appearance. This going out and coming in are both inevitable and essential to salvation. The doctrine of harmonious development is mischievous at least in the sense in which it is generally accepted and acted upon. Sinners, as we are, and wedded to this world's fascinations, we are ready to take advantage of this doctrine, and convert it into a most pernicious and accommodating principle of worldly advancement. That men should remain always in the midst of the world, acquire riches, seek honor, grow in knowledge, discharge duties to family and society, thrive in business, and harmoniously meet all the requirements of life without sacrificing anything, is a theory, and a specious theory it is. It is a picture, perfectly unreal and imaginary, having no counterpart in reality. Is this so-called harmony possible in a life already sold to the senses, paralysed by sin, and drawn far away into the regions of disorder and death? Can a broken soul grow beautifully and with all its parts complete? Can there be a fair adjustment of parts where some parts are abnormally inflated and have exceeded all natural proportions? Talk of peace in the land of sworn enemies—of harmony among conflicting elements! How can man give equal attention and attachment to this world and the next, when he is enslaved to the pleasures of this world? First subdue the senses, destroy carnality, drive away anger, lust covetousness, pride, and selfishness, and then talk of establishing harmony among the various departments of life. Let the disease die out before the whole body may realize the harmony and joy of health. Many years' worldliness and sin must bring about a reaction in the natural course of things. This reaction means a thorough distaste for the world, a retirement from its temptations, and a residence for self-discipline and education in the recesses of the heart. The Hindu at a certain period of his life solemnly retires from family and home to live in solitude in a remote wilderness. The natural man, as soon as he feels that he has served the world too much, runs away from the land of temptations which has ruined him, and hides himself for a time—where? in the inner retreat of the heart, and learns asceticism and sanctity. Whatever form this spirit of self-government, this spiritual self-mortification may assume it must come to every man sooner or later, who is anxious to attain purity and godliness. Every man must once in his life die unto the world if he wishes to live again in the Lord. This death of the lower life is true asceticism (bairagya); this is *banogaman* (retirement from the world.) But only for a time does the soul remain within itself, away from the world. When properly schooled and disciplined it comes out again self-possessed to do its work fearlessly and joyfully in the world. Then the regenerate man lives as one who has conquered the world and in whose life the body and the soul, God and the world have been harmonized.

BHAKTI TEACHINGS.

O BHAKTI learner! Know that Bhakti is only the true and tender love of the soul. The True, the Good, the Beautiful; these are the three seed-truths of Bhakti. These are the three sides of the nature of the Deity; they produce three corresponding sentiments in man's soul one after another; and the three sentiments in their turn comprehend Divine nature. Reverence for the True; love for the Good; enthusiastic devotion or inebriation in the Beautiful. The real exercise of Bhakti, however, ranges between the Good and the Beautiful. These two attributes of God form the basis of Bhakti, which grows upon them. Affection or love is the commencement of Bhakti, enthusiasm or inebriation is its maturity. Love is the seed, inebriation is the fruit. Love is the infancy, enthusiasm is the youth. But what about moral purity? Is there no morality in the ground of Bhakti? Nay true Bhakti is beyond the region of morality and immorality. The Bhakta can not be sinful. It is unnecessary to say that he must be holy. The deep truth of the matter is this. The ground of moral purity must be fully secured before Bhakti can begin. Let all sin first go away; let all moral duties be first discharged, and then only can the discipline of Bhakti commence. Unless a man's character be thoroughly good, he is unworthy to take up the question of Bhakti. But a man's character may be pure in two different ways. Purity may in some cases be only strict and rigorous self-discipline; in other cases it may be the result of the sweetness and tenderness of the soul. The latter is Bhakti. Its very beginning is joy. Bhakti grows on the soil of holiness. Bhakti comes with color and beauty in its wings. The outlines of a picture may be correct and good. But as in themselves those outlines are naked, harsh, dry and incomplete and when filled with warm coloring they become alive, soft, and charming; so a man's character may be good and pure but harsh and charmless, and it is only when he is adorned with the beauty of love, tenderness, and peace that his character acquires its fulness. Mere morality is not enough for Bhakti; but immorality makes Bhakti impossible. This bear in mind always. It is a most dangerous thing to say that a Bhakta can ever be immoral. It is never his custom to say first let me cultivate Bhakti, and I shall be pure afterwards. No. He eschews all sin before he begins Bhakti.

Now let us ask whence springs Bhakti? It springs from restlessness. Thou hast faith in God, thou dost faithfully perform all religious exercises, thou art good to thy neighbours, to thy kinsmen, true to all domestic and social relations; but the heart cries out in the midst of these things saying there is no rest for me in all this. Then the Giver of all truth finds it necessary to send a new dispensation. He sees His son hath no rest, and He wants to give him rest. Why should God's son suffer from the deep pain of restlessness in the heart? Peace is necessary, so is joy, so is love. Therefore the good God sends the dispensation of Bhakti. This is the sole reason of the Bhakti dispensation, and there is no other. The right question to ask is, have you real rest in God, in prayer, in the contemplation of the next world, in religion, in life? If you have not, you are not a Bhakta. Bhakti is in inverse ratio to peacelessness. The Bhakta says I long to behold the God of beauty, my soul weeps day and night for him. If you ask him why, he cannot give any reason. His restlessness is his whole reason. Ask him why he is delighted with his God, he can give no reason, his delight is his only reason. When the soul is once restless with the desire of beholding and loving God, give the man all the goods of this world, all its virtue, all its good deeds, and good names, and he will not be satisfied. He cannot account for his condition, he speaks, and cries like a child, nay like a fool. But yet awhile, and he is joyful again. His delight knows no bounds, he laughs, and is exceedingly glad, but can as little account for his joy. Bhakti therefore has been called *Ahaituki* or unreasoning.

Devotional.

BUILD up for me the cross O Lord whereon my earthly affections and desires may be nailed and sacrificed for thy glory. Make mine the peace that results from resigned self-sacrifice. Every relation whose source cannot be consciously traced to thee is the cause of endless trouble, and every wish that thou dost not bless is born to grieve the spirit. The load of trouble and grief that comes out of the weakness of the heart, teach me, O Lord, to bear with patience and meekness. Draw out the thorns in my flesh, even though the process will cause me to bleed exceedingly, and cure me from the deep disease of my soul.

> Happy are they that learn, in Thee,
> Though patient suffering teach
> The secret of enduring strength,
> And praise too deep for speech—
> *Peace* that no pressure from without,
> No strife within, can reach.

THE sorrow of thy righteous servants is turned into blessedness by thy compassion, O God of loving kindness. It is not true that thou feelest no sorrow, but the strength of perfect love converts it into the profound freshness of a new joy. Man's sufferings are great but they only can give him an insight into the depths of thy tranquility. Wound and mortify my spirit as thou wilt, only give me in the end the healing consciousness of thy sympathy.

> Oh, this is blessing, this is rest—
> Into thine arms, O Lord, I flee
> I hide me in thy faithful breast,
> And pour out all my soul to thee.

UPON those who look down upon me with scorn and disapprobation, God cause thy mercy to descend. Upon those who take pleasure to contradict, accuse, and humiliate me, send thy abundant grace. There are some who have spoken hard words to me, there are some who have ill-used such persons as I honor and love, there are some who have thrown me at a distance, O God bless them all, and reform their ways.

Brahmo Hymns

THE day is over, why are you sitting quietly, O my mind? What preparations have you made to cross the river of the world? The sun of your life is about to set, seeing you see it not; intoxicated with delusion you have lost the knowledge of truth. If you seek your own welfare take the shelter of Him who is the Captain of the vessel that will take you across the world, and who removes sin and sorrow.

The Brahmo Somaj.

WE have often expressed our views on the use of animal food. But still our correspondents write to make inquiries as to what Progressive Brahmos think on the subject. Well, once more let us say that we leave the use of animal food an open question. Those whose conscience it defiles and burdens should do without it at once. But this may not be the case with all.

AUGUSTINE'S CONVERSION.

(Concluded from last Sunday's Indian Mirror.)

But Alipius sitting close by my side in silence waited issue of my unwonted emotion. But when a deep consideration had from the secret bottom of my soul drawn together and heaped up all my misery in the sight of my heart, there arose a mighty storm bringing a mighty shower of tears. Which that I might pour forth wholly in its natural expressions, I rose from Alypius: solitude was suggested to me as fitter for the business of weeping; so I retired so far that even his presence could not be a burden to me. Thus was it then with me and he perceived something of it; for something I suppose I had spoken, wherein the tones of my voice appeared choked with weeping and so had risen up. He then remained where we were sitting most extremely astonished. I cast myself down, I know not how, under a certain fig-tree, giving full vent to my tears, and the floods of mine eyes gushed out an *acceptable sacrifice to Thee.* And not indeed in these words, yet to this purpose, spake I much unto thee: *and thou, O Lord how long? how long Lord, wilt thou be angry for ever? Remember not our former* iniquities, for I felt I was held by them. I sent up these sorrowful words. How long? how long "to-morrow and to-morrow?" Why not now? why not is there this hour an end to my uncleanness?

So I was speaking, and weeping in the most bitter contrition of my heart, when lo! I heard from a neighbouring house a voice as of boy or girl, I know not, chanting, and oft repeating, "Take up and read. Take up and read." Instantly my countenance altered, I began to think most intently, whether children were wont in any kind of play to sing such words: nor could I remember ever to have heard the like. So checking the torrent of my tears I arose; interpreting it to be no other than a command from God; to open the book and read the first Chapter I should find. For I had heard of Atony that coming in during the reading of the Gospel, he received the admonition as if what was being read was spoken to him, *Go sell all that thou hast, and give to the* poor, and thou shalt have treasures in heaven, and come and follow me: and by such oracle he was forthwith converted unto Thee. Eagerly then I returned to the place where Alypius was sitting, for there had I laid the volume of the Apostle, when I arose thence, I seized, opened, and in silence read the that section, on which my eyes first fell: *Not in rioting and drunkenness, not in chambering and wantonness, not in strife and envying; but put ye on the Lord Jesus Christ, and make not provision for the flesh,* in concupicience. No further would I read, nor needed I; for instantly at the end of this sentence by a light as it were of serenity infused into my heart, all the darkness of doubt vanished away.

Then puting my finger between or some other mark, I shut the volume, and with a calmed countinance made it known to Alypius. And what was wrought in him, which I knew not he thus showed me. He asked to see what I had read. I showed him and he looked even further than I had read, and I knew not what followed. This followed, *him that is weak in faith, receive,* which he applied to himself and disclosed to me. And by this admonition was he strengthened; and by a good resolution and purpose, and most corresponding to his character, wherein he did always very far differ from me for the better, without any turbulent delay he joined me. Thence we go in to my mother. We tell her she rejoiceth: we relate in order how it took place; she leaps for joy, and triumpheth, and blessed Thee, *who art able to do above that which we ask or think;* for she perceived that Thou hadst given her more for me than she was wont to beg by her pitiful and most sorrowful groanings. For Thou convertedst me unto Thyself, so that I sought neither wife, nor any hope of this world standing in that rule of faith, where thou hadst showed me unto her in a vision, so many years before. And Thou *didst convert her mourning into joy,* much more plentiful than she had desired, and in a much more precious and purer way than she erst required, by having grandchildren of my own body.

CONFESSIONS.

Literary.

MR. JOHN FORSTER, the biographer of Goldsmith, of Dickens, of Landor, of Swift, and the author of some works of much merit and research on the Puritan period of English history, died on Tuesday at his house in Palace Gate, Kensington, at the age of sixty-four. He was, in early years, a journalist, having been at one time a constant contributor to the *Examiner*, and at another, for about a year, the Editor of the *Daily News*, but latterly his literary work had been chiefly of a higher kind while the duties of a Commissioner in Lunacy occupied his hours of routine work till he resigned that office a year or two ago. He was a careful and an eminently sensible writer, who knew how to make biography thoroughly readable, though he could hardly command the delicate touch of the highest literary art. His life of Goldsmith is a fascinating book, and yet not all that such a subject, treated by one saturated with the love of Goldsmith's genius, might have made it. The higher biography requires for its perfection at least a few threads of poetic feeling, and this, with all his abilities, was apparently wanting in Mr. Forster, who knew well, however, when he could not portray his subjects to his own satisfaction, how to let his subjects portray themselves.—*Spectator.*

A Sanskrit Handbook for the Fireside, By Elihu Burrit. Mr. Burrit has attempted much, but has achieved less. His work is intended for young students, who, without outside help, are by means of its instruction to acquire ability "to read any classical work in Sanskrit with only the help of a dictionary." If it fall into the hands of a youth with a powerful genius for the acquisition of languages, it may perhaps achieve something like the result anticipated, but we fear the majority of the sanguine students who commence studying it, will fall far short of the expected goal. We have not much faith in any attempt to popularise the study of Sanskrit, and are pretty certain that the somewhat imperfect book before us will prove a failure.—*Friend of India.*

The Week

The Bishop of Madras is expected in this city shortly to take charge of the See of Calcutta.

CAPTAIN PRIDEAUX, the newly-appointed Political Resident, Persian Gulf, has left Calcutta, and is expected to reach Bushire on the 31st instant.

A LARGE and influential body of Native gentlemen waited at the Lahore Railway Station to receive Dr. Leitner on his return from Europe.

SIR JUNG BAHADUR will leave for Europe again in 1877. He intends visiting, among other places, Berlin, St. Petersburgh, Vienna, and Florence.

MISS CARPENTER delivered a lecture at Mahableshwar, and spoke highly of Poona and its institutions.

LORD LYTTON has left Alexandria for Suez to meet the Prince of Wales.

CALCUTTA will be 450 miles nearer to Bombay as soon as the Chuttisghur State Railway is completed. This line will connect Raipore with Nagpore, and be extented to Calcutta *via* Sumbulpore and Cuttack.

THE large sum collected in Tanjore to do honor to H. R. H. the Prince of Wales, is to be devoted to the establishment of a Medical College at Twadi in commemoration of H. R. H's. visit to India.

LATEST NEWS.

LIEUTENANT-COLONEL W. H. Beynon, Resident, Political Agent, Jeypore; Colonel J. A. Wright, Political Agent, Eastern States, Rajputana, and Colonel E. Thompson, Agent to the Governor-General at Murshidabad, have obtained respectively subsidiary leave for 30 days preparatory to furlough.

THE Colonel Chesney whose death has been reported by telegram, was not Colonel George Chesney, the author of the "Battle of Dorking," and Principal of Cooper's Hill College, but a brother of his—Colonel Charles Cornwallis Chesney. He was also a Royal Engineer and the author of several works—"Waterloo Lectures," "Campaigns in Virginia and Maryland" &c.

CAPTAIN C. A. BAYLAY, Officiating Political Agent, 3rd Class, will officiate for Colonel Beynon as Political Agent, Jeypore.

A PUBLIC meeting has been convened at Bombay to take suitable steps to commemorate the name of the late Mr. Merwanji Framji Panday.

MISS MARY CARPENTER arrived in Bombay on Monday last from Poona. She intends to leave for England by to-morrow's mail steamer.

THE Commission on the affairs of the Nawab Nazim has sent in its report.

MAJOR MONEY's appointment to the management of the Durbungah Raj has been confirmed.

MR. S. O. B. RIDSDALE becomes Secretary to the Chief Commissioner of Assam in place of Mr. Luttman Johnson, who gets a district.

IN recognition of the good services rendered to Government by Shadhun Chunder, Honorary Extra Assistant Commissioner in Assam, the Viceroy and Governor-General is pleased to confer upon him the title of "Rai Bahadur" as a personal distinction.

THE Vernacular papers published at Peshawur give currency to a rumour prevalent there, that some mines have been discovered at Cabul containing precious stones; the rumour would appear to have been confirmed on reliable authority. The color of the stones is said to be red, and the Amir sets a high value on them.

THE young Thakore of Bhownuggur, says the *Bombay Gazette* arrived in Bombay on Monday last, after completing the tour through India, on which he had started about four months ago under the guidance of Captain Nutt. His Highness was accompanied on his tour by a small personal suite, and saw most things of importance in the different towns and places which were included in the programme.

LORD NORTHBROOK will not only pay a visit to Sir William Gregory in Ceylon but also to the Duke of Buckingham, at Madras.

MR. C. J. LYALL, Under-Secretary in the Department of Revenue, Agriculture and Commerce, is going on leave for a month from the 1st of April.

MAJOR-GENERAL C. A. BARWELL, C.B., is gazetted as Chief Commissioner of the Andaman and Nicobar Islands, *vice* Major-General D. M. Stewart.

MR. BROUGHTON, the Government Quinologist at Ootakamand, who disappeared mysteriously about fifteen months ago, has, the *Madras Times* says, been heard of at last in New Zealand.

THE Maharajah of Travancore is said to be contemplating making a railway from Palamkota to Trevandrum.

A HALF mysterious half libellous paragraph, says the *Pioneer*, was lately published in Bombay about a Maharajah of the Punjab who was said to have turned Blue Beard and murdered various relations. His behaviour was supposed to have thrown the Government of India into much perplexity. When we put a plain interpretation on this cock-and-bull story, it loses, with its mystery, all its pobability. If our conjecture is right, we understand how this rumour spread, for the Maharajah, we mean, has many enemies. Their insinuations are contradicted, however, by the recent visit paid to the Chief in question by Sir Henry Davies, while the alleged appeal to the Viceroy and "the perplexity of the Government of India" seem to be altogether imaginary.

PUNDIT SURUP NARAIN, Native Assistant to the Agent to the Governor-General for Central India, is appointed to officiate as Political Assistant, 3rd Class.

THERE was a very large attendance of all classes (except Europeans) at the Bombay Town Hall on Tuesday last to listen to the lecture delivered by Swami Dayanad Saraswati on the "Aryans" and the history of Hinduism &c. The lecture was delivered in Hindustani.

LIEUTENANT-COLONEL J. W. W. Osborne, C.B., Political Agent, 1st Class, and Political Agent at Bhopal, is granted 3 months' privilege leave.

THE telegram informs us that on the reading of the Royal Titles' Bill a third time in the House of Commons a long and animated debate ensued, in which Mr. Disraele dwelt on the political reasons in favor of the Bill, referring especially to the advance made by Russia towards the frontier of India and to the recent conquests in Tartary. These facts being well-known throughout India the assumption of the title of Empress would be regarded as an unmistakeable sign of resolution to maintain our Empire. Mr. Lowe and Mr. Fawcett strongly censured M. Disraeli's allusion to the designs of Russia as both incautious and unwise. The bill was passed by 209 against 134 votes.

THE Parsi gentleman who superintended the illuminations at the Public Works and Post Offices, at Bombay, on the night of His Royal Highness the Prince of Wales' birthday, will shortly be made a "Khan Bahadur.

Calcutta.

ADDRESS TO MRS. PHEAR.

THE following address was read to Mrs. Phear at the house of Durga Mohun Dass, South Circular Road, by the former and present pupils of the Hindu Mohila Vidyalaya founded by Miss. Annet Akroyed. The address was read by Miss. Sharala Dass daughter of Babu Durga Mohun Dass

Dear Madam,—On the eve of your departure from India, we cannot forbear doing ourselves the pleasure of expressing to you our sincere gratitude for the interest you have taken in the cause of the education and improvement of the women of Bengal during the period of your stay in this country, and for your uniform kindness of manner towards its people. We cannot sufficiently express the warm feeling and regard which we entertain for you and your good husband. As Mr. Phear has, on the one hand endeared himself to the hearts of the people by the interest he has always taken in their welfare, by his genial manners and by his strict impartiality in the administration of justice, so you on the other hand, have entitled yourself to our respect and admiration by devoting yourself with unceasing energy to the female education and advancement. No English lady of your rank and position has, we believe, in this country ever been able to show that greatness of heart which you have exhibited, by devoting herself with such untiring zeal in this good work. Your noble heart was never found wanting in any way to help in promoting the cause of famale education. The good that you have done by your noble example in life to many of the women of our country, shall never be forgotten. By your example, many of us have now been able to appreciate the real duty of a woman's life; many a heart has glowed with feeling, and been imbued with a keener thirst for knowledge; and many of us have been able to understand how wide and extended is the sphere of a woman's action. We can make no adequate return for the benefit which you and Mr. Phear have done the people of this country—all that we can is to express to you the gratitude of our hearts, and our sincere thanks.

The kind feelings which you have always shown towards the pupils of the Hindu Mahila Bidyalaya, deserve here prominent mention, and our special gratitude. What that institution has been able to accomplish was owing in a great measure to your exertions and untiring devotion.

The tidings that you are bidding adieu to this land, and that the prospect is uncertain whether you return to us again, has conveyed to our hearts feelings of sorrow which we cannot find words to express. We shall look upon your departure as our common loss.

Although you will be far away from us, yet we earnestly hope and pray that the kind feelings which you have always entertained towards the men and women of our country shall not henceforth cease to exist. We have every reason to believe that you will, even from that distant land, try to do all that lies in your power to promote the well-being of the women of this country. It will be a great pleasure to us if you still remember us after you have reached your own land.

With the blessings of God on you, and with the tribute of our gratitude, we wish you a safe and happy voyage home. And we fervently pray that God will richly reward you for your many good deeds and your worthy life.

We have the honor to remain, Dear Madam, Yours with affection and gratitude, Sharna Prabha Bose, Sharala Dass, Hara Sundari Dutta, Sharna Moya Chatterji, Parbutty Sundari Bose, Benodmani Bose, Kadambini Bose, Girija Kumari Sen, Abala Dass.

THE Hon'ble Mr. and Mrs. Phear will leave for England on the 11th of April.

MR. J. H. B. WILKIS, late clerk to one of the Calcutta Magistrates, who was tried on a charge of forging the name of Captain R. Armstrong, now in England, to certain letters to Messrs. Kellner & Co., ordering some cases of brandy for the Mess at Dum Dum, has been convicted and sentenced to one year's rigorous of imprisonment.

OUT of 185 candidates who appeared at the last Junior Examination of the Calcutta Medical College, 79 have been successful. Only 13 candidates for the Senior Examination are passed.

IN recognition of the services rendered to Government by Babu Durga Narayan Banerji, Inspector on the Bengal Postal Establishment, the Viceroy and Governor-General is pleased to confer upon him the title of "Rai Bahadur" as a personal distinction.

ORDERS have been given, it is stated, for the *Tenasserim* to be in readiness by about the 7th proximo to convey Lord Northbrook to England. The public meeting at the Town Hall, in honor of his Lordship, takes place on the 8th.

BISHOP GELL of Madras, has taken charge of the See of Calcutta, and will, with those of his own Diocese, continue to perform the duties of the office until further notice. The Bishop purposes to hold a confirmation in Calcutta on the 6th April next. Dr. Gell has been fifteen years in India. The following notice of him appears in *Men of the Time* :—"Dr. Frederick Gell, son of the late Rev. Philip Gell, of Derby, was born in 1821, took his B. A. decree at Trinity College, Cambridge, in 1843, and soon afterwards became Fellow and Tutor of Christ College. Having been Chaplain to the Bishop of London, and one of Her Majesty's preachers at Whitehall, he, in 1861, was consecrated to the See of Madras." When at College, Dr. Gell was distinguished for his eminent piety, so much so that he was known among his fellow-students as "Pious Fred." He is said to be an accomplished Mathematician and a deep Theologian. He belongs to the Evangelical or "Low Church" party. Dr. Gell has made considerable progress in Telugu and Tamil. The appointment of the two Missionary Bishops, Drs. Caldwell and Sargent, was chiefly owing to Dr. Gell's suggestions.

THE 12th annual *conversaziones* of the Mahomedan Literary Society came off, as was announced, on the 23rd instant, at the Town Hall. There was a large gathering of the *élite* of the European and Native community. The Viceroy and the Lieutenant-Governor were both present. There were chemical and scientific experiments by Father Lafont, Mr. Pedler, and Dr. Kanie Lal Dey. Plants of various descriptions, architectural specimens and many other things were exhibited. Music was not wanting too. An address was presented on behalf of the Society to the Viceroy, to which His Excellency replied in fitting terms. A sad accident, however, marred in some degree the effect of the occasion. While Dr. Kanie Loll was making a chemical experiment, an explosion took place which, we are happy to say, ended in no serious hurt. We were extremely sorry to see that a number of gentlemen who were invited, were excluded from taking a part in the *conversazione* as they did not come in "proper dress."—[*Communicated.*]

Law

POLICE,—MARCH 25, 1876.

[*Before F. J. Marsden, Esq.*]

SERGEANT WALLS, of the Calcutta Police charged Mr. Gregory, Solicitor, with having, on the 13th instant, obstructed him in the execution of his duty. Mr. Carapiet, on behalf of the defendant, pleaded not guilty to the charge. The complainant stated that he had gone to the house of the defendant to serve a subpœna, issued at the instance of Mr. Joachim in the late case of enticement and adultery, on Mrs. Gregory, but that he had been refused admission on two separate occasions. On the third occasion he was obstructed by the servants, who would not allow him to enter the house. On demanding admission, Mr. Gregory asked him his name and wished to know on what business he had come. Being in his uniform, the complainant saw no reason for giving his name, but said that he had come to serve a subpœna on Mrs. Gregory. Afterwards, however, he gave his name, and left the subpœna with Mr. Gregory, whose wife was not at home at the time. The Magistrate, on the complainant's own statements, observed that the obstruction had not been caused by Mr. Gregory, but by his servants, and that it was not of such a nature as to demand the interference of the Court. The case was accordingly dismissed. Mr. Carapiet here informed the Court that the complainant, so far from being refused admission on the first two occasions, had actually entered the house, and peeped into every room—an allegation which he was in a position to prove. On the third occasion the servants did refuse admission, and this was because the defendant had given them instructions to them to allow no one to enter the house in the evening, as he generally saw his clients in the morning, and wished to enjoy the evening to himself.

Selection

OUR FAITH AND OUR EXPERIENCES.

[SUBSTANCE OF ANNIVERSARY LECTURE.]

I VERILY believe that, when Jesus Christ was about to leave this world, he made over the sacred portfolio of the ministry of his Church to the Holy Spirit. Every true believer must see in this arrangement heavenly wisdom, sagacity, foresight and loving kindness. It was indeed most important and desirable that the Prophet of Nazareth should do so. At that anxious hour when the light of the disciples—the light of their eyes and the light of their hearts, was about to pass away from their midst, when the great luminary that had been shining in the firmament of the religious world was about to set, and darkness and confusion threatened to swallow the world, when with trembling hearts the disciples were casting their last glance upon him whom they had always looked upon as their father and friend, their joy and hope,—aye even to-day the heart is perturbed as it looks back upon that gloomy scene of separation,—I say, at that solemn hour it was absolutely necessary that a successor should be announced. No true leader can bid adieu to his devoted followers without arranging for their future guardianship. It would be cruel to do so. And surely Christ with his loving and compassionate heart could not take leave of his weeping disciples without commending them into the arms of a fit successor. Did not their eyes as they tearfully looked up to him, indicate deep sorrow and utter helplessness, and did he not read within throbbing hearts most gloomy anxieties and forecasts about the future? Did not their dejected looks seem to ask,—Into whose hands, good shepherd, wilt thou consign the helpless sheep of thy fold?—Who will nurse and feed hereafter these thy children? And so Christ spoke in response naming him who was to sit in his place. But whom did he announce as the future minister of his Church and the future guide of his disciples? It was the Holy Spirit, and none other, "even the Spirit of truth which proceedeth from the Father." Let not your heart be troubled, said he to his disciples, neither let it be afraid; I will not leave you comfortless. Thus saying he described the functions of his great successor. He was to be their teacher, their comforter, their guardian and guide, their light and joy for ever. "I will pray the Father," said Jesus, "and he shall give you another Comforter, that he may abide with you for ever." "I have yet many things to say unto you," he added, "but ye cannot bear them now. Howbeit when he, the Spirit of truth, is come, he will guide you into all truth; and he will show you things to come." These are important utterances, fraught with deep meaning, which the world has yet to realize. Friends, was Christ's work over and his heavenly mission closed when the last mournful scene on calvary was enacted? Was everything really finished when Jesus uttered his last words, "It is finished?" No. His work was not completed. The great and glorious work of human redemption, so well begun by him, was far from being consummated. It needed to be supplemented and carried on to its final issue. The church he built was incomplete, and was very far from reaching its ideal. He had taught many truths indeed, but much yet remains to be taught, nor were the disciples yet prepared to receive any further lessons. A great deal of the new gospel of salvation which he had come to teach was yet veiled, but which could not be revealed as none seemed fit to receive it. More light the world needed for its redemption, but more light it could not bear now. Who was to give this new light? Who was to carry on and complete these sacred teachings which Christ began, for the benefit of his disciples and the world at large? Alas! Those lips were soon closed which after teaching much heavenly wisdom finished by saying. "I have yet many things to say unto you, but ye cannot bear them now." Who was to reveal to an anxious and sinful world these "many things"? The Holy Ghost, said Christ. The Living Spirit coming down from the Father Himself, and speaking in His name was to guide the disciples and the world "into all truth." To no earthly teacher, to no verbal message, are we referred for a fuller message of salvation. No apostle, however pure, no disciple, however wise, was named by Christ as his successor. He named the Holy Spirit in clear and unmistakable language as the future minister of his Church. The disciples were commanded to rely henceforth upon this Spiritual Guide for their future education and sanctification. Not in any outward Church, not from the lips of any human teacher, but in the dark chambers of the heart and beneath the feet of the Unseen and Infinite Spirit of God must they receive whatsoever they needed of wisdom, love and purity. In the days of tribulation and trial thy were to look up to Him as their comforter and friend. In moments of doubt and vacillation thy were to repair to Him as their teacher. In the season of scarcity and want thy were to seek the needful supply in His inexaustable store-house within. And when men persecuted them thy were to fight under Him as their Captain and bear witness to the truth in His name. They were to adore the Spirit, converse with the Spirit, learn of the Spirit, and be baptized by the Spirit with the spirit of truth. After enunciating solemnly and publicly this great doctrine of the succession, Christ made over his beloved disciples and calmly resigned his ministry into the hands of Him from whom he had received them. In a most solemn and touching prayer the loving Jesus said to his Father—"I have finished the work which Thou gavest me to do. Now I am no more in the world. Holy Father! keep through Thine own name those whom Thou hast given me. Sanctify them through Thy truth." And so the Heavenly Father as soon as Christ departed from the world, took all his devoted disciples under direct guardianship and inspiration of His Holy Spirit, and became unto them at once their guardian, comforter, teacher and saviour through His living Providence.

The most orthodox Christian divine need not be ashamed of so true and elevated a doctrine as this. Let no Christian think it unchristian to believe that the Holy Spirit of God is the true and living head of Christ's Church, who is the source of all inspiration now and for ever, and from whom a fuller revelation of saving truth is yet to come than what was vouchsafed to the world through Christ and recorded by the evangelists. In Christ's own words is to be found the best and most unimpeachable authority for such a doctrine. To the holy spirit of God then let all Christendom bow. Does not the entire history of Christianity bear testimony to the doctrine of God's spirit? Did not the Jewish Prophets proclaim in thrilling language the ancient Spirit-God of the universe? Did not Moses receive the Decalogue from the unseen God of Israel? Did not Daniel converse with that Holy Spirit? Did not Jeremiah and Isaiah hold communion with Him? Their was no material Divinity. To no visible idol were the prayers of their hearts addressed. To the Spirit they spoke and the Spirit replied to them. But why go back to Jewish history for evidence on this point? Was the Spirit-God recognized and worshipped, was His glory sung by Jewish Prophets alone? Later on we find Saint Paul speaking frequently and emphatically of the operations of God's Spirit in sanctifying and converting the human heart. "As many as are led by the spirit of God they are the sons of God." In the Epistles of Paul we find abundant and frequent testimonies to the action of the unseen spirit on the heart, testimonies which to this day constitute the main stay of the spirituality of the Christian church and nourish the souls of thousands of Christian devotees with spiritual food and comfort. But why do we go to the apostles and prophets of distant ages and climes in quest of the Spirit-God? The banner of the great spirit was not hoisted on Jewish and Christian ground alone.

(To be continued.)

ICE! ICE! ICE!

MADE IN FOUR MINUTES

THE PNEUMATIC ICE MACHINE

THIS IMPORTANT INVENTION IS CONSIDERED A BOON TO THOSE LIVING IN TROPICAL CLIMATES.

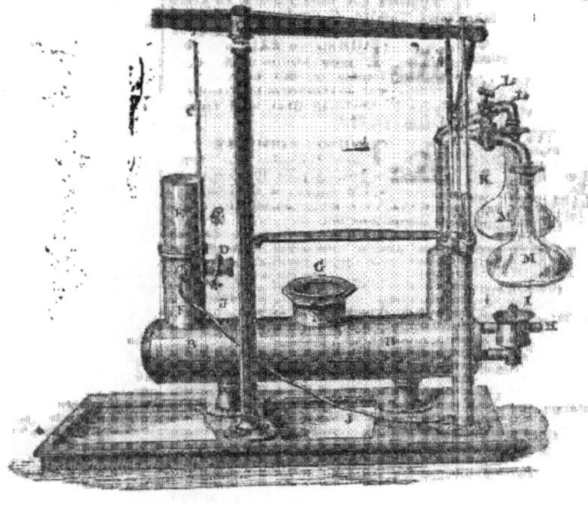

CAN BE WORKED BY THE MOST INEXPERIENCED HAND AND IS NOT LIABLE TO GET OUT OF ORDER.

From Rs. 175, each Machine complete.

MESSRS. ARLINGTON & CO.

AGENTS.

HAROLD & CO.,

3. DALHOUSIE SQUARE, CALCUTTA

HARMONIUMS.

Harold and Co., call attention to their unequalled stock of rich-toned Harmoniums made especially for India.

FROM RS. 90 TO RS. 900 EACH.

All kinds of Musical Instruments of the best description are always kept in Stock.

THACKER, SPINK AND CO.

INDIAN LAW.

ACTS of the LEGISLATIVE COUNCIL of INDIA. Annual Volume, uniform with Theobald's addition. 8vo. For 1873, Rs. 6. For 1874, Rs. 5.

BELL'S LAW of LANDLORD and TENANT as administered in Bengal. Second Edition. Royal 8vo. Rs. 7-8.

BENGAL CRIMINAL PROCEDURE; being a Translation of the Fourth Edition of Mr. H. T. Prinsep's Work. By Krishna Prosunno Bose. 8vo. (and Supplement containing Act XI of 1874) Rs. 5.

BONNERJEE'S HINDU WILLS ACT. With the Sections of the Indian Succession Act made applicable to the Wills of Hindus, &c. 8vo. Rs. 6.

BROUGHTON'S CODE of CIVIL PROCEDURE. With Appendix containing the Charters of the High Courts and Miscellaneous Acts. Fourth Edition. By C. J. Wilkinson, Esq. Royal 8vo. Rs. 22.

BROUGHTON'S DECLARATORY DECREES; being an extended Commentary on the Fifteenth Section of the Civil Procedure Code. 8vo. Rs. 4.

CHART of INHERITANCE ACCORDING to the Bengal School of Hindu Law. On Card. Colored Rs. 1-8.

CHART of SUCCESSION ACCORDING to the Suni School of Mahomedan Law. With descriptive Letter-Press. On Card, Colored. Rs. 2.

CHEVERS' MANUAL of MEDICAL JURISPRUDENCE for India, including an Outline of a History of Crime against the Person in India. Royal 8vo. Rs. 12.

COLEBROKE'S LAW of INHERITANCE According to the Mitakshara. Edited by Rajendro Missry. 8vo. Rs. 8.

COWELL'S HISTORY and CONSTITUTION of the Courts and Legislative Authorities. 8vo. Rs. 8.

COWELL'S INDIAN DIGEST: INDEX to the Reported Cases of the High Courts. Second Edition. Super-royal 8vo. Rs. 30.

COWELL'S LECTURES on HINDU LAW as administered by the British Courts, in India. 2 vols. 8vo. Rs. 20.

CROSTHWAITE'S LAND REVENUE LAW of the North-Western Provinces; being Act XIX of 1873, with Notes. Royal 8vo. Rs. 16.

CURRIE'S INDIAN LAW EXAMINATION Manual. 8vo. cloth. Rs. 7-8.

FIELD'S BENGAL REGULATIONS WITH chronological Table, Introduction, Notes and Index Rs. 21.

FIELD'S CHRONOLOGICAL TABLE of, and INDEX to, the Indian Statute Book. 4to. Rs. 21.

FIELD'S HIGH COURT RULES and CIRCULAR Orders, Civil and Criminal, from 1862 to 1871. With Indices. 2 vols. 8vo. Rs. 16.

FULL BENCH RULINGS, from the commencement of the High Court to 1868. Royal 8vo, cloth. Rs. 26. Part II separately. Rs. 16.

GOODEVE'S LAW OF EVIDENCE as administered in England, and applied to India. Royal 8vo. Rs. 10.

GOODEVE'S NEW EVIDENCE ACT I of 1872. With Notes, &c., showing Alteration in the Law. 8vo. Rs. 1-8.

KNOX'S CRIMINAL LAW of the BENGAL Presidency: Penal Code, Criminal Procedure, and all Miscellaneous Criminal Acts and orders. 2 vols. Royal 8vo. Rs. 20.

MACNAUGHTEN'S STAMP ACT. With Notifications, High Court Rulings, and Notes. 8vo. Rs. 3.

MACPHERSON'S LAW of MORTGAGE in Bengal and the North-Western Provinces. Fifth Edition by N. H. Thomson, Esq. 8vo Rs. 10.

MACPHERSON'S NEW PROCEDURE of the Civil Courts of British India, 8vo. Rs. 16.

MACRAE'S LAW of DIVORCE for INDIA. With Notes of decided Cases on all branches of the Law relating to Matrimonial Suits. Demy 8vo. Rs. 10.

India General Steam Navigation Company, Limited.

SCHOENE, KILBURN & Co.—*Managing Agents.*

ASSAM LINE.

NOTICE.

Steamers now leave Calcutta for Assam every Tuesday, Goalundo every Thursday and Doorooghur downward every Saturday.

THE Str. "MADRAS" will leave Calcutta for Assam, on Tuesday, the 28th Instant.

Cargo will be received at the Company's Godowns, Nimtollah Ghat, until noon, of Monday, the 27th.

THE Str. "CHUNAR" will leave Goalundo for Assam on Thursday, the 30th instant.

Cargo will be received at the Company's Godowns, No. 4, Fairlie Palace, up till noon of Tuesday, the 28th.

Goods forwarded to Goalundo for this vessel will be chargeable with Railway Freight from Calcutta to Goalundo in addition to the regular Freight of this Company.

Passengers should leave for Goalundo by Train of Wednesday, the 29th.

CACHAR LINE NOTICE

REGULAR WEEKLY SERVICE.

Steamers now leave Calcutta for Cachar and Intermediate Stations every Tuesday and Chattuck downward every Tuesday.

A Steamer and "FLAT" will leave Calcutta for Cachar on Tuesday, the 28th instant.

Cargo will be received at the Company's Godowns, Nimtollah Ghat, up till noon of Monday, the 27th.

For further information regarding rates of Freight or passage money, apply to,

4, Fairlie Palace, G. J. SCOTT,
Calcutta, 23rd March 1876. *Secretary.*

BABU BASANTA KUMAR DATTA,

Homœopathic Practitioner.

No. 20. Sunker Halder's Lane. Ahiritolah.

JUST ARRIVED
FROM ENGLAND.

MEDICINES, AND ALL REQUISITES, TO BE HAD AT—

DATTA'S HOMŒOPATHIC LABORATORY
No. 312, CHITPORE ROAD, BUTTOLAH, CALCUTTA.

BABU RADHAKANTA GHOSH

HOMŒOPATHIC PRACTITIONER,

12, College, Square.

Is practising here on moderate terms.

SMITH, STANISTREET & CO

Pharmaceutical Chemists & Druggists

BY APPOINTMENT

To His Excellency the Right Hon'ble
LORD NORTHBROOK, G.M.S.I.,
Governor-General of India,
&c. &c.

SYRUP OF LACTATE OF IRON.

Prepared from the original receipe. Lactate of Iron, in various forms of preparation, have been in use in France, and generally through the Continent of Europe, for some years past, and is highly esteemed as one of the most valuable Chalybeate Tonic Remedies yet introduced. The Syrup, being the most agreeable as well as convenient form of administration, is in most general use. It is a most valuable remedy in the following diseases:—Chlorosis or Green Sickness, Leucorrhœa, Neuralgia, Enlargement of the Spleen. In combination with quinine, it has also been very successfully used in the cure of fever, while to persons of delicate constitution, enfeebled by disease, it is invaluable. In bottles, Rs. 2 each.

SYRUP OF THE PHOSPHATE OF IRON Rs. 2 per bottle.

SYRUP OF PHOSPHATE OF IRON AND STRYCHNINE, Rs. 2 per bottle.

SYRUP OF PHOSPHATE OF IRON AND QUININE, Price Rs. 2-8 per bottle.

SYRUP OF PHOSPHATE OF IRON, QUININE AND STRYCHNINE, DR. AITKIN'S TRIPLE TONIC SYRUP,) Rs. 2-8 per bottle.

Smith, Stanistreet & Co.

Invite special attention to the following rates, the quality guaranteed as the best procurable:—

Pure Ærated Waters.

Made from Pure Water, obtained by the new process through the Patent Charcoal Filters.

			Rs	As.
Ærated plain (Triple Ærated), per doz.			0	12
Soda Water	ditto	"	0	12
Gingerade	ditto	"	1	[illegible]
Lemonade	ditto	"	[illegible]	[illegible]
Tonic (Quinine)	ditto	"	[illegible]	[illegible]

The Cash must be sent with the order to obtain advantage of the above rates.

!!! হুকা !!!
!!! HOOKAHS !!!

ENGLISH made Hookahs of various choice designs, colours and sizes ranging in price from Rs. 2 to 5 each, 60 designs to choose from. Apply to

BADANAUTH CHOWDRY,
2?3, Jorasanko.

যৌবনে যোগিনী ।

NEW HISTORICAL TRAGEDY

BY

GOPAL CHUNDER MOOKERJEE.

Price, Re. 1, postage 2 ans.

To be had at 5?, Grey Street, Shobabazar, and Sanskrit Press Depository.

NATIONAL COMPANY.

HOMŒOPATHIC CHAMISTS AND PUBLISHER

SUPPLY ALL KINDS OF

HOMŒOPATHIC MEDICINES, BOOKS CASES AND OTHER REQUISITES,

12 COLLEGE SQUARE,

Calcutta.

Printed and published by M. M. Bukkit, at the "INDIAN MIRROR" Press, No. 15, College Square, for the Proprietor.

The Indian Mirror.

SUNDAY EDITION.

VOL XV.] CALCUTTA, SUNDAY, APRIL 2, 1876. { REGISTERED AT THE GENERAL POST OFFICE. } [No. 78

CONTENTS.

Editorial Notes

THE National Indian Association does many useful things. One of these is that it organizes expeditions to interesting places, under the leadership of competent persons who explain all the objects and associations connected therewith. The writer witnessed one of a very interesting expedition to the Tower of London under the guidance of Mr. Henworth Dixon, who has written three volumes on the Tower. About the end of the last month, another expedition was organized to St. Paul's Cathedral when Cannon Gregory showed the party over the place, and explained everything. Many Indian gentlemen were present in the party.

THERE are few men who use the English language with greater mastery and skill than Dr Martineau. Yet Professor Tyndall in replying to his criticisms in the *Fortnightly Review* censures him for want of precision. The peculiar character of Dr. Martineau is shown when he owns the justice of the censure, and with humility acknowledges that his writing is deficient in precision and lucidity. He does this when the best part of the English press gives as its deliberate opinion that Professor Tyndall does not understand his own position and that Dr. Martineau has most unanswerably proved the inconsistencies of his statements.

THE following table may not be unacceptable to those who wish to classify sins and sinners, and also determine their own position in the moral world. We are apt to congratulate ourselves if we have only cast away the more serious forms of vice and crime, not remembering that evil in less hideous and more insidious forms still dwells within us. Men may have ceased to be murderers and adulterers, but they may still cherish covetousness and sensuality in their hearts, in their thoughts and desires. Those who have been delivered from these, may still be guilty before God of such sins as worldliness, insufficient realization of Divine presence, absence of attachment to the enemy, and other sins mentioned in class V. below. The table shows that continued growth in devotion faith and purity is necessary. In commending the table to our readers we do not say it is complete or exhaustive. It may be taken as a suggestive classification.

Class I.	Murder, Adultery, Perjury Theft, Assault, Fraud, Unbelief.
Class II.	Untruthfulness, Oppression, Misappropriation, Lustful eyes, Calumny, Revenge, Injustice, Unkind words, Blasphemy, Scepticism.
Class III.	Anger, Envy, Jealousy, Pride, Covetousness, Lustful excitement, Unkindness, Desire to tell untruth or otherwise [mislead, Unpunctuality, Hypocrisy, Misanthropism, Desire to be unjust. Unsteady belief.
Class IV.	Irregularity in prayer, Not going to church, Diversion of thoughts during prayer, Dryness of heart, Indifference, Despondency, Selfishness, Worldliness, Frivolity, Waste of time, energy and wealth, Unbrotherliness.
Class V.	Preferring the world to things spiritual, Not loving the enemy, Want of passionate attachment to God and man, Absence of enthusiasm, Insufficient realization of Divine presence, Distaste for sustained communion.

WILL the Christian community inform us what it is they conceive before them when they address their prayers to Jesus? They evidently ignore the possibility of seeing an Eternal and Incomprehensible Spirit, and they prefer an incarnate deity to the Invisible. We are ready to admit that man finds some comfort and consolation in approaching a personal and visible divinity, and recoils from a vast and unknowable spirit. But how can those who have never seen Jesus nor his likeness conceive him, or pray unto him. To us this is a problem which no amount of sophistry can solve. We have often thought of it, but have found no satisfactory solution. Men may speak of Christ as an historical character in the third person; they may revere 'him' and follow 'him.' But to sit in his presence and address him as 'thou,'—this seems morally impossible, unless we suppose there is a photograph or some other likeness to help a direct conception of the person Christ. In the absence of a knowledge of his features, the doctrine of his incarnation is of no avail. For of what profit is it to believe that he had a face, eyes, and nose, and ears if there are no means of realizing exactly these features? No man can conjure up a bodily Christ, by fancy or devotion, and say honestly that was the real Christ of history. And if the real body of Christ is not known, men in preferring an incarnate deity to the Spirit of God, prefer one unknown quantity to another. Amidst all this confusion connected with the metaphysics of Christ, his loving spirit is dear to us all. Whatever his face and features, his spirit must be loved and revered wherever his name has gone forth. The body-Christ is nothing; the spirit-Christ is all in all. To us Christ means nothing but an amiable and sweet spirit.

A LARGE library is a modern institution. People who have large libraries seldom read the books they possess. Formerly the case was different. Men owned a very small number of books, and read them so thoroughly that it was not safe to argue with them respecting the merits of any one. In fact books had to be copied with one's own hand, as the Pandits do in this country even at the present day. Half a dozen volumes would form a complete library. Ambassadors used to be sent from France to Rome to beg a copy of Cicero's Orations, or Quintilian's Institutes. A famous Abbot with incredible labor and expense got together a library of one hundred and fifty volumes, and this was considered a wonder. In 1494 the library of the Bishop of Winchester contained parts of seventeen books only! When he borrowed a Bible from a certain convent he had to give a heavy bond carefully drawn up that he would return the book uninjured. What a pity such bonds are not required from book-borrowers in these days, who never return anything they take away. When any one presented a book to a monastery, the gift was celebrated with great solemnity, the book was laid on the altar, and salvation was conferred on the donor, and when a new book was purchased, influential men were invited to be witnesses of the fact. "The Convent of Rochester," we are told, "every year pronounced an irrevocable sentence of damnation on any one who should dare to steal a certain Latin translation of Aristotle, or even obliterate a title." Such was the value of books when they were scarce, men were learned then, much more so than they are now, when there is such a glut of librabies everywhere. Possess a few books, but good ones, and what is more important read them thoroughly.

ENGLISH Unitarianism is definitely taking shape. The controversy on the subject of the name and uses of the Unitarian buildings proposed to be erected in London, is still fresh in the mind of the public. Though that controversy ended in the satisfaction of no party, still the far-sighted liberality of views expressed by Mr. Martineau, and his followers, considerably changed the position and spirit of Unitarianism in the minds at least of the rising generation of that community. One result of this change is observable in the controversy that greatly agitates the Unitarian body just now. There has been a proposal before the British and Foreign Unitarian Association for sometime to publish in England some of the works of Theodore Parker at the society's expense. A somewhat excited opposition is made to this proposal by a number of gentlemen who may be said to belong to the conservative section of the community, their objection being that Parker attacked Christianity, disowned the Christian name, and should not therefore find support or circulation among Unitarian Christians. The advanced school on the other hand are of opinion that Parker's works should undoubtedly be published by the Society, because though he did attack some forms of Christianity,—those that are more or less full of supernaturalism and superstition,—he never attacked Christ, but on the contrary always expressed the highest reverence for his character and teachings. Now the old question recurs, namely what is Unitarian Christianity? What is essential to that creed? It is very well-known that there are endless shades and grades of opinions among the Unitarians. There are men who admit a *very* large portion of the supernatural element in the New Testament; there are others again who throw almost the whole miraculous department of Christianity over board. All these men support the Unitarian Association, and have their representatives in the governing body of that institution. The utmost perplexity arises when such difference of views arises as on the present occasion. The conservative section is represented by the wealthy and socially influential members of the community, and the progressive section by the earnestness, intelligence, and youth in it. Though a separation seems often imminent a separation is exceedingly undesirable, it will weaken both parties, without benefitting the public at all. Under these circumstances let us hope some effectual compromise may be made which without interfering with the progress of freedom and toleration, will not unnecessarily shock the prejudices of the elder party. The Society, says the *Inquirer*, is founded on "broad principles," "How liberal the spirit on which the Society was formed, is evinced by the absence of all definition, whether of Unitarianism, or of Christianity. *To every man's conscience and good sense is it left to decide what is Unitarianism, and what is Christianity.*" If this be so why should there be so much opposition to the views of one who decided his Christianity for himself? We shall wait the issue of this controversy with interest.

SINS NOT COMMITTED

SINNER! thou art busy in atoning for the sins thou hast committed. But wilt thou not atone for such of thy sins as are not committed? Often must such startling questions press upon souls that have learnt to measure the enormity of hidden sins. The root of the tree of corruption lies within in all its hideousness and vileness. Only a few evil deeds, words, and thoughts appear outside as fruits. The root is not to be measured by the fruits. A few drops only come trickling down from the ocean of impurity in the depths of the heart. These alone are taken into account as sins both by those who are guilty, and those who sit as judges. The latter seek to punish them and prevent their recurrence; the former atone for them and try to be free from their bondage. All discipline both personal and social, all reformatory agencies among men are directed against the extermination of sins that are actually committed in thought, word, or deed. Cut the branches, that is the essence of the world's ethics. Rejoice if you have ceased to do and think evil,—that is the highest congratulation an unthinking world is capable of bestowing. Where the hand, the tongue, and the mind do no evil, there, there is paradise,—so says, earthly faith. Theism, unearthly and divine, proclaims a higher standard of purity. Accordiug to it there is much deeper evil than comes to the surface. One perhaps out of a hundred sins lying in man's heart is committed in actual consciousness; the remaining ninety-nine lie hid potentially. A man steals twice and thinks of doing so ten times. The world's highest morality would charge him with only twelve cases of theft. But these are no measure of the real source of all these sins, namely covetousness, which is perhaps, a hundred times more filthy and terrible than its dozen menifestations. It is the deadly viper that clings to the heart that we call sin, and until that is dead and gone, none should believe that evil has been thoroughly subdued. Sensuality, dishonesty, envy, pride, selfishness,—are these to be measured by their actual manifestations? They may not appear for months as sins in actual consciousness, and yet they are there. They are asleep, if not awake; but they are none the less real because asle p. Who among us is not proud or selfish? And yet who can measure his pride and selfishness, or count how many sins of either description he has actually committed? Will Heaven in passing judgment upon us, take notice only of the half a dozen proud and selfish thoughts and deeds which have defiled our lives? No. We may *feel* pride or envy only once in the day, but we *are* proud and *envious* the whole day. Selfishness may be excited into actual exercise two or three times every month, but it *dwells* in the heart throughout the month. Particular vicious inclinations and proclivities are called into play by certain circumstances which act as exciting causes; but whether excited or not they may dwell potentially in the heart. Man is responsible not merely for the sins he actually commits, but also for the seeds of sin, the passions and weaknesses he cherishes within. Sins, though not committed, and which perhaps will never be committed, are sins in our hearts if we are only capable of committing them. The question is not whether we are dishonest, jealous or covetous, but whether if temptations come we are likely to fall into these sins. Conscious strength is the measure of holiness, such strength as can overcome temptations. We must not only leave all sins we have committed, but likewise all those sins which we may commit, and which lie in the depths of our carnal nature in the form of conscious tendencies, or mere weaknesses. How difficult is it to be pure according to this high standard!

THE VIRGIN.

WHAT is there to admire in woman? Her beauty is often a snare and a vanity. Her affection is often selfish and worldly. Her fortitude is frequently no better than an instinct. It is woman's purity that is really deep and beautiful. Generally speaking women are *much more* pure than men. At least that is our experience in this country. It is the flattery, meanness, and wickedness of men that tempt them. Weak in body, deficient in the outward means of self-protection, Providence has gifted woman with moral safe-guards that effectually resist and overcome the lawlessness of man. We are fully aware of the fact that when woman is bad, she is *very* bad. But we know equally well that when she is good, she is *very* good. The majority of that sex, however, are neither very good nor very bad. They lead petty little selfish commonplace lives, whose principal occupations are living nicely, looking nice, seeing nice people, having nice husbands and children. The entire creation and all objects in it are characterized by two words *nice*, and *not nice*. We are not going to speak to-day of such highly respectable people, whose number, we are deeply sorry and alarmed to find, is spreading in this country very much. Those butterflies of pleasure daily burn in hundreds in the fire of the world's temptations and trials. The virgin does not come from their ranks. It is the modest tender purity which they worship in the mother of Christ, that we are here speaking of. The sweet cheerful holiness of heart, untemptable and unaware of the least stain of evil within, that makes the virgin. Is there any woman in our midst whose highest ambition in life is to show the example of the deepest and most glorious purity attainable? Blessed is that community in which there are such women. Everybody in the world marries, and gives in marriage. What glory is there in living as others live with family and friends, husband and brother, amidst worldliness and carnality? What glory is there in being rich, and having pleasures, and means of pleasure at command? Thousands have these and who knows of them? Wives become widows, and widows become wives, and the rich become poor, and the pleasure-loving become unhappy for life every day; and their number cannot be counted. What good do they do in the world, who remembers them, or cares to take the least notice of them? They live and die unknown, unsympathized with. Poor and petty is the heart of the woman who wants to be like one of them. On the contrary let there be one who profoundly aspires, earnestly struggles, and prays to glorify and elevate her sex by the example of her unselfishness, affection, and purity of life; let there be one who cheerfuly suffers with the suffering, weeps with the unhappy, rejoices with those who are humbly glad of God's mercies shown in due season; let there be one true daughter of God, a virgin who has consecrated her life to the service of her Father; and such a woman will be prized, honored, blessed on earth, and rewarded in Heaven with the crown of eternal joy. God is not our Father only, but our Mother also. The womanly tenderness of the Divine nature, the womanly wisdom, the stainless womanly purity, the womanly solicitude for all are but little known to the world. The highest, the profoundest, the most beautiful virginity is in our God. Our divine Mother is the only true Virgin, the mother of a yet undefiled in eternal purity. The fragrance and beauty of that virginity feel all things pure and good. Men have preached and shown in their lives the fatherhood, the manliness, the holiness of God. And now will no woman come forward, and show us the motherhood, the womanliness, the virginity of the Divine Being? Can there be an object of higher and holier ambition for her in existence? Will no Brahmo father devote his whole energy and attention to train up his daughters, and dear ones with this holy object? Before an imaginary Virgin, imaginary but not unpossessed of real and noble virtues, Christian countries have bowed for centuries; her place formerly lower, is now higher than the throne of her glorious son; in her name thousands of women, young, handsome, and wealthy have cheerfully renounced all hope of worldly happiness and renown for God's service and man's good; the name of Our Mother Mary breathes an odour of sweet sanctity and divine affection in many a sin-stricken, and sorrow-stricken Catholic home; the beautiful form of the Madonna and Child represents the masterpieces of Italian painting. It is all for the sake of an idea, the idea of the tender, modest, unworldly, unspeakably loving purity of God's nature. Will this idea find no representation in the Brahmo Somaj? If there be any woman in our midst who will take it up, cherish it in her heart, sacrifice all prospects of life before it, she will sanctify our homes, our hearts, and our churches. She will earn honor and glory, before which earthly crowns fade and shrink away. Let the Brahmo Somaj be but the mother of virgins, and she will be the home of holiness for all time.

REVIEW.

(From an English Lady.)

AN interesting article has appeared in the January number of the British Quarterly Review, to which it may, perhaps, be worthwhile to draw the attention of your readers. *The Hindu Woman Real and Ideal* is its name.

The writer in a forcible style speaks of the part played by woman in India in old days, judging by the touching stories of them in your classical literature, where the lovely characters of Sita and Savitri make such deep impression upon us, and give the highest examples of what womanhood is capable in any age or country.

A short quotation here will give the best notion of our auther's *Real* woman of the past.

"In Vedic times, to respect woman was not only thought to be right and proper, but was also enjoined as a sacred and most important duty. Hard out-door work was not to be apportioned to her, for her place was at the domestic hearth, making it happy by her presence, soothing man in his labors, consoling him in his sorrows, and moderating his reason by her wisdom. Man is commanded to protect her with tenderness and to please her with beautiful gifts. If he laughs at her sufferings, woe be unto him at his hour of need! If he despises her, 'he despises his mother.' If he takes advantage of her weakness to persecute her or despoil her of her property, he is guilty of an odious crime. If he incurs her curse, he will bring down the vengeance of God. A young girl is free to select the bridegroom of her choice, and her family is bound to provide for her a suitable dowry to which her brother is recommended to add out of his own portion, the finest heifer of his herd, the purest saffron of his cross, the loveliest jewel in his casket. Her husband should treat her with deference and consideration; he should be unto her amongst her children even as one of them."

Further on, and after mentioning the Mohomedan influence on Hindu Society and the subsequent seclusion of woman, the writer goes on to speak of Indian ladies of the present day, and to give charming extracts from letters of lady members of the Brahmo Somaj to an english lady friend. Perhaps we may be permitted again to quote, and from one of these.

"Dear English sister, having received your letter full of love, I gained indescribable joy. I never for one moment dreamt in my mind that it would be possible for me to receive so much kindness from a sweet sincere-hearted sister like you; all this is from the unasked for kindness of the merciful God. With gratitude do I bow at the feet of our Father, who is an ocean of tenderness, and through whose liberal kindness I have been able to enjoy such pleasure. Dear sister, I greet all of you with inward gratitude, you who strive so much for our good. To God do I pray that the Merciful Father may bring to pass the fulfilment of the good wishes of all of you for the happiness of the world. I hope that you will not fail to accomplish what you propose to do for your Indian sisters' good. How much friendship do you all give my dear husband; for that I from my heart render gratitude to you all. You are learning Bengali; seeing your handwriting, I was very much pleased, I have a great wish to learn English, but many things hinder me so much, I am not able to do it. When my dear husband comes back to our country, I think I shall be able to learn. I now study Bengali. In our country, acquirement of learning is very difficult for a female. There are no schools for young women. If her husband is near she may learn a little, or from a brother or other near relation a little may be learnt; otherwise it is not easy to learn anything. I formerly when my husband was close by, used to learn a little; now that he has to dwell in a foreign country I am not learning any thing. I do every day some household work, and in leisure time occasionally write and read. We with our own hands cook and prepare food for our relations. I am living with my near relations. Make known to me with whom you live? What more shall I say? I think the letters of the honored wives of—and—and others have pleased you very much, and my letter will not be like theirs, for compared with me they must be better taught. They are ladies living in the capital, and learning in the school for young ladies called the Female Normal School. Its otherwise with me who living in a village, learn by myself alone; therefore whether this writing will be able to give your mind a little joy, of that I cannot be sure; however this be, I send this little letter trusting to your kindness. If you accept it, I shall be happy? Sister, I now take leave, may God fulfil your good wishes!"

We are evidently left to infer from this, and other equally interesting extracts that modern daughters of India may be found, in no way unworthy successors of your classical heroines, and that the these letters show by their sweet words, fair promise for the future of your country. We could have wished for more details here as to the work of your church and of the school of thought in which these *real* women of the present were formed.

But in spite of this shortcoming the article is particularly satisfactory, coming as it does from an orthodox Christian, and one quite unconnected with your church, and therefore showing the wide-spread interest felt here in your countrywomen, and their efforts after higher education. One more extract, and we will end this short notice which by no means does justice to the article before us.

* * * "it is our plain duty without abating our own exertions" (for the good of India) "thankfully to welcome those of men, pure-minded, and courageous, whatever may be their religious opinions, who strive no less than we for the time when regenerate India shall give voice to the silent orison of every pious Brahman "greater than the sun, that sun's supremacy, God let us adore, which may well direct."

Provincial

ANNIVERSARY OF THE BOMBAY PRARTHANA SOMAJ.

[FROM OUR OWN CORRESPONDENT.]

BOMBAY, *the 22nd March* 1876.

I SEND the following few lines in connection with the Anniversary of our Somaj. Tuesday the 21st instant was the day of the Utsab. This, Utsab was celebrated for 4 days. On Saturday evening the proceedings commenced, and on Tuesday evening they ended. The proceedings were as follow:—There was a service on Saturday evening. It was conducted by Mr. Sadashiva Pant Kelker. He is a youngman full of energy and activity. In his sermon he alluded to the proceedings that were to follow, and urged the necessity of taking some bolder steps than what they had been accustomed to do. On Sunday morning there was text reading. At 2 P.M., in the afternoon of the same day a report in connection with the funds of the building was read. That was followed by a religious discussion, in which the members as well as the outsiders took part. The subject was the Vedas as the revealed books of God. Many spoke but few to the point. Mr. Shanker Pandurung Pandit who was in the chair, said that every one of us ought to study the Vedas, and if not, we should ask a Veda-knowing man in whom we may have confidence; and if our inquiry tended in favor of the Vedas we should take them as the true and revealed books of God. But we must inquire for ourselves. Mr. Shankur Pandurung Pandit is a great Sanskrit Scholar, and is shortly going to publish a translation of the Riga Veda Sanhita into Marhatti, English and Sanskrit. It is to be published in a pamphlet form. However, this has nothing to do with our present purpose. The discussion ended, and the usual Sunday evening service commenced at 6 P.M. in Gujrathi. As I do not understand that language I cannot give you the substance of it. On Monday morning there was individual prayer. Every member who liked, prayed. In the evening at 6 P.M., there was an English lecture. Mr Shanker Panduran Pandit was the lecturer. The subject was "The Aryan Sacrifices with special reference to our duties and faith." The lecture was very learned and instructive. He explained to us the different forms of sacrifices. He showed to us that the sacrifices as prescribed in the "Brahmans," were of later growth, and that the original sacrifices prior to the supremacy of Priesthood, were very simple and not intricate as those prescribed in the "Brahmans." Even the word "Yadnya" had a quite different meaning from what it was made to assume at the period of the supremacy of Brahmans. It meant only worship, not with garlands. In short, sacrifice meant nothing more than giving to god or gods the best of one's possessions. It was food (including the flesh of cow, sheep &c.) Our ancestors, the Rishis, asked from the gods rain, pastures for their cattle, &c. These were the most valuable things they asked from gods or goddesses. At that time there was nothing like officiating priesthood for offering sacrifices. However, as the wealth of our ancestors increased, things to be offered for sacrifice to gods also multiplied. But as yet there was no priestcraft. He cited many hymns from the Vedas in illustration of what he said. As the Brahmans became supreme in the land they were changed into something like special hymns to be chanted on the occasion of special sacrifices. This they did in order to assert their supremacy. Afterwards the holy thing was polluted so much so that human sacrifices came into practice. However, if this period be excepted the principle of sacrifices was not changed. In fact, the same principle was applicable to all the sacrifices in the world. Even the Christians maintained this principle. The King Harischandra made a sacrifice of his kingdom in order to fulfil a promise he had made. Rama suffered all the troubles of *banabas* (forestliving) for the fulfilment of his father's promise The great Saukhya Muni sacrificed his kingdom, and became founder of a religious system. The principle of *sutti* had the same origin. The martyrs of the reformation set a noble example of this principle of sacrifice. In short, wherever we see, we see that great things were not achieved without great sacrifice. The lecturer made an appeal in conclusion to the members and those assembled, to consider their religious condition, their political condition, and their social condition. He put to them three questions, and left the solution of those questions to themselves. These questions are as follow:—Is there any occasion for sacrifice? What have we to sacrifice? Are we prepared for sacrifice? If I have succeeded in giving you a clear idea of the lecture, you will see the importance of it. I need not describe it at length. I request the lecturer to publish his lecture in a pamphlet form. Thus ended the proceedings of Monday.

On Tuesday, the 21st instant, there was morning service. It was conducted by Mr. Chintamon Kunundiker As I was not present at the time, so I cannot give you the substance of it. In the afternoon a sort of nine years' history in the form of a report, was read by the Secretary of the Somaj. It was from the begining to the present period. The only thing worthy of notice in the report, was that the Somaj received an impetus from the visit of Babu Protap Chunder Muzumdar. Afterwards a hot discussion followed among the members themselves as to what progress they had made in the past nine years. All the members admitted that they had done nothing in the right direction, and if they had done anything at all, it was very little. They have postponed the discussion to next Sunday. At 6 P. M. the evening service was conducted by Professor Bhandaeker. There were separate hymns published for the day. The Somaj building was full of men The whole scene was very impressive. On one side of the pulpit there was the chorus party, and on the other there were ladies with shawls on and with their young ones. To my mind, there was nothing more convincing of the usefulness of congregation worship than the appearance of the Somaj on the evening of the 21st instant. The idea of so many men and women joining together to worship the one true god was a most delightful one. The text of the sermon was from "Bhagvatgita." It ran as follows:—"I will take incarnation whenever there will be any confusion about religion in the world." The learned Professor said that we need not take the literal meaning of the text, but the present state of the different religions of the world and a general craving for religious life are enough to demand attention from God; and therefore to remedy the evil God sent this Brahmo Dhurma through the instrumentality of his children. Now, Sir, I conclude and hope to see the day, to give you an account of the tenth anniversary of our Somaj, better in form and better in substance.

Devotional

O GOD, our Divine Mother, we pray to thee for the spotless spiritual virginity that dwells with thee for ever. Make all evil thoughts utterly foreign to me; wash out all the many stains of my heart; and cause all vile imaginations to be impossible. Enable me to devote all my days, and all my powers to thy holy service, and the good of mankind. Mine eyes, mine hands, mine mouth, my whole being wash thou clean, and void of offence. Our Mother as thou dost combine tenderness with purity, and art beautiful only in thy goodness, so cause my soul to be like unto thee. Let me honor sanctity in all, in men, and in women especially; let me bow in deep humility and reverence before those daughters of thine whom thou hast honored with the eternal virginity of thy nature.

THE saints above seem to say unto me,

O God, that my prayers are hollow and my communion unreal. Compared to their faith, their devotion, and their joy, my spiritual progress is as nothing. What I have known, and tasted of thy sweetness is but a drop compared to the ocean of blessedness in which they live immersed. Make this conviction strong, O my God, that it may curb my pride, and make me always humble. It is a pleasure to know how little I am when that knowledge is accompanied by the hope that even this my little life will expand into the fuller and heavenlier life of the saints above in the fullness of time, and that I shall live to be quite as happy as they are now.

WE pray unto thee, God of Love, for the welfare of all our opponents and enemies in the world, and of all those who hate and curse us. There are many whom we have irritated by our misdeeds and vices, our pride, and selfishness, and our insolence. Others have become our enemies because of our reformed faith and practices. Others dislike us because they do not know us and often misunderstand us. Father do good to all such men, and help us to forgive and forget their enmity. Teach us to love them as our brethren in spite of their antagonism. May we always bear in mind thy holy injunction that though others may be our sworn enemies we have no right to be enemies unto others!

Brahmo Hymns

BLESSED thy forbearance! Being the Holy God thou art seeing with thine own eyes while sitting before them, how great is the impurity of thy children. How dost thou always bear such indignity, being the Supremely Righteous Lord of the universe? In a twinkling of the eye thou canst destroy the wicked hypocrisy of a hundred infidels. Blessed be thy patience and forgiveness, thy generous dealings, thy loving chastisement. Thou knowest how to do good. For their welfare thou hast given thy children those inestimable treasures, conscience and freedom. As a witness thou art near us day and night, and yet I am bold to do evil, neither shame nor fear have I. Shame to our wicked lives; we hear not the words of such a friend.

LORD, what shall I give unto thee? All is thine; what is there that is mine? Thou art unfolding the flowers of love in the heart. Do thou accept them; they are thine.

How shall I say what sweet beauty I saw on entering the do rs of the heart. Wonderful, formless, not comparable; what shall I say of the sweet beauty I saw on opening the doors of the heart. I have seen that sight as difficult to see. Blessed be His mercy, blessed! With what joy I saw on opening the doors of the heart.

The Brahmo Somaj.

A BRAHMO Marriage was celebrated on last Thursday evening not far from our office. The bride-groom Babu GobURdhone Mullick is a Dispensary Compounder of Allahabad, and the bride Sreemati Dakhyani is about seventeen years old. We were very sorry to notice that the marriage ceremony was often interrupted by a great crowd of uninvited people from the neighbourhood who should not have been admitted into the house. The solemnity was marred, and it was with difficulty the rabble could be persuaded to disperse. The gentlemen entrusted with the arrangements of these marriages ought to remember always that the reform is still exceedingly unpopular, and therefore liable to rude interruption. In future we hope greater privacy and solemnity will be secured for Brahmo marriages.

IT is with sincere pain that we make room for the following appeal circulated among the members of the *Prarthana Somaj* of Bombay on the occasion of their late anniversary. Those who were present at that joyful gathering must have been as much pained as we are to read it. But we must confess with humiliation there is much truth in it. Though anonymous, there can be little doubt that it is the production of a member of the Somaj itself, one of the few perhaps who have found the courage to act according to their professions. May we hope it will do some good among those for whom it is intended!

AN APPEAL TO THE MEMBERS OF THE PRARTHANA SOMAJ.

Brethren,—Your Somaj is now nine years old. You have a beautiful building and you number amongst yourselves men of rank, reputation, education and wealth. You have for the last nine years preached outwardly the True and the Living God, you have professed to give up idolatry and break the abominable barriers of the caste system. You have besides this professed to learn and teach several other minor reforms for the salvation of the soul, and the regeneration of the sinful Hindu.

From the outward appearance of your place of worship, from the sermons preached from week to week, from your outward conduct and from your professions you ought to be quite a different set of people now.

But Alas! such is not the case. You are hypocrites. You deceive yourselves and the public. Perhaps, you are at a greater distance from the Almighty than those simple and innocent idolaters whose minds are not perverted and who, though misdirected, have pure faith and true devotion.

On the day of Judgment there will be no excuse for you to plead when you stand before the Creator and the Preserver of this Universe, God Almighty whom you could have loved and adored as the only Living and the True God.

From the recent Marriage ceremonies, the Small-pox processions and the Thread ceremonies, that some of you have celebrated, one cannot make out why you assemble at all in the House of God and pollute the pulpit and the seats in it. You are not Christians, you are not Mahomedans, you are not Hindus. Who are you then? Prarthana Somajists you are not. You say one way, and behave just the other way. I beseech you to see what I mean, I don't wish to insult you. I am not your enemy. I am really one who is grieved to see the unsettled state of the rule of conduct you pursue, one in words and just the other in practice. Brethren, in the name of the Almighty in whom the world lives, moves and has its being, I entreat you to come out as real reformers and worshippers of the God of the Universe, Omnipotent, Omniscient and All Love. Moral courage you have none, hypocrisy you have enough, you can deceive human beings, but God you cannot.

He reads your minds. Do you not bow down before idols? Do you not fear the brute force of superstition and Brahmanism? Do you not show a want of real love for truth which alone is the salvation of your human souls?

Break through the barrier of caste. Don't say that you have an old mother or father at home, who will be grieved. Look upon all men as your brethren, and eat and drink from all hands just as freely in public as you *do* in private. I entreat you to follow the dictates of your conscience in spite of trials, temptations and ex-communications. Reforms and particularly religious reforms, and more particularly the worship of the Living God requires a great sacrifice which, I assure you, you are not prepared to make.

All your movements are superficial for worldly good (if any there be) and for frail reputation. Great sacrifices were made by the reformers of Europe and India. I need not tell you that several were martyrs for the cause of reform. I emphatically assure you that you sadly want moral courage, and so long as this is wanting, your Somaj, your prayers, your sham devotion will never succeed.

Oh God send Thy Spirit to these Heathen Prarthna Somaj Reformers. May they have the courage to love Thee in private as well as in the public for Thy sake only. Amen.

MORAL COURAGE AND REFORM.

Literary.

IN the *Contemporary Review* for March, Mr. J. Dacosta, in an article on "Irrigation Works and the Permanent Settlement in India," argues in favor of extending the system of a permanent settlement of the land tax, which he contends has worked so successfully in Bengal, to the other provinces into which it has not yet been introduced. In the provinces in which the land revenue is subject to periodical revision, indigence, he says, is the normal condition of the ryots; there is apt to be a difficulty in collecting the revenue; and land is allowed to go out of cultivation, notwithstanding the irrigation works introduced by the Government.

OWEN MEREDITH (Lord Lytton), says the *Pioneer*, has a great example before him. Warren Hastings was a confirmed poet; the first thing he did every morning was to write a copy of indifferent verses, but for all that he was a splendid Governor-General.

BUTLER'S ANALOGY edited by Rev. Joseph Cummings, LL. D., D. D. of the Wesleyan University, and published by Nelson & Phillips, has been laid upon our table. It is just such a book as one who has had the benefit of the Dr.'s instruction in the class room would expect to come from his hands. He has relieved the text of some of its obscurities by breaking up and re-arranging the more difficult passages, and by valuable notes of his own and of other eminent critics of the work. The marginal titles are also very valuable. It will undoubtedly supplant in a large degree the older editions of this long used text book.

Scienti ic

SIR JHON LUBBOCK has been reading a paper at the Linnæan Society on ants. He was of opinion that ants did not possess the power of making communications about route and localities, that they had organs of smell but not of hearing, and that while they might care for a companion that died laden with food, as a rule they showed no affection for ants that had been immersed in water from one to ten hours.

A DEPUTATION recently waited upon the Duke of Richmond to urge the Government to afford increased support to scientific instruction. Another deputation invited Her Majesty's Government action to provide for the registration of qualified female medical practitioners.

Gleanings

RELIGION NOT A RESTRAINT.

PEOPLE talk about religion being a restraint upon men. In some senses, it is a restraint. But this is not its chief idea. There are in men certain destructive tendencies,—passions, appetites and inordinate affections which need the curb; and religion operates as a curb upon these and reins them in. But it has other and larger uses than this. Fetters and curbs and gags do not represent it. It plants more than it uproots. When the work of correction is ended, it has only just begun its operations in the soul—operations which will continue in force eternally. Negatives do not express religious duty. We love to think that religious life means the growth of all the faculties, and not a slow strangulation of them. Religion no more cramps a man than wings do a bird or fins do a fish. Piety is not a ship at anchor on a level sea; it is a ship in motion, with every sail set and swelling with wind and the waters around it crested with white. Christianity makes a man active vibrant, tense. Great injury has been done to religion by teaching people to regard it as a mild form of slavery, in which people consent to be tied up that they may not hurt themselves or others. But there is no such religion as this, at least in the New Testament. The gospel Christ taught, is a gospel of liberty. It is a stimulant to man's energies not a narcotic. It makes him a doer and not a hearer. "Why stand ye here all the day idle?"—*Golden Rule.*

LATEST NEWS.

MR. T. J. CHICHELE PLOWDEN, Officiating Under-Secretary to the Government of India in the Home Department, has obtained three weeks' privilege leave of absence. Mr. J. A. Bourdillon will officiate for him.

THE services of Colonel J. E. Gastrell, Superintendent of Revenue Surveys and Deputy Surveyor General, are replaced at the disposal of the Military Department.

MR. C. P. L. MACAULAY, of the Bengal Civil Service, is appointed to officiate as Under-Secretary to the Government of India in the Department of Revenue, Agriculture and Commerce during the absence of Mr. C. J. Lyall.

THE Viceroy and Governor-General is pleased to confer upon the under-mentioned gentlemen the title of "Khan Bahadur" as personal distinction:—Muhammad Hadi-ulla, Anwar-ul-Din, Abdul Ali, Shadi sons of the late Rashed-ul-Dowla, Bahadur, of the Carnatic family, and Muhammad Abdul Bari, Shadi grandson of the same gentleman.

DR. T. OLDHAM having resigned his appointment as Superintendent of the Geological Survey, Mr. H. B. Medlicott is appointed to succeed him.

A MEMORIAL has been submitted to the Bombay Government by the Sirdars and inhabitants of Las Beyla on behalf of the Jam of that place, who was deported from Sind to the Deccan some six years ago.

THERE is a rumour at Baroda that H. H. the Guickwar with H. H. Jamnabai and Sir T. Madhowrao were to have left Baroda for Bombay yesterday, for the purpose of meeting the new Viceroy on his arrival in Bombay, on the 7th.

THE principal speakers, in the House of Commons, who took part in the debate on the Queen's Titles' Bill, on the 9th March, were Mr. Disraeli, Sir G. Campbell, Mr. Gladstone, Sir Stafford Northcote, Mr. Forster, Mr. Smollett (who enthusiastically supported the bill), Mr. Anderson, and Lord Hartington.

LORD SALISBURY drew attention in the House of Lords to the selection of candidates for the Indian Civil Service on the 17th March.

THE Marquis of Lorne and the Princess Louise will be the guests of Sir Edward Thornton during their visit to the Centennial exhibition in Philadelphia, America.

THE Duke of Argyll said recently, in the House of Lords, that in a recent correspondence between his noble friend, the Secretary for India, and the Viceroy, the noble Marquis referred to a despatch which he, when Secretary for India, addressed to Lord Mayo, then Governor-General, on the subject of the relations between the Home Government and the Government of India. He begged to move for that despatch. The Marquis of Salisbury said there was no objection to its production.

HER IMPERIAL Majesty the Empress of Austria, travelling under the *incognito* title of Countess of Palfy, arrived in London on March 4, attended by the Countess Festetics and Baron Nopcsa, and others.

WITH the Parliamentary Papers just published, is a Copy of Dissent recorded by members of the Council of India upon Lord Salisbury's despatch to the Governor-General, of the 11th of November, 1875, relating to the Indian Tariff Act of 1875. The dissentient members are Sir E. Perry and Sir H. Montgomery. Sir E. Perry says: "I have already recorded my dissent to the telegram of the 30th of September last which stated disapprobation of Lord Northbrook's financial reforms, and in substance enjoined the abolition of import duties on cotton goods, and I did so on the ground that we had had no opportunity of considering the reasoning on which the Government of India proceeded. Now that I have read all the papers, I am decidedly of opinion that the course adopted by the Government of India was wise (with the exception, perhaps, of the new duty on raw cotton, which was a concession asked for by the Bombay Chamber of Commerce), and that the abolition of the import duties would inflict a loss on the revenue not easily reparable." . . . . . Sir H. Montgomery makes the following remarks:—"I, too, recorded a dissent to the telegram of the 30th of September, on grounds similar to those now stated by Sir E. Perry. I concur in his remarks regarding Lord Northbrook's budget arrangements, with the exception of the objections he raises to an income-tax."

H. M. S. *Orontes*, with Lord Lytton the new Viceroy of India, arrived at Aden, on Friday last, and sailed for Bombay at three in the afternoon of the same day.

THE House of Lords, on Thursday last, passed the second reading of the Queen's Titles' Bill.

Calcutta.

THE Census of Calcutta will be taken on the night of Thursday, the 6th instant. We hope the Native inhabitants of the town will give every facility to the taking of it. The Enumerators will first make lists of the houses in their respective blocks, and for this purpose they are authorised to ascertain the names of the occupier and owner of each house. Before Thursday next they will go round their blocks, and fill up the Householder's Schedule for every family, the head of which is unable to write English or Bengali. If a house-holder can write English or Bengali, and wishes to fill up his own Schedule, he can do so, and the Enumerator will supply him with the requisite forms for the purpose. On the night of the 6th April the Enumerators will go round again to each house, and correct their Returns, striking out the names of any persons who may be absent from the town on that night, and adding the names of any others who may have come to the town since the date of filling up the return. The names of women need not be mentioned. The Enumerators have been selected from among the residents of that part of the town where they will be employed in taking the Census, and they have been strictly enjoined to conduct themselves with civility and forbearance towards every one. To prevent imposition, moreover, each Enumerator has been furnished with a printed letter of appointment. Any complaint as to the conduct of an Enumerator should be addressed to the Secretary to the Justices. Persons omitting to give the information required by law, are liable to a fine of one hundred rupees.

THE P. & O. Co.'s S. S. *Assam*, Captain G. F. Cates, arrived in Bombay Harbour, on Wednesday last, from Suez with the English Mails of the 10th instant on board. The following is the list of passengers:—

From Southampton.—Col. and Mrs. Tytler and child, Major and Mrs. Boulton, Miss Pearson, Miss Wood, Mrs. R. E. Otto and infant, Mr. T. A. Crawford, Miss Donald, Mrs. E. Hart, infant and two children, Mr. W. H. Smith, Mr. T. W. Smith, Major E. W. Hercy, Mr. Blackett, Mr. Campbell, Mr. A. S. Kennard, Mr. J. Lewtas, Mr. W. C. Diblin, Dr. Holmes' servant.

From Malta.—Lieut. Hart, Lieut. Murphy.

From Venice.—Miss Campbell, Mrs. Cunningham, Dr. G. Bruce, Mrs. Hutchinson, Miss R. F. Stewart, Mr. J. D. Gordon, C. S. I., Mr. Richardson, Mr. Clarke, Mrs. Howell, infant and child, and European female servant.

From Brindisi.—Mr. Chrystie, Col R. Baker, Mr. A. Kelly, Mr. Stewart, Mr. Webster, Mr. A. Zella, Mr. Ashworth, Mr. Mair, Mr. D'Souza, Mr. Mahamet.

From Suez.—Mr. Ogilvie, Mr. E. Baker, Mr. H. Watanabe, Mr. R. Nakai.

From Ancona.—Mr. Balbi.

From Aden.—Surg. Waters, Mrs. Cassumbhoy and sister, Mr. Cassum, friend and two children, Mr. Mirza Amun, Mr. Ahmud bin Meain and three friends, Mr. Ahmurchund, Mr. Shurmurchund and friend Mr. Mootealal and four friends.

THE annual distribution of prizes to the pupils of the Balur Government Aided School, took place on Sunday, the 26th instant, at 7½ A. M. From the report read, it appears, that the late Babu Grish Chunder Ghosh, the Editor of the *Bengalee*, was the Secretary to the School. During his life-time the school was in the zenith of its glory. Owing partly to the ravages committed by the epidemic fever and partly to the utter neglect of the inhabitants of Balur, the school is at present in a very deplorable state. Its existence is now solely due to the exertions of Babu Chunder Nath Roy, the Head Master, and Babu Khetter Mohun Mullick, the Pundit of the School. When the distribution of prizes was over, Babu Nogendro Nath Bhadury delivered an eloquent address in English, pointing out the benefits of education and exhorting the inhabitants to unite in raising the school to a position which it once attained. He also laid great stress on the importance of moral training in private and public schools.—[*Communicated*].

A CORRESPONDENT writes:—"For the benefit of the Howrah Girls' School, the Howrah Native Amateur Theatrical Party are going to play on Saturday, the 1st April, on the Howrah Railway stage *Karani Darpan*, a drama, in which is depicted clearly the treatment, our fellow-brethren, the *Keranis*, receive at the hands of their European superior officers.

Public Engagement.

MUSICAL Evangelistic Service.—The Rev. Shib Chunder Bannerjea will deliver an Address in Bengali in the Free Church Institution, Nimtollah Street, to-morrow evening, 2nd instant, at 7 o'clock. Subject:—"The Ten Virgins." Hymns in Bengali, set to Hindu Music, will be sung.

Selection

ANNIVERSARY LECTURE ON "OUR FAITH AND OUR EXPERIENCES."

[*Continued.*]

INDIA sang the glory of the Eternal Spirit in the remotest period of pre-historic faith. Our nation has long been familiar with the *Param Atma*, the Supreme Spirit; and the light wherewith thousands of cultivated Brahmins recognise Him and adore Him throughout India is all their own, drawn from their own scriptures and their own sages. Ransack and search the ancient scriptures of the Hindus, and you will find the most sublime and beautiful conceptions of the Great Spirit scattered all over the ancient Vedas and the Vedanta, you meet with sparkling tex s pointing to Him Unseen. In India more than in any other country, in the Hindu scriptures more than in any other scrip ure, have the attributes of this Spiritual Divinity been elaborately and fully depicted. In fact it is in glowing descriptions of an all pervading Spirit-God that primitive Hinduism consists. Do not mis-understand me. I do not even take into account the numerous errors and absurdities, the pantheism and polytheism, the rites and ceremonies, which defile the primitive sacred literature of our race; far be it from me to vindicate them. I am not discussing the Hindu's scheme of salvation. But I speak of the central and towering truth of early Hinduism, the truth of the One Unseen Spirit. And here facts warrant enthusiastic advocacy. It is not mere patriotic fervor but truth, well attested truth, that leads me to admire the Hindu's conception of the eternal and bodiless spirit. Transport yourselves back to the Vedic age, when idol worship was altogether unknown, and you will be struck to find how the ancient *Rishis* communed devoutly and joyfully with the Supreme Spirit within the inner sanctuary. That wonderful book, the *Rig-Veda*, the earliest record of the Aryan faith, presents rich treasures of spiritual worship. How sublime are these texts! "Who knows the Primitive Person? Who is there that has seen Him, who is there that has revealed Him"? "He is the Father of our parents and is resplendent. He is even inherent in the indestructible world within. He is the only fountain of truth." "By His own might has the Lord established the mountains and caused the waters to flow downwards. He upholdeth the world, and by His own wisdom doth He keep the heavens above from falling down." The evidences of spiritual communion with Pure Spirit thicken as you come down to the later and more philosophical disquisitions known as the *Upanishads*. Everywhere in these books you meet the All-Holy Spirit; every page almost reveals Him. One feels weary as he wades through these volumes of philosophical spirit-worship, containing nothing but reiterated descriptions of the Supreme *Brahma*. How the *Upanishads* magnify the Supreme Spirit will appear from such striking passages as these. "He moves, He moves not; He is far, He is near too; He is within these, He also dwells without." "Smaller than the smallest is the Supreme Spirit, and greater is He than the greatest. He dwells in the hearts of living beings. He who is free from sorrows, perceives the Lord who transcends the senses, and beholds His glory through His Grace. He hath no hands and yet He holdeth; He hath no eye and yet He seeth; He hath no ear and yet He heareth." "He whom the Brahmins praise is the eternal *Brahma*." These precious treasures have we received from our venerable ancestors. Richer far than gold and silver is the doctrine of the Spirit-God, they have bequeathed unto us as a heavenly legacy. A God not of clay or stone, not fashioned by mortal hands, not spun of delusive fancy, but the real Spirit-God immanent in the universe and in the inmost soul, that God, recognized all over India as *Brahma*, we have received from our forefathers. Yes venerable *Rishis* and devotees of ancient India! at your holy feet modern India lays her humble tribute of gratitude for this priceless legacy! (Applause.) Gentlemen, was the God of our forefathers a mere metaphysical abstraction, a prolongation as it were into the outward universe of men's intellectual consciousness? Was their deity nothing but thin air or a mere romantic fancy? I emphatically say, no. It was the reality of God-head that our ancestors sought and worshipped. Did they renounce the world, its riches and pleasures, and honor in quest of some aerial phantom? Did they sacrifice their all for a fiction? Did they leave father, mother, wife and children, and go into solitary retreats but to indulge in a mere idea? No, that cannot be. If they erred at all, they erred in making too much of the encompassing reality of the Supreme Spirit, a reality they saw and felt and held joyfully, nay with passionate attachment in the inmost heart. In their prayers and addresses to the Deity, in their daily meditation and in all their varied spiritual exercises, we find neither fancy nor frenzy, neither abstract metaphysics nor lifeless theories, but a thrilling and direct intercourse with a burning reality. They did not dream, but they saw. They imagined not, but they handled the Great Spirit. To them God was as "a fruit held in the clutches of the hand,"—"*karatala nyasta amlaka vat.*" They also spoke of Him as a shining light, so vivid was their perception of His real presence. But the Spirit-God was not only a bright Reality to our forefathers, but He was also a Loving Personal Reality. Not only did they see Him with the eye of faith and by pure insight, but they also held Him in their hearts. In the *Rig-Veda* the Lord is spoken of as a friend "whose friendship is sweet." He is "a friend, a father, and the most fatherly of fathers,"—"Sakha, pita, pitritama pitrinam." Such an expression, quite unusual, as "the most fatherly of fathers," cannot fail to strike even the most prejudiced reader of the Hindu scriptures as offering most satisfactory evidence of the affectionate relations in which India's ancient devotees stood to their God. Nay their conceptions rose higher still and even recognised the motherhood of God. He is represented both as father and mother of mankind. "Twam hi na pita vaso twam mata." Let none then say that the ancient Hindus worshipped an abstract deity.

[*To be continued.*]

Advertisements

ALBERT HALL.

PATRON.

His Honor the Lieutenant Governor of Bengal

COUNCIL.

Hon'ble Sir William Muir, K. C. S. I.—*President.*
Rajah Rama Nath Tagore Bahadur C. S. I.—*Vice-President.*
Hon'ble Ashley Eden, C. S. I.
Archdeacon Baly.
Colonel H. E. L. Thuiller, C. S. I.
Maharajah Kumar of Bettiah.
Hon'ble Rajah Narendra Krishna Bahadur.
Rajah Komul Krishna Bahadur.
Rajah Joteendro Mohun Tagore Bahadur.
Babu Digumber Mitter C. S. I.
Hon'ble Nawab Ashgar Ali Bahadur, C. S.
Nawab Amir Ali Bahadur.
Moulvi Abdul Latif Khan Bahadur.
Manockji Rustomji Esq.
Babu Keshub Chunder Sen.

SUBSCRIPTIONS.

His Highness Maharajah Holkar ...	Rs.	8,000
His Highness Maharajah of Jeypore	"	5,000
His Highness Maharajah of Putialah	"	2,500
Maharajah Kumar of Bettiah ...	"	2,000
Rajah of Bhinga ...	"	1,000
Maharani Surnomoie, Cossim Bazar	"	1,000
Maharajah of Hutwa ...	"	500
Rajah Komul Krisna Bahadur ...	"	500
Rajah Joteendro Mohun Tagore ...	"	500
Hon'ble Rajah Narendra Krishna Bahadur ...	"	300
Sirdar Dyal Singh ...	"	200
Rajah Roma Nath Tagore Bahadur	"	200
Babu Shama Churn Law ...	"	200
Hon'ble Sir William Muir ...	"	100
Hon'ble Ashley Eden ...	"	100
Dr. Mohendro Lall Sircar ...	"	100
Babu Goonendro Nath Tagore ...	"	100

POSTAL NOTICES.

Mails for Persian Gulf for transmission per Steamer from Bombay will be closed at the General Post Office on Tuesday the 4th proximo at 7 P. M.

The next Overland Mail via Bombay will close at the General Post Office on Friday the 7th April 1876, by which mails for Mauritius, St. Denis, Reunion, Zanzibar, Mozambique, Delagoa Bay, Natal, Cape of Good Hope, the Comoro Islands, and Madagascar can be forwarded.

2. Book post and pattern packets must be posted on the 6 idem.

N. B.—The Letter Box will close at 7 P. M precisely, after which hour Overland letters, fully prepaid and bearing extra postage stamp of two (2) annas on each cover, will be received up to 7-30 P. M., or bearing an extra postage stamp of four (4) annas on each cover, up to 8 P. M.,

Printed and published by M. M. Rukhit, at the "Indian Mirror" Press, No. 15, Colleg Square, for the Proprietor.

The Indian Mirror.

SUNDAY EDITION.

VOL. XVI] CALCUTTA, SUNDAY, APRIL 9, 1876 {Registered at the General Post Office.} [No. 84

CONTENTS.

Editorial Note

MR. AND MRS. PHEAR have no reason left to complain of the ingratitude on the part of those who benefited by their friendship and good offices during their long sojourn in this country. Another meeting, and this time a more influential one, was held at the house of Mr. Manomohun Ghose, the Barrister, to bid them farewell on last Friday evening. There was a good number of Hindu ladies present. The European guests also mustered strong. His Honor the Lieutenant-Governor was present, as well as the Chief. Lady Muir, and a pretty large number of European ladies were there. The address read on the occasion we publish elsewhere. There was a very handsome present offered. The proceedings were satisfactory, and both Mr. and Mrs. Phear must have been exceedingly pleased by the sincerity of the good wishes shown to them by every one.

THE Hindu and European races instead of being united, are parting wider every day. The *Friend of India* assigns as reason of this the fact that the European population of India is continually increasing. Every Englishman who cares to move in society, finds plenty of his own countrymen to associate with. The company of Hindus therefore is not called into requisition. This may be a reason, but it does not account for the whole fact. The truth of it is Englishpeople find very little to please or interest them in Native society. Those of them who are disposed to patronize, or reform, or make researches, or gain converts, occasionally mingle with the people; but a man cannot always play the patron, or the reformer, or the antiquarian, or even the missionary. He wants some real relaxation and companionship, which in the case of an Englishman here, few but English men can supply. As for Hindu gentlemen we must do them the justice to say that they always look up to the acquaintance of Europeans as a high honor; but the latter, generally speaking, regard them with such ineffable condescension that it withers all free and genial sympathy, and social relationship on anything like a footing of equality is out of the question. Any advance on the part of a Hindu in this direction is either put down as an impertinence, or ignored as a piece of youthful folly. The sensitive and self-respectful among us knowing this state of things keep aloof; the ambitious and the self-serving, whose name is a ligion, flatter and sneak without reservation, and confirm the already strong opinions in the minds of Englishmen on the subject of our national chracter. Christian missionaries who mix with us to instruct and proselytise, will oblige us much if they say how many of them covet social equality with the heathen. How then is the union of the two races posible under such circumstances?

CASTE as a fixed social distinction we condemn strongly. Caste as a badge of individual superiority or inferiority we destroy. Caste as a religious institution we demolish. It is against the doctrine of the Brotherhood of Man, one of the two foundation stones of the Brahmo Somaj. If anything has distinguished socially the career of the Brahmo Somaj during the last forty years, it is our determined hostility to the distinction of castes. But one thing we cannot ignore. We cannot ignore the clans and families to which we belong; the race, and the generation of men and women from whom we have sprung. The descendant of Brahmin ancestors is a Brahmin physically, just as the descendant of Saxons is a Saxon, though morally and religiously he may degrade himself below or exalt himself above his forefathers. In this sense a man may call himself a Brahmin, or a Vysia, or Kaistha. He is certainly free to intermarry with other castes, and the Nativ Marriage Act has been passed to legalize such marriages. But he is also free to marry with his own caste, if he is so disposed, either in conformity to the principle of Natural Selection, or for the preservation of that social integrity which is sacrificed to a certain extent by promiscuous marriages. The difference of castes besides does mean the difference of habits and tastes, and not unfrequently intellectual, moral, and religious difference. The castes nearest each other resemble most, and the further they part, the wider the difference. Intermarriage though a duty in some cases, is not advisable always. In fact the law of intermarriages between castes, races, and nationalities must be most carefully regulated. From this point of view then, and from it alone, we may be said to regard the institution of caste if not with favor, at least with delicacy. And if some Brahmos of the Progressive School have mentioned their castes as well as their religion in the census returns, they have done so with this view. Others who have not done so, have not done so lest they be misunderstood, and taken to mean that they are Hindus by religion as the rest of the population.

TWO KINDS OF RELIGIOUS MEN.

BEHOLD the man whom the world has called religious. He is good, he is valuable, you cannot find fault with him. There is in him what you call "a harmonious development." His intelligence is clear and cultured, and capable of understanding the relations of things. His information is vast and varied, his observation is shrewd and extensive, his thoughtfulness deep. He can express himself with power and with taste, and his words it is pleasant and profitable to hear. His feelings too are fine and polished. They are easily awakened, and when they are awakened they can sometimes strike their kindred fire in other hearts. He has a glowing sense of Divine love, and understands also the sweetness of human relations. He has drunk deep of the piety of his forefathers, and delights to dwell upon the theology of poetry, as well as the poetry of theology. The pathetic, the glowing, and the sublime are to him sentiments most natural. In the performance of his duties he is faithful. A good husband, and a good father, he is just and generous to his neighbours, and true to those who are religiously ministered unto by him. His dutifulness is the result of strong conscientious struggle. He has cultivated his moral nature with the same painstaking exertion which characterizes his whole life His sympathies are large, catholic, and active. He is of much use to his friends, countrymen, and to the world at large. But he is nevertheless a worldly man. There are many like him everywhere.

Behold a man of a far different type. Men do not speak very well of him, and say that he might make himself more useful than he now is. At all events he is not what you would call a "harmonious development." Some parts of his nature are exceedingly prominent, others are not so prominent. His intellect does not show much sign of elaborate culture. His information is limited, and some of it perhaps wrong. His observations seem to be now and then common-place. He cannot express himself in epigrams, and is sometimes prolix, now and then repeats himself, and frequently speaks in figures and parables. Being peculiar, and obstinate in his peculiarities, he offends many. He is inattentive to the most gloried gifts of the world, and its feelings and moralities he holds but in light esteem. His lofty ideals people say are impracticable and foolish, they attract few, and retain the favor of fewer still. But his faith in his destiny is tremendous. He cares but little to meddle with the refinements, and so called relations of ordinary life; his intellect penetrates into deeper objects and relations; his eloquence dwells on scenes and purposes foreign to other men; his joys and griefs are solitary, few can measure them, few can understand them. His very religion is different from that of his fellowmen, the hidden meaning of his language and sentiments few comprehend. He learns out of Divinity. He teaches out of his life, and not merely out of his head, or heart. His life is a hundred times deeper than his word, all that he knows he does not say. He says he lives to make the world new, to create a new soul in men, to break down the ancient temple of the past, and build it again in three days. His piety means madness; his faith means sight and hearing; his purity means life and death in God. He has established unforeseen relations in human life; created new motives; discovered original ends of existence; new fields of happiness; explained, illustrated, and glorified the science of sorrow. His definition of sin is new, his definition of righteousness is new, he upsets all the long-established notions of men, and teaches what the people call strange doctrines. Not a jot or tittle of what he says he ever retracts; and allows nothing to remain unfulfilled. He confounds the wise; he humiliates the rich; he scourges the hypocrite; he exalts the meek; he gathers the sorrow-stricken, the weak and the sinful; he blesses the little children; and at last consummates the teachings of his life by the calmness and glory of his death.

Telegraphic Intelligence

Reuter's Telegrams.

LONDON, APRIL 7.

The Royal Titles Bill was read this evening in the House of Lords a third time. No amendments were introduced, and the Bill passed without a division.

Cambridge is the favorite in the betting on the Oxford and Cambridge Boat race, which takes place to-day, the latest odds being 10 to 3 on Cambridge.

The trial of Captain Kuhn, of the Steamer *Franconia*, has resulted in a verdict of guilty of manslaughter. Sentence has been deferred. Captain Kuhn contested the Jurisdiction of the Court, on the ground that the *Franconia*, at the time of the collision, was bound on a foreign voyage.

Correspondence.

MOODY AND SANKEY.

To the Editor of the *Indian Mirror*.

SIR,—He only is my best friend who will most kindly and clearly show me my faults, and convince me of sin. The sin of the mind,—we say not of the heart,—the sin of the mind is false doctrine. It is teaching my child, or my friend, what I have reason to suspect is not true. It is all the more sinful if I grieve away the spirit of God when it pleads with me, with "a still small voice," in my heart of hearts not to dishonor Him by teaching error, because the truth would not "bring peace" but division. It is because I love the work of the American Methodists, as thus far conducted in Calcutta, and wish it success in all godliness and honesty, that I send you the following from the *Unitarian Review* for Dec. 1875, and remain yours, as ever.

C. H. A. Dall.

[In "The Truthseeker," from Rev. J. P. Hopps of Glasgow,]

[Mr. Hopps has published a sermon on the effect of Mr. Moody's preaching in England.]

[Here is a portion of his extracts of a sermon heard with his own ears. We know, of course, that this is not the staple of all Mr. Moody's addresses, but we must look at what he sometimes says, with calm impartiality:—

"The sermon before me is his last on the subject (of Hell), but it is only one of many,—it is neither better nor worse than his others on the same subject. More than once—once, to my knowledge, in Manchester and once in London—he pictured good, beautiful girls in hell, not because they were wicked, but because, to use his favorite phrase, they were 'out of Christ,' or in plain English, because they could not agree with Mr. Moody, and accept what he told them about salvation by blood. He pictured those girls as given over by Satan in hell to the lusts of his devils, with not even a policeman to hear or help them. This 'young lady' who is weeping at Moody's door is not a wicked person; she is anxious and interested even, she would shudder if, in going home, a drunken man spoke to her: yet, in hell, 'libertines and drunkards and murderers' will be her 'companions,' if she fail to 'find Christ.' Why! Mr. Moody leaves us alone with shameful atrocity, unjustified and unexplained. When people are punished here on earth, even by imperfect men, they are punished for something, and their punishment has some relation to their offence. We should think it scandalous to punish a child as we punish a man: we should think it monstrous to punish the thief who steals a loaf of bread, as we punish the swindler who heaped up riches by forgery and lying. For a first offence we do not punish as for a second or a third. All kinds of considerations are introduced to make the sodes of justice true. Some young criminals are not even punished at all, but are sent to a reformatory—a kind of compulsory school; and, when they learn to do well, they are gladly admitted to the open world, and have free course amongst their fellows. Now, will any one tell me why this that is right with men should be all wrong with God? Why, even with wicked women who have to be imprisoned, it is our custom to keep them apart from 'libertines and drunkards and murderers;' and from one end of the country to the other there would be a cry of horror, if, in the obscurest prison even, the worst women were subjected to the horror of being turned loose and unprotected upon the society of the other prisoners, known to be 'libertines and drunkards and murderers.' That cry of horror would be a thousand times more intense, if, not the worst of women, but some 'young lady' prisoner, were subjected to that degradation, peril, and shame. Yet that is what Mr. Moody lays to the charge of the Almighty. It is he who has ordained the allotments of the future life; it is he who has declared that all who are 'out of Christ,' shall be damned; it is he who will turn beautiful young girls into hell, regardless alike of justice, humanity, or the credit of his own name or reign. What of the noble spirits of all ages and nations, the choice souls who on earth lived to teach the ignorant, save the fallen, restore the wandering, and help the weak? What has happened to them, that they seek and save no more? And what has happened to Jesus of Nazareth? On earth he went about doing good: he sought out the sinner, he spoke hopefully to the most despairing, he turned no sorry soul away. But what does Mr. Moody say? He says, in this sermon, 'You came here to-night to hear Mr. Sankey sing "Jesus of Nazareth passeth by," but bear in mind you will not hear that song in the lost world; or, if you do, it will not be true—he does not pass that way.' How does Mr Moody know? Or if he is right, I want to know why Jesus does not pass that way; I want to know if he has nothing to say about that young girl, and the 'libertines, drunkards, and murderers;' I want to know whether he is tired, or helpless, or hopeless. I want to know who is responsible for this most gigantic horror, that hell is supremely wretched, supremely hopeless, and full of cruelty, injustice, and crime, and that heaven makes no effort to mitigate, instruct, or save. Some one must be responsible for the hopeless misery of hell, and some one must be responsible for the horrible selfishness or inability of heaven; and it is an urgent question —who?

Who has given life to men under this horrible condition, that they shall have no real chance here, and then be shut up to hopeless inability forever? Who has made improvability a fact in this life only? Who has decreed that the first step, the first experiment of life shall determine its eternal character? Who is it that has so ordered things that, anywhere, the wish to improve shall be eternally denied? There is only one reply: it is this, so God has ordered it. Then I say plainly, if such a God there be, he is himself the arch-demon of the universe; his cruelty is unspeakable, his injustice is immensurable, his rule is the most detestable of tyrannies, his heaven is the scandal of universe, and it is shameful to be sav d.

'God help us to regard it all as a horrible nightmare! God help us to trust him, and to believe that hell is not eternally hopeless, that heaven is not eternally selfish. The poor soul stumbling from earth, confused and blind and harassed and ignorant, does not deserve to be thrust down to black nig t and horrible despair; and it surely cannot be sinful for me to think that the good God has provided for education and help and progress on the other side. To him I come, to him I cling, —my God, my Father, and my Friend. When I go to that unseen world, I look to see all his good and blessed ones employed in teaching and comforting and guiding the dark, the sorrowful, and the sinful; and when I think of heaven for myself I can only say, give me, O God, my humble place among the he lers and the helpers of the sick, the despairing, and the lost."]

Devotional

APPEAL to the sense of my soul, O Lord and there enable me to behold, and understand the hidden relations of things. The five senses delude and smother the soul, they misinterpret the objects and uses of life. The knowledge that comes through them comes with an appeal to the desire of enjoyment and possession. The relations which they would encourage are the short-lived earthly relations that surely cause misery. Even the religion they foster is the tainted religion of the world. O spirit supreme, teach me all knowl dge from within, cause me to foster the relations that are born and fed in the spirit; give unto me that spiritual religion that grows within the soul, that interprets all things, enjoys all things, there.

WITHOUT hope no man can live, hope is life's sustenance. But to centre any hope in man is to court sure disappointment. There is only one source from which the fulfilment of hope can come, and that is, O my God, thyself. Let me entertain such hopes only as thou dost justify, thou shalt bless them with fulfilment.

SOUL ASPIRATION.*

PRAYER is aspiration, or that beauty breathed in words, which ascends as silently as the perfume of flowers, prompted by the needs of the soul. And the attitude, the purpose of prayer when the soul turns inward, finding another sphere, where shutting out the world she may pour out the story of her needs, reaching higher and yet higher, until on tireless wing, she seemingly ascends to the great centre of life, whose fountains of light are ever sending forth their vitalising streams, with creation laid out before and creator all around, is more than beautiful—is sublime. Belonging to the inner sanctuary of the soul, true prayer can never be fully expressed in words. As spirit rises, it requires matter more and still more refined for manifestation; so thoughts, so prayers approaching the Divine become so pure and impersonal that earthly language is inadequate; the soul no longer speaks but feels, and blends in holiest communion with the infinite, and thus blending becomes conscious of its own infinity. Nor is this feeling altogether deceptive. The soul in self-communion, feels its immensity, its relation to the universe, and its illimitable future. And through prayer and meditation, the external universe partially reveals its inmost self, and another universe—that within—the subjective, opens in grandeur, seemingly limitless before the spirit vision.

We are strange beings, and our strangeness is an inexhaustible study. It is impossible to perfectly know one's self. In our every day lives we are as screw on rolling waters. While in the divine interior life we are as majestic as the gleaming heavens, and as much obey the fixed laws of destiny as the starry host above us. Prayer necessarily opens the gate to this inner life, for in silence and solitude we best know our dee est selves. In these precious moments of contemplation and aspiration, the soul's feelers reaching heavenward, the angels come around us in love, and silently ministering, imprint the kiss of holiness upon our up-turned brows, and we returned from this state of exaltation becalmed and at peace with all the world, feeling that the Infinite Father does all things well.

The influence of that angel kiss, remains as holy spell upon us, making our lives beautiful, and further inviting to our bosoms angel guest, giving us perpetual joy. From these moments of prayer standing on the mount of transfiguration we return with wonder at the contrast ourselves in the future—how vast! In the present objective world how insignificant. And yet an infinite future, all rainbowed and golden with promise, lies before us.

* This has been lying with us for sometime, it was sent to us by a gentleman. Not knowing whether it is an extract or an original production we did not publish it so long. But as some of the sentiments are good, we give it insertion leaving it open to criticism.

The Brahmo Somaj.

THERE will be collection in the Brahmo Mandir this evening

THERE was an annual devotional service in the family house of Babu Kanye Lal Pyne last evening. Some of the missionaries of the Brahmo Somaj were present, as well as a number of other Brahmos. Babu Kanye Lal Pyne belongs to the elder generation of Brahmos, and though by no means old, has been intimately connected with the Brahmo Somaj for about the last twenty-five years. He is still a zealous member of our cause.

WE wait with some interest to ascertain the results of the census as regards the number of Brahmos in Calcutta. This will be a work of considerable difficulty with the compilers. All Brahmos have not called themselves by that name. Some have written theists, others deists perhaps, and some non-Hindus. Those who have not signed the Brahmo covenant, an act by no means indispensable on the part of our fellow-religionists, hesitate to call themselves Brahmos. We are inclined to think that even the name Brahmo is not indispensable. The English word *theist* will do quite as well. Under such circumstance we hope Mr. Beverly will give proper instructions to the compilers to ascertain the number of those who subscribe to the faith of the Brahmo Somaj.

THE harsh, indelicate, and one might say almost defamatory handbills circulated among the members of the Prarthana Somaj on the occasion of their last Anniversary, are, we find, the productions of some young men connected with the movement, who have given little promise to outshine in moral heroism, or spiritual grandeur, those whom they so indiscriminately censure. We admit there is very great inconsistency in the Prarthana Somaj, and we regret the fact as sincerely as we can, but will rabid and senseless vilification cure the evil? If there is reasonable continued and strong agitation among the members on the subject, we may expect good results. But let the spirit of faultfinding, and vilifying be given up. It aggravates the disease, instead of abating it.

ASYLUM FOR ORPHANS & WIDOWS.

1. AN Asylum for Orphans and Widows is proposed to be established at Allahabad, under the auspices of the Northern India Brahmo Somaj with Branch Asylums at other places where efficient management can be ensured.

2. Orphans and widows of all castes and races will, so far as the funds of the Institution will permit, be admitted, under the following conditions, into the proposed Asylum, where they will receive necessary food, clothing, and comfortable accommodation, and be brought up in a respectable way.

Condition I.—That the candidates for admission into the Asylum be of good character, and prepared to subject themselves to such discipline as may be enforced by the Managers of the Asylum with a view to train them up as members of the Native Society.

Condition II.—That they be prepared to receive such secular, moral, and useful education (including instructions in the principles of theism), as may be prescribed for them by the Directors of the Asylum.

Condition III.—That they, or their lawful guardians, give an agreement to the effect that they (the candidates for admission into the Asylum) will not leave the Asylum unless on reasonable grounds, which may be accepted as sufficient by the Directors, until they obtain a certificate from the Manager of the Asylum of their having received sufficient amount of education befitting them for leading independent and respectable lives.

3. Children other than orphans, and women other than widows, will also be exceptionally admitted into the Asylum under the conditions stated in the preceding paragraph, and under the special sanction of the Directors in each case.

4. The caste prejudices of the inmates of the Asylum will not be interfered with, and they will be free to retain or renounce them at their will.

5. The Asylum will be supported by the aid that may be received from the public in the

shape of monthly subscriptions, donations, or other gifts.

6. Those who will render the Institution regular pecuniary aid, or exert themselves towards the furtherance of its object by obtaining pecuniary aid from others, or candidates for admission into the Asylum, or in any other way, will be the Members of the Institution.

7. An Annual Meeting of the Members will be held in every town, wherein an Asylum or Branch Asylum may be located, for regulating the affairs of the Asylum.

8. The Members will elect from amongst their body a number of gentlemen not exceeding twelve, and not less than four, to be the Directors of the Asylum, provided that at least half of the number of Directors elected be Members of the Brahmo Somaj.

9. The Directors will hold a Monthly Meetin for managing the affairs of the Asylum.

10. The Directors will elect from amongst them a Manager, with Assistant Managers, if necessary for the Asylum.

11. Directors will be elected every year, but the Managers of the Asylum and the Secretary of the Institution will hold their posts to an indefinite period, unless the Directors or the Members, respectively in a regular meeting, elect by majority of votes other gentlemen to succeed them.

12. The co-operation and aid of the generous public, as described in paragraph 5, is respectfully solicited. All communications should be addressed to the Secretary, who will acknowledge with thanks all remittances, howsoever small, and other aid that may be given to the Institution.

ALLAHABAD, The 27th January 1876. } NABIN CHUNDRA RAI, Honorary Secretary.

Scientific

An important advance has been made on one of the Parsi tramways, by propelling the car by means of compressed air heated as used by being passed through hot water. *Les Annales Industrielles* fully describes the arrangement made by M. Mekarski, by which he appears to have solved the problem of running a self-acting tram-car along street tramways, without smoke or steam.

Gleanings.

I AM THE LORD, I CHANGE NOT.

CHANGE not, change not to me, my God, I would that thou should'st be
To furthest worlds what thou hast been on this sad earth to me.
Though thou hast baffled sore my life, though thy swift-scourging rod
Hath left me spirit-scarred, I cry, change not to me, my God !

Change not to me for any change that o'er my soul may come,
When lips that dearly love thy praise in bitterness are dumb ;
Yea, when I love thee not at all, when from thy face I flee,
Let thy compelling love pursue—my God, change not to me.

When death hath wrought his awful change, and left the spirit bare
Thou didst hide me 'neath thy wings, thy mantling love prepare.
I am no other than I was when most thou didst prepare befriend,
I trust thee, Lord, for what thou wert, be changeless to the end.

I do not ask with sudden step thy purest heaven to win,
Be still, Most Merciful, all love-relentless to my sin,
Yea, Lord, make wholly beautiful what thou lovest so well
Burn out in me whatever defiles, burn out in fire of hell.
Let me but know thy voice, its word in all I will obey,
In outer darkness still most sure that thou wilt find a way
To bring thy banished to thyself, as thou didst bring of old
When thy sin wearied child, but thought on the forsaken fold.

Change not to me, in those far worlds, where all is strange and new,
Where can my stranger spirit rest, if thou art changed too !
As turns the child from alien crowd to the one kindred face,
To find that mother eyes make home in unfamiliar place.
So trembling must I turn to thee, the God whom I have known,
The God who in this lonely world hath never left me alone.
Do with me, Lord, whate'er thou wilt, so only thou wilt be
Forever, and forever more, what thou hast been to me.

The Truth Seeker.

LATEST NEWS.

THE *Delhi Gazette* announces that Babu Anghornath Chatterji, Station Gomastah, Commissariat Department, Agra, and permanent Gomashtah of the Camp and Howiskhana of His Excellency the Viceroy and Governor-General of India, and who was, as such, deputed by his Departmental superiors to carry on the duties of his Department with the late Camp of His Royal Highness, at Delhi, Agra, and the Terai, has been presented, by His Royal Highness, through the Assistant Quarter Master General, and the Executive Commissariat Officer, Agra, with a massive gold chain and a medal bearing the Royal Insignia, as a token of remembrance of his services at the late Camps of H. R. H.

MR. W. B. HENRY, the late Manager of Lewis' Dramatic Company, will proceed to New York with a view to organizing a new and extensive theatrical company with which he will visit India as soon as arrangements can be completed.

IT is proposed again to amend the Indian Registration Act.

THERE is an ice-famine at Madras, the supply of the Tudor Company being exhausted.

THE whole attention of our Government is now directed to Beluchistan. Something very serious is evidently in contemplation, and vigorous measures are being taken in every direction. Colonel Loch has been suspended from duty as Commandant of the Upper Scinde Frontier, for opposing the political officers.

THE Lieutenant-Governor of the Punjab is shooting with the Rajah of Nahun in his territory. He will not go to Simla before the 20th.

The services of Rao Bahadur Manibhai Jeshbai, Assistant Resident of Baroda, have been placed by the Resident at the disposal of the Durbar of Cutch in accordance with the dying wishes of the late Rao of Cutch. Mr. Manibhai has seen distinguished service in Guzerat.

THE 9th Regiment stationed at Baroda have heard on the very best authority that they are one of a number of regiments that are to from a Force for Egypt. The object of sending an army form India to Egypt would be probably merely as a demonstration to enforce the payment to England of Egypt Turkish tribute.

SIR FREDERICK HAINES, the new Commander-in-Chief of India, arrived at Bombay on Thursday last. Lord Napier of Magdala also arrived there on the same day. But we are sorry to hear his Lordship is too unwell to respond to the invite of the Byculla Club to a dinner. He will leave for England on Monday or Tuesday, if the *Orontes* can be got ready.

A SOCIETY for the Prevention of Cruelty to Animals has been established at Rangoon.

THE Prince of Wales arrived at Malta on Thursday last.

THE Thakur of Limri, with a small retinue, will leave Bombay for England by the Mail Steamer to-morrow.

A STATE dinner was given to Lord Lytton at Bombay, on Thursday last. No address was presented to him.

THE Rangoon Municipality proposes to borrow from Government Rs 90,000, for the purpose of erecting a new bazar.

THE law relating to copyright in India is about to be amended.

RUMOUR has found another fiancée for the Princess Beatrice, in the person of Prince Adolphus Frederick, of Mecklenburg Strelitz, the only son of the Grand Duke of Mecklenburg Strelitz, who married Princess Augusta, sister of the present Duke of Cambridge. The Prince is in his 28th year and is an officer in the celebrated Prussian Uhlans.

THE Peshawur correspondent of the Lahore journal confirms the report relative to the taking of Maimena. There appears to have been severe fighting and the loss on both sides to have been severe, some two thousand being numbered amongst the slain.

THE Native population of French India have received thanks from Marshal Macmahon for the addresses they sent him expressing their attachment towards the Government of France under the Marshal.

LORD LYTTON will leave Bombay for Calcutta to-day, and arrive here on Wednesday next.

THE annual exodus has begun. We announced the other day the departure of the Governor of Madras for the Neilgherries. The Governor of Bombay will leave for Mahableshwur next week, and Lord Lytton for Simla on the 20th or 22nd instant.

MR. J. W. WALKER, Acting Session Judge of Ahmedabad, gave his decision on Thursday evening in the Maharaj Libel Case of Ahmedabad which had been engrossing public attention in Guzerat for some months past. All the imputations made against the complainant, Kaliananand Purshotum Anand by the accused (the proprietor of the *Hitechu* paper of Ahmedabad) were considered by the Court as fully proved and substantiated by the oral and documentary evidence adduced for the defence, with the exception of the imputation as to the complainant being the principal in a certain case of theft, and for this last imputation the accused was fined the sum of Rs. 10.

MR. HORMUSJI JAMSETJI RUSTOMJI, a Parsi merchant of Kurrachi, will proceed to England and the Continent to extend his business connections, and thereby enlarge his sphere of operations.

THE services of Dr. R. M. Meiklejohn, late in medical charge of the Baghelcund Political Agency, are placed at the disposal of the Home Department, with effect from the date on which he may receive medical charge of the establishments of the Rajputana and Scindia Railways at Agra.

SHARAF-UD-DIN KHAN BAHADUR who has been placed by the Resident at Hyderabad in charge of the Office of Assistant Cantonment Magistrate at Secunderabad, will officiate as Political Assistant, 2nd Class, with effect from the date of taking charge, *vice* Sheik Hisam-ud-din, on privilege leave.

MR. D. KISHEN SINGH is appointed Assistant Accountant General, Madras.

CHOLERA has broken out in several of the Districts of Kattywar.

CAPTAIN BURTON, known as Hadji Abdullah, has left Bombay for Sind.

Calcutta.

ON Friday last His Honor the Lieutenant-Governor of Bengal honored Dr. Mohendrolall Sircar with a visit, at his residence, at Saukaritollah. The *Indian Daily News* says the visit was an "unexpected" one. We understand His Honor has subscribed Rs. 500 to Dr. Sircar's Social Science Association Fund.

AT next Tuesday's meeting of the Governor-General's Council, Lord Northbrook will make speech reviewing the course of legislation during his tenure of office as Viceroy.

The new Art Gallery will be open daily (except on Sundays) in the morning from 6-30 to 9-30, and in the afternoon from 3 to 6. Two mornings (Tuesdays and Thursdays) and one afternoon (Saturdays) in each week will be "public days"—admission free. The other days will be "Student's days," and to gain admission on those days the public will have to pay a small fee. For a day or two until certain details as to amount of fees to be charged, &c., &c., are settled and published, the Gallery will be open *free* in the mornings from 6-30 to 9-30, and in the afternoon from 3 to 6.

The Thwaytes' Memorial Fund at Hughly already amounts to Rs. 1,500.

The *Indian Daily News* complains that its Reporter was not permitted to be present at the inauguration ceremony of the Calcutta Art Gallery, on Thursday last. We do not know why so much secrecy was observed in this affair. No previous public announcement was made of the ceremony, nor were the members of the Press admitted to it. Strange.

The farewell address to Lord Northbrook will be presented at Government House, on Wednesday next.

The following Native Chiefs have already subscribed the sums mentioned opposite to their names, to the "Northbrook Memorial Fund":—Maharajah of Benares, 7,000 Rs.; Rajah of Bettia, 3,500 Rs.; and the Maharajah of Vizianagram 7,000 Rs.

A number of Hindu ladies and gentlemen as well as Europeans met at the house of Babu Manomohun Ghose, on Friday evening, to bid farewell to Mrs. Phear, proceeding home, and read the following address:—

TO MRS. PHEAR.

Dear Madam,—On the occasion of your departure from this country we desire to express to your on grateful appreciation of the arduous and disinterested labors of yourself and Mr. Phear in the cause of female education and social progress in Bengal. During your residence in this country, extending over a period of nearly 11 years, you have not only been always ready, as occasion offered, to devote your time and energies to every movement in aid of female advancement, but you have also endeared yourself personally to us by your uniform kindness and courtesy towards the people of this country. Notwithstanding the many difficulties in the way of social intercourse between the European and Indian races, you and your good husband have undertaken, with great success, the novel experiment of bringing them together in social life and thereby promoting a better understanding and closer sympathy between them than has hitherto existed. Nor is it possible to forget that in the peculiar circumstances of this country the work of female education has not unfrequently to be carried on without that cordial sympathy and co-operation from the general body of the people, which alone could render such a task grateful and attractive to a foreigner working for the good of a strange people. But in spite of all these drawbacks and obstacles, enough perhaps to damp the energies of any, but the most large-hearted philathropist, you and your good husband have been unremitting in your labors and unflagging in your zeal for the amelioration and social well-being of the people amongst whom you have resided for so many years. As Honorary Secretary to the "Hindu Mahila Bidyalaya," an institution which owed its continuance so long chiefly to your exertions, you have shown an example of disinterested labor and untiring energy which will be long and gratefully cherished by the women of Bengal, and though the institution has unfortunately, by reason of circumstances of an unavoidable or unforeseen nature, now ceased for a time to exist, it will never be forgotten that the experiment has been eminently successful, and whenever institutions of a similar character are established in future, the "Hindu Mahila Bidyalaya" will be regarded as their parent and model. It would be needless, even if it were practicable on this occasion, to enumerate the many and distinguished services rendered by yourself and Mr. Phear to the cause of female education and social advancement ever since your arrival in this country. There have been few projects or movements in Bengal in connection with those objects within the last 11 years, in which yourself and Mr. Phear have not taken an active interest and which you have not materially promoted by your labors. The extraordinary zeal, which has enabled you in a trying climate, and your husband amid the onerous duties of his high office, to bestow so much of your time and labors upon such a cause, has ever been a subject of wonder and admiration to the people of Bengal.

We have learned with deep regret that you are now about to depart from this country, though we hope it is not for ever, and have now assembled together to bid you farewell and to assure you that the women of Bengal will long cherish your names in their grateful recollection for the warm sympathy and active interest which you have always shown on their behalf. There are times when the emotions are too deep for utterance, and on this occasion we feel that every form of words which suggests itself to us is too weak to convey our sentiments. It is to be regretted that many Hindu ladies who would have been happy to be present here to-night are precluded by the customs of the country from doing so, but we can assure you that the feelings, which we have taken this opportunity to express, are shared in by the inmates of every zenana where your name is known.

In conclusion, we beg to wish you a pleasant voyage and health and happiness upon your return to your native land, and in bidding you farewell we venture to ask your kind acceptance of the humble token of our regard and gratitude, which is offered in the hope that it may serve to remind you sometimes of the many years you have spent amongst us and the many friends you will have left behind you.

We remain,
Dear Madam,

Your sincere and devoted friends,

7th April 1876.

Mr. Justice Phear on behalf of Mrs. Phear spoke a few appropriate words in reply.

PUBLIC MEETING IN HONOR OF LORD NORTHBROOK.

The public meeting held yesterday at the Town Hall in honor of Lord Northbrook, was presided over by Sir Richard Temple. It was attended mostly by Natives, there being only a sprinkling of Europeans. Some persons belonging to the Indian League, numbering only ten, opposed the passing of the first resolution, but they were hissed out; and the resolution was carried by acclamation. Among the opponents we may mention the following names:—Babu Monmothnath Mullick, Barrister-at-Law; Babu Sumbhu Chunder Mukhopadhya, the *quondam* President of the League; Babu Judunath Ghose, Head Master, Seal's Free College; and Babu Jogesh Chunder Dut, one of the Secretaries to the League. We have not heard of the names of the others. The following resolutions were passed:—

I. Proposed by Rajah Romanath Tagore, seconded by Sir Richard Garth and supported by the Maharajah of Vizianagram:—

That this Meeting desires to record its high sense of the eminent public services of the Right Honorable Lord Northbrook during his administration of British India, marked as that administration has been by a judicious management of the finances, by reduction of taxation, and consequent increased public confidence, by a liberal commercial policy, by humane and effective exertions to save the lives of millions of suffering people at a time of wide-spread distress from drought and scarcity, by a steady prosecution of measures of progress without excessive strain upon the national exchequer or violence to public feeling, and, generally by a loyal, considerate and conscientious exercise of the gracious behests of Her Majesty the Queen, contained in the Royal Proclamation for the Government of Her subjects in the East.

II. Proposed by Dr. Rrjendralala Mittra, seconded by Rajah Jotendromohun Tagore, and supported by Rajah Sivapersaud C. S. I. (on behalf of the Maharajah Benares.):—

That a Statue of the Right Hon'ble Lord Northbrook be erected in the City of Calcutta as a memorial of His Lordship's successful administration of the British Indian Empire.

III. Proposed by Babu Digumber Mitter C.S.I., and seconded by the Hon'ble Mr. Inglis:—

That the following address expressive of the sentiments of the community of Calcutta on His Lordship's administration of this country be presented to the Right Hon'ble Lord Northbrook:

[We omit the address for want of space.]

IV. Proposed by J. Bullen Smith Esq. C. S. I., and seconded by Rajah Suttyanund Ghosaul:—

That the following gentlemen be requested to wait in deputation upon the Right Hon'ble Lord Northbrook to present the Address.

Sir Richard Garth.
Hon'ble A. G. Macpherson.
Venerable Archdeacon Baly.
Hon'ble J. R. Bullen Smith.
Hon'ble G. C. Paul.
Hon'ble David Cowie.
Sir Stuart Hogg.
J. Pitt Kennedy Esq.
H. H. Sutherland Esq.
A. G. Apcar Esq.
Elias Gubboy Esq.
J. C. Murray Esq.
J. B. Knight Esq.
J. Jennings Esq.
J. Mackinnon Esq.
T. A, Vlasto Esq.
A. Ralli Esq.
G. M. Sturthers Esq.
Hon'ble H. Bell.
His Highness the Maharajah of Benares.
His Highness the Maharajah of Vizianagram.
Rajah Ramanath Tagore Bahadur.
Babu Degumber Mitter.
Rajah Jotindra Mohun Tagore Bahadur.
Hon'ble Rajah Narendra Krishna Bahadur.
Rajah Rajendra Narain Deb Bahadur.
Rajah Harendra Krishna Bahadur.
Rajah Suttyanund Ghosal Bahadur.
Babu Durga Churn Law.
Rai Rajendra Mullick Bahadur.
Babu Pannna Lal Seal.
Babu Joykissen Mukerji.
Babu Subuldass Mullick.
Babu Jodolal Mullick.
Babu Rajendralala Mittra.
Babu Chunder Kant Mukerji.
Kumar Grish Chunder Sing Bahadur.
Newab Amir Ali Bahadur.
Nawab Ashgar Ali Bahadur.
Prince Rohimuddin.
Prince Ferok Shah.
Hon'ble Mir Mahomed Ali.
Moulvi Abdul Lutif Khan Bahadur.
Manickji Rustomji Esq.
Revd. Dr. K. M. Banerji.
Babu Keshub Chunder Sen.
Babu Hem Chunder Kerr.
Hon'ble Kristodas Pal.

V. Proposed by F. Jennings Esq., and seconded by Moulvie Abdul Lutif Khan Bahadur.

That a committee consisting of the following gentlemen be appointed to receive subscriptions for the purpose of defraying the expenses of the Statue and carrying out the objects of the preceding resolutions:—

Sir Richard Temple.—*President.*
Sir John Strechey.
Sir Richard Garth.
Sir Henry Norman.
Hon'ble A. Hobhouse.
Hon'ble Ashly Eden.

Sir William Muir.
Sir Richard Meade.
Sir Henry Daly.
Sir Henry Davies.
A. C. Lyall Esq.
Hon'ble A. G. Macpherson.
Sir Stuart Hogg.
Venerable Archdeacon Baly.
R. B. Chapman Esq.
Mellville Esq.
Sir George Couper.
Sir Richard Pollock.
Hon'ble J. R. Bullen Smith.
Hon'ble David Cowie.
Hon'ble G. C. Paul.
H. H. Sutherland Esq.
J. B. Knight Esq.
F. Jennings Esq.
J. Pitt Kennedy Esq.
A. G. Apcar Esq.
J. C. Murray Esq.
Elias Gubboy Esq.
Manickji Rustomji Esq.
His Highness the Maharajah of Benares.
His Highness the Maharajah of Vizianagram
Raja Ramanauth Tagore Bahadur.
Babu Digumber Mitter.
Hon'ble Rajah Narendra Krishna Bahadur.
Rajah Rajendra Narain Deb Bahadur.
Rajah Harendra Krishna Bahadur.
Rajah Suttyanund Ghosal Bahadur.
Babu Durga Churn Law.
Rai Rajendra Mullick Bahadur.
Babu [illegible] Lall Seal.
Babu Joykissen Mukerji.
Babu Subul Das Mullick.
Babu Jodulall Mullick.
Babu Rajendrala Mittra.
Babu Chunder Kont Mukerji.
Kumar Gris Chunder Sing Bahadur.
Rajah Pramath Nath Roy Bahadur.
Maharani Surnomoyee.
Babu Kally Kissen Tagore.
Babu Annadapros.ud Roy
Newab Abdul Gunny Bahadur.
Newab Amir Ali Bahadur.
Newab Ashgar Ali Bahadur.
Prince Rohimudden.
Prince Ferrok Shah.
Hon'ble Mir Mahomed A'ly.
Moulvi Abdul Latif Khan Bahadur.
Babu Keshub Chunder Sen.
Hon'ble Kristodas Pal.

Hon'ble H, Bell. Raja Joteendra Mohun Tagore Bahadur.	*Members and Hony. Secretaries Ex-officio.*

(With power to add to their number.)

VI. Proposed by Manickji Rustomji Esq., and seconded by Babu Keshub Chunder Sen:—

That the Committee be requested to communicate with such parties as they may deem proper in Bombay, Madras, the N. W. Provinces, the Punjab, Oudh, the Central Provinces and other parts of the country with a view to invite them to join in the memorial to Lord Northbrook.

ACKNOWLEDGMENT.

The Loyal Hours, being a couple of Poems to welcome Their Royal Highnesses the Prince of Wales and the Duke of Edinburgh on their respective advents to India in 1875 and 1860. Written on behalf of himself and his fellow-countrymen. By Gooroo Churn Dutt, the author of the "School Hours." Calcutta 1876.

DOMESTIC OCCURRENCE.

BIRTH.

DAS.—At Vikrampore, thanah Moifutgunge, District Furridpore, Village Koniorpore, on Friday night, the 10th *Pous* corresponding with the 24th December, 1875, the wife of Babu Kailas Chunder Das, of a son.

Public Engagement.

MUSICAL EVANGELISTIC SERVICE.—The Rev John Hector, M. A., will deliver an address in the Free Church Institution, Nimtollah Street, on Sunday evening, 9th instant, at 7 o'clock, Subject.—"God's love to the world"—John iii. 16 Hymns in Bengali, set to Hindu Music, will be sung.

Law

POLICE.—APRIL 8, 1876.

[Before F. J. Marsden, Esq.]

MR. DICKENS, Magistrate, Northern Division, charged his sirdar-bearer with having cheated him out of several sums. The facts are these. On the 6th March, the accused, who had the sole management of his master's expenses, ordered the *chaprasi* to call a cart with straw. The *chaprasi* did so, and the bearer purchased the straw for Rs. 4, but charged Rs. 4-8 for it. In April the same thing was done, and the *chaprasi* informed his master of the fact. This time fraud was committed in the presence of both the syce and the coachman, who gave their evidence. The Magistrate sentenced the accused to six weeks' rigorous imprisonment.

Advertisements

THACKER, SPINK AND CO.

INDIAN LAW.

ACTS of the LEGISLATIVE COUNCIL of INDIA. Annual Volume, uniform with Theobald's addition. 8vo. For 1873, Rs. 5. For 1874, Rs. 5.

BELL'S LAW of LANDLORD and TENANT as administered in Bengal. Second Edition. Royal 8vo. Rs. 7-8.

BENGAL CRIMINAL PROCEDURE; being a Translation of the Fourth Edition of Mr. H. T. Prinsep's Work. By Krishna Prosunno Bose. 8vo. (and Supplement containing Act XI of 1874) Rs. 5.

BONNERJEE'S HINDU WILLS ACT. With the Sections of the Indian Succession Act made applicable to the Wills of Hindus, &c. 8vo. Rs. 6.

BROUGHTON'S CODE of CIVIL PROCEDURE. With Appendix containing the Charters of the High Courts and Miscellaneous Acts. Fourth Edition. By C. J. Wilkinson, Esq. Royal 8vo. Rs. 22.

BROUGHTON'S DECLARATORY DECREES; being an extended Commentary on the Fifteenth Section of the Civil Procedure Code. 8vo. Rs. 4.

CHART of INHERITANCE ACCORDING to the Bengal School of Hindu Law. On Card. Colored Rs. 1-8.

CHART of SUCCESSION ACCORDING to the Suni School of Mahomedan Law. With descriptive Letter-Press. On Card. Colored. Rs 2.

CHEVERS' MANUAL of MEDICAL JURISPRUDENCE for India, including an Outline of a History of Crime against the Person in India. Royal 8vo. Rs. 12.

COLEBROOKE'S LAW of INHERITANCE According to the Mitakshara. Edited by Rajendro Missry. 8vo. Rs 8.

COWELL'S HISTORY and CONSTITUTION of the Courts and Legislative Authorities, 8vo. Rs 8.

COWELL'S INDIAN DIGEST: INDEX to the Reported Cases of the High Courts Second Edition. Super-royal 8vo. Rs 30.

COWELL'S LECTURES on HINDU LAW as administered by the British Courts in India. 2 volls. 8vo. Rs. 20.

CROSTHWAITE'S LAND REVENUE LAW of the North-Western Provinces; being Act XIX of 1873. with Notes. Royal 8vo. Rs 16.

CURRIE'S INDIAN LAW EXAMINATION Manual. 8vo. cloth. Rs. 7-8.

FIELD'S BENGAL REGULATIONS WITH chronological Table, Introduction, Notes and Index Rs. 21.

FIELD'S CHRONOLOGICAL TABLE of, and INDEX to, the Indian Statute Book. 4to. Rs. 21.

FIELD'S HIGH COURT RULES and CIRCULAR Orders, Civil and Criminal, from 1862 to 1871. With Indices. 2 vols. 8vo. Rs. 14.

FULL BENCH RULINGS, from the commencement of the High Court to 1868. Royal 8vo. cloth. Rs. 26. Part II separately. Rs. 14.

GOODEVE'S LAW OF EVIDENCE as administered in England, and applied to India. Royal 8vo. Rs. 10.

GOODEVE'S NEW EVIDENCE ACT I of 1872. With Notes, &c., showing Alteration in the Law. 8vo. Rs. 1-8.

KNOX'S CRIMINAL LAW of the BENGAL Presidency; Penal Code, Criminal Procedure, and all Miscellaneous Criminal Acts and orders 2 vols. Royal 8vo. Rs. 20.

MACNAUGHTEN'S STAMP ACT. With Notifications, High Court Rulings, and Notes. 8vo. Rs. 3.

MACPHERSON'S LAW of MORTGAGE in Bengal and the North-Western Provinces. Fifth Edition. by N. H. Thomson, Esq. 8vo. Rs. 10.

MACPHERSON'S NEW PROCEDURE of the Civil Courts of British India, 8vo. Rs. 16.

MACRAE'S LAW of DIVORCE for INDIA With Notes of decided Cases on all branches of the Law relating to Matrimonial Suits. Demy 8vo. Rs. 10.

India General Steam Navigation Company, Limited.

SCHOENE, KILBURN & Co.—*Managing Agents*

ASSAM LINE.

NOTICE.

Steamers now leave Calcutta for Assam every Tuesday, Goalundo every Thursday and Debrooghur downward every Saturday.

THE Str. "ASSAM" will leave Calcutta for Assam, on Tuesday, the 11th instant.

Cargo will be received at the Company's Godowns, Nimtollah Ghat, until noon of Monday, the 10th.

THE Str. "SIMLA" will leave Goalundo for Assam on Thursday the 13th instant.

Cargo will be received at the Company's Godowns, No. 4, Fairlie Palace, up till noon of Tuesday, the 11th.

Goods forwarded to Goalundo for this vessel will be chargeable with Railway Freight from Calcutta to Goalundo in addition to the regular Freight of this Company.

Passengers should leave for Goalundo by Train of Wednesday, the 12th.

CACHAR LINE NOTICE

REGULAR WEEKLY SERVICE.

Steamers now leave Calcutta for Cachar and Intermediate Stations every Tuesday and Chattuck downward every Tuesday.

A Steamer and "FLAT" will leave Calcutta for Cachar on Tuesday, the 11th instant.

Cargo will be received at the Company's Godowns, Nimtollah Ghat, up till noon of Monday, the 10th.

For further information regarding rates of Freight or passage money, apply to.

4 Fairlie Palace, G. J. SCOTT,
Calcutta, 5th April 1876. *Secretary.*

BABU BASANTA KUMAR DATTA,

Homœopathic Practitioner.

No. 20, Sunker Halder's Lane. Ahiritolah.

JUST ARRIVED FROM ENGLAND.

MEDICINES, AND ALL REQUISITES TO BE HAD AT—

DATTA'S HOMŒOPATHIC LABORATORY
No. 312, CHITPORE ROAD, BOTTOLAH, CALCUTTA.

BABU RADHAKANTA GHOSH

HOMŒOPATHIC PRACTITIONER,

12, College, Square.

Is practising here on moderate terms.

SMITH, STANISTREET & CO.

Pharmaceutical Chemists & Druggists

BY APPOINTMENT

To His Excellency the Right Hon'ble LORD NORTHBROOK, G.M.S.I., Governor-General of India.

&c. &c.

SYRUP OF LACTATE OF IRON.

Prepared from the original receipe. Lactate of Iron, in various forms of preparation, have been in use in France, and generally through the Continent of Europe, for some years past, and is highly esteemed as one of the most valuable Chalybeate Tonic Remedies yet introduced. The Syrup, being the most agreeable as well as convenient form of administration, is in most general use. It is a most valuable remedy in the following diseases:—Chlorosis or Green Sickness, Leucorrhœa, Neuralgia, Enlargement of the Spleen &c. In combination with quinine, it has also been very successfully used in the cure of Fever, while to persons of delicate constitution, enfeebled by disease it is invaluable. In bottles, Rs. 2 each.

SYRUP OF THE PHOSPHATE OF IRON Rs. 2 per bottle.

SYRUP OF PHOSPHATE OF IRON AND STRYCHNINE, Rs. 2 per bottle.

SYRUP OF PHOSHATE OF IRON AND QUININE. Price Rs. 2-8 per bottle.

SYRUP OF PHOSPHATE OF IRON, QUININE AND STRYCHINE, DR. ATKIN'S TRIPLE TONIC SYRUP, Rs. 2-8 per bottle.

Smith, Stanistreet & Co.

Invite special attention to the following rates, the quality guaranteed as the best procurable:—

Pure Ærated Waters.

Made from Pure Water, obtained by the new process through the Patent Charcoal Filters.

			Rs	As
Ærated plain (Trible Ærated), per doz.		...	0	12
Soda Water	ditto	...	0	12
Gingerade	ditto	...	1	4
Lemonade	ditto	...	1	4
Tonic (Quinine)	ditto	,, ...	1	4

The Cash must be sent with the order to obtain advantage of the above rates.

!!! हुका !!!

!!! HOOKAHS !!!

English made Hookahs of various choice designs, colours and sizes ranging in price from Rs. 2 to 5 each, 60 designs to choose from. Apply to

RADANAUTH CHOWDRY,
373, Jorasanko.

হেমলতা যোগিনী।

NEW HISTORICAL TRAGEDY

BY

GOPAL CHUNDER MOOKERJEE.

Price, Re. 1, postage 2 as.

To be had at 50, Grey Street, Shobhabazar, and Sanskrit Press Depository.

NATIONAL COMPANY.

HOMŒOPATHIC CHAMISTS AND PUBLISHER

SUPPLY ALL KINDS OF

HOMŒOPATHIC MEDICINES, BOOKS CASES AND OTHER REQUISITES.

12 COLLEGE SQUARE,
Calcutta.

Printed and published by M. M. BUKSHI, at the "INDIAN MIRROR" Press, No. 15, College Square, for the Proprietor.

The Indian Mirror.

SUNDAY EDITION.

VOL. XV.] CALCUTTA, SUNDAY, APRIL, 16, 1876 { REGISTERED AT THE GENERAL POST OFFICE. } [No. 90

CONTENTS.

NOTICE.

Letters and all other communications relating to the literary department of the Paper should be addressed to "The Editor."

All letters on the business of the Press should be addressed, and all remittances made payable to the Manager of this Paper. Particular attention is solicited to this notice.

Subscribers will be good enough to give prompt notice of any delay, or irregularity in delivery of the Paper.

Editorial Notes.

THE Albert Hall scheme is likely to be a *fait accompli* very soon. The promoters have been spared the trouble of erecting a new hall. That commodious and most favorably situated house in College Square, which was formerly occupied by the Presidency College, has been taken up under the Land Acquisition Act, and we have no doubt that it will after undergoing the necessary alterations and improvements admirably answer the purposes of the Albert Hall. The Native community must feel profoundly thankful to Sir Richard Temple for the kind interest he has evinced and the valuable aid he has offered in this good cause. How glad we shall be to have a public hall and library in the Native quarter of the town!

OUR Sunday paper is patronized by some eminent lady-readers in England. We have a proposal to make before them. We propose that a book be written illustrative of the highest types of feminine character, as representing different ideals of life. What is, for instance, the highest type of religious womanhood, and what historical characters represent it? We may extend the right of illustration to popular literature, and find out how this ideal is set forth in the characters that fill our best novels and dramas. What is the highest standard of woman's morality, and how far historical and other characters approach it. Thus if different ideals be taken up and illustrated, the book will be most valuable especially in this country, where we require so much aid and illustration to develop the character of our young country-women.

BEFORE leaving the shores of India Lord Northbrook took occasion to assure the leader of our community of the deep interest he always felt in the Brahmo movement, though of course theologically he differed in opinion. He fully appreciated the high moral work undertaken by the Brahmos, and the progressive enlightenment they had been the means of diffusing in Native society in its present critical state of unsettlement and transition. His Lordship spoke most encouragingly of their efforts to suppress drunkeness and immorality, and lead Native youths into a better path. Lord Northbrook expressed his sincerest regret at the ravages of intemperance and the highly deleterious influence exercised by the Native stage on the morals of the rising generation through obscene plays, and prostitute actresses. We heartily honor the ex-Viceroy for such deep and unusal solicitude for public morals and trust our present Viceroy will continue the good work. Lord Northbrook may rest assured that he carries home the good wishes of all advanced Natives.

IN spite of so many opinions expressed on the subject of the Budhistic *Nirvan*, the subject is still exceedingly little understood. Generally speaking the belief is that *Nirvan* means annihilation. Burnouf, and Max Muller both insist on this view, and a host of minor authorities confirm the popular impression. That Buddha distinctly declares non-existence to be the destiny of the wise and the blessed, there is no doubt. But strange to say he predicates with equal distinctness *personality, purity, joy, wisdom, and permanence* of this state of non-existence. Non-existence is said to be of four kinds. That which has not existed, but may exist in the future; that which once existed, but is now no more; that which exists as the contrary of something else; that which is purely imaginary, and neither existed, nor can exist at any time. *Nirvan* belongs to the third order of non-existence. It exists as the contrary of certain states of being. It is the contrary of covetousness, or desire, or *Trishna*; it is the contrary of ignorance, or self-delusion, or *Avidya*; it is the cotrary of aversion, or cruelty, or *Himsa*; it is the contrary of all impermanent existence, and all phonomenal knowledge and joy that springs from the six organs of sense, or *Indryas*. Absence of all desire and *trishna* means purity; absence of all self-delusion and *Avidya* means wisdom; absence of all aversion means a heart full of joy; and absence of sense-knowledge, or *Rupa* means permanence. "*That* is personal, pure, permanent, and full of joy," says Buddha, "which is left after the six organs, and the six objects of sense, and the various kinds of knowledge are destroyed. Illustrious youth, when the world weary of sorrow, turns away and separates itself from the cause of all this sorrow, then, by this voluntary rejection of it, there remains that which I call the true self; and it is of this I plainly declare the formula, that it is permanent, full of joy, personal, and pure." This is *Nirvana*.

THE Unitarian controversy is over. The liberal party among English Unitarians must be said to have gained a considerable triumph, and the works of Theodore Parker are henceforth to be printed and published by the British and Foreign Unitarian Association. That society has thus launched into a new career from the beginning of the present year, and we hope and trust that career will continue in the future to be more liberal, and expansive, and inclusive. There is positive gain in Theodore Parker being recognized as a Christian by the most powerful Unitarian Christian organisation in the world. We hope the Unitarians of America will now imitate this example. Thus gradually the difference between Unitarian Christianity and pure Theism is ceasing to exist, and ere long the two systems may unite. There is only one fact which pains us greatly in connection with this controversy. This is the resignation of the worthy Secretary of the Association, the Rev. Robert Spears. He has been identified with the conservative party, and with its defeat he has laid down his office like an honorable minded Englishman. His attitude towards the Brahmo Somaj has been uniformly so friendly, nay so enthusiastic in its friendliness, that we view his disconnection with the society as a great loss to us, We know wherever Mr Spears is he will prove eminently useful to the Unitarian community, and may his career in the future be as honorable and prosperous as it has been in the past. Another curious feature in the controversy was the position taken by Mr. Martineau. In all previous Unitarian controversies he uniformly led the advanced party of progress, and almost all the reformers among the new party are his disciples and followers. But he was for compromise this time, and voted for the amendment which for an indefinite period of time would banish Parker's grandest work *viz.*, The *Discourse*, from the Unitarian book depot. We have no doubt Mr. Martineau had the best reasons for this course, but some of his pupils were obliged to take an opposite line of argument. And they triumphed.

SOME of the American Baptists are consistent in celebrating the Lord's Supper. They not only eat the sacramental bread, and drink the sacramental wine, but conclude the whole business with "the Sacrament of Feet-washing." To the other denominations this ceremony is unpopular, and they denounce it as senseless "literalism." In damp chilly whether this is certainly inconvenient, and pious men may thus catch cold through their religion, which no amount of piety may cure. But it is doubtless a part of the Last Supper, described in the thirteenth chapter of John. What can be more touching than when it is said: "And supper being ended, he riseth from supper, and laid aside his garments, and took a towel, and girded himself, and began to wash his disciples' feet." There is some real humiliation in it, and some real moral courage too, which no eating and drinking, however devout, does possess. A Protestant Bishop who witnessed the ceremony in a chapel of colored Baptists in South America, ironically describes it thus :—

The table was cleared of its fine linen and sacramental vessels, and revealed a plain white table, underneath which we had previously seen pails of water—or buckets, as they call them here. Off went the coat of the pastor. Off went a dozen other coats—those of his deacons, I presume. The whole church was in commotion. The basins began to fly. A brother stood behind the water-pails and dealt out a small gourdful to each basin, Brother and sister went on their knees before brother and sister. The shoe and stocking of the right foot was taken off, and a slight wash and wipe completed the ceremony. Then the one with the cleansed foot knelt and washed the cleanser's foot. They went among the pews, and it was as modest as such an act could be, Little children washed little children. The chief lady stood in the front of the communion-table, inspiring the scene with her sage, directing, evidently, the women. In dress and bearing she surpassed her sisters, and I supposed her the pastor's wife. She sat down on the seat fronting the pulpit and was washed and washed the washer. Her husband, the preacher—if his wife it was—toward the close took his seat on a bench under the pulpit, fronting the congregation, and took off a nice shoe and stocking, and had his foot cleansed by a clerical brother, who wore a long white apron. Then he arose, girded himself with the apron, and washed the other brother's foot. The water was only used for the two and then changed. Sometimes it looked hideously dirty; but usually not much so. It was evident that most had prepared for the occasion by private cleansing.

WAHABEEISM is considered by many to be the purest form of Mahomedanism. It is said to represent the spirit of Mahomed much more strictly than any other form of Islam. This is evidently the view of Palgrave, the great Arabian traveller, than whom Mahomedanism could not have a more determined enemy. With the obstinate and inveterate hostility of Mr. Palgrave to Mahomed and his religion, we have no sympathy, though some of his observations, we think, possess a large measure of truth. One of these is the attitude of Mahomedanism to popular pleasures and amusements. Wine of course is strictly prohibited; but tobacco is still more rigorously forbidden; and the same embargo is laid on painting, music, and all kinds of oriental imagery; there is even an anathema against bells. Commerce is positively discouarged. "He who twice embarks on sea is a very infidel." Agriculture too is denounced: "Angels visit not the house where a plough is laid up." This course taken by Mahomed is explained on the following ground. The Arabian prophet endeavoured most assiduously to cut off all bonds of sympathy between his followers, and those of neighbouring religions, lest the former by social influences and worldly friendships find the prominent peculiarities of their creed softened down, and in the end merge into other communities. Therefore he forbade among his disciples all those amusements and pursuits, which distinguish the rest of the world. "The history of ascetic brotherhood," observes Mr. Palgrave, "and secret sects in the East from the Durdanellea to the Indus, proves how near the verge of dissolution Islam was brought more than once by the indirect filtration of expansive ideas." Even among Mahomedans themselves all secular amusements and pursuits are forbidden. In common conversation almost every sentence is interlarded with the name of the Diety. Add to this the constantly recurring prayers, rites, and duties, the festivals, and constant gatherings at the Musjids. All this shows that the object of the Prophet was to remind his followers what religion and what organization they belonged to." The services are short, and not tiresome; but they come so often that they make the forgetfulness of the vocation of the Mahomedan impossible, and they always contain the quintessence of the Mehomedan doctrines so tersely and well, that in their very monotony they make it impossile for the Mahomedan to identify himself with the followers of another religion. These measures have most wonderfully preserved the integrity of Mussulman nations, but they have at the same time made those nations the most bigoted and unprogressive in the world.

OUR FAITH AND OUR EXPERIENCES.

(Continued.)

LET us now dismiss the past; let us take leave of ancient dispensations, and come down to see things as they are to-day. What is it that we see around us? The Theists of modern India, we see, are worshipping this Great Spirit-God, in their temples and also in their homes. They adore no visible divinity, but worship and serve the unseen and intangible Spirit of God. Strange it is, yet true, that for this they have been ridiculed and charged with attempting an impossibility. Even the educated of the present day have not hesitated to pronounce them thoughtless adorers of a metaphysical absurdity. The Infinite Spirit is said to be inconceivable and unknowable. Philosophy banishes the Infinite from the domain of thought, and places Him far above the reach of human thought and cognition. The very laws and conditions of thought rebel against a conception, however remote, of absolute and unconditioned Spirit. To think Him is to think Him away. God as a pure Spirit, whom neither the senses can apprehend nor the mind conceive, is altogether unknowable. Such is the verdict of the so-called philosophy of modern times. Against this startling and pernicious doctrine I desire to declare my most emphatic protest. It *is* possible for man in spite of the limitations of thought to think and realize pure Spirit. It is absurd to say that if we are to conceive Divinity at all, we must clothe Him with flesh, and invest Him with the form and attributes of humanity, so as to bring Him within the reach of our thought and sympathy. It is equally absurd to contend that if we abandon the idea of worshipping God in a human or other visible shape, we must as an inevitable alternative, rush into the regions of the absolutely unknowable. Universal experience proves that the finite soul can stand before and commune with the Infinite soul, "in spirit and in truth". In the consciousness of the true devotee the Divine Spirit shines as a reality, infinitely more real than the small realities of the world around us. (Applause) I speak not of possibilities only, but of veritable facts. The weak and credulous may bow before idols, the sceptical may complacently dismiss divinity from their minds as simply inconceivable, but the spiritually-minded have in all ages worshipped the Pure Spirit. Nay, they have even loved the unseen Spirit with the warmest and sweetest love. Reverently do I bow to the dictum of pholosophy that our finite intellect can not even by its highest stretch conceive the Infinite Mind, and that He must always remain an incomprehensible though admitted reality. Yet in the same breath and with equal reverence must I proclaim the fact that the higher spiritual nature of man clearly perceives and passionately lover a mere Unseen Presence and evinces as much vividness of perception and fervour of personal attachment as an idolater does to his idol, or a hero-worshipper to his hero. Do you not see this verified in the religious consciousness of modern India? The Theists in India, individually and as an organized community, have not only revived the worship of the ancient Spirit-God of the Aryans, but are found to be possessed in a great measure of the sentiments and feelings of later idolatry. It is not to be denied that Puranic or Idolatrous India has, with all her prejudices and superstitions and her vast Pantheon, peopled with millions of divinities, contributed to throw upon the Spirit-God of Aryan India, such charming colors as have made Him peculiarly dear to modern Theists. As we roll down the steam of our national history we are grieved to find how amidst successive changes a higher and purer faith has gradually degenerated into debasing forms of idolatry and superstiton, how in consequence of the later corruptions of Hinduism the country has gone down century after century in a course of moral and spiritual decadence. And yet marvellously has God's Providence evolved light out of all this darkness, truth out of all this evil. Out of evil cometh good. Out of idolatry have been extracted the sweets of Theism. It may seem strange, yet nevertheless it is true, that even the curse of idolatry has proved a blessing to us. To the myriad gods and goddesses of India, to the Mahabharata, the Ramayana, and all the legends of Hindu mythology we owe a debt of gratitude. It is these divinities, however unreal, that have called forth the varied affections of the Hindu mind. The worshippers of Rama and Krishna, whatever their errors, have worshipped their gods with hearts full of devotional feelings. The idolatrous Hindu lives in the midst of an unceasing flow of deep sentiments. Personal feelings towards a visible and personal divinity, the warmest sentiments, the sweetest feelings of gratitude, love, filial tenderness, and friendly communion abound in his heart.

HINDU WORSHIPPERS.

There are very few really sincere worshippers of Hindu deities, men who have disinterestedly devoted their whole life and energy to attain the perfection of their cult. But one or two such men may here and there be found. We are going to record our experiences of them. The immorality and grossness associated by European bigots with every form of idolatry in this country are not to be found in the really sincere. The dark errors and superstitions which Paganism is said to indicate, can be rarely detected in their conversation and belief. Most of their sentiments on the subject of practical piety are simple, tender, genuine, and most natural. But nevertheless they are the worshippers of idolatrous deities. Their opinions and ours are very different, most contradictory in many essential matters. There is not a word of exaggeration in all that we have said. We agree and disagree with them to a wonderful extent. Dr. Murray Mitchell, than whom we do not know a more orthodox, or a more genuine Christian in this country, once talking to a Brahmo of our acquaintance, thus concluded his conversation, "And you must allow me to say *it is a marvel to me that you are not a Christian!*" We have ourselves sometimes felt impelled to make a similar exclamation on reading books, and talking to people of other persuasions, and we have eminently experienced this feeling in communing with certain worshippers of Hindu deities. The three presiding deities of the Hindu pantheon are Vishnu, Shakti, and Shiva. The numerous incarnations of these three make up almost the whole Hindu mythology. Brahma, the abstract, subtle, attributeless, creative essence, has no cult peculiar to itself, no sect or following that belongs to it alone, and is represented by Prakriti or Shakti, the female principle in creation. The popular Hindu religion of the times, therefore, is classified under the three grand divisions of Vaishnavas, Shaktas, and Shivaites. No end of discussions there have been and no end of opinions have been expressed on the creeds and relations of these sects, opinions which it is not our object here to criticise, or even to notice. We see only three vital ideas represented by the sects, and their presiding deities. The Vaishnavas set forth the idea of love and faith. The Shaktas set forth the filial relation of children to the Mother. And the Shivaites contemplating on death, and self-renunciation, illustrate the principles of meditation and communion (Yoga), and unworldliness, and the worthlessness of bodily pleasures. We have plenty of Vaishnavas, and Shaktas in Bengal, and we can easily observe the operation of their principles around us. The great Chaitanya has developed the Vaishnava's religion in such a way that there can be no mistake about it. The tender devotion, the intense wonderful faith, the goodness and purity of life called forth by singing hymns to the sweetness and glory of the name of Hari at the time of Chaitanya and his disciples, are matters of history. There is little in the annals of religion anywhere that can excel these traits of the Vaishnava's piety. Then the religious genius of Ramprasad Sen, and others like him, has very touchingly illustrated how far filial relations with the Supreme Mother, whom they call Durga, Tara, and Kali, can be developed in the heart of the Shakta worshipper. Some of Ramprasada's popular songs, (who knows them not in Bengal?) breathe a serenity of child-like dependence, a sweetness of trust and self-surrender, a depth of wisdom and insight into the weaknesses, and desires of human life unsurpassed by any other hymns we have yet come across. That there is real profound religious excellence in such a system, no one who knows it can deny. To seek for the Shivaite we must go out of Bengal, to Bombay and Madras, into those vast tracts where the great Shunkararjya preached and propounded his doctrines, where the mighty masses of Shanyasis congregate on the banks of the Godavery at Nassick, or bathe and chant their sweetly composed verses in the streams of the Krishna. But Shanyasis in Bengal are known, and Shiva's attributes are not altogether foreign. The tigerskin, the ashes, and the necklace of bones, the long matted locks of dishevelled hair, the fondness for the resorts of silence and death, the fixed self-absorted, unchangeable posture of meditation, likened unto the snowy peak of the Dhavalagiri, these indicate the pursuits of Shiva, and the Shivaites. Shiva is the emblem of utter unworldliness, of unearthly simplicity and self-renunciation, of rapt communion that makes one unconscious of what is around him, an absorption in spiritual realities full of profound calmness and joy. In a word, Shiva is the emblem of Yoga. We have had the good fortune of meeting a man, who combines all these cults in his comprehensive soul. We have found him immersed at times in faith and love, singing, as Chaitanya sang, the sweetness of Hari's name. We have found him deep in the sentiments that inspired Ramprasad's voice in love and trust to the Divine mother, whose worship Bengal celebrates every year with national joy. We have observed him rapt and full of joy recounting the strange weird attributes of Shiva, sitting amidst scenes of death and solitude. Such idolatrous worshippers, however ignorant or supercilious men may denounce them, are to us objects of profound reverence. Their opinions and ours are divided as the poles asunder, but our souls seek the definiteness and reality of their worship, the vividness and clearness of their view of the Divine nature, and the relations thereof with our nature.

Correspondence.

PROFESSIONAL LIFE IN INDIA.

To the Editor of the *Indian Mirror*.

Bread-winning is just now uppermost in my thoughts. We must eat to live. Except a man work neither shall he eat. To earn the means of living for him and his, comes to every man, Bhaktas and Yogis not excepted,—as his *kismut*, his fate, his duty. In the sweat of thy brow shalt thou eat bread. And this, not as a cross or a curse but as a joy and a blessing. How shall I earn a livelihood? The varied answers to this question all centre in one which is clear as chrystal; *plant yourself on a want.* The world is full of wants. Give, and it shall be given to you. Supply, and you shall be supplied. Give good and get good. He that watereth shall be watered also himself. All need water, and need a bread, but man cannot live on bread alone, or on water alone. He has higher wants. He wants to love and be loved. Hence marriage and a home; a wife and children. He wants a just and wise protection of his home. This want is at once so large and so difficult to supply that a principal section of the best-taught men in every civilized community, plant themselves upon it. Here they thrive, and constitute a body of honored bread-winners, than whom, in every nation, none deserve better or win more; and these constitute, the Legal Profession. Again, sickness comes to all. From the hour of entering the world to the moment of leaving it, we are all instantly liable to want help in disease or accident. . . . Hence appears another band of learned and honored bread-winners, the Medical Profession. We need not name other professions, such as those of the Teacher, (who *per excellence* is the Professor), the Civil Engineer, the Artist, or the Merchant. But there is another professi n that has held its own in every age, and through all history,—planted on a perenial human want. It is that of the guardians and guides of worship,—the priests and the prophets,—the ministers and purifiers of religion. No deep study of human wants is needful, in order to discover that life,—national, social, individual,—is hopelessly crippled without religion. As readily may the body spare the grain-supplier, as the soul the supplier of religious light and food. Every man his own lawyer; every man his own doctor; every man his own house-builder; every man his own railway-constructor; his own teacher, Governor, ruler, and Church. These cries have just enough truth in them to captivate the thoughtless. No man of common observation, or maturity of mind, doubts, that the "student of divinity" builds on strong foundations when he wisely and persistently plants himself on the human want of religion; on man's need as a worshipper, lover, student and worker out of the will of God. Doubt what you will, but never doubt that man needs help in *that* department of his life. His want—I do not say of theology, important as that is,—but of worship, of holiness, of godliness, and of continual help from its faithful cultivators and professors, is not an open question. In all recorded life plainly appears this cardinal need. Especially in a people as worshipful as the Hindus, must this hunger be supplied. Bread or a stone, they will have;—meat or drug; the egg or the asp. Pastors or prisoners,—which shall it be? The paramount question, to-day,—the one question which most urgently demands an answer, the life-question, for the people of India, is this. Whence, for her, is to arise an honored profession, co-ordinate with her legal and medical professions, able and willing to take charge of her religious guidance and supply? Is India's old Brahmanical priesthood awakening to her new life; or willing or fit to nurse it? God knows. But it does not seem so. Are those who have been her priests welcoming the light that dawns upon her sure as sun-rise, and as irreversible? If not,—if not then will the All Merciful and all Bountiful, as to this need, let India starve? Up, men, and meet this famine. Tens of thousands will perish; they will do worse than eat their own flesh, before this want is fairly met. Happy he who not only believes, but knows that this want is real; and hastens out with its natural and God-meant rice and grain. Young man plant yourself betimes upon this want, and He who made man a religious being will see that your business prospers.

Yours &c.,
DALL.

TO CORRESPONDENTS.

A SUFFERER wants to know if there is any cure for short-sightedness, which is assuming "an alarming growth" among Bengali students. The use of spectacles by youngsters in their teens, is condemned.

CALLY PROSUNNO PALIT informs us that a Babu by name of Joynarain Bhuttacharji, will shortly deliver a lecture showing that Christianity is derived from Budhism.

MAN.—God is certainly not responsible for your actions. You talk blasphemy.

P. N. S. is anxious to know the benefits that this country has derived from the Prince of Wales' visit. The assumption of the title of Empress of India by the Queen is one. As to the rest we would refer our correspondent to the *Charivari*.

The Brahmo Somaj.

THE Bengali New Year was celebrated in the Brahmo Mandir early on thursday morning. Service began before six, and lasted till a quarter to nine. There was good attendance considering the day of the week, and the hour of the day.

THE anniversary of the Eatra Brahmo Somaj, a village to the West of Howrah, took place on Wednesday evening. And the anniversary of the Saukaritolah Brahmo Somaj was celebrated on Friday evening. Babu P. C. Mozumdar conducted the service on both occasions.

IT gives us some amusement to see the criticisms which our Christian friends make about our movement, and our principles in their journals. They have at last made the wise discovery that we are on the high way to Hinduism, because we make a copious use of such words as *Bhakti*, *Yoga*, *Byragya* &c. If we make use of English phraseology, which is necessarily Christian, we are directly accused of stealing all our doctrines and improvements from Christianity; if we make use of Hindu phraseology to express our sentiments we are at once denounced as rushing headlong into Hinduism. What can we do under such circumstances? We must either invent a new language for ourselves, or manage some how to survive the criticisms of our evangelical well-wishers. All things considered we prefer to abide by the latter course.

DR. ATMARAM PUNDURUNG, Secretary of the Prarthana Somaj Bombay, accompanied by his daughter, an unmarried young lady, and two sons, left Bombay for England by the last mail steamer. Dr. Atmaram is the most enlightened, and progressive Hindu in Bombay. We wish him, and his family a safe voyage, and prosperous sojourn in Europe.

Literary.

KHUDAYAR KHAN, the ex-ruler of Khokand, has been interviewed by a *Times* correspondent.

A NEW paper, called the *South Indian Post*, has been started at Negapatam "to represent the Southern districts of this Presidency."

IN *Vanity Fair* "Rasper" tells the following story: "A clergyman was 'turned down,' at Lady Combermere's Spelling Bee for spelling drunkenness with one 'n.' He shortly after returned to his parish, and found himself very coldly received by his parishioners. He sent for the parish clerk and asked him what was the cause. 'Well, Sir,' replied the man, 'a report has come down here that you was *turned out of a great lady's house in London for drunkenness*!'"

THE death is reported in the prime of life of Professor Siegmund, a German Orientalist of great distinction. The professor had the misfortune of falling down a precipice at Amathes, in Cyprus, where he was engaged in the excavations undertaken by the American Government. He died on the spot.

THE *Friend of India's* London correspondent warmly advocates the establishment of a London paper which should speak with independence and authority to the English nation on Indian politics.

BY far the most interesting article in the April number of the *Calcutta Review* is the one on "the 'Struggle for existence' of the English Press" in India, by Mr. W. Digby, the Editor of the *Colombo Observer*.

THE *Friend of India's* London correspondent while referring to the Prince of Wales' visit to India writes:—"The only literature evoked by the Prince's visit which has attracted many readers are the letters of *Punch's* correspondent. The rich and artistic use of 'local colouring' in these fine productions has been greatly applauded: the Native potentates who figure there have been everywhere acknowledged to be very much more interesting than the unpronounceable people who crowd together in the columns of the *Daily News*, or the *Times*. The Rajah of Pekkhuapri, and Sir Bars Berrijam are Eastern potentates we all fell an interest in; and Sir Jak Holkar, *the* Holkar, never appears upon the scene without being greeted with several rounds of applause."

MR. RICHARD HENRY DANA, nominated Minister to England in the room of General Schenck, is the author of the well-known book, "Two Years before the Mast."

MR. TREVENYAN'S "Life and Letters of Lord Macaulay" is to be ready at *Longmans'* on the 30th of March.

THE Royal Academy has elected the Right Hon. W. E. Gladstone, M.P., Professor of Ancient History, in the room of the late Bishop Thirlwall; and Sir Philip de Malpas Grey Egerton, M.P., Antiquary, in the room of the late Earl Stanhope.

DR. VON DOLLINGER is engaged in editing for publication, shortly to take place, the hitherto unpublished portions of the reports of the Council of Trent.

Latest News

DEATH OF THE MAHARAJAH OF PUTTIALLA.

WE deeply regret to announce the death of Maharajah Mahinder Singh of Puttialla. He went out shooting, and died of apoplexy. He has left two minor sons. He was born on the 16th September 1852, having been only ten years old at the time of his father's death. He succeeded to the *guddi* in February 1870. He was well educated for a Native Prince knowing English Persian and gurmukhi. His education was conducted by Professor Ramchunder. He married three wives. The lady last married, the daughter of Mian Mehtab Sing Dhaliwal of Dina, a relative of the Rajah of Furridkote, gave birth to a son on the 17th October 1867. He becomes the heir to the *guddi*.

THE Sindia Railway is intended to connect Agra with Gwalior. The principal work on it will be a large bridge over the River Chumbal. This Railway has only just been commenced, the contract for its construction having been recently given to Messrs. Glover and Co. of Bombay.

BOTH the Calcutta and South-Eastern and Nulhati State Railways are expected to be worked at a loss during the year 1876-77 owing to expenditure in India and England on rolling-stock and sleepers.

THE object of the Tirhoot Survey is to investigate and estimate for the construction of a Railway to connect Tirhoot and Northern Behar with the Northern Bengal Railway on some point between Rungpore and Julpigori.

A PROJECT for a Railway from Nagpore to Chuttisghur has for some years been under the consideration of Government, and has lately been submitted for the orders of the Secretary of State. An extension thence eastward through Raipore, Bilaspore and Korba to Ranedil, and on to Raniguuge, or some other suitable point on the East Indian Railway, will be made the subject of investigation when survey parties are available.

THE authority of the Secretary of State is now awaited to a project to extend the Railway from Ajmere through Marwar to Ahmedabad in the Presidency of Bombay and on sanction being received will be proceeded with as means become available by the completion of other projects.

THE Adhai-din-ka-Jhompra, a beautiful temple, in Rajputana, which was falling into decay, is to be restored under the direction of General Cunningham. The cost of restoration will be about Rs. 10,141.

THE Imperial grant assigned to Bengal for Civil Buildings, and roads in Budget orders for 1876-7, is Rs 4,55,900. Rajputana gets nearly as much to provide principally for the Mayo College at Ajmere.

THE Rajputana Railway has realised in 1875-76 Rs. 20,37,550, gross traffic earnings. The traffic seems to have grown rapidly.

THE Rangoon and Irrawaddy Valley (State) Railway from Rangoon to Prome, 161 miles, is expected to be opened throughout, in June 1877.

THE Northern Bengal Railway from Sara on the banks of the Ganges to a point at the foot of the Darjiling Hills, 203½ miles, is well on to completion. It is expected that a section of 75 miles will be opened for traffic during 1876-77, and the remainder of the line in the following year. Arrangements are being made for a steam-ferry over the Ganges and for the construction of a Railway about 13 miles in length from Poroda on the Eastern Bengal Railway to Damukdia opposite Sara.

MR. H. G. COWIE, B. A., received charge of the Offices of Accountant General, Central Provinces, and Deputy Commissioner of Paper Currency, Nagpore Circle, from Mr. J. Westland on the 31st March 1876.

THE designation of the office of "Judicial Commissioner of Assam" will from this date be "Judge of the Assam Valley Districts." Mr. W. E. Ward, C. S., is to officiate as such Judge during the absence on furlough of Colonel W. Agnew. Pending Mr. Ward's arrival, Colonel T. Lamb will officiate as Judge of the Assam Valley Districts.

IN recognition of the services rendered to Government by Faiz Mahammed, Extra Assistant Collector in Sind, the Viceroy and Governor-General is pleased to confer upon him the title of "Khan Bahadur," as a personal distinction.

WITH the exception of very slight and partial showers in Kurnul and Tanjore, no rain has fallen in the Madras Presidency. The drought has affected the supply of pasture in Kurnul, Tanjore, Malabar and Madura. In the last-named district, drinking water is said to be failing. Cholera is prevalent in most districts, and in Kurnul a considerable number of fatal cases have occurred. Cholera is also slightly on the increase in Mysore and Curg. The Bombay reports show a little rain in Dharwar, but none elsewhere. There has been a severe outbreak of cholera in Belgaum, and the disease is still prevalent throughout Kattywar and the Southern Maharatta Country.

WE learn from the *Madras Times* that the Madras Presidency has expended sixty thousand rupees more than Bengal on account of the reception of His Royal Highness the Prince of Wales and that the Government of India have called upon the Madras Government to explain the cause of such an excess, accompanying the same by vouchers in support of the excess.

MAJOR SANDEMAN is said to have been getting on very well in Khelat. His reception was satisfactory. The Khan's representative had met him, and every thing promised favorably for the success of his mission. It is expected he will be able to do something towards bringing about an understanding between the Khan, his Chiefs, and the Indian Government.

IT is reported to be the intention of the Bombay Government to abolish the office of pauper's attorney.

THERE is a rumour afloat, according to the *Jam-e-Jumshed*, that Mr. Mahadeo Govind Ranade, Subordinate Judge at Poona, will be appointed Judge of the Small Cause Court at Ahmedabad when Rao Bahadur Gopalrao Hurry Deshmukh retires on pension.

THE public meeting of the inhabitants of Bombay, for the purpose of protesting against the Bombay Revenue Jurisdiction Act, will be held at the Framji Cowasji Institute, Bombay, on Tuesday next.

Calcutta.

HIS EXCELLENCY the Viceroy and Governor-General of India has been pleased to make the following appointments on His Lordship's personal staff, with effect from the 13th instant:—

Lieutenant-Colonel O. T. Burne, C. S. I., to officiate as Private Secretary.

Staff Surgeon O. Barnett, of Her Majesty's British Medical Service, to officiate as Surgeon.

To be Military Secretary.

Colonel G. Pomeroy Colley, C. B., 2nd Foot.

To be Aides-de-Camp.

Captain G. C. Jackson, of the late 2nd Regiment European Light Cavalry.

Captain W. Loch, General List, Infantry, 3rd Squadron Officer, 19th Bengal Cavalry—(Temporary).

Lieutenant Lord W. L. De la P. Beresford, 9th Lancers.

Lieut. A. F. Liddell, of the Royal Artillery,—(Temporary).

Captain J. Biddulph, of the 19th Hussars,—(Extra.)

Ressaldar Major Khanan Khan, Corps of Guides, (Queen's Own).

To be Honorary Aides-de-Camp.

Lieutenant Colonel A. J. Hadfield, Madras Invalid Establishment.

Lieutenant Colonel J. W. W. Osborne, C. B., Madras Staff Corps, Political Agent, 1st Class, Gwalior.

Colonel J. C. Graves, C. B., Bombay Cavalry, Commandant, 3rd Bombay (Queen's Own) Light Cavalry.

Colonel R. Baigrie, C. B., Bombay Staff Corps.

Colonel F. R. Maunsell, C. B., Royal Engineers, Commandant, Corps of Bengal Sappers and Miners.

Lieutenant Colonel B. Walter, Bombay Staff Corps, Military Store-keeper and Commandant of the Calcutta Volunteers.

Lieutenant Colonel T. E. Gordon, C. S. I., Bengal Staff Corps, Commandant, Meywar Bheel Corps, and Ex-Officio Superintendent of Hill Tracts of Meywar, and 1st Assistant to Political Agent, Meywar.

Lieutenant Colonel C. J. Godby, Bengal Staff Corps, Commandant, 4th Punjab Cavalry.

HIS EXCELLENCY the Governor-General in Council is pleased to appoint the under-mentioned gentlemen to be Fellows of the University of Calcutta:—

The Honorable Romesh Chunder Mitter B. A., B. L.
The Honorable H. J. Reynolds, B. A., C. S.
Surgeon-General J. F. Beatson, M. D.
A. Colvin, Esq., C. S.
L. H. Griffin, Esq., C. S.
H. B. Medlicott, Esq., M. A., F. G. S.
F. S. Growse, Esq., M. A., C. S.
J. O'Kinealy, Esq., C. S.
M. S. Howell, Esq., B. A., C. S.
Surgeon-Major J. Elliott, M. D.
Surgeon-Major T. E. Charles, M. D.
Surgeon-Major H. Cayley, M. D.
Rajah Jotendra Mohun Tagore.
Rajah Jye Kishen Doss, C. S. I.
P. Hordern, Esq., B. A.
J. C. Nesfield, Esq., M. A.
Syud Ahmed Khan, C. S. I.
Munshi Ram Chundra.
Major J. Eckford, S. E.
B. Leslie, Esq., C. E.
V. Ball, Esq., M. A.
T. D. Ingram, Esq., L. L. D.
Thakur Gire Prasad of Baiswan.
H. Blochman, Esq., M. A.
Baba Khim Singh Bedi.
H. Roberts, Esq.

THE *Indian Charivari* of the 14th instant contains a portrait of Lord Lytton, our new Viceroy, and an appreciative notice of His Excellency.

ABOUT Rs 60,000 has been sanctioned by the Imperial Budget of 1876-7 for renewals and improvements to Government House, Calcutta.

SIR FREDERIC HAINES, the new Commander-in-Chief of India, arrived in Calcutta yesterday under the usual salute. His Excellency formally assumed command of the Indian Forces on the 10th instant.

MR. RIVERS THOMPSON, Acting Chief Commissioner of British Burmah, will most likely leave Calcutta for Rangoon to-morrow.

LORD NORTHBROOK left Calcutta yesterday in the *Tenasserim*. His Lordship will stop at Colombo for a few days, and be the guest of Sir William Gregory, the Governor of Ceylon.

IT may interest some of our readers to know that at Brown & Co's auction on Saturday last, the 8th instant, the following of Lord Northbrook's horses sold for the prices marked opposite their names. The four first were, it is said, bought for Lord Lytton:—*Kilmeston* Rs 2,000; *Feramors* Rs 1,040; *The Dean* Rs 1,250; *Mariner* Rs 1,000; *Little John* Rs 950; *Hotspur* 1,150; *Fop* Rs 1,150; *Cockmarn* Rs 450.

IT is considered not improbabe in England that the Rev. L. G. Mylne, tutor of Keble College, Oxford, who was recently nominated to the bishopric of Bombay, but who has not yet been consecrated, will be transferred to Calcutta, and that another appointment for Bombay will be made.

THE following notification about the Levee to be held by His Excellency the Viceroy, appears in yesterday's *Gazette of India*. 9-30 P. M. is rather an unusual hour for holding the Levee:—

Calcutta, the 13th April, 1876.—His Excellency the Viceroy and Governor-General will hold a Levee at Government House, on Wednesday, the 19th April 1876, at 9-30 o'clock P. M.

Gentlemen attending the Levee are requested to bring two cards with their names legibly written on each; one card will be delivered on entering Government House, the second to the Aide-de-Camp in waiting at the time of presentation.

Gentlemen purposing to attend the Levee are requested to send their cards to the Aide-de-Camp in waiting before 5-30 P. M. on the 17th April 1876, after which no cards can be received.

Gentlemen who have not already been presented at the Court of St. James' or at Government House, are requested to send their cards with their address and the name of the gentlemen by whom they are to be presented to the Aide-de-Camp in waiting with as little delay as possible.

The carriages of gentlemen (except such as have the Private Entree) attending the Levee will enter by the north-east gate, set down at the foot of the grand staircase, and pass out by the north or north-west gates.

By Command, G. Pomeroy Colley, *Colonel Mily. Secy. to the Viceroy.*

DURING the week ending Saturday, the 15th instant, the Calcutta Art Gallery was visited by 74 Europeans and 64 Natives. The Gallery is open to the public daily (except Sundays) from 6-30 to 9-30 A. M. and from 3 to 6 P. M.

ACKNOWLEDGMENTS.

Recollections of an ex-Detective of the Madras Police Force. Edited by Dr. White, Author of "British Policy in India" and "Letters to the Madras *Athenæum and Daily News* by a Native of India". Madras. 1876.

Pictures of England: Translated from the Telugu. Edited by Pothum Jana Kunnaiah Ragavin, a Hindu lady of Madras. Descriptive of her visit to Europe. Madras. 1876.

Public Engagement.

MUSICAL EVANGELISTIC SERVICE.—The Rev. George Kerry will deliver an address in the Free Church Institution, Nimtollah Street, on Sunday evening, 16th instant, at Seven o'clock. Subject—"The Foolishness and Power of the preaching of the Cross." Hymns in Bengali, set to Hindu Music, will be sung.

DOMESTIC OCCURRENCE.

BHUTTACHERJI.—On Wednesday, the 5th April, the wife of Babu Brojendra Chunder Bhuttacharji of Tundla, of a daughter.

Selection

COURAGE.

THE following sermon on the life of Dr. Howe was preached by the Rev. James Freeman Clarke in the Church of the Disciples, Boston, on Jan. 16, taking his text from Ephesians vi. 17: "And take the helmet of salvation and the sword of the Spirit":—

Among the Romans courage made the essence of all virtue. The word *virtus*, or manliness, or courage, was the same as our *virtue*.

Courage has not always considered a virtue among Christians. Not to fight, but to submit, was long supposed to be the chief duty of a religious man. The Christ himself was supposed to be made up of passive virtues—patience, submission, nonresistance, meekness, humanity. In all mediæval pictures he was represented as bowing down his head like a bulrush; standing mute, like the sheep that is sheared. And, through many centuries, the saint, *par excellence*, was the man who retired from the world and its evils to fast and pray, and save his own soul, instead of remaining in the world to fight with its evils, to resist its abuses, to meet falsehoods in the battle of honest argument, to make war against triumphant and powerful villany.

Not such the view of the apostle Paul. To him life was a long battle for right against wrong, for freedom against slavery, for humanity against all that would harm it. "Put on the whole armour, the panoply of God," says he. "Fight the good fight of faith." "Take the helmet of salvation and the sword of the Spirit." "Stand fast, quit you like men, be strong." "Son Timothy, war a good warfare." He meant every blow to tell. "I do not fight as one who beats the air," said he; when he struck he struck to hit. But it was a moral strife. He had no hostility to men, except when they represented principles. "We wrestle not against flesh and blood, but against wrong principles, against evil forces, against the influences which darken life, against triumphant wickedness, no matter how highly placed."

Nor was the goodness of Jesus merely or mainly passive. He went forth from the quiet air of his Nazarene home to attack the ruling principles and ideas of his time. The Pharisis were the rulers of the nation's mind, the guides of public opinion. He denounced and defied them. What was harder, he must disappoint all the expectations of the people. They hated the Romans, with their soldiers and tax-gatherers. He went to the house of the Roman Centurion to heal his child; he made a Roman tax-gatherer one of his apostles. They hated the Samaritans; he made a Samaritan the hero of his loveliest story. They were hungering for a Messiah who should lead them against the Roman power; he told them that his kingdom was not of this world. All the virtues of Christ were active, not passive. His love was active love, going about to do good. His piety was practical piety, resisting and opposing all formalism, all ceremonial worship, and calling on men to worship God in spirit and in truth. The life of Jesus was one long act of heroic courage.

If we distinguish between the essence of courage and its accidents, we shall see what an indispensable ingredient it is in all goodness. It is the power which makes us ready to encounter difficulties, meet opposition, go without delay or hesitation to each duty, attacking every task of life as soon as it presents itself, not shirking the work of to-day, or putting it off till to-morrow; being ready to speak the truth, whether men hear or forbear; standing by our convictions, though custom, authority, and friendship are all on the other side. This is courage; and without it, goodness is a sickly plant, virtue a pale shadow, religion a hollow decorum, exercising no influence, and deserving none.

The distinction usually made is between physical courage and moral courage. I prefer a different classification. I should make three kinds of courage—viz:—

1. Personal courage.
2. Moral courage.
3. Christian courage.

I do not like the phrase "physical courage," because this is often only insensibility to danger. In this sense, a stone would have more courage than a brute; a brute more courage than a man; a coarse and brutal man more courage than a man of thought and imagination. But insensibility, which plunges blindly into danger, does not deserve the name of courage. That alone is true courage which sees the danger, knows all the risk it must run, and yet is willing to encounter it. There is no courage in risking a peril to which we are insensible. If a man can truly say, "I never knew what fear was," he must also say "I never knew what courage was." The capacity of feeling fear is essential to all true courage. To feel fear and rise above fear—that is what we understand by courage.

Dr. Howe, then, as I judge, possessed in a high degree all the three kinds of courage of which I have spoken; and I will illustrate them all by the story of his life. Personal courage loves danger for danger's sake; not because it is insensible to it, but because it enjoys its excitement and stimulus. What a strange attraction have war and the tumult of battle for many men! This courage of the battle-field is shared with man by his faithful companion, the horse, who rushes with joy into the thick of the fray, not from insensibility to danger—for he is a timid and imaginative creature—but he is lifted, like man, above all fear by the strange fascination of the battle-field. Two thousand years ago this had been noticed by the author of the Book of Job, who said of the horse, "He saith among the trumpets 'ha' ha!' and smelleth the battle afar off." Dr. Howe, in this respect, was like one of the Knights of the Round Table. When he went to Greece to fight by the side of Byron; when he risked his life and liberty to help the Poles in their insurrection; when he stood by Lafayette in the streets of Paris in the struggle of 1830, there was mingled with his sympathy for human freedom something also of the *gaudium certaminis*—the delightful excitement of peril. But also there was the conviction that there was a principle at stake, and that this was the eternal conflict for the rights of man; and so the personal courage of the Knight was joined with the moral courage of the hero. He was ready to die, but only in a good cause—*non indecoro pulvere sordidum.*

This marks the difference between personal courage and moral courage. Personal courage gives the joy of conflict; moral courage adds to this a deeper joy, the satisfaction of fighting for truth, justice, freedom, humanity. It also enlarges the sphere of the battle; lifting it to the vast field where principles of truth and falsehood contend in the grand struggle of reason with reason. And so, when the anti-slavery controversy began in this country, it was easy to see where Dr. Howe would be. With his friends, John G. Palfrey, Horace Mann, Charles Sumner, Theodore Parker, John A. Andrew, Frank Bird, and others like them, his heart, voice, pen, purse, hand, were always given to the cause of the slave. How much he did in that cause few can tell, for he was a man who never spoke of his own past efforts or achievements. But it was always well understood that if any help was needed in that cause Dr. Howe could be relied upon. I only saw Captain John Brown twice—once in Charles Sumner's room in Hancock street; the other time it happened thus:—I met Dr. Howe in the street, one day, and he said, "Captain John Brown—Ossawattamie Brown—is in my office. He has a plan in view, and, if you would like to help him, he will tell you something about it." I went to the office, and Captain Brown was there alone. He described to me what he had done in Missouri, carrying away slaves from the frontier through Kansas and Nebraska, and said, "I intend doing the same thing on a large scale, elsewhere; but where and how, I keep to myself. My idea is to destroy the value of slave property along the border, and so drive slavery South." If John Brown, or any one else, had a blow to strike for humanity, he knew that he had an ally always ready in Dr. Howe.

ICE! ICE! ICE!

MADE IN FOUR MINUTES

THE PNEUMATIC ICE MACHINE

THIS IMPORTANT INVENTION IS CONSIDERED A BOON TO THOSE LIVING IN TROPICAL CLIMATES.

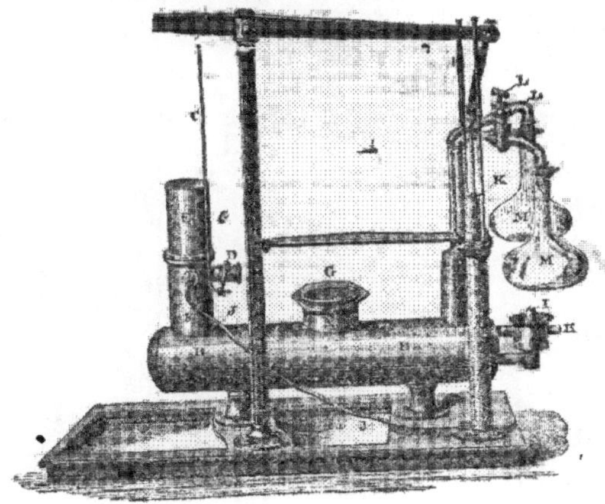

CAN BE WORKED BY THE MOST INEXPERIENCED HAND AND IS NOT LIABLE TO GET OUT OF ORDER.

From Rs. 175, each Machine complete.

MESSRS. ARLINGTON & CO.

AGENTS.

HAROLD & CO.,

3, DALHOUSIE SQUARE, CALCUTTA

HARMONIUMS.

Harold and Co., call attention to their unequalled stock of rich-toned Harmoniums made especially for India.

FROM RS. 90 TO RS. 900 EACH.

All kinds of Musical Instruments of the best description are always kept in Stock.

THACKER, SPINK AND CO.

No. 5, GOVERNMENT PLACE, CALCUTTA.

Just Published.

The Legislative Acts

Of the Governor-General of India in Council of 1876.

With Table of Contents and Index, 8vo., cloth, Rs. 5.

Our land and Revenue Policy,

IN NORTHERN INDIA.

By Charles James Connell, Esq., B.C.S.

8vo., Cloth. Rs. 5.

DESCRIPTIVE CATALOGUE OF THE

Reptiles of British India

BY W. THEOBALD, ESQ.,

Geographical Survey of India. 8vo., cloth, Rs. 10.

CATALOGUE OF THE

Land and Fresh Water Shells

Of British India.

BY W. THEOBALD, ESQ.,

Geological Survey of India. Quarto, Paper Cover. Rs. 6.

Poetry.

THE ODES of ANACREON, translated by Thomas Moore, with fifty-four illustrative designs by Girodet de Roussy, Ornamental cloth gilt, Rs. 8-4.

SWINBURNE.—Bothwell, a Tragedy, by Algernon Charles Swinburne, in two volumes cloth, 8vo, Rs. 8-14.

SWINBURNE.—poems and Ballads. By Algernon Charles Swinburne, 4th Edition, cloth, 8vo., Rs. 6-8.

SWINBURNE.—Chastelard, a tragedy, by Algernon Charles Swinburne, cloth, Rs. 5.

O'SHAUGHNESSY.—Lays of France, (founded on the lays of Marie), by Arthur W. E. O'Shaughnessy, cloth, 8vo., Rs. 7-8.

O'SHAUGHNESSY.—Music and Moonlight, poems and songs, by Arthur O'Shaughnessy, cloth, Rs. 5-6.

KINGSLEY.—Poems, including the Saints tragedy, Andromeda, songs; Ballads, &c., by Charles Kingsley (Collected Edition) cloth, Rs. 4-4.

FAY.—Lyrics and Idylls, by Gerida Fay, cloth, Rs. 2.

TENNYSON.—Queen Mary, a drama, by Alfred Tennyson, cloth, Rs. 4-4.

LOWELL.—The complete poetical works of James Russel Lowell, second Edition (with portrait), Rs. 5-6.

MILTON.—The poetical works of John Milton, with introduction and notes, by David Masson, M. A., L. L. D. professor of Rhetoric and English literature in the University of Edinburgh, 2 vols., Rs. 6-8.

TENNYSON.—The Cabinet Edition of Tennyson's poems, 10 vols., 18 mo., scarlet cloth, frontispiece to each vol., at Re. 1-12 each.

Vol. I.—Early poems.
„ II.—English Idylls and other poems.
„ III.—Locksley Hall and other poems.
„ IV.—Lucretius and other poems.
„ V.—Idylls of the King.
„ VI.— „ „
„ VII.— „ „
„ VIII.—The Princess.
„ IX.—Maud and Enoch Arden.
„ X.—In Memoriam.

INGOLDSBY LEGENDS, or mirth and marvels. By Thomas Ingoldsby, Esquire (new Edition), 3 vols., fcap., 8 vo., Rs. 7-8.

DERBY.—The Iliad of Homer rendered into English blankverse, to which are appended translations of poems, ancient and modern, By Edward Earl of Derby, ninth Edition, in two volumes, cloth, 8vo., Rs. 7-4.

MORRIS.—The Æneids of Virgil, done into English Verse, by William Morris, Author of "Earthly Paradise," second Edition, cloth, Rs. 10.

India General Steam Navigation Company, Limited.

SCHOENE, KILBURN & Co.—*Managing Agents.*

ASSAM LINE.

NOTICE.

Steamers now leave Calcutta for Assam every Tuesday, Goalundo every Thursday and Dibrooghur downward every Saturday.

THE Str. "LAHORE" will leave Calcutta for Assam, on Tuesday, the 18th instant.

Cargo will be received at the Company's Godowns, Nimtollah Ghat, until noon of Monday, the 17th.

THE Str. "ASSAM" will leave Goalundo for Assam on Thursday the 20th instant.

Cargo will be received at the Company's Godowns, No. 4, Fairlie Palace, up till noon of Tuesday the 18th.

Goods forwarded to Goalundo for this vessel will be chargeable with Railway Freight from Calcutta to Goalundo in addition to the regular Freight of this Company.

Passengers should leave for Goalundo by Train of Wednesday, the 19th.

CACHAR LINE NOTICE

REGULAR WEEKLY SERVICE.

Steamers now leave Calcutta for Cachar and intermediate Stations every Tuesday and Chattuck downward every Tuesday.

A Steamer and "FLAT" will leave Calcutta for Cachar on Tuesday, the 18th instant.

Cargo will be received at the Company's Godowns, Nimtollah Ghat, up till noon of Monday, the 17th.

For further information regarding rates of Freight or passage money, apply to

4 Fairlie Palace, **G. J. SCOTT,**
Calcutta, 12th April 1876. *Secretary.*

BABU BASANTA KUMAR DATTA,

Homœopathic Practitioner.

No. 20. *Sacker Halder's Lane, Ahiritolah*

HOMŒOPATHIC

JUST ARRIVED FROM ENGLAND

MEDICINES, AND ALL REQUISITES, TO BE HAD AT—

DATTA'S HOMŒOPATHIC LABORATORY

No. 312, CHITPORE ROAD, BUTTOLAH, CALCUTTA.

BABU RADHAKANTA GHOSH

HOMŒOPATHIC PRACTITIONER,

12, College Square.

Is practising here on moderate terms.

SMITH, STANISTREET & CO.

Pharmaceutical Chemists & Druggists

BY APPOINTMENT

To His Excellency the Right Hon'ble LORD NORTHBROOK, G.M.S.I.,

Governor-General of India.

&c. &c.

SYRUP OF LACTATE OF IRON.

Prepared from the original receipt. Lactate of Iron, in various forms of preparation, have been in use in France, and generally through the Continent of Europe, for some years past, and is highly esteemed as one of the most valuable Chalybeate Tonic Remedies yet introduced. The Syrup, being the most agreeable as well as convenient form of administration, is in most general use. It is a most valuable remedy in the following diseases:—Chlorosis or Green Sickness, Leucorrhea, Neuralgia, Enlargement of the Spleen &c. In combination with quinine, it has also been very successfully used in the cure of Fever, while to persons of delicate constitution, enfeebled by disease it is invaluable. In bottles, Rs. 2 each.

SYRUP OF THE PHOSPHATE OF IRON

Rs. 2 per bottle

SYRUP OF PHOSPHATE OF IRON AND STRYCHNINE, Rs. 2 per bottle.

SYRUP OF PHOSPHATE OF IRON AND QUININE. Price Rs. 2-8 per bottle.

SYRUP OF PHOSPHATE OF IRON, QUININE AND STRYCHNINE, DR. ATKIN'S TRIPLE TONIC SYRUP.) Rs. 2-8 per bottle.

Smith, Stanistreet & Co.

Invite special **attention** to the following rates, the quality **guaranteed** as the best procurable:—

Pure Ærated Waters.

Made from Pure Water, obtained by the new process through the Patent Charcoal Filters.

				Rs.	As
Ærated plain (Triple Ærated), per doz.			...	0	12
Soda Water	ditto	„	...	0	12
Gingerade	ditto	„	...	1	4
Lemonade	ditto	„	...	1	4
Tonic (Quinine)	ditto	„	...	1	4

The *Cash* must be sent with the order to obtain advantage of the above rates.

!!! হুকা !!!

!!! HOOKAHS !!!

ENGLISH made Hookahs of various choice designs, colours and sizes ranging in price from Rs. 2 to 5 each, 60 designs to choose from Apply to

RADANAUTH CHOWDRY,
373, Jorasanko.

(হেমলতা নাটক)

NEW HISTORICAL TRAGEDY

BY

GOPAL CHUNDER MOOKERJEE,

Price, Re. 1, [illegible]

To be had at [illegible] Grey Street, Shobhabazar and Sanskrit Press Depository.

NATIONAL COMPANY,

HOMŒOPATHIC CHEMISTS AND PUBLISHER

SUPPLY ALL KINDS OF

HOMŒOPATHIC MEDICINES, BOOKS

CASES AND OTHER REQUISITES.

12 COLLEGE SQUARE,
Calcutta.

Printed and published by M. M. RUDRA, at the "INDIAN MIRROR" PRESS, No. 15, College Square, for the Proprietor.

The Indian Mirror.

SUNDAY EDITION.

VOL. XV.] CALCUTTA, SUNDAY, APRIL 23, 1876. {Registered at the General Post Office.} [No. 95

CONTENTS.

NOTICE.

Letters and all other communications relating to the literary department of the Paper should be addressed to "The Editor."

All letters on the business of the Press should be addressed, and all remittance made payable to the Manager of this Paper. Particular attention is solicited to this notice.

Subscribers will be good enough to give prompt notice of any delay, or irregularity in delivery of the Paper.

Editorial Notes

THE British Indian Association, the Trades Association and the Mahomedan Literary Society have all presented Lord Lytton with addresses of welcome, and His Excellency has returned suitable replies. The Brahmo community in India beg to tender His Lordship a hearty loyal welcome, and sincerely pray that "a Power higher than any earthly power may help him to advance the moral and social interests of this great country. We respectfully urge upon His Lordship's attention these important subjects,—female education, liquor traffic, suppression of public obscenity, social harmony.

To be a Hindu ascetic in the fullest measure one must forsake his home and family. Yoga is not possible in married life. We do not endorse such a theory, though we are aware it prevails generally among students of Hindu theology, both here and in Europe. Shiva, of the Hindu triad, is recognised and worshipped as the very impersonation of the highest yoga and asceticism. And yet we are told he was extremely fond of his wife and children. When Narad went to Shiva to be indoctrinated he found him surrounded by his dear wife Parvati and his children on the Himalayas. It is also said in Hindu mythology that a certain worshipper of Vishnu on seeing Shiva's extreme attachment to his family, indignantly remonstrated against such worldliness on the part of one who professed to instruct the world in asceticism. Certainly from the example set by Mahadeva one must naturally infer that the arduous duties and holy pleasures of domestic life are not incompatible with the highest communion and self-denial enjoined by Hinduism. Such also is the teaching of modern civilization.

THERE are three complexions that characterize the present population of America, white, black, and red, and whites are unfortunately at enmity with all. Of course black and white are contraries everywhere, and nowhere more than in America, but as there is as little agreement between white, and red. The red man will never be a slave, he would much rather prefer to be exterminated. And many races of American Indians have been already exterminated in consequence. They have died out in irreconcilable enmity with the white man who is of course powerful. It appears the Quakers, to whom the Negroes owe so much, as any reader of Mrs. Stowe's novels knows, have for a long time undertaken the protection of the American Indian tribes. And we are told that "Friends" who are entrusted with the charge of Indian tribes, have every reason to be satisfied with the co-operation of President Grant's Government, "which is, in fact, the first Government in the history of the United States which has ever really recognised the *rights* of the Indians, or sent United States troops to protect them from the ravages of the whites."

THE Hindu word *Maya* is wonderfully expressive. It means but the sublimest and most refined form of worldliness. It is the spirit of selfishness (or *I, mine,* and *me* in the language of *Theologia Germanica*) extended over the whole sphere of human existence. A man first calls a thing *his*, and then gets attached to it. These attachments multiply as the relations of life multiply, till they settle, consolidate, and surround a man so that he is incapable of seeing and fulfilling his spiritual relations and duties. A man is blinded by *Maya*, he is deadened and deluded by it, and led unconsciously through the gates of sin to death. He gradually weaves the fatal web around himself, and death only cuts it asunder when too late. *Maya* in the sense that the world is a delusion we do not admit. *Maya* as an agent of God, a sort of sorceress sent from above to lure mankind to their ruin, we do not admit. But as the spiritual blindness generated by an infatuated attachment to worldly objects and relations, it is only too true. The best of men are not free from it, and the deepest forms of spirituality often get involved in the meshes which the soul has woven round itself. A man that is totally free from *Maya*, and is still faithfully discharging his duties in the world, unbound, yet kept in his appointed course by the spirit of God within him, such a man is worthy to be imitated, and admired.

A DISTINGUISHED Native gentleman was heard to whisper, on the occasion of the recent inauguration of the Art Gallery, "I don't understand a bit of these pictures. Upon my word I cannot say which is good. They are all the same to me. I have looked at them, and I confess I feel not the slightest interest in any of them." After a short while the Babu was no longer seen in the hall. Perhaps his feeling of unconcern grew into positive disgust, and he went away. We do not mean any disrespect to this gentleman, but we simply contend that he represents the feeling and taste of the general body of educated Natives in the matter of painting. Barring a few exceptions, our countrymen, in spite of their high English culture, do not seem to appreciate pictures. They say *Cui bono?* Well, pictures, besides pleasing the eye, have a wonderful moral effect upon the national heart. A picture gallery is an educator. By founding this institution Sir Richard Temple has proved a real benefactor of the people. But like every good institution it is in advance of the age; we mean, in India. Our countrymen have yet to appreciate it. Years must roll on before we see hundreds with enthusiastic excitement gather before a good picture, as they do in England. To all educated Natives we say—go and see the Art Gallery. Their feelings and tastes will be educated, and disciplined, as they study and enjoy the poetry of colors.

ONE must love God with intense love and yet revere his holy word with the profoundest loyalty. To carp at a single letter of scripture is infidelity, and is not tolerated, nay is resented in heaven. We have a beautiful anecdote illustrative of this truth in the Vaishnava books. A devotee could not bear to see in the Bhagvata a passage in which God is described as "bearing the burden" of his loving disciples, and he accordingly effaced that expression from the book. Shortly after this event two boys came to his house, and as he was absent, complained most piteously to his wife of the heartless cruelty of her husband, who, they said, had causelessly beaten and tortured them, and to verify their complaint pointed to several parts of their bodies which were profusely bleeding in consequence of the wounds thus received. This greatly affected the good wife, and though she repeatedly urged her husband's high character and the moral impossibility of his doing anything of the kind, they as often pressed upon her the truth of their charge. On her husband returning home she explained what had transpired. He was confounded for he was satisfied that he could never have perpetrated such a foul deed. After some difficulty and delay he found a solution of the mystery. With a pointed iron hook, he recollected, he had effaced certain objectionable words in the Bhagavata, and as that sacred book is identical with God Himself, Jagannath and Balaram had come to his wife in the guise of two little boys to complain of the cruel treatment, and, to show that by wounding the scripture he had wounded them personally. Yes the word of God is identical with God, and if we dishonor His injunctions and truths we dishonor His spirit. If we love Him we must accept and follow every word He utters in the inmost soul.

THE BRAHMIN AND THE SUDRA.

A BRAHMIN and a Sudra are theological fictions invented in priest-ridden Hindustan for obvious reasons. But in one sense they may be accepted as realities in the moral world. The distinction between a Brahmin and a Sudra if realized from a catholic and spiritual standpoint, will appear to be not only true, but to involve a most important principle. We shall presently explain what this principle is. In the first place it is generally admitted that man is commissioned to serve others with the utmost humility. He comes into the world, not to rule but to serve. However exalted his position may be, however great his learning, power or wealth, he is always a servant and never a master. He is a born servant; he is born to serve. Hence from his lowly position no amount of acquired power or knowledge can raise him. He must always continue to be where nature, by a sort of predestination, has fixed him. He may be a king, an emperor; he may be a saint, a prophet. Yet is he but a servant, destined humbly and submissively to serve mankind. Now, in Hinduism 'Sudra' is the word for a born servant, and it is a most expressive term. Indeed, no word can better express the uncomplaining lowliness, the abject posture, the lifelong submissiveness of a born servant. Every man then is a Sudra unto others. Who then is the Brahmin? Those who claim a high descent, who trace their ancestry to Brahma or God Himself are called Brahmins, and are deemed worthy of the highest respect and entitled to the most loyal services of those below. They may be poor, they may be ignorant, they may be the meanest of the mean, yea they may be vicious and immoral men. Yet are they to be honored and served. A portion of God's nature is said to dwell in their nature, and hence their sanctity cannot be destroyed. They are born God's children; in their very constitution is lodged Divinity. Their right to command respectful service is a birth-right, altogether indestructible, and not to be forfeited. They may be the worst and vilest of men, degraded to the level of brutes, so far as character is concerned. Yet are they masters, whom everybody is bound to serve and honor. This essentially Hindu idea may be applied to our relations to others. In serving a brother we must not take into account his merits or demerits; we must not withhold service on the ground of his moral weaknesses. Whatever his character or position, he is to be reckoned a superior person being in the master's position. However virtuous, and learned we may be, we must always consider ourselves to be in the inferior position of servants and slaves. This is true humility that we regard all men as Brahmins, on principle, and not out of mere fitful sentiments, and assiduously serve them as our masters. If men quarrel with us, and becomeour enemies, we must still serve them out of respect for their natural and irreversible position of masters. If they are inferior to us in knowledge, in social status, in wealth and power and honor, we must still feel that we are destined by nature to sit at their feet, and offer our humble services. We may be thoroughly convinced that many of those around us are bad men, and yet we must serve them under the conviction that by so doing we sanctify ourselves. Let us have the Hindu's simple faith that by feeding a Brahmin, washing his feet or otherwise serving him one goes to heaven. By serving the meanest among our brethren in an humble spirit we are sanctified and saved.

TYPES OF RELIGIOUS PROGRESS.

IT is necessary and natural for every man to think that his way to God is the only way, and there is no other. If he thought there were other ways, he should go to seek and find them, and his pursuit would end perhaps in finding no way at all, neither his own, nor any body else's. This description of exclusiveness, which in other words may be called the singleness of the spiritual eye, is indispensable. But the man of wisdom is very well aware that God's dealings with mankind have been various and manifold, and no one can define or ascertain the mysterious processes through which He draws his children to himself. Sufficient unto each is the dispensation under which he is called to be saved. But in the world there have been may dispensations, which cannot be denounced as false, unless falsehood is attributed to the very Source of all truth. It would require the infinite hardihood of bigotry to maintain that the followers of no other religion except one's own have been admitted into the blessedness of salvation, and that heaven is reserved only for subscribers to the articles of his own creed. The moment it is conceded that such as have not the law, are a law unto themselves, and that the uncircumcized gentile has the word of God written on the tablet of his heart, it is also admitted that there are different types of religious progress among mankind, each type representing the peculiar spirituality, the peculiar aspirations and character of individuals, or the community, race, and generation which they constitute. Hinduism embodies one type of religious progress, and Christianity embodies another. The ardent personal seeking of God, that ends in self-oblivion, the absorption of the spirit in a rapturous sense of union with the deity, that is the Hindu idea. The absolute surrender of self in faith and obedience to the will of God, the enthusiastic consecration of suffering and labor to the good of others in a Christlike spirit of meekness and love, ending in the perfect reconciliation of human will and affections with the spirit of holiness that pervades all things, this is the Christian idea. To compare these two ideas is not our province, even if we had the requisite fitness for the task. To us both the ideas are profound, both most edifying, equally acceptable, equally indispensable. The purely Christian type of religious development, however applicable to other countries and nations, and even if partly applicable to our own will be unsuited to the Hindu nation as a whole. The purely Hindu type of religion, however suitable to the people of India, and even if partly applicable to men of other nations, will not answer all the moral and spiritual wants that have been awakened in us here at the present day. Both have to be combined, in what measure, and according to what processes we cannot say, that being hidden in the purposes of Providence. Nor can we say that the future religion of India is to be merely the compound of Hinduism and Christianity effected by men who neither believe in the one nor in the other. Providence is never guilty of repitition, and the past, however full of striking analogies, cannot be re-enacted in the present. Heaven only knows through what mysterious processes the people of India are to be saved in the future, and what will be the exact form of religion that is destined to regenerate our millions. All we can say is that it will not ignore or be unfaithful to the past. And in so much the types of religious progress already presented to the world by Hinduism and Christianity, will not remain unrepresented. In one sense the past may be said to lie in our hands, because we can enter into the spirit and study the recorded experiences of the prophets and sages, who have, by their teachings and examples, embodied the typical progress of their times and religion. To realize their feelings, beliefs, motives, and spiritual experiences,—and how can we know what they were unless we are able to realize these—it is necessary to throw ourselves as much as possible into their circumstances, and cultivate the peculiar processes through which they went. This we are ready to admit is not perfectly practicable, because we cannot forget the changes of society, and the altered notions of life. But nevertheless the culture, the exercise, the circumstances can be partly reproduced. And to reproduce them as far as the altered conditions of existence will permit, is no unprofitable task. That this is a want in human society is evident in the revivals and re-actions that now and often disturb the otherwise unruffled flow of worldliness in religion. Such phenomena as the revival of monasticism, and the growing movement of ritualism in the Protestant Church, the assertion of Papal Infallibility in the Roman Catholic Church, Wahabeeism among the Mahomedans, of Kukaism among the Sikhs evidence the same necessity, we mean the reproduction of the primal type of religion among the degenerate followers of the present times. If the Brahmo Somaj is led to reconsider the primitive type of Hindu piety, of course discarding the errors incident to it, they are but true to the spirit of the age. The new disciplines, forms, and processes of spiritual exercise prescribed by Brahmo Missionaries for themselves, cannot but terminate in harmonizing the two types of religious progress which have had most influence in developing the faith and career of their church.

OUR FAITH AND OUR EXPERIENCES.

[*Continued.*]

SUCH exuberance of devotional sentiments has been bequeathed to us by our Puranic ancestors. Their errors and prejudices we pity, their idolatry and superstition we shun as darkness, but their intense love, reverence and faith we gratefully honor and imitate. If the ancient Vedic Aryan is enthusiastically honored to-day for having taught the deep truth of the *Nirakar* or the bodiless Spirit, the same loyal homage is due to the later Puranic Hindu for having taught religious feelings, in all their breadth and depth. In the age of Monotheism and Pantheism, in the days of the Vedas and Vedanta, India was all communion and inward vision. In the age of the Puranas India was all emotion. The highest and best feelings of religion have been cultivated under the guardianship of specific divinities to whom they were directed, and they have grown with wild luxuriance and in all imaginable varieties. With a deity before the eye to see and adore every good feeling of which man's nature or woman's nature is capable, has started into life and developed into full bloom. Holy fear, chaste affection, filial attachment, warm gratitude towards God, and charity, philanthrophy towards man, and the utmost kindness towards animals have grown profusely on Indian soil in the days of idolatry. Through this deluge of feeling the Spirit-God of primitive India has had to pass before reaching our souls. The most absorbing spiritual communion has come to us through a garden of fragrant sentiments, redolent of sweetness. Misunderstand me not, Gentlemen. I praise the Subjective, not the objective, the sentiment of the worshipper, not the object worshipped. False deities I disown and scornfully repudiate. But the wealth of sentiments, the sweet flowers of love I dare not ignore. The Hindu yields to none in religious passions, and these as loyal descendants and zealous patriots we must acknowledge and cherish with profound thankfulness. Fellow-Theists, ye have done well in accepting the Spirit-God of the ancient Hindu and the heart of the later Hindu. Let us rejoice that Providence has enabled us to do this. Let us rejoice that we are not roaming through a desert of dreary rationalism or dreamy Idealism with an unseen and shadowy vastness overhanging us, but that we are marching to the kingdom of love with a Real and Personal God fixed in the depths of our affections. No one can deny, even the casual observer cannot overlook the fact, that in the modern Theistic Church the feeling-element is most strong. Its excessive prevalance has led many a superficial critic to charge us with mysticism. What does this charge mean? Certainly it does not mean that our faith is dry and rationalistic and that we worship a shadow with heartless metaphysics. It means not the absence but the excess of devotional fervor. It is something that the accusers of modern Theism in India can not charge it with upholding and preaching the worship of a dry divinity. They rather accuse it of too much sentiment and too much love towards the Unseen Spirit. If Indian Theists err, they err on the side of exuberance, not want of feeling. It is the luxury not the scarcity of emotion that renders them liable to censure. Well then, let it be proclaimed that in the natural course of progress in this country a small band of Spirit-worshippers have sprung up, who can love the Invisible and Unknowable One with all the passionate love of an idolater. It will not do to say that these Theists simply love God. No, they can love the Unseen and Intangible Spirit as warmly, as tenderly as the idolator loves the tangible idol and the visible incarnation. Into the heart of the Indian Theists the Holy Spirit has come as a charming and captivating Personality, and His advent is being celebrated by hundreds of men and women in this land with all the poetry of enthusiastic love. Charming did I say? Yes, most charming is the Spirit of God. Were it not so, I would not say so to you. Let those that have eyes see that here in India though there is no visible divinity, no graceful form to please the eye and gladden the imagination, no heavenly voice speaking behind the clouds, the pure Spirit of God fascinates the hearts of worshippers by His unspeakable spiritual beauty. Hundreds around you revel in joy—a blessed sight—for having found a God who is unto them a good Good, a very good God, an excellent God, sweeter than sweetness. Is the Spirit God fascinating to the eye and dear to the heart? Modern Indian Theism solemnly replies—Yes.

Simple and short is the creed of this Church. Its entire faith may be evolved out of this natural consciousness of the living Spirit of God. Let me now proceed to analyze the Theist's creed.

The Interpreter

THE boldest language which a Hindu believer could employ in defence of the doctrine of toleration is to be found in Yogvashishtha, IV. 99, which says:—"Accept reasonable words even from a boy. Should even Brahma [of the Hindu triad] say anything unreasonable eschew it as grass." How wide the spirit of toleration here inculcated! Even if the gods teach error men should treat their sayings as worthless, and prefer to learn wisdom from boys. Nothing can be more catholic.

WE really do not know what it is to "patronize" Christ. We love him, and honor him and desire humbly to sit at his feet for instruction. But a Christian contemporary has been good enough to discover in us lately an odious habit. "The *Indian Mirror*, says he, has taken to patronizing Christ." We will have no Christian to judge us. But let Christ judge. Our contemporary after rebuking us goes on to say:—"Asceticism finds no sanction in the life of Christ." This must appear ridiculous to those who have read the gospels. He who "had not where to lay his head," who declared it wrong to take thought for the morrow, who sent his disciples to go about preaching without purse and provision, and whose charming poverty has been organized by the Roman Catholic Church into standing institutions, which are the wonder of ages,—surely he was an ascetic, aye the greatest of ascetics. Men of refinement in the West may not like asceticism and therefore do not wish to associate it with the character of Christ. But truth demands that he should be accepted as he was, and not as the rich and the fashionable world wish him to be. He was a *fakir*, a *byragi* of the highest type, and we delight to honor him as such.

Provincial

ANNIVERSARY OF THE BRAHMO SOMAJ AT GYA.

[FROM OUR OWN CORRESPONDENT.]

GYA, *the* 18*th April* 1876.

THE Ninth Anniversary of the local Brahmo Somaj, passed off on the 2nd instant rather quietly this year. By "quietly" I mean without much fuss and noise. From a month before the anniversary day, the Brahmos had been holding *Sankirtan* meetings every other evening by way of preparation for the advent of that auspicious day, until the arrival of the Brahmo Missionary, Babu Dina Nath Mozamdar, on Thursday, the 30th ultimo, from which date the *Sankirtan* meeting was held daily in the newly-built premises of Babu Omesh Chundra Sarkar in which the Missionary gentleman had put up. Though little outward excitement was manifested on the *Utsab* day by the Brahmos, yet one could hardly fail to read in their faces those marks of contemplative serenity and earnestness, which always characterise those who are sincerely anxious to better their spiritual condition. The solemn chanting of some sacred hymns in the Mandir announced the commencement of the *Utsab* at about 6 A. M. on the Anniversary day, after which the usual morning service was held till 10 A. M. After some three hours' respite the Brahmos re-assembled in their Mandir at 1 P M., and commenced religious conversation and interchange of spiritual experiences in their own lives. This lasted till about 3 P M, when the Missionary gentleman read portions of the Hindu scriptures in solemn musical Sanskrit, interpreting the same in Bengali also. This ended at 4 P. M., after which there was a respite for two hours. By 6 P. M. the Brahmos again assembled together, there being several Hindu and Brahmo ladies present on this occasion. And now commenced the evening *Sankirtan* accompanied with *Mridangas* and *Kurtals* (cymbals). The devout earnestness of some of the Brahmos as well as the sweet and touching hymns and sermon of the minister were really affecting ; but I regret to say that the audience was unusually thin this year, there being only a few outsiders present on account of the celebration of the Aunopurna Pujah on the same day at two different places in the station. The evening service was finished at 9 P. M. when the Brahmos dispersed, recounting within themselves the real benefits (if any) they had been able to secure at the *Utsab*. I have omitted to mention that at the suggestion of the Missionary gentleman, a small fund was collected for the distribution of clothes to the ragged and beggars here on the occasion of the Anniversary, and that although on the *Utsab* day a few such beggars only had received clothes, yet up to this day clothes are being daily distributed silently and without fuss or exhibition to the really needy, who are selected out of the swarming hosts of beggars with whom this ancient seat of pilgrimage abounds. It has been proposed to make a permanent charitable institution here with this small beginning, and with this view some tickets have already been issued to fit objects of charity.

From the day after the Anniversary until the 14th instant, when the Missionary gentleman left this for Bankipore, a regular *Sankirtan* meeting was held every evening in the house of Babu Omesh Chunder Sarkar, where the sweet voice of the Missionary as well as the solemn and sonorous sound of *Mridangas* and *Kurtal*, aided by the resounding echoes of the new building, drew together many an outsider. On Friday, the 7th instant, there was a Hindu prayer-meeting convened for the benefit of the Hindustanis who appeared to be highly satisfied with the Brahmic hymns sung in Hindi on the occasion, accompanied with a *Dholak*, according to their own national custom. In the morning of Sunday next, the 9th of April, the Namkaran ceremony of the son of our venerable brother, Harry Sunder Bose, took place at his place with great solemnity, the Missionary gentleman acting as minister on the occasion, when the Brahmos felt the beauty and holiness of worshipping the All-Merciful in the midst of a Brahmo family, and witnessed the rare sight (so far as the local Brahmos are concerned) of a really pious father praying with up-turned eyes and with the child in his arms to the Most High, for the future spiritual welfare of his son. So touchingly beautiful was this spectacle, that from some eyes it had actually drawn tears. The next evening (Monday) the Brahmos held a prayer meeting in a nice little mangoe-grove near the Gobachhowa Hill (so-called from the stony figures of a cow and calf to be found there), where with the serene, starry heavens over them, the songs of birds around them, the rising moon before them, the range of hills near these(holding the moon as it were on their top), and the stillness of the night surrounding them, broken now and then by a distant human voice—the Brahmos joined their hearts in prayer, meditation, and *Sankirtan*, lifting up their united voices with the noise of *Mridanga* and *Kurtal* till the neighbouring hills resounded. Last though not the least, was the prayer-meeting on the summit of the Rumsilla Hill, traversed over by a flight of steps constructed by your townsman, the late Krisnaram Bosu in the year 1702 Shakabda. Here the Brahmos assembled early in the morning of the 14th instant, with the full view of the distant city just enlivened by the rising sun, the sandy and meandering Falgu, the hills and hillocks jutting up here and there, and the cornfields all to the west and north. Here in the coolness of the morning breeze, the Brahmos prayed and sang fervantly, raising up their hearts gently "from nature up to nature's God," and enjoying an unearthly delight which seldom falls to their lot.

With the last prayer-meeting, I may say, ended the excitement of our Anniversary which generally continues so long as the Brahmo Missionary stays in the station ; for in the evening of that very day he left this for Bankipore by the mail cart, the Brahmos in a body escorting him to the Post Office whence the mail cart starts, as if the same were the Railway station of this place. As one permanent effect of our late Anniversary, I may mention the fact that the room in the newly-built house of Babu Omesh Chundra Sarcar, in which the Missionary gentleman during his short stay here, was accommodated has been set apart by him for religious purposes only, where the Brahmos have proposed to meet every evening for *Sankirtan*. For this, I need hardly add, the Babu is entitled to the heartfelt gratitude of his brother-Brahmos.

Cholera is raging here very fearfully, and a Bengali gentleman—a near relative of Roy Shyam Lall Mitter,—was carried away the other day within 12 hours, leaving a number of little orphan boys in this wide world. Great credit is due to a distinguished Pleader here, who with the co-operation of his brother, also a Pleader (but sometime a medical student) is saving numerous lives daily with homœpathic medicines. I may also mention that the medicines are distributed by him out of pure charity, and the labor and trouble he undergoes for the suffering humanity, is a labor of love only. Would that the other Brahmos here (the Pleaders above referred to being Brahmos) had thus rendered themselves practically useful, each in his own way, and thereby repudiated the charge of religious selfishness—verging almost upon sectarianism—brought against them by your correspondent sometime ago.

Devotional

BLESS our new Viceroy and Governor-General, God Almighty, and vouchsafe unto him such light and strength as may enable him to govern this country unto thy glory. Grant that he may rule justly and mercifully the millions thou hast entrusted to his care, promoting their material as well as moral prosperity.

WHERE is that home into which saints and prophets and all thy devoted servants have gone to enjoy rest and peace ever more? My heart longs to go there, and join that happy band. But I cannot. My time has not come yet. I am still enchained by sin and fettered by worldliness. My spirit is not free. My heart is not pure. Set me free, kind God, from the trammels of sin, and make my heart clean, that I may be worthy of the better land above. And when the time comes show me the way, that I may walk with thee into the mansions of light and joy,

WHERE is my beloved Christ, Lord? I wish to see him. And where is thy soul-intranced devotee, Chaitanya! Where is Socrates? Where are Janak and Sukdeb? Where are Nanak and Kabir? Where they are my heart wishes to be. They have won my affections, and I cannot live without them. But alas! my wicked heart cannot go there. Grant then, Merciful Father, that those holy and saintly spirits may come and abide in my heart. In their company I shall find heaven.

LOVING God, how sweet is it to love! how happy be who loves! I have tasted the sweets of love through thy grace. I pray I may learn at thy feet to love yet more warmly and tenderly. May my love grow and expand day after day, embracing friends and foes, men of my faith and country, and men of other persuations and countries, all sects and communities without prejudice? Teach me, Father, to love those who stand outside the pale of my love and sympathy, and grant that I may be more lovingly attached to those whom I love.

The Brahmo Somaj

THE new Prarthana Mundir at Ahmedabad will be opened on the 3rd proximo, at 8 A. M.

UNDER Lord Northbrook's instructions given on the eve of his departure from India, Mr. Locke, Principal of the Government School of Art, is getting a water color portrait of Babu Keshub Chunder Sen painted by the students of the institution. Already the portrait has made some progress, and will, it is hoped, be a success.

PRIVATE letters inform us that our English friends in England are somewhat anxious about the recent classification of Brahmo devotees. Even here we find a great deal of misapprehension on the subject. How can we expect then that foreigners at a distance will be able to form a right estimate of the movement? Besides we must wait for a fuller development.

THE two students of *yoga* and *bhakti* continue to receive instructions on alternate days from the minister. We are glad to hear the Upadhya, Pandit Gour Gobinda Rai, is translating the notes into Sanskrit verse.

THERE seems to be no prospect at present of sending out a missionary worker to Australia, in response to the invitation we noticed the other day.

THE *Tattwabodhini Patrika* publishes an interesting discourse read by Babu Satyendra Nath Tagore before the Kurrachi Brahmo Somaj.

THERE was some delay in commencing service in the Brahma Mundir on the occasion of the New Year's Day. This is very much to be regretted.

WE are sincerely glad to learn that arrangements have been made to pay off all the liabilities of the Mission Office. A religious institution, which encourages poverty and asceticism, should not encumber and paralyse itself with heavy liabilities, and always work according to its limited means. A debt is a curse, and is the root of many evils.

Correspondence.

To the Editor of the *Indian Mirror*.

SIR,—A certain editorial paragraph in a late issue of the Sunday *Mirror* on the subject of caste and intermarriage has, I am sorry to find, led to unpleasant reflections regarding our minister, both in Calcutta and the Mofussil, where I had occasion to spend a few weeks lately. I have made inquiries upon my return, and have the minister's own authority for saying that he is not responsible for the opinions expressed in the paragraph in question, and that so far as he is concerned he altogether ignored caste in filling the census returns of his house. I am also informed that when he was referred to for advice he seriously objected to Brahmos mentioning caste in the census returns. Caste is practically ignored in a community where intermarriages have taken place.

A MISSIONARY.

Literary.

THE *Pekin Gazette* has been established over 1,000 years and probably its present numbers are exact counterparts of the first it issued. It covers ten pages, four by eight inches, and has a yellow cover, on which its name is printed. It is the only Native paper circulating in a kingdom of 414,000,000 souls, and is exclusively confined to official notices.

Scientific

THE Government of India have desired the Chief Commissioner of Mysore to adopt such steps as he may deem expedient in preparing a list of objects possessing antiquarian interest in the Province of Mysore and Curg. The Chief Commissioner has already deputed Mr. B. L. Rice, the Director of Public Instruction, to prepare the list in question, with a descriptive account of the subject, from the information which the several Deputy Commissioners are directed to collect and submit to him.

Gleanings.

EVERY great fact of nature or society may be regarded as a parable, veiling yet suggesting spiritual realities.

IT is not the thing that we do, but the spirit that we work in, that tests our moral and spiritual condition.

EVENTS are the shells of ideas.

WHEN one has performed a good act, made a noble sacrifice, resisted temptation, or broken up a bad habit, nature looks more pleasant and peaceful. It sheds as it were, a benediction upon him in the sunshine, and whispers approval in the breeze. On the contrary, when he has committed any deed of shame he cannot look up unrebuked to the calm blue sky, or the majestic hills.

CHAPLIN.

THE Moslem roams the world from east to west,
And finds no alien clime, no hostile strand,
No loneliness in any desert land,
So he but knows by some unerring test
Which way lies Mecca. Then he is at rest.
Happy, on bended knee with outstretched hand
He prays; then rises girded to withstand
All foes; secure and honored, Allah's guest.
Hearts have their Mecca. Waters may be wide,
And mountains stretch across a continent,
The faithful from their worship to divide;
But love is leagued with every element.
The earth no secret from true love can hide;
True hearts their Mecca know and are content.—
[*The Independent.*

Latest News

WE are glad to learn that the Bustar affair is settled. The ryots are dispersing, and the troops are returning to Madras.

MR. G. G. DEY, C. S., has obtained a certificate of High Proficiency in Sanskrit, and a reward of Rs. 2,000, and Mr. W. Jenkyns, C. S., a certificate of High Proficiency in Persian and a reward of Rs. 2,000.

CHINESE enterprise is showing itself in another direction. A Chinese Banking Company is in process of formation. The capital is to be $2,000,000, in share of $100 each, nearly all of which have been already taken up by wealthy Chinese.

THE *Englishman* says that "the Indian grievance-mongers are rapidly becoming a recognised profession in England."

A RUMOUR reaches the *Pioneer* from Indore that H. H. Maharajah Holkar has determined to give all his establishments, his revenue, judicial, and ministerial officers, his army his household servants, in fact every one employed in his State, an advance of six months' pay, *subject to a deduction of* 10 *per cent for interest.*

THE services of Mr. C. P. L. Macaulay, Officiating Under-Secretary to the Government of India in the Department of Revenue, Agriculture and Commerce, are replaced at the disposal of the Government of Bengal with effect from the 22nd instant.

MAHOMED YESSIN KHAN is appointed an Attache to the Resident at Hyderabad.

THE services of Mr. H. T. Prinsep, late Officiating Judicial Commissioner of Mysore and Curg, are replaced at the disposal of the Government of Bengal.

SIR DINKAR RAO passed through Poona by the mail train on Monday last.

THE number of people who attended the *juttra* or pilgrimage at Jejuri, in the Poona District, is estimated at 30,000. The third class railway carriages were crowded with people. The roads from Sattara were thronged with companies of pilgrims carrying flags and in some cases, instruments of music.

THE reduced rates on Indian postage—six pence *via* Southampton and eight pence *via* Brindisi—may be expected to come into force on the 1st of July. Newspapers *via* Brindisi will cost two pence, and books three pence, per two ounces.

THE Native Munshis of the British Agents at Ladakh and Yarkhand are, at Lahore, busily preparing some of the official material for their masters.

MAHARAJAH HOLKAR'S Minister has adopted stringent measures for the suppression of cholera and small-pox, which prevail to a slight extent. A Medical Department will shortly be organised in Indore under a Native Surgeon.

THE Peshawar correspondent of the Lahore paper gives a rumour that the Afridis attacked the outpost of Cherat on the night of the 13th instant, adding that a force of all arms has since left Peshawar and proceeded towards the Khyber Pass.

THE Bishop of Madras, accompanied by his Domestic Chaplain, returned to Madras last Friday, in the Steamer *Eldorado* from Calcutta.

THERE has been but little rain in the Madras Presidency. Light showers have fallen in the parts of Kistna, Tanjore and Malabar. Heavy rain is much needed in Tanjore and Madura, where the water-supply is scanty. Cholera has been severe in Kurnul and Malabar. Cholera is also prevalent in parts of Mysore. There has been no rain in Bombay. Cholera continues in Kattywar, Guzerat and parts of the Southern Mahratta Country. Timely rain is reported from most districts in Bengal, and the preparation of the land for sowing is being briskly proceeded with.

FROM a resolution published in the *Gazette of India*, we gather that the average amount of Notes issued under the Indian Paper Currency Act outstanding at the end of each month during the year 1874-75 was Rs 10,67,04,071, being less by Rs 47,47,830 (4·45 per cent.) than the average of 1873-4 and by Rs. 2,19,36,296 (17·05 per cent.) than the average of 1872-3. Notes of the Allahabad and Lahore Circles for Rs. 2,58,41,005 were cashed in Calcutta under the peculiar provision of the law which makes the Government accept this obligation. The amount is rather less than the amount (Rs. 2,00,30,715) similarly encashed in the preceding year. The number of five-rupee notes in circulation is still small. The notes for Rs. 1,000 represent more than 60 per cent. of the whole amount outstanding, followed at a long distance by the notes for Rs. 10,000 representing 11 per cent., and for Rs 100 representing 10 per cent. The use of the Currency Offices as Agencies for the supply of small silver and copper appears to be creasing. The profits of the Department during the year were Rs. 19,80,151.

THE Lieutenant-Governor of the North-West Provinces will leave Allahabad for Nyni Tal this day.

No less than seventeen persons will be hanged on the 5th May for the murder of Mr. Margary.

TELEGRAPHIC advices received from Jacobabad state that Major Sandeman's party was attacked by cholera on the 10th instant, and that there were about thirty deaths. Major Sandeman pushed on to the Bolan Pass by forced marches. Since then an improvement has taken place, and there were only two admissions to hospital on the 14th instant.

THE death of Lord Lyttleton is announced by his own hand. He was for sometime the President of the East Indian Association, London.

THE *Englishman* is getting remarkably out-spoken. Our contemporary writes :—"The gun-grievances of the Maharajah of Burdwan no longer supply pabulum to Bengali editors, through whom they were wont to become the subject of fitful discussion in the Calcutta newspapers. His Highness has adopted the much more effectual advertisement of writing a gentlemanly letter to the *Times*, forwarding some pretty medals for the boys who behaved well in the affair of the *Goliath*, and thus secured the ear of the English public when the question of his status and ambition for a salute is again raised."

THE usual notification is published in the *Gazette of India* that the Viceregal Council will meet at Simla, until further notice.

IN a resolution published in the *Gazette of India* it is stated :—"Taking into consideration the length of the journeys, aggregating in all 4,829 miles, performed by His Royal Highness the Prince of Wales on Indian Railways, and the difficulties with which the Railway authorities had to contend, consequent on an augmented traffic at a time when efforts were needed to ensure the safety of the Royal train, and the personal convenience and comfort of His Royal Highness the Prince of Wales, the Governor-General in Council is pleased to record his high appreciation of the services rendered by the Railway officials of all ranks."

Calcutta

MR. SCONCE has returned from a month's furlough, and taken his seat as Third Judge of the Calcutta Small Cause Court.

MR. RICHARD VANGELDER, of the Inner Temple, London, has been admitted as a member of the Calcutta Bar.

LORD LYTTON left Calcutta for Simla last night. His Excellency is expected to arrive at Simla on or about the 25th instant.

SIR FREDERICK HAINES took his seat as an Extraordinary Member of the Governor-General's Council, on the 16th instant.

THE Levee held by Lord Lytton, on Wednesday last, at Government House, was attended by 868 European and Native gentlemen. Of the former there were 681, and of the latter 187 only.

FROM the 29th April till further notice, Parts I, IV, and V of the *Gazette of India*, and the Weather and Crop Report, will be published at Simla. After the 22d instant, all Notifications and other matter intended for publication in those Parts should be addressed to the Officiating Publisher at the station. Parts II and III and the Supplement will continue to be published in Calcutta.

DURING the absence of the Governor-General in Council from Calcutta the Officiating Secretary to the Government of India in the Military Department, Colonel A. B. Johnson, will have charge of that portion of the Home Department and of the Foreign Office which will be left at Calcutta.

THE rules for the examination of candidates to admission to the service of the Government of India in the Financial Department, and of officers in the Financial Department, are published in yesterday's official *Gazette of India*.

HIS EXCELLENCY the Viceroy and Governor-General in Council is pleased to recognize the appointment of Monsr. Eydoux as Consul General for France at Calcutta.

A LAC and a half has been paid by Government to the Asiatic Society, as compensation for the abandonment of the Society's claim, under Act XVII of 1866 to accommodation in the new Museum at Calcutta. The Society, therefore, will continue to occupy their present premises, and the compensation money will be invested at 5½ per cent.

IT is officially announced that the reform of the copper coinage, Calcutta, has been satisfactorily accomplished at a considerable expense.

SIR RICHARD TEMPLE will, we believe, leave Calcutta for Darjiling to-morrow.

DOMESTIC OCCURRENCE.

BIRTH.

SEN.—On Thursday 20th April, 1876, at 7-30 A. M. (at Manikgunge) the wife of Babu Chandi Charan Sen, 2nd Munsiff of Manikgunge, of a son.

MARRIAGE.

SEN.—At Pottuldangah, Calcutta, on Sunday the 16th April, 1876, corresponding 5th Bysack 1283 B. E., Mohendro Nath Sen, 2nd son of Dr. Nil Madhab Sen, to Srimati Heminta Devi, 3rd daughter of Babu Tarak Nath Sen of 9 Rutton Mistree's Lane.

Law

POLICE—APRIL 22, 1876.

[*Before F. J. Marsden, Esq.*]

THE following judgment was delivered this morning in the case in which Henry Wickley, an ordinary seaman of the American ship *Cromwell*, charged Captain Richardson, of the same ship, with having used criminal force towards him, and also with having assaulted him :

Mr. Marsden : In this case the facts elicited in the evidence before me are as follows : The complainant, Wickley, was, on the evening of Friday, the 14th instant, accused by the Steward of the *Cromwell* of having stolen a chicken. This Wickley denied at once. The Steward reported the matter to the chief officer, and no more passed on that day ; and both Wickley and the Steward subsequently went on shore. The following morning, Wickley, being still angry with the Steward, laid in wait for him, and, having caught him, struck him two or three blows. The chief officer interfered, and separated them ; and, leaving Wickley in the fore part of the vessel the chief officer and Steward went aft, the former reporting the fact to the Captain. On this the Captain directed the chief officer to call Wickley aft. This was at once done, and Wickley appears to have obeyed the call in a quiet and orderly manner. On his coming aft, Captain Richardson asked him what he had been doing to the Steward, Wickley answered, "I punched him for accusing me of stealing a chicken when I had not stolen one." On this the Captain at once ordered the chief officer to put Wickley in irons. This was at once done, Wickley offering no resistance whatever. Not content with this, the Captain ordered him to be triced up by the wrists to the mizzen-stays, and the chief and second officers triced him up in obedience to the Captain's orders, in such a manner that his toes barely touched the deck. Wickley thereupon raised his feet till he got them on to the fife-rail, evidently to ease the strain on his wrists. On seeing this, the chief mate triced him up still higher, till his toes barely reached the fife-rail ; there being some belaying pins on the fife-rail, Wickley managed to get his feet on them, so as to again ease his wrists, when the chief officer ordered the second mate to take away the belaying pins, so that Wickley was again left with his toes barely reaching the rail. While triced up, Wickley used very abusive language to the Captain, and the Captain struck him two or three times with a rope's end. In this painful posture he appears to have been kept for about half an hour, with no hat on his head, and exposed to the sun, which, Captain Mitchell states, was so strong that he had put a handkerchief under his own *sola topi* to protect himself from it. During this time Captain Mitchell, who happened to be passing the vessel in a boat, seeing a man triced up to the mizzen stays, went on board the *Cromwell*, and saw Wickley in the position described, and remonstrated, but with no effect, and was only ordered to leave the ship, which he was obliged to do. Shortly after Captain Mitchell left ; and, in consequence of a crowd having collected on shore and clamouring against what was taking place Wickly was taken down by the Captain, and lashed to a stanchion. From this he shortly afterwards made his escape, and managed to get on shore, and make his way to the police station with the handcuffs still on him, and made his complaint, and later in the day obtained a summons from this Court. Captain Mitchell in his evidence states that he saw Wickley at the Thannah, and that his hands were then perfectly livid and in such a state that he was unable to open them. On Wickley's being triced up to the mizzen-stays, he certainly used very bad language to the Captain which, I believe, was the cause of the Captain's striking him two or three times with a ropes end. But this assault with a rope's-end is, in my opinion, a question of minor importance. It is clear to me on the evidence that Wickley used no bad language whatever until *after* he had been triced up. These being the facts of the case, the conclusion I have arrived at is, that there was nothing whatever in Wickley's conduct to justify the Captain's treatment of him. When called aft, he was perfectly quiet; nay more, he did not even raise the slightest objection to the Captain's placing him in irons, which, considering that the vessel was in port, and the circumstances of the case, I hold the Captain had no right whatever to do. But the Captain went much further than merely placing him in irons, for he (the complainant) had been triced up in such a way that his toes barely reached the rails, and of this I am perfectly convinced from the fact of the man's hands being in such a livid condition when he reached the police-station. The tricing the man up in the manner described, was, in my opinion, nothing more or less than cruelty of the most cowardly and brutal description. He was not merely made fast to the stays to prevent his committing violence, but was suspended by the wrists for about half an hour, until his hands were perfectly livid. The thanks of the community at large are due to Captain Mitchell for the part he has taken in the matter, and I wish to mention that the evidence of the able seaman of the *Cromwell*, was most thoroughly straightforward and trustworthy. Having all regard to the strict discipline that must be kept upon board-ship, I should not be doing my duty were I not to inflict a substantial punishment in this case. The sentence of the Court is that Captain Richardson do undergo one month's rigorous imprisonment, and be fined Rs. 100 ; in default, 14 days' further imprisonment. The case brought by the Steward against Wickley will be dismissed.

ICE! ICE! ICE!

MADE IN FOUR MINUTES

THE PNEUMATIC ICE MACHINE

THIS IMPORTANT INVENTION IS CONSIDERED A BOON TO THOSE LIVING IN TROPICAL CLIMATES.

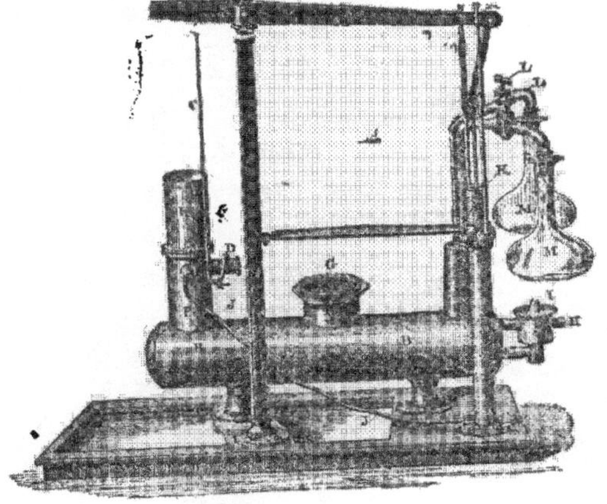

CAN BE WORKED BY THE MOST INEXPERIENCED HAND AND IS NOT LIABLE TO GET OUT OF ORDER.

From Rs. 175, each Machine complete.

MESSRS. ARLINGTON & CO.
AGENTS.

HAROLD & CO.,

3, DALHOUSIE SQUARE, CALCUTTA

HARMONIUMS.

Harold and Co., call attention to their unequalled stock of rich-toned Harmoniums made especially for India.

FROM RS. 90 TO RS. 900 EACH.

All kinds of Musical Instruments of the best description are always kept in Stock.

ALBERT HALL.

PATRON.

His Honor the Lieutenant Governor of Bengal

COUNCIL.

Hon'ble Sir William Muir, K. C. S. I.—*President.*

Rajah Rama Nath Tagore Bahadur C. S. I.—*Vice-President.*

Hon'ble J. F. D. Inglis.

Hon'ble Ashley Eden, C. S. I.

Hon'ble H. Bell.

Archdeacon Baly.

Colonel H. E. L. Thuillier, C. S. I.

His Highness the Maharajah of Vizianagram.

Maharajah Kumar of Bettiah.

Hon'ble Rajah Narendra Krishna Bahadur.

Rajah Komul Krishna Bahadur.

Rajah Jotendro Mohun Tagore Bahadur.

Babu Digumber Mitter, C. S. I.

Hon'ble Nawab Ashgar Ali Bahadur, C. S. I.

Nawab Amir Ali Bahadur.

Moulvi Abdul Lutif Khan Bahadur.

Manockji Rustomji Esq.

Babu Keshub Chunder Sen.

SUBSCRIPTIONS.

His Highness Maharajah Holkar ...	Rs.	8,000
His Highness Maharajah of Jeypore	„	5,000
His Highness Maharajah of Puttiala	„	2,500
His Highness Maharajah of Vizianagram ...	„	1,000
Maharajah Kumar of Bettiah ...	„	2,000
Rajah of Bhinga ...	„	1,000
Maharani Surnomoie, Cossim Bazar	„	1,000
Maharajah of Hutwa ...	„	500
Rajah Rama Nath Tagore Bahadur	„	250
Rajah Komul Krishna Bahadur ...	„	500
Rajah Joteendro Mohun Tagore ...	„	500
Hon'ble Rajah Narendra Krishna Bahadur ...	„	300
Babu Joykissen Mookerjee ...	„	250
Sirdar Dyal Singh ...	„	200
Babu Shama Churn Law ...	„	200
Hon'ble Sir William Muir ...	„	100
Hon'ble Ashley Eden ...	„	100
Dr. Mohendro Loll Sircar ...	„	100
Babu Goonendro Nath Tagore ...	„	100
Babu Ananda Mohun Bose ...	„	100
Babu Rajkissen Mookerjee ...	„	200
Babu Janoki Nath Mookerji ...	„	100

Printed and published by M. M. RUKHIT, at the "INDIAN MIRROR" PRESS, No. 13, College Square, for the Proprietors.

The Indian Mirror.

SUNDAY EDITION.

VOL XV.] CALCUTTA, SUNDAY, APRIL 30, 1876 { REGISTERED AT THE GENERAL POST OFFICE. } [No. 102

CONTENTS.

NOTICE.

Letters and all other communications relating to the literary department of the Paper should be addressed to "The Editor."

All letters on the business of the Press should be addressed, and all remittances made payable to the Manager of this Paper. Particular attention is solicited to this notice.

Subscribers will be good enough to give prompt notice of any delay, or irregularity in delivery of the Paper.

Editorial Notes

ENGLAND is said to be the greatest Mahomedan power in the world. This is of course in relation to the occupation of India by England. There are forty one millions of Mahomedans in this country, and in Bengal alone there are more Mossulmans than are ruled by the Sultan of Turkey, and the Khedive of Egypt together. It would be interesting to know the exact number of Mahomedans in the world, and what proportion they bear to the whole Mossulman population of India.

THE word Brahma Nirvan often occurs in the *Bhagavat Gita*. It means the cessation of all desires and all secular knowledge in God. There is little doubt that much is common between the Budhistic and Hindu use of the word, the main distinction being that while the Hindus merge the personality and desires of man in the supreme Essence of the Deity, the Budhists seem to be of the opinion that the extinction itself is productive of supreme peace and wisdom.

"A MISSIONARY" writing in our last Sunday's issue, adverts to views expressed in these columns sometime ago on the subjects of Caste and Intermarriage. He says that these views have given rise to unpleasant comments both in Calcutta and the Mofussil, where people conclude that Babu K. C. Sen is their author. "A Missionary" could have left it to us to contradict this unfounded impression. Not only was Babu K. C. Sen not the author of those views, but he did not know that they had appeared in the *Mirror*, till he read them sometime after their appearance. This is not mentioned here with the object of withdrawing, or even modifying in the slightest degree the remarks made by us on the subjects of Caste and Intermarriage. We do not believe anything has been said from which man of common sense can dissent. But yet for various reasons, we think, there ought to be no misunderstanding as to the authorship of the paragraphs we allude to.

WE publish elsewhere some extracts from the daily manual of the Budhist devotee, or *shaman*, the Sanskrit word being *Sramana*. Those extracts will show the profound spirit of love which inspires the devotions, and spiritual exercises of genuine Budhists. The *Pranam*, or obeisance to Budha, will prove the injustice of the common assertion that the Budhist admits no prayer, and no devout aspiration into his system. There is little in the devotional departments of other religions that can surpass in depth or tenderness the passage we have quoted. Nay it would be a strange contradiction to all human experience, and divine dispensations, if a system of faith that still enlists the largest number of mankind as its votaries, should win the spiritual adherence of millions without feeling the deepest spiritual appetites, those of prayer and communion, ingrained in the heart. There is much more in Budhism than Brahmos in general seem yet to be aware of, and when there is a revival in their midst at the present time of the past spirit of Hinduism, we hope some attention would be paid to a religion which inspite of its deficiencies, bears on it the evident marks of true wisdom, heavenly piety and divine approval.

WE must ask to be enlightened on what principle of Christianity, common sense, or decency is the universal use of nude female figures allowed in works of art that are admitted almost into every Christian art-gallery and household, and seen by men and women of all ages, tastes, and temperaments. Venuses and Appollos are good things in their way, and the peculiarly esthetic spirits and the archæologically inclined may inspect, and study and enjoy them. But in drawing-rooms, libraries, and places of domestic and public resort, we should like to know how the exhibition of naked figures, in all sorts of attitudes, is justified. Of course the superlatively virtuous among the world will cry out *Puris omnia pura*, and we will be condemned of secondhand Moodyism and puritanical prudery. But we should in sober earnest like to know how many young men and women standing together before a nude figure, can with pure minds and unabashed brow, exchange their criticisms on the work of art they see, and look each other in the face. To our minds this is a relic of the voluptuous Paganism of Rome and Greece, and has done not a little to undermine the practical purity of Christian morals.

THE protracted and somewhat undignified squabble in Parliament on the subject of the Queen's new title, seems to us people of India to be trivial and unnecessary. Endless references have been made both by the Government and the Opposition, to the feelings which the title would call forth in this country, and a great deal too much concern has been shown for our welfare. If the Bill had excited in the minds of the English people that interest in the affairs of India which never existed there, it would, perhaps, be a measure of importance to us. But that is not the case. It has been judged from a purely English point of view, and opposed on traditional and political grounds peculiar to England alone. We are glad of the new title, because it definitely associates the name of the Queen with this country, and shows some attachment and appreciation on the part of Her Majesty for her Indian dominions. Otherwise it is all the same to us whether she is called Queen or Empress. The moral effect of the title almost amounts to nothing. Mr. Disraeli is right when he says that it will suit the oriental imagination, and invest Her Majesty constitutionally with a dignity which the millions of her Indian subjects tacitly attribute to her already.

WE never meant to speak lightly of the blessed spirit of peace, purity, and consolation which an inward sympathy with the love and service of Jesus produces in the heart. Truly Christ's life was the life of obedience, but it was obedience perfected through the highest love, that love which merges opposing personalities into one, and fuses the irreconcilable elements of independant wills. Human will can perhaps conform to human will, when the trifling difficulties of circumstance, training, taste &c., are overcome. But how awful is the union of man's will, poor, ignorant, captive, and self-seeking as it is, with the infinite will of Him whose nature is so infinitely different from man's? Nothing can bring about such union but absolute, unconditional, perfect self-sacrifice. And how can such sacrifice be possible on the part of self-seeking man but through perfect love, that loses self in the depths of its Divine Object. Christ is the exemplar of such union, of such sacrifice, and such love. And therefore he says I and my Father one. They who believe in him, because they have been told to do so, because they fear they will go to hell unless they do so, because books teach them, opinions incline them, and circumstances force them to the belief, do not know Christ, however loud they may be in their Christian professions and begoted in their denunciation of others. But they who love with an intense passion of love—a passion they cannot define, that binds them in a double service to man and to God, a service that leads to suffering they cannot express—a suffering that leads and points to death as its inevitable end,—it is such men who without imagining a corporeal Christ, derive from sympathy with his spirit a peace that passeth understanding.

THE THING TO HOLD BY.

THE first thing to find out is what you hold by in the kingdom of God. Have you anything to hold by, is that which you hold by strong enough to keep you from falling when the trying time comes? Man holds by external and, or he lives by faith aids dependence in God alone. Faith points out external aids, and external aids increase faith. There are few who can live by faith alone. External aids again may multiply, and monopolize faith, attention, energy, and time, without leaving much margin for the cultivation of direct relations with the formless, and absolute spirit of God who transcends all worldly helps and supports. The golden mean of religion lies between the two. Yet to find out the mean is not in itself an easy thing. It is discoverable by him only who understands the relative value of both, and can strike out the harmony between them. Direct spiritual relations with the Deity when duly cultivated, tend to embody themselves in certain objects, without which the relations themselves often fade into unreality. Now for instance when we speak of loving God, we are at once reminded that we are not able to enjoy this mighty spiritual blessedness, unless we cultivate the habit of loving the smaller and more comprehensive souls wherewith we are surrounded in the world. And we know that when we are incapable of the latter action, we are much more incapable of the former. Take again the aspiration of becoming holy. Unless holiness is cultivated in certain definite relations of life, purity in the abstract is simply unattainable, or imaginary. The great secret of a truly pious life is that it has fastened itself upon certain objects, events, and circumstances which by the force of inviolable mental law can at all times, and under all difficulties safely carry it to the throne of Heaven. The helps and friendships, the books and the exercises that we often value so much, slip away from our hands at the moments of utmost need. The wise man will, amidst such irreparable losses, keep a few things, find a few men, rely upon certain external helps that by repeated experiments have been proved to be unfailing. But where can these be found? Faith and prayer when rightly indulged in point them out, nestle in them, and repeatedly illustrate the necessity of holding by them. With some it may be a man, with others it may be a book, with others again it may be certain relations. These form for him a surrounding world in which his spiritual life exists, an environment out of which he ought not under any circumstance to move.

SIR RICHARD TEMPLE AND THE ALBERT HALL.

IF Sir Richard is, as he is said to be, fond of popularity, it must be admitted in justice to him, that he can also stand a considerable amount of plain-speaking. During the last few years, whether as Finance Minister, or as Lieutenant-Governor, he, we believe, has been the best abused man in the country; and so far as popularity goes, he has done quite as much to lose it, and *has* perhaps as effectually lost it, as the most stubborn of his predecessors. If then inspite of the hard things said about him on all hands, and harder things could not be said than what these columns have sometimes contained, he still manages to keep up his affability towards every one, and, what is more, really goes about in every direction doing and encouraging to do good, certainly it ought to be conceded that his public acts are inspired by something higher than the mere love of popularity. When a popularity-hunter ceases, in the blindness and self-delusion of his favorite passion to be any longer popular, and discovers that people have found him out, his rage and mortification over-ride his temper and good sense; and a more unamiable misanthrope than him it is not easy to conceive. Sir Richard Temple is just the opposite of this. In connection with the late Income Tax, much more notably in connection with the recent Municipal Bill, and the various minor questions which it raised, His Honor has been assailed with a vigor, with a virulence, with an unanimity which would have ruffled the patience and tried the temper of any saint, if saints have been at all remarkable for patience and sweet temper. But Sir Richard Temple is there, just the same as before, planning *Rhotas* expeditions, and garden-parties, presiding at meetings, attending *soirees*, encouraging Prof. Monier Williams, Miss Carpenter, patronizing Babu Manomohan Ghose, patting the Indian League on the back, giving money to Dr. Sircar's Science Association, and rendering the most handsome aid to the Albert Hall movement. A man smarting under the sense of unpopularity could not do all this, and the hundred other things which His Honor is perpetually doing. It is with popularity, as with higher things:—He that seeketh and liveth to keep it, shall lose it in the end, and he that chooses to lose and sacrifice it shall regain and enjoy it in the world.

One popular thing, however, Sir Richard has really done. We mean his presence and speech the other day at the Inauguration of the Albert Hall. For more reasons than one we must congratulate the founders of that institution. We cannot run into an ecstacy over it just yet. We reserve our usual superlatives of eminence for that stage in its career when it has really commenced to be useful. What we can at present say is that the Albert Hall has made a good beginning. And if good beginning be any augury of future success, certainly the Albert Hall, unlike its London namesake, deserves to be successful. To secure a concensus of sympathy for a common end from the various sections of society, whose normal state is, what Mr. Darwin calls, "the struggle for existence," and, what is a much more difficult operation, to transform and condense that sympathy into hard cash, represented by the respectable figure of thirty thousand rupees, the whole process taking not more than six months, does seem to be promising. The founders do not seem to have gone to sleep over their project. And where there is such energy, success cannot be very far off. Looking next to the position of the persons by whom the institution has been made possible, who have spent their energy and their money over it, we find similar cause for congratulation. It is the object of the Hall to bring together different classes of society, and to promote friendly union and fellow-feeling among them. That this is no mere twaddle is evidenced by the substantial sums of money contributed by some of the highest and most powerful Native Princes towards the project. The

Maharajahs of Jeypore and Indore, when they are in Calcutta will naturally feel interested to come and see what use is being made of their valuable aid, and if they are satisfied, may be induced to continue that aid. Nor can they help being flattered by the significant notice taken of their donations by such a high functionary as the Lieutenant-Governor of Bengal, whose warm approval may be justly taken as the harbinger of a still higher approval in official quarters. But even if that be wanting, the gain to society will be immense if such heterogenus bodies as the Princedom of India, the British Indian Association, the Indian League, the Mahomedan Literary Society, the Parsis, the descendants of the Mysore family, the members of the Brahmo Somaj, the members of the Students' Association and others can be fused into social intercourse, in which all religious and conventional differences are to be studiously kept in the background. And if Sir Richard has not promised us large and liberal attendance on the part of Europeans, who "find the climate so exhausting," he has very distinctly told us that the leaders of the European community will not grudge us either their sympathy or their co-operation. And we believe he is right. When names like Sir William Muir, the Hon'ble Ashley Eden, Archdeacon Baley, not excluding that of His Honor himself, are among the subscribers, there is chance that European patronage will not be absent altogether. Sir Richard did good in paying that graceful compliment, which he knows so well how to do, to Dr. Sourindro Mohun Tagore, and to Hindu music in general by calling it elaborate and scientific. When a thing does not strike you as sweet, it is always safe to call it scientific, and if in the heart of his heart he did not think Hindu Music very sweet or inspiring, he expressed that feeling with equal delicacy and wisdom in the remark that Native gentlemen did not go into raptures over the music of their rulers. If Dr. Sircar's Association, and Science College become accomplished facts, we do agree with His Honor, that the wind will be very much taken out of the sail of the Albert Hall. But there will be plenty of other things left. There was a tone of earnest sincerity, and careful modesty in the concluding statements of the Lieutenant-Governor which was truly pleasing. In offering to teach us what he and his countrymen knew, Sir Richard said that his own people were learning still. We differ from Richard Temple in his many of his local and political views and we shall always point out this difference as explicitly as we can. But we think few will dissent from us when we say that so far as social accomplishments go, and the important art of respecting others and treating them with kind and delicate consideration, Sir Richard Temple remains unsurpassed by all those who have preceded him in the Government of Bengal.

Telegraphic Intelligence

Reuter's Telegrams.

LONDON, APRIL 28.

The proclamation declaring the Queen to be Empress of India was issued today. After recital, the proclamation declares that henceforth, so far as may be convenient on all occasions and instruments wherein the style and titles of Her Majesty are used, excepting charters, commissions, letters-patent, grants, writs of appointment, and similar instruments not operating beyond the United Kingdom, the following addition to the style and titles pertaining to the Imperial Crown of the United Kingdom, and its dependencies, shall henceforth be made in the Latin tongue *India Imperatrix*, in English *Empress of India*. The proclamation further states that all coinage shall continue to be lawful without the additional title until the Queen's pleasure is further declared.

Her Majesty has been pleased to confor a Baronetcy on Sir Bartle Frere.

The *Dunraven*, Captain Cane, bound from Bombay to Liverpool, has been lost in the Red Sea. The crew was saved.

The total amount tendered for the new loan of £4,000,000 was £8,600,000. Tenders at £102-8 will receive about 73 per cent. above in full.

In the House of Commons this evening, Mr. Eutace Smith moved for the appointment of a Select Committee upon the mode followed in relieving the sufferers by the last Indian famine. Government opposed the motion, which was rejected by 149 votes against 46.

Provincial

BERHAMPORE.

[FROM OUR OWN CORRESPONDENT.]

The 23rd April 1876.

I THINK it will give pleasure to you and your readers to know that a very laudable movement has been set on foot in this town. About two months since, a Total Abstinence Society has been established here by the energetic zeal of the Rev. W. B. Phillips, a Christian Missionary, who has lately arrived here from England. Some of the Native gentlemen have joined to assist him in carrying on the noble project. The first meeting of the Society came off, on the 2nd March last, at 7½ P.M., in the Hall of the L. M. S. School, Kingra. There was a large gathering of Native gentlemen. The business of the meeting was commenced by a prayer which was followed by a hymn, sung by a few European ladies present on the occasion. Mr. Phillips, the Chairman, then explained briefly to the meeting, the object that the Society proposed to carry out. To suppress the great evil of intemperance which is unfortunately causing the death of many people of this Station, is the chief and only object the Society has in view. Then followed, at intervals, short but impressive speeches both in English and Bengali on the evils of intemperance. The Rev. S. J. Hill and Babu Kali Krishna Chatterji spoke in Bengali, and the Rev. Nanda Lal Dass in English. The signing of the Pledge then began. A good many gentlemen present "solemnly and voluntarily pledged themselves, by the help of God, to abstain from all Intoxicating drinks and drugs, except when given as medicines by a Doctor." The meeting then broke up after prayers had been offered to the Almighty.

We hear that the second meeting of the Society will be held on Wednesday, the 26th instant, at 1½ P. M. in the Hall of the L. M. S. School. I shall try to give you an account of the proceedings of the meeting. In short, the meeting sits once in every 2 months. I cannot help mentioning here with heart-felt gratitude the names of the gentlemen who compose the Managing Committee of the Society, and consequently have taken an active part in the work. They are:—

Rev. W. B. Philips, *President.*

Babu Kali Krishna Chatterji, *Vice-President and Secretary.*

Rev. Nanda Lal Das, *Treasurer and a Member.*

Babu Sita Nath Bose,
" Atul Krishna Nag,
" Brajendra Nath Chatterji,
and a few of the young boys of the station. } *Members.*

A few words about the energetic President, I hope, will not be out of place here. Mr. Philips is a young man of amiable disposition and cheerful mind. Any one who has once come in contact with him, has been impressed with his noble and admirable qualities.

The local College is now ably managed by the Principal, Mr. Bellet. But we often hear students of the College classes complaining of the lectures they hear from their Mathematical Professor, but I am not sure whether it is a fact or not. Since the last few months a middle class English School has been opened very close to the College by some young men. I doubt not, this School will do and has done already a great injury to the College, as regards the numerical strength of some of the lower classes of the collegiate School. The College has already been reduced to a very small number of boys since the opening of an L. M. S School at Kingra. The educated guardians of the boys should compare the education their boys receive in a College with that in a private school, and try to improve the College by sending their boys to prosecute their studies in the collegiate School.

The heat has been again very intense here since about a fortnight. We had a small shower yesterday, which did not cool the atmosphere though.

Devotional

SPIRIT of God, All-seeing witness of the deepest thoughts that are unexpressed, guide a soul that has long looked up to thee in trust and reliance. Thou dost cause light to come out of darkness, and good to come out of evil. Confound all that is wicked in me, and turn my feelings and inclinations which are so easily misled into the paths of righteousness and thy holy will.

HELP me, O Lord, to find my place in thy Kingdom, teach me to discover the unfailing aids that surely lead to thee. My God, if my trust and dependence in thee be real, fasten them upon the right relations and duties of life. Let thy Providence be unto me embodied in real events and objects which preclude all doubt and question. When the time of trial comes, enable me to hold by that which thou hast pointed out to me. As thou art thyself ever infallible, so the ways appointed by thee are infallible.

LORD cause thy blessings to descend upon those to serve whom we labor and are always anxious. May the men and women unto whom we minister be aided and cheered by thy Spirit. Help to explain our counsels and actions to them, deliver them from the evil that is within them, and rightly establish our relations with them here and hereafter.

The Brahmo Somaj

A BOOK of Brahmo Gleanings, is likely to be published in England during the summer. It is to contain a number of articles, scraps, and prayers that have appeared in the *Mirror* from time to time, for spreading information about the Brahmo Somaj among the English public. We wish the project every success.

A STUDENT belonging to the Government Art School has published a number of lithographs of Babu Keshub Chunder Sen taken from a photographic likeness representing him in the posture of devotion. We hope it will find sale.

WE are glad to find that Mr. Shunker Punduring Pundit of Bombay, a gentleman of very high literary attainments, knowing several European languages, besides being a very distinguished Oriental Scholar, has begun to take interest in the Prarthana Somaj. He gave a sermon on the occasion of the last anniversary, which drew a good audience.

Literary.

BHATS and Charans, says the *Indu Prakash*, are the historiographers of Native sovereigns, and in Western India they are chiefly found in Kattywar and Kutch. Their collections of stories and anecdotes of the most renowned of Rajput Princes interspersed with songs and alliterations, are romantic and interesting. A Charan, named Desa Pitha, from Kattiawar, at present on a visit to Bombay, gave a recitation of this kind to a small party at Dr. Atmaram Pandurang's house Sunday before last, and the performance so delighted the audience that similar ones are being held at the houses of other gentlemen.

IT is proposed to start another weekly journal, in addition to the *Star of India*, in Rajputana.

MR. W. THEOBALD has compiled a descriptive catalogue of the reptiles of British India.

As an instance of the power of wonderful capacity of mind, it is said that a Native officer now in the Mysore Commission, has learnt off the whole of Johnson's Dictionary, any page of which he can repeat verbatim.

Scientific

LIEUTENANT CAMERON, the African explorer, has arrived in England in the steamer *Congo*. On his arrival at Liverpool, he was presented with an address from the Mayor and Corporation of that city, and was entertained at a banquet in the Town-hall. Lieutenant Cameron was attended by an intelligent little African boy, who had shared his travels. A considerable number of persons assembled at the landing stage to witness the arrival of the traveller, who was very heartily cheered. Lieutenant Cameron states that he reserves details of his journey for the Royal Geographical Society. He has supplied, however, some dates of his travels, which may be recalled. He left England in November, 1872, arriving at Zanzibar in January, 1873. In March he left for Kikoka, and formed a camp at Rehenneko on the 1st of May. In the August following he arrived at Unyanyembe, where the body of Livingstone was met. He turned towards the west in November, reaching Ujiji in February, and afterwards went round the south of the lake Tanganyika. The outlet of the river was discovered in May, 1874. Subsequently he crossed to Kasongo, and got to Nyangwe early in August. After that he had to go south to the Lualaba river. In November he arrived at the station of the Portuguese traders, where he was detained until June last. He reached Benguela on the 4th of November, 1875.

Gleanings

THE DAILY MANUAL OF THE SHAMAN.

ON awaking in the morning, let the Shaman sit up in a grave posture, and with a meditative heart, recite the following Gatha :—

"On first awaking from my sleep,
I ought to pray that every breathing thing
May wake to saving wisdom, vast
As the wide and boundless universe."

On hearing the convent bell, or striking it oneself, let all recite the following Gatha:—

"Oh! may the music of this bell extend throughout the mystic world,
And, heard beyond the iron walls and gloomy glens of earth,
Produce in all a perfect rest, and quiet every care,
And guide each living soul to lose itself in Mind Supreme"

On binding the sash :—

"On binding on the sash, I pray
That every living soul may closely bind
Each virtuous principle around himself,
And never loosen it or let it go."

On putting on the five garments, say :—

"Hail! robes of final and complete release
Fit robes for those whose happiness is unsurpassed :
I take these vestments to me reverently,
Forever and forever mine."

On bowing down before Buddah, say :—

"King of the law, the most exalted Lord,
Unequalled through the threefold world,
Teacher and Guide of men and gods,
Our loving Father, and of all who breathe,
I bow myself in lowest reverence, and pray,
That thou wouldst soon destroy the power of former works (*i.e.*, destiny.)
To set forth all thy praise,
Unbounded Time would not suffice."

CATENA OF BUDDHISTS SCRIPTURES.

Latest News.

IN the House of Lords, the Marquis of Salisbury declined to lay before Parliament the terms of dissent of Sir E. Perry and Sir H. Montgomery from his confidential telegram to the Indian Government in September 30, 1875.

THE Whips of the Liberal party in the House of Lords issued a circular, requesting the attendance of Peers to support Lord Shaftesbury's amendment to the Royal Titles Bill.

A PUBLIC meeting was held in the Free Trade-hall, Manchester, at which resolutions of sympathy with the Herzegovina insurgents were passed. Letters of concurrence were read from Earl Russell, the Bishop of Manchester, and several members of Parliament.

A SUM of £10,000 in specie has been recovered by divers from the wreck of the steamship *Schiller*, sunk off the Sicilly Islands.

THE semi-official Russian agency contradicts the rumours of the Emperor Alexander's ill-health, and says that His Majesty's plans for the ensuing summer have been decided upon.

THE Russian Press is urging the necessity of united action on the part of the Great Powers to induce the Ottoman Government to improve the condition of its Christian subjects.

A PUBLIC meeting was held in the city of London when, notwithstanding much interruption and opposition, several resolutions deprecating a change in the Royal titles were passed.

THE Emperor William being sick with cold, was unable to visit Queen Victoria at Baden-Baden. The Queen went to Darmstadt to visit the Prince and Princess Louis of Hesse, and returned in the evening to Baden-Baden.

TWO English financiers, Messrs. Stainforth and Ross are endeavouring to arrange at Constantinople for a conversion of the Turkish debt.

A PUBLIC meeting of Native gentlemen was held in the Julsah-i-tahsil at Lucknow, on Sunday last, to protest against the proposed Dramatic Performances Bill. About two hundred persons were present.

A CORRESPONDENT at Mandalay writes to the *Rangoon Times* that a European there has been urging on the King the advisability of improving and extending the cultivation of the tobacco plant, as a source of additional revenue.

THE line of State Railway from Indore to Mhow and Oojein, is to be opened for goods and passenger traffic from the 1st July next.

A SCHEME for placing a window in Rawul Pindi Church as a local memorial to Bishop Milman at the station where he entered into his rest, has been set on foot. It is proposed that it should be a Ladies' Memorial.

THE Government of the N. W. Provinces have purchased the Kumaon Iron Works at Kaladhungi near Nyni Tal.

THE Delhi Stone Slab, in commemoration of the blowing up of the Cashmere Gate, Delhi, is being erected by order of Napier of Magdala. On the inscription the plan of action is described, and it contains the names of the officers and men concerned, who were killed or wounded.

FRANCE and Italy are, it is said, arranging a loan for the Egyptian Government without reference to England, but there is reason to believe that the Khedive is making a final effort to induce the British Government to appoint a Commissioner.

MR. S. A. HILL, Professor of Physical Science, Muir College, Allahabad, has been appointed Meteorological Reporter to Government, N. W. P., vice Mr. J. Elliott, B. A.

THE Lahore journal hears that the Mahomedan sects of Terah have joined the Afridis; in fact, the whole of the tribes of the Peshawur frontier have determined to stand by them.

MR. JUSTICE BOULNOIS of the Punjab will probably take leave at the end of June or early in July.

THE Duke of Edinburgh has arrived in London from the Continent.

THE Empress of Austria has left England on her return to Vienna.

IN the House of Lords, Lord Shaftesbury moved his resolution for an address to the

Queen, praying Her Majesty to adopt another title than that of Empress, which, he proceeded to contend, was distasteful to English minds. The Lord Chancellor disputed the statement that public opinion was unfavorable to the assumption of a title that was to be restricted to India. The debate was continued by Lords Selborne, Rosebery, and Houghton in support of the resolution; and Lords Carnarvon, Middleton, and Faversham in opposition. Upon a division, the resolution was negatived by 137 to 91, and the Royal Titles Bill passed through Committee without amendment.

IN the House of Commons, Mr. Disraeli, in reply to Sir William Harcourt, said the title of Empress would be employed solely with reference to external affairs, and not to those of Great Britain.

A DEPUTATION headed by Mr. Lowe, M.P., had an interview with the Earl of Carnarvan to urge the legalisation in England of marriages with a deceased wife's sister contracted in the colonies, where such unions are lawful. Lord Carnarvon did not express himself very favorably towards the proposal.

A MAN in Northampton county, America, has contracted to ship 76,000 school slates to Japan.

THE wife of a Minnesota man has just obtained a verdict of $9,500 against a druggist of Decorah, Iowa, America, for selling liquor to her husband, under the stupefying influence of which he froze his hands and feet so badly as to require amputation.

THE Bombay Press, says the *Pioneer*, is calling upon the Local Government to visit with its displeasure Mr. Maneckji Cowasji Enti, District Deputy Collector and Magistrate of Surat. Mr. Enti, it appears, failed to sustain certain charges which he brought against his wife; and when, in a counter-suit, he was cast for alimony, he failed in his endevavours to escape payment. In the course of these proceedings, the Judge characterised Mr. Enti's conduct as "a base degrading conspiracy," and in open Court charged him with having committed" perjury," marking his displeasure by making him pay a double set of costs.

THE *Karnatika Prakasika* states that during the visit of Mr. Dalyell to Mysore recently, the Ranis of the palace expressed their several grievances to him personally, and among these the following connected with the young Maharajah's visit to Bangalore and Bombay:—*1st*, the absence of the usual caste mark on His Highness' forehead, both on his visiting the Prince of Wales and on the occasion of his Durbar at Bangalore (which the Ranis presume was intentionally done); *2nd*, the prohibiting of the *Vaidika* Brahmans invited to make the usual presentations at Durbar; *3rd*, the non-observance of the usual festivals in the temples in commemoration of H. H's visit; and *4th*, the want of consideration shown to the performers and others who were waiting at the gate of the Durbar Hall. The Chief Commissioner, it is stated, felt surprised, and made inquiries in the matter.

A GRAND DURBAR will be held by Lord Lytton at Delhi next cold season.

A CASE similar to that of Colonel Valentine Baker is now before the Lahore Magistrates. The accused is a driver on the S. P. and D. Railway, and the victim of the attempted outrage is a Bengali lady, "of no mean size and personal attractions."

THE *Statesman* learns that an address and memorial from the people of Ireland is about to be presented to the Maharajah of Jeypore in acknowledgment of the handsome manner in which the memory of the late Earl Mayo has been perpetuated by the Maharajah in the execution of the spacious hospital, statue, &c.

THE Albert Hall at Jeypore will cost about rupees six lacs. A correspondent of the *Statesman* says that besides the large spacious hall, there will be a billiard-room, reading-room, and a splendid library, an art collection, music room, theatre and bowling alley.

ACCORDING to Reuter's Telegram, in the House of Commons, on Thursday last, Mr. Disraeli refused to delay advising Her Majesty to proclaim the title of Empress. An adjournment of the House was then moved and a stormy debate ensued, in which Mr. Fawcett took the lead, party recriminations being freely indulged in. The Marquis of Hartington declined to assist Mr. Fawcett's motion, in consequence of the uselessness of doing so. Her Majesty the Queen has given her assent to the Royal Titles Bill.

Calcutta.

THE Zoological Gardens will be opened to the public on the 4th May next.

THE Native Cashier to the firm of Messrs. Turner, Morrison and Co. has levanted with Rs. 25,000 belonging to his employers. The Police are on his track.

MR. W. E. H. FORSYTH, Clerk of the Crown, has obtained six months' leave on private affairs. Mr. Macgregor has been appointed to officiate for him.

THE Presidency Banks Act will come into force from to-morrow. The registered holders of Shares and Stock in the present Bank of Bengal will be entitled to be registered as proprietors and holders of a like quantity of stock and a proportionate number of Shares, two Shares of Rs. 500 each being deemed equivalent to one Share of Rs. 1,000 in the present Bank.

THE Revd. B.T. Atlay, M. A., Chaplain of St. Paul's Cathedral, Calcutta, has been appointed to act as Commissary in Calcutta to the Bishop of Madras (at present exercising the jurisdiction and functions of the See of Calcutta) during the absence of His Lordship and the Ven'ble the Archdeacon from Calcutta.

ON the 17th instant, says the *Indian Church Gazette*, a meeting of the General Committee for the promotion of the Lahore Mission Memorial Bishopric, was held at Belvedere, under the presidency of the Lieutenant-Governor. There was a larger attendance. A working Committee was appointed to organise the scheme and establish local Committees in India and at Home for the purpose of promoting its object.

THE P. & O. Co.'s S. S. *Deccan*, Commander J. D. Gaby, arrived in Bombay harbour, on Wednesday last, from Suez with the English Mails of the 7th instant on board. The following is the list of passengers :—

From Southampton.—Mr. P. Rogers, Mr. Egerton, Major H. S. Anderson, Captain Tandy, Mr. J. Peate, Mrs. Summers and child, Mr. Evezard, Miss. Evezard, Lieut. H. R. Cook, Mr. E. W. Bullock, Mr. C. P. Witcombe, Mrs. Blaikie, infant, and child, Dr. J. O'Sullivan, Mr. G. Coxon, Mr. C. Coxon, Mr. Leslie, Mr. McKenzie, Mr. and Mrs. G. L. Elliott, Surgeon W. H. Briggs, Mr. J. Knowles.

From Venice.—Mr. and Mrs. Wynne, Mr. Coghlan, Dr. Cebter, Colonel Beauchamp, Captain Shakespear.

From Brindisi.—Lieut-Colonel Gulliver, Mr. D. M. Stewart, Mr. and Mrs. Keith, Captain F. P. Worthy, Mr. Quinemant.

From Marseilles.—Mr. Alexander Jappe.

From Aden.—Mr. Hirjibhoy Ardaseer.

WE regret to find the announcement of the death of Mr. B. Newman of the firm of Messrs. T. E. Thomson & Co, of this city, late a Justice of the Peace, at Galle.

WE are glad to find that the Bank of Bengal has reduced its rates one per cent all round. But the writer of the Money article in the *Englishman* says:—"Although the Bank of Bengal's rates have been reduced 1 per cent. to-day, it does not necessarily follow that they will continue to run down speedily till they reach an ordinary level. It must be remembered that the new Bank Act comes into force, on Monday, and with it the practical diversion of the great bulk of the Government balances from the assistance of trade. The Bank's rates are still very high, 10 per cent. demand—11½ thirty days, and 12½ sixty days, and to-day's reduction may be more properly attributed to principle than to expediency, the proportion of cash to liabilities having increased from 48¾ to 52¾ per cent."

MR. MANOCKJI RUSTOMJI, the Persian Consul in Calcutta and late a Sheriff of this city, finds himself honored with his portrait in the pages of the last *Charivari*.

THE Bengal Government has agreed to contribute an annual grant of Rs. 13,000 towards the purchase of buildings for an asylum in Calcutta for Natives afflicted with incurable diseases, on condition of the public contributing an equal sum.

THE total number of deaths in Calcutta during the week ending the 22nd instant, was 282. That during the previous week was 248. The largest number of deaths arose from cholera and fevers.

THE number of visitors to the Calcutta Art Gallery during the week ending Saturday 29th April, was 166, viz., 531 Europeans and 113 Natives. The Gallery is for the present open to the public daily (except Sundays) from 6-30 to 9-30 A. M., and from 3 to 6 P. M., but will be closed from and inclusive of the 8th May until further notice for re-arrangement consequent upon the return of some of the loan pictures to their owners.

Law

POLICE—APRIL 29, 1876.

[*Before F. J. Marsden, Esq.*]

MESSRS COOK & Co., through one of their assistants, charged a syce in their employ with the theft of a set of horse-clothing, valued at Rs. 10. The prisoner was also further charged by Mr. Hastings with stealing several pieces of wearing apparel belonging to him. He pleaded guilty to the former charge, and was sentenced to six weeks' rigorous imprisonment; but denied the latter, saying that he had bought the articles of wearing apparel from time to time from *bickri-wallahs*, but called no witness to support this allegation. He was found guilty, and, for this offence was sentenced to six months' rigorous imprisonment and a whipping of fifteen stripes.

MR. WILLIAM MORGAN HARRISON, second Engineer on board the S. S. *Busheer*, but at present officiating Chief, charged two Madrasis with having, on the 15th instant, in Chandney Choke Lane, assaulted him and wounded him, over his right eye. The defendants denied the charge, Mr. Cranenburgh appeared for the prosecution, and elicited of the witnesses that while the complainant was returning home from China Bazar, he was attacked in the dark by the defendants who were perfect strangers to him, and struck and relieved out of a pocket-handkerchief containing 4 Rs., and his hat. They were, however, not arrested there and then, but some short time after in the house of their countrymen. His Worship entertained some doubts as to their identity and gave them the benefit of it by discharging them.

Selection.

INTRODUCTION TO THE LANGHAM MAGAZINE.

THE Langham Magazine, in asking for a place in current literature, is happy in coming forward on claims of its own, and not in any sense as a would-be rival of existing monthly publications.

Its main purpose is one that has not yet been ostensibly adopted, although in various ways the ground which it hopes to occupy has been prepared and cultured by the Magazines which are already established.

The primary object of the Langham Magazine is to carry far and wide those blessed convictions—we should like to call them "truths," only that a becoming modesty forbids us to adopt a dogmatic phraseology—which are now tolerably well known under the name of "Theism;" convictions which are "blessed" in being in harmony with the Reason, the Conscience, and the Affections, and in affording to the human spirit the highest and surest consolations yet known by the sacred names of Faith and Hope.

These convictions have long been held and secretly cherished by religious souls in every Church, Sect and Denomination. But hitherto they have not been brought out in simple and systematic form for the benefit of the general public. Books there are of priceless value in which these convictions are enshrined, and our Magazine will tell its readers where these books may be found; but no effort has yet been made to bring these happy thoughts of God and man into the homes of England.

Moreover, this effort towards enlightenment is rendered necessary by two grave considerations: the one is that with the decline of belief in traditional orthodoxy, is rapidly passing away also all faith in God, all hope for man. The minds of many—especially of the young—are so stunned by the discovery that most of their early beliefs are no longer tenable that they have no spiritual energy left, no power to raise their hearts in trust and aspiration; religion itself seems to be a mockery and a delusion, and in casting it aside with undisguised scorn or with a more perilous determination to regard it with a total indifference, the young sceptics leave behind them all that gives light and strength to life, and enter the dark region of practical Materialism, where they are "without hope and without God in the world."

It is to serve such that we would write and plead. It is to rescue the priceless and imperishable elements of Religion from the wreck and ruin of traditionary beliefs. It is to build up a "most holy faith" on the *debris* of fallen superstitions. This is our one great hope—to give religion to those who have none; to show the sweet reasonableness of a pure and lively faith; to prove that not one charm of the past religion need be lost, but that all its moral powers are renewed with tenfold vigour, its devoutness exalted into a sublime passion, its consolations multiplied and rekindled with heavenly fire.

The other consideration to which allusion has been made as rendering the work necessary, is that all forms and degrees of unorthodoxy are by many erroneously supposed to be alike associated with impiety, immorality, gross materialism, pantheism—in short, are no better than atheism—and further, that unorthodoxy goes hand in hand with low political notions and schemes; that it is by nature seditious, anarchical, and generally lawless; that it is the threatening foe of monarchies and constitutions, the hinderer of law and order, the avowed advocate of innovation on time-honored morality, the secret destroyer of domestic peace, and the violator of the solemn sanctities of wedded life.

This huge misunderstanding prevails widely among our upper and middle classes; and some so-called Freethinkers have to thank themselves for much of the odious imputation. We have, however, to undo the mischief with what speed and ability we can summon. We have to rescue Theism from the not altogether unjust stigma put upon it by the "sorry rabble" which follow the army of seekers after truth. We look forward with some confidence to the recognition of the true place which Theism occupies, and of its entire independence of the lawlessness and vulgarity once attributed to its followers. Our magazine will have none for contributors but men and women of fine feeling and good taste, whose object will be to help on everything that is pure, honest, lovely, and of good report; and without condescending to the arena of party politics, will uphold the order and constitution of this realm, will honor the Queen and all in authority under her, and in these interests will encourage whatever changes in legislation or custom may seem desirable for the common wealth. As a mere act of justice to those in all ranks from the very highest to the lowest who are Theists at hearts, our magazine is, we might almost say, demanded of us, especially in this critical period of transition from old forms of thought to new. Bearing in mind these objects, we shall endeavour to set forth our convictions with the utmost clearness using great plainess of speech; writing indeed, so that children may learn the alphabet of of faith and hope; it will be our constant desire also to avoid giving needless offence or wounding susceptibilities by fierce controversy. Not that for one moment we shall tamper with what we believe to be truth, or adopt Shibboleths to win favor, or use ambiguous terms to disguise our honest thought. The solemnity of this responsibility we pray may be ever before us, guarding us from the guilt of unfaithfulness, and giving the fervor of absolute sincerity to our words.

We have chosen this form of pursuing the work we have at heart because, as religion is not the *whole* of human interest and duty, but rather the animating spirit which should pervade the whole nature and life, it is needful and wholesome to attend to the culture of all our other faculties likewise. Even amusement is thus to be recognised and sanctified by its association with religious thought.

Our magazine will therefore provide—to the very best of our resources—for human culture on all sides. *Nihil humani a me alienum puto* will be our motto, and thus the religion we love, and would fain teach to those who know it not, will not be forced down the throats of unwilling guests. If our words on this stupendous theme have no charm for them, they can regale themselves on the other and varied articles which each number will contain.

Although a notice respecting individual responsibility is printed conspicuously on our title-page, we would lay additional emphasis on the entire independence of each contributor. No one writer is to be held to endorse anything said by any of the rest. We have adopted this rule not merely as a necessary security for each contributor, but to give to each one in turn additional liberty to express his own convictions. Of course a certain measure of sympathy is already expressed by the act of co-operation, but it must not be misunderstood to imply more than the common aim and hope of *doing good*.

In collecting a staff of contributors (the list of whom is not nearly close), it was very gratifying to receive expressions of hearty sympathy from some of our most eminent men in Church and State. In several instances, ill-health or overwork has alone deprived us of very distinguished allies. We commend our work to the public in general, and to the critics in particular, because it is not a rival speculation, nor started with mercenary motives, not the offspring of factious opposition, still less of malice.

If our aims be not enough to disarm opposition, to banish bigotry and to silence prejudice, then we have not read our countrymen and country-women aright; we shall have given them credit for more earnestness and generosity than they deserve, and shall have earned the ridicule attaching to those who are indiscriminate in the scattering of their jewels. But we hope better things. The bias of the mind in the long run is always towards what is right and true; and although opposition may be encountered at the onset, it will only serve as a wholesome stimulus to renewed exertion.

All we ask for is a patient hearing and a candid judgment; assuring our readers that no money or labor shall be spared in their gratification if only we meet with that encouragement which the objects of the Langham Magazine deserve.

CHARLES VOYSEY

REGISTERED No. P

THACKER, SPINK AND CO.

BOOKSELLERS AND PUBLISHERS.

BY SPECIAL APPOINTMENT.

To H. E. The Viceroy and Governor-General.

ORIENTAL WORKS.

DIALOGUES ON THE HINDU PHILOSOPHY, comprising The Nyaya, The Sankhya, The Vedant; to which is added a discussion of the Authority of the Vedas. By Rev. K. M. Banerjea, 8vo, cloth. Rs. 8.

DIALOGUES ON THE HINDU PHILOSOPHY, freely rendered into Bengali with [illegible] By Rev. K. M. Banerjea, 8vo, cloth. Rs. [illegible]

[illegible] OF ENGLISH AND HINDUSTANI [illegible] used in [illegible] and other [illegible], and Scientific Manual of Words and Phrases in the Higher branches of Knowledge containing upwards of five thousand words not generally to be found in the English and Urdu Dictionaries. (New and cheaper edition). By Major H. G. Raverty, 8 vo. limp cloth Rs. 2-8.

IKHWANUS Safa; or Brothers of Purity, Translated from the Hindustani: By professor John Dowson, M. R. A. S. 8vo., cloth. Rs. 5.

INTRODUCTION to The Bengali Language: By the late Rev. W. Yates, D.D., Edited By J. Wenger. Elementary part. Containing a Grammar, a Reader, and explanatory Notes, with an Index and Vocabulary, large 8vo., cloth, Rs. 5.

INTRODUCTION to The Hindustani Language. Eighth Edition, Improved. By the late Rev. W. Yates, D. D., large 8vo., cloth, Rs. 6.

A MANUAL of ENGLISH and HINDUSTANI Terms, Phrases, &c., in the Roman character. By the Rev. Mohun Sudun Seal, 12mo., cloth, Rs. 1-12.

A SHORT INTRODUCTION to the ORDINARY Prakrit of the Sanskrit Dramas, with a list of Common Irregular prakrit words. By E. B. Cowell, professor of Sanskrit in the University of Cambridge, and hon. LL.D. of the University of Edinburgh, 8vo., cloth, limp, Rs. 2-8.

A GRAMMAR of the URDU or HINDUSTANI Language. By John Dowson, M.R.A.S. 8vo. cloth, Rs. 7-8.

The NEW TESTAMENT of our LORD and Saviour Jesus Christ; translated into the Burmese from the Original Greek, 8vo. leather, Rs. 1-8.

The PRINCIPLES of MURATHEE GRAMMAR. By the Rev. J. Stevenson, D.D. Third Edition, Rs. 6.

SYNOPSIS of the GRAMMAR of MODERN Arabic, with a Vocabulary, and Dialogues. By F.E.G. Hayes, 8vo., paper cover, Rs.2.

MODERN PERSIAN PHRASES. By an Officer of the Hyderabad Contingent. Revised; By Aka Meerza Zeinul Abideen Sheerazee. Large, 8vo. cloth, Rs. 4.

The POCKET HINDUSTANEE VOCABULARY. By an Officer of the Bengal Staff Corps, cloth, limp Rs.2.

A HAND-BOOK of SANSKRIT LITERature: with appendices descriptive of the Mythology, Castes, and religious sects of the Hindus. Intended specially for candidates for the India Civil Service, and Missionaries to India. By George Small, M.A., 8vo., colth, Rs 4-10.

A BENGALI GRAMMAR, by the late Rev. W. Yates. D.D., reprinted, with improvements, from his introduction to the Bengali Language. Edited by J. Wenger, small 8vo., cloth, Rs 1-5.

The STUDENT'S GRAMMAR of the HINDI LANGUAGE, by Rev. W. Etherington, 8vo., cloth, Rs 4.

A GRAMMAR and VOCABULARY of the Pooshtoo Language. By Captain John L. Vaughan. Large 8vo., paper cover, Rs. 4.

KHIRAD-AFROZ (The Illuminator of the Understanding). By Maulavi Hafizuddin. A New Edition of the Hindustani Text, carefully revised, with notes, critical and explanatory: By Edward B. Eastwick, F.R.S., F.S.A., M.R.A.S. Imperial 8vo., cloth, Rs. 19-12.

India General Steam Navigation Company, Limited.

SCHOENE, KILBURN & Co.—*Managing Agents.*

ASSAM LINE.

NOTICE.

Steamers now leave Calcutta for Assam every Tuesday, Goalundo every Thursday and Dibrooghur downward every Saturday.

THE Str "RAJMEHAL" will leave Calcutta for Assam, on Tuesday, the 2nd May.

Cargo will be received at the Company's Godowns, Nimtollah Ghat, until noon of Monday, the 1st proximo.

THE Str. "LAHORE" will leave Goalundo for Assam on Thursday the 4th May.

Cargo will be received at the Company's Godowns, No. 4. Fairlie Palace, up till noon of Tuesday, the 2nd proximo.

Goods forwarded to Goalundo for this vessel will be chargeable with Railway Freight from Calcutta to Goalundo in addition to the regular Freights of this Company.

Passengers should leave for Goalundo by Train of Wednesday, the 3rd proximo.

CACHAR LINE NOTICE
REGULAR WEEKLY SERVICE.

Steamers now leave Calcutta for Cachar and Intermediate Stations every Tuesday and Chattack downward every Tuesday.

A Steamer and "FLAT" will leave Calcutta for Cachar on Tuesday, the 2nd May.

Cargo will be received at the Company's Godowns, Nimtollah Ghat, up till noon of Monday, the 1st proximo.

For further information regarding rates of Freight or passage money, apply to,

4 Fairlie Palace, G. J. SCOTT,
Calcutta, 26th April 1876. *Secretary.*

BABU BASANTA KUMAR DUTT,
HOMŒOPATHIC PRACTITIONER
No. 20, Sastee Holder's Lane, Aheritolah.

A FRESH INDENT OF

HOMŒOPATHIC

Medicines and other Requisites
Have arrived from England.
Medicines, Books, Pamphlets;
Absolute Alcohol; [illegible] Camphor,
SPECIAL MEDICINES

For Suppressed, Laborious and difficult menses; Leucorrhœa.

For Hysteria; Spermatorrhœa; Dysentery; Diarrhœa; Cholera.

For Asthma; Pile; Pain; Sore and Diseases of the Children.

Ice, Lemonade, Soda and Tonic water always.

To be had at
DATTA'S HOMŒOPATHIC LABORATORY,
No. 312, CHITPORE ROAD, BUTTOLA, CALCUTTA
TERMS CASH.

Price List can be had on application.

BABU RADHAKANTA GHOSH
HOMŒOPATHIC PRACTITIONER,
12, College Square,
Is practising here on moderate terms.

SMITH, STANISTREET & CO.

Pharmaceutical Chemists & Druggists
BY APPOINTMENT
To His Excellency the Right Hon'ble
LORD LYTTON, G.M.S.I.
Governor-General of India,
&c., &c.

SYRUP OF LACTATE OF IRON

Prepared from the original recipe. Lactate of Iron, in various forms of preparation, have been in use in France, and generally through the continent of Europe, for some years past, and is highly esteemed as one of the most valuable Chalybeate Tonic Remedies yet introduced. The Syrup, being the most agreeable as well as convenient form of administration is a most [illegible]. It is a most valuable remedy in the following diseases:—Chlorosis or Green Sickness, Leucorrhœa, Neuralgia, Enlargement of the Spleen, &c. In combination with quinine it has also been very successfully used in the cure of Fever, while to persons of delicate constitution, enfeebled by disease it is invaluable. In bottles. Rs. 2 each.

SYRUP OF THE PHOSPHATE OF IRON Rs. 2 per bottle.

SYRUP OF PHOSPHATE OF IRON AND STRYCHNINE, Rs. 2 per bottle.

SYRUP OF PHOSPHATE OF IRON AND QUININE. Price Rs. 2-8 per bottle.

SYRUP OF PHOSPHATE OF IRON, QUININE AND STRYCHNINE (DR. ATKINS TRIPLE TONIC SYRUP,) Rs. 2-8 per bottle.

Smith, Stanistreet & Co.

Invite special attention to the following rates, the quality guaranteed as the best procurable:—

Pure Ærated Waters.

Made from Pure Water, obtained by the new process through the Patent Charcoal Filters.

				Rs.	As.
Ærated plain (Trible Ærated), per doz.				[illegible]	[illegible]
Soda Water	ditto	„	...	0	[illegible]
Gingerade	ditto	„	...	1	4
Lemonade	ditto	„	...	1	4
Tonic (Quinine)	ditto	„	...	1	4

The *Cash* must be sent with the order to obtain advantage of the above rates.

!!! হুকা !!!
!!! HOOKAHS !!!

ENGLISH made Hookahs of various choice designs, colours and sizes ranging in price from Rs. 2 to 5 each. 60 designs to choose from. Apply to

RADANAUTH CHOWDRY,
373, Jorasanko.

[illegible]।

NEW HISTORICAL TRAGEDY
BY
GOPAL CHUNDER MOOKERJEE,

Price, Re. 1, postage 2 ans.
To be had at 50, Grey Street, Shobhabazar, and Sanskrit Press Depository.

NATIONAL COMPANY
HOMŒOPATHIC CHAMISTS AND PUBLISHER
SUPPLY ALL KINDS OF
HOMŒOPATHIC MEDICINES, BOOKS
CASES AND OTHER REQUISITES.
12 COLLEGE SQUARE,
Calcutta.

Printed and published by M. M. BYSACK, at the "INDIAN MIRROR" PRESS, No. 15 [illegible], for the Proprietor.

The Indian Mirror.

SUNDAY EDITION.

VOL. XV.] CALCUTTA, SUNDAY, MAY, 7, 1876 { REGISTERED AT THE GENERAL POST OFFICE. } [No. 108

CONTENTS.

NOTICE.

Letters and all other communications relating to the literary department of the Paper should be addressed to "The Editor."

All letters on the business of the Press should be addressed, and all remittance made payable to the Manager of this Paper. Particular attention is solicited to this notice.

Subscribers will be good enough to give prompt notice of any delay, or irregularity in delivery of the Paper.

Editorial Notes

WE bitterly rue the day when the popular literature of the land connected nothing but unmitigated sensuality with the sacred subject of feminine beauty. The early associations fostered in the mind, imbibed unconsciously with the moral air we breathe in society, cling to the heart, and are seldom got rid of except by the most persistent devotions, and religious exercises. We are afraid very few Hindus are worthy to look upon the features of a femine countenance with the holiness of feelings that the subject ought to inspire in a religious heart. Perhaps very few men even among other nations have such feelings. Men of sensitive piety still keep away from women, and all things considered perhaps it is good they should. But the highest purity is not here certainly.

THE appointment of an Inspectress of female schools by Sir Richard Temple, must have given general satisfaction to all friends of female progress in Bengal. Often and often we recommended this measure to the Local Government, but no notice was taken of it. Neither Sir William Grey nor ever Sir George Campbell could be induced to take what evidently appeared to them to be a bold step. It was reserved for our present Lieutenant-Governor to introduce this reform, and we heartily thank him for it. A sound system of Zenana and public education under efficient Government supervision, will produce the best results which could be expected in the present state of Native society. If the Inspectress could act with the help and advice of a good Native Committe, many of the difficulties which now beset the work of female education will be removed.

ACCORDING to some wise critics the destiny of the Brahmo Somaj hangs on the arithmetic of the census returns. Our fate is entirely in the hands of Mr. Beverley. So we must anxiously look forward, and tremble in fear! We find ourselves, however, in an altogether different mood,—indifference if not complacency. We are not very much interested in the question of our numbers. And we shall say why. Supposing we had more than a thousand professing Brahmos in Calcutta, would that make us rejoice? They might not all be genuine believers. In the hour of trial half the number might recede. It is the number of faithful soldiers we are anxious to ascertain, and we are painfully conscious that their number is extremely small. Half a dozen men of the type of the fishermen of Galilee or the devotees of Navadwipa we want. Could Mr. Beverley show us that in the returns we would rejoice.

THE question is raised whether the life of Dr. Norman Macleod was not wasted, and his splendid talents frittered away. It is said by some that in choosing to be a Minister, he quite mistook his vocation, and that if he had pursued any other calling, say that of literature, his success and reputation would have been much greater. He never had any power of doing anything like justice to himself. Norman Macleod hated church politics, and kept as much as possible in the background when church affairs were discussed; but in other respects he was an ornament to the church. The breadth and profoundness of his views did a great deal to change many popular ideas on the subject of Christianity. The eloquence of his utterances in the pulpit is deservedly admired by all. His missionary activity also made him famous, and he travelled even to India where, during his short sojourn, everyone who had occasion to know him was delighted. It is said hundreds of working men gathered around him week after week, and when the funeral procession that carried his remains to their last resting place, had been moving on, one of those poor people exclaimed—"There goes Norman Macleod, if he had done no more than what he did for my soul, he would shine as the stars forever." Even his literary career, taken by itself, would confer honor and reputation on any other life, apart from the other things he did. Such a life cannot be justly characterized as a failure. It may, perhaps, be urged that Norman Macleod was too genial, too wide-minded, too highly cultured for a Scottish minister, and did not find the opportunities which any other profession would have placed before him, but there is the more reason in this that he should have chosen the church which gained so much by his connection.

IN Hinduism every teacher claims identity with God. "I and my Father are one" is altogether an Eastern idea, and one is astonished to find how largely it prevails among Hindu sages and preachers, and how even those among them who belonged to the ordinary class of instructors, and had not the remotest pretensions to the character of prophets, glibly and unceremoniously spoke of themselves as the very God when addressing their disciples. Hardly less remarkable is the fact that this identity they claimed only so long and so far as they actually taught others the principles of religion, and did not extend over their whole lives and character. They professed to represent the deity in the teacher, not in the man. They were not God incarnate, but only when they taught they professed to speak and teach in His name and authority. Their language often wore the character of intolerable audacity, blasphemy and arrogance, and many a reverent believer would certainly turn away from such language with disgust. A closer analysis would however, show that this apparent assumption of Divinity was only a deep matter of faith, and not conceit or self-sufficiency. There is evidently error in this pantheistic identification. But there is also a deep truth involved in it. Whatsoever truth comes from the *guru*, comes actually from God, he being only a medium of communication. "The words I speak are not mine, but the

Father's." The true teacher must forget, deny and ignore himself and never teach his own opinions or ideas, but communicate only divine wisdom and be, in all teachings, but the mouth-piece of God. So far, and so far only, the human teacher must humbly discard himself, and claim oneness with the Divine teacher.

WHAT does the charge of drifting back towards Hinduism mean? The charge has been brought against us, our leaders and missionaries, and all our advanced men; and it is desirable that we should both indignantly rebut it and soberly reply to it. When the Lord brought us away from the errors of Hinduism, from idolatry and caste, we gave them up as lies and parted with them for ever. To revert to them now, or even to show any tendencies in that direction, would argue fatal moral imbecility in us, and would clearly prove we were going back from light to darkness after twenty years' steady progress. We hate the idea of retrogression. To recede is to die. There is not a single man among the Progressive Brahmos who could at this time of the day think of tolerating idolatry, defending caste, discouraging intermarriages, or justifying the superstitious rites of Hindu domestic life; and if he did he would be branded and disowned as a renegade. But we must say that while we continue to detest even all leanings towards idolatry and caste with unabated repugnance, we are entering more deeply into the higher life of Hinduism; and our attachment becomes greater as we discover in the hidden mines of Hindu spirituality fresh inspiration, light and joy. Asceticism, *yoga*, *bratha*, daily scriptural readings, *Kirtan*, cooking one's own food, —these essentially Hindu ideas we are cultivating among ourselves with some degree of zeal now-a-days. But in doing so, one can easily see the Brahmos seek no convenience and compromise, but rather privations and self-denial. Nor do we see here any unworthy attempt to conciliate and win over the Hindus by putting on an appearance of Hindu sanctity. For it is known to many that the very men who have adopted these national modes of *sadhan* or discipline, are most uncompromising in their renunciation of caste and other evils of Hinduism, and do many things in public and private life which to an orthodox Hindu would appear to be nothing short of *mlechaism*.

MORE than a dozen Brahmica ladies visited the Art Gallery yesterday. Special arrangements were made with the Superintendent for the visit, and the gallery was placed at the pisposal of the ladies at the time when it is closed to the rest of the public. A pretty careful inspection was made over the rooms, and the ladies who, we believe, never saw a similar collection of good pictures before, enjoyed much of what their attention was directed to. The middle room of the upper floor was ofcourse most interesting. The Madonna No. 1 by Sassoferrato, presented by Lord Northbrook, was universally admired, and the attitude of devotion, was considered most sweet and natural. Next to that was esteemed the Holy Virgin by Carlo Dolci, the property of Kumar Grish Chunder Singh. In our opinion the latter picture is decidedly superior to the former. The inimitable grace of form and features, the pure simplicity of loveliness in the countenance, the subdued holiness, and humility of expression, all toned down by the conscious sweetness of piety which beams through the whole of this beautiful piece of painting, are rendered most faithfully by the softness and harmony of coloring, the delicacy of back ground, and the noble simplicity of drapery which invests the figure. The martyrdom of Saint Sebastian is not a subject for ladies to appreciate much. But the glorious lights and shades which characterize the genius of Murillo, the boldness, dignity and firmness of outline, could not but draw and rivet attention, and excite admiration for the manliness and faith of the great saint's sufferings. The *Kittens* in the landing room, and the Sunset on the Hughly are really fine. In the downstair rooms Sir Richard Temple's water colors called forth much remark, and one enthusiastic young lady pronounced His Honor's Valley of the Sutlege to be the finest piece in the room. Every one expressed surprise that a Lieutenant-Governor, and a somewhat hairy and prosaic one too, could draw such fine pictures. For aught we know, the ladies may have been moved to all this admiration by the interest which Sir Richard Temple takes in female education, but much of it must have been real, and His Honor will, we hope, appreciate the compliment.

THE LIFE OF DEVARSHI NARADA.

THE history of Narada's religious life as told by himself, in the Hindu scriptures, is a most interesting and instructive study. It furnishes valuable materials for reflection and aids to devotion, while it illustrates, in a remarkable manner, some of those high spiritual truths which we have often discussed in these columns as the essential principles of Theism. One is struck with wonder to find how centuries ago, and in the midst of idolatory and superstition, such happy thoughts, such heavenly truths rose, by simple natural processes, in the heart of a Hindu devotee. It is such instances of parallelism of thought and life that prove, beyond doubt, the universality of divine Theism. Creeds differ and nations disagree; but in the highest creed of love and devotion all nations and all sects agree. Let us now listen Narada's account of his own spiritual struggles and growth. In early life, says he, he used to serve the many Yogis and Rishis who came on pilgrimage to the place where he resided. They took pity on him, and were pleased with his services. In their company and service, and by hearing from their lips sacred words and music, the boy Narada grew up in the knowledge and love of God. On their recommendation he subsequently commenced to travel about. After traversing many cities and towns, and deserts he at last found himself in a dense jungle, wearied and exhausted by his long journeys. With the waters of an adjacent rivulet he quenched his thirst, and then after resting awhile under the shade of a large banian tree, he gave himself up to quiet meditation. Soon he was immersed in the ocean of love, tears rolled down from his eyes, and the Lord several times came and appeared in his heart. He was overwhelmed with the joy, and amid raptures unutterable he lost both himself and his God. Excited he rose up, and then composing his heart, he sat down and again began to meditate in the hope of again seeing the Lord. But he saw Him not, though he tried repeatedly, and his heart was sorely troubled. And then in solemn whispers the Lord said unto him,—"child, in this life thou shalt not see me again, for those who are not Yogis and are held in bondage by the senses, cannot see me. The reason why I have revealed myself once in thy heart is but to excite thy interest and love so that all thy worldly desires may thereby be extinguished. Go and serve good men, O Narada, and learn to fasten thy love on me. At last this carnal body of thine shall fall off, and thou shalt be mine. Wait patiently for that blessed time." At last that happy hour came in Narada's life, and his regenerated soul put on "holy divine body." Then Narada entered upon his sacred mission of going about singing the Lord's name, and whenever he sang, his beloved God came to him promptly as one invited. The story ends here. The devout reader must find in it much to gladden him, and confirm his own faith and experiences. The Lord may mercifully reveal Himself to a believer, but his own subsequent efforts are as necessary as Divine grace for his regeneration. The first revelation of the Lord's beautiful countenance is followed by darkness, in order that the dovout may feel the absence, and prayerfully realize Him again. The final result of all endeavours after holy life is an utter destruction of the carnal body. There is deep meaning in this. Salvation is to be achieved in the present life, and heaven should be sought and realized here. But this cannot be done so long as the senses are dominant and the carnal passions are strong. The whole body must be renewed spiritually, and out of its ashes must rise the *bhagavati tanu* or divine body, formed in God's spirit and in His image. This is regeneration.

OUR FAITH AND OUR EXPERIENCES.

(Continued.)

THERE are only three essential doctrines in Theism, the doctrine of God, the doctrine of immortality and the doctrine of conscience. These three constitute the Theist's creed. And yet they are not three doctrines, but one doctrine. They are the constituent elements of one idea, and must be accepted or rejected together. Whoever believes in the Infinite and Living Spirit-God must perforce accept, as a necessary part of that doctrine, the immortality and accountability of the human soul. The genesis of the doctrine of the great hereafter is deeply interesting. Theological students are in the habit of dissociating this doctrine from that of the God-head. There are some who altogether deny the next world while believing thoroughly in the existence of a Creator. This seems to me quite as illogical and absurd as to take one half and to disown the other half of the same truth. I question the wisdom of searching for separate proofs of the existence of the future world. What better proof can there be of our immortality than the fact of God's existence? He who believes in the Living God, has already tacitly believed in the next world. In fact the two doctrines are inseparably linked together in the depths of our being. The idea of immortality lies potentially in the idea of the God-head, and requires only to be evolved out of it. The Infinite Father above and the eternal home before, meet in one focus in the eye of the believing soul, and may be said to be apprehended together in man's natural consciousness. In natural religion, in Pure Theism, there can be no divinity without a future world, no immortality without a divinity. The intuitive eye raised above beholds God; directed forward it sees its future home in the next world. A father without a home, a home without a father, that is an anomaly against which nature rebels. A more philosophical analysis gives us as the last fact a deep sense of dependence, in which both these doctrines have their root. The soul naturally, and in the earliest dawn of religious consciousness feels that it depends, for life and for everything else, upon the living God. "In Him we live and move and have our being" is the primitive creed of the infant soul. And in this you see already the root idea of immortality. The soul feels that its life is in God, and will continue to be in God. I live in the Infinite Vital Power,—here you have the doctrine of God. I shall continue to live in that Power,—here you have the doctrine of immortality. If we have no life apart from God, we cannot but regard Him and our future existence as one integral fact. How can you separate the one from the other? Nay, by rejecting the doctrine of immortality, you virtually surrender all the important attributes of Divinity, and thus reject the true God. If we have no here*after* to supplement and complete our life *here*, God's wisdom, power, mercy and justice would all be gravely impugned, and we would in fact have an imperfect and finite deity to adore and honor. Believe that the dissolution of the body is the last chapter in the history of mans' life, and you banish the Great God from your theology. Thus both by positive and negative evidence all true believers are shut up to the alternatives of accepting at one and the same time, and as parts of one indivisible truth the doctrines of divinity and immortality. As the Lord enters the heart of the devout believer, He brings with him the future heaven, the house of "many mansions," where the moral world is completed, and where blessedness and glory everlasting awaits His children. If then you acknowledge him, you must believe in that heaven, and strive to live righteously here, that you may worthily enter your place hereafter. Yes, you must live well and righteously. The doctrine of duty is inseparably connected with the two doctrines already mentioned, and these three form one integral truth. In the believer's consciousness God, Immortality and Duty form an indivisible unity of faith. The idea of moral economy may be said to be made up of these three primary ideas. The moral law, the moral Governor and a life of moral discipline and recompense are all realized, three in one, trinity in unity, in human conscience, and none of these can be eliminated. How can he who solemnly realizes God and Eternity, trifle with the sacred obligations of duty. Daily and hourly must he feel his stupendous responsibilities to the great moral Governor. Purity and faith go together. Prayers without righteousness are a solemn mockery; devotion without morality is only a hypocritical trade Woe to the man who professing to be godly and devout, transgresses the dictates of conscience in practical life, and under carnal impulses violates the laws of truth, justice and charity. There can be no true belief in God unless it is accompanied by the assiduous and rigid performance of the varied duties of life. Theism recognises no faith, how devout and prayerful it may be, which is not connected with righteous life. Gentlemen, you see how simple is the Theists' creed. Worship the Spirit-God, believe in eternity and live righteously,—this is all that the theology of our Church teaches. Do you require a longer creed? Would you have a more elaborate theology? Do you seek salvation in multiplied articles of faith? Do you believe that you must go through endless folios of academic Divinity and traverse the vast field of historical theology before you reach heaven? Assuredly they who seek scholarship must read a great many books, and accumulate a great many doctrines and tenets. But he who seeks salvation will find all he needs in this simple creed. Saving faith lies in a nutshell.

Telegraphic Intelligence

Reuter's Telegrams.

LONDON, MAY 5.

The race for the One Thousand Guineas was won by Camelia, Allumetee being second, and Seine third.

LONDON, MAY 5, (MIDNIGHT.)

Mr. Cochrane this evening asked for the production of the papers relating to Khokand. Mr. Disraeli said that none existed. England's policy was frankness and firmness. The *entente* with Russia was never better. Russia has not regarded Her Majerty's new title of Empress as a menace; and Russia has equal right to conquer in Central Asia as England had in India.

ROME, MAY 5.

The Rubattino Company's Steamer *Asia*, with His Excellency Sir Salar Jang and suite, arrived here to-day. Sir Salar had an audience of the King and the British Ambassador, Sir Augustus Paget.

The Interpreter

IT cannot be that Christ had no love for his mother. He whose heart was full of philanthropic love for all mankind and was aglow with divine love, could not be hard or indifferent to a mother. And yet the following passage in Math. XII, 47-50, seems perplexing, and requires explanation:—

> Then one said unto him, Behold thy mother and thy brethren stand without, desiring to speak with thee.
>
> But he answered and said unto him that told him who is my mother, and who are my brethren?
>
> And he stretched forth his hand toward his disciples and said, Behold my mother and my brethren!
>
> For whosoever shall do the will of my Father which is in heaven, the same is my brother, and sister, and mother.

This is evidently one of those passages in the gospels which prove that Christ was a thorough ascetic. It was his asceticism alone that led him to speak in the above strain of his mother and brethren. His human heart no doubt always lovingly recognised these earthly relationships, but his superior ascetic heart, his divine love was drawn to heavenly relationships alone. He had no mother, no brother except those who did the will of his Father. There was his home, there his kinsmen. Asceticism merges the world with all its domestic and social relationships and interests in the absorving and vast realities of the spirit-world.

CHRIST said unto all "that labor and are heavy laden,"—"Come unto me, and I will give you rest." And in the very next sentence we find these words, —"Take my yoke upon you." There is no rest in Christ except by obeying him. Thorough obedience in all matters of religious and moral life is the only road to peace and eternal blessedness. There are many who purchase imaginary rest by simply reposing sentimental faith in Christ. They ought to remember that there is no real peace unless they cease to sin and fully obey Christ's commandments.

Correspondence.

THE LATE BISHOP MILMAN

To the Editor of the *Indian Mirror*.

SIR,—What is *Heaven*?—Heaven is rest, and it is not rest. Heaven is the rest of a bird on the wing; every muscle instinct with power, as it floats across the sky from zone to zone, unconscious of fatigue. If that be rest,—that intense and joyous life,—then Heaven is rest. Heaven is not the rest of a bird with its head under its wing; surrendering consciousness that it may, by rest, renew vitality. Heaven is vitality; renewed and at work. Heaven comes to us, saying "I am come that you may have life, and have it more abundantly." We read that, at Rawul Pindi, Bishop Milman "entered into his rest." Quere; into *Nirvana*? into the state in which an infant lies in its nurse's arms, either wholly unconscious, or smiling in its sleep? No: surely not. It is truer to say, especially of such an one as he, that, at Rawul Pindi, the Bishop *entered into life*. It was his life to be a worker. It almost seems as if his delight in work, his chief joy, took him from us before his time. Let who will, I cannot suppose him to be now at rest from that which he loved most, and enjoyed most; and to which he utterly abandoned himself in his holiest hours and most heavenly moods. Could Brahmins accept the indefatigable Bishop as a true Brahmin, we could pardon their saying, according to the simplest meaning of the words, that he had "entered into rest." So far Brahminism: so far Buddhism. But we look to the teachings of Christ for whatever is true in Hinduism, and for a yet higher, broader, truer word of God. "No more work for me, thank God!" Who can imagine Bishop Milman as entering the spirit-land with such an exclamation? We could sooner imagine his choosing for himself, among the many mansions or retreats of the house of Our Father, if not for his promenade,—at least for his office, a hall of co-operation, on whose door would be written "Positively no admission to idlers: no admission, here and now, except on business."

Yours &c.,

DALL.

Brahmo Hymns

WHAT more shall I say in praying to thee? All my words have been exhausted, and yet my heart is not changed. Thou seest everything within, who can deceive thee with words? Life of my life, what more shall I say, what else have I got to say? O my God, if my heart seeks thee, canst thou remain at a distance? Thou comest of thine own accord into the doors of the sinner. Therefore thy name is the Saviour of the fallen.

MY heart cries for thee. Wilt thou comfort my mournful life? Thou, Lord, art the ocean of love, the True God and Beautiful; cool the afflicted by pouring the sweets of peace. What shall I say of the secrets of my soul? Thou knowest my inward sorrow. Who else looks compassionately on the face of the poor?

WHY do I see all sides so sweet to-day? In the azure sky above I behold wonderous beauty, and within the heart myriad moons shine. The moon to-night showers sweet light; how much sweetness do the winds gently convey! By the auspicious advent of the Lord in the garden of the heart all the flowers of love have bloomed.

The Brahmo Somaj

WHY should there not be a theological class for young Brahmos? There are many in Calcutta and in our immediate neighbourhood, who could very well afford to spend an hour or two on Sunday for religious study and conversation. The seeds of unbelief, moral as well as theoretical, which are being sown broadcast at the present time, may fall into the minds of our young men, and take root there. If not removed early, the consequences may turn serious before long. To obviate this evil it has been proposed from this day to open a class for Brahmo young men. In the absence of a more suitable place the class will for the present sit in the school room of the premises No. 13 Mirzapore Street. It is hoped a fair number will be present.

Literary.

"THE Devil's Chain," the latest work of Mr. Edward Jenkins, M.P., author of "Ginx's Baby" and other prominent books, has had a very large circulation. The first edition of 5,000 was quickly disposed of; a second edition was sold on the day of publication; and a third edition, bringing the number up to 10,000 is about to be issued. Considering that the price of "The Devil's Chain" is five shillings, this is a very large circulation, and one that indicates a more than usually great interest in the important subject with which it deals—*i. e.*, the liquor traffic.

A HINDI "Sakuntala" will shortly be published by Mr. Frederic Pincott, and will, no doubt, be a valuable and welcome production for all who study this language.

THE *Athenæum* says M. A. de Biberstein Kazimirski has devoted a *brochure* of eighty-four pages—entitled "Specimen du Divan de Menoutchehri, poete Persan du Ve Siecle de l'Hegira," and printed at Versailles for private circulation only—to a notice of one of the oldest Persian poets who lived at the Court of Mahmud of Ghazni and of his sons, Masud and Muhammad. The "Divan" of Menutchehri has hitherto been very little known, and manuscript copies are rare. The King of Oudh's copy, described by Sprenger, perished in the mutiny.

SIR JOHN BENNETT, the watchmaker, has invented but not patented, a new word at a meeting of citizens of London held on the 31st ultimo to discuss the Royal Titles Bill, when he is reported to have said that "the people of England never dreamt of Emperor or Empress, or any such Disraelotic nonsense." Disraeli's recent conduct has created the want of such a word.

A GOOD anecdote is told of Lord Lyttelton whose death by his own hand we announced the other day. The "man of position," as *Vanity Fair* styled his Lordship, was known as the most illegible of writers, and when Lord Derby's Reform Bill was before the House of Lords, Lord Lyttelton proposed an amendment which no clerks of the House could read, but which on being interpreted by his Lordship was to the effect that no person should have a vote who could not read and *write*.

ANGLO-INDIAN newspapers have a curious habit of identifying themselves with the European section of their readers, and so, by implication, with the British nation, says the *Pioneer*. You can hardly take up one of these journals without reading of "*our* Native army," "*our* Indian subjects," and so on; as if the editors kept a Native army or an eastern kingdom on the press premises. The sooner this custom is dropped the better for the influence of Indian journalism. We do not deny that we fall into it ourselves sometimes; but it is wrong and stupid all the same. The more the Press of this country speaks with the common voice of India, the more attention will it win.

Scientific

SIR ARTHUR COTTON (who is now seventy-three years of age) writes to the London *Times* with reference to his connection with the North-West African expedition. He says that he had offered at first to go out with a party of two or three merely as an Engineer to give an opinion on the practicability of admitting the sea into the Desert. He is informed that his name has since been mixed up with a proposal to establish a settlement, and as those interested in it may suppose that he is in some measure a party to the organization of such a project, he asks us to state that the project is altogether out of his line, and that he offers no opinion concerning it.

Latest News.

DR. MYLNE, the new Bishop of Bombay, will leave England for his diocese on Ascension Thursday, the 25th May, and travelling *via* Italy, will arrive in Bombay when the first burst of the monsoon is over.

THE Puttiallah correspondent of the *Statesman* says, that a number of Calcutta tradesmen who are large creditors of the late Maharajah are now there to get their accounts settled. They left Calcutta immediately on hearing of His Highness' death.

THE boy Maharajah of Puttiallah is to be installed on the *guddi* by Sir Henry Davies shortly.

THE rarest collection of birds in India, is said to be found in Puttiallah. The late Maharajah went into large expense to get this collection.

IT is clear, says the *Delhi Gazette*, that our present Viceroy is not forgetful of his father's maxims. If our memory do not deceive us, one of the works of the Great Novelist concludes with the following: "The worst use you can put a man to, is to hang him." Such is evidently the present Lord Lytton's opinion, for the murderer of Tallygunge has obtained a reprieve at the eleventh hour. He was to have been hanged on the morning of the 4th May, when a telegram from Simla arrested execution. The sentence of death had been confirmed by the High Court, and a petition to the local Government for a reprieve had proved unsuccessful. It is not at present known whether the sentence has been commuted for one of transportation for life.

THE Commander-in-Chief of India has directed that a sword-knot shall be worn by all Native officers of Infantry regiments.

THE proposed Industrial School for Behar in commemoration of the Prince of Wales' visit, will be opened not at Pusa but at Bankipore. The Reception Committee have in hand Rs. 1,53,000 for the purpose, after defraying

Rs. 22,580 to meet the expenses for the reception given to H. R. H.

THE latest advices from Siam state that the bamboo tax levied by the Government brings in a large revenue. The bamboos are sold in clumps at 7½ cents for every two clumps, and purchasers are willing to enter into arrangements for their purchase, as they make a little profit in the article. The enterprising gentleman who for some time owned the Bankolein Printing office and issued the *Siam Advertiser* regularly, informed his "patrons, subscribers and friends," that it was his intention, after a pretty long stay in the country, to proceed to Europe and America. The publication of the *Advertiser* will not be interfered with. It is announced that the enterprising publisher's wife will "be in charge." The *Siam Government Gazette* continues to be issued once a week, every Sunday, the third volume having been completed. This publication was issued soon after the King returned to Bangkok from Calcutta, and it is said that this is one result of His Majesty's visit to India.

BAZAR Mohamed Amir Hussain, Khan Bahadur, a Riess of Mahmudabad, Panjab, offers a prize to the student who has passed most honorably the Arabic test in the B. A. Examination.

MR. R. B. SHAW, British Joint Commissioner at Ladakh, arrived at Lahore on Wednesday last.

CHOLERA has appeared in the Eastern Districts of the North-Western Provinces.

AN attempt was made to throw No. 10 Passenger Train off the line at Gaepura near Mirzapur, on the 4th instant.

ERAC, nephew of Tasakone, the late Panthay Governor of Moimein, who, with about thirty of his officers, died sword in hand in defence of the last stronghold of Panthay, has been most cordially welcomed by Yakub Khan, the Ruler of Kashgar, and appointed to a military command.

LORD LYTTON, we are sorry to find, has been suffering from a bilious attack since his arrival at Simla.

AN edict has been issued in Japan forbidding the practice of wearing swords by others than the military and police.

IT is expected that the Gulam Baba Cotton Spinning Mill at Surat, will be started by the end of June next.

A GOANESE at Bombay has been seventy-one times in jail, and the Magistrate in committing him to the Sessions of the Bombay High Court for a fresh offence, hoped that, under the 72nd conviction, he would be trasported for life.

THE telegram informs us that with reference to the denial given in the name of the Queen by Mr. Disraeli, Mr. Lowe has apologized and retracted the statement he made respecting two of Her Majesty's former Ministers having been requested to propose the new title for Her Majesty.

IN reply to a question in the House of Commons, on Thursday last, Lord George Hamilton explained that the new Indian four per cent. loan opened in London, was larger than the budget statement, because it had been found necessary to provide besides for Public Works, for the deficient yield of Secretary of State's Council Bills during the last year, and also, for a possible deficiency during the current year.

IN the House of Commons, on Thursday last, on Mr. James introducing a motion that the proclamation was inadequate to prevent the use of the imperial title in Her Majesty's dominions other than those appertaining to India, Mr. Disraeli agreed to fix Thursday next for the discussion of the motion as a vote of censure and want of confidence.

CHOLERA still prevails in Cashmere.

MR. GROSVENOR and party reached Tallfu on the 12th ultimo.

THE Escort under Jebb reached Bhamo on the 30th, and intended starting for the Chinese Frontier on the 3rd current.

THE *Indian Daily News* has been advised by wire that the weather at Madras is looking very suspicious.

A GREAT fire occured at Baroda last week and very valuable and substantial buildings, about one hundred and seventy-five in number, and almost all belonging to opulent sowcars, have been burned down to the ground. The exact loss is unknown, but many lacs of rupees worth of property must have been destroyed.

A GREAT fire has also occured at Agra. The loss of property is considerable. But no life has been lost.

ON payment of four times the ordinary rate a telegraphic message, it has been recently ruled, can be sent from one station to another in cases of "extraordinary emergency."

IN consideration of the gallantry, judgment, and general resources exhibited by Lieutenant Abbott, R. N., in the late operations on the Perak, while in command of a detachment of blue jackets, he has been granted by the Admiralty special leave of absence.

A CORRESPONDENT of the *Oudh Akhbar* informs that paper that a great storm passed over Rampore, and that an elephant was killed by a tree falling on it.

A CHRISTIAN female is employed to teach the Canarese language to the female convicts in the Central Jail, Bangalore, and much good is done by this means.

THE *Bangalore Spectator* hears on the most reliable authority that Mr. C. R. Saunders, C. B., will, on the expiration of his leave, return to India as Chief Commissioner of Mysore and Coorg.

Calcutta.

SILVER specie to the value of £225,000 is now on its way to Calcutta from London.

PURSUANT to Section 35 of Act XI of 1876, the Directors of the Bank of Bengal authorize the under-mentioned Officers for and on behalf of the Bank to sign the several documents and to do the several acts specified or mentioned in the said Section and required for the business of the said Bank :—

R. Hardie, Secretary and Treasurer.

J. Hector, Deputy Secretary and Treasurer.

J. Gordon, Chief Accountant and Deputy Secretary.

THE Rev. Dr. K. M. Bannerji has been appointed President of Graduates' Association, Calcutta.

A CASE has been instituted in the Magistrate's Court, Hughly, against the Government Pleader there, for presenting for registration a document insufficiently and unduly stamped.

THE Second Anniversary of the Bengal Gymnastic School, will take place this day at the garden-house of the late Babu Kashishur Mittra, Nundunbagan, 68 Upper Circular Road, at 5½ P. M. When and where Babu Nobogopaul Mitra will address the meeting.

OF late the local papers have been publishing many accounts of the vagaries and oppressions of the Calcutta Police. The most recent one is in connection with the working of the Contagious Diseases' Act. In Calcutta we have now two gentlemen belonging to the Civil Service as Commissioner and Deputy Commissioner of Police, who have had no special experience of the Police ; and Sir Stuart Hogg has also little time to look after his business as Commissioner of Police. The *Statesman* is quite right in his remark that "the executive head of the force in a great city like this, requires to be a man of very special and exceptional powers."

THE last Special General Meeting of the Justices had to be adjourned for a day because there was no quorum ; and the adjourned meeting was subsequently attended by not more than fifteen Justices including the Chairman and Vice-Chairman. The Justices are evidently smarting under a sense of wrong and injustice, and do not care to attend the meetings, now that the Corporation is about to die. But till the new Municipal constitution comes into existence, who is to take care of the interests of the poor rate-payers ? The Chairman may do any thing he likes, in the absence of all independent Justices. Certainly the rate-payers may well grumble, under the circumstances. The sooner the new Municipality is organised the better.

IN view, perhaps, of the approaching death of the Corporation of the Justices, the Collector and Treasurer, Babu Jogendro Narain Ghose, has tendered his resignation, which has been accepted, and the Justices have recorded their thanks to the Babu "for the valuable services rendered by himself, and, before him, by his father, deceased, as Collector and Treasurer to the Municipality for many years together." As a tentative measure to last till the end of the present year, two of the subordinates of the Babu, will, on increased pay, collect the rates of the city.

CALCUTTA is about to have a garden of "a quasi-public nature" (to use the words of Sir Stuart Hogg) at Chorebagan, now in course of erection by Rai Rajendro Mullick Bahadur at a cost of nearly a lac of rupees. The Municipality have sanctioned an expenditure of Rs. 1,556-4-11, for sewering the ditch north of this new Garden.

THE Calcutta Municipality are about to fill up the Bertolish Tank in Chitpore Road, as being conducive to health, since it is too small to have a supply of wholesome water throughout the year. The Municipality will do well to have all such tanks either filled up or re-excavated. They are the very hot-beds of disease. We may name some of them. One is to be found in Halliday Street, another in Machua Bazar Street and a third in Bhowany Churn Dutt's Lane. We beg to call the attention of the Health Officer to these tanks.

THE Government has refused to give the Justices any compensation for the Tramway, and they seem to have pocketed the refusal quietly, on the recommendation of Sir Stuart Hogg. This is too bad. The Hon'ble Babu Juggodanund Mukerji was right in insisting on Counsel's opinion being taken as to the legal remedies of the Justices against the Government ; but Sir Stuart Hogg of course combines in him everything. He is as good a lawyer as anybody, and his *dictum* is that "the Justices have no legal claim for compensation on Government." "When Sir Oracle speaketh, let no one ope his mouth."

THE Justices have recommended expenditure not exceeding Rs. 1,000, for extra establishment necessary for preparing Police and Lighting-rate Bills for 3rd quarter of 1876, which, under the new Municipal Act, would be due on the 1st July, and must be prepared before 1st June.

WE have received the report of proceedings of the Twenty-fourth Annual General Meeting of the British Indian Association, held on the 29th April last. We are sorry that want of space obliges us to do no more than make a few extracts from it this morning. We are glad to find that there was some discussion at the meeting on a subject to which we have several times referred in these columns of late. The report before us tells us that at the meeting "some conversations ensued as to the disadvantage in which the Indian community were placed in respect of Parliamentary legislation. Parliament now took a more active interest in Indian affairs than before, but the people of India had no opportunity of making known their opinions, views, and requirements. The Indian Bills introduced in Parliament were not published in the *Gazette of India* for general information, and no time was allowed to the Indian public for the discussion of these measures. Two important Bills were introduced in Parliament this year, one referring to pensions to Members of the Indian Council, and the other to the powers of the Indian Legislative Councils. The first has been passed into law, and the second would probably be passed shortly. It was worthy of consideration as to whether some means could not be devised by which an opportunity might be given to the Indian public to study Indian Bills introduced into Parliament before enactment into law." Dr. Rajendralala Mittra, in that true spirit of independence for which he is distinguished, said some rather blunt truths. Referring to the duties of the Association collectively and of the members individually, he observed :—"The only proper course for the Association was to follow that which it had hitherto followed—that straight course of duty, which required it to serve as the interpreter of the people to Government and of Government to the people, and this it should do with the sole object of securing good Government, without any fear of consequences or any sinister view of favor. It should always invariably, and on all fitting occasions, say its say modestly, respectfully, and constitutionally, but, at the same time, firmly and unflinchingly. It can justify its existence solely by so doing, and will well deserve to be abolished when it failed to do so. Some obloquy some misrepresentation, some abuse, it must be prepared to withstand, idle impatience and official arrogance will always denounce it as meddlesome and obstructive, but there was always sufficient number of men in high places who were willing to consult the wishes, wants, and feelings of the people, and from such men the Association is sure to have its due, for its honesty, straightforwardness, and disinterested devotion to duty, and what was true of the Association collectively, was equally true of the members individually. They could often serve their own ends—obtain situations for themselves or their relatives, favors and smiles from men in power, honors and rewards from high quarters, by adopting the policy of *ap-ka-waste*, and *johukum*, but by subscribing, for the sake of a radiant smile or hearty shake of the hand, to every thing they hear from men in power, without reference to the peculiar exigencies and condition of the people of this country ; they will betray the interests of their fellow-men, forfeit the respect of the good deprive themselves of the approbation of their conscience, and in every way render themselves unworthy of the position they hold in society. They had the choice, smiles and exerts, at the cost of sacrificing the interests of the nation, of all that is most sacred, on the one side, and the cause of truth, justice and one's country, but no smiles, on the other, and he hoped they would find no difficulty in making up their mind as to which to choose." The following gentlemen have been elected office-bearers of the Association for the current year :—

Raja Rommanath Tagore, Bahadur, C. S. I.,—*President.*

Babu Degumber Mitter, C. S. I., Hon'ble Rajah Narendrakrishna, Bahadur, Rajah Suttyanund Ghosal, Bahadur, and Rajah Harendrakrishna, Bahadur,—*Vice-Presidents.*

Members of the Committee.

Rajah Rajendranarain Deb, Bahadur.
Babu Joykissen Mukerji.
" Peerychand Mitter.
Dr. Rajendralala Mitra.
Babu Durgacharn Law.
" Debender Mullick.
" Rommanath Law.
" Jodulal Mullick.
Rajah Promothonath Roy, Bahadur.
Nawab Amir Ali, Bahadur.
Babu Punnalal Seal.
" Chunderkant Mukerji.
" Krishnamohun Mullick.
" Grishchunder Ghosh.
Kumar Grishchunder Sing, Bahadur.
Babu Subuldas Mullick.
" Pearymohun Mukerji.
" Tarrinychurn Bannerji.
" Dwarkanath Mullick.
Hon'ble Mir Mohamed Ali.
Kumar Kantichunder Singh, Bahadur.
Babu Norendranath Sen.
Nawab Ahmed Ali, Bahadur.
Babu Sreenath Dass.
And Hirjibhai Manickji Rustomji Esq.

Rajah Jotendromohun Tagore, Bahadoor,—*Honry Secretary.*

Hon'ble Kristodas Pal,—*Assistant Secretary.*

Public Engagement

A MEETING of the Mahomedan Literary Society, at the Calcutta Mudrussah, at 9 P.M. on Friday, the 12th May 1876. Lecture by C. H. Wood Esquire. On "*Chemistry of Common Salt,*" with Experiments.

Law

POLICE—MAY 6, 1876.
[*Before F. J. Marsden, Esq.*]

A MAHOMEDAN shoe-maker charged another with the theft of five pair of shoes on the 26th instant. The defendant, who appeared in answer to a summons, pleaded not guilty. The complainant stated that he had his shop in a bazaar, and that the defendant had his in another bazar on the other side of the road. On the day in question, the defendant, seeing the complainant with the shoes in his hand opposite his shop, snatched them away, and quietly walked into his shop. Proceeding at once to the local Thana, the complainant signed a charge against the defendant; and the Police, instead of going to the spot, and arresting the defendant, advised the complainant to apply for a summons. Two witnesses were called to support the above facts. For the defence it was urged that this prosecution was brought about because the defendant, who was formerly a tenant of the man owning the bazaar in which the complainant had his shop, had gone over to the opposite bazaar, and would not return, though the owner had used all means in his power to get the defendant and others back. These facts were admitted in cross-examination by the complainant and his witnesses. The defence further set up a plea of *alibi*, but could not establish it. The Magistrate fined the defendant Rs. 50, observing that it appeared to him quite clear that the defendant did snatch away the shoes, and that this was done as a pressure to induce the complainant to go over to the other bazaar. Rs. 10 of the fine was ordered to be paid to the complainant as compensation, the shoes not forthcoming.

PRIVATE WILLIAM GILBERT, of the 1-3rd Buffs, was charged with having deserted his regiment. From the evidence of a European constable it appeared that the defendant was arrested on board the *Viceroy*, by which vessel he had intended to leave the country. The evidence as to his identity being recorded, the Magistrate ordered the defendant to be taken to jail, there to await an escort from the military authorities, who would deal with him according to their law.

MR. HENRY TWIDALE applied for a warrant against the person of his servant for the theft of a gold watch and chain, valued at Rs. 300. The Magistrate granted a search-warrant. The accused is said to have gone to Hughly.

[*Before P. D. Dickens, Esq.*]

MR. ROSENBURGH, a contractor, was charged with having cheated several trading firms out of various sums of money. The witnesses not being present, the cases were remanded, the prisoner being enlarged on bail for Rs. 300 only.

Advertisements

ALBERT HALL.

PATRON.

His Honor the Lieutenant Governor of Bengal

COUNCIL.

Hon'ble Sir William Muir, K. C. S. I.—*President.*

Rajah Rama Nath Tagore Bahadur C. S. I.—*Vice-President.*

Hon'ble J. F. D. Inglis.
Hon'ble Ashley Eden, C. S. I.
Hon'ble H. Bell.
Archdeacon Baly.
Colonel H. E. L. Thuillier, C. S. I.
His Highness the Maharajah of Vizianagram.
Maharajah Kumar of Bettiah.
Hon'ble Rajah Narendra Krishna Bahadur.
Rajah Komul Krishna Bahadur.
Rajah Joteendro Mohun Tagore Bahadur.
Babu Digumber Mitter, C. S. I.
Dr. Rajendralala Mitra.
Hon'ble Nawab Asgar Ali Bahadur, C. S. I.
Nawab Amir Ali Bahadur.
Moulvi Abdul Lutif Khan Bahadur.
Manockji Rustomji Esq.
Babu Keshub Chunder Sen.

SUBSCRIPTIONS.

The Hon'ble Sir Richard Temple ...	Rs.	200
His Highness Maharajah Holkar ...	"	5,000
His Highness Maharajah of Jeypore	"	5,000
His Highness Maharajah of Putialah	"	2,500
His Highness Maharajah of Vizianagram ...	"	1,000
Maharajah Kumar of Bettiah ...	"	2,000
Rajah of Bhinga ...	"	1,000
Maharani Surnomoie, Cossim Bazar	"	1,000
Maharajah of Hutwa ...	"	500
Rajah Roma Nath Tagore Bahadur	"	500
Rajah Komul Krisna Bahadur ...	"	500
Rajah Joteendro Mohun Tagore ...	"	500
Hon'ble Rajah Narendra Krishna Bahadur ...	"	300
Babu Joykissen Mookerjee ...	"	250
Sirdar Dyal Singh ...	"	250
Babu Shama Churn Law ...	"	200
Hon'ble Sir William Muir ...	"	100
Hon'ble Ashley Eden ...	"	100
Dr. Mohendro Loll Sircar ...	"	150
Babu Goonendro Nath Tagore ...	"	100
Babu Ananda Mohun Bose ...	"	100
Babu Rajkissen Mookerjee ...	"	200
Babu Janoki Nath Mookerji ...	"	100
Hon'ble H. Bell ...	"	100
Babu Debendro Nath Bose ...	"	200

ICE! ICE! ICE!

MADE IN FOUR MINUTES

THE PNEUMATIC ICE MACHINE

THIS IMPORTANT INVENTION IS CONSIDERED A BOON TO THOSE LIVING IN TROPICAL CLIMATES.

CAN BE WORKED BY THE MOST INEXPERIENCED HAND AND IS NOT LIABLE TO GET OUT OF ORDER.

From Rs. 175, each Machine complete.

MESSRS. ARLINGTON & CO.
AGENTS.

HAROLD & CO.,

3, DALHOUSIE SQUARE, CALCUTTA

HARMONIUMS.

Harold and Co., call attention to their unequalled stock of rich-toned Harmoniums made especially for India.

FROM RS. 90 TO RS. 900 EACH.

All kinds of Musical Instruments of the best description are always kept in Stock.

Printed and published by M. M. REKHIT, at the "INDIAN MIRROR" PRESS, No. 15, College Square, for the Proprietor.

The Indian Mirror.

SUNDAY EDITION.

VOL. XV.] CALCUTTA, SUNDAY MAY 14, 1876 {Registered at the General Post Office.} [No. 114

CONTENTS.

NOTICE.

Letters and all other communications relating to the literary department of the Paper should be addressed to "The Editor."

All letters on the business of the Press should be addressed, and all remittances made payable to the Manager of this Paper. Particular attention is solicited to this notice.

Subscribers will be good enough to give prompt notice of any delay, or irregularity in delivery of the Paper.

Editorial Notes

WE are glad to learn that Maharani Surnomaye has contributed, besides a thousand rupees to the Albert Hall, an additional sum of two hundred rupees in aid of the Library and Reading Rooms connected with the Hall.

BETTER far is it to serve others than to do good to others, though apparently there is little difference between the two. In service there is humility, as one cannot serve without being in the lowly position of a servant. But in doing good to society one occupies the superior position of a benefactor, and in the highest philanthrophy and benevolence there may often be discovered the most disgusting pride and arrogance. To do good is to confer a fovor; hence it indicates always the pride of patronage. No such feeling is or can be cherished by the poor servant, who, however rich, learned or virtuous, must feel that he sits at the feet of those whom he serves by promoting their material or moral welfare. Better is *seba* than *paropakar*.

THE *Inquirer* has the following on Mr. Voysey's movement. It does credit both to the head and heart of the Unitarian organ:—"A contemporary, adopting the word 'Christian' as part of its title, has the following:—'The Voysey Fund.—We have received an appeal that £3,000 may be raised for a building for Mr. Voysey. The congregation has removed to a smaller hall. We wish no success to a ministry that endeavours to lower our esteem of the moral character of Jesus Christ.' The Christianity of this sentence is as curious as its literary construction. We are by no means at one with Mr. Voysey in his estimate of the character of Christ, but we do not therefore feel bound to despise his efforts to combat ignorance and superstition, and to raise up a nobler conception of God. Nor do we consider ourselves wanting in what is called 'allegiance to Christ,' when we desire Mr. Voysey God-speed in that work. It is a poor sort of Christianity that seeks to exclude all who cannot fight under the same banner."

WHAT is "cool self-love?" This highly important affection is said by Bishop Butler to be not only not against the Divine virtue of benevolence, but "perfectly coincident with it." Mr. Matthew Arnold, in contesting this serious blunder in Butler's psychology, contrasts it with the psychology of Jesus Christ which, he says, "without the least apparatus of system, is yet incomparably exacter than Butler's as well as incomparably more illuminative and fruitful." According to this psychology man has two selves, one higher and one lower. The one is self-love, the dersire of personal happiness, "cool" or "hot", according to individual training and temparament, but self-love all the same. The other is the love of God, or what is convertible with it, the love of humanity, the higher and impersonal self, which when mixed with the desire of happiness, and made to govern it, can make us truly happy. The habitual disposition to ask how a certain line of conduct will affect our own interests is at the opposite pole from all truly religious consciousness.

MAN is naturally a religious being. It is a cardinal truth of Theism that man's heart is not "bent on evil and only evil and that continually;" as too many Christians affirm;—but that it is quite as natural for man to be religious as to be thoughtful or affectionate or active in business; all of which imply conflict and victory. Theists recognise the need of trial, effort and self-discipline with God's help,—in setting the man on the back of his animal, to ride him manfully. Yet it is in the order of nature and not *against* nature, to keep the man above and the brute below. In the American correspondence in our latest copy of the *(London) Inquirer*, we notice a statement strongly corroborating the idea that religion, like business, will take care of itself; and that Government interference is no more needed in a civilized country, to build churches, than to build shops and warehouses for the people. Leave religion free, and it will grow like a plant. The statement in the *Inquirer* is this:—"When we (Americans) began the support of religious institutions on the purely voluntary principle, even such men as Judge Story prophesied that many of our churches would be closed. Yet what is the record? One hundred years ago, this country had 1,950 churches for three and a half millions; a church for every 1,704 persons. In 1870, with a population of thirty-eight millions, we had more than 72,000 church organizations *i. e.* a church for every 529 persons. Thus while the population has increased eleven-fold, the churches have multiplied thirty-seven fold. This surely does not look like a decay of religious institutions under the voluntary principle. The most enormous progress in numbers will be found among the Roman Catholics and the Methodists."

WHAT seek ye? To this question every body will doubtless return the following reply—Salvation. But salvation is a growth. It means ever-increasing holiness and joy. The highest salvation passeth our understanding and defies conception. Thank God, however, we have already seen and felt enough of heavenly reality and sweetness to realize a stage of salvation, which for the present would satisfy our best wishes, hopes and aspirations. Our heaven is a summing up of our highest spiritual experiences. At least this is the heaven which would satisfy our modest ambition at present, and when we have reached that we shall think of and seek a higher heaven. At some moment of our lives or other we have by Divine grace, realized each of the various sides of religious life in an eminent degree. We have prayed most devoutly, subdued our passions thoroughly, behaved towards others most generously and meekly, felt within the heart the highest flights of communion and rapturous love, and gone down into the deepest depths of humility, poverty and asceticism,—all this, however, at different times. We never were devout, lowly, pure-minded, philanthropic and truthful at one and the same time. When we were fortunate enough to cultivate intense love towards others, we perhaps found that self-centred and sustained devotion was ebbing away. Again in the midst of most fervent prayers practical righteousness was often deficient. Thus at different times different elements of religious life have been realized and enjoyed by us. What we wish is a simultaneous realization of *all* these elements. Instead of broken lights we desire now to have a full view of the sun of righteous life in its totality. We wish to gather together the scattered elements of goodness from our past life. What we have seen in parts and fragments we wish to realize as a whole. All the choice blessings showered by Heavenly grace upon us at different times require only to be accumulated. The rainbow colors of heaven the eye has already seen, would, if put together and adjusted, form a complete and charming picture of that holy land we so much wish. We need little in addition to what we have received. If only all the good things of our past life are reproduced in us as a harmonious whole we shall be content. The Brahmo must feel profoundly thankful to his God that he can find heaven in a mere summing up of the good things he has already tasted. Let him pray for light and strength that he may find such heaven on earth.

MR. WHEELER'S new history of the Mahomedan rule in India is favorably noticed. The contests between Hindus and Mahomedans are described in graphic language. Here is the battle of Somnath :—"Then Mahmud swore that he would destroy Somnath, and teach the idolators that there was no God but Allah and that Muhammad was his prophet. *And* he marched from Ghuzni to Multan with thirty thousand horsemen. *And* he gathered together thirty thousand camels and loaded them with corn and water; for beyond Multan the land was desert. *Now* when all was ready the Sultan went to Somnath. *And* on the way he sacked the city of Ajmir; for the Rajah of Ajmir and all his people had gone out of the city in great fear when they heard of his coming. *And* after this he saw many forts with idols inside, which were chamberlains and heralds to the god of Somnath, and as he went he destroyed them all. *And* the Sultan and his horsemen halted before Somnath on a Thursday. *Now* the temple was guarded like a fortress because of its treasures. *And* the waves washed three of its sides; and the fourth side, which joined on the main, was fortified with walls and battlements and manned with Rajputs. *And* when the Mussulmans galloped up, the Rajputs scoffed at them, saying: 'The god of Somath will destroy you all.'" We shall give the two following paragraphs as Mr. Wheeler writes them, for the narrative is worth completing. "On Friday the battle began. The Turkish archers drove the Rajputs from the battlements, whilst the swordsmen planted the ladder and climbed the walls, crying 'Allah Akber.' Then they fought the Rajputs with great slaughter until the night closed in and they could see no longer. On Saturday the battle was renewed. The Sultan prostarated himself upon the ground before all his army and prayed to God for victory. The battle raged in front of the gateway. The Rajputs fought like devils, but the believers gained the mastery. Many Rajputs ran into the temple, threw themselves down before the pillar, implored the God for help, and then ran back and perished sword in hand. At last the Rajputs saw that all was lost, fled to their boats, and put out to sea."

SECTS AND SECTARIANISM.

SECTS are not bad, but sectarianism is. Sects mean the embodiment of certain ideas, and essential characteristics of religion into distinctive institutions and opinions, prominent above others which are considered less essential. Sectarianism means hatred and disgust against men who hold opinions contrary to those held by one's self. Sects there must be in the world as long as some phases of truth will present themselves to some more strongly than to others. Because these will always attract a following, and none but sympathetic followers can foster and develop the tendencies that the peculiar religious characters of leaders show under circumstances proper to their time and place. The soldiers of God must fight under different banners organized, and must be led by the special genius of the captains under whom they are placed, but when men refuse to recognize other phases of truth than those which they have perceived, when the followers quarrel, and the leaders try to injure each other's case, the war instead of being carried on against the enemies of Heaven, becomes an internecine struggle, brothers shedding the blood of brothers; the fatal poison of sectarianism consumes the very life-blood of humanity. Religious aspirations, ideals, and plans of service, after a simultaneous growth for sometime, tend ultimately to classify themselves. Not that the religious scholar, versed in the thought, faith and piety of varying orders of believers in the world, is against the contemplative saint whose delight is the calm and quiet insight of divine truths in the depths of divine communion. Nor that the ardent practical missionary, eager and anxious to save souls, and intensely concerned to spread the glory of God, is against the sacred solitary devotee who by his intense piety, equally affects the life and the heart of men. Each of these four men will gather around them congenial spirits, who will under their respective leadings learn what each has to teach in his sphere. This is what happens every day in the world. But there is an unfortunate tendency generally manifested. The natural classification gives rise to the spirit of exclusiveness, and this is the mother of sectarianism. Exclusiveness lives and grows upon ignoring the virtues of those who exist beyond its pale. It is the self-consciousness of piety and religiousness attained by the system under which one enlists himself. The real difficulty is to reconcile, and harmonize ideals and aspirations which the more they develop and grow, tend to individualize themselves. Classification is a necessity of the human constitution, and repeats itself in every department of man's life. But unregulated classification cuts up society into pieces, and multiplies the already existing too many enmities and unpleasantnesses of the world. Judicious and well-regulated classification finds out, binds up, encourages, and very highly develops the deep and powerful characteristics of men, groups them, disciplines them, lays before them in the clearest manner possible their destiny, and serves in the sphere of religion the purpose which an efficient, well-organized, and patriotic army serves in the defence and well-being of the State to which it belongs. In the model commonwealth the different orders of workers, though so entirely different in the pursuits, duties, and gifts, work harmoniously. The Governor, the law-maker, the administrator, the judge, the soldier and the schoolmaster only help and perfect each other's work. They feel no antagonism, show no personal animosity; if they are men of average sense, there is no sectarianism, though there are so many sects. In the religious commonwealth, exactly the same thing may take place if men are only sensible and amenable to discipline.

The Interpreter

THERE is a beautiful passage in the Yogavashishta which reminds us of being all things to all men according to St. Paul. The text, in describing the characteristics of the regenerate saint, says :—"He who has found salvation in this life is a loving devotee in the company of loving devotees; he is cunning among the artful, a child among children; an old man among old men, and meek among the meek." Superficial observers may denounce this many-sided and changeable character, and attribute it to inconstancy and fickleness. But to the far-seeing eye it is nothing but nature's simplicity. The regenerated heart becomes true to nature, it is altogether natural, its thoughts and feelings, its outward bearings and conversation all shape themselves according to the atmosphere in which it is placed and the men with whom it has to deal. All types of goodness are in the regenerate man, child-like frankness, the old man's seriousness, wisdom that can conquer the world and love; and all these manifest themselves as occasion requires. Hence is it that all good men who are in the hands of God and are true to nature, are "all things to all men."

Correspondence.

CHRIST AND HIS MOTHER

To the Editor of the *Indian Mirror*.

SIR,—I have read with great interest your remarks on Christ's love for his mother. To tell you the truth, it is this point in the life of the great apostle which has often perplexed me. I cannot say that your explanation has freed me from the perplexity. If Christ was an ascetic, he was surely a most unnatural ascetic. It is true, as you say, that "asceticism merges the world with all its domestic and social relationships and interests in the absorbing and vast realities of the spirit world." Is that any reason, however, why Christ should behave so heartlessly towards his mother? There are ascetics and ascetics—cynical ascetics that feel a pleasure in trampling upon the world and its dearest, albeit most harmless objects, and godly ascetics that see in the love and goodness of the world the reflection of the Divine face. When Christ addressed his mother as "Woman," when he had not even a tender parting word for her while himself suffering the agonies of the cross, what shall we conclude but that his conduct was most unaccountable? I believe either that the English version of the Bible is incorrect or that Christ was an unnatural son. The former supposition may be true; but that the latter is true cannot be doubted when we consider that, throughout the four Gospels we find no instance of Christ respectfully accosting his mother, if we except only that closing scene in the drama where he entrusts the charge of his mother to the most beloved of his disciples. To love a mother is the most natural and beautiful act of a man's life; and if Christ had loved his mother, he would surely have, considering the fulness of his heart in all things heavenly, manifested it in more ways than one. This was what struck me while I was reading the life of that most charming apostle. I shall feel obliged by your enlightening me on the subject. Surely you have yourself confessed in many ways that one who is mad with God's love, is never satisfied unless he showers that love upon the whole world.

Yours obediently,
S.

A REBUKE.

To the Editor of the *Indian Mirror*.

SIR,—I am filled with regret as well as surprise to see, in your issue of the 7th instant, that you [We meant some Brahmos, and not we individually.—Ed. *I. M.*] are "cultivating the Hindu idea of cooking one's own food with zeal." My regret is that by taking the *hatabari* for the pen for at least two or three mortal hours every day, you would now find less time for catering for your poor readers than heretofore. My surprise is that an educated man like yourself, could find any thing holy in cooking one's own food any more than in buying one's own clothes &c. You have every right to enlist yourself as a moharrir of the Handial (earthen pot) department of your household, or be your own barber or,—but to talk approvingly of the first of these occupations with the evident object of getting converts, is certainly cruel on your part in this grilling weather, and places you in the not enviable position of the fox who had lost his tail.

Do you think that cooking curbs the animality and thereby aids devotion? Or your *receipe* is, sit by the fire for some time every day, and the spirit will be regenerated; only you advocate *cooking* on the "killing two birds with one throw" principle: Or you mean to say that the body should be mortified in some shape or other for our highest good? I wonder what remedy for the soul in the shape of torturing the body, would you prescribe for the poor sons of toil who daily cook their own food, bring their own water, and hew their own wood. For mercy's sake, hide your pill before them.

Mr. Editor, you are certainly burning at the wrong end of the candle, for instead of telling us to "cast off impure desires, to combat with our besetting faults," you advise us to do unmeaning things. Need I waste words to repeat a truism that we should nourish the body with all diligence and care to do the work which God has appointed for us, and that if we wilfully do anything which will compromise our health or shorten our lives, we commit slow suicide for which we shall be guilty before God and man.

You are pleased to talk of cooking one's own food as an essentially Hindu idea. Are not making vows in sickness, eating light food on certain days, bathing in the Ganges for cleansing our sins, as much Hindu ideas as your pet one? And because they are Hindu ideas, would any sane man countenance them? The fact is they are pure superstitions of popular Hinduism and are not the higher teachings of the Hindu Shastras. Toolsidass, the celebrated modern Hindu writer, in one of his renowned verses, ridicules the idea of becoming saints by bodily mortification. I cannot resist the temptation of giving a free translation of some of them:—

If ablution
Gives salvation,
Then they h've got it,
The finny race.
If eating fruits,
Or mealy roots,
It much boots
To mend our ways;
Lo! up the trees,
Sit true *rishis*
Your Sires, please,
As Darwin says.

Hoping you will give the above a place in your columns.

I remain,
Yours sincerely
A THEIST.

The 12th May 1876.

* We have let our correspondent say his very worst. We think he could have said it all in good spirit.—ED. *I. M.*

Brahmo Hymns

[TRANSLATED FROM BENGALI]

LORD, why wilt thou not have mercy upon me? When didst thou deny any of thy children thy grace? Whoever thirsting under sin and sorrow once calls upon thee with an aching heart, thou coolest him with the waters of the ocean of thy mercy. How many wicked children of thine do I see, but never have I heard of a forsaken child. If one guilty of a thousand sins, cries unto thee mournfully thou at once takest him upon thy lap as thy child.

MY heart loves thee. Therefore it pants for thee. There is joy in beholding thee, love rises in thy company, the heart is filled by enjoying thee, in thy touch there is salvation.

COME ye who wish to go to the regions of love. Come, come, come, come all. Neither sickness nor sorrow, sin nor suffering is there. There the heart is comforted by seeing the Loving God. Come with anxious hearts, come, come, come. How long will ye burn in the fire of worldliness? He who has given unto all life, youth and wealth, prostrate yourselves at His feet, weighed down with love.

The Brahmo Somaj

ORDINARY week-day Service will commence in the Mundir at 7½ P. M from this day.

WE hear of a family of blacksmiths in the village of Jungdbari near Mymensing, who have entered the Brahmo Somaj and commenced to preach and propagate their faith in the village with considerable success. Though belonging to one of the lower caste, with little wealth and education, they have gained much influence; they conduct divine worship in many houses, and are making satisfactory progress.

THE new garden house bought at Morepooker near Connaghur, for spiritual exercises and recreation, will probably be consecrated next week. It is to be named *Sadhan Kanan*.

THE minister's lectures to the two disciples on yoga and bhakti, which have been translated into Sanskrit, already number more than seven hundred Slokas. The *granth* when completed, may help many a Brahmo inquirer in the shape of a *Brahma Gita*.

BABU Protap Chunder Mozumdar will conduct Divine Service in the Mundir this evening.

BABU Nobin Chunder Ray, late of Lahore now living in Allahabad, has published an important book. It is a selection of text from the Vedas and Upanishads which establish faith in the One True God. The expositions of the texts are all in pure Hindi, of which language Babu Nobin Chunder is a master.

WE publish elsewhere an article that appeared in yesterday's *Friend of India*. Though written in very good spirit, and personally complimentary to our leader, we do not think it does justice to our movement. One truth the writer has, however, found out. We cannot be swallowed up by the form of orthodox Christianity that surrounds us. And we are not going to be swallowed by Hinduism either, if we can help it. At least a good many of us are conscious of the danger.

Literary.

THE *Indu Prakash* of Bombay, writes an unusually long article extending over five columns, on the late Pundit Vishnu Parashram Shastri, its Proprietor and Marhathi Editor.

THERE is as well-written article on "India's Expectations" in the April number of *Fraser's Magazine*.

THE last number of the *Indian Charivari* contains a protrait of the present young Gaekwar of Baroda, Syaji Rao. He has an intelligent appearance. He is a boy only of 12 years of age.

AFTER all not a Native of India but a Frenchman, (Mr. Barrier de Meynard) has been appointed to succeed the late Mr. Mohl, in the chair of Persian in the College of France.

THE *Athenæum* says that M. Garcin de Tassy has been elected head of a Commission for the publication of the works of the late M. Doudate de Lagree on Central Indo-China.

Scienti ic

AN hotelkeeper in Jermyn-street, St. James' London, died from the effects of sudden fright upon a weakened heart, he having in mistake drunk part of a poisonous lotion, which had become innocuous by evaporation.

IN France M. M. Victor Hugo and Louis Blanc addressed a meeting of working men on Easter Sunday, the subject of the meeting being to raise funds to pay the expenses of a deputation of *Ouvriers* to the Philadelphia Exhibition.

THE London correspondent of the *Bombay Gazette* writes:—"Your readers will be perfectly aware that while the archæological surveys of Bengal and Bombay are being carried out by General Cunningham and Mr. Burgess, very little has been done for Madras. A long correspondence has taken place on this subject between the Madras and the Supreme Governments, and an offer has just been made from the India Office of a salary and travelling allowances for a surveyor, but the sum mentioned is so very small that there is no immediate prospect of any competent person being tempted to undertake the duty."

DR. BURNELL left Negapatam by the S .S. *Goa* on the 3rd instant for Galle, *en route* to Java and other places in Batavia whither he proceeds on a tour with a view to study the Kawi inscription and other antiquities in Batavia and afterwards in the Straits of Malacca and amalgamate the results in the forthcoming second edition of his *Elements of South Indian Palæography*. His edition of the *Arsheyabrahmana* is already in the press.

THE Grand Duke Constantine of Russia has been elected an Honorary Associate of the Institution of Naval Architects, London.

Gleanings

HAFIZ is little understood even in the East. His analogies of wine are interpreted to mean gross sensuality, but even those who attribute such unworthy sentiments to Hafiz, can be ignorant of such passages as the following :—

While life is time, consent not, Hafiz,
That it should speed ignobly by ;
But strive thou to attain the object
Of thy existence ere thou die.
My soul is as a sacred bird, the highest heaven its nest,
Fretting within the body's bars it finds on earth no rest.
Lord ! to whom no one has in vain appealed,
Thou Judge and Agent, to whom all must yield,
Why should I tell to Thee my secret thought,
When nothing secret is from Thee concealed !

And, again, it is pleasant and refreshing to find in this writer ethical sentiments so sound and healthy as the following:—

Thou who never hast issued from the shrine of Sense,
How to Truth's high pathway can'st thou journey hence?
'Tis writ in golden characters upon the sapphire sphere;
Save noble actions, all things here
Shall not remain.
Plant thou the tree of Friendship only, so shall thy heart's desire bear fruit;
Uproot thou Hatred plant completely, or woes unnumbered thence may shoot.
So live thou here, that when thy life has fled,
No one may say of thee, "Thus man is dead."
Not one grain of the sheaves of life is shored by those who've trod
The pathwaw of mortality, and sown no seed for God.

Latest News.

MR. GLADSTONE, writing to a constituent at Greenwich, adheres to his former view, that the Income Tax should be abolished, and naturally adds his disapproval of its recent increase in England and the enlarged expenditure proposed by Mr. Disraeli's Government.

MESSRS DENT, PALMER, and Co. London, have given notice that they have been authorized to make payment of one-half the amount of overdue Coupons of the Turkish Loans of 1854 and 1871.

THE Vienna and St. Petersburg papers assert that the understanding between the Governments with respect to the affairs of Turkey is perfect, and that there is no fear of any collision. The German press view the prospect very differently, and affirm that the insurrection in Herzegovina and Bosnia and the military preparations of Servia are encouraged covertly by Russian agents.

MR LOWE M. P., spoke recently at a political dinner at Retford and severely criticized the recent acts of Mr. Disraeli's Government, but expressed his belief that their position was unassailable during the existence of the present Parliament.

GRAND preparations are being made at Cochin to receive the Roman Catholic Lord Bishop of Bombay.

GRAM is selling at 43 seers per rupee at Lucknow. At Sitapur it is selling at the rate of 55 seers per rupee.

THERE is still a good deal of small-pox in Poona ; chicken-pox also prevails extensively among children.

IT is stated that a library is shortly to be opened at Baroda, the foundation of which will be laid by Sir T. Madava Rao.

CHOLERA has made its appearance in Jeypore, Rajputana. Small-pox is also raging there.

MAJOR SANDEMAN has halted at Mastung to rest the troops forming his escort and to allow time for cholera infection to be shaken off. Another kaffila has passed safely through the Bolan Pass without any military escort.

A PUBLIC meeting will be held at Rangoon for the purpose of establishing a Volunteer Corps.

ADVERTISEMENTS of lotteries in newspapers are ordered to be suppressed in British Burmah too. All the local Governments are acting upon instructions received from the Supreme Government.

THERE will be a Railway from Rangoon to Mandalay.

THE *Bangalore Examiner* says that the Native gentlemen of the Mysore Commission are unfairly treated. Promotion is brisk among the European members of the Commission, but not so among the Native members who also draw much smaller pay than their Europeans colleagues. If this policy is followed in a Native State which is to be handed over, after a few years, to a Native Government on the Maharajah of Mysore assuming the age of majority, what are we to expect in the British territories ? All these subjects should be mooted in Parliament.

MOST serious charges are brought by the *Bangalore Examiner* against Colonel Malleson, the Guardian of the Maharajah of Mysore. The Mysore Maharajah's family are known to be great Hindus ; and Colonel Malleson is said to have, in direct defiance of those caste prejudices and social customs which the Government has pledged itself to respect in the case of the very meanest of its subjects, engaged a house at Ooty, one half for himself and his friends, and the other for the Maharajah and his suite. He is also said to force the young Maharajah and his brothers always to partake of refreshments with him. On the lads refusing, Colonel Malleson treats them to horse play by way of punishment. The result of all this has been that one of the young Princes has been compelled to leave Ooty for Mysore in a common cart. We do not know what necessity there was in taking the Princes to Ooty at all. The fact of it is that Colonel Malleson more than the Princes, was really desirous of spending a few days at Ooty, in this hot weather, and so they were made to accompany him.

THERE has been a debate in the House of Commons on the taking of Khokand by the Russians. It is evident the English are at last rousing to the necessity of guarding India against Russian aggression, and with this view there was a discussion on the question of the efficiency of the Native Army. Sir Henry Havelock was of opinion that the Native Army was in a rotten condition. But Lord George Hamilton replied that the Native Army was never in a more efficient state than now. Lord Northbrook seems to have lately sent despatches home on Military matters including the Minute written by Lord Napier of Magdala. These will be shortly produced in the House. It is proposed to increase the efficiency of the Native Army.

LORD LYTTELTON has committed suicide by throwing himself over the balustrade to the bottom of a well staircase. The jury returned a verdict of "Committed suicide from an unsound state of mind."

THE *Zastava*, a paper published in Austrian Croatia, states that the great majority of the Servain population is ready for the war, "come what may."

SIR SALAR JUNG, says the London correspondent of the *Bombay Gazette*, is expected in England in about ten days, and he will remain in the country for several months. Invitations are being prepared for him in most of the chief centres of provincial industry, and the first welcome that will be offered to him will come from Manchester.

THE Napier Memorial Committee has confided to its Vice-President, Mr. George Ricketts, C.B., the task of circulating notices and collecting subscriptions in the North-West Provinces.

A LETTER published in the *Times*, says the *Pioneer*, "gives a very sad account of the Czar of all the Russias. Sickly, and old before his time he is worried on every side. The death of his sister was a great blow. Then his sons are behaving badly; while outside the family circle, financial embarrassments and political complications make him long for the retirement that Charles the Fifth, and other great rulers sought before him. The Grand Duke Czarevitch and his wife would like to have a war with Germany, and some day such a war may break out ; but meanwhile *Messieurs les Tsachkendois*, with their constant annexations, are draining the resources of the Empire. No wonder if the Emperor craves a refuge from all his troubles; and, unless many rumours must be disbelieved, his abdication will not be delayed very long." But this, it must be remembered, is an *ex parte* statement. We should like to hear the other side.

THE number of cases of small-pox in Bombay, says the *Deccan Herald*, is surely though slowly decreasing. A month ago about fifty persons were dying daily of this disease, but the measures adopted by Mr. Pedder and other gentlemen to check it, have certainly much reduced the number of victims.

THERE has been another revolution at Muscat. Sayyad Turki is again made Imam, and Abdul Aziz is exiled to Kurrachi. The latter will receive an allowance granted to him by Sayyad Turki, to be deducted from the Zanzibar tribute.

THE Prince of Wales on his arrival in London, drove from the Railway Station straight to Buckingham Palace, where the Queen awaited his arrival. In the evening there was a grand gala at the Opera.

THE grand Vizier Mahmoud Nedim Pacha has been dismissed from his post as President of the Council of Ministers.

MR. W. H. JAMES' motion, in the House of Commons, on the 4th instant, for a vote of censure against Mr. Disraeli's Government in connection with the Imperial title for Her Majesty, was rejected by 334 votes against 226. So Mr. Disraeli has at every point met with complete triumph in this matter.

THE King of Burmah is doing every thing to strengthen his military arrangements. The work of the Mandalay Bund wall is being pushed on with vigor, ten thousand men being employed daily upon it. The four Italian gun-makers, brought out by the King, are to turn out fifteen rifled cannons a month for His Majesty.

Calcutta.

MR. W. R. FINK, Assistant Registrar, High Court, Original Side, has obtained two months' privilege leave of absence from this date.

THE Post Master of Calcutta sends us the following notice for publication :—

After Friday, the 26th May, 1876, the Overland Mail *viâ* Bombay will, until further notice, be closed at the Calcutta General Post Office on every Tuesday. The first Tuesday Mail will be on the 30th May 1876.

THE P. & O. Co.'s S.S. *Bokhara*, Commander W. D. Anderson, arrived in Bombay Harbour on Wednesday last, from Suez with the *English* Mails of the 21st ult. on board. The following is the list of passengers :—

From Southampton.—Capt. and Mrs. Rannick, Mrs. C. Lee, Mr K. McKean, Mrs. Le Ruez, Mr. and Mrs. Sowden and child, Mr. G. Hampton, Mr. H. Whyte, Miss Allen, Mr. E. Schmit, Mr. W. Entwistle, Mr. J. W. Smith, Mr. L. Smith, Lieut. G. R. Towsond, Lieut. C. R. Irving, Lieut. E. Nash, Lieut. E. S. May, Lieut. Sir G. V. Thomas, Bt, Lieut. C. M. T. Western, Lieut. G. F. A. Norton, Lieut. T. H. E. Acton, Lieut. R. E. Taylor, Lieut. R. C. Haines.

From Malta.—Maj. and Mrs. Harris.

From Venice.—Mrs. Borrodaile.

From Brindisi.—Mrs. Bidie, Mr. Master.

From Marseilles.—Mr. G. Emmens.

From Aden.—Mr. Cullsunbhoy Gangjee, 11 Natives.

THERE was a meeting of the Committee of the Bengal Temperance Society, yesterday at the Albert Hall, at 5 P. M.

Law

HIGH COURT.

ORIGINAL SIDE.

PEREMPTORY CAUSE BOARD

FOR

Monday the 15th May 1876.

BEFORE

The Hon'ble Mr. Justice Pontifex.

UNDEFENDED CASES.

Rammarain Doss & anr. v. Dobendra Nauth Mukhit & anr.—Shamoldhone Dutt

S. M. Nokoormoney Dassee v. Greesh Chunder Bhur & ors.—Joykissen Gangooly.

DEFENDED CASES.
(Final Disposal.)

Kaderkameenee Dossee v. Kirtee Chuder Mitter (*pt. hd.*)—Dutt & Mitter—Dover.

C. Koegler & ors. v. The Coringa Co., Ld (*pt. hd.*)—Pittar—Heckle.

Abdool Rohim v. Johora Bibee & ors.—Trotman & Watkins, Dhur & Mitter

Shahabzadee Fuckroonnjessa Begum v Shahzada Halemoozooman & ors.—Watkins—Goodall

Nocoor Chunder Bose v. Kally Coomar Ghose—Fink—T. N. Roys.

Grish Chunder Sen v. Ram Chunder Singhee—Leslie—Pearson.

Seetul Chunder Mallick v. Hurrolall Mitter & ors.—Carruthers—Chauntrell and Co., Swinhoe and Co.

Satcowrie Doss v. Pearymohun Doss and ors.—Watson—Dignam and Robinson.

Komulmoney Bewah v. Rajendronarain Moonshee and ors.—Shamoldhone Dutt—Bose and Dutt.

Ramnarain Chuckerbutty v. S. M. Siddessory Dabee—Beeby and Rutter—Hart.

Surroop Chunder Bhuttacharji v. Ramdoolall Nundy—Hart.

Dheerendronauth Bonnerji & anr. v. Raja Jotendromohun Tagore and anr.—Remfry—Chauntrell and Co. Swinhoe and Co.

POLICE—MAY 13, 1876.

[*Before F. J. Marsden, Esq.*]

KASIM ALI, the serang of the *Argyll*, who was yesterday remanded to jail on the charges of importing and transporting fire arms, and concealing and offering them for sale, was re-arraigned this day, and committed for trial at the Sessions, the Magistrate, on the application of Mr. Wigley, Solicitor for the defence, ordering the accused to be enlarged on his signing a recoginsance for Rs. 1,000, and finding two sureties for Rs. 1,000 each.

CAPTAIN CULLEN, master of the river-steamer *Colgong*, was charged by the Port Commissioners, through their harbour-master, Mr. Baring, with having on the 7th ultimo, off No. 4 Jetty, steamed up the river during flood-tide with the steamer *Colgong*, which was then towing the flat Ganges, an act which was an offence under rule 3, Section 17, Act XXII. of 1855. The defendant admitted the charge, but endeavoured to justify his conduct by saying that Mr. Baring himself subsequently given him permission to steam up the river during flood-tide. In answer to this Mr. Baring said that, he might have given the permission on the ground as safety. The Magistrate thought that, on the defendant's own admission, it was quite clear that he had broken a port-rule; but, taking all the circumstances into consideration, His Worship was of opinion that the ends of justice would be satisfied if the defendant were warned and discharged. His Worships hoped, however, that the offence would not be repeated, as it would not be dealt with leniently. The defendant was accordingly discharged.

Selection.

THE BRAHMA SOMAJ.

THE leader of the Brahma Somaj has long ago taken his place among the remarkable men of his time and country. As a religious leader and reformer, he has held an acknowledged position for years. His name is familiar to all who know anything about India. Though he is not founder of the theistic church of this country, he has brought it into its present position, and its history for several years past may almost be said to be the history of the mind of Babu Keshub Chunder Sen. As its leader,—we may without offence say, as its prophet, his name is well known in Europe and America and at the English antipodes. We should probably be correct to say that his reputation is rather an English than an Indian reputation. Though as a prophet he is not without honor in his own country, and has devoted adherents and admirers in Calcutta and many parts of India, the work he has done and is still doing for his countrymen, is perhaps better appreciated, and himself more warmly admired, by liberal-minded Englishmen and Americans than by any except an earnest and enlightened few in India.

It is not our purpose to analyse the character, or estimate the real worth of this distinguished man. We hardly rank ourselves among his most ardent admirers. But we admire his eloquence, we respect his character, and we set a high value on his work. But while we continue to esteem the man, and to look on his religious developments and his position as the leader of the Theistic Church of India as significant, we see in those developments and that position characteristics that, if we read history aright, are proofs that the religious school of which he is the head is not fitted to endure. It lacks the element of permanence, a human centre round which to revolve. It has neither a God incarnate, nor a prophet whose name can stand beside that of the deity in the creed. With neither an incarnate God or nor a prophet claiming honors almost, if not altogether, divine, no religion has been able, and no religion will ever, we believe, be able, permanently and on a vast scale to affect humanity, without lapsing into idolatry. A great religion cannot be built up on faith and sentiment without a great human person with whom that faith and that sentiment are intimately associated, any more than a great religion can be established on a basis of pure reason. The religion of the Hebrews is not an exception Their God dwelt among them in the tabernacle and temple, and they had their mighty prophets with whom God spake face to face as a man speaks to a friend. He went before them to battle, he gave them corn and wine, or he slew them with pestilence. The laws of the state and the rules that regulated their daily life public and private, were the very words of God. Such a God, believed in with an intensity of faith such as characterized the best life of the Hebrew people, with so distinct a personality, and attributes that were the greatest attributes of humanity magnified and glorified, was an object of faith almost as concrete and human as when he afterwards descended among men as the "Word made flesh." Whenever his personality faded into indistinctness the people lapsed into idolatry. And when it finally withdrew into the dimness of later times, the old Hebrew religion as a great and significant spiritual power in the world gave place to Christianity. In all the other great religions of the world we see either one great overshadowing human character, whose name, and works, and words form the vital enduring power that gives it permanent influence, or else we see it degenerating into idolatry. Even Christianity with its human Saviour has at different times and in different countries, had its purity defiled with corruptions of a strongly idolatrous character, and it is not too much to say that from the destructive influence of these corruptions, and from the blows of Time, and chance, and change, as well as from the unfaithfulness of half believers and the attacks of infidels and philosophers Christianity has been preserved and has been enabled to retain possession of its best truths by the faith of those in all ages to whom the present existence of a living, human Christ was no more doubtful than their own. It is remarkable how many students of Christianity have lost sight of the truth, that its power as a religion, and as a regenerating social force in the world lies not in its theology, nor in its social and political principles; but in the perpetual presence, or let us say the faith of all the best Christians in the perpetual presence and help of a living, sympathizing, human redeemer. It is true that Christ was "the founder of a new society," it is true that "the new society was potentially a world-wide one, a vast democracy in which Jew and Roman, slave and freeman, rich and poor, were on a footing of absolute equality"; but this society is cemented and endowed with everlasting vitality only by the presence in it in all ages of the Man who makes "the whole world kin." Christianity is Christ. It is not his theology, his morality, nor the great principles which he laid at the basis of Christian Society, but himself that is the foundation and life of the Christian Church.

Now, the Theistic Church of India has no great human name and life, to which peoples and generations may bow in reverence, and it seems destined to pass into a religico-philosophic school of few adherents, which will speedily lose its individuality among other schools of modern religious thought; or to pass away as a transient ripple on the still surface of Hinduism produced by the presence and power of Christianity.

Among the signs that we can discern indicate that Keshub Chunder Sen's great work as the prophet of a new religion is [illegible] done, we may mention the eclectic character of his teaching and his strong desire for a certain universality that is evident in those of his utterances which have lately come under our notice. We have nothing at present to say against eclecticism as such, but no eclectic philosopher or teacher has ever built up an enduring fabric and probably never will. The Brahma teaching is becoming more eclectic in its character daily

It seems really to aim at gathering up all that is good in all the religions and gradually piecing together a robe of many colors as the wedding garment of the Theistic Church of India. Christ and Confucius, Buddha, and the Brahmin sages and poets, ancient pantheists and modern Intuitionists are laid under contribution. Till lately, indeed, the teaching of Christ occupied so prominent and so large a place in the Brahma teaching, and the leaning towards Christianity was so strongly marked that many were inclined to look on Brahmoism as almost Christianity. The fact that it was so, was at once its strength and weakness. It caused Englishmen to take great interest in the new Church: it gave it its position in the eye of the world; it gave it its power as a radical society; it gave it all that is best in its theology and its morality, but Christianity without Christ is a system without a centre, whose grand characteristic is instability, and it may be said with considerable confidence that an honest attempt at reformation of the Hindu religion without so general an adoption of the doctrines and the very words of the Christian religion, might have better stood the tests of time and circumstance than Brahmoism is likely to do. It has been observed by those who watch the developments of doctrine in the Brahma Church that, of late the leaning back towards Hinduism has been as marked as the leaning forward towards Christianity formerly was. When the charge is made, as it has been made by some, that the Brahmas are relapsing to Hinduism, it is stoutly and indignantly denied; but whatever may be the final goal towards which the youthful Church on which so many high hopes were based, is tending, the effort to Hinduise the Christian doctrines it has embraced, and the effort to modernise and rationalise (some might prefer to say spiritualise), the old Hindu doctrines and practices, are the great apparent forces now struggling within it. It had gone over almost to Christianity; but when men were nearly ready to call it a Christian Church, it retired to a new and somewhat strange position. It stood on a lofty perch whence it professed to survey all the extent of Christianity on the one side and Hinduism on the other; it claimed the right and the faculty of selecting from both systems all that was good, and rejecting what was erroneous; mean-while it refused to be called Christianity, and scarcely less indignantly disclaimed the name of Hinduism, and asserted for itself a position among the independent churches of the century, under the name it now loves—the Theistic Church of India. Few things have been more remarkable in it for a considerable time, but increasingly of late, than its dread of being confounded with Christianity. A consciousness of the extent of its obligation to Christianity, made it all the more sensitive of slights to its individuality, and practically the protest "Not Christianity" has been one of the most conspicuous mottoes inscribed on the Brahma Somaj. And in the attempt to show the world that it is not Christianity it has been driven to assimilate itself much more than formerly to Hinduism. For instance, when the charge became common that the Brahmas, while denying that they were Christians, were obliged the borrow the language of Christianity in which to utter their beliefs and sentiments; a strange effort became evident, and is very noticeable at the present time, to make use as largely as possible of Hindu phraseology. The endeavour has all the appearance of morbid energy, to find a Hindu phrase for a notion formerly expressed by a Christian one, the authority of a Hindu sage for a truth hitherto treated as Christian, or a truth foolishly supposed to be a Christian monopoly, strangely disguised but still recognisably present in the garb of some ancient Hindu parable, practice or ceremony. Already it is becoming no less necessary to prevent the world from confounding Brahmoism with Hinduism than it formerly was to prevent it from confounding it with Christianity. And accordingly a lofty impartiality is affected, and, as we have already said, not only the two great systems already mentioned are borrowed from, but a readiness to accept hints of truth and aids to devotion from any religion or system of philosophy of any time or nation is paraded whenever opportunity can be found. The eclecticism, it may be confessed, is more apparent than real, but it is real enough to exercise its characteristic weakening influences. The attempt to make a new religion by combining the best elements of several religions has been tried before, and it has been tried before in India, but always with distinguished failure. The new religion lives and prospers for a time it may be, while the individual or individuals who gave it vitality are alive or vividly remembered, but it cannot survive the lifetime of many generations. It gravitates slowly but surely towards one or other system whose integrity is greater than its own, until at last it completely loses its individuality. Careful students of Brahmoism will probably be inclined to conclude that it is no longer in danger of being swallowed up by Christianity, but will exist for a considerable time as a reformed society of Hindus, and will gradually become indistinguishable among other social and religious forces which are apparently at hand in India.—*Friend of India.*

ALBERT HALL.

PATRON.

His Honor the Lieutenant Governor of Bengal

COUNCIL.

Hon'ble Sir William Muir, K. C. S. I.—*President.*
Rajah Roma Nath Tagore Bahadur C. S. I.—*Vice-President.*
Hon'ble J. F. D. Inglis.
Hon'ble Ashley Eden, C. S. I.
Hon'ble H. Bell.
Archdeacon Baly.
Colonel H. E. L. Thuillier, C.S. I.
His Highness the Maharajah of Vizianagram.
Maharajah Kumar of Bettiah.
Hon'ble Rajah Narendra Krishna Bahadur.
Rajah Komul Krishna Bahadur.
Rajah Jotendro Mohun Tagore Bahadur.
Babu Digumber Mitter, C.S.I.
Dr. Rajendralala Mitra.
Hon'ble Nawab Ashgur Ali Bahadur, C. S. I.
Nawab Amir Ali Bahadur.
Moulvi Abdul Lotif Khan Bahadur.
Manockji Rustomji Esq.
Babu Keshub Chunder Sen.

SUBSCRIPTIONS.

The Hon'ble Sir Richard Temple ...	Rs.	200
His Highness Maharajah Holkar ...	„	8,000
His Highness Maharajah of Jeypore	„	5,000
His Highness Maharajah of Puttiah	„	2,500
His Highness Maharajah of Vizianagram ...	„	1,000
Maharajah Kumar of Bettiah ...	„	2,000
Rajah of Bhinga ...	„	1,000
Maharani Surnomoie, Cossim Bazar	„	1,000
Maharajah of Hutwa ...	„	500
Rajah Roma Nath Tagore Bahadur	„	250
Rajah Komul Krisna Bahadur ...	„	500
Rajah Jotendro Mohun Tagore ...	„	500
Hon'ble Rajah Narendra Krishna Bahadur ...	„	300
Babu Joykissen Mookerjee ...	„	250
Sirdar Dyal Singh ...	„	200
Babu Shama Churn Law ...	„	200
Hon'ble Sir William Muir ...	„	100
Hon'ble Ashley Eden ...	„	100
Dr. Mohendro Loll Sircar ...	„	100
Babu Gonendro Nath Tagore ...	„	100
Babu Ananda Mohun Bose ...	„	100
Babu Rajkissen Mookerjee ...	„	200
Babu Janoki Nath Mookerji ...	„	100
Hon'ble H. Bell ...	„	100
Babu Debendro Nath Bose ...	„	200

HAROLD & CO.,

3, DALHOUSIE SQUARE, CALCUTTA

HARMONIUMS.

...old and Co., call attention to their unequalled stock of rich-toned Harmoniums made especially for India.

FROM RS. 90 TO RS. 900 EACH.

All kinds of Musical Instruments of the best description are always kept in Stock.

ICE! ICE! ICE!

MADE IN FOUR MINUTES

THE PNEUMATIC ICE MACHINE

THIS IMPORTANT INVENTION IS CONSIDERED A BOON TO THOSE LIVING IN TROPICAL CLIMATES.

CAN BE WORKED BY THE MOST INEXPERIENCED HAND AND IS NOT LIABLE TO GET OUT OF ORDER.

From Rs. 175, each Machine complete.

MESSRS. ARLINGTON & CO.

AGENTS.

Printed and published by M. M. RUKHIT, at the INDIAN MIRROR PRESS, No. 16, College Square, for the Proprietor.

The Indian Mirror.

SUNDAY EDITION.

VOL. XV.] CALCUTTA, SUNDAY MAY, 21, 1876 { REGISTERED AT THE GENERAL POST OFFICE. } [NO. 120

CONTENTS.

NOTICE.

Letters and all other communications relating to the literary department of the Paper should be addressed to "The Editor."

All letters on the business of the Press should be addressed, and all remittance made payable to the Manager of the Paper. Particular attention is solicited to this notice.

Subscribers will be good enough to give prompt notice of any delay, or irregularity in delivery of the Paper

Editorial Notes

THE *Sadhan Kanan* was duly opened and consecrated yesterday. It is a neat, small garden, and seems well adapted to the object in view. Some of our missionary brethren are staying there at present for spiritual exercises, and prayers are held every morning in a suitable place under shady trees.

Now that the Albert Hall is an accomplished fact, it is desirable that public sympathy and aid should be secured towards the formation of the proposed public library in connection with it. Besides inviting subscriptions, which we hope will be freely given in so good a cause, the Committee should ask the European and Native public to present all useful books and periodicals they may spare. Authors also may be asked to contribute. There are many in England, who, we are assured, would be glad to co-operate and assist in forming a really good public library for the benefit of the Native community.

AMONG the children of Brahmos the *brata* system may be, and has been in some instances, successfully employed for their moral education. As a class they are now generally neglected, there being no system and no place for affording them that special Brahmo training which they need. We would never teach boys and girls dogmas. Even a theological catechism we would put out of their way. Simple moral instructions and practical discipline we recommend. Let them set apart particular days and weeks for giving food to the hungry and drink to the thirsty, for serving thier parents, brothers and sisters, and also for tending birds and animals. Their tender hearts would develop beautifully under such a system of specific culture.

THERE is something note-worthy in the services held now-a-days among advanced Brahmos in Calcutta. Silent meditation occupies a little more time than it used to do heretofore. The change has been brought about in the natural course of progress, and must be accepted as an evidence of the growing spirituality of our Church. It is to be hoped the Brahmos utilize the few minutes set apart for meditation in the best manner possible, and really enjoy the high privilege of "seeing" the Lord, and holding secret communion with Him in the inner sanctuary, though in the midst of their friends and brethren.

A CERTAIN Native Prince who is not a whit better than other Native Princes in intellect and morality, but a shade less amiable, has been cried up by all manner of people, officials generally, for "his military genius, and the drilling and disciplining of his army." And it is recommended that other Native Princes should be advised to go and do likewise. We should very much like to know of what earthly use is the army of a Native Prince except as a costly, and somewhat dangerous toy, for which his hard pressed people have to pay. Is it held, that in case of a real disaster to the country, these bejewelled, indolent, sensual Maharajahs could undertake a day's hard work, or suffer a day's privations in the actual field of battle?

WE are sincerely glad to read that the friends of the late Mr. Vishnu Shastri are going to do honour to his memory. A meeting was held in the Prarthana Samaj rooms with this object, and though no report of the proceedings has yet reached us, we have little doubt the meeting was numerously attended, and efficient steps would be taken to perpetuate the name of a man who, next to Pundit Vidyasagar, has done most for the cause of the remarriage of widows in India. Pundit Vishnu Shastri was in his way a promoter of the theistic movement also, and took considerable interest in the Prarthana Samaj. The advocates of widow marriage in Calcutta ought, under the leadership of Pundit Iswara Chunder Vidyasagar, to convene a public meeting to express sympathy with the friends of Mr. Vishnu Shastri in Bombay. They ought not to be indifferent to this proposal because we make it. We suggest it because the thing may not have occurred to them, and the importance of the character and labors of the deceased they may not be aware of.

THE cause of Native industry is a sacred cause. The idleness, poverty, and the attendant misery and crime so often found among the lower classes both in towns and villages, cannot be removed by any means except habits of regular, sustained, and remunerative labor, such as industrial occupations can foster. The improvement and elevation of the masses will remain a hopeless problem until some amelioration in their present condition is effected by raising them to circumstances favorable to greater independence and self-respect. Religion too so far as it means reformation, can have no hold upon the lower orders under the existing state of things. We therefore have great sympathy with the circular letter issued by the secretaries of the society for the encouragement of Native Industry at Ahmedabad, to all the promoters of this cause throughout the country. They want statistics from all quarters to prove that by the introduction of foreign and machine-made goods at cheap rates into the country, Native manufacture of various kinds have ceased to exist, and others are fast dying out, and "the rising generation of the people is highly embarrassed for want of employment, and the necessary means of support." We hope this information will be supplied to them by every one in possession of the facts.

MR. NOWROJI FURDONJI of Bombay, who is really an active and well-meaning old man, though somewhat garrulous, and incorrect at times in his facts and conclusions, has had a cruel snubbing from Sir Frank Souter, the Bombay Commissioner of Police. Mr. Nowroji who is a member of the local Town Council, had made an unfortunate statement before that body. He said that in cases of fire in the Native Town, the Police received gratification in the shape of large sums of money from owners of property to be persuaded to make an effective use of the fire-engines to put out the conflagration. Mr. Nowroji was challenged by the Police Commissioner to produce his facts and substantiate this statement, which he failed to do, somewhat plaintively observing "that reports like these, in his humble opinion, should not be set aside, but should be borne in mind, and their truths tested on future occasions of fire." Sir Frank Souter at this comes down dreadfully upon the Parsi gentleman, accuses him of falsehood, calumny, impudence, libel, and winds up by saying "that such false and discreditable statements can only be attributed to the unfortunate imaginations of a diseased mind." Mr. Nowroji certainly committed a serious indiscretion by saying what he did; but the Police Commissioner by the miserable ill-temper and scurrility in which he has freely indulged in his letter, has by no means exalted the dignity of his position, or proved the gentlemanliness of his manners. It would be impossible on occasions to substantiate certain charges against the Police which every one knows to be undoubtedly true. If every Police officer were to fly out at the least imputation against the body of men under him, as if the Police were too sacred a subject to be spoken about by ordinary mortals, there would never be any hope of improvement.

EVIDENTLY there is nothing new in recent attempts to ridicule away poverty and asceticism from the Brahmo Somaj, nor is there any doubt that our Church will survive these unworthy scoffings. The rich, the well-to-do and the refined have always hated with intense hate every form of poverty, and shunned the society of the poor mendicant, and the mean ascetic. If those among us who consent to walk barefooted through the streets during the anniversary procession, or live on purely vegetable diet, or play on the *mrindnga* and the *gopi jantra*, or cook their own food, are reviled and laughed at they need not complain. For have not the poor in spirit been always treated with contempt? And if these men be educated and respectable they must be prepared for more fierce attacks, for then their offence is grave. We only hope that such opposition coming from thoughtless men of the world, will, by divine grace, serve to increase a hundredfold that spirit of lowliness which has just commenced to grow in our midst. Poverty when enjoined by Providence, must be reverently cherished as a heavenly treasure, and blessed are they who so cherish it amid the smiles of heaven, though the world deride and persecute them! If Brahmo leaders give up their vow of humble living, and like fashionable gentlemen "eat, drink and be merry," offering only a five minutes' prayer in the morning, we shall look upon them as the worst enemies of the Brahmo Somaj. But if they sacrifice wealth, health and even life itself in a truly ascetic spirit, their sorrow shall be the joy of their country, and their death its life. It is the fashion of our critics to insinuate that the men who cook their own food waste their time and energy. The charge is a fabrication, and those who prefer it ought to be ashamed of their own culpable ignorance. The men against whom it is levelled, far from wasting their time make the best use of it. Perhaps, we ought to state the facts of the case in order to remove all misconception from the public mind. As a rule three quarters of an hour only is the time spent upon cooking, and during all this time texts from sacred books are read, expounded and discussed by some men in the company. Those who have been present at such readings will testify that they have derived some of the highest scriptural lessons and the most valuable spiritual benefits in their lives upon such occasions. Is this a waste of time? No. The only other charge which deserves notice is that of saintliness. We are assured that the idea of appearing Hindu saints never entered into the heads of Brahmo missionaries. Cooking one's own food, is doubtless an essentially Hindu idea; and by adopting it in its integrity, one may pass for a saint or at least a pious devotee among Hindus. But let the world know that as practised among a few Brahmos, the thing is carefully divested of all Hindu sanctity. They do their cooking for simplicity and privation's sake, and for the good of their community; but they take care that they get no credit for it, for their evening meals are cooked by others, and besides whatsoever is given by others, even by Mahomedan hands, they take without hesitation. Can there be merit or sanctity in such *mlecha* practices? Let it not be supposed that we advocate cooking as a Brahmo duty, we do not even recommend it as a penance. It has nothing in itself of a religious character. We say this emphatically. But if certain persons adopt it with a view to cultivate simplicity of habits, and set examples of self-denial, we see nothing wrong in the thing.

IS BRAHMOISM LIKELY TO STAND?

No, say the Christians, and the Hindus say no; and though this loud negative has been continually dinned in our ears for a long series of years, it has been found that our religion has survived every such wise prognostication of death. The *Friend of India* in a really thoughtful and able article, attempts to muster the leading arguments that have lately been hurled against our movement, and to show in an exhaustive manner that Brahmoism as a spiritual instrument of elevation and progress, will never succeed. We admire our contemporary's dispassionate style of criticism, and feel, therefore, the greater pleasure in entering the lists against him. We cannot have too much friction in controversies relating to religion, for, sure enough, every such contact will make truth burn the more vividly, and therefore the more beneficially for the world. We are not going to enter into detail, but shall merely say that our contemporary would have written more correctly, if he had contemplated our position as a Brahmo, and not as a Christian. Sympathy in all respects is the key to mutual appreciation; and if the *Freind* had only known what our trials are, what our stand-point, in reference to the prevalent religions of the world, consists in, and what the process is by which we endeavour to make our way to the sympathies of different sects, without pledging ourselves distinctively to any particular party or banner, he would have succeeded in forming a correct picture of the future of the Brahmo Somaj. The position which our contemporary has taken, is such as is naturally taken by every Christian. But we wonder how the *Friend*, having grasped the fact that Brahmoism is essentially eclectic, could have missed the very point which would have brought him at once to a correct estimate of what such a religion must aim at. To say that the Brahmo Somaj is eclectic and at the same time that it proceeds upon a careful course of calculation of the effects, which an occasional leaning towards a particular religion might produce in the public mind, seems to be inconsistent. If a creed is eclectic and is determined to seek, accept and honor truth, wherever obtained, it naturally follows that it will always scan the sayings of all the great prophets and pick out whatever is sterling metal in their lives and utterances. That Brahmoism has done this consistently through a long series of years, is what is frankly admitted by every member of that church. When it was necessary for us to examine the Christian scriptures, we were struck with the rich mine of gold that underlay this much-abused religion. It was a duty incumbent on us to proclaim the beauty of the Christian ethics, and to hold out its founder as the most charming and perfect embodiment of faith and charity hitherto realised. Our Christian friends, however, would not admit this. On the contrary, they accuse us of having gone a far way towards being converted, and having discovered that we had gone too far, of having retracted in the end. On this ground they account for our present supposed leaning towards Hinduism as a mere shift for convincing the world that our ways were always straight, and never diverged towards Christianity. That this is a mistake, is apparent to every Brahmo. The wonder is how our Christian friends could have come to such a conclusion. For our part we are disposed to trace it to a mere misunderstanding of the nature and principles of eclecticism. The same principle which led us to guage the depths of Christianity, leads us now to search for treasures on the vast field of Hinduism, and may lead us before long through the fiery mazes of Islam. We are simply amused when we hear people calling us by different names accordingly as we traverse one or the other of the various fields of human experiences in faith and wisdom. Our principle is so simple that we cannot understand why people so persistently misconstrue it. We can understand one reason for it, and it is to be found in the fact that our opponents have never been brought to see the possibility, not to say the efficiency, of eclecticism as the only medium of faith and redemption. Indeed, the *Friend of India* maintains that a creed without a "human centre" will never stand. "A prophet" or "a God incarnate," or even a "human centre," according to our contemporary, is the "element of permanence" in a creed. This proposition leads to another premises, namely, that Brahmoism has no such "prophet," or "God incarnate" or even a human centre," and this is followed by the inevitable conclusion that Brahmoism shall not stand. This argument, plausible enough, fails in a most essential point. Our contemporary's major requires to be modified. If he had stated that all creeds which have a human centre, have lasted for a long time and that Brahmoism, having no such centre to boast of, will, therefore, *probably* not last. He would have been more logical and more within the reach of reason. The fact is, that while history has proved that creeds in a supernatural shape have retained the hold of the human imagination for a pretty long period, it has not yet proved that a creed without that shape will not last for an indefinite time. The case of Sikhism which our contemporary quotes, is not appropriate, for every student of history knows that the Sikhs honor Guru Nanak as a God-sent and inspired "prophet." Within the circle of our own knowledge we discover no instance of a purely theistic church having been organized to meet the spiritual wants and aspirations of the world. We believe that christ's Church, as established by him, was an essentially theistic conception, disfigured subsequently, alas! by the morbid fancies and superstitions of the centuries that immediately followed the death of that "unique" man. If Christ's church had been developed according to his conception, the Brahmo Somaj would not have been a necessity of the world. As it is, our church is an experiment, the first of its kind, and history has yet to prove whether it will be a success, or a failure. If it is true that God is the only God, that no prophet, however, brilliant or holy, can, without blasphemy, be said to usurp the rights and functions of the Supreme Maker; if it is true that the God whom we worship is a merciful God, in whom the whole world can live and move and have its being, and that all our wisdom and virtue is a direct reflection from His face; if it is true that the gradual advance of science renders supernaturalism less probable—then it follows, as night follows the day, that a system which eliminates all errors, which satisfies all needs, and which holds out all hopes, is a necessity of the times, and its usefulness is evident. Such a religion is that held forth by the Brahmo Somaj; and of its ultimate success, no man is entitled to speak with confidence. It is a God-send to our country, and as such it ought to receive the appreciation of all who believe in a living Providence.

OUR FAITH AND OUR EXPERIENCES.

(Continued.)

EXPERIENCE teaches us that, if men have deep and firm faith in the living God they have all that is essential to salvation. If you can realize the Great Spirit as an encompassing reality who is with you always, in your uprising and down-sitting, sitting with you at home, and moving with you abroad, conversing with you and animating your very life and activity; if you can feel the encircling and vivifying presence of such a God, you will need no supplimentary aid of dogmas and doctrines to carry you safely through life's dangers and temptations. The entire economy of religious life with its round of diverse duties, its details of doctrine and discipline, its rules of devotion, and the history of divine dispensations, is certainly very large; but the seed is extremely small out of which it grows. As the mighty tree with its huge trunk and thousand branches, which spreading in all directions give shade and comfort to many, lies potentially in a small seed; so volumes of theology and ethics lie hidden in a mustard seed of faith in the living God. Plant this seed in the heart, and by proper culture will come out of it, in due season, tender foliage, beautiful flowers, and sitting under its widespread and shady branches, ye shall gather and taste the fruits of immortality now and for ever (Applause.) Verily there is no creed, no doctrine but God. He is all in all. To the believer He is every thing, scripture, doctrine, church, and salvation. Why call ye the Lord your Saviour? Is He not our salvation too? What is salvation, but to believe and live in God Almighty? In the highest theology of the true believer God and Heaven are convertible terms. It is true, he seeks light for his mind, love for his heart, and purity for his soul, but all these he finds in God. If we read God we have our scripture; if we live in Him we have joy and holiness and salvation. Who cares about a distant heaven apart from God? Fancy may paint it with rainbow colors, and adorn it with all conceivable beauty and sweetness, and thus make it altogether a blissful and romantic abode high above the clouds. To the stern eye of faith this bright picture of elysium is visionary, a pleasant dream, a splendid fiction, nothing more. The wishes, fancies, and aspirations of all who live in the flesh, however religious they may be, will always fondly look forward to a land of joy where all the pleasant objects and relationships of this life have been transferred. But the decrees of Heaven are not as men's wishes. Nor do the spiritually-minded covet a dream-land agreeable to the senses. They do not, as others do, pray to God for heaven hereafter; they pray to God for life in God, and deem any other heaven an impiety and a sacrilege. To live day and night in the Lord, with thoughts, feelings, and deeds, all centred in Him alone, that is what they seek as their heaven. Blessed are they whose souls always, and in all circumstances dwell lovingly in the Lord, for they dwell in heaven. Indeed, there is heaven here as well as on the other side of the grave. Even in the midst of the pressing activities of business there is heaven. Even in earthly places shines the light of heaven. Are you engaged in the ordinary duties of domestic life surrounded by your family and children? Are you working at the clerk's desk in a mercantile office? Are you inditing in the cabinet chamber elaborate minutes on complicated economic questions upon which hangs the fate of millions? There, even there you may feel around you an encompassing heaven, if the heart is with God. Wherever you may be if the soul dwells in the All-Soul, you are in heaven! Say not of heaven, it is lo! here, lo! there, for it is within. If you keep near your God you cannot be far from heaven, for your God is your heaven. You do not repair to heaven, there to meet the Heavenly Father, but wherever the Heavenly Father is there surely is heaven. And where is He not? Above, below, here, there and everywhere is He. I turn to the right, He is here; I turn to the left, lo! He is here. How real, how sweet this presence! How thrilling, how solemn and holy! I tell you, brethren, in all seriousness, the spirit of your Father encircles you as a holy and sweet presence. To be conscious of this is heaven. Cultivate in the depths of the heart this consciousness of a holy and loving Father and Friend encircling you by His arms, and you will feel as if you are in the Holy of holies, and you will have nothing left to desire here or hereafter. It cannot be that you, who trust in the Great God and hold communion with Him, have never seen heaven. The truth is, we have seen it now and then, but have forgotten it and dismissed it from our thoughts and aspirations. Men often realize heaven during prayer and communion, but they lose it as soon as they enter upon wordly avocations, and lay aside religion and God. If we could, by proper culture, always keep alive the consciousness of the in-dwelling spirit of God, and cherish it in all places and amid the varied duties of life, we would assuredly live altogether in heaven. Seek then, my friends, to realize this spiritual heaven as a present reality, by living entirely in the Spirit-God, and banish all illusory dreams of a distant paradise above the clouds. Believe that God is heaven, and seek heaven in God. Remember that he is a true believer who seeks no other heaven but God. How beautifully is the Hindu idea of a true devotee set forth in the *Sreemat Bhagvata*. There the Lord describes His own devoted desciple in language such as this:—"My devotee is satisfied with me, and to him all sides breathe heavenly sweetness; his heart has been surrendered to me and he desires nothing besides me. Even salvation he desires not, and even the heavens above he despises." Such is the character of one of one whose heart is in the Lord, and who loves Him with such singleness of aim as to disdain not only all the kingdoms of the earth but even the Kingdom of Heaven above. He rejoices in God always, his Saviour and his Salvation too.

Now my friends, I have held up before you the ideal of our simple faith, a faith not novel, not original, it is the oldest of all creeds, and the simplest of all creeds. We believe in the one Spirit-God, in life eternal and in duty, three doctrines which again are summed up in one fundamental doctrine, life in God. Such is our faith. What are our experiences?

The Interpreter

A RELIGIOUS teacher, however clear his instructions may be, is sure to bewilder his disciples now and then upon important questions. They will occasionally trouble him with requests to throw light upon what he has most lucidly treated several times. And he will often find to his intense mortification and disappointment that he has been misunderstood, and that opinions and inferences have been formed out of his teachings which are directly opposed to his creed. Hence he is often heard to say. "So long have I been with you and yet ye have not known me." The teacher may be with his disciples for fifty years, continually enlightening and guiding them, and yet they know him not. To understand him rightly and fully the follower must be as he is. "O Keseva," says Arjuna in the Gita III. 2, "thy words are ambiguous, and confound my intellect. Thou hast praised deeds sometimes, and sometimes thou hast extolled knowledge. Tell me clearly whether it is deeds that save man or knowledge." If during his life-time the teacher is so much misunderstood, how greatly must his teaching be misrepresented after his death!

IT is not they that occupy high places in the religious world who are really superior men. Those who move in the humbler walks of life are often found to be the best of men, though their virtuous deeds are not proclaimed ostentatiously from house tops. The difference between leaders and followers, between clergymen and laymen, must not be held to be identical with the difference between saints and sinners. The distribution of honors among men is purely conventional and arbitrary. Those whom men honor, are not always they whom the Lord honors. His judgment is not based upon human approbation. Let us always remember that "many that are first shall be last; and the last shall be first," in the kingdom of heaven.

IN all ages and countries the devout have honored sorrow as their friend and educator, and borne testimony to the fact that they owed much of their progress to the effects of suffering. The heart is purified by tribulation. There would have been few prophets and great men in the world had there been no suffering. What Bitahavya rishi says, Yogavashishtha, 120, applies to the experiences of many. "O Sorrow," he says," I sought and found God because thou didst inflame me. Therefore thou art my Guru. I am thy disciple. Again and again I bow before thee."

Telegraphic Intelligence

Reuter's Telegrams.

BANQUET IN HONOR OF THE PRINCE OF WALES AND HIS SPEECH.

LONDON, MAY 20.

The Banquet given in honor of the Prince of Wales' return from India by the Corporation City of London, came off last evening at Gildhall, and was a most brilliant affair. Covers had been laid for 500 guests. His Royal Highness replying to the toast of the evening said, he looked back to his visit to India with the greatest gratification, and although his stay in that country was unhappily only a short one, he had gathered much valuable knowledge. His reception by all classes had been of the kindest and most hospitable description, and his own feelings could not sufficiently thank the Native Princes and peoples of India for the manner of his reception. Indeed, the kindness of his reception had left a lasting impression on his memory, and he felt sure it was a sign that the Indian Empire was not disloyal to the Queen. In concluding his speech His Royal Highness made a complimentary allusion to the Native Troops. The guests, at a splendid ball, which followed in a grand pavilion, specially erected at Guildhall yard, numbered 3,000.

Devotional

O GOD, I will not hate the rich, nor will I hate the poor. Give me a heart that shall love and respect all classes of men, and be partial unto none. What have the rich done that I shall abuse and revile them, and think them unworthy of heaven! Riches and poverty are both thy gifts, and both must be honored. There is nothing impure in either. Whether therefore men be rich or poor, grant O Lord, that I may serve all alike as thy children, and therefore my masters.

TEACH me to hide my deeper life, O my Father, so that men may not see it. Let not what I show be a measure of what I am; but mercifully grant that far above the devotion and piety which others see in my outward life, may be the real goodness of my heart which thou alone canst give and which mortal eye can never see. The roots of godliness can never bear to be exposed; they dry up if exposed. Therefore O God, keep my true self concealed within me, for if men see and praise it it will wither away through pride and arrogance. How often have I lost my best possessions because of popular applause! Kind Saviour, whatsoever cannot bear the gaze of others, whatsoever is really good and pure and heavenly in me, do thou conceal in the depths of my heart.

The Brahmo Somaj

THERE will be collection in the Mandir this evening after service.

DURING the minister's absence from Calcutta Babu Protap Chunder Mozoomdar will continue to conduct service in the Mandir.

WE deeply regret to record the death of Babu Bhugwan Chunder Dey of Commilla. He devoted his latter days to devotion and asceticism.

THE Indian *Evangelical Review* for April, devotes a good many of its pages to the discussion of Brahmo questions. The spirit in which this is done is not so decidedly hostile in the present number as in preceding ones. Our contemporary takes considerable pains to dive into the depths of the *Yoga* and *Bhakti* agitation, and master our principles regarding the classification of devotees. But he candidly confesses that neither "the meaning nor the purpose of these developments seems exactly clear" to him, and in a sort of despair he is prone to accept "the bold declaration" of the *Bengal Christian Herald* that the whole thing is accounted for by "a scheme on the part of the Progressive Brahmos for conciliating Babu Devendra Nath Tagore." This really is the best part of the joke, and perhaps, our conservative friends will laugh as heartily over it, as the progressives do. The *Indian Evangelical Review* will perhaps do well not to repose too much confidence in the "bold" things which the *Bengal Christian Herald* takes pride in saying. If, as the reviewer himself says, "the most temperate and considerate men among the Bengali Christians disclaim the *Bengal Christian Herald*, which professes to be the organ of that community, should that paper be taken as a fit representative of Brahmo matters? We never in these columns take the least notice of what the Native converts who write the *Bengal Christian Herald* say about the Brahmo Somaj, because we feel their "bold declarations" are about equally impotent in doing harm or good to our cause.

Scientific

INDIAN subjects, says the London correspondent of the *Bombay Gazette*, are not wanting in the Royal Academy Exhibition to be opened on Monday. In the collection of sculpture there is a model of the bronze statue of Lord Lawrence, by T. Woolner, R. A., which is to be erected in front of Government House, Calcutta. The ex-Viceroy is here represented in civilian dress, and his face is beardless as it was when he was in India. There is, however, among the pictures Val Prinsep's portrait of his Lordship as he now looks. This is a full length painting of his Lordship in his official uniform, and has been executed by direction of the Marquis of Salisbury. It will be hung by and bye at Government House, Calcutta. Millais' portrait of Lord Lytton, painted since His Excellency's appointment as Viceroy, hangs in the principal room of the Academy, and is "on the line." The marble statue of the last new Parsi Baronet, Sir Cowasji Jehangier Readymoney, by Woolner, is placed near the colossal figure of Lord Lawrence in the Central Hall. There is also a portrait by F. Leighton, R. A., of Captain Burton, the traveller who is now in India, and another by Miss Starr, of Mrs. Henry S. King.

CAPTAIN H. HANNA, B. S. C., has, we learn, patented an invention for certain improvements in the construction of ships of war, by which the inventor claims to have made the hull proof against "shot, rain, or even Whitehead's fish torpedo." Captain Hanna has also, it appears, invented novelties in motive machinery, in steering, in bilge pumps, and in hydraulic hoists.

Gleanings

NATURE takes a higher aspect from places where good and memorable deeds have been done, and it lends to them a deeper charm. It is enriched with rarer sanctity, it sheds more blessed dew upon the spot where the hero struggled, or the martyr perished, or the righteous sleep. Palestine will always be a "Holy Land."

God's work is freedom. Freedom is dear to his heart. He wishes to make man's will free, and at the same time wishes it to be pure, majestic, and holy.

GENIUS is the accumulated wealth of our humanity,—its most intense development concentrated at one point, and then with clearer expression and with mysterious power shot back to us across the galvanic lines of thought and feeling.

IT is a great thing, when our Gethsemane hours come, when the cup of bitterness is pressed to our lips, and when we pray that it may pass away,—to feel that it is not fate, that it is not necessity, but divine love for good ends working upon us.

Latest News.

MR. VENCATASAWMY NAIDU, the well-known merchant of Madras, is still very unwell, though a good deal better than he was a fortnight ago. His medical advisers have recommended him a sea voyage, and as soon as he gains a little more strength and is able to leave his bed, Mr. Vencatasawmy Naidu will in all probability take another trip to England.

A MADRAS paper has good reason to believe that Sir Bartle Frere, Bart, has the reversion of the Bombay Governorship from the doubtful year when it will be Sir Philip Wodehouse's time to retire. As Sir Bartle Frere is over 60 there must be much uncertainty as to the outcome of this proposal.

MR. TASKER is appointed Government Solicitor, Madras.

ON Wednesday, April 26, Mr. Forsyth, member for Marylebone, brought forward his motion, in the House of Commons, for admitting women to the Parliamentary franchise. It was defeated by a majority of 87, the figures being 230 against 152.

THERE is no news of great importance as to the Eastern Question. Russia and Austria appear to be acting together harmoniously, and the former has interfered to prevent Turkey from proclaiming war against Montenegro.

IN the House of Commons there have been three short discussions on the question raised by Mr. Fawcett's motion for an address to Her Majesty, praying her not to take the Imperial title. Mr. Disraeli declined to give Mr. Fawcett any opportunity for bringing it forward, and Lord Hartington expressed his opinion that no good could come from its discussion.

IN the Passion Week the Queen's bounty was distributed in sums ranging from 5s. to 7s-6d., to 200 aged poor people, principally cripples or blind.

IT has been resolved to form a temperance association of duly qualified medical men in England.

IT is rumoured that the Duchess of Edinburgh has purchased a splendid villa at the mouth of the Neva, and has ordered French upholsterers to furnish it.

IN the House of Commons, on the 24th April, Mr. Fawcett requested the Prime Minister to facilitate the discussion of his motion for an address to the Crown upon the subject of the Royal Titles Bill. Mr. Disraeli said he had previously made an arrangement for the discussion of the motion, but it had not been taken advantage of by Mr. Fawcett, and in the present state of Government business he could not undertake to give up an evening for a debate upon a subject already decided. Mr. Fawcett then said he would alter the terms of his motion so as to convey a direct censure upon the Government, and would then repeat his question.

THE Lieutenant-Governor of Bengal will give a ball at the "Shrubbery," Darjiling, on the 24th, in honor of the anniversary of the birth-day of the Queen.

IT is said that a tour has been planned for the Prince of Wales in Australia and New Zealand to take place in 1878, so that H. R. H. may be able to say when he is called to the throne, that he has travelled over every portion of his vast Empire.

UNWARNED by the admonitions of the *Jame-Jamshed* and other conservative members of the Guzerathi Press, the *Rast Goftar* in its last week's issue advocates a swimming bath for Parsi ladies after the model set by the European community.

A NUMBER of packages, described as agricultural implements, and sent from Bombay to China, have been discovered by the Bombay Custom House authorities to be munitions of war.

THE Civil Service grievances have been before the General Committee of the Indian Council, and have been referred thence to the Finance Committee, who were to make their report after the Easter Holidays.

THE Queen invested Sir Bartle Frere at Windsor Castle with the Grand Cross of the Bath, and Lord Suffield with the Knight Commandership of the Bath.

FRANCE and Italy have notified that they adhere to Prince Gortschakoff's memorandum. England, however, refuses to join.

RANI RANMABAI'S late interviews with Lord Northbrook and Lord Lytton has not been fruitless. Her Highness is said to have received an increase of her allowance from Rs. 6,000 to Rs. 12,000 a year.

THE steamer *Karruck* which left Calcutta for Chittagong with a large number of passengers, among whom was Mr. Monomohun Ghose, Barrister-at-law, had grounded at D'apres shoals, about 50 miles off the mouth of the Chittagong river. All the passengers have been saved.

LORD and Lady Lytton will give a Ball at Peterhoff, Simla, on the 30th instant.

THE Honorable Nawab Syud Ashgar Ali Diler Jung and his son have left Calcutta for Simla, where they are expected to arrive to-day.

COUNT MUNSTER, the German, and Count Schouvaloff, the Russian Ambassadors, have returned to London from their respective capitals.

THE Persian Ambassador in Paris has written a letter to an English newspaper, denying that there is any intention on the part of his Government to contract a loan in Europe.

THE Amir of Bokhara has informed the Russian Government that Shere Ali Khan of Affghanistan has occupied Maimaneh.

THE Emperor of Russia will be accompanied on this year's journey to Ems by a numerous diplomatic and military suite. Prince Gortschakoff, Baron Domini, Herr von Hamburger, Count Alexander Adlerberg, Generals Potapoff, Rileyeff Voyekoff, and Soltikoff are mentioned in the Russian press.

MR. GLADSTONE has written a letter, denying the report that the assumption of the title of Empress had ever been proposed to him by the Queen during his tenure of office as Prime Minister.

IT is stated that the health of Valentine Baker, late Colonel in the army, has become so impaired during his imprisonment that serious apprehensions are entertained by his friends.

MR. RIVSDALE has been appointed Secretary to the Chief Commissioner of Assam.

THE Bombay Mint has been placed under the direct administration of the Government of India.

Calcutta.

THERE will be a Subscription Ball held at the Town Hall, on the 24th instant, in honor of Her Majesty's birth-day.

THE Northbrook Testimonial Fund is progressing. The Hon'ble Rajah Norendra Krishna Bahadur, Rajah Jotendro Mohun Tagore Bahadur, Babu Degumber Mittra, C. S. I., and Cower Grish Chunder Singh have each subscribed Rs. 1,000 to the Fund.

A PUBLIC meeting will be held at Barranagore to-day to consider the Mofussil Municipalities Bill.

JUDUNATH GANGULY who was charged with the wilful murder of a woman at Kalighat with whom he was intimate, has been convicted of culpable homicide not amounting to murder, and sentenced to 10 years' penal servitude. By the way, we notice another murder has occurred at Kalighat. Four men are implicated in this case. They are said to have murdered one Behary.

THE P. & O. Co.'s S. S. *Ceylon*, Commander, Julius Orman, arrived in Bombay harbour on Wednesday last, from Suez, with the English Mails of the 28th ult. on board. The following is the list of passengers :—

From Southampton.—Surgeon Fanand, Surgeon Pedroza, Surgeon Clarkson, Surgeon Parker, Mr. Williamson, Mr. O'Brien, Mrs. Clayton, Mr. Chadwick, Mrs. and Miss. Yardley, child and 2 infants, Mr. Elder, Mr. Newhouse, Mr. Spedding, Mr. and Mrs. Doyle, Mr. Boods, Mrs. O'Brien.

From Venice.—Col. Mrs. and Miss. Nicholetts, Mr. H. Johnston, Mr. N. Waslekar.

From Brindisi.—Col. Prendergast, Capt. and Mrs. Brooke and child, Mr. N. Moller, Capt. Kinloch, Capt. and Mrs. Thorburn, Mr. T. Reid, Mr. W. E. Marshall.

From Aden.—Lieut. P. Hockin, R. N., Sergt. Burton, 22 Deck. Natives.

ANOTHER case of false personation is now engaging the attention of the Magistrate of the Northern Division. The case is considered to be interesting from the manner in which the offence was discovered. There are three defendants in the case. The first is a *chukri-wala*, or receiver of stolen property; the second a Durwan; and the third, a police-informer. The last two only are in custody, the first having escaped. It appeared that the last two defendants went to one Sital Chandra Shaha, a money-lender of Cotton Street, and told him that they wanted Rs. 60 on the mortgage of a tiled hut, which was situated at 26, Brijo Dadal's Street, and was jointly owned by them and one Madhub. The money-lender said that he was willing to advance the amount, and a mortgage-deed was accordingly drawn upon stamp-paper. But before advancing the money he expressed a wish to see the house, and accordingly accompanied the defendants to the place. Arriving at the spot, the defendants pointed out to the *chukri-wala* as the person whose name was Madhab. The *chukri-wala*, who was seated at the gate, said that that was his name, and that he wished to mortgage the house. At this time, a woman living in the house, who knew the money-lender, asked him what had brought him there. The money-lender told her that he had come to see the house on the mortgage of which he was to advance Rs. 60 to Madhub and others. She said that Madhab was not at all in need of money, as he was himself a wealthy man. At this time the real Madhub made his appearance, and the *chukri-wala* seeing him, ran away. Madhub told the money-lender that he did not need any money, and that the house was his sole property. The two defendants were, before they could escape, arrested by Madhub and Sital, and taken to the Thana. After recording the evidence, the Magistrate remanded the case.

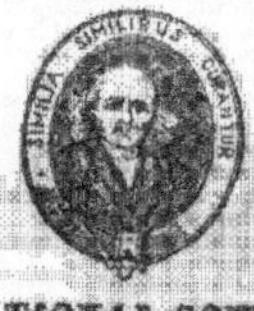

THE public meeting in Calcutta for an enquiry into the famine expenditure, will, we believe, be held on Saturday next.

Law

POLICE—MAY 20, 1876.

[*Before F. J. Marsden, Esq.*]

MR. L. BIBRA, an Engineer in the employ of the Calcutta Municipality, charged his cook with criminal misappropriation of Rs. 6-8. Mr. Bibra stated that his wife had given the defendant Rs. 6-8 on the night of the 10th instant to make bazar for the 11th, but that the defendant never returned. Upon this Mr. Bibra gave information to the Police, who arrested the defendant yesterday, and brought him to his master. The defendant said that he had received nothing from Mrs. Bibra, and that this charge was brought owing to his having left the service abruptly. The reason he assigned for leaving the service was this. Mrs. Bibra had given him Rs. 6 on the 9th to make bazar for the 10th. The cost of the purchases, however, came up to Rs. 8, and he accordingly asked her to pay him the amount in excess, Rs. 2. This she refused to pay, and he accordingly left the service without receiving any sum for making bazar for the following day. Mr. Bibra however, proved from the evidence of a bearer and a khidmatgar that the amount was paid to the defendant by Mrs. Bibra, she paying the Rs. 6 to him directly, and the eight annas through the bearer. In his defence the accused urged that he bore a good character, having been in the employ of Mr. Justice Macpherson, and now in the employ of Mr. Murray, Proprietor of a Boarding-house. The Magistrate, however, convicted and sentenced the accused to three months' rigorous imprisonment.

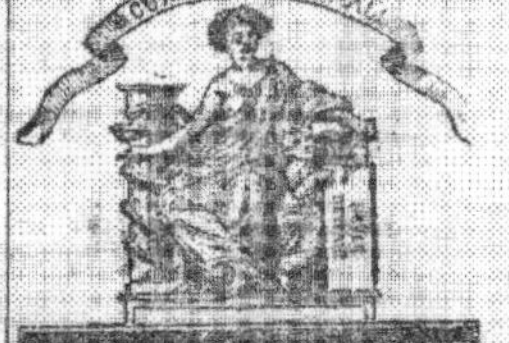

HAROLD & CO.,

3, DALHOUSIE SQUARE, CALCUTTA

HARMONIUMS.

Harold and Co., call attention to their unequalled stock of rich-toned Harmoniums made especially for India.

FROM RS. 90 TO RS. 900 EACH.

All kinds of Musical Instruments of the best description are always kept in Stock.

ICE! ICE! ICE!

MADE IN FOUR MINUTES

THE PNEUMATIC ICE MACHINE

THIS IMPORTANT INVENTION IS CONSIDERED A BOON TO THOSE LIVING IN TROPICAL CLIMATES.

CAN BE WORKED BY THE MOST INEXPERIENCED HAND AND IS NOT LIABLE TO GET OUT OF ORDER.

From Rs. 175, each Machine complete.

MESSRS. ARLINGTON & CO.

AGENTS.

BABU BASANTA KUMAR DUTTA,

HOMŒOPATHIC PRACTITIONER

No. 20, Sunker Holder's Lane, Aheritolah.

A FRESH INDENT OF

HOMŒOPATHIC

Medicines and other Requisities.
Have arrived from England.
Medicines, Boxes Books, Pamphlets ;
Absolute Alcohol ; Cholera-spirit Camphor.

SPECIAL REMEDIES

For Suppressed, Laborious and Difficult menses ; Leucorrhœa.

For Hysteria ; Spermatorrhœa ; Dysentery ; Diarrhœa ; Cholera.

For Asthma ; Pile ; Pain ; Sore and Diseases of the Children.

Ice, Lemonade, Soda and Tonic water always.

To be had at,
DATTA'S HOMŒOPATHIC LABORATORY,
No. 312, CHITPORE ROAD, BURTOLA, CALCUTTA
TERMS—CASH.
Price List can be had on application.

BABU RADHAKANTA GHOSH

HOMŒOPATHIC PRACTITIONER,

[illegible]

Is prastising here on moderate terms.

India General Steam Navigation Company, Ld.

SCHOENE, KILBURN & Co.—*Managing Agents.*

ASSAM LINE.

NOTICE.

Steamers leave Calcutta for Assam every Tuesday, Goalundo every Thursday and leave Dibrooghur downward every Saturday.

THE Str. "CHUNAR" will leave Calcutta for Assam on Tuesday, the 23rd instant.

Cargo will be received at the Company's Godowns, Nimtollah Ghat, until noon of Monday, the 22nd.

THE Str. "PATNA" will leave Goalundo for Assam on Thursday, the 25th instant.

Cargo will be received at the Company's Godowns, No. 4 Fairlie Palace, up till noon of Tuesday the 23rd.

Goods forwarded to Goalundo for this vessel will be chargeable with Railway Freight from Calcutta to Goalundo in addition to the regular Freight of this Company.

Passengers should leave for Goalundo by Train of Wednesday, the 24th.

CACHAR LINE NOTICE

REGULAR FORTNIGHTLY SERVICE.

Steamers now leave Calcutta for Cachar and Intermediate Stations every alternate Friday, and leave Cachar downward every alternate Sunday.

THE Str. "CALCUTTA" will leave Calcutta for Cachar on Friday, the 2nd June.

Cargo will be received at the Company's Godowns, Nimtollah Ghat, up till noon of Thursday the 1st proximo.

For further information regarding rates of Frieght or passage money, apply to.

4, FAIRLIE PALACE. G. J. SCOTT,
Calcutta, 29th May 1876. *Secretary.*

THACKER, SPINK AND CO.

MEDICAL AND SCIENTIFIC.

CLINICAL LECTURES on Diseases of the Urinary Organs, delivered at University College Hospital. By Sir Henry Thompson. Fourth Edition, large 8vo, cloth, Rs. 8-8.

The COMPLETE HANDBOOK of OBSTETRIC SURGERY, or, Short Rules of Practice in every Emergency, from the simplest to the most formidable operations, connected with the Science of Obstetricy. By Charles Clay, M. D. Third Edition, 8vo, cloth, Rs. [illegible]

The PRACTITIONER: A Journal of Therapeutics and Public Health. Edited by T. Lauder Brunton, [illegible] Vol. 15, [illegible] 8vo, cloth, Rs. 7-8.

ON CERTAIN ENDEMIC SKIN and other Diseases of India and Hot Climates generally. By Tilbury Fox, M.D., and T. Farquhar, M.D., including Notes, &c., with five plates, by H. V. Carter, M.D., published under the sanction of the Secretary of State for India in Council, 8vo., paper cover, Rs. 7-8.

DISEASES of MODERN LIFE. By Benjamin Ward Richardson, M. D., [illegible] F. R. S., cloth, 16mo, Rs. [illegible]

CHEMISTRY, ELECTRICITY, LIGHT. By J. H. Pepper, late Professor of Chemistry, and Hony. Director of the Royal Polytechnic Institution, with numerous Illustrations, cloth gilt, 12mo, Rs. 3-3.

The PHARMACOPŒIA of the Hospital for Diseases of the Throat, based on the British Pharmacopœia, 1867. Edited by Morell Mackenzie, M. D., Third Edition, small 8vo, cloth, Rs. 2-2.

A CLASS BOOK of CHEMISTRY, on the basis of the new system. By Edward L. Youmans, M. D., 8vo, cloth, Rs. 3-8.

A TEXT BOOK of ELECTRICITY in MEDICINE and SURGERY for the use of Students and Practitioners. By George Vivian Poore, M. D., 8vo, Rs. 6-2.

DOCTORS and PATIENTS ; or, Anecdotes of the Medical World and Curiosities of Medicine. By John Timbs, F. S. A., 8vo. cloth, Rs. 4-4.

A MANUAL of FAMILY MEDICINE for INDIA. By W. J. Moore. Published under the authority of the Government of India, 8vo. cloth, Rs. 6-2.

The USEFUL PLANTS of INDIA ; with Notices of their chief value in Commerce, Medicine, and the Arts. By Colonel Heber Drury. Second Edition, with additions and corrections, large 8vo. cloth, Rs. 5-6.

EXPERIMENTAL MECHANICS. A Course of Lectures delivered at the Royal College of Science for Ireland. By Robert Stowell Ball, M.A., with Illustrations, cloth gilt, Rs. 5-6.

YEAR-BOOK of FACTS in Science and the Arts, The ; 1876. Edited by Charles W. Vincent, F.R.S.E., F.C.S. (London) and Berlin, cloth gilt, 12mo, Rs. [illegible]

HISTORY AND TRAVELS.

The SEVENTH GREAT ORIENTAL MONARCHY or, The Geography, History, and Antiquities of the Sassanian or new Persian Empire. Collected and illustrated from Ancient and Modern sources. By George Rawlinson, M.A. Large 8vo, cloth, Rs. 20.

NEW HOMES for the OLD COUNTRY. A personal experience of the Political and Domestic Life, the Industries, and the Natural History of Australia and New Zealand. By George S. Baden Powell, with 40 Illustrations, large 8vo. cloth. Rs. 7-8.

HOMERIC SYNCHRONISM. An Inquiry into the Time and Place of Homer. By the Right Hon. W. E. Gladstone, M. P., cloth gilt, 16mo, Rs. 4-4.

NARRATIVES of the MISSION of GEORGE BOGLE to Thibet, and of the journey of Thomas Manning to Lhasa. Edited, with Notes, an Introduction, and Lives of Mr. Bogle and Mr. Manning. By Clements R. Markham, C. B., F. R. S., large 8vo. cloth, Rs. 15.

CHUNDER AND BROTHERS

25½ & 112 RADHA BAZAR, CALCUTTA.

TERMS,—Cash Strictly.

Printing Press, Paper and Materials

Columbian Super Royal size each unit	Rs.	506 0
" Royal " "	...	450 0
" Foolscap " "	...	275 0
" ½ Sheet Folio Post "	...	150 0
Albion Amateur to print [illegible] inch	...	70 0
Lithographic Printing Press, 15 inch	...	140 0
Copper plate do. do.	...	207 0
Iron Hot Press	...	180 0
[illegible] 30 inch	...	45 0
Ditto do. [illegible] inch	...	65 0
Roller and Frame, 6 inch	...	4 0
Do. do. 9 inch	...	5 0
Do. do. 12 inch	...	5 8
Expanding Roller Frame	...	8 0
[illegible]	...	27 0
[illegible]		
[illegible]		
[illegible]		
[illegible]		60 0
Chases [illegible]		
Springs for Albion Press.		
Paper Cutting Machines 15 inch	...	155 0
Shooting Sticks, brass tipped.		
Mallets Bagnals made.		
Card Board Cutting Machine	...	70 0

Also Celebrated Printing Inks

Of all [illegible] and Shades [illegible] Blue, Brown, Chocolate, [illegible] Purple, Red, Magenta, White and Yellow.—Price according to quality.

17th May 1876. CHUNDER & BROTHERS.

SMITH, STANISTREET & CO.

Pharmaceutical Chemists & Druggists

BY APPOINTMENT

To His Excellency the Right Hon'ble

LORD LYTTON, G.M.S.I.

Governor-General of India,

&c., &c.

SYRUP OF LACTATE OF IRON

Prepared from the original recipe. Lactate of Iron, in various forms of preparation, have been in use in France, and generally through the continent of Europe, for some years past, and is highly esteemed as one of the most valuable Chalybeate Tonic Remedies yet introduced. The Syrup, being the most agreeable as well as convenient form of administration is in most general use. It is a most valuable remedy in the following diseases ;—Chlorosis or Green Sickness, Leucorrhœa, Neuralgia, Enlargement of the Spleen, &c. In combination with quinine, it has also been very successfully used in the cure of Fever, while to persons of delicate constitution, enfeebled by disease it is invaluable. In bottles. Rs. 2 each.

SYRUP OF THE PHOSPHATE OF IRON Rs. 2 per bottle.

SYRUP OF PHOSPHATE OF IRON AND STRYCHNINE, Rs. 2 per bottle.

SYRUP OF PHOSPHATE OF IRON AND QUININE. Price Rs. 2-8 per bottle.

SYRUP OF PHOSPHATE OF IRON, QUININE AND STRYCHINE. (DR. ATKIN'S TRIPLE TONIC SYRUP,) Rs. 2-8 per bottle.

Smith, Stanistreet & Co.

Invite special attention to the following rates, the quality guaranteed as the best procurable :—

Pure Ærated Waters.

Made from Pure Water, obtained by the new process through the Patent Charcoal Filters.

				Re	As
Ærated plain (Trible Ærated), per doz.			...	0	12
Soda Water	ditto	"	...	0	12
Gingerade	ditto	"	...	1	4
Lemonade	ditto	"	...	1	4
Tonic (Quinine)	ditto	"	...	1	4

The Cash must be sent with the order to obtain advantage of the above rates.

Printing Materials.

MILLER AND RICHARD'S PRESSES, TYPES and all requisites always in Stock,

TERMS CASH.

EWING & CO.

Printed and published by M. M. RUKBIT, at the INDIAN MIRROR PRESS, No. 15, College Square, for the Proprietor.

The Indian Mirror.

SUNDAY EDITION.

VOL. XV.] CALCUTTA, SUNDAY MAY 28, 1876 { REGISTERED AT THE GENERAL POST OFFICE. } [No. 125

CONTENTS.

NOTICE.

Letters and all other communications relating to the literary department of the Paper should be addressed to "The Editor."

All letters on the business of the Press should be addressed, and all remittances made payable to the Manager of this Paper. Particular attention is solicited to this notice.

Subscribers will be good enough to give prompt notice of any delay, or irregularity in delivery of the Paper.

Editorial Notes

THE Rev. Nehemiah Goreh is about to proceed to England for a year.

THERE are three things which Roman Catholic asceticism recognises as essentials, poverty, chastity and obedience. Vaishnava asceticism forbids devotees who have renounced the world to approach three things,—a woman, a King and one's native city.

WE are deeply interested in the intellectual and moral advancement of the Mahomedan community, and therefore welcome with pleasure the *Madrasah Club Budget*, a monthly literary journal, published by the members of the Literary and Debating Club established in connection with the Calcutta Madrasah. In spite of imperfections, it promises to prove useful to those for whom it is intended, and deserves the utmost encouragement.

HIS HONOR the Lieutenant-Governor has kindly permitted the Committee of the new Science Association to commence operations immediately in the house in Bowbazar, purchased for them by Government, provided they fulfil the terms of His Honor's Minute within six months. We await with sincere interest and some degree of anxiety the evolution of a really feasible and efficient plan of promoting scientific education among Native youths. The Government has proved most liberal, the Rajahs and Zemindars have subscribed as generously. It now remains to be seen how such valuable contributions to the cause of science are taken advantage of by those for whom they are intended.

THE Ootterparah Hitakari Sabha continues to do its good work quietly and steadily. The thirteenth anniversary was celebrated at the house of the well-known Zemindar, Babu Rajkissen Mukerji, on Wednesday last. We regret that, owing perhaps to an accident, the most welcome feature of these anniversaries, namely a short Theistic prayer accompanied with hymns, was missed on the last occasion.

HABIT has been well described to be second nature. The Sultan of Turkey has been so accustomed to extravagance that though unable to pay his just debts, he still indulges in it. A Turkish official journal informs us that the other day a vast crowd of Turkish women, mostly widows, went to the Ministry of War and clamored for hours for pensions which have been long overdue. A day or two later, above a thousand workmen from Kadikeni beset the Ministry of Finance with shrieks and angry cries for their arrears. "While this is going on," adds the same journal, "we are coolly told that the Sultan, charmed by the big gun which Herr Krupp has presented to him, has ordered three more big guns at a cost of £25,000 per gun." Surely the condition of the Sultan calls for genuine pity. He is only going headlong into ruin. It is rather a remarkable fact that the two most important Mahomedan powers, the Governments of Turkey and Egypt, have at the same time got so heavily embarrassed in financial difficulties, through a course of reckless extravagance. Their sins will no doubt bring their own punishment.

WE have often been favored with words of sympathy and encouragement from appreciative men in England. But seldom do such words come from Englishmen in India. Hence it is that when they do come they are all the more valuable because unexpected. There are no doubt among the European community scattered in all parts of India, a few here and a few there, who really sympathize with our good cause and are even ready to help it. We can assure them that we greatly value their sympathy and good-will, and shall be delighted to hear any cheering words they may send. From a private letter lately received from a gentleman in upper India we extract the following, which will be read with interest by our Brahmo friends:—"I fully enter into all the grand and advanced views of the Brahmo Somaj for the good and welfare of mankind,—the only lasting ones, and to my mind the highest and most exalted notions men can grasp of his destiny here on earth. Your system is the very acme of civilization. It is a great pity the Brahmo Somaj is not more generally known. I have many friends in Australia (members of the Legislative Council) who are warm admirers of your faith. Why don't you send out missionaries? The good you would do, would be immense. I shall be proud to be of the smallest service to your good cause."

MISS SWAIN M. D., who left India a few days ago, has arrived in America; and the *Northern Christian Advocate*, an American journal, gives the following account of her work in this country:—"Miss Swain, M. D., after six years' service in India, has got home. She has superintended Bible readers in scores on scores of Zenanas; visited socially at these homes; taught and graduated in medicine a score or so of young Hindu women; established a Dispensary of great repute now among Natives and Europeans, and administered to ten thousand sick women and children, and talked to all of them as she could about a better balm than she had in her Materia Medica." Having said this much the Editor addresses his readers thus:—"Please don't crush out the little energy she may have left, nor make her 'talk himself to death' while informing home people about her work." Praise could not have been higher.—American energy, we must admit, is enormous; but the American way to estimate a Missionary's work is rather too business-like—too matter-of-fact to commend itself to our approval. A Missionary's work is to be measured not so much by its quantity as by its results.

WE are among those who dislike the distinction between missionaries and laymen. It is both unreasonable and harmful that a few should be allowed to constitute themselves a holy fraternity, and exact homage from masses sitting at their feet, as if sanctity, wisdom and devotion were all their birthright and their monopoly. Such invidious distinctions, more injurious if they are hereditary, dividing society into the heaven-born and the earth-born, and giving rise to all the evils of priest-craft, must be denounced by those who have read history. While setting our face, however, against the corruptions of the priestly ordinance, we cannot be blind to its moral necessity in the present state of society. If clergymen and missionaries have been found in some instances to abuse their trust and demoralize mankind, they are quite as necessary as a class as those trades and professions which are essential to the material security and welfare of society. The world may hate missionaries, but it is the world that causes such an order to grow at all. But for the world and its worldliness there would be no clergy. The missionary ordinance means nothing but *a protest against worldliness.* So long as men are worldly-minded and worship Mammon there must be missionaries. Nay their very covetousness, avarice, envy, dishonesty and lying create in society such a class as missionaries and preachers. If we could conceive a world which has ceased to be worldly and carnal, we may then and then only conceive the extinction of the missionary order. The remedy ceases to exist with the disease which calls it forth. Doctors and preachers exist by reason only of the existence of physical and moral diseases.

THEORY AND PRACTICE.

IN the autobiography of the late Mr. John Stuart Mill there is, we think, a passage in which that philosopher relates how he was taken to task on one occasion by his redoubtable father for venturing the oft-asserted expression that what is good in theory is not good in practice. And the elder Mill was surely right; for when a particular theory is once known or proved to be good, its very *goodness* or soundness implies that it is good for all practical purposes. To have a conviction is to say that the particular theory of which one is convinced, is such as can beneficially be applied to his own needs and acquirements. A good theory means one that is applicable to, and is co-extensive with, man's entire practical Nature; and in this sense, theory and practice are convertible terms. The greatest thinkers of the world have theorized and philosophized with the sole anxiety of offering a solution to the numerous wants of the human species. If they had known that their theories were so many sports of their imagination, fit to be published and laughed at by the world; if they had known that what they thought was not practicable, they would have ceased acting the role of philosophers and taken to more agreeable pursuits. A conviction of usefulness underlies every theory, and it is only when the world percieves that a particular theory answers all practical purposes that it calls it good. The most successful preachers and apostles are those that maintain this harmony between theory and practice; and those are the best teachers that illustrate by personal example what they preach. It will be an evil day for the world when this harmony is disturbed, when men theorize for the sake of pastime, and act as if they had no conviction, when hypocrisy is the order of the day and men divorce example from precept. Yet the prudence of the world prescribes a different philosophy. It has grown too sceptical of theories, hobbies and crotchets whenever in their usefulness, and in its supreme contempt for philosophy, has grown to an over-weaning confidence of its own wisdom and common sense. Surely the world is not to blame for this, for it is to the complete estrangement of example from theory as exemplified in the lives of many eminent thinkers and their disciples, that we are indebted for the havoc which this scepticism has committed among men's consciences. Conceive the demoralising effects of a body of religionists preaching one thing and practising another. We are ready to make every allowance for philosophers who depart from their doctrines. But to a religious disciple practice is life, and he who does not practise what he says, is a traitor to his cause. It is sad to think how the world's illogical maxim which we have been so long dwelling upon, otherwise called prudence, has compromised the best teachings of the best preachers. Consider the Sermon on the Mount, and has not the world with its usual patronizing smiles delivered itself of the opinion that what is embodied therein is too good to be practicable? Alas! that men's wickedness, which they have nick-named weakness, dallies in this way with even the most heavenly of things! It is a fact that such precious precepts which are left to us as a legacy that cannot be exchanged for the whole world with its treasures, have been allowed to be confined within the four corners of the sacred books, and are never permitted to influence men's lives. There have been philosophers, indeed, who have carried their crotchets to such a ridiculous extreme that they could not, in the name of common sense and reason, seriously practise what they professed. Bacon tells us of a philosopher who used to say that he considered life and death as just the same. "Why do you not then," said an opponent, "kill yourself?" "Because," he replied, "it is just the same." Such men are too ridiculous themselves to deserve our attention. There are others who are evidently mistaken, but who, nevertheless, do not think that they are so. These always deserve pity, and for ourselves we confess that we entertain also some respect for their conviction. We have to instance the Peculiar People who are now subjected to a series of harassing prosecutions in London for their belief in the sole-efficacy of prayer in the cure of bodily diseases. Gibbon mentions the Donatists of Africa who flourished in the middle of the fourth century, many of whom were so much possessed with the horror of life and the desire of martyrdom that they deemed it of little moment by what means, or by what hands, they perished. They would sometimes, we are told, rudely disturb the festivals and profane the temples of paganism with the design of being executed. They sometimes forced their way into the courts of justice and compelled the affrighted Judges to give orders for their immediate execution. Often they would stop travellers and oblige them to inflict the stroke of martyrdom by the promise of a reward, if they consented, and by the threat of instant death, if they refused to grant the favor. But these are mistaken men, and their views are apparent crotchets—at least the world detects their absurdities as soon as they are proclaimed. We are not speaking of these, but of views which the world has universally accepted as true and divine. We mean the precepts of Jesus, and the precepts of many religious devotees that strike a chord in every human soul. Why do men praise Christ, and yet do not venture to turn their left cheek when the right is smitten? Why do they serve God and mammon when only one is to be served? Why do men preach humility when they think it is true dignity to keep their heads erect? Why is it that Christians who show that their hearts are filled with the milk of Christian charity, still persist in inflicting kicks and blows upon the heathen Natives of India? Is not this discord between theory and practice—between righteous theory and unrighteous practice—the immediate cause of the failure of Christianity in this country? Verily, one must be a martyr to his conviction if he wishes to influence his fellow-men. Intellectual assent and practical dissent, or what is conveyed in a homely expression, mere prattle without practice, is the bane of the religious world. It is the foremost duty of the teacher to convince his disciples that what is good in theory, is invariably good in practice, or it is not good in theory at all. The Brahmo Somaj should especially direct its attention to this important formula, for there are evils which are already creeping into it, which directly tend to subvert the truth of the doctrine we allude to. We shall in our next try to expose these evils and show in what way its very existence depends upon the extinction of the fallacy which we have criticised in this article.

The Interpreter.

THE love of God disdains heaven, It finds its reward in itself. True love is its own reward. Heaven in the sense both of *nirvana* and a place of enjoyments, is strongly condemned in all Hindu scriptures that embody the gospel of love. The following striking passage is quoted from the *Bhakti-rasamrita Sindhu* :—"So long as that demon, the desire of heavenly pleasures and absorption reigns in the heart the joy of devout love is not realized."

CHRIST doubtless meant deep intercommunion when he said unto the Lord.—"Thou Father art in me, and I in thee." Here is a parallel passage in the *Gita*, which applies this important and beautiful principle to all devout children of the Lord :—"The band of devotees who worship me live in me and I live in them." Verily this consciousness of dwelling in God and God dwelling in us is heaven.

THAT blessed scene of Christ washing the feet of his disciples who would not like to see? "He riseth from supper, and laid aside his garments; and took a towel, and girded himself. After that he poureth water into a basin, and began to wash the disciples' feet, and to wipe them with the towel wherewith he was girded." John XIII 4 5. Most charming indeed is this picture of meekness and lowliness. Our weak and sinful hearts can hardly bear the thought of so great and heavenly a prohhet sitting like a servant at the feet of his disciples. May we hold up this example of humility and lowly service before us, that it may constantly rebuke our pride, and bring us down to the dust!

Provincial

DELHI.

[FROM OUR OWN CORRESPONDENT.]

The 20th May 1876.

BABU NOBIN CHUNDER ROY, delivered another lecture in Urdu, at the Delhi Society, on the "Progress of the Soul." The gathering was small as the day was stormy and cloudy. The zealous Pundit Bissen Nath, a member of the above Society, spoke a few words, after the lecture was over. He said :—"We should thank God that He out of his mercy sends such pious man amidst us for our spiritual welfare" &c., &c. Babu Nobin Chunder Roy requested the audience to convene a meeting where religious convesations might take place. Babu Nobin Chunder, though a layman, is doing much towards the propagation of Theism in the N. W. P. and the Punjab.

Correspondence.

AN EXPLANATION.

To the Editor of the *Indian Mirror*.

DEAR SIR,—With reference to your footnote on my letter which appeared in your issue of the 14th instant, I beg to state that it was no bad blood that impelled me to write, but a pure desire to combat an erroneous notion that was gaining ground in certain quarters. For months past, Babu Keshub Chunder Sen took to cooking his own food. As I love the Babu very much, I wish he would have spared himself the infliction. But as it was, the Babu was riding his hobby rather too hard, adding to it other curious forms of asceticism, as it was called, such as drinking water from an earthen glass and so forth. Now the Babu exercises a great influence, for good or for evil, over a pretty large circle of devoted and earnest admirers. He is born to be a fisher of men. Such is the charm of his countenance, such the power of his eloquence, such is the fervour of his devotion, such his broad intelligence, winning conversation and manners, that it seems, one has to go to him and be his bond-slave. It behoves the Babu to be very careful in what he says and does. I do not know whether the Babu gave any lecture on the value of the culinary art, but his followers were very much taken in by his example. Indeed, a respectable old Brahmo friend of mine gravely told me that cooking certainly does a great deal of good to the soul by repressing the lower nature. On my telling him that it causes pain and would make us ill, he replied that one cause of the longivity of our widows might be their devoti n to the duties of the Kitchen. My friend had not the least intention of acting the cook himself, but he would defend it tooth-and-nail for the simple reason that Keshub Babu was doing it. Men were alarmed at the new turn Keshub Babu was giving to Brahmo Dhurmo. Some uncharitable people went so far as to say that the Babu, with a view to teach parsimony to his missionaries, was setting them an example in his own person. I take the story for what it is worth. At any rate, it appeared to me that several well-meaning persons had imbibed a mistaken idea of purity, and that true religion was at peril. My surprise became great when I found the mania had reached (as I then thought) your editorial "we." I accordingly took my feeble pen to arrest the evil. I thought enquiry and doubt would arise, and open men's eyes to see things as they are, and that abler hands would come forward in the field.

Yours &c.,
A THEIST.

The 18th May 1876.

PRAYERFULNESS.

To the Editor of the *Indian Mirror*.

SIR,—A person who learns to love God, learns likewise to regard His affectionate children. As a layman he should never judge his religious preceptors, for the hatred which may accrue from such judgment will surely bring him his own ruin. The more he succeeds to pray fervently, the more he discovers the superiority and sincerity of his tutors; and the less he feels satisfied with his prayer, the less humble he grows. In consequence he claims his own superiority and dies. To be a first-class Brahmo he should always pray Him lovingly, tender his hearty thanks to Him for any happiness he enjoys, and to escape danger or any disaster he should now and then fathom the depth of his love towards God and His children.

The 19th May 1876. } Yours obediently,
S. C. D.

A REPLY TO AN ENQUIRY.

To the Editor of the *Indian Mirror*.

SIR,—Your correspondent "S" seems to think that Christ was wrong—indeed, his conduct is most unaccountable—in addressing his mother as "woman." It is for his special benefit that I write this letter. When Christ addressed Mary, his mother, as "woman," he wanted to put her in mind of his mission, he wanted to tell her that she was of the earth, earthy, and he was of heaven, and, above all, that the turning water into wine was something in which he and his father alone were concerned. Mary realized the force of the remark, and, saying unto the servants, "whatsoever he saith unto you, do it," kept quiet on that point. Besides this, it was a common mode address among the Jews of that time. I say *of that time* because I am not aware that the form of address question, is in vogue among the Jews of to-day.

Among the ancients "woman" was a term of respect, and was used in connection with *ladies of rank*. "S" will find the truth of my remark borne out by any ancient author, whose writings are still extant.

Yours &c.,
R.

The 18th May 1876.

The Brahmo Somaj

THE anniversary of the Konnaghur Brahmo Somaj takes place to-day. Babu Keshub Chunder Sen conducts service in the morning, and Babu Dijendra Nath Tagore in the evening.

THE anniversary service of the Gorifa Brahma Somaj takes place this morning. Babu Protap Chunder Mozumder conducted service.

ON the 20th instant, Saturday, the "Sadhan Kanan" was formally opened. The ceremony of consecration was short but impressive. In the course of the service the minister preached a short sermon on heaven being always and in all religions compared to a garden. During prayer he declared the ground consecrated, and asked the Lord to bless the water, the soil, the trees and plants, the flowers and fruits unto the good of all devotees who might use them. A procession was then formed and the guests moved towards the gate chanting the name of the Lord. The minister then uncovered the marble slab bearing the inscription "Sadhan Kanan," all present shouting with him *Brahma kripa-hi kevalam*" &c. The procession then traversed the garden chanting another hymn.

THE Ninth Anniversary of Salem Brahmo Samaj was celebrated on the evening of Tuesday the 11th April last, at the Mr. S. P. Narasimmulu Naidu.

Literary.

THE study of English is in future to be made obligatory in all the Marine Schools of Russia.

MR. A. C. LYALL, Agent to the Governor-General in Rajputana, is about to compile a Gazetteer of Rajputana.

MR. N. B. DENNYS, a Chinese scholar of some repute, has a volume in the press on "The Folk-Lore of China, and its Affinities with that of the Aryan and Semitic Races."

THE Editor of the *Calcutta Review* has taken a decided attitude against the author of the *Black Pamphlet*. He charges him with dishonesty.

MR. LAING MEASON has contributed an article on the "Indian Army" to the May number of *Fraser*.

YOUNG Lieutenant the Earl of Lord Mayo has just published an interesting book, entitled "A Narrative of Sports in Abyssinia; or the Mareb and Tackazzee." In this he recounts in a lively style his adventures in the fields of Abyssinia.

"KASHGAR, PAMIR AND THIBET" is the title of an article in the April number of the *Quarterly Review*.

AN article on "Lord Mayo's Indian Administration" appears in the same number of the *Edinburgh Review*.

MR. S. MCBEAN is the author of a work, just published, entitled *England, Palestine, Egypt, and India Connected by a Railway System*. It is, he says, "incumbent on us, as a nation, to resolve to carry out the entire length of line, at our own cost, from Scutari to Kurrachi, about 3,300 miles; and from Antioch to Ismailia, with branches to Damascus and Jerusalem, about 600 miles altogether." He looks forward to the day when trains will run from Calcutta to Pekin. But sixty millions is the money wanted for the construction of this Railway—a mere trifle.

THE late Lord Amberley's book on "Religious Belief" will shortly appear.

MISS COLENSO, daughter of the Bishop of Natal, is now publishing an interesting novel in the *Natal Colonist*.

M. RENAN contributes to the *Revue des Deux Mondes* of March 15, an article in which he describes the religious impressions of his earliest years. He speaks of himself as being still influenced by a faith which he no longer intellectually holds.

MESSRS. BLACKWOOD AND SONS announce the publication of a new work by the author of "The Battle of Dorking," entitled "The Dilemma."

Scientific

MR. A. MACPHERSON of Bombay will manufacture good burning gas from Native earth oil which, he asserts, will not only be considerably cheaper than the cost of the gas as at present supplied, but will also be of greater illuminating power. It has the further advantage of being non-explosive.

THE new disease, *Suraku Mariatha*, which has been raging in Madras, partakes much of the nature of Dengue. A patient first feels a sensation of tingling in the toes and soles of the feet very closely resembling what Englishmen commonly term 'pins and needles.' Shortly after this he experiences intense pain in the spinal column, and with this comes a sense of stiffness and weight in the whole of the body, accompanied by a dull heavy pain in the occipital region. Goat's dung, dried and powdered, and taken in small doses in a cup of water is said to be the best remedy.

THE authorities of South Kensington have opened a new room, expressly devoted to interesting art-treasures collected in Persia. The articles, consist of metal work, arms and armour, enamel on metal-gold and silver, personal ornaments, small objects in crystal, carvings in stone, books, manuscripts, paintings, woodwork, and papier mache, musical instruments; also specimens of silk, cotton, and woollen fabrics and embroideries, and a fine assortment of earthenware, wall tiles, and glass. The cases of glazed earthen-ware are likely to prove of great interest to collectors, who have had few like opportunities of familiarising their eyes with the rich and graceful designs and colors of Persian bowls, water bottles, and rice dishes. Some of the examples of glaze in blue, yellow, and green are quite fascinating in their gem-like purity and lustre. Over 700 specimens of pottery for the most part once in daily and hourly use among the Persians, serve to illustrate the elegant taste of that remarkable people, more especially their love of color. This feeling is no less manifest in the embroidery and needlework, in their depth, richness, and contrasts that startle by their intensity. An assortment of arms and armour ingeniously contrived and worked up to the completest finish, will attract the curious and informed in the art of war.

Latest News.

—ON the 4th May, in the House of Commons Mr. Fawcett gave notice that on the motion for going into Committee on the Indian Budget, he would move a resolution to the effect that, with the view of preventing further additions to the debt of India, especially having regard to the depreciation in the value of silver, no new works should be undertaken to necessitate the raising of fresh loans, and that the distinction in Budget estimates beewen ordinary and extraordinary expenditure should be discontinued.

—THE Poona Sarvajanik Sabha has called a public meeting to consider the steps that should be taken to present an address of congratulation to Her Majesty the Queen on Her Majesty's assumption of the title of Empress of India. The meeting has been called at the request of a large number of the Sirdars of the Deccan.

—SIR WILLIAM MUIR has accepted a seat in the Indian Council, and will leave India in November next. His service in this country has extended over 30 years. In him we shall lose a true friend of this country.

—As the Talukdars of Oudh were the first to suggest an Indian title for the Queen, the *Lucknow Times* suggests that they should present an address of congratulation to Her Majesty.

—AN Irishman at Lucknow is about to turn a Mahomedan.

—THE Duke of Buckingham, as a great *guest* of England, celebrated Her Majesty's Birth-day at Ootacamund, by giving an entertainment to all the local schools in the Hobart Park, which was followed by a grand display of fire-works in the evening.

—MR. RIVERS THOMPSON'S health is much improved. So Mr. Thompson has abandoned his intention of resigning the Chief Commissionership of British Burmah.

—WE are glad to hear that the Indian Legislation Bill is not likely to be passed during the present session of Parliament. Sir William Harcourt has given notice of his intention to oppose the passing of this Bill. The Bill, if passed, will complete "the reign of terror" in this country.

—THE house taken for Sir Salar Jung by the Duke of Sutherland, is at the corner of Hamilton Place, Piccadilly, and the rent is £1,400 for the season. It contains, says the *Bombay Gazette*, 40 rooms. The Nawab has been invited by the City of London to the Banquet in honor of the Prince of Wales' return, and will also visit Manchester on the invitation of the Chamber of Commerce.

—THERE is, says a London Correspondent, a disposition among two or three ex-Indians to raise a debate about the Bombay Revenue Jurisdiction Bill. The subject is being privately discussed with that object.

—MR. LOWE, says the *Home News*, having stated in a speech at East Retford that two Governments had successively declined to accede to a wish of Her Majesty's to introduce a bill, similar to the Titles Bill brought in by the present Government, Mr. Disraeli contradicted, on the authority of the Queen, in the House of Commons, on Tuesday, May 2, Mr. Lowe's assertion, and on Thursday, May 4, Mr. Lowe humbly apologised to Her Majesty from his place in Parliament for having adopted such calumnious gossip.

—THE London correspondent of the *Bombay Gazette* says:—"In connection with the Royal Titles proclamation, I may mention that it is currently stated you are to have a great demonstration over that document in India. I do not refer to any popular proceedings in regard to it, but to the official way in which it is to be made known to the people and the Princes of India. There is some talk here that when Lord Lytton begins his Durbars, this proclamation is to be made known with great pomp and circumstance."

—THE same correspondent says:—The salute given to Sir Salar Jung in Italy has bothered our authorities at home not a little. There is a strong feeling in certain high quarters that whatever guns Sir Salar Jung may be entitled to at home, the distinction of gunpowder should be limited to his native land. It will certainly jar against official feeling if the Prime Minister of a Foreign Prince is to recieve salutes in England, and notwithstanding the Italian precedent, I believe Sir Salar Jung will not be honored in that respect as he would wish. Italy, it should be remembered, rather likes to pay court to Eastern swells,—the Burmese mission and the Khedive's affairs, to wit.

—THE Prince of Wales is said to have declined to witness a bull-fight at Madrid, H. R. H. being the Patron of the Society for the Prevention of Cruelty to Animals, London. The London correspondent of the *Indian Daily News* asks:—"Was His Royal Highness, I wonder, not equally a patron of the Society for the Prevention of Cruelty to Animals when he witnessed the brutal wild-beast fight at Baroda?"

—DR MYLNE, the new Bishop of Bombay, is spoken of very highly.

—A PROFESSIONAL prisoner has been apprehended in the Central Provinces who by his own confession has been guilty of sixteen murders within the last four years. He is a Mahomedan. He spent eleven years and a quarter of his life in prison.

—THE success that has hitherto attended Major Sandeman's mission in Khelat, is attributed by a correspondent of the *Bombay Gazette* to money and coercion. It is apprehended the mission will eventually prove a bubble. The Khan of Khelat is represented to be a wicked man altogether.

—THE London correspondent of the *Englishman* observes that "feminine" fastness is increasing in England. Mr. Justice Hannan, in a late divorce case, remarked that there had of late years been a very marked change in the habits and manners of society, and that formerly woman would have shrunk from being seen with persons and at places in circumstances which were now thought nothing of. He spoke of the change with loathing. The advocates of female liberty in India should take note of the fact.

—LORD LYTTON granted private audiences, on Friday last, to the Maharajah of Jeypore, the Hon'ble Nawab Ashgar Ali Diler Jung of Calcutta, and to the Vakils of the Rajahs of Jhind and Nabha.

—THOUGH the advertisement of Lotteries have been ordered to be suppressed by Government, the results of some of the Derby sweeps are published. The first prize in the Umballa sweep is worth Rs. 41,000, the second Rs. 15,400 and the third, Rs. 5,100.

—THE assumption of the title of Empress of India by Her Majesty, is said to have given even the Beluch chieftains the greatest satisfaction.

—OUR Behar contemporary says that a portion of the redundant population of Behar will be drafted off to the Bhutan Dooars, where they will settle for good, being provided by Government with the necessary outfit for their colonial career.

—The Punjab Government has sanctioned an expenditure of about seven lacs in improving the water-supply of the city of Lahore, and an annual expenditure of Rs 20,000 for maintaining arrangements in working order.

—The effect of opening the Bolan Pass is said to have been to let loose a lot of hoards of Mussulman thieves to overrun India.

—The German Empress has paid a visit to the Queen, at Windsor Castle.

—*On dit* that Colonel Keatinge, the Chief Commissioner of Assam, is going on furlough, and that Mr. C. T. Buckland is to officiate as Chief Commissioner.

—On the 2nd May, Lord Selborne called attention, in the House of Lords, to the Royal Proclamation just issued, and expressed his opinion that its terms did not carry out the declared intention of the Government to limit the use of the title of Empress to India. The Lord Chancellor maintained that the engagement entered into by the Government had been completely fulfilled by the proclamation. On the same day several questions relating to the recent Royal Proclamation were put in the House of Commons and elicited replies from the Chancellor of the Exchequer and Mr. Disraeli, the latter explaining that it was intended that the new title should be used in military commissions.

—The Corporation of Dublin have used the title of Empress of India in an address of congratulation presented by them to Her Majesty on the safe return of the Prince of Wales from India.

—The Prince of Wales was designated the Emperor of India in the address presented to him by the Chelsea Vestry on his return from India.

—The attendance in the House of Commons when Sir George Balfour rose to speak, in the course of the debate on the Bengal famine, dwindled into only three, consisting of Mr. Eustace Smith, Lord George Hamilton and Mr. Grant Duff.

—It is much to be regretted that Mr. Disraeli has not kept faith with the British public in the matter of the Royal Proclamation. It was distinctly stated by him that the use of the title of "Empress of India" would be confined to India alone. Now the Proclamation, as issued, says that the addition of the Imperial style to the Royal titles shall be made "so far as conveniently may be on all occasions." There is a great deal of dissatisfaction in England in consequence. The effect of this bad faith on the part of the Premier, will, we are afraid, be worse still in India. England's honor is likely to suffer much in public estimation.

—The honor of G. C. S. Iship is said to have been conferred upon the Governors of Madras and Bombay for the accidental fact that they happened to be Governors of those Presidencies when the Prince of Wales visited India.

—The *Pioneer* hears that Mr. George Adams, the well-known London sculptor, has been consulting with the Master of the Mint, Bombay, about a new design for the rupee. This means, of course, that *Imperatrix Indiæ* is to be stamped on the Indian coinage.

—Mr. Nanabhai Haridas, LL. B., who has been appointed acting Judge of the Bombay High Court, in the room of Mr. Justice West, took charge of his office on Monday.

Calcutta.

At a public meeting, convened by the Indian League, at the Town Hall yesterday at 4½ P.M., for the purpose of presenting an address of congratulation to Her Majesty the Queen on her assumption of the title of "Empress of India," the Rev. K. M. Bannerji in the chair, the following resolutions were passed :—

Moved by Rajah Kamal Krishna Bahadur (by proxy), seconded by Prince Walla Gohur Shah, and supported by Babu Bhoyrub Chunder Bannerji. :—

I. That Her Majesty's assumption of the additional title of "Empress of India," formally defines the position of this country as constituting with its princes and people an integral member of the British Empire, openly exhibiting the British Crown as a visible and central object for the exercise of the national allegiance and loyalty, and thus drawing the people of India nearer to her throne than ever before, and the occasion is, therefore, well befitting an expression of national joy and satisfaction.

Moved by Babu Chunder Cumar Roy, seconded by Babu Anup Chand Mitter, and suported by Babu Amarendranath Chatterji :—

II. That an humble address of congratulation on the event mentioned in the 1st Resolution, be presented at the foot of the throne through the constitutional channels embodying the national joy and gratefulness on that event, and giving expression to those feelings of reverence and loyalty for Her Majesty's office and person and those hopes and aspirations for the future of India which the occaison is calculated to evoke.

Moved by Roy Shamasunker Chowdry Bahadur, seconded by Aushutosh Mullick, and supported by the Rev. Kally Churn Bannerji M. A :—

III. That the Council of the Indian League be requested to give effect to the preceding Resolutions asking the aid and co-operation of the following gentlemen : *viz*, H. H. the Maharajah of Burdwan, Rai Rajiblochan Rai Bahadur, Raja Baradakant Rai Bahadur, Babu Digamber Mitra C. S. I., Rajah Raj Krishna Sing Bahadur, of Susung, Dorgapur, Rajah Kumod Naryan Bhup Bahadur of Bisni, Rajah Kandepswar Bahadur of Assam, Rajah Kamal Krishna Bahadur, Rajah Luchmun Persad Gorgo Bahadur, Rajah Jogendra Nath Bahadur, Nawab Abdul Gunny, Moulvi Abdul Lutiff Khan Bahadur, Ray Luchmiput Sing Bahadur, Ray Dhunput Sing Bahadur, Babu Ananda Prasad Ray, and Babu Chunder Kumar Roy.

The Milman Memorial Fund amounts to Rs. 13,173.

Both a Parsi and a Chinese Dramatic Companies are giving performances in Calcutta.

We omitted to notice last week that some excitement had been caused in Calcutta by the Commissioner of Police prohibiting a Christian missionary from preaching by the side of the Course. We do not know why a Missionary should be prevented from preaching in a fashionable quarter of the city. Will the preaching defile the ears of "the fashion" of Calcutta.

The P. and O. Co.'s S. S. *Peshawur*, Commander G. A. White, arrived in Bombay harbour, on Tuesday last, from Suez with the English Mails of the 5th inst. on board. The following is the list of passengers :—

From Southampton.—Mrs. Onslow, Mrs. Madden and infant, Mrs. Baker, Mrs. Lazarus and ayah, Mr. Lazarus, Dr. Coombe, Capt. Kyle, Capt. and Mrs. Caldecott, 2 children and servant. Mr. Thomas, Mr. Macnaghton, Mr. Ware, Mr. Taylor, Mrs. Cope.

From Venice.—Col. and Mrs. Maude, Miss. Maude and servant, Rev. Mr. Stead, Mrs. Filgate, child and European and Native servant, Mr. T. Elliot, Mr. Hawkins.

From Brindisi.—Mr. Pierce, Mr. Sett, Dr. Anderson.

From Suez.—One Native.

From Aden.—Capt. A. R. Seton and servant, Mrs. Gallagher and 10 Natives.

THE BENGAL TEMPERANCE SOCIETY.

A meeting of the Executive Committee of the above Society, was held on the 13th instant, at 5 P. M., at the Albert Hall, the Rev. Mr. K. S. Macdonald, (one of the Vice-Presidents) being in the chair. The following amended rules were read and confirmed :—

I. That this Society is open to men of all classes. All persons above 15 years of age are eligible as members, provided they pay an annual subscription of not less than one Rupee and sign the printed declaration of the Society or otherwise make it clear that they are total abstainers, by signing or authorizing the Secretary to sign their names in a book of the Society kept for the purpose. The above rule does not preclude any person from signing the declaration.

II. That the members of this Society shall exercise all their influence severally and jointly to persuade their friends, relatives, dependants and others to abstain from the use of all wines and spirituous liquors except for *bona fide* medicinal purposes.

III. That the Society shall meet every three months or oftener, together with as many representatives of fraternities in and out of Calcutta as practicable.

IV. That the Executive Committee shall meet once a month or oftener, to deliberate on the general plan of operations and other matters connected with the Society ; and that the presence of six members shall form a quorum.

The following resolutions were then proposed and carried :—

I. That, on account of the resignation of Babu Ananda Mohun Bose M. A. as Secretary of Society, Babu Bhuban Mohun Sircar, the Assistant Secretary, be appointed as Secretary without an assistant.

II. That the following gentlemen be elected as members of the Executive Committee:—Babus Sasipada Bannerji, Bani Madhub De., M. A., Gurudass Bannerji M. A., Prannath Pundit, Nanda Krishna Bose M. A., Jogendro Nath Ghose and Chunder Nath Bose M. A.

III. That His Honor the Lieutenant-Governor of Bengal be requested to become the Patron of the Society.

IV. That printed sheets or pamphlets, containing extracts, translations or original productions in English, Bengali and Urdu languages demonstrative or illustrative of the evil effects of drinking, be distributed *gratis* or at very low prices, among all classes of the people and all other lawful and expedient means be taken for the purpose.

V. That efforts be made to revive the old fraternities, and organize new ones in different parts of Calcutta and also in the Mofussil for the furtherance of the Temperance Movement.

VI. That correspondence be opened with the various temperence organizations in this country as well as in England and America, and they be requested to co-operate with this Society and assist it with all their publications in the shape of tracts, journals, pamphlets &c.

VII. That the Government be applied to present the Society regularly with a copy of such of its publications as may be useful to this Society, and especially those connected with the administration of the Abkari.

VIII. That an active agency be organized to suppress public drunkenness, and to see the enforcement of the laws on all offences against the Abkari rules and regulations that may come to their knowledge, or which their searching enquiry may bring to light. In carrying their object the Society will have—

(1.) To secure the enforcement of existing laws tending to the repression of public drunkenness.

(2.) To seek improvement, legislation or admistration where either the one or the other is defective or inadequate.

(3.) To watch over the administration of the Abkari rules and regulations, and to represent to the proper authorities all instances of neglect, carelessness, irregularity or corruption.

(4.) To watch the conduct of the vendors and manufacturers of intoxicating drinks and drugs.

IX. That efforts to be made to establish a Temperance Library.

X. That a summary, of the proceedings of the Society from its commencement up to date, be printed and published.

NOTICE TO CORRESPONDENTS.

GIRINDRA MOHUN GUPTA sends us a complaint about obscene songs being sung at the Goldigi. He invites the attention of the Society for the Suppression of Public Obscenity to this evil. But that Society seems to have lost all vitality of late. What is its Honorary Secretary doing ?

NAGENDRA CHUNDER PALIT sends some particulars of a Police case in which a marriage in a Bengali family in Calcutta was attended by a serious affray. Some of the prisoners have been enlarged on bail, and a warraut have been issued for the apprehension of another. But the Police seem to be neglecting to arrest him.

TRUTH writes, though somewhat late in the day, as follows :—"On the eve of His Honor the Lieutenant-Governor's departure from Calcutta for the hills, Sir Richard Temple effected a very great social revolution which had baffled the attempts of the '*pioneers* of Indian Civilization,' I mean the missionaries, for a century The *elite* of Calcutta who raised so tremendous a howl against the Hon'ble Juggudanund Mukerji for his having tried the rather bold social experiment of admitting Englishmen into the Zenana, accepted, by a strange inconsistency, the hospitality of His Honor on board the *Rhotas*, and did not hesitate to partake of refreshments consisting of various sorts of sweetments &c., along with Mahomedans and Europeans for whom, of course, separate apartments were reserved, but on board the same ship. In this entertainment which was given publicly in broad daylight by Sir Richard Temple, and accepted by his guests, we understand the Editor of the *Hindu Patriot* and that of the *Amrita Bazar Patrika* who pretend to be the leaders of Hinduism, made themselves conspicuous by taking a very active part in it. Now these gentlemen were the first to condemn the Hon'ble Juggudanund for what he attempted and did in January last; and they were the first to evince an active interest in partaking of the hospitality of His Honor in broad daylight on board the *Rhotas*. The inconsistency of these gentlemen is a riddle to me, which I request you, Mr. Editor, to solve."

OUR UTTARASAN brings some most serious charges against the Tangail Police in the District of Mymensing; and calls for a public investigation into their conduct. He hopes His Honor the Lieutenant-Governor of Bengal will call upon the proper authorities to make this investigation.

R. seems to think that Mr. Fentiman and others are making an unnecessary fuss. He blames the Christian Missionaries, and writes thus :—" As matters now stand, I cannot but be heartily grieved. Some of the European Missionaries say, 'O, the kingdom of God cometh not with observation,' and then go *to sleep*. Others say, 'we have to write tracts and pamphlets, you know, and have hardly any time left for preaching to the common people,' and then *go out for a drive*. A third class say, 'we teach Philosophy, and cannot bother ourselves with the unlettered multitude,' and then *sit down to prattle with their little ones*. Such being the case, what *can* be done ? The very Missionaries are an obstacle to the preaching of the Gospel. That which passed at the last Missionary Conference should silence Mr. Fentiman once for ever."

R. complains of the mischief that is being done by a certain class of teachers in our public schools. He hopes that in the appointment of teachers, Government will take care to choose such men as are not ungodly. Ungodly teachers do an incalculable amount of harm. Lately a Head Master in charge of a Government School read an essay in which he pointed out that " animal life works like a machine, without the hand of God."

JUSTICE (Midnapore).—Your letter is libellous. Besides, it is not authenticated.

Law

POLICE—MAY 27, 1876.

[*Before F. J. Marsden, Esq.*]

MRS. MATILDA MACNAMARA, residing in Ensambagh Lane, applied for a summons against Mrs Olivia D'Rozario for having made use of abusive language towards her, and with having criminally intimidated her. The applicant stated that Inspector Ferris had called on the premises, where both she and the accused resided, with the view of ascertaining whether one Mr. Green resided there. She stated that she did not know, and, when asked by the Inspector to go and inform the people living on the upper floor, she stated that she was not on speaking terms with them, and desired him to make the inquiries himself. He accordingly went upstairs, and made the necessary inquiries. After he had gone, the accused blamed her for having told him things which she should not have said. She denied having said anything of the sort. Upon this the accused abused her in very foul language, and came down to her apartments with the object of assaulting her. The Magistrate granted the application.

Advertisments

ALBERT HALL.

PATRON.

His Honor the Lieutenant Governor of Bengal

COUNCIL.

Hon'ble Sir William Muir, K. C. S. I.—*President.*
Rajah Rama Nath Tagore Bahadur C. S. I.—*Vice-President.*
Hon'ble J. F. D. Inglis.
Hon'ble Ashley Eden, C. S. I.
Hon'ble H. Bell.
Archdeacon Baly.
Colonel H. E. L. Thuillier, C. S. I.
His Highness the Maharajah of Vizianagram.
Maharajah Kumar of Bettiah.
Hon'ble Rajah Narendra Krishna Bahadur.
Rajah Komul Krishna Bahadur.
Rajah Joteendro Mohun Tagore Bahadur.
Babu Digumbar Mitter, C. S. I.
Dr. Rajendralala Mitra.
Hon'ble Nawab Ashgar Ali Bahadur, C. S. I.
Nawab Amir Ali Bahadur.
Moulvi Abdul Latif Khan Bahadur.
Manockji Rustomji Esq.
Babu Keshub Chunder Sen.

SUBSCRIPTIONS.

The Hon'ble Sir Richard Temple ...	Rs.	200
His Highness Maharajah Holkar ...	"	8,000
His Highness Maharajah of Jeypore	"	5,000
His Highness Maharajah of Putiallah	"	2,500
His Highness Maharajah of Vizianagram ...	"	1,000
Maharajah Kumar of Bettiah ...	"	2,000
Rajah of Bhinga ...	"	1,000
Maharani Surnomoie, Cossim Bazar	"	1,000
Maharajah of Hutwa ...	"	500
Rajah Rama Nath Tagore Bahadur	"	200
Rajah Komul Kissen Bahadur ...	"	500
Rajah Joteendro Mohun Tagore ...	"	500
Hon'ble Rajah Narendra Krishna Bahadur ...	"	300
Babu Joykissen Mookerjee ...	"	250
Sirdar Dyal Singh ...	"	200
Babu Shama Churn Law ...	"	200
Hon'ble Sir William Muir ...	"	100
Hon'ble Ashley Eden ...	"	100
Dr. Mohendro Loll Sircar ...	"	100
Babu Goonendro Nath Tagore ...	"	100
Babu Ananda Mohun Bose ...	"	100
Babu Rajkissen Mookerjee ...	"	200
Babu Janoki Nath Mookerji ...	"	100
Hon'ble H. Bell ...	"	100
Babu Debendro Nath Bose ...	"	200

HAROLD & CO.,

3, DALHOUSIE SQUARE, CALCUTTA

HARMONIUMS.

Harold and Co., call attention to their unequalled stock of rich-toned Harmoniums made especially for India.

FROM RS. 90 TO RS. 900 EACH.

All kinds of Musical Instruments of the best description are always kept in Stock.

ICE! ICE! ICE!

MADE IN FOUR MINUTES

THE PNEUMATIC ICE MACHINE

THIS IMPORTANT INVENTION IS CONSIDERED A BOON TO THOSE LIVING IN TROPICAL CLIMATES.

CAN BE WORKED BY THE MOST INEXPERIENCED HAND AND IS NOT LIABLE TO GET OUT OF ORDER.

From Rs. 175, each Machine complete.

MESSRS. ARLINGTON & CO.

AGENTS.

CHUNDER AND BROTHERS

25½ & 112 RADHA BAZAR, CALCUTTA.

TERMS,—Cash Strictly.

Printing Press, Paper and Materials

		Rs.	
Columbian Super Royal size each sett	...	500	0
" Royal " "	...	450	0
" Foolscap " "	...	275	0
" ½ Sheet Folio Post "	...	150	0
Albion Amateur to print 7½×5½ inch	...	76	0
Lithographic Printing Press, 13 inch	..	140	0
Copperplate do. do.	...	200	0
Inunlist Press	...	180	0
Roller Moulds, Zinc, 36 inch	...	45	0
Ditto do. Iron, 36 inch	...	65	0
Roller and Frame, 6 inch	...	4	0
Do. do. 9 inch	...	5	0
Do. do. 12 inch	...	5	8
Expanding Roller Frame	...	8	0
Brass Rule & [illegible]	...	22	0
Brass Rules, [illegible] plain.			
Do. Waved dotted &c.			
Composing Sticks best gun metal			
English Goal Mould	...	65	0
Chases various sizes.			
Springs for Albion Press,			
Paper Cutting Machines 18 inch	...	100	0
Shooting Sticks, brass tipped.			
Mallets English made.			
Card Board Cutting Machine	...	70	0

Millthorp's Celebrated Printing Inks

Of all colors and Shades,—Black, Blue, Brown, Chocolate, Green, Lilac, Mauve, Pink, Purple, Red, Magenta, White and Yellow.—Price according to

May 1876. CHUNDER & BROTHERS.

SMITH, STANISTREET & CO.

Pharmaceutical Chemists & Druggists

BY APPOINTMENT

T His Excellency the Right Hon'ble LORD LYTTON, G.M.S.I.

Governor-General of India,

&c., &c.

SYRUP OF LACTATE OF IRON

Prepared from the original receipe. Lactate of Iron, in various forms of preparation, have been in use in France, and generally through the continent of Europe, for some years past, and is highly esteemed as one of the most valuable Chalybeate Tonic Remedies yet introduced. The Syrup, being the most agreeable as well as convenient form of administration is in most general use. It is a most valuable remedy in the following diseases:—Chlorosis or Green Sickness, Leucorrhœa, Neuralgia, Enlargement of the Spleen, &c. In combination with quinine, it has also been very successfully used in the cure of Fever, while to persons of delicate constitution, enfeebled by disease it is invaluable. In bottles. Rs. 2 each.

SYRUP OF THE PHOSPHATE OF IRON Rs. 2 per bottle.

SYRUP OF PHOSPHATE OF IRON AND STRYCHNINE, Rs. 2 per bottle.

SYRUP OF PHOSPHATE OF IRON AND QUININE. Price Rs. 2-8 per bottle.

SYRUP OF PHOSPHATE OF IRON, QUININE AND STRYCHINE (DR. ATKIN'S TRIPLE TONIC SYRUP,) Rs. 2-8 per bottle.

Smith, Stanistreet & Co.

Invite special attention to the following rates, the quality guaranteed as the best procurable:—

Pure Ærated Waters.

Made from Pure Water, obtained by the new process through the Patent Charcoal Filters.

			Rs.	As.
Ærated plain (Trible Ærated), per doz.		...	0	12
Soda Water	ditto	" ...	0	12
Gingerade	ditto	" ...	1	4
Lemonade	ditto	" ...	1	4
Tonic (Quinine)	ditto	" ...	1	4

The *Cash* must be sent with the order to obtain advantage of the above rates.

Printing Materials.

MILLER AND RICHARD'S PRESSES, TYPES and all requisites always in Stock,

TERMS CASH.

EWING & CO.

BURAL BROTHERS.

[ESTABLISHED IN 1870 A.D.]

JEWELLERS, GOLD AND SILVER-SMITHS AND WATCH-MAKERS,

BY APPOINTMENT

TO

His Excellency the Viceroy and Governor-General of India

AND

HIS HIGHNESS THE MAHARAJAH ADHIRAJ OF BURDWAN,

BURAL BROTHERS,

[illegible] Street.

BABU BASANTA KUMAR DUTTA,

HOMŒOPATHIC PRACTITIONER

No. 20, Sunker Halder's Lane, Aheritolah.

A FRESH INDENT OF

HOMŒOPATHIC

Medicines and other Requisities,
Have arrived from England.
Medicines, Boxes Books, Pamphlets;
Absolute Alcohol; Cholera-spirit Camphor.
SPECIAL REMEDIES.

For Suppressed, Laborious and Difficult menses; Leucorrhœa.

For Hysteria; Spermatorrhœa; Dysentery; Diarrhœa; Cholera.

For Asthma; Pile; Pain; Sore and Diseases of the Children.

Ice, Lemonade, Soda and Tonic water always.

To be had at

DATTA'S HOMŒOPATHIC LABORATORY,

No. 312, CHITPORE ROAD, BURTOLA, CALCUTTA

TERMS—CASH.

☞ Price List can be had on application.

THE BYABASAYI

(ব্যবসায়ী)

A MONTHLY VERNACULAR JOURNAL

of

AGRICULTURE, MANUFACTURE AND COMMERCE.

To combine the best features of the *Indian Agriculturist* and the *Statistical Reporter*, and to contain trust-worthy information, and suggestions of improvement of indigenous Agriculture, Arts and Manufacture. To be contributed by men who have special knowledge in these subjects. The *Byabasayi* will supply a long felt desideratum, and will be pre-eminently the journal for Landlords, Tenants and Merchants of Bengal. The annual subscription payble in advance is 2 rupees, exclusive of postage. Gentlemen desirous of subscribing for the paper are requested to communicate with the Editor,

SRINATH DUTT.

15, College Square, Calcutta.

THACKER, SPINK AND CO.

MEDICAL AND SCIENTIFIC.

CLINICAL LECTURES on Diseases of the Urinary Organs, delivered at University College Hospital. By Sir Henry Thompson. Fourth Edition, large 8vo. cloth, Rs. 8-8.

The COMPLETE HAND-BOOK of OBSTETRIC SURGERY; or, Short Rules of Practice in every Emergency, from the simplest to the most formidable operations, connected with the Science of Obstetricy. By Charles Clay, M. D. Third Edition, 8vo. cloth, Rs. 4-10.

The PRACTITIONER. A Journal of Therapeutics and Public Health. Edited by T. Lauder Brunton, [illegible] July to December, large 8vo. [illegible] Rs. 7-8.

On CERTAIN ENDEMIC SKIN and other Diseases of India and Hot Climates generally. By Tilbury Fox, M.D., and T. Farquhar, M.D., including Notes &c., with five plates, by H. V. Carter, M.D., published under the sanction of the Secretary of State for India in Council, 8vo., paper cover, Rs. 7-8.

DISEASES of MODERN LIFE. By Benjamin Ward Richardson, M. D., M. A., F. R. S., cloth, 16mo., Rs. 8-14.

CHEMISTRY, ELECTRICITY, LIGHT. By J. H. Pepper, late Professor of Chemistry, and Hony. Director of the Royal Polytechnic Institution, with numerous Illustrations, cloth gilt, 12mo., Rs. 3-8.

The PHARMACOPŒIA of the Hospital for Diseases of the Throat, based on the British Pharmacopœia, 1867. Edited by Morell Mackenzie, M. D. Third Edition, small 8vo. cloth, Rs. 2-2.

A CLASS BOOK of CHEMISTRY, on the basis of the new system. By Edward L. Youmans, M. D., 8vo. cloth, Rs. 3-8.

A TEXT BOOK of ELECTRICITY in MEDICINE and SURGERY for the use of Students and Practitioners. By George Vivian Poore, M. D., 8vo., Rs. 8-2.

DOCTORS and PATIENTS; or, Anecdotes of the Medical World and Curiosities of Medicine. By John Timbs, F. S. A., 8vo. cloth, Rs. 4-4.

A MANUAL of FAMILY MEDICINE for INDIA. By W. J. Moore. Published under the authority of the Government of India, 8vo. cloth, Rs. 6-2.

The USEFUL PLANTS of INDIA; with Notices of their chief value in Commerce, Medicine, and the Arts. By Colonel Heber Drury. Second Edition, with additions and corrections, large 8vo. cloth, Rs. 5-6.

EXPERIMENTAL MECHANICS. A Course of Lectures delivered at the Royal College of Science for Ireland. By Robert Stowell Ball, M.A., with Illustrations, cloth gilt., Rs. 3-6.

YEAR-BOOK of FACTS in Science and the Arts, The; 1875. Edited by Charles W. Vincent, F.R.S.E., F.C.S. (London) and Berlin, cloth gilt, 12mo., Rs. 2-8.

HISTORY AND TRAVELS.

The SEVENTH GREAT ORIENTAL MONARCHY or, The Geography, History, and Antiquities of the Sassanian or new Persian Empire., Collected and illustrated from Ancient and Modern sources. By George Rawlinson, M.A. Large 8vo. cloth, Rs. 20.

NEW HOMES for the OLD COUNTRY. A personal experience of the Political and Domestic Life, the Industries, and the Natural History of Australia and New Zealand. By George S. Baden Powell, with 68 Illustrations, large 8vo. cloth, Rs. 7-8.

HOMERIC SYNCHRONISM. An Inquiry into the Time and Place of Homer. By the Right Hon. W. E. Gladstone, M. P., cloth gilt, 16mo., Rs. 4-4.

NARRATIVES of the MISSION of GEORGE BOGLE to Thibet, and of the journey of Thomas Manning to Lhasa. Edited, with Notes, an Introduction, and Lives of Mr. Bogle and Mr. Manning. By Clements R. Markham, C. B., F. R. S., large 8vo. cloth, Rs. 15.

Printed and published by M. M. RUKHIT, at the INDIAN MIRROR PRESS, No. 15, College Square, for the Proprietor.

The Indian Mirror.

SUNDAY EDITION.

VOL. XV.] CALCUTTA, SUNDAY JUNE, 4, 1876 {REGISTERED AT THE GENERAL POST OFFICE.} [NO. 131

CONTENTS.

NOTICE.

All letters and communications relating to the literary department of the Paper should be addressed to the Editor. All other letters should be addressed to the Manager, to whom all remittances should be made payable.

Subscribers will be good enough to bring to the notice of the Manager any delay or irregularity in the delivery of the Paper.

Editorial Notes

THERE is evidently room for another Unitarian newspaper in England. The *Inquirer* and the *Unitarian Herald* are good in their way, but it cannot be said they represent all sections of Unitarian Society. The Rev. Mr. Spears, late Secretary to the British and Foreign Unitarian Association, is going to publish another weekly newspaper to be called "The Christian Life." "Several gentlemen of literary ability and high character," we are told in the prospectus, "have informed that their help may be counted upon." We wish the new undertaking every success. Mr. Spears has energy and resources enough to make it prosperous in every way.

WE are glad to find the editor of the *Friend of India* bears generous testimony to the educational progress which Brahmo ladies are making in connection with the Native Ladies' Normal School. Our contemporary has seen a long English letter, descriptive of a tour, which a young lady belonging to that institution wrote to a friend, and gives it as his opinion that the letter displays "a high degree of intelligence, and a facility for English composition which is rather above the average to be met with in the advanced classes of an English boarding school." We thank the *Friend of India* for his very flattering estimate, and though, we believe, Brahmo ladies are by no means making as much progress as they should, considering the advantages they enjoy, it is some comfort to find that the outside public sympathize with what little they *are doing*.

THERE is divinity in a genuine smile. It is God's choicest blessing to the human face, the only one that distinguishes it from the countenance of the brute. The deepest and purest feelings of the heart find their silent utterance in a smile. Its language the child understands, the savage understands, even some of the inferior animals understand. A smile sometimes gives an assurance, a consolation, which the most eloquent words fail to convey. A smile is an index to the man. You can often easily make out the character of a man by the way in which he smiles. The man who smiles not is an anomaly, one ought not to approach him, there is no knowing what he is. It is the sacred duty of everyone to smile when he can, even to smile with an effort. It is the duty of all men to create around them the genial atmosphere of smiles.

CANON LIDDON, considered by some to be the ablest and most eloquent of High Church divines, has been instructing his congregation in St. Paul's Cathedral on the nature and privileges of the Devil. His position seems to be that virtue and good men and Jesus Christ would not be complete without a Personal Devil for them all to fight and conquer. The bright side of religion is not bright enough without the dark background cast by the shadow of the evil one. This position is certainly artistic, and reduces the whole providence of the world into a certain school of painting that produces the greatest effect by mixing together only a sufficient proportion of black and white. Canon Liddon is of opinion that the Devil is not omnipresent, and as to omnisience Satan is very far from possessing that quality. We should really like to know the exact pretentions of the Evil One on these matters, seeing that he is often credited with more than is honestly his due.

MR. JOHN BRIGHT does not seem to be the champion of women. Just as Mr. Gladstone inspite of his towering genius ecclesiastical as well as political, is a believer in the old orthodox creed of the country, so Mr. Bright a great reformer as he has undoubtedly been, is an advocate of the old theory of the exclusion of women from their political rights. A Bill was not long ago introduced into Parliament, and defeated by a large majority. Mr. Bright among other reasons, stated that women themselves don't like to have a political position, and any suffrages extended to married women, could not be withheld from unmarried ones. These objections are said to be old-fashioned and equally applicable to all reforms alike. That women, the most educated among them, are not against it, is proved very well by the connection of the women's suffrage movement with such eminent pasonages as Miss Cobbe, Mr. Fawcett, Miss. Harriet Martineau, Mrs. Maclaren, and a number of other ladies equally reputed for their learning and ability. We have ourselves been personally present at women's suffrage meetings, and hearing the speeches made and the arguments adduced all by women, some of them quite young and handsome, we could not help the conviction that the softer sex in England at all events is quite as able to discharge their political responsibilities, as any of the sterner sex can possibly do.

WE did not know that the incident which occurred sometime back in the Brahma Mandir, we mean the discontinuance of sermons by the minister in consequence of the want of appreciation on the part of the congregation, should lead to such strange misconceptions in England. One Mr. Acomb lately published a paper in the *Free Press*, entitled "Wells—good, bad and indifferent," in which the following appears about the Brahmo Somaj:—"It is the religion of the New Church of India, which preaches a Gospel without Christ. What the human heart requires is a God it can love, and picture to itself, and hold fellowship with. Now, God manifest in the flesh, meets that want. A localised Deity is a necessity of our constitution. Instead of which the Brahmo Somaj proclaims God as a pure and lofty Spirit, unknowable, an abstraction cold as an iceberg, far away out of sympathy with sinful suffering men. Such doctrine only disappoints, and the thirsty one turns sadly away from a well without water. The last I heard of the Theistic Church of India was that the minister at Calcutta advised the closing of its preaching hall on account of the immorality of its members." We are glad that the mis-statement has been contradicted, as will be seen elsewhere.

THE Hindu idea of the accompaniments of the *shradha* ceremony we denounce, and must discourage as contratry to nature. Upon all occasions of the ceremony the chief mourner, as host, gives a feast to his guests, after the usual ceremony is over. We do not like this at all. The occasion is surely not one of rejoicing. Why then should there be a banquet with all its accompanying merriment and joviality at a time when the most solemn thoughts, if not melancholy sentiments ought to prevail concerning the departed? Nature and duty alike demand that when relatives meet once a year to honor the dead, they should have nothing but prayers and serious discourses, and renounce all pleasures and amusements. We say all this with a view to guard our Brahmo friends against imitating the Hindus in this matter, a practice which seems to be gaining ground in spite of reiterated protests on the part of those who wish to base religion upon natural instincts and sentiments. Feasting on the occasion of a *shradha*, though sanctioned by national customs, is inconsistent with nature and the high spirit of true religion, and we hope it will be discountenanced and put down.

CONSCIOUS merit reflects upon itself, and religion forms no exception to the rule. The religious man knows that he is religious, and cannot ignore the conviction. He must, he cannot but feel that he is unlike others, and others are unlike him. The contrast is most vividly realized in the rules of life. In the first place the fact that the religious man goes through certain forms and ceremonies enjoined upon him by his scriptures or his teachers, and other men either do not observe these, or feel excluded from observing them by natural incapacities, is a sufficient contrast between the two classes. In the second place the importance and sacredness attached by religious men, we mean the sincere among them, to the forms and rules they observe, and the indifference with which others are apt to regard the same, would add to the strength and distinctness of the contrast. In proportion as the conviction and faith of the religious man concentrate upon his own pursuits, his appreciation of pursuits foreign to his own grows feeble and ineffectual, and society settles down to the old classification of the priestly and secular classes. Now in real wisdom, genuine devotion, and the sterling purity of heart, such classification is not exactly possible, these spiritual attributes being unconfined by forms and human institutions. The priesthood of nature is a free, progressive, and universal institution. No one has the right of monopoly to it. In the case of men who rigidly adhere to rules and forms, and do so successfully, there is always the danger of a religious self-consciousness seldom wholesome to the growth and depth of the soul. In the thoughtless and less spiritually advanced, this danger is really great. In the case of men, on the other hand, who do not adhere to any definite principles of discipline and religious culture, there is always the danger of playing fast and loose with their convictions, so dissipating and enervating to the soul. And the conscious contrast between them and the disciplinarians only adds obstinacy to antipathy. The two classes are likely to fall out of sympathy with each other very much. Can there not be a union in devotion, purity of heart, faith in common principles, and such work as may be done together without jarring against special rules which may be adopted in special cases? We believe the problem requires consideration.

RAJARSHI JANAK.

OF Devarshi Narad we have already spoken, commending the interesting history of his conversion to all devout believers. Let us speak now of Rajarshi Janak, whose life stands out prominently in the Hindu scriptures by reason of his unique character of an ascetic householder. It is generally believed that Hinduism invariably sends away its votaries into the wilderness to learn and practise asceticism, if they are so inclined, and makes it obligatory on them to forsake family and home for ever. This is a mistake. The life of Janak is a protest against this erroneous assumption. Janak was not only a busy householder, beset with family cares and domestic duties, but he was a powerful king also. His dominion lay somewhere near the town of Mozufferpore, in Tirhoot, and its relics may still be found in Janakpuri, where large numbers of Hindus go on pilgrimage. In spite of the harassing cares and difficulties, the awful duties and responsibilities of royalty, Janak had attained a remarkably high stage of spiritual culture, and occupied an eminent position even among exalted Rishis. Far from hating him or treating him with contempt as a wordly man, the sages and saints of those days used to repair to him frequently for advice and guidance, for his fame as a Yogi had spread far and wide. Let those then who complain in these days of civilization and activity that the calm self-possession and deep communion of saints cannot be attained, in the midst of worldly engagements and trials, gather lessons from the life of Janak, and conclude from his actual experiences that the true devotee who relies wholly on Divine inspiration and help, can be extremely active in worldly business, and yet cultivate profound communion in a serene atmosphere in the depths of the heart. We are told in the *Yoga Vashishtha* that he had once started upon a pleasant excursion in spring to some romantic place, with his family and attendants. The beautiful scenery on all sides so greatly delighted and charmed him that he felt inclined to leave the party, and travel alone amid the beauties of nature. The refreshing and cool breeze and the lovely objects around, made his heart more and more tranquil and composed, and he fell into such deep sympathy and communion with nature that he lay for a time completely fascinated and absorbed. Deep silence prevailed within and without, and all was still. At last a sweet voice broke the silence. Whence came this voice he knew not. With speechless wonder and curiosity he looked about in all directions, but in vain. Who spoke, from where the strange voice emanated, remained a mystery. Janak listened with rapt attention, and the voice from heaven he then heard had the effect, we are told, of completely regenerating him. The voice went on in such strain as this:—"Him I worship who has no head, no limbs, who penetrates all, and who repeatedly says I AM." They who forsaking the Divinity that rules within as Lord of the heart, take shelter under other divinities, forsake the richest treasure in their possession in the hope of finding inferior treasures." "As Indra by his thunderbolt rends mountains, so conscience strikes and destroys the senses which are constantly inflamed by outward objects." These words enjoining the worship of the Invisible God in the hearts and the duty of obeying conscience above the senses, went deep into Janak's heart, and rebuked and mortified him greatly. He was full of remorse. He sent his retinue home, and then entered into a deep cave for solitary meditation. In deep agony he cried out as he reflected on his own worldliness and inconstancy. "Compared to the ocean of eternity my life is but a drop. That life I have wasted. How long shall my name endure, how long my kingdom? In the sea of the world I see only formidable waves of sorrow. The world is like a tree whose fruits, flowers and branches are our desires. I will destroy these desires, and will see that the tree of the world dries up." Such anguish and remorse brought wisdom in Janak's mind after some time, and then followed heavenly joy, which he thus expressed:—"Ah! I am now awake; my sleep is over. I have at last struck that thief with the arrow of asceticism who stole my best treasure from the heart, and for many years troubled me. Now I have found wisdom, and now I surrender myself to the Intelligent and Blissful Spirit." Janak's heart was completely subdued, and became thenceforth like deep, full and calm ocean. His old life ceased, and new life began to flow. Under Heaven's inspiration he then decided that in future he would desire nothing but God. He retained all the things he had, which a merciful Providence had bestowed upon him, and neither renounced what he had, nor panted for what he had not. Though an ascetic, he continued in the world as a dutiful householder. It is clear that Janak owed his conversion not to books, but to direct inspiration. The voice he heard was the heveuly voice of wisdom in his own heart. The process of sanctification that followed was natural. He did not rejoice immediately. He went through the fire of repentance, and after the full measure of self-condemnation and remorse came joy, new life and resignation.

Correspondence.

USE OF THE TERM WOMAN BY CHRIST.

To the Editor of the *Indian Mirror*.

DEAR SIR,—In your edition of some days ago I saw a letter concerning the use of the term "woman" by Christ to his mother. Perhaps the few following remarks may enlighten your correspondent. The term "y u v a c" in Greek is the equivalent of the Latin "domina," *lady*, and not of "mulier" woman—the Greek word translated "woman" in the Bible might just as easily have been translated "madam" or "lady." In fact, the word "y u v a c" has been frequently used to the wives of Kings, as any one acquainted with Greek will well remember. Christ cannot be classed as a harsh or unloving son when amidst the torments of the crucifixion he could yet remember her who stood by him to the last, and could provide for her a home with his best-loved disciple. The term woman is her highest title among Cristians, for she was the "woman," the second Eve whose seed bruised the serpent's head. For as by Eve's disobedience death came into the world, so by Mary's obedience ("behold the handmaid of the Lord") came life into the world. Christ spoke of himself frequently as the "Son of Man." His mother would never feel hurt by being called "woman," even were it not a respectful term which in the Greek sense it is. I regret that distance prevents my writing earlier.

Yours truly,
ALPHA.

THE BARAHANAGORE BRAHMO SOMAJ.

To the Editor of the *Indian Mirror*.

SIR,—A special prayer meeting of the Barahanagore Brahmo Somaj was held on Saturday, the 13th instant, at 7-30 P. M., in the hall of the "Barahanagore Institute." Babu Protap Chundra Mozumdar conducted the Divine Service on the occasion. About fifty men joined the meeting.

Yours &c.,
A TRUTH-TELLER.

Devotional

IT is not possible to obtain rest in the world, O Lord. Even the dearest and best in it think nothing of wounding us deeply. By Thy merciful dispensation, such wounds tend to do good to the soul, but they are often hard to bear. In the fulness of Thy mercy, grant that we may endure our lot with resignation and peace, and in perfect trust to thy beneficent purposes.

LORD vouchsafe to comfort me. Vouchsafe to be my friend and guide. Chasten my heart, sweeten it with Thy holy chastizement, and console me when I am heavily pressed.

UPON all widows and virgins O holy God, cause thy blessings to descend. Preserve them always in the light of thy purity, and let thy holiness be as a garment to their body and soul. Keep them safely away from the evil eye of bad men, from the speech and reach of thine enemies who seek the ruin of innocent souls. Let their reputation be always bright and untarnished like the rays of the sun, let their joy be always to worship thee, and be thy handmaidens. And may their pure influence be the remedy of such social evils and corruption as we find around thee.

The Brahmo Somaj

THE anniversary of the Bankipore Brahmo Somaj was celebrated on the 23rd ultimo. It is to be regretted that none of our missionaries could attend the anniversary festival at the above place nor the one lately held at Hazaribag.

AT Sukundia, a small village near Mugra, there was lately Hari Sankirtan got up by the Hindu residents to propitiate the deities and avert sickness. Day after day the procession went through the streets chanting certain idolatrous songs composed for the occasion. A few Brahmos seized the opportunity, and went forth singing Brahmo hymns, which were so much liked by the men and women of the village that every body joined the Brahmo procession and the Hindus themselves gave up their own Kirtan. Such is the triumph of simple Theistic devotion, which wins without the aid of logic and metaphysics.

THE hut of a poor milkman at Morepuker was, the other day, the scene of Brahmo Sankirtan and prayer. The heart of a poor Hindu woman present, was so much affected by the proceedings, that she immediately ejaculated a short prayer to the following effect:—"Lord have mercy on the poor. Thou art the Lord of the poor, &c."

A LITTLE child while bathing in a tank the other day, caught hold of his father's arm and then confidently said.—"What do I fear? I have taken hold of my father's arm." This is suggestive. How wise and pure we would be if we had such childlike trust!

BABU KESHUB CHUNDER SEN and the disciples who live with him in the little garden (*Sadhan Kanan*) he has recently purchased, live in a perfectly primitive style, and, in a very original style indeed. They all sit under the trees for their morning devotions which continue for seldom less than two hours and half, squatting on grass mats, pieces of rough woollen stuff, and tiger skins. Then they begin to cook their food which they finish eating by noonday time. Resting for half an hour, they engage in religious conversation which lasts for an hour. Then some of them do a little work, writing, reading, and otherwise employing themselves. In the afternoon they draw water, cut bamboos, make roads and pave them, plant, remove and water trees, construct their cabins, cleanse out various places, and are seen to work diligently in the hot sun, some with pieces of wet cloth on their heads, some bare-headed. Working till six they rest for half an hour again, and then retire for solitary devotions. When the evening is advanced, say by half-past seven, they sing Sunkirtan hymns, and issue out in a procession chanting through the Jungle-skirted village lanes, and usually enter a poor man's hut, there singing and praying for the benifit of the household. Babu Keshub Chunder Sen finds time amidst all these occupations to conduct his correspondence with Government officers and other big people, to arrange and take energetic measures for the progress and prosperity of the Albert Hall, and contribute to the newspapers. How long the present method of life will continue we can not say, but so long as it lasts it is interesting and instructive.

THE *Friend of India* has the following on our doctrines of spiritual life:—"We do not know the Brahmos enough to judge how far their daily life is consistent with their spoken and written teaching. We judge them by their words. And from their words we ought to infer that to them their religion is their chief possession,—in very truth their all. And their religion—still judging from their own account of it—is definable as *living in God* They do not profess to know His counsels from all eternity, they have no revelation of Him in infallible human speech to enable them to draw up a body of systematic divinity; they are not expressly informed of the exact nature of all his purposes with them either in this life or in the life to come; they do not know much *about* Him, but they profess to know *Him*. They believe that they live and move and have their being in Him; they feel and know that His presence encompasses them; when sacred emotions, such as are imperfectly described in language as light, joy, peace, and devotion in the soul, make their bosoms swell, they recognise in these emotions the presence of God. When thoughts that prompt to high endeavours after a spiritual life different from the common life of worldly men, rise within them they hear the voice of God. Thus they hear his voice, they feel his presence; and whether conscious of it or not, they believe that at all moments they are in Him and He in them, and their ideal of spiritual attainment is to be more clearly conscious of this than of any other fact whatever. We are not, we think, over-stating their belief when we say that they think it possible to be so completely absorbed in this consciousness of being *in God*, that they may become at such seasons almost, if not entirely, unconscious of everything else; and so their ideal of a perfect life is almost identical, perhaps if rightly understood, purely identical, with the old belief that man's highest destiny is loss of conscious individuality by absorption into the deity. To cultivate habits of life favorable to such self-oblivion, and to avoid, as far as the necessities of life permit, whatever is supposed to interfere with the soul's contemplation of the Divine Spirit, they seem to have agreed to call asceticism. The word is not used by them in the popular sense which English Protestantism has affixed to it. Whether they do well to use the word is doubtful; the thing as explained by themselves is surely not to be hastily condemned.

Literary.

Mr. W. T. Thornton of the India Office lately read a paper before the Society of Arts London, upon Indian Irrigation Works. Mr Thornton came to the conclusion that the evidence on the subject "must convince the most sceptical that, regarded as a whole, the investments of the Indian Government in Irrigation Works had hitherto been decidedly the reverse of unprofitable."

The London correspondent of the *Indian Daily News* says that "on addressing his constituents at the University of London, Mr. Lowe strongly attacked Lord Salisbury's proposal to grant £150 a year to those selected students for the Indian Civil Service, who would consent to go to a University for two years. Mr. Lowe had, he said, no objection to the students going to a university, but he objected to their being bribed with £150 a year to go to one."

Mrs. Lovett Cameron, wife of Lieutenant Cameron, the distinguished African traveller, has engaged to write a novel for the *Belgravia Magazine.* The title is "Juliet," and the first chapters appeared in the number for May.

"The Prince's Dream" is the title of "a fancy sketch or skit on the Royal Titles Bill," just published.

The London special correspondents who were out with the Prince in India, are going to flood us, writes the London correspondent of the *Bombay Gazette*, with permanent records of His Royal Highness' travels. Dr. W. H. Russell will have a book, Messrs. Forbes and Henty another, Mr. J. D. Gay, a third, and Mr. G. P. Wheeler, a fourth.

On May 6, a banquet to representatives of literature in its various branches, was given at the Mansion House, London, by the Lord Mayor and the Lady Mayoress. The guests, 250 in number, included Lord Houghton, Mr. Robert Browning, Mr. J. A. Froude, Mr. Anthony Trollope, Mr. Matthew Arnold, Sir Francis Doyle, Mr. Martin Tupper, Mr. Swinburne, Mr. Harrison Ainsworth, Mr. Tom Taylor, Admiral Sir Hastings Yelverton, G.C.B., Admiral Sir W. Edmonstone, M.P., Sir Henry Peek, M.P., Sir J. Eardley Wilmot, M.P., Sir C. Dilke, M.P., Mr. Gordon, M.P., Mr. Heath, M.P., Mr. E. Jenkins, M.P., Mr. Charley, M.P., &c. The usual loyal and patriotic toasts having been drunk, Lord Houghton replied for the House of Lords, and Sir Eardly Wilmot, M.P., responded for the House of Commons.

The death is announced of the celebrated philologer, Professor Lassen, of the University of Bonn, one of the founders of the modern study of Sanskrit and Sanskrit literature.

Scientific

We read that Earl Granville, the Chancellor, and Mr. Lowe, the representative in Parliament of the University of London, lately advocated the throwing open of the degrees in medicine of that university to women.

Gleanings

Let not therefore thy heart be troubled, neither let it be afraid! Trust in me, and put thy confidence in my mercy. When thou thinkest thyself farthest off from me, oftentimes I am nearest unto thee. When thou judgest that almost all is lost, then oftentimes the greatest gain of reward is close at hand. All is not lost when a thing falleth out against thee. Thou must not judge according to present feeling; nor so take any grief or give thyself over to it, from whencesoever it cometh as though all hopes of escape were quite taken away.

Think not thyself wholly left, although for a time I have sent thee some tribulation or even have withdrawn thy desired comfort; for this is the way to the kingdom of heaven. And without doubt it is more expedient for thee, and for the rest of my servants, that ye be exercised with adversities, than that ye should have all things according to your desires.

I know the secret thoughts of thy heart, and that it is very expedient for thy welfare that thou be left sometimes without spiritual enjoyments, lest perhaps, thou shouldst be puffed up with thy prosperous estate, and shouldst be willing to please thyself in that which thou art not. That which I have given I can take away, and can restore it again when I please.

When I give it, it is still mine, when I withdraw it, I take not anything that is thine; for every good and every perfect gift is mine. If I send thee affliction or any cross whatsoever, repine not, nor let thy heart fail thee; I can succour thee, and turn all thy heaviness into joy.

Imitation of Christ.

Latest News.

—Several Natives of India, who returned with the Prince of Wales are, says *Galignani*, at present to be seen on the Paris boulevards, where their rich coustumes attract much attention.

—Her Highness the Princess of Tanjore is said to have so progressed in her studies that she writes letters in the English language to her friends.

—Mr. Disraeli lately said in the House of Commons.—"I believe, indeed, that at no time has there been a better understanding between the Courts of St. James and St. Petersburgh than at the present moment, and there is this good understanding because our policy is a clear and a frank policy."

—Lord George Hamilton referring to the Native Army, in the House of Commons, quoted the words of some one whom he did not name, but whom he described as an authority, on the condition of the Indian Army. These words were: "Native regiments, in appearance, equipment, and *esprit de corps*, are simply magnificent."

—"The visit of the Empress of Germany, a clever woman, though a very ugly one, is supposed," says the London correspondent of the *Englishman*, "to have a political motive. She has had several confabulations with the Premier, and the Berlin Conferences on the Eastern question have fairly begun with the arrival not only of Count Andrassy, but of the Czar, in the Prussian capital."

—Here is an allusion to one of the numerous "scandals in high life" from a London gossiper:—"I hear that the excuse which Lady de la Zouche intends to offer for the martial infidelity which her husband alleges against her, is of a kind which will compel Sir James Hannen to hear it *in camera*. Lady de la Zouche was only married (at the age of twenty) last July to her husband, and the co-respondents in the case are the Earl of Mayo and Mr. Blunt. Lady de la Zouche is a daughter of Lord Saltoun."

—A Begum who, we are told by the *Koh-i-Noor*, is some relative of the Nawab of Rampore, intends leaving Agra soon for England to lay a claim before the Privy Council which she has against the above Nawab. Mr. Wilson, a Pleader, accompanies her.

—The Maharajah of Jeypore, who is now at Simla, is attended by 108 Sirdars, and accompanied by Rajah Pertap Sing, brother of the Maharajah of Jodhpore.

—A Superintendent for the Oriental College, Lahore, is wanted on a salary of Rs. 500 a month.

—The *Times of India* hears from Rawul Pindi that affairs at Kohat are in *statu quo*. The Afridis have cut the telegraph wires, but as there is another line through Sind, traffic has not been stopped.

—Dr. Bellew is at Simla, summoned there probably by the Viceroy for consultation respecting some political prospects not yet disclosed.

—Mr. Grosvenor's arrival at Mandalay has been reported to Government. The results of his mission, however, are not known at present.

—The Viceroy is expected back at Simla from Mushobra to-morrow.

—Lord Lytton's health has latterly much improved at Simla.

—It is believed, says the *Pioneer*, that Sir Louis Mallet, though considerably improved in health, is likely to resign his Under-Secretaryship at the India Office at no distant date.

—Mr. H. M. Plowden has taken his seat on the Chief Court Bench, Punjab, in the room of Mr. Justice Boulnois, who has obtained leave. Mr. Justice Boulnois, we understand, proceeds on a tour through Kulu to Simla, reaching this latter station about the middle of August next.

—A meeting of the Honorary Magistrates and Native Members of the Municipal Committee, Lahore, was held last week before whom the Deputy Commissioner conferred rewards and khillats on those Mohulladars and Chowdries who gave assistance to the vaccinators. Four vaccinators also received Rs. 20 each for their exertions.

—The Maharajh of Mysore will stop for six months at Bangalore, and spend the other six months at Mysore and Ootacamund respectively. The Maharajah was expected back at Mysore from Ooty on the 25th or 26th ultimo.

—The legacy of three lacs of rupees which was left by a Native of Pondicherry to the French Government by his Will, is to be applied towards the construction of a small line of railway which is to connect Pondicherry with the Madras railway line.

—The *Times of India* tells us that in one of the Rajputana States, administered by a well-known Native minister, a special commission consisting of three members, has been appointed to investigate charges of bribery and corruption preferred against some of the highest officials of the State. The special commission have taken in hand their preliminary work, and the whole city is in a state of agitation awaiting the result of the sittings. The European officers charged with the supervision of the proceedings of the State have, it is said, been informed of the action taken.

—The Bombay public, it is said, intend convening a public meeting to vote an address of congratulation to the Queen. The Bombay Corporation, they say, represented only some Parsis and not the public of Bombay.

—The Rangoon railway cannot possibly be opened for traffic to Prome before April of next year.

—An agitation is going on now amongst the railway servants in India to get some cessation of labor on Sundays. Some of the clergy have joined in a petition to the Home Boards of Directors, on the subject.

Calcutta.

The Coroner with a Jury held two inquests on Friday evening last. The first inquest was touching the death of a Native who had hanged himself in the Shampukur Section of the town; and the second was touching the death of a Native who was found floating in a tank in the Jorasanko Section of the town. The Jury returned verdicts in accordance with the evidence.

The P. & O. Co's *S. S. Travancore*, Commander W. B. Andrews, arrived in the Bombay harbour on Tuesday last, from Suez, with the English Mails of the 12th inst. on board. The following is the list of passengers :—

From Suez.—Mr. and Mrs. C. Hogg, Mr. Saunders, Mr. Bolman, Mrs. Chambers, Mr. Hardinge, Condr. Bather, Master Bather, Mr. G. Petter, Mr. J. Hayes.

From Brindisi.—Mr. Bulman.

From Alexandria.—Mr. Smale.

From Aden.—Surg. Major Grant, Col. J. 'A. Fuller, Miss Minto, Lieut. H. H. Brooke, 54 deck passengers.

THE thirty-fourth Hare Anniversary was held at the University Senate House, Calcutta, on the 1st June, 1876. About 150 persons were present. The Hon'ble Rajah Narendra Krisna Deb, Bahadur, in the Chair. The Hon'ble Chairman, after making a few prefatory remarks on the philanthrophy of the late David Hare, and the services he had rendered to the cause of Native education, introduced Dr. Mohendrolall Sircar to the meeting. The learned Doctor delivered an address, which was listened to with much interest. The Rev. Dr. K. M. Bannerji then proposed that the best thanks of the meeting be tendered to Dr. Mohendrolall Sircar for the able address he had delivered. This resolution was seconded by the Hon'ble Isshur Chunder Mitter, and carried by acclamation. It was then proposed by Babu Amarendronath Chatterji, seconded by Babu Gopi Kissen Mitra, and unanimously carried, that the thanks of the meeting be tendered to the Senate for allowing the meeting the use of the Senate House. After a vote of thanks to the Chairman the meeting terminated.

ACKNOWLEDGMENTS.

The Vedarthayatna, or An Attempt to Interprit the Veda. Bombay. 1876.

Nabab Serajud-dowla. An Historical Drama. By Lukhynarain Chuckerbutty. Calcutta. 1283.

Law

POLICE.—JUNE 3, 1876.

[*Before F. J. Marsden, Esq.*]

AN old thief was charged with having kidnapped a sweeper's child, aged about five years, and stolen some ornaments from his person. The child, it appeared, was playing about in a lane in Taltola with others of his age, when the accused, seeing him with ornaments, enticed him away a little distance, robbed him of his ornaments, threw him into a ditch, and ran into a house. The other lads, seeing this, raised an alarm, and the Police arrested the accused in the house. The case was, after the recording of some evidence, adjourned to Thursday next.

Selection

THE THEISTIC CHURCH OF INDIA.

TO THE EDITOR OF THE "FREE PRESS."

SIR,—I have just seen a paragraph in your paper by the Rev. W. J. Acomb, of West Bromwich, in which he says "The last I heard of the Theistic Church of India was that the minister at Calcutta advised the closing of the preaching hall on account of the immorality of its members." As a personal friend of the minister in question, permit me to give a decided contradiction to this injurious rumour, which is probably a distorted version of the following facts, which I condense from the *Indian Mirror*.

On Sunday, the 28th of November last, it was announced from Mr. Sen's pulpit, by deputy, that the minister would discontinue preaching for the present. The chief reason, as explained, was that the congregation "had not answered the expectations entertained of them as to the holiness and devotedness of life, and till the minister saw that his precepts were likely to be better obeyed, he would reserve them, and have that duty performed by some one else. This caused some sensation," and "two of the congregation offered up prayers indicative of humility and repentance." On the two following Sundays sermons were read by one or other of the Brahmo missionaries; but on the Sunday following, December 19th, the minister resumed his place in the pulpit (which he has retained ever since), and "the congregation felt relieved at the restoration of the old order of things." Mr Sen is intensely earnest, and it was evidently a vivid experience of that disappointment which all earnest pastors must know only too well—the disappointment at the slow *spiritual* progress of his flock—which induced his singular action. But "immorality," in common parlance, stand for gross sin, and this was not implied for a moment.

I may add that the idea of God as "unknowable, an abstraction, cold as an iceberg, far away out of sympathy with sinful suffering men," is one against which the Brahmo Somaj leaders protest quite as strongly as Mr. Acomb himself, though they do not hold with him, and with their idolatrous fellow-countrymen that "a localised deity is a necessity of our constitution." They would, however, entirely agree with Mr. Acomb that "what the human heart requires is a God it can love, and picture to itself, and hold fellowship with." And it is their firm and happy belief that they have found Him.

Yours faithfully,
SOPHIA DOBSON COLLET.
33, Hamilton Road, Highbury, London, N.
MAY 2nd, 1876.

BRAHMO SOMAJ, OR THEISM IN INDIA.

TO THE EDITOR OF THE "FREE PRESS."

SIR.—In the paper by the Rev. W. J. Acomb on "Walls—Good, Bad, and Indiff-rent," published in the *Free Press* of April 29th, the following statements are made with respect to the Brahmo Somaj (the Church of One God) of India :—

"The Brahmo Somaj proclaims God as an abstraction, cold as an iceberg, far away out of sympathy with sinful suffering men."

"Such doctrine only disappoints, and the thirsty one turns sadly away from a well without water."

"The Minister of the Theistic Church at Calcutta advised the closing of the preaching hall on account of the immortality of its members."

As I happen from a variety of circumstances to have given some attention to the aims and progress of the Theistic Church in India, I am anxious to correct the misrepresentations (no doubt unconcious on the writer's part) contained in these statements of the character and value of Indian Theism.

My desire that every sect of religionists should be fairly represented, if spoken of at all critically in a public paper, must be my excuse for writing in defence of the Brahmo Somaj.

I shall give authority for the statements I make, and quote from the sermons of the greatest living leader of the Theistic movement, passages illustrative of the religious teaching of Indian Theists.

In the *Times* newspaper of the 17th of last month a long letter, entitled "A Traveller's Impressions of India." was published. It was written from Bombay, by Mr. Monier Williams, Boden Professor of Sanskrit in the University of Oxford, and as he is our latest authority, and certainly trustworthy, I will quote his words He says: "In almost every large town there is a Samaj, or society of such men (Theists) whose creed would be expressed by the 1st part of the 1st article of the Church of England. They retain the name Brahma as applicable to the Supreme Being, but they regard Him as a Personal God, to be addressed by prayer as well as praise."

Now, to proclaim God as a "Person" to whom prayer and praise are believed to be acceptable, is surely a very different thing from proclaiming God as "an abstraction, cold as an iceberg, far away out of sympathy with sinful suffering men." The following is an extract from a sermon on "Regenerating Faith," preached on the occasion of the 38th anniversary of the Brahmo Somaj, at Calcutta by Chunder Sen :—

"Through faith we not only realize the Unseen Spirit, but dwell in Him, fear Him as an ever-present Witness and Governor, and love Him as a Father who never forsaketh us; and, in short, feel Him, in all places, and at all times, in our uprising and down-sitting, as an encompassing Presence not to be put by. Such realisation of Divine presence alone can effectively guard us against sin and temptation, and enable us to inhale purity as freely, easily, and naturally as we now inhale impurity in the atmosphere of the world. Do not preach to me dogmas and traditions, do not talk of saving my soul by mere theological arguments and inferences. These I do not want; I want the living God, that I may dwell in Him, away from the bustle of the world, and secure from its allurements. Nothing short of this can satisfy me, save me. That I may become godly, I must first feel my God to be the greatest and dearest reality—a reality dearer than father and mother and friend, dearer than wealth, and dearer than everything else."

This extract needs no comment, and it is only want of space that prevents my giving from the speeches of other Indian Theists equally clear proof that the Brahmo Somaj does not proclaim God as "an abstraction, cold as an iceberg, far away out of sympathy with sinful suffering men," but as "a God the human heart can love, and hold fellowship with."

The statement that the doctrine of the Theistic Church of India "only disappoints, and the thirsty one turns away sadly from a well without water," may either rest on facts which have come to the writer's knowledge, or may be a mere inference of his. If an inference, it is clearly an inference from wrong data, for the religious teaching of the Brahmo Somaj is not of the character he describes.

I assert on the strength of fact, not inteference, that Theism is *not* a "dry well."

I quote again from our latest authority, Professor Monier Williams. He says: "Education is causing a great upheaving of old creeds and superstitions throughout India, and the ancient fortress of Hinduism is in this way being gradually undermined. The educated classes look with contempt on idolatry, in fact the present condition of India seems very similar to that of the Roman empire before the coming of Christ. A complete disintegration of ancient faiths is in progress in the upper strata of society. Most of the ablest thinkers become pure Theists or Unitarians. Christianity has made most progress among people of low caste, and with some of the aboriginal tribes. Real conversions are certainly uncommon, nor will they, in my opinion, be more common until our religion is presented to the Hindus in that more simple Oriental form which originally belonged to it on its first foundation at Jerusalem."

Clearly to many of the intelligent Hindus, breaking away from ancient superstitions and idolatries, Theism is no "dry well," but a well of living water, and is preferred by them to that which has a "crimson dye." (!)

I cannot give now a detailed account of the opinions of Indian Theists with respect to the Bible, Christ, and Christianity, and it is perhaps sufficient to say that passages from the Bible are read in their religious services, that Jesus is accepted as a teacher of religion, and spoken of with reverence, affection, and enthusiasm, as the following passage from Chunder Sen's lecture on "Jesus Christ; Europe and Asia" will show :—

He says: "I have always regarded the Cross of Christ as a beautiful emblem of self-sacrifice unto the glory of God, one which is calculated to quicken the higher feelings and aspirations of the heart, and to purify the soul; and I believe there is not a heart, how callous and hard soever it may be, that can look with cold indifference on that grand and significant ymbol. Such honorable and disinterested self-sacrifice has produced, as might be anticipated, wonderful results; the purpose of Chist's noble heart has been fully achieved, as the world's history will testify. The vast moral influence of His life and death still lives in human society, and animates its movements. It has moulded the civilisation of modern Europe, and it underlies the many civilising and philanthropic agencies of the present day."

The gospel of modern Indian Theism is not, as I understand it, "a gospel without Christ." Testimonies have been frequently given by missionaries and travellers in India to the great religious value of the Theistic movement. The Rev. J. Smith, Baptist missionary in Delhi, said at a missionary meeting a few years ago: "The Brahmo Somaj is covering the whole ground of Christian morality, and there is a great deal of the spirit of Christ in all its leader's action. To a large extent this form of Theism has cleared the heavy atmosphere of Hinduism. God grant that Chunder Sen may be long spared to do in many parts of India what he has done in Calcutta."

To the fervent wish of the Baptist missionary I would utter a hearty amen!

The Brahmo Somaj is at the present day doing a noble work of a social as well as directly religious character. It is courageously protesting against those ancient forms of superstition which have hitherto so greatly retarded the moral growth of the people of India—superstitions which have degraded the lives of women, hindered the attainment of a condition of society in which true brotherhood should be recognised, and checked in many ways the growth of simple piety and manly virtue.

The Brahmo Somaj is a true Church of God, marked doubtless, as all other human societies are, by limitations and short-comings, but still engaged in a truly divine work, "about the Father's business," the destruction of superstition, the banishment of misery, the rectification of wrong, the establishing of truth, righteousness, and peace, the promotion of the highest welfare of mankind.

The leaders of this church are men of prophetic fervor, reminding us of the best of the Hebrew prophets; their enthusiasm, like that of Jesus of Nazareth, sustained by communion with God; their best loved work to bring their brethren to the worship and service of one true and living God, "Our Father in Heaven."

The statement with respect to the proposed dissolution of the Church at Calcutta "on account of the immorality of its members, which is clearly given as proof in fact of the correctness of the writer's opinion of the spiritual inefficiency of Theism, has been voluntarily corrected by Miss Collet, the editor of several Brahmo Somaj publications, and a personal friend of the minister of the Church at Calcutta, and whose letter will, I believe, be found in the letter column of this paper. I have only to add that the task of writing about the Brahmo Somaj, would have been a pleasanter one if it had not taken the shape of a criticism of a description of Indian Theism conscientiously, but as I think I have shown, mistakenly made.

Yours faithfully,

JOHN HARRISON.

Jesson Street, West Bromwich,

May 3, 1876. —*The Free Press.*

Advertisements

BURAL BROTHERS

[ESTABLISHED IN 1870 A.D.]

JEWELLERS, GOLD AND SILVER-SMITHS AND WATCH-MAKERS,

BY APPOINTMENT TO

His Excellency the Viceroy and Governor-General of India

AND

HIS HIGHNESS THE MAHARAJAH ADHIRAJ OF BURDWAN,

BURAL BROTHERS,

10, Hare Street.

India General Steam Navigation Company, Ld.

SCHOENE, KILBURN & Co.—*Managing Agents.*

ASSAM LINE.

NOTICE.

Steamers leave Calcutta for **Assam every Tuesday**; Goalundo every Thursday **and leave Debroo**ghur downward every Saturday.

THE Str. **"ASSAM"** will leave Calcutta for **Assam, on Tuesday, the** 6th instant.

Cargo will be **received** at the Company's Godowns, Nimtollah **Ghat, until** noon of Monday, the 5th.

THE Str. "SIMLA" will leave Goalundo for Assam on Thursday, the 8th instant.

Cargo will be received at the Company's Godowns, No. 4 Fairlie Palace, up till noon of Tuesday the 6th.

Goods forwarded to Goalundo for this vessel will be chargeable with Railway Freight from Calcutta to Goalundo **in addition** to the regular Freight **of this** Company.

Passengers should **leave** for Goalundo by Train **of** Wednesday, the 7th.

CACHAR LINE NOTICE

REGULAR FORTNIGHTLY SERVICE.

Steamers now leave Calcutta for Cachar and Intermediate Stations every alternate Friday, and leave **Cachar downward every alternate** Sunday.

THE Str. "LUCKNOW" will leave **Calcutta for Cachar on** Friday, the **16th instant.**

Cargo will be received at the Company's Godowns, **Nimtollah Ghat, up till noon of** Thursday the 15th.

For further information regarding rates of Freight **or** passage money, apply **to.**

4, FAIRLIE PALACE. Calcutta, 2nd June 1876. } G. J. SCOTT, *Secretary.*

THE BYABASAYI

(ব্যবসায়ী)

A MONTHLY VERNACULAR JOURNAL

of

AGRICULTURE, MANUFACTURE AND COMMERCE.

To combine the best features of the *Indian Agriculturist* and the *Statistical Reporter*, and to contain trust-worthy information, and suggestions of improvement of Indigenous Agriculture, Arts and Manufacture. To be contributed by men who have special knowledge in these subjects. The *Byabasayi* will supply a long felt desideratum, and will be pre-eminently the journal for Landlords, Tenants and Merchants of Bengal. The annual subscription payble in advance is 2 rupees, exclusive of postage. Gentlemen desirous of subscribing for the paper are requested to communicate with the Editor,

SRINATH DUTT.

15, *College Square, Calcutta.*

Printing Materials,

MILLER AND RICHARD'S PRESSES, TYPES and all requisites always in Stock,

TERMS CASH.

EWING & CO.

!!! হুকা !!!

!!! HOOKAHS !!!

ENGLISH made Hookahs of various choice designs, colours and sizes ranging in price from Rs. 2 to 5 each, 60 designs to choose from Apply to

RADANAUTH CHOWDRY,

373, Jorasanko

HOLLOWAY'S PILLS

How to Enjoy Life

Is only known when the blood is pure, its circulation perfect, and the nerves in good orders. The only safe and certain method of expelling all impurities is to take Holloway's Pills, which have the power of cleansing the blood from all noxious matters, expelling all humours which taint or impoverish it, thereby purify and invigorate and give general tone to the system. Young or old robust or delicate, may alike experience their beneficent effects. Myriads affirmed that these Pills possess marvellous power in securing these great secrets of health by purifying and regulating the fluids and strengthening the solids.

BABU BASANTA KUMAR DUTTA,

HOMŒOPATHIC PRACTITIONER

No. 20, Sunker Haldar's Lane, Aheritolah.

A FRESH INDENT OF

HOMŒOPATHIC

Medicines and other Requisities.

Have arrived from England.

Medicines, Boxes, Books, Pamphlets;

Absolute Alcohol; Cholera-spirit Camphor.

SPECIAL REMEDIES

For Suppressed, Laborious and Difficult menses; Leucorrhœa.

For Hysteria; Spermatorrhœa; Dysentery; Diarrhœa; Cholera.

For Asthma; Pile; Pain; Sore and Diseases of the Children.

Ice, Lemonade, Soda and Tonic water always.

To be had at

DATTA'S HOMŒOPATHIC LABORATORY,

No. 212, CHITPORE ROAD, BURTOLA, CALCUTTA

TERMS—CASH.

☞ Price List can be had on application.

SMITH, STANISTREET & CO.

Pharmaceutical Chemists & Druggists

BY APPOINTMENT

To His Excellency the Right Hon'ble

LORD LYTTON, G.M.S.I.

Governor-General of India,

&c., &c.

SYRUP OF LACTATE OF IRON

Prepared from the original recipe. Lactate of Iron, in various forms of preparation, have been in use in France, and generally through the continent of Europe, for some years past, and is highly esteemed as one of the most valuable Chalybeate Tonic Remedies yet introduced. The Syrup, being the most agreeable as well as convenient form of administration is in most general use. It is a most valuable remedy in the following diseases:—Chlorosis or Green Sickness, Leucorrhœa, Neuralgia, Enlargement of the Spleen, &c. In combination with quinine, it has also been very successfully used in the cure of Fever, while to persons of delicate constitution, enfeebled by disease it is invaluable. In bottles. Rs. 2 each.

SYRUP OF THE PHOSPHATE OF IRON Rs. 2 per bottle.

SYRUP OF PHOSPHATE OF IRON AND STRYCHNINE, Rs. 2 per bottle.

SYRUP OF PHOSPHATE OF IRON AND QUININE. Price Rs. 2-8 per bottle.

SYRUP OF PHOSPHATE OF IRON, QUININE AND STRYCHNINE, (DR. ATKIN'S TRIPLE TONIC SYRUP,) Rs. 2-8 per bottle.

Smith, Stanistreet & Co.

Invite special attention to the following rates, **the quality guaranteed as the** best procurable :—

Pure Ærated Waters.

Made from Pure Water, obtained by the new process through the Patent Charcoal Filters.

				Rs	As
Ærated plain (Trible Ærated), per doz.			...	0	12
Soda Water	ditto	„	...	0	12
Gingerade	ditto	„	...	1	4
Lemonade	ditto	„	...	1	4
Tonic (Quinine)	ditto	„	...	1	4

The *Cash* must be sent with the order to obtain advantage of the above rates.

CHUNDER AND BROTHERS

251 & 112 RADHA BAZAR, CALCUTTA.

TERMS,—Cash Strictly.

Printing Press, Paper and Materials

Columbian Super Royal size each nett	Rs.	500 0
„ Royal „ „	...	450 0
„ Foolscap „ „	...	275 0
„ ½ Sheet Folio Post „	...	150 0
Albion Amateur to print 7¼ × 5¼ inch	...	70 0
Lithographic Printing Press, 13 inch	..	140 0
Copper plate do. do.	...	200 0
Iron Hot Press	...	130 0
Roller Moulds, Zinc, 36 inch	...	45 0
Ditto do. Iron, 30 inch	...	65 0
Roller and Frame, 6 inch	...	4 0
Do. do. 9 inch	...	5 0
Do. do, 12 inch	...	5 8
Expanding Roller Frame	...	8 0
Brass Rule & Lead-cutter	...	22
Brass Rules, 3 to 6 to 4 to pica plain,		
Do. Waved dotted &c,		
Composing Sticks best gun metal.		
English Lead Mould.	...	65 0
Chases various sizes.		
Springs for Albion Press.		
Paper Cutting Machines 18 inch	...	100 0
Shooting Sticks brass tipped.		
Mallets English made.		
Card Board Cutting Machine	...	70 0

Mitthorp's Celebrated Printing Inks

Of all colors and Shades,—Black, Blue, Brown, Chocolate, Green, Lilac, Mauve, Pink, Purple, Red, Magenta, White and Yellow.—Price according to quality.

15th May 1876. CHUNDER & BROTHERS.

Printed and published by M. M. RUKHIT, at the INDIAN MIRROR PRESS, No. 15, College Square, for the Proprietor.

The Indian Mirror.

SUNDAY EDITION.

VOL XV.] CALCUTTA, SUNDAY JUNE, 11, 1876 { REGISTERED AT THE GENERAL POST OFFICE. } [No. 137

CONTENTS

NOTICE.

All letters and communications relating to the literary department of the Paper should be addressed to the Editor. All other letters should be addressed to the Manager, to whom all remittances should be made payable.

Subscribers will be good enough ***to bring to the notice of the Manager any delay or irregularity*** *in the delivery of the Paper.*

Editorial Notes

IN the April number of the *Evangelical Review*, which is a fair average publication, there is an article on the English speaking Natives of Upper India which is simply a covert attack on the Brahmo Somaj. We have no right to expect an immunity from the severe and hostile criticisms of our Native Christian friends, as that seems to be the only consolation left to them in the midst of their internal disorder and disagreements, but, we believe, we have some show of right to expect that gross and glaring misrepresentation of facts should be as far possible avoided in such attacks. In respect of the Brahmo Somajes in Upper India the writer has made statements simply untrue. We are ready to believe he was misinformed, but in that case he should, perhaps have written less dogmatically and triumphantly.

MR. W. J. ACOMB publishes a rejoinder in the *Free Press*, in which he replies in a facetious and indignant spirit characteristic of his school, to the replies of Miss Collect and the Rev. J. Harrison. Here is a remarkable specimen of his queer logic. Miss Collect said, in the letter which we reproduced the other day, that the congregation of the *Mandir* did not "answer the expectations entertained of them as to holiness and devotedness of life" by the minister. Mr. Acomb replies:—"I am a plain man, accustomed to call a spade a spade, and claim that a want of holiness and devotedness may be correctly stigmatised as immorality!" *Ergo* the Brahmos are "immoral" men, because their minister thinks they have not attained a sufficiently high standard of holiness and devotion. If Mr. Acomb himself were tried by the measure of purity enjoined in the gospel of Christ, surely he would be convicted of gross immorality.

BHAKTAMAL is the name of an obscure and ill-printed publication which those who care anything about the spirit of the Hindu religion, must read in order to be able to form any idea of the piety, self-sacrifice, devotedness and brotherly love which must have characterized the heads and followers of certain Hindu sects mostly Vaishnavite. The book was originally composed in Hindi, in Birjvakha verses by Nabhaji, a great Vaishnava leader himself. The Bengali translation is by Krishnadass Babaji. The book contains biographical sketches of eminent Bhaktas both male and female. The versification however is barbarous, and some of the passages objectionable. What we propose is that a new edition of this really noble book should be got out by some enlightened man able to write good verse, who can exercise sound, moral discretion as to what passages should be retained and what discarded in the existing book. The undertaking, if carried out, will be as beneficial as profitable.

THE wonderful change brought into the soul as the immediate effect of prayer, must always remain a marvel to those who have felt it. The highest sense of purity is not only realized but retained by a heart which is naturally unholy. The hard and heedless man is transformed into the humble and loving saint, and that within a short time. The change where it takes place is itself marvellous, though it may not be lasting. How to make it lasting is the great and all-important problem of religion. There is an abnormal overstraining of the soul, an unnatural excitement of fear and faith, a religious insanity, so to call it, which drowns all common sense, and sets the man shrieking in pious hysterics. We do not mean this kind of excitement, its continuance would be a disaster to society. We mean the calm Godward upheaving of the soul in prayer which descends upon the earth again with the sun-light of joy and holiness on its breast, joy so deep, holiness so exalted that heaven seems to dawn in the earth for those who acquire the blessedness of possessing them.

THERE is a profoundly oriental and malancholy romance in the deposition and death of Sultan Abdul Aziz, the late Sultan of Turkey. The man upon whose freakful fancy hung yesterday the fate of hundreds of thousands and the peace of Europe, who by his rapacious extortions made himself the dread of his subjects and the object of wrath to the whole world, is silently removed to-day from his mighty seat of power. He abdicates his throne, and none knows the reason why. And the next day he puts an end to his existence with a calmness and philosophical resignation which would not have disgraced a Socrates or a Seneca. There is a mystery about the whole matter which the newspaper telegrams have not explained, and perhaps never shall. The fury and fanaticism characteristic of a Mahomedan revolution, in a semi-barbarous country like Turkey, are not here. The rancour and violence of party spirit manifested even in the most civilized and Christian countries on like occasions, have not been heard of. There has been a stillness, a placidity, a self-possession in the whole affair that breathe the spirit of ancient stoicism more than any other modern event of the same importance. A great tyrant who set the whole world in mighty convulsions, chooses to step aside from his throne, sits down, bleeds himself with his own hand, and sinks into the ground dead. Another man quietly comes to fill up his place by his will. The world is saved a sea of blood by the voluntary death of one man. There is a strange solemnity and pathos in all this.

THERE is not a single book from which one can arrive at any definite idea as to the number of existing Hindu sects in India. Wilson's "Hindu Sects" is the only exhaustive treatise on the subject, but it was written nearly a century ago, and compiled from materials older still. Since then several Hindu sects have grown and disappeared, or so materially altered their aspects and principles that they can hardly be recognized for what they are described in the book named above. Babu Akhay Kumar Dutt's *Upasak Sampraday* is such a close imitation of Dr. Wilson's treatise on the subject, that the only advantage of its publication seems to be the fact of its being written in the Bengali language. It might have appeared fifty years back without rendering any difference in the facts and descriptions given in it at all necessary. There is not a word giving us any idea of the teeming and multiplying sects of Guzrat and the Punjab. Even such prominent sects as the Tukaramists of the Deccan, and the Kukas of the Punjab are not there. We do not mean to find fault with Babu Akhay Kumar Dutt's book. He is an invalid, and has not had the means or the time to gather fresh information on the subject he writes upon. But we do require an exhaustive and reliable book on the various religious sects of India. Is there no one among our learned countrymen who can supply us with one?

WHETHER the religion of the Brahmo Somaj is making sufficient progress in this country or not may be problematical. But all honest witnesses will bear testimony to the somewhat singular fact that this religion is becoming more and more difficult every year. Our own experiences tell us the same thing. Perhaps, the public expect to hear from us, that we Brahmos are getting nearer our ideal heaven. However paradoxical it may be, the truth is we are becoming more and more conscious of our distance from God, the kingdom of heaven. As we ascend, higher hills than those we have left behind present themselves to our view, and we find we are much further from the highest peak than we had formerly thought. We certainly know more of God, worship, immortality and salvation now than we did before; and yet we are becoming more painfully conscious of our ignorance. The fact is we did not know enough of our faith a decade back. Fresh pathos of duty and joy, devotion and communion are daily opening before us of which we had perhaps only a dim and distant glimpse, and we have hardly completed one round of spiritual discipline and culture when we are summoned to enter upon another sphere altogether new. Not that our religion changes and grows, but our ideas and views are expanding. We thank and bless God that He has vouchsafed unto us a faith which appears more and more difficult of attainment as we grow in years, and which as it presents greater difficulties, holds out also deeper joys and sweeter felicities to its votaries.

THE Indian friends of the Rev. Robert Spears, the late Secretary to the British and Foreign Unitarian Association, will be glad to hear of the handsome way in which his services to the Unitarian community for the last eleven years, are going to be acknowledged by a number of Unitarian gentlemen. A fitting testimonial is going to be given to Mr. Spears, and with this object a fund has been opened. The plan proposed to be adopted is that "a sum of money should be raised to be presented to Mr. Spears, or invested for the benefit of him and his family." The subscriptions, as advertised in the *Inquirer*, already amount to £1,436 4s, and of course more money is expected. Among the subscribers we find the names of Unitarian leaders of all classes. Mr. Samuel Sharpe, the well-known Hebrew scholar, represents the party of orthodox Unitarians, and comes forward with a subscription of £50. Mr. Samuel Courtauld who represents the extreme party of liberal thinkers, and may be better identified, we believe, with Theists than with Unitarians, comes forward with the handsome amount of a hundred pounds. Then we find Mr. Martineau, the Bucktons and Luptons of Leeds, the Lawrences of London, the Carpenters, and such other names as Mr. Steinthal, Dr. Sadler, Mr. Samuel Sharpe, and the Misses Swanwick. Altogether sympathy with Mr. Spears is as universal and warm as could have been expected by his most devoted friends. We are glad this is so. Our differences with the theology held by Mr. Spears are really great, but his heart has been so broad, warm, and many-sided, that we rejoice his value is thus appreciated by the community to which he belongs.

THE controversy about miracles will never cease. It is now admitted by all sensible people that the power of working miracles, granting that any one ever possessed such power, would not in itself be divine, because it has been believed in all ages, and by all workers of mircles, that the power of working them can be possessed by bad men, by false prophets, and the enemies of God, quite as much as by good men, and the friends of religion. The gift of miracle-working therefore, unless we believe in devils and demigods, either resolves itself into the possession of great knowledge of the laws of nature and their operations, or the possession of such very unusual power, as can by its superior exercise, control, and modify the action of the laws of nature. The writer in the *Quarterly Review*, whose views the *Spectator* endorses, believes in the power of working miracles in this sense, further observing that the power is only exercised to bring about a change of destiny in an individual or in a nation, in fact that its exercise is dependent on the production of vastly important moral results. It is then said that miracles from such a point of view do not involve the infraction of natural laws, but only introduce new conditions into those laws by action of the Supreme Will, so as to impress upon their operations a significance, a moral purpose, a great religious lesson which otherwise they could not convey. The forces of nature involve each other. The chemical forces assume the mechanical laws, but add such new conditions to them as to make the effects entirely different; the vital laws like wise assume the chemical; and the laws of the will add in the same way such conditions upon physiological laws as to bring about completely new effects. "And so too supernatural events assume the laws of all the laws of all that we call natural phenomena as their basis, and involve only new controlling principles which greatly modify their issue." This view is certainly ingenious, only the new conditions and principles are conjectural, and themselves stand in need of proof. Also it remains to be proved that the introduction of such new conditions into the working of external nature, is essential towards producing those spiritual changes, the changes of destiny in individuals and nations which religion must effect in effecting the revolution of human society. As we conceive religion is all-powerful in its own legitimate sphere to produce by its internal vitality, the changes which men's characters and destinies need.

EAST AND WEST.

IN the nature of things nations must be true to their types. The marked characteristics of races must repeat themselves, and develop as generations multiply. In the working out of the law of evolution where the most prominent peculiarities fail to be consorted together, the peculiarities grow less and less marked in the course of time, and ultimately disappear. The disappearance means the destruction of national character, if not the extermination of the race. The modern Jews, Greeks, and Romans illustrate this truth. We Hindus, also partially illustrate it, though in our case it must be said the disappearance of national peculiarities has not been complete, and the consequent loss of national character, therefore, not final. There has been evident decay, real and terrible, and we are sometime struck with amazement how in older times such mighty geniuses, philosophical, literary, and religious, sprang from such materials as now form the inner and outer constitution of Hindu society. But there is before us the obstinate fact. Hindu society has not very materially changed, at least in Western and Northern India, but the genius of the nation, its internal vitality, is all but gone. We can yet appreciate and go into the depths of the old Aryan types of character, the unspeakable and ingrained peculiarities of Hindu nationality strike within us at times a strange response, the aroma of our sacred antiquity now and then sets our brain and blood aglow, and for the time we feel all our wants satisfied in the endless affluence of our ancient ideas and utterances. We feel all this; the types and the peculiarities are there. Only we fail to repeat them. They have very nearly ceased to be the elements of our character, we have almost lost the power of propagation. The few remaining embers of the old national character are being stamped out very fast by an aggressive Western culture which in its conquering fury is blind to the claims of every other thing besides itself. The West is simply swallowing up the East. The West is swamping the exquisite structures of Eastern thought and faith under a torrent of utilitarian and scientific civilization, the ultimate stages of which are best represented by Mr. Mill's "Three Essays on Theism," and Professor Tyndale's Belfast Address. India must consent to be buried alive, or reassert its vitality. How can this be most effectually done? If it be admitted as a fact that the old susceptibilities still lie latent in our character, and are aroused in intense flashes when we come in contact with what was really great and noble in the past, they can be developed by culture. We want a thoroughly oriental, or let us say Hindu culture. Putting aside for the time all foreign influences, all conventional, illegitimate, non-descript methods, if we adopted for the time strict systems of national culture, the ancient Aryan elements in our character would certainly develop, and unbury for our use those antique treasures of thought and worship, of faith and inspiration, which might once more put our nation on its primeval footing of progress and originality. It is useless and somewhat shameless to be continually vapouring about our past greatness, and doing nothing so far as we are ourselves concerned, to revive it. But on the other hand it must be observed that the ancient times cannot come back again. If Manu trod the soil of India once more we would not consider ourselves bound to accept from him a fresh code of social polity or religious observances, unless he undertook to change his own principles very materially. Vyas and Vasista would meet in us strict and determined antagonists if they tried to impose their old views upon the population of India. Our needs are new, our views have progressed, our principles have left the old prescribed limits. We cannot afford to dispense with the West. The practical instincts, the steady energy, the undaunted and undying firmness, the ever-active ever-beneficient struggle for society, the fearless protest and war against oppression and wrong whereever found, the scientific ardour, the deep regard for life and comfort, so peculiar to the West, these we cannot dispense with. We cannot push by the strong arm of Europe supporting us in the midst of our weakness and decay, and find the step or the steadiness to walk by ourselves. Our present religion and morality owe more to the influence of Europe than we can express. It is there we find the model of national life, the types of national character, and though our nation must be very differently constituted indeed from theirs, we can not deny they have struck within us the kindred fire of humanity, to be kindled and developed according to the materials and elements at our disposal. "I have longed to set your Asiatic jewls in a Western frame," writes a friend from England," it is not in me to sit down content while such grand and beautiful elements of life and thought as the Brahmo Somaj presents, are worked out so imperfectly as is often the case. The East and the West need each other. You need our practical determination, and we need your reverent devoutness." Yes, so we do. Let each of us work within our sphere in faithfulness to our capabilities and ideals, to our history, antecedents, and faith, and in the end there must come to be the grand fusion of gifts and humanities set down thus in prophetic language.—"And they shall come from the East and the West, and the North and the South, and sit down in the Kingdom of God."

OUR FAITH AND OUR EXPERIENCES.

(Continued.)

HERE my heart trembles and my mind seems to falter. In truth, I cannot speak of our Experiences except with some degree of diffidence and hesitation, sorrow and shame. I have told you, my friends, that the Eternal Spirit-God is guiding us into all truth. It is He who has called us, animated and bestirred our hearts, guided and cheered us in our daily struggles and conflicts with the temptations of life. At home the Spirit-Father, the Spirit-Mother feeds us, and with tender care watches over our interests and keeps us under a most loving and unwearied guardianship. In the Church the Spirit-Pastor preaches to us, gives us holy council whereby the Soul is enlightened and sanctified. In the battle-field of daily life, where a thousand deadly foes have to be confronted and vanquished, the Spirit-Captain with thrilling commands guides our movements and saves us from danger. Thus at all times the encompassing Spirit of God is our guide, refuge and comforter. We know no other master, we have no other guardian. Sure it is that we are marching under His guideuce. But marching whither is the question? Whither is the spirit of God leading progressive India? Is He leading us more and more to what you call the Brahmo Somaj? I say emphatically, no. That Heaven is leading us onward to His holy Church, it would be base infidelity to deny. You dare not deny that India is marching towards the Kingdom of Heaven. But the Brahmo Somaj, as it is, is not God's holy Church; it has no semblance whatever of the Kingdom of Heaven. Verily, verily, this Brahmo Somaj is a rediculous caricature of the Church of God. Such an assertion may startle many here present, but it is nevertheless true. I would not traduce or misrepresent my own Church. Surely, it is not expected of me that I should in the least underrate or disparage the Brahmo Somaj. May I feel I am partial to my own Church. And who is not? I love my Church, because all my best hopes for time and eternity are centred there. I cling to it affectionately, because my God has called me to it for my salvation and my country's, and I will fight for it because there is Divine truth in it. But I cannot suffer my partiality and fondness to run into blind bigotry and untruthful partizanship. Whatsoever in my Church God has hallowed by His sacred touch, let me honor and justify; but whatsoever in it is of man, carnal and earthy, I would be foremost in denouncing. I honestly tell you that this Church, I see before me to-day, known as the Church of *Brahm* or the Supreme God, satisfies not my own ideal of the true and living Church of God. It is, indeed, a pleasure to see men and women forsake idolatry and gather together in the Brahmo Somaj. And in their beaming countenances there is evidence enough of a desire to know truth and of a striving after a better life. Then again these Brahmo Somajes are multiplying in different parts of the country, year after year, and thus extending the domain to light, and diminishing the area of darkness, unbelief and corruption. All this is real and cheering, and cannot fail to make us rejoice exceedingly. And yet I say these Brahmo Somajes and the men thereof are far from attaining the high standard of truth and goodness they profess. From old anscestral errors they have indeed gone far away, and are on the way to the true Church. But they have errors and weaknesses, sins and iniquities, of which they must be ashamed. They have, by their ignoble practices, dishonored their noble faith. Their own experiences are a melancholy commentary upon their creed. Their forty years' history is a sad and discouraging tale of how ignominiously men behave in their actual lives in spite of their lofty professions. If, gentlemen, you wish to see a community where men have conspired to ignore their faith, sacrifice their consciences and rebel against Heaven's ordinances, witness this Church which has proudly set itself up in this country as the very type of God's Church. Our experiences must be disappointing and discouraging to those who seek a high order of purity in our community. Let us turn to our moral history, and analyze our character, and I should be surprised if we did not unanimously confess with sorrow and shame our ten thousand sins and short-comings. The question is not, whether you are guilty of gross crimes and vices, but whether you have attained that high purity of character which your religion enjoins. Can you combat and vanquish the temptations of the world? Is there strength enough in your hearts to crucify the flesh? Is your power of will such that evil, of whatever form and degree, must succumb to it? Do we find every evening that the day has been spent honestly and righteously, and that nothing impure has polluted the hand of the heart? If our deeds and words are pure, are our thoughts and wishes altogether clean? As we pass in review our daily experiences, how much alas! there is to excite sorrow, remorse and self-condemnation. Charity, justice, meekness, forgiveness, veracity, philanthropy,—are these virtues to be found in an eminent degree among the men of our Church? Surely we have not given India what we promised. We are not an example unto our countrymen and countrywomen. There is not enough love of truth in our intellectual pursuits and speculations. There is not enough brotherly love among our community. There is not enough purity in our lives. Ah! my friends, that all embracing catholicism for which we wish the world to give us credit is sadly wanting in us. We are narrow, sectarian and exclusive..

Correspondence.

LETTER FROM MUSSOORIE.

To the Editor of the *Indian Mirror*.

BROTHER,—Yesterday, Sunday, we met at the house of Babu Bissonath Roy of Lucknow, who, as you remember, was present at our late Anniversaries in Calcutta. We were thirteen in all; and, by a unanimous vote, are to meet there again next Sunday. There are in all about 25 Babus in Mussoorie. . . . There was a felt joy among us in the discovery that the possibilities of Jesus under God were simply and altogether human. And, that what God has done, in him, God may do again, in others of his children: though Jesus stands now, among men, *facile princep*, *first* on the list of our benefactors. His *spirit* was present at our meeting, realizing our dear Keshub's brave assertion that India's chief joy is and must be, "the spirit of Christ." It (he) spoke to us from heaven and said "I have given you an example that ye should to do to others what I have done for you; and greater things than I have done ought ye to do, never forgetting that what man can, can man. I am a man who has told you the truth that I have heard of God." "God loves you quite as well as he loves me. Holy Father, keep, in thine own love, these seekers of truth, in the spirit of truth, that *they* may be one as we are." Such was the tone of our meeting. One who was present said: "I quoted once, to a dying mother, the words ascribed to Job, as he cast himself upon God, and said, 'Though He slay me, yet will I trust in Him.'" "Ah, but, Charlie," she replied, "I once heard Dr. Holley say that the book of Job was a poem." To her, a poem was something like a fiction. "Grand-mother," he replied, "if these words dropped from a bleeding human heart, and yours is a human heart, why care for the wrapper in which the Father has sent us this triumph of faith! They utter the clear voice of faith triumphant in death. As such let us feed on them, with thanksgiving, and be strong." This personal incident prefaced a remark on "*The consolatory discourse*," as it is called, *i. e*, the converse of Jesus with his faithful few, at their last meal together, before his death. What was said of this, must close my present letter. It was asserted with apparently general consent,—the Jesus' words to his disciples, at the table of their last supper with him, filling five chapters of St. *John's* gospel, *viz*: from the 13th to the 18th—give us the *spirit*—the religion—of a divine life;—the voice of a true salvation just as "*The Sermon on the Mount*," (filling chapters 5, 6, 7, of *Matthew's* biography of Jesus,) gives us the *morality* of the true eternal life. "The Consolatory Discourse" sheds down the very glow of heaven into our valley of the shadow of death. This it does with a warmth and brilliancy, that dazzles and over-shines all the tapers of intellectual and historical criticism that men can bring around it. Sitting in the full glory of this light,—which when fairly pondered, makes the glorious death-scene of Socrates but as a lamp to the lightning,—we care little for the question as to how it reached us. However important, that matter falls into shadow. *How we got* this light to illumine the dark way out of life into life,—who cares? Here is the light. Who *wrote* the Gospel biography of Jesus ascribed to John?—To me it matters not. *How I got* the wealth I hold in undoubted possession, I leave to the lawyers. 'Tis their business. That I have the money and am its actual and rightful possessor, is the thing for me. * * * Such was the drift of part of our conversation which, by a unanimous show of hands up, we renew next Sunday.

Yours &c.
DALL.

CHRIST AND HIS MOTHER.

To the Editor of the *Indian Mirror*.

SIR,—In last Sunday's *Indian Mirror* I see a reply to a letter which appeared in your paper four weeks ago, and I shall feel obliged if you will allow me, even at this late date, to bring forward the following for the consideration of your first correspondent.

However courteous may have been the Greek term used by Christ in addressing his mother, it is very evident that on the few occasions of which we hear of Mary in the Gospels, Christ's language expresses separation between himself and her. One is struck by this, and asks why it was, that the tender and loving Jesus so spoke and acted, for he was dutiful as a boy, (see Luke 2 51-52) and he must have been the support of his mother and her family, working as a well-known carpenter in Nazareth. (Matt. 13, 54-56 and Mark 6, 3.)

Your correspondent cannot understand what would seem to be coldness to his mother on the part of Jesus, whom he describes as a "charming apostle." But those who in the lowly son of man recognize the son of God, who was soon to return to "the bosom of the Father," to the glory which he had with Him before the world was, (John 17.) easily find one, at least, very strong reason for Christ's speaking as he did.

Did not the Lord Jesus Christ cast his eye down the long ages of the future and see those who called themselves "Christians" bowing down by millions to Mary, and appealing to her as the mediator, instead of to Himself? Did he not see images of the "Virgin" set up in the place of Venus? Did his eye not scan the paintings in what should have been the house of God, and read the words of Scripture written beneath, which referred to himself as the Saviour, misapplied to Mary? Did he not see the countless shrines with votive offerings to the mother who was supposed to care? Did he not see the word of God itself withheld from the people, denounced and burned down even to our day in Spain and Mexico, because its teachings showed the traditions of the Church of Rome to be contrary to the will of God? The Lord Jesus who "knew what was in man," must have foreseen the overwhelming amount of sin that would be committed in this wordship of Mary, or "Mariolatry."

Perhaps, your correspondent has never been brought into contact with the teaching of the various Churches which recognize tradition and "the voice of the Church" as of equal authority with the Holy Scripture, and thus like the Jews of old teach for doctrines the commandments of men (Mark 7. 7.)

What Church that took the word of God for its lamp and guide, could have fallen into the errors of the Greek, Armenian, Russian and Roman Catholic Churches? Seemingly ignorant of the loving heart of Jesus, they go to Mary as to a sympathizing mother, though there is not one word in Scripture which tells us to pray to Mary, or gives us the least hope that she can hear, or answer, or intercede. Indeed, I think if devout Mary could come back, mortal, to earth again and see all the dishonoring of God through her name, it would break her heart.

The following is from Gardner's "Faiths of the World;" "Pius IX in his encyclical letter of date 1846, says: In order that our Most Merciful God may the more readily incline his ear to our prayers, and may grant that which we implore, let us ever have recourse to the intercession of the most holy Mother of God, the Immaculate Virgin Mary, our sweetest mother, our mediatrix, our advocate, our surest hope and firmest reliance, than whose patronage nothing is more potent, nothing more effectual &c. &c. In 1854 His Holiness issued a decree declaring the immaculate conception of the Virgin to be henceforth an article of faith in the Romish Church. She is henceforth to be taken out of the category of sinful mortals and ranged among sinless beings."

Hodge in his "Systematic Theology" says of the doctrine of *Mary's being born herself without sin*. "This question was undecided at the meeting of the Council of Trent" (1545). The controversy went on, therefore, after the Council of Trent very much as it had done before, until the present Pope, himself a devoted worshipper of the Virgin, announced his purpose to have the Immaculate Conception of the Mother of our Lord declared. This purpose he carried into effect; and on the 8th December 1854, he went in great pomp to St. Peters at Rome, and pronounced the decree that the "Virgin Mary from the first moment of conception by the special grace of Almighty God in view of the merits of Christ, was preserved from all stain of original sin."

Eleven years ago, in the harbour of Civita Vecchia in Italy I saw a newly painted steamer, the Italian title—strange one for a ship—which shone out in gilt lettering was the "*Immaculate Conception!*"

What need there is for all who would know what the doctrine of Jesus Christ is, to keep close by the word of God! If your correspondent will read through the Gospel of John, I think he will see that if Christ is not *Divine*, he has no right to be considered even a "charming apostle." We understand now those Jews who would not believe in Christ's divinity, crucified him for what they considered "blasphemy." But we, believing the Scripture which cannot be broken, honor the Son even as we honor the Father. (John 5. 25.)

CALCUTTA, The 8th June, 1876. } I am, Sir, Yours, A CHRISTIAN.

Devotional

GRANT unto me O Lord, a pure mind that is assured in confidence upon thy approval, and I seek no more. Grant unto me a clear conscience that lives in the atmosphere of thy holiness, and I shall be satisfied. I would seek not the approbation of men, and fear not much the evil words men delight to utter, only suffer me to be faithful in the service to which thou hast called me. The strength that thou dost bless a good conscience with can defy the hardness and injustice of the world's treatment. Enable me in all circumstances to preserve my heart undefiled.

MY son rest securely in me, be assured of my love and protection, and abide in safety. Do not call up thy fears and suspicions, let not thy imagination delude thee, when I am at hand to succor and rescue thee. No one that put his trust in me, did ever suffer. No one that wept at my feet was ever given up. I am nigh unto thy troubled heart, despair not; my right hand is ready to save thee, why shouldst thou sink?

MY God, my Saviour, who is so gracious as Thou? A word from thee is like the water of life and joy to me. Thy promise is the rock of ages. My Father, I would abide safely in thee even when my soul misgives, I will put my trust in Thee when my best friends in the world have failed me. The readiness of Thy right hand to shield me is like a fortress of strength to me that defies the wrath of sin, and hardness of the world. I bless Thee, and would do Thy work cheerfully.

IN the darkness of solitude, in the depression of melancholy O thou God of light, visit me. Visit me in the still hour of evening when there is no one near, visit me in the gloomy hour of midnight when the world is buried in gloom. Visit me again when I totter alone on the brink despair and when distrusting doubts take away from me the staff of my existence. When the fear of death, of desertion, of homelessness, of poverty, of degradation stares me in the face, and fills me with fright, good, good Master, be not far. Fear not, I am with thee always.

The Brahmo Somaj

THE new Brahmo Mundir at Noakhali has been consecrated and opened.

AN interesting Brahmo marriage was celebrated in Dacca on the 1st instant. The bridegroom Babu Ambica Churn Sen is lecturer of Chemistry in the Krishnagur College, and is about twenty-six years of age. He is of the Vaidya caste, and is altogether a promising young man. The bride, Sudakhina Ganguli, is a pupil of the Dacca Normal School perhaps the most shining pupil there. She is about seventeen years old, and comes from a high Brahmin Kulin family. The marriage was celebrated with some *eclat*, all sections of Dacca society, Christian, Mahomedan, and Hindu being present. Dr. Robson, the Inspector of Schools, and Mr. Livingstone, a Professor of the local College, were present. Babu Kanty Chunder Mitter presided over the ceremonial, and Babu Bango Chunder Roy over the devotional part of the proceedings. We wish the newly married couple every happiness and prosperity.

UNDER the auspices of Babu K. C. Sen, the Brahmo missionaries are now learning in right earnest the methods by which the truths and the spirit of their religion can be successfully carried into the midst of the poor and the masses in the country. For a whole week they have been issuing in evening processions from the *Sadhan Kanan*, and visiting the houses of the poor people of Morepukur, there to sing hymns and offer prayers of such a nature as may affect their simple uneducated hearts. May divine blessing descend on such noble and good effort!

THE following appears in the *Friend of India*:—An admirer of Babu Keshub Chunder Sen, writes eloquently from the Punjab in praise of the Babu's "philosophical religion, solid doctrines, and spiritual teaching." We refrain from shocking the modesty of Keshub Babu by publishing our correspondent's letter in full. He differs from the opinion we recently expressed as to the future of Brahmoism and thinks it is destined to be the universal religion—the "Common Church" of mankind. Prophets disagree.

AN interesting devotional meeting was held in the Bharat Asram on the morning of the 24th May last. The service commenced exactly at 4½ A. M., and concluded at 6 A. M. The ladies of the house, some of whom had been acting up lately according to a prescribed discipline, entered the place of service each with a lighted lamp in one hand and garlands of flowers in the other. The room which was quite dark before became somewhat obscurely lighted by these lamps which were placed underneath the flower pots and plants arranged in the middle of the room. After service the ladies put the garlands round each other's necks, and exchanged mutual salutations. Everything looked exceedingly graceful and natural, and the ceremony, it is hoped, produced wholesome influence on the minds of those who joined it. Devotional and other readings commenced at 8 A. M. The ladies provided and served out refreshments to each other.

Literary

AN American book entitled "The Mysterious Island" by Jules Verne, is just out. This wonderful work contains the adventures of five Union prisoners of war, who escaped from Richmond during 1865, in a captured Balloon! They are blown about for days, like a feather, by a wild tempest, and at last are cast upon a desert island in the Pacific Ocean.

MAJOR R.D. OSBORNE'S "Islam under the Arabs," is just published by Messrs Longmans & Co.

BALLARD'S "True Tales about India, its Native Princes, &c," is just issued.

Municipal London. By Joseph I. B. Firth, LL.B. (Longmans.)—Mr. Firth expresses the subject of his book thus:—"London Government as it is, and London under a Municipal Government." It is an indictment formidable in every way (the volume runs to nearly eight hundred full-sized octavo pages) of the present order of things, especially of the proceedings of the Corporation of London, and suggestions for a reformation. It is impossible to go into details, but some of Mr. Firth's figures may be quoted. "The Corporation pays in salaries between £60,000 and £70,000 per annum, and in wages between £110,000 and £120,000." That is sufficiently startling. And then among minor items, "more then £1,000 has been spent upon the City State Coach during the last ten years." As it makes but one journey in the year, that is a somewhat heavy charge. It would scarcely be fair to those whom the author attacks to specify his charges. Let it suffice to say that they are such, so grave, and supported by so much *prima facie* evidence, that they must be answered.—*Spectator.*

MESSRS. SAMPSON, LOW AND CO., are issuing an interesting "Monthly" for 1s 6d. It is called "Men of Mark," and each number contains three beautifully executed photographs of contemporary celebrities. There is a short biography attached to each portrait. The first number contains portraits and lives of Lord Lytton, Judge Hudleston and Mr. Plimsoll. The work is said to be a charming production.

ANOTHER new paper, to be called the *Punjab Courier*, and to be published twice a week, is to be started at Lahore on the 1st of August next.

WE have received a copy of the *Indian Standard*, a small daily pice paper, just started at Lucknow.

AN extra number of the *Graphic* has been published as a souvenir of the visit of the Prince of Wales to India. It consists of sixty-eight pages, the greater portion of which are devoted to the best illustrations which have appeared from time to time in the *Graphic* of the most noteworthy scenes during the progress of the Prince through India.

THE dispute between Professors Muller and Whitney is widening and deepening. The *Academy* refused to publish Professor Whitney's last letter: but it found a place in the *Examiner* and in the *Nation* (the American paper), together with much accessory matter, tending to convict Professor Max Muller of double dealing of no ordinary kind. The dispute has reached Germany, so that a general *expose* is going on. Boehtlingk has told Max Muller in a German pamphlet to adhere to the truth, and to abstain from complimenting him, as his praises can give him (Boehtlingk) no pleasure, and do him no honor! The controversy is certainly waxing warm.

MR. A. C. LYALL, Agent to Governor-General for Rajputana, is, it is reported, about to compile a Rajputana Gazetteer.

IT is announced that Mr. Gladstone is writing a paper on "Modern Religious Thought." It will appear in the *Contemporary Review* for June.

IT seems that Lieutenant Cameron is to receive ten shillings for every copy of his book sold; and since ten thousand have already been ordered to be printed as a first edition, that will give him £5,000 down. Colonel Baker only gets three shillings a copy for his "Clouds in the East"; and Fred Burnaby has taken a different course from either, and is to have a lump sum of £750 for his work on Khiva.

Scientific.

IT is estimated that if one minute be given to the examination of each article in the Philadelphia Centennial Exhibition, it will take five months, at ten hours each day, to get through.

EMPRESS VICTORIA has signified her intention of contributing a number of articles made by herself and members of her family, to the Philadelphia Exhibition. The list comprises twenty-six etchings by the Empress, and two table napkins of her own spinning; a banner screen embroidered by the Princess Beatrice; a table cloth embroidered by the Princess Louise of Hesse, and the Princess Christian of Schleswig-Holstein; and four drawings of flowers, by the Princess Louise, (Marchioness of Lorne.)

A FYZABAD correspondent of the *Indian Standard* notes the receipt by the local museum of a "petrified turtle," found in a bed of kunkur. It was presented by Mr. Gennoe, of the Opium Department.

SOME very ancient statues have been discovered at Bulrampore which are being carefully dug out.

Latest News

—ON May 19, Sir George Campbell was to have called the attention of the House of Commons to the relations between the Colonial Office and some Crown and other colonies situated in tropical regions, with especial reference to the treatment of Asiatic immigrants.

—MR. DISRAELI has granted a pension of £100 a year to the widow of Shirley Brooks, for many years, Editor of the *Punch* and *Home News*.

—THE favorite relaxations of the late Mr. A. T. Stewart, the American millionaire, were reading books on theology and searching for a classical origin of English words.

—CAPTAIN K. C. PYE, R. E., Manager, Rajputana State Railway, is granted one month's privilege leave, with effect from the 29th May 1876.

—MAJOR O. ST. JOHN, R. E., Principal of the Mayo College at Ajmere, has been granted privilege leave for one month.

—THE Rev Dr. Thoburn, has already arrived in America. He is now at Belaire, Ohio.

—THE Prime Minister of Japan will visit America soon.

—THE King of Dahomey has refused to pay the fine imposed upon him for outrages on British subjects. He has invited the British Commodore to his capital, promising to pay him there in powder and shot.

—THE Princess of Wales, accompanied by her two sons, was present at an entertainment to the school-children in Sandringham School, illustrative of the Prince of Wales' recent Indian visit.

—THE Royal Titles Act has already given rise to a "question" in the law courts. Vice-Chancellor Hall was asked on Wednesday whether or not it would be necessary to state the new title in a writ intended to be served in Germany? His Honor refused to give an opinion, and referred the querist to the Records and Writs Office. A clerk in that Office will, therefore, be asked to settle the question.

—A MEETING of members of the National Indian Association took place at the Society of Arts, London, on May 15, to hear Miss Carpenter give some account of her recent visit to India. The chair was taken by Mr. Samuel Morley, M.P., who stated that he presided on that occasion with the greatest pleasure, if only to show his respect and admiration for their dear friend, Miss Carpenter, whose exertions in the cause of Indian female education deserved, in his opinion, their greatest admiration and gratitude. Young English ladies, said the lecturer, could not do better than prepare themselves at home and proceed to India in the educational mission. In answer to questions Miss Carpenter was happy to state that Mahomedan schools were being formed in parts of India. Mirza Pir Buksh, a Mahomedan, thanked Miss Carpenter for her lecture. After some warmly eulogistic observations from Mr. H. Pratt, the Chairman proposed a hearty vote of thanks to Miss Carpenter for her admirable address. It must be admitted, he said, that we had very much neglected India, and that it would be wise to do something to stimulate public opinion in its favor.

—MR. PEDDER has resigned the Municipal Commissionership of Bombay. There is some probability of Sir Frank Souter, the Commissioner of Police, Bombay, being elected to that important post.

—THE new Bishop of Bombay and his Chaplain left Southampton by the P. and O. steamer, on June 8.

—THE Prince Imperial well shortly make a tour through North America. The idea of the journey, which is strongly supported by General Fleury and the Prince himself, has been opposed by the once omnipotent M. Rouher, while the Empress has been neutral in the matter.

—THE Pope completed his eighty-fourth year, on Saturday, the 13th May, having been born on May 13, 1792.

—IN consequence of several English travellers having penetrated into remote parts of the Russian Empire, where it is not desired that they should appear, orders have now been issued by the Russian Government that all foreigners on crossing the Russian frontier, shall report themselves to the Consul of their country, who will be held responsible for their subsequent movements.

—MR. W. G. McIVOR, Superintendent of Government Cinchona Plantations, died at Ootacamund, after a brief illness.

—SIR JOSEPH FAYRER'S friends of the Indian Medical Service, entertained him at dinner at St. James' Hall, London, in recognition of his having attained the honor of knighthood, and also of his safe return from India.

—THE presents received by the Prince of Wales from the Native Princes of India are to be exhibited at South Kensington at one penny a head.

—THERE is a report at Peshawur that a Camp of Exercise, on a small scale, will probably, be held at Hasn Abdal, next cold season.

—THE Prince of Wales' collection of Indian animals are being exhibited at the London Zoological Gardens at one shilling for each visitor.

—THE *Englishman* says that the Acting Agent of the East India Railway Co., having heard that dissatisfaction is felt by the employes of the Locomotive Department, has requested Government to appoint an officer to hold an independent enquiry into the complaints of the men, and that Captain Wallace, R. E., has been deputed to this duty. The enquiry will commence at Allahabad to-morrow morning.

—THE Prince of Wales held a brilliant levee at St. James' Palace, London, when besides the Thakore of Limri, there were presented two Resaldars of the 11th Prince of Wales' Own Bengal Lancers, who, the following day, went to Windsor, and were received by the Queen. So says the London correspondent of the *Englishman*.

—MR. GROSVENOR will not proceed to Simla, but the whole of his party were to have left Rangoon for China *via* the Straits yesterday. It is said he was not admitted to see the King of Burmah at Mandalay.

—IT seems to be pretty well settled (the *Athenæum* says) that another change of some importance, besides the reduction of the limits of age announced in Lord Salisbury's recent Minute, will be made in the regulations affecting candidates for the Indian Civil Service. A smaller amount of knowledge of Oriental languages and dialects than has hitherto been required in the further examinations will be exacted, as the number of subjects prescribed is to be diminished and a portion of the studies of the candidates will be deferred till their arrival in India.

—IT is stated that the Duke of Edinburgh will shortly be promoted to the rank of Rear-Admiral.

—SIR FRANK SOUTER, KT., C.S.I., took his seat for the first time as a member of the Town Council, Bombay, on Wednesday last.

—SIR BARTLE FRERE and Lord Suffield have been honored with the Knight Grand Cross of the Order of the Bath, and Mr. Francis Knollys, the Prince of Wales' Private Secretary, has been elevated to the companionship of the same order.

—ON Friday last, a horse belonging to Mr. Charles, residing at the new Civil Station, Allahabad, seized his syce by the back of the neck and galloped about, shaking him until life became extinct. The brute then dropped the body at the entrance to the compound, and retired quietly into his stable.

—THE London correspondent of the *Bombay Gazette* says that the reported value of the presents which the Prince of Wales has received from the Native Princes, has been greatly exaggerated.

—SOME quarrelling has taken place between the Sunni and Shias at Delhi, and the Deputy Commissioner has had to take measures to preserve the peace. All preaching in the streets has been prohibited.

—IT is reported that Colonel J. W. Younghusband, C. S. I., of the Punjab, is likely to be created a K. C. S. I.

—THERE was a heavy fall of hail in the Rawul Pindi district last week. Two Natives are said to have died from injuries received from the hail during the storm.

—A WEEKLY Hindu *Anjuman* is about to be started in Gujran-wala in the Punjab, under the auspices of Rai Gopal Dass, Judicial Assistant Commissioner.

—A. M. PLATZ who belongs to an old Austrian family, has laid a wager that he will ride from Vienna to Paris in a fortnight on the back of a camel which he has brought from Africa.

—COLONEL GEORGE CHESNEY, Principal of the Civil Engineers' College at Cooper's Hill, has retired on full pay.

—ACCORDING to *Allen's Indian Mail*, Sir Lewis Pelly is probably expecting to be the first Chief Commissioner of Sind upon the completion of the Indus Railway, and the retirement of Sir W. L. Merewether from the present Commissionership.

—MR. R. F. CAMPBELL, the Senior Magistrate of the Madras Police Court, delivered over charge of his office to Mr. Srinivasa Row last week. Till a successor is appointed, Major Weldon and Mr. Mahomed Yusuff will assist Mr. Srinivasa Row, in the Madras Police Court.

—THE present pay of the Chief Commissioner of Mysore is Rs. 4,166-10-8, and his "sumptuary allowance" Rs. 500, but, according to the *Bangalore Spectator*, Mr Saunders comes out with a personal allowance of Rs. 1,000 which will bring his total salary up to Rs. 5,666-10-8.

—THE Hon'ble Mr. Gibbs has left Mahableshwur for Sattara.

—THE Commander-in-Chief and the Governor of Bombay were expected to arrive at Poona on Wednesday last.

—THE Governor-General's Council will probably meet soon at Simla to consider bills for remedying effects of the Privy Council's decision in the Bhownugger cession case.

Law

POLICE—JUNE 10, 1876.

[*Before F. J. Marsden, Esq.*]

A *Mali* charged a Native with the theft of a jack-fruit from a tree in 17, Theatre Road. The *Mali* and his witnesses stated that the defendant was caught on the tree with the jack in his hands, and made over to the Police. The defendant stated that certain boys had shot a bird on the tree, and had sent him to fetch it. After he had climbed the tree in order to get down the bird, the *Mali*, picking up a jack which was lying down, put it into his hands, and raised a hue and cry. It appearing, however, that the jack was freshly broken, the Magistrate, in the absence of any proof for the defence, sentenced the accused to fourteen days' rigorous imprisonment.

Advertisements

Printed and published by M. M. RUKHIT, at the INDIAN MIRROR PRESS, No. 15, College Square, for the Proprietor.

The Indian Mirror.

SUNDAY EDITION.

VOL. XVI.] CALCUTTA, SUNDAY JUNE, 18, 1876 { REGISTERED AT THE GENERAL POST OFFICE. } [No. 143

CONTENTS.

NOTICE.

All letters and communications relating to the literary department of the Paper should be addressed to the Editor. All other letters should be addressed to the Manager, to whom all remittances should be made payable.

Subscribers will be good enough to bring to the notice of the Manager any delay or irregularity in the delivery of the Paper.

Editorial Notes

A BENGALI gentleman, erewhile an enthusiastic member of the Brahmo Somaj, now studying science and philosophy in Germany, purposes to return home, travelling by foot through Europe and Asia, and studying the manners and customs of the countries through which he walks. Such an enterprise, if performed, will develop a new phase of character in our young countrymen, and give further evidence of their capabilities.

THE tables are turned. Religion bribes Science in Europe, Science bribes religion in India. The officer in charge of the Great Trigonometrical Survey in Madras, wanted to conduct his scientific operations from the top of a high Hindu temple. The Brahmins mustered in large numbers at the gate, and noisily objected to the installation of the theodolite over the heads of the gods underneath. Major Branfill, the officer in charge, then offered money to defray the expenses of expiatory ceremonies rendered necessary for the surveying work upstairs. Thousands of rupees were asked and given. Thus science performed her operations, and religion her purification, and everything went on smoothly because there was plenty of money to pave the way. What say the rigid Christian officials to this sort of arrangement?

OUR learned and revered theistic sister Miss Frances Power Cobbe, is engaged just now in a work exposing the injustice and inhumanity of these painful experiments on living animals which are understood by the word Vivisection. While science is on the one hand making its votaries callous to all the nobler sentiments of spirituality and faith, it is on the other hand making them callous to the sentiments of pity and humanity, for the terrible sufferings which it inflicts on dumb and helpless brutes. Who knows but that the rage for scientific experiments may some day develop into the Vivisection of human beings. If the law against cruelty of animals does not apply to pain caused by scientific experiments, why should the law against causing grievous bodily hurt to human beings apply in the case of similar scientific investigation, when the men who suffer are paid or persuaded to consent to the suffering?

ALL missionary work, undertaken in the right spirit, must produce good effect. But the effect is definite in certain cases, and not definite in others. A missionary may cast abroad the seeds of truth and righteousness on all sides, and may have no opportunity in his life-time to gather the harvests he has richly deserved. And there may be another who does all this, and at the same time finds the means, by Divine grace, of training up two or three souls according to the highest standard of truth and purity he may possess. Perhaps, every one who undertakes the duties of a missionary, should pay attention to both these branches of good work. Let him go where he is called if his spirit urges him far and near. But let him also do the Master's work at home training up and maturing in goodness a few souls entrusted to his care. The legacy of the spirit must be left behind to the many and to the few; to the many in future and undeveloped goodness, to the few in definite forms of righteousness and truth.

IF suspicion is once engendered in the minds of religious men and friends against each other, and if that suspicion be of such a nature that they do not venture to open their minds on the subject, the cause of brotherhood and mutual good will really arrive at a crisis. Open and loud protests against mutual deficiencies, arguments, and hot discussions do not perpetrate half the mischief that silent, secret, unjust suspicions do. The oldest and deepest friendship is undermined. The tenderest relations are ruptured and no community of feeling or action is possible when the foul influence of this unholy distrust once infects the heart. It tells upon a growing brotherhood like an unspoken curse marring the effects of the highest teaching, and chilling the influences of the noblest discipline. Men upon whom an unholy suspicion is fastened, labor under a dead weight whose depressing influence few can estimate. If religious men cannot love each other let them at all events esteem each other as honorable men who fear God, and want to serve Him with sincerity.

HOW far are expressions of bitterness allowable in religious discourses? Religion is a sweet thing, but it is a sad thing too sometimes, and at other times it is a bitter reality, carrying its disagreeable sensations into the very core of man's being. Upon some, and upon all on certain occasions, religion sheds its profound sweetness so full of consolation amid the trials and sorrows of life. Upon others, and all men at times come within that category, religion inflicts a bitterness which tinges and influences their whole character. When religion itself produces different impressions at different times, it is only natural to expect that the teachers and expounders of religion should make use of different expressions to suit different occasions. No one should think that nothing but sweet words can come out of the preacher. Sour and caustic words, scalding where they fall, and leaving a long and lasting impression of pain must come at seasons. It is this occasional sourness which makes the sweetness, when it comes, still more sweet.

"LIKE Cadmus the men of letters and philosophy" are said to be "sowing dragon's teeth, whence an armed host will rise to destroy, they think, all religious belief. But as in the fable an invisible hand will throw a stone in their midst, and make them fight with one another, till none but a few remain, and these would assist in building the city of God." This prophecy, the observers of the times say, is not likely to be fulfilled. The men of philosophy do not show much sign of misunderstanding each other, nor do they delight to indulge in unmeaning prascology which conceals the facts they mean to give expression to. So far as they deal with observed and ascertained truths in nature, they are not likely to fight with each other, but have been, and still are pretty unanimous. And their mission is not "to build the city of God." Let the defenders of religion recognize honorably and bravely the rights of the opposing host, take them by the hand, and associate with them in an amicable and humble spirit in building the new Jerusalem. "It will not be by the hostility of negative creeds," says a writer in the *Spectator*, "but by the discriminations of a brooding faith, that the destructive doubts of the day will be resolved."

STRICT and scrupulous honesty in shop-keeping is unhappily a rare virtue in India, and in fact anywhere in the world. But among our countrymen honorable, virtuous, righteous tradesmanship is all but unknown. Foreigners who go to our bazaars to make purchases, return with the worst opinion possible of our national character. If there is any intelligent and hard-working Brahmo ready to deliver his fellow countrymen from this unhappy reputation, let him read the career of Mr. A. T. Stewart of New York, a tradesman who leaves at his death forty millions sterling, the greatest fortune ever amassed by a single individual. The whole secret of his wonderful success in business is the strict and unflinching truthfulness of his dealings with his customers. "In these days of reckless speculation, fraudulent bankruptcy, and cheats and shams of every kind, he set his face like a flint against them all, dismissed every salesman who was found mis-representing goods or wheedling purchasers, and made it as safe for the most inexperienced child to approach his counters as for the most adroit bargainer." Mr. Stewart's custom was, therefore, unrivalled and he won a marvellous fortune!

IF all that is said be true of Lord Lytton in regard to the action His Excellency has taken on the subject of the grant of Rs. 12,000 made by the Lieutenant-Governor of the N. W. Provinces to the Roman Catholic Chapel at Allahabad, the Viceroy possesses a more unsectarian mind and a greater breadth of sympathy than usually falls to the lot of great Indian functionaries. The story according to a local contemporary's version is this. Sometime ago the authorities of the Roman Catholic chapel applied to the Local Government for a grant of money on condition of keeping five hundred free seats for British soldiers. Sir John Strachey forwarded the application to Calcutta wishing to know whether the money should be paid from imperial or from provincial funds. Being told that the Government of India could not advance the sum he ordered his own Government to pay it. The wrath of the imperial officials at this was great. They were of opinion that Sir John, by living long among the heathen, had forgotten his duties to his religion, and to the Reformation. It was an unheard of desecration of Protestant money to pay it in aid of a Roman Catholic Chapel and accordingly a thundering minute against His Honor's false liberality was indited, circulated, and put into the hands of the printer. As a matter of form the final proof-sheets were submitted to the new Viceroy for sanction. But Lord Lytton, to the surprise of all, not only did not accord his sanction, but indulged in such a strong minute against the eminently Protestant statement and the orthodox sentiments contained therein, that some believe the ministerial bigwigs entertain great apprehensions for His Excellency's soul. It is a statesman with European experience only, who is new to the country and its traditions, that can find the courage and the principle to snub little-minded bigotry like this in high official circles.

THE EXCOMMUNICATED.

EXCOMMUNICATION is a necessity of human nature. It is good for him who suffers it, and for those who inflict it. Real excommunication is seldom experienced, it does not fall to the lot of ordinary men. There are few men who are truly alone in their sorrow, and in their joy, who think it vain to seek, because they never can get sympathy. The severance of sympathy is almost always relative and never complete. Where it does approach completeness, there you see the sublimity of suffering. To the man who never had caste, nor relations, who has been born and bred to a life of ignoble selfishness and indifference to all the world, the man who has neither parents, nor brothers, nor sisters, nor friendships, nor deep and tender relations, to such a man excommunication means nothing. To the man who has no work to do, and does not want to have any, who understands only his present comfort and security, and wants freedom from every manner of interruption, to him excommunication is no suffering. The dull and the apathetic, the hard-hearted and the self-centered, what care they for excommunication? But the sensitive and affectionate, the man of many friendships and relations, the man who has once tasted of human affection and good will, it is he who feels the keen edge of the knife when sympathies and ties are cut away. The man who has work to do, and nobody would have him work, who would call others his friends, and take his own beloved ones by the hand, but they shun him and think his association polluting, or at rare intervals extend to him the benefit of their distant patronage, that man of all men suffers the penalty of being excommunicated. It is when those who have been most tenderly and persistently served, at whose hands you cannot think you have deserved any cruelty, when those turn away from you, and would not vouchsafe a little kind word, or even a look of sympathy, you feel how alone you are in the world. Sitting for hours, working, musing, sighing, hoping with no one beside you, the whole world flitting past without taking the least notice of you, as if you scarcely are in the land of the living, your affection unreceived and forgotten, your work and services ignored, your past blotted out in scorn from men's memory, your future dark and stark staring you in the face, it is then that you feel you are alone in the world. Watching by the bed side of the sick, awake when others are sleeping, tearful when others are glad, struggling, wrestling, being overwhelmed whith a whole world of familiar faces and friendly hands around, yet none ready to help, you feel you are really alone in life's wilderness. An exile in your own birth-place, homeless while you are so near home, unwept for when all know your deep sufferings, poor when you know you might have been rich, the load of dishonor fastened around your neck, you feel what it is to be excommunicated. Pity is due to the poor, medicine to the sick, and comfort to the sorrow-stricken, but to thee who art excommunicated, nothing is due. No one owes any duty to *thee*. You pass in the streets so well-known to you, but they know you there no more. In the old dear house-hold—the scene of so much affection and sacred joy, your presence produces a chill. Where you go men no longer smile. And if you have dear ones who who cannot be parted from you, they suffer with you, and sometimes more than yourself. You can bear your own misery you think, and you can calmly contemplate the inevitable end of it all, but the anticipation of their future strikes a new agony and dismay into your soul. But one moment's reflection will lay open the blessedness of this state. Who can pray so well as the excommunicated man? Who understands the sacredness of human sorrow so deeply as he. To whom, and to what does the whole soul turn, when the world shuts its doors so completely against him? Is there no new no profound source of sympathy unlocked to the excommunicated, when all other sources of comfort are closed? The relations of the alone to the Alone are then only realized in fulness. The soul seldom begins to leave off the vanity of human affections until these affections are withdrawn from it, and seldom appreciates the reality, depth and beauty of Divine love. Nothing but utter friendlessness can teach us the supreme friendship of Heaven. Excommunication which means social death, represents to us very nearly the end of all human relationship. It disembodies the soul in the body, and gives us all the coselation we deserve to get in the spiritual world where the highest promises are for them that mourn and are poor in spirit.

THE BRAHMO SOMAJ AND A GROWING EVIL.

[COMMUNICATED.]

HISTORY has borne repeated testimony to the painful fact that wherever there has been a complete divorce between man's religious belief and his practice, there has been a corresponding degradation in his morals. Even the highest spiritual exercises have not been a proof against individual depravity. On the contrary, where men soar the highest, they sink the lowest into the deepest pit of corruption. The case of modern Vaishnavaism will illustrate our position. We know of no creed where spirituality is cultivated to a greater extent, yet there is none where we meet with greater sensuality. The fact is, the higher the doctrine, the greater the discredit which man's natural wickedness brings upon it. There are some creeds, such as Hinduism, which are capacious enough to hold all that is good and evil in the world; and in them it requires no great effort to preserve a strange equilibrium between theory and practice. The highest and the lowest patterns of excellence are to be found in Hinduism, to regulate the fancies and to check the inordinate aspirations of the soul. To be a Hindu of the ordinary type, requires no sacrifice or heroism. That religion is ambitious of little, and it requires little of its followers. But the difficulty is increased, as soon as you come across an uncompromising creed. *All or none; thorough; not partial*—is the unmistakable motto of Brahmoism. What is to be accepted must be accepted thoroughly; what is to be done, must be done entirely, such is the law of our religion. There can be no half measures in the Brahmo Somaj, or if there are any, they must be considered as so many disadvantages and defects in our movement. It is greatly to the credit of our church that, up to this moment, our leaders and prominent members have preserved a purity, which has led even our stoutest opponents to identify it with every conception of goodness and true nobility. People expect the utmost saintliness and moral excellence in a Brahmo; and they would never have indulged in this expectation, if they had not seen the possibility of such goodness in the lives of many individual Brahmos. We allude to this fact with the greater pride, because we know that we are not indulging in a vein of self-gratulation or vanity, but merely consider the point necessary with a view to elucidate our future. And here we must confess that we tread on a delicate ground. The standard of our ethics and the excellence of our creed, have of late developed themselves to so high a pitch that we are perfectly justified in feeling an honest pride in its progress and rapid development. But query—is this growth accompanied by a corresponding elevation in morals? We should feign say, *Aye*, though sober truth requires that we should say *No*. Let not our friends frown, nor our enemies malign. Truth must be told, even when it wounds one's self-esteem. Our opinion is that the Brahmos have arrived at a certain stage of excellence, but beyond that and for a large number of years, there has been a painful stagnation. Let our Brahmo readers take note of this fact, for, conceal it as we may, it *is* a fact. There may be a fancied security in the present excel-[illegible] with every community, whose watchword is progress, not to advance is to recede. In this sense, is it not true that the Brahmo Somaj has receded a great deal? We appeal to the life of every individual Brahmo, and, say, is it worthy of man's confidence and of God's? Is there not too much fickleness, too much indolence, too much ease in our community? Is it not true, that while a few—a very few—have been preaching and practising truth, the vast majority of the Brahmos are lamentably lagging behind, unable to follow their leaders, though not unwilling to confess their inability? Are not the vast tracts in the Mofussil a dull, dreary waste of spiritual decay and weakness? We point to these sad features in the hope that our voice will be heard. The trumpet of danger should be kept blowing from every mouth, when the energies of the whole community require to be roused from their present torpor. What, it may be asked, is the cause of the present stagnation? The reply is simple. We say, it is the gulf which is daily widening between our theory and our practice. Day by day a conviction is growing among our Brahmo friends that the truths which our minister preaches, are not for them. Query again—are they intended for the missionaries? If so, are they duly practised? Let this question be honestly answered, for we respectfully declare that it is upon a satisfactory answer to this question that the interests of the Brahmo Somaj mainly depend. Not that the lay Brahmos are entirely absolved from their responsibilities and obligations; but they seem to enquire whether the truths that are preached every Sunday, have been exemplified in the lives of those that have devoted themselves to the service of religion. Nay, they seem to doubt also that these truths have at all been practised. Such doubts and such inquiries may be unreasonable; but the very fact that they have arisen, seems to show the danger of our position. The present difficulty is not a little aggravated by the fact that as time goes on the missionary body is being gradually cut off from the rest of the community. A secret circle is being formed, and this circle is being narrowed and closed till the community at large can feel no sympathy with, nor evince any appreciation of its labors. Meetings of our church where the missionaries formerly had the opportunity of meeting their Brahmo friends, are now rare; and so far as missionary visits to the Mofussil are concerned they are often now few and far between. This stagnation in the generality of the Brahmos and their separation from missionaries, are the two causes which may produce infinite mischief in the future. But both of these are to be attributed to the same sources, *viz*, the inconsistency of our lives. There is *no* higher duty at the present moment than to [illegible] there is no [illegible] approaching danger, preach the perfect compatibility of theory with practice. We have studied the present position of our church with some degree of attention, and our belief is that the danger we have indicated is real, and no less fatal than it is real. It behoves every Brahmo to throw off his torpor and inactivity, and it behoves every missionary to cast off his exclusiveness, and let the two combine to check the progress of the growing evil.

MOFUSSIL.

Correspondence.

CHRIST AND HIS MOTHER.

To the Editor of the *Indian Mirror*.

SIR,—I am much obliged to your several correspondents for their answers to my queries on the subject of Christ's attitude towards his mother. I cannot say that I have been satisfied; but in a matter such as this, even discussion is good and may be productive of benefits to all.

I do not intend to comment upon the assertions of your correspondents regarding the use of the term "woman" in Greek and in Hebrew. For aught I know, its meaning may have been what your correspondents aver. But my contention is not merely about the use of a certain word in Greek or Hebrew. Did Christ love his mother? Did Christ love her as a dutiful son would? If so, why do we find so few traces of his attachment in his life as furnished to us by his disciples? Whatever Christ felt he felt in abundance. It never rained but poured—this may be said of every emotion that filled the heart of Christ, which he employed in refreshing abundance for the benefit of his disciples. Now if Christ had loved his mother as warmly and ardently as he loved his disciples, as divinely as he loved the world, should we not have obtained more proofs of such an affection in his actions? Should he not have, for instance, washed her feet on that touching occasion when he also washed the feet of his disciples? I repeat that if he had felt this attachment, he would surely have manifested it in more ways than one—it may not be in the form I have indicated, at least in a thousand different ways. And if we assume the negative answer, namely, that he did not love his mother as he ought, to what circumstances are we to ascribe it? Most of your correspondents assert that he did love her; and I take the liberty to say, that the simple etymology of the word 'woman' does not satisfy me. It is only your last correspondent, "A Christian," who agrees with me in believing that

Christ was cold to his mother. The term 'woman' may be one expressive of respect and endearment; but if we contemplate the whole scene, does it not become clear that Christ purposely eliminated his mother from the list of those he called his own? "A Christian" argues that Christ was purposely cold because he clearly anticipated that Mary would in future ages be worshipped by Christians, and it was with a view to prevent this that he forbore any mention of his mother, and avoided attaching any importance to the relation he bore to her. If such had been his motive, I must say that the means which he adopted, utterly failed to answer his purpose. For Mary was and is still being largely worshipped by Christians, and the world shows no sign of being freed from [illegible] argues that as a divine being Christ knew what was to come, and he merely wanted to prevent the future by abstaining from mentioning the importance of his mother while alive. I think that as a divine person Christ should have found a more efficacious and potent remedy to prevent the future evil.

You will thus see, Sir, that none of your correspondents have yet been able to satisfy me on the subject, and I shall be glad if your correspondents condescend to throw further light upon it.

Yours Obediently.
S.

To the Editor of the *Indian Mirror.*

DEAR SIR,—The paragraph in your issue of the 4th instant regarding the daily doings in the *Sadhan Kanan*, was no doubt dictated by the best of motives. But sometimes men may do harm under excellent motives. You give Babu Keshub Chunder Sen and his followers credit for what they are doing. It seems to me, however, that there is nothing extraordinary in their proceedings, and that what they have been homely doing in their well-chosen retreat, does not deserve public praise. Cooking one's own food, making roads, drawing water *&c.*, are not such rare phenomena among poor devotees as to call for flattering comments; and none, I am sure, would blush so much under these comments as the Babu himself. As for the Babu's keeping up correspondence with high officials and sending contributions to newspapers, I am credibly informed that it is rarely that he does so.*

A VOICE FROM MOREPUKER.

The 16*th June*, 1876.

Devotional

CAUSE thy blessings to descend O Lord upon the uncared for children of thy servants, the little boys and girls, for whose training few take much care. Turn our hearts in mercy to their welfare, and teach us to take pains for their good. Suffer these little ones to grow up in the path of virtue, and in the knowledge of thy ways. Bring them up according to the wisdom of thy providence, and the law of thy loving kindness, and let them be faithful to the lives and convictions of their parents.

VISIT the excommunicated and poor in their loneliness O Lord, and cheer their cold desolation. Teach us to give pity and love whence peace of mind has fled, and to speak sweetly unto those who suffer in mind and body. To the homes of misery teach us to bring consolation, to the bed of sickness comfort, and always stand by the oppressed and deserted.

KINDLE in me, O holy Spirit, the flame of purity and piety wherewith I may kindle it in those souls who are around me. Create in [illegible] sweetness and peace of which I may partake with others. Lord, let my thoughts and feelings be better than my words, my actions better than my feelings and thoughts, and my life better and purer than anything I can outwardly do.

The Brahmo Somaj

THE anniversary service of the Rampore-hat Brahmo Somaj was conducted by Babu Deno Nath Mozumder, on Wednesday last.

A NEW *Brata* comprising eight moral injunctions, has been undertaken by our friends in the *Sadhan Kanan*, for the period of a month.

THE spirit of religious discipline may now be said to be entering our community, not a moment too soon. The laxity of life and habits which is so prone to enter into a theistic body, the members of which do not recognize any definite authority of tradition or scripture, must be remedied by such rules and ordinances as may regulate daily actions, desires, and feelings. Brahmo Missionaries are many of them submitting to such rules, and nonmissionaries too in certain instances prefer to abide by them. Brahmo ladies should imitate their example as readily and cheerfully as they can.

ON the 2nd June last the anniversary of the prayer meeting at Jeypore in Rajputana was celebrated. Our young friend and brother Babu Krishna Behari Sen, the Principal of the local College, conducted the services. His sermon was stirring and eloquent. We are glad he is utilizing his powers in so many ways at Jeypore. After service a number of the lame and blind people of the city were fed. A charitable fund has been established in connection with the Somaj.

THE death of the minister of the Cooch-behar Brahmo Somaj, Babu Koylash Chunder Roy, is reported. The *Dhurmatattwa* says that he was an enthusiastic Brahmo at one time, and at the time of death his strong religious sentiments did not desert him. We should have liked to find fuller details of the death. It is really encouraging to find that Brahmos can thus retain the peace of their mind at the time of death.

MISS COLLET wishes very much to obtain all the materials of the life of the late Sridharalu Naidu, the Brahmo Missionary of Madras, the recollection of whose painful death three years ago is still so fresh in our minds. We don't know how far Sridharalu's brother is able or willing to furnish such materials. Mr. Sringaravalu Mudeliar of Mylapur, Madras, who has been Secretary to the Southern India Brahmo Somaj for a number of years, is perhaps better able to help Miss Collet. We shall be very glad to be communicated with either by Mr. Sringaravalu, or any other gentleman who is in possession of the facts required.

MISS COLLET'S book of Brahmo Gleanings is not likely to be out till next October, when English people return to town from their midsummer holidays. Miss Collet says she will be very glad to receive literary contributions from Brahmo ladies. This ought to be a hint to our sisters who live in Calcutta, or in the *Mofussil*. There seems to be little difficulty now to get a good translation of Bengali into English in London.

WE are unfeignedly glad to hear the educational success which our friend and brother Babu Prosonno Cumar Roy, is achieving in England. The degree of Doctor of Science has been conferred upon him by the University of Edinburgh, and high encomium of his attainments is pronounced by the Examiner. He is going up shortly, we believe, for the D. S. C. examination of the London University, which is considered to be one of the most difficult examinations in the world. Babu Prosonno Cumar Roy has been, whether here or in England, a most sincere and enthusiastic Brahmo, and if with all his scientific attainments he can keep his faith and enthusiasm unabated, which we have great hopes he will, he will be really an acquisition to his church.

Literary

"OUR Indian Empire, the History of the Wonderful Rise of British Supremacy in Hindustan," by the Rev. Samuel Norwood, B.A., Head Master of the Royal Grammar School, is the title of a new London publication.

"THE Anglo-Indian Prize Poems of the Crown Perfumery Company, being Contributions of Indian and English Authors upon the Royal visit to India" is being sold by Messrs. Hamilton Co., 31 and 32 Paternoster Row, London. An *Edition de Luxe* of these Poems will appear in a few days.

"FIVE months in India with the Prince of Wales" is announced by Allingham, the London publisher.

MESSRS. H. FROWDE and Co., of the Oxford University Press Warehouse, Paternoster-Row, London, have just published a new edition of the Book of Common Prayer, which is a marvel of compactness and legibility. The little book weighs less than 2¼ ounces, and is printed on unbleached India paper, which, though necessarily slight in material, is remarkable for toughness.

THE *Indian Spectator*, a new Native paper started at Bombay, indulges in the following dream:—"An editor, great man!—how can he be approached, what can he be like? We enter the office with trembling steps, and with faltering speech ask for the—the—never mind who. At last we see him, we have shaken hands; the first awe has gradually vanished, and we begin to use our eyes. And what do we find? A half-starved man with dim eyes and sunken cheeks, poring over piles of newspapers and journals, making a mark here and an extract there, sipping brandy between intervals, often biting his very fingers for vexation, writing, perhaps, under some cruel attack of an adversary, and making up a

---

* We did not mean to give credit to any one in the paragraph alluded to, and do not remember to have made any "flattering comments" such as need induce any body "to blush." Our correspondent has no doubt written from "the best of motives," but it strikes us he has done harm by drawing attention to, and disclaiming credit which no one ever meant to give. Extraordinary or not the style of living is "primitive," and that was all we said. ED.—*I. M.*

volume (which is, perhaps, quoted the next day all over the town) with a difficulty, which an editor or a writer for the press alone can imagine. Out of office also the poor editor, notably in India, has no rest. He must attend public meetings, make speeches and maintain his reputation. Indeed, the office of an editor **is no** sinecure. He is denied all the luxuries **of life;** he toils at all hours; he reads, not for **pleasure but** from compulsion; and thinks **himself well off,** if he is not damned."

Scientific.

—The *Levant Herald* says that Mr. Gladstone contemplates a visit to the plains of Troy in the autumn to explore the site of Dr. Schliemann's discoveries.

Dr. Schliemann has written to the *Academy* that he had just obtained a new firman for two years for Troy, and was to proceed there on the 5th of May to build some frame-houses, so as to be able to continue the excavations on the 21st instant.

Gleanings and Incidents

In the collection called the Ocean of the rivers of stories by Somadeva we read of a merchant who had embraced the religion of Sugata and shewed great respect to the Buddhist monks. His young son, however, despised his father, and called him a sinner. 'Why do you abuse me?' said the father. The son replied. 'You have abandoned the law of the Vedas, and followed a new law which is no law. You have forsaken the Brahmans, and worship the Sramanas. What is the use of the Sugata religion, which is followed only by men of low birth, who want to find a refuge in the monasteries, who are happy when they have thrown away their loin cloths and shaved off every hair on their head: who eat whatever they please and perform neither ablutions nor penances?'

The father replied: 'There are different forms of religion: one looks to another world, the other is intended for the masses. But surely true Brahmanism also consists in avoiding of passion, in truthfulness, kindness towards all beings, and in not recklessly breaking the rules of caste. Therefore you should not always abuse my religion which grants protection to all beings. For surely there is no doubt that to be kind cannot be unlawful and I know no other kindness but to give protection to all living beings. Therefore if I am too much attached to my religion whose chief object is love, and whose end is deliverence, what sin is there in me, O child?' However, as the son did not desist from his abuse, his father took him before the king, and the king ordered him to be executed. He granted him two months to prepare for death. At the end of the two months the son was brought before the king again, and when the king saw that he had grown thin and pale he asked for the reason. The culprit replied that seeing death approach nearer and nearer every day, he could not think of eating. Then the king told him, that he threatened to have him executed in order that he might know the anguish that every creature feels at the approach of death, and that he might learn to respect a religion which enforces compassion for all beings. Having known the fear of death he ought now to strive after spiritual freedom, and never again abuse his father's religion.

The son was moved, and asked the king how he could obtain spiritual freedom. The king hearing that there was a fair in the town, ordered the young man to take a vessel brimful of oil, and to carry it through the streets of the town without spilling a drop. Two executioners with drawn swords were to walk behind him, and at the first drop being spilled, they were to cut off his head. When the young man, after having walked through all the streets of the city, returned to the king without having spilled one drop, the king said:—'Did you to-day, while walking through the streets, see anybody?' The young man replied: 'My thoughts were fixed on the vessel and I saw and heard nothing else.'

Then the king said: 'Let thy thought be fixed in the same way on the Highest! He who is collected, and has ceased to care for outward life, will see the truth, and having seen the truth, will not be caught again by the net of works; thus I have taught you in few words the way that leads to spiritual freedom.'—*Max Muller's Lectures.*

Beneath a sandal tree a woodman stood
And swung the axe, and as the strokes were [laid
Upon the fragrant trunk, the generous wood
With its own sweets perfumed the cruel blade.
[illegible]
With light from heaven, a nature pure and [great,
Will place its highest bliss in doing good,
And good for evil give, and love for hate.
—*William Cullen Bryant.*

Latest News

—In Banda there were 95 cases of cholera and 80 deaths for the week ending 3rd May.

—The *Pioneer* is sure of inactivity this Simla season in all matters relating to Frontier or Central Asian politics.

—The monsoon has fairly burst over the western coast of Ceylon.

—The *Behar Herald* hears that Babu Kedarnath Bannerji, Government Pleader, Mozufferpore, will give a grand entertainment to the European gentlemen and ladies resident in the district on the occasion of a marriage in his family.

—The famine contract cases in Tirhoot have, after all, says the Behar paper, been compromised, it being settled that the profits should be equitably devided between Proprietors and Managers. The evidence adduced has brought to light some strange facts in connection with the late famine, and the internal economy of the Indigo Factories.

—Sir John Kaye is much better.

—Mr. Rivers Wilson has left Egypt for England, and will not enter the service of the Khedive.

—The death is announced of Mr. W. L. Heeley, of the Bengal Civil Service in England. He was for sometime the Inspector-General of Prisons and the Registrar-General of Assurances in Bengal.

—Mr. G. Pothecary of the Public Works Department in Bengal, is also dead. He was for sometime the Engineer to the Justices of Calcutta.

—Inouye Kawori of Japan is said to be entrusted with a special mission to several foreign countries, and he will leave Japan in June next.

—It is reported that a Japanese Consulate is to be established in London.

—Outrages are reported to have been committed on Christians in the Province of Szechuen in China mainly caused, it is said, through the circulation of an anti-foreign memorial by the Literary Chancellor of the district.

—From the American papers to hand it appears that the agitation against the Chinese in California has increased in force, and a day or two ago a telegram was received here stating that the newly-arrived Chinese are exposed to great dangers, and the Chinese in the service of foreigners have all been dimissed.

—The Chinese ascribe the wreck of the *Kwangtung* to the fact of an ill-fated ourang-outang being on board.

—After all, it appears, it is not a son but a daughter that is born to Scindia. Disappointment is His Highness' fate. It is the Mujhi Malnani (daughter of the Sawunt Warri Chief,) married to Scindia last year, who has been delivered of the daughter.

—The South Indian Railway from Madras to Chinglepat, will not be opened till the 1st of September.

—Murderous outrages are taking place in Constantinople. On the night of the 15th instant, whilst Ministers were assembled in Council of Midhat Pasha, the new Grand Vizier, a recently dismissed Officer of the Turkish Government having entered the Council room armed with a revolver suddenly shot dead Hussein Pasha and Rachid Pasha, Ministers of War and Foreign Affairs, also seriously wounded Kaiserei, Minister of Marine, besides killing an Aide-de-Camp of the Grand Vizier, and a servant of Midhat. The assassin was arrested.

—The Puttiallah paper states that on the 5th instant the ceremony of giving a name to the heir of the Puttiallah *guddi* was duly gone through. The name given to him is Maharaj Kwour Teka Rajundur Singh Bahadur.

—Cholera of a mild type has appeared at Morar.

[illegible]
at home as the new Admiral for the Mediterranean fleet.

—A little incident in connection with the Prince of Wales' visit to India, does not seem to be generally known. We are all aware that there were great doubts as to the Prince's physical ability to bear the climate of this country. In the course of the medical consultations held upon this point, we are told that a practical test was applied. Under direction of the Doctors, the Prince was placed in a conservatory heated up to Indian point, in order to ascertain his powers of endurance. He held on bravely for a time it seems; and rather liked the sensation than otherwise. But eventually he fainted clean off. This was a great check upon the medical imagination, as may be supposed, and the Prince himself was staggered for a time, and the expedition was nearly all off. But resuming the experiment—we presume with more success—His Royal Highness eventually resolved to brave the peril.

—Sir T. Madhava Rao, K. C. S. I., has been pleased to give orders for the opening of a school at Baroda for the Christian children there.

—Mr. Saunders, the new Chief Commissioner of Mysore, intends, according to a Bangalore paper, to proceed very shortly to Mysore, to obtain the opinion of the Ranias to the permanent location of His Highness the Maharajah at Bangalore until the attainment of his majority.

—It is rumoured that Messrs. Mackinnon, Mackenzie and Co., the managing agents of the B. I. S. N. Company at Calcutta, have advised Messrs. Binny and Co., the Madras agents of the Company, of their intention to start a line of steamers between Madras, Singapore, and Hongkong. Hitherto all the traffic between Penang, the Straits, and China has been the monopoly of the P. & O. Company.

—It is the Queen's intention to appoint the Prince of Wales and the Duke of Connaught (Prince Arthur) personal Aides-de-Camp to Her Majesty. Her Majesty will also appoint the King of Hanover (Duke of Cumberland) to a Generalship in the British Army.

—Sir George Campbell's bill for throwing open the judgeships, was the subject of a count-out in the House of Commons, the other night. Mr. Dunbar and Mr. Leith have declared war against it, and it is feared it must fall through.

—Two of the tigers which have just been lodged at the London Zoological Gardens from the *Serapis* are named "Moody" and "Sankey," and those titles are pasted up on labels either over or opposite to their dens. Some of the Americans in London are much incensed at it.

—The London correspondent of the *Bombay Gazette* hears that Sir Salar Jung has already been overwhelmed with numberless applicants to look after his interests. One well-known public man offered Sir Salar his services in regard of the Berars to bring the subject forward in Parliament, and in fact to do all that was necessary to compel the restitution of those districts. Sir Salar administered him a quiet but very justifiable rap on the knuckles.

—The Duke of Connaught is to be married to his cousin, the daughter of the ex-king of Hanover, who is at present on a visit to England.

Calcutta.

MR. W. R. FINK, Assistant Registrar, High Court, Original Side, has obtained fifteen months' leave of absence on medical certificate from the 22nd of May last. Mr. E. A. Nott is appointed in his place.

THE P. & O. Co.'s. S. S. *Venetia*, Commander G. J. Babot, arrived in Bombay harbour on Wednesday last, from Suez with the English Mails of the 26th ult. on board. The following is the list of passengers :—

From Southampton.—Mr. Edgiston, Mrs. Barron, Mr. Leman, Mr. Sherman, Six Chinese, Lieut. G. Keigwin, R. N.

Mr. Moliter, Major. Wood, Mr. J. Scroggie, Mr. E. Johnson.

From Aden.—Mr. B. Dinshaw, Mr. J. Winckler.

THE following arrangement of the business of the High Court will take effect from Monday, the 19th instant, the date of Mr. Justice Jackson's departure on privilege leave :—

1st Bench.—The Chief Justice and Mr. Justice Mitter.

2nd Bench.—(Patna group).—Mr. Justice Kemp and Mr. Justice Birch.

3rd Bench. (Rajshahye group.)—Mr. Justice Macpherson and M. Justice Morris.

4th Bench. (Burdwan group.)—Mr. Justice Markby and Mr. Justice MacDonell.

5th Bench (Presidency group.)—Mr. Justice Glover and Mr. Justice Ainslie.

Original Jurisdiction.—Mr. Justice Pontifex.

Insolvent Court (the first Tuesday in each month.)—Mr. Justice Macpherson.

Privy Council Department.—Mr. Justice Markby.

English Department.—Mr. Justice Glover.

English Committee.—The Chief Justice, Mr. Justice Kemp, Mr. Justice Glover, Mr. Justice Macpherson, and Justice Ainslie.

DOMESTIC OCCURRENCE.

DEATH.

GHOSE.—At Rishra, on Friday the 16th June 1876, the mother of Prosunno Cumar Ghose.

Selection.

THE THEISTIC CHURCH OF INDIA.

TO THE EDITOR OF THE *Free Press.*

SIR,—In reply to your critical correspondants, Miss Collet and Rev. J. Harrison, allow me to say that I am afraid there was too much truth embodied in my reflections upon the Theistic Church of India, if one may judge from the anxiety of its friends to explain them away.

With reference to my fair opponent, Miss Collet, with all courtesy allow me to point out to her that she has simply proved my case. She admits that in consequence of the congregation of Theists, or Brahmos, under the ministry of Chunder Sen, not having "answered the expectations entertained of them as to holiness and devotedness of life, he had threatened to withhold his services. Now, I am a plain man, accustomed to call a spade a spade, and claim that a want of "holiness and devotedness" may be correctly stigmatised as "immorality." I have been hitherto in favor of the Women's Suffrage movement, but if Miss Collet fails to perceive that she has confirmed my statement, I shall be disposed to follow John Bright into the other lobby, though I cannot help thinking that she sees it as clearly as I do.

In reply to the other statements common to both Miss Collet and Mr. Harrison, I beg to say that their rose-colored picture of Brahmoism reminds one of some of the railway advertisements of ambitious watering places. We find when you reach Takeinton, that instead of the half not having been told us, we have been sold. Mr. Harrison's picture stands thus: "The Brahmo Somaj is a true Church of God, marked doubtless, as all other human societies are, by limitations and shortcomings, but still engaged in a truly divine work, 'about the Father's business,' the destruction of superstition, the banishment of misery, the rectification of wrong, the establishing of truth, righteousness, and peace, the promotion of the highest welfare or mankind."

The description given of it last month at Exeter Hall by the Rev. T. Morgan, Baptist missionary from India, reads thus : "The modern Vedantists, or Brahmos, of which sect Kesub (Chunder Sen) is the head, asserts that volume of nature tells us all that we want to know of the nature of God, and of the future destiny of man. These men repudiate Christ, the atonement, revelation ; they are bitter, inveterate enemies of Christianity. I see nothing in them that is favorable. They are [illegible] commanded by the devil himself, like a broad phalanx determined to oppose Christianity, and they have told me over and over again they are going to convert us. They are far more formidable enemies to Christians than the old othodox Hindu."

Sir, I beg to submit these two sketches, and say "Look on this picture, and then on this," and judge for yourself. Mr. Harrison's was evidently derived from the prospectus of the new Church of India a few years since; Mr. Morgan's embodies the facts as evinced in 1876. He is "the latest authority." Venice, when approached by sea, gives out sweet music that floats across the blue waters with heavenly effect. Distance lends enchantment to the scene. But approach nearer, and the horrible discord of pandemonium salutes the ear. Application obvious.

Objection is also taken to my estimate of Theism as "a dry well." Now, the matter stands thus : I have experienced the saving truth of Christ crucified for years. I have drunk of this life-giving stream with delight. I speak that which I do know. Like all ministers, I read up the current literature of the day. Among other things, have studied Theism as represented in Chunder Sen's Essays and Sermons from which Mr. Harrison quotes so freely, and my deliberate conviction is, that in dealing with the heart's necessities it is a miserable failure. We ask for bread, and lo, a stone. We look for positive truth, and behold "words, words, words." We seek water, but froth is offered instead. I repeat that "the thirsty soul turns sadly away as from a well without water." My opponents have liberty to form their own conclusions and I claim the same.

My dictum, "a localised Deity is a necessity of our constitutions" was also attacked by my friends. In reply to their objection, I venture to put against them Lord Macaulay, who thus endorses my view: "The history of the Jews is the record of a continual struggle between pure Theism supported by the most terrible sanctions, and the fascinating desire of having some visible and tangible object of adoration. Judaism scarcely ever acquired a proselyte. God, the uncreated, the incomprehensible, the invisible, attracted few worshippers. A philosopher might admire so noble a conception; but the crowd turned away in disgust from words which presented no image to their minds. It was before Deity embodied in a human form, waking among men, partaking of their infirmities, leaning on their bosoms, weeping over their graves, slumbering in the manger, bleeding on the Cross, that the prejudices of the synagogue, the doubts of the academy, the pride of the portico, the farces of the Lictor, and the swords of thirty legions were humbled in the dust."

Now, I am not "a philosopher," the people for whom I write and preach are not philosophers, and when I declair by pen or voice that the incarnation of God was the crowning proof of Divine love and the greatest boon ever bestowed upon the race, I am but expressing the sentiments of the mass of mankind. The common people, who have little faith in a sublimated ethereal essence, heard the Son of God gladly. "To Him shall be the gathering of the nations." I admit freely that the incarnation of God was, *inter alia*, a concession to human weakness. Other methods had failed. Last of all He sent His Son. Will Miss Collet and Mr. Harrision join with those who cast Him ont of the vineyard and slew Him! I trust not.

In concluding my answer, allow me to admit that Theism is infinitely superior to Heathenism. I only object to it when it pr sumes to take the place of Christianity. Of course Mr. Harrison will concede that excellence is relative. To a Hindu, coming from the degrading superstitions and heavy penalties of his ancient faith, Theism must present a great charm, and in his new-born enthusiasm he would shout "Euraka" just as travellers in Wales when they have climbed a pretentious looking hill shout "Snowdon," only to find that the chief among mountains towers a thousand feet above them. To those who know better it sounds childish in the extreme to hear that Brahmos favorably compare Theism with Christianity pure and proper. Before America was discovered, on the Spanish medals were inscribed the Pillars of Hercules and the motto, "ne plus ultra" (no more beyond); afterwards it was altered to "Plus ultra" (more beyond). That motto I commend to Theists and their friends.

I remain, yours faithfully,

W. J. ACOMB.

Highfields, May 9, 1876.

—Free Press.

Advertisements

ICE! ICE! ICE!

MADE IN FOUR MINUTES

THE PNEUMATIC ICE MACHINE

THIS IMPORTANT INVENTION IS CONSIDERED A BOON TO THOSE LIVING IN TROPICAL CLIMATES.

CAN BE WORKED BY THE MOST INEXPERIENCED HAND AND IS NOT LIABLE TO GET OUT OF ORDER.

From Rs. 175, each Machine complete.

MESSRS. ARLINGTON & CO.
AGENTS.

HAROLD & CO.,

3, DALHOUSIE SQUARE, CALCUTTA

HARMONIUMS.

Harold and Co., call attention to their unequalled stock of rich-toned Harmoniums made especially for India.

FROM RS. 90 TO RS. 900 EACH.

All kinds of Musical Instruments of the best description are always kept in Stock.

SANTIPORE

THE Str. "JUMNA" will leave Calcutta, Hatkhola Ghaut, on the following dates in June and July, 1876.

12th, 16th, 20th, 24th and 28th June.

2nd, 6th, 10th, 14th, 18th, 22nd, 26th, and 30th July.

HINDU MONTHS.

31st Joisto.

3rd, 7th, 11th, 15th, 19th, 23rd, 27th, and 31st Assar.

4th, 8th, 12th, 16th, 20th, 24th, 28th, and 32nd Sraban.

For further particulars apply to

ALICK APCAR, JR.,
19, Pollock Street.

BURAL BROTHERS

[ESTABLISHED IN 1870 A.D.]

JEWELLERS, GOLD AND SILVER-SMITHS AND WATCH-MAKERS,

BY APPOINTMENT

TO

His Excellency the Viceroy and Governor-General of India

AND

HIS HIGHNESS THE MAHARAJAH ADHIRAJ OF BURDWAN,

BURAL BROTHERS,
10, Hare Street.

BABU BASANTA KUMAR DUTTA,
HOMŒOPATHIC PRACTITIONER
No. 20, Sunker Halder's Lane, Ahiritolah.

A FRESH INDENT OF

HOMŒOPATHIC

Medicines and other Requisities,
Have arrived from England.
Medicines, Boxes, Books, Pamphlets;
Absolute Alcohol; Cholera-spirit Camphor.
SPECIAL REMEDIES.

For Suppressed, Laborious and Difficult menses; Leucorrhœa.

For Hysteria; Spermatorrhœa; Dysentery; Diarrhœa; Cholera.

For Asthma; Pile; Pain; Sore and Diseases of the Children.

Ice, Lemonade, Soda and Tonic water always.

To be had at

DATTA'S HOMŒOPATHIC LABORATORY.

No. 312, CHITPORE ROAD, BURTOLA, CALCUTTA

TERMS—CASH.

☞ Price List can be had on application.

Printing Materials.

MILLER AND RICHARD'S PRESSES, TYPES and all requisites always in Stock.

TERMS CASH.

EWING & CO.

SMITH, STANISTREET & CO.

Pharmaceutical Chemists & Druggists

BY APPOINTMENT

To His Excellency the Right Hon'ble

LORD LYTTON, G.M.S.I.

Governor-General of India,

&c., &c.

SYRUP OF LACTATE OF IRON

Prepared from the original recipe. Lactate of Iron, in various forms of preparation, have been in use in France, and generally through the continent of Europe, for some years past, and is highly esteemed as one of the most valuable Chalybeate Tonic Remedies yet introduced. The Syrup, being the most agreeable as well as convenient form of administration is in most general use. It is a most valuable remedy in the following diseases:—Chlorosis or Green Sickness, Leucorrhœa, Neuralgia, Enlargement of the Spleen, &c. In combination with quinine, it has also been very successfully used in the cure of Fever, while to persons of delicate constitution, enfeebled by disease it is invaluable. In bottles. Rs. 2 each.

SYRUP OF THE PHOSPHATE OF IRON Rs. 2 per bottle.

SYRUP OF PHOSPHATE OF IRON AND STRYCHNINE, Rs. 2 per bottle.

SYRUP OF PHOSPHATE OF IRON AND QUININE. Price Rs. 2-8 per bottle.

SYRUP OF PHOSPHATE OF IRON, QUININE AND STRYCHNINE, (DR. ATKIN'S TRIPLE TONIC SYRUP,) Rs. 2-8 per bottle.

Smith, Stanistreet & Co.

Invite special attention to the following rates the quality guaranteed as the best procurable:—

Pure Ærated Waters.

Made from Pure Water, obtained by the new process through the Patent Charcoal Filters.

				Rs.	As.
Ærated plain (Trible Ærated), per doz.			...	0	15
Soda Water	ditto	„	...	0	12
Gingerade	ditto	„	...	1	4
Lemonade	ditto	„	...	1	4
Tonic (Quinine)	ditto	„	...	1	4

The *Cash* must be sent with the order to obtain advantage of the above rates.

NOTICE

MAKHON LOLL GHOSE.

No. 91, Radhabazar, Wholesale and Retail Stationer, Account Bookseller, &c.

Begs to invite the attention of the Public to an Invoice of Commercial and Fancy Stationery of all sorts which he has recently received, and which he is disposing of at moderate prices. He has been long in the Trade, and presumes he has always afforded every satisfaction to the several merchants here who have constantly favored him with orders. Any Moffusil orders accompanied with remittances shall be promptly attended to.

Just Received

AN Invoice of Mathematical Instrument Boxes, Color Boxes, Drawing Pencils and various other requisites in Stationery. They are priced very moderately for speedy sale.

H. C. GANGOOLY & CO.,
24, Mangoe Lane, Calcutta.

!!! হুকা !!!

!!! HOOKAHS !!!

ENGLISH made Hookahs of various choice designs, colours and sizes ranging in price from Rs. 2 to 5 each, 60 designs to choose from. Apply to

RADANAUTH CHOWDRY,
373, Jorasanko.

CHUNDER & BROTHERS,

25½ & 112, RADHA BAZAR,
CALCUTTA,
FOR CASH ONLY.

G. AND F. MILTHORP'S

CELEBRATED

PRINTING INKS of all Colours and Shades.

Black, per lb. Rs. 0-8, 0-12, 1-0, 1-8, 2-0, 2-8, 3-0, 4-0 and 5-0.
Blue Azure, per lb. Rs. 3-0.
„ Brilliant „ „ 3-0, 4-0, 5-0, 7-0.
„ Light „ „ 7-0.
„ Mazarine „ „ 7-0 and 9-8.
„ Ultramarine „ 1-8, 2-0 and 2-8.
Brown, per lb. Rs. 1-8, 2-0, 2-8 and 7-0.
Chocolate „ „ 3-0.
Green „ „ 3-0 and 7-0.
Gold (preparation) per lb. Rs. 1-0.
Lilac, per lb. Rs. 7-0.
Mauve, per lb. Rs. 2-8, 3-0, 9-8 and 12-0.
Pink, „ „ 9-8.
Purple, „ „ 9-8.
Red, „ „ 1-8, 2-0, 2-8, 3-0 and 7-8.
„ Magenta, per lb. Rs. 2-8, 3-0, 10-0 & 12-0.
White, per lb. Rs. 2-8, 3-0 and 12-0.
Yellow, Golden, per lb. Rs. 7-0.
„ Lemon, „ „ 3-0.
„ Medium „ „ 3-0.
„ Orange „ „ 3-0 and 7-0.
Varnish, *best*, for lowering Inks, per qrt. Rs. 3-0.

C. & BROS. having made special arrangements with some respectable Manufacturers in England, are now in a position to offer at moderate prices, PRINTING INKS, PRESSES, &c., recently arrived, which, for their superior quality and low rates, are expected to afford satisfaction.

To orders of 50lbs. Coloured and 200lbs. Black Inks and upwards, a liberal allowance will be given for cash only. Anything relating to printing, happening not to be in stock, can be ordered out from England at English price *plus* expences and 5 per cent. extra.

To prevent disappointment, early applications are requested.

5th June, 1876.

India General Steam Navigation Company, Ld.

SCHOENE, KILBURN & Co.—*Managing Agents.*

ASSAM LINE.

NOTICE.

Steamers leave Calcutta for Assam every Tuesday, Goalundo every Thursday and leave Debrooghur downward every Saturday.

THE Str. "MIRZAPORE" will leave Calcutta for Assam, on Tuesday, the 20th instant.

Cargo will be received at the Company's Godowns, Nimtollah Ghat, up till noon of Monday, the 19th.

THE Str. "MADRAS" will leave Goalundo for Assam on Thursday, the 22nd instant.

Cargo will be received at the Company's Godowns, No. 4 Fairlie Place, up till noon of Tuesday the 20th.

Goods forwarded to Goalundo for this vessel will be chargeable with Railway Freight from Calcutta to Goalundo in addition to the regular Freight of this Company.

Passengers should leave for Goalundo by Train of Wednesday, the 21st.

CACHAR LINE NOTICE

REGULAR FORTNIGHTLY SERVICE.

Steamers now leave Calcutta for Cachar and Intermediate Stations every alternate Friday, and leave Cachar downward every alternate Sunday.

THE Str. "LUCKNOW" will leave Calcutta for Cachar on Friday, the 30th instant.

Cargo will be received at the Company's Godowns, Nimtollah Ghat, up till noon of Thursday the 29th.

For further information regarding rates of Freight or passagemoney, apply to

4, FAIRLIE PLACE,
Calcutta, 16th June 1876.

G. J. SCOTT,
Secretary.

Printed and published by M. M. RUKHIT, at the INDIAN MIRROR PRESS, No. 15, College Square, for the Proprietor.

The Indian Mirror.

SUNDAY EDITION.

VOL. XVI.] CALCUTTA, SUNDAY JUNE 25, 1876 { REGISTERED AT THE GENERAL POST OFFICE. } [NO. 149

CONTENTS

NOTICE.

All letters and communications relating to the literary department of the Paper should be addressed to the Editor. All other letters should be addressed to the Manager, to whom all remittances should be made payable.

Subscribers will be good enough to bring to the notice of the Manager any delay or irregularity in the delivery of the Paper.

Editorial Notes

THE cause of Temperance steadily prospers in spite of opposition. It is a striking fact that on board Her Majesty's ships there are no less than 151 temperance societies with 5,000 members.

THE number of places of worship in England and Wales connected with the Establishment, is said to be 18,000 or 19,000 while those of other churches number 28,000. The Methodists of the Old Connection have 7,500, the United Methodists 1,210, the New Connection 417, Primitive Methodists 6,245, Congregationalists 4,113, Baptists 3,217, Roman Catholics 1,661, and Unitarians 320.

IT seems that Christian missionaries in India are sometimes obliged to use the school master's rod to promote piety and check misbehavior among their "flock." The well-known missionary among the Santhals, Mr. Skrefsrud, writes to a contemporary to say:—"I found a Christian half drunk, and I gave him a most merciless thrashing there and then before all the heathen, and it has done him a world of good." Muscular Christianity is helpful after all, at least in India.

WE cannot contemplate the prospect of Sir William Muir's early retirement from the service except with the deepest regret. He has won universal respect no less by his distinguished official career than by his sincere and earnest Christianity. A good Christian in the service is rare, and therefore all the more valuable. Men like Lord Lawrence, Sir William Muir and the late Sir Herbert Edwardes, have done almost as much to elevate and sanctify British rule in the East as the best and most self-denying missionaries.

PUNDIT DYANUND SARASWATI has compiled a book of rituals from the original Vedas for the celebration of domestic and social incidents for the use of those who are not prepared to conform to the existing idolatrous observances on the subject. The Pundit is really earnest for the suppression of idolatry, and the energy he manifests, and the self-sacrifices he undergoes to carry out his objects, would be indeed worthy of imitation in any community. We are informed that Mr. Hurry Chand Chintamon of Bombay has celebrated the funeral ceremonies of his late father according to the Vedic ritual prescribed by the learned Pundit.

THE profound spiritual insight, and depth as well as originality of thought which intensely sensitive and sympathetic natures are capable of, was best shown perhaps in the case of the late F. W. Robertson of Brighton, whose sermons are considered to be such treasures by all denominations of Christians in England. He died of a disease brought about by offended feelings created by disagreement with the vicar of Brighton who refused to sanction the nomination of a successor whom he had chosen. Mr. Robertson was exceedingly cheerful and exceedingly gloomy by turns. His despondency at times was unmanly, while at other times the hope, the light of living faith and thoughtfulness he created among his congregation, can be matched by few things that other religious ministers have done in this century.

WORDS of sincere sympathy and deep regret are due to the friends and relatives of the late Mr. Vencataswami Naidu from us. The deceased gentleman was uniformly a warm friend to our cause, and our missionaries who have travelled to Madras, must bear witness to the hospitality and kindness he always showed to them. Mr. Vencataswami Naidu's death is a calamity to the educated community of the Southern Presidency, where the number of the truly educated is so small. Mr. Vencataswami was not a member of the Brahmo Somaj, but we always counted, and justly counted upon him as our friend. An essentially self-made man, he filled with grace and dignity the position which he occupied. His removal creates a gap in the Native society of Madras which cannot be easily made up.

THERE is no such thing in heaven or earth as *Nirguna Brahma*,—divinity devoid of attributes. It is a philosophical absurdity; it is an inconceivable myth altogether. The shrewd metaphysical Hindu makes, indeed, too much of this thing, a pure abstract essence *minus* all qualities. His pantheistic creed glories in a deity who is simply an all-pervading spirit, and who cannot possibly possess any attributes, however exalted, without sinking into humanity. The Theist rejects such an idea, it is true, but in one sense he too clings to a *Nirguna* Divinity. He knows there can be no deity devoid of attributes, but he believes that sometimes the Lord should be realized in consciousness as a mere Presence, a Real and Vivid Presence, and nothing more. There can be no *Nirguna* God, but there may be and is such a thing as the *nirguna* contemplation of God. Those who have experienced this, know it is a precious privilege and a great joy.

SOME people say to us,—your missionaries are wordly-minded men, they covet riches and renown, and are quite as fond of pleasure and convenience as other people. There are others again who say,—your missionaries are ascetics, they are low and mean, and are always foolishly inflicting upon themselves severe penances and privations. Such mutually adverse criticisms remind us of the story of the old man, his son and the ass, and only serve to confirm our utter repugnance to human judgment in matters of faith. To follow man's caprices and opinions is to ruin the soul. We say to our missionary brethren,—Be deaf to what man says; disregard and shun the wisdom that comes from man. And follow steadfastly the voice of God, whatever the consequences may be. Not to follow earthly guides is the way to salvation.

THE public are naturally impatient to see a good practical beginning made of the Albert Hall concern. No tangible progress is yet visible, and since the inauguration hardly anything has been done beyond accommodating a few small public meetings. There are, we understand, reasons for the delay, which ought not, therefore, to be construed into apathy or lukewarmness on the part of the projectors. The matter lies now in the hands of the Collector, who has to go through all the legal processes prescribed by the Act (X of 1870), with a view to come to terms with the owners of the premises, and issue the usual award. The Committee must wait for the award before taking any further steps towards the furtherance of the undertaking. We are glad to hear that His Honor the Lieutenant-Governor continues to take unabated interest in the Hall, and it is not likely that the final settlement of the matter will be delayed much longer, if the subscribers pay their respective subcriptions at once. The Government is ready to pay its share immediately.

THE London *Inquirer* publishes an interesting report of the welcome sermon preached by Dean Stanley, at Westminister Abbey upon the safe return of the Prince of Wales, his text being the first verse of Psalm CXXII. Touching India, the Dean said:—"A fresh responsibility had been laid upon the nation by the recent visit paid to India. Every crying need for spiritual help, every just complaint, every high aspiration from those distant shores ought henceforth to find more ready access to their hearts; every act of grace or courtesy which they had shown, or might show, towards those subject-races; every firmer grasp on the eternal principle, justice and charity, that they could exhibit towords them, would henceforth strike with a double force on those who were drawn to them by the bonds of personal regard or personal knowledge. Every deed of good or ill that they should perform anywhere, was henceforth enacted not only in 'the fierce white light that beats upon the throne,' but in the presence of the gazing 'eyes and listening ears of peoples, of kindreds, and of nations which no man could number.' 'I was glad when they said unto me, we will go into the house of the Lord.'"

MISS CARPENTER gave an account of her recent visit to India, at a meeting of the National Indian Association, held on the 15th ultimo, at the Society of Arts. Referring to the Bethune School she justly remarked;—"There was a splendid building, calculated to accommodate two or three hundred children, but it contained only a few children of the higher Native class. She hoped that this exclusive system would be relaxed, and a proper normal school established." We are not aware there are any "hideous" Hindu temples in India, though certainly one could point to hideous looking gods and goddesses. But Miss Carpenter is reported to have observed that "during her travels she had seen many hideous Pagan temples but in Bombay," she continued, "one devoted to the worsnip of the one true God. In Ahmedabad, also, a temple to the one true God had been erected by a Native gentleman, and in it a pure worship was regularly celebrated. Native ladies actually delivered addresses in advocacy of the worship of the one true God, and the feeling against Paganism was perceptibly spreading." Miss Carpenter evidently meant the Brahmo Somaj, and ought to have mentioned it.

THE MARY AND THE MARTHA OF OUR HOUSEHOLDS.

"MARTHA is cumbered with much serving." She has to look to the whole household alone. Her sister Mary will not help her. Mary always loves to sit at the master's feet, and hear and speak of the things of the Kingdom of Heaven. She does not like that her sister Martha should always busy herself with the perishable goods of this world, although she knows these be often necessary and useful. Marthas we have in our midst, almost in every household, but very few Maries. There are not many women in these days among the rising generation who would sit at the feet of their fathers and masters for hours together, talk and hear of heavenly things with rapt wonder and attention, anoint the feet of those they revere, and wipe them with their hair. On the contrary there are a good many who are worked and wearied with household care, and have neither the time nor the wish to attend to anything else. Almost every woman is a Martha in her sphere. But occasionally we do meet with natures in which the idea of moral and spiritual development, over and above that of practical and detailed service, is seen to predominate. On the other hand in the midst of hard-working and practical natures, one often detects many distinct veiws of depth, tenderness, and spirituality which we wish we knew how to develop and cultivate. The fact is that the two types of character which Mary and Martha respectively illustrate are seldom found to exist mutually distinct and independent. They mix and mingle almost in every female life with which we come in contact. Mary in Martha, and Martha in Mary is what we frequently see. Active, practical, domestic service forces itself upon every woman so naturally, and in accordance with all the present laws and arrangements of society, that she has seldom any choice given her to select any other line of life. But the growth of spiritual goodness, and the deeper and heavenlier susceptibilities of the feminine nature so few of us appreciate, or understand, that the gifts and faculties relating thereto are left unnoticed and uncultivated, and are not unoften treated with discouragement and condemnation.

THE SPIRIT OF THE AGE.

[COMMUNICATED.]

WHEN jesting Pilate asked, "What is truth?"—We are told that he did not stay for an answer. We are sure that if one wanted us to define what the spirit of the age means, he would as willingly not stay for an answer. The spirit of the age is one of those vague expressions that are better conceived than defined. We know what it means, and though we cannot define it, we know what the spirit of the present age denotes. It implies what was never conceived in the past, nor anything that we fain hope to see realized in the future. In one word, the spirit of the age seems to be anything but transcendental. All notions of ultimate causes and the essence of things are decried as the unwholesome fancies of a disordered brain. The spirit is given up as a delusion, while the fleeting phenomena of the outward world, are accepted as solid realities. In politics men have given up the doctrine of the divinity of kings; in science God has been banished to a region of repose where his own laws seem to persecute and oppress Him. In philosophy the autological distinctions between matter and mind are considered as distinctions without a difference; while in religion God is everywhere being chased to make room for law—the immutable, unalterable, and supreme law. The essentially materialistic tendencies of our speculations have given a tone to our life and a motive to our exertions which signally differ from the spirit, which actuated our fore-fathers. He is a safe reformer and guide who takes us along the current of the prevailing tendencies. To wear the cloak which is prescribed by the latest fashion, gives you a status and respectability which is a passport to fame and utility. Blessed is he who follows the times and does not lead them. Happy were it if the world did not require the services of martyrs and leading geniuses. How much blood would be spared, how much agony and persecution averted, if the world did not stop its progress now and then, and require the exertion of some men to push it on. Yes, the world is a vexatiously slow coach which requires to be occasionally governed, coaxed, and chastised. Unhappy he who so governs, coaxes, and chastises! Such a man is never popular, and his measures are never swallowed unless moistened and diluted with his blood. Gentle reader, when we say this, you ought to think we are alluding to the present times and to the present state of our society. The opinions which we have always broached in these columns, the proceedings which we sanction, the sacrifices which we approve, are such as can never be liked by you. The present age is one of scepticism, of material comforts and civilization. Our countrymen are mad after wealth, ease and happiness. Religion to the majority of people must be a luxury in or'er to be entertaining and attractive. The picture which it holds out of man's state in this world and his bliss in the next, must be such as is painted by the master-hand of an artist who knows of no shades to bedim his productions. Is the standard which we proclaim as the ideal of the Brahmo world of such a nature? We regret to anticipate the verdict which is sure to be returned. No, no, no!—this is the emphatic negative which greets our query from all sides. The minister of our Church wants to establish a heaven upon earth, and he wishes us to forego the world that we may be sure of the former. We are told to eschew all idle pleasures and betake ourselves to humble cells for our hermitage. We are desired to chasten spirit by the infliction of a simple mode of living. While the world talks of the unknowable God, the minister asks us to look within and see Him. Philosophers, they say, have laid conscience safely at rest, while our minister is not satisfied unless he makes every one of his disciples *hear* the buzzings and whispers of the troublesome "demon." Sufficient unto the senses are the things that we see, hear, and feel. But our minister proceeds further, and he says, that we ought to see what our eye hath never seen, hear what our ear hath never heard, and feel what our touch hath never felt. Yea more. To realize these he wants us to leave our actual pleasures and sensations and take to pursuits which require us to sacrifice our comforts and bodily conveniences. Impossible! angrily affirms the age. Should such teachings then be discontinued? Is the Brahmo Somaj to be made a bed of roses? Is our whole code to be one of rose water morality, that shifts and bides and flows as the breeze of current opinion directs it? Listen to what we say, again, gentle reader. A man who has an idea to preach, is never dismayed by threats. The truths which he holds are for you, whether you accept them or not; and if you think that your opposition will frighten him, or your inconveniences will melt him, or your appeals for compromise will deter him, you are greatly mistaken. We are not ashamed to proclaim our own conviction. We know, and we do hold, that the truths which have been proclaimed from these columns, and which have come with so bewitching an effect from the pulpit of the Brahmo Mandir, are a God-send in the present state of our society, without which there can be no salvation for our country. And it is because we know this, it is because we know that our souls are better than our flesh, that our country's cause is better than our individual comforts, and that a blissful future depends only upon a painful present—that we invite our countrymen to shake off their lethargy and acknowledge the good tidings which we proclaim. We know that our position is very unfortunate, and that in the discharge of our manifold duties we shall become, as we have already partly become, unpopular with our countrymen. The minister of whom we are so proud to-day, will probably be hissed and hooted, cursed and hated to-morrow. We know that, and he knows it too. But there is no thwarting the truth. Reformers and prophets have always gone against the current, and they have uniformly reached the fountain-head of their inspiration. History bears ample testimony to this. When the adultress was brought before Christ for judgment, did that sublime prophet obey the spirit of the age, and act the part of a trimmer by concealing what he knew to be an unpopular truth? Let him cast the first stone who is pure in heart—this was his reply, and it made his opponents furious against him. We can count numerous examples, but this will suffice as showing what the greatest prophet of the world did under the most trying circumstances. We hold this spirit to be the spirit of true reformers. A teacher must not obey, but be obeyed. He does not sail with the wind, but against it. He shuns popular applause, and never courts it. Let our readers mark. It is in no spirit of self-glorification that we have dwelt so long upon what we conceive to be the true mission of the present leaders of our Church. We mean to say that those in the midst of our Church that are convinced of certain truths, are determined to preach and practise them, be the results what they may; and it is the manifest duty of every Brahmo, instead of rebelling against their leaders, to investigate the matter calmly and prayerfully, honestly and hopefully, before they come to a final conclusion.

OUR FAITH AND OUR EXPERIENCES.

(*Continued.*)

IN short we are unworthy in every respect of the religion we profess. Is it not said in all the streets of India that our Church has not fulfilled the high expectations raised in the minds of men, both here and in other parts of the world? Do not thousands, pointing the finger of scorn and contempt at us, say,—Lo! these are they that have belied their professions, and are hypocrites and infidels in the guise of reformers? Does not disappointed India, after being tantalized for years by our hollow professions, cry shame on us, unworthy Brahmos? Surely we cannot affect to be deaf to the vote of censure universally passed upon us by an intelligent and honest public. Nay our own consciences convict us. So there is condemnation within and without, and we cannot ignore the festering sore, however much we may try to hide it. Far be it from me to flatter my own Church or my own people. Far be it from me to purchase the smiles of an ignorant public with the price of untruthful self-glorification. Let our weaknesses and shortcomings, our wickednesses and iniquities be confessed and proclaimed, and let the world see us as we are, and when we are weighed in the balance and found wanting let us be condemned as we ought to be. If we have proved untrue to our God, our faith and our conscience, let generation after generation continue to condemn and rebuke us with deserved severity. Ah! we all of us need stern reproof and chastisement that we may be corrected and chastened. Would you believe that there is not throughout the length and breadth of Brahmo India a single man or woman who has yet been saved? We have yet *to be* saved. We are marching towards salvation, but are very far from it. The Kingdom of Heaven is before, not behind. There is not one among us who can say, I have been saved. We are all in the bondage of iniquity, every one of us. There is none fully redeemed, no, none at all. We are being sanctified by Divine grace, it is true, and every year finds us marching slowly towards our heavenly home, yet are we terribly unclean, and are far, very far from that home.

Let us turn to our missionary experiences. How far have we succeeded in spreading truth among our countrymen? Small indeed is the measure of our success in this direction. For if the honest truth must be told, believe me, the masses of India yet remain outside our movement. We have not touched them. We have made little or no impression upon them of our holy faith. But a ray of hope comes from another quarter. Among the womanhood of India the influence of our Church is beginning to be felt in a marked manner. Behold the sister is following in the wake of the brother, and the wife is treading in the footsteps of the husband. The number of these Theistic ladies is extremely small. In all India you will not find more than a handful of those who have boldly cast away idolatry, and who daily worship the Spirit-God with faith and love. Yet in this small band of female Theists every patriot must find a significant fact, and a power not to be despised. If woman's tender heart has been touched and won by theism, all objections on the score of its so called metaphysical dryness melt away, and its charming simplicity and sweetness are established beyond all doubt. Yes, the soft heart of the Hindu woman has been acted upon in a remarkable manner by the spirit of God. You see her sitting side by side with her husband, and offering the purest and highest devotion to the invisible God, and singing the sweet and captivating hymns of our Church with a loving and joyful heart. It is a marvel that our faith, so eminently spiritual and philosophical, and devoid of all tangible symbols, has commended itself to the simple, untutored hearts of Indian women, simply because of the sweet gospel of Divine love it teaches. Let us praise God for this, and let us rejoice that the handful of our country-women whom the Lord has brought into our Church, will be the means of organizing happy theistic homes, and training up their children and children's children in the love of the True God.

You will perhaps ask me now what success we have achieved among the educated classes. What is the number of those in the higher and more cultivated ranks of society who have joined the Theistic Church? I know not. The number may be small or large according to the standard of faith and character we may apply. But of this I can assure you that among the educated and enlightened Natives of India, barring those on the one hand who have formally embraced Christianity in some form, and those on the other hand who have either through doubt or worldliness sold themselves to unbelief, materialism or positivism, all the others, and their number is legion, who have any interest in religion, and are alive to the deeper interests of their souls, all such men, I say, are with us.

Correspondence.

AN ENQUIRY.

To the Editor of the *Indian Mirror*.

SIR,—My father who is a strict Brahmo always brings me treatises on religious subjects. I read them with great pleasure. I often get my doubts about many difficult things cleared by him. I have now been reading a treatise on the "Existence of Sins." The author of the treatise has given many reasons to prove their existence. But Mr. Editor, as I have fallen in a great difficulty I ask you—"is there anything like sin?"

My female knowledge and experience tell me that there is no sin. My words may be proved to be just by considering the fact, namely, that the soul is a part or portion of God, and that whatever we do is done by God. Therefore, if we do any sinful act, it is done by God. But God who is full of truth cannot sin; therefore there is no sin.

If you or any of your readers enlighten me upon this matter, I will remain ever thankful.

CALCUTTA, The 23rd June. } Yours &c., GIRINUNDINI.

Devotional

POVERTY and humility, vouchsafe, O God unto thy devoted servants. The world wishes it not, but rather that they should serve thee and Mammon both. Asceticism is hateful to the world, for it is of heaven heavenly. There are thousands among religious men who are as the upper ten, and though pious, never sink below the line of respectability. They mix with the aristocracy, and are partial to those in high places. The poor they shun, and all that pertains to poverty. Train up devotees, we beseech thee, who shall be friendly to the poor, and shall honor the surroundings of poverty, so that the largest and most despised section of thy children may have patrons and friends in them. Who will befriend and minister unto the poor if thy devotees do not look to them? Good God, grant for the sake of the poor that the more advanced devotees may be perfectly poor in spirit and life.

IN the inner sanctuary there is no turmoil Lord; neither strife nor sorrow is there. How pleasant is it to dwell with thee there and enjoy serene communion! Let the world clamour and pierce the sky with its terrific war-cries, nothing can disturb the harmony and peace of the soul that is hid in thee. Let clouds and storms darken and distract the outward universe, my heart shall lie sweetly absorbed in thine infinite joy.

THOU in me, and I in thee, this, this, O Eternal Spirit, is my heaven. No other heaven do I seek. Grant, Lord, that I may always find myself immersed in thee, and thy spirit rooted in the depths of my heart. In such profound intercommunion thy unworthy child shall find joy unutterable.

THESE flowers, ah! so beautiful and tender, made by thy hand, have fascinated me, and I cannot resist their attractions. It is for their sakes that I cannot leave this sweet retreat. The rose and the jessamine on either side seem to say—'Go not,' and I cannot go. Dear Lord, may these heavenly flowers teach me love and purity!

The Brahmo Somaj

ON Thursday last the anniversary of the Bhowanipore Brahmo Somaj was celebrated by our conservative brethren, who deserve credit for having kept up, though not in a flourishing condition, one of the oldest Somajes in Bengal.

THE Secretary of the Mymensing Brahmo Somaj has written to the Secretary of the Brahmo Somaj of India, requesting that measures might soon be adopted for getting a Brahmo Marriage Registrar appointed by Government in that district, under Act III of 1872.

A NUMBER of Brahmo marriages are likely to be solemnized in the course of a few weeks in Calcutta.

THIS evening service will be conducted by the minister in the Mandir.

IN consequence of continued rains the *Sadhan Kanan* has proved somewhat unfavorable to spiritual exercises in open ground, and our missionary friends staying there may be subjected to some degree of inconvenience in these days. It is in consequence of these difficulties that the ancient Hindus adopted the rule of *Chaturmashaya*, and took shelter elsewhere during the four rainy months.

Literary

THE Lord Mayor entertained the representatives of Literature at a public dinner at the Mansion House this day week, the speeches at which can hardly be regarded as an accession to the literature on behalf of which they were delivered. Lord Houghton compared the men of Letters and the men of the Press to the Lords and Commons of Literature, the former holding the chief rank, and the latter the chief power,—which was an ingenious but hardly an accurate comparison, as not only do a great many Lords sit in the Commons, or Commoners in the Lords, but it is a great deal more usual, we suspect, for Lords to go down into the Commons than for the Commoners to be elevated to the Lords. Mr. Froude recalled an ancient banquet, in which there "was a porpoise at one end of the table and a sturgeon at the other;" and Mr. Sala, having pledged himself to remember "long, joyfully, and with heartfelt gratitude," the compliment paid to literature by the Lord Mayor,—a promise lightly made, we fear, and perhaps, by this time, lightly broken,—recounted with somewhat quaint candour, in answer to the toast of "The Drama," his own dead failure in producing a burlesque. Men of literature had better enjoy themselves in private, if they cannot give us better gleanings than these. City hospitalities, apparently, do not invigorate the brain.—*Spectator*.

Scientific.

THE anniversary meeting of the Royal Geographical Society was held in Burlington Gardens on May 22, Sir H. Rawlinson in the chair. The founder's medal for the year, for the encouragement of geographical science and discovery, was presented to Lieutenant V. L. Cameron, R. N., for his journey across Africa from Zanzibar to Benguela, and for his survey of the southern half of Lake Tanganyika. Sir Henry Rawlinson, in his address, pointed out that the scientific results of Lieutenant Cameron's journey had induced the Council to award him one of the gold medals of the year; for his essential merit was as an observer, and he had furnished the Society with a series of over 5,000 observations for latitude, longitude and elevation. The extreme accuracy and skill with which he had used his instruments pointed him out as a model to all future travellers whose lot might be cast in the unexplored regions of the earth. Sir Rutherford Alcock was elected president for the ensuing year; Sir Henry Rawlinson, Sir Bartle Frere, and Admiral Milne, vice-presidents. In the evening the annual dinner took place at Willis' Rooms.

MR. COTTERILL, son of the Bishop of Edinburgh, has left Liverpool on his mission of African exploration.

Gleanings

IT is false that the will can naturally regulate itself according to sound reason.

The will without God's grace can do nothing else than what is unreasonable and evil.

It does not, however, follow that the will is by nature evil, that is, is the nature of the evil one, as the Manicheans taught.

The will is not free to act if the good is presented to it.

It standeth not in the will of man to will and not to will whatever is presented to it.

This assertion is not contrary to that of St. Augustine, when he says,—'There is nothing so much in the might of the will as the will itself.'

Friendship is no virtue of nature, but of prevenient grace.

There is naught in nature save a certain craving for God. This very passion for God becomes evil and the fornication of the spirit. It is not true that this passion becomes good through the virtue of hope. Hope cometh not out of desert but out of a passion which taketh away desert.

On the side of man there goes nothing before grace save an unsuitableness, yea, a rebellion.

In one word, nature has neither a pure reason nor a good will.

We are not masters of our actions from beginning to end, but servants (Against the Philosophers).

We do not become righteous when we do what is good; but when we become righteous we do what is good. The whole ethical doctrine of Aristotle is the deadliest foe of the divine grace. It is an error to say that

Aristotle's notion of the highest good is not contrary to Christian doctrine. It is an error to say that without Aristotle no man is a theologian. It is truer to say that no man is a theologian unless he is without Aristotle. To say as men commonly say, "a theologian who is no logician is a rash heretic," is rash and heretical. It is a vain phantasy to speak of a logic of belief.

No syllogistic form harmonizes with divine things. In one word, the whole of Aristotl places again theology, is as darkness against light. However, it is a doubtful point whether the Latins rightly understand Aristotle. It would have been good for Christendom if Porphyry with his universals, had never been born. The best known definitions of Aristotle point to nothing, and no one becomes wise through them.

The grace of God is not torpid or dead, but a living, moving, and active spirit. The omnipotence of God itself cannot decree that a man should do any work of friendship or love, the grace of God not being present therein.

God cannot receive man without the grace of God, which maketh righteous.

The work of God's law can be done (outwardly) without the grace of God.

The law of God cannot be fulfilled (in the man himself) without the grace of God.

The law and the will are two foes, which without the grace of God, can never be brought into harmony.—*Luther.*

Latest News

—A LONDON special telegram sent to the *Bombay Gazette* says:—"In future legislative changes, financial or other, may be initiated in the Viceroy's Council but not carried through without communication with the Secretary of State for India in England."

—THE same telegram states:—Considering the loss caused by the depreciation in the value of silver, Lord Salisbury cancels his instructions for the immediate reduction of the cotton duties.

—THE Bank of Bombay has again reduced its rates of interest and discount one per cent. all round.

—AN official notification has been issued at Bombay announcing that His Excellency the Governor of Bombay will hold a Levee at the Council House, Poona, on Monday, the 26th instant, at 5-30 P. M.

—COLONEL MALLESON has not been dismissed. The new arrangement carries out his own recommendations.

—THE *Indu Prakash* of Bombay notices several cases of wanton and unprovoked assault by Europeans upon Natives at Bombay having occurred in the course of a fortnight. The two most recent ones are the following:—Mr. W. E. Hamblet, of the Tudor Ice Company, who assaulted a Mahomedan purchaser of ice, was fined Rs. 5, and Mr. John Forward, of the Bombay Education Society's Press, who assaulted a Hindu compositor, was fined Rs. 10.

—IT appears to have provoked a deal of remark in London that Sir Bartle Frere did not attend either of the Prince of Wales' levees, or the ball and banquet given to the Prince at the Guildhall.

—THE Taxing Officer of the Bombay High Court will have an assistant on a salary of Rs. 1000 per month.

—AS an illustration of how things go on occasionally in some of the Native States, it is related that Kaluba, the illegitimate son of the Jam of Nowanugger, ordered the Magistrate of the place to be seized and dragged through the public streets, and while being so taken along, he was being beaten and kicked, simply because the poor Magistrate asked a *Khowas* or menial of Kaluba, who was charged with assault to furnish security for his appearance when required. He was afterwards rigorously imprisoned by Kaluba. The Jam on hearing of the imprisonment, ordered immediately the Magistrate's release. His Highness is said to have spent a few months ago nine lacs of rupees in securing Kaluba's right to succession to the *guddi*, he not having had issue by any of his wives.

—HERE is the freak of a Mofussil Hazur. The Magistrate of Patna it is said by the *Behar Herald*, has been prosecuting a man of the name of Monilal for presenting to him an application for an appointment on one anna stamp paper instead of, as the Magistrate contends, an eight anna stamp. The man has been put upon his trial, under the Penal Code, for attempt at cheating. This is exactly one of those things which make the British rule most unpopular.

—MR. PAYNE, the Solicitor of Bombay, has addressed a letter to the *Bombay Gazette* with reference to the scene in the Cochin Court in which he figured. He says the report published in the *Cochin Argus*, was erroneous and one-sided. He considers that Mr. Gantz offered him gross insult by the remark he had made that the witness who was being examined was looking at his Counsel, and that signs were being made to him. He was bound to resent such insult. He adds:—"On my stating deliberately that it was a falsehood, Mr. Gantz in effect repeated the charge still more excitedly, and I then told him, and not the Court, in pretty strong language (unjustifiable, I admit, in a Court of Justice) my opinion of him. Mr. Gantz then asked the Judge to take notice of what I had said. The Judge after a pause told him he was the aggressor, and had brought it on himself and declined to interfere, and he reminded him of, and rebuked him for, having used improper language the day before to the witness. Shortly afterwards I spontaneously apologised to the Court expressing my regret that I had been betrayed into a loss of temper in a Court of Justice." The case brought by Mr. Gantz against Mr. Payne, was withdrawn on the following paper being read in open Court:—"Mr. Gantz having stated in Court and out of Court that his remarks with regard to the signs being made did not apply in any way to Mr. Payne, Mr. Payne entirely withdraws all his remarks which he made as regards Mr. Gantz, and expresses his regret for having made them." Mr. Payne denies most emphatically that he used the expressions "black soor" or "blackguard." Mr. Payne confesses that he is "not of a temper to stand an insult quietly. What has caused him the greatest pain and regret is that the affair should have occurred in a Court of Justice."

—THE Rajah of Nahun has arrived at Scindia has abandoned his intention of going there, but Nabha is expected in a few days.

Calcutta.

THE Milman Memorial Fund already amounts to Rs. 16,117-8. At Madras the Duke of Buckingham has subscribed Rs. 500, and the Bishop of Bombay, Rs. 1,000 to the Fund.

THE *Indian Daily News* understands that the Hon'ble V. H. Schalch will not take leave before November next. Mr. Dampier is likely to succeed him.

SIGNOR MASSA proposes to bring out an Italian Opera Company again next cold season. The expenses are estimated at Rs. 95,000. But only Rs. 40,000 have up to this time been subscribed.

DR. BOYES SMITH, the Principal of the Calcutta Medical College, has returned from Madras by the Steamer *Pekin*.

COLONEL MALLESON, the late Guardian to the Maharajah of Mysore, arrived in Calcutta, on Friday last, *en route*, we believe, to England.

THE P. & O. Co.'s S. S. *Siam*, Commander N. W. Hasleweod, arrived in Bombay Harbour, on Wednesday last, from Suez with the English Mails of the 2nd instant, on board. The following is the list of passengers:—

From Southampton.—Mr. F. Blake, Mr. Rilkie, Mr. Ellis, Mr. C. E. Ryanne.

From Venice.—Mr. S. E. Shillwin.

From Brindisi.—Col. J. C. Wood, Mr. A. F. Woodburn, Mr. J. T. Fleet, Mr. E. C. Gordon, Mr. Curwen, Mr. G. Cheetham, Major Lang.

From Aden.—Lieut. A. Curfeild, Mr. F. Blockley, Five Natives.

THOUGH the new Municipal Act comes into force on the 1st July next, the election will not take place till the 1st of September, but the register of voters and qualified candidates must be completed by the 15th of July.

Selections.

THE THEISTIC MOVEMENT IN INDIA.

TO THE EDITOR OF THE *Free Press.*

SIR,—In support of the testimony to the highly moral and religious character of the Theistic movement in India, furnished in the two letters which appeared in your last issue, permit me to quote from a speech made by the Rev. W. Burgess, at the annual meeting of the Wesleyan Missionary Society, held at Exeter Hall, on the 1st inst. That gentleman said—

"The formation of the Brahmo Somaj is an undoubted result of Christianity acting upon Hinduism—not quite the result we could wish for, but one we have reason to be thankful for. This new faith has taken a determined stand against caste, and there is no heart here to-day but would wish it Godspeed. It has declared a crusade against idolatry; here we are one in truest sympathy. It has lately made organised endeavours to ameliorate the position of the Hindu widow, and we all wish well to such a movement. Their success is ours. Every achievement is a victory for the Master. There is a danger, in our desire to see a certain result, of overlooking what God has already wrought. All light comes from the Master, and if among the noble Brahmos there is a jewel fallen from the Crown of Christ, we must not discard it because we find it in surroundings unharmonising with our preconceived opinion; but stoop to pick it up and place it in its true setting. The tendency of the Somaj is towards Christianity, and the day is coming, I believe, when they will turn to the Cross, and, giving heed to the soft whisper, 'Come unto me,' find soul satisfaction in Jesus."

Whether the Brahmos will in the future, as Mr. Burgess believes, accept Christianity as expounded by the orthodox churches, is very problematical. They have, however, already imbibed the spirit of Christ's teaching, and their faith as delivered to us by Chunder Sen, the great apostle of Indian Theism, has for its chief constituents the vital and imperishable elements of our own religion. So far from being the "dry well" Mr. Acomb wishes to make it out to be, it is a well of which the springs are becoming stronger and more abundant, and the streams from it by-and-bye will extend in all directions throughout the empire, purifying the nation's worship from the deadly taint which the gross and idolatrous practices of ages have engendered, and which the water made "crimson" has not been able, in any degree, to remove.

How high the institution has recently risen in public estimation may be judged of from the fact that at the annual meeting of its members, held in Calcutta in the 3rd week in January last, there were present representatives from 26 Brahmo Somajes, the congregation numbering about 500, among whom were the Lieutenant-Governor of Bengal, the Lord Bishop of Calcutta, and other ministers of the Christian Church.

Surely, if these whom I have named, being as they are in the midst of the people to whom this gospel is preached, and therefore eminently qualified to judge as to the effect produced by it upon the heathen population, think it well to aid the movement by their presence on such an occasion, no statement which disparages the influence for good of the institution, and in which the morality of its members is impeached, should be credited by us for a moment, except upon authority the most unquestionable. There are doubtless to be found, among those who have labored there as Christian missionaries, some who, with but little discernment and little capacity for apprehending the conditions under which orthodox Christianity may or may not be easily promulgated, and failing to meet with the success they anticipated, have come to regard Theism as an obstruction to the spread of orthodox religion, and therefore endeavour to bring it into disrepute by magnifying its imperfections; but those who, from their knowledge of the people and and of the Theistic system of religion are most competent to speak upon the question, have propounded Theism to be the mightiest agency now operating in India for the social, moral, and religious elevation of the nation.

I am, Sir, yours respectfully,
A CHRISTIAN.

West Bromwich, May 10, 1876.

TO THE EDITOR OF THE *Free Press.*

Sir,—Your readers who took the trouble to read the letters written by Miss Collet and myself, to correct certain misrepresentations of the Theistic Church of India, in the Rev. W. J. Acomb's articles on "Wells," would be surprised to find him saying, in his reply last week, "My dictum," "a localised deity" is a necessity of our constitution, "was also attacked by my friends." The simple truth is, that I never mention that dictum, and Miss Collet refers to it only in the following words: "They (the Brahmos) do not hold with him, and with their idolatrous fellow-countrymen, that a localised deity is a necessity of our constitution." Does he call this "attacking" his dictum? My object in writing, Sir, was not to attack any theological dictum of Mr. Acomb's, but to defend the character of the teaching and work of noble men against his unfounded accusations. He might, therefore, have spared himself the trouble of quoting Lord Macaulay's remarks on Jewish Theism, and of stating his own theological opinions. The question is not "Theism v. Orthodoxy" but "what is the character of the religious teaching of the Brahmo Somaj, and the value of its work in India?"

Mr. A.'s theological dicta would have passed by me unquestioned as far as your paper is concerned, but I felt bound to defend the teaching and work of a part of the Church of God against misrepresentations, which at first I was willing to believe were unconsciously made. His letter last week obliges me to return to the defence. He informs us that he "reads up the current literature of the day, and has studied Theism as represented in the essays and sermons of Chunder Sen." This information must increase the surprise of your readers that he should have told them that "the Brahmo Somaj proclaims God as an abstraction, cold as an iceberg, far away out of sympathy with sinful, suffering men." They must be still more surprised to find that after saying there is "much truth embodied in his reflections upon the Theistic Church of India," and that I am "anxious to explain them away," he makes no attempt to show that he has truly described the religious teaching of that Church. As a student of Theism he is, of course, familiar with its characteristic ideas of God, and we might reasonably expect him, therefore, to support the statement he made by quotation of a passage in which God is spoken of as an ice-cold, unsympathetic abstraction. He makes no such quotation. Your readers must form their own conclusion.

Mr. Acomb suggests that I have fashioned a "rose-colored picture of Brahmoism" out of the materials of "the prospectus of the New Church of India, a few years since." He quotes a passage from the speech of the Rev. T. Morgan, Baptist missionary from India ("the latest authority") as proof that your readers "have been sold." Happily there are Christian missionaries in India who, while believing that Christianity contains higher truth than Theism, see in the Brahmo Somaj "a true Church of God, engaged in a truly Divine work," and who must be deeply grieved to find this Church spoken of, by a professed servant of Christ, as "a new regiment commanded by the devil himself."

The Rev. W. Burgess, Wesleyan missionary from India, said in Exeter Hall, on the 1st of this month:—"The formation of the Brahmo Somaj is an undoubted result of Christianity acting upon Hinduism—not quite the result we could wish for, but one to be thankful for. This new faith has taken a determined stand against caste, and there is no heart here to-day but would wish it "God speed." It has declared a crusade against idolatry; here we are one in truest sympathy. It has lately made organised endeavours to ameliorate the position of the Hindu widow, and we all wish well to such a movement. In these things we are one at heart. Their success is ours. Every achievement is a victory for the Master. There is a danger, in our desire to see a certain result, of overlooking what God has already wrought. All light comes from the Master, and if among the noble Brahmos there is a jewel fallen from the crown of Christ, we must not discard it because we find it in surroundings not harmonising with our preconceived opinion; but stoop to pick it up and place it in its true setting. The tendency of the Somaj is towards Christianity, and the day is coming, I believe, when they will all turn to the Cross, and, giving heed to the soft whisper, 'Come unto Me,' find soul satisfaction by believing in Jesus."

Permit me to add to this testimony that given by Sir Richard Temple in his "Minute on the Administration of Bengal for 1874-5": "Their leaders (the Brahmos) are earnest men of excellent repute; the doctrines of the sect appear to have an excellent effect upon the lives and conduct of its members. The number of strict professing Brahmos is apparently not great, but the number of those who are Brahmos in mind and heart is said to be very considerable. Whether that be so or not, it appears that opinions and sentiments identical with or similar to those of the professed Brahmos are spreading among the educated classes of Hindus in these provinces, and this is a very important circumstance."

Now, Sir, I have contented myself with a statement of facts, as I did in my last letter, for Mr. Acomb's relation of personal religious experience, and his statements of theological opinion do not concern me; and your readers must now judge which "picture of Brahmoism" is true to fact.

Mr. Acomb warned off your readers from Theism as a "dry well," asserting that its idea of God is an unsympathetic "abstraction," attempting to prove that it is spiritually inefficient, if not worthless. He now indorses Mr. Morgan's description of the Theistic Church in India, as composed of men "who repudiate Christ," are "bitter, inveterate enemies of Christianity," "a new regiment commanded by the devil himself, like a broad phalanx, determined to oppose Christianity." Surely this is not language we should have expected from men, who must have discerned the spirit of Christ, amid large varieties of thought, the essential elements of religion in men of various creeds and churches. To say that the Brahmo Somaj "preaches a gospel without Christ," "repudiates Christ," is not true, except to those who assert that Christ is not preached unless their conception of Him is proclaimed. Let the opening sentence of Chunder Sen's anniversary lecture, delivered on the 24th of January last, be sufficient disproof of such charges: "I verily believe that when Jesus Christ was about to leave this world, He made over the sacred portfolio of the ministry of His Church to the Holy Spirit." Is this the language of a man who "repudiates Christ?"

My own deliberate conviction is that the religious future of India is bound up with the Brahmo Somaj; I look on the Brahmos as fellow Christians; and it is because the men and their work have appealed to my inmost sympathies that I have written in their defence. "To bring the soul into direct communion with the everlasting God, to flood the human spirit with the light of His presence, and strengthen the moral nature for the performance of duty amid all the engagements of life—this is their self-imposed and noble task. May their success be equal to the purity and earnestness of their faith."

Yours faithfully,
JOHN HARRISON.

Jesson Street, West Bromwich,
May 17th, 1876.

[We feel it necessary to close this correspondence at once.]—ED. *F. P.*

—*Free Press.*

Printed and published by M. M. RUKHIT, at the INDIAN MIRROR PRESS, No. 15, College Square, for the Proprietor.

The Indian Mirror.

SUNDAY EDITION.

VOL. XV.] CALCUTTA, SUNDAY JULY, 2, 1876 } REGISTERED AT THE GENERAL POST OFFICE. { [NO. 155

CONTENTS.

NOTICE.

All letters and communications relating to the literary department of the Paper should be addressed to the Editor. All other letters should be addressed to the Manager, to whom all remittances should be made payable.

Subscribers will be good enough to bring to the notice of the Manager any delay or irregularity in the delivery of the Paper.

Editorial Notes.

SIR RICHARD TEMPLE has wisely avoided giving needless offence to people's religious feelings by allowing the Juggernath Car at Mahesh to be drawn. The local authorities had ordered the prevention of the practice. The Ruth festival is the most popular in the neighbourhood, and the joy of the people is not so much in the drawing of the car as in the fair, the buying and selling and the merriments around.

THE ladies, Mrs. Woodrow and Miss Chamberlain, who recently examined the pupils of the first class of the Native Ladies' Normal School under the Indian Reform Association, have, we are informed, furnished their reports. The remarks they make on the attainments and manners of the young ladies examined are highly encouraging. We hope the managers of the Institution will publish their annual report, and embody in it opinions of the examiners and others as to the progress made during the past year.

AMONG those who may expect to go to heaven Mahomed enumerates seven kinds of men. Those who in early youth devote themselves to the service of God. Those who bind themselves in love and friendship in the name and for the sake of God. Those who weep in secret before the throne of God. Those who sitting in the throne of kings, can do full justice to all. Those who from the time they enter the Musjid till the time they leave it, are wholly absorbed in the ideas which the Musjid ought to inspire. Those who can in the name of God resist the amorous solicitations of rich and beautiful women. Those whose left hands do not know the charities they give with their right.

SCEPTICAL thinkers and evolutionists profess great contempt for the character of savages. Mr. Mill most broadly puts down in his Three Essays on Theism that barbarian nations are great liars. From what facts this conclusion is drawn we are not told, for we know to a certainty that among many savage tribes in India certain virtues of a high order such as truth and chastity prevail to a very remarkable degree, much more so decidedly than among persons who boast of their civilization. It is a truth that the advent of Europeans, and our high class town-educated Hindus, has spoiled the morals of the rude and simple people of the hills and frontiers. Dr. Livingstone used to say that "the only new point of morality which he had to teach African Pagans, was not to have more than one wife." The moral department of human nature, like other departments, is susceptible of great improvement and change, but it is positively wrong to say that so far as existing civilization goes, civilized men are in all points morally superior to savages. There is such a thing as primeval and uncorrupted morality which the latter possess.

PROFESSOR NEWMAN in his article on "National Religion" in the May number of the *Langham Magazine* criticises the assertion of Lord Macaulay that the Hindu religion is so bad as to have no good tendencies at all. We do not agree with Mr. Newman when he says that this is true when we interpret the creed from the legendary fables of Hinduism. The legends of Hinduism, like various other religious legends admit of different interpretations, but granting that some of them are really bad, a great many are so decidedly noble and beautiful that it is only those who do not understand them through ignorance and prejudice like Lord Macaulay that can call their tendencies in any sense vile. Are not the *Ramayana*, the *Mahavarata* and most of the Purans full of the most interesting and edifying anecdotes? Professor Newman however writes the following passage on the general moral influence of Hinduism:—"The earnest Native reformers of the Hindu faith, the successors of Rammohun Roy, insist that in uncorrupted quiet districts the total influence of Hinduism produces many beautiful and lovely virtues. Indeed an English ex-judge from India has lately uttered among us a pungent declaration, that he has nowhere seen eminent 'Christian' virtue in practice, except in remote districts of India which Europeans have not yet corrupted."

THE Jews of England are not the Jews of India. Of the latter we know so very little that we would not venture to express an opinion about them. But the Jews of England, nay of all European countries almost, are not as flourishing as the rest of the community, but in charity and humanity are not the inferior of any. The Jew labors under a great many disadvantages from which others are comparatively free, and not the least formidable among these, is the bad repute in which they are universally held in Europe. But nevertheless they spend large sums in charity. There are ninety charitable institutions belonging to Jews in London alone, and a Jew spends from five to tenfold as much as his Christian neighbours. We take the following from Mr. Voysey's magazine:—"Charity accompanies into this world the child of Jewish lowly life. The mother receives medical advice and material comforts; the father obtains a gratuity; the infant, if a boy, when he grows up, is educated, apprenticed to a trade, started in life. The man is tended when sick, pensioned when old, buried when dead; and his family are provided for, during the week of confined mourning, when Jews do not work. Girls also enjoy similar advantages; various societies distribute marriage portions to the successful maidens who draw lucky numbers; and if their natural protector is called away and leaves them aged and destitute, different asylums provide them with a shelter for their declining days. Finally, a number of miscellaneous institutions surround the poor Jew throughout life, cheering him during trouble, befriending him when in need, watching over his moral and spiritual welfare, and endeavouring to elevate his material and mental condition."

THE author of "The Devil's Chain," himself a Member of Parliament, dedicates his book to Sir Wilfrid Lawson than whom there can not be a more valiant defender of the cause of Temperance. The book itself is an exposure of the evils of intemperance. The dedication is as follows :—

My dear Lawson, I dedicate this book to you, not as a token of adhesion to all your opinions, but as a tribute of sympathy with you in your gallant fight with a terrible evil, and of admiration for your pluck. At a time when this latter virtue has grown weak on front benches, it is refreshing to find it vigorous below the gangway. A man who cannot be driven from a frank expression and profession of the truth he holds within him, either by the crackling laughter of a select few or the outcry of the mob, is in these days a rare work of God, the which, when one sees it, he feels bound to bless heaven for, and to take hopeful courage for humanity. Perplexed between the extremes of a disease at once so complicated and outrageous as that which you work so hard to remedy, I do not attempt in this book to prescribe the purge. My aim is here—as it was in 'Ginx's Baby'—rather to exhibit in rude, stern truthful outlines the full features and proportions of the abuses I would humbly help to remove. It is a great thing done if we can get people to think about the reality, bearings, and size of an evil; and in spite of the exposures, through the press, of the dismal fruits of traffic in drink, I find men going about, and dining comfortably, and voting steadily, in utter disregard of their fell, disastrous, and diabolical effects. I cannot acquit myself of having too long done the like. I have therefore tried to bring into one small picture a somewhat comprehensive view of these evils, in the hope of rousing some men of quiet digestion out of their apathy, and so of aiding your noble work. No one knows better than you that there is not an incident in the ensuing pages which is not unhappily, not only possible, but probable. In no case have I represented here any individual, yet, I do not doubt that I shall be credited with intentional personalities. No better evidence could be afforded of the extent and variety of the evils against which you so righteously protest.

FOR BRAHMO PARENTS.

MAY we ask if Brahmo parents have begun to think earnestly of the marriage of their sons and daughters? Of course they will answer in the affirmative. But the question we have asked is not answered quite so easily. Much has been said on the subject of marriage, its object and its ideal; marriage ceremonies have been improved and reformed; early marriages are being slowly done away with; all this we admit. But we ask what is being done to train up children in such a way that when they grow up they may make happy and virtuous families. Brahmo boys and girls are fast growing up, and as girls become marriageable much sooner than boys, the question becomes daily more and more serious as to where to find suitable husbands for them. In the first place Brahmo children are not properly educated, then their moral training is not taken into due consideration, and then in the third place little thought is spent on their religious education. Brahmo parents who do take any trouble with the education of their boys and girls, entertain so very high expectations on the subject of their marriage, that these have little chance of fulfillment. These expectations are naturally shared in by those on whose behalf they are entertained, and matches become still more difficult.

To begin with the remedy of this evil, certain wrong ideas on the subject of education will have to be removed. There is a false fashionable standard of teaching accomplishments, inculcated by a second hand European civilization which is totally foreign, inapplicable to the society around. This imparts mischievous inflated ideas to which no practical realities can correspond. They make the teaching of sound and wholesome ideas about life distasteful, and young people grow up in utter ignorance of the real trials and duties that await them. Those, therefore, who have the training and guardianship of the sons and daughters of Brahmos in their hands, must take care to see that the education they get be thoroughly true and practical, removed as far as possible from the showy useless refinements which have commenced to make the youth of this country to be conceited and self-conscious. The most judicious and careful moral training will have to be given to form the right habits and feelings. The ways of thinking among Brahmos in general are neither strictly Hindu, nor do they conform to any standard known in this country or elsewhere. Under this circumstance it is but natural their children should be untaught to cultivate their best moral feelings, and grow up as other children grow up in the transition state of society in the land, without any definite rules of conduct whatever before them. Simplicity, meekness, purity, and gentle habits of domestic usefulness ought to be inculcated by the best and most unremitting efforts. It should be early taught that strict and pure morals are of incalculably greater value than the most showy social and intellectual accomplishments, that genuine happiness in life does not lie in fashionable refinements and outward appearances, but in virtuous and well-disciplined habits of personal and domestic economy. And above all a real and suitable religious training should be attended to as a supreme necessity. It always pains us to discover that Brahmo parents give so little importance to this point. Does it never occur to them that considering the circumstances around, some of their children may never be married, that their daughters may have to live and die as old maids, and that the vicious society in the midst of which they live, may slander and malign them. Add to all this the real danger arising from the temptations and snares on all sides, and they will see the pre-eminent necessity of teaching them holiness and devotion, the fear and the love of God when their hearts are tender and susceptible.

With one practical suggestion we shall conclude. Let wishes and expectations in the mind of young men be moderated as much as possible. They must not be made to think so highly of themselves that may be misled to entertain the mischievous wish of marrying beyond their station in life, and the expectations of worldy happiness to which they have no real claim.

OUR FAITH AND OUR EXPERIENCES.

(Concluded.)

I ADMIT they do not all profess to be Brahmos. Not a few among them even hate the Brahmo name. Nay are hostile to many of our doctrines and movements, and look upon many of our teachings and practices as altogether false. With intense bitterness they treat me and my colleagues as their enemies, and seldom lose an opportunity of obstructing our work in various ways. Yet are they with us, fellow-members of the National Theistic Church. They may not subscribe to all the details of our theology, but its fundamental principles,—divine unity, man's immortality and accountability they fully accept; idolatry they detest and abjure. Hence, if not in name, in spirit they are all Brahmos. (Applause.) That they object to the Brahmo name is perfectly immaterial, so long as they think, believe and act as Theists. Verily there is no fascination in that name. I myself would at this very moment disclaim it if needed. It is enough that these thousands and tens of thousands of educated Indian youths, here and in other parts of India, acknowledge and worship the One Spirit-God whom we glorify. They are our brothers and sisters in faith; they are co-workers with us in God's vineyard. They are all engaged, more or less, in up-building the true church in India. They are all doing our work, yes, every one of them. Those among them who deny us, revile us, oppose us, know not alas! what they are doing. They unconsciously, others consciously, are being led by the hand of Providence towards the true Theistic Church of the future. Under different names and different colors, they are all marching in the same direction, under the guidance of the same Divine Captain. Whatever our differences and peculiarities, we are moving on like a great army under the banner of Theism. We are moving on, did I say? Those who are not fully with us, may be said to be gradually advancing towards our Church. But are *we*, who have established ourselves upon a definite faith and are members of an organized church, are we too moving on? Then, you will perhaps say, our faith is uncertain, we have not yet found the truth, our light is in the future, and we are only groping in the dark, moving on, if haply we may find the truth. Ah! my friends, stagnation is not redemption;

there is no glory in standing still, but in marching on. If you ask me whether we have succeeded after forty years in crystallizing our doctrines, opinions and beliefs into a fixed creed, I say, no. Nor do we mean to do so. To be shut up amid hard barriers of dogmas is not the heaven we seek. To walk steadily on in free air and open light is our heaven. Who would stumble midway in his God-ward course with the huge mill-stone of lifeless dogmas hanging round his neck? Now I tell you plainly we do not mean to stand where we are. Have we not found the truth? We have, but we need more. Have we not seen the light? Yes we have, but how it shines unto the perfect day, we have yet to see. Dew drops of heavenly joy and peace, have we gathered and tasted, but the vast ocean of Divine joy still surges before us. Therefore we mean to go further and further under the guidance of God, in the path of ever-incerasing wisdom, love, purity and joy, never satisfied with what is achieved, but always panting and struggling for fresh acquisitions. Our scripture is not closed, but fresh Chapters are being written, and added year after year. What the Lord will reveal to us ten years hence who knows save He? We thank Him for the revelation. He has already vouchsafed unto us, but more He will yet reveal as He has told us. Towards fuller light we shall, therefore, prayerfully and reverently press forward. March on, my friends, and do not stand still as conservatives. Even if your prospects be gloomy and frightening do not ignominiously run away. Face the cannon's mouth like a true and brave soldier, and die the martyr's death, rather than surrender the banner of truth to the enemy. Hindu Brethren, Christian friends, pray, fervently and unceasingly pray for our welfare. Pray, that the Lord may direct our steps. If you think we are in error, commend us to Him who removeth all error. If you think we ought to move in better paths, ask the True Guide to direct us. We shall not be guided by you, your shibboleths you need not impose upon us. Yet give us the benefit of your friendly and anxious prayers, and continually beseech the Merciful Father to lead us wheresoever there is truth. Let the devout and good of all nations bless us with their sympathy and prayer. Is not the path of the religious reformer in this country full of thorns, and will not dire difficulties beset his work for many years to come? Those who engage themselves in such a work must be prepared for the worst, and pay the price of their own life-blood for every inch of ground they win. Amidst the gloom and terror of such trying work, it is indeed natural that the workers, a small and feeble band, should seek sympathy and help among friends. But if such sympathy be not forthcoming, let the Lord's will be done. Let truth triumph in the midst of agony, bloodshed and death. Rest assured that the persecuted shall be justified at last, and God's devoted servants and faithful ambassadors, though reviled, hated and trampled by men, shall receive the crown of glory in heaven. Fellow theists, whether men smile or look frowningly upon you, whether they praise or persecute you, you must honor all, friends and foes alike, and go on humbly discharging your duty to your country and to your God, and learning truth even from those who strike you. Let us remember that our Church is small and is in its infancy. Let us look upon our Hindu and Christian brethren as our elders, and humbly sit at their feet to learn those things in which they excell us. Brethern, check all desire of vain glory. Cast away proud antagonism and sectarian malice. In a candid and lowly spirit confess your faults and shortcomings, and freely give credit to other Churches for all the solid truths and excellent virtues which adorn them. And to you, gentlemen, who for one reason or another, are antagonistic to us, I would say one word before I resume my seat. Do you not remember the advise of Gamaliel, that great counsellor among the Jews, concerning the apostles. "Then stood there up one in the counsel, a Pharisee, named Gamaliel, a doctor of the law, and said unto them, Ye men of Israel, take heed to yourselves, what ye intend to do as touching these men. . . . And now I say unto you, Refrain from these men, and let them alone: for if this counsel or this work be of men, it will come to naught: but if it be of God, ye cannot overthrow it; lest haply ye be found even to fight against God." Christians, Hindus, Mahomedans, Bhudhists, and men of other religious denominations, however hostile ye may be to these men, the Brahmos, ye should refrain from them and let them alone. Ye may rest assured that if their teachings and their work be of men, they shall surely perish, and the Lord Himself shall confound His enemies. But if the work they are doing be the Lord's work it is utterly beyond your power to discomfit them, however formidable ye may be. Ye shall not stand against the Almighty. Do not fight against these people, for by so doing ye may be fighting against God Himself. Therefore I say, "refrain from these people." That the country has been convulsed by some mysterious spiritual force you dare not deny. What is it that like a mighty wind drives these men, some here, some there, in the various cities of India, in a state of spiritual excitement, towards a better place which the eye hath not seen? Why this onward rush of small groups of pilgrim soldiers in different parts of the country? Whence all this enthusiastic devotion among people who have no outward revelation, no articles of faith, no visible church authority to bind or sustain them? Verily verily this mighty wind is the breath of God Almighty. Do you despise and ridicule our Church because it is a small thing, and therefore cannot be from God? Remember that with God Almighty nothing is impossible, and that out of little things hath He always achieved wonders among the nations of the earth. There is no power surely in numbers, but in the spirit of God. If half a dozen young men were imbued with the Holy Spirit, what would they not achieve? What wonders would happen in these days if the Lord were to say, as He did of old, "on my servants and on my hand-maidens I will pour out in those days of my Spirit?" Remember the day of Pentecost, when "suddenly there came a sound from Heaven as of a rushing mighty wind, and it filled all the house where they were sitting." With such a general outpouring of the Holy Ghost, with such an outburst of apostolical enthusiasm, like "a rushing mighty wind," a handful of God's devoted servants will certalnly work wonders in India. Will not our Heavenly Father vouchsafe unto our country a pentecostal shower of His saving grace?

Lord, Bless Thy work here and strengthen Thy servants that truth may triumph in this land. Teach us love, that we may love each other in spite of differences of opinion. Gather all races and tribes, Kind God, in Thy fold, wherever it may be.

And now my Brethern, I commend you to my God and your God. May He bless you all for ever (applause).

Provincial

CUTTACK.

[FROM OUR OWN CORRESPONDENT.]

The 23rd June, 1876.

I PROMISED to tell you something about the Utkal Brahmo Somaj at Cuttack, which I hope, may not be quite uninteresting to your Brahmo readers. This is a subject, however, on which I should like it far more to say too little, than to say too much. I need hardly premise that the Utkal Brahmo Somaj does, by no means, deserve a prominent notice, as having done more work or as being more advanced than many other Somajes in India. The truth is there are few Brahmo Somajes so low in spiritual progress as the Somaj in question. The Somaj, as it is, is a poor caricature of what it ought to be. The organization is as defective as could be imagined. There is hardly any spiritual union among the members. There is no mutual service so far as I am aware. In short, judged by the standard of Brahmoism as has been revealed unto the world, nay as has been attained in other places, the Utkal Brahmo Somaj is scarcely deserving of the name. Yet if we compare the present with the past, we find much ground for hope even in an institution like this. There seems to be a mighty force at work, which the wickedness of men cannot counteract. The Utkal Brahmo Somaj has been in existence for 6 or 7 years, and during that time, though its progress has not been very encouraging, it has yet undergone many changes for the better. Those who have watched it for the last 5 or 6 years, will bear me out in saying that as at present constituted it is quite a different thing from what it was. Though it was at first more numerously attended than now, most of the members were mere school-boys, with no clear conceptions about the religion they professed, and though now and then some degree of zeal and earnestness was manifested, it could not be relied upon. Most of them have since left the Somaj, perhaps for ever. When Babu Aghurnath Gupta, the well-known Brahmo Missionary, visited Orissa, he found the Somaj in a miserable condition, both internally and externally. There were only half a dozen of Brahmos, or thereabouts, and among them there was scarcely one who had attained to a pretty high standard of faith and life. Even this, I must say, was an improvement on the past. The Brahmo Somaj was no long looked upon as a place of amusement. Some pressure had now been brought to bear on the members for improving their life and character. Some idea of the sacrifices which religion entails on its followers, had been presented to men. The consequence was, many had withdrawn, and the Somaj had been reduced almost to a skeleton. So Aghur Babu found it. His lectures and sermons, and, above all, his life and example exerted a very wholesome influence among the members of the Utkal Brahmo Somaj, most of whom were for the first time made acquainted with *living* prayer, as distinguished from a mere uttering of words to one's self. One of them, an elderly person, still acknowledges, in feeling terms, his indebtedness to the Brahmo Missionary for having, for the first time, opened his eyes to true prayer. When Aghur Babu came daily prayer was a thing very rare among the Brahmos here. In the *Sangat* which was held every week no question was so often repeated as that wheather or not the members had prayed regularly during the previous week. The answer was in most cases in the negative. Many regretted some, perhaps, explained their inability, or simply apologized for it; but for all that, every succeeding week only repeated the sad experience of the past. Since Aghur Babu's departure, the members of the Utkal Brahmo Somaj began to pay more attention to daily prayer than they had ever done. When our revered Missionary, Babu Protap Chunder Mozumdar, came down to Cuttack, the local Brahmos, though few in number, and at best lukewarm in religious matters, were yet more prayerful than their former selves. Our good Missionary was, however, much disappointed by what he saw, and well he might. Not that the Brahmos did not receive him well, but that he saw few or none among them who were zealous enough in the cause of religion. There was no yearning for spiritual life among those for whose especial benefit he had come, and this grieved him very much. It is a matter for congratulation to the Utkal Brahmo Somaj, that there is more striving for spiritual progress now than there has ever been. Daily prayer is no longer a rare thing among them. Some time ago some of them signed a resolution to the effect that they would do everything that they believed to be calculated to promote their spiritual welfare, and desist from doing whatever they believed to be contrary to the will of God. This was followed by another by which some members bound themselves to remain faithful to God and His Church for ever. More is expected to be done in that direction, which, though it may not possess any great value, when considered in itself, is still a sign of the change which has happily come over the Somaj. The Somaj building also bids fair to be completed or to be at least fit for use ere long. Subscriptions have been set on foot, and the work will be resumed in a day or two. It is true that want of funds was the main cause that prevented the completion of the Somaj building so long. But it is also true that the Brahmos did not feel so intensely, as they do now, the want of a permanent place for public worship. I do not mean to give the Somaj any credit for the present earnestness (comparatively speaking) among the members. How long this will last and how far it will carry the Brahmos remains to be seen. Of late there has been some increase in the weekly attendance, but that is not so important a point as internal progress. One faithful servant of God is of more service to the world than a thousand so called worshippers. What I have said about the Utkal Brahmo Somaj, naturally gives rise to some general reflections which I reserve for my next.

Devotional

AM I not a thief and a robber, O God? Have I not stolen this body, wealth and all my earthly possessions, which are all due to my brethren, and retained them for my own use? Every penny I possess, every drop of blood in my body belongs to others, and I cannot use it as mine own. Lord, teach me to consecrate my body and mind and all I have to the service of my brother and sister.

AMID plants and trees, flowers and fruits the heart remains pure and happy, and easily learns simplicity, humanity and asceticism. Amid family cares and engagements and the bustle and business, the trials and temptations of society, it is hard, very hard, my God! to become godly. But as thy child must serve society, and achieve purity in the battle-field of life, grant Father, that in the rural retreat, amid the beauties of nature, I may be fitted by true communion for the duties and trials of social life.

The Brahmo Somaj

AN Institution like the Bharat Asram has been established, at Dacca, by Babu Bungo Chunder Roy, the local Brahmo missionary. We take the following from the *East* :—"Last Wednesday the East Bengal *Asram* was formally opened in the house where some Brahmo families were so long residing and worshipping the Living God with the object of establishing here so important an institution as Asram. An institution without a local habitation and a name is admittedly no institution whatever, and as such it fails to produce the desired result. It was practically seen that although great exertion has been made, and many measures have been taken to arrive at the result by simply dwelling and worshipping together without giving a name to the Institution, it failed to produce the effect, at least in the same degree as it should have otherwise done. There was celebrated an *Utsab* on the occasion, which was very deep, very impressive and very instructive. It was very interesting to hear some ladies and girls varying in age from 60 to 12 years offering very sincere and pathetic prayers. We wish the institution all prosperity, and hope it will prove successful under Divine influence.

LAST Sunday the minister of the Brahma Mandir discoursed on Secret Wealth. As in the world so in the Kingdom of God, what the truly wealthy display outside of riches and power and greatness, is not a measure of their real opulence. What they possess far exceeds what they show. By far the largest quantity of his riches the worldly man carefully conceals in the bank or the safe. So the true devotee, however fervent his outward prayers and remarkably self-sacrificing his charities, hides the treasures of his goodness in the recesses of his heart. True devotion, true love and true charity are things that cannot be shown. They are deep and invisible realities, known only to the all-searching eye of God.

WE ought to realise fully the significance of the three great institutions we have now in our midst, the Bharat Asram, the Brahmo Niketan and the Sadhan Kanan. Each is important and useful in its own way, and cannot be superseded by the others. While recognising the high mission of the Kanan, we must not be blind to the merits of the other institutions; nor must we think they are lately thrown into the shade by the growth of this new institution. If they could all be included in the same plan and made to work harmoniously the best results would be achieved.

BABU PROTAP CHUNDER MOZUMDAR will conduct divine service in the Mundir, this evening.

THEOLOGICAL CLASS.

Sunday May 7, 1876.

(*First Day's Lesson.*)

MODERN unbelief or scepticism is reducible under three principal heads so far as the grounds on which it establishes itself are concerned. (I) Physical, or Scientific grounds; (II) Metaphysical, or mental grounds; and (III) Moral grounds based upon the adjustment of good and evil in the world.

(I) *Physical Grounds of Unbelief* may be subdivided into (a) The Theory of Creation or the genesis and classification of such phenomena and objects as meet us in the world. (b) The Theory of Forces or the nature of the active principles which induce all the changes observable in natural phenomena.

(II) *The Metaphysical Department of Unbelief* is mainly concerned with the theory of causation necessarily involving analogies between the creation and the administration of the world, and the origin and management of human affairs. And in the second place it undertakes an investigation into those natural ideas otherwise called first principles, *a priori* beliefs, intuitions, upon which the faith of all mankind is more or less established.

(III) *The Moral Department of Unbelief* is exclusively concerned with those difficulties in the arrangements and providence of the world which meet us everywhere in the seemingly insufficient balance between happiness and misery, vice and virtue, good and evil.

Theory of Creation. The old notion of the creation of the world by an abrupt fiat of God's will is, we believe, philosophically and scientifically untenable. We take it to be a demonstrated fact that the world in all its stages has been the effect of an incalculable series of pre-existing changes. The first link of that chain is beyond the experience and calculation of man. But that the original elements were created and combined through a process which we cannot realize or reason upon, we take as a first principle. In acknowledging this inability and assuming this fact, we lose nothing. Even the most materialistic theory of the origin and development of the world is not free from assumptions quite as great, but much more gross. Unless we believe that there are two eternities, or what is equally absurd, unless we believe that the material world is identical with the Divine Being, we must come to the conclusion that the world had a beginning, and that beginning had its origin in God. The arguments from design, power, goodness, holiness which have survived all the attacks of materialism and unbelief, tend only to confirm that position.

In reasoning upon the subject of the creation of the universe, therefore, the Theist finds his position to be clearly intermediate between the two extreme theories of the eternity of matter on the one hand, and the sudden appearance of the *cosmos* with all its present laws and developements out of the depths of the Divine Being on the other. The Theist thus arrives at a practical reconciliation of the vexed questions of the evolution of matter and the creation of the Universe by divine agency; and the balance is preserved between the ancient faith of mankind and the latest discoveries of science. To sum up, let us briefly repeat that we do not pretend to discover either the first links in the chain of material developements, nor do we profess to foretell their ultimate consequences. But nevertheless we hold it equally certain that the origin and the initial developements of the universe must have taken place in the mysteries of the Divine will; that its maintenance is attributable to the ever active impulses of the same will; and that its ultimate destinies also lie involved therein to be shaped and developed in future according to the infinite purposes that are noticeable in the present and past.

Literary

M. Renan has published a volume of "Dialogues et Fragments Philosophiques." The Dialogues, which form the larger part of the book, were written at Versailles, in May, 1871. M. Renan says that he hesitated for a time to publish them, as they bear the impress of the terrible crisis through which France was then passing.

Amongst Messrs. Macmillan and Co.'s latest publications we notice Mr. Grant Duff's "Notes of an Indian Journey." According to the *Saturday Review* these 'Notes' are full of pleasant remarks and illustrations, borrowed from every kind of source. In an appendix Mr. Grant Duff states his opinions about India with the utmost frankness. This addition to the volume is most valuable. It is full of thought, both true and new. There is no petty [illegible], no optimism about it. What the writer thinks he says, and what he thinks has been clearly and carefully thought out.

Privy Councillor Grigorieff, Professor of Oriental History and Dean of the Faculty of Oriental Languages at the University of St. Petersburg, has been elected President of the Committee of Organisation of the third International Congress of Orientalists, which is to meet this summer at St. Petersburg. Professor Robert Douglas, of London, has been designated as the Committee's corresponding member for England.

"India and Lancashire" is the title of an article in the June number of the *Fortnightly Review*. The writer is Mr. R. Raynsford Jackson.

The Athenæum and Daily News, the oldest paper, we believe, in Madras, has lately become the property of the Hon'ble J. G. Coleman.

The valuable Library of the Rev. Dr. Wilson is to be purchased by the Bombay University.

Next winter (says the *Athenæum*) the Semitic Languages Tripos at Cambridge, the scheme of which was settled some two or three years ago, will, for the first time, be actually in operation, as there will probably be a couple of candidates in Hebrew and Syriac. Oriental studies are beginning to take root in the University. Trinity has given two scholarships for Sanskrit, both obtained by pupils of the City of London School, where Sanskrit has been taught—and well taught—for some time. Last April St. John's offered a 50l. scholarship in Sanskrit or Arabic, but met with no response. At Corpus, the Brotherton prize is, at stated intervals, awarded for Sanskrit, and is open to all graduates of the University under the standing of M. A. Queen's College also, under the able guidance of its President and Professor Wright, is doing its best to foster legal studies.

It has been noted as marvelous, that four of England's most famous ecclesiastical disputants and leaders at the present day, were colleagues and firm friends during their college days at Oxford. The eldest was John Henry Newman, then came Edward Pusey, next Henry Edward Manning, and youngest of all William Edward Gladstone. They were all strong sympathisers in the religious movement of that day, which was giving more prominence to the Catholic element in that strange mixture, the established Church of England, and took a deep interest in the controversies of the time. It is over forty years since then. The varying results are known. Manning is Cardinal Archbishop of English Romanism; Pusey has almost a similar eminence among the Catholics who still remain in the Anglican Church; Newman is the devout and able, but secluded theological champion of Roman Catholicism; and Gladstone is crowning his days by an equally able championship on the opposite side, the only one of the four who has developed towards Protestantism, and that only till of late.—*Lucknow Witness.*

Scientific

Regarding the scheme for an Indian Museum on the Thames Embankment, the London correspondent of the *Bombay Gazette* writes: "I referred some time ago to a scheme which was on foot for establishing an Imperial Museum for India and the Colonies, on the Thames Embankment. The matter has now assumed a tangible form, and is being pressed upon the attention of Government by the Royal Colonial Institute and the Royal Asiatic Society. The life and soul of the business is Dr. J. Forbes Watson, who has just published a very able pamphlet, setting forth the advantages of such a scheme and such a site. The project is a great blow at the Cole party who are not only hoping to retain the Indian Museum at South Kensington, but to add a number of Colonial Museums to it. South Kensington is all very well for pleasure-seekers and west-[illegible], but these are not the class of persons who are likely to take advantage of such a practical Museum as that which Dr. Watson seeks to place close to the official quarter, and within a stone's throw of the law courts and the City. The majority of the Cabinet, for it has now become a Cabinet question, are in favor of the scheme, but the main difficulty is that of finding the money. . . . I may add, too, that Dr. Watson's plan has found so much favor in the Provincial towns that several of the Chambers of Commerce have given it their support, and I doubt not that if the Government cannot afford to give the site that a movement will be started for raising the necessary money by public subscription.

Gleanings

There was an account in the papers, the other day, of a man who showed that he had the spirit of Martyr Stephen in him. His name was Joseph Robbins. He was a bridge watchman on a railway. He was murdered by a neighbour who wanted to get his money. The murderer was caught directly after. During the trial he made this confession in open Court:—"I knew that Robbins had just received his month's wages, and I resolved to have his money. I got a shot gun and went to the bridge. As I came near to the watchhouse, on looking through the window, I saw Robbins sitting. His head and shoulders only could be seen. I raised the gun, took aim and fired. I waited a few minutes to see if the report of the gun had alarmed any one, but all was still. Then I went up to the watch-house door, and found Robbins on his knees praying. Very plainly I heard him say, 'Oh God, have mercy on the man who did this, and spare him for Jesus' sake.' I was horrified; I did not dare to enter the house; I could not touch that man's money. Instead of this, I turned and ran away, I knew not whither. His words have haunted me ever since." This man had the very spirit of Jesus. And it was knowing and believing the truth in Jesus which put this spirit in him. The truth that can do this for us is the best of all truth.

Buddha said:—"There are difficult things in the world—Being poor to be charitable; being rich and great, to be religious; to escape destiny; to repress lust and banish desire; to see an agreeable object and not seek to obtain it; to be strong without being rash; to bear insult without anger; to move in the world (to touch things) without setting the heart on it; to investigate a matter to the very bottom; not to contemn the ignorant; thoroughly to extirpate self-esteem; to be good, and at the same time to be learned and clever; to see the hidden principle in the profession of religion; to attain one's end without exultation; to exhibit in a right way the doctrine of expediency; to save men by converting them; to be the same in heart and life; to avoid controversy."

Latest News

—Another Native Chief has arrived at Simla—the Nawab of Maler Kotla.

—In the House of Commons, on Thursday last, replying to a question of Mr. Lowe, Lord George Hamilton said that a despatch of the Marquis of Salisbury to the Governor-General of India, embodying proposals for the mitigation and prevention of the recurrence of the block in promotion in the Covenanted Civil Service was before the India Council, and would be forwarded to India in a few days.

—Sir Henry Ramsay, Commissioner of Kumaon, it is said, is going to England for six months.

—It is stated at Hyderabad that two relatives of Sir Salar Jung, Nawab Nasir Nawaz Jung and Ghulam Jung, who went with the Prime Minister to England, may be soon expected to return to India, as the climate in England does not agree with them.

—A Zenana is said to be established at Baroda at a cost of Rs. 10,000.

—His Grace the Duke of Buckingham and family were the guests of Sir Walter Morgan for a few days last week at Conur.

—Mr. Marshall, the Collector of Customs, Chittagong, is said to have died, through official or rather civilian persecution, for which that place has now become famous.

—Major Sandeman was suffering from fever on the 11th and 12th instant; his negotiations with the Khan of Khelat have consequently been interrupted.

—A lady of the Baroda House, Jebanbai Saheb Gaekwar, in a rather quaintly written letter addressed to some of our contemporaries, calls for an enquiry into the alleged arbitrary proceedings of Mr. Melvill and of Sir T. Madhava Rao. But the charges she brings against them are very vague. Every lady of the Baroda family seems to have a grievance of her own.

—The Alpha Gold Minning Company in Wynaad, Madras, is said to have as yet proved a failure. The Company is reported to be largely in debt.

—A number of the leading mercantile firms of Bombay, have joined in a project for forming a Joint Stock Company to embark in the Central Asian trade. The new Company is to be floated in Bombay, under the auspices of one of the leading and longest established firms of that city.

—The Puna Sarvajanik Sabha has addressed a letter to the East India Association, London, on the subject of the Indian Civil Service, with a view that the Association may bring to the notice of Lord Salisbury the modifications necessary with special reference to Native candidates, in the proposed new rules regulating the admission to the Indian Civil Service.

—Sir Richard Temple has expressed his willingness to give a site close to the Patna College for the proposed Industrial Institution at Bankipore. His Honor is prepared to give a Government grant in-aid to the amount of Rs. 6,000 a year, on condition that the subscriptions invested in Government securities yield at least an equal sum. The Institution will be under the supervision of the Principal of the Patna College.

—The *Swadesh Mitra* complains that there is so little moral courage among the educated Natives of Bombay that the Widow Re-marriage Association there exists only in name.

—Aden is gradually becoming an asylum for the oppressed Arabs who are by degrees being driven from their homes by the Turks. It is believed that the number of Arabs in the settlements cannot be less than 9,000.

—The proposed Agricultural College at Sydapet in Madras is about to be opened.

—An appeal has been lodged by the G. I. P. Railway Company against the judgement given in the action of the Begum of Bhopal.

—Mr. E. B. Peacock, Assistant Commissioner, is transferred from the Gurgaon to the Montgomery District.

—A rather severe shock of earthquake was felt at Mussuri about 2 P. M. on the 17th instant. The shock lasted for 10 seconds.

—A telegram received from Constantinople in Paris on the 4th June, announced that the Sultan Abdul Aziz had "stabbed himself with a dagger in the region of his heart." He died at the Tcheragan Palace at 10 o'clock in the morning. He was buried at Mahmoud the Second's tomb in the evening.

—A person is accused of having made away with a large sum of money, the proceeds of Lottery tickets in aid of the Allahabad Seminary sold by him. About six thousand rupees have been misappropriated by him.

—There was a fall of hail at Rajnagar, Punjab, on the 18th instant, and several heads of cattle are reported to have been struck by lightning during the storm.

—Sir George Couper will assume the Lieutenant-Governorship of the N. W. P., on the 18th instant. Mr. Inglis will take charge of his appointment in Oudh also on the same date.

—The Manchester folks are very busy in getting up petitions for the repeal of the import duty on cotton levied in India, and are said to have already obtained more than 10,000 signatures.

—The plague in Bagdad has ceased.

—Difficulty is felt in the immediate settlement of the Puttiallah administration, owing to the hostility between the Punjab Rajahs and others to Kalifa. A strong feeling exists amongst the Sikhs and Mussulmans on this question, which will probably restrain the Punjab Government from issuing final decision for some time.

—General Biddulph has successfully opened the Hill Home at Mussurie, with 46 soldiers' children, and has obtained a volunteer lady superintendent.

—The Natives of India resident in London desired to present an address to Sir Salar Jung. But Sir Salar was too ill to receive it.

Calcutta.

The passenger train and service on the Chitpore Branch of the Eastern Bengal Railway will be discontinued from the 20th instant. Probably the line has proved a failure.

The Chairman of the Calcutta Municipality has prepared a list of over 13,000 individuals whom he believes to possess a right to registration, and yesterday forms of application for registration and certain other papers, were forwarded to every person on the list. Any one who receives no such communication from the Municipal Office may apply for registration and, if refused, may appeal from the Chairman's decision to that of a Police Magistrate.

The P. and O. Co.'s steam-ship *Assam*, Commander G. F. Cates, with the Overland Mails of June 9th, arrived in Bombay Harbour on Tuesday last. She left Suez on the 18th at 11 P.M. and Aden on the 21st June at noon. The following is the list of passengers:—

From Southampton.—Mr. G. F. Price, Capt. W. G. Sharpe, Mr. W. Main, Mrs. Pilot and Infant, Mr. A. Houston, Mr. G. T. Nixon, Mr. W. Ingram.

From Brindisi.—Mt. Williams, Mr. Logan, Col. Davidson, Mr. McKee, Mr. G. Wingrove, Mr. Richardson, Lt.-Col. Iredell, Major Neville, Mr. Macfarlane, Capt. Azir N. Shah, Hon. W. E. Noel.

From Aden.—Mr. M. D. H. Larpent.

The rate of conversion of Indian into sterling money for Overland Money Orders has been charged to 1*s.* 7½*d.* per rupee.

The Senate of the University of Calcutta will proceed, in the month of August next, to the election of a Tagore Law Professor for such term as the Senate may approve.

Mr. G. Nevill, Assistant Secretary, &c., of the Indian Museum, has been granted privilege leave for two months and eight days from the 5th June 1876.

M. Trillard, the Governor-General of the French Settlements in India, accompanied by his Chief Secretary, M. Cave, Captain Corne, and by M. Carrial, Ingenieur Colonial, is expected to visit Chandernagore, by the end of this month.

The drawing of the Chandernagore Lottery in aid of the sufferers from the late inundations in France, will take place on the 19th August next. The French Government guarantees the drawing.

Sir Richard Temple is expected to arrive in Calcutta in about a fortnight more. His Honor will, after a short stay, leave for Chittagong again.

ACKNOWLEDGMENT.

Report on the Progress of Education in the Mahomedan Anglo-Oriental College at Allygurh. For the last seven months of 1875. Benares, 1876.

Selection.

WHAT THEY SAY.

BY SUSAN HARTLEY.

What does the brook say, flashing its feet
Under the lilies' blue, brimming bowls,
Bright'ning the shades with its tender song,
Cheering all drooping and sorrowful souls?
It says not, "Be merry," but, deep in the wood,
Rings back; "Little maiden, be good, be good!"

What does the wind say, pushing slow sails
Over the great, troubled path of the sea;
Whirling the mill on the breezy height,
Shaking the fruit from the orchard tree?
It breathes not, "Be happy!" but sings, loud and long,
"O bright little maiden, be strong, be strong!"

What says the river, gliding along,
To its house on far-off Ocean's breast;
Fretted by rushes, hindered by bars,
Ever weary, but singing of rest?
It says not, "Be bright!" but, in whispering grave,
"Dear little maiden, be patient, be brave!"

What do the stars say, keeping their watch
Over our slumbers, the long, lone night;
Never closing their bonnie bright eyes,
Though great storms blind them, and tempests fright?
They say not, "Be splendid!" but write on the blue,
In clear silver letters, "Maiden, be true!"

—*St. Nicholas for May.*

Advertisements

ICE! ICE! ICE!

MADE IN FOUR MINUTES

THE PNEUMATIC ICE MACHINE

THIS IMPORTANT INVENTION IS CONSIDERED A BOON TO THOSE LIVING IN TROPICAL CLIMATES.

CAN BE WORKED BY THE MOST INEXPERIENCED HAND AND IS NOT LIABLE TO GET OUT OF ORDER.

From Rs. 175, each Machine complete.

MESSRS. ARLINGTON & CO

AGENTS.

HAROLD & CO.,

3, DALHOUSIE SQUARE, CALCUTTA

HARMONIUMS.

Harold and Co., call attention to their unequalled stock of rich-toned Harmoniums made especially for India.

FROM RS. 90 TO RS. 900 EACH.

All kinds of Musical Instruments of the best description are always kept in Stock.

Printed and published by M. M. RUKHIT, at the INDIAN MIRROR PRESS, No. 15, College Square, for the Proprietor.

The Indian Mirror.

SUNDAY EDITION.

VOL. XVI.] CALCUTTA, SUNDAY JULY, 9. 1876 { REGISTERED AT THE GENERAL POST OFFICE. } [No. 161

CONTENTS.

NOTICE.

All letters and communications relating to the literary department of the Paper should be addressed to the Editor. All other letters should be addressed to the Manager, to whom all remittances should be made payable.

Subscribers will be good enough to bring to the notice of the Manager any delay or irregularity in the delivery of the Paper.

Editorial Notes.

THE *Standard* understands that the Bishopric of Calcutta has been offered to the Rev. J. Moorhouse, Bishop designate of Melbourne. But it is not likely he will accept it.

WE are glad to be informed that Miss Brink, the lady doctor, who has taken the place of the late lamented Miss Seelie, has consented to deliver elementary scientific lectures to the pupils of the Native Ladies' Normal School. The subject to be taken up at for the present will be human physiology.

WE are glad to learn that already some books have been received as presents for the Library attached to the Albert Hall. Dr. J. Muir, of Edinburgh, has kindly presented a copy of his "Religious and Moral Sentiments from Sanskrit Writers." The Hon'ble Sir William Muir has presented the following valuable works:—Nabatati Hind or Indian Botany in Urdu; Sukla or White Yajur Veda. It is to be hoped that these examples will be followed by other European gentlemen here and in England.

THE following appears in an American paper:—"The Rajah of Travancore is obliged to fast on the day of the great festival at Susindram until the sacred cars have been dragged around the temple. The intelligence that the rite has been performed is conveyed to him by telegraph. A very curious adaptation of European science to Hindu superstition." But the conveyance of thousands of Hindu pilgrims, month after month, to Benares and other "holy" cities in Upper India is a more extended and systematic adaptation of European science to Hindu superstition. The application of steam to Juggernath's unwieldly car is not unlikely in these days of rapid progress.

IN the June number of the *Truthseeker* the Rev. Mr. Page Hopps writes an article on India and the Hindu in which he exposes the absurdity of looking down upon the population of India as a race of "benighted Pagan." He calls this "an impertinence, and an absurdity," and asks if the annual expenditure of £600,000 which Great Britain makes on Foreign Mission, is not a misapplication of money. When Mr. Sen came here, says Mr. Hopps, some years ago, as an Indian, I really believe our city magnates thought he was an Indian chief, and a great dignitary actually *did* ask me whether he could speak so as to be understood; and expressed considerable surprise when I told him that the ministers of Glasgow would do well to hear him, if only to get a lesson in exquisite English exquisitely spoken.

WE fully agree with the *Friend of India* in condemning all sorts of sensational writing, such as occur now and then in Brahmo publications. Religious enthusiasm, no doubt, drags our friends at times beyond the limits of moderation. With reference, however, to the particular passage in the anniversary address which our contemporary criticises, we must confess his inference is far-fetched, and the mischief he predicts quite imaginary. Every zealous Brahmo has been heard to speak of persecution in the same strain, his idea being that should there be violence and bloodshed even then the true believer must not yield, not that there is actually any attempt in these days to sacrifice one's life for the sake of faith. Keep your powder dry, be ever ready to lay down your life for truth,—surely we need such reminder, though we are living quietly and happily under the British Government.

AN Organization somewhat Similar to the *Bharat Asram* has arisen in England. The *Spectator* notices it, and criticizes it. There has arisen close to the St. James Park Station of the District Railway within the last year a fantastic building, in a Brobdignagian style of architecture, a dozen storeys high. Here Mr. H. A. Hankey has spent, or is spending, a quarter of a million of money to induce Englishmen to abandon the axiom that each man's house is his castle, by showing how man had better abide in flats than in either houses or castles; and in educating a select number of our upper classes in the theory and practice of a refined Socialism. There are, or are to be, 250 sets of appartment, each set distinct at an average rent of £100 a year; but with a common kitchen, common coffee-room, saloon, and reading-room, servants supplied by the management, and fixed charges for everything. The experiment is a very interesting one, and ought to succeed, tried on such a scale, amid a population which affords such an area for experiment as that of the wealthier, unsettled classes of London. The main difficulty will, we imagine, arise in the organisation of service. The Briton may relinquish his regard for his house, but will hold longer to the wish to have his own household about him.

WE purposely abstain from saying anything on the unfortunate relations that exist between the two races of the rulers and ruled. From a somewhat long experience we find it produces little good to tell people of the faults which they do not mean to correct, and in which they take a sort of glory. It has been simply unavailing to try to impress upon certain Englishmen the duty of being humane and considerate to the people of this country, who are so decidedly inferior to them in many respects, and therefore deserve the more patience and forbearance. Now they find the Prince of Wales and his friends have taken up the side of the people, and think it worthwhile on great State occasion to speak of "the mean whites in both services who think it exhibits British 'spirit' to speak of the Natives of India as 'niggers.'" There are large number of Englishmen, it would seem, who do not like such allusions, and the *Pioneer* represents their feelings when it says that the Prince has been ungrateful for what his countrymen are here did to entertain him. This is exactly the charge brought against our people when they venture to point out the ill-treatment to which they are subjected, but it will not exactly stand against the Prince of Wales. He can afford to speak the truth on the matter, and if any one can influence the British nation on Indian subjects at this moment, it is the Prince of Wales.

IN the course of our thoughts and reflections the other day it occurred to us that men ought not to look forward to heaven for the reward of such virtues as have been rewarded in this life. The moral economy of the Just God shuns double recompense. It is not fair, and we have no right to expect it. The servant who has once received his wages should not again claim the same. There are many things in the good man's life and character which subject him to cruel annoyance and persecution at the hands of an antagonistic world. Yet on the other hand, there are certain things which the world appreciates and honors and freely rewards. They who pray fervently, deal honestly, are meek, charitable and truthful, receive considerable praise and honor among men. This in most cases is enough reward, and ought to be taken as such. Heaven guarantees no reward for these mere superficial phases of Godly life, which buy sufficient honor in this world's market. It is those deep things of regenerate life which this world cannot or does not honor, and must, therefore, pass unrewarded into the next world, it is these that shall be blessed with joy and honor in heaven. It is hence the duty and interest of pilgrims to eternity not to rest content with amassing too many of those outward virtues which are honored on earth. They should deligently acquire day after day the deeper treasures of the spirit.

THE love of children is a blessed and beautiful instinct with which all are not equally gifted. There are few men, at least we have never known any, who thoroughly hate children, but cases are not unfrequent in which infant life is contemplated only from the standpoint of the occasional inconvenience which it causes. Certain unmarried gentlemen decidedly object to the neighbourhood of children, certain married gentlemen who are fathers, positively dislike all other children except their own, and certain young ladies married and unmarried, take it to be a grievous insult when the probability of their ever becoming mothers is discussed in their presence. On the other hand there are men, young, middle-aged, and old, who are in perpetual love with children, to whom a child's smile has a never-ending brightness of sunshine in it, and a child's lawless utterances an inexhaustive well of sweetness and philosophy. We donot know whether this instinct is more fully developed in men or in women, perhaps it is common to both the sexes alike varying in manifestation, but equal in depth. The world of children is where every man who is weary and hard worked at times wants to go—a world of sweetness, trust and simplicity, innocence, liberty and tenderness. The man that loves children, is sure to be loved by them. "It is the child within in the man," as Lord Granville recently said, that is in love with children, and with which children are in love. Let us be in perpetual sympathy with the truly childlike.

"OTHERS mocking said,—These men are full of new wine." These words, the readers of the Bible are aware, were spoken of the apostles. So serious was the accusation understood to be, and outward appearances so decidedly favored it, that Peter felt constrained to "lift his voice" against it, and to stoop to such an argument as this to silence calumny,—"For these are not drunken, as ye suppose, seeing it is but the third hour of the day." No one, of course, would for a moment believe that the apostles needed any such pleading to rebut the silly charge of drunkenness. Yet it is clear that there must have been something in their conduct which called forth so strange a charge. If they were not drunk, were they seemingly so? Did they look and behave as if they were drunk? They did. Too much devotion produces the effects of "new wine." The love of God, as we have often said, inebriates the heart. The familiar expression—*intoxicated* with the sweets of Divine love, surely involves deep meaning. And it was evidently this spiritual intoxication that led to the charge of drunkenness. The truly devout are "drunken," and no wonder men jestingly speak of them as such. Sometime back our remarks vindicating religious intoxication called forth sharp comments both here and in England. Our critics evidently misunderstood us. It is to be hoped the above Biblical incident will render clear to them what we meant, and persuade them to admit with us that when men are influenced by the Divine Spirit they do strange things, so that the world in amazement cries out,—These are either drunk or insane.

THE Duke of Somerset while addressing the House of Lords in favor of the practice of Vivisection, spoke of the *aggregate* suffering caused to animal life by means other than scientific investigations, and seemed to argue that when no protest was made against such suffering, the cry raised against experimenters and students was unreasonable. It cannot be denied that the callousness to suffering and death, caused by the sinful wantonness of shooting and hunting in which ninety-five Europeans of every hundred indulge with wonderful thoughtlessness, does furnish a sort of excuse to those who inflict pain with the professed object not of pleasure but of profit to themselves and the whole of mankind. But it is hardly necessary to observe that heartlessness in one department of life does not justify heartlessness in another; and the aggregate of small sufferings in many cases can be no subject of comparison with the intensest pain deliberately inflicted in a few. It seems as if flogging a number of school boys for petty offences, a practice reprehensible enough in itself, is tantamount to flaying one of them alive for doing something really bad, and that the former act would justify the latter. A few dozen pigeons shot in cold blood at Hurlingham would be painful enough to think of, but it can neither be any palliation, nor any argument for cutting open the brains and nerve centres of a slightly smaller number of living dogs and cats, and watching the course of exquisite misery by exposing them to the action of slow or powerful poisons. The Duke of Somerset has acquired an unenviable reputation for cynicism by defending vivisection in the House of Lords. Lord Shaftesbury, whose humanity has been the noblest ornament of his useful career along with others fought for the Government Bill, and fought with success.

THE MANY-SIDEDNESS OF MAN.

IT is wonderful to think how vastly men disagree! If all the disagreements that there are amongst us were developed and understood, we would have to throw up in despair every attempt at social organization. The ground of agreement in the midst of so much that is jarring is, it may be admitted, large, and it is also curious to think that constituted as we are with strange differences separating man from man, we should have so much that is common to all. The probabilities of disunion, we suspect, are not seen from the point of aggreement, nor does the extent of possible unity clearly appear when men are discussing the differences that make them so unlike. May it not be for this reason that at the early formation of a church the apostles do not perceive the seeds of future disaggreement they unconsciuusly sow in the profusion of their zeal and devotion, and that the bitter disagreements of sects have never been reconciled, and seem as if they never shall be? What are we think of such disunion? Is it irreconcilable, radical, ineradicable, a part and parcel of nature itself, or is it but the mistaken view, a superficial estimate of an untried region, an unsounded depth of man's being? Seeing below the surface it would appear that what men call differences, are not grounds of disunion, but only so many different sides of the vast and mighty unity which human nature in its aggregate represents, that unity which is the ideal sonship of God, divided, so to say, in tens of thousands of fragments, each filling and individualizing a soul. The souls so filled, so shaped, form so many members, so many sides of the future family in which mankind must in the end be re-united. Unfortunately human builders seldom recognize the individualities they deal with, they rarely see the adjustment of the sides, or the modes by which, if applied, they would fit in, and form the unity whereof they are parts. Self-seeking and interested men understand this principle of adjustment much less, and the many-sidedness of man is a subject admitted in theory, but most imperfectly understood and applied in practice. Every soul, especially among those who feel, called to accomplish a great purpose, is a marvel of divine genius, a master piece of workmanship capable of performing momentous functions in organized life. But the great misfortune often times happens to be that men exaggerate their differences, think them to be irreconcilable, and drift into despair. If any unity is possible, it is only possible in the midst of differences, because it is many-sided minds alone that can represent the varying wants and aspirations of society. Every man thinks his sphere of life to be the only rational and possible one, unable or unwilling to see anything beyond, and incapable to understand what is seen in a foreign province. Thus human life becomes narrow and little and exclusive. There are some men who can grasp a great many sides of man's nature, and include them all under an organization which is extensive enough to embrace them. They fear not the so called differences, and are not discouraged by disagreeing temperaments and tastes. On the contrary, they see in all this many-sided variety in the midst of which true union is possible. In divine nature there are more sides than we can ever understand. Being His children we inherit peculiarities that lie in the Parent nature. We understand not each other. He understands all of us. He can be gracious therefore when we are sullen. He builds still while we would give up the house in despair; He can reconcile when we brood over the petty enmities of life. To Him the intricacies and subtleties of His work are best known, and He can reconize sides, adjust and fit them in, when we weep and declare that the machinery has broken to pieces. Let us look up to Him to understand human nature, and deal with it effectively. Let us study and understand His character so that we may know and feel our way towards human unity.

HAFIZ.

SWEET Hafiz! What precious thoughts and sentiments has he left behind to instruct and ennoble us! The heart is really enamoured of his charming *guzals*, and is delighted to read them over and over. We commend the following gleanings from his precious book to our readers :—

O morning zephyr, if you go to my Friend's country bring me the fragrace of His hair. I swear I will offer my life with profound thankfulness if you fetch any glad tidings from my Friend. Should you fail to secure admission into His temple, then bring me dust from His gate for cleansing my eyes.

Do not try to dissuade or threaten me with the words of reason. That Kotwal, reason, has no power in *my* dominion; he cannot arrest me.

The traveller, who has known the path that leads to the liquor shop, deems it a sin to knock at the doors of any other house. He who has entered the liquor shop knows by the merits of the glass he drinks the deep secrets of the house of devotion.

Hafiz is scattering drops of tears from his eyes. Haply the bird of Vision [perception of the Lord] will be tempted to fall into my trap.

When tears fall like rain from my eyes, it seems that the lightning of my prosperity gone away long ago will soon reappear.

When Hafiz becomes unconscious [after drinking excessively the sweets of devotion] he does not reckon the wealth and dominion of the highest king worth even a grain of wheat.

This goblet of wine, do thou brighten, O Guide, with sparkling wine, and then say the object of my life is achieved.

O thou ignorant of the taste of my wine, thou knowest not. In the goblet of wine I see the countenance of my Beloved reflected.

How shall I express myself? Yesterday I lay unconscious and very bad [through excessive spiritual drink] in the liquor shop. What glad tidings did the messenger of the spiritual kingdom bring to me then!

He who has become a faquir in thy lane does not pray even for eight heavens.

Although devoted love has made me bad, it has fertilized the depths of my life and produced harvest.

Roza, the time for fasting is over, *ecd* is come. The heart rejoices in the distellery wine is being fermented. Now is the time to seek wine.

Correspondence.

CASTE MARK FOR THE BRAHMO.

To the Editor of the *Indian Mirror*.

SIR,—It is a peculiar feature of the Hindus that they wear some marks or other indication of the religion to which they belong, and therefore if they find any one without these marks it is natural for them to conclude (it may not be true in this country because Hindus here scarcely wear anything on their forehead) that he is not a Hindu. Here it is very difficult to make out whether a Native gentleman is a Hindu or a Christian unless we know him. But in the South you can find out, by the different marks which men wear, even the particular religious community to which a particular man belongs. Therefore, in such countries every one is a Christian or a Musulman who does not wear such marks. Therefore if the Brahmos in such parts do not wear any such marks, they will, no doubt, be looked upon either as Christians or as Mussulmans, and if they wear such marks they will be looked upon as Hindus. Here one is in a dilemma, that is, if he wears marks he will be a Hindu and if he does not he is either a Christian or a Mussulman in the estimation of the people. Here if they do a certain thing, they are guilty; if they do not do it, they are guilty. Under these circumstances anything by way of advice with reference to this, will not be uninteresting to them. The sooner they are informed as to what they should do and what they should not do, the better.

I am Sir yours,

N.

Devotional

THINKING and being are closely connected. If I think often of the world, its temptations and pleasures, I become worldly; if I think of heaven, I must be heavenly-minded. But how seldom, O my God, do I think of heaven! That sweet and charming picture of heaven which thou hast shown me to-day, do thou always hold up before me. How happy that devoted group of thy loving children gathered round thy feet! Oh how happy! Father, may I constantly think of their heavenly joy and seek it!

FATHER, dear Jesus loved thee, and he loved thee so intensely that he said, "I and my father are one." O God, teach me that singleness of heart, that obedience of will and child-like trust which Jesus, thy son, possessed in abundance. May I love thee as he loved thee!

O how difficult it is to be poor! I have tried, I have struggled, but poverty, sweet and heavenly poverty is far from me. Lord, I have entered the hermit's cottage, and put on his rude tattered raiment, and I eat and live in a lowly style. Yet am I not poor. My heart is yet the heart of a rich man, proud, haughty and fond of the pleasures and luxuries of the world. O God humble my spirit, and make my heart poor and lowly.

WHY do I fancy, O God that there is such a being as 'I' with independent rights and possessions on earth? I, as an independent master, do not exist except in my own imagination. If I exist, O Lord, it is only as a born slave whose every thing is sold and therefore belongs to others. Help me, Father, to realize this my true position, and to feel deeply that not my earthly possessions and even ego itself belong to those around me.

The Brahmo Somaj

IN consequence of the excessive rain which took place on Sunday last the attendance at the Mundir was very small. The congregation numbered about forty.

WE take the following remarks on the anniversary lecture from the *Friend of India* :—"The *Mirror* has given us by Sunday instalments the lecture on *Our Faith and Experiences* delivered in the Town Hall by Babu Keshub Chunder Sen. While we cannot approve of all it contains, there is much in it, we admire, and much in it that all earnest men whether Christians, Theists or by whatever name known, would do well to lay to heart. Yet there is in some parts of it a want of sobriety, which we believe to be more in the language than in the meaning, but which, however explicable, is neither good nor safe. We shall give one extract where the exaggeration of language covers a meaning which is perfectly comprehensible to us who are acquainted with the circumstances under which the speech was delivered, and the principal immediate objection to it is that it is slightly sensational in tone But we may pay the speech the compliment of considering it as material which the future historian of British India will eagerly use, when he wishes to gather evidence as to the state of the country and chiefly its religious condition under our rule in the latter part of the nineteenth century. What will the historian in some future century make of the following, and how will he reconcile it with other testimony showing that universal peace and toleration, and liberty of speech and action were allowed to all religions under our rule? 'Is not the path of the religions reformer in this country full of thorns, and will not dire difficulties beset his work for many years to come? Those who engage themselves in such a work must be prepared for the worst, and pay the price of their own life-blood for every inch of ground they win. Amidst the gloom and terror of such trying work it is indeed natural that the workers, a small and feeble band, should seek sympathy and help among friends. But if such sympathy be not forthcoming, let the Lord's will be done. Let truth triumph *in the* **midst** *of agony, bloodshed, and death.* Rest assured that the persecuted shall be justified at last, and God's devoted servants and faithful ambassadors though reviled, hated and trampled by men, shall receive the crown of glory in heaven.' Contemporaries know well enough what all that means, but the future historian might fairly infer from it that when Lord Northbrook was Viceroy of India, members of the Brahmo Somaj were persecuted to blood and death. The rhetorical gain is not worth the exaggeration of language, which may be mischievous."

OUR Dacca missionary, Babu Banga Chunder Ray, has gone to Mymensingh to celebrate the anniversary of the Branch Brahmo Somaj there. He is shortly expected back at Dacca as he will have to solemnize a Brahmo marriage there.

Literary

THE *Academy* says that the story of the late Mr. Margary's journey from Shanghai to Bhamo and back to Manwyne, which, as told in his journals and letters, will be published very shortly by Messrs. Macmillan and Co., and will be supplemented by a valuable epilogue on our relations with China from the pen of Sir Rutherford Alcock, K.C.B. The book will also contain a route map, practically new to geographers of the country, through which Mr. Margary passed.

MR. HUTTON, former editor of the *Hurkaru*, and more recently of the *Englishman* has, we see it stated, just returned to Calcutta in the capacity of correspondent to the *Pall Mall Gazette* and London *Standard*.

MR. GLADSTONE again contributes to the *Contemporary* for June. The subject is "The Courses of Religious Thought."

DR. SHORTT, of Madras, has ready for the press a comprehensive work on Indian Snakes.

THE London Association of Correctors of the Press, at a late meeting, made arrangements for the production of "a dictionary of doubtful and disputed words," which will shortly be published.

IN the last numbers of *All the Year Round* are two papers on soldiering and Railway travelling in India, the latter from the pen of Mr. Meason, the Special of the *Echo*.

SOME of the clergy at Colombo are preparing to publish on the first of each month, and under the sanction of the Bishop of the diocese, a church paper, to be called the *Ceylon Diocesan Gazette*.

THE late Lord Amberley's "Analysis of Religious Belief" is just issued. The London correspondent of the *Englishman* says:—"A very audacious, as well as singular, book it is. Strange to say, the work is issued with the sanction of Lord Amberley's mother, the Countess Russell, who appends a half apologetic, half laudatory notice of the writer and what he has written."

MR. ALEXANDER ALLARDYCE, late Editor of the *Ceylon Times*, who has already published several charming Indian stories in *Blackwood's Magazine*, has a novel in the press, and lately he has been contributing largely to the English magazines. He has left journalism, and taken to the less laborious if less profitable field of magazine literature.

Scientific.

THE Governor of Turkistan has established a Museum at Balkh.

SEVERAL foreign naval powers are directing their attention to the practicability of establishing telegraph stations in mid-ocean, by which messages can be sent from one part of the sea along the line of the cable to the terminal point on shore, and *vice versa*, so that communication with iron-clads, mail-steamers, and other vessels, when out at sea, may be established. One invention for carrying out this scheme consists of a hollow sectional column with a base plate attached by ball and socket, joint, which column is lowered into the water and anchored rigidly to the ground. The branch cable is coupled to the main cable and carried along the column to the surface of the water, to be there connected with instruments on board the vessels. By this invention it is proposed to control naval and strategical movements, while a ship in distress could communicate her exact position, the nature of her disasters, and thus procure assistance.

Latest News

—THE real causes of Colonel Malleson's resignation are said by a Mysore correspondent of the *Bangalore Examiner* to be the following:—The defacing of caste-marks on our Maharajah's forehead at Bangalore and Bombay; the Bangalore Durbar; the Tea party at Ooty which necessitated His Highness' brother suddenly leaving for Mysore, unattended, in a country bullock cart; and the arduous and unexampled riding lessons taught to the juvenile Rajah in the shola of Ootacamund.

—A MAHOMEDAN priest named Syed Abdulah attended by a few followers, has been preaching in the Madras Presidency against certain ceremonies which are usually performed by Mahomedans. Some of the followers are armed with swords, rifles &c.

—COLONEL BURNE, C. S. I., Private Secretary to Lord Lytton, remains in India for a year, at the end of which time he will return to his duties at the India Office. So says the *Vanity Fair*.

—SIR JOHN STRACHEY leaves India on the 25th instant. There is a probability of Sir John returning in November or December next.

—WAR preparations seem to be in active progress in England. Before the mail of the 16th June left, orders had been received at Portsmouth, directing all the troopships to be got ready for immediate use, in case of an emergency.

—WOMEN clerks are now employed in Insurance Offices in England. Many operators and clerks in the Telegraph Offices there are also women.

—THE *Delhi Gazette* which attacked the Maharajah of Jeypore most cruelly the other day, now appears as the apologist of Maharajah Scindia!

—THE Society for Promoting Christian Knowledge, has given £5,000 to the Bishop Milman Memorial Fund. The Lambeth Conference supports the scheme.

—THE *Delhi Gazette* mentions a probability of the See of Calcutta being offered to the late Bishop's Chaplain, the Rev. Mr. Jacob.

—BISHOP MYLNE of Bombay, who has been successful in obtaining men, has been equally successful in obtaining the help of a staff of ladies. They will be in connection with the Wantage Institution.

—MR. REYNOLDS, Barrister-at-Law, is to be appointed Law Lecturer of the Punjab University.

—THE London correspondent of the *Indian Daily News* is informed that Mr. Smollett, M. P., is preparing a formidable indictment against the Indian P. W. D. This indictment Mr. Smollett intends to prefer when the Indian Budget is under discussion in the House of Commons, and his attack will be supported by Mr. Fawcett and other M. Ps. who have special knowledge of Indian matters.

—THE Directors of the Bank of Bombay will declare a dividend for the year ending 30th June last, at the rate of 10 per cent. per annum; 2¼ lacs will be carried to reserve fund, which will then amount to 20 lacs; Rs. 20,000 will be written off cost of premises; Rs. 10,000 will be carried to bad and doubtful debt account.

—THE repairs on the G. I. P. Railway are finished. The trains come in very regularly now. The floods have abated below the Ghauts.

—GHULAM JILANI, Prime Minister to H. H. the Maharajah of Kapurthala, has been dismissed from office. Haji Walinlah has been appointed Judge, and Tehsildar, Aziz Buksh, Magistrate of Kapurthala.

—DENGUE has made its appearance in Quilon, Madras. About sixty persons have been admitted in hospital.

—DR. MYLNE, the new Bishop of Bombay, has arrived at Bombay with his Chaplain. His installation took place on Thursday last.

—THE articles exhibited at the second yearly exhibition of Native arts and manufactures, now opened at Poona, have says the *Indu Prakash*, improved both in quality and number.

—BABU JODUNATH MUKERJI, the Government Pleader at Hazaribaugh, who has been created a "Rai", is told by the *Indian Statesman* of Bombay that he should be ashamed of the title, for "Rai", in Mahratti, means "silly or half-demented fellow."

—DINBAI, the Parsi widow, has appealed to the Bombay High Court against the sentence of death passed upon her by the Sessions Judge of Tanna for the murder of her infant child.

—A PORTION of the G. I. P. Railway line **has been damaged** by floods in consequence **of the heavy rain on** Saturday last.

—THE female students of the Madras Medical College were present at the last anniversary of that College and sat with the male students. They are four in number and their names are:—Mrs. Mary Scharlieb, Miss S. Mitchell, Miss D. White and Miss N. Beale. They are in the first year of their study and are reported to have taken great interest in their work and to have made commendable progress.

—BOMBAY is very anxious to see an Agricultural College established like that lately opened at Sydapet in the Madras Presidency. Bengal is not less anxious. Sir Richard Temple ought to take the hint.

—THE Prince of Wales' Indian presents will be exhibited in the Indian Museum, South Kensington, on the 22nd July. The Princess of Wales has also allowed the presents made to Her Royal Highness by the young Guckwar, Scindia, and others to be exhibited, and they will be arranged in special cases apart from the Prince's presents. The public exhibition of these collections was a spontaneous suggestion of the Prince of Wales himself.

—MR. SYDNEY P. HALL has been commanded by the Queen to paint in oil the heads of the two Native Officers Mahomed Afzul Khan and Anup Sing, who accompanied the Prince of Wales from India, and to make a water-color sketch of their orderlies.

—THE Bank of Bombay has reduced its rates of interest and discount one per cent. all round.

—JUMSU, the Parsi cook, who buried Dinlal's infant, was tried separately last week at Tanna, before Mr. Coghlan and three assessors, on charges of adding and abetting infanticide. He has been convicted and sentenced to twelve months' rigorous imprisonment.

—A RUMOUR has reached the *Bangalore Examiner* that Lord Lytton has resigned the Viceroyalty, and will proceed to Europe as early as possible. Considering his Lordship's delicate state of health, combined with the probability that his services are needed in Europe in connection with the present crisis in Turkish affairs, it is just possible, says our contemporary, that the information is correct.

—Anup Singh, *Aide-de-camp* to the Prince of Wales, writes home to his friends that he has discovered Paradise, and by no means wishes to return to the dull routine of duty with his regiment. He has written his name in the Queen's album, and sat to many pictures.

—THE London correspondent of the *Indian Church Gazette* says :—"There are two pictures, or rather portraits, in which people of India are interested. One of Lord Lytton, and the other of Dr. C. Macnamara, which is destined eventually to adorn the walls of the Native Hospital at Calcutta. The one of Lord Lytton is easy and certainly a striking likeness. I leave the one of Dr. C. Macnamara for Eastern criticism. I do not think they will be disappointed in its truthfulness."

Calcutta.

THE College Square Tank (Goldigi) is now being used for bathing purposes by the public.

IT is rumoured, says the *Indian Daily News* that Colonel Tennant, the Mint Master of Calcutta, intends to proceed on short privilege leave, and that in that case Dr. Busteed, the Assay Master, is likely to act for him.

MR. ANDREWS' Royal Skating Rink was opened at No. 16, Chowringhi, Calcutta, last night.

MR. JOHN VANSOMEREN POPE, B. A., of the Guckwar's High School, at Baroda, and formerly of Mysore, has been appointed a Professor of the Presidency College, Calcutta, *vice* Mr Rogers who joins the Patna College. Mr. Pope's appointment to the Patna College is cancelled. Mr. Pope is a son of the late Dr. Pope of Bangalore. He is highly spoken of.

DOMESTIC OCCURENCE.

BIRTH.

GHOSH.—At Lahore, on 11th July 1876, the wife of Baboo Brojo Lall Ghosh of Halishahar, Assistant Surgeon and Teacher, Lahore Medical School, of a daughter.

Selections.

THE MINISTER'S WIFE.

BY MRS. M. A. HOLT.

MANY of the best of our Church people are often a little uncharitable toward our minister's wives. They generally look for a certain amount of perfection, which they seldom find—and they expect more than one weak woman can usually do. The results are that they are disappointed by their own unreasonableness, and the minister's wife bears all the blame, and is looked upon as unworthy of the position that she occupies.

It is true that she occupies a high and important position, and her influence is almost as far reaching as that of the pastor, and with this knowledge our people seem to think that she should take certain positions in the Church and in society, without reference to her home surroundings, or her fitness to feel them.

Many of our pastor's wives are burdened with large families, and it is a great tax upon their physical strength to attend to home duties alone. And all know that it would not do for our minister's wife to neglect any branch of domestic affairs. It would be a very unexcusable fault, in spite of any plea, in the eyes of our good sisters of the Church, who often neglect their own household matters to a very great extent. It does seem a little hard that our minister's wives cannot be excused for neglect of duty upon the same grounds that other ladies may, yet such are the rules of society and of the Church, and so they must be borne.

Then beside being a perfect housekeeper, she must be a worker in all the various departments of the Church. She must be the principal actor in the sewing society, the Church fair, or in fact, any enterprise that occurs. She must take her place in the Sabbath-school and in the prayer-meeting. While others are kept at home by slight reasons, the pastor's wife cannot be excused by any occurrence.

She must be a perfect lady also, and be able to shine in any society. She must be able to exhibit at any time a degree of intelligence that can only be acquired by study and constant observation. An uncultured mind would be a a very serious drawback to the wife of the itinerant.

Then how closely she is watched in regard to her personal appearance. She must have a remarkable degree of judgment and discretion to know just when and where to smile and look serious. Some people have a strange prejudice against a quiet smile, while others ignore a serious look.

"I know that I shall not like Mrs. W———, because she looks so cross," said one about the new pastor's wife. She judged very hastily and falsely, for Mrs. W——was one of the sweetest spirits that we ever meet with in this life. We all learned to love her very dearly in a short time, and forever within our hearts there will be a sunny glow of radiance that was created by her quiet presence. It is not always right and best to judge one by the smile or look of seriousness that may rest upon the face.

It also requires a great amount of discretion to be able to dress rightly. People's taste vary in this matter also. Many have a strange abhorence to a simple flower upon the hat, or anything else that is in keeping with fashion. Perhaps in this respect the minister's wife is criticised the most severely. She must be a model of neatness without a particle of display. This is quite a difficult matter to arrange, and so minister's wives often fail, like the rest of us.

"It is a perfect shame for our minister's wife to wear such a gay hat," one said not long since. "I Don't see how she can do it, occupying the position that she does," the indignant speaker went on.

"It was a present to her, and she wears it for the sake of those who gave it to her," was the quiet reply.

"Oh that is it, I supposed she bought it," was the critic's reply.

"Let us be sure that we have reason to condemn before we judge so severely," was the answer.

Christian brother and sister be charitable toward your pastor's wife. She is human like all of us. Do not look for perfection in weak humanity, for it cannot be found. Do all you can to help, sustain your pastor and his wife. Give them your sympathy and love if nothing else. These alone go a great ways in smoothing the rough places in life.

They have burdens to bear, without condemnation from you. There are crosses and shadows awaiting them at every step, and it is your duty to encourage them in every possible way.—*Northern Christian Herald.*

THE STORY OF BUDDHA.

BY REV. J. ALABASTER.

BUDDHA means "The Wise," and a great number of Buddhas have appeared to enlighten the world. The Buddha to whom is traced the origin of Buddhism, was born in Kapila, about one hundred miles north from Benares. His father, Suddhodana, was a king, his mother, Maia, a princess, the refined product of numerous transmigrations. During a previous existence she made a costly offering to a Buddha, and prayed to become the mother of a future Buddha.

She finally appeared as Maia, a virgin, possessing the sixty-four Brahmanical marks of womanly perfection, and constant in charity and piety, and in due time was married.

Buddha, her promised son, had been many times born on the earth, and during countless ages had desired to become a Buddha, that he might "redeem all teachable beings sunk in the great ocean of evercircling existence, and lead them to the jewel ed realm of happiness, the immortal Nirwana."

Untold ages had he been in the Tushita heavens, where all who are to become Buddhas pass the last stages of angelic life. As the time of his advent approached, forty thousand angels of ten thousand worlds gathered about him entreating him to accomplish his birth and "redeem all beings from the four seas of existence. Accordingly he looked down upon earth, selected the time, continent, country, caste and mother, that should give him birth, and, surrounded by angels, descended to the beautiful Nanthawan gardens, where were trees covered with angelic flowers and fruits, whose branches were filled with birds of heavenly plumage and song, and where were lotus lakes with sweet-scented lilies, and stairs leading thereto overlaid with gold and jewels.

As he came, earth shook, the worlds vibrated while light gleamed along the universe, and prodigies occurred—the blind saw, the dumb spake, the deaf heard, the crippled became straight, prisoners were loosed, people all forgot their anger and spake kindly, the flames of hell grew faint, the sky rained flowers, the winds blew soft and balmy, the heavens were dotted with lotus flowers, and the air was filled with music—such was the Conception of Buddha.

When he was born a great council of Brahmans declared he would become "an omniscient Buddha of the world," and he was named Sidharta. He become a beautiful and accomplished boy, amazed his teachers, did marvellous things, took no part in the plays of childhood, and was inclined to solitude and meditation. It had been told his father that Sidharta would become either a universal king or a Buddha; and he determined to prevent the later and secure the former. The king selected for his son a beautiful princess thinking that a wife would turn him from his solitude, but nothing hindered his meditations or turned him from the wants and woes of man. Continually would he say, "Nothing is stable on earth; nothing is real; life is a spark produced by the friction of wood, it is lighted and is extinguished, we know not whence it came or whither it goes; it is like the sound of a lyre, and the wise men ask in vain from whence it came and whither it goes; there must be some supreme intelligence where we could find rest; if I attained it, I could bring light to man; if I were free myself, I could deliver the world." Neither palaces nor thrones, nor royal honours, the wish of his parent nor the lovliness of his royal wife, could dissuade him from his desire to be a Saviour of men; and finally came what are called "The Four Visions," that settled his course of action. One day in his royal chariot, inlaid with jewels, carpeted with the skins of lions and tigers, and drawn by magnificent steeds, he set out to visit his flower gardens and lotus lakes, passing out of the east gate.

On the way he saw an old man, blear-eyed, toothless, deaf, hollow-cheeked, bald, bent, endeavouring to support his tottering form with a crutch. Having never witnessed such a sight, and supposing this some exceptional case of infirmity, he asked his charioteer who the old man was; and was told, this is the common lot of men who live to be eged. In great sadness, Sidharta returned home without seeing his gardens.

At another time he rode toward his pleasure garden through the south gate, and there lay a man suffering from illness, growling in agony, parched with fever, and weeping and groaning continually, while he was covered with mud and tormented with swarms of flies. "Who is this?" The charioteer assured the prince, that sickness, pain and trouble, are the common lot of man, and again they turned back. A third time Sidharta was on the way to his gardens, when, as he passed out of the west gate he saw a corpse on a bier, surrounded by weeping, mourning friends, who tore their hair in their grief and cast dust upon themselves. Once more he questioned his charioteer as to the meaning of this strange sight, and finding death the lot of all, exclaimed, "O woe to the youth, youth, which must be destroyed in old age! Woe to health, which must be destroyed by so many diseases! Woe to this life, where a man remains so short a time. If there were no old age, no disease, no death; if these could be made captive forever!" Turning back once more, he determined to seek how to accomplish man's deliverance. Finally, as one day he passed out of the north gate he saw a mendicant whose dress and manner were so different from other men, he appeared calm, dignified, devoted, and carried an alms, dish. "Who is this?" The coachman replied, "A man in holy orders, a man of the highest merit: he has renounced all pleasures, all desires, and leads a life of austerity; he tries to conquer himself; he has become a devotee; without passion, without envy, he walks about asking for alms." The prince determined to adopt the life of a mendicant; and one night when about thirty years of age, mounting his splendid steed, he took his flight, and reached a spot by the river Anoma, where he exchanged his royal robes for the garb of a monk, and gave his horse to his attendant to take back to the city. A monument in after years marked this spot.

Sidharta journeyed on and came to the dwellings of hermits, learned all he could from them, yet was unsatisfied; he found a noted Brahman, but inquired in vain for the deliverance he sought; plunging into the great Uruela forest, he gave himself to solitude and penance for six years, and was visited by five noted Brahmans who were waiting his achievement of the Buddhahood. But, convinced that the knowledge he sought must be attained in some other way, and rising grandly above the Brahmical austerities, he began to frame a system of his own. Then came his trial—his temptation in the wilderness—in ecstatic visions the greatness of his spiritual empire appeared to him, and the purifying influence of his doctrines; but the daughters of Mara, the Evil one, came against him with all their fury, and then Mara himself with a legion of evil spirits and the terrifying sound of a hundred thousand thunders, a very onslaught of apollyon, so that the good angles that guarded Sidharta fled in terror, and he was left alone with Mara. The furious warriors of his Satanic majesty crowded upon him, wild beasts gnashed at him, mountains reeled and fell headlong at his feet, and the air was filled with deadly powers, yet Sidharta sat invulnerable upon his throne of virtue and merit, unmoved by the hosts of hell, until they were swept away by a torrent of waters, when he was at once compassed by legions of comforting angels; and in that night, after this great victory, Sidharta arrived at the infinite knowledge, the cause of all the changes and evils in life, being individual existence, to be corrected by the destruction of belief in the existence of self: thus did Sidharta attain the Buddhahood. For a long time he kept his knowledge, but finally went to Benares, the Oxford of India, and became a public teacher, dying at the age of seventy. Various dates are assigned the origin of Buddhism, the most probable being about 550 years before Christ; and to-day it numbers from four to five hundred millions of followers, or over one-third of the population of the globe, extending over Siam, Burmah Anam, Thibet, Ceylon, a ll portions of India, China and Japan as well as other parts of Asia.

Buddha, then, is a name of historical importance, Buddhism, a religion worthy profound study. Points of resemblance in the story of Buddha as told in full, and that of Christ are numerous, as that, each had a previous existence, each came a light into the world, each left great glory in the heavens and came to earth, each became incarnate for man's good, each was born of a virgin, each came of a royal lineage and of the warrior caste or tribe, each was born amid signs and wonders on earth and in sky, each was remarkable in youth, each passed through temptations of supernatural character, at the close of which he received the ministration of angles, each was tempted by the proffer of universal empire, and each chose to become the humble teacher of men, each lived lives of great self-denial and voluntary proverty, each passed a lay period of thirty years, each went into seclusion before appearing as a public teacher, as have so many great teachers—Moses in Horeb, Elijah at Cherith, John in the desert Paul in Arabia, Jesus in the wilderness, and each was a reformer of an effete and over-burdened ritualistic faith, as was Zoroaster against the old Vadic legalism, Darius against the Magian formalism, Confucius against the obsolete Chinese faith, Luther against the Papacy. Buddha raised his protest against the burdensome ceremonial of Brahmanism. Who can fail to hear in the story of Buddha the sound of that long, earnest, universal groan of the race for redemption. But between Buddha and Christ how great the contrasts; the former giving man at best a religion of negations that shuns the risk of suffering in life, and ends in nihilism at death, the latter teaching how men may meet suffering and conquer it, pass through death and have life "more abundantly;" Buddha sacrificed for man, Christ died; Buddha reposes all the good that man can hope for in himself alone unaided of God, Christ sets before man a divine and spiritual power that energizes his feebleness. How all the efforts and doctrines of Buddha pale before these glorious announcements of Him who came in Bethlehem of Judea—the Sent of God—who declared, "I am the way, the truth, and the life," "I am the living Bread," "I am the light of the world;" and who stands at the head of a sorrowing, crushed, and sinning race with the invitation. "Come unto me all ye that labor and are heavy laden, and I will give you rest." Truly, all nations, all people, the world's great Teachers have sought what Sidharta searched for in the wilds of India—God and Rest—yet in vain; but man is not to be disappointed, for as Haggai says, "The Desire of all nations shall come."

HAROLD & CO.,

3, DALHOUSIE SQUARE, CALCUTTA.

HARMONIUMS.

Harold and Co., call attention to their unequalled stock of rich-toned Harmoniums made especially for India.

FROM RS. 90 TO RS. 900 EACH.

All kinds of Musical Instruments of the best description are always kept in Stock.

ICE! ICE! ICE!

MADE IN FOUR MINUTES

THE PNEUMATIC ICE MACHINE

THIS IMPORTANT INVENTION IS CONSIDERED A BOON TO THOSE LIVING IN TROPICAL CLIMATES.

CAN BE WORKED BY THE MOST INEXPERIENCED HAND AND IS NOT LIABLE TO GET OUT OF ORDER.

From Rs. 175, each Machine complete.

MESSRS. ARLINGTON & CO.,

AGENTS.

BABU BASANTA KUMAR DATTA,
HOMŒOPATHIC PRACTITIONER
No. 20, Sunker Haldar Lane, Ahiritolah.

FRESH INDENT OF

Medicines and other Requisities,
Have arrived from England.
Medicines, [illegible]
Absolute Alcohol; Chloro-spirit Camphor.
Special Remedies.
For Suppressed, Laborious and Difficult [illegible]; Leucorrhœa.
For Hysteria; Spermatorrhœa; Dysentery; Diarrhœa; Cholera.
For Asthma; Piles; Pain; Sore and Diseases of the Children.
Ice, Lemonade, Soda and Tonic water always.
To be had at
DATTA'S HOMŒOPATHIC LABORATORY,
No. 312, Chitpore Road, Buttolla, Calcutta
TERMS—CASH.
☞ Price List can be had on application.

!!! हुक्का !!!
!!! HOOKAHS !!!

English made Hookahs of various choice designs, colours and sizes ranging in price from Rs. 2 to 5 each, 60 designs to choose from. Apply to

RADANAUTH CHOWDRY,
375, Jorasanko

How to Enjoy Life

Is only known when the blood is pure, its circulation perfect, and the nerves in good order. The only safe and certain method of expelling all impurities is to take Holloway's Pills, which have the power of cleansing the blood from all noxious matters, expelling all humours which taint or impoverish it, thereby purify and invigorate and give general tone to the system. Young or old robust or delicate, may alike experience their beneficent effects. Myriads affirmed that these Pills possess marvellous power in securing these great secrets of health by purifying and regulating the fluids and strengthening the solids.

Just Received

An invoice of Mathematical Instrument Boxes, Color Boxes, Drawing Pencils and various other requisites in Stationery. They are priced very moderately for speedy sale.

H. C. GANGOOLY & Co.,
24, Mangoe Lane, Calcutta

NOTICE
MAKHON LOLL GHOSE.

No. 91, Radhabazar, Wholesale and Retail Stationer, Account Bookseller, &c.

Begs to invite the attention of the Public to an invoice of Commercial and Fancy Stationery of all sorts which he has recently received, and which he is disposing of at moderate prices. He has been long in the Trade, and presumes he has always afforded every satisfaction to the several merchants here who have constantly favored him with orders. Any Mofussil orders accompanied with remittances shall be promptly attended to.

BURAL BROTHERS

[ESTABLISHED IN 1870 A.D.]
JEWELLERS, GOLD AND SILVER-SMITHS AND WATCH-MAKERS,

BY APPOINTMENT
TO
His Excellency the Viceroy and Governor-General of India
AND
HIS HIGHNESS THE MAHARAJAH ADHIRAJ OF BURDWAN,

BURAL BROTHERS,
10, Hare Street.

India General Steam Navigation Company, Ld.

SCHOENE, KILBURN & Co.—*Managing Agents.*

ASSAM LINE.
NOTICE.

Steamers leave Calcutta for Assam every Tuesday, Goalundo every Thursday and leave Debrooghur downward every Saturday.

THE Str. "CHUNAR" will leave Calcutta *via Matabanga* for Assam, on Tuesday, the 11th instant.

Cargo will be received at the Company's Godowns, Nimtollah Ghat, up till noon of Monday, the 10th.

THE Str. "RAJMEHAL" will leave Goalundo for Assam on Thursday, the 13th instant.

Cargo will be received at the Company's Godowns, No. 4 Fairlie Place, up till noon of Tuesday the 11th.

Goods forwarded to Goalundo for this vessel will be chargeable with Railway Freight from Calcutta to Goalundo in addition to the regular Freight of this Company.

Passengers should leave for Goalundo by Train of Wednesday, the 12th.

CACHAR LINE NOTICE
REGULAR FORTNIGHTLY SERVICE.

Steamers now leave Calcutta for Cachar and Intermediate Stations every alternate Friday, and leave Cachar downward every alternate Sunday.

THE Str. "COLGONG" will leave Calcutta *via Matabanga* for Cachar on Friday, the 14th instant.

Cargo will be received at the Company's Godowns, Nimtollah Ghat, up till noon of Thursday the 13th.

For further information regarding rates of Freight or passage-money, apply to,

4, FAIRLIE PLACE. } G. J. SCOTT,
Calcutta, 8th July 1879. } *Secretary.*

Printing Materials

MILLER AND RICHARD'S PRESSES, TYPES and all requisites always in Stock,

TERMS CASH.
EWING & CO.

SMITH, STANISTREET & CO.

Pharmaceutical Chemists & Druggists

BY APPOINTMENT
To His Excellency the Right Hon'ble
LORD LYTTON, G.M.S.I.
Governor-General of India,
&c. &c. &c.

SYRUP OF LACTATE OF IRON

Prepared from the original recipe. Lactate of Iron, in various forms of preparation, have been in use in France, and generally through the continent of Europe, for some years past, and is [illegible] one of the most valuable Chalybeate Tonic Remedies yet introduced. The Syrup, being the most agreeable as well as convenient form of administration is in most general use. It is a most valuable remedy in the following diseases:—Chlorosis or Green Sickness, Leucorrhœa, Neuralgia, Enlargement of the Spleen, &c. In combination with quinine, it has also been very successfully used in the cure of Fever, while to persons of delicate constitution, enfeebled by disease it is invaluable. In bottles. Rs. 2 each.

SYRUP OF THE PHOSPHATE OF IRON Rs. 2 per bottle.

SYRUP OF PHOSPHATE OF IRON AND STRYCHNINE, Rs. 2 per bottle.

SYRUP OF PHOSPHATE OF IRON AND QUININE. Price Rs. 2-8 per bottle.

SYRUP OF PHOSPHATE OF IRON, QUININE AND STRYCHNINE (DR. AITKIN'S TRIPLE TONIC SYRUP.) Rs. 2-8 per bottle.

Smith, Stanistreet & Co.

Invite special attention to the following rates the quality guaranteed as the best procurable:—

Pure Ærated Waters.

Made from Pure Water, obtained by the new process through the Patent Charcoal Filters.

				Rs	As
Ærated plain (Trible Ærated), per doz.			...	0	12
Soda Water	ditto	"	..	0	12
Gingerade	ditto	"	...	1	4
Lemonade	ditto	"	...	1	4
Tonic (Quinine)	ditto	"	...	1	4

The *Cash* must be sent with the order to obtain advantage of the above rates.

CHUNDER & BROTHERS,

25½ & 112, RADHA BAZAR,
CALCUTTA,

TERMS,—CASH STRICTLY.

Cash Boxes of sizes with & without Chubbs locks.
Railway Bags, of Carpet, Leather &c.
Overland trunks of leather.
Scarborough trunks of sizes.
Brass Candlesticks of sizes.
Cricket Bats & Balls.
Chinese Canisters, Square & round.
Compendium of Games of sizes.
Bulleye Lantern, Japanned.
Hand Lamp ENGLISH, for Table & Wall.
Mathematical & Surveying Instruments.
Drawing & Painting Materials.
Color Boxes of sizes & descriptions.
Magic inkstand in large variety.
Inkstands with & without stands of sizes &c.
Playing Cards of different patterns.
Brass Padlocks of sizes.
Water Cocks (brass) for Iron and lead pipes.
Iron & Lead pipes of sizes.
Note & Letter paper of all sizes & qualities.
Foolscap, Demy, Medium, Royal paper &c.
Printing Papers of sizes &c.
Steel Pens, Quills, Pencils.
Writing Inks, of all colors & sizes.
Bank Books, Pocket Book &c &c.
Fancy & Useful Articles.

CALCUTTA
The 30th June, 1879. } CHUNDER & BROTHERS.

Printed and published by M. M. RUKHIT, at the INDIAN MIRROR PRESS, No. 15, College Square, for the Proprietor.

The Indian Mirror.

SUNDAY EDITION.

VOL. [illegible] CALCUTTA, SUNDAY JULY 16, 1876 { REGISTERED AT THE GENERAL POST OFFICE. } No. 167

CONTENTS.

NOTICE.

All letters and communications relating to the literary department of the Paper should be addressed to the Editor. All other letters should be addressed to the Manager, to whom all remittances should be made payable.

Subscribers will be good enough to bring to the notice of the Manager any delay or irregularity in the delivery of the Paper.

Editorial Notes.

ANY attempt to revive the study and practice of ancient Hindu medicine must have our hearty sympathy. We, therefore, hail with pleasure an excellent Bengali translation of a portion of the well-known standard medical work, *Susruta*, a copy of which has been kindly sent to us for review. We hope to review it hereafter.

THE *Vaishnavas* classify love to God under five heads. The first of these is *Santa*, the profound calmness that fills the mind on contemplation of the blessedness of Divine nature, and His greatness and glory in nature without. The second is *Dasya*, the dependence which the servant feels upon his master. It is subdivided into filial love whereby man feels glorified in God, and into the loyalty of the slave who honors and glorifies his Lord. The third is friendship *Sakhya* in which man places the utmost confidence and trust in his Divine Friend, and can walk with Him safely under all circumstances. The fourth that is *Batsalya*, is a form of Divine mercy, and is not clearly distinguishable from the other relations in their fulness and detail. The fifth is *Madhurya* or perfect inebriation of the soul in Divine beauty and love. This is taken to be the highest state of devotional blessedness, and is attained in very rare instances. It will be seen that in the main the classification is accurate and nearly complete. A great part of it may be adopted by all reasonable theists.

As if their excesses in the horrible practice of vivisection are not enough, the council of the Medico-Chirurgical Society, and other medical gentlemen who assembled at a *soiree* lately, have signed a memorial to be presented to the House of Lords for the purpose of transforming Lord Carnarvon's Bill for setting limitations to the exercise of vivisection, into one for the promotion of that inhuman practice. They propose the virtual withdrawal of all restrictions imposed by the present Bill upon the terrible experiments made by medical students and others upon the bodies of living animals. We may just observe here that the concensus of public opinion against the practice of vivisection is something very extraordinary. At a general meeting, held not long ago in the Westminister Palace Hotel, prominent part was taken by persons whose theological relations are most radically discordant. The chair was taken by the Earl of Shaftesbury, the head of the Low Church party. Cardinal Manning and the Marquis of Bute, the highest representatives of Romanism in Great Britain, sat at the chairman's righthand. On his left there was the Bishop of Gloucester, and about a yard from him was our friend the Rev. Charles Voysey! Miss Frances Cobbe is Honorary Secretary to the Society.

SUCCESS is a happy thing, it is universally wished for, because it is another name for reward. But success is a shallow thing, and very often does it not spoil him upon whom it attends? Failure is not happy, it is never desired, never praised, it conceals within itself profound and acute pain. But failure is a deep thing; it humiliates, torments, perhaps kills him whom it visits; yet it purifies, ennobles, deepens, softens, and in the end glorifies. Failure in the greatest of human missions means struggle, thought, watching, waiting, prayer, self-sacrifice, and perhaps death. Failure in life-time means endless success after death. Failure in the world of truth, beauty, love, and holiness means the utter impossibility of rendering in outward symbols the inlying inspired ideal of the soul. It is the conception of the spirit that findeth and can find no utterance. The prophet's inward vision of blessedness will find its counterpart in heaven, and when the kingdom of heaven descends upon the world; till then he must content himself with the cry "It is within." He fails, it is true, before men, but he fails with his Divine Master whose purposes men may cross and delay, but whose will in the end shall achieve the glorious triumph to which all human destinies infallibly point.

GEORGE SAND is a name in French literature as eminent, if not more so, than George Eliot in English literature. Both are women, both are novelists, both are literary geniuses, both are popular, and unpopular in about the same degree on account of their capricious, and we must say, somewhat unsound ideas on the subject of individual and social morality. George Eliot is solid, philosophical, cynical, and melancholy. Her stories are not half so attractive as her sentiments, and observations of human, and especially feminine nature. George Sand is brilliant, mystical, ravishing, and most beautiful in her stories. Her productions fascinating to the imagination, are morally very dangerous. George Sand (Madame Dudevant) is just dead at the ripe age of 72. George Eliot (Mrs. Lewes) who is not far past middle age, is still living and writing.

THE future of Mahomedanism in Europe is really becoming a serious question. With the Christian provinces in the Turkish Empire in furious and determined rebellion, a new Sultan, by no means celebrated for the strength and wisdom of his character, just occupying the throne, the army half-disatisfied, the feelings of the population divided, and the sympathies of the first class powers in Europe strongly in favor of the insurgents, Turkey looks as if a terrible dismemberment of her dominions is not far off. On the other hand the Khedive of Egypt is all but a bankrupt, he has suffered a most calamitous defeat of his troops in Abyssinia, and it is seriously discussed after the recent financial *coup de main* of Mr. Desraeli, whether Egypt should not be reduced to the condition of a British feudatory State. Demoralized and impoverished, surrounded by dissatisfied subjects and unfriendly neighbours, the Mahomedan kingdoms of Europe give signs that before long they must crumble away in their moral decay. But it will be urged with reason that Christian countries are not free from evil, and if the Mahomedanism of Turkey and Egypt deserves to die, the Christianity of certain Christian countries we could name, does not surely deserve to live.

A VAST and truly monster-assembly gathered at Hyde Park on the 5th of the last month, to make a demonstration in favor of Sir Wilfrid Lawson's Permissive Bill which was to have come on for its second reading in the House of Commons on the 14th ultimo. The multitude that presented itself is estimated at between 50,000 to 1,20,000 souls, the largest Temperance gathering ever held in Great Britain we think. Though the day was a muddy, misty, rainy day the vast concourse slowly wound it way though the Thames' Embankment with bands, banners, and decorations, and slowly formed itself in Hyde Park were addresses were delivered among others by Sir Wilfrid Lawson himself, and Cardinal Manning, denouncing the fatal progress of drunkenness in the land, and condemning the policy of Government in thrusting spirit-shops upon parishes where the vast majority of rate-payers felt these shops to be dreadful sources of crime and misery. If proprietors refuse to have beer-houses in their estates, said Cardinal Manning, why should rate-payers allow them to be established in their parishes? Whether Sir Wilfrid's Bill is made law in this session of Parliament or not, there is no doubt that the measure can no longer trifled with by Government. Sufficient praise can not be accorded to Sir Wilfrid for his wonderful persistency and heroism in carrying the measure through bitter opposition and gainst powerful vested interests to its present stage. He is the worthy leader of a worthy cause, and may it prosper and succeed is the wish and prayer of every one who has the good of mankind at heart.

THE sentiments expressed by our influential contemporary of the *Hindu Patriot* on the subject of the Juggernath car drawing at Mahesh, seem to have caused considerable irritation in official circles. On the other hand the arbitrary, and unnecessarily harsh interdiction on the part of the Magistrates has undoubtedly created very strong feelings in the minds of the people. We are perfectly well aware that any desire of instituting a system of religious persecution was entirely absent from the minds of the Magistrates, but they ought to have known that undue harshness, and the interdiction of the procession would be most naturally construed in that light. That they have no sympathy with the religion of the people is admitted on all hands, and when to that absence of sympathy is added the prohibition of a religious festival which has been celebrated by the people from time immemorial, how are people to interpret such conduct? It will not do to throw the whole blame on the proprietor of the car. The car was his, but not the festival, and if the Magistrates in their ostentatious regard for the safety of the multitude, imposed restrictions and exacted conditions which he thought were unecessary, high-handed, and unjust, he had every right to let the matter alone, and send the people home with any feelings they chose to carry with them. It was for the Magistrates to reflect on the probable consequences of their interdiction, and if they have become unpopular by their unwise measure they have themselves to thank for it. We must, however, do them the justice to say that it is perfectly wrong to attribute any motive of religious persecution, though their unwisdom is open to many and very obnoxious interpretations.

ATTITUDES OF PRAYER.

WE must under no circumstance forget ourselves while in prayer. That is to say we ought always to bear in mind the distance between us, and the perfect spirit of God whom we address. In one sense it is true that nothing can be nearer than He is to us, He being the very life of our lives. In another sense it is equally true that nothing can be more distant than He, between Him and ourselves there being the inconceivable difference of infinity. The conscious harmony of these two relations constitutes the secret of the right attitude of prayer. Contemplating His nearness, the sameness or rather the similarity of His nature to ours and consequent intimacy of relationship, there comes to spring a familiarity, both in language and sentiment, which is as unreal as unbecoming. We often humanize God to such an extent that we all but lose sight of His divinity. Father, mother friend are sweet endearing words, but applied unreflectively, sentimentally, and without a due appreciation of the truths they convey, they shut out from our view the Supreme nature, as it is in its reality. This perhaps makes religious exercises easy, and yields speedy satisfaction to us as to our own progress in what we call spirituality; but the awful face of the Spirit is veiled in impenetrable gloom before the presumptuous littleness of our vision. Our piety becomes but a mass of soft-sounding sentences with very little underneath it but a superficial sentiment or two.—On the other hand the soul is perfectly lost in the contemplation of the immensity of Divine nature. To think of the infinite distance of His being from ours, His awful, wonderful, dreadful attributes as compared to our pitiful miserable humanity, makes all approach to him impossible and drowns every effort and hope of ever attaining to a full or even an adequate knowledge of His being. The very deepest reverence of our hearts becomes painfully unworthy of the majesty of Divine righteousness and power, and we become annihilated, as it were, in the glory of that unspeakable Presence. The weakening though tender sentimentalities of certain sects, the anthropomorphic puerilities of others, betray as much want of insight into the soul of truth in this matter, as the wild though grand pantheism of that philosophic devotion for which this country has been celebrated, and the unnatural thirst after annihilation and absorption into the Deity manifested by not a few of the reflective among mankind. The golden harmony must be discovered, or we ourselves run the imminent risk of drifting into some extreme of the soul's attitude in prayer, and finding it too late to recede.

With different persons the attitudes of prayer must differ more or less. With one class of men the prevailing attitude should be that of the convicted sinner towards the God of holiness whom he has offended, and from whom he hopes for salvation and peace. In service, in conversation, in meditations, in devotions, the prevailing posture of the soul must be one of genuine but secret lowliness and self-hatred. Rules and exercises ought to be fixed upon, and gone through in private that may help to induce this necessary state of the mind. The display and the talkativeness in which self-imposed repentance is so apt to indulge itself, must be carefully avoided. There is another class of persons, women especially, with whom the sense of sin cannot be a predominent feeling, for the simple reason that never being exposed to any serious temptation, they have never been guilty of any serious offence. Their attitude towards Heaven must be different. If they are of an active and serviceable disposition, the relationship of the servant to the Master can be impressed upon their minds with considerable benefit. Active service in the name and for the pleasure of the glorious Master, will perhaps recommend itself most readily to their nature, and they shall find both joy and purity in doing what little they can to accomplish the purposes of their Lord in heaven. Actual and important work, with definite rules to bind them to it, must be found for them, and in daily devotions they ought to approach their Deity as the august Master whose salt they eat. A few there may be of this description of people whose hearts delight to hear the discourse of divine love, and who are as ready with their service, as with their affection. To them the lessons of divine Fatherhood may be slowly and carefully expounded, so that as each fresh truth is perceived, the soul may find and rejoice to find nearer and more glorious vision of the Supreme Parent's love. Care should be taken that any discourse on eternal love may not be wasted on unwilling and immature hearts, but speech and sentiment may lead step by step to recognize in reality that God is love. This crowning truth when perceived, gives a sweetness to the soul's attitude in prayer and in practical life, which blossoms and fructifies into relations of nameless beauty. The servant attains to the sonship, the Master becomes the loving Father; the wills unite, and the hearts unite. There sounds through the ages, with the prolonged and profound music of paradise, the unmatched utterance "I and my Father are one"—"He that hath seen me hath seen my Father." This does not by any means exhaust the subject of the soul's attitudes. We might say more on the sublime in the spiritual world, the rapt up lifted gaze of wonder into the depths, heights, and mysteries of creative will and purpose, the God within glorified in the infinite without. But we have said enough for to-day.

THE IDEA OF DUTY.

THE greatest dullard and dunce of this century has got by heart the ordinary duties and obligations of humanity. Every one knows that it is his duty to do a certain thing and that it is forbidden to him to do another. Yet how many men practise what they profess, and avoid what they ought not to do? The world has formed a ready excuse for this almost general deviation from the paths of duty. It is not easy to practise what one professes, and on this principle men's actions are easily explained away. This is a false estimate of human nature, and we protest against it with our whole heart. It is not that men cannot, but they will not, do what they think to be right. The blame lies not with their want of power, but their want of will. Ordinary human nature wants to grovel and wallow in the mire of their foul desires and vicious inclinations. Men can easily do good if they will, as easily as they do evil. It is a melancholy truth that this will is not adequately aroused by the system of education which is in vogue at the present day. How to provide it with a proper complement of moral impulse is the problem which every education must have in view yet we are sorry to say, that this impulse is systematically ignored whenever it is proposed to imbue the character of any considerable section of a community with a deep tinge of morality.

Whatever the methods proposed to influence the mind in this direction, it is obvious that every knowledge and therefore every inducement to practise what we know to be true, should begin with self. 'Know thyself' is a truth propounded two thousand years ago; yet how slightly has it been appreciated by society at large. The lives of great men remind us that there can be no genuine excellence which is not based upon a thorough knowledge of self. To know what I am and what I am not, is the only clear way to superiority. When one knows his real position among his fellowmen, the road before him is open and unobstructed by those heaps of rubbish, which men call by the names of conceit, vanity and presumption. Life is short, but our work is vast; and in the vast generality of cases we find that the larger portion of a man's life is spent in the preparatory and almost useless work of exempting the mind from pitiful delusions and errors. This would not have been possible, if men had been born with a due sense of their position. As it is, one half of our life is spent in supreme conceit, another fraction in vain regrets and sighs, and only a small portion is left for the the affairs of the next world. The Hindu Scriptures have accommodated themselves to this trait of human nature, and have provided that every person should devote only the last fraction of his life to God, thus squandering the rest away upon the vain pomp and circumstances of this life. Is not, however, man capable of striking out the right path as soon as he gets the possession of his senses and reason? Is it not easy to be righteous and godlike, if I do but know what I am, whence I have come, for what purposes am I born, or how I am related to others? This knowledge, if repeatedly and duly presented before the mind, is sure to bring along with it a knowledge of its relations. If I know that I am a rational being, having parents and relatives to whom I owe many duties and who in return owe many duties to me, that there is a God who stands to me in the relation of Father, King, Guide, and Protector and to whom, as such, I owe innumerable duties myself—such knowledge will engender a strong sense of duty in our minds. What is required in any system of education, is this constant presentation of my relation to myself, to others, and to God; and as sure as it is that this familiarity will create in the end a belief in our obligations, even so will this belief create with it a real will and impulse to discharge those obligations. Now, moral truths are nothing but such obligations, and moral education is nothing but the creation of an impulse to carry them out. One may be well tutored like a parrot to repeat whatever truths may be required of him, but to be of use they should always be presented to his mind as so many truths for himself. "This is a truth and this truth is for me and none else" this belief should be fostered in the mind of every student of morality. In other words every duty should be studied in reference to self. Men generally take it for granted that all duties are for other men, and not for themselves. If a teacher admonishes his hearers on any department of their obligations, each one of them seems to exclude himself from the list of those whom the teacher wishes to benefit. This exclusion of self, this vanity, this sense of inordinate superiority—is the weakness of all men, and it is this feeling which system of moral education should try effectually to suppress.

Correspondence.

THE STATE OF THE MADRAS BRAHMO SOMAJ.

To the Editor of the *Indian Mirror*.

SIR,—What is it that keeps up the spirit of a religious man and that of the community of which he is a member? Among many other necessary qualities, I mention earnestness and enthusiasm. Where there is no earnestness and enthusiasm, there everything goes backward. This is true of all; of students, of professional men. But we cannot expect every one to be earnest and enthusiastic. It is the presence of these qualities in one or in a few that keeps up the spirit of the rest. In this part of India leaders, eminent and earnest, now and then or at stated intervals, add a kind of impetus to the exhausted, drooping, sinking energy of their followers. Hence if there are some men cold and indifferent to their creed, there are others to animate them.

Madras which has been justly called "benighted," stands opposing all reform whether social or moral, and therefore demands the presence of a competent leader almost immediately. The introduction of Western thought has, no doubt, opened the eyes of the Madrasis, but they all, as a rule, seem to be afraid of speaking out what their convictions are in morals and religion. Look at an educated Native gentleman of Madras, you will see the three caste stripes on his forehead. Judging from his outward appearance, you will call him a "*pucca*" Hindu. A few moments' conversation with him will easily convince any one that his inward and outward persons are as different as night and day. Native gentlemen of Madras seem to be guided by the vicious principle "whatever others do, do ye also likewise." This may be a good principle in its own way, but when strictly practised it will end in hypocrisy. Of course, persons who cannot think for themselves, may find nothing offensive in this principle; but those who can think for themselves if they wish to carry it out, will be compelled to act a double part. They must say yes, when their better judgment says, No; thus it will be unsafe to follow this principle.

The present tendency of the young men of Madras is towards Nihilism. The cause of this tendency is not far to seek. For the young and unmoulded minds, easily imbibing the destructive thoughts of sceptical writers from books prescribed for the higher University Examinations, spread the imbibed poison wherever they go. This is sufficient to show that Theism makes no progress. It is not Theism, but Atheism that seems to make rapid progress there. Under these circumstances true religion cannot make her way in the south. Persons who once professed Theism, persons who exhibited a good deal of fire in them, persons who regularly preached in the Samaj, the place of worship where all once met; what has become of them? Religion does not interest many; the fire that was once stirred up by an accident is now quenched; the preachers now have gone to different parts of the country (not of course to preach); and the place of worship is unused.

If the Parent Samaj wishes the prosperity of the Daughter Samaj, it is high time for her to send competent persons to sow the seeds of Theism in a soil which was once found to be barren. I say this is the proper time, because the abortive notions imbibed by Native gentlemen, have not sunk very deep into their hearts. They had to learn these because they had to reproduce them in the University examinations; and they have only seen one side of the picture, and the other side is not shown to them and therefore they do not appreciate it. Two or thee weeks' lectures by a competent missionary are sufficient to act like a dose of healing medicine in their minds.

I am, Sir, Yours.
A THEIST OF SOUTHERN INDIA.

Devotional

ONLY the soul's pure gladness of life in thee is real, O my God, all else, all else is deeply false. I have seen the noble human face in the bloated ugliness of approaching death, the unspeakable foulness and contortions of the last disease, and it all passed away soon into gloom and unconsciousness. I have seen the sun-lit beauty and healthful fragrance of innocent youth before it passed away into sickness, decay, and old age. It is all so sadly unreal and deceiving! My God, what miserable mockery is man's hope, of life and joy but in thee? Suffer me to be secure in thee, no other safety I seek. Enable me to feel what cheerfulness I am worthy of only with thee and in thy service.

THE grace of holiness, my Merciful Saviour, I entreat thee to bestow. I have longed before thee for the holiness of flesh and the holiness of spirit. and neither of these is yet mine. Untainted and washed out by thy redeeming mercy let me approach thy feet, how can I draw near to thee with uncleanness still clinging to my heart? For the living waters of thy ever-glorious righteousness my spirit thirsts, thou dost know, O Holy Spirit, vouchsafe to show me the salvation wherein the soul becomes pure for ever.

FOR the honor and welfare of thy neglected daughters I once more lift up my feeble hands in prayer to thee, O our common Father, suffer all thy servants to plead for those who cannot plead for themselves. The delicacies and depths of woman's nature thou alone hast sounded and dost know. We who profess to teach them are ignorant, vain and unrighteous. Teach them, and give them the light of sober wisdom and piety that they may know and do the work for which thou didst send them here. Enlighten us also that we may not be harsh and unfeeling where we should be kind and sympathetic, that we may not be indulgent and weak where we should be stern and unbending. Above all teach us by truthfulness and purity, and a loving disposition to help, and aid each other in going to thy home in heaven.

The Brahmo Somaj

OUR minister was again laid up with fever last week, this being the fourth attack he has had in the course of about six weeks. He is now better.

THE anniversary of the Rampore Hat Brahmo Somaj was celebrated the other day.

THE Brahmo missionaries who have been living in the *Sadhan Kanan* may now be expected back in town.

THE members of the *Prarthana* Somaj Bombay seem to be anxious to secure the services of a resident missionary who will stay with them for years, learn their language, and be a thorough Mahratti in habits. We hope some one will come forward.

Gleanings

THE *MYNA* AND THE CROW.

(Translated From Sheikh Sadi.)

A *Myna* was once shut up with a crow in a cage. The *Myna* was always vexed at the idea of sharing his cage with the ugly crow, and frequently addressed him thus:—How horrid you are to look at. Your conduct is always bad, and every one despises you. You are as unlike to me as the east is to the west. If any on has a sight of you in the morning, his dya-daw of joy is turned into the sunset of sorrow. It becomes you to live with others who are as bad as yourself. But I think no living being in this world is so unfortunate as to be fit to live with you.

It is very curious that the crow too was equally unhappy to be in the same cage with the *Myna*. He was always stroking his legs in sorrow and vexation and speaking to his companion:—What misfortune! Does this mean thing deserve the honor of dwelling with me? Is a *Myna* worthy to dance with a crow on the garden wall? Bad company is like imprisonment to the virtuous. Of what fault I am guilty that God has compelled me to live with such a vain, vile, foolish, low-bred, and excessively talkative creature as this *Myna*? O thou mean miserable bird! If thou ever goest to heaven, it is far preferable to other people to walk down to hell to avoid you.

Moral—If superior people dislike the company of their inferiors the latter only return that compliment with compound interest.

M.

Literary

MR. GLADSTONE has undertaken to write the essay on Lord Macaulay in the forthcoming number of the *Quarterly Review*, suggested by Mr. Trevelyan's life of the late statesman.

MR. MARGARY'S Journal and Letters, which are announced for speedy publication by Messrs. Macmillan, will be supplemented by a valuable Epilogue from the pen of Sir Rutherford Alcock, K. C. B., treating fully the question of the British commercial and political relations with China.

A BOOK is announced with the title of "Our Indian Empire; the History of the Wonderful Rise of British supremacy in Hindustan." By the Rev. Samuel Norwood, B. A., Head Master of the Royal Grammar School, Whalley.

MAJOR W. W. KNOLLYS was to have contributed to the new number of the *New Quarterly Magazine* a paper on "Our Disasters in Afghanistan."

DR. BURNELL'S new work "On the Aindra school of Sanskrit grammarians; their place in the Sanskrit and subordinate literature," is just out.

MESSRS. HIGGINBOTHAM & Co., of Madras, are, with characteristic energy, preparing a lithographed map of the seat of war in Turkey. As the country is very little known, the map should meet with a ready sale.

"THE Eastern Question. Also, The Turks: their Character, Manners, and Institutions, as bearing on the Eastern Question" is the title of a work by H. A. Munro-Butler-Johnstone, Esq., M. P. The publishers are James Parker and Co., 377 Strand, London.

—AT the Oxford Commemoration held on June 24, Prince Leopold, Lord Northbrook, Sir Salar Jung (who was prevented by indisposition from being present), Sir James Francis Davis, Lieutenant Cameron, and others, received the hon. degree of D.C.L.

Latest News

—SIR SALAR JUNG was entertained to a dinner by the Prince of Wales.

—THE Russian Embassy to Kashghar consisting of a Captain of the Turkistan Staff and three officers, was to cross the Cashmere frontier early last month.

—REFERRING to the several petitions against the oppressions of the Simla Municipality, sent to the Punjab Government, the Lahore paper says:—"The petitioners ought to have borne in mind that the Municipality is in want of money, which must be got somehow in order to render the Vice-regal summer residence wholesome and pleasant; and so as loyal, trusty subjects of the crown, they ought to have evinced greater public spirit, paid up without demur, and respectfully and deferentially offered further and larger contributions towards effecting this desirable object."

—PROFESSOR WELLS, the aeronaut, now at Lahore, seems to think that the improvements lately made in Balloons are of such a nature that Balloons may now be employed for the transport of large bodies of troops with armament, &c., and from personal examination which the Professor made in 1874 of the War-Balloons under construction by the Russians at St. Petersburg, he is impressed with the belief that the time is not far distant when Russia will be able, and will more than probably do so, descend on British India over the mountains in Balloons with 100,000 warriors, and thinks that the British Government should make preparations to meet such a contingency.

—MR. E. D. DICKSON, Physician to the British Embassy at Constantinople, says that the Plague has spread into Persia, and that unless Government take the utmost precautions, it might even break out in India. The symptoms observed are those of true Plague—a malignant fever accompanied by glandular swellings.

—SIR SALAR JUNG had a degree conferred on him by the Oxford University, but was incapacitated by his late accident from receiving it in person.

—THE *Nord*, of Brussels, in a recent article says:—"The language held by the English Ministers and the comments of the British Press show that England desires the pacification of the East by means of a real improvement in the lot of the population. One may congratulate oneself upon seeing the English Cabinet enter upon this path and Russia especially will approve its so doing, for it matters little to her by whom the improvement of the unbearable position of the Christian population in the East is brought about. If the English Cabinet lay claim to the initiative, it may rely beforehand upon the sympathies and approbation of the Russian Government and of all the other Powers."

—A BALL was given a few evenings ago by Her Majesty the Queen to the tenants and servants at Balmoral. Her Majesty joined in the dance.

—A DEPUTATION from Stratton, consisting of the Rev. S. E. Lyon and Messrs. Charles Henry and William Prin, William and George Ewens, waited upon Lord Northbrook, on June 19, at his residence, Hamilton-place, Piccadilly, for the purpose of presenting an address of hearty welcome to his Lordship on his return to his home from his mission as Viceroy and Governor-General of India. His Lordship, in returning thanks, expressed his sincere gratification at being so warmly welcomed by his own friends at Stratten.

—SIX CHINESE Companies have prepared a memorial, to be forwarded to the President of the United States, giving an argument on their side of the question on Chinese emigration, and the present anti-Coolie movement.

—FATHER HYACINTHE (M. Loyson) who is now in London, delivered his second address "On the Prospects of Christendom," in the presence of Mr. Gladstone and other distinguished persons.

—THE mode of suicide adopted by the late Sultan, appears being imitated by others tired of life. We read that a commission agent at Liverpool has been remanded upon a charge of attempting suicide by opening the veins of his arm.

—IN the House of Commons, Mr. Macdonald and Mr. Burt presented petitions objecting to further grants to the Royal Family until a full statement had been made of their personal incomes.

—THE Rajah of Nabha gave an entertainment to Lord Lytton at Simla. Nautches were given and a *burra khana* too. The *Pioneer's* Simla correspondent fancies "that during the visit Lord Lytton paid him, [the Rajah] about a week ago, something must have been said by His Excellency to the effect that he would like to see a Native Nautch." And hence, it is believed, the Nautches. We should like to know how Lord Lytton liked them.

—THE extreme heat in the Punjab has been followed by such tremendous downpours that a portion of the country has been flooded and the railway communication interrupted. A large number of houses have fallen at Lahore, several lives have been lost and more injured. Large quantities of gram have been destroyed too.

—IT is not yet certain when Sir Henry Davies will leave Simla. His Honor, it appears, will prolong his stay there.

—IT is reported that the Afridis have successfully raided village Shekhon in British territory, carrying off nearly one hundred head of cattle.

—THE language of the St. Petersburgh press is still very excited, Ministerial papers leading the van, and surpassing even the Slavophil and more independent journals. One specimen from the *Golos* will suffice:—"England's idea of achieving victory without power and shot is simply ridiculous. Or is England bent upon war with Russia? In such a case England had better look out for more useful allies than Spain, who really is not an adversary worthy of our notice; but times have changed since 1853. France, who saved England in the Crimean War, now ranks foremost among her adversaries. We shall throttle Turkey before the eyes of England. Unless Russia is opposed by other Powers than Spain and Great Britian she will not allow the rebellion in the Balkan Peninsula to be put down."

—ONE Syed Agha Husain, a merchant from Khorasan, delivered an address in Persian on his travels in Central Asia at the last anniversary meeting of the Patna Mahomedan Literary Society. Mr. Metcalfe, the Commissioner of Patna, was present.

—DISSATISFACTION of the Czar and of Prince Gortchakoff at recent events in Turkey, has become greatly modified, and there is no reason to apprehend any hostile movements.

—THE visit of the Emperor of Russia to the Chateau of Reichstadt is to be made at the special invitation of the Emperor of Austria.

—MR. GROSVENOR has sent his report respecting the murder of Mr. Margary to the British Government.

—THE St. Petersburg *Herald* declares that there is every prospect of Russia not being diverted from her chosen path by Great Britian.

—THE Cetigne correspondent of the *Moscow Gazette* says that the Turks in Bosnia have unfurled the green flag, indicative of a Holy War against all Christians.

—A COLLECTION of sketches in water-colors, taken from life in Bombay and Bengal by Mr. William Taylor during the Indian tour of His Royal Highness the Prince of Wales, is now on view at the Dickinson Gallery, New Bond Street, London. These productions have little, if any, merit as works of art. They are not so much pictures as pictorial memoranda, having but slight reference to incidents of royal travel, and relating for the most part to groups of Natives, temples, trees, and some of the more obvious scenes and objects which attract attention in Hindustan.

—THE Prince of Wales has written a letter announcing his intention to visit the Brussesl Exhibition in next August and September.

—THE friends of the Earl of Northbrook celebrated his return home from India by a banquet and reception to his Lordship on the 28th June last.

—THE Begum of Bhopal has obtained a decree for Rs. 15,263 against the Great Indian Peninsular Railway Company, for damages sustained by Her Highness by the loss of goods in transit from Bombay to Hurda.

—THERE is a rumour in the North-West, says the *Statesman*, that Lord Lytton is not likely to remain in India beyond November next, and that Sir John Strachey is spoken of as his probable successor.

—SIR JOHN STRACHEY leaves for Almora on the 28th.

—YAKUB BEG, the Kashgar Envoy, is expected daily at Srinuggur.

—A CHARGE has been laid before the Magistrate of Allahabad against Mr. Purcell, late of Allahabad, for criminal breach of trust of Rs. 6,000, and an attempt at cheating, in connection with St. Joseph's Seminary Lottery. Mr. Purcell is on bail for Rs. 5,000.

—MR. H. RIVETT CARNAC takes three months' leave in September, and Mr. F. M. Halliday, Collector of Gya, officiates as the Benares Opium Agent.

—HASSAN, the Circassian, who assassinated Hussein Avni Pasha and Raschid, the Turkish Ministers of War and Foreign Affairs, on June 15, has been hung. The motive of the act is believed to have been personal rather than political.

—ANOTHER Wynaad Gold Mining Company is proposed, after favorable prospecting. The capital is to be four lacs sterling.

—MR. DISRAELI stated, in the House of Commons, on the night of June 22, that the European Powers, though differing on many points, were agreed as to the wisdom of not putting any undue pressure on the new Sultan and his Government.

—MUCH satisfaction is felt in England with the foreign policy of Mr. Disraeli's Government.

LORD SALISBURY paid a visit to Sir Salar Jung at his residence in Piccadilly, London.

Calcutta.

THE Hon'ble H. Bell has consented to be one of the Vice-Presidents of the Social Science Association during the current year in the room of Dr. J. Ewart, proceeded to England on furlough.

WE have been assured seriously, says the *Indian Daily News*, that Sir Richard Temple entertains so high an opinion of the services of some of the Justices who have been prominent members of "Her Majesty's opposition" at the Municipal Board, that in the event of their failing to be returned by the burgesses of any ward, he purposes to nominate them to the commission, in order to secure to the city their valuable services. Some of the names of the parties to be so honored were mentioned to us.

A MEETING was held last evening at the Town Hall to finally decide the question as to having an Italian Opera here in the ensuing cold season.

THE Chief Justice has drawn up a Minute upon the Subordinate Judicial Service, which will shortly be submitted to Government.

THE P. & O. Co's, S. S. *Zambesi*, Commander A. Symons, arrived in Bombay harbour on Wednesday last at 12-30 A. M., from Suez with the English Mails of the 23rd ult. on board. The following is the list of passengers.

From Venice.—Capt. Oldham, M. A. J. Oldham.

From Brindisi.—Mr. Floyd, Mr. O'Callaghan, Major Vibart, Lieut. C. W. Douglas, Major C. S. Blair, Mr. H. F. White, M. Peaker, Mr. and Mrs. Harlow, Col. Dillon.

From Southampton.—Mr. and Mrs. Osborne, Maj. Steward, Mr. T. Robinson, Mr. J. S. Davis, Vety. Surg. Paton, Bamdr. Langlands, Mrs. Langlands, Sub-Comdr Cogan.

From Aden.—Mr. E. H. Stone, Surg. Maj. J. F. Keith.

THE Harrish Chunder Mukerji Library was opened yesterday in No. 18, British Indian Street, at 4-30 P. M., Rajah Romanath Tagore presided.

ACKNOWLEDGMENT.
Calcutta Magazine for July 1876.

Selection.

DEAN STANLEY.

THE Dean is a handsome man of sixty, with an appearance at once dignified and suave, and courtly, graceful manners. He is the favorite of royal and other great persons. He was sent to St. Petersburg to perform the Protestant part of the marriage service of the Duke and Duchess of Edinburgh, and he was entertained in a very succession of imperial and royal palaces on his way home. He stands as a sort of medium between our English literature. When the Queen wished to have a talk with Thomas Carlyle, and it was not quite certain that the rugged old philosopher would endure being trotted out even for the gratification of royalty, it was Dean Stanley, I believe, who managed the affair. The Queen coming to this house, and Mr. Carlyle being induced to drop in there "promiscuous," as Mrs. Gamp might say. It was Dean Stanley who came to the rescue of John Stuart Mill when the latter, at one of the Westminister elections, was charged by the journal which is owned by the London ginshop-keepers and whisky-sellers with atheism, or blasphemy, or something of the kind. It was Dean Stanley who allowed Max Muller to give lectures in Westminister Abbey and American preachers to preach there. All this makes some people very angry. They insist that the Dean is a mere hunter of titles or seeker after popularity. Especially are some rigid Churchmen offended by the catholicism of his ways with regard to other sects. They cannot understand why a Church of England clergyman should take part in any manner of religious service with Newman Hall or have anything to do with Spurgeon. Not long since Dr. Stanley delivered an address in the town of Bedford, on the occasion of the unveiling of a monument to John Bunyan; and very furious were some of the extreme Churchmen because a Dean of Westminster had paid such homage to a Dissenter. Dr. Johnson said of Isaac Watts that he wished everybody could imitate him in all things except his non-conformity; but there are some fierce Churchmen in whose minds the bare fact of the non-conformity extinguishes all merit and leaves nothing to be imitated. A newspaper specially devoted to the interests of the Church of England was so angry because of the tribute paid by the Dean of Westminster to the merits of the Dissenter Bunyan that it sarcastically recommended the raising of a statue of the Devil, and intimated its belief that Dean Stanley would be found ready to pronounce the eulogy.—*The Galaxy.*

Advertisements

MUNICIPAL ELECTION.

The following questions have been put by several persons to the Chairman, and as the replies given may be of use to the public, they are published for general information.

QUESTION.—1. If a person sleeps beyond the town and suburbs of Calcutta, but personally works for gain in Calcutta, and has an office in town, is he a resident of Calcutta within the meaning of Sections 4 and 7, of Act IV. (B. C.) of 1876, and if otherwise qualified, may he vote for the election of Municipal Commissioners, and may he stand for election as a Municipal Commissioner?

ANSWER.—1. The Chairman considers that the term "resident," as used in the Sections quoted, should be liberally interpreted, and is therefore of opinion, that as the High Court and Small Cause Court can entertain suits against a person who either dwells or personally works for gain within the limits of their jurisdiction, it is fair to hold, that a person sleeping out of town, but paying rates and taxes in town, and daily doing business in town, is qualified to vote and to stand for election as a Municipal Commissioner.

Q. 2. With reference to the words in Section 8 "who shall have paid on his own behalf and not otherwise," may an agent or attorney vote for his principal?

A. 2. A mere agent or a person voting under a power of attorney cannot, in the Chairman's opinion, come under the definition of a person paying on his own behalf, but a Trustee under a Will or Settlement who is solely responsible for the management of a property is entitled to vote—as the property is for the time being vested in him.

Q. 3. If a joint undivided Hindu family of 4 males each holding a 4 anna's share in a property has paid Rs. 100, as rates in the name of the head of the family, is each member entitled to vote?

A. 3. Yes, each member is entitled to vote, as he has paid Rs. 25 on his own behalf through the head of the family.

Q. 4. May a voting paper be signed by an attorney on behalf of his principal?

A. 4. No. As there is nothing in the Act sanctioning the vote by a proxy or an attorney.

By the Rules published by Government, voting papers may either be sent on the 1st September to the Polling Officer, or delivered in person. In the former case, the signature of voter must be attested by a respectable witness, and in the latter case, the voter must sign in the presence of the Polling Officer.

Q. 5. If a person has paid Rs. 20 as rates in Ward No. 1, and Rs. 10 as rates in Ward No. 12, may he vote in both Wards No. 1 and No. 12?

A. 5. No. He cannot vote in both Wards Nos. 1 & 12, but by Section 8, he may vote either in Ward No. 1 or Ward No. 12, or the Ward in which he resides or the Ward in which his place of business is situated.

ROBERT TURNBULL,
Secretary to the Corporation of the Town of Calcutta.

ALBERT HALL.

PATRON,

His Honor the Lieutenant Governor of Bengal.

COUNCIL,

Hon'ble Sir William Muir, K. C. S. I.—*President.*
Rajah Rama Nath Tagore Bahadur C. S. I.—*Vice-President.*
Hon'ble J. F. D. Inglis.
Hon'ble Ashley Eden, C. S. I.
Hon'ble H. Bell.
Archdeacon Baly.
Colonel H. E. L. Thuillier, C. S. I.
His Highness the Maharajah of Vizianagram.
Maharajah Kumar of Bettiah.
Hon'ble Rajah Narendra Krishna Bahadur.
Rajah Komul Krishna Bahadur.
Rajah Jotendro Mohun Tagore Bahadur.
Babu Digumber Mitter, C. S. I.
Dr. Rajendralala Mitra.
Hon'ble Nawab Ashgur Ali Bahadur, C. S. I.
Nawab Amir Ali Bahadur.
Moulvi Abdul Lutif Khan Bahadur.
Manockji Rustomji, Esq.
Babu Keshub Chunder Sen.

SUBSCRIPTIONS.

The Hon'ble Sir Richard Temple ...	Rs.	200
His Highness Maharajah Holkar ...	"	8,000
His Highness Maharajah of Jeypore	"	6,000
His Highness Maharajah of Putialah	"	2,500
His Highness Maharajah of Vizianagram ...	"	1,000
His Highness the Maharajah of Cooch Behar ...	"	1,000
Maharajah Kumar of Bettiah ...	"	2,000
Rajah of Bhinga ...	"	1,000
Maharani Surnomoie, Cossim Bazar	"	1,000
Maharajah of Hutwa ...	"	500
Rajah Roma Nath Tagore Bahadur	"	250
Rajah Komul Krishna Bahadur ...	"	500
Rajah Jotendro Mohun Tagore ...	"	500
Hon'ble Rajah Narendra Krishna Bahadur ...	"	300
Babu Joykissen Mookerjee ...	"	250
Sirdar Dyal Singh ...	"	200
Babu Shama Churn Law ...	"	200
Hon'ble Sir William Muir ...	"	100
Hon'ble Ashley Eden ...	"	100
Dr. Mohendra Lall Sircar ...	"	100
Babu Goonendro Nath Tagore ...	"	100
Babu Ananda Mohun Bose ...	"	100
Babu Rajkissen Mookerjee ...	"	200
Babu Janoki Nath Mookerji ...	"	100
Hon'ble H. Bell ...	"	100
Babu Debendro Nath Bose ...	"	200

BURAL BROTHERS

[ESTABLISHED IN 1870 A.D.]

JEWELLERS, GOLD AND SILVER-SMITHS AND WATCH-MAKERS,

BY APPOINTMENT

TO

His Excellency the Viceroy and Governor-General of India

AND

HIS HIGHNESS THE MAHARAJAH ADHIRAJ OF BURDWAN,

BURAL BROTHERS,
10, Hare Street.

HOLLOWAY'S OINTMENT

How to Enjoy Life

Is only known when the blood is pure, its circulation perfect, and the nerves in good order. The only safe and certain method of expelling all impurities is to take Holloway's Pills, which have the power of cleansing the blood from all noxious matters, expelling all humours which taint or impoverish it, thereby purify and invigorate and give general tone to the system. Young or old, robust or delicate, may alike experience their beneficent effects. Myriads affirmed that these Pills possess marvellous power in securing those great secrets of health by purifying and regulating the fluids and strengthening the solids.

THE INDIAN MIRROR

The Cheapest Daily Paper

IN

INDIA

AND

Having an Extensive Circulation.

SUBSCRIPTIONS.

(IN ADVANCE.)

	Town.				Mofussil, Including Postage.		
Yearly	... Rs. 12	0	0		Rs. 23	0	0
Half yearly	... " 6	8	0		" 11	8	0
Quarterly	... " 3	8	0		" 6	0	0
Monthly	... " 1	8	0		" 2	8	0

Cash sales, One Anna per copy.

Sunday Edition.

Per Annum ... ... Rs. 6

MOFUSSIL SUBSCRIBERS.

Per Annum ... ... Rs. 4 10 8

Via Southampton.	£ S. D.	Via Brindisi.	£ S. D.
Per Annum	0 18 9	Per Annum	1 7 6

Cash sales, Two Annas per copy.

RATE OF ADVERTISING.

First insertion, 8 lines and under, 1 Rupee.

Second and succeeding insertions, 2 Annas per line.

For Advertisements which are to be inserted for a considerable time special contracts may be made on application to the manager.

Domestic Occurrences	Non-Subscribers ...	1 Re.
	Subscribers ...	8 As.
Public Engagement each insertion ...		1 Re.

FOR SALE.

AT THE BRAHMO SOMAJ OF INDIA

MISSION OFFICE,

No. 13, Mirzapore Street.

	Rs.	As.	P.
Brahmo Pocket Diary, 1876 ...	0	2	
Behold the Light of Heaven in India ...	0	8	0
Sacred Anthology ...	2	0	0
Last Days of Rajah Ram Mohun Roy ...	1	0	0
Essays, Theological and Ethical ...	0	12	0
Historical Sketch of the Brahmo Somaj	0	4	0
Jesus Christ, Europe and Asia ...	0	3	0
Future Church ...	0	3	0
True Faith ...	0	2	0

ICE! ICE! ICE!

MADE IN FOUR MINUTES

THE PNEUMATIC ICE MACHINE

THIS IMPORTANT INVENTION IS CONSIDERED A BOON TO THOSE LIVING IN TROPICAL CLIMATE.

CAN BE WORKED BY THE MOST INEXPERIENCED HAND AND IS NOT LIABLE TO GET OUT OF ORDER.

From Rs. 175, each Machine complete.

MESSRS. ARLINGTON & CO

AGENTS.

HAROLD & CO.,

3, DALHOUSIE SQUARE, CALCUTTA.

HARMONIUMS.

Harold and Co. call attention to their unequalled stock of rich toned Harmoniums made especially for India.

FROM RS. 90 TO RS. 900 EACH.

All kinds of Musical Instruments of the best description are always kept in Stock.

Printed and published by M. M. RUKHIT, at the INDIAN MIRROR PRESS, No. 15, College Square, for the Proprietor.

The Indian Mirror.

SUNDAY EDITION.

VOL. XVI.] CALCUTTA, SUNDAY JULY 23 1876 {Registered in the General Post Office.} [No. 173

CONTENTS.

Editorial Notes.

THE New Testament Revision Company have proceeded to the Epistles to the Philippians and the Thessalonians.

THE *Christian Life* is doubtless a success. We commend it to all interested in liberal thought and spiritual progress. The number before us is creditably got up, and is highly promising.

THE English papers announce the establishment of a new religious association in London, called the Anglo-Israel Association, whose only object seems to be to "develope and disseminate the truth of the proposition that the Anglo-Saxon race is descended from the lost tribes of Israel." Can the advancing world take any real interest in a question like this?

MISS ANNA SWANWICK'S able and interesting paper on "Evolution and the Religion of the Future" read at a recent meeting of the Liberal Social Union, appears in the last number of the *Contemporary Review*. The *Inquirer* congratulates the members of the British and Foreign Unitarian Association on the election of this accomplished lady of the Committee of the Association.

THE cause of liberal religion in Germany is represented by the party whose representative, Dr. Carl Manchot of Bremen may be said to be. Their cause is the cause of Theism in Germany. They are being persecuted by the orthodox party. The following about them is from the *Inquirer*:—

Our liberal friends in Bremen have recently held the annual meeting of their local Protestant Association. The number of members has increased about one hundred during the past year, and now stands at three hundred and thirty. The income has risen in like proportion, and the funds are in quite a flourishing state. The courses of lectures delivered under the auspices of the Association during the winter have been highly appreciated, and by this and other means much sound and valuable information on the ecclesiastical questions of the day has been widely disseminated. At the annual meeting Dr. Carl Manchot delivered a most interesting and carefully prepared address on the operation of the new Civil Marriage laws in Bremen. The Provincial Association for North-west Germany, which holds its annual meetings at Harburg on June 7 and 8, has been scurvily treated by the Church authorities of that town. These, being apparently afraid of the desecration of the building under their care, by the presence of Liberal Christians within its walls, have refused the use of the church for the opening service on June 7, when Pastor Buck, of Hamburg, was to officiate. This was naturally called forth an indignant protest from the members of the local association of Harburg, and efforts are still being made to induce these too faithful guardians of the sanctuary to depart from a course which is felt by all right-thinking people to be so unfraternal and inhospitable, and even so un-Christian as to bring disgrace on the whole community. "The Church authorities and the Consistory" (says the *Protestant ablatt*) "will speedily find that though they may have control over the iron, wood, and stone of the church, the Spirit of God dwells where it will.

THERE are not a few who for obvious reasons industriously conceal their devotional feelings, and feel ashamed to show them lest men should question their intellectuality and accuse them of the weakness of being too emotional. By so doing they often stifle their better feelings and impulses, a danger we must all guard against. This point has been clearly dealt with by a Unitarian writer, in a London paper, from whose observations we extract the following lines:—"The fault is our own. We have not done full justice to our religion; when we have felt its power we have too often been ashamed to show our feelings; shrinking from fanaticism we have assumed in manner an indifference we do not experience; anxious to be reasonable we have sometimes ignored the emotional. As in our public services we have aimed at having our singing in good taste rather than at having it congregational, vigorous and hearty, our sermons correct in manner rather than powerful in matter, our chapels acceptable to a refined few rather than thronged by a mixed multitude; so, in our personal demeanour, we have been too much afraid of manifesting our religion openly we have been reticent till the unexpressed feeling has lost its power. We have not experienced in ourselves, and therefore have not manifested to the world the full strength and beauty of the truths we hold and the emotions they produce. The fault is not in our religion but in ourselves. We have the truths, and in part at least we feel their power, and if ever the time comes when we speak out these truths as they deserve, when we proclaim to the world the Gospel of Love, and do full justice to the inspiring hopes and promises it contains, and let them move our hearts, and through us the hearts of others, as they should, then will it be seen that our Christianity has a way to the general heart and an influence over the general life, which may make it the salt of the earth."

ONE of the charges which Mr. Gladstone prefers against the Theist, in his able article in the *Contemporary*, is that he does not "profit by the vast capital which has accumulated by the labor and experience of his race." This is just the reverse of actual facts. For surely there is none in the religious world who is so anxious, diligent and devoutly earnest a student of the wisdom and experiences of other sects as the Theist. The Reverend J. Page Hopps, of Glasgow, has, we see, addressed a reply to Mr. Gladstone, contradicting the charge, from which we extract the following:—"The Theist, on the contrary, is precisely the man who *does* profit by the religious accumulations of the race, who *does* inherit these accumulations up to the latest moment of his own career, who *does* leave an inheritance of fresh thought and feeling to his successors, and who, so far from simply leasing a religious house made to his hands by Catholic or Protestant builders, feels it to be his duty and delight to use up the old material in providing a home adapted to the needs of to-day. The Theist is absolutely free to do this, and he is a Theist simply because he declines the order of Catholicism and Evangelicalism—to learn nothing and forget nothing. He holds that the rich accumulations of religious thought in nations other than the Hebrew, and in connection with religious experiments other than Chistian, *should* be profited by; he holds that the last eighteen hundred years have added much to our grounds of knowledge, to our material, to our methods, to our light, to our capacity, and even to our possibilities of reverent and worthy conceptions of Deity; and he, therefore, declines to abide by some old things and decides to hold by many things that are new. In other words, he declines to do the very things you say he does; he declines to neglect the "vast capital which has been accumulated by the labour and experience of his race;" he declines to refuse to inherit from his predecessors and to leave nothing to his successors; he declines to simply renew the lease of the old house for his life.

THE distribution of prizes to the pupils of the Native ladies Normal school passed of successfully yesterday. Among those present we noticed Mr. and Mrs. Woodrow, Mrs. Reynolds, Mrs. Grant, Miss Williams, Mrs. Wheeler, Mrs. Wilson, Mrs. Simmons, Mrs. M. Ghose, Miss. Chamberlane, Miss. Brink M. D., Father Lafont and Rev. K. M. Banerji and the Rev. C. H. A. Dall. His Honor the Lieutenant-Governor gave away the prizes. A brief account of the school with a report of the last year's operations was given by Babu Protap Chunder Mozumder. We give below the substance of the remarks made by Sir Richard Temple at the conclusion of the proceedings. Ladies and Gentlemen,—I am glad to have been able to come here. The aspect of the place is pleasant, the aspect of the gathering is also pleasant. The progress made by the young ladies of the School has been satisfactory which is proved by the readings and recitations we have heard and the pieces of composition shown to us. The hand-writing has been excellent, and the matter good, I am glad to say this is not the first institution of its kind, and in such institution Hindu ladies acquire knowledge and improvement. It is a matter of congratulation that Hindu ladies are thus making progress. Though my friend opposite, the Director of Public instruction, does not think that female education is making sufficient progress in this country, we cannot but think that some progress is being made. This school shows that some good work has been done, and though it is not much, it is solid and real. When gentlemen and ladies, both Native and European, as we see here present take active interest in the cause of such institutions, they cannot but do good work. And especially when such men as Babus Protap Chunder Mozumder and Keshub Chunder Sen whose ability and eloquence and religious fervour are so well known, devote themselves to the work, we may hope for very good results. But the managers of the school ought not to be satisfied with what they have done, they ought to do more. Though the school is connected with the Brahmo Somaj, I think they gladly admit pupils from the other communities. (cry of yes yes) I believe Brahmo ladies take more readily to education than other Native ladies, but I have no doubt that this dissimilarity will disappear in due course of time. I am very glad that Government grant has been extended to the school by which its usefulness ought to increase. And before I depart I must say that the managers and supporters of the school may rest assured that their work and their objects will no where meet with more sincere and cordial sympathy than in the present Lieutenant-Governor of Bengal (cheers.)

CAN MEN SEE GOD?

"BLESSED are the pure in heart for they shall see God" here Christ evidently speaks of the perception of God as a future recompense of purity Such perception is not vouchsafed even to the highest purity of character in this life, but is reserved as a reward in after life. We are not told that the pure in heart do see the Lord; they "shall see the Lord." If this doctrine were fully developed it would come to mean that the infidel does not see God, nor the worldly-minded, nor the sensual, nor the iniquitous, nor even the saint. It is only the dis-embodied spirit of the saint that can hope to see the Lord face to face in the realms of eternity. So far as this world is concerned the perception of the Invisible God must accordingly he declared an impossibility without questioning the profound wisdom of this Christian doctrine or doubting in the least its logical soundness, we still hold such perception to be possible in the present life. In a higher sense, we admit, the privilege of seeing God is possible only in the exalted consciousness of purified humanity in the life to come; but in the lower sense, it is unquestionably within the reach of ordinary faith in the present life. We cannot see Him as the pure and regenerate shall see Him in heaven; yet surely we can see Him, as the trusting child sees the loving parent, or as the opened eye perceives instinctively and without an effort the object before it. How can a sinner see as the pure-minded alone can see? How can seeing the Holy Spirit be realized on earth as it is in heaven? Nevertheless the sinner on earth, a worm though he be, can and does see God with the eye of faith. In fact, by seeing we mean faith. Faith in our theology signifies nothing but an immediate apprehension of the unseen realities of the spirit-world. Whoso has deep and vivid faith in God sees Him. He may be a sinner, he may be a worldly-man, he may have ten thousand imperfections, he can see the great spirit if he has only living faith. Anything like perfect perception is not possible except where there is purity of character. But to ordinary perception nothing is essential save faith. He among us who has said with all the emphasis of direct apprehension, "Thou art" has seen God. Those who are more spiritually-minded than others, whether naturally or by training, possess an advantage in this respect which cannot be ignored or undervalued. The greater a man's faith, the keener his insight, and the more spiritually-minded he is, the more vivid is his perception of God. The power of seeing Divinity denotes only the power of saying with the whole heart and soul, "Here is my God."

Provincial

CUTTACK.

[FROM OUR OWN CORRESPONDENT.]

The 14th July 1876.

I BEG to offer a few thoughts in continuation of what I said in my last. I do not pretend to give your readers anything new, but I mean simply to lay before them what I consider as deserving of serious reflection. With a few exceptions, all the Mofussil Brahmo Somajes with which I happen to be acquainted are more or less in the same predicament: they are all of them making a very slow progress, so slow as hardly to be perceptible. If we inquire into the causes, we shall perhaps find them to be the same. The progress of a Somaj is identical with that of the individual members collectively, and that again depends in a great measure on the life and example of the *leading* members. Where the Minister or other prominent members of a Somaj betray a want of earnestness and living faith, and live a life at best indifferent, no great improvement can be reasonably expected. The article which lately appeared in the *Dharma Tattwa* on this subject, was a very thoughtful one, and a suggestive one too. One great disadvantage which a Mofussil Somaj very often labors under, is the want of a competent Minister. In point of spiritual progress, which ought to be the chief thing to determine the choice of a Minister, there is often found no difference between him and the congregation at large. In faith and spirituality he may be as low as his brother-worshippers, though he may happen to be superior to them in learning or experience, or to occupy a more respectable position in society. A Brahmo Somaj without a *living* Brahmo (I mean of course one spiritually living) is apt to grow every day more indifferent about religion, and to mistake the mere externals for solid virtue. The doctrines and tenets of Brahmoism, to which every body has a free access, if he would only take the trouble to read the theistic publications, are to such Brahmos of no practical importance, as if the truths of religion were simply to be *heard* and *remembered* and not followed in every-day life. To learn things by rote is admittedly a bad thing; but nowhere it is so bad as in religion. A Brahmo having a mere second-hand knowledge of spiritual truths is a very pitiable sight; one who makes such knowledge the measure of his spiritual progress is infinitely more pitiable—nay, painful; yet such self-deception is not a rare phenomenon among the Mofussil Brahmos. I do not mean to speak disparagingly of the Mofussil Brahmos. I sincerely believe that the *second-hand knowledge* of which I have spoken, is sometimes mistaken for spiritual improvement, and a Brahmo thinks he has nothing more to *learn* when he is well versed in Brahmo theology. Thus we see that this second-hand knowledge instead of making us humble, has a tendency to make us self-sufficient and arrogant. We do not even hesitate to place ourselves on the same level with those whose spiritual culture has extended over many years. To suppose that a person who has been for years together a devoted servant of God and a pilgrim in the spirit world, has nothing to give us, clearly implies a belief that there is no such thing as spiritual progress, and that all that it is possible for one to do in religion is to learn a few doctrines by heart, and to repeat certain prayers and hymns from day to day, and to keep up a decent exterior. It would sometimes do a Brahmo a great amount of good to unlearn what he has learned at second hand, and to cease to give himself credit for what he has *heard*. We have not so much to hear and *remember* as to *live*. "Religion," said Mr. Dall in one of his letters to the *Mirror*, "is life, and life is growth." Where there is no inward growth, there is no religion. A Brahmo may be considered as having gained one step in spiritual progress when he can feel that in spite of what he knows of Brahmoism he stands very low, and there are many who are decidedly superior to him. To acknowledge the superiority of another in words is one thing; to feel it, a quite different thing. The latter can only be when we have been accustomed to make a distinction between the doctrines and opinions, on the one hand, and life and spiritual growth, on the other. A Brahmo Somaj in which the members look for spiritual excellence in their Minister and in one another cannot fail to improve day by day. In this low state of spiritual advancement we must take many things upon trust; but we must not stop there. Let us realize them in our own lives. To remain satisfied with the information furnished by our elders, is our chief drawback which the sooner we can remove the better.

Correspondence.

A NATIVE LADY'S DOUBTS AND DIFFICULTIES.

To the Editor of the *Indian Mirror*.

SIR,—I am going to pen a few lines about something which seems very mysterious to me, hoping you will do me the favor of inserting them in a corner of your valuable paper.

I have gone through some portion of the New Testament and have found reason to admit that Jesus Christ was one of the best of men, and his doctrines praiseworthy in the extreme. So far so good. But what is the necessity of a mediator (as he is called) to go to the foot of the throne of the Beneficent Father? Perhaps some Christian would say that if we required to call on a gentleman, we must first apply directly to the *doorman* who will introduce us to the gentleman. But, I think, this is not the case with the Heavenly Father. For who wandering over distant countries, and suffering every kind of hardship, wants a letter of introduction to his father when he returns home after a long absence?

I shall deem it a great favor, Mr. Editor, if any one of your Christian readers explains clearly, through your paper, the necessity of a mediator to be saved.

I remain Sir, yours &c.,
BHUBUN MOHINI DASSI.

The 3rd July, 1876.
BHOWANIPUR.

Devotional

GREAT God, enable me to feel how small I am. In thy majestic presence I am but a worm crawling on the earth, a mere grain of sand. Let me hide myself in shame under an over-powering sense of my utter worthlessness. What am I, O God, before thee? I am as nothing. Lord teach me humility.

O THIS wicked and miserable individuality! Grant, O God, that I may soon be free from it. I would merge my proud self in thee and in the community. I would have no distinct and selfish personality; I would not live for myself, but for the world. Teach me, my Father, to live in mankind and for the good of mankind. May I be absorbed in humanity's cause. Lord root out self and selfishness, and make me one with those around me.

The Brahmo Somaj

A CHRISTIANI Catechist of Chinsurah has just publicly renounced Christianity, and joined the Brahmo Somaj at Burrisal.

THE Anniversary of the Utkal Brahmo Somaj came off on the 2nd instant. In addition to the morning and evening service there were reading of theistic texts, meditations and prayers, hymns &c., in the afternoon. The sermon preached on the occasion was "Humility as an Attribute of God." Most of those present were moved and edified by it. Two gentlemen formally accepted Brahmoism on the occasion. The *utsab*, we are informed, had never been so successful as it was on the last occasion.

ON Sunday, the 16th instant, exactly a month after her demise, Babu Prosunno Coomar Ghose, of Moropooker, performed the *shradha* ceremony of his mother. Besides the relatives of the Babu, a number of Brahmos from Calcutta and Connaghur and almost all our Brahmo missionaries were present on the occasion. After the usual service the minister Babu Bijai Krishna Gossami joined by two other missionaries, seated on either hand, chanted together a number of Sanscrit text, bearing on our obligations to parents, on death and immortality. Babu Prosunno Coomar then offered a prayer invoking Divine blessing on the soul of his departed mother, which was followed by benediction. The Babu then stood up, with his brother, and announced certain charities in honor of their deceased mother. The Upadhaya Babu Gour Gobinda Rai read a list of the charities, which embraced all classes and creeds, and were of an eminently catholic character.

THE Bangalore Brahmos met at the house of their Secretary, Mr Ramaswamy Chetty, and resolved to erect a Mandir at Pettah. The sum of Rs. 400 was collected at the meeting.

WE are glad to see the Southern Presidency is coming out bravely in the matter of practical social reforms. At Bangalore a Brahmo, occupying a high and respectable position in Hindu society, had the courage to perform the funeral rites of his deceased wife in accordance with Brahmic principles. Mourning was kept up for a fortnight, during which there was regular daily prayer. On the last day special service was held, of a most solemn and impressive character, the attendance being extremely large. We should like to know the nature of the reformed funeral rites observed on the occasion.

Literary

MR. ARCHIBALD FORBES of the London *Daily News*, and Mr. Henty of the *Standard*, have proceeded to Servia as "Specials" of those papers.

THE London *Daily News* published a biography of the late Miss Harriet Martineau, which that lady had herself written for that journal in the year 1855 in view (as the London correspondent of the *Indian Daily News* tells us) of what she then thought to be her rapidly approaching end! Miss Martineau contributed more than two thousand leading articles to the London *Daily News*, besides endless contributions to other magazines and reviews. Miss Martineau was consulted for many years by the most eminent politicians (including more than one Prime Minister) upon current political events. Miss Martineau, it is said, "inspired" the policy of more than one English Cabinet.

A BOOK, called "The Prince of Wales in India; being a complete Narrative of his Royal Highness's Travels, from the Time he Left London till his Return to Portsmouth. By George P. Wheeler, of the Inner Temple, Special Correspondent of the *Central News*," is about to appear in a few days.

SOME one who professes to know all about the New York papers has been appraising the money value of them, in the *Cincinnati Gazette*. He says that the *Herald* is worth £400,000, the *Times* £200,000, the *Tribune* the same less a mortgage, the *World* £60,000, the *Journal of Commerce* £160,000, the *Evening Express* £50,000, the *Evening Post* £140,000, the *Commercial Advertiser* £30,000, the *Evening Mail* £20,000, and the *Sun* £40,000.

Latest News

—THE London correspondent of the *Bombay Gazette* says:—The Prince of Wales is so highly gratified that his collection of presents are proving so popular—in fact, they are the chief sight of London—that he has given direction for the exhibition to be kept open till the end of September in order that persons coming up from the country may have an opportunity of seeing them. Many of your Bombay readers will be glad to hear that Dr. Birdwood's services in connection with this exhibition and with the purchase and selection of the presents taken by the Prince to India, have been recognised by His Royal Highness, who has just presented Dr. Birdwood with a massive gold pencil case, handsomely jewelled with emeralds and rubies. There is also some prospect of the more important public services which Dr. Birdwood rendered during his residence in Bombay being rewarded by the India Office.

—As a proof how hard up the Russian Treasury is at present, a London correspondent cites the following instance:—Some time ago the Imperial Government wanted the telegraph line to Siberia duplicated, and this was undertaken by the same contractor who had originally constructed it. The cost was £500,000 and the contractor has been trying for six months to get his money, as yet without success.

—MR. HAMILTON the Magistrate of Puna, was entertained on the evening of Sunday last by the Vakils of Puna, at the residence of Mr. Kasinath Purshram Gadgil.

—GOLD has decreased in value in Bombay to twenty rupees and eight annas a tolah.

—SEVERAL of the embroidery and lace workers of Puna have been thrown out of employment on account of the rise in the value of gold, and the price of lace remaining the same.

—MAJOR HOLROYD has returned to India, and he is about to take over charge of the Directorship of Public Instruction, Panjab, at Delhi, from his officiating *locum tenens*, Mr. C. Pearson, who proceeds at once on two and a half months' privilege leave to Cashmere.

—A LARGE number of mules, sent by the Amir of Cabul, have arrived at Peshawur; and it is rumoured that they are intended for the carriage of a subsidy of 20 lacs of Rupees which, it is asserted, the Amir has demanded from the British Government! Another story regarding them is that they are to take back goods which the Amir has purchased from Seth Ala Buksh, Merchant.

—A CAPTAIN of the 63rd Regiment has killed a lion in the Gir, Kattywar.

—WE hear some of the Native inhabitants of Delhi propose to set up a Spinning and Weaving Mill.

—MR. POGSON, the Astronomer to Government at Madras, has predicted that the rainfall in the Madras Presidency will be very light this year, and still lighter next year.

SIR HENRY DALY has returned from Simla to Indore.

—THE *Indian Church Gazette* hears a rumour that the See of Calcutta was, after the refusal of the Bishop Designate of Melbourne to accept it, offered to some one at Cape Town.

—THERE is every probability that the £10,000 which is being raised in the diocese of Winchester to found an Indian See, will be devoted to a Bishopric in Burmah.

—THERE will be no Camp of Exercise in the Bombay Presidency next cold season.

—*On dit* that the Maharana of Oodeypore is to be married to a daughter of the Maharajah of Kishengurh.

—AN underwriter from Lloyd's is now in Galle, having been sent out to prosecute enquiries as to the causes of the late shipwrecks on that coast.

—LORD TAVISTOCK, heir to the Dukedom of Bedford, is about to be married to the second daughter of Lord Somers, whose mother was a Miss Prinsep, a name well known in India.

—THE Bank of Bombay has again reduced its rates of interest and discount one per cent all round.

—THE unparalleled feat of a lady walking 100 miles in less than a period of 24 hours, was accomplished by Mrs. J. L. Wiltshire, of the City-hall, Auckland, Australia, between half-past 8 o'clock on Friday evening and 20 minutes past 8 o'clock on Saturday evening.

—A FAREWELL Ball was given by the residents of Lucknow to Sir George and Lady Couper on the 20th instant.

—A LUCKNOW paper says:—"Our readers are already aware that the property of the late Mumtaz Mahal is in litigation. The Begum was originally a Hindu, but was converted unto Mahomedanism after her marriage with King Nasir-u-din Hyder. A Hindu brother of the deceased claims the property, and an adopted daughter of the Begum disputes the claim. The case has been filed in the Civil Judge's Court, and clever lawyers have been engaged on both sides. The question is whether a Hindu brother can inherit the property of a Mahomedan sister.

—COLONEL WILLOUGHBY OSBORNE, Political Agent, Bhopal, leaves for England by the next mail steamer. Colonel Kincaid officiates during Colonel Osborne's absence.

—MAJOR-GENERAL Sir Henry Ramsay, Commissioner of Kumaon, has been granted privilege leave for three months.

—MISS C. DURRAY of London, is engaged upon a bust of Sir Jung Jung.

—SIR PHILIP WODEHOUSE, Governor of Bombay, retires early next year. Sir Arthur Hamilton Gordon will be the next Governor. He is the fourth son of the late Earl of Aberdeen, and brother of Lieutenant-General Sir Alexander Hamilton Gordon, who, some few years ago, commanded the Puna Division of the Army. Sir Arthur has been Lieutenant-Governor of New Brunswick, Governor of Trinidad, and Governor of the Mauritius, in all of which appointments he was very popular. He is now Governor of the Fiji Islands, and will be moved thence to Bombay early next spring.

—THE Prince of Wales' medals, intended for presentation to the Native Princes and Chiefs which have lately arrived from England, (says the *Indian Daily News*) have been made over by the Foreign Department to the Calcutta Mint for the purpose of having the names of the recipients engraved upon them. They are about sixty-one in number, *viz.*, sixteen of pure standard gold, each weighing about eight sicca weights, and forty-five medals of pure silver.

—SIR SALAR JUNG will be back in Hyderabad by September or the beginning of October next.

—PRIVATE theatricals took place at Government House, Simla, on Wednesday night. The "Porter's Knot," the only piece on the programme, was admirably played.

—THE *Indian Public Opinion* informs us that an Envoy or Agent of the Russian Government is reported to have reached Cabul *pardu*, and to have had several secret audiences with the Amir Sahib who has received and treated him with honorable kindness and condescension and has shown him much favor. The object of the Russian Agent is believed to be to obtain a binding and reliable pledge of the Amir's neutrality in the affairs of Merv, the people of which had solicited the Amir's aid, on both religious and political grounds, in resisting the Russians; but obviously the Russian Agent has some ulterior object in connection with Russian progress in Central Asia.

—SIR J. STRACHEY will give over his Government to Sir G. Couper, at Lucknow, on Wednesday next, Sir G. Couper immediately afterwards proceeding to his new province—an arrangement, slightly irregular, but sanctioned for Sir J. Strachey's convenience.

—MR. INGLIS leaves Simla in a day or two for Oudh.

—MAJOR SANDEMAN'S negociations with the Khan of Khelat are progressing well.

—THE Russian Government is reported to have issued stringent and general orders to the merchants and traders of Khokand, Samarcand and other places within their recent conquests, directing that they shall, within six months, dispose of all the English calicoes, piece-goods and broad cloths, in their possessions, and shall for the future refrain from importing English goods into Russian territory.

Calcutta.

THE Directors of the Bank of Bengal have again reduced their rates of interest and discount one per cent all round.

THE P. and O. Co.'s S. S. *Malwa*, Commander P. S. Tomlin, arrived in Bombay harbour, on Tuesday last, at 5 P. M. from Suez with the English Mails of the 30th ultimo on board. The following is the list of passengers:—

From Southampton.—Mr. G. F. M. Grant, Mr. Lumsden, Capt. and Mrs. C. M. Beynon, Capt. and Mrs. Pollock, Mr. Bedford, Mr. Beresford, Mr. Sohrabji Eduji.

From Brindisi.—Mr. H. Prinsep, Genl. Burlinge, Mr. Josephs, Major T. Wakefield Mr. E. C. Morgan, Mr. J. M'Gregor Mr. J. W. Chisholm, Mrs. Gamble, Col. and Mrs. Playfair, Mr. and Mrs Banyard, Mr. J. A. Bourdillion, Mr. and Mrs. Watson, Major W. R. M. Holroyd.

Aden.—Thirteen Native deck passengers.

DOMESTIC OCCURENC

Birth.

GHOSE.—On Sunday, the 9th July 1876, the wife of Babu Aghor Nath Ghosh of Bairampur, Bongong Sub-Division, District Nuddia of a son.

Birth.

WIFE of Ram Chundra Trimbuk Raji of a daughter on the 7th July 1876, at Kaladgi, Bombay Presidency.

Law

HIGH COURT.

ORIGINAL SIDE.

PEREMPTORY CAUSE BOARD

FOR

Monday, the 24th July, 1876.

BEFORE

The Hon'ble Mr. Justice Phear,

(Reference.)

Punchcowry Mull v. Sooney Poddar—Hart—Moses.

BEFORE

The Hon'ble Mr. Justice Pontifex.

UNDEFENDED CASES.

Ashootosh Dhur v. Hem Chunder Chunder and ors.—Nemy Chund Bose Remfry.

Ashootosh Dhur and anr. v. Hem Chunder Chunder and ors.—Nemy Chund Bose—Remfry.

Set Sultan Chund Bhunsale v. Punchanun Bysack—Pittar—Gregory.

Kissorymohun Roy and ors. v. Muddoosoodun Bonnerji and ors.—Pittar—1st deft, person, P. D. Dutt.

Hurraykristo Doss and anr. v. Satcowrie Doss and ors.—Watson.

DEFENDED CASES.

(Final Disposal.)

Tariny Churn Bose v. Jeesraj and ors.—Dutt and Mitter—Gillanders.

Chundersekur Mookerjee v. F. F. Wyman (pl. ad.)—Paliologus—Orr and Harriss.

Sreekissen Doss & anr. v. Mohunlall & anr.—Cassell—Moses.

Ram Chunder Ghose v Tincowrie Raha & ors.—T. N. Roys.—Ghose & Bose, P. N. Bose.

Ram Chunder Shaw v. Rajmohun Dutt & ors.—Hart.—Promothonath Bose.

Mocoondomonary Shaw v. Sutrolall Shaw and ors.—Carruthers—Pittar, Gray and Co.

Dunnoo Babu v. Chunnoo Babu—Trotman and Watkins—B. M. Dos.

Baney Madhub Roy v. Bholanath Pyne and ors.—M. N. Holdar—Dhur and Mitter.

Amelia Madden v. G. F. Smith—Leslie—Fink.

S. M. Rukhomoney Dossee v. Tariny Churn Bonnerjee—Remfry—Berners and Co.

A. A. Massa v. A. H. Gowenlock—Hart—Gray and Co.

Advertisements

CALCUTTA MUNICIPALITY.

THE attention of the public is invited to Section 135 of the Calcutta Municipal Consolidation act IV of 1876, by which all latrines and water closets, now supplied, or hereafter to be supplied with water, shall be provided with a cistern of such size and description as the Commissioners shall direct. All such cisterns shall be put up at the cost of the Owner of the house or land so supplied with water.

ROBERT TURNBULL,
Secretary to the Corporation of the Town of Calcutta.

How to Enjoy Life

Is only known when the blood is pure, its circulation perfect, and the nerves in good order. The only safe and certain method of expelling all impurities is to take Holloway's Pills, which have the power of cleansing the blood from all noxious matters, expelling all humours which taint or impoverish it, thereby purify and invigorate and give general tone to the system. Young or old robust or delicate, may alike experience their beneficent effects. Myriads affirmed that these Pills possess marvellous power in securing these great secrets of health by purifying and regulating the fluids and strengthening the solids.

NOTICE.

INFALLIBLE SPECEFICS FOR ASTHAMA, CONSUMPTION, COLIC, GONORRHŒA AND SPERMATORRHŒA !!!

I AM the son of the late Titaram Paul of Midnapore, who, the public is well aware, was acquainted with specific medicines for the above diseases. I fully learnt the mode of preparing those medicines from my late father, and have cured many people of Midnapore, Calcutta, Hughly, and other places since his death, as the annexed testimonial will shew. Any one wishing to be treated by me can apply to me, care of the Manager of the Indian Mirror.

WOOPENDRA NATH PAUL.

MY father was ailing from asthma for a long time. He had recourse to various sorts of treatment, but none of them proved effectual. At last he regularly used the medicine of Babu Upendra Nath Pal, and was, within a month, freed from all disorders. My own experience leads me to admit that the medicine of Upendra Babu is especially efficacious in cases of Asthma.

HEM CHANDRA BHATTACHARJYA,
Editor of Balmiki Ramayana.
AND
Asst. Secretary, Adi Brahmo Somaj.

28th Baisak,
1798 Sakabda.

ALBERT HALL.

PATRON.

His Honor the Lieutenant Governor of Bengal

COUNCIL.

Hon'ble Sir William Muir, K. C. S. I.—*President.*
Rajah Rama Nath Tagore Bahadur C. S. I.—*Vice President.*
Hon'ble J. F. D. Inglis.
Hon'ble Ashley Eden, C. S. I.
Hon'ble H. Bell.
Archdeacon Baly.
Colonel H. E. L. Thuillier, C. S. I.
His Highness the Maharajah of Vizianagram.
Maharajah Kumar of Bettiah.
Hon'ble Rajah Narendra Krishna Bahadur.
Rajah Komul Krishna Bahadur.
Rajah Joteendro Mohun Tagore Bahadur.
Babu Digumber Mitter, C. S. I.
Dr. Rajendralala Mitra.
Hon'ble Nawab Ashgar Ali Bahadur, C. S. I.
Nawab Amir Ali Bahadur.
Moulvi Abdul Latif Khan Bahadur.
Manockji Rustomji Esq.
Babu Keshub Chunder Sen.

SUBSCRIPTIONS.

The Hon'ble Sir Richard Temple	...	Rs.	200
His Highness Maharajah Holkar	...	"	8,000
His Highness Maharajah of Jeypore		"	5,000
His Highness Maharajah of Putialah		"	2,500
His Highness Maharajah of Vizianagram	...	"	1,000
His Highness the Maharajah of Cooch Behar	...	"	1,000
Maharajah Kumar of Bettiah	...	"	2,000
Rajah of Bhinga	...	"	1,000
Maharani Surnomoie, Cossim Bazar		"	1,000
Maharajah of Hutwa	...	"	500
Rajah Roma Nath Tagore Bahadur		"	200
Rajah Komul Krisna Bahadur	...	"	500
Rajah Joteendro Mohun Tagore	...	"	500
Hon'ble Rajah Narendra Krishna Bahadur	...	"	300
Babu Joykissen Mookerjee	...	"	250
Sirdar Dyal Singh	...	"	200
Babu Shama Churn Law	...	"	200
Hon'ble Sir William Muir	...	"	100
Hon'ble Ashley Eden	...	"	100
Dr. Mohendro Loll Sircar	...	"	100
Babu Goonendro Nath Tagore	...	"	100
Babu Jadulol Mullick	...	"	100
Babu Ananda Mohun Bose	...	"	100
Babu Rajkissen Mookerjee	...	"	200
Babu Janoki Nath Mookerji	...	"	100
Hon'ble H. Bell	...	"	100
Babu Debendro Nath Bose	...	"	200
Babu Annoda Prosad Roy	...	"	100

Just Received

AN invoice of Mathematical Instrument Boxes, Color Boxes, Drawing Pencils and various other requisites in Stationery. They are priced very moderately for speedy sale.

H. C. GANGOOLY & Co.,
24, Mangoe Lane, Calcutta

NOTICE.

MAKHON LOLL GHOSE.

No. 91, Radhabazar, Wholesale and Retail Stationer, Account Bookseller, &c.

BEGS to invite the attention of the Public to an Invoice of Commercial and Fancy Stationery of all sorts which he has recently received, and which he is disposing of at moderate prices. He has been long in the Trade, and presumes he has always afforded every satisfaction to the several merchants here who have constantly favored him with orders. Any Moffusil orders accompanied with remittances shall be promptly attended to.

THE INDIAN MIRROR

The Cheapest Daily Paper IN INDIA AND Having an Extensive Circulation

SUBSCRIPTIONS,
(IN ADVANCE.)

	Town.	Mofussil, Including Postage.
Yearly	... Rs. 13 8 0	Rs. 23 0 0
Half yearly	... " 6 8 0	" 12 8 0
Quarterly	... " 3 8 0	" 6 0 0
Monthly	... " 1 8 0	" 2 8 0

Cash sales, One Anna per copy.

Sunday Edition.

Per Annum ... ... Rs. 5

MOFUSSIL SUBSCRIBERS,

Per Annum ... ... Rs. 6 10 0

Via Southampton.	£. S. D.	Via Brindisi.	£. S. D.
Per Annum	0 18 9	Per Annum	1 7 0

Cash sales, Two Annas per copy.

RATE OF ADVERTISING.

First insertion, 8 lines and under, 1 Rupee.

Second and succeeding insertions, 2 Annas per line.

For Advertisements which are to be inserted for a considerable time special contracts may be made on application to the manager.

Domestic Occurrence [illegible]	Non-Subscriber ...	1 Re.
	Subscriber ...	8 As.
Public Engagement each insertion		...1 Re

THE POSITIVE GOVERNMENT SECURITY LIFE ASSURANCE COMPANY, "LD."

Capital, £500,000, with power to increase
AN UNIFORM RATE OF PREMIUM FOR THE WHOLE WORLD
And for all Professions or Employments.
NO ENTIRE FORFEITURE OF POLICIES,
And Lapsed Policies revived without Fine.

Surrender Value of Policies (being 40 per cent. of Premiums paid) fixed at time of effecting the Assurance.

POSITIVE NOTES, OR PAID-UP POLICIES, ISSUED
On each Payment of Premium being made,
ALL NET PREMIUMS INVESTED IN GOVERNMENT PAPER AT COMPOUND INTEREST,
And lodged with Official Trustee to meet claims.

As an outer fortification to the system, £20 out of every £100 paid as capital, is invested in consols in trust, and forms a guarantee fund, which can only be made available on the improbable consequence of a sudden mortality effecting the ordinary life funds of the Company.

Assurances effected in Five different Forms

Whole Life Policies, with payment of Premium, ceasing, at the option of the Assured, after 5, 10, 15, 20, 25, or 30 years.

Whole Life Policies, with Premiums payable during continuance of life.

POLICIES FOR JOINT LIVES payable at decease of the First which shall fail of Two Lives.

POLICIES FOR SHORT TERMS of from 1 to 12 years.

ENDOWMENT POLICIES payable at 50,55,60 or 65 years of age, or earlier in the event of, death.

POLICIES in force, upwards of £1,00,000 (One Million Sterling)

ANNUAL Premium Income, £50,000

A. B. ANTRAM, Manager;
6, Old Court House Street, Calcutta.

POSTAL NOTICE.

Mails for France, Foreign Europe *via* France, the intermidiate Ports, Mauritius and China, for transmission per French Mail Steamer "*Himan*" will be closed at the General Post Office on Saturday, the 29th July 1876, at 7 P. M.

HAROLD & CO.,

3, DALHOUSIE SQUARE, CALCUTTA.

HARMONIUMS.

Harold and Co., call attention to their unequalled stock of rich-toned Harmoniums made especially for India.

FROM RS. 90 TO RS. 900 EACH.

All kinds of Musical Instruments of the best description are always kept in Stock.

ICE! ICE! ICE!

MADE IN FOUR MINUTES

THE PNEUMATIC ICE MACHINE

THIS IMPORTANT INVENTION IS CONSIDERED A BOON TO THOSE LIVING IN TROPICAL CLIMATES.

CAN BE WORKED BY THE MOST INEXPERIENCED HAND AND IS NOT LIABLE TO GET OUT OF ORDER.

From Rs. 175, each Machine complete.

MESSRS. ARLINGTON & CO.

AGENTS.

India General Steam Navigation Company, Ld.

SCHOENE, KILBURN & CO.—*Managing Agents.*

ASSAM LINE.

NOTICE.

Steamers leave Calcutta for Assam every Tuesday, Goalundo every Thursday and leave Debroo-ghur downward every Saturday.

THE Str. "PROGRESS" will leave Calcutta *Via Mutlah* for Assam, on Tuesday, the 25th instant.

Cargo will be received at the Company's Godowns, Nimtollah Ghat, up till noon of Monday, the 24th.

THE Str. "PATNA" will leave Goalundo for Assam on Thursday, the 28th instant.

Cargo will be received at the Company's Godowns, No. 4 Fairlie Place, up till noon of Tuesday the 25th.

Goods forwarded to Goalundo for this vessel will be chargeable with Railway Freight from Calcutta to Goalundo in addition to the regular Freight of this Company.

Passengers should leave for Goalundo by Train of Wednesday, the 26th.

CACHAR LINE NOTICE

REGULAR FORTNIGHTLY SERVICE.

Steamers now leave Calcutta for Cachar and Intermediate Stations every alternate Friday, and leave Cachar downward every alternate Sunday.

THE Str. "CALCUTTA" will leave Calcutta *via Matabanga* for Cachar on Friday, the 28th instant.

Cargo will be received at the Company's Godowns, Nimtollah Ghat, up till noon of Thursday the 27th.

For further information regarding rates of Freight or passage money, apply to

4, FAIRLIE PLACE, } G. J. SCOTT,
Calcutta, 12th July 1876. } *Secretary.*

BABU BASANTA KUMAR DATTA,

HOMŒOPATHIC PRACTITIONER

[illegible]

FRESH INDENT OF

HOMŒOPATHIC

Medicines and other Requisites,
Have arrived from England,
Medicines, Boxes, Books, Pamphlets;
Absolute Alcohol; Cholera-spirit Camphor.

SPECIAL REMEDIES

For Suppressed, Laborious and Difficult menses; Leucorrhœa.

For Hysteria; Spermatorrhœa; Dysentery; Diarrhœa; Cholera.

For Asthma; Pile; Pain; Sore and Diseases of the Children.

Ice, Lemonade, Soda and Tonic water always.

To be had at

DATTA'S HOMŒOPATHIC LABORATORY.

No. 312, CHITPORE ROAD, BURTOLA, CALCUTTA

TERMS—CASH.

☞ Price List can be had on application.

NATIONAL COMPANY.

HOMŒOPATHIC CHEMISTS AND PUBLISHERS

SUPPLY ALL KINDS OF

HOMŒOPATHIC MEDICINES, BOOKS

CASES AND OTHER REQUISITES.

12, COLLEGE SQUARE,

Calcutta.

Printing Materials

MILLER AND RICHARD'S PRESSES, TYPES and all requisites always in Stock.

TERMS CASH.

EWING & CO.

NOTICE.

A QUARTERLY MEETING of the Bengal Social Science Association will be held at Belvedere, on Monday next, the 24th July 1876, at 5 P.M.

The Hon'ble Sir Richard Temple, Bart. K.C.S.I., President of the Association, will preside.

PAPERS WILL BE READ.

"*On the Economic Museum.*" By the Hon'ble Mr. Justice Phear.

"*On Some Results of the late Census of Calcutta.*" By H. Beverley Esq., C.S.

"*On a few facts concerning Village life.*" By the Hon'ble Baboo Issur Chunder Mitter Roy Bahadoor.

All Ladies and Gentlemen interested in the objects of the Association are invited to attend.

ABDOOL LUTEEF,
Hony. Secretary.

Hats, Hats, Hats!!!

C. C. DASS & CO.

SOLA HAT MANUFACTURERS,

74, Radhabazar.

Just opened new Invoices of Silk and Felt Hats and Hawke's Patent Helmets.

CHUNDER & BROTHERS,

25½ & 112, RADHA BAZAR,

CALCUTTA,

TERMS,—CASH STRICTLY.

Cash Boxes of sizes with & without Chubbs locks.
Railway Bags, of Carpet, Leather &c.
Overland trunks of leather.
Scarborough trunks of sizes.
Brass Candlesticks of sizes.
Cricket Bats & Balls.
Chinese Canisters, Square & round.
Compendium of Games of sizes.
Bulleye Lantern, Japanned.
Hand Lamp English, for Table & Wall.
Mathematical & Surveying Instruments.
Drawing & Painting Materials.
Color Boxes of sizes & descriptions.
Magic inkstand in large variety.
Inkstands with & without stands of sizes &c.
Playing Cards of different patterns.
Brass Padlocks of sizes.
Water Cocks (brass) for Iron and lead pipes.
Iron & Lead pipes of sizes.
Note & Letter paper of all sizes & qualities.
Foolscap, Demy, Medium, Royal paper &c.
Printing Papers of sizes &c.
Steel Pens, Quills, Pencils.
Writing Inks, of all colors & sizes.
Bank Books, Pocket Book &c &c.
Fancy & Useful Articles

CALCUTTA }
The 30th June, 1876. } CHUNDER & BROTHERS.

BURAL BROTHERS

(ESTABLISHED IN 1870 A.D.)

JEWELLERS, GOLD AND SILVER-SMITHS AND WATCH-MAKERS,

BY APPOINTMENT

TO

His Excellency the Viceroy and Governor-General of India

AND

HIS HIGHNESS THE MAHARAJAH ADHIRAJ OF BURDWAN.

BURAL BROTHERS,
10, Hare Street.

THEISTIC BOOKS,

FOR SALE.

URDU.

Rahut Hakiki	Rs.	0 3 0
Nizam Konif		0 2 0
Kasaful Ilham		0 2 0
Kholasa, of [illegible] ...		[illegible] 1 0

HINDI.

Upasana Padhati	Rs.	[illegible] 1 0
Bonai [illegible] or Hymn book ...		[illegible]
Tut Bodh		[illegible]
Upanashid Sar		[illegible]
Dharm Dipika		[illegible]

ENGLISH.

Claims of so called Revealed Religion ...	Rs.	[illegible]
New [illegible]		[illegible]
Living God		[illegible]
Higher and Lower Virtue ...		[illegible]

Apply to the Secretary,
BRAHMO SOMAJ OF THE PUNJAB,
Lahore.

SMITH, STANISTREET & CO.

Pharmaceutical Chemists & Druggists

BY APPOINTMENT

To His Excellency the Right Hon'ble

LORD LYTTON, G.M.S.I.

Governor-General of India,

&c., &c.

SYRUP OF LACTATE OF IRON

Prepared from the original receipe. Lactate of Iron, in various forms of preparation, have been in use in France, and generally through the continent of Europe, for some years past, and is highly esteemed as one of the most valuable Chalybeate Tonic Remedies yet introduced. The Syrup, being the most agreeable as well as convenient form of administration is in most general use. It is a most valuable remedy in the following diseases:—Chlorosis or Green Sickness, Leucorrhœa, Neuralgia, Enlargement of the Spleen, &c. In combination with quinine, it has also been very successfully used in the cure of Fever, while to persons of delicate constitution, enfeebled by disease it is invaluable. In bottles. Rs. 2 each.

SYRUP OF THE PHOSPHATE OF IRON Rs. 2 per bottle.

SYRUP OF PHOSPHATE OF IRON AND STRYCHNINE, Rs. 2 per bottle.

SYRUP OF PHOSPHATE OF IRON AND QUININE. Price Rs. 2-8 per bottle.

SYRUP OF PHOSPHATE OF IRON, QUININE AND STRYCHINE. (DR. ATKIN'S TRIPLE TONIC SYRUP,) Rs. 2-8 per bottle.

Smith, Stanistreet & Co.

Invite special attention to the following rates the quality guaranteed as the best procurable:—

Pure Ærated Waters.

Made from Pure Water, obtained by the new process through the Patent Charcoal Filters.

			Rs	As.
Ærated plain (Treble Ærated), per doz.		...	0	12
Soda Water	ditto	„ ..	0	12
Gingerade	ditto	„ ...	1	4
Lemonade	ditto	„ ...	1	4
Tonic (Quinine)	ditto	„ ...	1	4

The *Cash* must be sent with the order to obtain advantage of the above rates.

!!! हुका !!!

!!! HOOKAHS !!!

ENGLISH made Hookahs of various choice designs, colours and sizes ranging in price from Rs. 2 to 5 each, 60 designs to choose from. Apply to

RADANAUTH CHOWDRY,
373, Jorasanko

Printed and published by M. M. RUKHIT, at the INDIAN MIRROR PRESS, No. 15 College Square, for the Proprietor.

The Indian Mirror.

SUNDAY EDITION.

VOL. XV.] CALCUTTA, SUNDAY JULY. 30, 1876. { REGISTERED AT THE GENERAL POST OFFICE. } [NO. 179

CONTENTS.

NOTICE.

All letters and communications relating to the literary department of the Paper should be addressed to the Editor. All other letters should be addressed to the Manager, to whom all remittances should be made payable.

Subscribers will be good enough to bring to the notice of the Manager any delay or irregularity in the delivery of the Paper.

Editorial Notes.

WE have been requested to acknowledge the receipt of a large box of books presented to the Brahmo Somaj of India by the British and Foreign Unitarian Association. We have great pleasure in making this announcement. The books are very valuable, and if carefully perused, will greatly help young Brahmos in the formation of their faith and principles.

DR. SIRCAR'S Science Association was inaugurated with due *eclat* yesterday afternoon. His Honor the Lieutenant-Governor presided. A large and influential audience gathered, and crowded the place. Some of the scientific men of the city were also present. The inaugural address as announced, was delivered by Dr. M. L. Sircar himself. He explained some of the Forces of Nature by experiments, which were popular, and we dare say well-understood, and showed clearly that some of them were convertible. He admited that our primary motion of force proceed from the phenomena of human volition. Towards the end of his lecture he paid merited compliments to the Editor of the *Hindu Pariot*, Father Lafont, to the Lieutenant-Governor, and to his countrymen in general for the great help they had all rendered towards the formation and inauguration of his scientific scheme.

THE late Commander-in-Chief has written to the Secretary of Army Temperance Society from Trieste, congratulating him on the effects of Teetotalism in the army. Referring to the statistics of crime Lord Napier says that the crimes committed by Teetotallers are virtually none. There are now 1466 Teetotallers in the English army in India. And "there can be no doubt that the action of the Society has exercised a most beneficial influence, and the Society deserves the warmest encouragement as long as its action continues to be as discreetly directed as at present." The Society's operations have been hitherto entirely subordinate to the moral control exercised by the commanding officer over the regiment. This is no doubt wise. But what is the Society to do when commanding officers happen to be men who are against the principles of total abstinence from intoxicating liquors?

OUR co-religionists of Bombay seem really earnest to invite Babu Keshub Chunder Sen on a short visit to their city for the benefit of the local Prarthana Samaj. There is some agitation on the subject we find, and two letters, evidently written by men outside the Samaj, have appeared in the Bombay *Statesman*. The hopeful feature in the agitation is that gentlemen outside the circle of members to the Prarthana Samaj are prepared to help towards the successful carrying out of the project of inviting Babu Keshub Chunder. We hope the present earnestness will take effect before long, and as the Babu's time of annual tour is approaching fast, arrangements will be made with the view of securing his presence in Bombay for however short a period of time. For we have no doubt it will do signal and lasting good to the Prarthana Samaj.

WE are perfectly sure there are not many among the European community in India like the man and woman who have been figuring under the name of Mr. and Mrs. Lacey in the Bombay Police Court. These people, who brought a disgraceful charge against Mr. Arbuthnot, the Collector of Bombay, have been proved to have characters very bad indeed. Throughout the whole country, in almost every city, Mr. Lacey has made himself guilty of serious offences such as perjury and forgery, and Mrs. Lacey seems to be hardly better than her husband. The facts elicited during the course of cross examination in the Police Court, were so scandalous that Mr. Lacey had to withdraw the charge of adultery brought against Mr. Arbuthnot. That there was an acquaintance between the latter and Mrs. Lacey is evident, though how far that acquaintance extended it is difficult to say. No one can reasonably doubt now that the Laceys are truly extraordinary in their career of wickedness, and in the interests of society thanks are indirectly due to Mr. Arbuthnot for pushing on the case so far. It would have been better, however, if the special charge, preferred against Mr. Arbuthnot had been sifted to the bottom, and the general public had been convinced by sufficient evidence that this gentleman is perfectly innocent of everything that approaches to undue familiarity with Lacey's abandoned wife. So far as the evidence has gone, we have only to infer Mr. Arbuthnot's innocence from the previous wickedness of the wretched people who prosecuted him with the evident object of extorting money.

WE hope the following affecting story is true. It shows the tender piety which many a widow humbly cherish in their desolate homes, unknown to every one save God:—A clergyman, says the *Rock*, was sent for to visit a young girl who was seriously ill. She was the only child of her widowed mother. The illness proved fatal, and the once hapy wife and mother was left in poverty and desolation. A few days after her child's funeral, the widow called and requested to see the clergyman. After some little hesitation, she put into his hand a small packet, containing money, which she begged he would give to some society which was sending the Gospel to the heathen world. He opened the parcel, and, to his amazement, counted out £20. He at once remonstrated with the widow, told her that, gaining her precarious living as a laundress, she surely ought not to give so large a sum. With great modesty she urged him to take it, and then said: "How I come to have this large sum is just this; when my child was born, I thought she'll live to get married some of these days, and I thought I would begin to put by a little sum to be a store for her then, I began that day with sixpence. You know what happened last week. Well, I thought to myself, the heavenly Bridegroom has come, and He has called her home to be His bride; and

I thought, as he has taken the bride, it is only right He should have the dowry."

A COMPARISON between the relative pay and expenses of a Protestant Missionary and a Roman Catholic Missionary, suggests curious reflections. The facts are supplied by the *Madras Mail* :—

A European Missionary of the Church Missionary Society, appointed in England, who is married, and has children, receives free passage for himself and family and an outfit allowance of Rs. 300 for himself, 230 for his wife, Rs. 300 for a child under three years of age, and Rs. 50 for a child over that age. On his arrival in India he is entitled to a local outfit allowance of Rs. 700 for a house, furniture, &c., and a a monthly salary of Rs. 216, if posted to the Mofussil, or of Rs. 230 at the Presidency, plus Rs. 12-8 per mensem for each child under ten, and Rs. 18-12 per child above ten years of age. When a son of his arrives at fifteen, or a daughter at sixteen years of age, a fixed payment made by the Society for his son or her settlement in life. At stations where there is no house belonging to the Society for his use, he receives house rent varying from Rs. 33 in the Mofussil to Rs. 80 at the Presidency He can also draw Rs. 15 per mensem for a moonshee, which must "not be continued beyond five years without special sanction." When he travels out of his district he receives travelling allowance for himself and family, calculated on a scale slightly in excess of the necessary expenditure. He is permitted to go home on furlough at intervals on sick certificate, when his passage and that of his family to and fro is paid, together with an outfit grant; and subsistence allowance is granted him while at home. And should he become permanently disabled provision is made for him, and, after his decease, for his widow and family, as far as the means of the Society permit. It cannot be said that the Society overpays its missionaries; but it is very evident that a Protestant Missionary in this country represents an expenditure many times in excess of that involved by a Roman Catholic Missionary. * * * * * * * *
The salary of Catholic Missionaries ranges from Rs. 20 to Rs. 50 per mensem according to length of service; and it is wonderful how some of them contrive to subsist on even less than the smaller of these pittances. There is an old missionary at Pondicherry who is said to have supported himself, his servant, and his dog on Rs. 7 per mensem for many years. None of the missionaries at Pondicherry receive more than Rs. 22½ per mensem, as a regular salary, plus an occasional rupee for performing Mass and a little altar wine and altar bread.

MA'YA—OR THE DOCTRINE OF SELF-DELUSION.

THERE is no English word, we are aware of, which expresses half so well the self-deception whereto all men are subject, as the Sanskrit word *Máyá*. Hindu pietists say that a divinely-ordained principle of hallucination governs all the affairs of the world, enters into all the thoughts, feelings, desires, and mutual relations of mankind. The wheel of this is supreme hallcination is perpetually revolving; and men, women, children, events, objects, the whole world, tied blindfold to it, perform the unceasing gyrations of life, death, and endless change. Once in the whirlpool few can get out of it. *Máyá*, impersonated as the typical woman, leads, lures, binds, blinds, stupifies the senses of the soul, and draws humanity down into the fathomless depths of destiny. God himself is considered not free from it, but that the creation of the world is the result of the influence of *Máyá* upon Divine nature. It is self-delusion all, supreme ignorance on the part of positive being of every description. This transcendental nihilism which culminates in the pantheistic abstractions of the *Vedantas*, the Brahmo Somaj has long discarded. But there is a soul of truth in it that we can not but recognise.

Into the constitution of every man there is seen always to enter a strange element of forgetfulness of the real nature of things. Persons and objects are taken for what they are not, and not taken for what they are. Every one interprets the world through the medium of self, and calls men, women, and things by names which belong not to them, views them in relations that are foreign to their nature, and clings to them with a warmth of affection and energy, singularly evanescent, though loud in professoin of permanence. The all-absorbing pursuit of what is for instance called business-life, zealously, regularly, unceasingly followed, which crowds our roads, rivers, markets, banks, public offices, that leads some men to wealth, some men to bankruptcy, most men nowhere at all, leaves no time even to think once of God in the day, is found to cease with the first attack of illness, and to vanish in the thin air with the prospects of approaching death. Yet men do walk in the same track whether they really want money, or whether they do not, led by an irresistible influence over which they have no control! The pursuits of life were made for man, and not he for them, but he is now bound very nearly doomed to pursue what others pursue, by hidden laws and associations that force him onwards till he dies. The loves, the friendships, the relations that float like waves on the surface of society, that play around the nature of men, grown up, old, and young, that dissolve away and are renewed ever so often, that are tender and violent by turns, and continually create circumstances and needs as artificial and as short-lived as they, whence do they come, whither do they tend? We know that at least most of them are perfectly unreal, but we yield ourselves to them all the same, and we are the playthings of our own passions. Remorseful and self-reflective we brood upon the ill-spent past, wondering that we have been so weak, or so bad, not more strong-minded, not better masters of our own situation. But the future is only the prolongation of the past, and the weakness of the weak is as much self-delusion, as the strength of the strong-minded. Why what fatal halluciation is this that would make us do what we do not like, and not let us do what we wish? Where happiness itself is illusory, and the estimate of human perfection is deceitful, will not everything that tends thereto and rises therefrom, be deceitful also? Man thus weaves around himself a network of complicated ideas and relations, every one of which is founded upon a mistake. Other men help towards the confirmation of these mistakes, society is a whirlpool where the mistakes of many revolve round the common centre of self-love. So there is a strange influence by which men move about in their ordinary places in life. The world itself is real, the relations of life are real, human duties and obligations are real. But the ideas men form about them from the point of view that self-love supplies are unreal, and in this unreality whole humanity is sublmerged. It is only knowledge of the Supreme Reality that can change the character of the unrealities of life, and bring out the hidden soul of truth from the surrounding masses of falsehood. It is therefore said that those who know Him, in Him know themselves, and all things as they are, and grieve not. The renunciation of self only can remove the blindness that covers all things with the heavy coating of darkness. The strange self-delusion in the midst of which men have willingly placed themselves, is the cause of a thous and vices and errors. It is the God of Truth alone who can deliver s.

Correspondence.

MR. DALL'S REPLY TO THE QUERY OF "BHUBUN MOHINI DASSI."

To the Editor of the *Indian Mirror*.

SIR,—Allow me to reply to a question in your issue of July 23rd, regarding the necessity of a mediator in our prayers to the Father. This question makes the burden of a letter from our sister Bhubun Mohini Dassi, which you have entitled "A Native lady's Doubts and Difficulties." It is put with a brevity and distinctness that honor at once her head and heart. She says she has gone through "some portion" of the New Testament. Has she read, in the four gospel, John's account of the last table interview of Jesus with his apo stles? If so, will she look once more at verses 23, 26, 27 of the sixteenth chapter of that gospel? Nothing can exceed the plainness with which Jesus first bids those he loves, never to pray to him, and then tells them theyt should not of necessity, give him their petitions to carry up to God, his father and their father Jesus commands all who love God to speak to Him:—and speak to Him directly and immediately, with no person whatever between the finite petitioner and the Infinite Hearer. What Christian, of any sect or church, can deny the word of Jesus himself And what does he tell us? He says to Peter and John and the others, "you say you do not understand me. The day is coming when you will understand me." "In that day" [John 16; 23 v.] ye shall ask me nothing . . . ask the Father!" "He will give it to you." I conceive that Jesus never imagined that a follower of his could be guilty of the sin of praying to him as the most High God. His words "*ye shall ask me nothing*" distinctly cover that blasphemous act with a prohibition clear as words can make it. "Ask me nothing;" neither as principal, nor as intermediary : neither as God nor as mediator. "Ask me nothing." This thought, this command is clear as day-light. But, to make assurance doubly sure, the ever-truthful Jesus reiterates the truth (v. 26) in the following declaration : "I say not that I will pray the Father for you ;" be your mediator in prayer I will not ;—"I need not be." And why ? Because "the Father himself loveth you." "He seeketh such" as love the light "to worship Him." What can please a Father better than to have a loving child run into his arms ?—No ; "I say not that I will pray the Father for you ;"—except as any child of God may pray for another. At times you need me. Ask me then, and I will come to your aid. There are times when you do not need me ; and then I will not put myself forward as your mediator. Why should I ?—Cannot,—ought not a child to speak to his own father ? Yes. At such times "I say not that I will pray the Father for you" (v. 27) "for the Father himself loveth you." Go directly to Him. Ask pardon and strength of God in the name of all that is good and right. Ask, if you choose, in my name, who have shown you, and realized, under all human limitations,—so much that is right and good and holy. I will help you all I can; while others are helping you all they can.—Yes : ask in my name, in my spirit ; but "*ask me nothing;*" nor look to me to pray the Father for you, when your love and faith are strong enough to move you confidingly to pray for yourself.—So I hear Jesus speak ; saying that mediators as teachers, guides, friends, parents, helpers and good shepherds, are God-sent blessings, all through our lives ; and yet that there can be no real spiritual manhood or womanhood until the growing child of God has learned to walk, ; to go to and fro, upon his own feet, without a nurse, a priest or a mediator.

Yours,

DALL.

P. S. Let nothing I have said herein, conflict with my favorite battle-cry of Theism, "God our Father, Man our brother, Jesus our guide" by which I mean our guide to heaven, our highest Benefactor, rallying Centre, and Commander-in-Chief.

C. D.

Devotional

LORD, I am about to engage myself in my daily work. As worldly business perverts the understanding, deadens spiritual susceptibilities and aspirations, excites avarice, cupidity, jealousy, pride and all the baser passions, I humbly surrender myself to thee, and beseech thee to deliver me from these evils. I cannot venture to enter the regions of worldy trials and temptations without invoking thine aid. Help me God.

MY friends complain, O my God, that I do not attend sufficiently to the wants of my wife and children. If I neglect my duties to them I am guilty before thee. But my conscience tells me that in this matter I practise the rule of resignation. My wife and children are in thy hands. My life is in thy hands. Teach me to believe that I ought not to think anxiously about our food or raiment. May we trustingly worship thee and serve thee, and leave all the rest with thee.

The Brahmo Somaj

THERE will be *sankirtan* every evening in the Brahma Mandir, from this day till Sunday, the 20th proximo, when the Bhadro festival takes place. It will be held in the portico, so that both those in the Mandir and passers-by in the streets may hear. This evening *sankirtan* commences half an hour before service, that is, at 7 P. M.

WE have been requested to state that the minister's connection with the *Indian Mirror* and the *Sulav Samachar* as Proprietor ceases on and after the 1st August.

THE revival of the Brahmica Somaj is talked of. The institution did much good to the ladies of the Brahmo Somaj, in the early days of their spiritual life. Whether it will succeed now is problematical. But there is no doubt that our ladies need special sermons and services, adapted to their peculiar wants and difficulties.

ANOTHER Brahmo marriage under Act III of 1872 was solemnized at Dacca, on Wednesday last. Two of our missionaries proceeded there to assist at the ceremony. The bridegroom is Babu Juggut Chunder Doss, B. L., Extra Assistant Commissioner, Tezpore, Assam. The bride, Srimati Soudamini Gupta, second daughter of Babu Kali Narain Gupta, and sister of Babu Krishna Govinda Gupta, C. S. Upwards of five hundred persons were present on the occasion as guests amongst whom were the leading Native gentlemen of the city and a few European gentlemen. We understand that the bride was a pupil of the local Adult Native Ladies' School, and is now 16 years of age.

THEOLOGICAL SCHOOL.

PRESERVATION OF THE WORLD OR PROVIDENCE.

CREATION cannot be said to have stopped. The preservation of the Universe means fresh creation every day. The materials and laws out of which the world is reconstructed they continually. had preexistence of course, and in that sense the preservation of the world may be said to be a pure process of transformation ; but the Active and Combining Principle out of which these materials have their composition, birth, growth, is clearly beyond the possession and thought of man. It is this active principle that may be said to constitute the creative agency in God, but of this more anon. Every thing decays and out of the decay new existences spring into being. The Universe is full of death and birth, youth and old age. Its maintenance and preservation mean but the remodification of the inexhaustible store of materials out of which it is constructed. In going to seek the deep causes of this preservative redevelopment of things we arrive most certainly at a number of seconday active principles, which though intangible in themselves and invisible on the surface, are the causes of the origin and preservation of things, their decline and decay, and their transformation into new life. These important agents in the providence of the world are called by the simple name of *Forces*. The forces of nature have long been the prolific source of human faith and unbelief, and all manner of theories about Divine government and the self-preservation of the world,

The forces of Nature are divisible into certain heads such as, Mechanical, Chemical, Vital &c. These forces are the active principles of all the change that we see around, Unseen themselves they are continually seen in their manifestations and their essential character eludes the purely material scrutiny of the scientific man In this sense, therefore, the forces of the Universe are admitted to be hyperphysical in their nature and essence. They do not come within and are not exhausted by the rigorous law of phenomena that confines all things within the limits of co-existence and succession. There is evidently something more in them. "The word force," says Mr. Grove, "and the idea it aims at expressing, might, indeed, be objected to by the physical philosopher as representing a subtle mental conception, and not a sensuous perception or phenomenon. To avoid its use, however, if open to no other objection, would be so far a departure from recognized views as to render language scarcely intelligible." So there is no help for scientific men but to recognize the forces of nature as the original principles of all phenomena. The origin of the forces, therefore, will explain the whole order, providence and preservation of the Universe.

Forces are many in number, so far as their scientific classification goes Nature is supplied with sources of power corresponding to the number of products which she displays. And the difference in the effects is attributed to the difference in the originative principles. The classification of the Natural Sciences has been in accordance to the old classification of the forces of nature. But the progress of scientefic research has made it clear that the classification is essentially defective. Forces have been known to merge into each other and their intimate co-relation is oftentimes physically and mentally inseparable. The phenomena of electricity and magnetism, of heat and light are often known to proceed from common principles which in certain stage of their development are therefore convertible. This experience about the forces of nature, leads to simplify the old classification and suggests the idea that all these forces disguise within them an identity of power which [shapes itself into different causes in accordance to the nature of the effects which it has to produce. In fact, so far as the consciouness of force goes, no other theory seems to be tenable Force as apart from the mechanical fact of an impulse communicated by one body to another, represents a consciousness of effort and the possession of an independent agency to produce changes only realizable in the department of the human mind. "The energy of volition," says Dr. Carpenter, "communicates itself to the motory nerves, these again hand over the stimulus to the muscular fibre, by whose contraction some mechanical movement is produced"—a motion which can be transmitted, undiminished from body to body through an indefinite space of time. So far as human experiences go the plurality of forces is a mistake. There is but one force behind all phenomena—the prolific cause of infinite changes, and that force is in the will of an intelligent being. If then all the active principles in creation that give rise to the laws and facts, which science enumerates, be resolvable into an all-pervading and all-governing Mind and the *will* which that Mind exercises, we are not far from a rational and theistic philosophy as to the providence and preservation of the world. Thus both science and religion prove the Divine mind and *will* to be the originating cause of all causes, and prove nature as carrying out His infinite purposes of goodness and truth towards all creatures.

Literary

On the first of July, there was published, in Florence, the first part of a magazine, which is to be issued twice a month, called the *Bollettino Italiano degli Studii Orientali*. The founders of the new periodical are the Professors of Oriental languages in the Istituto di Studii Superiori—D. Castelli, Professor Extraordinary of Hebrew; Fausto Lasinio, Professor of Arabic; A. Severini, Professor of Chinese and Japanese; C. Puini, Professor adjunct; A. De Gubernatis, Professor of Sanskrit. Prof. De Gubernatis is the editor; the sub-editor, to whom communications should be addressed, is Dr. Puini. The subscription is 10s. a year, and Messrs. Trubner will receive English subscriptions.

THE priests of the East Shinshu sect of Buddhists in Japan have become zealous for the propagation of their religion and a thorough acquisition of its tenets. They have accordingly selected two of the most promising of their novices, who are to be sent first to England to study Sanskrit, and subsequently, when sufficiently advanced in that language, proceed to India, and there make themselves thoroughly conversant with the doctrines of the sect as taught in the home of Buddha. A number of novices are also to be sent to China to pursue their studies there.

THE Moormen of Colombo "in view of their rising importance and the present position of affairs in Turkey," have established a newspaper, published in the Tamil vernacular. It is designed *Puthinalankari* which being freely interpreted, means. "The Embellished Lady of News."

THE Oriental Congress at St. Petersburg having invited the Anjuman-i-Punjab, Lahore, to depute a representative to the Congress, the Anjuman lately solicited His Honor the Lieutenant-Governor to move the Government of India to send their President, Dr. G. W. Leitner, Principal of the Government College, Lahore, as the delegate of India in that assembly. The Punjab Government have written in reply to say that "there is no intention on the part of the Punjab Government to send officially any officer to represent the Province as suggested in the Anjuman's letter; but the Lieutenant-Governor is quite aware of the qualifications of Dr. G. W. Leitner, President of the Anjuman, to represent it with credit at St. Petersburg, and should the Society desire to depute him on their behalf, paying his expenses as proposed in the 6th para of their letter, His Honor the Lieutenant-Governor would be prepared to ask the Government of India to grant Dr. Leitner such special leave as may be necessary for the time of his absence." Dr. Leitner has refused to accept any money from the Anjuman, and says that it is too late now to avail himself of the offer of the Punjab Government.

Gleanings

FROM HINDU DEVOTEES.

(Translated from the Bengali.)

RAM CHARAN.

THE body is the temple of Rama. The earnest desire to know Him is his *arati*, and to remember always is true prayer. No *puja* is like that of always remembering God and no votive offering is like self-surrender. Renounce your pride and make yourself humble, then God will accept your offerings. He who understands that his body is a temple and Rama is the tutilary God of it, is fully satisfied. Do not wish to gain any reward if you have done any good work, but try to be happy by being always content, kind to those who are poor and good and peaceful. Always be truthful, renounce your anger, and carefully guide your tongue. Recite the name of Rama in the mind and try to know him. Be void of all desire and be content; be merged in the sea of Divine communion. The *Fakir* who drinks the nectar of Divine love, always clings to God with his heart. He does not live in vain. Whether he is asleep or awake he never forgets God, and he rules over his passions, forgives every one and checks carnal affections and undue desires. He never prays to any one except Rama, and if the thirty-three million Gods is angry with him he does not care about it.

Man dresses himself in beautiful and perfumed clothes, and proudly walks in the world. Though his outward appearance is very nice, yet his mind is unclean. He is puffed up with vanity when he looks into the looking glass, but he does not know that his body will be annihilated at last and the beautiful coating of skin which hides the uncleanliness of his mind will be destroyed.

He whose bed is the rock, whose seat is the sky, whose arms are his pillow and who eats out of earthen pots, is the true *Fakir*. He is the lord of the four quarters of the globe. No one disregards him. It is true he lives by begging, but kings and peasants both respect him.

TOOLSI DASS

THE Clouds send down thunder, lightnings and hail-stones, yet the *Chataka* never looks to any other directions for its drinks but to the clouds.

There are many rivers and seas in the world, but *Tulsi* says that to the *Papia* except the waters of the star *Swati* all other water is like dust.

Latest News

—THE Bank of Bombay has again reduced its rates of interest and discount one per cent. all round.

—MISS BRITAIN has been delivering an address at the Prayer Meeting Room in the Cantonment, at Trichinopoly, on the subject of Zenanas.

—THE *Rast Goftar* of Bombay earnestly recommends those Natives in search for employment to enter themselves as students at the Agricultural College on the Sydapet Farm, Madras, established under the superintendence of Mr. A. Robertson, of the Farm. The *Rast's* Editor has been at some pains to enquire further into the matter, and Mr. Robertson, in his letter of reply, assures our contemporary that "the climate of Sydapet and neighbourhood is one of the most healthy in India."

—A MEETING of the Anjuman-i-Punjab took place at the Sikha Sabha Hall at Lahore, in order to take into consideration Lord Salisbury's speech at the Cooper's Hill College. In this speech Lord Salisbury made use of the following words:—"There was one drawback which had a tendency to increase the distance between the governing and the governed. From conversation which he had had with several gentlemen who were on the staff of H. R. H. the Prince of Wales during his recent visit to India, they had brought home a painful impression that there was a coldness between the two races; he urged, therefore, the necessity of welcoming the entry of Natives into the covenanted service rather than grudging them that privilege."

—A SLIGHT shock of an earthquake was felt at Peshawur on Saturday, the 22nd instant, at 2 P.M., but no damage was caused.

—THE Rajah of Nabha paid a state visit to His Honor the Lieutenant-Governor at Simla, on the evening of the 21st July.

—BISHOP MECRIX returns from Cochin to Bombay immediately. The Syro-Roman Catholic dispute is settled. The Bishop promises the appointment of a Syrain Bishop.

—RAJ NARAIN DASS has been appointed to act as Judge of the Lucknow Small Cause Court in the room of Captain Pitcher.

—THE Jeypore correspondent of the *Indian Public Opinion* says that Saidu Sing, Nazim of Jeypore, has been dismissed from office by the Maharajah of Jeypore for an act of indecency in public Durbar, and that Thakur Bogi has been appointed in his room; also that a forest official is accused of having wounded a Chaprasi on the arm with his sword.

—A RUSSIAN Envoy, armed with credentials from the Russian Governor of Turkistan, has arrived at Cabul, but the *object* of his mission is not yet apparent.

—KHAN-KHANAN KHAN, the A. D. C. of the Viceroy, who lately visited the Amir of Cabul for the purpose of delivering a letter from the Viceroy to the Amir, returned some time ago, says the Lahore *Public Opinion*. It has leaked out that the purport of the said letter was a request to establish two British Missions in Afghanistan, and to depute an English Medical Officer specially to Cabul, whose medical services would be available to the Amir, who however has declined the request on political grounds, after consulting Akhund Mullah Mushk Alum of Ghuzni, who is one of his principal and most trusted spiritual advisers, and in whose sincerity and disinterestedness the Amir has the highest confidence.

—THE Amir of Cabul has celebrated the marriage of his grand-son, Ahmed Ali Khan (the son of the late Sirdar Mahomed Khan, the former heir-apparent) with great *eclat* and festivities.

—THE Amir of Cabul's military strength is now reported to be about 100,000 men under arms distributed into—67 Regiments of Infantry, 30 Batteries of Artillery of sorts, 20 Regiments of Cavalry; and it is asserted that he has raised the pay of the private soldiers to 7 Rs. each per man per mensem.

—A SOLDIER of the Amir of Cabul's regular army having robbed and murdered a traveller, he was crucified by the special order of the Amir as a deterrent example to others.

—A MEETING of the Anjuman-i-Punjab took place on Thursday evening last, at which the following matters were discussed:—

1. Rudeness of Railway subordinates to Native passengers.
2. Inadequacy of the punishment awarded by Mr. Leeds, Magistrate of Agra.
3. Conversion of the Anarkali Book Club into a Free Public Library.
4. Address of Congratulation to Her Majesty the Queen on her adoption of the title of Empress of India.
5. Deputation to the Oriental Congress at St. Petersburgh.
6. Reply to Government regarding Mr. Dew's proposal to adopt the Roman characters for the Indian alphabets.

—MR. H. PRINSEP, late Acting Judicial Commissioner of Mysore, returned to India form three months' leave to England in the *Malwa*.

—MESSERS CHALK AND TURNER, Solicitors, Bombay, have addressed a letter to the local papers to state that they did not undertake the scandalous Lacey case without careful enquiry, and that they afterwards resolved to withdraw from it as soon as the sense of professional duty would permit. When they applied for the summons on the 10th inst. (which they did to the Magistrate in his private room), they had no knowledge of the character of the principal parties, but they had—

1.—The information of Lacey.
2.—The deposition of his wife.
3.—The deposition of their coachman.
4.—Eleven letters written by the defendant Arbuthnot to Mrs. Lacey.
5.—The statement of Forward.
6.—Notes of other corroborative evidence.

—THE Bombay High Court was closed on the 24th instant out of respect for the memory of Mr. Dhirajlal Mathuradas, the late Government Pleadar at Bombay. Before closing the Court Sir Michael Westropp, the Chief Justice, expressed his great regret at the loss sustained by the death of Mr. Dhirajlal. He had been practising for the last 25 years, and was very popular. Sir Michael referred to "his highly straightforward and honorable conduct."

—THE King of Siam has opened a new Mint at Bangkok.

—THREE villages are said to have been swept off and several lives lost by the floods near Dinapore.

—COLONEL GEORGE CHESNEY has not been appointed as successor to Sir William Muir.

—THE Maharajah of Bhurtpore is about to visit Simla, where he is expected on the 15th of the next month.

—THE Anjuman-i-Punjab offers to buy the books of the Lahore Book Club and present them to Lahore as a free public library. Already the Anjuman has started a free Native Library in the city.

—THE Burdwan epidemic fever is said to have ceased to trouble the inhabitants of that District.

—SPECIAL prayers are being offered up by the Mahomedans in the Mosques at Bombay in behalf of Turkey.

—THERE is a report that Tao, the Chinese General, has committed suicide, owing to the rout of his army by the forces of Yakub Beg of Kashgar.

—THE *Kowaid Mumbai*, Bombay, says that the notorious Damodhur Punt, a Baroda celebrity, a few days ago, wrote a letter to one Rao Saheb Gujanund Wittul, a member of the Baroda Police, in which the following assertions are made:—"But I find that your kind regards for me have so much lessened. But you ought to keep them as you did before, because I have done all these things relying upon you. And although I am here still I rely upon you. And this be, as it is I received twelve hundred rupees on account of my *warshasan* [annual allowance]."

—MESSRS. GROSVENOR, Davenport and Baber arrived at Hongkong by the French mail on the 25th June *en route* for Shanghai, where they will be met by Sir Thomas Wade, who has left Peking for that port. No information could be elicited from them as to the Mission.

—IT would appear that the Government of Baroda intend to give greater attention to the requirements by young men of the province of the fine arts. Sir Madava Rao has procured from Madras many copies of Lord Napier's lectures.

Calcutta.

MR. TURNBULL, the energetic Secretary to the Municipality, has prepared an alphabetical index to the Municipal Act.

AT the last meeting of the Bengal Social Association, held at Belvedere, on Monday last, Mr Justice Phear read an able and exhaustive paper on the Calcutta Economic Museum, to the advancement of which Mr. Phear contributed so largely. Mr. Phear complained of the want of co-operation and assistance on the part of the District Officers in Bengal in promoting the cause of Economic science. Mr. H. Bell who proposed a vote of thanks to Mr. Phear, defended the District Officers against this charge. Mr. Bell alluded to the hard work done by them. His Honor the Lieutenant-Governor "was, for his own part, not disposed to pity the over-worked Collectors when they were engaged in the task of collecting specimens for the Economic Museum, because he considered it to be the essential duty of these officers to be well acquainted with the natural products of the Districts of which they were in charge, and to give all necessary information on the subject," and he also hoped that the Native gentlemen would render all the assistance in their power to the Economic Museum. The Rev. Dr. K. M. Banerji and others spoke of the great obligation of the Bengal Social Association to Mr. Phear for his valuable co-operation. The services of Mr. Phear to this country both as a citizen and as a Judge also received most honorable mention. "In losing Mr. Phear," Mr. Bell said, "we should not only lose a most conscientious, painstaking, and able Judge, but we should lose a man who was always ready to devote his time and abilities to all questions that concerned the prosperity and well-being of the country." His Honor the Lieutenant-Governor observed "no Judge ever commanded the confidence of European and Native alike as Mr. Justice Phear did." His Honor added:—"He thought he might safely count Mr. Phear among the many Englishmen who had done their best for the welfare of the country in which they lived—such as David Hare, Drinkwater Bethune, Lyall and D. L. Richardson (cheers); and he was sure they would all join in bearing testimony to these services." Though we most readily and gladly acknowledge the value of the services rendered by Mr. Phear to this country, and yield to none in our admiration of that distinguished gentleman, we cannot go the length of including Mr. Phear in the same category with Mr. David Hare. But His Honor now and then indulges somewhat in hyperboles. Did we not notice it the other day in the case of Sir Stuart Hogg?

A TELEGRAM from London to the *Pioneer* states that Mr. J. S. White, late Advocate-General of Bombay, succeeds Mr. Justice Phear at the Calcutta High Court.

MR. J. B. ROBERTS declines to be elected a Municipal Commissioner of Calcutta.

WE are requested to announce for the information of the Bethune Society and the public in general, that a special meeting of the Society will be held at the Theatre of the Medical College to-morrow, the 31st instant, at 8½ P. M. to take into consideration the best means of commemorating the eminent services rendered to the Society by its retiring President, the Hon'ble Mr. Justice Phear.

THERE will be a special meeting of the Ootterparah Hitakari Sabha this day, at 3 P. M., to meet the Hon'ble J. B. Phear.

THE following report has been issued by the Directors of the Bank of Bengal:—Although there has been no activity in trade during the past half-year high rates of interest have prevailed. The decline in the value of silver, and the continuous and heavy fall in Sterling Exchange, which led to the partial suspension of the sale of the Secretary of State's bills on India, had the effect of disorganizing the local money market.

The half-year opened with the Bank's minimum rate of interest at 4 per cent., which was advanced by successive steps until on 13th April, it stood at 11 per cent.; towards the end of that month it was reduced to 10 per cent., and further reductions followed, the half-year closing with the rate at 7 per cent.

The net profits for the 6 months at Head Office and Branches, amount to Rs. 13,62,711-6-0; this sum, with Rs. 3,594-4-6 brought forward from last half-year, makes a total of Rs. 13,66,305-10-6, which the Directors have dealt with as follows:—

I.—In payment of a Dividend at the rate of 10 per cent. per annum... ...	Rs. 10,00,000 0 0
II.—Transfer to Reserve Fund	2,00,000 0 0
III.—To provide for depreciation in the Bank's Investments in Government Securities	98,620 2 2
IV.—Transfer to Bad Debt Fund...	25,000 0 0
V.—Carried forward to the Profit and Loss Account of next half-year ...	32,685 8 4
	Rs. 13,66,305 10 6

During the half-year the Directors have closed the Mirzapore and Mirzapore Branches which were no longer profitable.

Since 1st May the Bank has been working under the provisions of the "Presidency Banks' Act XI of 1876." On that date the Government ceased to be a Shareholder, and in pursuance of the arrangement mentioned in the Directors' last report, the shares for 22 lacs held by Government were taken over by the Bank and shares for 20 lacs cancelled, thus reducing the Bank's capital to 2 crores of rupees, represented by shares of Rs. 500 each, which are divisible into half-shares, and convertible into Stock.

The Agreements for the conduct of the Government business at Calcutta and at the Bank's Branches have been concluded and the Directors have satisfaction in stating that the term of the Agreement for the conduct of the Government business at Calcutta has been fixed at 10 years. The Agreements for the conduct of the Government business at the Branches are subject to termination on 3 months' notice from either party.

At the Annual General Meeting in August, Mr. R. A. Lyall and Mr. J. J. Guise retire from office as Directors, but are eligible for re-election, and offer themselves accordingly. Auditors will have to be elected for the ensuing year, and their remuneration fixed. Mr. H. Roberts and Mr. H. W. I. Wood, the present Auditors, also offer themselves for re-election.

The Directors annex the usual half-yearly statements of accounts, together with the report of the Auditors.

BOARD OF DIRECTORS (IN THE ORDER OF ROTATION).

J.J. Guise, Esq., of Messrs. Gisborn & Co.
R.A. Lyall, Esq, of Messrs. Lyall, Rendie & Co.
J.F. Ogilvy, Esq., of Messrs. Gillanders, Arbuthnot & Co.
The Hon'ble J. R. Bullen Smith, C.S.I., of Messrs. Jardine, Skinner & Co., President,
W.T. Berners, Esq., of Messrs. Ashburner & Co.
The Hon'ble David Cowie, of Messrs. Colvin Cowie & Co., Vice-President.

ACKNOWLEDGMENTS.

Notices of Sanskrit MSS. By Rajendralala Mitra LL. D. Published under orders of the Government of Bengal. Volume III, Part IV. Calcutta.

Calcutta University Mathematical Papers, Part II. First Examination in Arts Papers with Solutions. By P. Ghosh, Lecturer, Cathedral Mission College. Calcutta. Thacker Spink and Co.

Law

HIGH COURT.

ORIGINAL SIDE.

PEREMPTORY CAUSE BOARD

FOR

Monday, the 31st July, 1876.

BEFORE

The Hon'ble Mr. Justice Pontifex.

UNDEFENDED CASES.

Goorooddoss Ghose v. Sheik Assadur Rohoman and ors—Lew—P. C. Mookerji.

J. O. Moses v. Ameer Ally Khan—Dover—Sen & Farr.

Jadub Chunder Burrah Muddock v. Deenonath Mondle & anr—Promothonath Bose.

Hafeezoonissa Bibee v. S. M. Gungamoney Dossee—Bose and Dutt—Ghose and Bose.

Moorleydhur Sen v. Shurfoonissa Begum and anr.—Farr.

W. C. Trotman and anr. v. Gholam Hyder Khan and anr.—Watkins.

DEFENDED CASES.

(Final Disposal.)

Amelia Madden v. G. F. Smith(pt. hd)—Leslie Fink.

S. M. Rakholmoney Dossee v. Tariny Churn Bonnerjee—Remfry—Berners and Co.

A. A. Mass v. A. H. Gowenlock—Hart—Gray and Co.

Sreegopal Misser and anr. v. Purbutty Beeby and anr.—Carapiet—Joykissen Gangooly.

Toylockonauth Multylol v. Dwarkanauth Biswas—Dutt and Mitter—Bose and Dutt.

Tariney Churn Bose v. Rampersaud and anr.—W. C. Bonerjee—N. N. Sen.

Bolasseram Sing Ameenh v. Sewram Doss—Dignam and Robinson—Gillanders.

Shaik Sefatoollah and ors. v. Nundo, Mohun Shaw and anr.—Nobin Chand Burral—B. M. Dass.

Roy Latchmeput Singh v. Meer Asruff Ally—Beeby and Rutter—Carruthers.

Kalleesundun Paul and Another v. Upendronarain Nundy and ors—P. N. Bose—Bose and Dutt.

Matilda Casella v. S. M. Ganodamoye Dossee—Francis—Grees Chunder Ghose,

Advertisements

MUNICIPAL ELECTION.

NOTICE is hereby given that the list of qualified voters and the list of persons qualified to be elected as Commissioners under Act IV (B. C.) of 1876 has this day been posted up at the Police station in each Ward, at the Town Hall, and at the Municipal Office, in the manner prescribed by Section 19 of aforesaid Act.

The following statement gives the number of qualified voters in each Ward.

Ward No.	Voters.	Ward No.	Voters.	Ward No.	Voters.
1	419	7	225	13	127
2	787	8	429	14	92
3	400	9	393	15	79
4	431	10	182	16	25
5	512	11	286	17	30
6	642	12	165	18	17
	3191		1680		370
			Grand Total		5241*

The number of persons qualified to stand for election as Municipal Commissioners is 438.

A copy of the list of persons qualified to be elected as Municipal Commissioners will be forwarded to each voter, and each person qualified to be elected as a Commissioner will receive a copy of the list of qualified voters.

R. TURNBULL.
Secretary to the Commissioners.

The 31st July 1876.

* The actual total number of voters as shewn in the General Register is 4996. The difference is owing to persons entitled to vote in more Wards than one being entered in each Ward in which they are entitled to vote.

NOTICE.

MAKHON LOLL GHOSE.

No. 91, Radhabazar, Wholesale and Retail Stationer, Account Bookseller, &c.

BEGS to invite the attention of the Public to an Invoice of Commercial and Fancy Stationery of all sorts which he has recently received, and which he is disposing of at moderate prices. He has been long in the Trade, and presumes he has always afforded every satisfaction to the several merchants here who have constantly favored him with orders. Any Mofusil orders accompanied with remittances shall be promptly attended to.

ALBERT HALL.

PATRON.

His Honor the Lieutenant Governor of Bengal

COUNCIL.

Hon'ble Sir William Muir, K. C. S. I.—*President.*
Rajah Roma Nath Tagore Bahadur C. S. I.—*Vice-President.*
Hon'ble J. F. D. Inglis.
Hon'ble Ashley Eden, C. S. I.
Hon'ble H. Bell.
Archdeacon Baly.
Colonel H. E. L. Thuillier, C. S. I.
His Highness the Maharajah of Vizianagram.
Maharajah Kumar of Bettiah.
Hon'ble Rajah Narendra Krishna Bahadur.
Rajah Komul Krishna Bahadur.
Rajah Joteendro Mohun Tagore Bahadur.
Babu Digumber Mitter, C. S. I.
Dr. Rajendralala Mitra.
Hon'ble Nawab Ashgur Ali Bahadur, C. S. I.
Nawab Amir Ali Bahadur.
Moulvi Abdul Lutif Khan Bahadur.
Manockji Rustomji Esq.
Babu Keshub Chunder Sen.

SUBSCRIPTIONS.

The Hon'ble Sir Richard Temple ...	Rs.	200
His Highness Maharajah Holkar ...	„	8,000
His Highness Maharajah of Jeypore	„	5,000
His Highness Maharajah of Putiala	„	2,500
His Highness Maharajah of Vizianagram ...	„	1,000
His Highness the Maharajah of Cooch Behar ...	„	1,000
Maharajah Kumar of Bettiah ...	„	2,000
Rajah of Bhinga ...	„	1,000
Maharani Surnomoie, Cossim Bazar	„	1,000
Maharajah of Huttwa	„	500
Rajah Roma Nath Tagore Bahadur	„	200
Rajah Komul Krisna Bahadur ...	„	500
Rajah Joteendro Mohun Tagore ...	„	500
Hon'ble Rajah Narendra Krishna Bahadur ...	„	300
Babu Joykissen Mookerjee ...	„	250
Sirdar Dyal Singh ...	„	200
Babu Shama Churn Law ...	„	200
Hon'ble Sir William Muir ...	„	100
Hon'ble Ashley Eden ...	„	100
Dr. Mohendro Loll Sircar ...	„	100
Babu Goonendro Nath Tagore ...	„	100
Babu Jaduloll Mullick ...	„	100
Babu Ananda Mohun Bose ...	„	10C
Babu Rajkissen Mookerjee ...	„	200
Babu Janoki Nath Mookerji ...	„	100
Hon'ble H. Bell ...	„	100
Babu Debendro Nath Bose ...	„	200
Babu Annoda Prosad Roy ...	„	100
Babu Digumber Mitter ...	„	100

Ulcerations of all kinds.

There is no medicinal preparation which may be so thoroughly relied upon in the treatments of the above ailments as Hollways Ointment. Nothing can be more simple and safe than the manner in which it is applied, nothing more salutary than its action on the body, both locally and constitutionally. The Ointment rubbed round the part affected enters the pores as salt penetrates meat. It quickly penetrates to the core of the evil and drive it from the system,

Just Received

AN invoice of Mathematical Instrument Boxes, Color Boxes, Drawing Pencils and various other requisites in Stationery. They are priced very moderately for speedy sale.

H. C. GANGOOLY & CO.,
24, Mangoe Lane, Calcutta.

FOR SALE.

AT THE BRAHMO SOMAJ OF INDIA

MISSION OFFICE.

No 13, Mirzapore Street.

	Rs.	As.	P
Brahmo Pocket Diary, 1876 ...	0	8	0
Behold the Light of Heaven in India ...	0	6	0
Sacred Anthology ...	2	0	0
Last Days of Rajah Ram Mohun Roy ...	1	0	0
Essays, Theological and Ethical ...	0	2	0
Historical Sketch of the Brahmo Somaj	0	4	0
Jesus Christ, Europe and Asia ...	0	3	0
Future Church ...	0	3	0
True Faith ...	0	2	0
Brahmo Somaj Vindicated ...	0	2	0
Popular Tracts, Nos. 1 to 4 ...	0	2	0
Destiny of Human Life ...	0	2	0
Reconstruction of Native Society ...	0	1	0
Welcome Soiree in England ...	0	1	0
Lecture on Inspiration ...	0	4	0
Essential Principles of Brahma Dharma	0	1	0
Proceedings of the Marriage Law meeting at the Town Hall ...	0	2	0
Theistic Annual 1872 ...	0	8	0
Ditto Ditto 1873 ...	0	8	0
Ditto Ditto 1874 ...	0	8	0
Ditto Ditto 1875 ...	1	0	0
Ditto Ditto 1876 ...	1	0	0
Lecture on Progress of Theism ...	0	2	0
Ditto Age of Enlightenment ...	0	3	0
Lecture on Marriage Law ...	0	2	0
Ditto on the Jains ...	0	2	0
Man the Son of God ...	0	1	0
Order of Service ...	0	1	0
Prayers for Different Occasions of Life	0	2	0
Theistic Devotions ...	0	5	0
Epistles to the Theists in India ...	0	0	0
Lecture on Prayer ...	0	1	0
Ditto Alcohol ...	0	1	6
Practical Sermons of Rev. Dr. Carpenter	0	12	0
Memoir of Rev. Dr. Carpenter ...	0	12	0

THE INDIAN MIRROR

The Cheapest Daily Paper

IN

INDIA

AND

Having an Extensive Circulation

SUBSCRIPTIONS,
(IN ADVANCE.)

	Town.			Mofussil, Including Postage.		
Yearly ...	Rs. 13	0	0	Rs. 23	[illegible]	[illegible]
Half yearly ...	„ 6	8	0	„ 11	8	0
Quarterly ...	„ 3	8	0	„ 6	0	0
Monthly ...	„ 1	8	0	„ 2	8	0

Cash sales, One Anna per copy.

Sunday Edition.

Per Annum ... ... Rs. 5

MOFUSSIL SUBSCRIBERS.

Per Annum ... ... Rs. 6 10 0

VIA SOUTHAMPTON. £. S. D.	VIA BRINDISI. £. S. D.
Per Annum 0 18 9	Per Annum 1 7 0

Cash sales, Two Annas per copy.

RATE OF ADVERTISING.

First insertion, 8 lines and under, 1 Rupee.

Second and succeeding insertions, 2 Annas per line.

For Advertisements which are to be inserted for a considerable time special contracts may be made on application to the manager.

Domestic Occurrences	Non-Subscriber ...	1 Re.
	Subscriber ...	8 As.
Public Engagement each insertion	...	1 Re

ICE! ICE! ICE!

MADE IN FOUR MINUTES

THE PNEUMATIC ICE MACHINE

THIS IMPORTANT INVENTION IS CONSIDERED A BOON TO THOSE LIVING IN TROPICAL CLIMATES.

CAN BE WORKED BY THE MOST INEXPERIENCED HAND AND IS NOT LIABLE TO GET OUT OF ORDER.

From Rs. 175, each Machine complete.

MESSRS. ARLINGTON & CO.

AGENTS.

HAROLD & CO.,

3 DALHOUSIE SQUARE, CALCUTTA

HARMONIUMS.

Harold and Co., call attention to their unequalled stock of rich-toned Harmoniums made especially for India.

FROM RS. 90 TO RS. 900 EACH.

All kinds of Musical Instruments of the best description are always kept in Stock.

THEISTIC BOOKS.

FOR SALE.

Urdu?

Rahut Hakiki	Rs.	0	3	0
Nizam Komi	...	0	2	0
Kasufal Ilham	...	0	2	0
Kholasa, of, Asool Brahm Dharm	...	0	1	0

HINDI.

Upasana Pudhati	Rs.	0	1	0
Bhani Putrika or Hymn book	...	0	1	0
Tut Bodh	...	0	8	0
Upanashid Sar	...	0	8	0
Dhurm Dipika	...	0	0	6

ENGLISH.

Claims of so called Revealed Religion	Rs.	0	2	0
New Life	...	0	0	6
Living God	...	0	1	0
Higher and Lower Virtue...	...	0	1	0

Apply to the Secretary,
BRAHMO SOMAJ OF THE PUNJAB,
Lahore.

NATIONAL COMPANY.

HOMŒOPATHIC CHEMISTS AND PUBLISHERS
SUPPLY ALL KINDS OF
HOMŒOPATHIC MEDICINES, BOOKS
CASES AND OTHER REQUISITES.
11, COLLEGE SQUARE,
Calcutta.

BABU BASANTA KUMAR DATTA,

HOMŒOPATHIC PRACTITIONER
No. 20, Sunker Halder's Lane, Ahiritolah.

FRESH INDENT OF
Medicines and other Requisites,
Have arrived from England.
Medicines, Boxes, Books, Pamphlets;
Absolute Alcohol; Cholera-spirit Camphor.
SPECIAL REMEDIES.

For Suppressed, Laborious and Difficult menses; Leucorrhœa.

For Hysteria; Spermatorrhœa; Dysentery; Diarrhœa; Cholera.

For Asthma; Pile; Pain; Sore and Diseases of the Children.

Ice, Lemonade, Soda **and Tonic water always.**

To be had **at**

DATTA'S HOMŒOPATHIC LABORATORY,
No. 312, CHITPORE ROAD, BURTOLA, CALCUTTA
TERMS—CASH.
☞ **Price** List can be **had on application.**

NOTICE.

INFALLIBLE SPECEFICS FOR ASTHAMA, CONSUMPTION, COLIC, GONORRHŒA AND SPERMATORRHŒA!!!

I AM the son **of** the late **Titaram** Paul of Midnapore, who, the public **is** well aware, was acquainted with **speci**fic medicines for the above diseases. **I** fully learnt the mode of preparing those medicines from my late father, and have cured many people of Midnapore, Calcutta, Hughly, and other places since his death, as the annexed **testi**monial will shew. Any one wishing **to** be treated by me can apply to me, care of the Manager of the Indian Mirror.

WOOPENDRA NATH PAUL.

MY father was ailing from asthma **for** a long time. He had recourse to various sorts of treatment, but none of them proved effectual. At last he regularly used the medicine of Babu Upendra Nath Pal, and was, within a month, freed from all disorders. My own experience leads me to admit that the medicine of Upendra Babu is especially efficacious in cases of Asthma.

HEM CHANDRA BHATTACHARJYA,
Editor of Balmiki Ramayana,
AND
Asst. Secretary, Adi Brahmo Somaj.

28th Baisak,
1798 Sakabda.

BETHUNE SOCIETY.

A SPECIAL meeting of the *members and well wishers* of the above Society will be held at the Theatre of the Medical College on Monday, the 31st of July instant, at the hour of 5½ P. M., in honor of its retiring President, Mr. Justice Phear. His Honor the Lieutenant Governor is expected to be present.

26th July 1876.

GREESH CHUNDER MITTER,
Honorary Assistant Secretary,
Bethune Society.

CHUNDER & BROTHERS,

25½ & 112, RADHA BAZAR,
CALCUTTA,
TERMS,—CASH STRICTLY.

Cash Boxes of sizes with & without Chubbs' locks.
Railway Bags, of Carpet, Leather &c.
Overland trunks of leather.
Scarborough trunks of sizes.
Brass Candlesticks of sizes.
Cricket Bats & Balls.
Chinese Canisters, Square & round.
Compendium of Games of sizes.
Bulleye Lantern, Japanned.
Hand Lamp ENGLISH, for Table & Wall.
Mathematical & Surveying Instruments.
Drawing & Painting Materials.
Color Boxes of sizes & descriptions.
Magic Inkstand in large variety.
Inkstands with & without stands of sizes &c.
Playing Cards of different patterns.
Brass Padlocks of sizes.
Water Cocks (brass) for Iron and lead pipes.
Iron & Lead pipes of sizes.
Note & Letter paper of all sizes & qualities.
Foolscap, Demy, Medium, Royal paper &c.
Printing Papers of sizes &c.
Steel Pens, Quills, Pencils.
Writing Inks, of all colors & sizes.
Bank Books, Pocket Book &c &c.
Fancy & Useful Articles.

CALCUTTA } CHUNDER & BROTHERS.
The 30th June, 1876. }

India General Steam Navigation Company, Ld.

SCHOENE, KILBURN & CO.—*Managing Agents.*

ASSAM LINE.
NOTICE.

Steamers leave Calcutta for Assam every Tuesday, Goalundo every Thursday and leave Debrooghur downward every Saturday.

THE Str. "SIMLA" will leave Calcutta *Via Matabanga* for Assam, on Tuesday, the 1st August.

Cargo will be received at the Company's Godowns, Nimtollah Ghat, up till noon of Monday, the 31st instant.

THE Str. "PROGRESS" will leave Goalundo for Assam on Thursday, the 3rd August.

Cargo will be received at the Company's Godowns, No. 4 Fairlie Place, up till noon of Tuesday the 1st proximo.

Goods forwarded to Goalundo for this vessel will be chargeable with Railway Freight from Calcutta to Goalundo in addition to the regular Freight of this Company.

Passengers should leave for Goalundo by Train of Wednesday, the 2nd proximo.

CACHAR LINE NOTICE.
REGULAR FORTNIGHTLY SERVICE.

Steamers now leave Calcutta for Cachar and Intermediate Stations every alternate *Friday*, and leave Cachar downward every alternate Sunday.

THE Str. "LUCKNOW" will leave Calcutta *via Matabanga* for Cachar on *Friday*, the 11th August.

Cargo will be received at the Company's Godowns, Nimtollah Ghat, up till noon of Thursday the 10th proximo.

For further information regarding rates of Frieght or passagemoney, apply to,

4, FAIRLIE PLACE, | G. J. SCOTT,
Calcutta 27th July 1876. | *Secretary.*

Hats, Hats, Hats!!!

C. C. DASS & CO.

SOLA HAT MANUFACTURERS,
74, Radhabazar.
Just opened new Invoices of **Silk and Felt** Hats and Hawke's Patent **Helmets.**

SMITH, STANISTREET & CO.

Pharmaceutical Chemists & Druggists
BY APPOINTMENT
To His Excellency the Right Hon'ble
LORD LYTTON, G.M.S.I.
Governor-General of India,
&c., &c.

SYRUP OF LACTATE OF IRON

Prepared from the original receipe. Lactate of Iron, in various forms of preparation, have been in use in France, and generally through the continent of Europe, for some years past, and is highly esteemed as one of the most valuable Chalybeate Tonic Remedies yet introduced. The Syrup, being the most agreeable as well as convenient form of administration is in most general use. It is a most valuable remedy in the following diseases:—Chlorosis or Green Sickness, Leucorrhœa, Neuralgia, Enlargement of the Spleen, &c. In combination with quinine, it has also been very successfully used in the cure of Fever, while to persons of delicate constitution, enfeebled by disease it is invaluable. In bottles. Rs. 2 each.

SYRUP OF THE PHOSPHATE OF IRON Rs. 2 per bottle.

SYRUP OF PHOSPHATE OF IRON AND STRYCHNINE, Rs. 2 per bottle.

SYRUP OF PHOSPHATE OF IRON AND QUININE. Price Rs. 2-8 per bottle.

SYRUP OF PHOSPHATE OF IRON, QUININE AND STRYCHINE. (DR. ATKIN'S TRIPLE TONIC SYRUP.) Rs. 2-8 per bottle.

Smith, Stanistreet & Co.

Invite special attention to the [illegible] the quality guaranteed as the best procurable:—

Pure Ærated Waters.

Made from Pure Water, obtained by the new process through the Patent Charcoal Filters.

				Rs	As.
Ærated plain **(Treble Ærated), per doz.**			...	0	12
Soda Water	ditto	„	...	0	12
Gingerade	ditto	„	...	1	4
Lemonade	ditto	„	...	1	4
Tonic (Quinine)	ditto	„	...	1	4

The *Cash* **must be sent with the order to obtain advantage of the above rates.**

BURAL BROTHERS,

[ESTABLISHED IN 1870 A.D.]
JEWELLERS, GOLD AND SILVER-SMITHS AND WATCH-MAKERS,

BY APPOINTMENT
TO
His Excellency the Viceroy and Governor-General of India,
AND
HIS HIGHNESS THE MAHARAJAH ADHIRAJ OF BURDWAN,
BURAL BROTHERS,
10, Hare Street.

Printing Materials

MILLER AND RICHARD'S PRESSES, TYPES and all requisites always in Stock,
TERMS CASH.
EWING & CO.

!!! हुका !!!
!!! HOOKAHS !!!

ENGLISH made Hookahs of various choice designs, **colours and** sizes ranging in price from Rs. 2 to **5 each, 60** designs to choose from. Apply to

RADANAUTH CHOWDRY,
373, Jorasanko

Printed and published by M. M. BOSE, at the INDIAN MIRROR PRESS, No. 15, College Square, for the Proprietor.

The Indian Mirror.

SUNDAY EDITION.

VOL. XV.] CALCUTTA, SUNDAY AUGUST, 6, 1876. { REGISTERED AT THE GENERAL POST OFFICE. } [No. 185

CONTENTS.

NOTICE.

All letters and communications relating to the literary department of the Paper should be addressed to the Editor. All other letters should be addressed to the Manager, to whom all remittances should be made payable.

Subscribers will be good enough to bring to the notice of the Manager any delay or irregularity in the delivery of the Paper.

Editorial Notes.

WE are glad to learn that the needful amount of money has been deposited in the office of the Collector of 24-Pergunnahs, as desired by Government, to enable him to complete the purchase of the site for the Albert Hall. As soon as the award is issued the committee hope to commence operations.

A CERTAIN Sunday in the month of June is set apart to make collections in every Church throughout England on behalf of the sick and suffering in hospitals, and it is called Hospital Sunday. Thousands of pounds are collected in the churches, chapels, meeting houses, synagogues, and even roadsides of London. The money so collected is devoted to the improvement of the hospitals. Every one pays his quota, Dissenters, Churchmen, Jews and all. In some years the collections are larger than in other years. It is a beautiful custom, and ought to be introduced into every country.

THERE is said to be a religious revival among the deaf and dumb of certain European countries, the lead being taken in Belgium. One of them has been converted from Roman Catholicism into a more rational creed, and he has been able to influence other unfortunates like him so wonderfully that there is in other European countries a great religious agitation. Of course it is known to our readers that in Europe the deaf and dumb are taught to speak by certain signs. And we are told in connection with this revival, a deaf and dumb preacher communicates his fervid sentiments by such earnest and strangely demonstrative gesticulations, that it is not only interesting but positively delightful to watch him in his silent discourses.

THE Jews have begun to modify even their religious customs in Christian countries. Now nothing is so more rigidly enforced by Jewish custom as the observance of the Sabbath. And yet we learn that the Israelites of New York have agreed to hold Sunday services. Religion is to be considered philosophically and ethically, and all disputed points to be discussed from a strictly scientific point of view. Their Saturday services are to be retained still. We need scarcely point out the fact that the Jews in Christian countries call their religion pure Theism.

HOW is it that we no longer hear of widow marriages under the Act among professed Hindus of the advanced school, headed by Pandit Iswar Chandra Vidyasagar? If the movement has not collapsed, there is evidence enough to show that the zeal of the Native public is ebbing away. Besides, it is a well-known fact that there is hardly a single instance of a widow marriage in a high and respectable Hindu family. It is to be deeply regretted, if true, that the helpless Hindu widow has now fewer friends to compassionate her distress than she had when the Act was passed. Is there no prospect of renewed zeal in this direction?

THE *Langham Magazine*, of which Mr. Voysey has had the editorial charge, seems to have failed, and is not published any more. We are really sorry for this. English theists do require an organ, and the *Langham* which was started with that object, did never strike us, we must say, as very promising. But nevertheless we wished it success and prosperity in hopes of future advancement. And now we are informed it is dead from want of funds. Though we find our friends, some of as active and philanthrophic as ever, we wish that the majority of the other theists should have asmuch enthusiasm and vigor as they. The premature collapse of the *Langham Magazine* is we are afraid partly owing to certain obnoxious views expressed by Mr. Voysey on Slavery, a matter on which English public opinion seems to be considerably agitated since the controversy on the notorious Fugitive Slave Circulars.

THE relations between Russia and England are not likely to be placed on a very improved footing in consequence of the attitude of the two contries towards the revolutions and disturbances now taking place in the Ottoman Empire. While many Russian officers have come forward to take important commands in the insurgent army of Servia, Montenegro, a pretty large number of English officers are said to have offered their services to the army of the Sultan. Besides, the policy of the present Government is deeply suspected to be in favor of Turkey, while the views of the Russian Government on the subject are known all the world over. We must say we do not much believe in the stories of Turkish excesses in the Christian provinces. No doubt, there is some oppression such as follows the putting down of an insurrection in any part of the world. How did the British soldiery behave in the N. W. Provinces after, and in the midst of the Mutiny?

CORPORAL punishment in schools has now grown to be such an inveterate and immemorial custom, that even those who do not approve of it do not know how to get rid it. The boys are perfectly familiarized with it by early training and tradition, and always expect it in case of delinquency. If it is withheld, and nothing substituted in its place, they take it as undue leniency, or perhaps weakness on the part of the teacher, of which they are seldom slow to reap the utmost advantage. How can strict discipline be enforced without the birch-rod and rattan? In the school connected with University College, London, Mr. Horton, the Headmaster, has adopted successfully the following method:—Should a boy be disobedient or behave ill, the only consequence to himself is that he is told to carry home to his parents or guardians the master's written report of the fact, and to bring back the paper the next day to the master with the parent's signature to it, showing that it has been read. That censure is found to be quite sufficient for its purpose, and is rarely resorted to. We are not sure how far this method will do in this country.

LORD LYTTON'S famous resolution in the Fuller case is a triumph of justice and humanity over oppression, and equality over race and color. A moral triumph like this makes the whole nation rejoice. The Viceroy has by this one act won the loyalty and affections of the Native population, and administered a wholesome warning to all Europeans who may not be disposed to treat the poorer Natives with becoming kindness. But unfortunately our congratulations are embittered by certain unpleasant reflections. We are sorry to find this case has already provoked race feelings on either side, and opened old and disagreeable sores, which should have been allowed to heal up. The Press, both Native and European, has a most important duty to discharge at this season. Let it not inflame race-antagonism by angry and wholesale denunciations and bitter invectives. Why should individual and exceptional cases, why should Fullers and Meareses and Kirkwoods be allowed to disturb the harmony which generally prevails between the two races, and which is so essential to the prosperity and well-being of both. Is not this the time when our contemporaries should show the magnanimity of forbearance and kindness, and throw oil over troubled waters?

THE spirit of imitating Europe which has even entered into the indeginous arts and industries of India, has no where met with a more signal condemnation than in the criticisms which which public journals of England contain of the presents made in this country to the Prince of Wales, and which His Royal Highness is exhibiting in the galleries of the South Kensington Museum. Where the taste, and workmanship, and design are exclusively Indian, unmeasured praise is lavished on the articles exhibited. We hear of "the marvellous tracery," the gold and the enamel "so harmoniously delightful to the imagination," the swords, and shields, so "splendid in their inutility," the couchant tigers, the climbing apes, the forest foliage, and the elephants with the cunning ruby eyes. There is rapture in every line of the criticism. Where the design is European, the taste is Western, and the workmanship is mongrel, unspeakable vulgarity is attributed to the unfortunate presents, and the hint is broadly given that they ad be thrown out of the window. The claret jugs, and egg-cups, the tea-services, and wash handstands, the muffineers, and candelabras inspire an unpatriotic disgust in the breasts of the critics, and they call it all exceedingly barbarous. This is suggestive, and shows what refined European taste expects of the growing civilization of India. The tastes and customs of Europe reproduced in India do but belie the great trust which Europeans repose in the genius and instinct of elegance possessed by the imaginative and artistic Hindu.

WHAT the future of the new political Association lately opened in Calcutta will be, it is difficult to divine. But if men and movements are to be judged by the motives and intentions which dictate them, the Native public must thank and encourage the projectors, and wish them Godspeed. The dumb millions require to be represented, their rights and interests demand constant agitation, their grievances need redress. Agents should be deputed to visit provincial stations and distant villages, and inquire into the wants and requirements of the tenantry. They must go and see with their own eyes the condition of the poor ryot in his humble cottage, and hear the tale of his misery from his own lips. If with facts thus elicited, a number of disinterested and earnest men would, by constitutional agitation and other means, work for the political and social advancement of the masses, great results will be achieved in time. If only a small fraction of such reform is all that the new Association now contemplates and quietly succeeds in accomplishing hereafter, it will have done enough to deserve the thanks of our patriots, as well as rulers. Let the projectors keep clear of ostentation and self-seeking; let them work in a manly, honest and truly benevolent spirit, and they shall have their reward. We must say we have not as much faith in their capacities and resources as we have in their motives and intentions. They must give some evidence of their power before they can hope to inspire public confidence. The opposition they called forth from other political parties at the very outset, as well as the welcome accorded to them by the Press, should both stimulate their exertions in the righteous cause they have undertaken. No work can be more sacred than befriending the poor.

MISS HARRIET MARTINEAU, whose name and fame have extended to every country where English is read, died on the 27th of June, and a short autobiographical memoir of the eminent lady appeared in the London *Daily News* of which she was a most frequent, and a most valued contributor. We wish we had space to publish the whole of that sketch, but as that is impossible we content ourselves with an extract. Miss Martineau was born in 1802, and was, therefore, seventy four years of age when she died. She retained all her mental faculties unimpaired to the last, and took the most active interest in all literary political, and social questions from what "she called the verge of the horizon of human existence." She was partially deaf, and generally in a weak state of health, but her literary and political activity was wonderful. She was immensely popular, and enjoyed the intimacy and confidence of some of the highest and noblest members of English society. A pension £150 was fixed upon her by Government, and her name placed on the Civil List in 1842. She wrote on all manner of subjects religious, social, political, philosophical literary, novels and &c., &c. Her chief works were the twenty-five volumes of her Illustrations of Political Economy, and her translation and abridgment of Auguste Comte's positive philosophy. She is the author of ninety-nine volumes, fifty of these being treatises on political subjects, most ably written; the others are on various subjects, six of them being religious, about fourteen social, nearly a dozen novels, and the rest miscellaneous. Besides these she wrote endless reviews, essays, letters, pamphlets, and poems. She was also a most indefatigable contributor to the newspapers and periodicals, her articles to the *Daily News* alone numbering 1,642. She wrote various articles in the *Westminister Review*, *Edinburgh Review*, *Cornhill*, *Macmillan*, *Quarterly*, *Once a Week*, *Spectator*, *Chamber's Journal*, and various other English and American publications. Harriet Martineau was the sister of the Rev. James Martineau. A worthy sister to a worthy brother was she.

THE SOLITUDES OF LIFE.

LET us count out the solitudes of life. Freedom from the presence of men is not pain. It is often a relief, it is a recreation amidst the noise and disturbance of our daily life. The soul wants to be alone that it may enter into the deep spiritual repose of which the world is such an enemy. The soul wants to be alone and far away from the irritations, excitements, bitternesses, and temptations of others' speech and presence. The solitude of the chamber of meditation in which the recluse lives is a world of profound realities for him. He would not part it for the loudness and enthusiasm and self-forgetful rapture of the hall of pleasure. The air of his native solitude is pure and strengthening to the son of God. The solitude of sorrow is no less sacred. The down-cast eye, the deep and suppressed sigh, the broken and crushed affections, seek to be alone, away from the world's rude gaze. There is a heart's pain that refuses human consolation; there is a profound affliction for which no remedy can be found in man's sympathy; the soul bleeds and no one can bind up the wound; the soul weeps and no one can wipe its tears; and the man of sorrow retires to his solitude, and cries unto his God. Intrude not, therefore, into the sacredness of deep sorrow which is averse to human approach. The solitude of sickness is also very intense. The suffering that no one can understand, the sleeplessness that no one can share, the fears that are the offspring of disease, the dreams that oppress the head, the visions that scare the sense, and the untold anxieties, and wretchedness, and helplessness of the sickbed all these must be met alone. The unrelived silence of the night that seems as if it would never end, the tediousness, idleness, listlessness of the long long day; the hasty formal visits of friends; the monotonous and unvarying attention of those who wait; the cold unconcern of the doctor, in whom all hopes are centered; all these combine to create a desolation around the bed of sickness, the solitude of which none can understand. And when disease slowly brings in the prospects of death, does not that solitude become still more striking and awful? What can be more solitary than death? Of all other sufferings there is some recorded experience which fellow-suffers have left behind them; but in the dark solitude of death there is not a single light which may cheer the fading eye. When every familiar object fades away, when every familiar face seems to sink in gloom, when every familiar thought proves to be a vanity, when every familiar feeling becomes a source of pain, then only a man is truly alone!—That unknown, unfelt, secret solitude which is hidden for every one of us in the bosom of the Eternal. Blessed he who is prepared to enter into that world alone with his God.

Let us now turn our eye to solitudes in other the walks of life. Let us search the solitudes of character. Behold the loneliness of the man of secret strength who thinks alone, and his thoughts are known to none except as he chooses to let them out. His actions are all planned in the secret of his heart, and no one knows of them but by their results. His aspirations and hopes are always locked within the far off recesses of his soul, and invisible to all but his God. For human sympathy he never expressed a longing, for human aid he never expressed a prayer, for human opposition he never expressed a fear. His weaknesses unknown and unexpressed, his strength is secret and unmeasured. He lives within the depths of his being alone. Behold the solitude of another man who craves for man's sympathy and gets it not, who offers his sympathy but it is not received by any one; who weeps for others, himself unwept. His nature nestles around the hearts of those that surround him and they understand him not; his plans are for others, they heed him not. His highest ideal is either unrecognised, or recognised and passed over in silence; his highest thoughts are preached in vain. Men hear them, but give them not a moment's reflection. His deepest utterances create but a faint echo and then die away in silence. The world within his heart has no counterpart in the world where he lives. His men and women are different from those that he sees about him. And therefore he lives alone, he thinks alone, he feels alone, and is altogether a being of solitude. There is only one other kind of loneliness of which we shall speak before we close. It is the loneliness of temptation. Our deepest and dearest friends do not understand our hearts. Amidst the intricacies of his motives and feelings man lives alone. The thoughts that becloud his best moments are known to no other. The vileness that clings to his holiest affections is imperceptible to any other touch but his own. And the fever that rages in him sometimes is beyond the reach of cure, such as man may propose. Covered before every other eye his naked deformity is an offence before the pure witness of his God. Unsearched and beyond the search of his follow beings, he stands condemned before the throne of Heaven. Men's praise and blame matter nothing to him who in the solitude of his temptation looks up to heaven only for help. He has no friend but the friend of the poor and falling; he has no home but the bosom of his Saviour; he has no strength but the mercy of the Infinitely Good; he has no rescue but the right hand of the Lord.

Such are some of the solitudes of life, yet let us not feel alone when we feel solitary, for our Father is always near at hand.

Correspondence.

MAYA; ITS TRUTH AND ITS ERROR.

To the Editor of the *Indian Mirror*.

SIR,—I read with pleasure a well-written article on *Maya*, "self-delusion", in your last Sunday's issue. The exposition given of it taken as a whole, is satisfactory. Still I lay it down with a feeling that the *Maya* riddle is not wholly solved herein. There is an apparent, though surely not intended contradiction between the opening affirmation that *Maya* is divinely ordained, and the writer's closing statement that, it is "a strange self-delusion in the midst of which men have willingly placed themselves." For the honor of man, this should be cleared up. Again, for the honor of God another confounding statement should be made clear—especially in a paper devoted to pure theism—that, namely, wherein the writer says that, "we cannot but recognise a soul of truth in the pantheistic abstractions of the Vedanta, long since discarded by the Brahmo Somaj, that God himself is not free from (Delusion) *Maya*, but that the creation of the world is the result" (the proof) "of its influence upon him." I suppose sound Brahmos, everywhere, regard it as a damnable error of old Hinduism that the Infinite God can be misled, or can purposely cheat and deceive His children; tell them lies and then punish them for believing what He says. "Let God be true and every man a liar," is a more theistic way of looking at it; and as much more sensible as it is more theistic. I bear in mind that the root of the word *Maya* is *Ma*; and if I be correctly informed,—a good son, in this land, frequently and fondly calls his mother not only *Ma* but *Maya*. Again, my unforgettable talks with the Rajah Radhakant make me sure that all love, all desire, is identified by orthodox Hindus with *Maya*; so that *Maya* when addressed to a mother, ceases to mean deceiver, and means one who loves me—or the object of my love or desire to bless. Had my friend Samuel Johnson, the honored author of "Oriental Religions," enjoyed a score of years of personal intercourse with Hindus, he would hardly have missed, as I think he has, in his rich chapter on *The Vedanta*, the fact that "*Maya*" can be applied to the purest possible affection. Was it not Hinduism's injustice to the heart, in favor of the soul, its condemnation of feeling as injurious to worship, Hinduism commanding man to kill all feeling that justified the use of Buddhism! Such was the demand of the Heart five hundred years before Christ; and the neglected reform of Chaitanya, Tukaram and other heroes of the heart a few centuries ago. Nor need I add that it is a cardinal doctrine of that religion whose typal prayer begins "Our Father who art in heaven" that God can feel and desire to bless. God as a Lover, is an arch-heresy and a lie, to pure Hinduism. To orthodox Hinduism, as I understand it, the Buddha is a liar, and Jesus is a liar, and Chaitanya is a liar, and God is a liar, in just so far as one or other of these declares he is a lover of men, a lover of souls or a lover of good and of doing good. Brahma, the Infinite One, (so Radhakanta told me) did not create,—could not have created the world. No, no; it was Brahma, and Brahma lost the gift of immortality, first person of the *trimourti* though he be, by this *raja goon*, this element of rage, this *desire* to create. Desire is impossible to the Most High; says the orthodox Hindu. Thus we have a distinctly two-fold application of the word *Maya*. It means deceit and it means feeling. Because the God of truth loves and thinks and works. He is not therefore a cheat and a deceiver; says the Brahmo Somaj. Neither are the odours of the mountain rose, nor the colors of the evening sky sent by Him to deceive his children. We should all enjoy the sweets of life as helps to heaven, and not as lures to hell. Neither should gold and gems draw us in any other direction than to true *nirvana* (rest and joy) in the Infinite Bounty and Beauty of Brahma, the only One. In the *Dabistan* we read "the *Maya* of the Vedantists is the magic of God, the universe is his playful deceit." Explain it as we may, this talk dishonors God and is dangerous to man; for whom truth and the whole truth, and nothing but the truth is salvation, present and eternal. Only as affection, and as love without deceit, is *Maya* predicable of God. *Maya* as "delusion," *Maya* as cheating belongs not to the Omniscient and All Holy. 'Tis a fully exploded error that God is the author of evil, *i. e.*, of any absolute wrong. All God does is right and makes for righteousness—what once *seemed evil* turns out to be discipline. Parable:—Custard and mustard are both yellow and their names sound alike. Both are put on dinner tables. A child fond of sweets, says 'Give me some mustard.' 'No, my darling! it is not good for you; it will bite your tongue,' says Grandpa. 'No it won't,' says the little man, 'Give me some! I will have it!' 'Is it so, my boy?' says Grandpa, and after vain efforts to dissuade and fool the ignorant and foolish one, he says—"Well, Jamie, come here!" Jamie opens wide his mouth for a spoonful of mustard. 'It will teach him a lesson for life,' says the good disciplinarian. So down goes the mustard into the tender mouth which gets blistered and burned. Without *Maya* or magic or cheating, but simply in the way of needed discipline comes the lesson from a wise and righteous father. If the man-child *will* have the mustard, let him taste it, for his good.

Yours,

DALL.

SANKIRTAN UNDER THE PORTICO OF THE BRAHMA MANDIR.

DEAR SIR,—As duly announced in your paper, our revered brother missionaries of the Brahmo Somaj of India, have, from Sunday last, begun to chant the name of the Lord, every evening under the portico of the Brahma Mandir. I regret to say, that it is only to last until the coming *Utsab*, which takes place on the 6th of Bhadra. Within so few days, this practice has begun to wield vast spiritual influence over our hearts. Yourself as well as your numerous readers are aware that the majority of our congregation hav to work hard in the several educational and other public institutions of the metropolis, and you may well understand, how these sacred and sweet hymns chanted by such who are specially gifted, act upon the hearts of those, who come quite exhausted and heavy-laden from the fields of their labor. The name of the Lord is in itself sweet and sanctifying to every believer; but here it enters into our souls with several additional charms. First, it comes from the lips of those who, we trust, are striving with their fullest energies, to be holy or in other words, to do the Will of their Heavenly Lord. Secondly, it is chanted in a place which is connected with a world of our more sacred and dear associations. Under these circumstances, I cannot imagine the existence of any Brahmo who will not gladly agree with me to pray to the minister of the Mandir to extend this holy practice throughout the whole year. It is, dear Sir with this object in view that I address you these few lines. I must also request the proper authorities that the *Sankirtan* may commence at a time before the sunset when it will be convenient for all classes of people to attend. Special attention must be had to secure the attendance of those gentlemen who work in the offices, colleges and the schools.

Yours,
A METROPOLITAN.

Devotional

THOU hast appointed thy servants, O Lord, to build one house, and not many houses. But they are building each a seperate house for himself, because they do not agree, and condemn each other's building. Father, in this disagreement we see our pride, selfishness, and infidelity. There is one dispensation of which we are parts, one body whereof we are members, and in one house, O God of providence, hast thou called us to dwell. May we have such faith and such union!

O GOD, anger is a fit of passion, which though subdued for a time, returns as soon as exciting causes appear. I have tried these twenty years to control it, but thou knowest, Master, that I have shamefully failed. Even now, though I have prayed so long provocation upsets my temper and makes me think of revenge. When I first came unto thee, my Saviour, I brought unto thee a most unclean and vindictive heart. Thou hast taught me forbearance, but the root of the evil in me is not yet gone, and when trials come I cannot stand. Teach me such love that I may altogether subdue my evil passions.

THERE is a beauty in thy face, dear Lord, which has fascinated thy devoted saints above. Even to this sinner thou hast partly revealed it, but my heart thou hast not yet won. O how hard and currant is my heart. If I see thee continually shall I not love thee? Yes.

IN the gardens of the world all species of flowers have been numbered and classified. But in thy garden in heaven new species grow, which none ever saw before. Sweet ideas and sweet joys spring up, not only fresh flowers on the same tree, but fresh species of flowers, they like of which the heart never saw. Who knows what new light and joy thou wilt send to-morrow to thy humble worshipper?

The Brahmo Somaj

THE Bhadro Utsab, or the anniversary festival in commemoration of the opening of the Brahmo Mandir, will take place on Sunday the 20th instant. As usual, service commences early in the morning and continues till evening.

THE evening *sankirtan* near the gate of the Mandir is a success, although it is not numerously attended. The attendance varies from twenty to forty. What interests us most is that many if not all of these men belong to the poorer classes, who on their way home from their daily business, pause awhile to hear the chanting of God's name. The singing is on the whole well conducted, and proves impressive.

IT will be somewhat disappointing to Christian missionaries to learn that after all the returns of the census regarding the strength (or rather the weakness) of the Brahmo community, which they so lustily *wished* to believe to be accurate, are a pure fiction, as we repeatedly said at the time. Our brethren were often warned not to rely on the figures, but as often they asserted with dogged obstinacy and unfairness that there were only ninety Brahmos in all Calcutta! The late census, we believe, raises the figure to about 500. Probably this number excludes all who, though Brahmos in faith, call themselves Theists or Monotheists. And then again the junior members of a family are in many cases, for obvious reasons, not returned as Brahmos by the elders. However, we are glad that the untruth in which many seemed to delight, has been disproved authoritatively.

WE have received the July number of *Theological Review*.

Scientific

DR. CALDWELL, Bishop of Tinnevelly, has been continuing his excavations at Korkei and Kayel in the Tinnevelly district. The only things discovered were small fragments of Indian pottery at the former place, and of China and Arabia at the latter. The reverend doctor found no traces of the Greeks in his research, but he believes many traces of the great antiquity of the place exist. The *Indian Church Gazette* is glad to learn that Dr. Caldwell has been thus engaged, as it apparently refutes the statements which have recently been put forth about his health.

Gleanings

FROM HINDU DEVOTEE.

THE *Durbesh* who is void of all desire, is always happy. Whether you remain in one place or go about hither and thither, never be idle to labor for salvation. Whether you are awake or asleep do not be selfish. Whether you keep your hair long or shave your head, it does not matter. He who is void of all worldy desire, is only always happy. Try to do good to others and keep your mind as white and soft as the honey-comb. Keep your eyes always fixed to the ground. Be truthful and patient, and be careful to dance dexterously without slipping once your foot.

The Fakir who has seen the beauty of the Merciful Being, remains absorbed entirely all the twenty-four hours of the day. His spirit came from an unexplored region to take shelter in the gross elements of body, and when he sees the miseries of the world his spirit retires to its unexplored home again. As long as he lives in the hostellery of the earth he pays all the tributes due, but he is perfectly void of desire, and surrenders his self to God alone. He travels in this world without anxiety, seeks alone for his beloved God, and gives alms to the poor. He with love and unselfishness helps all people, and shows them the path to heaven and salvation from death. Ramcharan says, the Fakir who is so good and whose heart is thus free from all worldly thoughts, being contented with every thing that comes. Such a Fakir has but little following in the world. Heaven is his resting place, there he sees and feels his God. Ramcharan says such a Fakir as labors hard to see the unspeakable presence of that Being in the temple of his body, men do not understand his secret heart.

Latest News.

—IT is likely that the Viceroy will leave Simla about the 15th of October. He goes to Cashmere and afterwards inspects the Sind and Punjab frontier.

—THERE is a good deal of dengue at present in Lucknow.

—SIR ANDREW CLARKE is said to have prepared a scheme for the re-organisation of the Public Works Department, which is to come into force about next December.

—SIR MADHAVA RAO has opened, in the name of the Guickwar, a school for European and Eurasian boys and girls at Baroda, under charge of a European master and mistress.

—A BRANCH railway will connect Ghazipore with the E. I. R. line at Dildarnugger.

—A PRISONER at Agra who was sentenced to transportation for life by Mr. Keene, the Judge, calmly removed one of his shoes, and "sent it flying" at the Judge, who as calmly "lobbed" it, and placed it on his desk! One of the the Sudder Court Judges in Calcutta Mr. Rattray, met a similar fate some years ago.

—MISS FLORENCE EMILY SOPHIA BIRCH, Mr. Arthur Birch and Miss Constance Alice Birch, in recognition of the services of their father, the late Mr. J. W. W. Birch, British Resident at the Court of Perak, and in consideration of the sad circumstances in which they are placed by his untimely death, have each been allowed from the Civil List a pension of £75.

—THE remains of the late Lord Hastings, who was struck down by jungle fever while out-shooting on the Annamally Hills and died in the Travellers' Bungalow at Tanjore in December last, are to be conveyed to England immediately.

—HIS HIGHNESS the Maharajah Dhulip Sing is disposing of that portion of his collection of jewellery which was formed at the Court of Lahore by his father, Runjit Sing, the late possessor of the celebrated Koh-i-noor diamond, and has entrusted it to Messrs. Frazer and Hans, of Regent-street, for that purpose.

—THE *Whitehall Review* says:—The following must be taken for what it is worth. It is stated that Her Imperial and Royal Highness the Dutchess of Edinburgh has written a strong and very urgent letter to the Queen, complaining of the attitude of England towards Russia, and begging Her Majesty to request Dr. Disraeli and the Earl of Derby to be less bitter in their references to her father's empire.

—WE regret to hear that Mr. George Norton, the late Advocate-General of Madras, is dead.

—COLONEL BAKER, whose term of confinement expired on the 29th of June last, has already received and accepted the offer of a high command in the army of the Porte, and will immediately proceed to Turkey to commence his new career.

—THE Prince of Arcot intends visiting England.

—ON July 7 His Royal Highness the Prince of Wales honored Sir Salar Jung with his company at dinner at his house in Piccadilly. The guests—some thirty in number—asked to meet His Royal Highness included the Maharajah Dhulip Singh, the Lord Chancellor, the Marquis of Salisbury, the Lord Chamberlain, the Earl of Northbrook, Lord Halifax, Lord Lawrence &c. Previous to dinner a Durbar was held strictly according to the usual Eastern ceremonial, and Sir Salar Jung presented His Royal Highness with the customary nuzzur of 101 gold mohurs; this was touched by His Royal Highness and then returned. Such Native members of Sir Salar's suite as were entitled to be presented, then came forward (their names being announced by Mr. Fitzgerald, A. D. C. to the Secretary of State for India) and presented their respective tributary nuzzurs. The Durbar room was decorated with gold embroidered carpets, for the manufacture of which the Nizam's State is famous.

—TWO Russian officers, accompanied by a Tartar Russian servant have, the *Indian Public Opinion* says, arrived at Cabul on a mission to the Amir, the object of which is not yet known, but it is surmised that their instructions are to induce the Amir to consent to the residence of a duly accredited Russian Political Agent at Cabul, and to pledge himself to non-interference in the affairs of Russian Turkistan.

—THE Akhund is said to have issued strict orders, prohibiting British subjects and servants from being permitted to enter the Swat Valley on any pretence whatsoever; and has directed that they be turned back, and that if they do not profit by the option of returning unharmed, they should be brought before him for punishment.

—THE *Delhi Gazette* hears that the leading members of the Agra bar, both Native and European, are about to call a public meeting to protest against wanton interference with the administration of justice, and to protect courts of law from the "contempt" necessarily arising from it.

—THE anti-Christian movement in China, especially in Szechuen, still continues, many converts having, it is reported, been murdered, and a still larger number plundered.

—A NUMBER of pupils of the *Kaisei Gakko* left Japan on the 25th ultimo, in order to complete their education in Europe, eight proceeding to England and two to France.

—THE *Delhi Gazette* publishes a long letter from Mrs. Fuller, detailing all the facts of the case and the antecedents of the deceased syce. It is evident that the violence used by him was "very slight indeed."

Calcutta.

THE address adopted at the meeting of the British [illegible] Society last Monday, will be presented to Mr. Justice Phear, by a deputation from the Society on Tuesday next. An advertisement appears elsewhere.

AT a public meeting of the Native inhabitants of Calcutta, held at the Beadon Street Pavilion, on Thursday last, in honor of Mr. Justice Phear, Prince Rahimuddin was voted to the Chair. The first resolution which ran as follows, was moved by Dr. K. M. Banerji:—"That, in the opinion of this meeting, the eminent services which the Hon'ble Mr. Justice Phear has rendered to the country, both as a Judge and as a public benefactor, call for a general expression of gratitude from the whole Native community." The Resolution was seconded by Dr. Kanailal De, Rai Bahadur. The next resolution, moved by Moulvi Abdul Latif Khan Bahadur, was as follows:—"That the country loses in him an upright, able, and conscientious Judge, possessed of uncommon energy and indefatigable application, who, for his independence, learning, and a high sense of justice, has enjoyed the confidence and esteem of all sections of the community." The Resolution was seconded by the Rev. Kally Churn Banerji. Kumar Surendro Nath Deb then moved a resolution for the appointment of a committee to raise the necessary fund for perpetuating the memory of Mr. Justice Phear, in such a manner as the fund so raised may permit, and for inviting the friends and admirers of Mr. Justice Phear to co-operate with them. Babu Kalimohun Das, moved:—"That the following address [we omit the address for want of space] be adopted, and that a deputation be appointed to present it to Mr. Justice Phear, at such time and place as he may appoint." The address expresses a hope that the Home Government of India may recognise the wise policy of finding a position for Mr. Justice Phear by which his opportunities of doing good to India will be continued.

HENRY M. JONES, for some time Proprietor of the *Oriental Figaro*, who filed his petition of insolvency, has been sworn and discharged. The debts due by insolvent were Rs. 21,120-2-8. The assets were as follows:—Interest in land, Rs. 1,500; debts owing to insolvent, Rs. 2,721-2-10. Excepted articles, Rs. 235. A Mr. Howard induced Mr. Jones to take up the *Oriental Figaro*, of which the former was for sometime the proprietor. The principal creditor who entered a position was Mr. Smith, of the City Press, who had a claim for printing the *Figaro* amounting to over Rs. 500. The debt due by the insolvent to Mr. Smith was partly made up of a sum of money due on account of the printing of the *Oriental Figaro*, and partly of a sum paid by Mr. Smith to a bailiff of the Small Cause Court, to release the insolvent from arrest.

RAM RAO *alias* Vencutty Rao, a Native of Vizagapatam, who was charged with cheating, and thereby inducing Mr. Hallsart, the Jeweller in Old Court House Street, to deliver to him several gold watches and chains, has been found guilty and sentenced by Mr. Justice Phear to four years rigorous imprisonment. The prisoner represented himself as the agent of the Maharajah of Travancore. The evidence of the Maharajah was taken at Trevandrum under commission.

JOHN IRVINE *alias* Johnson *alias* Crawford *alias* Evans, a young East Indian, pleaded guilty, to a charge of cheating Messrs. W. Hurst & Co., of this city, out of two cases of brandy, and also with forging the name of one Brown to an order on Messrs. Mackinnon Mackenzie & Co. He was sentenced by Mr. Justice Phear to seven years' transportation.

TARUK NATH MUKERJI, a clerk in the service of Mr. Wood, Barrister-at-Law, stands charged by Bishen Nundy, a Uriah, with having, in the months of January and February last, cheated him out of Rs. 12 and 16-8, respectively, by falsely representing himself to be a Vakil.

THE rate of conversion of Indian into sterling money for Overland Money Orders has been changed to 1s. 7½d. per rupee.

ALL the public offices will be closed on Saturday, the 19th instant, on account of the Hindu festival *Janmo Ostomy*.

THE Annual General Meeting of the Proprietors and Shareholders of the Bank of Bengal will be held at the Bank on Wednesday, the 23rd instant, at 3 P.M., for the transaction of the following business:—

I.—To receive the Directors' report and the accounts up to 30th June 1876.

II.—To elect two Directors in room of Mr. J. J. Guise and Mr. R. A. Lyall who go out by rotation, but who are eligible for re-election.

III.—To elect two Auditors and to fix their remuneration.

THE P. and O. Co.'s S. S. *Surat*, Commander Geo. C. Burne, arrived in Bombay Harbour, on Wednesday last, at 9 A. M., from Suez with the English Mails of the 14th ult. on board. The following is the list of passengers:—

From Southampton.—Rev. J. and Mrs. Slater, Master Slater, child, and ayah, Mr. and Mrs. E. Harwood and two children, Mrs. S. Harwood, Mrs. H. Richards and child, Mr. and Mrs. A. P. Agg, Mr. and Mrs. Bramhall, Mr. W. Price, Mrs. Mills, Miss Peters, Mr. Laughlin, Mr. Willock, Mr. R. W. Bulman.

From Venice.—Mr. J. W. Laing, Mr. J. C. Oman.

From Brindisi.—Dr. H. Johnstone, Mr. W. B. Cunningham, Mr. F. N. Thorowgood, Mr. and Mrs. W. Robinson, Mr. H. J. Sparks, Mr. G. Lyell, Lieut. F. T. Romilly, Mr. T. Benson, Mr. Rowell.

YESTERDAY at ½ past 1 P. M., the Attorneys of the High Court waited on Mr. Justice Phear, in the Court House, and presented him with their farewell address contained in a handsome casket, made by Mr. Jalibert, the Jeweller. The address was read by Mr. W. F. Gillanders, as the most senior member of the profession. Mr. Phear in a feeling speech in reply, said it afforded him no ordinary gratification to receive such evidence of the appreciation of his services as a Judge from the Attorneys of the Court who of all others had the best opportunities of judging of his judicial career, and whose testimony was, therefore, the more valuable. He spoke in highly complimentary terms of the Attorneys of the Court who, he said, were in comparison equal in ability, intelligence and honesty to the Attorneys of any other Court either in England or India. The Attorneys had been of great assistance to him in the administration of justice on the Original Side of the High Court, and he thanked them warmly for it. If he had sometimes been over-exacting in his relations with the Attorneys, it was with the best of intentions and for their own good and for the good of the suitors, the responsibilities of the Attorneys being always very great.

THE following was Mr. Justice Phear's reply to the address presented to him by the Ooterpara Hitakari Sabha:—He said their words were really much too kind. They had been led by their good feeling towards him to exaggerate the little service he might have rendered them. He was only too glad if his small exertions had been of any help or use to them and to other cognate workers for the welfare and progress of their country. Placed as he had had the honor of being in a high position of responsibility in the administration of the country, and at the same time a foreigner strange to all their ways, it had been his business to learn, as much as his narrow opportunities admitted, of the circumstances and conditions of their social life. Without this he could not do what he had been sent to the country to do. Thus situated in the midst of them, eagerly working out their own progress and development, it was impossible for him to stand by an apathetic spectator. Their kind words were much more than an adequate reward for the little part he had taken with them. On behalf of Mrs. Phear and himself he thanked them cordially for them. The great misfortune they had always felt was that the two peoples could not get nearer to each other. The immense difference in their daily habits and ways of life and of social traditions, made a great gap between them. It was to be hoped that time would lessen this. Nothing would tend more to bridge it over than timely expressions, such as the present, of kindly appreciation of all efforts, however feeble, at co-operation. He was much obliged to them for giving him the occasion of the distribution of prizes to the girls of affiliated schools as the opportunity for bidding them good-bye. He felt that it was particularly incumbent on them, as well-wishers of their country, not to slacken in their endeavours to advance the cause of female education. Their Association had already done good service in this direction, and he was confident they would continue to do so. They would do him the justice to remember that he had never advocated any one particular form or fashion of education. He had always declined to pledge himself to anything of the kind. He did not believe in any royal road to perfection. Their Association had a method of its own and was evidently doing true work. There were others again—he saw one of the most earnest among them then in the room—who had taken up the task at, he might say, a stage in front of them and were working with great success. It was because he saw the efforts at promoting female education taking so many different directions that he still believed in the vitality of the movement. The promoters of these various plans were not in antagonism with each, but were striving by different roads to attain the common end, and he doubted not that eventually very sensible symptoms of progress would be apparent. He could not recall what he had said elsewhere of his disappointment at the smallness of the advance which had actually been made within the period of his own observation; still he always thought and he continued to think that the movement was alive, was real. It would conform, of course, to the customs and habits of the people. It should not be an introduction from the outside. But he felt sure that the young men of the present generation who would be the old men of the next, would not be satisfied that their wives, sisters, and daughters should remain so far removed from themselves in education as they now generally are. He dwelt on the happy effects of female culture in England, and warned them against forming their opinion of English women from such books and satirical publications as commonly reached their hands here. He asked them at least to suspend their judgements till they could themselves come to England and see what domestic life there actually was. If they would do this, he should have no fear for the results. He pressed all who could, to come to England, and he for one promised to give them a hearty welcome.

And lastly he spoke of his great interest in the Association. He hoped notwithstanding the separation of time and distance, they would still consider him as among them. He should always be glad to be continually informed of their proceedings.

Mr. Phear ended by reiterating on behalf of Mrs. Phear and himself of their sincere thanks. The reward was ampler than the desert.

Selection.

HARRIET MARTINEAU.

BORN, 12TH JUNE, 1802. DIED, 27TH JUNE, 1876.

In ripened age, amid the tears of kindred, and the regrets of friends, the powerful and the independent spirit of Harriet Martineau has departed to encounter those mysteries which abide within the veil. The descendant of a Huguenot surgeon, Dird Martineau, of Dieppe, who preferred expatriation to conformity on the revocation of the Edict of Nantes, she nobly sustained the family reputation thus begun, illustrating it not only by a genius of rare breadth and freshness, but by a courage in opinion which never faltered, and a brave encounter with life's ills and hardships, full of capacity and strong in resource, and, to the last, instinct with high resolve. Among the remarkable women of this century it is scarcely possible to point to a more remarkable name than hers. The literary world of Europe, just fresh from laying its chaplet of immortelles on the grave of George Sand, hears the sad news from the quiet knoll at Ambleside, and knows that yet another of the greater names of modern authorship is severed from the band of living workers, and belongs now to history.

A red brick house, still standing in Magdalen-street, Norwhich, was the birthplace of a brother and sister, who, whatever their divergences of career and of speculation, had many great gifts in common, and among their points of likeness were always characteristically akin in the possession of a pure, lofty, and undaunted spirit. If to James Martineau we proudly turn as the most brilliant illustration of the genius of our special household of faith, let us not be slow to remember that the strenuous virtues and fine qualities of Harriet Martineau—better known, perhaps, to the world at large—were moulded in the same nursery of souls heroic. It is touching to recall that there was a time when the authoress of the beautiful hymn "Lord Jesus Come" was but a little way from sharing the life a [Unitarian preacher; it is worth repeating that her first striking success in literature was the series of three Prize Essays, contributed early in 1830, on the "Introduction and Promotion of Christian Unitarianism among the Roman Catholics, the Jews, and the Mahomedans," when by three distinct sets of judges the commanding merits of Harriet Martineau's work were distinguished.

To enumerate the long and weighty list of her contributions to the literature of this country, from her "Devotional Exercises for the use of Young Persons," in 1823, to her "Biographical Sketches," in 1868, is not our present purpose. The catalogue testifies not only to an indomitable industry, but to an insight equally at home with the "Traditions of Palestine," the "Feats on the Fiord," and the later social and political history of her own country. Be it enough to call to mind those charming stories, the "Illustrations of Political Economy," as of all her literary labors at once the most original in idea, the most attractive in execution, and supplying the most solid basis for her permanent fame.

A volume of later religious inquiry, issued in conjunction with a still living writer, both surprised and saddened a large public, in addition to private friends, owing to the vast distance of speculation by which she now separated herself from positions of belief once loved and defended. Of this we simply record the honorable fact, that in negation she showed herself as frank and candid as she had been open in her adherence to an unpopular faith. It is not ours, in solemn presence of the dead, to assume vain airs of playing infallibility. Strong in our own conviction of the firm basis of an immortal hope, we rejoice to think that a Father's arms were open to receive this brave spirit as it soared beyond the clay to the realm where the crude surmises of belief and unbelief are alike swallowed up in the Light Eternal.

Tried with many trials, refined through suffering, enabling her to look out from her enforced retirement with eager sympathy for the struggles and warm anxiety for the welfare of her kind, the religion of Harriet Martineau may have parted with its theological ground, but it never lost its saving hold on heart and life.—*The Christian Life.*

HARMONIUMS.

Harold and Co., call attention to their unequalled stock of rich-toned Harmoniums made especially for India.

FROM RS. 90 TO RS. 900 EACH.

All kinds of Musical Instruments of the best description are always kept in Stock.

ICE! ICE! ICE!

MADE IN FOUR MINUTES

THE PNEUMATIC ICE MACHINE

THIS IMPORTANT INVENTION IS CONSIDERED A BOON
TO THOSE LIVING IN TROPICAL CLIMATES.

CAN BE WORKED BY THE MOST INEXPERIENCED HAND
AND IS NOT LIABLE TO GET OUT OF ORDER.

From Rs. 175, each Machine complete.

MESSRS. ARLINGTON & CO.

AGENTS.

BABU BASANTA KUMAR DATTA,
HOMŒOPATHIC PRACTITIONER
No. 20, Sunker Haldar's Lane, Aheritolah.

FRESH INDENT OF
Medicines and other Requisities,
Have arrived from England.
Medicines, Boxes, Books, Pamphlets;
Absolute Alcohol; Cholera-spirit Camphor.
SPECIAL REMEDIES
For Suppressed, Laborious and Difficult menses; Leucorrhœa.
For Hysteria; Spermatorrhœa; Dysentery; Diarrhœa; Cholera.
For Asthma; Pile; Pain; Sore and Diseases of the Children.
Ice, Lemonade, Soda and Tonic water always.
To be had at
DATTA'S HOMŒOPATHIC LABORATORY.
No. 3/1, Chitpore Road, [illegible] CALCUTTA.
TERMS CASH.
Price List can be had on application.

THEISTIC BOOKS.
FOR SALE.

URDU.

Rahut Hakiki	Rs.	0	3	0
Nizam Komi	...	0	2	0
Kasuf.l Ilham	...	0	2	0
Kholasa, ol, Asool Brahm Dharm	...	0	1	0

HINDI.

Upasana Padhati	Rs.	0	1	0
Benai Putrika or Hymn book	...	0	1	0
Tut Bodh	...	0	8	0
Upanishid Sar	...	0	8	0
Dharm Dipika	...	0	0	6

ENGLISH.

Claims of so called Revealed Religion ...	Rs.	0	3	0
New Life	...	0	0	6
Living God	...	0	1	0
Higher and Lower Virtue ...	...	0	1	0

Apply to the Secretary,
BRAHMO SOMAJ OF THE PUNJAB.
Lahore.

NATIONAL COMPANY.
HOMŒOPATHIC CHEMISTS AND PUBLISHERS
SUPPLY ALL KINDS OF
HOMŒOPATHIC MEDICINES, BOOKS
CASES AND OTHER REQUISITES.
12, COLLEGE SQUARE,
Calcutta.

NOTICE.
INFALLIBLE SPECEFICS FOR ASTHAMA, CONSUMPTION, COLIC, GONORRHŒA AND SPERMATORRHŒA!!!

I AM the son of the late Titaram Paul of Midnapore, who, the public is well aware, was acquainted with specific medicines for the above diseases. I fully learnt the mode of preparing those medicines from my late father, and have cured many people of Midnapore, Calcutta, Hughly, and other places since his death, as the annexed testimonial will shew. Any one wishing to be treated by me can apply to me, care of the Manager of the Indian Mirror.

WOOPENDRA NATH PAUL.

MY father was ailing from asthma for a long time. He had recourse to various sorts of treatment, but none of them proved effectual. At last he regularly used the medicine of Babu Upendra Nath Pal, and was, within a month, freed from all disorders. My own experience leads me to admit that the medicine of Upendra Babu is especially efficacious in cases of Asthma.

HEM CHANDRA BHATTACHARJIA,
Editor of Balmiki Ramayana.
AND
Asst. Secretary, Adi Brahmo Somaj.

28th Baisak,
1798 Sakabda.

SMITH, STANISTREET & CO.

Pharmaceutical Chemists & Druggists
BY APPOINTMENT
To His Excellency the Right Hon'ble
LORD LYTTON, G.M.S.I.
Governor-General of India,
&c., &c.

SYRUP OF LACTATE OF IRON
Prepared from the original receipe. Lactate of Iron, in various forms of preparation, have been in use in France, and generally through the continent of Europe, for some years past, and is highly esteemed as one of the most valuable Chalybeate Tonic Remedies yet introduced. The Syrup, being the most agreeable as well as convenient form of administration is in most general use. It is a most valuable remedy in the following diseases:—Chlorosis or Green Sickness, Leucorrhœa, Neuralgia, Enlargement of the Spleen, &c. In combination with quinine, it has also been very successfully used in the cure of Fever, while to persons of delicate constitution, enfeebled by disease it is invaluable. In bottles. Rs. 2 each.

SYRUP OF THE PHOSPHATE OF IRON Rs. 2 per bottle.

SYRUP OF PHOSPHATE OF IRON AND STRYCHNINE, Rs. 2 per bottle.

SYRUP OF PHOSPHATE OF IRON AND QUININE. Price Rs. 2-8 per bottle.

SYRUP OF PHOSPHATE OF IRON, QUININE AND STRYCHINE. (DR. AITKIN'S TRIPLE TONIC SYRUP,) Rs. 2-8 per bottle.

Smith, Stanistreet & Co.
Invite special attention to the following rates the quality guaranteed as the best procurable:—

Pure Ærated Waters.
Made from Pure Water, obtained by the new process through the Patent Charcoal Filters.

				Rs	As.
Ærated plain (Treble Ærated), per doz.			...	0	12
Soda Water	ditto	„	...	0	12
Gingerade	ditto	„	...	1	4
Lemonade	ditto	„	...	1	4
Tonic (Quinine)	ditto	„	...	1	4

The Cash must be sent with the order to obtain advantage of the above rates.

NOTICE.
MAKHON LOLL GHOSE.
No. 91, Radhabazar, Wholesale and Retail Stationer, Account Bookseller, &c.

BEGS to invite the attention of the Public to an Invoice of Commercial and Fancy Stationery of all sorts which he has recently received, and which he is disposing of at moderate prices. He has been long in the Trade, and presumes he has always afforded every satisfaction to the several merchants here who have constantly favored him with orders. Any Mofusil orders accompanied with remittances shall be promptly attended to.

Printing Materials
MILLER AND RICHARD'S PRESSES, TYPES and all requisites always in Stock,
TERMS CASH.
EWING & CO.

!!! হুকা !!!
!!! HOOKAHS !!!

ENGLISH made Hookahs of various choice designs, colours and sizes, ranging in price from Rs. 2 to 5 each, 60 designs to choose from. Apply to

RADANAUTH CHOWDRY,
575, Jorasanko

Bethune Society.

A DEPUTATION of the members and well-wishers of the above Society, will meet at the Town Hall, on Tuesday the 8th instant, at 12½ P. M., precisely to proceed from thence to Mr. Justice Phear's residence at No. 7, Harrington Street to present to him the Society's Address.

Gentlemen wishing to join the Deputation are respectfully invited to attend at the house and place appointed.

GUNESH CHUNDER MITTER,
Hony. Asst. Secy. Bethune Society.

5th August 1876.

CHUNDER & BROTHERS,
35½ & 112, RADHA BAZAR,
CALCUTTA,
TERMS CASH STRICTLY.

Cash Boxes of Sizes with & without Chubbs' locks.
Railway Bags of Carpet, Leather &c.
Overland trunks of leather.
Scarborough trunks of sizes.
Brass Candlesticks of sizes.
Cricket Bats & Balls.
Chinese Canisters, Square & round.
Compendium of Games of sizes.
Bulleye Lantern, Japanned.
Hand Lamp ENGLISH, for Table & Wall.
Mathematical & Surveying Instruments.
Drawing & Painting Materials.
Color Boxes of sizes & descriptions.
Magic inkstand in large variety.
Inkstands with & without stands of sizes &c.
Playing Cards of different patterns.
Brass Padlocks of sizes.
Water Cocks (brass) for Iron and lead pipes.
Iron & Lead pipes of sizes.
Note & Letter paper of all sizes & qualities.
Foolscap, Demy, Medium, Royal paper &c.
Printing Papers of sizes &c.
Steel Pens, Quills, Pencils.
Writing Inks, of all colors & sizes.
Bank Books, Pocket Book &c. &c.
Fancy & Useful Articles.

CALCUTTA,
The 30th June, 1876. } CHUNDER & BROTHERS.

India General Steam Navigation Company, Ld.

SCHOENE, KILBURN & Co.—*Managing Agents.*

ASSAM LINE.
NOTICE.

Steamers leave Calcutta for Assam every Tuesday, Goalundo every Thursday and leave Debrooghur downward every Saturday.

THE Str. "ASSAM" will leave Calcutta Via Mutabunga for Assam, on Tuesday the 8th instant.

Cargo will be received at the Company's Godowns, Nimtollah Ghat, up till noon of Monday, the 7th proximo.

THE Str. "SIMLA" will leave Goalundo for Assam on Thursday, the 10th instant.

Cargo will be received at the Company's Godowns, No. 4 Fairlie Place, up till noon of Tuesday the 8th.

Goods forwarded to Goalundo for this vessel will be chargeable with Railway Freight from Calcutta to Goalundo in addition to the regular Freight of this Company.

Passengers should leave for Goalundo by Train of Wednesday, the 9th.

CACHAR LINE NOTICE
REGULAR FORTNIGHTLY SERVICE.

Steamers leave Calcutta for Cachar and Intermediate Stations every alternate Friday, and leave Cachar downward every alternate Sunday.

THE Str. "LUCKNOW" will leave Calcutta via Mutabunga for Cachar on Friday, the 11th instant.

Cargo will be received at the Company's Godowns, Nimtollah Ghat, up till noon of Thursday the 10th proximo.

For further information regarding rates of Freight or passage money, apply to

4, FAIRLIE PLACE, } G. J. SCOTT,
Calcutta, 2nd August 1876. } *Secretary.*

Printed and published by M. M. RUKHIT, at the INDIAN MIRROR PRESS, No. 6, College Square, for the Proprietors.

The Indian Mirror.

SUNDAY EDITION.

VOL. XVI | CALCUTTA, SUNDAY AUGUST, 13. 1876 | REGISTERED AT THE GENERAL POST OFFICE. | No. 191

CONTENTS.

NOTICE.

All letters and communications relating to the literary department of the Paper should be addressed to the Editor. All other letters should be addressed to the Manager, to whom all remittances should be made payable.

Subscribers will be good enough to bring to the notice of the Manager any delay or irregularity in the delivery of the Paper.

Editorial Notes.

IT seldom fell to the lot of any Englishman in India to return home with so many addresses or with such unanimous expressions of sympathy and good-will from all classes of the community, as has been the case with Mr. Phear. The fact is creditable to both parties. It evinces sincere philanthropy on the one hand, and true esteem and gratitude on the other. In the present case more than in any other, has it been proved that to every Englishman who loves and serves India with a generous heart, the nation will accord the tribute of its love and gratitude.

THE Rev. Mr. Jardine is going to publish eighteen letters for the English-speaking youth of the country. Of course Mr. Jardine will write all about Bramic Intuitions, Theisim, Hinduism, and other matters. He is making appeals to Christian gentlemen for aid, which we hope he will get. Pandit Nehemiah Nilcant, we believe, wrote similar letters, and Dr. Murray Mitchell also. These letters may be very good, but we hear they are not read by any one. Mr. Jardine, we dare say, will be able to persuade the young men of his school to read his letters, but seeing the fate of similar publications from abler men than himself, we think his undertaking will not be very succful.

SOME time ago we expressed our surprise and regret that Miss Carpenter should have made the erroneous statement at Madras, as reported in the papers, that the leader of the Brahmo Somaj did not meet with a cordial welcome at the hands of the English public in England until the National Indian Association, founded by her at the time, gave him the benefit of its patronage and hospitality. We are glad to learn, upon reliable authority, that it was the reporters who made the absurd mistake. Miss Carpenter is said to have remarked to her friends that it was utterly impossible that she could have said anything of the kind. The whole passage, we understand, was struck out in the revised report which she sent to Bristol from Madras, and which subsequently appeared in the Journal of the National Indian Association.

HOW very little of what people hear do they understand! We have experienced that even when spoken to by men of thought and depth, we have frequently failed to understand them. Not that the words used have been very hard or unintelligible, but it is exceedingly difficult to construe a man's words from his own point of view. What is said or written is understood through the feeling and mood of mind in which we happen to be at the particular moment when we hear it. And as no two men agree in their feelings and states of mind at any given moment of time, mutual misunderstanding becomes almost inevitable. Misunderstanding does not mean the act of putting a disagreeable interpretation upon what we hear, but an agreeable interpretation also when nothing agreeable and complimentary is meant. We are often strangely mistaken in our agreements as our disagreements with men. If all that is said or done, were seen and understood exactly in the sense in which it is said and done, our estimate of men and our mutual relations would come to be very different. Unless there is a perfect seeing into each other, or something very near it, frequent communications with men become very often the source of discomfort and mischief. Men rarely express outwardly what they feel, and what a pity that even when they *do* express themselves, we do not understand them! Unless there is understanding among religious men, can there be brotherhood?

IT is gratifying to observe the interest which Lord Northbrook continues to feel in the "millions in India." At the entertainment given in his honor by the Mayor of Winchester, His Lordship is reported to have made the following excellent remarks in the course of his speech:—"I received to-day, gentlemen, a letter from Rajah Romanath Tagore, in which he said that he hoped I would, now that I was at home, remember the millions in India, and raise my voice if it was ever necessary, on their behalf. I felt when I read that letter, and I feel now, that so far from having worked too hard when in India I have not done perhaps, what I might have done for the millions that were for the time to some extent committed to my care. Taking India altogether, those millions of India are a people who commend themselves most entirely to the affections of those who govern them. (Cheers.) I do not think there exists a more contented people, a people more ready to obey to the letter, and feel confidence and trust in those put over them. (Hear.) All do their duty to their relations and friends in times of difficulty, and all live peaceably one with another. (Applause.) There is no man, I venture to say, who has had charge of a district of India, and has had to deal with the Natives of that country, who will not say the same as I am saying now—no man who has had charge of a district who does not go away with a feeling of affection for the Natives of India—a feeling which remains with him during his life. (Cheers.) My connection was not so close as that, but I have known men I am proud to call friends in India, men with traits of character which make me respect and love them, and I certainly shall not belie the opinion which my friend Rajah Romanath Tagore has of me, and shall not forget the millions that I have governed for fours years. (Cheers.)"

WE publish elsewhere a very good article from the *Spectator* on Miss Harriet Martineau's short autobiography in the *Daily News*. The article does not attempt to give any elaborate description of Miss Martineau's life and character, but points a very important and peculiar feature of her mind, namely the rigid impartiality of her self-estimate. It is impossible while reading the autobiography in the *Daily News* to think that Miss Harriet Martineau could have written it. There is a sentimental self-depreciation in certain people speaking about themselves which tends to produce, or perhaps it is meant to produce, an impression exactly contrary to what the words imply. There is an angry and violent self-denunciation indulged in by others equally uninteresting, untasteful, and sometimes very disagreeable to the uuconcerned public. On the other hand there is a secret self-esteem in some people's confessions about themselves, a cool confidence in their own powers and judgments, which few but themselves could have chosen to entertain. As to "the grotesque vanities" kept away in hidden corners in the minds of many men of culture, and fed upon in private when other eyes are not upon them, we do not allude to them at the present moment. Miss Martineau was free from all these faults. Hers was a cold, passionless view of her own merits and demerits as a writer, which would be strange in men, and in women, so far as we know, unexampled. She criticizes herself in detail and in principle, from a general point of view, and from a special point of view, with that thorough, severe, and sometimes painful impartiality, that cold, hard, intellectual analysis which only unfavorable critics with much ability, and a sincere desire to be honest are sometimes seen to possess. Even the *Saturday Review* itself admires Miss Harriet Ma tineau.

RELIGIOUS GENIUS.

SAY what we might in favor of the theistic doctrine of revelation, the light of Heaven directly received by every soul, it cannot be denied that of late years the gift of genius has been possessed far less in the department of religious life and thought, than in other departments of human pursuit. Take science for instance, or take literature and art at the present day, and the manifestations of genius are more numerous, and far more prominent than in the sphere of religious development. This might have induced an author fond of such sweeping generalizations as Mr. Buckle to pass the opinion that none but young men of weak constitutions, and enervated intellects ever choose to enter into the profession of religion. Place on one side such men as Herschel, Davy, and Faraday; or as Darwin, Huxeley, Tyndal, Mill and Spenser; such men as Wordsworth, Coleridge, and Southey or Carlysle, Emerson, and Tennyson, or Thackeray, Dickens and Ruskin; such women as Mrs. Somerville, George Elliot, and Harriet Martineau; and on the other side place the names of those whose religious utterances, and spiritual culture can claim a corresponding degree of eminence. Do not the latter look very much poor and insignificant in comparison? At the present day names such as Dr. Newman, Cardinal Manning, and Dr. Pusey, or men like Mr. Maurice, Dean Stanley, and the much-lamented Mr. Robertson of Brighton deservedly stand in very high repute, and Mr. Martineau on behalf of the neglected sect of Unitarians may claim an equal eminence. But perhaps with the exception of Dr. Newman, very few of them would be entitled to the position of what may be called religious genius. They are writers, scholars, historians, theologians, and many of them very good ministers. But that is all. F. W. Robertson's sermons do indeed coruscate often with the gleams of true genius, and a depth of spiritual emotion very rare indeed in the cold Western nature; and Mr. Maurice lifts us from the low platform of materialistic scepticism and muscular Christianity to the sublime regions of the piety of the Fourth Gospel; and Mr. Martineau quietly accompanies us through green and noble pastures of thought to the sun-lit summits and cool mountain-breezes of a higher and better world. All this we admit, and for what they, and others like them, have taught us, we feel more grateful than we can express. The pursuit of religion so difficult in ordinary circumstances, has become familiar and profitable under their guidance. But the fire of genius that burns and sanctifies, creates conflagrations and spreads far and wide, and affects mighty masses of men, *that* is absent. The light of European piety, like the effulgence of the Polar sky, is an extensive illumination without corresponding heat. A George Fox, or a John Wesley working among the unlettered and humble, possessed more of the true stuff, though not a very large amount of the cold light whose market value is so great at the present day. Religious men often labor under the strange mistake that religion without scholarship would not be passable before the tribunal of truth, and that without acquaintance with Thomas Aquinas, Lucretius, and the Stagyrite, one cannot be admitted to the select circle in heaven. Now it has sometimes seemed to us that in true genius there is always a back ground of ignorance, conscious confessed ignorance, before which, and by the negative effect of which, the light of Heaven shines forth with the greater glory and intensity. There is in such genius, so it has appeared to us, a clearness, a straight and direct vision of ultimate ends, which looks not unoften like narrowness and exclusiveness. The roughness, readiness, fearlessness, and singularity so completely opposed to what in social cant will be called culture, the familiarity which strongly savours of the vulgar sometimes, so very much against the modern canons of propriety, may distinguish the genius. We cannot say we have been always enamoured of the utterances of Mr. Spurgeon, or out and out admirers of the Moody and Sankey system of eloquence; but Messers Spurgeon, Moody and Sankey will find tens of thousands to hear them, and build Metropolitan Tabernacles for them, while Mr. Stopford Brooke has no chapel in which to sermonize on the Theology of Poetry, and Mr. Newman Hall's church is built for him by the friends whom he visited and lectured in America. We are admirers of both these last-mentioned gentlemen, and specially of the former; but religious genius is very different from what they posses. Dean Stanley invited Prof. MaxMuller to lecture in Westminister Abbey, a bold and unusual step, and the good Dean himself seldom withholds his eloquence whenever there is a statue to be unveiled, or a funeral sermon to be read. Canon Kingsley, John Bunian, and Dr. Priestly make no difference to him; and Bishop Colenso acted as nobly as wisely when he declined, though asked, to preach in Westminister Abbey, all these are good men and true, but we seek in vain for any vestige of spiritual genius in these quarters. Genius in literature, art, and science means thought, discovery, and research; it means imagination, emotion, and the grasp of mind. Not that these gifts are foreign to religion; but religious genius means a deep, all-absorbing and secret life more than anything else. It is not so much to think and feel in paths untrodden before, as to be dragged into a vortex of life as strangely dissimilar to the ways of the world as the life of the Manicheans and the Astrologers was to that of St. Ambrose, or the profession of Rhetoric to that of Augustine. Now in St. Augustine such genius culminates in a passion of piety, now in Chaitanya it culminates in faith and love; in St. Xaviour it reaches the extremity of self-sacrifice, and in Mahomet the extremity of zeal for presolytism and the destruction of infidility, in Thodore Parker the destruction of untruth. But in all these men the genious was a *character* which filled them wholly, which preyed upon their health and rest, led them about like a strange and uncontrollable influence they knew not whither. It is curious to note how men of religious genius have uniformly inveighed against the principle of free personality, and it is positively wrong to single out Martin Luther for his eccentric sayings on this particular point. From the days of St. Paul, and him whom St. Paul recognized as his divine master, to those of the German Mystics, from the time of Sakya Singha as he sat under the emblamatic Bo tree in the Nepal Terai, to that of the writers of the Bhagavat Gita, among the Vaishnavas of Bengal, and the Sufis of Persia, and the Vedantists of Guzrat, spiritual self-destruction, or rather self-immersion has been the doctrine of all doctrines. Every great religious genius has borne repeated testimony to the pre-eminent necessity of merging all self-will, self-indulgence, self-consciousness in the supreme fact of life in Divine Life. It is living the life divine, loving on the model of divine love, dying to do the divine will that creates and constitutes true greatness here. Because in these days the tendency has been reversed entirely, because self-consciousness and self-reliance form the passport to eminence and ease, because men are of opinion that as in other matters so in religion, genius means only thought and sentiment, with the average and recognized quantum of ethical and spiritual life, therefore the gift of religious genius is being slowly withdrawn, and religious men sink into the level of mediocrity, and suffer from comparison with the votaries of Science and Art.

Correspondence.

WORSHIP OF THE GHOO-GHOO

To the Editor of the *Indian Mirror*.

SIR,—Theism is eminently just, impartial, charitable; and only asks to be judged by its fruits. It has no prejudices. God's love and purity, copyable by man,—God's discoverable wisdom and imitable methods of working, furnish its creed; and it needs no other. Its only remaining need is organisation, centralisation, union in the guidance of the fittest; in the leadership of the most worthy, to victory over its enemies, the enemies of God and man; carelessness, ignorance, animality and surrender to the lower self. Theism, as the Science of Religion, though an infant science, has already seen that the "heathen" world quite as much as the Christian has, on the whole, made the best of its opportunities; and is eager for improvement. The "heathen" is as glad as the Christian to get good; and the highest good, True Religion. Theism as fraternity, says, that all truth needs all truth and every man wants his neighbor's sympathy and co-operation.

"All are needed by each one;
Nothing is good or true alone."

"Worship this," said the Rajah Radhakant to me, one morning, clapping his hand upon a pillar of the veranda. "This is God. God is all, and all is God. Worship what you will, you can't go wrong; for everything is God." "No, my dear friend," I replied, "God is not brick and mortar, God is a spirit; and all that worship Him must worship him in *spirit*, if in truth." 'But how does spirit commune with man except through form?' was evidently in his mind. Idolatry to him was but the visible, tangible expression of spirit answering to spirit. Blameless in theory, ruinous only in its practical results. At the moment two Ghoo-ghoos, garden-doves, ring-doves, flew into the veranda, and up to the cornice in which they had their nest. "Ah, I have you now!" he said, "God is a spirit; but you worship these! Christians worship these! Holy-ghost! Holy-ghost! Ghoo-ghoo; do you not worship the Ghoo-ghoo? Did God not descend in bodily form as a Ghoo-ghoo?' I could not deny that I had seen what a large numerical majority of Christians declare to be 'God the Holy Ghost,' 'the only God,' 'the Most High—chiselled in marble in bodily form as a dove,—or painted in dove-color, in many a 'Christian' Church, both in Europe and America. Though the *pran pratistha* is never performed upon the dove, nor the magic blessing which puts God into holy wafer, believed by Christians, to be the tangible, "real presence" of God. Yes he had caught the Christian, at his idol, in the worship of the water, if not also of the Ghoo-ghoo,—and there was no escape. Christian and Hindu were alike idolators. In self-defence I could not but tell the leader of orthodox (trinitarian, idolatrous) Hinduism, the good and sincere idolator and Pantheist that I was not a Pantheist;—I was a Theist;—that as to those just described I was neither of one party nor of the other. To me neither Ghoo-ghoo or wafer was God; God in "real presence;" though anything God had made might be used as a teacher or suggester of God's love and peace. . . . . How then did I explain the descent of the Holy Ghost, escape ghoo-worship, and still call myself a follower of Christ?

My answer to this question as a 'Christian' theist, must close this letter.—I said that Jesus,—to clear his mind from its last earthly hope,—and confirm his resolve to tell the truth and die for it, solemnised this cleansing, this purpose pure as heaven, by the rite of baptism. Who should administer it but the foremost of living prophets, the one baptizer, John the Baptist. Jesus leaves his mountain home, and by a journey of 70 or 80 miles reaches the banks of the river where John was baptising, and hundreds were confessing their sins, and being pledged to a new and pure and holy life. John at first declines the office deciding, from all that he knew of Jesus, and spiritually discerned to be in him, that Jesus was the manlier man of the two, the godlier soul.—Jesus insists, argues, gives his reasons, till finally John yields and consents to perform the rite. Throughout the ceremony Jesus was wrapped in earnest prayer. Every door and portal and avenue of his soul was thrown open to "the descending God," of power, peace, purity. By a divinely natural and impartial law of His own government, God could not but come in. He did come in. But that triumphal entry could not be told, be outlined except in figures. The symbol of peace and purity, in all tongues, what is it? The dove. In any after-revealing by Jesus of what he experienced on this occasion how could he avoid this figure? To encourage his friends to a like self-surrender, for God and man, Jesus, as the spirit of wisdom, moved him in various ways and on several occasions essayed to tell of the unspeakable joy, tried to impart the incommunicable bliss and welcome of that hour of self-consecration. 'Ask and ye shall receive,' he said. 'Seek and ye shall find; knock at the Gate of heaven and it will be opened to you.' I knocked and it was opened to me at that hour. I saw heaven open, and its white angels descending upon me. The very love of peace came and nestled in my soul.' . . . Of course it was a spirit-dove. Of the four biographers, three, Mathew, Mark and Luke say, 'twas Jesus alone who saw the dove They name no other witness. The fourth evangelist adds that the Baptizer, John, had, with Jesus a consentaneous realization that God's peace came upon him. John saw it in Jesus' eye, his face, his glorified, extatic demeanor. John knew enough of his cousin's life and purpose to read heaven in his soul. None saw an outward bird-form, resembling that Ghoo-ghoo on the Rajah's cornice. Such a Holy Ghost is a correspondence and nothing more.

Yours,
DALL.

Devotional

LORD, I cannot pray unto thee, day after day, for the removal of the same vicious habit, unless I am a hypocrite and a confirmed sinner and really unwilling to part with favorite sins. One sincere prayer, uttered before thee, out of the depths of the heart, is capable of overcoming even the most inveterate sin, such is the power of true prayer, such the power of thy saving grace. How is it then that though I have prayed a hundred, yea a thousand times, my sins are not yet gone, my heart is still estranged from thee. Grant, O God, that my prayers may not be vain repetitions, like those of a hypocrite.

LORD, let thy blessing descend in showers upon the Bharat Asram. Though imperfect, and mismanaged by those into whose hands thou hast entrusted it, it has, so far as it has proved true to thee, conferred great benefits upon those who have taken shelter in it. Here the homeless have found a home, and the helpless wanderer in life's path has here found rest. Make it, Kind God, more and more a sweet home and a place of education and discipline unto its inmates.

More humility vouchsafe unto me, O my Father. Pride is my bitterest enemy. It defiles my heart as nothing else can, and shakes the very foundations of faith, love and purity. I think I am humble if I can only bow reverently before thee and acknowledge my nothingness. Thus I deceive myself. Before my brother and sister I cannot bring down my arrogant head. The dust of their feet I do not yet accept as the means of my salvation. Crush my pride hard as stone, and make me humble and meek.

O GOD, I glorify tears. They are my friend and helper. In them I find light and strength and joy. If my eyes are dry I apprehend danger, for all my enemies seeing that the time is favorable to them begin to attack me. With tears in my eyes I see through them the rainbow colors of heaven, and rejoice. Grant me Lord, tears of love for ever.

The Brahmo Somaj

THE Brahmica Somaj meets at the Bharat Asram, in the hall of prayer, twice every week. Four sermons have been preached in easy and homely Bengali, adapted to the female mind, on the following subjects:—(I) The Real God, (II). The Beautiful God, (III) Our Future Home (IV) Our Beautiful Future Home.

THE daily *sankirtan* continues to excite interest and draw crowds of people. So many as fifty or sixty persons are now and then seen gathered. The singing is enthusiastic and effective. Hymns in the *oula* tune, which is extremely popular, with the accompaniment of the *ektara*, may, we think, be advantageously introduced on alternate days.

YESTERDAY the first anniversary of the opening of the Chinsura Brahmo Mandir was celebrated, service being conducted by Babu Amrita Loll Bose.

WE understand that the Brahmo Gita will be chanted on the occasion of the Utsab on Sunday next. Babu Grish Chunder Sen will read a paper on "Spiritual Friendship" translated from the Persian.

Gleanings

HE who avoids the battle of life, remains weak and unready, and only he who contends for the mastery wins the crown.

No man knows the genuineness to his convictions until he has sacrificed something for them.

God's beneficence streams out from the morning sun, and his love looks down upon us from the starry eyes of midnight. It is his solicitude that wraps us in the air, and the pressure of his hand, so to speak, that keeps our pulse beating. O! it is a great thing to realize that the Divine Power is always working; that nature in every valve and every artery, is full of the presence of God.

Courage is always greatest when blended with meekness; intellectual ability is most admirable when it sparkles in the setting of a modest self-distrust; and never does the human soul appear so strong as when it foregoes revenge and dares to forgive an injury. There can be no true manliness without gentleness, mercy, and love. There only superficial strength in him who can do but not endure.

What is prayer without love but the mockery of lofty compliment, or the awe and agony of servile fear? Love is the very life of the best things, and without it they are mere bodies, dead and empty.

To-morrow may never come to us. We do not live in to-morrow. We can not find it in any of our title deeds. The man who owns whole blocks of real estate and great ships on the sea, does not own a single minute of to-morrow. To-morrow, it is a mysterious possibility, not yet born. It lies under the seal of midnight,—behind the veil of glittering constellations.

Living Words.

Literary

MR. P. H. P. GORDON, late Editor of the *Madras Athenæum*, has died in England.

THE honorary degree of D. C. L. voted by the Convocation of the University of Oxford to Sir Salar Jung, at the recent commemoration, was conferred on him in person at Oxford on July 24th.

WE are glad to hear good accounts about the health of Mr. M. Maclean, the Editor of the *Bombay Gazette*. "There is no reason to suppose that he will not be able to return to India in the course of a few months."

DR. SCOTT's "Village Life in India," is well spoken of.

A PHILADELPHIA correspondent declares Rowell's American newspaper building in connection with the Centennial Exhibition to be a Native enterprise of which the Americans may all be proud. Files of over eight thousand papers are kept, and a pleasant notice invites every one to "step in and see a newspaper from home." The lower floor is devoted to the pigeon-hole files, and a gallery around the sides contains four pretty little rooms and two long rows of desks for the use of the journalists. One of the rooms, intended for ladies, is furnished entirely with wicker furniture, and overlooking the little lake, makes a most charming retreat on a hot day.

AN article on the "Rajput States of India," has appeared in the July number of the *Edinburgh Review*.

MR. EDWARD STANFORD of London has published the following:—"Russia—Map of the Acquisitions of Russia in Europe and Central Asia, since the Accession of Peter I. to 1876. By J. Arrowsmith," and also "Central Asia—Map of Central Asia. Constructed from the latest English and Russian Documents. By John Arrowsmith. With Additions and Corrections to the Present Time. Extending from Peshawur, in India, to Orenburgh, on the limits of European Russia; and from Teheran, in Persia, to Chuguchak, on the frontier of China, including all the recent English and Russian Explanatory and Military Surveys," &c., &c.

MESSRS. CHAPMAN and Hall have published Lord (Robert) Lytton's "Fables in Song."

ADOLPH FREDERIC STENZLER, Ph. D., Professor of Oriental Languages in the University of Breslau, has edited the "Institutes of Gautama."

Scientific

THE *Moniteur Industriel Belge* states that a locomotive without furnace, has commenced running in Paris on one of the tramways. It has a reservoir of superheated water, which furnishes a constant supply of steam for moving the vehicle. On another line of tramways an ordinary steam locomotive is at work. It is like a small omnibus in shape and size, containing a boiler. The furnace is out of sight, and fed with coke and charcoal. The draught of the furnace is kept up by a supply of compressed air.

PROF. HUXLEY will visit America this summer, and has promised to deliver at least three lectures before leaving for England.

QUEEN EMMA, of the Sandwich Islands, has sent to the Philadelphia Centennial Exhibition some cloaks made from the bark of the bread-fruit tree. They look like tissue paper and are as tough as an ulster.

Latest News

—SEVERAL wealthy Natives of Bangalore have among themselves subscribed Rs. 20,000 for the sole purpose of encouraging the sale of Indian-made cloths and have for this purpose opened a shop in the heart of the Pettah, where a great variety of the country-made stuff is exposed for sale.

—THE Amir of Bokhara received an imperial ukase from the Emperor of Russia, directing him to collect supplies and carriage for the Russian troops employed in Central Asia. The Amir has accordingly set to work energetically to carry out the order.

—SEVERAL of the leading men of Swat waited upon the Akhund to report that the Afridis had sought their aid against the British, and to inquire his wishes in this respect, and his opinion as to whether it would be a lawful crescentade against infidels within the meaning of the Koran. The Akhund replied that they might please themselves about fighting against British, but that no "Jehad" or religious war could be lawful in which the contending parties on either side were not headed by Kings.

—THE cruelties now being committed by the soldiery in Turkey are horrible. We hear of soldiers cutting Christian infants in pieces and throwing these pieces into the air to catch them on the points of their swords.

—BABU NOBIN CHUNDER ROY, Deputy Examiner of Public Accounts, N. W. P., has been appointed Pay Master of the Rajputana State Railway. His head-quarters will be at Agra.

—SOME of the Bombay Native papers are already agitating that Mr. Dadabhai Naoroji should be nominated to the Bombay Legislative Council.

—THE picture of the young Gaikwar of Baroda, entrusted by Sir Madava Rao to the artist, of the First Prince of Travancore is nearly completed. It is a life-size painting of a half figure of the young Prince in full Court dress.

—THE case in which a Native butler at Madras was charged with attempting to commit adultery with his mistress, was concluded at the Sessions on the 8th instant. The butler was sentenced to six months' rigorous imprisonment.

—HEAVY floods have occurred at Mangalore. Many miles of property have been washed away and hundreds rendered houseless. There is great destitution among the poor people.

—AT Simla, says the *Bhaskur News* of the 31st ultimo, a young European gentleman has forsaken the religion of his forefathers, and become a devotee in accordance with the rites of Hinduism. He is now living in the house of a Brahmin, who has become his moral preceptor, with a view to bring him up as a regular *fogi* or devotee, before he sets out on his intended pilgrimage to the shrines of the different Hindu deities.

—THE London *Guardian* is informed that the bishopric of Calcutta has been offered to the Rev. Alfred Blomfield, and has been declined by him. It was said to have been previously offered to Drs. Farrar and Moorhouse without better result.

—IT is stated that the proposed new Indian bishopric, the seat of which will be at Lahore, will probably be coferred upon the Rev. Francis Baring, M.A., who has been for some time past laboring as a missionary in the Punjab, and is now in England. He is a son of the Bishop of Durham.

—SIR GEORGE CAMPBELL is expected to deliver a Parliamentary protest against the discussion of the Indian Budget being relegated to the fag-end of the Session.

—ON July 15, at Dunrobin Castle, Sir Salar Jung received addresses presented by deputations from the Town Councils of Inverness, Dingwall, Tain, and Wick. Inverness was represented by the Provost, two baillies, and town clerk; Dingwall by the Provost, two baillies, and town clerk; and Tain and Wick, each by the Provost and two baillies. The reception was held in the drawing-room, each deputation being introduced in succession by the Duke of Sutherland; and in reading and presenting the addresses they generally referred with satisfaction to the visit to England of Sir Salar Jung, to whom a hearty welcome was given, as the guest of an honored and patriotic nobleman.

—SIR RICHARD TEMPLE received an address from the inhabitants of Bancurah and also some *slokas*, the composition of a local Pundit; to which His Honor gave suitable replies. His Honor held a *conversazione* at which the elite of the Native society were present.

—THE bridge over the Sutlej is broken.

—A rail was taken out of the E. I. Railway line near the Assensole Station, with the intent to throw the Down Mail Train. Happily danger was averted.

—ON Friday last we read that a "large congregation of Mahomedans, more than the usual number, assembled at the Jumma Musjid, Bombay, and after the sermon and prayers were over, the priest prayed for the recovery of Sultan Murad, in the Arabic language, and the people cried aloud, 'ameen, ameen' at the end of every sentence, and blessings were offered.

Calcutta.

THE P. and O. Co.'s S. S. *Geelong*, Commander C. Fraser, arrived in Bombay Harbour, on Wednesday morning last, from Suez with the English Mails of the 21st ult. on board. The following is the list of passengers :—

FROM SOUTHAMPTON.

Mr. W. Searle — Mr. and Mrs. J. Rumicorn.
Mr. G. Carter

FROM BRINDISI.

Mr. G. G. Arbuthnott — Mr. G. Jeffores
Mr. J. Kindersley — Capt. Hay.
Mr. W. Ryan

FROM SUEZ.—Mr. J. Robinson.

FROM ADEN.

Miss O'Grady — Eleven Natives.

MR. E. J. TREVELYAN, Barrister-at-Law, has been nominated as Tagore Law Professor for the following year.

THE funeral of the late Mr. Justice Glover, at Galle, was attended by Military and Civilian gentlemen and by the local Bar.

"THE *Indian Daily News* hears that the Board of Directors of the East Indian Railway have voted Rs. 40,000 to the family of the late Mr. Cecil Stephenson, Rs. 80,000 to Mr. J. D. Nond, Secretary to the Board, and Rs. 22,000 to Mr. George Sibley.

THE Hon'ble V. H. Schalch retires in March next.

DOMESTIC OCCURRENCE.

BIRTH.

BOSE.—On the 7th July 1876, at Jamalpore, E. I. Railway, the wife of Babu Ashutosh Bose of a son.

Original Poetry.

THE SONG OF LIFE.

A maiden sat, and sang, and sang
The whole of the livelong day ;
Both lip and brow were deck'd with smiles,
And this was her roundelay :—
"Oh, life is long, and love is strong,
The world is kind and true ;
Oh, life is long, and love is strong :
Somebody come to woo."

The maiden sat, and sang, and sang
The whole of the livelong day ;
And young love paused, as you may wear,
To list to her roundelay.
She sang "Oh life and love are strong,
The world is kind and true ;
Oh, life is long, and love is strong ;
Somebody come to woo !"

And still the maiden sat and sang
Thro' each long summer day ;
And her blithe young voice grew blither yet,
As she sang this roundelay :—
"Oh, love is long and deep and strong,
My world is kind and true ;
Oh, life is long, and love is strong,
Since both have come to woo.

The maid was wed, yet still she sang
Blessing her bridal day,
Her own glad heart and life's dull sands
Making a roundelay.
"Oh, life is long and love is strong,
The world is kind and true,
Oh, *death* is strong tho' love be long
And age creeps on to woo."

Years fled—and other maidens sang,
With hearts as light and gay ;
The mother she sat apart and croon'd
This trembling roundelay :—
She sang, "Oh, life and love are strong,
And heaven is kind and true :
Its life is long, its love is strong,
And *Death* is near to woo.

EMILIE SEARCHFIELD.

Selection.

HARRIET MARTINEAU'S AUTOBIOGRAPHY.

THE epitomized autobiography which Miss Martineau deposited with the *Daily News*, to be published immediately after her death, and which appeared in that journal on Thursday, is a true literary curiosity. We have always maintained that cultivated persons, in this conscious age of ours, are less under delusions about themselves and their own capacities than it is the fashion with satirists to assume. Very few, it is true, or probably none, understand themselves completely, and very many, possibly all, retain in hidden corners of their minds baseless little vanities, sometimes of a very grotesque kind. But a very large number indeed weigh their own powers, as distinct from their own character, very accurately, know exactly what they can do and cannot do, and are able to judge their own minds *ab extra* as they would judge those of third persons. If they make mistakes, it is in the direction of self-depreciation, of a distrust which sometimes is consistent with an appearance of vanity on the very subject on which they know themselves to be weak. Vanity, and particularly visible vanity, is often a mere parade of armour over the weak place, and men are constantly soothed by flattery directed to the qualities which, as they recognise, with humorous contempt alike for the flatterer and themselves, they do not possess. Here, for instance, was a middle-aged woman of fifty-three, who had for ten years resided almost in solitude in the Lake country, who was visited mainly by worshippers, who had had, for a woman, considerable literary and political success, and who was by no means of the very first order of intellect. She was a nervous woman, too, who all her life had mistaken a weak heart and a liability to nervous exhaustion for imminent heart-disease,—a temperament perhaps the most unfavorable of all to true self-knowledge. Yet she sits down and writes a newspaper biography of herself and her work, so coldly judicial, so severely passionless, so harsh, indeed, in some respects, that had it not been her own work, the Editor of the *Daily News* would have been charged with a mocking hardness for giving it publicity so soon after her death. He would hardly have ventured to write of her efforts at fiction the sentence we have italicised :—"None of her novels or tales have, or ever had, in the eyes of good judges or in her own, any character of permanence. The artistic aim and qualifications were absent ; she had no power of dramatic construction ; neither the poetic inspiration on the one hand, nor the critical cultivation on the other, without which no work of the imagination can be worthy to live. Two or three of her 'Political Economy Tales' are, perhaps, her best achievement in fiction,—*her doctrine furnishing the plot which she was unable to create*, and the brevity of space duly restricting the indulgence in detail which injured her longer narratives, and at last warned her to leave off writing them. It was fortunate for her that her own condemnation anticipated that of the public. To the end of her life she was subject to solicitations to write more novels and more tales, but she for the most part remained steady in her refusal. Her three volumes of 'Forest and Game-Law Tales' and a few stories in *Household Words*, written at the express and earnest request of Mr. Dickens, and with little satisfaction to herself, are her latest efforts in that direction." That is a perfectly just judgment, with these exceptions,—that Mr. Martineau had some faculty of suggesting, though none of analysing character ; and that she had a strange, almost inexplicable power of touching, in most prosaic and unimaginative fashion, the springs of pathos and pity. Reading some of her Poor-Law stories is like standing by the death-bed of a hungry woman, and leaves a sensation almost of physical. She had not, however, the artistic touch, and her fictions, though they did good work in their time, will all moulder away forgotten in ancient libraries.

That a writer should despise some division of his writings is, however, no unfrequent phenomenon. Defoe never dreamed that he was to live for ever through "Robinson Crusoe," and many a statesman has hoped, like Richelieu, to survive by his wretched poems, but Miss Martineau judged all her work with the same coldly unfavorable eye. She says of her first book on America, that she was carried away by sympathy with some American statesman, and "the book is not a favorable specimen of Harriet Martineau's writings, either in regard to moral or artistic taste. It is full of affectations and preachments, and it marks the highest point of the metaphysical period of her mind." She is equally severe on herself as a historian. Her book, "The History of the Thirty Years' Peace," will live some years, as the only brief and readable collection of the annals of the period, and it brought her much popularity ; but she reckons it in her biographical sketch at nearly its true value :—"Without taking the chronicle form, this history could not, from the nature of the case, be cast in the ultimate form of perfected history. All that can be done with contemporary history is to collect and methodise the greatest amount of reliable facts and distinct impressions,—to amass sound material for the veritable historian of a future day,—so consolidating, assimilating and verifying the structure, as to do for the future writer precisely that which the lapse of time and the oblivion which creeps over all transactions, must prevent his doing for himself. This auxiliary usefulness is the aim of Harriet Martineau's history, and she was probably not mistaken in hoping for that much result from her labor." Of the most serious defect of the book its absurd over-estimate of that showy politician Canning, she was probably unaware, as she was also unaware that her theological writings contributed positively nothing to the stock of ideas in the world. She seems, in her biographical sketch, to make an exception in their favor to an estimate more harshly true, perhaps, than woman ever yet passed upon her own performances and powers :—"Her original power was nothing more than was due to earnestness and intellectual clearness within a certain range. With small imaginative and suggestive powers, and therefore nothing approaching to genius, she could see clearly what she did see, and give a clear expression to what she had to say. In short, she could popularise, while she could neither discover nor invent. She could sympathise in other people's views, and was too facile in doing so ; and she could obtain and keep a firm grasp of her own, and moreover, she could make them understood. The function of her life was to do this, and in as far as it was done diligently and honestly, her life was of use, however far its achievements may have fallen short of expectations less moderate than her own." If any proof were wanting of the lucidity of vision and expression which are the only powers she claims, this sketch alone is sufficient to afford it ; and it will suggest to most men also that she must have possessed another power,—that judicial faculty which is so often wanting in men and women of genius, and is so seldom lacking to any high order of ability. That faculty will give a high interest to the posthumous work we are promised, the Autobiography to which she devoted two years, and which, fearing lest her executors should be blamed for some statements in it, she herself passed through the Press. Considering the number of personages she knew, her utter freedom, as it appears from this sketch, from self-interested prejudice, and her considerable political knowledge, this should be a book of great interest, even though it does not tell us very much of the inner nature and ideal life of Miss Harriet Martineau.—*Spectator.*

Advertisements

ALBERT HALL.

PATRON.

His Honor the Lieutenant Governor of Bengal

COUNCIL.

Hon'ble Sir William Muir, K. C. S. I.—*President.*

Rajah Rama Nath Tagore Bahadur C. S. I.—*Vice-President.*

Hon'ble J. F. D. Inglis.
Hon'ble Ashley Eden, C. S. I.
Hon'ble H. Bell.
Archdeacon Baly.
Colonel H. E. L. Thuillier, C. S. I.
His Highness the Maharajah of Vizianagram.
Maharajah Kumar of Bettiah.
Hon'ble Rajah Narendra Krishna Bahadur.
Rajah Komul Krishna Bahadur.
Rajah Joteendro Mohun Tagore Bahadur.
Babu Digumber Mitter, C. S. I.
Dr. Rajendralala Mitra.
Hon'ble Nawab Ashgar Ali Bahadur, C. S. I.
Nawab Amir Ali Bahadur.
Moulvi Abdul Latif Khan Bahadur.
Manockji Rustomji Esq.
Babu Keshub Chunder Sen.

SUBSCRIPTIONS.

The Hon'ble Sir Richard Temple		Rs.	200
His Highness Maharajah Holkar	...	„	5,000
His Highness Maharajah of Jeypore		„	5,000
His Highness Maharajah of Putialah		„	2,500
His Highness Maharajah of Vizianagram	...	„	1,000
His Highness the Maharajah of Cooch Behar	...	„	1,000
Maharajah Kumar of Bettiah	...	„	2,000
Rajah of Bhinga	...	„	1,000
Maharani Surnomoie, Cossim Bazar		„	1,000
Maharajah of Hutwa	...	„	500
Rajah Roma Nath Tagore Bahadur		„	200
Rajah Komul Krishna Bahadur	...	„	500
Rajah Joteendro Mohun Tagore	...	„	500
Hon'ble Rajah Narendra Krishna Bahadur	...	„	300
Babu Joykissen Mookerjee	...	„	250
Sirdar Dyal Singh	...	„	200
Babu Shama Churn Law	...	„	200
Hon'ble Sir William Muir	...	„	100
Hon'ble Ashley Eden	...	„	100
Dr. Mohendro Loll Sircar	...	„	100
Babu Goonendro Nath Tagore	...	„	100
Babu Jadulall Mullick	...	„	100
Babu Ananda Mohun Bose	...	„	100
Babu Rajkissen Mookerjee	...	„	200
Babu Janoki Nath Mookerji	...	„	100
Hon'ble H. Bell	...	„	100
Babu Debendro Nath Bose	...	„	200
Babu Annoda Prosad Roy	...	„	100
Babu Digumber Mitter	...	„	100

Ulcerations of all kinds.

There is no medicinal preparation which may be so thoroughly relied upon in the treatments of the above ailments as Holloways Ointment. Nothing can be more simple and safe than the manner in which it is applied; nothing more salutary than its action on the body, both locally and constitutionally. The Ointment rubbed round the part affected enters the pores as salt penetrates meat. It quickly penetrates to the root of the evil and drive it from the system.

NOTICE.

INFALLIBLE SPECIFICS FOR ASTHAMA, CONSUMPTION, COLIC, GONORRHŒA AND SPERMATORRHŒA!!!

I AM the son of the late Titaram Paul of Midnapore, who, the public is well aware, was acquainted with specific medicines for the above diseases. I fully learnt the mode of preparing those medicines from my late father, and have cured many people of Midnapore, Calcutta, Hughly, and other places since his death, as the annexed testimonial will shew. Any one wishing to be treated by me can apply to me, care of the Manager of the Indian Mirror.

WOOPENDRA NATH PAUL.

BABU UPENDRA NATH PAL.

Sir,

You will be glad to hear that the painful asthama under which I was suffering for the last three years and through which I was nearly brought to the brink of death, has been perfectly cured through your treatment. I was laid under the care of several able Doctors and *Kabirajes*, but every treatment on their part proved a failure on me. God bless you and let your cure spread over those who are suffering under the same wretched circumstances.

SURYA COMAR MAZUMDAR

CALCUTTA,
SCHOOLER, SMITH, AND CO.
The 30th August 1875.

THEISTIC BOOKS.

FOR SALE.

URDU.

Rahut Hakiki	...	...	Rs.	0	3	0
Nizam Komi	...	...	...	0	2	0
Kasnfal Ilhau	...	...	...	0	2	0
Kholasa, ol, Asool Brahmo Dharm			...	0	1	0

HINDI.

Upasana Pudhati	...	...	Rs.	0	1	0
Benai Patrika or Hymn book			...	0	1	0
Tut Bodh	...	...	...	0	8	0
Upnashid Sar	...	...	...	0	8	0
Dhurm Dipika	...	...	...	0	0	6

ENGLISH.

Claims of so called Revealed Religion	...	...	Rs.	0	3	0
New Life	...	...	...	0	0	6
Living God	...	...	...	0	1	0
Higher and Lower Virtue	...		...	0	1	0

Apply to the Secretary,
BRAHMO SOMAJ OF THE PUNJAB,
Lahore.

NOTICE

MAKHON LOLL GHOSE.

No. 91, Radhabazar, Wholesale and Retail Stationer, Account Bookseller, &c.

BEGS to invite the attention of the Public to an Invoice of Commercial and Fancy Stationery of all sorts which he has recently received, and which he is disposing of at moderate prices. He has been long in the Trade, and presumes he has always afforded every satisfaction to the several merchants here who have constantly favored him with orders. Any Mofussil orders accompanied with remittances shall be promptly attended to.

ESTABLISHED 1833.

H. C. GANGOOLY & CO.

STATIONERS, DIESINKERS, ENGRAVERS, PRINTERS, LITHOGRAPHERS & CO.

24, Mangoe Lane, Calcutta.

Cash prices of the following :—

	Rs.	As.	Rs.
Whatman's Drawing paper double elephant sizes (40 X 27) each ...	0	7	
Mathematical Instrument, Boxes	2	8 to	1
Color Boxes	0	4	„

Drawing pencils, Drawing and Mapping steel pens and various other requisites in stationery.

BABU BASANTA KUMAR DUTTA,
HOMŒOPATHIC PRACTITIONER

No. 20, Sunker Halder's Lane, Ahiritolah.

FRESH INDENT OF

Medicines and other Requisites,
Have arrived from England.
Medicines, Boxes, Books, Pamphlets;
Absolute Alcohol; Cholera-spirit Camphor.
SPECIAL REMEDIES.

For Suppressed, Laborious and Difficult menses; Leucorrhœa.

For Hysteria; Spermatorrhœa; Dysentery; Diarrhœa; Cholera.

For Asthma; Pile; Pain; Sore and Diseases of the Children.

Ice, Lemonade, Soda and Tonic water always.

To be had at

DUTTA'S HOMŒOPATHIC LABORATORY

No. 312, CHITPORE ROAD, BURTOLA, CALCUTTA.

TERMS—CASH.

Price List can be had on application.

THE

INDIAN MIRROR PRESS

Is Ready to Undertake to Print
BOOKS AND JOB WORKS
OF ALL DESCRIPTIONS,
VIZ :—
Price-Currents, Circulars, Labels,
Letter-Heads, Tables,
STATEMENTS, BILLS, CHEQUE
IMPORTS, EXPORTS,
And all other kinds of Form,
AND
ALL SORTS OF TICKETS AND CARDS
WITH NEATNESS & DESPATCH,
and at very Moderate Rates.

All communications &c. to be addressed to the Manager, "INDIAN MIRROR" Press, 15 College Square.

THE INDIAN MIRROR

The Cheapest Daily Paper
IN
INDIA
AND
Having an Extensive Circulation

SUBSCRIPTIONS,
(IN ADVANCE.)

		Town.				Mofussil, Including Postage.		
Yearly	... Rs.	13	0	0	Rs.	23	0	0
Half yearly	... „	6	8	0	„	11	8	0
Quarterly	... „	3	8	0	„	6	0	0
Monthly	... „	1	8	0		2	6	0

Cash sales, One Anna per copy.

Sunday Edition.

Per Annum ... ... Rs. 5

MOFUSSIL SUBSCRIBERS.

Per Annum ... ... Rs. 6 10 0

Via Southampton.	£. S. D.	Via Brindisi	£. S. D.
Per Annum	0 18 9	Per Annum	1 7 6

Cash sales, Two Annas per copy.

ICE! ICE! ICE!

MADE IN FOUR MINUTES

THE PNEUMATIC ICE MACHINE

THIS IMPORTANT INVENTION IS CONSIDERED A BOON TO THOSE LIVING IN TROPICAL CLIMATES.

CAN BE WORKED BY THE MOST INEXPERIENCED HAND AND IS NOT LIABLE TO GET OUT OF ORDER.

From Rs. 175, each Machine complete.

MESSRS. ARLINGTON & CO

AGENTS.

HAROLD & CO.,

3, DALHOUSIE SQUARE, CALCUTTA

HARMONIUMS.

Harold and Co., call attention to their unequalled stock of rich-toned Harmoniums made especially for India.

FROM RS. 90 TO RS. 900 EACH.

All kinds of Musical Instruments of the best description are always kept in Stock.

CALCUTTA

106, Bowbazar Street.

DR. H. C. SARMA'S

CELEBRATED.

MEDICINE FOR DEBILITY

(NERVOUS)

Brought on by indulgence in irregular habits, effects of previous diseases, loss of power of limbs, weakness or loss of memory, absent mindedness, irritable temper, disposition of the mind to displeasure at trifles, want of attention towards business, despair at finding no relief from treatment &c. &c. &c.

Price with postage &c. Rs. 5.

Particulars of disease and directions for despatch received from patients [illegible] distance.

DR. SARMA'S FEE.

In cases of Debility (nervous) Rs. 16 per visit, } In
For advice at Home......... Rs. 16 ... } Town
Out of Town Rs. 500 per Day.

HEEM-SAGAR OIL.

The best remedy for Headache arising from overstudy, intellectual occupation, overthinking, mental anxiety and weakness, as well as heat of head from living in hot places.

It cools the head and produces very agreeable sensation. Removes Dandriff as well as all other impurities from the head. Promotes the strength and growth of the hair and prevents its premature falling-off.

Price per 4 ounce phial...	Rs.	2	0 0
Postage &c.			10 0

MEDICINE FOR LEPROSY.

Price with Postage &c. Rs. 5.

OIL FOR LEPROSY.

And Inveterate Skin Diseases.

Price per 8 ounce phial...	Rs.	2 0	0
Postage &c.	„	0 12	0

CELEBRATED.

INDIAN TOOTH POWDER.

Strengthens loose teeth, alleviates pain of, and **prevents bleeding** from Gums, cleanses the mouth, **corrects its putrid odour and cures** ulceration of **the Gums without blackening the Teeth.**

Price per packet	**Rs.**	**0 4 0**
Postage &c., for 4 packets ...	**„**	**0 5 0**

CELEBRATED.

TONIC OIL.

Imparts vigour and **tone to the paralyzed or relaxed parts of the** Human **system—Restores** proper **circulation of** blood to **weak and inactive parts.**

Price for four ounce phial.	**Rs.**	**1 0 0**
Postage &c.		0 10 0

HAIR PRESERVER.

Will restore grey hair to its original colour.

It acts directly upon the roots of the hair, removes dandriff, prevents premature falling-off of the hair, and promotes its growth and strength giving it Lustre and Health of Youth.

It also produces a cooling and soothing **effect** upon the head.

Price, for 4 ounce phial ...	Rs.	1 0 0
Postage &c.		0 10 0

Copy of Letter received from Raja Chundernath Roy Bahadoor of Nattore.

*Wellesley Street, No. 18, Motts Lane, 29th **March** 1874.*

MY DEAR HURSUKH BABU,—I shall thank you to send me another phial of your "*Excellent Hair Restorer.*" In fact it has done me a great benefit **and** I should like to have more of it. It **has** disabused **me** (young as I am) of old age.

Your's Sincerely
C. N. of *Nattore*

CELEBRATED.

MEDICINE FOR BALDNESS.

Will certainly cure baldness if applied on the **bald portion,** night & morning according to directions given **in** the adjoining direction paper

Price per two ounce **phial**	Rs.	1	**0 0**
Postage &c.		**„**	**6 0**

SMITH, STANISTREET & CO.

Pharmaceutical Chemists & Druggists

BY APPOINTMENT

To His Excellency the Right Hon'ble

LORD LYTTON, G.M.S.I.

Governor-General of India.

&c. &c.

SYRUP OF LACTATE OF IRON

Prepared from the original receipe. Lactate of Iron, in various forms of preparation, have been in use in France, and generally through the continent of Europe, for some years past, and is highly esteemed as one of the most valuable Chalybeate Tonic Remedies yet introduced. The Syrup, being the most agreeable as well as convenient form of administration is in most general use. It is a most valuable remedy in the following diseases:—Chlorosis or Green Sickness, Leucorrhœa, Neuralgia, Enlargement of the Spleen, &c. In combination with quinine, it has also been very successfully used in the cure of Fever, while to persons of delicate constitution, enfeebled by disease it is invaluable. In bottles. Rs. 2 each.

SYRUP OF THE PHOSPHATE OF IRON Rs. 2 per bottle.

SYRUP OF PHOSPHATE OF IRON AND STRYCHNINE, Rs. 2 per bottle.

SYRUP OF PHOSPHATE OF IRON AND QUININE. Price Rs. 2-8 per bottle.

SYRUP OF PHOSPHATE OF IRON, QUININE AND STRYCHNINE (DR. ATKIN'S TRIPLE TONIC SYRUP.) Rs. 2-8 per bottle.

Smith, Stanistreet & Co.

Invite special attention to the following rates the quality guaranteed as the best procurable:—

Pure Ærated Waters.

Made from Pure Water, obtained by the new process through the Patent Charcoal Filters.

				Rs	As.
Ærated plain (Treble Ærated), per doz.			...	0	12
Soda Water	ditto	„	...	0	12
Gingerade	ditto	„	...	1	4
Lemonade	ditto	„	...	1	4
Tonic (Quinine)	ditto	„	...	1	4

The *Cash* must be sent with the order to obtain advantage of the above rates.

MUDHOO SUDUN PAUL & CO.

120, RADHA BAZAR,

CALCUTTA.

Tea! (Assam) Tea!

TRADE M. MARK.

In 1lb. and 2lb. Tins

Pekoe Tea	2lb. Tin, Per Tin	Rs.	3 4
„ Flowery	„	„	3 8
„ Souchong	„	„	2 8
Family Mixture	„	„	2 4
Canepoi	„	„	2 0
Imperial Mixture with China ...		...	3 0
China Rose Pauchong ...		...	2 8

The above in 1lb. Tin at half the respective prices, plus two annas extra.

BURMAH CIGARS.

No. 1 per 100	Rs.	1	0
„ 2 „		0	12

HUNTLEY AND PALMER'S BISCUITS.

Albert, in Tins of 2 lb each	Rs.	1	8
Arrow Root, ...	„	1	4
Mixed, ...	„	1	8

Indian Chutnies, Castor Oil, Candles, Kerosine Oil, China Preserves, Perfumery, Domestic Medicines, and other stores always in stock and offered at lower rates than other Houses.

Catalogue to be had on application,
MUDHOO SUDUN PAUL & Co.

Oriental Gas Company Ld.

THE price of Gas in Calcutta and Howrah is reduced to Rs. 5 per 1,000 feet.

Printing Materials

MILLER AND RICHARD'S PRESSES, TYPES and all requisites always in Stock,

TERMS CASH.

EWING & CO.

India General Steam Navigation Company, Ld.

SCHOENE, KILBURN & CO.—*Managing* ***Agents.***

ASSAM LINE.

NOTICE

Steamers leave Calcutta for **Assam every Tuesday,** Kooshtea every Thursday and **leave Debrooghur** downward **every** Saturday.

THE Str. **"AGRA"** will leave Calcutta *Via Mutabunga for Assam,* on Tuesday the 15th instant.

Cargo will be received at the Company's Godowns, Nimtollah Ghat, up till noon of Monday, the 14th.

THE Str. "ASSAM" will leave Kooshtea for Assam on Thursday, the 17th instant.

Cargo will be received at the Company's Godowns, No. 4 Fairlie Place, up till noon of Tuesday the 15th.

Goods forwarded to Kooshtea for this vessel will be chargeable with Railway Freight from Calcutta to Kooshtea in addition to the regular Freight of this Company.

Passengers should leave for Kooshtea by Train of Wednesday, the 16th.

CACHAR LINE NOTICE

REGULAR FORTNIGHTLY SERVICE.

Steamers leave Calcutta for Cachar and Intermediate Stations every alternate Friday, and leave Cachar downward every alternate Sunday.

THE Str. "COLGONG" will leave Calcutta *via Mutabunga* for Cachar on Friday the 25th instant.

Cargo will be received at the Company's Godowns, Nimtollah Ghat, up till noon of Thursday the 24th.

For further information regarding rates of freight or passage money, apply to

4, FAIRLIE PLACE, } G. J. SCOTT,
Calcutta 10th August 1876. } Secretary.

CHUNDER & BROTHERS,

25½ & 112, RADHA BAZAR,

CALCUTTA.

TERMS,—CASH STRICTLY.

Cash Boxes of sizes with or without Chubbs locks.
Railway Bags, **of Carpet,** Leather **&c.**
Overland trunks **of leather.**
Scarborough trunks of sizes.
Brass Candlesticks of sizes.
Cricket Bats & **Balls.**
Chinese Canisters, Square & round.
Compendium of Games of sizes.
Bulleye Lantern, Japanned.
Hand Lamp ENGLISH, for Table & Wall.
Mathematical & Surveying **Instruments.**
Drawing & Painting Materials.
Color Boxes of **sizes &** descriptions.
Magic inkstand in large variety.
Inkstands with & without stands **of sizes &c.**
Playing Cards of different patterns.
Brass Padlocks of sizes.
Water Cocks (brass) for Iron and lead pipes.
Iron & Lead pipes of sizes.
Note & Letter paper of all sizes & qualities.
Foolscap, Demy, Medium, Royal paper &c.
Printing Papers of sizes &c.
Steel Pens, Quills, Pencils.
Writing Inks, of all colors & sizes.
Bank Books, Pocket Book &c &c.
Fancy & Useful Articles.

CALCUTTA } CHUNDER & BROTHERS.
The 30th June, 1876. }

Hats, Hats, Hats!!!

C. C. DASS & CO.

SOLA HAT MANUFACTURERS,

74, *Radhabazar.*

Just opened new Invoices **of Silk and Felt** Hats and Hawke's Patent Helmets.

!!! হুকা !!!

!!! HOOKAHS !!!

ENGLISH made Hookahs of various choice designs, **colours and sizes, ranging in price from** Rs. 3 to **5 each, 60 designs to choose from.** Apply to

RADANAUTH CHOWDRY,
373, Jorasanko.

Printed and published by M. M. RUKHIT, at the INDIAN MIRROR PRESS, No. 6, College Square, for the Proprietors.

The Indian Mirror.

SUNDAY EDITION

VOL. XV.] CALCUTTA, SUNDAY AUGUST 20, 1876 { REGISTERED AT THE GENERAL POST OFFICE. } [NO 197

CONTENTS.

NOTICE.

All letters and communications relating to the literary department of the Paper should be addressed to the Editor. All other letters should be addressed to the Manager, to whom all remittances should be made payable.

Subscribers will be good enough to bring to the notice of the Manager any delay or irregularity in the delivery of the Paper.

Editorial Notes.

THE usual *Bhadrotsub* of the Brahmos will be celebrated to-day from 7 A. M. to 9 P. M. May Divine grace make the festival successful towards refreshing and fructifying the souls of our brethren and sisters who come to attend it!

MR. VOYSEY'S congregation has been removed, we find, from St. George's Hall to Langham Hall. The latter can hold as many people as the former, and has been obtained, we believe, at a cheaper rent. The congregation continues to be as numerous as before, and the proceedings have not much variation. Mr. Voysey ought to make the cause of Theism a strong cause, so that it may survive his labors and efforts when he has ceased to work. Personal sympathy with him and his views ought to be quite separate from the progress and organization of Theism on a sound basis, and according to sound principles. He is the avowed representative of our cause in England, and we naturally expect a great deal from him.

THE Unitarians are not at all satisfied with the views expressed by Mr. Gladstone in his late contribution to the *Contemporary Review* on the subject of Unitarianism. They think he confounds religion with dogmatism and ecclesiastical systems, and ignores the recent transitions of opinion and faith amongst the thoughtful in all countries. Mr. Gladstone's religious essays, considered from a religious point of view, are not very highly spoken of. He writes on these subjects as a statesman, to whom the connection between the political and ecclesiastical constitution is a matter to be considered in relation simply to the interests and precedents which the question involves. The wishes, tastes, civil and moral rights of the population on the one hand, law, custom, and the political tendencies of the times on the other hand, seem to decide every thing.

WE believe in no country as in India, men occupying very high positions of wealth and honor suddenly sink down into utter poverty and destitution. A single lawsuit, a single speculation mania, the insolvency of a single bank would involve hundreds of the rich and luxurious into a state of abject misery from which they are never to rise in this life again. In other countries it is the dishonest and the idle who suffer in this way, because for the truly unfortunate there is ready help at all times. Here, however, the innocent and the guilty sink into a common doom and there is nobody to rescue them. It is by no means an uncommon sight to see the man who was a master of lacs not long ago, begging for alms among people who grudgingly bestow their charity upon him. The purse strings of our rich men are so often held in the hands of officials and others, extracting large donations for purposes with which the doners have no sympathy whatever, that they have very little inclination left in them to confer charities in quarters where compassion may be now and then excited. Payments of money at volunteer rifle matches, horseraces, and the like are simply degrading when there is so much misery that remains unalleviated in the very bosom of our society.

THE act of suicide, in these enlightened days, still retains its primitive barbarism. If a man is bent upon destroying himself, why should not self-destruction be rendered as scientific, as refined, as painless, and even as esthetic as possible. Hanging, poisoning, drowning, throat-cutting, and blowing out the brains breathe the ancient spirit of Vandalism and heathenish fury. The Americans who are really going ahead of the world, though they get so little credit for it, are solving this problem, as they have solved so many other problems of destruction. A gentleman in the state of Indiana of the name of James Moore, made as good and enlightened provisions for his suicide as any educated Christian may be expected to do. "He got a sharp axe, weighted it with iron bars, made it revolve on hinges fixed in the floor of his room, and strapped himself so under it that when it fell it would strike his neck. He had tied it back by a cord, and placed a lighted candle so that in a given time it would burn down to the cord, and he had placed his head in a box containing cotton-wool saturated with chloroform. Of course he became and remained insensible, and when the candle severed the cord, the impromptu guillotine severed his head from his body without any alarm or fear to himself. That was an efficient suicide of its kind. We suppose the reason why one so seldom hears of such cases is, that suicide usually implies hatred of life quite too passionate to take into account the pangs of death."

ENGLISH opinion is strongly agitated upon the subject of England's interference in the present affairs of Turkey. So far as the views of the Ministry on the subject are concerned, it cannot be doubted that there are decided leanings in favor of Turkey. But the public at large are well nigh infuriated at the reported atrocities committed by Turkish soldiers upon the Christian population in Bulgaria, and the other provinces where the rebellion has broken out. Thousands of the innocent and defenceless have been massacred; young women "were regular articles of traffic, and sold publicly in the villages;" cart-loads of the heads of girls and children were carried about with the Turkish regiments, and seventeen such heads were fixed on lances to strike terror into the population. Mutilations of the living, dismemberment of the dead, and dishonor to women are attributed to the Turks. We are at a loss how far we may believe these accounts. Surely Mr. Disraeli says his official information does not bear out the horrible reports in the newspapers. That fanatical Mahomedan soldiers, as much fanatical Christian soldiers, are capable of doing infernal things, we all know in India, but the English public should think twice before taking any decisive action on the sensational accounts of newspaper correspondents. Turkey is very hard pressed, and her political position demands sympathy, while the barbarities of her soldiers demand strong and unqualified condemnation

THE Sisters belonging to the Loretto Convent who have charge of the Entally Orphanage, resort to effective modes of punishment when they find the girls under them negligent, or uncleanly, or disobedient. Lately there appeared in a contemporary's columns a letter commenting on these modes of punishment. The Lady superior of the Convent writes in defence of the Sisters, and says that one of the girls being uncleanly, and her head being "crowded with vermin," she was shaved. Now shaving a girl's head, even for uncleanliness, is, we think, an injudicious operation, because hair to a woman, to use a Biblical metaphor, is like the breath of her nostrils. We know severe fits of hysterics to which young ladies have been subject, have been marvellously cured by summary threats of shaving. We make an extract from the letter of the Lady Superior to show the punishment administered to another girl :—

A little before this, A. B. had been suffering from itch and had therefore been removed to the Orphan's Infirmary, where, on becoming better, she asked for and obtained the temporary care of a little babe, who was also in the Infirmary. She soon grew tired of her charge, and considerably injured the child by giving it sour milk and keeping the vessels destined for its use unwashed, allowing the fresh food to mingle with the stale. The sister repeatedly remonstrated with her about these negligences, and on two occasions punished her for them by slapping her hands, not with the post, but with the small tester of an infant's bed. She likewise, for the same reason, tied a small copper *handy* round her neck for two hours, and placed her on a seat in a passage where the sisters might see her going to their different duties. The *handy* was used for warming milk for the infant.

THE REGION OF SILENCE.

THE common saying is that "still waters run deepest." Human language is indeed eloquent and beautiful in its varied music. But there are inward experiences whose depth is inexpressible by anything man can say, and therefore he had best say nothing about them. From the early days of mythology man's conceptions have been grander and more profound than what his words could convey, and he tried to express by symbols the unspeakable mysteries perceived by his soul. One such symbol often carries more meaning than many volumes of theology will. Symbolism thus embodies the silence of the soul. The region of silence is where the soul is merged in the profoundness of its inward being and experiences. The deepest faith is silent. It cannot explain itself, it cannot justify itself before men ; there are so few who have had real faith, and those few have always kept it so secret, that language furnishes no equivalents to the spirit's trust in the unseen. Besides we cannot construe and formulate our faith to ourselves, the moment we try to put it into a logical and verbal garb it seems to deteriorate, and fall far short of it secret genuineness and integrity. Nay even if adequate words are found, the expression of what is most sacred and profound in ourselves seldom creates a corresponding conviction in the hearer's breast, and creed becomes cant, and the holiest and most cherished faith of the prophet is mouthed by the vulgar with an unfeeling effrontery which saddens as much as it demoralizes. The deepest under-current of faith, therefore, remains and must always remain unuttered. Faith goes from heart to heart like the waves of electricity, unseen, and undetected by sounds, but most potent and most thrilling in its effects Silence and trust, therefore, go hand in hand, and silence, perhaps the silence of death, seals the victory of trust. The king who has faith in his heaven-descended dignity, is clothed in tatters, crowned with thorns, and plied with questions before the mock-tribunal of the world, but he prefers to remain silent. They kill him it is true, but beneath the tree on which he dies his enemies carve his royal title on the tough wood, and when remonstrated with say *quod scriptum est, scriptum est.*

Men say love is eloquent. Perhaps when affection finds speech its words, are sweet. But that is rare, affection cannot utter itself, and not unoften scorns that task. Ever flowing inwards it shrinks from the gaze of the unloving, and even from the gratitude of the loved ones, and consents to hide itself in meekness and silence. Not only unrewarded, but persecuted by those whom it wants to benefit, the love of the godly shuns the vanities of speech and expression, and imitates its divine prototype in the secrecy and solitude of its existence. Deep devotion, profound humility, utter resignation, real philanthropy, and all the other deepest feelings of the heart live in the region of silence.

Correspondence.

To the Editor of the *Indian Mirror*

SIR,—It will be news to your readers, if they have not made the discovery themselves, that the last two Brahmo Marriages under the Civil Marriage Act took place on days marked in the Hindu Almanac as specially auspicious for that purpose. For the latter of these another lucky day had been fixed, but the ceremony was postponed. How would the Brahmos account for these "strange coincidences"? Will they say they were merely accidental?*

It is also worthy of note, that on these as well as on almost all previous occasions when a Brahmo was married to a Brahmo, the nuptials were held at night time. Must we impute this also to chance, for men must choose between day and night, or have the Brahmos found out that after all our forefathers were not fools who prohibited marriages by day?

The 14, *August* 1876 } Yours truly, ANTI-HUMBUG.

* The coincidence never struck us, or the parties concerned in these marriages before our ingenious correspondent pointed it out.—ED. *I. M.*

CONDITION OF THE BRAHMOS.

The Editor of the *Indian Mirror*

Sir,—I have observed with much regret the present spiritual status of the general Brahmos. It is one of absolute stagnation, there seems to be a stoppage of even sort of mental activity. Attempts have been and are being made by the fathers of our church, but apparently to no purpose. Utsabs after Utsabs have rolled over without much affecting the Brahmos, they go and come, and there is an end of the matter.

It may be asked, what is (rather what can be) the cause of this stupor. Stupor implies self-forgetfulness, and self-forgetfulness implies want of self-examination. It is not necessary to say much on the point, consciousness is the only test of humanity He who does not consciously exist, and simply is drifted by the mercy of chance, is not humanly existing.

Perhaps the Brahmo will say that he *does* think, but still he is where he is. These two statements are not reconcilable. If one is conscious of his condition, he is compelled by the necessities of his better nature to improve it. There may be some persons who cannot *help* being where they are. These are as a rule, slaves to some gross habits. Their number is very small among the Brahmos, they live in eternal torment of the fear of public disclosure. The state of things, however cannot long last with them, sooner or later, but *surely*, they *shall* come out It needs not that their crimes be brought home to them, and then they leave at once.

It is of the other class of Brahmos, those who *pass* their lives in average morality that I am speaking. Let them answer this question. Are they well?—Is the routine method of life the be-all and end-all of their existence? To say *yes* is unreasonable, and to say no, equally if not more so. It cannot be that going to office, eating, sleeping &c. is *all* they need care for. If it be all, the difference of humanity from animals disappears. To say that they think and consciously exist, and at the same time to say that their physical necessities are all they need think about, is to ignore the substance for the sake of the accident,—to think of the body and not to think of *thing* which *makes* them *think*.

The other side of the case is,—does the world deserve *so much* consideration? In reply it may be said that there is nothing else which is deserving of *more* consideration. This is assuming too much. It is not fair, not having seen a *thing*, to reject *prima facie*, all the testimony of those who have seen it. It is alone they who have explored both the *seen* and the *Unseen*, that have any right to compare.

The conclusion therefore is, that eating sleeping &c. is not *all* that is to be cared after, and that there is a region which is of more interest than this world. If this be admitted it follows that the man, (*only* caring after his physical necessities) must say that he is not what he should be. This is what is said by those who say *no* to the question proposed before—"Are they well?" It may now be very naturally asked, why do they not then try to be better? The is the plight in which the Man of God has found the Man of the World, from the beginning down to the present time. Brahmos cannot—none can answer this question. "I know I am wrong but———" means I will continue wrong. I invite the Brahmos to come forward, and assert before the public in the same breath that they are Brahmos and that they know they are wrong, and desire to continue as they now are.

Yours &c.
A BRAHMO.

Devotional

GRANT, O God, our Father, that all hearts may be united in peace and good will before thy altar to-day. Grant that the sacrifice of our tears and prayers may be acceptable to thee, and sanctified through our fraternal love for each other. Grant O God of peace, that brother may forgive the offences of brother, and sister may embrace sister in the holiness of their sacred relationship, and all may assemble in thy house without the least ill-feeling to celebrate thy goodness, and rejoice over thy blessed name.

SUFFER me O Lord, to lie low at thy feet, and be very humble. My pride has offended both men and women, and humiliated me much in my own estimation. I have been a bad example and I have perverted those whom I should have taught to be meek. For all this, righteous God, chastize me severely, and create in me that poverty of spirit which wills often to conciliate those whom my conduct has hardened. Bless me so that I may cease to be a stumbling block in the way of thy children to thy house, and rather be a help to them in their need.

CAUSE thy blessings to descend, O Lord, upon mine enemies, upon the men and women who have hated me, slandered me, persecuted me, and used me spitefully. I seek their true welfare at thy hands, because their unkindness has often done me the greatest good. Behold, O my God, I am but a poor sinner, and deserve much severity at the hands of men. If their severity has been at times exercised when I was not prepared for it, I cannot complain, because they have as often withheld their punishment when my conduct fully called for punishment. Cause thy grace to visit mine adversaries, those who hold different ideas and opinions from myself, those whose faith is different from my own, those who condemn my ways of action, and entertain a very low estimate of my worth and work. Merciful Lord, teach me tolerance, large-heartedness, and the love of all men.

The Brahmo Somaj

THE members of the National Indian Association in London are most of them our personal friends. They take a warm and active interest in the Brahmo Somaj, though, as a body, being pledged to the principle of religious neutrality, they cannot manifest that interest in their proceedings. We wish we knew the actual number of the sympathizers with our movements both in London, and in other parts of the British Isles.

THREE Brahmica ladies were present at the Wednesday Evening Service in St. Paul's Cathedral. They were exceedingly interested with what they saw and heard and though the chanting and singing were partly unintelligible to them in the absence of hymn books, they were very much impressed with the novelty and solemnity of the whole service. We wish they could be shown over the Cathedral, and everything explained to them.

A NUMBER of Brahmos have arrived in Calcutta from other parts of the country to be present at this day's festival. The largest number of arrivals are from East Bengal. The proceedings of the *Utsab* are to be as the following.

Hymns ...	From 7	to 7-30	A.M.
Morning Service ...	„ 7-30	„ 10	„
Midday Service ...	„ 1	„ 1-30	P.M.
Reading of Discourse	„ 1-30	„ 2	„
Chanting of Brahma Gita	„ 2	„ 3	„
Meditation	„ 3	„ 4	„
Prayers and Hymns	„ 4	„ 5	„
Popular Hymns ...	„ 5	„ 5-30	„
Sankirtna	„ 5-30	„ 6-30	„
Evening Service ...	„ 7	„ 9	„

BABU DURGA DOSS ROY of Dacca has published a Bengali pamphlet on *Byragya* in vindication of the modes of asceticism adopted by some of the missionaries of the Brahmo Somaj of India. The arguments of the writer are supported by free quotations from Hindu scriptures.

IT has been resolved by the Managing Committee of the East Bengal Brahmo Somaj to open a Night School for giving moral instructions to the alumni of the schools at Dacca.

Gleanings

LAST WORDS OF MAHOMED TO HIS DISCIPLES.

GREAT joy and lasting prosperity be yours. May profound peace rest on you. May God protect you all in the midst of mutual friendliness far from the evils of separation. Heaven's grace be sent unto you and may that grace be with you at all times.

In fear and danger may Divine shelter cover you. May the Lord help you and protect you in all circumstances. May God increase your glory and His grace be your companion. May He take you as His own, lead you to the path of virtue and place you under His glorious shelter.

May God keep you safe from breach of duty and evil. May the inexhaustible store of His mercy be your provision. Resignation, patience and fear of God these are my last precepts to you all. I commit and commend you to God and make Him guardian over you. By pride and conceit do not injure the servants of God, do not open the door of trouble and oppression in his kingdom. God said he has mansions of eternal bliss for those who are not proud.

Bayit Akoorkita.

THE heart too often like the cement of the ancient Romans, acquires hardness by time.

OH, the matchless power of silence! There are words that concentrate in themselves the glory of a life-time; but there is a silence that is more precious than they. Speech ripples over the surface of life, but sinks into its depths. Airy pleasantness bubbles up in airy pleasant words. Weak sorrows quiver out their shallow being and are not. When the heart is cleft to its core, there is no speech or language.

BY taking good care of our own vineyard, we learn how to help others in the care of their vineyard. If you cannot raise grapes in your garden, you cannot raise them in mine.—*Talmage.*

"ONE would think," said a friend of the celebrated Dr. Samuel Johnson, "that sickness and the view of death would make men more religious." "Sir," replied Johnson, "they do not know how to go about it. A man who has never been religious before, no more grows religious when he is sick, than a man who has never learned figures can count when he has need of calculation."

THE Rev. John Newton was one day called to visit a family that had suffered the loss of all they possessed by fire. He found the pious mistress, and saluted her with, "I give you joy, madam."

Surprised, and ready to be offended, she exclaimed, "What! joy that all my property is consumed!"

"Oh, no," he answered; "but joy that you have so much property that fire cannot touch."

A MAN of deep religious experience is always effective. I care not how poor his voice is, or how uncomely his countenance, or how awkward his gestures, or how shabby his clothes, or how lame his grammar.

Literary

MR. HENRY DURAND, Attache, Indian Foreign Office, has just published in England his paper on "Central India in 1857," being an answer to Sir John Kaye.

ON the return of the Supreme Government to Calcutta, the Indian Copyright Act is to be revised.

THE following gentlemen have been appointed Examiners for the forthcoming Examinations of the Punjab University College:—In Arts, *English*—Professor E. Lethbridge, Krishnaghar; *Arabic*—Professor Blockmann, Calcutta; *Sanskrit*—Professor Thibaut, Benares; *Persian*—Maulvi Kerim-uddin, Amritsar; *Hindi*—Babu Navina Chandra Rai; *Urdu*—Pandit Moti Lal, Extra Assistant Commissioner; *History and Geography*—E. O'Brien, Esq., C. S.; *Mathematics*—Dr. Center; *Physical Science*—Professor J. Elliot; *Philosophy and Political Economy*—J. G. Cordery, Esq., C. S. For Oriental Diplomas, *Sanskrit*—Babu Mahesh Chandra Nyaratna; *Arabic*—Professor Blochmann; *Persian*—Maulvi Obeydulla. In Law—Mr. H. M. Plowden, Mr. C. H. Spitta, Mr. P. D. Bullock and Mr. H. B. Powell. In Civil Engineering—Major A. M. Lang and Rai Kanhya Lall, C. E. The viva voce Examiners in the above subjects are respectively (in Arts) Messrs. Bullock, Khalifa Hamid-uddin, Pandits Rishi Kesh and Guru Parshad, Rai Kanhya Lal, Pandits Moti Lal and Munshi Muhammad Latif, Dr. Behari Lal, Dr. Steinmagel, Dr. Center, Syud Amir Shah; (in Orientals) Pandits Bhagwan Das, Maulvi Zia-ud-din and Fakir Syud Kamar-ud-din, Nawab Nawazish Ali Khan and Maulvi Muhammad Hussain; (in Law) Messrs. Plowden, Spitta, Bullock and Powell, and (in Civil Engineering) Rai Kanhya Lal.

SANSKRIT scholars may be glad to know that Dr. Ernst Haas' "Catalogue of Sanskrit and Pali Books in the Library of the British Museum" is now ready. The compiler, who holds the chair of Sanskrit in the University College, London, has produced a most useful book, something more indeed than a catalogue, for the descriptive details make it a valuable work of reference.

Mr. Dacosta, late of the firm of Ashburner &c. Co. of Calcutta, whose deep interest in the cause of good government of India is so well-known, is about to publish a pamphlet in London on the Financial Condition of India. It will contain a *preface*, written by Sir George Campbell and Sir Charles Wingfield.

Professor Monier Williams is expected to visit India again this winter. He is said to be writing a work on the religious systems and sacred places of India, to complete which it will be necessary for him to make a tour in the Madras Presidency.

It is stated that the Editors of the leading European and Native journals in India will be specially invited and entertained by the Viceroy in a special camp to be provided for them at the Grand Durbar to be held at Delhi on the 1st January 1877.

Scientific

The Emir of Zeila has received the member of the Italian Geographical Society's expedition to Central Africa inhospitably, refusing them tents, and forcing them to encamp under a blazing sun. Victor Emmanuel's presents for the King of Shoa are already damaged by insufficient transport. The Italian Government demands explanations from the Khedive.

Latest News

—Another son of the Queen, H. R. H. the Duke of Connaught, will come to India next cold weather, and remain a year or so in the country, some of his time being passed at Simla or one of the hill stations. The Duke's visit to the East is to form part of the practical military Education he has been going through for some years past.

—Sir John Strachey is named as likely to succeed Sir William Muir, as Finance Minister of India.

—It is officially announced that His Excellency the Viceroy will hold a Grand Durbar at Delhi on the 1st January next for the purpose of proclaiming the new title of the Empress of India, and the gracious sentiments which have induced Her Majesty to make this addition to Her title, specially to mark Her interest in this great dependency of Her Crown and Her confidence in the loyalty and affection of the Princes and peoples of India. The ceremony will be on a magnificent scale. A body of about 14,000 troops, detachments from each Presidency will be present, under the personal command of His Excellency the Commander-in-Chief. A telegram from Simla says all the Governors, Lieutenant-Governors, heads of administrations, Princes, Chiefs, and Nobles from all parts of India will be invited to be present. Orders in council will be issued suitable to the historical importance of the occasion, which it is expected will be met by public rejoicings and demonstrations of loyalty. Lord Lytton will make his public entry into Delhi the day after Christmas. All public offices will be closed for one week.

—Captain Kincaid, Assistant Political Agent, First Assistant to the Agent of the Governor-General, Rajputana, has gone to Bhurtpore as Political Agent.

—Lieutenant Marshall, Assistant to the Agent of the Governor-General, Rajputana, has been appointed Guardian to H. H. the Maharao Rajah of Ulwar, and joined his charge at the Mayo College, Ajmere.

—The yearly vacation of the Chief Court of the Punjab has begun.

—Babu Futtehnarain Singh of Benares is dead.

—Mr. C. A. Elliot, Secretary to the North-West Government, returns from furlough in January, and till then Mr. B. Colvin continues to officiate.

—Captain Molloy has started for Srinuggur to meet the Yarkand Envoy, but no news has been received of the Envoy's arrival there.

—The *Indian Tribune* says Benares received a visit from the Hon'ble Mr. Clifford, son of Lord Clifford.

—Colonel Dillon, late Military Secretary to the Commander-in-Chief, returns in November to assume command of the 4th Battalion of the Rifles. There are prospects of his early obtaining a brigade.

—Lord Northbrook delivered another speech at Falmouth, in which he declared that the supposition that the British policy towards the Turkey might affect the British Power in India, was purely imaginary. Lord Northbrook approved of the decision of Government not to attempt a remedy to counteract the fall of silver.

—On Sunday last, prizes were distributed at Bombay by His Highness the Sanglikur to the respective exhibitors of the Native Art Exhibition. There were in all thirty prizes, amounting in value to about two hundred and fifty Rupees, and thirteen certificates were also granted to the exhibitors.

—At Coimbra (Portugal) the students, exasperated by the severe examinations and the many reproofs administered to them, created a disturbance. The soldiers were called out. The students threw stones at them. Upon this the soldiers charged and fired. One man was killed, and several wounded on both sides.

—Mr. Fawcett gave notice that on the 31st July he would ask the Under-Secretary of State for India, whether considering that when the Indian Budget was introduced in Calcutta in March last, the loss to India by exchange on transactions with London was estimated at £2,332,000 for the current year, and as that there has since been a considerable further fall in the rate of exchange, whether he is able to inform the House at what amount the loss to India is now estimated. And, further, to inquire whether he can state the aggregate amount which has been spent by the Government on State Railways in India up to the present time.

—The *Daily Telegraph* says that at a meeting of the Bar, at which all the circuits were represented, it has been agreed that special fees for counsel going off their circuit shall in future be altered—that any junior can go off his circuit on either side for 50 guineas, and any Silk Gown for 100. The old rule previous to this arrangement was that no junior could hold a brief on another circuit than his own under 100, and a senior under 300 guineas.

—The ice famine continues to exist in Bombay with painful rigour.

Selections

A BISHOP ON MODERN MERCY.

In preaching in London to the deaf and dumb at St. Saviour's Church Oxford Street, the Right Rev. Dr. Magee, Bishop of Peterburgh, after eloquently speaking of the attributes of the divine mercy, asked whether in this nineteenth century in Christian England, which seemed so saturated with this feeling of mercy, and where there appeared to be no lack of merciful help to those who needed it, there were not some who stood in need of the supernatural grace of mercy? Let them see how far the mercy of God differed from the mercy of man. God's mercy was uniform; there was no capriciousness nor eclecticism in it. The barbarity of the heathen had so far passed away from men in the present day that the general sense of the community abhorred and reprobated cruelty. They were now free from cruelty; but were they always merciful in their dealings with their fellow men? Were they merciful in their judgment of their fellow men? Did they strive to believe even against appearances that the act which they reprobated was not as evil as it appeared, or that it might be done under a temptation they could not measure? Were they merciful in their speech? Did they, when speaking or writing a criticism, take or not take a pleasure in making it as harsh and sharp and as pungent as they could make it? Did they in their works of modern literature, in their criticisms on political matters, in their newspapers, in the judgments they passed even upon literary works, or upon politics or upon the social life of others—did they strive to speak charitably? Was it not rather a gratification to the person himself who wrote, and was it not often a gratification to the world who read, and did not both enjoy the criticism when it was sharp, pungent, and clever, and seasoned with all that was malicious to wing it to its mark like a feather winging the poisoned arrow home? Then were they merciful in their consideration for others as employers to employed? Did they act in a spirit of mercy to those over whose lives they had got a power in places of industry, in shops and business? Were they careful and considerate of the feeling and mindful of the circumstances of those over whose lives God had given them a power for their happiness? Surely there was in this great need for "thoughtful" mercy.—*Indian Church Gazette.*

SOME CHILDREN'S STORIES.

"In the dear old days of 'once upon a time,' there seemed to be less room in the world for children than is made now for them, and there were more people who took their perverseness into consideration as well as their pretty ways." To not a few among us these "dear old days" are still real; "the golden mist of years" is not yet thick enough to veil from us the sad fact that we were then, *qua* children, of insignificant importance, that we were spoken of as "only" the children (what has become of that objectionable word now?), and were liable to snubs from proverbs of an unflattering nature and conceived in a most unsympathetic spirit,—nay, that our subjection was so abject, that we failed even to recognise the injustice of such treatment. Those days are gone, and with a sigh over vanished discipline, and a passing grudge (well expressed by Thackeray in one of the *Roundabout Papers*) at the youngsters who are made so much more comfortable than ever we were, we turn to new fashions, and join in the "spoiling," over which we shake our wise heads, as over a weakness, unknown when we were young. In those days of wholesome discipline lived the Favell children. They were taught to know their place, and that that place was not—as in the case of the pet dogs of the old county lady—wherever they chose to go. Their lives were hemmed in by restrictions, and darkened, at times, by well-meaning severity; but narrow boundaries (gardeners tell us) have their use in the rearing of young growths, and not a few children now-a-days feel, with the poet, the tiring urtars of "unchartered freedom" and "the weight of chance desires." The old conditions, according to our own memory and the experience of the Favell children, proved by no means destructive to the happiness of childhood, or to the development of its quaint fancies and bright humours.

We say the "experiences" of the Favell Children, for we altogether decline to accept them as fictitious. Keen and loving study of real individuals could alone, we think, have produced such delicate shading of character, such life-liked touches of childish nature as delight us in these "three little portraits." We believe implicitly in them from the moment we are introduced into the "Lumber Palace," that enchanted ground where nothing is that seems, where empty toy-chests are banqueting-halls or summer residences for people of quality, and where rush chairs hide under their unpretending exterior "potentialities beyond the dreams of" even fairy godmothers. Here Dorothy is explaining to her elder sister Pearl how in her married home there shall be no books, and how none of her children shall go to school, when the door opens, and six-year-old Geoff enters with a lighted fire-basket, requesting a guy to be made quick, as he wishes to enjoy himself. Debarred of this enjoyment, he takes to fishing for mice with a crooked pin and a bit of soap, bidding Dorothy hold her tongue, for "how could a mouse bite, if it heard talking." "Geoff" is the "curled darling" of the family, who, in open opposition to all moral laws, "looks prettiest when he is cross and contrary," but has the saving grace to be very angry if he is told so. Pearl, of eleven, is grave and reticent, her strong feelings, and passionate impulses get her often into disgrace with the worthy lady who has charge of the motherless family. Poor Mrs. Druse! to her children meant worry, and "though fully determined to do her duty by the particularly trying specimens of them whom she had in charge, she did not take into consideration that all the pleasantness, as well as much of the profit, of having duty done by one depends on its being done in love;" and in Dorothy—bright little, loquacious Dorothy—so dull at her lessons, so swift in mischief, so gentle and submissive, yet so untameable, Mrs. Druse—good conscientious commonplace Mrs. Druse—found a character completely incomprehensible. Dorothy's great desire is to be a woman of business, but, alas! her businesses are always "wrong businesses," and bring in their train dire disgrace. One such, we must quote. Rag dolls are to be made:—

"Dorothy gave very particular directions about the dolls. They were to be her friends, and she was to name them. She wanted two families, the Ox family and the Slew family. There were to be three daughters in each,—Ann, Ban, and Segalia Ox, and Wilherem, Bitherem, and Pelerina Slew. Mr. Ox's name was to be Moorebias; Mrs. Ox would not require one, as her daughters would call her mama, her husband would say 'my dear' to her, and her letters would be addressed 'Mrs. M. Ox.' The Slew family were to be titled 'Lord and Lady Brutus Slew.' Pearl object to these names. She would have chosen some less odd, not say prettier, but Dorothy declared earnestly that no other names would do, for the reason that they would not suit the characters of her new friends. 'But Ban and Segalia, and some of the others, are not names at all,' argued Pearl.—'They must be names, if people are named them,' replied Dorothy, with such quiet firmness that Pearl submitted to her.—'Why must each family have exactly three daughters?' asked Pearl.—'Because they are to be friends; and don't you see, Pearl, that there must be a companion each for the daughters, as well as for the parents.' Ann Ox was made of pink calico, and was considered pretty. Her sisters, being of speckled stuff, had not such bright complexions. Bitherem was brown, Wilherem of a greenish-yellow, and Pelerina spotted. As black calimanco was all that was reserved for the manufacture of Lady Slew, she was supposed to be a negress. Pearl worked very hard, and the two families were soon nearly completed. 'Run down, Doro, and get some ink for their faces.' But Dorothy was in despair over a deplorable difficulty. Lady Slew could not have a face. Ink would not show upon black calimanco. 'Her ladyship's features can be marked with our hopscotch chalk,' said Pearl. —'Marked features,' said Dorothy, catching at words she had heard used by people, and had not understood; 'does that mean that a person has his features marked with anything —blackened, yellowed, or painted? Those clowns at the circus had marked features, hadn't they?' Pearl laughed as she explained to Dorothy what the phrase meant." Dorothy ran off, but returned with blacking instead of ink, and having eagerly watched the marking of Lord Brutus's face, retired with him into a corner; here she was so long and so suspiciously quiet, that Pearl feared some mischief was in the air. Investigation brought out the fact that Lord Brutus had been growing a fine pair of whiskers:—

"Where did you get those bristles from, Dorothy?—'They are broom-hairs,' answered Dorothy; 'I cut them out of such a nice new broom.'—'Oh, Dorothy, and you have cut such a quantity, the broom must be spoiled! Mrs. Druse will be so angry when Taylor finds it out.' Dorothy turned pale, and looked sorrowfully at the bewhiskered nobleman she was holding."

The conversation which ensues between these interesting newly made families, the unfortunate obstinacy of Bitherem Slew and the brilliant talent of Ban Ox; how they were taking airings in the garden till, meeting with Mrs. Druse, they were all ignominiously expelled under the general name of scarecrow rags; how the feelings of dear Lady Slew and kind Mrs. Ox were "hurt by such rude remarks," is told with a humorous simplicity that takes us into the very world where children live, "where truth that is and truth that seems blend in fantastic strife." Here is Dorothy, meditating over a snail:—

"'Don't say poetry, Pearl,' Dorothy interrupted. 'Look at this snail; I have been watching it poke its thick neck out of its shell. I wonder how it can get back, there seems no room for more snail; I wonder who this snail is.'—'Who it is, Dorothy?'—'Yes, I should like to know who it is.'—'You should learn natural history; I mean to.'—'Natural history would not tell me who this snail is. It looks like an Emma Jane; I wonder if it has any friends, and if it is kind or ill-natured.'"

At another time, she confides to Pearl her terror at the Parish Beadle:—

"He is bald, and I can't help looking at him, and thinking what a large, ugly nose he has; and then, I remember about the she-bears that slew forty-and-two children, because they mocked a bald prophet."

Dorothy is a dunce, and gets into sad trouble over her lessons. She is wilful, too, and often in mischief, but the skill with which the lovable, childish nature is shown beneath, will, we would fain hope, give the excellent, practical Mrs. Druse of real life some aid in deciphering the little enigmas that so often baffle and provoke them and show them how to guide by love rather than fear. "I should not mind," says poor Dorothy, "being a child, if people were as pleasant to me as Mr. Mayfield is; but when one has the most disagreeable things said to one, it quite spoils life!"

The *Fossil Children*, story without a plot and without an end, as it is, is a great advance on the earlier tales by the same writer. *Master Gregory's Cunning*, and its companion tales, are nice little child's stories of a moral turn, simply and pleasantly written; but only one—the *Story of a Leaf*—is in any way remarkable; it is imagined and worked out in the very spirit of Anderson.—*Spectator*.

ALBERT HALL.

PATRON.

His Honor the Lieutenant Governor of Bengal.

COUNCIL.

Hon'ble Sir William Muir, K. C. S. I.—*President*.

Rajah Roma Nath Tagore Bahadur C. S. I.—*Vice-President*.

Hon'ble J. F. D. Inglis.
Hon'ble Ashley Eden, C. S. I.
Hon'ble H. Bell.
Archdeacon Baly.
Colonel S. E. L. Thuillier, C. S. I.
His Highness the Maharajah of Vizianagram.
Maharajah Kumar of Bettiah.
Hon'ble Rajah Narendra Krishna Bahadur.
Rajah Komul Krishna Bahadur.
Rajah Jotendro Mohun Tagore Bahadur.
Babu Digumber Mitter, C. S. I.
Dr. Rajendralala Mitra.
Hon'ble Nawab Ashgar Ali Bahadur, C. S. I.
Nawab Amir Ali Bahadur.
Moulvi Abdul Lutif Khan Bahadur.
Manockji Rustomji Esq.
Babu Keshub Chunder Sen.

SUBSCRIPTIONS.

The Hon'ble Sir Richard Temple	...	Rs.	200
His Highness Maharajah Holkar	...	,,	8,000
His Highness Maharajah of Jeypore		,,	5,000
His Highness Maharajah of Puttiala		,,	2,500
His Highness Maharajah of Vizianagram	...	,,	1,000
His Highness the Maharajah of Cooch Behar	...	,,	1,000
Maharajah Kumar of Bettiah	...	,,	2,000
Rajah of Bhinga	...	,,	1,000
Maharani Surnomoie, Cossim Bazar		,,	1,000
Maharajah of Hutwa	...	,,	500
Rajah Roma Nath Tagore Bahadur		,,	200
Rajah Komul Krisna Bahadur	...	,,	500
Rajah Jotendro Mohun Tagore	...	,,	500
Hon'ble Rajah Narendra Krishna Bahadur	...	,,	300
Babu Joykissen Mookerjee	...	,,	250
Sirdar Dyal Singh	...	,,	200
Babu Shama Churn Law	...	,,	200
Hon'ble Sir William Muir	...	,,	100
Hon'ble Ashley Eden	...	,,	100
Dr. Mohendro Lall Sircar	...	,,	100
Babu Goonendro Nath Tagore	...	,,	100
Babu Jadulall Mallick	...	,,	100
Babu Ananda Mohun Bose	...	,,	100
Babu Rajkissen Mookerjee	...	,,	200
Babu Janaki Nath Mookerji	...	,,	100
Hon'ble H. Bell	...	,,	100
Babu Debendro Nath Bose	...	,,	200
Babu Annoda Prasad Roy	...	,,	100
Babu Digumber Mitter	...	,,	100

ESTABLISHED 1833.

H. C. GANGOOLY & CO.

STATIONERS, DIE-SINKERS, ENGRAVERS, PRINTERS, LITHOGRAPHERS & CO.

24, Mangoe Lane, Calcutta.

Cash prices of the following :—

	Rs.	As.		Rs.
Whatman's Drawing paper double elephant sizes (40×27) each ...	0	7		0
Mathematical Instrument Boxes	2	8	to	18
Color Boxes ...	0	4	,,	5

Drawing pencils, Drawing and Mapping steel pens and various other requisites in stationery.

MUDHOO SUDUN PAUL & CO.

120, RADHA BAZAR, CALCUTTA.

Tea (Assam) Tea

TRADE M. MARK

In 1lb. and 2lb. Tins.

Pekoe Tea	2lb. Tin. Per Tin	Rs.	3 4
,, Flowery	,, ,,	,,	3 8
,, Souchong	,, ,,	,,	2 8
Family Mixture	,, ,,	,,	2 4
Chempoi	,, ,,	,,	2 0
Imperial Mixture with China ...			3 0
China Rose Pauchong ...			2 8

The above in 1lb. Tin at half the respective prices, plus two annas extra.

BURMAH CIGARS.

No. 1 per 100 Rs. 1 0
,, 2 ... 0 12

HUNTLEY AND PALMER'S BISCUITS.

Albert, in Tin of 2lb each Rs. 1 8
Arrow Root, ... ,, 1 4
Mixed, ... 1 5

Italian Chesnuts, Castor Oil, Candles, Kerosine Oil, China Preserves, Perfumery, Domestic Medicines, and other stores always in stock and offered at lower rates than other Houses.

Catalogue to be had on application,

MUDHOO SUDUN PAUL & Co.

DENONAUTH DEY AND SONS,

NO. 80, CLIVE STREET.

GODOWNS, NO. 34, MACHOOA BAZAAR STREET.

CALCUTTA.

IMPORTERS OF

METALS, IRONMONGERY, HARDWARE, TEA GARDEN TOOLS, CHUBBS' LOCKS AND SAFES, RODGERS' CUTLERY,

Carpenters', Blacksmiths', Coopers', Engineers', Builders' and Planters' Tools.

SADDLERY,

STEAM, GAS & WATER-FITTINGS,

PAINTS, OILS, MARINE STORES, &c., &c.

Priced Catalogues supplied on application, at Rs. 2 each.

MAKHON LOLL GHOSE.

No. 91, Radhabazar, Calcutta,

BEGS to invite the attention of the public to several consignments of commercial and fancy stationery of all sorts, including account books of all sizes, made of handmade and machine made paper, by steamers recently arrived, and which he is disposing of at moderate prices. He has been long in the trade, and presumes he has always afforded every satisfaction to the numerous merchants here who have constantly favored him with orders. Mofussil orders accompanied with remittances shall be promptly attended to.

CALCUTTA,
The 18th August 1876. } M. L. G.

THE INDIAN MIRROR

The Cheapest Daily Paper

IN

INDIA

AND

Having an Extensive Circulation

SUBSCRIPTIONS,
IN ADVANCE.

	Town.	Mofussil, Including Postage.
Yearly	... Rs. 12 0 0	Rs. 20 0 0
Half yearly	... ,, 6 8 0	,, 11 4 0
Quarterly	... ,, 3 8 0	,, 6 0 0
Monthly	... ,, 1 8 0	2 5 0

Cash sales, One Anna per copy.

Sunday Edition.

Per Annum ... ... Rs. 5

MOFUSSIL SUBSCRIBERS.

Per Annum ... ... Rs. 6 10 0

VIA SOUTHAMPTON.		VIA BRINDISI.	
	£ S. D.		£ S. D.
Per Annum	0 18 9	Per Annum	1 2 0

Cash sales, Two Annas per copy.

RATE OF ADVERTISING.

First insertion, 8 lines and under, 1 Rupee.

Second and succeeding insertions, 2 Annas per line.

For Advertisements which are to be inserted for a considerable time special contracts may be made on application to the manager.

Domestic Occurrences { Non-Subscriber ... 1 Re. / Subscriber ... 8 As.
Public Engagement each insertion ... 1 Re.

Printing Materials.

MILLER AND RICHARD'S PRESSES, TYPES and all requisites always in Stock.

TERMS CASH.

EWING & CO.

THEISTIC BOOKS.

FOR SALE.

URDU.

Rahut Hakiki	Rs.	0	3	0
Nizam Komi	...	0	2	0
Kamfal Ilham	...	0	2	0
Kholasa, of, Asool Brahm Dharm ...		0	1	0

HINDI.

Upasana Pudhati	Rs.	0	1	0
Bunni Putrika or Hymn book	...	0	1	0
Tut Bodh	...	0	8	0
Upasashid Sar	...	0	6	0
Dharm Dipika	...	0	0	6

ENGLISH.

Claims of so called Revealed Religion	Rs.	0	3	0
New Life	...	0	0	6
Living God	...	0	1	0
Higher and Lower Virtue ...	...	0	1	0

Apply to the Secretary,
BRAHMO SOMAJ OF THE PUNJAB,
Lahore.

THE INDIAN MIRROR PRESS

Is Ready to Undertake to Print

BOOKS AND JOB WORKS

OF ALL DESCRIPTIONS,

VIZ :—

Price-Currents, Circulars, Labels, Letter-Heads, Tables, STATEMENTS, BILLS, CHEQUE IMPORTS, EXPORTS.

And all other kinds of Form,

AND

ALL SORTS OF TICKETS AND CARDS

WITH NEATNESS & DESPATCH,

and at very Moderate Rates.

☞ All communications &c. to be addressed to the Manager, "INDIAN MIRROR" Press, 15 College Square.

PERFUMERY VICTORIA

Rigaud and Co.

8, RUE VIVIENNE,

PARIS.

Patronized by the French fashionable circles, and dedicated to the elegant Indian society.

Special articles recommended to the Indian public for their quality, elegance and exquisite perfume :—

GENUINE YLANGYLANG PREPARATIONS.

SOAP, POMADE, OIL, TOILET WATER, POWDER, COSMETIC.

GENUINE JAPANESE POWDER FOR THE TOILET.

Superior to all other rice powders.

EXTRACT OF YLANGYLANG and MANILLA BOUQUET.

The two favourite perfumes, distilled from the flowers of the Ylangylang (unona odoratissima). Their fragrance is unequalled by anything hitherto known. they impart to the handkerchief the most grateful perfume ; in short, they far exceed the Jockey Club, Violet, and other extracts.

KANANGA,

A New Japanese Perfume.

The fashionable perfume, obtained from the flowers of the Kananga (pyrus japonica) and just imported by Messrs. Rigaud and Co.

KANANGA,

A New Japanese Toilet Water.

An admirable toilet fluid. An agreeable substitute for the most esteemed kinds of Eau de Cologne and Toilet vinegars. Purchasers must be careful to refuse all bottles not accompanied by our trade-mark and signature.

MIRANDA OIL

and

MIRANDA POMADE.

Composed of tonic substances of a very rich perfume. They are invaluable for promoting the growth and beauty of the hair.

MIRANDA SOAP

Possesses the most delightful and persistent fragrance, and imparts to the skin a velvety softness. Being entirely free from alkali, this soap cannot injure the skin. A single trial will prove that it contains every desirable quality.

RIGAUD'S DENTORINE.

A dentifrice elixir of unequalled virtues. Sweetens the breath, strengthens the gums, and preserves the teeth from decay.

SOLIDIFIED DENTIFRICE CREAM.

This new, elegant, and delightful preparation imparts a dazzling whiteness to the teeth, hardens the gums, and is entirely free from the inconveniences of the various powders, which frequently contain acids injurious to the enamel of the teeth.

SOAPS.

Very finest quality for the toilet and the beauty of the skin.

CASHEMION,

Ylangylang
Velontine
Fashion
Violette le grand
Glycerine

LAITUE.

New perfumes for the pocket handkerchief,

Essence of Cleopatra
Azalia
Bella Paquitte
Malagenta
Lyre de la ville
Bouquet de Cachemire

The Essence of Cologne water of Rigaud & Co. is the most agreeable and the best rated. We highly recommend the Cassie Cologne de la mode of the Tuileries.

—*Princes* which are much asked for by the high life.

AGENT, MOORE & Co.,
Calcutta.

HAROLD & CO.,

3, DALHOUSIE SQUARE, CALCUTTA

HARMONIUMS.

Harold and Co., call attention to their unequalled stock of rich-toned Harmoniums made especially for India.

FROM RS. 90 TO RS. 900 EACH.

All kinds of Musical Instruments of the best description are always kept in Stock.

ICE! ICE! ICE!

MADE IN FOUR MINUTES

THE PNEUMATIC ICE MACHINE

THIS IMPORTANT INVENTION IS CONSIDERED A BOON TO THOSE LIVING IN TROPICAL CLIMATES.

CAN BE WORKED BY THE MOST INEXPERIENCED HAND AND IS NOT LIABLE TO GET OUT OF ORDER.

From Rs. 175, each Machine complete.

MESSRS. ARLINGTON & CO.

AGENTS.

CALCUTTA

106, Bowbazar Street.

DR. H. C. SARMA'S MEDICINE FOR DEBILITY

(NERVOUS.)

Brought on by indulgence in irregular habits, effects of [illegible] diseases, loss of power of limbs, weakness or loss of memory, absent-mindedness, irritable temper, disposition of the mind to displeasure at trifles, want of attention towards business, despair at finding no relief from treatment &c. &c. &c.

Price with postage &c. Rs. 5.

Particulars of disease and directions for despatch required from patients residing at a distance.

DR. SARMA'S FEE.

In cases of Debility (nervous) Rs. 15 per visit. } In
For advice at Home... ... Rs. 10 " " } Town

Out of Town Rs. 500 per Day.

INDIAN TOOTH POWDER.

Strengthens loose teeth, alleviates pain of, and prevents bleeding from Gums, cleanses the mouth, corrects its putrid odour and cures ulceration of the Gums without blackening the Teeth.

Price per packet ...	... ...	Rs. 0 4 0
Postage &c., for 4 packets	...	" 0 5 0

TONIC OIL.

Imparts vigour and tone to the paralyzed or relaxed parts of the Human system. Restores proper circulation of blood to weak and inactive parts.

Price for four ounce phial.	... ...	Rs. 1 0 0
Postage &c.	... ...	0 10 0

HAIR PRESERVER.

Will restore grey hair to its original colour.

It acts directly upon the roots of the hair, removes dandriff, prevents premature falling-off of the hair, and promotes its growth and strength giving it Lustre and Health of Youth.

It also produces a cooling and soothing effect upon the head.

Price, for 4 ounce phial ...	Rs.	1 0 0
Postage &c.	"	0 10 0

Copy of Letter received from Raja Chundernath Roy Bahadoor of Nattore.

Wellesley Street, No. 18, Motts Lane, 29th March 1874.

MY DEAR HURRISH BABU,—I shall thank you to send me another phial of your "*Excellent Hair Restorer.*" In fact it has done me a great benefit and I should like to have more of it. It has disabused me (young as I am) of old age.

Your's Sincerely
C. N. of *Nattore*

MEDICINE FOR BALDNESS.

Will certainly cure baldness if applied on the bald portion, night & morning according to directions given in the adjoining direction paper.

Price per two ounce phial	Rs.	1 0 0
Postage &c.	"	6 0

HEEM-SAGAR OIL.

The best remedy for Headache arising from over-study, intellectual occupation, over-thinking, mental anxiety and weakness, as well as heat of head from living in hot places.

It cools the head and produces very agreeable sensation. Removes Dandriff as well as all other impurities from the head. Promotes the strength and growth of the hair and prevents its premature falling-off.

Price per 4 ounce phial...	Rs.	1 0 0
Postage &c.	"	0 10 0

MEDICINE FOR LEPROSY.

Price with Postage &c. Rs. 5.

OIL FOR LEPROSY.

And Inveterate Skin Diseases.

Price per 8 ounce phial...	Rs.	2 0 0
Postage &c.	"	0 12 0

NATIONAL COMPANY.

HOMŒOPATHIC CHEMISTS AND PUBLISHERS

SUPPLY ALL KINDS OF

HOMŒOPATHIC MEDICINES, BOOKS,

CASES AND OTHER REQUISITES.

12, COLLEGE SQUARE,

Calcutta.

CHUNDER & BROTHERS,

24 & 112 RADHA BAZAR,

CALCUTTA.

TERMS,—CASH STRICTLY.

Cash Boxes of sizes with & without Chubbs' locks.
Railway Bags, of Carpet, Leather &c.
Overland trunks of leather.
Scarborough trunks of sizes.
Brass Candlesticks of sizes.
Cricket Bats & Balls.
Chinese Canisters, Square & round.
Compendium of Games of sizes.
Bulleye Lantern, Japanned.
Hand Lamp English, for Table & Wall.
Mathematical & Surveying Instruments.
Drawing & Painting Materials.
Color Boxes of sizes & descriptions.
Magic inkstand in large variety.
Inkstands with & without stands of sizes &c.
Playing Cards of different patterns.
Brass Padlocks of sizes.
Water Cocks (brass) for Iron and **lead pipes.**
Iron & Lead pipes of sizes.
Note & Letter paper of all sizes & qualities.
Foolscap, Demy, Medium, Royal paper &c.
Printing Papers of sizes &c.
Steel Pens, Quills, Pencils.
Writing Inks, of all colors & sizes.
Bank Books, Pocket Book &c &c.
Fancy & Useful Articles

CALCUTTA, } CHUNDER & BROTHERS.
The 30th June, 1876. }

India General Steam Navigation Company, Ld.

SCHOENE, KILBURN & CO.—*Managing Agents.*

ASSAM LINE.

NOTICE.

Steamers leave Calcutta for Assam every Tuesday, Kooshtea every Thursday and leave Dibrooghur downward every Saturday.

THE Str. "MADRAS" will leave Calcutta *Via Mutlabunga* for Assam, on Tuesday, the 22nd instant.

Cargo will be received at the Company's Godowns, Nimtollah Ghat, up till noon of Monday, the 21st.

THE Str. "AGRA" will leave Kooshtea for Assam on Wednesday, the 23rd instant.

Cargo will be received at the Company's Godowns, No. 4 Fairlie Place, up till noon of Monday the 21st.

Goods forwarded to Kooshtea for this vessel will be chargeable with Railway Freight from Calcutta to Kooshtea in addition to the regular Freight of this Company.

Passengers should leave for Kooshtea by Train of Tuesday, the 22nd.

CACHAR LINE NOTICE.

REGULAR FORTNIGHTLY SERVICE.

Steamers leave Calcutta for Cachar and Intermediate Stations every alternate Friday, and leave Cachar downward every alternate Sunday.

THE Str. "COLOONG" will leave Calcutta *via Mutlabunga* for Cachar on Friday, the 25th instant.

Cargo will be received at the Company's Godowns, Nimtollah Ghat, up till noon of Thursday the 24th.

For further information regarding rates of Freight or passagemoney, apply to,

4, FAIRLIE PLACE, } G. J. SCOTT,
Calcutta 16th August 1876. } *Secretary.*

!!! हुक्का !!!

!!! HOOKAHS !!!

ENGLISH made Hookahs of various choice designs, colours and sizes, ranging in price from Rs. 2 to 5 each, 60 designs to choose from. Apply to

RADANAUTH CHOWDRY,
573, Jorasanko.

Hats, Hats, Hats!!!

C. C. DASS & CO.

SOLA HAT MANUFACTURERS,

74, Radhabazar.

Just opened new Invoices of Silk and Felt Hats and Hawke's Patent Helmets.

SMITH, STANISTREET & CO.

Pharmaceutical Chemists & Druggists

BY APPOINTMENT

To His Excellency the Right Hon'ble

LORD LYTTON, G.M.S.I.

Governor-General of India,

&c., &c.

SYRUP OF LACTATE OF IRON.

Prepared from the original receipe. Lactate of Iron, in various forms of preparation, have been in use in France, and generally through the continent of Europe, for some years past, and is highly esteemed as one of the most valuable Chalybeate Tonic Remedies yet introduced. The Syrup, being the most agreeable as well as convenient form of administration is in most general use. It is a most valuable remedy in the following diseases:—Chlorosis or Green Sickness, Leucorrhœa, Neuralgia, Enlargement of the Spleen, &c. In combination with quinine, it has also been very successfully used in the cure of Fever, while in persons of delicate constitution, enfeebled by disease it is invaluable. In bottles. Rs. 2 each.

SYRUP OF THE PHOSPHATE OF IRON Rs. 2 per bottle.

SYRUP OF PHOSPHATE OF IRON AND STRYCHNINE, Rs. 2 per bottle.

SYRUP OF PHOSPHATE OF IRON AND QUININE. Price Rs. 2-8 per bottle.

SYRUP OF PHOSPHATE OF IRON, QUININE AND STRYCHNINE, (DR. ATKIN'S TRIPLE TONIC SYRUP.) Rs. 2-8 per bottle.

Smith, Stanistreet & Co.

Invite special attention to the following rates the quality guaranteed as the best procurable:—

Pure Ærated Waters.

Made from Pure Water, obtained by the new process through the Patent Charcoal Filters.

				Rs	As.
Ærated plain (Treble Ærated), per doz.			...	0	12
Soda Water	ditto	"	...	0	12
Gingerade	ditto	"	...	1	4
Lemonade	ditto	"	...	1	4
Tonic (Quinine)	ditto	"	...	1	4

The *Cash* must be sent with the order to obtain advantage of the above rates.

BABU BASANTA KUMAR DUTTA,

HOMŒOPATHIC PRACTITIONER.

No. 20, Sunker Halder's Lane, Ahiritolah.

FRESH INDENT OF

Medicines and other Requisites.
Have arrived from England.
Medicines, Boxes, Books, Pamphlets;
Absolute Alcohol; Cholera-spirit Camphor.
SPECIAL REMEDIES.

For Suppressed, Laborious and **Difficult** menses; Leucorrhœa.

For Hysteria; Spermatorrhœa; Dysentery; Diarrhœa; Cholera.

For **Asthma; Pile; Pain; Sore and Diseases of the Children.**

Ice, **Lemonade, Soda and Tonic water al**ways.

To be had at

DUTTA'S HOMŒOPATHIC LABORATORY

No. 312, CHITPORE ROAD, BURTOLA, CALCUTTA

TERMS—CASH.

☞ **Price List can be had on application.**

Oriental Gas Company Ld.

THE price of Gas in Calcutta and Howrah is reduced to Rs. 5 per 1,000 feet.

Printed and published by M. M. RUKHIT, at the INDIAN MIRROR PRESS, No. 6, College Square, for the Proprietors.

The Indian Mirror.

SUNDAY EDITION.

VOL. XV.] CALCUTTA, SUNDAY AUGUST, 27, 1876. { REGISTERED AT THE GENERAL POST OFFICE. } [No. 203

CONTENTS.

Editorial Notes.

WE have been favored with a copy of "The Romance of Language," a lecture delivered by Babu Krishna Bihari Sen, M. A., Principal Maharajah's College, Jeypore, before the Students' Debating Society in that city. The price is only two annas a copy.

LALLA RALLA RAM has set a noble example to his Punjabi brethren, by getting his son married according to reformed nuptial rites. It is true he has not adopted the form observed by the Brahmos in this part of the country. We must however congratulate him on having succeeded in reforming the rites which prevail among the Punjabis, and setting his face against the pernicious customs and idolatrous ceremonies with which they are associated.

THE Brahmo missioneries seem determined to incorporate into their system all the spirit and truth of Vaishnavism. They are most steady just now in singing, hearing, and learning Vaishnava hymns. They are going into the bottom of the system of religion that originated with Chaitanya. If religion is to be made popular in Bengal, and sweet and accessible to all, some of the enthusiasm, meekness, and tenderness of Chaitanya's followers, as they must have been in former times, must be adopted. Vaishnaism without its grosser elements, contains a large and valuable mine of spiritual wealth.

IT is said that since Mr. Moody Sankey commenced to preach in New York there has been a considerable increase of cases of insanity in that part of America. It is some compliment to the preaching powers of these wonderful apostles of Methodism that men run mad so soon after hearing them. There is power here no doubt, though this power be somewhat misguided. The effect produced is generally by giving vivid and material representations of the horrors of hell, and the sufferings that are caused in this life by the excess of sinfulness. A drama, we are told, is being enacted in one of the theatres illustrative of the Last Judgment written mostly in scriptural language. No doubt this has produced much sensation, but we put to reasonable and thoughtful Christians themselves to decide if such representations are proper, and reverent to the spirit of the religion they profess.

THE inhuman war between Turkey and her subject provinces is still continuing, and no one can say where, how, or when its end is to be. The Turks look determined to defeat and punish the insurgents, though circumstances show that is by no means an easy task to accomplish. On the other hand her Christian subjects, who have no doubt had to suffer from fanatical injustice and outrage to which Mahomedans are so prone everywhere, and especially at those places where there power is absolute, also look pretty resolute. The rebellion is well and extensively organized, and there seems to be no doubt now that if not the Russian Government directly, large numbers of Russians are actively aiding, and personally exerting for the cause of Servia and Monte Negro. The great European powers keep a sharp and very watchful lookout, for their interference may be called for at any time. If the misguided Turks will cease from their barbarous and blood-thirsty excesses, they are sure to get the sympathy, and possibly the speedy aid of the English nation.

In Madras it is not always safe on the part of Christian Missionaries to attack the philosophy of Hinduism. A Rev. Mr. Slater tried lately to prove that the religion of the Hindus discouraged right action and practical goodness, and knowledge or *Gyan* is pointed out as the path of salvation. A Hindu gentleman, a man of learning and position who was present when this statement was made, did not agree in this opinion. He pointed out that the *Gyan Yoga* of Patangali, and the *Karma Yoga* were reconciled in the *Bhagavat Gita*, the most popular and the most revered book among Hindus at the present day. Asceticism and contemplation were to be alike blended in the duties of daily life. He pointed out that Hindus were not averse to works, or they would not build temples, Anna Chutters, Ghauts, and perform penances and pilgrimages which cost time, trouble, and money alike. Certainly there have been two schools in Hindu theology or there would not arise any controvesy between the relative merits of *Gyan* and *Karma*; but among the community at large the two doctrines are naturally blended to some extent.

WE have heard complaints regarding certain portions of the Brahma marriage ceremony. The chief point objected to is the long interval of silence which follows the declaration of consent, and during which the bridegroom and bride are led into the female apartments for *stri achar*, and subsequently into a side-room for registration under the Act. During this time the guests get tired, and there is nothing to engage their attention till the return of bridegroom with the bride. Such a break in the course of the ceremony must be inconvenient. To obviate this some would have the registration either before the service or after the entire marriage ceremony is over. Either course would be objectionable. The point was lately referred to the minister, and it has been decided that with a view to shorten the interval complained of the bridegroom and the bride will simply sign the Declaration form prescribed by the Act, in the presence of the Registrar. After this commences the nuptial ceremony begining with the minister's query,—"Wilt thou——take unto thyself——as thy wife?" After the conclusion of the ceremony the Registrar's Certificate will be duly signed and delivered. The words "I [*A*] take thee [*B*] to be my lawful wife (*or* husband)," which according to the Act must be pronounced "in the presence and hearing of the Registrar and witness," have been incorporated into the marriage service, and the Registrar shall in future be asked to attend to those words particularly in the course of the ceremony.

IT is to be regretted that our esteemed brother, the Editor of the *Tatwabodhini,* has shown himself incapable of rising above the popular fallacy which prevails among not a few unthinking Brahmos regarding the recent classification of Theistic students. Like them, he too is of opinion that the classification is sure to foster exclusivism and one-sidedness, and must prove injurious by leading some men into one sphere of religious life to the exclusion of others. Our contemporary contends that "equal attention" must be paid to the different elements of faith. This would bring all humanity to the dead level of uniformity, a thing evidently quite contrary to the economy of nature, and opposed to the experience of ages. That every man should throughout his life grow in wisdom, love, devotion and purity, and that it would be a sin to neglect any of these, no Theist would deny. This is a "first truth" in Theism. But while growing in all these, some men must cultivate specially particular gifts with which nature and early training have markedly endowed them. The venerable minister of the conservative branch of the Brahmo Somaj has, all along his career, shown in his character the three elements, *yoga, bhakti* and *karma*; yet every body knows that in his later life meditation towers above all. Is this special cultivation unnatural or wrong?

ALMS GIVING is a delicate and difficult subject. That indiscriminate alms-giving is not a virtue, and leads to much evil no one can doubt. In European countries where habitual pauperism and moral degradation are nearly synonymous, the evil is much greater than in India, where poverty and alms-taking may mean in certain cases perfect respectability. Miss Octavia Hill of London, who has made many efforts to improve the condition of the poor by bettering their dwellings, read a paper on this subject before the Liberal Social Union. She condemns alms-giving as such, her opinion being "that the poor are not one attom richer or better for the alms that reach them; that they are distinctly worse." It is not against immediate and temporary relief that this philanthropic lady has to say anything. In cases of sudden poverty, and immediate pressure as in sickness, calamity, famine &c. food, money, and clothes must be given to relieve immediate suffering; but even in such cases great care should be taken that such aid does not produce moral degradation. Miss Octavia Hill seems to be in favor of organized, and public systems of charity which relieve poverty, but keep up self-respect and dignity of character in the sufferer by getting them to do a certain amount of work for what they get, and do not trust upon them the humiliation of receiving direct charity for petty and every day wants. When immediate and ready help is reserved for emergent cases of sudden and unlooked for suffering, indirect charity has most of the moral advantages on its side.

THERE is a school of English poetry called the Fleshly School. It was Mr. Robert Buchanan who gave this characteristic name to a class of present-day poets, the gross sensuality of whose productions has threatened to vitiate the taste of the rising generation of England. Chief among this school are Messrs. Rossetti and Swinburne whose writings Mr. Robert Buchanan criticized five years ago in the columns of the *Contemporary Review,* the sharpness and vigor of which had such an effect upon public opinion that, 'The Fleshly School of Poets' were expelled from the Circulating Library of Mr. Mudie, and their publishers repudiated all connection with them in future. There is no doubt a power and sort of genius is observable in some of the obnoxious poems of Mr. Swinburne, and Mr. Buchanan speaks of him thus: "Let Mr. Swinburne burn all his French books, go forth into the world, look men and women in the face, try to seek some nobler inspiration than the smile of harlotry, and the shriek of atheism, and there will be hope for him. Thus far he has given us nothing but borrowed rubbish, but even in his manner of giving there has been something of genius." Smarting under the sense of disgrace thus inflicted on them Mr. Swinburne, and his friends have villified and attacked Mr. Buchanan in various ways, till he was compelled to seek the aid of law. In an action for libel brought by him in the Court of Common Pleas, Mr. Buchanan gave a signal check to his enemies. The jury gave a verdict for the plaintiff with damages £150. In delivering sentence the presiding judge observed that if Mr. Swinburne, Mr. Dante Rossette, and Mr. Morrison had written nothing it would have been better, and if their works are committed to the flames, the world would be a gainer by the loss. Some of our very good writers in Bengal are unmitigated disciples of the Fleshly School. They abjure gross and open obscenity in their writings, but there is so much of debasing and treacherous animalism at the bottom of their productions, that they would be less harmful if their immorality was more pronunced and evident. But there is no public opinion here to check this evil. Even open obscenity receives the sanction of most of our leaders of society.

THE separation of loving souls is always a painful and profound subject. When the parting takes place by Divine will, in the vow of obedience, for the sake of service, and the good of others, when its intense pain and desolation are borne in holy meekness and silent resignation, the spectacle calls into existence and strongly moves the deepest and most mysterious sympathies of the observer We never know what we are capable of unless we stand face to face sometimes with the profound sufferings of men and women whose affections wrenched and lacerated, bleed to death in our presence. The hand of Providence is seen to strike down to the dust the very best of the sons of men, and to turn their joy into intense sorrow. And yet the strangest part of such tragedy is that the sufferer still retains the sunlight of cheerfulness on his face. Such inward peace really passeth understanding. But it shows how far away from the everyday scenes of worldly joy and sorrow is the region of the stillness of true trust and tranquility. It shows the hollowness of the current ideas of happiness and unhappiness, laying bare the fruitfulness and the profound meaning of sorrow. The Budhist legends say that joy and suffering are sisters who live very close, and invariably point to each other, when either of them is sought. Somebody was singing the other day the feelings of Kousalya, (Rama's mother) when her celebrated son on the eve of ascending to his paternal throne, presented himself in the anchorite's humble garb about to proceed on his long self-inflicted exile in the wilderness. And he sang also of the feelings of Sachi (Chaitanaya's mother) when the prophet of Nuddea, the brilliant and beautiful young man, renounced the world, and dressed as the poorest devotee, forsook home and wife for ever, to preach the doctrine of Bhakti and salvation to the sin-stricken millions of this land. And we could not but call back to mind the dying son of God on the cross, the first who ever died for the cause of the love of God and man, as he saw his stupified mother among the little crowd of friendly faces that met for that sad bitter parting, pointed her to his most beloved disciple, and directed her henceforth to regard him as the substitute of her murdered son. The sorrows and sufferings of the world are indeed very strange, but the glorious meaning which they involve is stranger still. Pity that we do not contemplate on it oftener.

THE VINE AND ITS BRANCHES.

OUTSIDERS, and especially those with a hostile cast of mind, cannot find what there is in the Brahmo Somaj which people make so much of. If it is the monotheism of the movement, there has been monotheism in the world very often, and there are many men both in and outside of India holding very nearly the same news as the Brahmos. If it is social improvement, the Brahmos are not the only men who are trying to reform their country. Why then should the Brahmo Somaj be thought of so much, and what have the Brahmos themselves to say regarding the peculiar claims of their movement upon the public attention? This question is a very important one. Now those whose advocacy is inspired by the theology of the Brahmo Somaj, or whose sympathy has been created and kept up by some of the practical reforms introduced by it, have a very superficial insight indeed, into the life and principles of that institution. It is all very good to patronize the candid spirit of truth-seeking which Brahmos manifest, all very kind to encourage them for trying to raise a national church in place of the decaying errors of Hinduism, and the foreign errors and innovations which evangelical Christianity is trying to import into the country. We take such encouragement for what it is worth, and it is worth much amidst the bitter hostility which the orthodox of all classes have manifested from time to time. But it does not by any means touch the actual facts of the case.

The Brahmo Somaj is a manifold agency. It is an influence, which contains within itself various processes, and embodies itself in various institutions religious, moral, social, educational, and to a certain limit political also, having for their common object the elevation and regeneration of the individual, and the corporate life of Hindu society. The Brahmo Somaj aspires to shew the way of salvation to its followers and to the nation at large, not through the shibboleth of certain dogmas and sectarian formulas, but by broadening, deepening, purifying and spiritualizing all the various currents of life in which man's thoughts, wishes, and actions have commenced to flow at the present time. The religion of the Brahmos embraces all the principal concerns of individual and social existence, and its institutions are formed accordingly. Now these institutions, though all of them do not *look* religious from the outside, some but may be viewed in a completely secular and worldly light, are in fact so many essential embodiments of the faith and spirituality of the Brahmo leaders. Every institution with which the Somaj identifies itself, is unavoidable to it; it is the necessary result of spiritual light and growth; it is the manifestation of that Supreme, Inward Force, which constitutes the whole vitality of the movement, and involves its prosperity or its downfall. As the Brahmo Somaj professes to owe its existence to the will and inspiration of the God of truth, if this profession be genuine, the institutions, processes, and disciplines wherein its existence as a body is involved, are equally the results of Divine will and inspiration. Either the Brahmo Somaj is entirely a man-made and humanly-supported movement, and everything connected with it is the offspring of human speculation and fancy, destined as all human conceits are destined, to be swallowed up in the decay which comes upon the efforts of men slowly, but with a fatal certainty; or the different departments of the Brahmo Somaj which mean the essential ideas in which the movement divides itself, must be admitted to be the portions and sides of one great plan revealed in prayerful and devoted hearts who have long waited and watched to know the purposes of Heaven for the regeneration of this land. The man whose faith beholds in all the various branches of the Brahmo Somaj the deep and glorious phases of Divine purpose and will, the man whose spiritual insight beholds the marvellous adaptability of the several divisions of the work to the wants, sorrows, and purification of our race, is indeed a believer in Providence, in the wisdom and mercy of God. If there are any such men in the Brahmo Somaj, they understand the special claim of their church upon the outside world; they can very reasonably, and with the utmost firmness devote their whole life to the furtherance of the movement. Nay how can the various institutions and ideas of the Brahmo Somaj subsist without men to serve to represent them and devote their lives to them? There is the vine and the branches around it. There is the chief servant, with the other servants around him. If they faithfully represent their cause, and devote themselves truly; true and faithful men will find no difficulty to give them the tribute of trust and obedience. And when the men and the institutions, the movement and its departments are considered together, and when they are all illumined by the light of Divine appointment, faith recognizes in them the house with its many mansions. This is what some Brahmos term the Dispensation of the day.

Correspondence.

DIFFIDENCE IN PROVIDENCE.

To the Editor of the *Indian Mirror*.

SIR,—Confidence is the life of society. A social organization cannot exist without mutual help among its members, and this mutual help becomes an impossibility if confidence is eliminated. Were man to believe in every instance after taking all the *pros* and *cons* of the case into consideration, and after satisfying all the little doubts of his sceptical heart, he would never come to believe. Practical work requires immediate nay instantaneous belief, without which all business would be brought at once to a full stop. If one is to analyse every ingredient, every time the dish is laid before him with a view to knowing whether it is poisoned, he will never end by eating. Existence would then become an unbearable burden. Man is obliged, therefore, to yield this immediate belief in spite of himself.

But it is very curious and much to be regretted that this man so docile in all transactions relating to his *self*, to his physical and social concerns, should prove so untractable with God. Strange perversity of the human heart! As soon as it comes in the spiritual region, it begins to unfold all its wicked cunning and little trickery, that it has kept reserved in its dealings with humanity, that it might be the more effectively discharged against God. When the question is whether one is to trust his neck to the barber's razor, he at once becomes human by answering in the affirmative, but when it comes to believing in his *own God*, he cannot afford to concede his little stock of confidence.

There are three kinds of unbeliefs. First the unbelief of an atheist. I exclude here all those who are atheists for convenience, who really believe but are obliged to profess otherwise that they may be left to pursue undisturbed their career of iniquity. I speak only of those who would fain welcome a God, but are forced to disbelieve in the absence of all positive proofs. Unbelief is a matter of intellectual necessity with them. These are most hated by the theists though they deserve not this treatment. They are to be heartily pitied for the unhappy conclusions they have been forced to come at. The second kind of unbelief is that of the rationalist. He goes a step in advance of his brother and concedes the existence of the deity, but cannot believe in His Personality. His position, however, is virtually the same as that of the atheist. To accept the fact of existence without at the same time accepting the equal if not greater fact of Personality is for all practical purposes totally useless. Still he is to be pitied as his learning will not let him what he would otherwise gladly do, believe in an Intelligent Mechanic. The third kind of unbelief is that of the theist. The first two are *pardonable*, the last *heinous*. For with the Brahmo it is not a deplorable intellectual necessity that he cannot help succumbing to, but an unpardonable unauthorized arrogant believing in himself more than in his God. He seems to think that God is All-Wise in a general *vague* sense, but in the particular and practical region of his self, he himself is a far more competent judge. God cannot take so perfect a care of his family and affairs as he himself. He would just charitably concede to this God (theoretically) a short of general and unmeaning providence. But practically would much rather like to be left master in his own little sphere. This is believing one thing and proclaiming by action another, virtually not believing at all—believing in the Mercy, Wisdom and All-Powerfulness of God and acting as if God is incapable of taking a more minute, a more living and a *more perfect* care of His World. His God who loves him infinitely better than his *selfish self*, and who is infinitely more anxious for his soul than his hardened self, cannot take as much care of his affairs, as is necessary, and he himself *can*. God, whose wisdom is perfect, and the highest wisdom of the world is but a partial unveiling of the minutest part of whose wisdom, cannot select the best means to compass his highest good—and he *can* himself. Further and worse, God who is All Mighty—whose lightest breath would be sufficient to crush millions and millions of universe, has not the power to attend to the minute wants of his little insignificant self—and he himself has. O God, look at the *arrogant* presumption and *wicked* self sufficiency of thy *little creature*!!! O to unlearn all our wicked learning that we may repose with perfect confidence on that Infinite Love, that Infinite Wisdom and that Infinite Perfection.

Yours &c.,

A BRAHMO.

The 26th August, 1876.

The Brahmo Somaj

In consequence of an attack of vertigo the minister was prevented from conducting morning service on the occasion of the Utsab on Sunday last. He managed however to attend the Mandir, and found strength enough to take part in the afternoon and evening services.

There were seven persons, three of them from Gouriffa, who were formally admitted into the Brahmo Somaj on Sunday last, in the course of the evening service.

The marriage of Babu Satyapria Deb, son of Babu Shib Chunder Deb of Connaghur, takes place on Thursday next. A revised *padhyati* has been prepared for the occasion, which will be published hereafter in the form of a pamphlet. It is accompanied by a Sanskrit translation, which will no doubt be of some service in Bombay, Madras, and Northern India.

Divine service commences in the Brahma Mandir, at 7 P. M., this evening.

Gleanings

O my brother, cast not away thy confidence of making progress in godliness; there is yet time, the hour is not yet past.

Why wilt thou defer thy good purpose from day to day? Arise and begin in this very instant, and say, Now is the time to be doing, now is the time to be striving, now is the fit time to amend myself.

When thou art ill at ease and much troubled, then is the time of earning thy reward.

Unless thou doest violence to thyself, thou shalt never get the victory over sin.

Thomas A Kempis.

Where shall I find God? Only one step beyond thyself.

Inscription on a temple of Isis at Said:—"I am that which has been, which is, which will be, and no one has yet lifted the veil which covers me."

Sacred Anthology.

Literary

The *Times of India* charged the *Bombay Gazette* with "being mortgaged to Natives." The *Gazette* most indignantly denies the charge. The unseemly squabbles between the Bombay dailies are a scandal to Indian journalism.

A Delhi paper states that the Maharajah of Joudhpore in Rajputana, has offered large rewards for the detection of newspaper correspondents with a view to punishing and deterring them.

Scientific

According to the *Poona Observer* recent experiments made in India, have proved that roasted coffee is one of the most powerful disinfectants, not only rendering animal and vegetable effluvia innocuous, but actually destroying them. A room in which meat in an advanced state of decomposition had been kept for sometime, was instantly deprived of all smell on an open coffee-roaster being carried through it, containing a pound of newly-roasted coffee. In another room the effluvia occasioned by the clearing out of a cesspool was completely removed within a half minute by the use of three ounces of fresh coffee. The way coffee is used as a disinfectant, is by drying the raw bean, then pounding it in a mortar, and afterwards roasting the powder upon a moderately heated iron plate until it assumes a dark hue. The coffee, however, must be pure, as chiccory possesses no deodorizing power.

We take from the *Journal of the Telegraph* a few valuable observations on the subject of lightning-rods. The insulation of lighting-rods, says the *Journal*, is a grave error, because the insulators to some extent arrest the flow of currents of rarified electricity, which it is the true function of the lightning-rod to facilitate. On the other hand, the insulator amounts to nothing as a barrier against a discharge of lightning, which can either pass through it or leap the short distance between the rod and the building. The prejudice in favor of insulators arises from a misapprehension. Strictly speaking, there are no non-conductors; but that term is applied to substances which conduct very imperfectly and are subjected to violent disruptive effects when a shock of electricity passes through them. To prevent a discharge from leaving the rod and passing through the building, something more must be done than to attempt to keep it out by erecting such flimsy and insignificant barriers as insulators. The rod must be arranged so as to present points for the reception and discharge of electricity at the extremities of the building, both above and below, and the different terminations in the ground must be connected by rods lying across the roof, so that lightning can be provided with a path in an horizontal direction, which, being continuous, will be preferred to any series of detached masses of conducting matter contained within the building.—*Popular Science Monthly.*

We read in the *Celestial Empire*, a Shanghai paper, that the members of Her Majesty's Diplomatic and Consular Services have erected a monument in memory of the late Mr. Margary in the narthex (portico) of the Cathedral. It is a shield, carved in marble, and bears the following inscription:—

THIS TABLET IS ERECTED IN TOKEN OF AFFECTIONATE ESTEEM BY THE SENIORS AND COLLEAGUES OF THE LATE
AUGUSTUS RAYMOND MARGARY,
OF THE
BRITISH CONSULAR SERVICE IN CHINA.
He had successfully completed a difficult journey through China to Burmah, and was murdered, when returning, at Manwyne in Yunnan,
on the 21st February 1875.
"QUIT YE LIKE MEN"
I. Corinthians, XVI., 13.

Latest News

—The *Punjab Courier* says that it is probable the S. P. and D. Railway Engineers will have altogether to abandon the present Sutlej Bridge and build another on a different site.

—At the end of the year the Thakore of Morvi who has just left the Rajkoomar College, having attained his age of majority, will set out for his Indian tour, to give a finishing touch to his education. Captain Humphrey is likely to be appointed his travelling companion.

—There is good reason now to hope, we are told by the *Celestial Empire*, that the famine in the North of China will be arrested.

—The following Resolution of the Bombay Government was issued on Tuesday last:—

His Excellency the Nawab Sir Salar Jung, G.C.S.I., is expected to arrive in Bombay by the P. and O. Company's steamer *Pera*, on Thursday, the 24th instant at 10 A.M., and will be received on landing at the Apollo Pier by the Resident, Under-Secretary, and the Oriental Translator to Government.

2. A Guard of Honor will be in attendance and a salute of 17 guns will be fired on His Excellency's landing.

3. The Marine Department will make the necessary arrangements for the disembarkation of His Excellency and suite.

—A meeting was held some time ago at Bombay to organize or provide for the reception of subscriptions to be forwarded to Constantinople, in aid of the Turkish war with the Servians. We are now told that on every Friday in the mosques at Bombay after the noon service, a special prayer is said for the restoration of the health of Sultan Murad, and the quick return of peace and prosperity to the Turkish Empire.

—Sir T. Madhava Rao has, it is stated, sanctioned the expenditure of Rs. 1,25,000 for effecting repairs on "Dubhoi Castle" in Baroda State.

—The Puna Sarvajanik Sabha, a body whose public activity, we are told, contrasts favorably with the comparative supineness of kindred associations in Bombay, is about to memorialise the Viceroy on the subject of mitigating the punishment awarded by law in cases of female infanticide.

—The *Behar Herald* understands that judgment has been passed in the great Ticcari Case by Mr. Bignold, Officiating Judge of Gya. The claim related to 7 annas of the Ticcari Raj. The claimant was Mussummat Rajankour, widow of Babu Pertab Sahi of Chitterpur in Benares, said to have been adopted in *kritrima* form by Rani Sanedkuor, the younger widow of Rajah Modenarain of Ticcari, and lately in possession of 7½ annas of his estate, Babu Ran Bahadur who is the nearest agnate of the Ticcari Rajahs holding the entire estate of the late Rajah Modenarain, under an Ekrarnamah executed by Rani Osmedkuor, the elder widow. Mussummat Rajankuor's suit has been dismissed. Another suit relating to 8½ annas of the same property instituted by Lal Babu of Gorakpur, who alleges himself to have been adopted (also in *kritrima* form) by Rani Osmedkuor is now pending in the Gya Court.

—We have already announced that the Punjab Chief Court has been closed on account of the annual vacation. The Allahabad High Court will be closed from to-morrow. Sir Robert Stuart, the Chief Justice, and Mr. Justice Spankie go to Mussurie. Mr. Justice Oldfield to Almorah, and Mr. Justice Turner remains at Allahabad for the performance of criminal and other emergent business.

—The Maharajah of Bhurtpore arrived at Simla, on Thursday last.

—The King of Dahomey threatens the massacre of the Europeans in his territory.

—The newspaper agitation against Mr. Kirkwood has, we are glad to see, not been without effect. He has been removed from the 24-Pergunnahs to Jessore.

—Lord Ebrington has lately been on a visit to Central India for sporting purposes.

—The *Behar Herald* learns on good authority that Mr. Metcalfe, on making over charge of the Commissionership of this division to Mr. Bayley, will officiate as Inspector-General of Police, Bengal, *vice* Mr. Hankey who goes on leave for six months.

—It is said that Rajah Jay Kissen Dass has come to Allahabad with the express purpose of calling a public meeting of the inhabitants of Allahabad to raise subscriptions for the proposed statue of Sir William Muir.

—The minor Maharajah of Durbhunga has come to Bankipore. The object of his visit is not known.

—The prospects of crops in the Durbhunga district, have, the Behar paper learns, not changed much for the better. The relief operations started in those places have been, however, finally closed.

—The *Pioneer* announces, as an astounding fact for its Native readers, that Lord Nothbrook has, on his return home, become a squadron officer in one of Her Majesty's Yeomanry regiments, and that at the late inspection of the Hampshire troops, he was inspected by his own Military Secretary, Colonel Earle.

—Burdwan has for sometime been the scene of trial of a great *cause célèbre*. A most extensive will case has been going on between the widow of the late Babu Chekonl? Roy, the Zemindar Chuckdist, of and his nephew. Already it is said a lac of Rupees has been spent on this litigation by both parties. The Maharajah of Burdwan, however, is trying his best to bring about an amicable settlement.

—This year it is feared that there will be a famine in many parts of the Bombay presidency.

—It is definitely fixed that the Duke of Buckingham will visit Travancore in the middle of October. The Resident has gone to Courtallum, and will accompany the Duke on his visit to Travancore.

—Major Playfair, late Superintendent of the Hazaribaugh Penitentiary, who was tried by a Court Martial in Calcutta on a charge of "falsifying the records of the Jail," has been honorably acquitted. He was dismissed by the Bengal Government on a representation made by Mr. H. S. Beadon, C. S. Through the interposition only of the Secretary of State that Major Playfair got the opportunity of being tried by a Court Martial to clear his character.—Here is again a case of Civilian zulum. Mr. Beadon, as the son of an Ex-Lieutenant-Governor, thought he was too great a man to be able to do any thing with impunity. Sir Richard Temple also does not cut a good figure in the case. It is said he readily lent his ear to the representation of Mr. Beadon, because Major Playfair was appointed Superintendent of the Hazaribaugh Penitentiary by his predecessor in office, between whom and Sir Richard, it is supposed, there does not exist quite a friendly feeling.

At the annual conference of the representatives from the principal States of Kattywar, the following propositions were passed:—

The appointment of an Assistant Educational Inspector for Kattywar and Kutch, at a monthly expense of Rs. 1,000, was sanctioned.

The appointment of a Geological Surveyor on a yearly expenditure of Rs. 20,000, is sanctioned for two years.

The establishment of the Training College at Rajkote, which was tentative up to this time, has been made permanent.

The Racket Court in connection with the Rajkumar College is to be rebuilt at an expense of about Rs. 8,000.

—The Puna Fine Arts Exhibition was opened by the Governor of Bombay yesterday.

Calcutta.

A few days ago one of our correspondents questioned the right of Babu Sishir Cumar Ghose, the Editor of the *Amrita Bazar Patrika*, to be elected as a Municipal Commissioner of Calcutta. Our readers must have noticed an advertisement of the Municipality which appeared in yesterday's *Mirror*, pronouncing the Babu to be disqualified either for election as a Commissioner or as a voter in Ward No. I. How could he then register himself as a person qualified to be elected as a Commissioner and also to vote in Ward No. I? The Calcutta correspondent of the *Indian Tribune* seems to throw some light, on the subject, though we do not know how far his statement is true. He writes:—"In Shampuker Ward it is stated that one of the candidates thirsts so much for the civic honor that, in order to make up the amount of rates and taxes to Rs. 50 (the minimum sum which a person must pay as a rate or tax to become eligible to stand a candidate for the election) he has included the taxes and rates which are paid by a friend of his for his own property and with which the candidate has no concern whatsoever. An enquiry is being made as to the above by the Chairman, Sir. Stuart Hogg."

The Calcutta correspondent of the *Indian Tribune* writes:—"The High Court has given judgment in the Tippera Raj case. The judgment is against the claimant, *i. e.* the plaintiff in the case. He claimed the Raj, which consists partly of an independent territory and partly of a Zemindary under the British Government, on the ground that he, as the son of the late Rajah Eshan Chunder Manikya, was the preferential heir to succeed to the throne. One of the pleas set up by the defendant was that the British Courts had no jurisdiction to try a case which involved a question of title to an independent territory. The other objection had reference to the legitimacy of the claimant and the family custom as to succession. Mr. Justice Macpherson held that the British Courts had jurisdiction to try a suit of this nature. In fact the Tippera Rajahs from the earliest times on various occasions submitted to the jurisdiction of the Municipal Courts of British India, and it was too late now for them to raise a question of that kind. He further held that the plaintiff was the legitimate son of the late Rajah, but that under the family custom defendant was entitled to succeed as late Rajah previous to his death, had appointed the defendant as the Jobraj, a title by virtue of which the defendant was entitled to succeed to the throne. The litigation, it is estimated, has cost the parties more than 4 lacs of Rupees.

We are requested to announce that the next meeting of the "Bunga Bhasa Samalochoni Sava" will be held to-day at 4½ P. M., in the Albert Hall, when Babu Rajkristo Roy will deliver a lecture on "The Ancient Commerce of Indian." Babu Shivnath Shastri, M. A., will preside.

DOMESTIC OCCURRENCE.

BIRTHS

CHACKRAVARTY.—On Friday, the 18th August 1876, at 5-30 A. M., the wife of Babu Shib-Krishna Chackravarty of Lucknow, of a daughter.

GHOSE.—On Friday, the 11th August 1876, 8-45 P. M., at Dehara Doon, the wife of Babu Cally Mohun Ghose, of a son.

Miscellaneous.

RUNNING IN DEBT.

I DWELL on this point, for I would deter other from entering that place of torment. Half the young men in this country, with many old enough to know better would go into business—that is, into debt—to-morrow, if they could. Most poor men are so ignorant as to envy the merchant or manufacturer, whose life is an incessant struggle with pecuniary difficulties, who is driven to constant "shinning," and who, from month to month, barely evades the insolvency which sooner or later overtakes most in business; so that it has been computed that but one man in twenty of them achieves a pecuniary success. For my own part I would rather be a convict in the State Prison, a slave in a rice swamp, than to pass through life under the harrow of debt. Let no young man misjudge himself unfortunate, or truly poor, so long as he has the full use of his limbs and faculties, and is substantially free from debt. Huger, cold, rags, hard work, contempt, suspicion, unjust reproach, are disagreeable, but debt is infinitely worse than them all. And if it had pleased God to spare either or all of my sons to be the support of my declining years, the lesson which I should most earnestly seek to impress upon them is, "never run in debt." Avoid pecuniary obligations as you would pestilence or famine. If you have but fifty cents and can get no more for a week, buy a peck of corn, parch it and live on it, rather than owe a dollar! Of course, I know that some men must do business that involves a risk, and must give notes or other obligations and I do not consider him in debt who can lay his hands directly on the means of paying, at some little sacrifice, all he owes; I speak of real debt—that which involves risk or sacrifice on one side, obligation and dependence on the other—and I say from all such, let every youth humbly pray God to preserve him ever more.—*Horace Greeley.*

LETTERS IN FRIENDSHIP.

LETTERS are an invaluable sustainer of friendship, but no friendship can live on them. It is a delusion that a mere correspondence, whether daily, monthly or weekly, can supply the aliment for a lively, tenacious, thorough friendship; there must be a personal intercourse. For one reason the letters, to be intimate and unrestrained, and written in any mood and upon the spur of the moment, cannot fail now and then to jar upon the receiver. When two people talk they are alive to each other's state of temper and feeling. No one can guess the condition of his friend at the time he receives his letter. It may be written on impulse and read in weariness or in a testy mood. Or if cheerful a jest falls on a sore place. A snub may be detected where none was meant, a thought written under the presence of strong feeling may be misunderstood. Letters cannot attempt to supply the place of conversation between two vigorous minds without making room for some of these hitches; and if the topics of the letters never touch on delicate themes, never approach points where there may be a difference of opinion, then they do not keep friendship alive at the proper heat. All great friendships live in personal intercourse, and therefore it is that there are so few of them; and therefore that they do not remain unimpaired and in full strength to old age.—*Blackwood.*

TENDENCIES OF BESETTING SINS.

ITS tendencies. Some are steadily prevailing over the besetting sin. Some do fight a good fight. As they look back over the course of years, they can truly say, after the fashion of John Newton: "I am not what I ought to be; I am not what I hoped to be. But I am not what I used to be. By the grace of God I am what I am."

Modern physicians judge of the progress of a disorder by the prevailing temperature of the body. The patient complains of discomfort and languor and a parched tongue. But the little thermometer which has been laid under his arm, and near his heart which showed 103° on yesterday, reads 101° to-day. The doctor thanks God, and takes courage. And so, even if we are not in appearance stronger and happier than we were, still are we in the way of recovery, if, according to the test of daily life and temper, the heat of anger, or covetousness, or sensuality, has sensibly abated.

But it may be otherwise. It may be that the besetting sin is on the increase. My conscience tells me it is harder for me to give or to forgive than when I received my first communion. In my habits of devotion I am less punctual and diligent than I used to be. "Oh, that I were as in months past, as in the days when God preserved me! When His candle shined upon my head, and when by His light I walked in darkness; as in the days of my youth, when the secret of God was in my tabernacle!"

How vain it is to turn our eyes away from the truth, whatever it may be. There can be no better employment than to find out all that can be known by each one of us, touching the sin which doth so easily beset him. Be this our prayer:

That which I see not, teach Thou me. If I have done iniquity, I will do so no more.—Bishop Lay.

THE WIT OF A DOG.

WINKS, for his part, after an hour or two of it got bored with the levity of the conversation, and rustled about so that he was put out of the carriage, to run for the benefit of his health. He went along for a mile pleased enough, gathering dust in clouds about him. But when he intimated a desire to be taken in, the boys, hard-hearted beings! laughed in the face of Winks. "A run will do you good, old fellow," said Dick, with cruel satisfaction. A short time afterward, I am sorry to say, a dreadful accident, nature unknown, happened to Winks. He uttered a heart-rending shriek, and appeared immediately after, making his way toward the carriage, holding up one feathery paw in demonstrative suffering. The anxious party stopped immediately, and Winks made his way towards them, laboriously limping and uttering painful cries. But when, all a-dust as he was, this hypocrite was lifted into the carriage, holding up the injured member, and was laid upon the softest cushion to have it examined, words fail me to express the sardonic grin with which he showed his pink white teeth. There was no more the matter with the little villain's paw than with yours or mine.—*Our Dumb Animals.*

ICE! ICE! ICE!

MADE IN FOUR MINUTES

THE PNEUMATIC ICE MACHINE

THIS IMPORTANT INVENTION IS CONSIDERED A BOON TO THOSE LIVING IN TROPICAL CLIMATES.

CAN BE WORKED BY THE MOST INEXPERIENCED HAND AND IS NOT LIABLE TO GET OUT OF ORDER.

From Rs. 175, each Machine complete.

MESSRS. ARLINGTON & CO.

AGENTS.

HAROLD & CO.,

3, DALHOUSIE SQUARE, CALCUTTA

HARMONIUMS.

Harold and Co., call attention to their unequalled stock of rich-toned Harmoniums made especially for India.

FROM RS. 90 TO RS. 900 EACH.

All kinds of Musical Instruments of the best description are always kept in Stock.

CALCUTTA

106, Bowbazar Street.

DR. H. C. SARMA'S

MEDICINE FOR DEBILITY

(NERVOUS.)

Brought on by indulgence in irregular habits, effects of previous diseases, loss of power of limbs, weakness or loss of memory, absent-mindedness, irritable temper, disposition of the mind to displeasure at trifles, want of attention towards business, despair at finding no relief from treatment &c. &c. &c.

Price with postage &c. Rs. 5.

Particulars of disease and directions for despatch required from patients residing at a distance.

DR. SARMA'S FEE.

In cases of Debility (nervous) Rs. 16 per visit. } In
For advice at Home........ Rs. 10 „ „ } Town

Out of Town Rs. 600 per Day.

INDIAN TOOTH POWDER.

Strengthens loose teeth, alleviates pain of, and prevents bleeding from Gums, cleanses the mouth, corrects its putrid odour and cures ulceration of the Gums without blackening the Teeth.

Price per packet	... Rs.	0 4 0
Postage &c., for 4 packets	... „	0 5 0

TONIC OIL.

Imparts vigour and tone to the paralysed or relaxed parts of the Human system. Restores proper circulation of blood to weak and inactive parts.

Price for four ounce phial.	Rs.	1 0 0
Postage &c.		0 10 0

HAIR PRESERVER.

Will restore grey hair to its original colour.

It acts directly upon the roots of the hair, removes dandriff, prevents premature falling-off of the hair, and promotes the growth and strength giving it Lustre and Health of Youth.

It also produces a cooling and soothing effect upon the head.

Price, for **4 ounce phial** ...	Rs.	1 0 0
Postage &c.	„	0 10 0

Copy of Letter received **from** Raja Chunder Nath Roy Bahadoor of Nattore.

Wellesley Street, No. 13, ***Motts Lane,*** *28th March* **1874.**

MY DEAR HURISH BABU,—I shall thank you to send me another phial of your *"Excellent Hair Restorer."* In fact it has done me a great benefit and I should like to have more of it. It has disabused me (young as I am) of old age.

Your's Sincerely

C. N. of *Nattore*

MEDICINE FOR BALDNESS.

Will certainly cure baldness if applied on **the** bald portion, night & morning according to directions given in the adjoining direction paper

Price per two ounce phial Rs.	1	0	0
Postage &c. „		6	0

HEEM-SAGAR OIL.

The best remedy for Headache arising **from over-study,** intellectual occupation, over-thinking, mental anxiety and weakness, as well as heat of head from living in hot places.

It cools the head and produces very agreeable sensation. Removes Dandriff as well as all other impurities from the head. Promotes the strength and growth of the hair and prevents its premature falling-off.

Price per 4 ounce phial...	**Rs.**	**1**	**0**	**0**
Postage &c.	**„**	**0**	**10**	**0**

MEDICINE FOR LEPROSY.

Price with Postage &c. Rs. 5.

OIL FOR LEPROSY.

And Inveterate Skin Diseases.

Price per 8 **ounce phial...**	Rs.	2	0	0
Postage &c.	„	0	12	0

Oriental Gas Company Ld

THE price of Gas in Calcutta and Howrah is reduced to Rs. 6 per 1,000 feet.

MAKHON LOLL GHOSE.

No. 91, Radha Bazar, Calcutta.

BEGS to invite the attention of **the** public to several consignments of commercial and fancy stationery of all sorts, including account books of all sizes, made of handmade and machine made paper, by steamers recently arrived, and which he is disposing of at moderate prices. He has been long in the trade, and presumes he has always afforded every satisfaction to the numerous merchants here who have constantly favored him with orders. Mofussil orders accompanied with remittances shall be promptly attended to.

CALCUTTA }
The 18th August 1876. }

BABU BASANTA KUMAR DUTTA,

HOMŒOPATHIC PRACTITIONER

No. 20, Sunker Halder's Lane, Ahiritolah.

FRESH INDENT OF

Medicines and other Requisites.
Have arrived from England.
Medicines, Boxes, Books, Pamphlets;
Absolute Alcohol; Cholera-spirit Camphor.
SPECIAL REMEDIES.

For Suppressed, Laborious and Difficult menses; Leucorrhœa.

For Hysteria; Spermatorrhœa; Dysentery; Diarrhœa; Cholera.

For Asthma; Pile; Pain; Sore and Diseases of the Children.

Ice, Lemonade, Soda and Tonic water always.

To be had at

DUTTA'S HOMŒOPATHIC LABORATORY

No. 312, CHITPORE ROAD, BURTOLA, CALCUTTA

TERMS—CASH.

☞ List can be had on application.

THEISTIC BOOKS,

FOR SALE.

URDU.

Rahut Hakiki	Rs.	0	3	0
Nizam Komi	...	0	2	0
Kamfal Ilham	...	0	2	0
Kholasa, ol, Asool Brahm Dharm...		0	1	0

HINDI.

Upasana Padhati	Rs.	0	1	0
Bonai Patrika or Hymn book	...	0	1	0
Tut Bodh	...	0	8	0
Upanishid Sar	...	0	8	0
Dharm Dipika	...	0	0	6

ENGLISH.

Claims of so called Revealed Religion	Rs.	0	3	0
New Life	...	0	0	0
Living God	...	0	1	0
Higher and Lower Virtue ...	...	0	1	0

Apply to the Secretary,

BRAHMO SOMAJ OF THE PUNJAB,

Lahore.

Printing Materials.

MILLER AND RICHARD'S PRESSES, TYPES and all requisites always in Stock,

TERMS CASH.

EWING & CO.

NATIONAL COMPANY.

HOMŒOPATHIC CHEMISTS AND PUBLISHERS

SUPPLY ALL KINDS OF

HOMŒOPATHIC MEDICINES, BOOKS, CASES AND OTHER REQUISITES.

12, COLLEGE SQUARE,

Calcutta.

Rivers Steam Navigation Co. Limited.

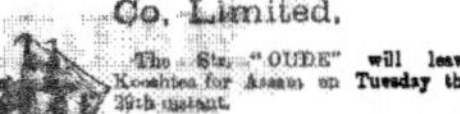

The Str. "OUDE" **will leave** Kooshtea for Assam on **Tuesday the** 29th instant.

The Steamer "BENGAL" will leave Calcutta for Assam on 10th September.

For Freight or Passage, apply to

No. 1 LYONS RANGE, } MACNEILL & Co.,
25th August 1876. } Agents.

India General Steam Navigation Company, Ld.

SCHOENE, KILBURN & Co.—*Managing Agents.*

ASSAM LINE.

NOTICE.

Steamers leave Calcutta for Assam every Tuesday, Kooshtea every Thursday and leave Debrooghur downward every Saturday.

THE Str. "RAJMEHAL" will leave Calcutta *Via Matabhunga* for Assam, on Tuesday, the 29th instant.

Cargo will be received at the Company's Godowns, Nimtollah Ghat, up till noon of Monday, the 28th.

THE Str. "LAHORE" will leave Kooshtea for Assam on Thursday the 31st instant.

Cargo will be received at the Company's Godowns, No. 4 Fairlie Place, up till noon of Tuesday the 29th.

Goods forwarded to Kooshtea for this vessel will be chargeable with Railway Freight from Calcutta to Kooshtea in addition to the regular Freight of this Company.

Passengers should leave for Kooshtea by Train of Wednesday, the 30th.

CACHAR LINE NOTICE.

REGULAR FORTNIGHTLY SERVICE.

Steamers leave Calcutta for Cachar and Intermediate Stations every alternate Friday, and leave Cachar downward every alternate Sunday.

THE Str. "SUCCESS" will leave Calcutta via Matabhunga for Cachar on Friday, **the** 8th September.

Cargo will be received at the Company's Godowns, Nimtollah Ghat, up till **noon of** Thursday the 7th proximo.

For further information **regarding rates of Frieght** or passagemoney, apply to.

4, FAIRLIE PLACE. } **G. J. SCOTT,**
Calcutta 24th August 1876. } ***Secretary.***

MUDHOO SUDUN PAUL & CO.

120, RADHA BAZAR,

CALCUTTA.

Tea! (Assam) Tea!

TRADE M. MARK.

In 1lb. and 2lb. Tins.

Pekoe Tea	2lb. Tin,	Per Tin	Rs.	3	4
„ Flowery	„	„	„	3	8
„ Souchong	„	„	„	2	8
Family Mixture	„	„	„	2	4
Cataper	„	„	„	2	0
Imperial Mixture with China ...	...	...	...	3	6
China Rose Pouchong ...	...	...	...	2	8

The above in 1lb. Tin at half the respective prices, plus two annas extra.

BURMAH CIGARS.

No. 1 per 100 Rs. 1 0
„ 2 „ „ 0 12

HUNTLEY AND PALMER'S BISCUITS.

Albert, in Tin of 2 lb each Rs. 1 [illegible]
Arrow Root, ... „ [illegible]
Mixed, ... „ 1 8

Indian Chutnies, Castor Oil, Candles, Kerosine Oil, China Preserves, Perfumery, Domestic Medicines, and other stores always in stock and offered at lower rates than other Houses.

Catalogue to be had on application.

MUDHOO SUDUN PAUL & Co.

!!! हुक्का !!!

!!! HOOKAHS !!!

ENGLISH made Hookahs of various choice designs, colours and sizes, ranging in price from Rs. 2 to 5 each, 60 designs to choose from. Apply to

RADANAUTH CHOWDRY,

[illegible], Jorasanka.

Printed and published by M. M. RUKHIT, at the INDIAN MIRROR PRESS, No. 6, College Square, for the Proprietors.

The Indian Mirror.

SUNDAY EDITION.

VOL. XV.] CALCUTTA SUNDAY SEPTEMBER 3, 1876 {Registered at the General Post Office.} [No. 209

CONTENTS

Editorial Notes.

CERTAIN remarks which lately appeared in the *Friend of India* regarding the prospects of the Brahmo Somaj have called forth a clear and forcible reply in the columns of the London *Inquirer*.

A CURIOUS meeting was recently held at Cheltenham to honor a clergyman for having fearlessly renounced the doctrine of endless punishment. For this honorable and bold step which he had taken, he was publicly presented with a purse of gold amounting to £10-10s! Surely the renunciation of the terrible theory of eternal torments is far more precious than ten guineas.

THE Rev. Father O'Neill, of the mission of St. John the Evangelist, an ultra-ritualistic, semi-apostolical Portestant sect which is very close indeed to the Curch of Rome, is urging the duty of a friendly relationship between the Protestant and Catholic Missions in this country, because, says he, both of them are saving creeds. Will the Roman Catholic authorities in India admit this of Protestantism, and the Free Church of Scotland Missionari s of the Society of Jesus?

THE English papers report an extraordinary will case in which it came out that the testator was a total disbeliever in all religion, revealed or otherwise, and he also repudiated the existence of a God. He was however a believer in the transmigration of souls. He would not allow his servant to flog a dog, as his notion was that the soul of his grand mother was destined to dwell in a dog at some period or other. His fixed idea was that he was destined to be a fox at some remote period. How the Hindu would rejoice to see his favorite doctrine of transmigration find disciples in England!

IT is said that Christian missionaries are considerable gainersby the fall in the value of silver. They draw their pay in England, and a stated sum in pounds sterling is worth a great deal more in rupees in India now than in former days. The *Friend of India* thinks that a missionary's salary is only supposed to be subsistance allowance, and as prices have risen here, he might be allowed the benefit of the profit by exchange which at present seems to go to swell the balance in hand of the Society at home. It would of course be open to the missionary to draw his whole salary at home and have it remitted to India, thus getting the full advantage to himself, but this would be contrary to the spirit, if in accordance with the letter, of his engagement, and would be rather sharp practice for a man of his profession.

So there has been a second revolution in Turkey. Murad Pasha whose dissipation in former life has made him a hopeless imbecile, has been deposed, and his brother Hamid has been proclaimed Emperor. People say that the new man is no better than those who have preceded him. In the meanwhile the Insurrection rages in the provinces as much as ever, and the excesses of the demoralized soldiery are being strongly resented in every European country. There is no money in the Exchequer, and the Government revenue is exceedingly slow to come from the interior. Meetings are being held in London by influential men to demonstrate the public feeling against any support "material or moral," that the British Government may be disposed to lend to Turkey. Altogether the prospects of the Ottoman Empire look dismal. We should like very much to hear what our enlightened Mahomedan fellow subjects have to say to this state of things in the head quarters of Islamism. We hope they do not identify themselves with the practices of Mossulman soldiers in Bulgaria. The Circassians seem to be the worst offenders in this respect.

A LITTLE persecution often does good. The marriage of Babu Kalinath Bose's daughter was to have come off on Thursday last, at his ancestral dwelling house, and friends had received invitation letters to that effect. Just two days before the appointed day his brothers conspired to prevent the marriage from taking place at the above house which they thought would be defiled by an un-Hindu marriage. Thus cut off from kith and kin almost at the last moment, the Babu, nothing daunted, sought the assistance of his Brahmo friends, who at once rallied round him, and by such prompt and hearty co-operation as the trying occasion called forth, made all needful arrangements. The Lord helped and strengthened them, and the marriage proved a complete success. There were nearly two hundred guests, among whom were to be found not only all the leading and advanced Brahmos, but also a good number of enlightened Hindus and even orthodox Brahmins, who were all greatly pleased with the national though reformed nature of the nuptial rites observed on the occasion. Great credit is due to Babu Shib Chunder Deb of Connaghur, the father of the bridegroom who in his old age has displayed a rare and remarkable amount of moral courage, which cannot fail to influence his youthful countrymen, and help the advancement of our cause. Altogether the event is a moral triumph for which we cannot feel sufficiently thankful to Providence.

FOR the edification of the unscientific world, the *Spectator* has given a specimen letter written by John Hunter, the great authority on the subject of Physiology, to Dr. Jenner equally great in the medical profession, illustrative of the humanity which characterizes the experiments performed upon living animals in the interests of science. "If you could make some experiments" writes Dr. Hunter on the increased heat of inflammation, I should be obliged to you, I have made some, but I am so much hurried that they are but imperfect. To give you an idea of such experiments, I first introduced the thermometer into the anus of an ass, then I injected a solution of corrosive sublimate, above a pint, which it threw out very soon. Some hours after I threw in another, and about twelve hours after,' I again introduced the thermometer. The same experiment might be made upon a dog. I opened the thorax of a dog between its ribs, and introduced the thermometer. Then I put some lint into the wound, to keep it from healing by the first intention, that the thorax might inflame, but before I had time to try it again (from the hurry of business) my dog died, which was on the fourth day. . . . . If these experiments will amuse you, I should be glad they were made, but take care you do not break your thermometer in the dog's chest." Such, and perhaps much worse are the experiments to defend which some of the eminent medical men of England have leagued themselves in opposition to the Vivisection Bill. The notable sentiments in the above letter are the great anxiety for the safety of the thermometer, and the feeling of "amusement" which the experiments are calculated to evoke. The picture is simply harowing.

THE subject of intemperance among the Santhals has, it seems, excited some interest in England, and the apathy of the Local Government has called forth adverse comments. The *Manchester Guardian* has the following:—"In Bengal officials and journalists are discussing the social condition of the Santhals with some degree of warmth. Our dusky fellow-subjects are fallen into evil habits, drunkenness being their chief vice. The Lieutenant-Governor has been strongly urged to adopt energetic measures, and the United Kingdom Alliance will be glad to hear that their principles find wide support in India. The Santhals, it is submitted, ought to be brought under a stringent system of prohibition. In no other way, it is alleged, is the curse of the country to be struck at with effect. These representations have failed to move Sir Richard Temple to action in the direction desired. He declines to attempt the suppression of alcohol, and doubtless for the sufficient reason that, issue what decrees he might, drinking would go on as before. The peasantry are to a large extent their own brewers and distillers, and if they are to be converted into habits of temperance some other method than official coercion must be resorted to. This is Sir Richard Temple's view, and he invites the missionaries and others who are interested in the people, to try what can be done by good counsel and the force of a good example. Some of our Indian contemporaries seem disgusted at what they appear to consider the feeble policy of the Lieutenat-Governor. They would apparently have recourse to much stronger measures; and the missionaries, it need hardly be said, are of the same way of thinking. One of these gentlemen tells a story which ought to become popular at Alliance meetings. 'I once passed a liquor shop,' he writes, 'where I found a Christian half drunk, and gave him a most merciless thrashing there and then before all the heathen, and it has done him a world of good. A Calcutta journal applauds this method of dealing with inebriates; but it may be pointed out that it would probably be found much too hazardous a process for general adoption even in India.' To thrash the Christian who was half drunk was, we must say, a strong measure If thrashing were best, we should suggest that the missionary try it on the Christian who made the other Christian drunk by selling him the liquor. Sir Richard Temple is evidently in the same fog as enwraps so many of our own legislators. We hope that in the end he will unite with the officials and journalists who invoke prohibition for the Santhals, and that finally they and he will come to see that what is best for the heathen Santhals is also best for all Christian people."

THE SURFACE AND DEPTH OF LIFE.

THERE are some men whose opinions are easy to find out. Within a short time we know all about them. Their whole life is on the surface. They have little more within them than what they say and do. Not only is the present state of their lives readily ascertained, but even their hopes and aspirations are perceived without difficulty. It is oftentimes pleasant to mix with such men. Their thoughts readily respond to what is said to them, and very little concealment is practised on those thoughts. In fact they cannot rest until they have made known the condition of their minds. This is a common type of character. It may be considerably improved, and good may be made to come out of it. But the surface shows a great deal of tendency to increase and widen, and the depth remains very much the same. Thoughts and feelings take a wide range in the mind; knowledge, experience, and instruction have good effect on the soil of the heart, and outwardly there is a greenness and culture in every phase of the man's character. People seldom care to go deeper, and the man himself takes slender pains to analyze and discover the underlying motives and principles.

There are other men really difficult to get at. Talk with them ever so long, associate with them, even long acquaintance fails to give anything like a sure insight into their real opinions and feelings in certain matters. A quiet and habitual reserve veils the operations of their minds from the outsider's gaze. It is felt directly you come in contact with them, that there is a great deal below what you see on the surface. Their thoughts and feelings do not grow on the outside of their nature, and send the roots of influence within, but grow at the bottom and then send up their indications to the surface. They tardily respond to what they hear from others; they shew little of what is called teachableness of spirit; make very slight concessions to the opinions that surround them; and seem altogether to exist in a secret sphere of their own being. A wide range of views and feelings is not observed, on the contrary there are clear symptoms of narrowness, and one might say at times of bigotry. The outside is somewhat rough, the culture, if it exists, is not seen very well on the surface. This type of character does not appear to be quite pleasant. The surface of the character is exceedingly limited. But those who have insight into human nature, see great depth below the narrow exterior. It is a whole mine of moral and religious wealth under the hard crust of an unfurrowed, and unadorned character. Every thing goes deep, every thing grows deep, every thing works in the midst of secrecy and depth. How very few are there with whom religion is a secret, who live safely and quite beyond the world's criticisms within the hiding places of their faith. What is religion worth if it is not a refuge for those who flee from the world, and what is a refuge worth in which your enemies can discover you easily. When the treasury is found, will it not be soon drained and exhausted, by those who draw upon it? When your treasure-trove is secret and deep, no man can rob you, or molest you. Therefore have a great depth rather than a great surface to your character.

Correspondence.

TRUE RELIGION.

To the Editor of the *Indian Mirror*

SIR,—True Religion is the aim of every honest seeker; and the day is come when men care less for the name than for the thing. Goodness, godliness is what we want. God's church is the only one men care to join. If Theism means godliness, we want it; and if not, not. If the Brahmo Somaj means the church of God, of the one without a second, we join it, and if not, we will look elsewhere. Right living is true religion; and all life, deserving of the name, is religious. Nothing good is secular. Nothing right is other than divine. Every organization, creed and sacred rite and custom, whether Christian, Hindu, Moslem, Zoroastrian, Confucian or Brahmo, is worthless, except in so far as it increases manliness and godliness and ennobles life.—Your last Sunday *Mirror* declares that the venerable minister of the conservative branch of the Brahmo Somaj, has all along his career shewn in his character the three elements [of life,] *Yoga*, *Bhakti* and *Karma*. Again in the same paper, on another page, it is said that recently in Madras, a Hindu gentleman, a man of learning, at a public meeting, pointed out that the *Gyan Yoga* and the *Karma Yoga* were reconciled in the *Bhagavat Gita*, the most popular and the most revered book among Hindus at the present day.—Let me say as a Theist, and one who has entered Theism—the city of God—by its Christian gate,—that I deeply and truly rejoice in the discovery here, alive and growing on what Christians call "heathen," *i. e. non-Christian* ground,—all the essential elements of true religion. As to their culture, and healthiness of growth, that is another question. The [illegible] tree of God's planting [illegible] they [illegible] of light and heat, of soil and moisture, of pruning and free air,—is open to inquiry. But I thank God that if not [illegible] [illegible] them, and holds them to be the most precious of all plants indigenous to the soil of India. What plants are [illegible]? These God-sent feeders and [illegible] of [illegible]? I answer,—bearing in mind that life is what we make it,—and that these elements of Life will be, to a large extent, what we make them to be,—that these [illegible], as you give them, are Love, Aspiration, Knowledge and Work. They are Joy in God, surrender to God, search for God and the Service of God. On the human side these same *Bhakti Yoga, Gyan* and *Karma*, are Affection, Reverence, Study and Firmness of will. They are, or may become in every Brahmo,—in every true man,—all that their original discoverers and revealers,—grand old Aryans as they were,—saw in them singly; and when united and harmonized as we are called of God to harmonize them, they may give us a completed chart of Life and Free Religion as much grander than *their* fondest ideal, as the last issued map of the world, now in the hands of young India, is grander and truer than the Vedic map of the world, with its (prophetic) *four* Ganges; and seven ocean rings and Mount Meru in the centre, 200,000 feet high. Yes: I rejoice with joy unspeakable, to find growing in India the four cardinals of truth absolute; its north, south, east and west;—in a word, the totality of a divine life, which my elder brother, set forth as the fullness of God *in* man and *for* man; *religion* so true as to fill with godliness, *i.e.*, with love, faith, wisdom and holy power, "all man's heart, and all his soul, and all his mind, and all his will." What is *Bhakti*? Can it be better told than in the extatic words of Charles Wesley.

"Thou hidden love of God, whose height,
Whose depth, unfathomed, no man knows,
I see from far thy beauteous light,
Only I sigh for thy repose;—
My heart is pained; nor can it be
At rest,—till it find rest in Thee!"

What is *Yoga*? can it be more simply uttered than in one of the most widely sung of all hymns:—

"Nearer, my God, to Thee!
—Nearer to Thee:
E'en though it be a cross
That raiseth me;
Still all my song shall be
Nearer my God to Thee;
—Nearer to Thee!—"

What is *Gyan*?

"Ye worship, ye know not what; come know what you worship." And again, "know the truth and Truth shall make you free."

And what is *Karma*?

"*Do the will* of God and ye shall know of the doctrine of God." "Not he that says, but he that does. Not he that saith (to Jesus) Lord Lord, but he that doeth the will of the Lord of Life,—he is, God's true child, I a son of God."—*Love* with all your heart, *Bhakti*; *worship* with all your soul, *Yoga*; inquire with all your mind *Gyan*; *govern* and serve with all your might, *Karma*. Carry all these faculties of feeling, trust, thought and strength, up and up, more and more forever, to the lovable glorious, discoverable and ever active One. Make yourself a true lover, believer, thinker and doer of the blissful, holy, wise and mighty Will, and your neighbor, your friend, your child, your servant, make him *the same*: "this is the first commandment" of true religion. This twofold fidelity to all the human and divine possibilities of your own life and of the *lives* [illegible] you,—there is no higher duty or destiny of man nor truer religion of God.

Yours,
DALL.

THE MINISTER'S ANNUAL TOUR OF INSPECTION AND THE AJUDHIA BRAHMO SOMAJ.

To the Editor of the *Indian Mirror.*

SIR,—As I hear Babu Keshub Chunder Sen, the chief minister of the Progressive Brahmo Somaj, and the leader of the Brahmo community, is soon to leave Calcutta on his annual visit to the Mofussil Brahmo Somajes, I earnestly hope he will favor this station with his presence which is most desirable at this moment, as the spiritual condition of the local Brahmos is really deplorable and heart-rending. Indeed, some of the Brahmos have gone so far as to give up the habit of daily prayer, and become such that it is difficult to say whether they were and are Brahmos, unless any body knows that their names are still on the list of members. In fact, they are not so much fond of their religion and Somaj as they are of theatrical performances which have become the source of ruin to many young men. I wish and pray Almighty God will soon raise these brothers from their spiritual death. May the All-merciful God bless their souls.

I hope and trust the minister will not deny us his presence.

Yours &c.,
A VOICE FROM LUCKNOW.

BRAHMO HOSPITALITY.

To the Editor of the *Indian Mirror.*

SIR,—May I be allowed, through the medium of your widely-circulated journal, to thank the noble-hearted Chowdhry Brothers, who on all occasions of *Utsub*, held in the Brahmo Mandir, freely and most generously expend a large sum of money to provide refreshments for their Brahmo brethren, many of whom they persuade to go to their house, which is close by, to partake of the delicacies prepared for them.

This seasonable supply of food is certainly a great boon to the Brahmos, particularly to those who come from great distances, and who do not like to stay away during the day from any part of the proceedings.

Yours obediently,
S. C. D.

The 22nd August, 1876.

Devotional

ON the outcast sinner, O my gracious Savior, cast thine pitying eye. Cast thine forgiving glance upon him who has made himself vile and abhorred of men. Let thine face shine upon him in the midst of his degradation; soften towards him; the hearts of those whom he has injured let him not altogether die in misery. My God, my God, are we not all of us sinners; has not every one of us outraged the majesty of thy law in thy presence for which we are punishable? Why then should I hate the brother sinner because in the world's estimation his transgressions have been greater than mine? Hold the degraded and the outcast within the safe shelter of thy mother's bosom; give them hope, and give them peace, give them purity, and deliver them from further trials.

THY dealings with me, O Lord, have been as just as merciful. To think of what thou hast done for me in the past, softens the hardest heart, and overpowers the strongest scepticism. Thou knowest my natural, my innate worthlessness, and the vices and follies of which I have been repeatedly guilty, are patent before thine eye. Yet in spite of all this thou hast lifted me up and through a long series of years hastied me forward from happiness to happiness, from virtue to virtue. [illegible], O my ever good Master, make the confession of thy goodness and my ingratitude. Let me read back the history of thy dealings, and the book of thy dispensations, and humbled, and enlightened, believe and declare there is no one like unto my God.

How lonely and disconsolate is the world to those who are truly sorrowful. Nobody understands the heart's ache, and those who know of it, pass it by. Thou alone, O my God, feelest for those who suffer silently. Cause the sorrows which thou dost send to cleanse and chastize my soul, spare me not until thou hast made me what I should be. O Lord, humble down the head that proudly sets itself up, and make thy gracious wounds to penetrate the most unhealthy parts of the soul. Thou Supreme Healer no man dies whom thou hast undertaken to cure. And if the world shall prove to be an indifferent spectator of my pain, teach me only to be more firm, and more faithful.

WE wish to serve thee O God, with united hearts, as a family having one head, as a regiment under one Commander. It is good to work together in thy service, and it is a great pleasure too. There cannot be greater joy or success than when thy servants unitedly carry out thy heavenly purposes on earth. Lord give us love, draw us together more firmly in thy service.

KIND God, have mercy upon us whose thoughts wander about during prayer. How often we have endeavoured to collect our thoughts and yet as often do they run astray. The sweets and benefits of concentrated and sustained communion we have not yet succeeded in realizing. Help us Lord so to control our minds that they may not be disturbed by a single foreign thought during prayer and meditation.

The Brahmo Somajes

ON Thursday last the marriage of Srimati Sarat Cumari Bose, daughter of Babu Kalinath Bose, was solemnized in accordance with Brahmo rites, at 61, Upper Circular Road. The bridegroom, Babu Satya Priya Deb, is the son of Babu Shib Chunder Deb of Connaghur, who has so highly distinguished himself by a long career of usefulness, both as a Brahmo and a philanthropist. The bride was brought up in the Native Ladies' Normal School, and has completed the age of fourteen years. Both families are highly respectable, and occupy a distinguished position in society. The house was elegantly furnished and tastefully decorated, and the guests numbered about two hundred. Among those present there were Dr. Rajendralala Mitra, Babu Peary Chand Mitra, Babu Grish Chunder Deb, Babu Cally Churn Ghose, Babu Radhica Prosunno Mukerji, besides the leading members of the Brahmo community. Divine service commenced at about 8-30 P. M., and was conducted by Babu Bijoi Krishna Goswami, assisted by Babu Gour Govinda Rai, Upadhyaya, and Babu Aghor Nath Gupta. The service and the nuptial ceremony altogether occupied an hour, after which the guests partook of a splendid dinner. The registration took place in a side room after the *stri achar*.

Literary

THE City Press, Calcutta, has just published a handsomely got-up book entitled, "Remarkable Criminal Trials in Bengal" by Lex. We shall notice it at leisure.

THE Native Christians of Travancore have recently started a journal of their own, called the *Travancore Times*.

THE name of Mr. John Dacosta, prefixed to a pamphlet on "the Indian Budget for 1876," which is addressed to "Members of Parliament, holders of Indian stock, and other Englishmen interested in our Indian Empire," will carry weight (says the *Home News*) with those of his readers who can identify the late senior partner in a Calcutta firm with a well-known and able writer on Indian financial topics.

THE *Chambers' Journal* for August contains an article on "Mistaken Ideas of India."

"A Run through Kattywar, Junagurh," is the subject of an article in the August number of *Blackwood's Magazine*.

An article on "the French in Cochin China" appears in the *Fraser's Magazine* of this month.

Scientific

AFTER a silence extending to thirteen months, tidings have at last reached England from Mr. Stanley. The African traveller and his followers, it appears, narrowly escaped massacre by the treacherous Natives of Bambireh after leaving King Mtesa's territory, for which treachery severe punishment was subsequently inflicted upon the savages. Mr. Stanley had twice visited, but not navigated, the Albert Lake, and in his despatches he describes a remarkable mountain named Gambaragara on the cool uplands of which a tribe of pale-faced people live. Mr. Stanley expected to reach Ujiji last month.

Latest News

—THE G. I. P. Railway line has been washed away by the rain at Amroli near Surat.

—THE *Indian Church Gazette* understands that Mr. Street, R. A., the eminent architect, is preparing a design for a monument to be erected over the grave of the late Metropolitan, at Rawulpindi. The work will be carried out in Agra, at the express wish of the late Bishop's family.

—THERE are some prospects of another dock being built in Bombay.

—A FEMALE gymnast, known as Madame Lulu, while performing on the trapeze at Dublin, missed the bar and fell from a considerable height, but her injuries are not dangerous.

—A MAHOMEDAN of the Pathan caste, named Mahomed Gul Mirza Ahmed, at Bombay, has cut off the ears and nose of his wife.

—A CLERICAL paper, published in Paris, asserts that it has been ascertained that a conspiracy has been formed at Rome for the lay election of a Pope at the next vacancy.

—THE present summer is the hottest known in Spain since the commencement of the century. In Madrid, at the end of the Session, the heat was so intense that several Deputies left the House fainting and completely overcome. A telegram now lies on my table, received yesterday, which runs thus:—"Madrid, August 4.—The heat is so fearful that whole families are flying to watering-places and baths. The rest sleep in their balconies, and keep themselves alive by use of enormous fans. In Seville people began to sleep in the street to such an extent that the city authorities had to prohibit the practice.

—EIGHT hundred Mormons left New York on the Pennsylvania Railroad for Salt Lake City on Monday evening. Some of them had as many as eight wives.

—WOMEN teaching in the schools of St. Louis, America, receive the same salaries as men.

—ANOTHER report is gaining currency that though Sir John Strachey will return to India, he will not resume the Government of the North Western Provinces, and that he will take up the portfolio of Finance Minister in succession to Sir William Muir.

—MR. KIRKWOOD has already left the 24-Pergunnahs for Jessore.

—AN examination of candidates for the Civil Service of India will be held in London on the 30th of next month, and candidates must by February 1, produce the usual evidence of their legality to the Civil Service Commissioners.

—IN the House of Lords, upon a motion for the production of official documents relating to the duties on cotton goods imported into India, Lord Northbrook assured the House that there had been no divergence of opinion between the Government of India and the Secretary of State. The Marquis of Salisbury, confirming this statement, added that the supremacy of the Home Government must be maintained. Lord Napier of Magdala thought it essential that the authority of the Governor-General in Council should be maintained, although a power of control must be retained by the authorities in this country.

—THROUGH the Maharajah of Johore's influence the Maharajah Lela, Pandut Indut, and others charged with complicity in the murder of the late Mr. Birch, have surrendered to the Governor of Straits Settlements.

—AT Berne, on Wednesday, a young Russian lady fired two shots at Prince Gortschakoff, son of the Prime Minister at St. Petersburg, and himself Russian Minister to Switzerland. The Prince was not hurt, and the young woman was arrested.

—INFANTICIDE is carried on to an alarming extent in London, and during the past few days the bodies of two infants, one aged three and the other four months, have been found in the West-end.

—IT is said that mosquitoes are pretty numerous in some London hotels, having been imported in the luggage of Americans.

—THE horse which the late Emperor Napoleon rode at Sedan, and which was purchased by the Duke of Sutherland, broke his leg a few days since in Scotland, and had to be shot.

—A NECKLACE is being exhibited in a jeweller's window in Bond-street, London, worth £25,000. It is, however, stated that diamonds, like silver, are depreciating in value.

—THE King and Queen of Greece and the Emperor and Empress of the Brazil have left London for the Continent.

—IN the House of Commons, Lord George Hamilton, in reply to Sir P. O'Brien, said it was not the intention of the Government to give effect to the suggestions of Dr. H. V. Carter embodied in his report relative to leprosy and leper asylums in Norway with reference to India. They have directed further inquiry to be made in India with a view to ascertain the correctness of the conclusions at which Dr. Carter had arrived.

Calcutta.

THE Honorable the Chief Justice has, with the approval of His Excellency the Governor-General in Council, appointed Mr. E. A. Nott to officiate as Assistant Registrar of the High Court, Original Side, during the absence of Mr. W. B. Fink on leave, or until further order.

THE P. and O. Co.'s S. S. *Khiva*, Commander C. G. Perrins, arrived in Bombay harbour on Wednesday last, at 3 o'clock, from Suez with the English mails of the 11th instant, on board. The following is the list of passengers:—

From Southampton.—Mr. E. Parker, Miss Taylor and two sisters, Capt. Gilden, Col. J. Preston, Mr. T. Norcross, M. J. C. McLaren, Mr. G. W. Forrest, Col. A. P. Elleridge, Mrs. L. Moore, Mr. L. Moore, Mr. W. West.

From Brindisi.—Mr. G. Pores, Mr. and Mrs. T. Nelson, Mr. J. Taylor, Mr. Nelson's two daughters, Dr. Ireland.

From Aden.—Mr. and Mrs. McDonald and 2 children, Mrs. Morod and 2 children, Captain Cargill.

THE Calcutta Court of Small Causes will be closed, on account of the Dusserah holidays for three weeks from the 23rd instant.

YESTERDAY at the half-yearly meeting of the Bhowanipore Students' Association held in the Hall of the Bhowanipore London Missionary Society's Institution, Babu Surendro Nath Banerji B. A., delivered a lecture on "Chaitanya." The Revd J. P. Ashton M. A., the President of the Association, took the chair.

WE observe from an extract in the *Indian Daily News*, which we reproduce below, that His Honor the Lieutenant-Governor has been pleased to reconsider the decision he had previously come to in Mr. Kirkwood's case. "His Honor remarks that Mr. Kirkwood cannot but know the importance which the Government attaches to the attempt to accustom the people to local self-government, and its desire to evoke something like public spirit amongst them, and an interest in the management of Municipal affairs. The Lieutenant-Governor views, therefore, with the gravest displeasure, Mr. Kirkwood's efforts to thwart these intentions at Chittagong. Mr. Kirkwood must know that it is a subject of constant regret with the Government, that the people shew so little interest in these proceedings, and apathetically or differentially leave their conduct entirely to the Civilian Magistrate who presides, ex officio at the Board.

"Instead of rightly valuing the interest shewn by the Native members of the Board at Chittagong in these proceedings, and encouraging the just independence of views shewn by Babu Lal Chund Chowdry, Mr. Kirkwood subjected the Babu to the outrage described in these papers, and proceeded finally to arrest him upon charges purely fanciful, and produced entirely by a diseased sense of his own importance.

"The Lieutenant-Governor feels obliged to remove Mr. Kirkwood from his office, and can hold out to him no hope of early re-employment."

The present action of the Government of Bengal, however brought about is worthy of its dignity, and we congratulate Sir Richard Temple on the manliness with which he has shaken off his natural prejudices in favor of an offending member of his own service. At the same time, we hope that the censure and the humiliation, to which Mr. Kirkwood has been justly subjected by removal from office on account of his conduct to Babu Lal Chund Chowdry, may be considered a sufficient punishment, and that he may be allowed an early opportunity of showing that he has profited by the lesson he has received on this occasion. If we have written strongly in this particular case, it is only because we think that the character of the British administration in India is tarnished by an unequal treatment of the European and Native subjects of the Queen.

Miscellaneous.

GOD NEVER FORGETS.

A DEAR little boy was very sick. His father and mother prayed many times that he might get well again.

One night, when very ill, he asked, "Isn't God so busy sometimes, helping everybody, that he forgets such little boys as I?"

"No my darling," said his mother; "God never forgets. He cares every moment for his own dear children, who are to live with him always in heaven. Even if he should take you from us, it would not be because he forgets you, but because he is thinking of you, and doing what will be the best thing for you and us."

"O mama, I'm so glad God never forgets me!" said the sick child. "I won't forget him, if I can help it, ever." After a few days the boy began to get well, and he said, "God didn't forget me, did he mama?"—*Bombay Guardian.*

Selection.

THE WHOLE DUTY OF WOMAN FROM A CHINESE POINT OF VIEW.

(*From the Pall Mall Budget.*)

The other day a learned Judge, charged with adjusting the more serious differences that arise between married couples, delivered a long disquisition on the marked change that has taken place of late in the habits and manners of young persons of the softer sex. Ladies, in his opinion, are gradually assuming a freedom of action and demeanour from which a little while ago they would have shrunk with wholesome aversion. Unfortunately, however, he indicated no remedy for this state of things, although few persons are better qualified to offer advice upon a subject so closely connected with domestic happiness. Had he the requisite leisure he might employ it with advantage in the compilation of a work similar to one which, it seems, enjoys high favor among the Chinese. It is known as the "Nuu Shun; or, Instructions to Women," and has lately been brought home to us in a French translation.

In this popular *vade mecum* the whole duty of woman is set forth with all the minuteness of detail dear to the natives of the Celestial Empire. At the beginning young ladies are cautioned how needful it is for them to observe the duties of politeness, to implicitly regard the injunctions of their parents, never to act from caprice, and to learn to make due distinction between persons of different positions. Young girls are, moreover, enjoined always to preserve a seemly demeanour, not to look round while walking, invariably to retire when male visitors make their appearance and, above all, not to regard the latter too curiously. They are prohibited from going to the pagoda, counselled always to be provided with a lantern when unavoidably out at night, and enjoined to rise in the morning at cock-crow. Hilarity is evidently not considered becoming, giggling young ladies being but little esteemed by the Chinese. Neither is garrulity approved of, gossips creating, we are assured, not only mischief among others but ample annoyance for themselves.

Reading and conversation are treated of at length. "If," says our mentor to his diciples, "you do not read the book of saints and sages how will you know the rites, the duties, the four virtues, and the three obediences"—namely, of the young girl towards her parents, of the wife towards her husband, and the widow towards the eldest of her sons? And he cites the example of Isoun, who threw herself against the sword that threatened her husband; of the mother of Ao, who, being too poor to buy books, taught her son to read by tracing letters on the sand; and of other worthy examples. "Women," he observes, "should know how to keep accounts in order to be capable of managing household," a circumstance well understood out of China. And women, he insists, "should study books of filial piety and morality in preference to amatory poetry, should not store their memories with songs and anecdotes, nor listen to relations of romances;" in other words, should eschew Mudie literature. He is evidently sensible of the difficulties of the task he seeks to impose, for he observes that "effort upon effort must be made to follow these injunctions." "The merit of a woman," remarks this Celestial Solomon, "consists, above all, in being reserved, and not meddling too much in other people's business. A man should not speak of his home affairs, nor a woman of outside matters." "There are circumstances," he admits, "under which a woman ought to speak;" but he advises her to do so "with softness and moderation, and never to let bad or angry words escape her." The Chinese golden rule that "to speak little is a fine accomplishment," will be unwelcome to European or Transatlantic belles with a reputation for brilliant small talk; but in these days of lath and plaster villas the wisdom of the recommendation that if a visitor is in the drawing-room the mistress of the house should be careful not to speak too loud in the kitchen" will be very generally recognized.

Our Chinese mentor expresses himself briefly but to the point on matters relating to the toilette, and English husbands will certainly approve of his maxims: "Study simplicity and neatness. If you are painted and dressed in bright-colored garments, men will stare at you. Do not use rouge and powder every day. Be not too fond of gold, silver, pearls, and jade—all very expensive articles. Be careful of your embroidered and silk attire, and do not wear it excepting when necessary." A careful woman will dress usually in cotton stuffs, but we are not so sure that she "ought not to throw them aside even when they become soiled." She might wash them at least.

Parental respect is strongly inculcated. "The brother and sister though of different sexes, owe the same respect to their parents; they should behave towards them both morning and evening in an amiable manner, ask them if they are warm or cold, bring them their food, and supply them with new shoes when necessary; the must obey their orders and endure their anger without replying." A young lady when grown up and married is enjoined not to forget the benefits she has recieved from her parents. "Once or twice a year she ought to ask her husband's leave to go and see them." Nothing is said, however, on the subject of return visits on the part of the mother-in-law. Ample directions are given as to the bride's behaviour towards her husband and the members of his family. "From the remtest antiquity to the present time the rule in marriage is that the husband commands and the wife obeys. In all matters it is the husband who will decide, and it is the duty of the wife to conform to his decision." Not only is the wife to obey her husband, but she is to be even more attentive and respectful to his parents than towards her own. "She must inquire after their health night and morning, help them to go in and out, always meet them with a smiling countenance, obey their orders, bring them food and drink at appointed times and joyfully offer to wash their clothes, caps, and sashes. She must furnish them with new shoes, new clothes, and new blankets, fulfil all their wishes without delay, and make every effort to satisfy them. Your new parents," she is told, "have the right to scold you if you are in the wrong," and under such circumstances she is only at liberty to reproach herself, and not to utter a single word against them. Younger sisters residing with their married brothers are enjoined neither to hate nor deceive their sister-in-law, and if the latter have faults, they are to conceal and not divulge them. For it is remarked that "young girls are too fond of telling everything, thereby causing serious misunderstandings."

A very delicate section, but one which has no application in this country, is that treating of "the consideration to be shown towards the second wife." If the first wife has not the happiness to have birth to a male child, the husband chooses a person whom he loves, in order to have a son who will continue his race. In these circumstances, remarks the sage, it does not do to give way to sentiments of jealousy, for it is necessary that all who live in the same house should mention amicable relation. But he concludes by recording the sad fact that "now-a-days great discussions exist between first or and second wives. Out of a hundred first wives scarcely more than one or two are of a mild and affable character." For this reason he considers it all the more necessary to impress upon such of his fair readers as have to yeild their places to second wives the desirability of controlling the feelings.

The rules laid down for the management of children are very few. They are to be kept clean, they are not to be allowed to eat and drink gluttonously nor to play too much for fear of contracting idle habits; and whenever a visitor arrives the girls are to be sent away and the boys only presented. Here also there are rules for summoning servants of both sexes. Their master is to exhibit towards them a serious air, and to forbear jesting with them on any pretence; but if they have committed a fault they are on the first occasion to be called to account—on the next they may be beaten. Paterfamilias, after reprimanding his butler for making too free with the '32 port, is afterwards justified in kicking him downstairs. The calculating wisdom of the Celestial crops out in the advice given to feed servants well, "since if you are sparing of their food they will be sparing of their exertions." As regards one's neighbours the having of a good understanding with them is held up as "a magnificent thing," and elsewhere "unity between neighbours" is proclaimed to be an "inestimable jewel."

The section devoted to "woman's work," may possibly not find favor in the eyes of the advocates of woman's rights. Chinese women are enjoined to rise early, since "as spring is the most favorable season for the work of the year, so is the dawn for that of the day." They are, moreover, bidden to take care of the hemp and the mulberry trees; to spin with zeal silk and cotton for their own use; to learn to cut out and make their own garments, and not to have recourse to assistance elsewhere; to wash these when they get soiled in order not to become an object of repugnance to others; while such leisure time as they can find is to be devoted to making shoes for their husbands, and children, their fathers and mother-in-law. Mr. Buckmaster and other professors of the school of cookery will be pleased to learn that in China the care of the kitchen is regarded as one of the first of the wife's duties. Morning and evening she has to prepare the necessary dishes of fish, meat, soup and vegetables, taking care that they are neither too salt nor too sour, and that the cups and plates are always clean. When a guest arrives tea and hot water are to be at once served, the one for internal, the other for exeternal use. The wife is enjoined always to fall in with her husband's wishes when it is a question of pressing a visitor to stay to dinner. On such occasions the eatables and drinkables are to be the best the house can afford, although we are assured that is of little moment what is offered if it is only offered if it is only offered with politeness. And no doubt it is true that "the husband of a woman who knows how to receive a visitor, is certain of being well received elsewhere."

A concluding section of the work relates to the libations and offerings accorded to the dead. Mourning for a husband and for a father or mother-in-law lasts for three years. During this time the wife has to wear garments unhemmed at the bottom, and of a sad color. To laugh in the presence of funeral hangings exposes the offender to universal contempt. "In spring and autumn offerings have to be made to the dead, and this established rule is not to be lightly disregarded." "The procelain utensils reserved for this purpose must be of the best quality and scrupulously clean." The wife is required to prepare all with her own hands, "letting her zeal testify the sincerity of her sentiments." Conjugal fidelity is expected of her not only during her husband's lifetime but after his decease. She is enjoined to emulate the virtuous heroines of antiquity—the wife of Ven-tchang, who ... of nucre to disfigure herself; the spouse of Wang, who cut off her nose to escape a ... ; the lady of Koung-Kiang, who ... a boat of cypress wood;" and the ... who refused to quit her husband's tomb. Finally, she is told "not to imitate faithless women who transgress their duties, but to keep to her heart, hard as stone and ..., always pure."—*Pall Mall Budget.*

Advertisements.

HAROLD & CO.,

3, DALHOUSIE SQUARE, CALCUTTA

HARMONIUMS.

Harold and Co., call attention to their unequalled stock of rich-toned Harmoniums made especially for India.

FROM RS. 90 TO RS. 900 EACH.

All kinds of Musical Instruments of the best description are always kept in Stock.

ICE! ICE! ICE!

MADE IN FOUR MINUTES

THE PNEUMATIC ICE MACHINE

THIS IMPORTANT INVENTION IS CONSIDERED A BOON TO THOSE LIVING IN TROPICAL CLIMATES.

CAN BE WORKED BY THE MOST INEXPERIENCED HAND AND IS NOT LIABLE TO GET OUT OF ORDER.

From Rs. 175, each Machine complete.

MESSRS. ARLINGTON & CO.

AGENTS.

CALCUTTA

166, Bowbazar Street.

DR. H. C. SARMA'S

MEDICINE FOR DEBILITY

(NERVOUS.)

Brought on by indulgence in irregular habits, effects of [illegible], loss of power of limbs, weakness or loss of memory, absent-mindedness, irritable temper, [illegible] of the mind, or displeasure at trifles, want of attention towards business, despair at finding no relief from treatment &c. &c. &c.

Price with postage &c. Rs. 5.

Particulars of disease and directions for despatch required from persons residing at a distance.

DR. SARMA'S FEE.

In case of Debility (nervous) Rs. 1 per visit. } In
For advice at Home........ Rs. 10 ,, } Town

Out of Town, Rs. 500 per Day.

INDIAN TOOTH POWDER.

Strengthens loose teeth, alleviates pain of, and prevents bleeding from Gums, cleanses the mouth, [illegible] edour and cures ulceration of the Gums without blackening the Teeth.

Price per packet ...	...	Rs. 0 4 0
Postage &c., for 4 packets	...	,, 0 5 0

TONIC OIL.

Imparts vigour and tone to the paralyzed or relaxed parts of the Human system. Restores proper circulation of blood to weak and inactive parts.

Price for four ounce phial.	... ...	Rs. 1 0 0
Postage &c.	... ...	0 10 0

HAIR PRESERVER.

Will restore grey hair to its original colour.

It acts directly upon the roots of the hair, removes dandriff, prevents premature falling off of the hair, and promotes its growth and strength giving it Lustre and Health of Youth.

It also produces a cooling and soothing effect upon the head.

Price, for 4 ounce phial	...	Rs. 1 0 0
Postage &c. ...	...	,, 0 10 0

Copy of Letter received from Raja Chundernath Roy Bahadoor of Nattore.

[illegible] Street, No. 18, [illegible] Lane, 28th March 1876.

MY DEAR HURREESH BABU,—I shall thank you to send me another phial of your "*Excellent Hair Restorer.*" In fact it has done me a great benefit and I should like to have more of it. It has dismissed me (young as I am) of old age.

Yours Sincerely,
C. N. of *Nattore*

MEDICINE FOR BALDNESS.

Will certainly cure baldness if applied on the bald portion, night & morning according to directions given in the adjoining direction paper.

Price per two ounce phial Re.		1 0 0
Postage &c.	,,	8 0

HEEM-SAGAR OIL.

The best remedy for Headache arising from overstudy, intellectual occupation, over-thinking, mental anxiety and weakness, as well as heat of head from living in hot places.

It cools the head and produces very agreeable sensation. Removes Dandriff as well as all other impurities from the head. Promotes the strength and growth of the hair and prevents its premature falling-off.

Price per 4 ounce phial ...		Re. 1 0 0
Postage &c., ...	...	,, 0 10 0

MEDICINE FOR LEPROSY.

Price with Postage &c. Rs. 5.

OIL FOR LEPROSY,

And Inveterate Skin Diseases.

Price per 8 ounce phial ...		Rs. 2 0
Postage &c.		,, 0 12

Rivers Steam Navigation Co. Limited.

The Str. "OUDE" has left Kooshtea for Assam on Tuesday the 29th instant.

The Steamer "BENGAL" will leave Calcutta for Assam on 10th September.

For Freight or Passage, apply to

No. 1, Lyons Range, } MACNEILL & Co.,
28th August, 1876. } Agents.

India General Steam Navigation Company, Ld.

SCHOENE, KILBURN & Co.—*Managing Agents.*

ASSAM LINE.

NOTICE.

Steamers leave Calcutta for Assam every Tuesday, Kooshtea every Thursday and leave Debrooghur downward every Saturday.

THE Str. "CHUNAR" will leave Calcutta *Via Mutchanga* for Assam, on Tuesday, the 5th September.

Cargo will be received at the Company's Godowns, Nimtollah Ghat, up till noon of Monday, the 4th proximo.

THE Str. "RAJMEHAL" will leave Kooshtea for Assam on Thursday, the 7th September.

Cargo will be received at the Company's Godowns, No. 4 Fairlie Place, up till noon of Tuesday the 5th proximo.

Goods forwarded to Kooshtea for this vessel will be chargeable with Railway Freight from Calcutta to Kooshtea in addition to the regular Freight of this Company.

Passengers should leave for Kooshtea by Train of Wednesday, the 6th proximo.

CACHAR LINE NOTICE
REGULAR FORTNIGHTLY SERVICE.

Steamers leave Calcutta for Cachar and Intermediate Stations every alternate Friday, and leave Cachar downward every alternate Sunday.

THE Str. "SUCCESS" will leave Calcutta via Mutchanga for Cachar on Friday, the 8th September.

Cargo will be received at the Company's Godowns, Nimtollah Ghat, up till noon of Thursday the 7th proximo.

For further information regarding rates of Freight or passage-money, apply to,

4, FAIRLIE PLACE, } G. J. SCOTT,
Calcutta 30th August, 1876. } *Secretary.*

NOTICE.

A MEETING of the Subscribers, on the Ramgopal Ghose Memorial will be held at the rooms of the British Indian Association, No. 18, British Indian Street, on Friday, the 8th September for the purpose of receiving accounts, and making necessary arrangements for carrying out the Memorial.

TARINEY CHURN BANNERJEE,
RAJENDRA DUTT,
Hony. Secretaries.

Oriental Gas Company Ld.

THE price of Gas in Calcutta and Howrah is reduced to Rs. 9 per 1,000 feet.

TO THE MEMBERS OF THE BRAHMO SOMAJ OF INDIA.

The undersigned has the pleasure to announce that he has received a large supply of Mr. T. Scott's Theistical publications which can be obtained at English price exclusive of postage, namely, from As. 2 to Rs. 2.

A List of the Pamphlets can be had on application to

MR. V. C. MOONESWAMY MOODELIAR
Lascar's Line,
Bangalore.

FOR SALE.

HOUSE and Premises No. 71, Ponchanon Tollah Lane, Harkatagolly (including the ground, measuring 4 cottahs, 6 chittacks, and 35 feet.) Apply to P. B. Pyne, Cashier, *I. D. News.*

BABU BASANTA KUMAR DUTTA.

Homœopathic Practitioner.

20, *Shaker Holder's Lane, [illegible].*

FOR STUDENTS AND PRACTITIONERS SERIES IN BENGALI—PICTORIAL.

১। নতুন-[illegible]

২। নতুন-[illegible]

Published Monthly.

Subscription for each copy 6 as.
Advance Subscription for 12 copies 3 Rs.
Postage 6 as.

For Females and Family men,

Family Guide in Bengali.

Subscription for each copy 2 Ans.
Advance Subscription for copies 1 Re. 4 Ans.
Postage 6 Annas.

Letter should be addressed and all remittances made payable to the manager at—

DATTA'S HOMŒOPATHIC LABORATORY.
No. 312, CHITPORE ROAD, BUTTOLAH, CALCUTTA.

SMITH, STANISTREET & CO.

Pharmaceutical Chemists & Druggists

BY APPOINTMENT

To His Excellency the Right Hon'ble

LORD LYTTON, G.M.S.I.

Governor-General of India,

&c., &c.

SYRUP OF LACTATE OF IRON

Prepared from the original recipe. Lactate of Iron, in various forms of preparation, have been in use in France, and generally through the continent of Europe, for some years past, and is highly esteemed as one of the most valuable Chalybeate Tonic remedies yet introduced. The Syrup, being the most agreeable as well as convenient form of administration is in most general use. It is a most valuable remedy in the following diseases:—Chlorosis or Green Sickness, Leucorrhœa, Neuralgia, enlargement of the Spleen, &c. In combination with quinine, it has also been very successfully used in the cure of Fever, while to persons of delicate constitution, enfeebled by disease it is invaluable. In bottles. Rs. 2 each.

SYRUP OF THE PHOSPHATE OF IRON Rs. 2 per bottle.

SYRUP OF PHOSPHATE OF IRON AND STRYCHNINE, Rs. 2 per bottle.

SYRUP OF PHOSPHATE OF IRON AND QUININE. Price Rs. 2-8 per bottle.

SYRUP OF PHOSPHATE OF IRON, QUININE AND STRYCHINE (DR. ATKIN'S TRIPLE TONIC SYRUP.) Rs. 2-8 per bottle.

Smith, Stanistreet & Co.

Invite special attention to the following rates the quality guaranteed as the best procurable:—

Pure Ærated Waters.

Made from Pure Water, obtained by the new process through the Patent Charcoal Filters.

				Rs.	As.
Ærated plain (Treble Ærated),		per doz.		0	12
Soda Water	ditto	,,	..	0	12
Gingerade	ditto	,,	...	1	4
Lemonade	ditto	,,	...	1	4
Tonic (Quinine)	ditto	,,	...	1	4

The Cash must be sent with the order to obtain advantage of the above rates.

Printing Materials.

MILLER AND RICHARD'S PRESSES, TYPES and all requisites always in Stock,

TERMS CASH.

EWING & CO.

Printed and published by M. M. RUKHIT, at the INDIAN MIRROR PRESS, No. 6, College Square, for the Proprietors.

The Indian Mirror.

SUNDAY EDITION.

VOL. XV.] CALCUTTA, SUNDAY SEPTEMBER 10, 1876. { REGISTERED AT THE GENERAL POST OFFICE. } [No. 215

CONTENTS.

NOTICE.

All letters and communications relating to the literary department of the Paper should be addressed to the Editor. All other letters should be addressed to the Manager, to whom all remittances should be made payable.

Subscribers will be good enough to bring to the notice of the Manager any delay or irregularity in the delivery of the Paper.

Editorial Notes.

DR. MUIR has presented to the Albert Hall Library his valuable work entitled "Sanskrit Texts," in five volumes.

IT is to be regretted that the Brahmo Somaj of India has yet sent no reply to the letter from Australia suggesting the extension of our mission there. We are, however, glad to learn that it is after all not unlikely that one of our missionaries may visit that part of the world.

WE see no reason why the preachers and missionaries of the Brahmo Somaj going out occasionally on visitation tour, should not be allowed to travel free on the railway lines in India. We believe Christian Missionaries enjoy the privilege, and it is but just that it should be extended to Brahmo preachers especially as there are many Brahmos in the Railway Service who stand in need of their ministrations. It is to be regretted that no application was ever made to the East India and other Railway Boards in the matter.

THERE are men who honestly believe that the growing regard for Chaitanya which is so clearly observable among the more devout Brahmos, means a proportionate lack of attachment to Jesus Christ. Are we to believe that one must take away so much love and reverence from Christ in order to give due homage to the prophet of Nuddea? Why should loyalty to one prophet mean rebellion against another? Such conflict is not possible in catholic Theism, which on principle honors all prophets. Dear Jesus is as dear and sweet to the genuine Brahmo heart now as he was before. In the really attractive Brahmoism of the present day Chaitanya only sweetens the deep holiness of Jesus, and softens pure faith into a tender passion.

THE *Dietetic Reformer*, the organ of the Vegetarian Society in England, announces with sincere regret the death of Mrs. Newman, the beloved wife of Professor F. W. Newman, President of the Society, and one of the most distinguished leaders of the Theistic movement in modern times. The melancholy event is announced in the following words:—"On Sunday morning, 16th July, 1876, a blessed saint breathed her last: Maria, the loved and loving life-companion for more than forty years of F. W. Newman; who, though sensible of deep loneliness, yet, in the fixed and sure conviction that death in its due season equally with life is a gift to man from the Most High, resigns the wife of his bosom gratefully and trustingly to the bosom of her God." The Brahmo community must sincerely sympathize with their respected brother, Professor Newman, in his sad bereavement.

WE love the Englishman who in the face of unpopularity and odium, and unbiassed by race prejudices, loves our nation. Bombay may well be congratulated on having such a man in Mr. Wordsworth, the able Principal of the Elphinstone College. This gentleman writes to the *Bombay Gazette* a most interesting epistle on the proper treatment of Native servants by Europeans, which does credit to his generous English heart. Here are words which are as truthful as they are noble:—"It is quite possible to have good and attentive servants here without the use of the whip as it is in England. The persons who systematically resort to that degrading method in this country, do so because they think that they are aobve the law, and because they know, as the bully takes care to know, that their victims are physically incapable of resistance. Such conduct is rightly stigmatised as cowardice; though, by a singular hallucination, the offenders appear to regard themselves as exceptionally manly." The *Bombay Guardian* in noticing the subject justly mentions "the fear of God" as one of the things needed in masters. Our contemporary says:—"There are not a few families where from one year's end to another, there is nothing whatever to show the servants that their masters ever bow the knee to God. A Native servant will not be likely to have much respect in his heart for one who appears to him to be utterly destitute of religion."

VOLUME IV of the ninth edition of the Encyclopœdia Britannica, just out, devotes an entire page to a short historical narrative of the Brahmo Somaj, which is evidently, as the initials indicate, from the pen of Mr. W. W. Hunter. It notices two schisms in our community. "About the year 1850," says the writer, "some of the followers of the new religion discovered that the greater part of the Vedas is polytheistic, and a schism took place, the advanced party holding that nature and intuition form the basis of faith." The secession of the "Progressive" body is thus noticed:—"For long the Brahmas did not attempt any social reforms. But about 1860 the younger Brahmas headed by Babu Kesub Chundra Sen, tried to carry their religious theories into practice by excluding all idolatrous rites from their social and domestic ceremonies, and by rejecting the distinction of caste altogether. This, however, the elder members opposed, declaring such innovations to be premature. The theoretical schism now widened into a visible separation, and henceforth the two parties of the Brahmos were known as the Conservatives and the Progressives. The progressive Brahmas or as they call their church, the Brahmo Somaj of India, have made considerable progress. They have built a chapel in Calcutta, which is crowded every Sunday evening; and they encourage the establishment of branch Somajes in different parts of the country. The number of avowed Brahmas probably does not exceed 3,000, but the greater part of the educated Natives of Bengal sympathize more or less with the movement."

THE THEORY OF EVIL.

IN his posthumous work on Religion John Stuart Mill dicusses the problem of evil, and stumbles on the Manichæan doctrine as the most logical and by far the most satisfactory explanation of the mystery. We chanced to read the other day a good account of the sect in the confessions of St. Augustine, and we shall attempt to reproduce it in a brief shape. A casual reading will be enough to convince the reader of the absurdity of the doctrine and the wrong-headedness which made it one competent to take the place of the theistic solution of the problem. Manes borrowed his system from the religion of Persia, which in his day was Zorastrianism. It combined the principles of good and evil as the basis, form and constitution of the world. The world, according to him, is an incessant struggle between the two principles; and what is benevolently contrived by the bounteous God or Good, is being everlastingly thwarted and counteracted by the devil or Evil. The theory of creation according to this view, is curious, though we admit by no means more absurd than the story as developed in the book of Genesis. We mean that both are unintelligible, unless we take the latter to be a beautiful and sustained allegory Manes held that in the beginning God was entirely separate from matter, and to use the words of St. Ausgustine, He knew not of it, nor it of Him. His abode was the North, East and the West, while matter inhabited the South. Many ages after there was a civil war among the particles of matter, the consequence of which was that some of these atoms pursued, and some were pursued by others till they arrived at the boundaries of God's Kingdom, which was light, matter being darkness all over. Seeing the light which they considered to be a glorious prize, they wished with their whole host to war against and seize it. The Civil dissension having been put an end to by the common prospect of a glorious prize, they united their forces and went to fight against the light. But God was far craftier than they. He dreaded the attack and determined to defeat their designs by pleasant tricks. Taking a portion of light He used it as a sort of bait and hook for matter. The latter eagerly stretching itself upon it, swallowed what was sent and was thus bound. Thus God was compelled to create the world. "matter," says our authority, "in itself confused and at strife, was held together by the presence of this good influence, but the influence itself suffered from being thus combined with what was radically evil." The world is thus darkness or matter *plus* a small portion of light or Good. The human soul is the principal portion of the light mingled with the world. It is always good, while matter, with which it is incorporated, is wholly bad. This is the origin of evil, according to Manes. The problem is—how is the soul to be delivered from its imprisonment? That which belongs to God is suffering contamination from its contact with matter, and all virtuous men who try to please God, please Him by endeavouring to set the soul free from its impurities. This can be done only by avoiding all things connected with matter. The chief duty of a Manichæan is, therefore, to avoid confining the substance of God in matter, as for instance, in every child born, a portion of this substance is supposed to be so confined, and in each successive generation more closely combined than ever. Marriage is thus with the followers of Manes no better than fornication and, as such, was strictly prohibited. Riches bind down the soul in attachment to the world and therefore it is their duty to vow poverty and abstain from worldly honors. But their most amusing doctrine related to the use of food. The Manichæans did not eat flesh because the divine substance had fled from it; nor did they eat eggs. They did not also drink wine, saying it was the Gall of the prince of darkness. According to them herbs and trees live, and both feel and grieve when injured, and shed tears when wounded. They thought it unlawful, therefore, to clear a field even of thorns and condemned agriculture as implying guilt of manifold murders. These are their words. "It is better to be an usurer than an husbandman. Whoso cuts the earth with a furrow, harasses the members of God; whoso plucks a herb from the earth, harasses the members of God; whoso plucks an apple harasses the the members of God." You may ask how did these people manage to live? Manes contrived to return a clever answer. He divided his sect into the Elect and the Hearers. The former were the elder Manichæans; they did not work and look for all food to be brought for their use by the latter, who were forgiven for their murders. It was the Hearers that brought the food to their elders, that ate flesh and cultivated fields, and, if they would, had wives. When about to eat bread the Elders first prayed and thus addressed the bread: "I neither mowed thee, nor ground thee, nor kneaded thee, nor cast thee into the oven; but another did these things and brought to me. I eat guiltless." The Hearers certainly deserved heaven for their disinterestedness in committing so many murders for the sake of their Elders, and rich was the reward which was held out to them. They were promised resurrection, and when they were born again, they became the Elect; or if they deserved better they entered into melons, cucumbers or other food, that they might be eaten by the Elect and thus freed. As it is, no spark of the divine constitution entered in fruits, could be freed unless the same were eaten by the Elders. If others ate them the divine substance became only the more confined therein. It was the duty, therefore, of every Manichælan to see that all fruits in the world were eaten by the Elders. This led to a horrible conclusion. "As it was by the Elect that the divine substance in fruits was detached and as it became fixed if others ate them, it was sin to give food to a hungry person, not of this sect." The Manechæans were forbidden to give an infidel bread or food or fruits or even water. Among them it was a hateful thing to pity the poor, and they would rather that men should starve and die than that they should compel the lawful Elders to minister to matter. Such was the creed of Manes, absurd in itself though not more horrible than absurd, yet precisely the thing, which so astute a philosopher as John Stuart Mill did not fail to recommend as far more satisfactory and logical than theism. Such are the vagaries of the intellect!

THE LAST FESTIVAL.

WHAT furnishes us with matter for much congratulation is the solidity and deepening character of the devotion that is being introduced among the advanced section of our Brahmo brethren. In the *Utsab* celebrated the other day this was the most prominent feature. The attendance from morning till night kept a uniform standard, being as numerous, reverent, and attentive as could be desired. The *Sankirtun* was singular in its sustained enthusiasm, and the effect it produced was great and general. We have seldom witnessed such effect before. The silent communion or *Dhyan* which lasted an hour, was astonishing in its undisturbed solemnity. There were about three hundred persons then present, and the stillness was so complete and breathless, so to say, that the slightest rustle of the breeze could be heard. The good minister's prelude to it unfolded to the attentive worshipper a whole world of new spiritual experience. Some, at any rate, for the first time, learnt and felt what *Dhyan* in the Brahmo Somaj meant. Why should he not say, what no one can say, the revelations that followed in his soul amidst the depth of the silence and thrilling solemnity that came after his preliminary utterances? And the hymns, how nobly were they sung? The popular hymns especially were very good. Can the congregation of the Brahma Mandir sufficiently express their sense of gratitude to the good man who month after month, anniversary after anniversary, benefits them, exalts them first by putting his sweet devotional experiences in beautiful verse, and then singing the same with a voice as sweet and beautiful. May he be long spared to us. We know many will respond to this wish. The mid-day proceedings which are generally somewhat dull, were not dull this time. The few short sentences written, we believe, by the minister, took the audience by surprise. The quaint ideas, in words still more quaint, and the great meaning they embodied all broke upon the mind with a novel and somewhat strange effect not unmixed with feelings of amusement. It is difficult to render that sort of thing into English, but take this:—My family is like a *potla* (wayfarer's bundle). To carry it wearies the shoulder; to leave it behind is impossible. Or this:—Thy clothes are perfumed? Yes, because I am just coming from the company of holy men. Thy clothes stink. Yes, because I live in the neighbourhood of *Muchees* (tanners of hide). Or this:—Men say I am getting old, they count my years forward—one, two, three, four. I say I am getting young, I count my years backward—four, three, two, one. We shall not multiply more instances here. Babu Grish Chunder Sen does us real service by translating those beautiful pieces from the Persian. His subject this time was "Religious Friendship from Shekh Sadi." His style, his reading, and the spirit he throws into the thing, are always successful. And we must thank him for it all. The *Brahmo Gita* which is a Sanskrit translation of the recent *Yoga* and *Bhakti* teachings, was chanted by three of our Sanskrit-knowing Missionaries, who have also been special disciples in those branches, we mean Pundits Bijoy Krishna Goshami, Gour Gobind Roy, and Aghur Nath Gupta. The short mid-day service was conducted by the last-named gentleman, with spirit and deep sincerity. There was a sigh and sentiment of relief when the minister ascended the pulpit for evening service, because there was some fear lest a substitute might be appointed! We need not describe the service. Every body knows how it is when it is in his hands. One thing, however, he must explain. He must explain how when a man is touched and prostrated with pain, his whole head sick his whole body, feeble the previous night, the very next morning he rises, and sits up for twelve hours together amidst the heat of an intense crowd, amidst a feverish excitement, that would exhaust the energies of a healthy man. Have we not some right to be told, we who have been in the Brahmo Somaj now for a long time, what is it that cools and heals the head when other remedies have failed, that soothes and invigorates the heart when the tender ministrations and watchful care of friends have failed, and makes a feeble prostrate frame stronger and more enduring than that of a powerful man. For so it was. The sorrow and consternation of the people were great when they were told their minister could not be present. Their surprise was equally great when at the end of the somewhat long morning service, he stood up at some undiscovered spot, and poured out a prayer, pure, sweet, still as a Himalayan fountain springing amidst the freshness of the silent verdure from the deep bosom of the everlasting rocks. The proceedings closed in the night as they had begun in the morning amidst joy, thankfulness and hope stretching out to the far future.

Provincial

SALEM, MADRAS.

[FROM OUR OWN CORRESPONDENT.]

THE Theistic Church at Salem was established some ten years ago, under the name of the "Veda Somaj" by Mr. Subburayelu Chetty, B.A., B.L., and was in a flourishing state for a few years, during which time a collection was made of about 700 Rs. to erect a Mandir in a central part of the town, but the sum was misappropriated by certain individuals after the death of Mr. Subburayelu. The Somaj was then entrusted to the well-known preacher, Mr. Darasawmy Iyengar, who left for Madras shortly after. On his departure the meetings of the Somaj ceased to be held for sometime. In the year 1871 the name of the Somaj, under the leadership of Mr. P. Narasimmulu Naidu, was changed into "Brahmo Somaj." At the same time a "Free Brahmo Reading Room" was opened in the very heart of the town, but it was closed within a short time owing to the insufficiency of the funds. The Somaj then used to meet once a week. Some of the members of the Somaj published some theistic books of which one is "Parisutha Visista Thivaitha Deepica" or "the Light of Pure Theism," another is "The Present State of India" and so forth. These two publications were circulated among the Native community in the Presidency. Indeed, it is a pity that not a single Brahmo Missionary has paid a visit to the church here, though it has been in existence for more than some 10 years. The hearty thanks of the Salem Brahmos are due to the Revd. Mr. Dall who has done some good to the Somaj. Now the members meet once a week for prayers and for theological discussions, that is, on every Sunday afternoon. For want of a better building the Somaj used to meet in a small house of our friend, Mr. Narasimmulu. The younger men of our schools and colleges now and then come and ask,—Is there any thing in the newspapers about Brahmoism? Where is Keshub Babu? How is he getting on? When shall we see his noble face? Where shall we get his portrait? and so on. I am also glad to state that the proceedings of the last Sunday meeting are worth reporting. On that day an aged Mahomedan (Wahabi) well versed in different scriptures, was present at the meeting and put a few such questions as—What is Brahoism—theism—pantheism—atheism &c., &c.?—and these were readily answered by our friend, Mr. Narasimmulu. The meeting lasted for some 5 hours, and there were also two Unitarian Christians namely, Mr. Paul and Mr. Aaron and also a good many Brahmos. The meeting dissolved after a short and heart-stirring prayer by our friend, Mr. Narasimmulu. It seems that the members are in urgent need of a suitable building and of the services of a Brahmo Missionary.

Devotional

O GOD, I magnify and praise thy unbounded love it is true, but I feel that I must now and then minify thy mercy and try to realise only that much of it which has been actually experienced by me in my life. That thou art infinitely good I believe in theory only, but I cannot conceive its vastness. Teach me to feel thy love as it is vouchsafed unto me in small measure from day to day and grant that I may hold and enjoy it as a sweet reality.

IN my attempts to acquire new truths, I am apt to forget old lessons. Grant O my Saviour, that my interest in the old testament of thy dealings with me may continue unabated and ever fresh. Grant that I may now and then call to mind all those truths and joys which thou didst confer upon me in days gone by, and learn to love and worship thee as my Friend and Guide for ever.

The Brahmo Somaj

THE usual monthly service in the Brahmo Mandir takes place this morning.

THE Brahmo Mandir needs slight repairs, and we hope the matter will receive the attention of the congregation before it is too late. The organ too is out of order, and must be immediately repaired. Altogether the repairs would cost about a thousand rupees.

BABU DEBENDRA NATH TAGORE came down from the hills lately, and returned after spending only three or four days in Calcutta. His stay was so short and so quiet that few could go and pay their respects to him. It is said that he came to settle certain points in connection with an important lawsuit.

SOME of our missionaries, as usual will leave Calcutta during the ensuing holidays, and proceed on their annual tour, visiting the provincial Brahmo Somajes. Nothing is as yet decided as to their movements. But it is more than probable that one of our missionaries will go as far as Dehra Doon and Mussurie. Another will visit all the important stations along the E. I. R. line in Bengal and Behar. Another will be sent to the eastern districts. There will also probably be a band of itinerant preachers, who will go about singing in villages and towns near the metropolis.

Gleanings

THE DYING WORDS OF SOVEREIGNS AND STATESMEN.

George II: O, God, I am dying. This is death! Cardinal Beaufort: What! is there no bribing death?

Cardinal Ximenes: In thee, Lord, have I trusted.

Emperor Vespasian: An Emperor should die standing.

Julian the Apostate: O Galilean, thou hast conquered.

Caliph Omar: Testify this for me at the day of judgment.

Lady Jane Grey: Lord, unto Thy hands I commend my spirit.

Queen Elizabeth: All my possessions for a moment of time.

Maria Theresa: I do not sleep. I wish to meet my death awake.

Anne Boleyn: It is small, very small indeed. (Clasping her neck.)

Frederick V. of Denmark: There is not a drop of blood on my hands.

Louis XIV. O, my God, come to my aid, make haste to succour me.

Augustus Cæsar: Farewell, Livia, and ever remember our union.

Emperor Severus: I have seen all things, and all things are of little value.

William the Silent: O, my God, have mercy on my soul! O, my God, have mercy on this poor people.

Mary Beatrice, of Madena: Pray for me and for the king, my son, that he may serve God faithfully all his life.

Mary Antoinette: Lord enlighten and soften the hearts of my executioners. Adieu, forever, my dear children. I go to your father.

Isabella of Arragon: Do not weep for me, nor waste your time in fruitless prayers for my recovery; but pray rather for the salvation of my soul.

Henry II: O shame! O shame! I am a conquered King! a conquered King! Cursed be the day on which I was born, and cursed be the children I leave behind me.

Empress Josephine: I shall die regretted. I have always desired the happiness of France. I did all in my power to contribute to it. I can say with truth that the first wife of Napoleon never caused a tear to flow.

Cyrus the Great: Adieu, dear children, may your lives be happy! Carry my last remembrance to your mother; and for you my faithful friends, as well absent, receive this last farewell, and may you live in peace.

Cardinal Wolsey: If I had served God as diligently as I have served the king, he would not have given me over in my gray hairs.

WARNING VOICE.

CAUTIOUSLY, carefully
Ponder your way;
Patiently, prayerfully
Live day by day.
Toil for God zealously;
Choose the good part,
Watching most jealously
Over your heart.
Trifle not needlessly,
Precious is time;
Waste it not heedlessly;
Folly is crime.
Pleasures love sparingly,
Oft they enthral,
Tamper not daringly,
Lest you should fall.

Ludlow.

Literary

A NEW Malay Dictionary, in Malay and French, has been lately published by M. L'Abbe Favre, who resided for many years in the Indian Archipelago. He has adopted the system of representing each letter of the Native alphabet by a single letter of the French alphabet.

THE London Conservative newspaper, the *Hour*, has ceased to exist.

Scientific

A MR. THOMAS ROUTHLEDGE, who has had some experience in the use of bamboo as a paper making material, has applied for and is likely to get a large grant of forest land on the Kala Nuddi (Carwar) for the scientific cultivation of the bamboo for this purpose.

THE *Deccan Herald* is glad to see the progress made by the Natives of Puna in good and useful directions. Our contemporary has frequently referred to the industrial works going on in Puna, and he is glad to notice now that they are cultivating the fine arts and sciences. Some of them have for some time past been practising the arts of painting and photography.

Latest News

—THE Paris correspondent of a contemporary states that M. Henri Cernuschi, the Italian millionaire, is making a tour of the capitals of Europe, to get up a general agitation in favor of a gold and silver currency. He is very sanguine in the ultimate success of the cause of bimetallism. M. Cernuschi thinks that India, and British commerce with the East generally, will force England to enter into the Latin monetary union, and accept silver equally with gold in the proportions of 15½ of the latter metal to one of the former as a legal tender.

—AN English contemporary reports that a great feat of speed and endurance in bicycling has been performed by Mr. Stanley Thorpe, of Hertford, who rode from Highgate Archway to York, a distance of 195½ miles, in 22½ hours.

—SIR GEORGE CAMPBELL on the 31st ultimo asked the Secretary for War if it was true that he had proposed to reduce the service of European regiments in India to half the present term; and, if so, whether regard would be had to the military and financial necessities of India before any such plan was adopted, and full opportunity would be given to the Indian authorities to express their opinion on it. Mr. Hardy answered that no such proposal had been made, nor would it be made without consultation with the Indian authorities.

—IT is stated that the Assistant Dewan of Baroda has been removed from his post on a charge of accepting bribes. Both this functionary and his evil genius, a Shastri, have been placed under custody.

—THE Rajah of Faridkote has left Simla *en route* for his own State.

—THE *Aftab Punjab* publishes an exaggerated account of the late railway accident at Nowrungabad near Jhelum, in which the Editor states having heard that the railway officials made away with upwards of 100 bodies of the Purbeah Coolies killed in the collision by putting them in bags and sinking them in the river Jhelum!

—THE *Times* in a leading article upon Lord Northbrook predicts that, ere many years are over, his Lordship will be found occupying high political office in England.

—THE Maharajah of Rewah has gone to Indore.

—ONE of the Akhund of Swat's disciples came to Peshawar for a Native Physician to attend upon the Akhund at Swat. The latter's health is in a most precarious state, and is causing considerable anxiety among the border tribes.

—A DESPATCH has been sent by the India Office to the Government of India dealing with the question of the block of promotion among the civilians in the N. W. P.

—THERE is not the slightest foundation for the persistent rumours about Lord Lytton's intention to resign office.

—THE *Times* says that "there are no independent Princes in India."

—DR. BALFOUR left Madras for Europe yesterday.

—IT is believed that under Rao Sahib Narayen Bhayi as the Head, and Mr. Shriram Bhikaji as his Assistant, the Educational Department of Berar will flourish.

—AT a dinner given at Mysore in honor of the Duke of Buckingham, the Maharajah proposed the health of Her Majesty, and the Duke proposed that of the Maharajah, who responded by proposing the health of his distinguished guest.

—DR. HARVEY, Civil Surgeon at Simla, accompanies the Viceregal party as medical officer during their approaching tour. Lord Lytton's children will remain behind.

—THE Lieutenant-Governor of the Punjab positively leaves Simla for Lahore *en route* to Murri to-morrow.

—IT is rumoured that Sir Henry Daly is about to retire.

—THE proper name of Jebanbai Saheb Gaekwar is Radhabai. Jebanbai is an assumed name.

—ONE of the Sikh Officers who accompanied the Prince of Wales to England, has come back. His name is Duffadar Narain Sing of the 11th Bengal Lancers. The other man Ressaldar Anup Sing is still in England.

—THE Gaekwar will bring his gold and silver guns to Delhi and a very large following.

—THE Governor of Bombay's State Ball will take place on Wednesday, the 27th instant. Invitations have been already issued for it.

—THE Central Asian Trading Company's goods have reached Ladakh by this time. The Company's agent, Mr. Dalgleish, is being well treated in Yarkand, and is just now very busy sending down horse-loads of goods.

—THE Judicial Commissioner of Oudh and some seven or eight principal Talukdars of that province will, says the *Indian Tribune*, shortly proceed to Simla in connection with the Oudh Land Revenue and Laws Bills, now pending before the Legislative Council.

—A PROPOSITION is before the Madras Government for the amalgamation of the Registration Office and the General Stamp and Stationery Offices, to be placed under the Hon'ble V. Ramiengar. It is considered that by the amalgamation a saving to Government of about Rs. 5,000 per annum will be effected.

—THE statement that Mr. John Bruce Norton would visit India again is contradicted. Mr. Norton has written to a Native gentleman at Madras that it is not his intention to visit India again.

—THE Civilian at Mussurie who has absconded after swindling several people, is Mr. Walter Macleane.

—ONE Lieutenant Colonel Galloway was sentenced lately by the Cantonment Magistrate of Lucknow to a fine of Rs. 50, or in default to one month's imprisonment, for assaulting his wife's ayah. He appealed against this sentence to the High Court N. W. P., but it has been dismissed, and the Cantonment Magistrate's sentence confirmed.

—LORD NAPIER OF MAGDALA has left England for Hamburg.

—HEAVY floods have occurred at Kampti in the Central Provinces.

—THE *Bombay Gazette* understands that the first annual Baroda Progress Report has been sent in to the Government of India. It is said to contain a record of great improvements in the condition of that State.

—A CORRESPONDENT of the *Pioneer* says that the coming durbar at Delhi is not looked upon with favor by the Chiefs in Central India. Holkar last year visited Calcutta, and had the Prince of Wales as his guest at Indore, and expended, as he says, a lac of rupees; and now again he is called on to proceed to Delhi in state. It will come hard too on the other Chiefs from these parts as they cannot attend without having so many followers, who want clothing and feeding. Dhar is liberal-hearted and will not care, but Rutlam, Jowrah, the Dewas chiefs and Bundelcund chiefs can ill spare the coins.

Calcutta.

THE P. and O. Co.'s S. S. *Venetia*, Commander G. S. Baker, arrived in Bombay harbour, on Tuesday last, at 6 o'clock, from Suez with the English mails of the 18th August on board. The following is the list of passengers:—

From Suez.—Major Crispin, Mrs. Payne, infant and ayah, Mr. J. Stewart Condr and Mrs. Courtenay, Mr. and Mrs. Scroggie and 3 infants, Mr. Winterbottom, Mr. Poynter.

From Aden.—Mr. Dadabhoy Edulji and 14 Natives.

Miscellaneous.

POOR GIRLS

THE poorest girls in the world are those who have never been taught to work. There are thousands of them. Rich parents have petted them; they have been taught to despise upon others for a living, and are perfectly helpless. If misfortune comes upon their friends, as it often does, their case is hopeless. The most forlorn and miserable woman on earth belongs to this class. It belongs to parents to protect their daughters from this deplorable condition. They do them a great wrong if they neglect it. Every daughter should be taught to earn her own living. The rich as well as the poor require this training. The wheel of fortune rolls swiftly round—the rich are very likely to become poor, and the poor rich. Skilled to labor is no disadvantage to the rich, and is indispensable to the poor. Well-to-do parents must educate their daughters to work; no reform is more imperative than this.—*Southern Christian Advocate.*

Selection.

PROSPECTS OF THE BRAHMA SOMAJ

THE article on the probable future of the Brahma Somaj, which appeared in a recent number of the *Friend of India*, has deservedly attracted a good deal of notice. It is written in a candid sprit, aims to appreciate this movement justly, points out its source of weakness, and touches besides on some matters of the highest interest and importance to English Unitarians and Theists, as well as to those of India.

The writer begins by speaking in high terms of the present leader of the Brahma Somaj. The importance of his work, and the sincerity and ability with which he carried it on, are cordially admitted. At the same time it is frankly allowed that Chunder Sen himself and the work he is doing, are better appreciated by liberal-minded Englishmen and Americans than by any except an earnest and enlightened few in India. Having paid this well-deserved tribute to the character and aims of Chunder Sen, the writer goes on to express his doubts of the permanence of the religious school of which he is the head. The Theistic Church of India has, he thinks, no future before it. "It lacks the element of permanence, a human centre round which to revolve. It has neither a God incarnate, nor a prophet whose name can stand beside that of the Deity in the creed. With neither an incarnate God nor a prophet claiming honors almost, if not altogether divine, no religion has been able, and no religion will ever, we believe, be able permanently, and on a vast scale, to affect humanity, without lapsing into idolatry." What the writer means by idolatry he does not explain. Idolatry we take to be this—the putting in the place of the Highest one who is not the Highest, and rendering to this secondary one the worship and honor due to the Highest alone. Has the belief in an incarnate God saved the nations from this idolatry? Has it saved Christendom from idolatry? What is orthodox Christianity but idolatry—the worship of one, as God, who lived and died as a man? What is Roman Catholicism but idolatry—the putting in the place of God, as objects of the trust, reverence and devotion, the Saints, the Virgin, and her Son? So far from the belief in an incarnate or anthropomorphic Diety being a protection or safeguard against idolatry all history shows it is the very step that leads to it. The teacher or prophet is conceived of as God incarnate, and then is worshipped with divine honors. The glory of God is given to another, and that is idolatry. The furthest remove from this seems to us a Theism like the Brahma Somaj. It keeps all secondary objects of reverence in their subordinate place, and brings it to prominence the one God and Father of all. It interposes no mediation between God and man; sets up no barrier to the spirit's free access to the Deity, makes every worshipper his own priest, and his own heart his altar. Instead of leading to idolatry we are told to say the universal diffusion of this faith would banish it from the earth.

Whether this faith will "ever be able permanently, and on vast scale, to affect humanity," is quite another question. It may be true that a great religion cannot be built upon faith and sentiment without a great human person with whom that faith and that sentiment are intimately associated. It may be true that the faith of the multitude needs "a human centre round which to revolve." In the present stage of the world's religious progress, and for ages to come, this help may be needful. But this human personality is only a means to an end—a leader on the soul's way to God—a pioneer in the path of heavenly aspiration. Theism does not disdain the help of the great religious leaders of mankind; it only refuses to put any one in the place of God; to regard any one, however exalted or noble his self-sacrifice, as a substitute for human sinfulness, or a mediator between God and the human soul. It is willing to learn of all and reverence all, but it looks to God before all, and trusts in Him only. We are quite prepared to admit that this may not be sufficient for the present needs of the multitude, but we maintain it is the loftiest and purest idea of religious thought. In place of all inferior names it gives us the name of God; instead of an idle ceremonialism it upholds the spiritual worship of the Holy One; for a narrow sectarianism it gives us universal charity. Perhaps it is too pure, too lofty for general acceptance. It may be true, as Mr. Greg, we believe, has said in one of his works, that for a religion to be acceptable to the mass it must not be too abstract, pure or spiritual, but must be alloyed with a certain amount of anthropomorphism and superstition; must appeal to the senses, must clothe itself in a sensuous form, wear an attractive dress, and abound with mystery and sensationalism. If these features are wanting its appeal is unheeded, and its theology fails to win its way to the common heart. For so many ages has religion been presented to the nations in forms more or less corrupt, that when divested of its corruptions it has been unsuited to the vitiated taste acquired by centuries of priestly rule and false teaching. The corrupt taste rejects the unadulterated food. It must have dogmas and anathemas, ceremonies, rites, and mysteries, or it is unable to recognise the presence of religion! This, we believe, is the true explanation of the slow progress of rational religion in the world. Men love darkness rather than light because they have been accustomed to the darkness so long. Their mental organ of vision has become depraved, and in consequence the truth looks like error in their eyes. Hence a pure Theism is rejected, while a corrupt Christianity finds ready acceptance by the multitude. The educator and the teacher of science must prepare the way for the rational religionist. It is their task to disseminate the knowledge which undermines superstition and conduces to the reception and appreciation of enlightened religious thought.

With regard especially to the Brahmo Somaj the writer in the *Friend of India* augues its decline principally from two causes—First, because it has "no great human name and life to which peoples and generations may bow in reverence," that is to say, it keeps clear of the hero worship, which is the highest incentive to idolatry, puts no great human name on a par with the Divine. Secondly, because its teaching "is becoming more eclectic in its character daily;" that is, it gives exceptional prominence to no one teacher of religious truth, makes no one the Saviour for all, but is willing to learn from all, and profit by the wisdom of all. "It seems really to aim at gathering up all that is good in all the religions, and gradually piecing together a robe of many colors as the wedding garment of the Theistic Church of India." If this is the head and front of its offending, we can only say, we wish other Churches were guilty of the same offence. We desire to see the good there is in each frankly recognised by all. But the *Friend of India* says:—"The attempt to make a new religion by combining the best elements of several religions has been tried before in India, but always with distinguished failure." We regret to learn this. Will the world never arrive at a truly catholic conception of religious truth? Must the walls of partition between sect and sect each with representative teacher, endure for ever? Will the Sectarianism of exclusive Churches never give place to a religion for humanity, to a Church embracing in a holy brotherhood the good and the true of all lands? Is the ideal too lofty for attainment by human society? We are inclined, with the progress of education and intelligence, to hope better things, both for India and the world.—*Inquirer.*

Advertisements

P. W. FLEURY & CO.,

BUILDERS, ENGINEERS, AND SCIENTIFIC INSTRUMENT MAKERS.

No. 44, Free School Street.

WE beg to intimate that we have been engaged in the above line of business for the past 20 years, and trust that our Constituents will continue to favor us with their work, which will meet with prompt attention on our part.

In connection with buildings, we undertake the erection and repairing of machinery at moderate charges; as also execute all descriptions of Iron and Brass work.

We can assure the Public that we undertake the repair and erection of Houses, and the laying of Water-supply Pipes on moderate terms, and guarantee to keep all the water-pipes and brass fittings supplied by us in good working order for three years, free of extra charge. We also guarantee to keep dwelling-houses' roofs water-tight for three years, free of extra charge, for such houses as we have repaired.

For purposes of illumination, we prepare our patent Chromatic Transparencies representing Coat-of-Arms, Landscapes, Scenery, &c., at prices, ranging from Rs. 80 to 300 each, according to size and design.

FOR SALE.

Light! Light!! Light!!!

Electric Light Apparatus, complete, worked with a battery of 50 large cells, on Bunsen's principle	500	0
Ditto ditto, with 40 cells, smaller size ...	400	0
Ditto ditto, with a powerful 44-cell Cast-Iron Battery, on Callan's principle ...	300	0
Lime Light Apparatus, complete, with Iron Gas-holder, and Copper Retort ...	150	0
Oxy-Hydrogen Light Apparatus, with safety Jets, 2 iron Gas-holders, and Retorts, complete	200	0
Hink's Patent Duplex Wall Lamps, with chimney	5	8
Ditto Duplex Lamp, with chimney and globe	7	8

Patent Leblanche Battery

For constancy, durability, and cleanliness, this battery is unequalled; price for each cell, with chemicals	3	8
Bunsen's Galvanic Battery, 9 inches, by 4 inches	7	8
Magneto-Electric Machine, with single magnet	14	0
Prismatic Compass 3-inch, in a lid leather case, by Elbot, *second hand*	22	0
Ditto, 4-inch, by Simmons, *second hand* ...	30	0

P. W. FLEURY & Co.,
No. 44, FREE SCHOOL STREET.

ESTABLISHED 1833.

H. C. GANGOOLY & CO.

STATIONERS, DIE-SINKERS, ENGRAVERS, PRINTERS, LITHOGRAPHERS &c.

24, Mangoe Lane, Calcutta.

Cash prices of the following :—

	Rs.	As.	Rs.
Whatman's Drawing paper double elephant sizes (40×27) each ...	0	7	0
Mathematical Instrument Boxes	2	8 to	16
Color Boxes	0	4 „	5

Drawing Pencils, Drawing and Mapping Steel pens and various other requisites in Stationery.

MUDHOO SUDUN PAUL & CO.

120, RADHA BAZAR,

Tea! (Assam) Tea!
TRADE M. MARK.
In 1lb. and 2lb. Tins.

Pekoe Tea, ... 2lb. Tin, Per Tin Rs.		3	4
„ Flowery ... ... „ „ „		3	8
„ Souchong ... ... „ „ „		2	8
Family Mixture ... ... „ „ „		2	4
Caper ... ... „ „ „		2	0
Imperial Mixture with China		3	0
China Rose Pauchong		2	8

The above in 1lb. Tin at half the respective prices plus two annas extra.

BURMAH CIGARS.

No. 1 per 100 Re. 1 0
„ 2 „ „ 0 12

HUNTLEY AND PALMER'S BISCUITS.

Albert, in Tin of 2 lb each Re.	1	6
Arrow Root, ... „	1	4
Mixed, ... „	1	8

Indian Chutnies, Castor Oil, Candles, Kerosine Oil, China Preserves, Perfumery Domestic Medicines and other stores always in stock and offered at lower rates than other Houses.

Catalogue to be had on application,
MUDHOO SUDUN PAUL & Co.

MAKHON LOLL GHOSE.

No. 91, Radha Bazar, Calcutta.

BEGS to invite the attention of the public to several consignments of commercial and fancy stationery of all sorts, including account books of all sizes, made of handmade and machine made paper, by steamers recently arrived, and which he is disposing of at moderate prices. He has been long in the trade, and presumes he has always afforded every satisfaction to the numerous merchants here who have constantly favored him with orders. Mofussil orders accompanied with remittances shall be promptly attended to.

CALCUTTA }
The 18th August 1876. }

DENONAUTH DEY AND SONS,

No. 80, CLIVE STREET.

Godowns, No. 24 Machooa Bazar Street.

IMPORTERS OF METALS, IRONMONGERY, HARDWARE, TEA GARDEN TOOLS,

CHUBBS' LOCKS AND SAFES, RODGER'S CUTLERY

Carpenters', Blacksmiths', Coopers', Engineers', Builders' and Planters' Tools.

SADDLERY, STEAM. GAS & WATER-FITTINGS,

PAINTS, OILS, MARINE STORES, &c. &c.

Priced Catalogues supplied on application, at Rs. 2, each.

NOTICE! NOTICE!! NOTICE!!!

A

GRAND HIGHEST BIDDER AUCTION SALE

AT

T. F. BROWN AND CO.'S

ON SATURDAY, THE 16th SEPTEMBER 1876.

COMMENCING AT 11 O'CLOCK PRECISELY.

A VALUABLE COLLECTION OF HORSES, CONVEYANCES, HARNESS, SADDLERY, AND STABLE GEAR

WILL BE OFFERED

WITHOUT RESERVE.

☞ Early descriptions of lots intended for this sale are solicited.

T. F. BROWN & CO.
Auctioneers.

ICE! ICE! ICE!

MADE IN FOUR MINUTES

THE PNEUMATIC ICE MACHINE

THIS IMPORTANT INVENTION IS CONSIDERED A BOON TO THOSE LIVING IN TROPICAL CLIMATES.

CAN BE WORKED BY THE MOST INEXPERIENCED HAND AND IS NOT LIABLE TO GET OUT OF ORDER.

From Rs. 175, each Machine complete.

MESSRS. ARLINGTON & CO

AGENTS.

HAROLD & CO.,

3, DALHOUSIE SQUARE, CALCUTTA

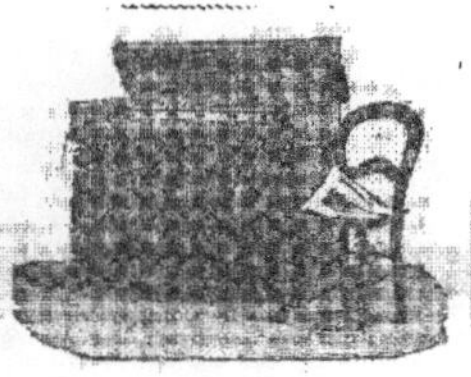

HARMONIUMS.

Harold and Co., call attention to their unequalled stock of rich-toned Harmoniums made especially for India.

FROM RS. 90 TO RS. 900 EACH.

All kinds of Musical Instruments of the best description are always kept in Stock.

CALCUTTA

106, Bowbazar Street.

DR. H. C. SARMA'S

MEDICINE FOR DEBILITY

(NERVOUS.)

Brought on by indulgence in irregular habits, effects of previous diseases, loss of power of limbs, weakness or loss of memory, absent mindedness, irritable temper, disposition of the mind to displeasure at trifles, want of attention towards business, despair at finding no relief from treatment &c. &c. &c.

Price with postage &c. Rs. 5.

Particulars of disease and directions for despatch required from patients residing at a distance.

DR. SARMA'S FEE.

In cases of Debility [illegible]
For advice at Home [illegible]

Out of Town Rs. 50 per Day.

INDIAN TOOTH POWDER.

Strengthens loose teeth, alleviates pain of, and prevents bleeding from Gums, cleanses the mouth, corrects its putrid odour and cures ulceration of the Gums without blackening the Teeth.

Price per packet ... ... Rs. 0 4 0
Postage &c., for 4 packets ... „ 0 5 0

TONIC OIL.

Imparts vigour and tone to the paralysed or relaxed parts of the human system—[illegible] proper circulation of blood in weak and inactive parts.

Price for four ounce [illegible] Rs. 1 0 0
Postage &c. ... 0 10 0

HAIR PRESERVER.

***Will restore grey** hair to its original colour.*

It acts directly upon the roots of the hair, **removes dandriff,** prevents premature falling-off of the hair, and promotes its growth and strength giving it Lustre and Health of Youth.

It also **produces a cooling and soothing** effect **upon the head.**

Price, for 4 ounce phial ... Re. 1 0 0
Postage &c. ... ... „ 0 10 0

Copy of Letter received from Raja Chundernath **Roy Bahadoor of Nattore.**

***Wellesley Street, No. 18, Molls Lane, 29th** March*
1874.

MY DEAR HURREISH BABU,—I shall thank you **to send me another phial of your "*Excellent*** *Hair* ***Restorer.*" In fact it has done me a great** benefit and **I should like to have more of it. It has** disabused **me (young as I am) of old age.**

Your's Sincerely

C. N. of *Nattore*

MEDICINE FOR BALDNESS.

Will certainly cure baldness if applied **on the** bald portion, night & morning according **to directions** given in the adjoining direction paper.

Price per two ounce phial Rs. 1 0 0
Postage &c. „ 6 0

HEEM-SAGAR OIL.

The best remedy for Headache arising from over-study, intellectual occupation, over-thinking, mental anxiety and weakness, as well as heat of head from living in hot places.

It cools the head and produces very agreeable sensation. Removes Dandriff as well as all other impurities from the head. Promotes the strength and growth **of the hair and** prevents its premature falling-off.

Price per 4 **ounce phial...** Re. 1 0 0
Postage &c. ... ... „ 0 10 0

MEDICINE FOR LEPROSY.

Price with Postage &c. Rs. 5.

OIL FOR LEPROSY.

And Inveterate Skin Diseases.

Price per 8 ounce phial... Rs. 2 0
Postage &c. ... ... „ 0 12

BEST BURMAH SEGARS.

The undersigned respectfully begs to call the attention of Consumers and Dealers to the following Segars which are made of the choicest leaves and are of superior quality; guaranteed free and pleasant to smoke:—

No. 1	per 100	Rs.	1	0	0
„ 2	„ „	„	0	12	0
„ 3	„ „	„	0	10	0
Dolly Varden,	„	„	1	4	0
Sedans	„ „	„	1	2	0
Babington	„ „	„	1	2	0
Trichinopolly,	„ „	„	1	8	0

Liberal discount allowed to wholesale purchasers.

All descriptions of Oilman's stores, Preserved Provisions and Tea to be had at moderate prices.

BONOMALLY SHAW.
[illegible] *Radha Bazar*

BABU BASANTA KUMAR DUTTA,
HOMŒOPATHIC PRACTITIONER
No. 20, Sunker Haldar's Lane, Ahiritolah,

FRESH INDENT OF
Medicines and other Requisites
Have arrived from England.
Medicines, Boxes, Books, Pamphlets;
Absolute Alcohol; Cholera-spirit Camphor.
SPECIAL REMEDIES.

For Suppressed, Laborious and Difficult menses; Leucorrhœa.

For Hysteria; Spermatorrhœa; Dysentery; Diarrhœa; Cholera.

For Asthma; Pile; Pain; Sore and Diseases of the Children.

Ice, Lemonade, Soda and Tonic water always.

To be had at
DUTTA'S HOMŒOPATHIC LABORATORY
No. 312, CHITPORE ROAD, BURTOLA, CALCUTTA
TERMS—CASH.
☞ List can be had on application.

CHUNDER & BROTHERS.
25½ & 112, RADHA BAZAR,

STATIONERY in all its varieties.
PRINTING PRESSES, Inks & Materials.
LITHOGRAPHIC PRESS & Materials.
BOOK BINDING Materials &c.

NOTICE.

INFALLIBLE SPECIFICS FOR ASTHMA, CONSUMPTION, COLIC, GONORRHŒA AND SPERMATORRHŒA!!!

I AM the son of the late Titaram Paul of Midnapore, who, the public is well aware, was acquainted with specific medicines for the above diseases. I fully learnt the mode of preparing those medicines from my late father, and have cured many people of Midnapore, Calcutta, Hughly, and other places since his death, as the annexed testimonial will show. Any one wishing to be treated by me can apply to me, care of the Manager of the Indian Mirror.

WOOPENDRA NATH PAUL.

BABU UPENDRA NATH PAL.

SIR,

You will be glad to hear that the painful asthma under which I was suffering for the last three years and through which I was nearly brought to the brink of death has been perfectly cured through your treatment. I was laid under the care of several able Doctors and *Kobirajes*, but every treatment on their part proved a failure on me. God bless you and let your cure spread over those who are suffering under the same wretched circumstances.

SURJA COOMAR MAJUMDAR.

CALCUTTA,
TANTANEAH,
The 30th August 1876.

BURN & CO.

RANEEGUNGE Fire bricks **are the best Fire** Bricks known;—superior to Ramsay's.
9 Rs. per 100.

Fire clay, 40 Rs. per Ton.

Glazed Stone **ware,** Drainage pipes of all sizes

BURN & Co.,
7, Hastings Street, Calcutta.

Oriental Gas Company Ld

THE price of Gas in Calcutta and Howrah is reduced to Rs. 5 per 1,000 feet.

!!! हुक्का !!!
!!! HOOKAHS !!!

English made Hookahs of various choice designs, [illegible] from Rs. 2 to 5 [illegible] from. Apply to

RADANAUTH CHOWDRY,
373, Jorasanko.

India General Steam Navigation Company, Ld.

SCHOENE, KILBURN & Co.—*Managing Agents.*

ASSAM LINE.
NOTICE.

Steamers leave Calcutta for Assam every Tuesday, Koosthea every Thursday and leave Dibrooghur downward every Saturday.

THE Str. "MIRZAPORE" will leave Calcutta *Via* Mutlah for Assam, on Tuesday, the 12th instant.

Cargo will be received at the Company's Godowns, Nimtolah Ghat, up till noon of Monday, the 11th.

THE Str. "CHUNAR" will leave Koosthea for Assam on Thursday, the 14th instant.

Cargo will be received **at the Company's Godowns,** No. 4 Fairlie **Place, up till noon of Tuesday** the 12th.

Goods forwarded to Koosthea for this vessel will be chargeable with Railway Freight from Calcutta to Koosthea in addition **to** the regular Freight **of** this **Company.**

Passengers should leave for Kooshtea by Train of Wednesday, the 13th.

CACHAR LINE NOTICE
REGULAR FORTNIGHTLY SERVICE.

Steamers leave Calcutta for Cachar and Intermediate Stations every alternate Friday, and leave Cachar downward every alternate Sunday.

THE Str "LUCKNOW" will leave Calcutta *via Mutubanga* for Cachar on **Friday, the 15th** instant.

Cargo will be **received** at the Company's Godowns, Nimtolah Ghat, up till noon of Thursday the 14th.

For further information regarding rates of Freight or passage money, apply to,

4, FAIRLIE PLACE, Calcutta 8th September, 1876. } C. J. SCOTT, *Secretary.*

Rivers Steam Navigation Co. Limited.

The Str. "OUDH" has left Kooshtea for Assam on Tuesday the 29th instant.

The Steamer "[illegible]" will leave Calcutta for Assam on 10th September.

For **Freight** or Passage, apply to

No. 1, LYONS RANGE, 25th August, 1876. } **MACNEILL & Co., Agents.**

TO THE MEMBERS OF THE BRAHMO SOMAJ OF INDIA.

THE undersigned **has the pleasure to announce** that **he** has **received a** large **supply of** Mr. T. Scott's Theistical publications **which can** be obtained **at English** price **exclusive of postage,** namely, **from As.** 2 to Rs. **2.**

A List of the **Pamphlets can be had on application** to

MR. V. C. MOONESWAMY **MOODELIAR**
Lascar's Line,
Bangalore,

Printed and published by M. M. RUKHIT, at the INDIAN MIRROR PRESS, No. 6, College Square, for the Proprietors.

The Indian Mirror.

SUNDAY EDITION.

VOL XVI.] CALCUTTA, SUNDAY, SEPTEMBER 17, 1876. {REGISTERED AT THE GENERAL POST OFFICE.} [No. 221

CONTENTS.

NOTICE.

All letters and communications relating to the literary department of the Paper should be addressed to the Editor. All other letters should be addressed to the Manager, to whom all remittances should be made payable.

Subscribers will be good enough to bring to the notice of the Manager any delay or irregularity in the delivery of the Paper.

Editorial Notes.

WE are glad to find that some of the Christian Missionaries in and out of Calcutta, are trying to point the evils of child marriage among Hindus. There is an article on the subject in the last number of the *Evangelical Review.* The influence of Christian Missionaries among the Hindu population is unfortunately exceedingly small, but still it is hoped the agitation will do some good.

THE utter corruption of the state of Roman society at the time when Stoicism under Seneca flourished in Rome, throws very powerful light on the moral conditions in the midst of which the foundations of the Christian faith were laid by the great contemporaries of Seneca, namely Jesus and Saint Paul. The glory of the character of the latter is drawn in full grandeur when we reflect on the surrounding gloom which enveloped them. In last Thursday's lecture on Seneca the Stoic, it was attempted to elucidate this fact from an historical point of view.

THE *Friend of India* with its characteristic Broad Church liberality, observes that "the English Thirty-nine Articles, and Confessions of Faith must for ever cease to interpret the New Testament for the Indian. It may even be that we—sometimes over-logical—Westerns shall yet in religious things find the relative position of the Hindu and ourselves completely changed, and see ourselves meekly learning from him how very simple, beautiful, and powerful over the life is that faith which we have laid in metaphysical labyrinths." This is exactly what we ourselves would have said. Christianity as a metaphysical creed Europe has for eighteen centuries tried to develop and realize. The work of evolving the simple faith of Christ in practical life, as a sweet and living reality, is reserved, in the economy of Providence, for the Hindu.

AT a public meeting at Falmouth a few days before the last Mail left, Lord Northbrook, speaking of the future religion of India, said:—"The day would come when we should give to India the inestimable blessing of a true religion. He did not think it would be right or fair for a Government to use the taxation of a country for the teaching of a certian form of religion to the children of the country. Rightly, the propagation of Christianity in India had been left to the Christian sects, some of which, he was happy to say, had been very successful, not so much with educated Indians, however, as where they came in contact with the aboriginal inhabitants in the interior. He had himself visited a part of the country where he believed the Native Christians numbered 25,000." After referring to the work of the Brahmo Somaj, the noble Lord went on to say that he did not think that any of the Indians would embrace Christianity in any of the numerous forms in which it was now brought before them by European sects. "He believed they would go further back, and get rid of much of the dogmas which had overlaid the foundations of Christianity for nearly 1800 years, and some of us might live to see them adopt a form of Christianity more nearly approaching the simplicity of the Apostolic Church than any which now existed."

THE *Friend of India* deplores the importation of immoral newspaper information into this country:—"It is easy to fancy the oriental over whose social life the European claims such an immense superiority, pointing the finger of scorn at a civilization which produces such women as Mrs. Bravo and Mrs. Rippingall, and such men as Captain Moore and other heroes of the Divorce Court; nor is it possible to escape the reflection, that the publicity given in these times to such scandal, must have a very material influence in widening that gulf between the races which the Prince of Wales, Lord Salisbury and others have so markedly deplored. Lord Campbell, once upon a time, brought in an act to restrain the dissemination of the Holloway Street school of literature and art, and it seems to us almost as if all the unsaleable stock which remained over that ordinance had been gradually cast into the Indian dust hole for such stuff ever since, so great has been the accumulation of nauseous stories and vicious literature in the India of this day. It does not make that sort of writing the better that it purports to be the news of Paris or London gathered by a corresponding moralist, nor is it much of an apology for the importation of these wares, that a paper as morally bad as *Vanity Fair* is perused by dwellers in Belgravia. What is inexcusable is, there should be literary scavengers of our own people and blood at home, to render Englishmen contemptible in the eyes of the Natives by reason of that garbage which they pick out of the London and Paris gutters for the adification of all Hindustan.

EVERY Brahmo marrying under Act III of 1872, is bound to declare that he does not profess the Hindu religion. This evidently implies that he must solemnly and unequivocally assert his total renunciation of Hinduism. To such un-Hinduizing of one's self not a few among us of conservative tendencies take exception. Why unnessarily cut yourself off completely from the Hindu community ?—they ask. Why deny nationality and kinship, and assume the position of an alien and an outcast ? In fact there are many who denounce the Marriage Act for this reason, and do all in their power to oppose its adoption. We rather look upon this particular clause in the Act as its vital and crowning point, and regard the circumstances which led to its adoption, as altogether providential. We verily believe that the Brahmo Somaj has thereby been saved, just in time, from falling into that vast and all-absorving vortex of Hinduism, which by its treacherous tolerance has swallowed almost all the reform movements in the country and eventually crushed and absorbed every system of religious and social reform that came trustingly too near its hidden rocks. The Brahmo Somaj, its men and resources, its power and influence, are as nothing compared with Hinduism, and who can say that it will not some day be swallowed up by the ancient and established faith of the land? Such absorption is inevitable, unless our people guard their church carefully against the danger. The claim in question in the Marriage Act will serve as an effective safeguard. It is a strong and mighty chain whereby the Brahmo Somaj, carried far away from the Hindu religion, has safely tied itself to a non-Hindu position, from which the most impetuous currents of reactionary conservatism will not be able to drive it. The progressive Brahmo cannot relapse to-morrow into Hinduism, for he legally declares himself to-day as a non-Hindu.

THE Rev. Mr. Dall's letter published in our issue of Sunday, the 3rd instant, repeats the old doctrine of Harmony in Life, which has often been discussed in these columns, and which is one of the admittedly essential principles of Theism to which every Brahmo is bound to adhere loyally. Neither love nor knowledge, nor work should be neglected, but all the elements of character must grow under careful and comprehensive culture, so that many-sided humanity may be perfected in each individual and collectively in society. This doctrine of harmony does not, as some suppose, clash with the theory of classification to which we recently drew attention. Every man must attain true manhood, complete in all its parts, and yet half-a-dozen individuals may be selected and intended by nature for special education over and above the average general training. Every man must in some measure be a *yogi* and a *bhakta* and a *sebak*. To ignore any of these elements of spiritual life would be morally wrong. But some men here and there tower above the rest owing to the extraordinary prominence of special qualities. Some are *yogis* not because *yoga* is all in all with them, and means the absence of *bhakti* or *karma*, but because above the highest love and practical righteousness that is possible in their lives, they have carried their peculiar and excessive natural aptitude for prayer and devotion. Such men the world needs, for they show, and they alone can show practically, how far particular elements of spirituality may be developed. Was Jesus wanting in any of the elements of character? And yet was he not an ascetic in order that the world might renounce worldliness and attain life eternal through asceticism? Let every son of God improve his humanity completely, neglecting nothing. Let those few whom Providence selects for special purposes, undergo special training in a devout spirit.

RENUNCIATION AND RETENTION.

IT is somewhat amusing to see how some men try to deceive God by a show of penances, religious exercises, and orthodox opinions, while they do not rectify, and do not *mean* the rectification of their lives. Equally amusing it is to see other men who try to deceive the world by enjoying all its pleasures and taking part in all its excitements under the high sounding, though now-a-days common place, profession that their religion forbids nothing, and tolerates all the good things of life, provided one can be temperate in his self-indulgence. Among the many characters so graphically drawn by John Bunyan, there is perhaps none so instructive as Mr. Facing-Both-Ways, the highly intelligent person who sincerely tries to outwit his God and his fellowmen, and succeeds in the end to deceive no one but himself. He fancies all the time that people regard him as excessively pious, while their estimate of his worth is even below what he would in strict justice deserved, and he is self-complacent with the idea that his devotions and piety are very much admired in heaven, while they are seldom in their utter unreality, even allowed to reach the throne of the Holy of holies. But the religion of almost the world well is this kind of double-service to God and Mammon. To the genuine devotee, and even to the man who yet merely aspires to serve his Master with a manly singleness of purpose, the question is sometimes very plainly put as to whether then he is prepared to "Renounce all things, and follow Me." This question may be stifled long, it may be explained away, it may be shirked, but if you are sincere, if you have passed a certain stage of progress in religious life, it shall come often so that evasion is impossible. It is felt that upon a satisfactory answer to this question hangs the whole future life; nay not another step forward is possible without some determination one way or the other. If it is *not* meant to devote the whole of what is called life, what portions of it are to be reserved for self? If the whole *is* meant for God why retain this, that, and the other against His will? When the consciousness dawns upon one that this, that, or the other is retained in violation of Divine command, with what face can another prayer be offered, and any aspiration be fostered of another single step in advance? There has been but one answer to this question in the case of faithful men, and they have renounced the world. This is specially noteworthy in the case of great religious teachers. They never lived in the world in the sense that we do. Some of them renounced it completely. If we try to follow their examples at the present day with any amount of strictness, as some religious sects have done and eminently some orders of the Roman Catholic Christian community, we are at one set down as arrant ascetics, whose examples and precepts are sure to poison the happiness and pervert the faith of honest men. Nor is renunciation in the old sense of the word now *possible*. Self-imposed asceticism is as hurtful as self-indulgence, with this difference that while self-indulgence seldom obtains any credit before the religious world, artificial pains and penances foster within the heart a vanity, the venom of which is very malignant indeed. On the other hand if we do not attempt to follow them, but live up to the standard of worldy religious life reconciling facts and courses of action that are in their nature irreconcilable, we stand arraigned before the tribunal of conscience, and feel self-condemned and unable to make the progress that we feel to be indispensable. How then can the difficulty be solved. This is the problem which the Brahmo Somaj has proposed to itself at the present day. Our leaders have reached that condition of mind in which they feel they cannot retain their favorite enjoyments and desires. Leave all things and follow Me, is a command daily heard. Do thy duties amidst all those circumstances wherein I have placed thee; is equally felt to be the will of the Supreme. What we must do to prove faithful to both these commands remains to be seen. It is something to meet with the admission that neither our penances nor our pleasures have been of the right description, neither our asceticism nor our protest has been of the right nature. What we must do, and how we must proceed to renounce sternly what God forbids, and retain what really comes from Him, will have to be determined by future experiences. The right impulses are within us, but the right means have not always been taken. May the guidance from above, be accepted by us in fidelity and trust; may the right standard of self-sacrifice be reverently and permanently adopted; and may the God of truth reveal unto our hearts what we have been unable to find out.

Correspondence.

THE REVEREND DR. JARDINE'S INTRODUCTORY LETTER.

To the Editor of *Indian Mirror*.

SIR,—The first of the series of letters to be published by the Rev. Dr. Jardine is just out. It has been very cleverly or rather masterly written; the spirit of the writing is excellent and worthy of a Christian Missionary. Although I am neither a believer of the Gospel nor a follower of Christ, yet I could not help reading the letter with great attention and with more than ordinary interest. The Rev. gentleman has very carefully avoided to condemn unmeritedly any thing not consistent with his own idea of religion. Staunch and enthusiastic Missionaries in their fervour of religious ardour and zeal, sometimes injudiciously make use of strong expressions in attacking those who in the their opinion are held as sceptics; but the Rev. Dr. Jardine's tone writing is admirable, and the letter has doubtless been written with the feeling and heart of a sincere Christian Missionary. I anxiously expect that the subsequent numbers will be as excellent as the first. I doubt not you have received a copy of the letter. In case you have not, I beg to send you one, and request that you will take such notice of it as you think best.

Yours &c.,
A. P. C.

EVER-LIVING PRINCIPLES, EVER-DYING SYSTEMS.

To the Editor of the *Indian Mirror*.

SIR,—Major Osborn denounces Mahomedanism as "one of the most atrocious systems that ever afflicted mankind." The Editor of the *Index*, a New England weekly journal devoted to Free Religion, I mean Mr. Francis E. Abbott, opens his "Impeachment of Christianity" with the words, "Christianity is the great *system* of faith and practice organized in the Christian Church;" and then condemns that system "in the name of human intelligence of human virtue, of the human heart, of human freedom, and of humanitarian religion." Viewing Christianity as an organized and articled system, he thinks, that "such is substantially the only definition of it which will abide the test of time." Why not accept it as a vitalizing principle? If I understand Mr. Birch, he welcomes Mahomedanism not as a system, but as an upholder of principles; such as charity to man, trust in God, sorrow for sin, justice, righteousness, fidelity to kindred, and, above all, that principle of principles, the infinite holiness and absolute unity of the divine nature. Theodore Parker, Freeman Clarke and others in opposition to Mr. Abbot, regard Christianity "not as a religion, but Religion"; and the least encumbered declaration of absolute principles; the purest known outflow of the spirit of God into humanity; the divine life brought down into the human, in the life of Jesus, in a manner, and to a degree, altogether unique in history. Mahomed saw the life of Christ to be a life purer than his own; while he condemned, and wisely too, every system of Christianity that prevailed around him. Now is Christianity a system? or is it an unceasing revelation of divine principles; of spiritual light, warmth, electricity, vitality, love, faith, wisdom, power, righteousness? As I see it, the pure theism of Jesus (my Brahmoism)—is not a theory of love, a covenant of faith, a contract of salvation by blood, a dogma of atonement by substitution of one man's holiness for another's sin. The glory of Brahmoism is its catholicity, its refusal to be a system, codified, fixed, limited, defined, stereotyped, formulated, walled in, fenced and fortified, by the temporary use of a certain age, against the temporary outs. Major Osborn is too clear-headed a man not to see that as every sect of Christians has a system of its own,—so the various and conflicting sects of Mahomedans, the Shias, Sunnies, Sufis, [illegible], have many and conflicting systems. Legions of systems are ever rising in emergencies, and falling to pieces when their work is done. If needed, in one age, they become rubbish and rottenness in another. They certainly need to be well looked after lest they prove nuisances, pollute the air, and breed disease and death. Read Channing on Creeds, and settle, once for all, the difference between Theology and Religion. See the danger of donning the shackles of a system, like Calvinism for instance; good, very good, in its time, as a weapon offensive and defensive; but to-day fulfilled, disbelieved, dishonored, gone. Some men like our good brother Dyson will have it that Brahmic Dogma is equivalent to Brahmoism. They seem not to see that what chiefly characterises "Progressive" Theism, is its dropping its dogmas, from season to season, as a growing tree drops its leaves. It would not be "Progressive" Brahmoism were it tied to a system, or to a book, or to the recorded word of any one man. It would be a dogma,—a system if it received not to grow with growing humanity, and accept the novel circumstances and fresh needs of every succeeding age. Not being a system but a life, it rejoices in the recorded triumphs of every great soul; and following as its present leader, captain and guide, that one, of all religious leader, who has, not dogmatized the best,—but—lived, loved and prayed; and said and done the best. I follow the man who has most truly realised a divine life under human limitations; my daily life of joy and sorrow; of hope and fear; of light and darkness; of weakness and of triumph. Let it never be forgotten that a system, however good, can never be more than the clothing of a principle. Sure as time, the best of systems grows old and wears out. Only principles have life. As a soul to a body, so is a principle to a dogma. There be Christian idolators of a hundred different systems of Christianity; *i. e.*, of the life and love of Jesus; but which he never systematized beyond a cry or a phrase; such as the Kingdom or state of God; God in man, God and his righteousness.

Mahomed, in the course of his life and during the publication of his 114 Suras,—the Koran,—accepted many systems; though not as many as Moslems have to-day. Can Islam discard its old systems, and re-clothe its principles in new ones, such as this age, and the Living God command? That is the question.

Yours,
DALL.

Devotional

LORD, like other good things poverty too ebbs away from the heart after a time unless it is duly and prayerfully watched. As the world guards riches, may I, Merciful Father, be enabled through thy mercy to guard my highest treasure on earth, my poverty and lowliness of spirit. Grant that I may be as diligent and prayerful in acquiring as in keeping that treasure.

SALVATION is in the eye, O my God. Therefore I beseech thee to purify my eyes, and give me the power of seeing things in their true light. Teach my eyes to see the hollowness and unreality of the riches and pleasures of the world, and turn with joy to thee as the only Reality I ought to love. May I by looking constantly at thy holy face sanctify my eyesight altogether, and learn to cast pure glances upon all objects and persons. Dwell in my eye, my Father.

The Brahmo Somaj

THE Dacca Brahmos celebrated their anniversary festival on the 3rd instant. Service was conducted by Babu Bungo Chunder Roy. A new feature of the music on the occasion was the strange yet harmonious combination of such instruments as the guitar, the tomtom, the tumbura and the ringing cups.

WE are glad to learn from friends who have seen the institution that, the Asram established at Dacca is very well managed so as to reflect great credit on the local Brahmos. It is even said that it is superior in internal economy and the poverty and discipline imposed on the inmates, to the Bharat Asram in Calcutta. There are many reasons why we should feel grateful to our brethren in the capital of Eastern Bengal.

AS Brahmoism is removing many of the obsolete and exceptionable customs and practices prevalent in Hindu society, it is to be hoped that the various modes of addressing persons in letters should be revised and improved. We do not approve, for instance, of the word *Pujaniya*. It means 'adorable,' and applies only to Divinity. *Bhaktibhajan* is preferable.

THE 'namkaran' ceremony of the infant daughter of Babu Ananda Mohun Bose was celebrated with due *eclat* last evening, at his residence, 11 South Circular Road.

THE third anniversary of the Brahmo Niketan was celebrated yesterday and the day before in the upper hall of the Niketan. The morning service yesterday was conducted by Babu Keshub Chunder Sen.

THEOLOGICAL CLASS.

Sunday, June 25th, 1876.

The greatest difficulties have always encompassed the subject of final causation. The controversy is old as undecided. From the days of Plato and Aristotle it has come down to our time and the results must be said to be as unsatisfactory as ever. That there are causes to all the effects otherwise called phenomena of the outer world, has indeed been always accepted as an axiom. The difficulty lies only in the analysis of the nature of these causes. Is causation no more than a sequence of phenomenal changes observable through the processes of scientific discovery? Or is there a necessary or inseparable connection between effects and causes? In assigning the cause of a phenomenon do we or do we not predicate the fact of a latent power in the cause to bring about the change which in common language is called to be its effects. The fact of the matter is, the whole conception of a *cause* lies involved in the conception of the power which it is universally believed to possess. The idea of causation, therefore, is inseparable from the idea of power. The next question is—How is power realised? Since in enumerating natural phenomena science is not authorized nor entitled to recognize anything except the co-existence, sequence, and resemblance of facts, and the laws whereby these are regulated, and since the co existence, sequence and resemblance of phenomena could not under any circumstances convey the idea of power; whence is this idea obtainable, where and what is its type? The idea of power then into which the subject of causation is resolvable, is not recognisable in the operations of outward nature as such, but emerges primarily in human consciousness. It is man's mind only that is conscious of the possession of power. Taking away this subjective conception from the human mind, it is impossible to realize or recognize the fact of power elsewhere in nature. We involuntarily humanise the universe by attributing to it the possession of power of which we are conscious in our own minds. Power is considered to be essentially in the sense of effort, towards the production of certain changes. And by an easy and natural analysis we detect the sense of effort in the will of man. The *will*, therefore, is the original type of power, and the last cause of the whole series of changes that constitute the chain of causation in reference to its own sphere of operation. All causation then so far as human consciousness is concerned, and that is the sole standard of Philosophy (at least in the present state of human existence) is resolvable into direct volition. The devine will thus becomes the all-sufficient cause of the origin and preservation of the universe, and retain matter and in mind to produce the great changes which history, religious, secular or scientific—attempts to record. Spiritually perceiving this crowning fact of philosophy, the Apostle exclaimed—"In Him we live and move and have our being."

Sunday, July 23rd, 1876.

The analogy between the administration of human affairs and the economy of the universe, is always a delicate and difficult subject. Agreeing in the original type of its constitution, the will of man disagrees almost entirely with its source and archetype in the minor operations and details of its ordinary existence. So far as the original and primitive act of volition is concerned, no effects human or superhuman can ever take place without it. In the first stage of causal change, therefore, the direct and distinct act of volition in God or in man must be present. Here the analogy between divine and human power concentrates all its force. At the very next stage, however, the differences begin. Divine volition is never self assertive. It communicates itself through the medium of complicated agencies and economies, every one of which outwardly bears the impress of perfect immutability and pre-ordained courses of action. Passing through such a long and changeless channel of immutable laws and fixed organisms, the original act of the creative will disguises its individuality and personal character, and the results with which nature surrounds us of the action of cosmical arrangements, are distinguished by nothing so much as by their material unconsciousness and impersonal uniformity. These arrangements are what scientific men call the laws of the universe, and their perfect changelessness and mathematical certainty seem to preclude the popular idea of a conscious and free will in the original source of creation. Among men, however, the rationale of affairs is different. Human beings are known from the rest of organic nature by their prominent and self assertive existence. The manliness of man consists in imposing his will upon the rest of the creation. He is more or less of a man inasmuch as he can make others more or less subservient to the freedom of his wishes. If there is a complicated channel of intermediate action through which human will passes into its outward expression of deeds, that channel does not belong to humanity. It is placed at his disposal, its forces are at his command to a certain extent, but they are not his, and the intermediate process between volition and act is as brief as it is unconscious. Thus man proves his will by the quickness and clearness of personality which stamps upon all his acts, and thus the Divine Being conceals His personality in the arrangements of the creation.

Sunday July 30 1876.

THE dispute at the present day is whether religion is entitled or not entitled to be considered as a branch of science. Even religious men themselves are not certain of the scientific position of religion. And then as for scientific men they, not excluding such as have retained their belief in divine truths notwithstanding the all-absorbing influence of their scientific investigations, have unanimously denied to every form of religion anything like a logical or scientific basis. Materialistic thinkers fail to detect the vestiges of mind or character in the domain of phenomena that come within the recognition of physical observations and experiments. And metaphysicians remove the knowledge of eternal objects beyond the conditions of thought. The great opponents of the knowledge of supersensible realities in the outward world, have been the eminent thinkers of the inductive school, and the apostles of the philosophy of the unconditioned, dating their origin from the career of Sir W. Hamilton, have removed religion out of the pale of mental philosophy. The latest developments of these two schools being Mr. John Stuart Mill on the one hand and Mr. Herbert Spencer on the other. The great argument against the scietific soundness of religion has been the absence of any facts within human nature and without it, upon which the religious belief of mankind would build a satisfactory foundation. Religion is charged with unwarrantable assumptions of truth which cannot stand the test of reasoning or thought. Religion is quietly handed over to the department of *faith* on the one hand, which in philosophical parlance means little short of arrant ignorance, and on the other hand to *emotion* which at best is a pardonable weakness of human nature. If faith means the acceptance of certain conditions of thought without adequate or conclusive reasoning, then the ignorance which it involves is not peculiar to religion alone, but lies at the bottom of all possible knowledge. Natural philosophy owes its existence to the observation and contemplation of certain objects in space and in time, with the necessary basis or substratum of what is technically called substance. The three conditions of thought by which natural philosophy becomes at all cognisable and an object of reasonable pursuit, are space, time and substance. An object that is not in space, that is not in time, and that has no substance, is perfectly unthinkable. But what are space, time and substance? Are they thinkable beyond the relations which they bear to outward objects? What conceptions can we form of space without the limits of being, of time; without the limits of existence, of substance; without the limits of qualities? When, therefore, these three indispensable conditions of thought and existence are not only not the results of reasoning and proof, but decline to come within the province of human knowledge or contemplation, are they not assumptions as distinct and positive as any which we may ever think of? Coming to the department of mental philosophy we likewise find that the existence of the mind itself and the elementary axioms of thought elude the laws of reasoning. And travelling into the region of moral science, the fundamental distinctions between right and wrong, between good and evil are equally arbitrary and assumptive. Religion, therefore, in establishing herself upon certain fundamental and necessary conceptions, does not lose her title, if she can otherwise make it good, of consulting a separate department of science by herself.

Gleanings

As the eye requires the light, and is incomplete without it so does the human soul crave, so is it not only incomplete, but inexplicable, without God and immortality.

THE weak sinews become strong by their conflict with difficulties. Hope is born in the long night of watching and tears. Faith visits us in defeat and disappointment, amid the consciousness of earthly frailty and the crumbling tombstones of morality. The best and the bravest man is the man who, amid all thronging realities of life, endeavors to conform to an ideal rectitude. Those who have accomplished great things, who have stood in advance of the age and dared to rebuke it, and who have overcome the world, have lived from sanctions that are above the world.

He that said, in the Gospel, "I fast twice a week," was a pharisee: he that can tell how often he hath thought on, or prayed to God to-day, hath not meditated nor prayed enough.—DONNE.

Literary

THE *Pall Mall Budget* is very severe upon a book called "Shells from the Sands of Time," which has recently been written by the Dowager Lady Lytton. It says:—"It is beyond a reviewer's powers to convey an adequate notion of the style of contents of this volume of essays. A book containing more than 200 pages, and written by a lady who has not ability, may possibly contain some passages that are worth reading, but they are in few in number. Quotations are numerous, and occasionally the reader will meet with an amusing anecdote."

A STATISTICAL Account of Bengal, by W. W. Hunter, B. A., LL. D., Director-General of Statistics to the Government of India, is just out. It consists of accounts of the following Districts:—

Vol. I. 24-Pergunnahs and Sundarbans.
Vol. II. Nuddea and Jessore.
Vol. III. Midnapore, Hughli and Howrah.
Vol. IV. Burdwan, Bankura, and Birbhum.
Vol. V. Dacca, Bakarganj, Faridpore, and Mymensing.

IT is proposed to start a first-class Anglo-Indian Magazine in Calcutta. The services of some well-known writers have been secured for its pages.

Latest News

—IT is reported that famine in a mild form will, in all probability, rage in parts of Mysore.

—MONSIEUR LE COUNT DESBASSYNS DE RICHEMONT, who represents the French establishments of India in the Assembly at Versailles, desiring to leave a perpetual proof of his benevolence and devotion to the good of the puplic, after the example of his father, intends with the co-operation of the Bishop of Pondicherry, to establish, at Pondicherry, a hospital exclusively destined for very old people of all religions.

—THE Maharajah of Bhurtpur is inviting all Simla society to a ball "to meet their Excellencies the Viceroy and Lady Lytton" on Friday, the 15th.

—THE new Yarkund Envoy was to arrive at Simla, on Friday last. A house has been taken for him by the Government of India.

—NUMBERS of ladies and gentlemen are leaving London for the purpose of acting as nurses to the wounded at the seat of war.

—THE Prince of Wales returned to England on August 24 from a continental trip. He has visited the Brussels Exhibition.

—THE French and Italian newspapers have contained several articles highly complimentary to Mr Disraeli and congratulating him on his elevation to the peerage.

—THE King of Dahomey threatens to kill all the Europeans he can lay hold of, as soon as hostilities commence against him.

—MR. MACLEANE, the Civilian, who has absconded from Mussurie, is said to have been a man of humble origin, but undoubtedy talanted. A widowed mother will deplore the end of her son whose beginning of life was one so full of promise. He is supposed to have gone to join his wife, known to have once been a French actress.

—COLONEL MALLESON'S leave having expired, his services have placed at the disposal of the Military Department.

—THE King of Dahomey has seized several European residents at Whydah, and threatens to kill them, should his territory be invaded by the British forces

—THE HON. R. Carington has issued an address to electors of Buckinghamshire as a Liberal candidate for the vacancy caused by Mr. Disraeli's elevation to the peerage.

—THE Earl of Beaconsfield has issued a farewell address to his late constituents in Buckinghamshire.

Calcutta.

WE hear that Syed Abdul Rohaman, of Jahanpore in the district of Furridpore, an ex-student of the Calcutta Madrassa, intends going to England in October next to study for the Bar. We wish him success.

THE judgment of Mr. A. F. Maclean, the district Judge of the 24-Pugunnahs, in the case of Babu Prem Chand Burul *vs.* Babu Kalichurn Ghose, the Collector of the 24-Purgunnahs under Act X. of 1870 (the Land Acquisition Act) was revised by the High Court last week on appeal, and they allowed an additional sum to that awarded by the Collector, Mr. Williamson, the Assessor and the Judge.

THE Hon'ble T. C. Hope will be the President of the Conference on Prison Discipline to assemble this winter at Calcutta. The local Governments have not yet named their representatives.

THE Railway Conference at Calcutta will, says the *Pioneer*, assume large proportions most likely. It will not be a committee sitting round a table, but a congress divided into sections for the discussion of the various questions to be brought forward. As yet no certain arrangement has been made as to who will preside. Sir Andrew Clarke would seem to be the natural president for an assembly of which he can hardly fail to be the guiding spirit, but possibly the new Finance Minister will be chosen to open the proceedings; at all events two or three members of Council will take in part these.

THE P. and O. Co.'s S. S. *Lombardy*, Commander W. A. Seaton, arrived in Bombay harbour on Tuesday last, at 11 o'clock, from Suez with the English mails of the 25th August on board. The following is the list of passengers:—

From Southampton.—Mr. E. Knight, Capt. Riddell, Mr. B. J. Sellerin, Capt. Highmoor, Mr. and Mrs. D. Joscelyn, Mr. R. C. Laughlin, Miss. L. Stamp, Miss. M. Mason, Mrs. E. Rochell, Mrs. Corrbett, Capt W. H. Ashe, Mr. and Mrs. Vollet.

From Venice.—Mr. and Mrs. Max Densc, Mr Chapman,

From Brindisi.—Mr. W. Mellor, Mr. Bussier, Col Malcolmson, Mr. H. C. Robertson, Mr. Foster, Mr. Allaruckhia.

From Aden.—Col Penn, Mr. J. M. Campbell.

WE hear on reliable authority that the Lieutenant-Governor has written to some of the leading Native and European gentlemen of Calcutta asking them to allow themselves to be appointed by Government as Municipal Commissioners.

ACKNOWLEDGMENT.

The Rent Question. By Parboti Churn Roy, Deputy Collector, Deerah Settlement, Dacca and Furridpore. Calcutta. 1876.

DOMESTIC OCCURRENCE.

BIRTH.

ROY.—At Bombay, on the 3rd of September 1876, the wife of Babu Rajani Nath Roy, of a daughter.

Miscellaneous.

BE KIND TO THE AGED.

AGE, when whitening for the tomb, is a worthy object of reverence. The passions have ceased—hopes of self have ceased. They linger with the young and pray for the young—and O, how careful should the young be to reward them with tender affection and the warmest of love, to dismiss the tide of ebbing life! The Spartans looked on reverential respect for old age as a beautiful trait of character. Be kind to those who are in the Autumn of life, for you know not what sufferings they may have endured, nor how much of it may still be their portion. Do they seem unreasonably to find fault or murmur? Allow not your anger to kindle against them; rebuke them not, for doubtless many have been the crosses and trials of earlier years, and pherhaps their dispositions, while in the Spring-time of life were less flexible than your own. Do they require aid? Then render it cheerfully. Forget not that the time may come when you may desire the same assistance from others that you render to them. Do all that is needful for the old and do it with alacrity, and think not hard if much is required at your hands, lest when age sets its seal on your brow and fills your limbs with trembling, others may wait unwilling, and feel relieved when the coffin has covered you forever.—*Selected.*

Advertisements

P. W. FLEURY & CO.,

BUILDERS, ENGINEERS, AND SCIENTIFIC INSTRUMENT MAKERS.

No. 44, Free School Street.

We beg to intimate that we have been engaged in the above line of business for the past 20 years, and trust that our Constituents will continue to favor us with their work, which will meet with prompt attention on our part.

In connection with buildings, we undertake the erection and repairing of machinery at moderate charges; as also execute all descriptions of Iron and Brass work.

We can assure the Public that we undertake the repair and erection of Houses, and the laying of Water-supply Pipes on moderate terms, and guarantee to keep all the water-pipes and brass fittings supplied by us in good working order for three years, free of extra charges. We also guarantee to keep dwelling-houses' roofs water-tight for three years, free of extra charge, for such houses as we have repaired.

For purposes of illumination, we prepare our patent [illegible] Transparencies representing Coat-of-Arms, Landscapes, Scenery, &c., at prices, ranging from Rs. 50 to 200 each, according to size and design.

FOR SALE.

Light! Light!! Light!!!

Electric Light Apparatus, complete, worked with a battery of 50 large cells, on Bunsen's principle	500	0
Ditto ditto, with 40 cells, smaller size ...	400	0
Ditto ditto, with a powerful 44-cell Cast-iron Battery, on Callan's principle ...	300	0
Lime Light Apparatus, complete, with Iron Gas-holder, and Copper Retort ...	150	0
Oxy-Hydrogen Light Apparatus, with safety Jets, 2 iron Gas-holders, and Retorts, complete	200	0
Hink's Patent Duplex Wall Lamps, with chimney	5	8
Ditto Duplex Lamp, with chimney and globe	7	8

Patent Leblanche-Battery

For constancy, durability, and cleanliness, this battery is unequalled; price for each cell, with chemicals	3	8
Bunsen's Galvanic Battery, 9 inches, by 4 inches	7	8
Magneto-Electric Machine, with single magnet	14	0
Prismatic Compass 3-inch, in a lid leather case, by Elliot, second-hand	22	0
Ditto 4-inch, by Simmons, second-hand ...	30	0

P. W. FLEURY & CO.,
No. 44, FREE SCHOOL STREET.

ESTABLISHED 1833

H. C. GANGOOLY & CO.

STATIONERS, DIE-SINKERS, ENGRAVERS, PRINTERS, LITHOGRAPHERS &c.

24, Mangoe Lane, Calcutta.

Cash prices of the following :—

	Rs.	As.		Rs.
Whatman's Drawing paper double elephant sizes (40×27) each ...	0	7		0
Mathematical Instrument Boxes	2	8	to	16
Color Boxes ...	0	4	"	5

Drawing Pencils Drawing and Mapping Steel pens and various other requisites in Stationery.

MUDHOO SUDUN PAUL & CO.

120, RADHA BAZAR,

Tea! (Assam) Tea!

TRADE M. MARK.

In 1lb. and 2lb. Tins.

Pekoe Tea ...	... 2lb. Tin, Per	Tin Rs.	2	0
" Flowery ...	... "	"	"	3	8
" Souchong ...	... "	"	"	2	0
Family Mixture ...	... "	"	"	2	4
Campoi ...	... "	"	"	2	8
Imperial Mixture with China	...	...	...	3	4
China Rose Pauchong ...	...	...	...	2	8

The above in 1lb. Tin at half the respective prices, plus two annas extra.

BURMAH CIGARS.

No. 1 per 100 Rs. 1 0
" 2 " 0 12

HUNTLEY AND PALMER'S BISCUITS.

Albert, in Tin of 2 lb each Re 1 6
Arrow Root, ... " 1 4
Mixed, ... " 1 8

Italian Chartolles, Castor Oil, Candles, Kerosine Oil, China Preserves, Perfumery, Domestic Medicines and other stores always in stock and offered at lower rates than other Houses.

Catalogue to be had on application,

MUDHOO SUDUN PAUL & Co.

CHUNDER & BROTHERS.

25½ & 112, RADHA BAZAR,

STATIONERY in all its varieties.
PRINTING PRESSES, Inks & Materials.
LITHOGRAPHIC PRESS & Materials.
BOOK BINDING Materials &c.

!!! হুকা !!!

!!!HOOKAHS!!!

ENGLISH made Hookahs of various choice designs, colours and sizes, ranging in price from Rs. 2 to 5 each, 60 designs to choose from. Apply to

RADANAUTH CHOWDRY,
378, Jorasanko.

MAKHON LOLL GHOSE,

No. 91, Radha Bazar, Calcutta.

BEGS to invite the attention of the public to several consignments of commercial and fancy stationery of all sorts, including account books of all sizes, made of handmade and machine made paper, by steamers recently arrived, and which he is disposing of at moderate prices. He has been long in the trade, and presumes he has always afforded every satisfaction to the numerous merchants here who have constantly favored him with orders. Mofussil orders accompanied with remittances shall be promptly attended to.

CALCUTTA
The 18th August 1876.

How to Enjoy Life

Is only known when the blood is pure, its circulation perfect, and the nerves in good orders. The only safe and certain method of expelling all impurities is to take Holloway's Pills, which have the power of cleansing the blood from all noxious matters, expelling all humours which taint or impoverish it, thereby purify and invigorate and give general tone to the system. Young or old robust or delicate, may alike experience their beneficent effects. Myriads affirmed that these Pills possess marvellous power in securing these great secrets of health by purifying and regulating the fluids and strengthening the solids.

NOTICE.

INFALLIBLE SPECIFICS FOR ASTHMA, CONSUMPTION, COLIC, GONORRHŒA, AND SPERMATORRHŒA!!!

I AM the son of the late Titaram Paul of Midnapore, who, the public is well aware, was acquainted with specific medicines for the above diseases. I fully learnt the mode of preparing those medicines from my late father, and have cured many people of Midnapore, Calcutta, Hughly, and other places since his death, as the annexed testimonial will shew. Any one wishing to be treated by me can apply to me, care of the Manager of the Indian Mirror.

WOOPENDRA NATH PAUL.

BABU UPENDRA NATH PAL.

SIR,

You will be glad to hear that the painful asthma under which I was suffering for the last three years and through which I was nearly brought to the brink of death has been perfectly cured through your treatment. I was laid under the care of several able Doctors and *Kobirajes*, but every treatment on their part proved a failure on me. God bless you and let your cure spread over those who are suffering under the same wretched circumstances.

SURYA CUMAR MAZUMDAR.

CALCUTTA,
TANTANEAH,
The 30th August 1875.

THEISTIC BOOKS.

FOR SALE.

URDU.

Rahut Hakiki	Rs.	0	3	0
Nizam Kend	...	0	2	0
Kasufat Ilham	...	0	2	0
Khulasa of Asool Brahm Dharm	...	0	1	0

HINDI.

Upasana Paddati	Rs.	0	1	0
Brahm Patrika or Hymn book	...	0	1	0
Tat Bodh	...	0	8	0
Upanishad Sar ...	...	0	8	0
Dharm Dipika	...	0	0	6

ENGLISH.

Claims of so called Revealed Religion	Rs.	0	2	0
New Life	...	0	0	6
Living God	...	0	1	0
Higher and Lower Virtues ...	...	0	1	0

Apply to the secretary,
BRAHMO SOMAJ OF THE PUNJAB,
Lahore.

CALCUTTA

166, Bowbazar Street.

DR. H. C. SARMA'S

MEDICINE FOR DEBILITY

(NERVOUS.)

Brought on by indulgence in irregular habits, effects of previous diseases, loss of power of limbs, weakness or loss of memory, absent-mindedness, irritable temper, disposition of the mind to despondency at trifles, want of attention towards business, despair at finding no relief from treatment &c. &c. &c.

Price with postage &c. Rs. 5.

Particulars of disease and directions for despatch required from patients residing at a distance.

DR. SARMA'S FEE.

In cases of Debility (nervous) Rs. 16 per visit. } In
For advice at Home ... Rs. 10 " } Town

Out of Town Rs. 500 per day.

INDIAN TOOTH POWDER.

Strengthens loose teeth, alleviates pain of, and prevents bleeding from Gums, cleanses the mouth, corrects its putrid odour and cures ulceration of the Gums without blackening the Teeth.

Price per packet ... ... Rs. 0 4 0
Postage &c., for 4 packets " 0 5 0

TONIC OIL.

Imparts vigour and tone to the paralyzed or relaxed parts of the Human system—Restores proper circulation of blood to weak and inactive parts.

Price for four ounce phial ... ... Rs. 1 0 0
Postage &c. 0 10 0

HAIR PRESERVER.

Will restore grey hair to its original colour.

It acts directly upon the roots of the hair, removes dandriff, prevents premature falling-off of the hair, and produces [illegible] strength giving Lustre and Health of Youth.

It also produces a cooling and soothing effect upon the head.

Price, for 4 ounce phial ... Rs. 1 0 0
Postage &c. ... ... " 0 10 0

Copy of Letter received from Raja Chundernath Roy Bahadoor of Nattore.

Wellesley Street, No. 18, Motts Lane, 29th March 1874.

MY DEAR HURRISH BABU,—I shall thank you to send me another phial of your "*Excellent Hair Restorer.*" In fact it has done me great benefit and I should like to have more of it. It has disabused me (young as I am) of old age.

Your's Sincerely

C. N. of *Nattore*

MEDICINE FOR BALDNESS.

Will certainly cure baldness if applied on the bald portion, night & morning according to directions given in the adjoining direction paper

Price per two ounce phial Rs. 1 0 0
Postage &c. " 6 0

HEEM-SAGAR OIL.

The best remedy for Headache arising from over-study, intellectual occupation, over-thinking, mental anxiety and weakness, as well as heat of head from living in hot places.

It cools the head and produces very agreeable sensation. Removes Dandriff as well as all other impurities from the head. Promotes the strength and growth of the hair and prevents its premature falling-off.

Price per 4 ounce phial... Rs. 1 0 0
Postage &c. ... ... " 0 10 0

MEDICINE FOR LEPROSY.

Price with Postage &c. Rs. 5.

OIL FOR LEPROSY.

And Inveterate Skin Diseases.

Price per 8 ounce phial... Rs. [illegible]
Postage &c. ... ... " 0 12

BABU BASANTA KUMAR DUTTA,
HOMŒOPATHIC PRACTITIONER
No. 20, Sunker Halder's Lane, Ahiritolah.

FRESH INDENT OF

Medicines and other Requisites.

Have arrived from England.

Medicines, Boxes, Books, Pamphlets; Absolute Alcohol; Cholera spirit Camphor, SPECIAL REMEDIES.

For Suppressed, Laborious and **Difficult** menses; Leucorrhœa.

For Hysteria; Spermatorrhœa; Dysentery; Diarrhœa; Cholera.

For Asthma; Pile; Pain; Sore and Diseases of the Children.

Ice, Lemonade, Soda and Tonic water always.

To be had at

DUTTA'S HOMŒOPATHIC LABORATORY
No. 312, CHITPORE ROAD, BURTOLA, CALCUTTA

TERMS—CASH.

☞ List can be had on application.

SMITH, STANISTREET & CO.

Pharmaceutical Chemists & Druggists

BY APPOINTMENT

To His Excellency the Right Hon'ble

LORD LYTTON, G.M.S.I.

Governor-General of India,

&c., *&c.*

SYRUP OF LACTATE OF IRON

Prepared from the original recipe. Lactate of Iron, in various forms of preparation, have been in use in France, and generally through the continent of Europe, for some years past, and is highly esteemed as one of the most valuable Chalybeate Tonic remedies yet introduced. The Syrup, being the most agreeable as well as convenient form of administration is in most general use. It is a most valuable remedy in the following diseases:—Chlorosis or Green Sickness, Leucorrhœa, Neuralgia, enlargement of the Spleen, &c. In combination with quinine, it has also been very successfully used in the cure of Fever, while to persons of delicate constitution, enfeebled by disease it is invaluable. In bottles. Rs. 2 each.

SYRUP OF THE PHOSPHATE OF IRON Rs. 2 per bottle.

SYRUP OF PHOSPHATE OF IRON AND STRYCHNINE, Rs. 2 per bottle.

SYRUP OF PHOSPHATE OF IRON AND QUININE, Price Rs. 2-8 per bottle.

SYRUP OF PHOSPHATE OF IRON, QUININE AND STRYCHNINE (DR. ATKIN'S TRIPLE TONIC SYRUP.) Rs. 2-8 per bottle.

Smith, Stanistreet & Co.

Invite special attention to the following rates the quality guaranteed as the best procurable:—

Pure Ærated Waters.

Made from Pure Water, obtained by the new process through the Patent Charcoal Filters.

			Rs.	As.
Ærated plain (Treble Ærated),	per doz.		0	12
Soda Water	ditto	" ...	0	12
Gingerade	ditto	" ...	1	4
Lemonade	ditto	" ...	1	4
Tonic (Quinine)	ditto	" ...	1	[illegible]

The Cash must be sent with the order to obtain advantage of the above rates.

TO THE MEMBERS OF THE BRAHMO SOMAJ OF INDIA.

THE undersigned has the pleasure to announce that he has received a large supply of Mr. T. Scott's Theistical publications which can be obtained at English price exclusive of postage, namely, from As. 2 to Rs. 2.

☞ List of the Pamphlets can be had on application to

MR. V. C. MOONSAWMY MOODELIAR,
Lascar's Line,
Bangalore.

BURN & CO.

RANEEGUNGE Fire bricks are the best Fire Bricks known;—superior to Ramsay's.

9 Rs. per 100.

Fire clay, 40 Rs. per Ton.

Glazed Stone ware, Drainage pipes of all sizes.

BURN & Co.,
7, Hastings Street, Calcutta.

Rivers Steam Navigation Co. Limited.

The Str. "BENGAL" will leave Kooshtea for Assam on the 21th Current.

The Steamer "BURMAH" will leave Calcutta for Assam on 21st Current.

For Freight or Passage, apply to
No. 1, Lyons Range, } MACKINNON & Co.,
12th September, 1876. } Agents.

India General Steam Navigation Company, Ld.

SCHOENE, KILBURN & Co.,—*Managing Agents*

ASSAM LINE.

NOTICE.

Steamers leave Calcutta for Assam every Tuesday, Kooshtea every Thursday and leave Dibrooghur downward every Saturday.

THE Str. "ASSAM" will leave Calcutta *via Mutlahunge* for Assam, on Tuesday, the 19th instant.

Cargo will be received at the Company's Godowns, Nimtollah Ghat, up till noon of Monday, the 18th.

THE Str. "MIRZAPORE" will leave Kooshtea for Assam on Thursday, the 21st instant.

Cargo will be received at the Company's Godowns, No. 4 Fairlie Place, up till noon of Tuesday the 19th.

Goods forwarded to Kooshtea for this vessel will be chargeable with Railway Freight from Calcutta to Kooshtea, in addition to the regular Freight of this Company.

Passengers should leave for **Kooshtea** by Train of Wednesday, the 20th.

CACHAR LINE NOTICE
REGULAR FORTNIGHTLY SERVICE.

Steamers leave Calcutta for Cachar and Intermediate Stations every alternate Friday, and leave Cachar downward every alternate Sunday.

THE Str. "LUCKNOW" **will leave** Calcutta *via Mutlahunge* **for Cachar** on Friday, the 22nd instant.

Cargo will be received at the Company's Godowns, Nimtollah Ghat, up till **noon** of Thursday the 21st.

For further information regarding rates of Freight or passage money, apply to,

4, FAIRLIE PLACE, } G. A. SCOTT,
Calcutta 12th September, 1876. } *Secretary*

R. K. GHOSH'S

HOMŒOPATHIC DISPENSARY.

No. 1, *Gour Mohun Mukerjee's Street, Simla.*

CALCUTTA,

HOMŒOPATHIC Medicine; Medicine chests of sizes,—containing **medicine in tube phials**; Homœopathic Books, tracts and pamphlets (English and Bengali); Dr. Rubini's "Saturated spirits of Camphor,"—(the best preventive and cure for cholera where medical aid is not available); and other Homœopathic requisites are sold here at a moderate price. Terms **cash**, Mofussil orders are promptly executed.

R. K. GHOSH,
Homœopathic Practitioner,
Manager

Printing Materials.

MILLER AND **RICHARD'S PRESSES, TYPES** and all **requisites always in Stock,**

TERMS CASH.

EWING & CO.

Oriental Gas Company Ld.

THE price of Gas in Calcutta **and Howrah** is reduced to Rs. 5 per 1,000 feet.

Printed and published by M. M. BUKHT, at the INDIAN MIRROR PRESS, No. 6, College Square, for the Proprietors.

The Indian Mirror.

SUNDAY EDITION.

VOL. XV.] CALCUTTA, SUNDAY SEPTEMBER 24 1876. [REGISTERED AT THE GENERAL POST OFFICE.] [No. 227

CONTENTS.

NOTICE.

All letters and communications relating to the literary department of the Paper should be addressed to the Editor. All other letters should be addressed to the Manager, to whom all remittances should be made payable.

Subscribers will be good enough to bring to the notice of the Manager any delay or irregularity in the delivery of the Paper.

Editorial Notes.

A NOVEL feature in the system of missionary life now adopted by the missionaries of the Brahmo Somaj, is the combination of self-culture (*Sadhan*) and preaching. Our missionary brethren are going abroad with the object of combining the discipline under which they have put themselves with the work of laying before others the truths they have obtained.

FROGS, we find, are to be exempted from the protection afforded by the Vivisection Bill. The eminent scientific men in England have extorted that concession from their Government. We wonder what prescriptive right scientific men have to torture poor frogs when the rest of the animal creation can claim and obtain immunity from the ruthless knife of the vivisector. Surely humanity in England has not risen above discreditable compromise.

MR. GLADSTONE'S exposition of Unitarian Chistianity, though somewhat overdrawn, is certainly not so very incorrect as some Unitarian gentlemen would have us suppose. Mr. Gladstone describes the Unitarians as a body of men "in which the individual, growing toward maturity, instead of accepting and using the traditions of his fathers until his adult faculties see ground to question it, is rather warned against such acceptance,as enhancing the difficulties of impartial choice." This is surely incorrect, and perceptibly overdrawn. The Conservative Unitarian knows how to quarrel for his theology as much as any Nonconformist; and the advanced Unitarian, though he would not accept a very definite creed, would still train up those under him according to his clear and well-ascertained convictions, leaving however a free and wide margin for individual faith and opinion to develope. Every Unitarian, so far as we are informed, is trained according to the traditions of his fathers, though nobody is suffered to persecute him if he outgrows them in his maturity. The Unitarians are certainly the most progressive sect in Christendom.

THE will, with two codicils, of Miss Harriet Martineau contains some interesting particulars, and one of these is that neither in the will, nor in the autobiography, the slightest mention is ever made of the Rev. James Martineau, her brother, and the most illustrious of the whole family. Her property amounted to about £10,000, besides the house, books, and manuscripts about which various arrangements and bequests are made. The property is to be equally distributed among her brothers, and their children. She leaves most positive injunctions that none of the private letters she ever wrote are to be published on any account. But the most characteristic feature in the will is the following: "It is my desire (she says) from an interest in the progress of scientific investigation, that my skull shall be given to Henry George Atkinson, of Upper Gloucester-place, London, and also my brain, if my death should take place within such distance of his then present abode as to enable him to have it for purposes of scientific observation." By the second codicil, dated October 5, 1872, this direction is revoked; 'but (the codicil proceeds)' I wish to leave it on record that this alteration in my testamentary directions is not caused by any change of opinion as to the importance of scientific observation on such subjects, but is made in consequence merely of a change of circumstances in my individual case."

IT is a difficult thing to say what makes a sermon interesting. We would have a sermon from everybody who mounts the pulpit; if the sermon is omitted we think we have been deprived of a long-estblished right; and still we reserve to ourselves the previlege of voting sermons as the most unmitigated bores that we have ever had to deal with. Sermons says the *Spectator* "are by their name a bugbear to a great portion, and that often the most cultivated portion of society. We grumble at our weekly share of them, we resent the imposition of an additional five minutes as a grievous personal wrong. There is nothing which we are so anxious to cut short or slip out of by any pretext, and yet, strange contradiction, not even the successful player, whose aim is our amusement, has half so great a hold on us as the preacher, when one happens to come in our way. The art, if we may call it by that name, suffers not from any fault of its own, but from the unspeakable incapacity of the mass of its practitioners. A true Preacher, a man endowed with the real faculty of religious exposition or exhortation, wherever he finds himself, will find an interested audience. Stupidity, wrong-headedness, dull folly, clever levity, every intellectual sin which belongs to man, have done their best to blunt the tools of the religious orators, and take his powers from him but they have beeen unsuccessful. The fury of the stupor into which we are lashed or lulled every Sunday by our own individual local tormentor floats away like a cloud, whenever the real possessor of the gift makes his long ed-for appearance. The sermon is the embodiment of everything that is most wearisome and tedious: the sermon is the most highly appreciated of human productions. No two things can be more contradictory or more true."

THE *Friend of India* in discussing the question of violence used by Englishmen against the people of this country, asks whether the cause of such violence lies in the mental constitution of the Englishman as Englishman, or whether it exists outside his mind, in the tendencies which Indian climate, Indian society and antecedents are calculated to foster, in the constitution of a conquering race. If the former be the case, then all Englishmen are potentially guilty of the same offence, and no one has the right to criticize his neighbour. If the latter be true then Englishmen who leave at home may very well congratulate themselves on their escape from the conditions and tendencies of Anglo-Indian life, while Anglo-Indians themselves may plead social, moral and climatic necessities in justification of their violence, the impulses to which are irresistible. Whatever the force of logic be in either of these arguments, we think both the reasons assigned above are true to a certain extent. There is an impatience in Anglo Saxon character which is easily inflamed into wrath whenever the inexactness, dilatoriness, listlessness, and stupidity in which Indian servants so universally excel, are brought in contact with it. In many matters the nature of the mild Hindu is just the opposite pole to the nature of the sanguine Anglo-Saxon. A struggle at times becomes almost inevitable, and of course the weakest goes to the wall. There are some Englishmen in India, we know, who understand this circumstance, and adapt themselves to their Native fellow-subjects in a way that is most likely to develope the latent faculties of the latter. There are others again who think violence is the best remedy for weakness and dulness of intellect, and by indulging in their favorite passion they bring dishonor and disrepute to the good English name in India.

FROM the letter of the *Daily News'* Special Commissioner, who writes from the scene of action, extracts are made to show the havoc which the Turks have made in some parts of the disaffected provinces. The following description relates to a village called Batak in Bulgaria. After riding through heaps of skulls and skeletons, most of them belonging to girls, some with the tattered clothing still left on them, the writer and his party came upon roofless houses, dismantled walls, and crumbling door-steps. Within the shattered walls of the first house we came to, was a woman sitting on a heap of rubbish, rocking herself to and fro, wailing a kind of monotonous chant, half sung, half sobbed, that was not without a wild discordant melody. In her lap she held a babe, and another child sat beside her patiently and silently, and looked at us as we passed with wondering eyes, She paid no attention to us; but we bent our ear to hear what she was saying, and our interperter said it was as follows:—'My home, my home, my poor home, my sweet home, my husband, my husband, my poor husband, my dear husband: my home, my sweet home,' and so on, repeating th same words over and over again a thousand times. In the next house were two engaged in the same way; one old the other young, repeating words nearly identical, "I had a home and now I have none; I had a husband and now I am a widow; I had a son and now I have none; I had five children and now I have one," while rocking themselves to and fro, beating their heads and wringing their hands. These were women who had escaped from the massacre, and had only just returned for the first time, having taken advantage of our visit or that of Mr. Baring to do so. They might have returned long ago, but their terror was so great that they had not dared without the presence and protection of a foreigner, and now they would go on for hours in this way, "keening" this kind of funeral dirge over their ruined homes." There is a talk of mediation on the part of the great European powers, a short armistice has been concluded, and peace between Servia and Turkey is not improbable. In the meanwhile much excitement prevails in England on the subject, and the indignation felt against the Government for its tacit support of Turkey is all but unanimous.

INWARD CAPACITY.

WE often make the mistake of supposing that our spiritual gifts are nearly inexhaustible, that we can pray any length of time, love God in a very large measure, and cherish unbounded affection for our fellowmen. Laboring under this mistake we go to expect from others that which we imagine ourselves to be quite capable of. Being disappointed in this expectation, we bitterly complain of the deficiency of other men. But they wonder to find us complaining, when we are sadly wanting in the virtues whose absence in others we are apt to deplore. We then for the first time perhaps come to understand that we have very real and practical deficiencies, and are a good deal pained to see ourselves as others see us. The fact is that the inward capacity for love and faith in us is exceedingly limited. The church of God continually demands from us more than we can give under our present circumstances, and since we have so little of the genuine article, we try to makeup for our want by tendering unreal and counterfeit coin. We are apt to think that our sentiments, words, and the discharge of routine duties are quite enough, and will satisfy the world; and we are hence justified in cherishing any amount of expectation as to what others should do to us. The very best among men even need often be reminded that there is a secret measure of spiritual capacity, short of which the world instinctively refuses to receive anything. Any amount of fine talk is but empty air, and is felt as such by those who are not blinded by the over-weening self-love of the talker to form a right estimate of the high-sounding utterances. Any amount of fine sentiment is as chaff before the practical requirements of men *wanting* to be saved. Even the habitual acts of service and self-discipline wherein we rejoice, are no index to the real inward capacity of the man who performs them. The inward capacity of genuine love and faith in ordinary men increases very slowly. This may be partly because of the low standard of spiritual excellence set before us by the world; partly owing to the absence of ambition in men to seek more of the inward and the true, than of the outward show, because silence, depth, and the grace of retirement are so little appreciated in any community. But whatever be the causes assigned, the fact is undeniable that our inward capacity is small, and shrinks into utter insignificance before the perpetual demands of our friends. We are vainly angry because we find others not aswering to our expectations, when we do not answer these expectations ourselves, if entertained by others of us. The best course for all would be to deepen and increase our inward capacity. The measure of our words may remain for a long time what it now is, nay even we may keep invariable our sentiments, and service; but it is pre-eminently important that our hearts should contain more of love, more of faith, more real and profound spirituality than we have hitherto possessed. The world has always esteemed *being* more than *doing*.

Correspondence.

THE MODE OF SITTING IN THE MANDIR

To the Editor of the *Indian Mirror*.

DEAR SIR,—I do not know what the majority of the members of the congregation of our Brahmo Mandir think of the Anglo-Indian fashion of sitting on benches at the time of their worship in the Mandir instead of the old, but comfortable way, in which our forefathers used to sit at the time of their sacred Puja. I for one prefer the old fashion of squatting on the floor just as the good old Hindus do, to that of reclining on benches with boots or shoes on, and my reason for this is that the one appears to be more comfortable than the other; besides it very much conforms to the popular notion of the Hindu race which form the majority of the congregation of the Mandir. I beg, therefore, to suggest that if, in the opinion of the authorities of the Mandir, the change it question be feasible, I would respectfully urge that it should be introduced as soon as possible. My simple proposal is this:—That the space beyond the marble platform before the pulpit may be set apart with a view to make accommodation for those who prefer to sit squatting, at the time of worship, and this could easily be done, by taking off the benches from the place indicated and substituting railing in rows to make it look nice and prevent intrusion. As regards the safety of the shoes question which may be raised as one of great objection to this innovation, I beg to say that those who wish to have their worship done in a proper and comfortable manner, will think of their shoes themselves or allow their shoes to take care of themselves.

You are no doubt aware, Mr. Editor, of the arrangement existing in the Calcutta Somaj. But I regret to observe that though a place has been set apart there in the way suggested, there is hardly any egress to those who wish to avail themselves of it, except to a chosen few. I think the arrangement of the Calcutta Somaj may well be introduced in our Brahma Mandir with this necessary modification that the admission thereto may be more free and not by election. I send these few hasty lines for the consideration of the Managing Committee of the Mandir.

Yours &c.,
R.

SERMONS IN THE MANDIR.

To the Editor of the *Indian Mirror*.

SIR,—A marked change has come over our Minister lately. One that regularly hears him in the Brahma Mandir, must have observed the change, a happy one, in our dear Minister. Hitherto his thoughts were confined to this world and its people; but now they have been directed to another world, the world hereafter, the Heaven and those who live in it. This change has been clearly observed from the last Utsab. The Minister's prayer on the Utsab morning, of which you spoke, in high terms in the concluding part of the article, headed, "The Last Festival" that appeared in your paper, clearly proved the change of which I am speaking. It appeared in the *Dharma Tatwa* of the 16th Bhadro last, and one who wishes to know the full particulars of this change should peruse it. The sermons in the Mandir for the last few Sundays that followed the Utsab, also speak of things in heaven. How the devotees of God in heaven praise Him; how they are dancing, diving, swimming, and playing in the ocean of happiness vouchsafed to them by our Great Father; how anniversaries are held every day in heaven, where there is no day, no night, no January and no August—the two months in the year when the two anniversaries of the Brahmo Somaj are held respectively; how and when we shall meet with those heavenly devotees, who have long left this worldly scene; how in our Utsab, every year, we realize in some degree the happiness they enjoy; how, when in the warmth and enthusiasm of our devotions, prayers, and *Sankirtans*, the merciful Father holds before the mind's eye the inexpressibly beautiful picture of heaven, and thus allures us for that day when we shall be like them and for that place where we shall meet them; how to realize True Friendship and Love in this world, we can see from the picture the True Friendship and Love of those devotees in heaven. These are some of the points dwelt on by our revered Minister.

Yours &c,
S. C. S.

VIVISECTION.

To the Editor of the *Indian Mirror*.

SIR,—In the editorial notes of one of your recent issues I read some cruel experiments on living animals made by John Hunter, an eminent physiologist. Equally cruel and inhuman experiments on the poor dumb creatures are every day increasing. It was the other day when I was passing by the large theatre of the Calcutta Medical College that I saw a dog was being forcibly dragged up to the theatre. On enquiry I came to know that an experiment was to be made by Dr. Laurie, Professor of Physiology, showing the inefficacy to keep up circulation when the heart ceases to beat, by artificial respiration, and naturally I had a curiosity to see the experiment. The dog was first put under chloroform and then the Professor opened the trachea or air-passage of the animal and connected it with an apparatus for supplying air to keep up the heart's action by artificial respiration. He then opened the thorax between the ribs and saw that the heart stopped beating. The dog died! He then made similar experiments with three other dogs which all shared the same fate. Not content with this, he again killed two other dogs this morning. Such, Mr. Editor, are some of the indirect means of depriving the life of perfectly innocent creatures in the name of science, and such are some of the instances illustrative of the humanity which characterises the experiments on living animals. Really and truly, Mr. Editor, it is high time now for the medical practitioners to put a stop to the increasing mania of vivisection and especially the excruciating pains which accompany these experiments.

Yours obediently,
A SYMPATHISER.

PERSECUTION.

To the Editor of the *Indian Mirror*.

SIR,—The Sunday Edition of the *Mirror* of the 27th August having announced that three persons from Gouripha have been formally admitted into the Brahmo Somaj on the occasion of the Bhadra Utsab, the event has created a great sensation in this village. Persecution and opposition come from all sides. We have been threatened with excommunication, and our Somaj has been declared an "Ass House"! Let the foolish persons who thus blaspheme the name of God, have the full benefit of their foolishness, and let us calmly and patiently put up with their ridicule and the torments they are causing us. True faith ever works out her plan very secretly, and builds up her stronghold in a different manner, and with different ingredients.

GOURIPHA, } Yours &c.
The 30th August 1876. } A BRAHMO.

Devotional

(AFTER ST. AUGUSTINE.)

LORD, what shall I say of thee. Thou art *unknowable* and yet *knowable*. Thou art without shape and figure yet most beautiful. Thou art immutable yet thou appearest in various aspects to thy children. Absolute and the only Lord of the universe, yet every individual subject of thy kingdom is a free being. Thou workest without noise. How busy art thou yet how calm and peaceful, how strict and immovable yet how tender and reconcilable; unapproachable yet accessible to any one that seeks thee. Almighty yet Thou art subject to the necessity of thy God-head. Omnipresent but ever absent, ever near and ever distant. The Universe cannot contain thee, yet thou art present fully in every object. Thou art ever anxious for every individual, yet thou appearest the most unconcerned spectator of the world. Infinite is thy abhorrence of sin, yet thou dwellest in the soul of a sinner. Exacting monarch yet most liberal. Extremely worldly, having so large a family and immense possessions, yet thou art the greatest ascetic. August and great, yet thou personally attendest to the comforts and welfare of the minutest and mean. Thou art most uncompromising yet accommodating. What shall I say of thee, Lord! May my feeble voice stop, my little mind benumbed, and my soul lost in thy wonderous immensity from where no travellers ever returns. (*Communicated.*)

The Brahmo Somaj

OUR revered minister left Calcutta with his family on Friday last for Ghazipur, and the N. W. Provinces. He is to be in that city for sometime to recover his impaired health, and to take rest after his many labors and anxieties in Calcutta. Though we know it is not his nature to be inactive anywhere, and though however employed, he is never unmindful of the interests and welfare of his church, still we venture to hope our friends and brethren at Ghazipur will give him as much repose as possible. The good wishes and love of the congregation of the Brahma Mandir follow their minister wherever he happens to be, for in spirit he is with them always. Babu Prosonno Cumar Sen accompanies the minister.

BABU AUGHORE NATH GUPTA has proceeded to Debra Dhoon. The retreats and natural advantages of that place and its immediate nearness to the Himalayas give great facilities for such meditation, and spiritual excercises as have been chosen by him as his special line. He will minister to the wants of the Brahmos of Debra Dhoon, whence he is to proceed to Lahore.

BABU GRISH CHUNDER SEN has left again for Lucknow to prosecute his Persian and Arabic studies which have been so beneficial in supplying us all with the ample spiritual wealth that lies within the different departments and developments of the Mosulman religion.

We are told by an Anglo-Indian gentleman who very strongly sympathizes with the movement of Mr. Voysey, that the information received by us some time ago as to the somewhat obscured prospects of Mr. Voysey's congregation is not correct, that the congregation is strong and hopeful as ever, and that the defunct *Langham Magazine* will be soon revived and placed on an improved footing under the name of the *Langham Review*.

THEOLOGICAL CLASS.

Sunday August 13, 1876.

THE fundamental ground of religion, therefore, is perfectly as sound as the fundamental grounds on which other departments of science base themselves. The question now presents itself as to what this fundamental ground consists of, on which religion makes her position good; or, in other words, what are the elementary convictions, *a priori* principles, or intuitions if you will, which lie at the very foundation of the universal faith of mankind. In the first place philosophers on mature deliberation, have finally concluded that without the instinct of causality, that is to say, the inherent belief that every phenomenon proceeds from a pre-existing source, and is caused by the efficiency thereof, the knowledge of phenomena and the knowledge of Being would not be possible. In the second place the knowledge of self which, says Des Cartes, is the only direct and fundamental knowledge whereupon philosophy establishes her superstructure (a position that remains uncontradicted by all the subversive speculations of the most eminent materialistic thinkers, and is distinctly admitted, among others, by professor Huxley) necessarily implies, and is made possible by the potential, if not always actual, knowledge of a Being beyond the precincts of the existence of self. In the third place the moral consciousness, or as Emanuel Kant says, the Practical Reason of mankind enforces upon itself the existence of a supreme law of duty, which man's consciousness, if its credibility is at all to be relied upon, is compelled to recognize. The perception of an outward intelligence that lurks at the root of all existence that is cognizable, forms also in the fourth place, another fundamental law of thought, though the necessary belief in Being beyond the confines of self may be said to involve it. Now, as these initial judgments of the human consciousness are not pronounced one after another as the problems of existence present themselves for solution before the soul of the infant, but occur, if they occur at all, simultaneously as a practical synthesis upon which all the future notions and convictions of human reason must proceed, the natural result of that synthesis is a natural and universal faith in a Being of some kind higher than human nature, possessing such attributes as his existence under such circumstances may involve. It is altogether an error foreign to the purposes of a rational Theism, to suppose that the consciousness of Divine existence and attributes is drawn upon man's soul in all its completeness with the very first stir of the faculties of his inner nature. It is altogether erroneous to hold that the *a priori* principles of religion, any more than the *a priori* principles of other departments of science, are found ready made, and only formulated within the regions of man's spiritual being, and thus out of this primitive code of Theistic philosophy, all the doctrines of rational religion are derived at once by a mechanical and unconscious process of the Theist's mind. The attacks of the antagonists of Theism in this country would be possible and worthy of some consideration, if such a view of "Brahmic Intuitions" were entertained for a single moment. But the attacks are abused, and because the opinions which those attacks try to controvert, are held to be most absurd. The enemies of Theism, therefore, fight with the spectres which their own imaginations have conjured up, and if any victory is gained in this fruitless battle, that victory neither makes Theism a loser nor a gainer. It is only the elementary materials out of which a divine philosophy is constructed by experience, by contemplation and all the many aids which surround the religious man in life, we find existing as instincts in our religious consciousness. If these materials are well-used, placed under favorable circumstances, surrounded by normal conditions of development, they grow into a rational system of faith. If the contrary happens, they certainly do not perish, but assert their existence by strange, unnatural and sometimes grotesque manifestations of which the mythologies of the world furnish unnumbered specimens. And as tribes of savages have been known to exist without the conceptions of the plainest relations of numbers and magnitudes with the strangest ideas about right and wrong, and the most unreasonable theories about the phenomena and events of the world, so numerous specimens of human nature may here and there be met with, with painfully erroneous opinions and the most utterly mistaken faith about the existence and attributes of the Deity and about His relations with mankind.

Gleanings

It matters little to what pole of doctrine the intellect swings, if the heart hangs unpenetrated and untouched.

Many a stripling considers his excesses as the crackling of the ethereal flame, the dross of inspiration and as essential to the part which he has assumed as the "eye in a fine frenzy rolling." It generally happens, however, that his achievements are limited to the darker hemisphere of genius. He exhibits little of Sheridan save his recklessness, and nothing of Byron except the gin and water. It has been said that "the defects of great men are the consolation of the dunces," but they are also the sorrow of the truly wise who in the very proportions of the achievement, detect the greatness of the aberration. And it is idle to say that there is any necessary connection between the achievement and the aberration while Milton sings to us from the gates of Paradise, we know that the essential inspiration of genius flows not from turbid fountains; and while Newton treads upward among the stars, it is evident that might and comprehensiveness of mind need not the feculent leaven of passion.

The safety and happiness of society flow out from the recesses of private principle.

The wild bird that flies so lone and far has somewhere its nest and brood. A little fluttering heart of love impels its wings, and points its course. There is nothing so solitary as a solitary man.

CHAPLIN.

Literary

The stock-in-trade consisting of steam printing presses, type cases, office furniture, &c., of the printing and publishing establishment, lately known as the *Indian Statesman* of Bombay, have been resold for Rs. 4,600. The machinery of the steam press by W. Conisbee, alone fetched the sum of Rs. 1,850 being purchased by Mr. Dadabhoy, proprietor of the Eagle Printing Press, Bombay; the remainder of the property was put up in small and convenient lots, and it is expected that the whole of the effects will have fetched nearly Rs. 6,000. The bidders were principally Borahs, and parties connected with the Bombay printing presses.

It is proposed to start a first-class Anglo-Indian Magazine in Calcutta. The services of some well-known writers have been secured for its pages.

In consequence of the holidays perhaps, the October number of the *Calcutta Review* makes its appearance in advance. This should be a lesson to those Indian periodicals which are always getting heavily into arrears. The contents of the present number are :—In the Nizam's Country; British Burmah in 1874-75, by H. L. St Barbe B. C. S.; Egyptology; Ancient Indian Metaphysics, by Professor A. E. Gough M. A.; Our Land Revenue Policy in Northern India, by C. H. T. Crosthwaite B. C. S.; The Last of the British Bards by James Hutton; The Opium Revenue, by D. W. K. B.; The Indian Political Department; The Nine-Lakh Chain; or the Maru Feud. By W. Waterfield C. S.; Critical Notices &c.

In connection with the Circular of the 17th July last issued at Bangalore announcing certain rewards for Sanskrit offered by Mr. A. S. Raghavachar, it has been notified at the request of that gentleman, that in honor of the assumption by Her Most Gracious Majesty of the title of Empress of India on the 1st of January next, he has made arrangements for commencing the presentation of the said rewards, on the results of the University examinations, to be held in December next.

The Misses Garrett, Mr. Fawcett's sisters-in-law (who have adopted house furnishing and decoration as a profession) have a work in the press entitled "Suggestions for House-Decoration in Painting, Wood-Work and Furniture."

Lord George Campbell, one of the sons of the Duke of Argyle, is about to publish "Unscientific Letters from the *Challenger*."

Mr. James Routledge, late Editor of the *Friend of India*, has completed a work, entitled "Chapters in the History of Popular Progress in England."

Latest News

—Referring to the Fuller case a correspondent of a contemporary says, that the late Lord Mayo was also satisfied as to the existence of the abominable practice "of striking Natives, as will be seen from the following extract from his Minute on record, expressing his own opinion and feelings about the nefarious practice:—"I must take this opportunity of expressing my opinion as to the abominable pratice of striking Natives. It is a detestable and abominable crime, and ought, in my opinion, to be visited with the most severe punishment."

—The *Aftab Punjab*, a vernacular paper published at Lahore, states that on the 14th an English officer, who was walking out with his wife on one of the public roads at Kohat, was set upon and killed by a gang of the recusant Afridi tribes. The information is not corroborated, and is *primâ facie* a canard.

—A letter from Bellary to a Madras paper says:—"Famine is very close on our heels. Prices of food are rapidly rising. No rain has fallen. Relief works have been started in various parts of the districts, and looting the bazaars is probable. The authorities are prepared for the worst."

—The first shipment of horses of the season from Australia has arrived at Madras and the usual spectacle of landing the animals can be witnessed daily.

—It has been discovered that the Municipal revenues of Madras have for several years, been gradually decreasing.

—The Bombay branch of the Amalgamated Society of Railway Servants, have resolved to remove Mr. Atkins from the Secretaryship of the Association.

—A report is current in London to the effect that the Indian Government are about to establish a mission to Herat.

—Lord Crichton has administered a severe horse-whipping to a Russian at Boulogne, for an indignity to one of his sisters.

—The proposed Ajmere and Ahmedabad Railway is about to be commenced.

—The Amir of Cabul has appointed Mahomed Hashum Khan to be the Finance Minister of his State.

—To avoid giving offence to the official class, the Anjuman-i-Tehzib, Multan, has given up the idea of preparing a list of the Fuller-type cases that have occurred, in the Multan District and its vicinity.

—On the occasion of the birth-day of the Maharajah of Jeypore, His Highness after the State dinner, made a little speech, touching on the custom of the Rajputs to eat out of the same dish and divide their food with each other. He said that from the most ancient times the occupation of the Rajputs caused sympathy with their clansmen to predominate over every other social feeling, so that they all regarded each other as brothers, and brotherly feeling could not be better expressed or more effectually cherished than by eating together in this manner.

—Abdul Hamid, the new Sultan, is a younger son of the late Abdul Medjid, and was born on the 22nd of September, 1842. He has consequently not yet completed his thirty-fourth year.

—Sir Bartle Frere will be present at the Delhi Assemblage on a special mission, and afterwards take up the Governorship of Bombay.

—It is now almost certain that Sir John Strachey is to be the future Finance Minister of India.

—The London correspondent of the *Indian Daily News* says, that the impression in England is that Lord Lytton is "a man at the end of a wire," that is, in his relation to Lord Salisbury.

—The Delhi Camp will assemble on the 23rd December and break up on the 5th January.

—A number of Shravaks are said to have left Bombay for Puna to present a petition to His Excellency the Governor, regarding the proceedings of the Thakore of Pulitana.

—Mr. Dadabhoy Nowroji is going to England to look after the affairs of his firm in London.

—The Mahomedans of Bombay have at a meeting of the Anjuman-i-Islam resolved to raise a subscription for the relief of the Turks wounded and the widows and orphans of those killed in the war.

—The Maharajah of Rewah has returned from Indore.

—The Viceroy is said to have opened the Fine Arts Exhibition at Simla with a witty speech.

—Rama Swami, the Travancore artist, has won the prize for the best figure subject in the Simla Exhibition.

—The Queen has been pleased to give the Countess of Mayo "The Ranger's Lodge," Greenwich Park, Blackheath, as a place of future residence.

Calcutta.

The P. and O. Co.'s S. S. *Venetia*, Commander W. B. Hall, arrived in Bombay Harbour, on Tuesday last, at 8 o'clock, from Suez with the English Mails of the 1st September on board. The following is the list of passengers:—

From Brindisi.—Rev. E. Eberschweiler, Rev. H. Güldmeister, Mr J. Fraser, Mr. McNabb, Mr. Alexander, Mr Kelly, Mr Macpherson, Mr. Kelbey, Mr. Black.

From Southampton.—Major Tyndall, Mr. and Mrs. Dick and child, Mr. J. Wood, Mrs. Mitchell and infant, Mr. Lefroy, Newton, Mr. Newton, Mr. Cooper, Captain Maltby.

From Aden.—Mr. Hossein Cabb, Mr. Syed Rahman.

Mr. W. E. H. Forsyth, Clerk of the Crown, High Court, has obtained three months' leave in extension of the leave granted to him by the Court's Notification, dated 25th April 1876.

FROM and after the 4th October 1876, the Money Order Office, Calcutta, will be located in the Paper Currency Office, No. 1, Dalhousie Square.

ACKNOWLEDGMENTS.

AN Address delivered at the Inaugural Meeting of the Dacca Branch of the National Indian Association by Tarini Kumar Ghose B. A., Deputy Magistrate, Dacca.

The Calcutta Review for October 1876.

Particulars regarding the Second Election for Ward No. 2, Calcutta, held on the 13th September, 1876.

The Madrasah Club Budget for September 1876. Calcutta.

Miscellanea.

AUTOMATONS.

ONE of the barbarities invented by the tyrant Nabis, King of Sparta, was a figure representing his wife Apega, magnificently dressed.

Whenever the king wished to extort money from any one he would at first converse pleasantly with him, portraying the danger to which Sparta was exposed from her many enemies, the great sums of money expended upon the gods, and for the good of the public.

If his words failed, and money was not lavishly offered the king would turn and say, "Probably the talent of persuasion is not mine; but I hope Apega will be able to persuade you." At these words the figure appeared. Nabis taking her by the hand, raised her from the chair, and led her to his guest. The hands, arms and breast of the machine were stuck with sharp iron points, concealed under the clothing. The pretended Apega embraced the unhappy victim, folding him in her arms, and clasping him to her bosom, while he uttered the most piercing cries. Many a poor victim of the cruelty of Nabis came to his death by the embrace of that awful machine.—*Wide Awake.*

Selection.

MORAL DIALOGUE.

(This dialogue is made up of the weekly moral lessons given to the boys of the first three classes of the Calcutta School.)

A.—Look at the world around us. How fair and beautiful it looks, full of laws and arrangements, full of light and sweetness, fit for reasonable creatures to dwell in!

B.—Yes, the world is a fair and good world that we see on all sides, but do you know that there is another world equally, if not more, fair?

A.—What is it?

B.—There is a moral world in which man lives, just as much as there is a world of matter that surrounds him.

A.—Where is the moral world?

B.—My friend, it is in man's thoughts, words, and deeds which are within his heart. Though the moral world is not seen, it is known by the outward lives of men that are seen, and it is exemplified by the words which we apply to express the qualities of things also seen by the eye around us.

A.—I do not understand you, pray explain more fully.

B.—Do you not call some men's action *fair* and other men's actions *ugly*? Are not some men's lives *beautiful*, and other men's lives *foul* and some men's motives *straight* and *clear*, whereas other men's thoughts are *crooked*, *impure*, and *bitter*? And thus you apply the words used to express the qualities of things which are seen, to express the qualities of the moral world which is not seen *without* but *within*.

A.—But are there arrangements and rules as clearly laid down in the moral world as in the earth where we live?

B.—Oh yes. There are laws in the world within us as clear and strong as those which we see around us. If you break these laws you become miserable and lose your place among your fellowmen. If you keep these laws you become happy, and are loved and honored by others.

A.—Prove that you say by an example.

B.—Behold the example of that unfortunate prince the late Gaekwar of Baroda. By breaking the laws of goodness and morality he made himself disliked by his people, lost the health and strength of his mind, and being led from bad to worse, was at last removed from his kingdom, and made unhappy for life. If this can happen to a prince, how much more happen to common people like ourselves!

A.—I understand you now. But how am I do know the laws of moral life?

B.—You will know them by a good moral education, which is unfortunately so much neglected in our public schools. Belive me, to have a pure character, to have sound and noble moral principles is as much object of man's life as the acquirement of knowledge.

A.—Certainly. But I do not see always much impurity or wickedness in the lives of my friends who are taught in public schools.

B.—Men's characters are not always seen outside, it is within the heart that immorality finds its seat. Unless the heart is made pure by good and effective moral precepts, how can it be blameless? Impurity within is sure some day to find its way out in life and action. Let us try therefore to be sweet, good, and beautiful *within*, as well as without.

A.—By what do we know the laws of the moral world, and distinguish its beauty?

B.—There is an eye in the heart of the moral man by which he sees light from darkness, finds out the rules of good actions, and distinguishes right from wrong. That eye you know, is Conscience. It opens in the heart as other powers open, it begins its action very early in life, and the boy, who by moral education is early taught to walk by its light, lives to grow a wise and happy man.

A.—Give me an example of the action of conscience in early life.

B.—Have you heard the name of Theodore Parker—a great and worthy American who tried to abolish slavery, and fight for his faith? When he was a boy of four years, he was one day walking in his father's farmyard. Coming near a pond he saw a large frog, which had just got out of the water, quietly basking in the sun on the moist earth. Young Theodore, like many other boys of his age, took up a stone, and was about to hit at the poor frog's head. But something within seemed suddenly to cry "Boy it is wrong!" He was so much startled by this voice within his heart that the stone fell his hand, and the frog escaped into the water. Theodore quickly ran to his mother, and asked what it was that said, "Boy, it is wrong." His mother fondly took him in her arms, kissed him, and said—"My son, it is the voice of God in the soul of man. If you heed it, it will grow and become clear, and you will be good and happy by your obedience. If you heed it not, it will become weaker and less distinct, and you will be unhappy and exceedingly wretched in the end." Young Theodore obeyed this Voice of God in his heart, and he died wise, good, happy and honored by all.

Advertisements

DOORGA POOJAH SALE!!!

T. E. BROWN & CO.

PURPOSE HOLDING

AN EXTRA UNRESERVED AUCTION SALE

On Saturday, the 30th Instant.

Description of lots intended for this Sale are solicited.

No lots be received except those

TO THE HIGHEST BIDDER.

T. E. BROWN & CO.,

AUCTIONEERS.

P. W. FLEURY'S

HALL OF OPTICAL ILLUSIONS

AND

PEPPER'S GHOST,

No. 62, WELLESLEY STREET.

THE most pleasing, startling, and wonderful Optical Illusion of the day, the Ghost which has enjoyed the greatest popularity in the Royal Polytechnic Institution at London for many years, will be produced with several variations.

EXHIBITION OF

Views of His Royal Highness the Prince of Wales'

Journey through India.

Splendid Photographic Views of Cities, Palaces, Waterfalls, Copies from paintings of the celebrated Artists of Europe and Chromatropes magnified by lenses and Illuminated by powerful Oxy-Hydrogen Lights.

A beautiful Transparency representing the much-admired

AGRA TAJ

AND

MOUNT VESUVIUS

will be exhibited with pleasing dioramic effects

&, &, &

Performance at 8-30 P. M.

ON MONDAY, 25TH SEPTEMBER.

ON TUESDAY, 26TH „

Reserved Seats	... ...	Rs. 2 0
Unreserved Seats	... ...	Re. 1 0

SEWING MACHINES.

BRADBURY & Co.'s celebrated Prize Medal, Domestic and Manufacturing Treadle and Hand.

PEARSON'S Wax-thread Larness Machine.

Sole Agents in India—MULLER & Co.

☞ Sub-Agents wanted.

KNITTING AND DARNING MACHINES,

COTTONS, SILKS, LINEN THREAD,

And all Machine requisites, and extras.

Price lists, free on application.

SMITH, STANISTREET & CO.

Pharmaceutical Chemists & Druggists.

BY APPOINTMENT

To His Excellency the Right Hon'ble

LORD LYTTON, G.M.S.I.

Governor-General of India.

&c., &c.

SYRUP OF LACTATE OF IRON

Prepared from the original recipe. Lactate of Iron in various forms of preparation, have been in use in France, and generally through the continent of Europe, for some years past, and is highly esteemed as one of the most valuable Chalybeate Tonic remedies yet introduced. The Syrup, being the most agreeable as well as convenient form of administration is in most general use. It is a most valuable remedy in the following diseases:—Chlorosis or Green Sickness, Leucorrhœa, Neuralgia, enlargement of the Spleen, &c. In combination with quinine, it has also been very successfully used in the cure of Fever, while to persons of delicate constitution, enfeebled by disease it is invaluable. In bottles Rs. 2 each.

SYRUP OF THE PHOSPHATE OF IRON Rs. 2 per bottle.

SYRUP OF PHOSPHATE OF IRON AND STRYCHNINE, Rs. 2 per bottle.

SYRUP OF PHOSPHATE OF IRON AND QUININE. Price Rs. 2-8 per bottle.

SYRUP OF PHOSPHATE OF IRON, QUININE AND STRYCHNINE (DR. ATKIN'S TRIPLE TONIC SYRUP,) Rs. 2-8 per bottle.

Smith, Stanistreet & Co.

Invite special attention to the following rates the quality guaranteed as the best procurable:—

Pure Ærated Waters.

Made from Pure Water, obtained by the new process through the Patent Charcoal Filters.

				Rs	As.
Ærated plain (Treble Ærated), per doz.				0	12
Soda Water	ditto	„	...	0	12
Gingerade	ditto	„	...	1	4
Lemonade	ditto	„	...	1	4
Tonic (Quinine)	ditto	„	...	1	4

The Cash must be sent with the order to obtain advantage of the above rates.

THE 'PATENT PERPETUAL FOUNTAIN.'

TABLEEPERGNE OR CENTRE PIECE,

FOR SCENT OR FOR PUREWATER WATER

In Richly Electro-Silvered Ware, [*One of the Greatest Novelties of the day.*]

Cash Price Rs. 175.

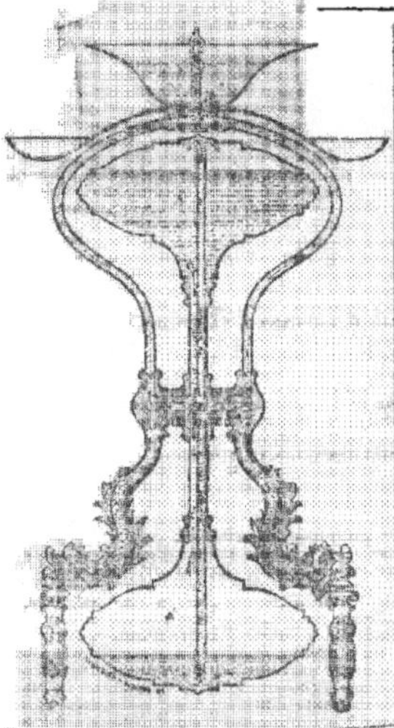

N. B.—The annexed drawing is not a correct representation of the Plated Table Fountains which A. & Co. have for sale. The drawing is only given to show the internal arrangements of the Apparatus and attention is invited to the following description:—

OBSERVE.—A, Al, are two cisterns or reservoirs which are connected together by pipes or tubes B, Bl, C, Cl, mounted on a hollow axis of motion D, surrounding a fixed conical pipe E, having suitable passages F, G, H, therein communicating with the pipes or tubes B, Bl, C, Cl, and I, and with the jet pipe J.

To put the fountain in operation water is poured into the dish or basin K until the lower reservoir is filled and the opening Il is covered. The cisterns or reservoirs A, Al, are then turned on their axis of motion, so as to place the filled cistern or reservoir A at the top when the water therefrom will flow to a level in the jet pipe J, and the water in the basin or dish K by passing down the pipes or tubes I and Bl into the lower cistern or reservoir Al, rises in such lower cistern or reservoir Al and forces the air out therefrom through the pipe or tube Cl, passage F, and tube H, into the upper part of the cistern or reservoir A, where it presses upon the surface of the water therein and forces it out therefrom through the tube C, passage H, and jet pipe J, until all the water in the upper cistern or reservoir A has passed through the jet pipe J and into the lower cistern or reservoir Al by the pipe I passage G, and pipe Bl, when by turning the cistern or reservoirs A, Al, on their axis of motion until the cistern or reservoir Al is at the top, the action of the fountain will be continued; the pipes or tubes B, Cl, which had previously been air passages now becoming water passages, and the pipes or tubes Bl, C, now becoming air passages which had previously served for the passage of water. By these improvements the necessity for alternately filling and emptying the cisterns or reservoirs A, Al, is obviated.

MAKHON LOLL GHOSE.

No. 91, Radha Bazar, Calcutta.

BEGS to invite the attention of the public to several consignments of commercial and fancy stationery of all sorts, including account books of all sizes, made of handmade and machine made paper, by steamers recently arrived, and which he is disposing of at moderate prices. He has been long in the trade, and presumes he has always afforded every satisfaction to the numerous merchants here who have constantly favored him with orders. Mofussil orders accompanied with remittances shall be promptly attended to.

CALCUTTA
The 18th August 1876.

ESTABLISHED 1833

H. C. GANGOOLY & CO.

STATIONERS, DIE-SINKERS, ENGRAVERS, PRINTERS, LITHOGRAPHERS &c.

24, Mangoe Lane, Calcutta.

Cash prices of the following :—

	Rs. As.	Rs.
Whatman's Drawing paper double elephant sizes (40×27) each ...	0 7	0
Mathematical Instrument Boxes	2 8 to	38
Color Boxes	0 4	5

Drawing Pencils, Drawing and Mapping Steel pens and various other requisites in Stationery

NOTICE

INFALLIBLE SPECIFICS FOR ASTHMA, CONSUMPTION, COLIC, GONORRHŒA SPERMATORRHŒA AND DYSENTRY!!!

I AM the son of the late Titaram Paul of Midnapore, who, the public is well aware, was acquainted with specific medicines for the above diseases. I fully learnt the mode of preparing those medicines from my late father, and have cured many people of Midnapore, Calcutta, Hughly, and other places since his death, as the annexed testimonial will shew. Any one wishing to be treated by me can apply to me, care of the Manager of the Indian Mirror.

WOOPENDRA NATH PAUL.

BABU UPENDRA NATH PAL

SIR,

You will be glad to hear that the painful asthma under which I was suffering for the last three years and through which I was nearly brought to the brink of death has been perfectly cured through your treatment. I was laid under the care of several able Doctors and *Kobirajes*, but every treatment on their part proved a failure on me. God bless you and let your cure spread over those who are suffering under the same wretched circumstances.

SURYA CUMAR MAZUMDAR

CALCUTTA,
TANTANEAH,
The 30th August 1876.

Oriental Gas Company Ld.

THE price of Gas in Calcutta and Howrah is reduced to Rs. 5 per 1,000 feet.

Rivers Steam Navigation Co. Limited.

The Steamer "BURMAH" left Calcutta for Assam on 22nd Instant and will leave Gauhati on 27th Instant.

The Steamer "NETUL" will leave Calcutta for Assam on 6th proximo.

For Freight or Passage, apply to

1, LYONS RANGE,
22nd September, 1876.

MACNEILL & Co.,
Agents.

India General Steam Navigation Company, Ld.

SCHOENE, KILBURN & CO.—*Managing Agents.*

ASSAM LINE.

Steamers leave Calcutta for Assam every Tuesday, Kooshtea every Thursday and leave Dibrooghur downward every Saturday.

THE Str. "SIMLA" will leave Calcutta *via Matabanga* for Assam, on Tuesday, the 26th instant.

Cargo will be received at the Company's Godowns, Nimtollah Ghat, up till noon of Monday, the 25th.

THE Str. "ASSAM" will leave Kooshtea for Assam on Thursday, the 28th instant.

Cargo will be received at the Company's Godowns, No. 4 Fairlie Place, up till noon of Tuesday the 26th.

Goods forwarded to Kooshtea for this vessel will be chargeable with Railway Freight from Calcutta to Kooshtea in addition to the regular Freight of this Company.

Passengers should leave for Kooshtea by Train of Wednesday, the 27th.

CACHAR LINE NOTICE
REGULAR FORTNIGHTLY SERVICE.

Steamers leave Calcutta for Cachar and Intermediate Stations every alternate Friday, and leave Cachar downward every alternate Sunday.

THE Str "COLGONG" will leave Calcutta *via Matabanga* for Cachar on Friday the 6th October.

Cargo will be received at the Company's Godowns, Nimtollah Ghat, up till noon of Thursday the 5th proximo.

For further information regarding rates of Freight or passage-money, apply to,

4, FAIRLIE PLACE,
Calcutta 21st September, 1876.

G. J. SCOTT,
Secretary.

How to Enjoy Life.

Is only known when the blood is pure, its circulation perfect, and the nerves in good order. The only safe and certain method of expelling all impurities is to take Holloway's Pills, which have the power of cleansing the blood from all noxious matters, expelling all humours which taint or impoverish it; thereby purify and invigorate and give general tone to the system. Young or old robust or delicate, may alike experience their benignant effects. Myriads affirmed that these Pills possess marvellous power in securing these great secrets of health by purifying and regulating the fluids and strengthening the solids.

Printing Materials.

MILLER AND RICHARD'S PRESSES, TYPES and all requisites always in Stock.

TERMS CASH

EWING & CO.

HAROLD & CO.,

3, DALHOUSIE SQUARE, CALCUTTA

HARMONIUMS.

Harold and Co., call attention to their unequalled stock of rich-toned Harmoniums made especially for India.

FROM RS. 90 TO RS. 900 EACH.

All kinds of Musical Instruments of the best description are always kept in Stock.

CALCUTTA

166, Bowbazar Street.

DR. H. C. SARMA'S

MEDICINE FOR DEBILITY

(NERVOUS.)

Brought on by indulgence in irregular habits, effects of previous diseases, loss of power of limbs, weakness or loss of memory, absent-mindedness, irritable temper, disposition of the mind to displeasure at trifles, want of attention towards business, despair at finding no relief from treatment &c. &c. &c.

Price with postage &c. Rs. 5.

Particulars of disease and directions for despatch required from patients residing at a distance.

DR. SARMA'S FEE.

In cases of Debility (nervous) Rs. 16 per visit. } *In*
For advice at Home......... Rs. 10 " " } *Town*

Out of Town Rs. 500 per Day.

INDIAN TOOTH POWDER.

Strengthens loose teeth, alleviates pain of, and prevents bleeding from Gums, cleanses the mouth, corrects its putrid odour and cures ulceration of the Gums without blackening the Teeth.

Price per packet ... ... Rs. 0 4 0
Postage &c., for 4 packets ... " 0 5 0

TONIC OIL.

Imparts vigour and tone to the paralyzed or relaxed parts of the Human system—Restores proper circulation of blood to weak and inactive parts.

Price for four ounce phial. ... ... Rs. 1 0 0
Postage &c. 0 10 0

HAIR PRESERVER.

Will restore grey hair to its original colour.

It acts directly upon the roots of the hair; removes dandriff, prevents premature falling-off of the hair, and promotes its growth and strength giving it Lustre and Health of Youth.

It also produces a cooling and soothing effect upon the head.

Price, for 4 ounce phial ... Rs. 1 0 0
Postage &c. ... ... " 0 10 0

Copy of Letter received from Raja Chundernath Roy Bahadoor of Nattore.

Wellesley Street, No. 18, Motts Lane, 29th March 1874.

MY DEAR HURISH BABU,—I shall thank you to send me another phial of your "*Excellent Hair Restorer.*" In fact it has done me a great benefit and I should like to have more of it. It has disabused me (young as I am) of old age.

Your's Sincerely

C. N. of *Nattore*

MEDICINE FOR BALDNESS.

Will certainly cure baldness if applied on the bald portion, night & morning according to directions given in the adjoining direction paper

Price per two ounce phial Re. 1 0 0
Postage &c. " 6 0

HEEM-SAGAR OIL.

The best remedy for Headache arising from over-study, intellectual occupation, over-thinking, mental anxiety and weakness, as well as heat of head from living in hot places.

It cools the head and produces very agreeable sensation. Removes Dandriff as well as all other impurities from the head. Promotes the strength and growth of the hair and prevents its premature falling-off.

Price per 4 ounce phial... Re. 1 0 0
Postage &c. ... ... " 0 10 0

MEDICINE FOR LEPROSY.

Price with Postage &c. Rs. 5.

OIL FOR LEPROSY.

And Inveterate Skin Diseases.

Price per 8 ounce phial... Rs. 2 0
Postage &c. ... ... " 0 12

BURN & CO.

RANEEGUNGE Fire bricks are the best Fire Bricks known;—superior to Ramsay's.

9 Rs. per 100,

Fire clay, 40 Rs. per Ton.

Glazed Stone ware, Drainage pipes of all sizes.

BURN & Co.,
7, Hastings Street, Calcutta.

BABU BASANTA KUMAR DUTTA,
HOMŒOPATHIC PRACTITIONER,
No. 20, Sunker Haldar's Lane, Ahiritolah.

FRESH INDENT OF

HOMŒOPATHIC

Medicines and other Requisites.

Have arrived from England.

Medicines, Boxes, Books, Pamphlets; Absolute Alcohol; Cholera-spirit Camphor.

SPECIAL REMEDIES.

For Suppressed, Laborious and Difficult menses; Leucorrhœa.

For Hysteria; Spermatorrhœa; Dysentery; Diarrhœa; Cholera.

For Asthma; Pile; Pain; Sore and Diseases of the Children.

Ice, Lemonade, Soda and Tonic water always.

To be had at
DUTTA'S HOMŒOPATHIC LABORATORY
No. 312, CHITPORE ROAD, BURTOLA, CALCUTTA.

TERMS—CASH.

☛ List can be had on application.

!!! হুকা !!!

!!! HOOKAHS !!!

ENGLISH made Hookahs of various choice designs, colours and sizes, ranging in price from Rs. 2 to 5 each, 60 designs to choose from. Apply to

RADANAUTH CHOWDRY,
378, Jorasanko.

CHUNDER & BROTHERS,

25½ & 112, RADHA BAZAR,

STATIONERY in all its varieties.
PRINTING PRESSES, Inks & Materials.
LITHOGRAPHIC PRESS & Materials.
BOOK BINDING Materials &c.

Printed and published by M. M. RUKHIT, at the INDIAN MIRROR PRESS, No. 6, College Square, for the Proprietors.

The Indian Mirror.

SUNDAY EDITION.

VOL. XVI.] CALCUTTA, SUNDAY, OCTOBER 1, 1876. {REGISTERED AT THE GENERAL POST OFFICE.} [No. 232

CONTENTS.

NOTICE.

All letters and communications relating to the literary department of the Paper should be addressed to the Editor. All other letters should be addressed to the Manager, to whom all remittances should be made payable.

Subscribers will be good enough to bring to the notice of the Manager any delay or irregularity in the delivery of the Paper.

Editorial Notes

THE proposed railway from Ghazipore will, we understand, be connected with the E. I. Railway at Dildarnagore, and not Zumaneah.

WE are glad to learn that the Collector of the 24-Pergunnahs has at last been enabled to come to terms with the owners of the Albert Hall premises, and that he has already completed the purchase in due form for Rs. 23,000, the amount originally asked for by the owners.

LORD NORTHBROOK has written an excellent letter to our esteemed friend, Rajah Romanath Tagore, which breathes throughout the spirit of genuine philanthropy and kindness, and proves his Lordship's continued interest in the welfare of our country.

WE are glad to find the Rev. Mr. Spears, late Secretary to the British and Foreign Unitarian Association, doing so well at Stepney, where he is minister to a congregation of the common people. The building has been considerably improved, and as Mr. Spears says it "is seldom that a Unitarian Chapel proves too small for its members." Mr. Spears's paper too, the *Christian Life*, is prospering very well. It is the third Unitarian newspaper we believe in England.

IF the Mahomedans persecute the Christians in Eastern Europe at the present time, the latter in their turn have for a long time persecuted the Jews, and seem quite willing to continue the persecutions now. The sole reasons for this are the creed of the Jews and their success in business. "The implacable animosity of the Jews" has been excited, and more than half the European world is bitter against the Christians of Roumania and Servia. "It is hopeless," says the *Spectator*, "to reason with a prejudice of this kind, but there ought to be brains enough among Roumanians and Servians to see that the total abolition of Jewish disabilities would do as much for the Christians of Turkey, as a great victory."

THERE appeared sometime ago a letter in our columns drawing attention to the fact that the Brahmos have commenced to celebrate their marriages in the night time in imitation of the Hindu custom on that subject. The Brahmos were accused of the tendency of becoming idolatrous. A friend of ours in Bombay seeing this letter, wrote to us privately to say that the ceremony of marriage in the night time is so far from being a Hindu custom that a large number of weddings in the Bombay Presidency take place during the day. It is quite a matter of indifference to the Hindus in Western India whether a marriage takes place during the night or day. This is perfectly sensible, and we see no reason why some Brahmos, if they think fit, perform their weddings according to the same liberal rule. Of course marriage in the night possesses certain advantages which performed in the day time will not have, but in the case of not a few, day time will have certain peculiar advantages also.

WE are glad to find that the Liberal Social Union of London is still going on very well. It may be said to be a sort of social counterpart to the Langham Congregation of Voysey, but the Liberal Social Union has a wider scope. Mr. Moncure Conway writing on this Society in one of the American papers, (Mr. Conway's letters in American papers have excited a good deal of attention at different times) says:—"The Society is made up of persons whose names have to be proposed by two members, and then balloted for by the whole society. Exclusions are not unfrequent. There is a vigilant committee, a darkly-consulting council of ten, who take care that the society does not suffer from an invasion of bores or vulgarities. The members are persons of culture, generally of the learned professions, and there are especially many very charming and gifted ladies. But the most noted thing about the society is the fact that it has united several hundred gentlemen and ladies for purposes of reciprocal culture, to be promoted by the reading of papers on religious and social problems, and discussions of the same, and by conversation, and that it has done this without drawing any line whatever of a limitary kind as to opinion or race. There are Atheists, Theists, Christians (Churchmen, Swedenborgians, Unitarians, and one or two Congregationalists), Parsees, Brahmos, Brahmins, Japanese, Buddhists, and a large number of Jews. The society has existed ever since anno 1 one of the infallibility of the Pope, and has never had a breath of discord or unpleasantness among all the varieties of belief and humanity. Having myself been a member of it from its first meeting, I can testify that this strange harmony among so many elements is not merely outward but genuine."

A MAN's enemies are said to be of his own household, and surely theological opposition does not seem to be an exception to the rule. It is evident that the Unitarians of Boston are much more bitterly opposed to Theodore Parker, and the publication of his works than the conservative members of the British and Foreign Unitarian Association in London. The *Christian Register* which is the organ of the former body thinks that Parker lost no opportunity to express his contempt for the Unitarian Association, its management, and its publications. The estimate of Parker's writings is thus given :—

We do not believe it is true that Mr. Parker ranks next to Channing in his claims upon the gratitude of all liberal Christians. The influence of James Martineau has been much more powerful in behalf of our cause throughout the world. A single book of James Freeman Clarke's has been read more eagerly and attentively by "Evangelical" ministers and divinity students, and has occasioned a much larger number of valuable conversions to liberal Christian theology than Mr. Parker's writings. These, with all their conceded merits, are too intemperate, dogmatic and illiberal in their treatment of opponents to disarm prejudice or obtain calm and favorable attention to his thoughts. Indeed, to place Mr. Parker above such peers as Dr. Hedge, Dr. Furness, Dr. Sears,

Dr. Bartol, and other able champions of freedom in religion, as if his writings alone have the strongest claims upon our gratitude, is to make a distinction which is as unjust as it is invidious. And we do not believe that there is an increasing demand for his writings. Whether for good or evil, their work is mostly done. His influence, instead of waxing, is evidently waning. Its height was reached some time ago, and no efforts, whether systematic or spasmodic, can prevent its steady decline in the future. His taste and temper are often offensive to conservative lovers of freedom, truth, and justice, while many modern Radicals have advanced beyond sight of his position, or look far down upon his obsolete methods. Only a small minority of our clergymen can now be considered Parkerites or Parker Unitarians. Most of our younger men have found better leaders, and do not wish to be labelled with his name. A good sized volume of selections would contain all of his writings that are either interesting or profitable now, and unless some such "boiling down" is done at an early day another generation will see them hopelessly out of print.

THE following is a much fuller extract from the speech of Lord Northbrook at Falmouth than the one we published a few issues back relating to the spread of Christianity in India :—

In India, where they had to deal with millions of people of different religions, it would be a great evil if the Government, as such, was to connect itself with any particular religious belief, or regarded it as its duty to inculcate upon the inhabitants of India any particular form of faith. It was this fundamental error which lost the great Mogul emperors their power in India. He furthermore entirely agreed with those who thought that it was not right for the Government to teach religion in their schools in that country—not that he undervalued the advantages of combining religion with education in any Christian country, but because he believed that it would not be right for the Government to make any attempt to bring the Hindus and Mahomedans from a different religion to their own, and further, because there would be difficulties almost insuperable in the way of teaching heathen children the Christian religion in any school connected with the Government. Therefore—and he thought rightly so—the efforts for the spread of Christianity in India had been confined to the voluntary exertions of the missionaries, of all denominations. He should be deceiving his hearers if he went so far as to say that, in his opinion, at the present time, these missionary efforts had produced any very tangible result amongst the educated Hindus and Mahommedans. He was afraid that the actual results up to the present day were by no means commensurate with the efforts that were made in that direction; but, on the other hand, where the missionaries had come into contact with some of the aboriginal tribes they have met with great success. In one part of the centre of India he had himself seen two large churches which he was told were filled on Sundays by the villagers of the neighbourhood, and he believed that the number of Christians in that part of India amounted to something like twenty-five thousand people. He had seen the same success attending the missions in other parts of India, and he believed that the service of the missionaries in those parts had been productive of the best results. He believed too, that as education spread in India, and as that education destroyed—as it must destroy—any real belief in the Hindu religion, the masses of the educated Hindus would find some one who would lead them to embrace Christianity in large numbers; but he did not believe they were likely to embrace Christianity in any of the precise forms presented to them now by the different religious communities existing in Europe. On the contrary, his own opinion was that they would go further back, and get rid of much of the dogma which had overlaid the foundations of the Christian religion for the last eighteen hundred years, and that eventually there would be seen in India a form of Christianity more nearly approaching the simple doctrines of the early Christians than either the Roman Catholics, the Church of England, the Wesleyans, or, perhaps, any other religious sect that existed in the present day.

THE English papers received by yesterday's Mail contain accounts of the preliminary meetings and actual opening of the Third International Congress of Orientalists, now in session at St. Petersburg. On the 30th of August, the organizing Committee met the foreign Orientalists who, as corresponding members, were present. But it does not appear that their number was very large. London was represented by Mr. Douglas of the British Museum, Professor of the Chinese Language and Literature in King's College. It is to be regretted that some how or other there was not a single German Orientalist present. The members of the Organizing Committee are the following gentlemen, all Russians :—His Excellency Dr. Basil Grigorief, Imperial Privy Councillor, Professor of the History of the East, and Dean of the Faculty of Oriental Languages in the Imperial University of St. Petersburg ; Mr. Patkanof, Armenian Professor in the same University ; Mr. Chwolson, Professor of Hebrew, Chaldi, and Syriac in the same University ; Mr. Kuhn, *attaché* to the Governor-General of Russian Turkestan for the purpose of archæological researches ; Baron Osten-Sacken, formerly Vice-Director of the Asiatic Department at the Russian Foreign Office, now Director of Internal Affairs at the same Ministry ; and Messrs. Dorn and Veliaminof-Zernof, members of the Imperial Academy of Sciences at St. Petersburg in the department of Mussulman languages and literatures. On the 1st September the opening sitting of the Congress was held in the Grand Saloon of the Imperial University. Dr. Grigorief delivered an eloquent inaugural discourse, giving a hearty welcome to the foreign Orientalists. Mr. Scheter, first dragoman to the French Government, Administrator of the Special School at Paris for the Living Oriental Tongues, responded warmly as the representative of France. Baron Osten-Sacken, as Secretary General of the Congress, read the report of the Organizing Committee. Afterwards the election of the Presidents and Vice-Presidents of Sections was confirmed, and Professor Grigorief was definitively elected President of the Congress. Grouped in a picturesque semi-circle at the bottom of the saloon, were representatives of about a dozen different Asiatic nationalities, arrayed in their Native garb. The Emperor of *Brazil* was present, having enrolled himself as a member of the Congress under the name of Dom Pedro de Alcantara. We regret to see that Russia has been so selfish as to confine the transactions of the present Congress to Russian Asia alone. It is, therefore, no little disappointment to India and other important Eastern countries. We expected grand results from the Oriental Congress; but now, it seems, its objects are different from those which we originally supposed them to be. The *World* takes precisely the same view of it as we did only the other day. Our contemporary says :—"The Russians are certainly astute, for they take without giving. They visit England and India, study all great public works, military and civil, and familiarise themselves with the arcana of local science ; but when asked for a similar courtesy in return, they decline to allow the foreigner to take notes of Kronstadt, or accompany an expedition to Khiva. And now, seeing their way to picking the brains of the world, they have advertised as the subject for the St. Petersburg Congress, 'Central Asia,' tabooing only 'administration,' 'politics,' and 'commerce.' That is to say, everything that might be useful to an aggressive Power will be received with thanks, but anything likely to illustrate its position or proceedings is forbidden."

SPIRITUAL DECADENCE.

SOMETIME ago we tried to point out that the Budhistic idea of Nirvan is not so atrocious as is generally thought. It is the awkwardness of European thought that cannot construe the profound, passionless, though we must admit exceedingly abstract phases of Eastern spirituality. To-day we are going to examine the principle of Budhistic transmigration. Now in the very beginning we must say we do not agree with all that the Budhists hold on the subject of transmigration. But the principle from which they derive their doctrine is singular, and deeply true. The idea is this :—Good men, whose righteousness is the result of a certain course of religious culture and struggle, enjoy the beneficent results of that righteousness for a certain length of time, and then the lamp of their goodness begins to wane. If their hearts are not continually replenished, and their culture is not uniformly sustained, if goodness is not multiplied upon goodness, and holiness does not increase without measure, the spirit suffers a slow decadence, the lustre of the soul fades by contact with the world, and the good man degenerates into a very ordinary, and perhaps an inferior type of humanity. And thus the Devas, glorious "souls of the spiritual (Arupa)" world, "for the present absorbed in ecstacy," may again be born in the carnal life in a very questionable shape, and "the Saints (Devas) of the material (Rupa) world, after leaving their pure abodes will again become subject to desire, and eventually return to birth in hell." Does not such spiritual decadence take place almost every day within our religious experience? "Let him that thinketh he stands take heed lest he fall." And such falls, considered in the highest sense are recorded repeatedly even in the life of the very best among men. Impermanency in spiritual progress is considered by the Budhists to be identical with "the circle of transmigration," and the confusion which men constantly make between the spiritual and material (Rupa and Atman) is said to form a very powerful element in the futility and impermanency of our fancied religious life. The highest and most refined shades of what is in its ultimate analysis material blend off so gradually, and one might say almost imperceptibly, into imagined spirituality —and who but a very few is perfectly free from imagination here—that the confusion seems all but inevitable. Misapprehending what is material and impermanent for that which is ever-lasting, man is inflamed with desire, his spirituality evaporates, his soul is in *dukha* (sorrow) like "a house in flames," he degrades himself into lower sphere of life, thus suffering transmigration, and being born to carnal life as "a bird or a beast." "The wise man," says the *Satdharma Pundarika*, and "escapes from the burning house by various methods, and overleaps the boundaries of all the worlds, and all the births." "The bodies of Devas," we are told, "are perfectly pure, and without any polluting quality; they are, moreover, bright and glistening; their hearts are ever full of joy; and there is no disturbing influence to interrupt their happiness. And yet because the fire of lust oppresses them, there are five signs of decadence visible when their term of happiness is drawing to an end. 1. The flowers when on their heads begin to decay. 2. Their eyes begin to roll about (as if in anticipation of change) 3. The lustre of the body begins to fade. 4. A moisture exudes from their arms. 5. They listlessly absent themselves from their proper places." When the flower of divine grace that rests upon the head of the holy man has once begun to decay, when he looks about for a change in life, for other joys than what his religion accords to him, then the blessed lustre of his spirit becomes gradually dim and faint, till he keeps away from the place that naturally belongs to him under the divine dispensation. When he does all this his fall is not far distant and he may suffer transmigration into a low, irreligious, and animal life. Let us be watchful that the evil signs may not be detected in any one of us.

Correspondence.

THE JOYS OF HEAVEN.

To the Editor of the *Indian Mirror*.

DEAR SIR,—Your correspondent, S. C. S, (*Mirror*, 24th instant) speaks of the things in heaven. Yes, they are blessed realities. How we sing with rapture the hymn:—

"There is a happy land,
Far, far away
Where saints in glory stand,
Bright, bright as day.
O! how they sweetly sing,
Blessed is our Saviour King,
Loud let His praises ring,
Praise, praise for aye.
Bright is that happy land
Beams every eye;
Kept by a Father's hand
Love cannot die."

But, Mr. Editor, allow me to say that a true worshipper of God should "live in God, for God and with God" and should love for God alone and not for the good things that God will give him here or hereafter. God should be all and all unto him. He should enjoy God every moment as it comes to him, and do the will of his Father. His business is with the present, wherein he will find fresh proofs of God's beauty and grace, and should never draw on his imagination to give zest to his love of God. As he should not lift up the veil of the future to think what God will give him a few years hence, so he will never think of his future life, resting contented that God will do best for him in that state as He pleases. "To have no will of its own is the best disposition for a child." May we, with child-like trust, confide in Him for what He will choose to give us. May we long for nothing, but Him and Him alone.

God does not allure us to love Him by the prospect of how we shall enjoy Him with the saints in heaven. A true lover of God seeks Him for Himself alone; he says unto his beloved:—"Thy name is as precious ointment poured forth, therefore do the virgins love Thee." Surely the "bribe of heaven" should not allure us unto virtue or even unto God.

The joys of heaven (black-eyed Houris, or other pleasures, all the same) are the baits which the true worshipper should avoid in his course through life. The Gita (II. 43) depreciates the heaven-mongers and inculcates *Bhakti* or "joy in God" as the only means of attaining Him. The joys of earth or heaven which God will give us, should not be the sauce to our devotion.

As poor sinners, can we say that our bodies are the only barriers to our entering the society of saints in heaven, and joining the anniversaries that are held there day and night? Do we not remember the words that find an echo in our hearts, "Be faithful unto death, and I will give you the crown of Life?" Have we devoted ourselves unto God, and are we His in thought, word and act so that when we die, our Father shall say unto us "my lost ones are found"? Indeed, we should prepare ourselves for heaven, and not think arrogantly of enjoying its joys as soon as we enter its gates.

Let the following prayer of a true believer be ours:—"May I never forget that I am in thy sight; may I always think and act in thy presence to the end that when summoned to appear at the tribunal of my Judge with the whole world of spirits I may not be constrained to flee from before the face of the Holy of holies."

Yours &c.,
A THEIST.

The 30th September 1876.

Devotional

THOUGH grown in years, I am, O God, my Father, I am as a child before Thee. Give me the power to feel as a child. Take away this crookedness from my heart, and this impurity. The hardness that is within me is not worthy of thy child, and this self-relying worldly prudence which does not look up, and does not depend upon thee. I have been in the holy company of children, and felt their innocence and their simplicity. O Lord, it brings sorrow and shame into my heart to see that I am not equal to one of them in love and artless goodness. Make me as holy, as simple, as loving, and as dependent as a child.

THERE is no increase within my soul, O God, my holiness and my love do not grow. The slow and imperceptible advance that there is in all human nature, does not satisfy me amid the great trials of my life. Enable me to feel that Thou art in me always, and that I am pure and tender in Thee. Without constant increase of love and heavenly purity, life loses all its warmth and fragrance. Cleanse and soften everything that is within, and let me grow in the inward gifts.

The Brahmo Somaj

ON Sunday last, the sermon preached in the Mandir was on the subject of Light and Darkness. It was attempted to illustrate that as it is the deep darkness of night that reveals to us myriads of the most brilliant worlds in the firmament, and the dazzling light of the day only conceals them from our view, so the light of this world or in other words, our love of worldly felicity spoils our internal vision, and thus makes us unfit to discover the glorious and most beautiful realities of the spiritual kingdom, which are distinctly unveiled only to those who are in the midst of the darkness of the world; that is, those for whom all carnal lights have ceased to glow. Such men have become utterly blind to the enjoyments of this world, and their eyes are awakened to the glory of the next.

BABUS TRAILOKYA NATH SANYAL, Dino Nath Mozumdar and Woomа Nath Gupta have left Calcutta to preach in the neighborhood of some of the stations on the E. I. Railway line.

BABU BANGA CHUNDER ROY has proceeded to Mymensing to celebrate a Brahmo marriage there.

ON Wednesday last, special prayer meetings were held in the house of Babu Ananda Chunder Nundi in commemoration of the annual festivals which he used to enjoy in his native village in Kaligacha. The service in the morning was conducted by Babu Protap Chunder Mozumdar, and that in the evening by Babu Gour Govinda Roy.

BABU GOUR GOVIND ROY has proceeded to Cumarkhali to celebrate the anniversary of the local Brahmo Somaj there, which takes place to-day.

BABU AMRITA LAL BOSE went to celebrate the fourth Anniversary of the Hatkhola Chandernagore Brahmo Somaj. There was an open air meeting on last Friday evening, and so also throughout yesterday in connection with the anniversary festival.

BABU PROTAP CHUNDER MOZUMDAR has proceeded to Krishnagar, where he is expected to stay for about a fortnight.

BABU DINO NATH MUZUMDAR on his way to Rampore Haut stopped for two days at Chandernagore where he performed the namkar n ceremony of the son of Babu Dino Nath Chakerbutty. More than a hundred persons, both male and female, who were invited on the occasion, evinced great interest in the ceremony, and did justice to the dinner served to them.

ON Sunday last, Babu Keshub Chunder Sen conducted the service in the Ghazipur Brahmo Somaj. The service was performed partly in Bengali and partly in Hindi. Nearly a hundred persons were present on the occasion. The Somaj holds its weekly meetings in the house of Lala Hurbanslal, an old gentleman nearly eighty years of age.

Gleanings

THE who trusts in the word of God knows that he will find nothing in the material universe but the will of God.

Life is a crucible. We are thrown into it, and tried. The actual weight and value of a man are expressed in the spiritual substance of the man. All else is dross.

No condition is unfavorable to virtue, where virtue is.

That is the sublimest condition into which a man can come when he perfectly surrenders to God his will, and does what He likes because he likes to do God's will.

The great crises of man's existence do not consist primarily in changes of place, or of external fortune, but in changes of state or inward condition.

I CONSIDER myself as the most wretched of men, full of sores and corruption, and who has committed all sorts of crimes against his King; touched with a sensible regret, I confess to Him all my wickedness, I ask His forgiveness, I abandon myself in His hands, that He may do what He pleases with me. This King, full of mercy and goodness, very far from chastising me, embraces me with love, makes me eat at His table, serves me with His own hands, gives me the key of His treasures; He converses and delights Himself with me incessantly, in a thousand and a thousand ways, and treats me in all respects as His favourite. It is thus I consider myself from time to time in His holy presence.—*B. Lawrence.*

GOD, has infinite treasure to bestow and we take up with a little sensible devotion, which passes in a moment. Blind as we are, we hinder God, and stop the current of His graces. But when He finds a soul penetrated with a lively faith, He pours into it His graces and favours plentifully; there they flow like a torrent, which, after being forcibly stopped against its ordinary course, when it has found a passage, spreads itself with impetuosity and abundance.—*Ibid.*

LIFE is real! Life is earnest
And the grave is not its goal.
Dust thou art, to dust returneth,
Was not spoken of soul.

Not enjoyment and not sorrow;
Our destined end or way;
But to act, that each to-morrow
Find us further than to-day.

Let us, then, be up and doing
With a heart for any fate
Still achieving, still pursuing
Learn to labor and to wait.

Longfellow.

Literary

CAPTAIN BURNABY will publish a book about Central Asia.

SERIOUS personal differences are reported between the British Ambassador at Constantinople and Mr. Galienga, the *Times'* correspondent at that part.

MR. WALTER of the *Times* has gone to New York, on a pleasure trip.

DR. FIELD of the New York *Evangelist*, who visited India a short time ago, has, after a tour round the world, arrived in America.

THE HON. W. E. Robinson, formerly editor of the New York *Tribune*, is preparing a book upon the "Origin and Source of the American people." In it he intends to show that Irishmen and their descendants form a large majority of the present population of America, and in all departments of the history of that country have acted the most prominent parts.

A CORRESPONDENT of the *Bombay Gazette* says that the Amalgamated Society of Railway Servants in India has advanced the editor of the *Railway Service Gazette* of Jubbulpore Rs. 10,000, in order to have an organ in which to ventilate their grievances.

Scientific

THE business of the British Association commenced on the 6th September last, at Glasgow. In the evening the President, Professor Andrews, of Belfast, delivered the opening address, in which he traced the progress of scientific discovery during the year. A vote of thanks to the President was proposed by the Duke of Argyll, seconded by Professor Sir William Thomson, and carried by acclamation. On the 7th addresses were read in the various sections—by Sir William Thomson on Physical Science, by Professor Young on Geology, and by Sir George Campbell on Economic Science and Statistics. Among those who read papers were Professor James Thomson, Mr. James Croll, and the Duke of Argyll.

WE learn that the Salicylic Acid treatment of Cholera which was introduced by Surgeon Major Boustead of the Bombay Army, has been extensively tried in Cashmere and other places by both medical men and intelligent Native gentlemen outside the profession with unexpected good results.

THE *Academy* of September 2 contains an interesting account of a literary and archæological excursion in Java by Mr. A. Burnell. Mr. Burnell agrees with Dr. Cohen Stuart in his opinion that it is to Southern India that the former Hindu civilisation of Java must be traced. In conclusion, he says:—"The number of statues to be seen everywhere, the inscriptions and endless ruins, show that Central Java must once have been a wonderfully successful Indian colony. The richness of the soil may have helped, but it is impossible to avoid the conclusion that the Brahmins and Buddhists were more successful, in every way, with the Polynesian Javanese than they have been with the low-type Dravidians of Southern India."

Latest News

—THE amount subscribed in the Madras Presidency to the Mitchell Memorial Fund now amounts to Rs. 6,156.

—THE Duke of Buckingham, the Governor of Madras, has received an advance of Rs. 6,000 to pay his expenses in attending the Delhi Assemblage. But how is the present retrenchment policy of the Government of India to be reconciled with the enormous expenses to be incurred in the Delhi Assemblage?

—THE Abyssinian envoy at Cairo is arranging for peace. He has brought to the Khedive three horses.

—A WOMAN in new York is under arrest for "cruelty to her husband."

—A SKATING RINK is to be established at Madras.

—THE great bridge on the Holkar State Railway over the Nerbudda will be opened on the 5th of October by H. H. Holkar. Special trains will run from Khundwa and Choral for the convenience of the guests who will be invited to a grand breakfast in honor of the event.

—MISS SWAIN, M. D., of India is now at Castile, New York, having been quite ill again; and is now unable to travel or enjoy much but her quiet room.

—THE Italian Minister, the Marquis of Mantegazza, has been found guilty of forging the names of King Victor Emmanuel and Prince Humbert to a number of bills, and sentenced to eight years' penal servitude.

—THE King of Dahomey has made all the Europeans at Whydah prisoners, and declares that if 10,000 Englishmen be sent to fight him, none shall return to tell the tale.

—THERE is some proposal of offering the portfolio of Finance in Turkey to an Englishman, Mr Foster, the Director of the Imperial Ottoman Bank. Mr. Foster, exercises considerable influence on the mind of the Grand Vizier, Mehemed Rushdi, and it is believed that owing to his recommendation that Colonel Valentine Baker has been offered a commission on the Staff of the Turkish Army, with the rank of Brigadier-General.

—THE Duke of Connaught has arrived at Vienna, and will be present at the Military Manœuvres, accompanied by the Crown Prince.

—THE Duke of Edinburgh left Besika Bay, on the 6th instant, and will pass through Constantinople on his way to the Crimea.

—FOR the convenience of persons corresponding with India, and Australia, *via* Brindisi, postage stamps of the value of 8d. have been issued in England.

—MAHARAJAH SCINDIAH has sent his congratulation to Her Most Gracious Majesty the Queen on the assumption of the title of Empress through the Political Agent; moreover, to show his feelings of loyalty, he has proposed to give an entertainment to the British Officers and soldiers stationed at Moror in the new building named the "Indur Bhuban."

Calcutta.

WE regret to hear of another death—that of Mr. C. H. Wilson of the firm of Messrs. F. Smyth and Co. Mr. Wilson was a Justice of the Peace, and was liked by all who knew him.

THE Perseverance Ice Company have again commenced operations.

SOME Hindu lads showed their skill in gymnastics during the Pujah, at the mansion of Rajah Harendra Krishna.

MR. DICKENS, the Magistrate, will resume his seat in the Police Court to-morrow.

WE are glad to note that there has been a sudden rise in the price of silver. This will have a good effect on the exchange.

WE fully sympathise with the writer in the *Pioneer* when he refers to the present condition of Calcutta in the following terms:—"Calcutta is terribly dreary. Every office and shop is closed, and the place is deserted by every one who can afford time and money for a holiday. One almost feels inclined to commit a crime and seek a lodging in the jail, where there is at least no want of company. In the course of an evening walk, a face one knows is now a rare God-send, and is heartily welcome. For those who can get away, the Durga Pujah holidays are a great institution, but those who cannot get away have a most melancholy time of it in Calcutta."

THE Calcutta correspondent of the *Pioneer* writes:—"If there is a reform wanted in India, it is a reduction of the Calcutta High Court Durga Pujah holidays. Here there are two Vacation Judges always in Calcutta. One of **them** might take a sessions during the vacation. High Court Judges **in** Calcutta are rarely overworked. The Chief Justice only **sits** four **days in the** week, and one of the **Puisne Judges, I believe,** adopts the same practice. **There is sometimes** one Judge sitting on Saturdays, **but** all the others have a holiday on Saturdays. Besides the hardship to prisoners, civil suitors who are entitled to some consideration are put to very great inconvenience by the long vacation. If the Court was made for the Judges there would be some excuse for the present long holiday, but I always thought that the Court and the Judges were made for the suitors." Why is not a portion of the Durga Pujah holidays allowed during the hot weather when people need rest most? As regards the two Vacation Judges, one of them has already gone to Madras holiday-making.

The P. and O. Co's s.s. *Hydaspes*, Commander Bennoldson, arrived in Bombay harbour, on Wednesday last, at 6 o'clock from Suez with the English mails of the 8th September **on board.** The **following is** the list of passengers:—

From Southampton.—Lieut. Byves, Mr. C. Hastings, Mr. Leishman, Mr. and Mrs. Carr, Mrs. G. Randall, Mr. and Mrs. Barlow, Mr. T. Harris, Mr. Robinson, Mr. F. Kennedy, Mr. R. B. Arch, Mr. F. Lean, Mr. R. Greaves, Mr. R. Mellison, Capt. Thornhill, Mr. W. Huck, Madame Loux.

From Venice.—Mr. Simson, Mr. W. B. Jones, Major Brown, Lieut. Robinson, Lieut. Sawyer.

From Brindisi.—Mr. W. B. Medlicot, **Mrs** French, Capt. Palmer, Mr. Campbell, **Mr.** Hoornby, Mr. Cartwright.

From Aden.—Deood and friend.

DOMESTIC OCCURRENCE.

BIRTH.

BOSE.—On Friday, the 22nd September 1876, at about three A.M. the wife of Babu Durga Kumar Bose of Sylhet, of a son.

Advertisements

P. W. FLEURY & CO.,

BUILDERS, ENGINEERS,
AND
SCIENTIFIC INSTRUMENT MAKERS.
No. 44, Free School Street.

WE, beg to intimate that we have been engaged in the above line of business for the past 20 years, and trust that our Constituents will continue to favor us with their work, which will meet with prompt attention on our part.

In connection with buildings, we undertake the erection and repairing of machinery at moderate charges; as also execute all descriptions of Iron and Brass work.

We can assure the Public that we undertake the repair and erection of Houses and the laying of Water-supply Pipes on moderate terms, and guarantee to keep all the water-pipes and brass fittings supplied by us in good working order for three years, free of extra charge. We also guarantee to keep dwelling-houses' roofs water-tight for three years, free of extra charge, for such houses as we have repaired.

For purposes of illumination, we prepare our patent Chromatic Transparencies representing Coat-of-Arms, Landscapes, Scenery, &c., at prices, ranging from Rs. 80 to 340 each, according to size and design.

FOR SALE:

Light! Light!! Light!!!

Electric Light Apparatus complete, worked with a battery of 50 large cells, on Bunsen's principle	500	0
Ditto ditto, with 40 cells, smaller size ...	400	0
Ditto ditto, with a powerful 44-cell Cast-iron Battery, on Callan's principle ...	300	0
Lime Light Apparatus, complete, with Iron Gas-holder, and Copper Retort ...	150	0
Oxy-Hydrogen Light Apparatus with safety Jets, 2 Iron Gas-holders, and Retorts, complete	200	0
Hink's Patent Duplex Wall Lamps, with chimney	5	8
Ditto Duplex Lamp, with chimney and globe	7	8

Patent Leblanche Battery

For constancy, durability, and cleanliness, this battery is unequalled; price for each cell, with chemicals	3	8
Bunsen's Galvanic Battery, 9 inches, by 4 inches	7	8
Magneto-Electric Machine, with single magnet	14	0
Prismatic Compass 3-inch in solid leather case, by Elliott, second hand	22	0
Ditto, 4-inch, by Simmons, second hand ...	30	0

P. W. FLEURY & Co.,
No. 44, FREE SCHOOL STREET.

NOTICE.

INFALLIBLE SPECIFICS FOR ASTHMA, CONSUMPTION, COLIC, GONORRHŒA SPERMATORRHŒA AND DYSENTRY!!!

I AM the son of the late Titaram Paul of Midnapore, who, the public is well aware, was acquainted with specific medicines for the above diseases. I fully learnt the mode of preparing those medicines from my late father, and have cured many people of Midnapore, Calcutta, Hughly, and other places since his death, as the annexed testimonial will shew. Any one wishing to be treated by me can apply to me, care of the Manager of the Indian Mirror.

WOOPENDRA NATH PAUL.

BABU UPENDRA NATH PAL.

SIR,

You will be glad to hear that the painful asthma under which I was suffering for the last three years and through which I was nearly brought to the brink of death has been perfectly cured through your treatment. I was laid under the care of several able Doctors and *Kobirajes*, but every treatment on their part proved a failure on me. God bless you and let your cure spread over those who are suffering under the same wretched circumstances.

SURYA CUMAR MAZUMDAR

CALCUTTA,
TANTANEAH,
The 30th August 1875.

BURN & CO.

RANEEGUNGE Fire bricks are the best Fire Bricks known; — superior to Ramsay's.

9 Rs. per 100.

Fire clay, 40 Rs. per Ton.
Glazed Stone ware, Drainage pipes of all sizes.

BURN & Co.,
7, *Hastings Street, Calcutta.*

LIGHT! LIGHT!! LIGHT!!!

PATENT PORTABLE AIR GAS MAKING APPARATUS,

SUITABLE FOR

Churches, Chapels, Schools, Country Mansions, Private Houses, Railway Stations, Barracks, Manufactories, Collieries, Mills, Offices, &c., &c.

THIS *simple* and *effective* Gas-making Apparatus supplies a want long felt of having Gas at places where no Gas Works exist. It may be introduced without any more trouble than the simply affixing of any ordinary Gas meter, and is about the same size for the same number of lights. The *piping* and *fitting* arrangements are in every respect the same as for the use of ordinary Gas. The *cost* of the Gas produced is about the same as is charged for ordinary Coal Gas, and the light produced is *more brilliant* and of *a greater illuminating power*; it is also *free from the impurities of Coal Gas*. The Gas, if used with the Patent Burner, is of great heating power, and hence suitable for cooking and heating purposes, or in manufactories for soldering, &c. The apparatus is PORTABLE; there is NO DANGER WHATEVER (ordinary care being used when filling it); the Gas is PRODUCED IN AN INSTANT WITHOUT ANY FIRE OR OTHER ARTIFICIAL HEAT.

Further particulars may be obtained from MESSRS. EDWARD THOMSON & CO., Contractors for Drainage, Water and Gas, who are appointed Sole Agents for the above apparatus, which can be seen working any week day between the hours of 6 A.M., and 6 P.M., at their place of business.

39, *BENTINCK STREET, CALCUTTA.*

3, DALHOUSIE SQUARE, CALCUTTA

HARMONIUMS.

Harold and Co., call attention to their unequalled stock of rich-toned Harmoniums made especially for India.

FROM RS. 90 TO RS. 900 EACH.

All kinds of Musical Instruments of the best description are always kept in Stock.

Rivers Steam Navigation Co. Limited.

The Steamer "BURMAH" left Calcutta for Assam on 22nd Instant and has left Goalundo on 27th Instant.

The Steamer "NEPAUL" will leave Calcutta for Assam on 6th proximo.

For Freight or Passage, apply to

1, LYONS RANGE, 22nd September, 1876. — MACNEILL & Co., Agents.

India General Steam Navigation Company, Ld.

SCHOENE, KILBURN & Co.—*Managing Agents*

ASSAM LINE.

NOTICE.

Steamers leave Calcutta for Assam every Tuesday, Kooshtea every Thursday and leave Debroogurh downward every Saturday.

THE Str. "SIMLA" will leave Calcutta *Via Matabanga* for Assam, on Tuesday, the 26th instant.

Cargo will be received at the Company's Godowns, Nimtollah Ghat, up till noon of Monday, the 25th.

THE Str. "ASSAM" will leave Kooshtea for Assam on Thursday, the 28th instant.

Cargo will be received at the Company's Godowns, No. 4 Fairlie Place, up till noon of Tuesday the 26th.

Goods forwarded to Kooshtea for this vessel will be chargeable with Railway Freight from Calcutta to Kooshtea in addition to the regular Freight of this Company.

Passengers should leave for Kooshtea by Train of Wednesday, the 27th.

CACHAR LINE NOTICE

REGULAR FORTNIGHTLY SERVICE

Steamers leave Calcutta for Cachar and Intermediate Stations every alternate Friday, and leave Cachar downward every alternate Sunday.

THE Str. "COLGONG" will leave Calcutta *via Matabanga* for Cachar on Friday, the 6th October.

Cargo will be received at the Company's Godowns, Nimtollah Ghat, up till noon of Thursday the 5th proximo.

For further information regarding rates of Freight or passagemoney, apply to,

4, FAIRLIE PLACE, Calcutta 21st September 1876. — G. J. SCOTT, *Secretary*.

ESTABLISHED 1833

H. C. GANGOOLY & CO.

STATIONERS, DIE-SINKERS, ENGRAVERS, PRINTERS, LITHOGRAPHERS &c.

24, Mangoe Lane, Calcutta.

Cash prices of the following :—

	Rs.	As.	Rs.
Whatman's Drawing paper double elephant sizes (40×27) each ...	0	7	0
Mathematical Instrument Boxes	2	8 to	16
Color Boxes	0	4 ,,	5

Drawing Pencils, Drawing and Mapping Steel pens and various other requisites in Stationery

DENONAUTH DEY AND SONS,

No. 80, CLIVE STREET.

Godowns, No. 24 Machooa Bazaar Street.

IMPORTERS OF METALS, IRONMONGERY, HARDWARE, TEA GARDEN TOOLS.

CHUBBS' LOCKS AND SAFES, RODGER'S CUTLERY Carpenters', Blacksmiths', Coopers', Engineers Builders' and Planters' Tools.

SADLERY, STEAM, GAS & WATER-FITTINGS,

PAINTS, OILS, MARINE STORES &c. &c.

Priced Catalogues supplied on application, at Re. 2. each.

R. K. GHOSH'S

HOMŒOPATHIC DISPENSARY.

No. 1, *Gour Mohun Mukerjee's Street, Simla.*

CALCUTTA.

HOMŒOPATHIC Medicine; Medicine chests of sizes,—containing medicine in tube phials; Homœopathic Books, tracts and pamphlets (English and Bengali); Dr. Rubin's "Saturated spirits of Camphor,"—(the best preventive and cure for cholera where medical aid is not available); and other Homœopathic requisites are sold here at a moderate price. Terms cash. Mofussil orders are promptly executed.

R. K. GHOSH,
Homœopathic Practitioner,
Manager.

Oriental Gas Company Ld.

The price of Gas in Calcutta and Howrah is reduced to Rs. 5 per 1,000 feet.

BEST BURMAH SEGARS.

The undersigned respectfully begs to call the attention of Consumers and Dealers to the following Segars which are made of the choicest leaves and are of superior quality; guaranteed free and pleasant to smoke :—

No. 1	per 100	Rs.	1	0	0
,, 2	,, ,, ...	,,	0	12	0
,, 3	,, ,, ...	,,	0	10	0
Dolly Varden	,, ,, ...	,,	1	4	0
Sedans	,, ,, ...	,,	1	2	0
Babington	,, ,, ...	,,	1	2	0
Trichinopolly	,, ,, ...	,,	1	8	0

Liberal discount allowed to wholesale purchasers.

All descriptions of Oilman's stores, Preserved Provisions and Tea to be had at moderate prices.

BONOMALLY SHAW,
128, *Radha Bazar.*

BABU BASANTA KUMAR DUTTA,

HOMŒOPATHIC PRACTITIONER

No. 20, Sunker Hulder's Lane, Ahiritolah.

FRESH INDENT OF

HOMŒOPATHIC

Medicines and other Requisites.

Have arrived from England.

Medicines, Boxes, Books, Pamphlets;
Absolute Alcohol; Cholera-spirit Camphor.
Special Remedies.

For Suppressed, Laborious and Difficult menses; Leucorrhœa.

For Hysteria; Spermatorrhœa; Dysentery; Diarrhœa; Cholera.

For Asthma; Pile; Pain; Sore and Diseases of the Children.

Ice, Lemonade, Soda and Tonic water always.

To be had at

DUTTA'S HOMŒOPATHIC LABORATORY

No. 312, CHITPORE ROAD, BURTOLA, CALCUTTA

TERMS—CASH.

☞ List can be had on application.

CALCUTTA

106, Rowbazar Street.

DR. H. C. SARMA'S

MEDICINE FOR DEBILITY

(NERVOUS)

Brought on by [illegible] irregular habits, effects of [illegible] loss of power of limbs, weakness or loss of memory, [illegible], irritable temper, [illegible] of the mind to displeasure at trifles, want of [illegible], despair at finding no relief [illegible] &c., &c.

Price [illegible]

[illegible] for despatch [illegible]

[illegible]

In cases of Debility (nervous) Rs. 30 per visit. } In
For [illegible] Rs. 10 " } Town

Out of Town Rs. 500 per Day.

INDIAN TOOTH POWDER.

Strengthens loose teeth, alleviates pain of, and prevents bleeding from Gums, cleanses the mouth, corrects its putrid odour and cures ulceration of the Gums without blackening the Teeth.

Price per packet ...	...	Rs. 0 4 0
Postage &c., for 4 packets	...	" 0 5 0

TONIC OIL.

Imparts vigour and tone to the paralyzed or relaxed parts of the Human system.—Restores proper circulation of blood to weak and inactive parts.

Price for four ounce phial.	...	Rs. 1 0 0
Postage &c.	...	0 10 0

HAIR PRESERVER.

Will restore grey hair to its original colour.

It acts directly upon the roots of the hair, removes dandriff, prevents premature falling-off of the hair, and promotes its growth and strength giving it Lustre and Health of Youth.

It also produces a cooling and soothing effect upon the head.

Price, for 4 ounce phial ...	Rs.	1 0 0
Postage &c.	"	0 10 0

Copy of Letter received from Raja Chundernath Roy Bahadour of Nattore.

Wellesley Street, No. 18, Motts Lane, 29th March 1874.

MY DEAR HURISH BABU,—I shall thank you to send me another phial of your "*Excellent Hair Restorer.*" In fact it has done me a great benefit and I should like to have more of it. It has disclosed me (young as I am) of old age.

Your's Sincerely

C. N. of *Nattore*

MEDICINE FOR BALDNESS.

Will certainly cure baldness if applied on the bald portion, light & morning according to directions given in the adjoining direction paper

Price per two ounce phial Rs.	1	0	6
Postage &c.	"	6	0

HEEM-SAGAR OIL.

The best remedy for Headache arising from over-study, intellectual occupation, over-thinking, mental anxiety and weakness, as well as heat of head from living in hot places.

It cools the head and produces very agreeable sensation. Removes Dandriff as well as all other impurities from the head. Promotes the strength and growth of the hair and prevents its premature falling-off.

Price per 4 ounce phial...	Re.	1 0 0
Postage &c.	"	0 10 0

MEDICINE FOR LEPROSY.

Price with Postage &c. Rs. 5.

OIL FOR LEPROSY.

And Inveterate Skin Diseases.

Price per 8 ounce phial ...	Rs.	2 0
Postage &c.	"	0 12

THE 'PATENT PERPETUAL FOUNTAIN,'

TABLEEPERGNE OR CENTRE PIECE.

FOR SCENT OR FOR PUREWATER WATER.

In Richly Electro-Silvered Ware. [*One of the Greatest Novelties of the day.*]

Cash Price Rs. 175

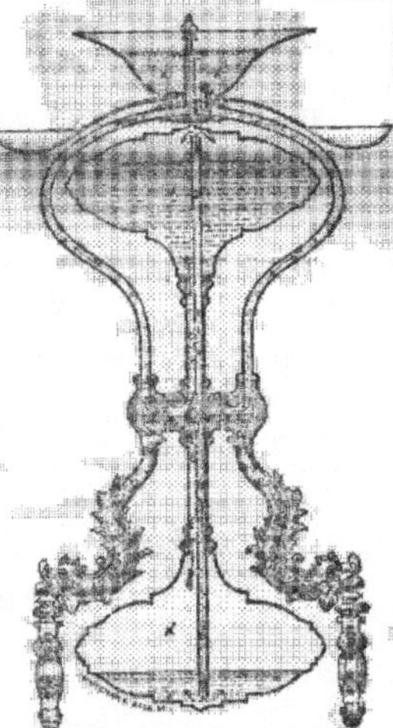

N. B.—The annexed drawing is not a correct representation of the Plated Table Fountains which A. & Co. have for sale. The drawing is only given to show the internal arrangements of the Apparatus and attention is invited to the following description:—

OBSERVE—a, a1, are two cisterns or reservoirs, which are connected together by pipes [illegible]

To put the fountain in operation water is poured into the dish or basin K until the lower reservoir is filled and the opening f1 is covered. The cisterns or reservoirs a, a1, are then turned on their axis of motion, so as to place the filled cistern or reservoir a at the top when the water therefrom will flow to a level in the jet pipe J, and the water in the basin or dish K by passing down the pipes or tubes I and a1 into the lower cistern or reservoir a1, rises in such lower cistern or reservior a1 and forces the air out therefrom through the pipe or tube c1, passage F, and tube B, into the upper part of the cistern or reservoir a, where it presses upon the surface of the water therein and forces it out therefrom through the tube C, passage H, and jet pipe J, until all the water in the upper cistern or reservoir a has passed through the jet pipe J and into the lower cistern or reservoir a1 by the pipe I passage G, and pipe a1, when by turning the cistern or reservoirs a, a1, on their axis of motion until the cistern or reservoir a1 is at the top, the action of the fountain will be continued; the pipes or tubes B, c1, which had previously been air passages now [illegible] tubes B1 C, now becoming air passages which had previously served for the passage of water. By these improvements the necessity for alternately filling and emptying the cisterns or reservoirs a, a1, is obviated.

SMITH, STANISTREET & CO.

Pharmaceutical Chemists & Druggists

BY APPOINTMENT

To His Excellency the Right Hon'ble

LORD LYTTON, G.M.S.I.

Governor-General of India.

&c., &c.

SYRUP OF LACTATE OF IRON

Prepared from the original recipe. Lactate of Iron, in various forms of preparation, have been in use in France, and generally through the continent of Europe, for some years past, and is highly esteemed as one of the most valuable Chalybeate Tonic remedies yet introduced. The Syrup, being the most agreeable as well as convenient form of administration is in most general use. It is a most valuable remedy in the following diseases:—Chlorosis or Green Sickness, Leucorrhœa, Neuralgia enlargement of the Spleen, &c. In combination with quinine, it has also been very successfully used in the cure of Fever, while to persons of delicate constitution, enfeebled by disease it is invaluable. In bottles. Rs. 2 each.

SYRUP OF THE PHOSPHATE OF IRON Rs. 2 per bottle.

SYRUP OF PHOSPHATE OF IRON AND STRYCHNINE, Rs. 2 per bottle.

SYRUP OF PHOSPHATE OF IRON AND QUININE. Price Rs. 2-8 per bottle.

SYRUP OF PHOSPHATE OF IRON, QUININE AND STRYCHNINE (DR. ATKIN'S TRIPLE TONIC SYRUP,) Rs. 2-8 per bottle.

Smith, Stanistreet & Co.

Invite special attention to the following rates the quality guaranteed as the best procurable :—

Pure Ærated Waters.

Made from Pure Water, obtained by the **new process through the** Patent Charcoal Filters.

				Rs.	As.
Ærated plain (Treble Ærated),	per doz.			0	12
Soda Water	ditto	"	...	0	12
Gingerade	ditto	"	...	1	4
Lemonade	ditto	"	...	1	4
Tonic (Quinine)	ditto	"	...	1	4

The Cash must be sent with the order to obtain advantage of the above rates.

THEISTIC BOOKS,

FOR SALE.

URDU.

Rahat Hakiki	...	...	Rs.	0	3	0
Nizam Korat	...	...	...	0	2	0
Kasaful Ilham	...	...	...	0	3	0
Kholasa, of, Ascol Brahm Dharm ...				0	1	0

HINDI.

Upasana Pudhati ...		...	Rs.	0	1	6
Brual Putrika or Hymn book			...	0	1	0
Tut Bodh	...	...	...	0	8	0
Upanishid Sar	...	...	...	0	8	0
Dhorm Dipika	...	...	...	0	0	6

ENGLISH.

Claims of so called Revealed Religion	...	...	Rs.	0	3	0
New Life	...	...	...	0	0	6
Living God	...	...	...	0	1	0
Higher and Lower Virtue...			...	0	1	0

Apply to the Secretary,

BRAHMO SOMAJ OF THE PUNJAB,

Lahore.

Printing Materials.

MILLER AND RICHARD'S PRESSES, TYPES and all requisites always in Stock.

TERMS CASH.

EWING & CO.

Printed and published by M. M. ROKHIT, at the INDIAN MIRROR PRESS, No. 6, College Square, for the Proprietors.

The Indian Mirror.

SUNDAY EDITION.

VOL XV.] CALCUTTA, SUNDAY, OCTOBER 8, 1876. | REGISTERED AT THE GENERAL POST OFFICE. | [No. 238

CONTENTS.

NOTICE.

All letters and communications relating to the literary department of the Paper should be addressed to the Editor. All other letters should be addressed to the Manager, to whom all remittances should be made payable.

Subscribers will be good enough to bring to the notice of the Manager any delay or irregularity in the delivery of the Paper.

Editorial Notes

THE departure of a Hindu Sannyassi from Bombay for England by the last Mail, testifies amply to the progress that India is making socially in these days. The name of the Sannyassi is Rasidar Bawah. He has gone with Dadabhoy Nowroji in the same steamer. It is said the object of his visit to England is to see Maharajah Dhulip Sing. The expenses of his journey will be paid by a Hindu Merchant of Bombay.

AT last the vacant see of Calcutta is about to be filled up. The telegram informs us that Archdeacon Johnson of Chester has already accepted the see. We pretend not to know much of Archdeacon Johnson, but if he be the very Rev. G. H. S. Johnson M. A., F. R. S., who was for sometime the Dean of Wells, he will be a fit successor to the late Bishop Milman. The very Rev. G. H. S. Johnson won high honors in mathematics in Queen's College, Oxford. He is well-known as a mathematician, and is the author of a "Treatise on Optics." He was for sometime the Savilian Professor of Astronomy in the Oxford University.

WE are glad to hear that the Report of the Calcutta Native Ladies' Normal School will be out very soon. It will consist of a *resumé* of the operations of the last few years; the reports of the European ladies who examined the classes in different branches; an abstract of the proceedings of the last annual assembly on the occasion of the distribution of prizes; and a few specimens of the English composition of the young ladies that were read before His Honor the Lieutenant-Governor. A statement of accounts is appended to the Report. We hope the public will come in aid of the School after the publication of the Report.

SIR CHARLES DILKE has startled English nation by instituting a parallel between the Turkish atrocities in Bulgaria and the British actrocites in the N. W. Provinces in the memorable year of the Indian Mutiny. He condemns English public opinion which was inert when Christians oppressed the Hindus, but is awakened when Mahomedans oppress Christians. We must say that Sir Charles Dilke has somewhat shot beyond the mark. Surely the conduct of British soldiers, on the testimony of English historians themselves, *was* savage and brutal, but then the offence which had been received was also savage and brutal. Nor were their excesses on a scale that might be compared with the doings of the Turks. But what British soldiers did in 1856 in putting down the Indian Mutiny was bad enough.

BENJAMIN FRANKLIN is stigmatized by many Christians as a Deist. He had doubts of the divinity of Christ, and he repudiated many other dogmas of orthodox Christianity. But he was nevertheless a very pious man. The *Independent*, an American paper, publishes some of the opinions and sentiments of the closing years of his life in a recent number. "During the last two years of his life he had not two mouths in all of freedom from pain. No repining ever escaped him. Even when the intervals from pain were so short that his words were frequently interrupted, I have known him to hold a discourse in the sublimest strain of piety. The warmest, the tenderest love cheered the last day of one who, if God is love, was as like God as any man then alive." Here is what Franklin writes about his own religious views:—"Here is my creed. I believe in one God, the Creator of the universe. That he governs it by his providence. That he ought to be worshipped. That the most acceptable service we render to him is doing good to his other children. That the soul of man is immortal, and will be treated, with justice, in another life, respecting its conduct in this. These I take to be the fundamental points in all sound religion; and I regard them, as you do, in whatever sect I meet with them."

SOME people more or less connected with the Brahmo Somaj, seem to be laboring under an exceedingly wrong idea on the subject of the Brahmo Missionary system. They think that our Missionaries may anytime set themselves up as a religious hierarchy oppressing men's private lives and outriding their convictions and conscience, that they may constitute themselves into a privilaged class burdening the whole community by their exactions. The facts are otherwise. Brahmo Missionaries far from setting themselves up, purpose to devote themselves to the service of their fellow-brethren by consigning their whole existence to learn and practise holy truths. They have left all other work to work for the Brahmo Somaj, with the simple purpose of being able to help those who have fewer opportunities than they have in this direction. They cannot say they have been able to discharge this duty satisfactorily, but they continually aim and struggle with that object in view. They have nothing to exact from the community. They are most grateful for the help, material and moral, which the Brahmos have offered them at all times. But they depend upon their Heavenly Master for their support and success. Instead of being exacting, they wish to be ready always to meet the exactions which the brethren of their church may desire to make upon their time and energy. No, they do not want to set themselves up, but to be set down for the service of God and man.

WHEN one thinks it worth while to express oneself in a certain language, it is quite to be desired that this should be done correctly, and with some elegance. But there is a fictitious taste always tending to rise which places disproportionate importance upon the manner of using a language. At present among our young countrymen there is an insufferable pedantry on the subject of using the English language. Every one who can write and speak English with tolerable accuracy at the present day, thinks that he has reached the very goal of his destiny. A perpetual attempt is kept up to disseminate false ideas on the matter of the glory of using the language of our conquerors with fluency. The result manifests itself in the extravagant statements and exhibitions made in print and in speech illustrative of the state of public feeling on the point. So much false value set upon superficial expertness in a foreign tongue, without any corresponding estimation of the solid worth of truth, sentiment, and principle, whether ethical or religious, is simply demoralizing to the generation in the midst of which we live. We do not despise the power of language; on the contrary we think it to be an essential and a noble gift. But language as apart from character, reality and a worthy aim, is simply so much jingling of false and hollow metal. First matter, then manner. First have all the worth of the character of the Englishman, or of the Hindu, either, and then you can wield the English language with effect

---

THE Englishman's abstract love of justice is wonderfully witnessed in the celebrated Bravo case which has ended in such a *fiasco*. Mr. Charles Bravo died amidst violent symptoms of poisoning which, it is as likely as not, may have been self-administered with the object of suicide. But as there was doubt on this point an enquiry was ordered by the Home Secretary. After considerable expense and worry on the part of Government, and on the part of Mrs. Bravo and her friends, no satisfactory conclusion was arrived at. There was a white heat of excitement from one end of the country to the other, and people's sympathy was as much excited on one side, or on the other as in the celebrated Tichborne case. At the failure of the first inquiry, a second is insisted upon. The sense of justice of the whole nation seems to have been awakened. The whole affair suggests in our minds the thought as to what would be done in this country if a similar case were to happen. How many deaths take place even in Calcutta about which dark suspicions are awakened in men's minds but nobody cares about them; and in the Mofussil how very much worse is the case! Our sense of Justice thus gets gradually weakened and inert, and when it is time for action, we have not the nerve to bestir ourselves. Strict and unflinching inquiry into crimes and lawlessness of every kind, educates the moral character of the entire nation. But in India every thing is more formal than actual, and though our rulers and administrators be impartial and conscientious, the machinery and the moral sense of Government are weak and cumbersome.

THE education of girls is a moot point in these days. The general maxim that can be laid down is, educate a girl for all the stations of life she can fill. A woman is by nature prone to acts of benevolence and hospitality. Educate your girl's benevolence by bringing her face to face with suffering, and teaching her how to relieve it. Teach her to be solicitous, and thoughtful for others' comfort. Let her learn to work to make others happy. A woman is naturally prone to religion. Cultivate her fear and love of God early. Teach her the simple lessons of goodness and piety, and let her reverence for holy things be awakened betimes. A woman's intelligence is generally fine and clear. Get her to learn a few things well, and be furnished with general information on important matters. Her unemployed time, teach her to spend in reading and writing. A woman is above all a domestic being. Her domestic education must not on any account be neglected. A woman that cannot make her home restful, sweet and comfortable, must always remain a useless creature, and a thorn in the flesh. No amount of fine intelligence and outward grace can compensate for the absence of laborious and skilled domestic habits. Let all young women who are under education of any sort, take careful note of this. The tendency at the present moment is decidedly in the direction of making a clever doll of a girl, a pleasantness to the eye, but a trouble to the heart. Taste and grace, and intelligence and refinement we appreciate, but a young woman of moderate circumstances who has not the nerve to work steadily four hours out of every twelve for her home and husband is a fool, and will cut a sorry figure in the world. Let, therefore, steadiness in habits of domestic usefulness and work be taught to our girls by all means; let them learn to be good wives, and good mothers, faithful to all their duties.

WORTHY old Hindu gentlemen, in fact, all Hindus more or less, stand aghast at the strange ideas which European moralists of the town entertain on the subject of cruelty to animals. A friend of ours the other day, had his horse suddenly taken ill. It was a fine little animal, and as he did not want to lose it, he sent it to one of the best livery stables for the veterinary surgeon to examine it, and cure it if possible. The reply soon came that the horse was incurable, but the authorities of the stables detained it with the benevolent object of killing the beast for a consideration. The proprietor insisted upon having his horse back, got it treated, and cured by a Native, and it is now in as splendid condition as ever before. Another gentleman had an old horse, which was somewhat lame, but served him well, and was strong enough. One fine morning the agents of the Society for the Prevention of Cruelty to Animals pounced upon the horse and *gari*, and dragged both into the Police compound. The owner got the Magistrate to inspect the horse, but he pronounced it unserviceable. Whereupon the agents of the Humane Society directly wanted to have the animal shot, and with that object sent it to one of the livery stables. This time the stable-authority proved more merciful than the Society for the Prevention of Cruelty to Animals, said that the horse did not deserve to be killed, and advised that it should be let loose in some garden in the suburbs. What Hindu gentlemen do not understand, is that humanity-mongers should desire so thoughtlessly to take the life of innocent brutes, when they profess so much horror to see them suffer from ordinary ailments. The Hindu cannot reconcile with his notions of mercy the conduct of condemning an animal to die when it can yet live for many years, perhaps with some amount of the suffering. Lameness is always considered by him less horrible than death.

CHRISTIANITY and Mahomedanism seem now to be pretty much at war with each other. The great movement in England in denouncing the Turkish atrocities, has been followed by a counter-movement in India among its Mahomedan population for the expression of sympathy with Turkey. The English people, it is evident, were far from prepared for such a thing. In the course of the debate in Parliament on the Royal Titles Bill, some of the members had no hesitation in declaring that the Mahomedans of India cared very little for the Sultan of Turkey. They thought that the followers of Islam in India divided their homage between the Akhund of Swat and the Shah of Persia. Lord Northbrook on his return from India, also assured the English public that the Indian Mahomedans took very little interest in the fate of Turkey. It is now even believed by not a few Englishmen in England that if the British Government in India maintained its reputation for good Government, the Mahomedans here would not trouble much about the fate of Turkey. But the public meetings of the Mahomedans lately held in Bombay, Peshawur and Calcutta have belied the conjectures of the British public. The tie of religion —the greatest of all ties—seems to be so strong among the Mahomedans all over the world that their sympathy with each other cannot be mistaken for a moment. It is not likely that their sympathy will be less than that exhibited by the Christians in England for those in Bulgaria. In the meantime, the British Ministry, in its present situation, will find itself placed on the horns of a dilemma. The British public has already pretty freely given vent to its feelings of horror, indignation and grief at the excesses committed by the Turkish soldiery upon the Bulgarian Christian, and has spoken too loudly to make its voice heard. But the British Ministry has a delicate task to perform. It knows that the driving of the Turks out of Europe, as the British public demands, means the possession of Turkey by ambitious Russia. England has always done more for Turkey than any other Power of Europe, in order to save the Sublime Porte from Russian grasp. If she now withholds protection and support from Turkey, all that the blood and treasure that she has hitherto given for Turkey will go for nothing, and only assist Russia in gaining all her much-prized objects. When the British Ministry further comes to receive the petitions of the Mahomedans of India on behalf of Turkey, it will find its difficulty still further aggravated to satisfy the British cry for the destruction, as is reported, of 65 Christian villages and of 15,000 Christian men, women and children. At the sametime, England must maintain her good name for humanity and justice. She who has always been the first at least in India, to put down outrages and cruelties, cannot allow herself to follow the un-English policy of supporting oppression, murder and rapine. She cannot desist from punishing atrocities at which Mr. Gladstone says—Hell itself might blush. But the Englishmen must guard against one thing. They must not be led away by passion. As Mr. Grant Duff says they should keep their heads cool. We do not much approve of the language used by some speakers at the indignation meetings held in England in connection with Turkish affairs. One gentleman spoke of "kicking the Turks into the Black Sea," and he used other words which are highly offensive to Mahomedanism. Then again we find distinguished ecclesiastics indulging in violent anathemas upon the Turks. Bishop Myine of Bombay has been found fault with for criticising rather too sharply the conduct of the Disraeli Ministry in connection with this Turkish question. But Bishop Myine, it appears, has only caught the contagion from his compatriots in England. The Rev. C. H. Spurgeon went so far as to offer a special prayer in the Metropolitan Tabernacle, beseeching God to cause the Turks to be defeated for the atrocities they had committed!" Be that as it may, England and India, at this time, present two extremes. While the British public have been condemning, in unmeasured terms, Turkish atrocities, protesting loudly against Her Majesty's Government continuing its support and countenance to Turkey declaring openly Turkey to be unworthy of a place in the civilized world, asking vehemently for the recall of Sir Henry Elliot, the British Consul at Constantinople, and praising highly the Special Correspondent of the London *Daily News* for exposing Turkish barbarities, the Mahomedans of India have been holding meetings to sympathise with Turkey and to call upon England to support the sublime Porte in every way in her power.

UNOBSERVED TENDENCIES.

TENDENCIES are unconscious. The roots and developments of character must lie deeper and further than the reach of self-reflective analysis. A man may be a good critic of others, but he is very rarely an impartial critic of himself. The cause of this is not pride always, it is in superficial characters only that pride is the cause of self-forgetfulness. But the very personality of man prevents the detection of hidden tendencies, whithin which his character grows for better or for worse, and ultimately settles itself. The eye that sees the whole universe cannot see itself. The man that knows his own mind about everything is very rare. No autobiography can be fully complete or just, neither Harriet Martineau's, nor John Stuart Mill's. It is for this reason good sometimes to see ourselves as others see us. To have our unobserved tendencies explained by really thoughtful men that take an interest in us, is indeed a rare privilege. If there is mutual confidence, no friendly communication is more profitable. But such confidence is unfortunately rare. We dare not tell our friends what we think of them. Things are easily enough said in their absence, or in their presence when we have lost our temper. But to lay bare the secret tendencies of character, which are sooner seen by the outsider than by the man whom they belong to, in a friendly and earnest spirit, we do not seem to be at all prepared.

Certain tendencies grow unobserved in the midst of individual circumstances. The company a man is obliged to keep constantly; the work which a man has undertaken to do; the ideas with which he has frequently to come in contact; the obstacles he has to deal with and subdue; the reading and relaxations which he must sometimes seek, unconsciously produce in him tendencies which unless they are noticed by lookers-on, and corrected so far as need be, will grow and mature themselves into hard elements of character, good or bad, according to the nature and antecedents of the man. Most careful must each man be in choosing and guiding his circumstances. He should, as often as he can, throw himself into the midst of opposite influences to those which his immediate surroundings are likely to exercise upon his mind. For instance, those who live surrounded by secular occupations and companions always, should now and then seek to associate as exclusively as possible with men whose occupations, thoughts, and characters are devoted to spiritual matters only. And religious men may very profitably to themselves at times step out of their exclusive sphere to see how the world outside is going on, and what may be learnt there.

There is another very important thing which brings about the development of tendencies. Every man accepts certain moral principles, notions of good and bad, proper and improper. These are modified very much by the nature, habits, and requirements of the individual who adopts them. Now, moral principles in themselves are few and simple enough. Applied to the feelings, desires and convictions of men as fostered by education, they become exceedingly complex and very generally produce tendencies which, if not checked and directed, will assume serious forms, and harden themselves into peculiarities, and not unoften, into vices also. Strange acerbities of temper, wonderful instances of narrowness and hardness of heart, unaccountable eccentricities, sometimes very blameworthy indeed, and serious blots are formed in men whose general principles of moral life are laudable and quite unexceptionable. But the wholesome influences of their characters are neutralized by certain over-grown tendencies parent to all others except to themselves. Moral principles, however, firm and exalted, require the constant watchfulness of impartial and impersonal observation, to watch them as they operate on character, and no one need feel safe as to the practical manifestations of his life if he has nothing but his principle to back him. He needs human correctors always.

But the most formidable source of unobserved tendencies has yet to be pointed out. Nothing moulds the character of a man so much as the religious attitude of his being. Now whatever may be the outward semblance of agreement between man and man, there is little doubt that so far as the history of the world yet goes, every one has a secret religion of his own. Faith, prayer, contemplation, experience, self-discipline, the influence of example, all exercise a joint influence upon the peculiar temperament and susceptibilities of each man, send down roots of conviction and principle within the depths of his heart, and throw out on all sides branches, and shoots of tendencies that become sturdier the longer they remain, each of them in time the mother of many roots and branches independently. A man's tendencies,—and what truly religious man has them not?—are the unfailing growth of the generous vitality within him. They have an equal proneness to be good or bad in every case. When well and faithfully directed they are never bad. When carelessly and prayerlessly suffered to grow they are seldom perfectly wholesome; frequently they lead to serious evil. Sects, unfortunate facts as they undoubtedly are, are the results of misdirected religious vitality. And so long as religion remains a living thing, so long sects will have a *tendency* to multiply. Every religious tendency when it grows into a principle, must embody itself when the tendencies of men who believe in the same religion have assumed the shape of principles; unless there is a power that combines them and creates within them a real, deep, and intense warmth of sympathy, these principles will seek their determinate embodiments, and when embodied will clash against each other. Religious tendencies, therefore, must be watched much more carefully than other tendencies, and demand a much more effective co-operation The more of religious life infused into a system, the more of earnestness there is in it, the more pronounced will the individual tendencies of those be who believe in it. And the more enthusiastic they are, the more devoted and self-sacrificing, the less will be their probability of their discovering and correcting their own tendencies. The sword is always hanging over the head of the religious man. The nearer he is to goodness, the more closely does evil track in his heels. In furthering the cause of his own regeneration how often does he forget the community that is directly or indirectly dependent upon his care! In trying to benefit the community he loses himself. O, that the unobserved tendencies of every religion were watched and pointed to him by his friends, that the tendencies of all were mutually understood and appreciated, and that the God of goodness were acknowledged and honored by each in his individual aspirations and destiny!

Devotional

EXPLAIN to me, O my God, the doctrine of the communion of saints. The best and truest men have gone to thee from this world of sin and sorrow, to dwell with thee in joy and blessedness for ever. Their company I seek, O Lord, next to thy holy company. Though they are absent thou canst make me dwell with them in spirit now and then and profit by their sanctifying and gladdening presence. Grant me this privilege for thy mercy's sake.

IF there are deep and secret messages which thou wouldst communicate to me for my soul's benefit, draw me, O Loving Guide, into some hidden place, and there reveal the glad tidings. Tell me where thou wilt speak to me, on the top of the hill or the banks of the river or in a rural retreat, and I will be there at the appointed time and wait for thy heavenly voice. O God, I wish to be instructed by thee in the deeper counsels of heaven.

SHALL we meet in heaven, O Lord. Thou sayst we shall, if we are united in spirit here on earth. It grieves us to find there is no such loving union among us, and that, therefore, there is little prospect of our forming one loving family in heaven. Give us, Kind God, such love and purity as shall knit us together for time and eternity in thy holy house.

WHY shall I feel dejected and humiliated if men revile and abuse me? Rather should I feel thankful unto thee, O Lord, that men are teaching me to be humble and lowly by their kind, though apparently unkind treatment. Teach me, my God, to feel my unworthiness.

The Brahmo Somaj

THE *Utsab* in connection with the ninth Anniversary of the Lucknow Brahmo Somaj will take place to-day, according to the following programme. Babu Aughornauth Gupta has gone there to celebrate the occasion. There will be a distribution of *atta* and *dall* to the poor.

MORNING.

Hymns	from 6 to 6½
Divine Service	from 6½ to 9

AFTERNOON.

Religious Conversation	from 1 to 3
Reading from Scriptures and Text Books	from 3 to 4
Meditation and Prayers	from 4 to 5
Explanation of *Slokas* from the *Gita* &c.	from 5 to 6

EVENING.

Hymns	from 6½ to 7
Divine Service.	from 7 to 9

THE *Utsab* of the Hyderabad (Sindh) Brahmo Somaj, was celebrated on Sunday, the 17th September last. Our Hyderabad correspondent writes:—"The attendance at the Morning Service which was conducted in the vernacular language of the country (Sindhi) was large. The Service commenced at 7 and lasted till 9. The subject of the Sermon was "Faith in God." All went away pleased with what they heard. The mid-day proceedings consisted of readings from *Bhagavat Gita*, the Granth and the Christian and Mahomedan Scriptures and *Kirtan*. At 3 P. M., prayers were offered by individual members (Sindhi and Dekani.) From 4 to ten minutes passed 5 o'clock there was service and a sermon on the "Growth of Life" in Marhathi. The evening Service was conducted in the English language, and ended with a sermon on, the "Importance of Religion to Man." There were 4 Europeans present on the occasion. The proceedings closed as they had begun, amidst joy and thanksgivings, and each returned home a wiser and and happier man."

ON Sunday last Babu Bejoy Kishen Goswami conducted service in the Brahma Mandir. The subject of the sermon was "What is True Worship?" True worship, he said, is an attitude of the soul in which it feels the nearness of God. The very vernacular term *upasana* is derived from a Sanskrit root, which with the prefix *upa* means to sit close by some one. Hence *Brahmopasana* means to sit close by the Supreme Spirit. He also said that whoever tastes the sweets of truly worshipping God or, in other words, enjoys the nearness of Divinity, feels naturally inclined to move every day onward to heaven or to place his soul in such a position as it may feel itself nearer to the Object of Worship.

OUR correspondent at Chandernagore informs us that on Friday, the 29th September, the *Nagar Sangkirtan* in connection with the Fourth Anniversary of the Chandernagore Hatkholah Brahmo Somaj took place. On the same day, our Missionary, Babu Amritalall Bose, delivered an open air address on the field of Lal Dighi. The subject was:—"Salvation in this age may be obtained by *Nam Sadhan* alone." About 500 men were present on the occasion, including some respectable inhabitants of the place. Some Native Sepoy guards of Chandernagore were so charmed with the address that repeated applauses came from them. The next day, Saturday, the *Utsab* took place. Babu Amritalall Bose delivered in the morning a sermon on "Sadhan." There were readings from various scriptures by Babu Gopalchunder Ghose of Sibnagor in the afternoon. The evening service was conducted by Babu Amritalall Bose. Some of the prayers offered by him were so pathetic that, our correspondent informs us, many Brahmos and Brahmicas present were moved to tears. On Friday, the 3rd instant, upwards of 300 beggars were supplied with rice.

ON Sunday and Monday last, there were open-air meetings at Chinsurah and Shahagunge, Babu Amrita Lal Bose delivered lectures on both occasions. There were at Chinsurah nearly 500 persons and at Shahagunge nearly 200 persons present. A correspondent informs us that the lectures were heard with rapt attention and repeated applauses.

Gleanings

SORROW does not predicate annihilation, but development.

THE weak sinews become strong by their conflict with difficulties. Hope is born in the long night of watching and tears. Faith visits us in defeat and disappointment, amid the consciousness of earthly frailty and the crumbling tombstones of mortality.

Literary

SIR LOUIS MALLET is writing a pamphlet on the Silver Question.

Latest News

—MR DADABHOY NOWROJI left for England by the steamer which left Bombay on Monday last. He has got a large mercantile firm in London.

—THERE will be fire-works at Delhi on the occasion of the Imperial Assemblage, costing about Rs. 30,000. Messrs Brock & Co of London have got the contract for the same.

—IT is said that public executions will be abolished in India.

—BOTH the Ahmednugger and Sholapore districts in the Puna Presidency, are threatened with a serious famine. In Sholapore, the Government School is vacant, merely because the pupils have gone to seek bread wherever they can find it.

—IT is apprehended that serious disturbances will take place on the death of the Akhund of Swat. The Lahore *Public Opinion* says:—"The Mullahs are opposed to the selection by the Akhund of his younger son as his successor, on the ground that he is much too young and also of too peaceable a disposition to be relied upon for the furtherance and support of the cause of 'Islam,' which is now seriously threatened by the aggressive progress and designs of Nazarene infidels. They are, therefore, agitating, and using their influence, to secure the popular election of the eldest son immediately on the occurrence of the expected demise of the Akhund."

—A RANGOON paper says that four pariah vessels have arrived there lately with some 600 passengers, "the greater portion of whom are women, destined to be sold as mistresses to their countrymen."

—THE King of Burmah will send eight Burmese youths to England, Russia, Italy, and New York, to study languages, and attend large manufacturing works.

—SOME of the robbers implicated in the atrocious Ahmednugger Mail robbery have been apprehended. One of them turns out to be a village Policeman.

—THE construction of the State Railway from Ajmir to Ahmedabad, is not to be undertaken by the Public Works Department, but let on contract.

—PUNDIT DYANUND SARASWATI is still at Lucknow.

—HER Highness the Begum of Bhopal intends to build *Serais* for travellers at all the chief places of her State.

Calcutta.

DENGUE seems to have made its appearance again in Calcutta. What with the *Suraka Mari* and the Dengue, existence in Calcutta at the present moment is getting almost unbearable. The *Suraka Mari*, it appears, has caused great alarm to the Native community. Several cases of death are reported. Have the Homœopathic Doctors got any remedy for it?

THE contract for the pyrotechnic exhibition, to take place in Calcutta on the New Year's Day in honor of the Queen's assumption of the Imperial title, has been given to Messrs. Brock & Co., of Crystal Palace, London, at a cost of 25,000 Rs.

THE *Statesman* understands "that Sir Stuart Hogg goes home in March next, and that Mr. Peacock will have the refusal of the vacant appointment. In the event of not accepting it, it will probably be offered to Mr. Bell or Mr. T. B. Lane." We shall be glad of Mr. Peacock's appointment. But as regards the two last-named gentlemen, one is as good as the other.

THERE are whisperings of a cyclone taking place in Calcutta. Atmospheric disturbances are apprehended in the Bay of Bengal.

THE Coroner will hold an inquest in connection with the late frightful accident on the River, on the 12th instant.

Advertisements

LIGHT! LIGHT!! LIGHT!!!

PATENT PORTABLE AIR GAS MAKING APPARATUS,

SUITABLE FOR

Churches, Chapels, Schools, Country Mansions, Private Houses, Railway Stations, Barracks, Manufactories, Collieries, Mills, Offices, &c., &c.

THIS *simple* and *effective* Gas-making Apparatus supplies a want long felt of having Gas at places where no Gas Works exist. It may be introduced without any more trouble than the simply affixing of any ordinary Gas meter, and is about the same size for the same number of lights. The *piping* and *fitting* arrangements are in every respect the same as for the use of ordinary Gas. The *cost* of the Gas produced is about the same as is charged for ordinary Coal Gas, and the light produced is *more brilliant* and of *a greater illuminating power*; it is also *free from the impurities of Coal Gas*. The Gas, if used with the Patent Burner, is of great heating power, and hence suitable for cooking and heating purposes, or in manufactories for soldering, &c. The apparatus is PORTABLE; there is NO DANGER WHATEVER (ordinary care being used when filling it); the Gas is PRODUCED IN AN INSTANT WITHOUT ANY FIRE OR OTHER ARTIFICIAL HEAT.

Further particulars may be obtained from MESSRS. EDWARD THOMSON & CO., Contractors for Drainage, Water and Gas, who are appointed Sole Agents for the above apparatus, which can be seen working any week day between the hours of 6 A.M., and 6 P.M., at their place of business.

39, *BENTINCK STREET, CALCUTTA.*

P. W. FLEURY & CO.,

BUILDERS, ENGINEERS,

AND

SCIENTIFIC INSTRUMENT MAKERS.

No. 44, Free School Street.

We beg to intimate that we have been engaged in the above line of business for the past 20 years, and trust that our Constituents will continue to favour us with their work, which will meet with prompt attention on our part.

In connection with buildings, we undertake the erection and repairing of machinery at moderate charges; as also execute all descriptions of Iron and Brass work.

We can assure the Public that we undertake the repair and erection of Houses and the laying of Water-supply Pipes on moderate terms, and guarantee to keep all the water-pipes and brass fittings supplied by us in good working order for three years, free of extra charge. We also guarantee to keep dwelling-houses' roofs water-tight for three years, free of extra charge, for such houses as we have repaired.

For purposes of illumination, we prepare our patent Chromatic Transparencies representing Coat-of-Arms, Landscapes, Scenery, &c., at prices, ranging from Rs. 80 to 300 each, according to size and design.

FOR SALE.

Light! Light!! Light!!!

Electric Light Apparatus, complete, worked with a battery of 50 large cells, on Bunsen's principle 500 0

Ditto ditto, with 40 cells, smaller size ... 400 0

Ditto ditto, with a powerful 44-cell Cast-iron Battery, on Callan's principle ... 300 0

Lime Light Apparatus, complete, with Iron Gas-holder, and Copper Retort ... 150 0

Oxy-Hydrogen Light Apparatus with safety Jets, 2 iron Gas-holders, and Retorts, complete 200 0

Hink's Patent Duplex Wall Lamps, with chimney 5 8

Ditto Duplex Lamp, with chimney and globe 7 8

Patent Leblanche Battery

For constancy, durability, and cleanliness, this battery is unequalled; price for each cell, with chemicals 3 8

Bunsen's Galvanic Battery, 9 inches, by 4 inches 7 8

Magneto-Electric Machine, with single magnet 14 4

Prismatic Compass 3-inch in solid leather case, by Elbot, *second hand* 22 0

Ditto 4-inch by Simmons, *second hand* ... 30 0

P. W. FLEURY & Co.,

No. 44, FREE SCHOOL STREET.

SEWING MACHINES.

BRADBURY & Co.'s celebrated Prize Medal, Domestic and Manufacturing Treadle and Hand.

PEARSON'S Wax-thread Harness Machine.

Sole Agents in India—MULLER & Co.

☞ Sub-Agents wanted.

KNITTING AND DARNING MACHINES,

COTTONS, SILKS, LINEN THREAD,

And all Machine requisites, and extras.

Price lists, free on application.

DENONAUTH DEY AND SONS,

No. 80, CLIVE STREET.

Godowns, No. 24 Machoon Bazar Street.

IMPORTERS OF METALS, IRONMONGERY, HARDWARE, TEA GARDEN TOOLS.

CHUBBS' LOCKS AND SAFES, RODGER'S CUTLERY, Carpenters', Blacksmiths', Coopers', Engineers, Builders' and Planters' Tools.

[illegible], STEAM, GAS & WATER FITTINGS,

PAINTS, OILS, MARINE STORES &c. &c.

Priced Catalogues supplied on application, at [illegible] each.

HAROLD & CO.,

3, DALHOUSIE SQUARE, CALCUTTA

HARMONIUMS.

Harold and Co., call attention to their unequalled stock of rich-toned Harmoniums made especially for India.

FROM RS. 90 TO RS. 900 EACH.

All kinds of Musical Instruments of the best description are always kept in Stock.

Rivers Steam Navigation Co. Limited.

The Steamer "BURMAH" left Calcutta for Assam on 22nd and Goalundo on 27th September.

The Steamer "NEPAUL" will leave Calcutta for Assam on 10th Current.

For Freight or Passage, apply to

1, Lyons Range, 4th October, 1876. MACNEILL & Co., Agents.

India General Steam Navigation Company, Ld.

SCHOENE, KILBURN & Co.—*Managing Agents*

ASSAM LINE.

NOTICE.

Steamers leave Calcutta for Assam every Tuesday, Kooshtea every Thursday and leave Debrooghur downward every Saturday.

THE Str. "MADRAS" will leave Calcutta *Via Matabanga* for Assam, on Tuesday, the 10th instant.

Cargo will be received at the Company's Godowns, Nimtollah Ghat, up till noon of Monday, the 9th.

THE Str. "PATNA" will leave Kooshtea for Assam on Thursday, the 12th instant.

Cargo will be received at the Company's Godowns, No. 4 Fairlie Place, up till noon of Tuesday the th.

Goods forwarded to Kooshtea for this vessel will be chargeable with Railway Freight from Calcutta to Kooshtea in addition to the regular Freight of this Company.

Passengers should leave for Kooshtea by Train of Wednesday, the 11th.

CACHAR LINE NOTICE

REGULAR FORTNIGHTLY SERVICE.

Steamers leave Calcutta for Cachar and Intermediate Stations every alternate Friday, and leave Cachar downward every alternate Sunday.

THE Str. "SUCCESS" will leave Calcutta via Matabanga for Cachar on Friday, the 20th instant.

Cargo will be received at the Company's Godowns, Nimtollah Ghat, up till noon of Thursday the 19th.

For further information regarding rates of Freight or passagemoney, apply to,

4 FAIRLIE PLACE, Calcutta 6th October, 1876. G. J. SCOTT, *Secretary.*

BABU BASANTA KUMARA DATTA,

HOMŒOPATHIC PRACTITIONER

No. 20, Sunker Haldar's Lane, Ahiritolah.

LONDON AGENT

MRS. HENRY TURNER & CO.

FRESH INDENT OF

HOMŒOPATHIC

Medicines and other Requisites.

Arrives every month from England

Medicines, Boxes, Books, Pamphlets; Absolute Alcohol; Cholera-spirit Camphor.

SPECIAL REMEDIES.

For Suppressed, Laborious and Difficult menses; Leucorrhœa; Hysteria.

For Spermatorrhœa; Dysentery; Diarrhœa; Cholera.

For Asthma; Pile; Pain; Sore and Diseases of the Children.

Ice, Lemonade, Soda and Tonic water always.

To be had at

DATTA'S HOMŒOPATHIC LABORATORY

No. 312, CHITPORE ROAD, BURTOLA, CALCUTTA

TERMS—CASH.

☞ Price List can be had free on application.

R. K. GHOSH'S

HOMŒOPATHIC DISPENSARY.

No. 1, *Gour Mohun Mukerjee's Street, Simla.*

CALCUTTA.

HOMŒOPATHIC Medicine; Medicine chests of sizes,—containing medicine in tube phials; Homœopathic Books, tracts and pamphlets (English and Bengali); Dr. Rubin's "Saturated spirits of Camphor,"—(the best preventive and cure for cholera where medical aid is not available); and other Homœopathic requisites are sold here at a moderate price. Terms cash. Mofussil orders are promptly executed.

R. K. GHOSH,
Homœopathic Practitioner,
Manager.

NOTICE.

INFALLIBLE SPECIFICS FOR ASTHMA, CONSUMPTION, COLIC, GONORRHŒA SPERMATORRHŒA AND DYSENTRY!!!

I AM the son of the late Titaram Paul of Midnapore, who, the public is well aware, was acquainted with specific medicines for the above diseases. I fully learnt the mode of preparing those medicines from my late father, and have cured many people of Midnapore, Calcutta, Hughly, and other places since his death, as the annexed testimonial will shew. Any one wishing to be treated by me can apply to me, care of the Manager of the Indian Mirror.

WOOPENDRA NATH PAUL.

BABU UPENDRA NATH PAL.

SIR,

You will be glad to hear that the painful asthma under which I was suffering for the last three years and through which I was nearly brought to the brink of death has been perfectly cured through your treatment. I was laid under the care of several able Doctors and *Kobirajes*, but every treatment on their part proved a failure on me. God bless you and let your cure spread over those who are suffering under the same wretched circumstances.

SURJA CUMAR MAJUMDAR.

CALCUTTA, TANTANEAH, *The 30th August* 1875.

BURN & CO.

RANEEGUNGE Fire bricks are the best Fire Bricks known;—superior to Ramsay's.

9 Rs. per 100.

Fire clay, 40 Rs. per Ton.

Glazed Stone ware, Drainage pipes of all sizes.

BURN & Co.,
7, *Hastings Street, Calcutta.*

REGISTERED No 97.

DR. H. C. SARMA'S

MEDICINE FOR DEBILITY

(NERVOUS.)

Brought on by indulgence in irregular habits, effects of previous diseases, loss of power of limbs, weakness or loss of memory, [illegible] irritable temper, disposition of the mind to displeasure at trifles, want of attention towards business, despair at finding no relief from treatment &c. &c. &c.

Price with [illegible] Rs. 5.

Particulars of disease [illegible] for despatch required from patients [illegible].

DR. SARMA'S FEE.

In cases of Debility (nervous) Rs. 16 per visit. } In
For advice at Home....... Rs. 10 " } Town

Out of Town Rs. 500 per Day.

INDIAN TOOTH POWDER.

Strengthens loose teeth, alleviates pain of, and prevents bleeding from Gums, cleanses the mouth, corrects its putrid odour and cures ulceration of the Gums without blackening the Teeth.

Price per packet ...	Rs. 0 4 0
Postage &c., for 4 packets	" 0 5 0

TONIC OIL.

Imparts vigour and tone to the paralyzed or relaxed parts of the Human system.—Restores proper circulation of blood to weak and inactive parts.

Price for four ounce phial. ...	Rs. 1 0 0
Postage &c.	0 10 0

HAIR PRESERVER.

Will restore grey hair to its original colour.

It acts directly upon the roots of the hair, removes dandriff, prevents premature falling-off of the hair, and promotes its growth and strength giving it Lustre and Health of Youth.

It also produces a cooling and soothing effect upon the head.

Price, for 4 ounce phial ...	Rs. 2 0 0
Postage &c.	0 10 0

Copy of letter received from Raja Chundernath Roy Bahadoor of Nattore.

Wellesley Street, No. 13, Moia Lane, 29th March 1874.

MY DEAR [illegible] BABOO,—I shall thank you to send me another phial of your "*Excellent Hair Restorer.*" In fact it has done me a great benefit and I should like to have more of it. It has disabused me (young as I am) of old age.

Yours Sincerely

C. N. of Nattore

MEDICINE FOR BALDNESS.

Will certainly cure baldness if applied on the bald portion, night & morning according to directions given in the adjoining direction paper

Price per two ounce phial Rs.	1 0 0
Postage &c. "	0 6 0

HEEM-SAGAR OIL.

The best remedy for Headache arising from over-study, intellectual occupation, over-thinking, mental anxiety and weakness, as well as heat of head owing to living in hot places.

It cools the head and produces very agreeable sensation. Removes Dandriff as well as all other impurities from the head. Promotes the strength and growth of the hair and prevents its premature falling-off.

Price per 4 ounce phial...	Rs. 1 0 0
Postage &c.	" 0 10 0

MEDICINE FOR LEPROSY.

Price with Postage &c. Rs. 5.

OIL FOR LEPROSY.

And Inveterate Skin Diseases.

Price per 8 ounce phial ...	Rs. 2 0
Postage &c.	" 0 12

THE 'PATENT PERPETUAL FOUNTAIN.'

TABLEEPERGNE OR CENTRE PIECE,

FOR SCENT OR FOR PERFUMATED WATER.

In Richly Electro-Silvered Ware, [*One of the Greatest Novelties of the day.*]

Cash Price Rs. 175.

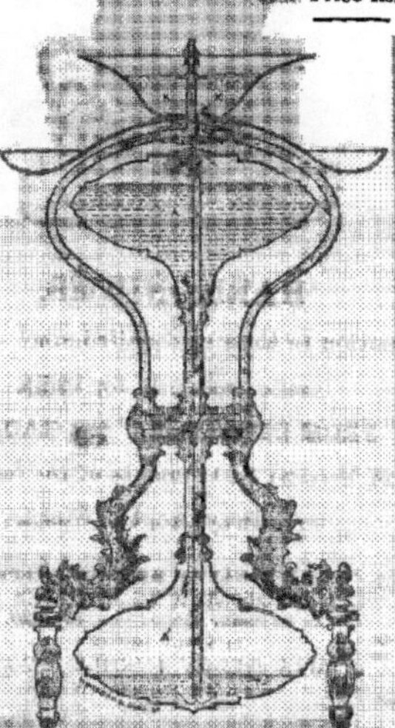

N. B.—The annexed drawing is not a correct representation of the Plated Table Fountains which [illegible] have [illegible]. The drawing is only given to show the internal arrangement of the Apparatus and attention is invited to the following description:—

[illegible] A, A1, are two cisterns or reservoirs which are connected together by pipes [illegible] axis of [illegible] central plug [illegible] C, C1 [illegible].

To set the fountain in motion the water is poured into the dish or basin [illegible] until the lower reservoir is filled and the [illegible] covered. The cisterns or reservoirs A, A1, are then turned on their axis of motion, so as to place the filled cistern or reservoir A at the top when the water therefrom will flow to a level in the jet pipe G, and the water in the basin or dish E, by passing down the pipes or tubes I and I1 into the lower cistern or reservoir A1, [illegible] in such lower cistern or reservoir A1 and forces the air out therefrom through the pipe or tube C1, passage F, and tube B, into the upper part of the cistern or reservoir A, where it presses upon the surface of the water therein and forces it out therefrom through the tube C, passage H, and jet pipe F, until all the water in the upper cistern or reservoir A has passed through the jet pipe F and into the lower cistern or reservoir A1 by the pipe I passage [illegible] and pipe I1, when by turning the cistern or reservoirs A, A1 on their axis of motion until the cistern or reservoir A1 is at the top, the action of the fountain will be continued; the pipes or tubes B, C1, which had previously been air passages now becoming water passages and the pipes or tubes B1, C, now becoming air passages which had previously served for the passage of water. By these improvements the necessity for alternately filling and emptying the cisterns or reservoirs A, A1, is obviated.

SMITH, STANISTREET & CO

Pharmaceutical Chemists & Druggists

BY APPOINTMENT

To His Excellency the Right Hon'ble

LORD LYTTON, G.M.S.I.

Governor-General of India,

&c., &c.

SYRUP OF LACTATE OF IRON

Prepared from the original recipe. Lactate of Iron, in various forms of preparation have been in use in France, and generally through the continent of Europe, for some years past, and is highly esteemed as one of the most valuable Chalybeate Tonic remedies yet introduced. The Syrup, being the most agreeable as well as convenient form of administration is in most general use. It is a most valuable remedy in the following diseases:—Chlorosis or Green Sickness, Leucorrhoea, Neuralgia, enlargement of the Spleen, &c. In combination with quinine, it has also been very successfully used in the cure of Fever, while to persons of delicate constitution, enfeebled by disease it is invaluable. In bottles. Rs. 2 each.

SYRUP OF THE PHOSPHATE OF IRON Rs. 2 per bottle.

SYRUP OF PHOSPHATE OF IRON AND STRYCHNINE, Rs. 3 per bottle.

SYRUP OF PHOSPHATE OF IRON AND QUININE. Price Rs. 2-8 per bottle.

SYRUP OF PHOSPHATE OF IRON, QUININE AND STRYCHINE (DR. ATKIN'S TRIPLE TONIC SYRUP,) Rs. 2-8 per bottle.

Smith, Stanistreet & Co.

Invite special attention to the following rates the quality guaranteed as the best procurable [illegible]

Pure Ærated Waters.

Made from Pure Water, obtained by the new process through the Patent Charcoal Filters.

				Rs	As.
Ærated plain (Treble Ærated),		per doz.		0	12
Soda Water	ditto	"	...	0	12
Gingerade	ditto	"	...	1	4
Lemonade	ditto	"	...	1	4
Tonic (Quinine)	ditto			1	4

The *Cash* must be sent with the order to obtain advantage of the above rates.

MUDHOO SUDUN PAUL & CO.

120, RADHA BAZAR.

Tea! (Assam) Tea!

TRADE M. MARK.

In 1lb. and 2lb. Tins.

Pekoe Tea	2lb. Tin,	Per Tin	Rs.	3 8
" Flowery	"	"	"	[illegible] 8
" Souchong	"	"	"	2 0
Family Mixture	"	"	"	[illegible] 4
Campoi	"	"	"	[illegible] 8
Imperial Mixture with China	...	...	...	3 4
China Rose Pouchong	...	...	...	2 8

The above in 1lb. Tin at half the respective prices, plus two annas extra.

BURMAH CIGARS.

No. 1 per 100	Rs.	1 0
" 2 "		0 12

HUNTLEY AND PALMER'S BISCUITS.

Albert, in Tin of 2 lb each	Rs	1 6
Arrow Root, ...	"	1 4
Mixed, ...	"	1 5

Indian Chutnies, Castor Oil, Candles, Kerosine Oil, China Preserves, Perfumery, Domestic Medicines and other stores always in stock and offered at lower rates than other Houses.

Catalogue to be had on application.

MUDHOO SUDUN PAUL & Co.

Oriental Gas Company Ld.

THE price of Gas in Calcutta and Howrah is reduced to Rs. 5 per 1,000 feet.

Printed and published by M. M. BUKSHI, at the INDIAN MIRROR PRESS, No. 6, College Square, for the Proprietors.

The Indian Mirror.

SUNDAY EDITION.

VOL XV.] CALCUTTA, SUNDAY, OCTOBER 15, 1876. { REGISTERED AT THE GENERAL POST OFFICE. } [NO. 244

CONTENTS.

NOTICE.

All letters and communications relating to the literary department of the Paper should be addressed to the Editor. All other letters should be addressed to the Manager, to whom all remittances should be made payable.

Subscribers will be good enough to bring to the notice of the Manager any delay or irregularity in the delivery of the Paper.

Editorial Notes

WE understand that Pundit Dayanund Saraswati, the distinguished Vedic reformer, intends proceeding to England. He is now engaged in studying English at Lucknow. The Pundit's visit will no doubt excite considerable interest among Oriental scholars in England, and in the continent.

THE mad Sultan of Turkey Murad V. who succeeded his equally mad and much more guilty uncle, has been deposed, which he ought to have been long ago. Abdul Hamid has been selected in his place, and no one seems to know what he is likely to turn out. The *Spectator* thinks he "will prove a strong, self-willed, fighting barbarian of the old type, whose first act will be the execution of some of the reformers." The hostility of the London press has been so great against the present Turkish Government, that its statements cannot be accepted without much hesitation.

THE lamented death of Mr. Woodrow will be felt by many Native gentlemen as a personal bereavement. Though some of his notions were peculiar, the sterling and genuine goodness of his heart could not be mistaken. Many poor students and Pundits are indebted to his kind offices, and his charity was often secret and effective. In the welfare of the rising generation of Hindus Mr. Woodrow took a sincere interest, and wherever there was any meeting or assembly, called together by the educated or the young, and Mr. Woodrow was asked to attend, he was surely there. His leanings towards missionary agencies in educational matters were clear and decided, and some of his views on social questions were such as we could not agree with. He was, perhaps, not so well fitted to be a Director of Public Instruction, as Professor, or Principal of a College, but there cannot be the least doubt he was an able man, and there is not another like him in the Education Department.

THE retirement of one of the most eminent political leaders of the age, Mr. Gladstone, from public life, suggests serious reflections as to the future of religious leaders, ministers, and missionaries. It seems natural that a life of unusual excitement, struggle, anxiety and labor should seek relief in retirement in old age. Wherever there is excessive labor such as a leader of men must undergo, a general relaxation is sure to follow, as something inevitable in the course of nature. To this law of reaction humanity submits in all departments of mental activity. Such of the leaders and missionaries of the Brahmo Somaj as are straining their nerves and muscles, and exhausting their energies and resources in the Master's work, seem to us destined to retire from the hardships of public ministry in their latter days. Let it not be supposed, however, that we recommend absolute retirement. Every covenanted servant in God's kingdom is bound to serve society to the end of the chapter; to neglect all social duties and enjoy absolute repose in a distant retreat, during the latter years of life, would be selfishness under the cloak of religion. All that nature requires is more joyful and undisturbed communion with God, and less hard work as life ebbs away.

THE Principal of Elphinstone College, Bombay, Mr. Wordsworth, is accused by the *Lucknow Witness* of making "open attacks upon Christianity, and indeed upon the foundations of all religion." This is a serious charge against an educational officer, and ought to be explained. But it is so vague, and is supported by so many expressions of ill-feeling on the part of our Methodist contemporary that we are obliged to accept his statement with some caution. What are the open attacks upon Christianity which Mr. Wordsworth has made, and how do they sap "the foundations of all religion?" The foundations of what is called Christianity in this country, and the foundations of "all religion" are by no means identical, and unless we are more clearly told of the nature of Mr. Wordsworth's offence we cannot join issue with him like the *Lucknow Witness*. It is also necessary to know whether that gentleman's religious speculations are in any way connected with the discharge of his official duties, or entirely independent of the same. If the former be the case, then, of course, his attacks upon Christianity, as much as upon any other religion, would be really condemnable; otherwise as a private individual, he can, we think, entertain any views he likes, and express them temperately before the public for rational criticism and discussion. Not knowing what these views are we speak simply from an abstract view of the case, and it is as likely that we may agree with Mr. Wordsworth, as that we may differ from him in *toto*.

PROFESSOR F. W. Newman has publicly joined the Unitarian body, and become a member of the British and Foreign Unitarian Association. The 'wherefore' of this rather remarkable step will, no doubt, be differently interpreted by different persons; and to some Professor Newman will appear to have compromised his position by abandoning his broad Theism for a narrow and a distinctively Christian creed. There is nothing, however, in his letter to Miss Anna Swanwick, published in the *Inquirer*, which would warrant such an assumption. In his *Apologia*, the Professor indicates no change of views, no theological or religious conversion, no progression or retrogression from cherished principles. He evidently stands exactly where he did. He does not in the least narrow his former position as a Catholic Theist by joining a small sect. His regard for Unitarianism amounts only to this, —"I esteem it to be the real and fertile germ of that wider and more blessed religion which shall permeate all nations and unite them in love of truth and in mutual esteem." The Professor seems to say in the above letter, though he does not distinctly state it, that it is not he who has gone over to the Unitarian body, but it is the Unitarian Church that has after successive and steady advances come over to him and identified itself with his well-known creed. The question, however, still remains,—why does he at all join the ranks of the Unitarians if he is just what and where he was; *cui bono?* It seems to us that Mr. Newman has often felt some degree of loneliness in his exalted but isolated theological position, especially since his late sad bereavement, and he very naturally seeks sympathy and co-operation. Mr. Newman's soul, like every body's soul, needs a Church next to God. We need the Great One above us, to hear our prayers and accept our love; and then we need brothers and sisters, around us, to join with us, as a family of fellow-worshippers, and fellow-servants, in His house. The Father and His family, we require both. We all feel the need of an associated and organized body of co-religionists, so that in their company, we may not only find comfort and strength for ourselves, but also adequate power and resources for effectively spreading the light of our faith among others. In England especially the need of co-workers must be deeply felt by our Theistics friends, who unfortunately occupy an isolated position, and lack the advantages of solid and organized labor. Nothing could be more hopeful than a combination of scattered Theistic forces in a powerful association like the Unitarian body.

AT Ghazipur, about four miles from the Native city, lives a Hindu Yogi, who though not a famous devotee, has during the last ten years lived quietly in a dark underground cell, hid beneath a temple dedicated to Rama and Sita. The temple, a decent and neat little structure, situated on the banks of the Ganges, and surrounded by a small garden, commands a most favorable position, and looks sacred and romantic enough to remind one of the Asrams of our ancient Rishis. Inside the temple is something like an ordinary glass case, in which are arranged half a dozen well dressed dolls representing Rama and Sita, Krishna and Radhika, with a small punkah swinging overhead, and lanterns and kerosine lamps of the latest fashion hanging round the deities. At the foot of the shelf on the left hand side is a trapdoor, which covers the passage to the cell. The passage is large enough to admit a man in a sitting posture, and the cell, which no body else has seen, is said to be far enough to be beyond the reach of all noise and disturbance. The Yogi goes down this narrow and frightfully dark passage, fastening the trap door from below. There he lives in his cell, shrouded in utter darkness, for hours, days, and even weeks together, absorbed in meditation, coming out only now and then for occasional intercourse with the outside world. When or what he eats, when he performs his ablutions in the river, all this is a mystery, which few have been able or have cared to solve. The Yogi himself, however, does not pretend to work miracles. He says he eats when he gets anything to eat, and seems to resign himself wholly to his God. There is an adjacent hamlet from which, it is believed, people bring him now and then food to eat. A coarse woollen sheet hanging down to his feet is all the raiment be puts on throughout the year. Whenever he makes his appearance, numbers of Hindus on receiving the intelligence come pouring in from all sides. They find him seated in the temple, incessantly pulling the punkah in the glass case by means of a long chain attached to it. Why he has selected this mode of serving his deity is not known. While thus engaged he would go on conversing with his visitors, and answering their questions. Neither a profound Shastri, nor a sentimental quietist, he speaks pleasantly, respectfully, and without affectation. His countenance is most serene, his attitude meek and humble, his words simple and modest. On being questioned about his faith and communion he invariably talks of the worthlessness and wretchedness of his soul, his deep ignorance and ungodliness. He says he knows nothing of communion or the love of God and would fain seek light from those among his visitors who would thus favor him. Some of our friends who lately went to visit him, were greatly impressed with the Yogi's exemplary meekness and humility. He is simple as a child.

IT may not be known to the general public that the condition of the Bethune Girls' School has been somewhat precarious for sometime. The late Director of Public Instruction applied for the sanction of the Government of Bengal to make over the whole management of the institution to Miss Brittain of the American Zenana Mission with the hope that this lady, who is exceedingly, energetic that she might altogether convert the School into a more prosperous concern, might be allowed a free expression to her religions views, and make a more becoming use of the splendid building in which it is located. Sir Richard Temple who has we believe, more than once expressed his dissatisfaction that a building which can accommodate six hundred pupils should be devoted to the use of sixty, did not exactly go the length of making over the institution bodily to the Lady Superintendent of the American Mission, but recommended the Director to consult the School Committee as to what portion of the premises might be placed under the disposal of Miss Brittain to be used as he thinks best. Now the Committee, composed of Native gentlemen entirely, and some of them of the orthodox type, strenuously object to the idea of locating a school of high class Hindu girls with such female pupils as a missionary lady might choose to bring together, in the same building. If the innovation is insisted upon, they threaten to resign in a body, which, we think, means the withdrawal of all the girls who attend the School. The School is, we believe a Government School and if it is against the policy of Government to mix secular and religious agencies together in the education of boys, are there not much graver reasons to follow the same policy strictly in the education of girls? Female education is still unpopular in the country, and any religious prejudices injudiciously excited will only intensify that unpopularity. But we must say we want to see a better use made of the Bethune School building than at present.

LIGHTS IN DARKNESS.

WHAT is so glorious in creation as light? We hail it with our birth in this world, we hail it every morning, untired with its all-revealing lustre. Everything that is hidden, stands disclosed by the touch of light,—beauty, color, order, the mysteries and laws of nature. Light calls us to action, to enjoyment, to mix with each other in the varied occupations and obligations of life. Everything that is bright, cheerful, prosperous, living, and replete with exalted relationship is compared with light. Just the opposite may be said of darkness. It conceals every thing, disfigures, blackens, buries within its depths all that is fair. We dare not walk, we cannot work, we fear to stray out in darkness. Everything that is sorrowful, disastrous, dead, unprospering is compared with darkness. Day and night are the two things emblematical of the fortune, and misfortune of man.

Well, but there are great many things which light darkens and destroys, of which we get no intimation when the glory of the sun dazzels, inebriates, and bewilders us. These are revealed and pointed out to us by darkness. These are lights in darkness. There are many suns and moons which shine not when shines upon us the light of the day. There are many worlds and many systems which are hidden away, and for a time destroyed before our vision when the little world in which we live is full of its daily glare and noise. There is a repose and tranquility, a solitude and a profound life which belong to darkness. The midnight is the revealer of the ineffable glories of the high heavens; the midnight is the time for wisdom, for contemplation, for communion, for entering into the mysteries of other worlds.

If from the outer world we come into the inner, we find the same meaning in darkness, only in an intenser form. When the sun of the world's fortune shines upon us, when circumstances are favorable, when men are approving, and brightness is on all sides, of course we are happy, and our nature gets ample aids and opportunities to grow. The generous virtues of the mind and heart show themselves; warm sympathies develop, we feel we are having the very best of life. But after a while the sky begins to lower, the evening shades fall thick, the brightness fades, and darkness falls upon the face of nature. Then shine out one by one the clear and solitary lights of the soul's firmament. The man is called out to watch and observe alone. The darkness thickens, but the lights brighten and multiply. This world, its joys and sorrows are forgotten in the glory of the greater worlds that burst forth into view. Deep repose fills every thing. The tranquility and refreshment that are sought but never found in the glaring superficial light of worldly prosperity, steep the soul in the midst of solitude and darkness.

HOW OLD ARE WE.

"MEN count their age from 1, 2, 3, 4, &c., but the age of religious life ought to be counted as 4, 3, 2, 1." This is what our minister said in the Brahma Mandir on the occasion of the last Utsab. The idea is suggestive, and we are tempted to dwell upon it at some length. We wonder why people celebrate the anniversaries of their birthday with so much zest and rejoicing. Is it a matter of self-gratulation that a man should year after year be hastening towards the grave?—that on the other side of fifty he is less able than hitherto to enjoy the luxuries, and bid defiance to the infirmities of life?—and that his hair should turn gray, his teeth, hitherto pearl white, should be conspicuous by their absence, and the sockets of his eyes sunk and sunk till the eyeballs become a lifeless jelly? The love of life is so strongly inherent in our nature that we would rather shrink from the contemplation of its close than take a pride in its gradual decline. Talk to an old man of his approaching death, and his eyes will start from their spheres, and his hairs stand on end in all the moods of horror, real and imaginary. We know of old men who consider every mention of death in their presence as a gross insult, and an unpardonable breach of etiquette. Yet the same man who remonstrates against the unmannerliness of the rising generation, is found to put on his holiday dress, and clad in his best, celebrate himself, and lustily desire others of his kinsfolk and friends to celebrate his sixtieth birthday with a gust and enthusiasm which is perhaps not quite explicable. Every Hindu rejoices in his birthday. The lower and middle class Hindu will get a new cloth, and set at large the traditional *koee* in a deep well. The aristocratic Hindu will have his gala day, when what with Nautches, balls, illuminations and fireworks, the whole earth is made to swing merrily round in glee for another birthday added to his life. The royal Hindu will have all his salutes fired, all his presents given, all his devotions observed, and will have not only merriment himself, but cause its electric force to thrill the loyal hearts of the population at large. *Vanitus vanitatum!*—Sayeth the moralist. Is the salute a birthday one, or is it the last trumpet? Is the rejoicing for all the time past, or all the time to come? Does the eye shed tears of joy or sorrow? Alas, that there is so much innate folly in our nature, when men easily convert a subject of mourning into one of laughter! The stern philosophy of our natural religion would lead a man to rejoice that so much of his period of probation in this world has been served, and that the day of final release from the world and its vanities is near. But how many of our countrymen are able to contemplate death with the dark spectacles of philosophy? It is all right in the closet, where scholastic abstruseness and mystic gloom bedim any man's vision; But in the busy haunts of men, in the forum, in the market place, in the ordinary affairs of every day life, what is death but a ghastly spectre to disturb and terrify men? No. We are foolish, all of us, to rejoice in that for which we should mourn. Wisdom lies in another direction—even in counting our age backward as 4, 3, 2, 1. Let us explain what we mean. The advance of age means so much time wasted in visionary pleasures and useless dreams, so much vitality lost, energy misspent, and talents misoccupied; it means all that is selfish and selfseeking; it means the misuse of God's gifts, the wilful postration of man's natural strength; it means more than everything else complete suicide. Whereas let a man advance in wisdom, let him serve God and continue to be His steadfast servant for ever, let him utilise his life to the best of his power, and he will seek that far from being encumbered with age, he becomes younger and more youthful instead, and that the more his eyes grow dim, his hands stiff, and his hearing impaired, the more clearly he is enabled to profit by his inner perfections. His mind's eye penetrates through eternity; his faith gives him a strength not his own; his hopes render him as buoyant as a young man in the bloom of life, and his words become as clear and refreshing as if they are gushing out of the perinial fount of wisdom. It is true of men and of societies. It can never be true that our dear church whose anniversary we celebrated the other day, will grow older and decay with the lapse of years, as old men do. On the contrary every year will add to its strength, every industrious bee of its hive will gather fresh sweets from the flowers; and the concentrated strength and piety of years will go on fructifying, till the whole becomes too deep rooted to fear the passing blasts of time. And so also with every individual man. He is fifty years old, you say? Evidently you mistake: he ought to be fifty years young. The more he gathers wisdom, the more youthful he becomes; and confronting eternity altogether, he may truly say that his life is yet to begin. He is ever young, ever strong, and ever fresh. All his wisdom teaches him that he is a child. To be sure he has forgotten his Arithmetic. He does not end his care when he is three score and ten, but renews it as a child just come out of its mother womb. Would that we were all children! A worldly man rejoices in his anniversary, because, foolish soul! he grows old, sees the approach of death. A man of the spirit, on the other hand, rejoices because he sees that every year he is becoming more of a child. The former rejoices because his life is withering away before the blast of age; the latter is glad because even winter is unable to destroy its blossoms, and discolor its freshness. What a difference between the two! Do the Brahmos feel this freshness and youth growing upon them upon every approach of their anniversary?

Correspondence.

THE REVIVAL OF THE SANGAT, PROPOSED

To the Editor of the *Indian Mirror*.

DEAR SIR,—Many would think the repetition of the very old common saying that "every thing grows by cultivation," is as unnecessary as every such thing should be. But at present the condition of the Brahmos of Calcutta is so dismal that I cannot but call their attention once more to it. In all my remarks I exclude the revered leaders of the progressive section of our Church—there is no denying of the fact that they are making rapid strides in their spiritual course. I do not say anything regarding the other section of our Church. I mean to apply these remarks to the congregation of the Brahmo Somaj of India. Perhaps I carry with me the opinion of every one when I say that the general body of the Somaj is lagging much behind. As far as my limited knowledge goes, I fail to find that the spirit of religion has very perceptible growth in it. No one will deny that when friends meet, they are most likely to converse on religious topics. Should their religious feelings be prominent, such conversations are as well the fruits as the means of spiritual growth. But the truth must be told; in our midst the most prolific subjects of conversation are not the things of spiritual but of this world—so much so that even in the holy precincts of our *Mandir* such conversations are not unfrequent occurrences, immediately before and after the service. On the other hand, the only institution in which religious subjects were discussed, I mean the *Sangat*, has long died out. Conversation not only keeps up the pious fervour but it also fosters our social feelings; so that with the decay of the religious intercourse, the bond of religious sympathy is being gradually severed, and persons, once friends, are now growing indifferent, if not strange to one another. I should very much like to see the revival of that useful institution, the *Sangat*, where persons who scarcely see one another in the course of a month may meet at least once a week. To mention nothing of the harvest our elders reaped from it, we ourselves must have seen, in the days of the *Sangat*, that from almost every meeting we carried something to let us remain contented during the next week. There the ignorant had their first lessons, and the learned renewed their passed impressions; there the indolent imbibed the spirit of activity and the active that of steadiness; there the grovelling sceptics removed their doubts, and the believers learnt to be faithful; there the cheerless destitute contracted their best friendships and the happy friends met together to forget the sorrows of separation. In short, it was the nursery where the infants were bred to be children and the children to be boys; it was the school where the boys were educated to be young and young to be men, it was the world where men found friends and friends met to learn to encounter successfully the hardships of life; and, lastly, it was the pulpit which taught men to be old and the old to smooth their path to death. For the growth of individuals and the community that institution seems indispensable to me. There were struggle, vitality, growth, sympathy, co-operation, and every thing when the Samaj existed. But alas! What now? Let us be up again, and grow by cultivating mutual sympathy and help.

I remain yours &c.,

A MEMBER OF THE LATE *Samaj*.

AN ENQUIRY.

To the Editor of the *Indian Mirror*.

SIR,—Will you, or any of your numerous readers, kindly let me know, through the medium of your columns, if there is any book on Brahmoism, printed in the Nepaulese language, and can be had at the Calcutta Mission Office, and oblige.

Yours &c.,

A NEPAULESE BRAHMO.

LOHAGHAT, PUNKABARIE.

No such book is to be had.—ED. *I. M.*

Devotional

THE distress of poverty, O God, threatens to press upon my mind very much sometimes. I am often inclined to feel humiliated and ashamed because of my want of means. Sweeten my heart, my good Father, when the wants of the world tend to depress me; for my livelihood and comfort teach me to depend upon thee entirely; and when the sufferings of those whom I love are about to make my soul sorrowful, give me the consolation of feeling that thou art my Father, my portion, my wealth for ever. Thou who hast the support of all creatures in thy hands, support me in the midst of my loneliness and poverty.

"THOU art always the same, O my merciful Lord," it is only I who am different at different times. Glorious and beautiful in thy protecting love when I rise from my act of loving prayer, thou art loving and protecting as ever when I have ceased to love thee, when my heart is hard and unfeeling as a stone. Thy relations with me never change, it is only my relations with thee that change so often. And in the unsteadiness of my heart I feel as if thou art changed to me. Help me, my Father, so that even when my heart is as a stone, I may still trust in thy never-changing love and goodness. What love and trust thou dost inspire in me, make it constant, so that in all states I may fondly and firmly rely and live in thee.

SUSPICION and hard usage seem to make the world very dark. Deliver my heart, O God, from the evil suspecting and ill-using others although I may not agree with them. Teach me to treat all men with sweetness, respect, and delicacy, and whatever be the return I get, let me bear it meekly and with dignity, as thy servant.

The Brahmo Somaj

THE anniversary of the Luckow Brahmo Somaj was celebrated on Sunday last with great *eclat*. The Somaj-building, not yet having come to a state of completion, the festival took place in the premises of Babu Nobin Chunder Chukerbutty. The large and spacious hall which was appropriated for this purpose was tastefully decorated with garlands of flowers. Morning and evening services were conducted by Babu Agore Nath Gupta. The mildness and pathos of the morning service were contrasted with the fervor and enthusiasm of that of the evening. The sermon preached by the minister in the morning was on *Joga* (hearing, seeing and touching God). It was very eloquent, pathetic, and impressive, and had an electrical effect upon the congregation. The sermon in the evening was on "What should we want before we go home"? "Permanent Communion with God" was the reply to this query. In the morning the minister also explained the spirit of true asceticism by expounding the meaning and spirit of scriptural texts. *Dyhan* (meditation) was the topic of religious conversation in the afternoon. Many practical hints were suggested for its *Sadan*. The distribution of *Ata, Dal* and pice to the helpless and poor (of whom about 600 were assembled) took place after the morning service was over.

BABU DEBENDRO NATH TAGORE has not, we understand, gone back to the hills, but is at present staying at Serampore. Hafiz is said to be now his favorite study.

PUNDIT DAYANUND SARASWATI delivered a public lecture at Lucknow, on Saturday, the 30th ultimo. In the course of the peroration the learned Pundit bestowed high eulogium on the leader of the Progressive Brahmos, and spoke in terms highly complimentary of the efforts made by the Brahmo Somaj to promote the worship of the One True God.

BABU AGHORE NATH GUPTA has left Agra for Lahore. Some of the Brahmos accompanied him to the Railway station to see him off. Babu Grish Chunder Sen, another Missionary of the Brahmo Somaj, has gone to Agra from Ghazipur.

BABU KESHUB CHUNDER SEN has been unfortunately taken ill again at Ghazipur. He is better now however. We are not sure that the difficulties and inconveniences of travelling will be beneficial to his present state of health. He requires perfect rest and quiet with very watchful and affectionate attendance. Outside Calcutta, we fear these advantages are not easy to acquire.

THE Kristnaghur Brahmo Somaj is one of the oldest Somajes in India. It was established more than forty years ago. But the old members for various reasons have either severed their connection with it, or been dispersed in different parts of the country. For sometime past it has been kept up by youngmen. The Somaj building is a decent and spacious hall, but it is not half-filled at the Sunday service. This is unfortunate. Of late Babu P. C. Mozoomdar who has seen there, tried to call the Brahmos together. His visit was short, but he was very encouragingly received by the local community. There were daily morning services, and public services also in the Somaj. There was a sort of *conversazione* where the *elite* of Krishnaghur assembled, and had a pleasant talk on various subjects. There was besides a public lecture in the spacious hall of the local College, where about two hundred and fifty people were present. Mr. Lethbridge, the learned and accomplished Principal of the College, though a Christian, takes warm interest in our movement. He not only let our missionary the use of the College hall, but personally took part in the proceedings. Mr. Lethbridge is deservedly popular among all sections of the Native public in Krishnaghur.

Gleanings

A VAIN man is not one with a dignified consciousness of his own personality, but rather one with a nervous solicitude about himself,—a fear that he shall not be noticed enough; with a half-suspicion that he may be a sham, a counterfeit, and, therefore, an extra endeavor that its clink and jingle shall be heard in the world.

IF we would induce others to act virtuously, it will prove more effectual to show them their capacities than to expose their weakness; to attract them by a fairer ideal than to terrify them by pictures of misery and shame.

WHATEVER may be our condition in life, it is better to lay hold of its advantages than to count its evils.

HE is a miserable being who has no resources of enjoyment within himself, but depends entirely upon foreign suggestion; who, in fact, must run away from himself, and pitch into the waves of superficial excitement a perpetual whirl and glitter that drowns all personality, and sweeps away soul and sense.

WE want not time to serve God but zeal; we have not too much business, but too little grace.

HOLY Greenham often prayed that "he might keep his young zeal with his old discretion."

HEARERS are of four sorts: the sponge, which swallows up everything; the funnel, which allows that to escape at one end which it receives at the other; the filter, which allows the liquor to escape, and retains the dregs; the seive, which rejects the chaff and retains nothing but the wheat.—*Jewish Proverb.*

Literary

"NAKED truths of naked people: being an account of expeditions to the Lake Victoria Nyanza and the Makraka Niam-Niam, West of the Bahr-el-Abiad (White Nile)". By Colonel C. Chaille Long, of the Egyptian Staff, is about to be published in London. The chief expedition was to Lake Victoria Nyanza, and the author gives a graphic account of a residence of some weeks at the court of King Mtesa some months before the arrival there of Mr. H. M. Stanley.

THE Lahore correspondent of the *Indian Public Opinion* states what we know to be a fact:— "The managers and proprietors of the Urdu papers generally pay visits to the Rajahs and Native Chiefs of this country with the object of getting some money or rewards from them; the Chiefs who comply with their demands are safe, and those who do not, are maligned in the most abusive language."

Scientific

A COUPLE of fishes brought from Sherman Colorado (says an American paper), have received the name of walking fishes. They have four legs, which they use on land, and double up when in the water.

—PROFESSOR NORDENSKJOLD'S expedition to Jenissick, by the Arctic Ocean, has safely returned to Norway. It has demonstrated that Siberia can be reached by sea.

—AT a meeting of the Administrative Council of the Italian Geographical Society an account was given of the recent movements of Italian explorers in Central Africa.

Calcutta.

MR. J. SUTCLIFFE, M. A., Principal of the Presidency College, has been appointed to officiate as Director of Public Instruction *vice* Mr. H. Woodrow M. A., deceased.

MURDER among the lower class of Europeans **in Calcutta, is** assuming an epidemic form. **Several cases are** reported. The latest ones **are the following** :—John Thomas, a private **in the 12th Regiment, stationed at** Fort William, **is charged with having** attempted to **murder one William Watson,** another private, **by dis charging a loaded rifle at him.**

James Walker, one of the crew of the *Wallace* ***Town* is** charged by his second officer, Norman McLeod, with having stabbed him **in** the mouth with a knife, and afterwards bit **off** a portion of his nose. The two Greeks named Mario Peter and Peter Melos, concerned in the late tragedy enacted at Colvin Ghaut in connection with an English sailor, named Gamble, since dead, have been committed to the Sessions to take their trial.

THE public offices will be closed **on** account of the Kali Pujah till Tuesday next.

THE following **is the** substance of some papers we received yesterday from Sir Stuart Hogg, the Commissioner of Police:—The Viceroy and Governor-General in Council having desired that the occasion of the Proclamation of the assumption of the Imperial title, by Her Majesty the Empress **of** India, should be celebrated in the principal **towns** of British India with appropriate rejoicings, and to this end the Government of India having granted a sum of public money in aid of the local efforts which will be made for the above object, His Honor the Lieutenant-Governor of Bengal has been pleased to assign a sum of Rupees fifteen thousand out of the amount placed at his disposal for the purpose, to be spent in the Town of Calcutta. It has been decided that the sum of Rs. 15,000 which has been so allotted by His Honor for Calcutta, should be expended in a Pyrotechnic display on the Maidan. **Sir Stuart Hogg, the** Commissioner **of Police, has accordingly made arrangements with Messrs Brock & Co. of the Crystal Palace,** London, **for a** display **of fire-works on the** 1st of January 1877. The public bodies and the leading members of the European and Native community of Calcutta are **re**quested to aid and join, with the Government, in promoting public rejoicings on the occasion in question. We have no doubt they **will** be too glad to do so.

THE number of deaths in Calcutta during the week ending the 16th September, was 233; during the week ending the 23rd September it was 195; and during the week ending **the** 30th September it was 191. So, it appears, **the** rate of mortality has been lower and lower **every** week, in spite **of** the so-called outbreak **of the** *Sarkis Mari*.

Latest News

—SIR JOHN STRACHEY has accepted the Ministership of India.

—A PORTION of the Gaekwar's troops, fully equipped, has left the capital for Delhi, on foot.

—PRAYER was offered for the success of the Turkish arms, and, also, for a seasonable fall of rain in Puna, at the public meeting of the Mahomedans at Puna.

—THERE are great apprehensions of scarcity at Dharwar, in the Bombay Presidency.

—AMONG the visitors now at Ooty is the Rajah of Nelambur.

—SIR A. ARBUTHNOT temporarily takes over the office of Finance Minister from Sir William Muir.

—A PUBLIC meeting of both Europeans and Natives was held at Puna on Thursday last, in order to concert measures for the relief of the poor ryots who are on the brink of starvation in the famine-stricken districts, in the Bombay Presidency.

—THE Puna Municipality have determined to open grain shops in Puna where the poor people may have supplies of grain at a more reasonable rate than at the Bunnias' shops on account of the Bombay Famine.

—GARIBALDI has written a letter to Mr. Arthur Arnold, in which he says he does not see any solution of the Eastern Question except by the passing of the Turks across the Bosphorus.

—IN England meetings still continue to be held to protest against Turkish misrule. The two most important of them took place in London and at Glasgow.

—the Duke of Argyll delivering a bitter invective against the Government at the latter.

—BARONESS BURDETT-COUTTS, Lord Coleridge, and Mr. Gladstone have written letters on the subject of the above demonstration."

—ON Sept. 20, Lord Beaconsfield made a speech at the annual dinner of the Buckinghamshire Agricultural Association, in which he explained his reasons for retirement from the House of Commons, traced the progress of events in the East, and indulged in much humorous invective against Mr. Gladstone.

—THE only Anglo-Indian paper at Madras which supports the Duke of Buckingham's action on the Weld case, is the *Athenæum and Daily News*. It takes a rational view of the whole question.

—SIX Burmese youths will proceed to Italy to be educated. The King of Ava is said to be more partial to the Italians than to the English.

—PRINCE HASSAN, the son of the Khedive of Egypt, was taken a prisoner by an Abyssinian chief, and not released until a ransom was paid.

—THE following was the Viceroy's reply of the Oudh Talukdars' address, presented at Simla:—"Talukdars of Oudh,—It is with sincere pleasure that I receive the address you have now presented to me; and I esteem myself fortunate in having had this favorable opportunity of meeting a body of noblemen and gentlemen whose attachment to British rule finds, in the terms of your address, such loyal and emphatic expression. The testimony you bear to the prosperity and social order now prevailing in the province of Oudh, and your recorded appreciation of those blessings, afford me the liveliest gratification; and I rejoice to receive from you the welcome assurance that the ties of confidence and affection which bind you to the Throne of our beloved Sovereign, have been rendered indissoluble by the sedulity of those efforts which the Government of India has made, is making, and will continue to make in maintenance of the privileges and promotion of the welfare of all classes of the population of Oudh. I am especially pleased to learn from your own lips that the important measures which have just passed into law, and which have benefited so much by your valuable criticisms, are calculated, in your opinion, to contribute to the general well-being of the province.

I **need** not assure you that the peculiar **so**cial institutions and agricultural conditions **of** the ancient and important province of Oudh, **to** which you have called my attention, will always **be** scrupulously respected by the Government of India, which can never be indifferent either to the rights and interests you so worthily represent, or to the sentiments and feelings of any class of the loyal population **of this** cherished portion of Her Majesty's Indian Dominions. The extent to which the administration of the North-Western Provinces may be **more** closely associated with that of Oudh, in **a man**ner conducive to the interests of the **two ter**ritories, and **at** the same time with due regard to those considerations to which I have referred, is a question now engaging my attention; and in the careful examination **of** it, I will not fail to give due weight to the views embodied in your present address."

Selection.

PROFESSOR F. W. NEWMAN AND THE BRITISH AND FOREIGN UNITARIAN ASSOCIATION.

MISS ANNA SWANWICK has placed in our hands for publication the following letter from Professor Newman, which will be read, we are sure, with very general gratification:—

To Miss Anna Swanwick.

My Dear Friend,—I write to you because you are on the Council of the Unitarian Association, **to request** that I may be admitted **as a member**. Since **I** have so long stood aloof **(never** with any hostile feeling), it seems right **to say** why I have changed my course.

Last summer I learned with warm interest that the decision against the Rev. Peter Dean was reversed, and that the members of the Association in London were cordial to the Rev. R. Rodolph Suffield. Now, to my still greater pleasure, I learn that the members gathering to London from all England, have twice decided **to accept** the **work** of Theodore **Parker for circulation, and to spend** money **upon them. I do not write as attaching** any extraordinary importance **to the** three persons whom I name for honor, but believing them to be tests of an important principle.

You know me well enough **to** be **aware** that I love the *spirit* of Christianity, while I cannot admit its *letter*. I doubt whether anything has been either uttered nobler than the noblest words in the New Testament, or any characters have lived more lovely and angelic than numbers of Christians who have **shaped** their course and fed their minds on select **precepts of** these Scriptures and of the older **Hebrew** writings. I regard the great problem of modern religion to be, how to hold fast the spiritual sentiment which the best Jews and best Christians hold in common, without re-establishing that slavish law of the letter which abundant experience proves to be pernicious when accepted, pernicious also by driving intellectual persons into an unbelief often deplorable. I have lamented the apparently inevitable antagonism of the Creed which has been the Creed of the future. It seemed as though (as at the Reformation in the sixteenth century, so now again) society would have a necessary convulsion; and that no bridge could be built for transition from the Old to the New. But I now see a happier course already begun, largely as a result of the peculiar combination of high qualities in my honored friend, Dr. James Martineau,—whose clear thought and purely devout sentiment have sunk into the hearts and minds of so many younger Unitarian Christians,—a most auspicious enlargement of view prevails in this select body. I now think I may esteem it to be the real and fertile germ of that wider and more blessed religion which shall permeate all nations, and unite them in love of truth and freedom and in mutual esteem; by maintaining and developing devout reverence, love, and trust in *a God who designs and rules and loves and pities*; also by maintaining Christian doctrine concerning marriage and purity; without enforcing any such dogmas as robust intellects cannot admit. Ever since I knew what Unitarians are, I have honored them; I now ask admission into their ranks.

August 2. FRANCIS WM. NEWMAN.

—*Inquirer.*

LIGHT! LIGHT!! LIGHT!!!

PATENT PORTABLE AIR GAS MAKING APPARATUS,

SUITABLE FOR

Churches, Chapels, Schools, Country Mansions, Private Houses, Railway Stations, Barracks, Manufactories, Collieries, Mills, Offices, &c., &c.

THIS *simple* and *effective* Gas-making Apparatus supplies a want long felt of having Gas at places where no Gas Works exist. It may be introduced without any more trouble than the simply affixing of any ordinary Gas meter, and is about the same size for the same number of lights. The *piping* and *fitting* arrangements are in every respect the same as for the use of ordinary Gas. The *cost* of the Gas produced is about the same as is charged for ordinary Coal Gas, and the light produced is *more brilliant* and of *a greater illuminating power*; it is also *free from the impurities of Coal Gas.* The Gas, if used with the Patent Burner, is of great heating power, and hence suitable for cooking and heating purposes, or in manufactories for soldering, &c. The apparatus is PORTABLE; there is NO DANGER WHATEVER (ordinary care being used when filling it); the Gas is PRODUCED IN AN INSTANT WITHOUT ANY FIRE OR OTHER ARTIFICIAL HEAT.

Further particulars may be obtained from MESSRS. EDWARD THOMSON & CO., Contractors for Drainage, Water and Gas, who are appointed Sole Agents for the above apparatus, which can be seen working any week day between the hours of 6 A.M., and 6 P.M., at their place of business.

39, BENTINCK STREET, CALCUTTA.

P. W. FLEURY & CO.,

BUILDERS, ENGINEERS,

AND

SCIENTIFIC INSTRUMENT MAKERS,

No. 44, Free School Street.

We beg to intimate that we have been engaged in the above line of business for the past 20 years, and trust that our Constituents will continue to favor us with their work, which will meet with prompt attention on our part.

In connection with buildings, we undertake the erection and repairing of machinery at moderate charges; as also execute all descriptions of Iron and Brass work.

We can assure the Public that we undertake the repair and erection of Houses and the laying of Water-supply Pipes on moderate terms, and guarantee to keep all the water-pipes and brass fittings supplied by us in good working order for three years, free of extra charge. We also guarantee to keep dwelling-houses' roofs water-tight for three years, free of extra charge, for such houses as we have repaired.

For purposes of illumination, we prepare our patent Chromatic Transparencies representing Coat-of-Arms, Landscapes, Scenery, &c., at prices, ranging from Rs. 50 to 300 each, according to size and design.

FOR SALE

Light! Light!! Light!!!

Electric Light apparatus, complete, worked with a battery of 50 large cells, on Bunsen's principle	500	0
Ditto ditto, with 40 cells, smaller size ...	400	0
Ditto ditto, with a powerful 44-cell Cast-iron Battery, on Callan's principle ...	300	0
Lime Light Apparatus, complete, with Iron Gas-holder, and Copper Retort ...	150	0
Oxy-Hydrogen Light Apparatus with safety Jets, 2 iron Gas-holders, and Retorts, complete	200	0
Hink's Patent Duplex Wall Lamps, with chimney	5	8
Ditto Duplex Lamp, with chimney and globe	7	8

Patent Leblanche Battery

For constancy, durability, and cleanliness, this battery is unequalled; price for each cell, with chemicals	3
Bunsen's Galvanic Battery, 8 inches by 4 inches	7
Magneto-Electric Machine, with single magnet	14
Prismatic Compass 3-inch, in a lid leather case, by Elliot, *second hand*	25
Ditto, 4 inch, by Simmons, *second hand* ...	35

P. W. FLEURY & Co.

NO. 44, FREE SCHOOL STREET.

How to Enjoy Life

Is only known when the blood is pure, its circulation perfect, and the nerves in good order. The only safe and certain method of expelling all impurities is to take Holloway's Pills, which have the power of cleansing the blood from all noxious matters, expelling all humours which taint or impoverish it, thereby purify and invigorate and give general tone to the system. Young or old, robust or delicate, may alike experience their renovating effects. Myriads affirmed that these Pills possess marvellous power in securing these great secrets of health by purifying and regulating the fluids and strengthening the solids.

DENONAUTH DEY AND SONS,

NO. 80, CLIVE STREET.

Godowns, No. 24, Mathoora [illegible] Street.

IMPORTERS OF METALS, IRONMONGERY, HARDWARE, TEA GARDEN TOOLS.

CHUBBS' LOCKS AND SAFES, RODGERS' CUTLERY, Carpenters', Blacksmiths', Coopers', Engineers' Builders' and Planters' Tools.

SADDLERY, STEAM, GAS & WATER-FITTINGS,

PAINTS, OILS, MARINE STORES &c. &c.

Priced Catalogues supplied on application, at Rs. 2. each.

ARLINGTON & CO.,

3, B DALHOUSIE SQUARE, CALCUTTA.

THE 'PATENT PERPETUAL FOUNTAIN,'

TABLE EPERGNE OR CENTRE PIECE

FOR SCENT OR FOR PUREWATER.

In Richly Electro-Silvered Ware. [*One of the Greatest Novelties of the day.*]

Cash Price Rs. 173

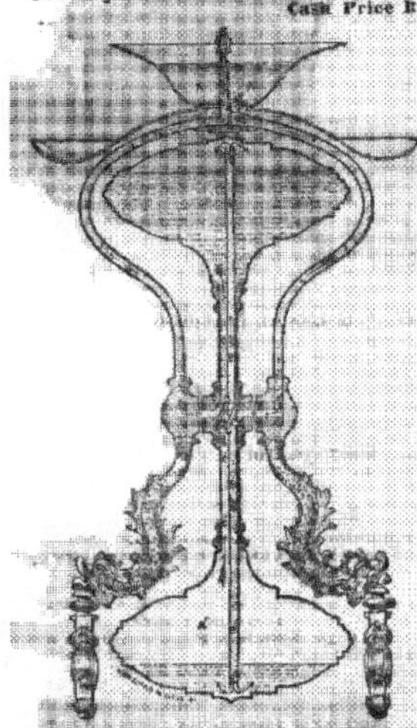

N. B.—The annexed drawing is not a correct representation of the Plated Table Fountains which A. & Co. have for sale. The drawing is only given to show the internal arrangements of the Apparatus and attention is invited to the following description :—

OBSERVE.—A, A1, are two cisterns or reservoirs which are connected together by pipes or tubes B, B1, C, C1, mounted on a hollow [illegible] plug G, having suitable passages F, G, H, therein communicating with the pipes or tubes B, B1, C, C1, and I, and with the jet pipe J.

To put the Fountain in operation water is poured into the dish or basin K until the lower reservoir is filled and the opening I1 is covered. The cisterns or reservoirs A, A1, are then turned on their axis of motion, so as to place the filled cistern or reservoir A at the top when the water therefrom will flow to a level in the jet pipe J, and the water in the basin or dish K by passing down the pipes or tubes I and B1 into the lower cistern or reservoir A1, rises in such lower cistern or reservoir A1 and forces the air out therefrom through the pipe or tube C1, passage F, and tube B, into the upper part of the cistern or reservoir A, where it presses upon the surface of the water therein and forces it out therefrom through the tube C, passage H, and jet pipe J, until all the water in the upper cistern or reservoir A has passed through the jet pipe J and into the lower cistern or reservoir A1 by the pipe I, passage G, and pipe B1, when by turning the cistern or reservoirs A, A1, on their axis of motion until the cistern or reservoir A1 is at the top, the action of the fountain will be continued; the pipes or tubes B, C1, which had previously been air passages now becoming water passages, and the pipes or tubes B1, C, now becoming air passages which had previously served for the passage of water. By these improvements the necessity for alternately filling and emptying the cisterns or reservoirs A, A1, is obviated.

Printing Materials.

MILLER AND RICHARD'S PRESSES, TYPES and all requisites always in Stock,

TERMS CASH.

EWING & CO.

CHUNDER & BROTHERS.

25½ & 112, RADHA BAZAR,

STATIONERY in all its varieties.
PRINTING PRESSES, Inks & Materials.
LITHOGRAPHIC PRESS & Materials.
BOOK BINDING Materials &c.

MAKHON LOLL GHOSE.

No. 91, Radha Bazar, Calcutta.

BEGS to invite **the attention of the** public to several consignments of commercial and fancy stationery of all sorts, including account books of all sizes, made of handmade and machine made paper, by steamers recently arrived, and which he is disposing of at moderate prices. He has been long in the trade, and presumes he has always afforded every satisfaction to the numerous merchants here who have constantly favored him with orders. Mofussil orders accompanied with remittances shall be promptly attended to.

CALCUTTA
The 18th August 1876. }

ESTABLISHED 1833.

H. C. GANGOOLY & CO.

STATIONERS, DIE-SINKERS, ENGRAVERS, PRINTERS, LITHOGRAPHERS &c.

24, Mangoe Lane, Calcutta.

Cash prices of the following :—

	Rs.	As.		Rs.
Whatman's Drawing paper double elephant sizes (40×27) each ...	0	7		0
Mathematical Instrument Boxes	2	8	to	16
Color Boxes	0	4	,,	5

Drawing Pencils, Drawing and Mapping Steel pens and various other requisites in Stationery.

THEISTIC BOOKS,

FOR SALE.

URDU.

Rahut Hakiki	Rs.	0	3	0
Nizam Komi		0	2	0
Kasaful Ilham		0	2	0
Kholasa, of, Asool Brahm Dharm ...		0	1	6

HINDI.

Upasana Padhati	Rs.	0	1	0
Bensi Patrika or Hymn book ...		0	1	0
Tut Bodh		0	8	0
Upanishid Sar		0	8	0
Dhurm Dipika		0	0	6

ENGLISH.

Claims of so called Revealed Religion	Rs.	0	3	0
New Life		0	0	6
Living God		0	1	0
Higher and Lower Virtue		0	1	0

Apply to the Secretary,
BRAHMO SOMAJ OF THE PUNJAB,
Lahore.

SMITH, STANISTREET & CO.

Pharmaceutical Chemists & Druggists

BY APPOINTMENT

To His Excellency the Right Hon'ble

LORD LYTTON, G.M.S.I.,

Governor-General of India,

&c. &c.

SYRUP OF LACTATE OF IRON.

Prepared from the original recipe. [illegible] of Iron, in various forms of preparation, have been in use in France, and generally through the continent of Europe, for some years past, and is highly esteemed as one of the most valuable Chalybeate Tonic remedies yet introduced. [illegible] the most agreeable as well as convenient form of administration is in more general use. It is a most valuable remedy in the following diseases :—Chlorosis or Green Sickness, Leucorrhœa, Neuralgia, enlargement of the Spleen, &c. In combination with quinine, it has also been very successfully used in the cure of Fever, while to persons of delicate constitution, enfeebled by disease it is invaluable. In bottles, Rs. 2 each.

SYRUP OF THE PHOSPHATE OF IRON Rs. 2 per bottle.

SYRUP OF PHOSPHATE OF IRON AND STRYCHNINE, Rs. 2 per bottle.

SYRUP OF PHOSPHATE OF IRON AND QUININE. Price Rs. 2-8 per bottle.

SYRUP OF PHOSPHATE OF IRON, QUININE AND STRYCHNINE. (DR. ATKIN'S TRIPLE TONIC SYRUP,) Rs. 2-8 per bottle.

Smith, Stanistreet & Co.

Invite special attention to the following rates the quality guaranteed as the best procurable :—

Pure Ærated Waters,

Made from Pure Water, obtained by the new process through the Patent Charcoal Filters.

				Rs.	As.
Ærated plain (Treble Aerated), per doz.			...	[illegible]	15
Soda Water	ditto	,,	...	[illegible]	12
Gingerade	ditto	,,	...	1	4
Lemonade	ditto	,,	...	1	4
Tonic (Quinine)	ditto	,,	...	1	4

The Cash must be sent with the order to obtain advantage of the above rates.

BURN & CO.

RANEEGUNGE Fire bricks are the best Fire Bricks known ;—superior to Ramsay's.

9 Rs. per 100.

Fire clay, 40 Rs. per Ton.

Glazed Stone ware, Drainage pipes of all sizes

BURN & Co.,
7, Hastings Street, Calcutta.

MUDHOO SUDUN PAUL & CO.

120, RADHA BAZAR,

Tea ! (Assam) Tea !

TRADE M. MARK.

In 1lb. and 2lb. Tins.

Pekoe Tea	... 2lb. Tin, Per Tin	Rs.	3	8
,, Flowery	... ,, ,, ,,		3	8
,, Souchong	... ,, ,, ,,		2	0
Family Mixture	... ,, ,, ,,		[illegible]	[illegible]
Campoi	... ,, ,, ,,		[illegible]	8
Imperial Mixture with China	... ...		3	4
China Rose Panchong	... ...		2	8

The above in 1lb. Tin at half the respective prices, plus two annas extra.

BURMAH CIGARS.

No. 1 per 100	Rs.	1	0
,, 2 ,, ,,		0	12

HUNTLEY AND PALMER'S BISCUITS.

Albert, in Tin of 2 lb each.	Rs.	1	6
Arrow Root, ...	,,	1	4
Mixed, ...	,,	1	4

Indian Chutnies, Castor Oil, Candles Kerosine Oil, China Preserves, Perfumery Domestic Medicines and other stores always in stock and offered at lower rates than other Houses.

Catalogue to be had on application.

MUDHOO SUDUN PAUL & Co.

Printed and published by M. M. RUKHIT, at the INDIAN MIRROR PRESS, No. 6, College Square, for the Proprietors.

The Indian Mirror.

SUNDAY EDITION.

VOL. XV.] CALCUTTA, SUNDAY, OCTOBER 22, 1876. {REGISTERED AT THE GENERAL POST OFFICE.} [No. 250

CONTENTS.

NOTICE.

All letters and communications relating to the literary department of the Paper should be addressed to the Editor. All other letters should be addressed to the Manager, to whom all remittances should be made payable.

Subscribers will be good enough to bring to the notice of the Manager any delay or irregularity in the delivery of the Paper.

Editorial Notes

WE as Brahmos have, in the name of our community, to accord a cordial welcome home to Dr. Prosunno Kumar Rai, of the London and Edinburgh Universities, in both of which he took his degree of Doctor of Science with high honors. He landed in Calcutta on Monday last amongst a crowd of expectant friends who warmly greeted him. Dr. P. K. Rai is a staunch and enthusiastic Brahmo, and with a wide philosophic and scientific culture he combines the theist's warm and simple faith. May he by the grace of God be instrumental in advancing the cause of truth, wisdom, and righteousness in his own fatherland.

THE *Friend of India* gives an interesting review of the book of Mr. Thoburn on Bannu. From the review it seems one of the most pleasant and interesting books ever witten. The insight it shows into the mysteries of Pathan life, the custom, the folklore, and the theories on natural phenomena, are highly instructive and amusing. Our contemporary extracts many instances, out of which we take the following :—

One day old Maharajah Runjit Singh, the Lion of the Punjab, received in Durbar a deputation of Hindus and Mahomedans, and presented each with magnificent "*Khilats.*" Amongst the presents to the former was a silver cow, and to the latter a silver pig.

A year after, the two deputations again visited him, and he asked the Hindus what they had done with their cow. They hung down their heads, and admitted they had melted it down and divided its silver amongst themselves.

"And what have you done with your pig?" said the monarch to the Mahomedans.

"Oh!" said they; "we threw the unclean beast into a drain as soon as we got to our homes."

When the Maharajah found that this was true, he fined the greedy Hindus all round, but rewarded the Mahomedans.

THE Mahomedan notion on the subject of earthquakes resembles the Hindu idea very much, and the two traditions must, we think, spring from the same source :—

An earthquake is caused by the cow, on whose horn the world is poised, changing the burden from one horn to another. When God made the earth, he placed it on a cow's horn, and the cow on the back of a fish, and the fish on a stone, and the stone on—well, God knows what. *That* has not been revealed to man. Some think that when the earth trembles, it is owing to the cow, which supports it, shaking herself, and not shifting the earth from one horn to the other. Whilst the quaking goes on, the Marwats rush out of their houses, and call to each other, "Come to Mecca! Come to Mecca!" But as soon as the motion ceases, their desire to go on a pilgrimage subsides also.

THE late Prime Minister of Cashmere, Dewan Kirpa Ram, was a typical Hindu. He was faithfully devoted to the interests of his master, and though now and then exacting in his behaviour towards the subjects, for a Native State he was a just and prudent statesman. The last act of his life is thus described by our Lahore contemporary who has by no means been friendly to the late Dewan.—"It appears that Dewan Kirpa Ram, the late Prime Minister of Cashmere, distributed all his property to the poor, a few hours before he expired. His wife even offered all her jewels for the purpose, but these, as well as a few horses for the personal use of the son, were allowed to be kept by the family. There is no doubt that, with very grave errors which we have unhesitatingly exposed at the time, the late Dewan was a great patron of learning, and himself a distinguished Oriental Scholar, combining the rare attainment of eminence alike in Sanskrit, Persian, and we believe also Arabic. He was also a most generous man, but his administration of Cashmere was oppressive. He is succeeded, as we are told, by his son, Dewan Anant Ram, who certainly in some respects has an illustrious example to follow." For a man of Dewan Kirpa Ram's position and wealth, this last act of self-sacrifice is simply glorious. From this our readers will get some glimpse into the spirit which genuine Hinduism fosters.

OUR accomplished Viceroy has paid a fitting tribute to the career and qualifications of our Finance Minister Sir William Muir, who is about to resign his present office. With Sir William Muir departs from India perhaps, the last representative of a generation of Indian civilians who combined with brilliant abilities and noble worth, a friendly and fatherly interest in the millions of men and women over whom they exercised a mighty power all but irresponsible, and very difficult to keep always uncontaminated from abuse. Sir William Muir has shown a noble example not only of the combination of deep and genuine scholarship with the discharge of arduous public duties, but an example still more illustrious of the combination of high political life with a moral purity and religious fervor very rarely met with in this country. And when we say that such a fervid and pure character has been adorned with a spirit of toleration, a catholic concern in the welfare of all sects, sexes and communities alike, we have given only a feeble sketch of the many virtues that have graced the long career of forty years during which Sir William Muir has taken part in the administration of India. We Brahmos feel a personal obligation to him for all that he has done to further some of our movements, and the distinguished consideration he has always shown to the head of our community. All classes of Native Society here and in the N. W. Provinces ought to unite in bidding a cordial, appreciative, enthusiastic farewell to Sir William Muir.

PROFESSOR HUXLEY is lecturing in America, where large numbers of people no doubt flock to hear him. But the evangelical element is as intolerant in America as elsewhere in the world. The *Independent*, a New York journal, which is orthodox enough, even takes exception to some of the language applied to Professor Huxley :—"Professor Huxley's address at Buffalo was happy in that it said nothing very unpleasantly. The welcome, however, which he gets from Bishop Coxe, of Buffalo, is not very cordial. The Bishop says : 'We regret to see those who profess and call themselves Christians going out of their way to pay attention to Prof. Huxley, the molecule philosopher. Mr. Huxley has gone out of his way to insult the faith of Christians and the civilization of evangelized nations. As a scientist he might deserve a high position; but as a gratuitous assailant of revelation he has forfeited his claim to the respect of believers. An intellectual suicide, who talks of laws and systems while he recognizes no lawgiver, and rejects an intelligent creator, demands our pity; but, if it is only the fool that says in his heart 'There is no God,' it is the dictate of propriety to leave consummate folly to find society with itself.' Now this is outrageous. Professor Huxley is, at least, a remarkably able naturalist. As such he deserves honor, whether he be a Christian or a Pagan. His philosophy appears to us insufficient and hostile to Christianity, but we do not see why he may not honestly hold it, and be no liar in his professions that he is in search of the truth. It will not pay to scold those who differ from us."

ENGLISH UNITARIANISM AND ENGLISH THEISM.

IN noticing not many months ago the somewhat painful controvercy that marked the proceedings of the British and Foreign Unitarian Association in regard to the printing and circulation of Theodore Parker's works, a controversy that somewhat unexpectedly resulted in the signal victory of liberal principles, we made this remark:—"Thus gradually the difference between Unitarian Christianity and pure Theism is ceasing to exist, and ere long the two systems may unite." The most striking corroboration that could have been furnished to this opinion is found in the fact of the formal reception of Professor F. W. Newman into the governing body of the English Unitarians. That Professor Newman has not renounced any of his well-known religious views in going to join the Unitarian Association, is evident enough in his letter to Miss Swanwick which we published last Sunday. That the Association has made no new or unprecedented concession in admitting him into their body, is equally evident when their late decision to publish and circulate Parkers' works is remembered, and further when we count how many men of almost the identical opinions held by Mr Newman there are on its council. Without the least compromise of principle on either side, the gain on both sides has been immense. English Theism, we believe, has no better representative in the world than Francis William Newman, and English Unitarianism, uncertain and unsettled as that creed has been from a long time, is represented, if it is represented anywhere, by the British and Foreign Unitarian Association. And when the representatives thus unite, is it very unreasonable to predict that the systems they represent shall also unite in no distant day? The great advantantage to Unitarianism that may be expected under the present policy of coalition, is the strong and decided sympathy of all rational religious thinkers with the struggles and progress of the advanced school of Unitarian theology. The Unitarian Church, it is very well-know, is divided into two sections, one of which is orthodox and conservative, keeping up as many of the old traditions and usages as possible, and vigorously trying to stem the tide of new-fangled ideas and innovations. The other section is liberal and progressive to such an extent that properly speaking there is very little in their theology distinctive of the position which they hold apart from the Free Christian and Theistic communities that are prospering and multiplying in England. The conservatism of the orthodox school shades and grades itself into so many nicely distinguished orders of thought and sympathy, that it gradually blends itself with the tendencies of the advanced section. So, therefore, the whole machinary of Unitarian thought and belief works in the direction of emancipating the mind from traditional fetters, and theological subservience. But the organization is firm and real, tending to become more and more extensive and real as the principles of the body widen in sympathy and scope, and as men of such peculiar moral and religious eminence as Mr. F. W. Newman are invited to join it. A whole host of men will gladly accord their sympathy and admiration to the British and Foreign Unitarian Association for the liberality and cordiality with which they have commenced to associate themselves with those from whom they differ very materially in theological matters.

On the other hand the gain to the cause of English Theism will be great. Because say what we might in favor of it, there cannot be a question that Theism in England has not yet been able to organize itself on a strong and well-recognized basis. A lonely theist like Mr. Newman, or Miss Cobbe can at present look to our organized movement for that personal sympathy and co-operation which solitary and unpopular religious souls must expect everywhere, and nowhere more than in the strongholds of orthodox Christianity. We do not by what we say mean to cast any slur on the parallel movement of Mr. Voysey or Mr. Conway. But they labor under certain disadvantages which cannot be removed just now. Men like Mr. Newman seeking to work in any extensive scale for the religious good of mankind, want to connect themselves with large fields of work where intelligence, spirituality, social refrom, progressiveness and practical energy are combined in an equal measure. Those English theists who can find these advantages among Unitarians find it a great gain to join them on an independent ground. As for ourselves in India we though sympathizing with all must keep our position quite separate.

Correspondence.

TRANSMIGRATION

To the Editor of the *Indian Mirror*.

SIR,—The spirit of eclecticism may, perhaps, be carried too far, and my apprehension is roused by the perusal of a recent article of yours on transmigration. Now there may be, for aught we know, a grain of truth in this doctrine; and, indeed, you may see in it more than meets an ordinary eye. But is the truth discernible to an eclectic that which is held by the vast majority of men believing in transmigration? If not, it is useless, I contend, to extract such sunbeams out of cucumbers. You may have said that such (I mean the view enunciated by you) *ought* to be the doctrine of transmigration. But to say that there is truth in the doctrine in the form in which it is believed in by Hindus, is to say what is not a fact. The truth, said to exist in the doctrine, is neither that contemplated by its first propounders nor that held by their disciples at the present day I believe, therefore, that to speak in the form you have done, would be misleading, as it would create an impression that there is more that is common to theism and pantheism than is at first experienced; and, believe me, Sir, I would not have said so much, if I had not been impressed with the mischievous extent in which the doctrines of pantheism are believed in from one end of India to the other. Outside Bengal it is not polytheism but pantheism against which theism has to wage its great warfare. Can this be done unless we see the monster in the face, and expose its hideous deformities? If there is any truth in the doctrines of transmigration and *nirvana*, it is more generally found in the philosopher's closet than elsewhere. With reference, therefore, to all such attempts at extracting good out of evil, I ask,—*cui bono*!

Yours Obedently,
B.

Devotional

WHICH have I in the world, O my God, but thee? There are many I would call dear, and near, and for whom I would willingly toil and suffer. But in the real darkness and distress of life, at the moment of real trial and separation, who stands with me but thou? My God, I am alone, and have only thy righteous mercy on my side. Show me the right way to behave towards my fellowmen, show me the way by which I may cease to be a trouble unto others. If it please thee manifest unto me in spirit the brothers and the sisters, the fathers and the mothers, the friends and the helpers whom I may call my own in calling thee my own.

THOUGH I be in constant want teach me yet, O my God, to take away my heart from the thought of worldly riches. Let holy poverty sweeten my soul to trust in thee more fully, and resign my all in thy hands.

WHY should I fear man's condemnation, O Holy God, when thou dost acquit me in the court of conscience. And why should I feel elated by other's praise when thine awful voice convicts me of guilt. I pray unto thee for the light and rest of a pure conscience. I cannot claim that others will give me rest, I cannot claim the right of human approbation, for even if I deserved it all, it would harden me, and lead me away from thee. My Father, bless me, that delivered from my many sins, I may stand in humble innocence before thy face. Fear and sorrow, care and humiliation cease when I stand justified within the embrace of thy sanctifying love.

CAUSE thy manifold blessings, O Lord, to descend upon the heads of those who have fallen into disease or destitution by faithfully working as thy servants. Suffer thy unspeakable peace to enter into those hearts that are aching with anxiety for others' good. Upon those who labor far from home and friends in thy vineyard, cause all blessing and success to descend. Let thy suffering servants feel soothed by thee at all times.

The Brahmo Somaj

VERY likely Babu Keshub Chunder Sen leaves Bhagalpur for Calcutta within the course of a week.

ON Sunday last Babu Gour Govind Roy conducted the monthly nothing service in the Mandir. And the evening Service was conducted by Babu Bejoy Kissen Goswamy. The latter clearly pointed out in the course of his sermon that the only and all powerful attraction which the Brahmo Somaj holds for its members is sweet and true worship of God. Without it, he said, there is no hope of the stability of any Brahmo life. He who has discovered in the Object of his Worship a perennial fountain of ever holy and ever fresh joy, will never secede from the Brahmo Somaj; but will endure to the last.

THE anniversary of the Serampore Brahmo Somaj takes place to-day. Babu Protap Chunder Mozoomdar is expected to conduct the morning service on the occasion.

THEOLOGICAL CLASS.

Sunday, September, 3rd 1876.

THE most profound scepticism of which human nature is capable, finds its home in the moral world. Man's intellectual difficulties certainly disturb his faith and warp his action to a great extent. But if his practical instincts are clear and strong, the clouds of his mind are often kept in abeyance. But when moral judgments are perverted, and doubts have arisen to confound the distinctions of good and evil, the intellect sympathises with the heart, the moral nature misleads both, and utter bewilderment in motives and practical life is the result. At the present day when happiness forms the sole standard of good, and pain is set down as synonymous with evil, the most alarming conclusions have been arrived at from the arrangement of facts in the outer world, and specially from the phenomena of sentient life. These conclusions have been partially suggested by the speculations of writers on Natural Theology like Paley and Brown, who have uniformly endeavoured to prove Divine Goodness by the superficial adjustments of the material creation to the nervous system of man, without trying honestly and vigorously to cope with the problem of suffering and evil. The fact of the existence of a single evil is as important towards unsettling our dependence on Divine Beneficence, as an incalculable amount of the same element. If that which is immoral, be it much or be it little, is found conformable to the just and righteous administration of the world's affairs, human life loses its best and strongest motives for sacrificing itself and suffering in the cause of an ideal goodness. The position, therefore, of maintaining the irreproachable, uncompromising, rigid, and unfaltering purity on the part of Providence, towards the moral government of the world is forced upon us. With the righteousness of our Moral Governor, stands or falls the possible righteousness of man. We have thus only stated our difficulty. Let us see how far we can meet it.

VINDUVASHINI THE WIDOW*

(FROM REAL LIFE)

IN a village near Calcutta there lived a rich family, and Vinduvasini was the favorable child of that family. She was very young, very handsome, her face was full of noble expression, and there was always a calmness and sweetness of look in her large eyes. Everyone loved her for her good qualities, and sweet disposition. Unfortunately she was married to a person who was unworthy of her in every respect. He was fond of drink and a bad man. Vinduvashini knew all this, but loved her husband nevertheless as a dutiful wife, though she was very unhappy for him. She always made attempts to conceal his faults from others and tried her utmost to make him better, but in vain. Her husband never improved. Vindu did not complain of her lot to any one. She had a beautiful little child, a boy two years old. When she saw that all her attempts failed regarding her husband, she did not impart to any one her sorrow, but cheerfully spent her days in nursing her child. She also tried to forget her unhappiness by doing her duties towards her widowed mother, and trying to do all she could to help and do good to her neighbours. Everybody who knew her felt for her, and loved her. But she was always silent about her sorrow. Only her mother discovered that at night, when every one in the house was deep in slumber, Vindu used to sit for hours together at the window, and sometimes in her sleep her pillow used to be wet with tears.

Vinduvasini now seldom saw her husband, for he lived in town. One day the news came that he had an attack of cholera, and then the next day came the startling message, that Vindu's husband was no more. At this the whole house was filled with loud lamentation. But by and by it ceased. Those who wept, smiled again. Everything took its former course. It seemed as if everybody had forgotten that Vindu had ever a husband! Only Vindu's heart remained the same. One month thus passed away. In the second month late one night when the rest of the household were fast asleep, Vinduvasini rose from her bed softly. She took out all her jewels from a box that was in the room and put them one by one upon the delicate person of her child, stopped and gazed at him tenderly a few minutes, as if for the last time, then tied her keys in the corner of her mother's dress, and at last noiselessly glided out of the house.

All around her was pitch dark. She went through the silent lanes, by the hedge and bush, by the pond and marsh she went, and under big trees amidst the shelter of whose leaves the birds slept, and now and then fluttered their wings in their dreams as she passed. All creation was insensible in sweet repose but there was no rest for one being only, and that was the young Hindu widow. But she fearlessly continued her march steadily going towards the river-side. She did not heed anything, to her the whole world was dead. She thought her own life worthless without her husband.

Thus at last Vindu reached the banks of the wide Gunga. It being the rainy season the river was full and swollen, and very broad. The sound of breaking banks was heard resounding in the solemn stillness of the night, and the stream rushed, and the waves made a noise that seemed full of sorrow to the widow's ears. The dogs barked at the *ghat*, and the shrill cry of the jackals was heard at intervals. On the big trees numbers of glow-worms were shedding their quiet lustre. Far far from the banks one or two little solitary boats were rowing over, everybody asleep inside, only the helmsman awake, breaking the silence around by snatches of some old, sad, country song.

In the midst of all this the poor young widow sat weeping on the bank. The night breeze cooled her heated brow, but what could cool her broken heart! She sat there for a long time,—how long, no one can tell; and then she disappeared—where no one can tell. Early in the morning when people came to bathe in the river, no one saw her. In her home when they became aware that she was missing, men were send to make a search, but they brought no tidings of Vindu. All hearts were filled with grief her mother went well-nigh mad, her child always asked after her, went about to look for her, and not finding her cried. The whole village was a scene of sorrow, because they all thought Vinduvashini had gone after her husband into the other world. Has she found him?— The boatmen who were on the river that night said that far towards the morning they saw a figure clad in white sitting on the overhanging bank. It was there for a long time, when suddenly there was a splash on the water as if some heavy thing had fallen. And after that they saw and heard nothing more. The figure in white (it seemed a woman's figure) had gone, and with it the part of the bank on which she was sitting.

The river is flowing below the old village still, the wind is playing with the waves, the leaves of the trees are making a sweet and soft song to the wind, but Vinduvasini's home is deserted and dark. If you ask the boatmen they would point even now with feelings of awe and sorrow to the place where Vinduvashini, the widow, entered the wide bosom of mother Gunga.

* Translated from Bengali by a lady, pupil of the Native Ladies' Normal School, and revised by the Editor.

Literary

IT is said that Dr. Browne, who was at one time in the service of the Bombay Municipality, is the Editor of that scurrilous anti-Native journal started at Madras, called the *European*.

Latest News

—SIR GEORGE COUPER is away on a tour through Almora and Ranikhet.

—THE Sonepore Races have been postponed till November, the 16th.

—ONE of the sons of the Khan of Khelat has died of cholera.

—SIR RICHARD TEMPLE has telegraphed to Lord Salisbury to send out some more education-wallahs forthwith.

—COLONEL A. D. DICKENS, C. B., Deputy Commissary General, is dead.

—THE *Times of India* hears on good authority that His Excellency the Viceroy has invited Sir Jamsetji Jejibhoy, Mr. Ardaser Hormusji Wadia, Sir Mungaldas Nathubhoy, and the Hon'ble Mr. Sorabji Shapurji Bengali to attend the Viceregal Durbar in Delhi in January next. The invitations have been sent through the Bombay Government.

—A HOTEL, called the "The Empress Hotel," is to be opened at Delhi by Hanty & Co. in connection with the Durbar.

—MR. ABDUL KHADAR, Assistant Commissioner, has been appointed to officiate as Town Magistrate of Mysore, during the absence of Colonel Renton at Bangalore as Military Secretary to the Chief Commissioner, in the room of Major R. G. Stewart. He is highly spoken by the Mysore papers.

—IT is stated that at Pusagaon, and also in other talokas in the Deccan, several persons have already died of starvation.

—THE *Pioneer* says:—"Lord Lytton has brought to the treatment of his foreign affairs a greater love of secresy—fostered by his diplomatic training—than any previous Viceroy has ever displayed before."

—MR. HALSEY, Officiating Commissioner of Customs, N. W. P., is lying in a very critical state at Agra.

—SOME signal marks of favor will be bestowed on the Native Chiefs at the Delhi Durbar.

—SIR SALAR JUNG, who is much better, has managed to get out and pay his first visit to the Nizam at a perfectly private Durbar.

—MR. BERTOLA, a tradesman of Simla, has been fined 90 rupees for striking a Native orderly.

—THE *Bombay Gazette* reports one death from starvation at Sholapore. He had gone to the Collector's Office to seek for relief, but he died close to the Cutcherry from exhaustion.

—LORD LYTTON has ruled that officials proceeding on privilege leave whose salary is below Rs. 200, can obtain an advance not exceeding two months' salary.

—SIR RICHARD MEADE has written a very eulogistic minute on the Educational report, prepared by Mr. Narayan B. Dandekar, Director of Public Instruction, Berars.

—SIR RICHARD MEADE on his return from the Imperial Assemblage will visit the Berars.

—IT is said that the Governor of Bombay in consequence of the famine in the Deccan, has abandoned his intended visit to Delhi, to be present at the Imperial Assemblage there.

Calcutta.

MR. RATTRAY, the most unjustly degraded Superintendent of Police, Chittagong, is shortly expected in Calcutta.

THE second inquest into the circumstances connected with the recent explosion on the river, will take place to-morrow at 4 P. M. We hope the Coroner and the Jury will be more careful this time in eliciting facts.

A ROYAL BENGAL TIGER, being a present from Mr. C. T. Metcalfe of Bankipore, has been added to the Zoological Gardens.

DR. LYNN who is astonishing the public with his spiritual manifestations, will be present at the Imperial Assemblage. It is said he is a great linguist, and the *Pioneer* suggests he should be taken into the Bengal Education Department.

COLONEL WALTON, of the Calcutta Volunteers, has been appointed to the command of the Volunteer Battalion which is to be formed from detachments of the several volunteer corps throughout India and embodied at Delhi at the Imperial Assemblage.

Selection

MAHOMED AND MAHOMEDANISM.*

DIPLOMATS and other Russophobists are trying to reassert that, after all, there was some ground for Lord Palmerston's belief that the dry bones of the Turkish Empire might still have some life in them. We have no such expectation. We say of the Turkish Khalifate as Mr. Carlyle said of the Romish Papacy, in those days when young enthusiasts looked for something to come of the reforms of the earlier years of Pio Nono, that when a kettle is nothing but rust, you can not scour it to any purpose. But just as we are not of those who say that because the Papacy is out of date as a European suzerainty over churches and States, therefore Christianity is itself out of date, so neither are the intrinsic truth and the practical worth of Mahomedanism, as one of the religions of the world, decided to be nothing in themselves, and to us, by our conclusion—or by the judgment of events—as to the Ottoman Khalifate. And therefore these lectures by Mr. Bosworth Smith are as opportune as interesting for all who care to learn, in that popular form which such lectures of a thoughtful as well as learned man can give, the facts of the Mahomedan religion as they were and are, and not merely such as they seemed to the eyes of mediæval prejudice, and still seem to those who try the habits of life and thought of semi-barbarous Oriental races by the strictest standards of European civilisation. We believe many of Mr. Smith's readers would have been glad if he had credited them with less knowledge of the life of Mahomed himself, and have given more directly many of its incidents to which he has only alluded. But his estimate of the character of Mahomed is clearly defined as that not of the mere impostor to which the Christian apologists of the eighteenth century reduced the diabolic Mahomed of the Crusaders and their successors; nor of a wise statesman but religious imposter of that type which the sceptics of the eighteenth century evoked from the depths of their inner conciousness; nor yet one of a third kind of imposters, conceived by our feebler moralists to have begun life in honest faith, but to have adopted religious deceptions to supplement a teaching which they found would not triumph over the ignorance and vice of the multitude by its own force. He was none of these, as Mr. Smith maintains, but a true prophet, a man sent from God with a message to those to whom he came, yet who, like other prophets and reformers, was a man of his own race and time, sharing more or less in the infirmities and the imperfect belief of his brethren, even while he was fulfilling his mission of raising them above their former selves. Mr. Smith reminds his readers that in order to form a candid judgment on the more difficult question of the career of Mahomed, "they need, above all things, the historical sense which does not apply the standard of the nineteenth century to the seventh, of Europeans to Asiatics, or of a high civilisation to semi-barbarism; and which is content to balance the evil against the good, without requiring a verdict, either for an absolute acquittal or an uncompromising condemnation." Mr. Smith's method, as he says elsewhere, is that of the "Science of Comparative Religion." The forms which this "Science" has taken from the earliest times are very various. It endeavoured to elucidate the fortunes of Prometheus, and the events of the siege of Troy; it was in controversy between Sennacherib and Hezekiah; it tempted Gibbon to sacrifice historical accuracy to epigrammatic smartness, when he imagined a period in which all religions were equally true to the people, equally false to the philosopher, and equally useful to the statesman; and in our own day it has found exponents who maintain that all religions are more or less subjectively true, more or less admirable fruits of human sentiment and imagination, though with no objective reality outside the mind which projects them. But Mr. Smith's science has more regard to the facts, has more claim to the name of science, than these last.

The superiority of Christianity in kind, and not merely in degree, does not—as Mr. Smith maintains, on the evidence of the Koran, and of the history, ancient and modern, of what Islam has done and is doing—does not shake his position that Mahomedanism is a true religion, a real relation between God and man, and a religion by which it seems to have been, and still to be, possible to establish that relation with races whom Christianity has not succeeded in influencing. Though the Koran represents God as a Sovereign, not as a Father, it represents him as a Sovereign who is merciful and compassionate, as well as just and holy; who hears prayer, and gives strength to those who ask it and who trust him. The so-called "fatalism" of Islam, if it be fairly judged by seeing what it was in the creed of Mahomed himself and his worthiest followers, is found to be the same absolute trust in God which characterised the Jews of old and the Puritans and Covenanters in later times, and which they all alike expressed in words of fatalism, but in deeds of manliest self-assertion. The laws and institutions of Mahomed raised the Arab tribes from their low condition of barbarous idolatry, polygamy, and moral and intellectual ignorance, though they made many concessions—as did those of Moses—for the hardness of their hearts, and at their best fell Short of our highest European standards in the nineteenth century. Though the Gospel did not teach, as the Koran did, that faith in God could be enforced by the sword, yet the practice of Christian kings and priests, as well as people, in the middle-ages, differed in this respect from that of the Mahomedans, only in the greater humanity with which the latter carried on their religious wars.

If, as we believe, civilisation and culture have their roots in true religion, there must have been such true religion to produce such Mahomedan sovereigns as were once seated on the thrones of Bagdad, Seville, and Granada, and of Agra and Delhi. And if we come to our own times, there is—as Mr. Smith shows, with very interesting details, which we can hardly do more than refer to—a great work of Mahomedan reformers and missionaries carried on in India and China, but still more in Africa, with all the marks of piety, and zeal, and self-sacrifice, which belong to the true reformer and missionary among Christians. In Africa, Mr. Smith says, Mahomedanism is spreading itself by giant strides almost year by year, and not, as of old, by the sword, but by earnest and simple-minded Arab missionaries. No sooner is Islam embraced by a Negro tribe, than polytheism, sorcery, and human sacrifices disappear; the general moral elevation is most marked; hospitality becomes a religious duty; drunkenness, from the rule, becomes the exception; chastity, within the limits prescribed by the Koran, becomes one of the commoner virtues, and such a desire for education springs up that newly-converted Mussulmans will travel long distances to obtain it in its higher forms. Mr. Smith does not conceal that there is a darker side of his subject, yet he shows that there are many races of mankind to whom—in their actual and probable future condition—Mahomedanism seems to be more congruous than Christianity. On the complicated problem which such a belief involves, as to the exact limits up to which Mahomedanism is true—a faith comes from God, and not merely a blind seeking after God—and in what way this lower faith may hereafter come into harmony, and so into unity with the Christian faith, Mr. Smith touches, but scarcely done more than touch. We could not expect him to do more in a course of popular lectures, but it is a problem of which neither the difficulty nor the importance can be easily over-stated.

* *Mahomed and Mahomedanism.* Lectures delivered at Royal Institution of Great Britain in February and March, 1875. By R. Bosworth Smith M.A., Assistant-Master in Harrow School, &c. Second Edition, revised and enlarged. London; Smith, Elder, and Co, 1876.

3. The Chairman to lay on the table Memo. by Health Officer, submitting vital statistics of the Town for the months of July and August 1876.

4. The Chairman to lay on the table letter from Government of Bengal, forwarding copy of a letter from the Government of India, in the Department of Revenue, Agriculture and Commerce, communicating the observations of His Excellency the Governor-General in Council on the administration Report of the Calcutta Municipality for the year 1875.

5. The Chairman to move, under Section 43 of Act IV, (B. C.) of 1876, that the dates and hours for holding Quarterly and Ordinary Meetings be fixed by the Commissioners.

6. The Chairman to submit letter from Government of Bengal, forwarding copy of a letter from Government of India, Financial Department, communicating the sanction of His Excellency the Governor-General in Council, to the grant of the Loan for Rs. 1,45,000 applied for by the Commissioners for construction of four new filters. The present Loan to be considered as a part of the existing 4½ per cent. Water Supply Loan.

7. The Chairman to lay on the table Statement of Accounts for the month of August 1876.

ROBERT TURNBULL,
Secretary to the Corporation.

21st October, 1876.

Printed and published by M. M. RUKHIT, at the INDIAN MIRROR PRESS, No. 6, College Square, for the Proprietors.

The Indian Mirror.

SUNDAY EDITION.

VOL XV.] CALCUTTA, SNUDAY, OCTOBER 29, 1876. {Registered at the General Post Office.} [No. 256

CONTENTS.

NOTICE.

All letters and communications relating to the literary department of the Paper should be addressed to the Editor. All other letters should be addressed to the Manager, to whom all remittances should be made payable.

Subscribers will be good enough to bring to the notice of the Manager any delay or irregularity in the delivery of the Paper.

Editorial Notes

WE publish elsewhere an extract in which Dr. Sexton speaks of his experiences in that condition of mind wherein he considered the existence God "a closed question." The unrest and yearning of the soul to believe and put its confidence in a Supreme and All-wise power are very truly set forth.

THE Arch Bishop of Canterbury has come down upon Theism in the course of a charge which he delivered at Croydon during an Episcopal Visitation. His attack was based upon the old notions of the Deist's creed, because His Grace recognizes no distinction between Deist and Theist. Mr. Voysey on behalf of Theism answers the accusation in a letter to the *Times*. We believe Mr. Vosey has accomplished his task satisfactorily.

WHEN the heart and the moral sense of a great and noble nation are aroused, it is a grand spectacle to see. And surely the strongest feelings and moral impulses of the British nation have been set ablaze by the events in Bulgaria. The man who can be said to have had the largest share in awakening his countrymen to their sense of duty is Mr. Gladstone. His influence upon the heart and conscience of the nation is simply wonderful. Mr. Disraeli is clever no doubt, and cautious, and has extraordinary insight into human nature, but when the higher principles of national character come to be dealt with, he is silently put by and his great rival enjoys the confidence of all men.

No one knows what the upshot of the present agitation in England against the Bulgarian horrors will be. So far as may be gathered from the signs of the times, we do not think Egland will go to war with the Turks, though there seems to be little doubt that some measures will be enforced on the Ottoman Empire to prevent the repitition of similar scenes in its Christian provinces. No doubt much of the present agitation is owing to the long-established prejudice against Mahomedanism that prevails in England and other Christian countries, and if there is a war, it will to some extent assume the shape of a *jehad* for the purpose of exterminating the Mossulman religion in Europe. And begots will warmly exult over such an event. It is to be hoped the common sense of Englishmen will prevent such an interpretation being put upon their preceedings at the present crisis.

WHILE in England theists are condemned as heretical, in France they are set down as mad. M. Bertel, a successful barrister in Paris, made a provision in his will to dispense with the ordinary Roman Catholic rites at his burial. The will began as follows :—

I firmly believe in One Supreme God, in the immortality of the soul of man, and in a return to everybody according to his works beyond the grave ; and I remit with confidence into the hands of God the spirit I have received from him ; but, having repudiated the official worship as inadequate to effect the happiness of humanity, and as opposed to the needs and aspirations of the age, it would be inconsistent on my part to claim the assistance of the ministers of any of these creeds to honor my obsequies. My express and decided will therefore, is, that my funeral be conducted civilly.

Mr. Bertel's sister applied for the rejection of the will on the ground that the passage quoted above proved insanity on the part of the testator. The Court of Appeal happily sustained the will, though it passed severe comments on a civil burial, and characterized M. Bertel as a man given to "all the most absurd and most noxious vagaries." If M. Bertel's sentiments constitute madness before the modern Festus who presides over the Court of Appeal in Paris, more than half the world at the present day has gone mad.

CAN there not be greater unity among the Brahmos than at present ? Are not the differences among them very trivial and transient, such as may be easily removed if they feel the necessity of united and organized action ? Alas, that personal misunderstanding should lead in any case to a neglect of the vital interests of the church, and the community ! Let all Brahmos feel that their cause is the cause of truth, and though the individual workers may often find reason to differ amongst themselves, the cause must have the loyalty of every one. He that is disloyal to *that*, is disloyal to the highest and best interests of himself, and is traitrous to his God besides. A common and warm fidelity to the great common cause is sure to produce effective and deep harmony in the end. When men determine to deny themselves, can they quarrel over their individual idiosyncracies while truth and salvation are at stake ? Wherever there is holiness let us rally round that, wherever we find wisdom and goodness and love there let us continue to be. Let individual tastes and feelings be put in the background entirely, mutual forgiveness and toleration be carefully cultivated, small differences and accidental disunion be forgotten, and then let us see whether harmony, enthuiasm, and united action will not reign amongst Brahmos of all classes. We rejoice to find signs of this in the Brahmo community of Calcutta.

WE doubt very much whether the Rev. Lal Behari Day has gained anything by his long letter to the *Friend of India*. The reverend gentleman, who is the editor of the *Bengal Magazine*, allowed one of his contributors, apparently a very zealous Christian, to make the statement that "the champions of infidelity are a hundredfold more numerous than Christians in the Government educational service." The *Friend of India* naturally concludes that Mr. Day, who is a notoriously zealous Christian himself, and also a professor in one of the Government Colleges, thus enjoying a double experience, must be of the same opinion as his contributor on this point, or he would not allow such a sweeping charge to appear in his magazine. The Rev. Lal Behari Day, sincerely frightened lest the authorities of Education Department should come down upon him one fine morning, tries to make a lengthy apology in the columns of the *Friend*. He says that, like the editor of the *Contemporary Review*, he is not responsible for the opinions of his contriouters. We cannot, we are sorry to say, view the *Bengal Magazine* in the same light as the *Contemporary Review*. The comparison is ungraceful. To say nothing of its position and abilities, of the *Contemporary* the principles and the line of policy by which it is guided, and the relations of the editor with his contributors are very well known. Besides against each article the full name of the writer is inserted and he seldom dreams of indulging in such personal reflections upon the conscience and creed of his neighbours as those in which Mr. Day's contributor rejoices. If every journalist were to be a midwife, and bring out into his columns what anonymous individuals chose to give birth to, journalism would not be a very respectable occupation. But that is not all. Mr. Day's friend insinuates that the champions of infidelity, being unconscientious, freely express their views before their pupils in Government Colleges, while the Christian professors, whose delicacy of conscience is great, remain silent as to their religious views. To apologize for this injustice done to the free-thinkers, Mr. Day says that the Christian professor enjoys equal liberty, and there is nothing to prevent him, whenever any occasion offers, from declaring to his pupils the excellency of Christianity. It would be a very good thing for us to have religious propagandists for our professors, if there was not so much fuss made by Government on the subject of religious instruction in state colleges. But under the existing policy of neutrality, it is a surprise certainly to be told by Mr. Day, who speaks from equal experience with Wordsworthian professors as well as Zealous Chritian professors, that between the two sets the Government policy of educational neutrality is turned into a dead letter, and a sham. Is there no one to look to this?

SPIRITUALISM seems to have suffered a shock in England. Dr. Slade has been for some time the hero of the system in the British metropolis, and he has impressed many men of eminence, like Dr. Carpenter for instance, with the success of his *seances*. His accustomed line of spirit manifestations has been to place a slate close against the table with a bit of pencil under it, and press it so that nothing can come between the slate and surface of the table on which it lies. Within a short time a scratching noise, as of writing, would be heard, and the slate being removed a message would be found ready written on it. This style of spirit-writing excited wonder, and was widely talked abroad, and many men of intelligence were attracted to test the truth of it. Dr. Lankester among others went to Slade's with Sergeant Cox, and Dr. Donkin of the Westminister Hospital. Here are Dr. Lankester's own words:—

I watched Slade very closely during these proceedings, which were repeated several times during my interview last Monday, paying no attention to the raps, gentle kicks, and movements of the table, of which I will say nothing further than that they were all such as could be readily produced by the medium's legs and feet. I simulated considerable agitation and an ardent belief in the mysterious nature of what I saw and heard. At the same time I was utterly astounded to find the strongest reason to believe that, with the exception of the first message, which was written by Slade underneath the slate with (I believe) one finger of the hand which was holding the slate, the rest of the messages, which were longer and better written were cooly idited on the slate by Slade while it was resting on his knee, concealed from my view by the edge of the table, and that the slate was subsequently placed by him in the position where the sprit-writing was to take place with the message already wirtten upon it.

Dr. Lankester, being determined to test the truth of his hypothesis, went with scientific friends to Dr. Slade again, and this is what happened:—

As on last Monday, so to-day, Slade allowed me to hold the slate against the table in order to receive the spirit writing, saying that the spirit would probably write more distinctly for me than for him. The slate had been cleaned, and was now declared by Slade to be devoid of writing, but writing was to appear on it in the usual way accompanied by the scratching noise of the pencil. There had been the usual delay and fumbling on Slade's part when I put out my hand and immediately seized the slate away, saying, "You have already written on the slate. I have watched you doing it each time." And there, sure enough, was the message already written, as I had anticipated.

Summons has been taken out against Dr. Slade under the Vagrancy Act to prosecute him for defrauding the public. His friends are gathering funds to pay for his defence.

THE INFLUENCE OF IMAGINATION ON RELIGION.

WE believe the power and action of the mysterious faculty which, in the absence of a better word, is called imagination, are as yet but imperfectly understood. There are some who deem it a serious offence to be charged with imaginativeness. There are others who consider that the deficiency of imagination is a serious blemish, and can seldom form a character really noble and deep. While to great numbers of men the meaning of the word is very vague, and includes almost everything which they do not understand. It is necessary in the first place for religious men to bear in mind that if there really be any such power in the human mind as imagination, it is not meant to be an organ of falsehood, but is at least as much connected with the discernment and acquisition of truth as any other faculty with which our complicated nature is furnished. If this be admitted it is necessary in the second place to remember that the history of religion in the world, as well as the religious history of individuals, prove that the influence of imagination on religious systems and personal piety has always been very great, and can scarcely be disconnected with any lengthened course of serious speculations and progress in religious truth. It being conceded then that the operations of this mysterious faculty are traceable almost universally in the department of religion, we must try to find out what the nature of these operations is, where it acts normally and healthily, where it is a danger and a snare.

In a word, we conceive the function of imagination to lie principally in forming an idea of the unseen and unknown from the nature and relations of things seen and known. It deals, therefore, in its higher occupations, with the ideal, with the spiritual, with the unseen world of beauty, truth, character, wisdom, and will. No field is foreign to it, neither art, nor philosophy, neither speculation, nor invention, neither poetry, nor practical life. And religion having always to adjust the unseen relations of the human and divine, and to establish the profound and unfamiliar principles of realities, affections and character which do not come within the ordinary range of man's worldly life, religion always comes more or less under its influence. As it is the seen which supplies the basis of the unseen, imagination can never work without the help of facts; and the more correct and deep the insight into facts, the greater probability there will be for the influence of that faculty leading us to the discovery of truth, and the real relations of things. And conversely, the less deeply we observe facts, and the less perfectly we understand their import and tendency, the greater danger there will be for the influence of imagination leading us to untruth and monstrous conclusions. Take an instance of this. The savage reflecting on natural phenomena with his unaided eyes and untrained powers of thought, will, by the action of his imaginative faculty, arrive at the most grotesque and unreasonable notions both about the Authorship, and the laws of the universe. The man of enlightened thought and faith gazing on the very same facts, will, by the chastened influence of his imagination, be led to the most truthful and sublime insights into the relations of spirit and matter, and discover whole realms of beauty and reality opened out to him. Applied to the phenomena of moral, social, and spiritual life, this instance will yield varied results, all going to prove that the influence of imagination is harmful or healthful according as the materials upon it sits in operation, are real, or otherwise, and are rightly or wrongly observed. If then in the sphere of your religious life you cannot dispel the influence of imagination, (and it would really be a dangerous experiment to try to do so) be careful to gather undoubted truths by the faculty of faith, ponder over and assimilate these realities, and then it will be no harm, but positive gain if your imagination healthily works thereon. This being so, the influence of the imaginative faculty depends for its right action very much on the laws of association, for our knowledge and the interpretation of objects and their relations is, as every body knows, governed by those strange and powerful laws.

Imagination in this manner works upon the ideas associated with realities quite as much, or perhaps more than upon realities themselves because the essential nature of the latter is so difficult to find out. It is not only necessary therefore that we should understand facts, but the right accessaries of facts also that our imagination may be chaste and healthy. Religious men and irreligious men, virtuous men and vicious men, the more imaginative they are, the more constrained they are by the associated ideas which the objects they are concerned with involve. The laws of association prey upon every faculty, but upon no part of the mind so much as upon the religious imagination. If these associations are good the imagination is helped forward, if they are bad there are dreadful struggles in the heart.

From what we have said above let it not be inferred that we view imagination in any sense as the organ, or the test of religious truth. Faith on the part of man, grace on the part of God produce realities, and their right view in the soul. If faith and devotion are strong, if the grace from above be abundant, the influence of imagination is a very great help. Faith leads imagination, and imagination helps faith in discovering unseen realities. Faith discovers realities, and imagination describes them, but the description not unoften aids the discovery. Because the prophet's insight of faith is deep and piercing, because the enlightening influence of the Holy Spirit is always his guide, therefore his imagination is also illumined, and his inward vision clothes itself forth in glorious conceptions and warm colors of which the revelations of all religions are full. Without the faith and the inspiration, the imageries would be extravagant and false ; without faith and grace they are and have been misleading to all who have received them. With a faithful insight into divine things and human destinies such as genuine prayerfulness, and the answering benediction of Heaven can inspire the imagination pourtrays unspeakable realities in speech and form, in sentiment and attitude, exalting and holy to all who come within the reach of its influence. On the whole, we think, the influence of imagination on religion has been harmful and wholesome in about the same extent, and among other problems, it will always remain a problem as to how the religious imagination may be trained aright.

WHAT A MINISTER REQUIRED OF HIS DISCIPLES.

Believe that ye cannot love me if ye do not love one another.

Live as poor men with the utmost simplicity, so that your poverty may be an example unto the world.

Above all things let thy heart be free from pride, anger, lust and envy.

Regard thine own life as thy highest gospel.

Let every offence against thy brother be followed by an apology.

Borrow not.

Honor the rich and the poor, the wise and the illiterate, for they are all God's children.

Thou shalt not be fond of the company of women.

Thou shalt not sleep nor indulge in frivolous talk when I or others in thy company discourse on sacred topics.

Thou shalt not publish in my name things which are not mine.

Thou shalt not in any wise hinder my placing my doctrines and institutions before the world unmixed and pure.

Believe no work to be thy mission unless thou hast performed it devotedly for at least a quarter of a century.

Every day thou shalt offer fresh prayers.

Deceive not thyself with too much singing, for the voice without the heart is a snare and is blasphemy.

Remember that holy love is salvation.

If ye are not as one united and loving family, ye are not fit to preach love unto others.

Devotional

I humbly confess, O my God, that I have made a great mistake in my life. I have always believed that I should, and that I could serve thee and the world conjointly. Alas! I now feel I have deceived myself. He who serves thee must renounce worldliness altogether, and love thee exclusively. Help me then, dear Saviour, to make thee the only object of my affection, the ever shining and beloved neck-lace of my heart.

A pretty little bird, flew away from yonder tree across the path of my vision. I adressed it as thy messenger, O loving God, and asked if it had any message from heaven for me. It spoke not, yet was I comforted. I devoutly trust O Lord, thine inspiring dove will some day bring me glad tidings from above.

When the world was young, they say, birds and beasts spoke, and all material objects too. They speak still, O God, if only my soul is young enough as a child to understand them. They speak indeed with charming eloquence to the believing heart. Does not the moon speak? Do not the roses speak? Yes, sayst thou, O God. Grant that I may always joyfully converse with nature.

(Communicated.)

I have learnt the English language, O my God, and through it have learnt to admire the philosophers, the statesmen, and the great generals of Europe, but why have I not learnt to sufficiently admire the meek and faithful Jesus, the devoted Paul, and the God-inebriated Augustine. Is it of little moment, my God, to have lived such lives, to have preached such truths, and to have thus died in believing? In vain have I taken so much care to enlighten my understanding, in vain have I consumed my midnight oil on works of philosophy and science, if I am still blind to the beauty of such lives. My God, my blessed Father, open thou my soul to truth and spiritual loveliness.

A Prayer for a missing brother.

I pray to thee, O my God, for my missing brother, he who was so great in his piety and devotion, and in his thorough renunciation of the world. He touched the inner chords of our soul by his glowing hymns, and taught many a wandering soul the sweetness of thy love. But now, when the time for working together in thy vineyard is come we miss him, O Father, and he is not amongst us. Why should he, who was honest, so fervent, and so noble be led astray, and I who am so fickle, so weak, and so worthless remain to sigh and pray for him. O restore him, almighty God, for his place is vacant in thy house. We miss him in our place of worship, in our feasts and festivals, yea in our family circle. Restore him, merciful Father, that we may once more join our voices, and sing the victory of thy all-conquering love!

The Brahmo Somaj

Babu Protap Chunder Mozumdar conducted service in the Mandir on sunday last. In the course of his sermon on silent and private devotions he emphatically declared that it is not so much anything outward that disturbs our solitary communion with the Father of Spirit as it is the unregenerate or worldly minded self which like a hidden demon breaks our peace when we are alone and sacrilegiously disturbs our sacred silence. He said as it is impossible to enjoy the serene pleasures of devotion in the din and clamours of a busy town under the full blaze of a meridian sun, so it is equally absurd to expect the enjoyment of undisturbed communion with the absolutely silent Deity when there is within the heart the mad excitement of hot and clamorous passions. In human life and also in the course of every solar day, he pointed out there are two stages which are symbolical of the majestic charms of silence. Silence reigns over the cradle and also over the grave. The infants as well as those who are to leave the world are speechless. But they are not without deep and secret feelings within their bosoms. The sublime calm of silence, likewise pervades the begining and the close of each day and they are most conspicuous in a calm and quiet country place. These symbols of nature suggest that we should put out the flames of our carnal desires, and drown the clamours of our excited passions in order to hold real and silent communion with God.

About three pounds worth of books have been purchased in London for the Sindh Brahmo Somaj. The books have been selected by a friend of ours in London, and will be generally useful. The Secretary of the Sindh Brahmo Somaj is requested to make a speedy remittance to us here that the money may be sent by the next mail to London. The books are expected to arrive in Calcutta by the time of the next anniversary.

Babus Gour Govinda Roy and Banga Chunder Roy have proceeded to Mymensingh to celebrate a Brahmo-Marriage there.

Babu Siva Nath Shastri conducted the evening service on the occasion of the Seventh Anniversary of the Chuna Puker Brahmo Somaj, which took place on Friday last.

Babu Aghore Nath Gupta has now proceeded to Jhang, after having celebrated the anniversary of the Lahore Brahmo Somaj.

Literary

We are glad to hear that there will be a change in the editorial management of the *Indian Charivari*, for the paper really requires a change. We hope the Editor will turn over a new leaf, and make the paper a honor instead of a disgrace to Anglo-Indian journalism.

COMMANDER CAMERON has nearly completed his forthcoming book "Across Africa." It will be profusely illustrated, and embellished with a map taken from Commander Cameron's own notes, and will be published by Messrs. Daldy Isbister and Co., early in November.—*Academy*

Latest News

—MR. Halsey, the *Pioneer* hears, is out of danger.

—THE Empress of Brazil has arrived at Constantinople.

—THE Hon. A. Rivers Thomson, Chief Commissioner of British Burmah, has given Rs. 500 to the Milman Memorial Fund.

—MR. W. E. FORSTER, M. P., having returned from Turkey, addressed a meeting at Bradford upon the subject of relief to the suffering Christians in the European Provinces, whose distress he described as being very great.

—IT is understood that Mr. Valentine Baker, formerly Colonel of the 10th Hussars, is at present at Constantinople, where he is engaged in the Bureau of the War Minister.

—THE German Press, in commenting upon the numerous public meetings in England to denounce the Turkish barbarities, refer to Mr. Schuyler's description of the Russian campaign in Central Asia, where dreadful cruelties were committed by the Russian troops.

—THE Resident of Hyderabad has engaged for the Nizam, and his nobles the well-known Metcalfe Estate at Delhi, which has lain in ruins ever since it was sacked and pillaged by the Gujurs of Chandrawal in 1857 when the mutiny first broke out. The rent to be paid is sixty-five thousand rupees. The Nizam will bring with him a large number of ladies; half the big house is to be partitioned off for them, and a regular zenanah constructed.

—AGENTS from the different Chiefs are flocking in daily to Delhi to engage houses and buy carriages and horses. Prices are rising, and there is a great demand for everything, from houses down to tubs.

—AVARICE has prompted certain house-owners at Delhi to oust their regular tenants.

—THE line between Muzaffurpur and Somastipur, on the Tirhut (State) Railway, will be opened for traffic on the 1st proximo.

—A CORRESPONDENT writing from Patna to the *Englishman* says:—"The Bombay and Madras famines appear to have affected the grain markets on this side of India already, as prices have been going up steadily."

—BRITISH BURMAH will spend 10,000 Rs. in rejoicings on the 1st of January on the occasion of the Proclamation.

—MR. F. C. DACKER, the Secretary to the Executive Committee appointed to make arrangements for the Delhi Durbar, notifies as follows:—"Persons desiring space for private Camps on the occasion of the Imperial Assemblage, to be held at Delhi on the 1st January 1877, are requested to apply to the Secretary to the Imperial Assemblage, Executive Committee, Delhi. No answers will be sent to such applications, but they will be duly registered, and all requirements will be complied with as far as may be practicable."

—WE are sorry to learn from our Gya correspondent that Mr. Langdon, Assistant Magistrate in charge of the Nowadah Sub-Division, was killed by a tiger the other day. While holding his Court he heard of the approach of the tiger in the vicinity of the Court premises, and he at once rushed out with his loaded double-barelled gun to kill the animal. But he missed the aim, and the tiger sprang upon him with lightning speed, and seized him by the arm, neck and thigh, grinding some of his bones in a fury and smashing even his arm with its teeth! His remains were brought to Gya, and buried on the 25th instant.

Calcutta.

THE *Indian Daily News* "understands that the first meeting of the Viceregal Council at the Presidency, will be held about the 15th proximo, when in all probability the bill to extend the jurisdiction of Presidency Magistrates will be taken up and discussed."

ACCORDING to the *Bharut Shangskarak*, an unpleasant scandal is being talked about in Assam, in which a Mr. Akin, a planter, and the Deputy Commissioner of the district in which his estate is situated, are likely to come to grief; the former for seducing a girl from the protection of her father, a Native Christian, living in the compound of an American Missionary; and the latter for refusing to take up the complaint against Mr. Akin. The case has come under the notice of Colonel Keatinge and is now before the Judicial Commissioner of Assam.

MR. T. BRUCE LANE, the Secretary of the Board of Revenue, is named by the *Englishman* as the most probable successor to Sir Stuart Hogg, as Chairman of the Calcutta Municipality. We give our decided veto to the appointment. We shall state our reasons on another occasion.

THE Calcutta correspondent of the *Indian Tribune* writes:—"It is said that the proposal of Sir Richard Temple about the formation of appeal benches, has been approved of by His Excellency the Viceroy and is likely to come into force from 1st January next. We would be in a position to know better and more on the return of His Honor to the metropolis, as in that case a Bill must be introduced in and pushed through the Council this Session."

WE are glad to announce that Nobin Chunder Bannerji returned from the Andamans to Calcutta by the *Sattara* on Friday last. Since his arrival he has been receiving the hearty congratulations of his countrymen, and is being visited by hundreds of people. He was yesterday taken to the Deputy Commissioner of Police for his final release, and was followed by an immense crowd of spectators, all eager to catch a glimpse of him. Most of them, however, were disappointed, as the crowd was too great. Nobin left Calcutta for the Andamans in October 1873. His character in the Andamans is described by Major Barwell, the Chief Commissioner and Superintendent of the Nicobars and Andamans to have been "very good indeed."

THE Police Court building will shortly be in the hands of the masons for repairs. The Court will for the time being hold its sittings at the Town Hall.

A most cold-blooded murder was committed yesterday at about noon in the Bowbazar section of the town. A young Bengali, named Issur, residing in Gopee Mohan Bose's Lane, severed his wife's neck with a dao. He was arrested red-handed on the spot, and made over to the Police. The body of the unfortunate woman was removed to the Police dead-house for the usual post-mortem examination.

Selection.

DR. SEXTION ON SCEPTICISM.

A LARGE congregation was attracted to Augustine Independent Church, Clapham-road, on Sunday morning, it having become known that Dr. Sexton would explain the reasons which led to his renouncing infidelity, and accepting Christian truth. The discourse was a careful analysis of modern Atheism, and received additional force, coming as it did from one who so long held a foremost place in the ranks of Scepticism. Dr. Sexton based his remarks on the words, "Without God in the world" (Ephesians ii. 12) It is impossible, said the preacher, for a man, in the strictest sense, to be altogether without God in the world, and the chapter, carefully read, revealed the fact that a man who is out of Christ is without God in the world. The aliens referred to by the apostle were not entirely without God. There are, however, various classes of people in the world who come under the designation of being without God in the world. In the first place, there are those who deny the existence of God altogether. This is a very small sect. Atheism—even were it not absurd, which it is even, though it did not drive us back at every step when we attempt to investigate it—is so opposed to the instincts of man, that it is not likely to make much progress in the world. Human beings even in a savage state have a vague notion of the supernatural. Atheism is absurd and irrational, because there must be a cause for every effect. The scientific philosophy of the day says that all nature is simply a manifestation of force, that what is called spirit has no existence, that what is called matter is probably also non-existent and that all we know is the operation of the forces such as life, heat, light and motion. Where does this line lead us? The form of force which was in existence first must have been the highest, and have contained within itself all other forces. The highest form of force must be intelligence, and there can be no intelligence without consciousness. Thus we have infinite intelligence and infinite personality, which is only another name for God. The masses of mankind do not deny God altogether, but say He is not a person. If the personality of God is got rid of, we merge into Pantheism, and are altogether without God in the world. Another school of men hold that there *may be* a God. This school includes such men as Tyndall and Huxley, and Dr. Sexton himself held the same views for twenty years. Then comes the school of Positivists, who cannot conceive of God, but are driven to find an object of worship somewhere else. Even Comte, the founder of the school, discovered that everywhere men will worship. There is in the mind of the sceptic a tendency to pray and bow down before a superior power. He (the speaker) had felt this again and again when overwhelmed with trouble, and had almost instinctively cried to God, and then would rebuke himself by saying, "There is no God." This shows where human nature would lead us. Comte saw this, and invented a religion known as the worship of humanity in the abstract whatever that might be. Dr. Sexton said he had a hundred times put the doctrine of the existence of God aside as a closed question, and there would immediately come back in his soul an overwhelming pressure of the problem, compelling him to investigate it anew. The problem is one which demands solution, and cannot be got rid of. The Positivists tell us that law has produced everything, but they never ask themselves What is this law? There must be behind this phenomenon called law an agent which is capable of producing it, and what they call law may be what men call God. To enthrone God in law, or embody Him in the whole universe, or worship Him in the abstraction, is practically being "without God in the world." What does this being without God involve? The state of mind of the unbeliever is of the most lamentable character, and is full of painful anxiety and doubt. It is of no moment whether there be a God who created the universe ages back; but the great question is, If there be a God, what is the relation man sustains to Him, and what is the duty on the part of man which arises out of this? What man wants is a God he can realise and lay hold of. It is absurd to say Atheists meet death philosophically. To say there is no world to come places man in an inferior position to the brutes of the field. The horror of sinking into non-being had risen before the speaker till he shuddered at the very thought, and envied the beetle as it crawled along with no aspiration for a future life. The creeping loose, did not release death; wherefore have we been endowed with this longing for another life, if we are to sink into a grave and be forgotten? In conclusion, Dr. Sexton asked What is the remedy for all this? The apostle explains that being without God is being out of Christ. The man is struck dumbfounded who attempts to realise what God is. We must come to the one grand truth, the truth of truths, that God was in Christ reconciling the world unto Himself. That is the only conception of God which is of value to mankind.—*Christian World.*

Advertisements

SMITH, STANISTREET & CO.

Pharmaceutical Chemists & Druggists

BY APPOINTMENT

To His Excellency the Right Hon'ble

LORD LYTTON, G.M.S.I.

Governor-General of India,

&c., &c.

SYRUP OF LACTATE OF IRON

Prepared from the original recipe. Lactate of Iron, in various forms of preparation, have been in use in France, and generally through the continent of Europe, for some years past, and is highly esteemed as one of the most valuable Chalybeate Tonic remedies yet introduced. The Syrup, being the most agreeable as well as convenient form of administration is in most general use. It is a most valuable remedy in the following diseases:—Chlorosis or Green Sickness, Leucorrhœa, Neuralgia, Enlargement of the Spleen, &c. In combination with quinine, it has also been very successfully used in the cure of Fever, while to persons of delicate constitution, enfeebled by disease it is invaluable. In bottles. Rs. 2 each.

SYRUP OF THE PHOSPHATE OF IRON Rs. 2 per bottle.

SYRUP OF PHOSPHATE OF IRON AND STRYCHNINE, Rs. 2 per bottle.

SYRUP OF PHOSPHATE OF IRON AND QUININE. Price Rs. 2-8 per bottle.

SYRUP OF PHOSPHATE OF IRON, QUININE AND STRYCHNINE.(DR. ATKIN'S TRIPLE TONIC SYRUP,) Rs. 2-8 per bottle.

Smith, Stanistreet & Co.

Invite special attention to the following rates the quality guaranteed as the best procurable :—

Pure Ærated Waters.

Made from Pure Water, obtained by the new process through the Patent Charcoal Filters.

				Re	As.
Ærated plain (Treble Ærated), per doz.				0	12
Soda Water	ditto	„	...	0	12
Gingerade	ditto	„	...	1	4
Lemonade	ditto	„	...	1	4
Tonic (Quinine)	ditto	„	...	1	4

The *Cash* must be sent with the order to obtain advantage of the above rates.

R. K. GHOSH'S

HOMŒOPATHIC DISPENSARY,

No. 1, *Gour Mohun Mukerjee's Street, Simla,*

CALCUTTA.

HOMŒOPATHIC Medicine; Medicine chests of sizes,—containing medicine in tube phials; Homœopathic Books, tracts and pamphlets (English and Bengali); Dr. Rubin's "Saturated spirits of Camphor,"—(the best preventive and cure for cholera where medical aid is not available); and other Homœopathic requisites are sold here at a moderate price. Terms cash. Mofussil orders are promptly executed.

R. K. GHOSH,
Homœopathic Practitioner,
Manager.

NOTICE.

INFALLIBLE SPECIFICS FOR ASTHMA, CONSUMPTION, COLIC, GONORRHŒA SPERMATORRHŒA AND DYSENTRY!!!

I AM the son of the late Titaram Paul of Midnapore, who, the public is well aware, was acquainted with specific medicines for the above diseases. I fully learnt the mode of preparing those medicines from my late father, and have cured many people of Midnapore, Calcutta, Hughly, and other places since his death, as the annexed testimonial will shew. Any one wishing to be treated by me can apply to me, care of the Manager of the Indian Mirror.

WOOPENDRA NATH PAUL.

I HEREBY certify that my youngest son suffered from Asthma from his fifth to his eleventh year and was wholly cured by the Medicine of Babu Woopendra Nath Paul.

RAJNARAIN BOSE,
President of the Adi Brahmo Samaj.

CHUNDER & BROTHERS.

$25\frac{1}{2}$ & 112, RADHA BAZAR,

STATIONERY in all its varieties.
PRINTING PRESSES, Inks & Materials.
LITHOGRAPHIC PRESS & Materials.
BOOK BINDING Materials &c.

BABU BASANTA KUMARA DATTA,

HOMŒOPATHIC PRACTITIONER

No. 20, Sunker Halder's Lane, Ahiritolah.

LONDON AGENT

MRS. HENRY TURNER & CO.

FRESH INDENT OF

HOMŒOPATHIC

Medicines and other Requisites;
Arrives every month from England.
Medicines, Boxes, Books, Pamphlets;
Absolute Alcohol; Cholera-spirit Camphor.

SPECIAL REMEDIES.

For Supposed, Laborious and Difficult menses; Leucorrhœa; Hysteria.

For Spermatorrhœa; Dysentery; Diarrhœa; Cholera.

For Asthma; Pile; Pain; Sore and Diseases of the Children.

Ice, Lemonade, Soda and Tonic water always.

To be had at

DATTA'S HOMŒOPATHIC LABORATORY

No. 312, CHITPORE ROAD, BURTOLA, CALCUTTA.

TERMS—CASH.

☞ Price List can be had free on application.

DENONAUTH DEY AND SONS,

No. 80, CLIVE STREET.

Godowns, No. 24, Machooa Bazaar Street.

IMPORTERS OF METALS, IRONMONGERY, HARDWARE, TEA GARDEN TOOLS.

CHUBBS' LOCKS AND SAFES, RODGER'S CUTLERY Carpenters', Blacksmiths', Coopers', Engineers, Builders' and Planters' Tools.

SADDLERY, STEAM GAS & WATER-FITTINGS,

PAINTS, OILS, MARINE STORES &c. &c.

Priced Catalogues supplied on application, at Rs. 2. each.

Printing Materials.

MILLER AND RICHARD'S PRESSES, TYPE and all requisites always in Stock,

TERMS-CASH

EWING & CO.

HAROLD & CO.,

3, DALHOUSIE SQUARE, CALCUTTA

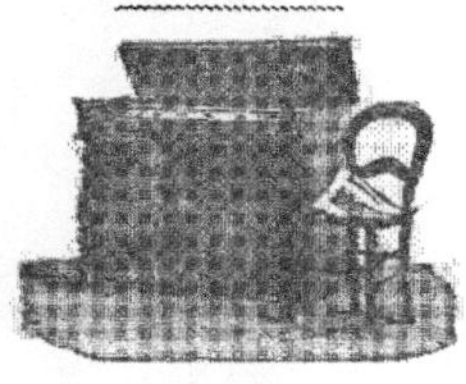

HARMONIUMS.

Harold and Co., call attention to their unequalled stock of rich-toned Harmoniums made especially for India.

FROM RS. 90 TO RS. 900 EACH.

All kinds of Musical Instruments of the best description are always kept in Stock.

CALCUTTA

106, Bowbazar Street.

DR. H. C. SARMA'S

MEDICINE FOR DEBILITY

(NERVOUS.)

Brought on by indulgence in irregular habits, effects of previous diseases, loss of power of limbs, weakness or loss of memory, absent-mindedness, irritable temper, diversion of the mind to displeasure at trifles, want of attention towards business, despair at finding no relief from treatment &c. &c. &c.

Price with postage &c, Rs 5.

Particulars of disease and directions for despatch required from patients residing at a distance.

DR. SARMA'S FEE,

In cases of Debility (nervous) Rs. 16 per visit. } In
For advice at Home... Rs. 10 " " } Town

Out of Town Rs. 500 per day.

INDIAN TOOTH POWDER.

Strengthens loose teeth, alleviates pain of, and prevents bleeding from Gums, cleanses the mouth, corrects its putrid odour and cures ulceration of the Gums without blackening the Teeth.

Price per packet ... ... Rs. 0 4 0
Postage &c., for 4 packets ... " 0 5 0

TONIC OIL.

Imparts vigour and tone to the paralyzed or relaxed parts of the Human system—Restores proper circulation of blood to weak and inactive parts.

Price for four ounce phial, ... Rs. 1 0 0
Postage &c. ... " 0 10 6

HAIR PRESERVER.

Will restore grey hair to its original colour.

It acts directly upon the roots of the hair, removes dandriff, prevents premature falling-off of the hair, and promotes its growth and strength, giving it Lustre and Health of Youth.

It also produces a cooling and soothing effect upon the head.

Price, for 4 ounce phial ... Rs. 1 0 0
Postage &c. ... ... " 0 10 0

Copy of Letter received from Raja Chundernath Roy Bahadoor of Nattore.

Wellesley Street, No. 18, Mott's Lane, 29th March 1874.

MY DEAR HURRISH BABU,—I shall thank you to send me another phial of your "*Excellent Hair Restorer.*" In fact it has done me a great benefit and I should like to have more of it. It has disabused me (young as I am) of old age.

Your's Sincerely

C. N. of *Nattore*

MEDICINE FOR BALDNESS.

Will certainly cure baldness if applied on the bald portion, night & morning, according to directions given in the adjoining direction paper

Price per two ounce phial ... Rs. 1 0 0
Postage &c. ... ... " 0 6 0

HEEM-SAGAR OIL.

The best remedy for Headache arising from over-study, intellectual occupation, over-thinking, mental anxiety and weakness, as well as heat of head from living in hot places.

It cools the head and produces very agreeable sensation. Removes dandriff as well as all other impurities from the head. Promotes the strength and growth of the hair and prevents its premature falling-off.

Price per 4 ounce phial ... Rs. 1 0 0
Postage &c. ... ... " 0 10 0

MEDICINE FOR LEPROSY.

Price with Postage &c. Rs. 5.

OIL FOR LEPROSY.

And Inveterate Skin Diseases.

Price per 8 ounce phial ... Rs. 2 0
Postage &c. ... ... " 0 12

S. C. GUPTA'S

DIARRHŒA PILLS

SEVERAL years of experience in private practice have proved these pills to be most efficacious in obstinate cases of Non-inflammatory, Infantile, Choleric, Chronic and all sorts of Diarrhœa, and in all cases of Indigestion, Dyspepsia, Flatulence caused by disturbance of the digestive function.

Sold in Boxes containing 12 pills with full directions for use :—

Price ... ... Re. 1 0 per box
" with postage ... " 1 4 "

To be had of DURGA DASS GUPTA, care of the Manager, Indian Mirror, Calcutta.

BEST BURMAH CIGARS.

The undersigned respectfully begs to call the attention of Consumers and Dealers to the following Cigars which are made of the choicest leaves and are of superior quality; guaranteed free and pleasant to smoke :—

			Rs.		
No. 1	per 100	Rs.	1	0	0
" 2	" " ...	"	0	12	0
" 3	" " ...	"	0	10	0
Dolly Varden	" " ...	"	1	4	0
Sedans	" " ...	"	1	2	0
Babington	" " ...	"	1	2	0
Trichinopolly	" " ...	"	1	8	0

Liberal discount allowed to wholesale purchasers.

All descriptions of Oilman's stores, Preserved Provisions and Tea to be had at moderate prices.

BONOMALLY SHAW,

128, *Radha Bazar*.

PRIZE MEDALLISTS

For Excellency of Workmanship.

J. M. EDMOND & CO.,

27—28, BENTINCK STREET,

ESTABLISHED 1833.

Cabinet Makers, Upholsterers,

AND

Billiard Table Manufacturers.

Houses completely furnished. Furniture designed and made to order.

ESTIMATES given for all kinds of Carpentering, Painting, Polishing, Gilding, and General Repairs; Marble Polished, Moulded, and Chased; Picture Frames made.

J. M. EDMOND & Co. in soliciting a continuance of public patronage, beg to say they have ready for sale specimens of Ebonized and Gold Oxford style of Fancy Chairs, and are prepared to execute orders for other Furniture in the same style.

J. M. EDMOND & Co.'s New Show-Room is now replete with New Heraldic Style of Dining-room Chairs, and Rustic Chairs, Telescopic Dining Tables, with Patent Table Expanders, and a variety of finished Furniture.—Orders solicited.

BURN & CO.

RANEEGUNGE Fire bricks are the best Fire Bricks known ;—superior to Ramsay's.

9 Rs. per 100.

Fire clay, 40 Rs. per Ton.

Glazed Stone ware, Drainage pipes of all sizes

BURN & Co.,

7, *Hastings Street, Calcutta.*

ARLINGTON & CO.,

3 B DALHOUSIE SQUARE, CALCUTTA.

THE 'PATENT PERPETUAL FOUNTAIN.'

TABLE EPERGNE OR CENTRE PIECE.

FOR SCENT OR FOR PUREWATER WATER.

In Richly Electro-Silvered Ware, [*One of the Greatest Novelties of the day.*]

Cash Price Rs. 175.

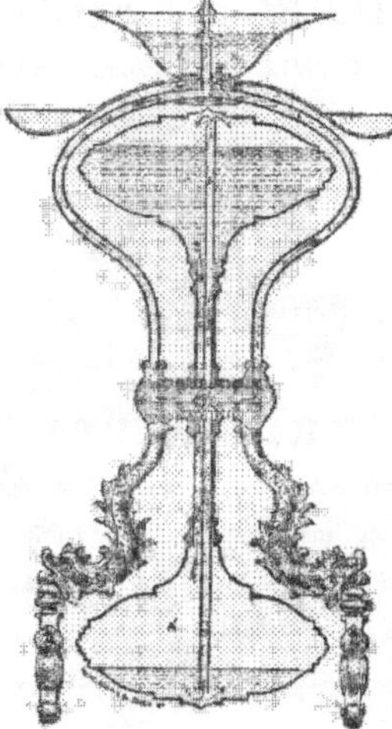

N. B.—The annexed drawing is not a correct representation of the Plated Table Fountains which A & Co. have for sale. The drawing is only given to show the internal arrangements of the Apparatus, and attention is invited to the following description :—

OBSERVE.—A, A1, are two cisterns or reservoirs which are connected together by pipes or tubes B, B1, C, C1, mounted on a hollow axis of motion D, surrounding a fixed conical plug E, having suitable passages F, G, H, therein communicating with the pipes or tubes B, B1, C, C1, and I, and with the jet pipe J.

To put the fountain in operation water is poured into the dish or basin K until the lower reservoir is filled and the opening II is covered. The cisterns or reservoirs A, A1, are then turned on their axis of motion, so as to place the filled cistern or reservoir A at the top, when the water therefrom will flow to a level in the jet pipe J, and the water in the basin or dish K by passing down the pipes or tubes I and B1 into the lower cistern or reservoir A1, rises in such lower cistern or reservoir A1 and forces the air out therefrom through the pipe or tube C1, passage F, and tube B, into the upper part of the cistern or reservoir A, where it presses upon the surface of the water therein and forces it out therefrom through the tube C, passage H, and jet pipe J, until all the water in the upper cistern or reservoir A has passed through the jet pipe J and into the lower cistern or reservoir A1 by the pipe I, passage G, and pipe B1, when by turning the cistern or reserviors A, A1 on their axis of motion until the cistern or reservoir A1 is at the top, the action of the fountain will be continued; the pipes or tubes B, C1, which had previously been air passages now becoming water passages, and the pipes or tubes B1, C, now becoming air passages which had previously served for the passage of water. By these improvements the necessity for alternately filling and emptying the cisterns or reservoirs A, A1, is obviated.

Printed and published by M. M. RUKHIT, at the INDIAN MIRROR PRESS, No. 6, College Square, for the Proprietors.

The Indian Mirror.

SUNDAY EDITION.

VOL. XV.] CALCUTTA, SUNDAY, NOVEMBER, 5, 1876. { REGISTERED AT THE GENERAL POST OFFICE. } [No. 262

CONTENTS.

NOTICE.

All letters and communications relating to the literary department of the Paper should be addressed to the Editor. All other letters should be addressed to the Manager, to whom all remittances should be made payable.

Subscribers will be good enough to bring to the notice of the Manager any delay or irregularity in the delivery of the Paper.

Editorial Notes.

THE season for making pilgrimages and the performance of miracles for Roman Catholic world has arrived. Thousands of pilgrims from all parts of Europe have proceeded to Lourdes, the place of pilgrimage, where in "the grotto" there is a wonder working spring dedicated to Virgin Mary. The water of the spring still produces miracles giving speech to the dumb, and sight to the blind. The Pope has blessed the pilgrims formally, and expressed the consolation which His Holiness feels at their presence.

FROM the publication of statistics it appears that there are 4,513,000 Christians to 3,450,000 Mahomedans in European Turkey, and the wonder of it is that the former should be subjected to the miserable rule of the dominant minority. The ladies of Europe have interested themselves in the cause of the oppressed Christians, and a memorial has been presented to the Queen by English ladies for the mitigation of the atrocities. And the ladies of Moscow have presented the Russian Ambassador at Constantinople a splendid embroidered banner in acknowledgment of his services to the Christians of Bulgaria.

A WESLYAN gentleman of Bombay, who seems to have more money in his pocket than common sense in his head, lays down the challenge that he will pay 10,000 Rs. to any one who will undertake to prove the truth of the Roman Catholic religion. We do not know if this challenge has been accepted, or ever will be. But in case it is accepted who will undertake to decide whether the Roman Catholic religion has been proved true or not? Will the arbiters be Weslyans, or Catholics? Such exhibitions of enthusiasm show only the unfortunate condition to which sectarian narrowness and hostility at which religious denominations have arrived in the present time.

AUGUSTE COMTE'S theory of logical consistency in all attempts and measures for a new social organization, though plausible, is impracticable. In the first place the logical faculty is not deep, penetrating, or powerful enough to take congnizance of all aspirations and latent relationships in man's nature. In the second place, though in the end all doctrines and principles which really embody truth, must harmonize, that harmony is hidden under strong appearances of conflict. The simultaneous action of contradictory principles in human society, therefore, must not be condemned until a better clue is found to the hidden harmonies of truth, justice, and goodness that pervade the depths of our nature. Underneath the apparent conflicts of circumstances and motives, there lies a profound harmony of principle and truth which few can discover. Those who discover it are the real benefactors of society.

EVERY religion which has aimed at organization has aimed at unity. Some religious systems are so highly organized that their experience on the subject of unity is exceedingly valuable. Unity is the universal aspiration of the highest forms of humanity. But nevertheless unity there has not yet been in the world. There have been various principles tried in the world for the production and maintenance of unity, but dissensions have not ceased, but broken out afresh. Even in our own community, small as it is, this has been our experience. And such experience has been more and more widely realized in more extensive organizations. After some reflection on the point, we feel inclined to say that any principle of unity, if, when applied to actual circumstances and practical difficulties, it tends to break out in repeated disunions and multiplied dissensions, must either be deeply fallacious in itself, or must be very seriously misapplied and misunderstood. So far as practical purposes go, the misapplication is as mischievous as the fallacy, and in either case the great end of unity is equally defeated. The fine and noble axiom of the Roman Catholic Church on the subject is: *in necessary things, unity; in doubtful things, liberty; in all things, charity.* The most difficult part of the business in matters of social adjustment and relation, is to agree what things are *essential*, what things are *doubtful*, and what things are *purely individual*.

IT is a most difficult thing to explain to others who don't feel it, the marvellous influence of works of real art upon the mind. It penetrates the feelings and faith more than any outward emblem, except, perhaps, "the human face divine." Mr. George Ticknor, a highly accomplished American gentleman, whose memoirs have been just published, bears testimony, among hundreds of others, to the influence of a picture gallery. He visited the Dresden gallery, and thus speaks of the Sistine Madonna of Raphael:—"From looking at a collection of thirteen hundred pieces an hour or two, I cannot, of course, say anything; but of the effect of one piece upon my unpractised eye I cannot choose but speak, for I would not willingly lose the recollection of what I now feel,—I mean the picture called the Madonna di San Sisto'. . . . I had often heard of the power of fine paintings, and I knew that Raphael was commonly reckoned the master of all imitation, and that this was one of the highest efforts of his skill, but I was not prepared for such a vision. I did not before imagine it had been within the compass of human talent to have formed a countenance of such ideal beauty as the Madonna's, on which a simple smile would have seemed earthly and unholy; or a child like Jesus, where the innocence of infancy is consecrated and elevated, but not marred in any of its natural sweetness and fascination, by the inspiration of the divinity which beams forth in the mild but fixed earnestness of his looks."

THE Report of the Native Ladies' Normal School for the year 1875-76 is out. The progress which the pupils have made since its establishment both in their studies, and in the art of teaching, has been shown. Those who began with the study of P. C. Sircar's

Fifth Book of Reading in the year 1871, are now studying Shakespeare, Wordsworth, Addison, and the best English authors. The School began with a single pupil teacher, and there are four now teaching the girls' classes. Mrs. Woodrow who examined the first class in English says:—"I consider they have made great progress in English, and I was especially pleased at their answers in English Grammar. Grammar is often considered a dry, and uniteresting study, therefore it shows that these young ladies have not only been carefully taught, but that they have brought their intellect to bear upon the subject, enabling them to understand its various niceties." Miss Chamberliam who examined them in Arithmetic says:—"I might here remark that in all the Bengali Girls' Schools I have seen, I have invariably found the pupils not so advanced in Arithmetic as in their other studies." On the occasion of the last distribution of prizes two of the young ladies read little pieces of composition, which they had written in the ordinary course of their school lessons, before the Lieutenant-Governor. One of these was on the "Duties of an Unmarried-woman," from which we have great pleasure to quote the following lines:—"An Unmarried-woman ought not be too attentive to her dress, simple and tasteful dress is best for her. Her personal habits ought to be neat and clean. Idleness is very injurious to her, she must be always active and diligent. She must not sleep in the day time, but must go to bed soon, and rise early. She ought not to be self-indulgent in matters of food. Modesty is the fairest jewel that adorns a young woman best, nothing is so disgusting as to see her rude, coarse, and impolite. Her mission is to comfort those who are in pain and anxiety, in sin or agony; indeed, she is qualified by nature for acts of love and kindness to the unfortunate and suffering members of the human family. She does not hesitate to perform a hospitable action, she is not haughty, but always gentle and amiable. She is unselfish, and sacrifices her own desire to comfort her fellow creatures. Whatever be the inconvenience to her, she is always ready to assist the needy. Her life is not her own, but to her God she has devoted it." The second paper was on a livelier subject, namely, The People whom I like, and whom I don't like." We quote the following lines from it:—"I like lively, playful, and lovely children. They should be neat and clean also. A child, even if he is not beautiful, if he is neat, clean, and lively, looks much lovelier than a child who is handsome, but sullen and dirty; always crying; wanting to eat though not hungry; going to no one, and who does not like to play. I love those friends and companions who are unselfish, and who understand my mind; help me in my difficulties; who can cheer my heart when it feels lonely, or when it is sad; and who can feel with me. How I dislike them who pretend to be affectionate, but truly do not love me at all; who are only my companions when I am at ease, but shun me when I am sick or sorry, and who are impatient and vexed with me for little things. When I am angry without trying to bring back my peace of mind or let me alone, they become provoking, and make me more cross." All this shows that some of the pupils are at all events making good progress. We wish to recommend the school to the notice and patronage of the public. It is an unfamiliar and unpopular undertaking, and should receive the encouragement which it deserves.

WHAT IS RELIGION?

IT will be thought somewhat late in the day to ask this question. But we reflect so little upon the true meaning of religion, and misunderstand each other so readily, that only attempt at occasional explanation will not be thrown away.

Religion is an Idea. Certain views of the nature of the Divine Being, certain views of human nature, and of the relations between God and man, as well as between man and man, embody themselves into an intense and glowing idea in great souls. The pressure of this idea is so great that it changes and recasts all the ordinary concerns of life, and shapes itself forth in doctrines, sermons, precepts, prayers, litanies, and rituals of which every religion is externally full. Now so long as men have an outward and an inward life, the inward must find its way to the outward, and the verbal and doctrinal manifestations alluded to cannot be avoided. But these may modify considerably, and be so far unlike each other in different stages of development, that superficial observers may conclude there has been a radical revolution. The fact is that if the soul does not remain stagnant, but proceeds continually in the direction of the attainment of blessedness and perfection, its views of Divine nature, beauty, love, and holiness make corresponding advance; and the expressions thereof in doctrine and in devotion seem different from what they seemed before. Those of us who remain always where we have been in the past, whose standpoint seldom changes, because we scarcely throw ourselves into the attitudes, and do not give sufficient time or attention to see even that there are any attitudes in the midst of which the relations between the devotee and his Deity, between the worshipper and his fellow-worshippers appear much more exalted, and exceedingly different from what they were formerly seen to be, cannot be easily reconciled with the difference, and think that the change comes from strange and unnatural peculiarities. And therefore the heavenly-minded have been always set down as mad by the worldly. But be that as it may, we must admit that religion thus stands for an idea, which in turn represents certain phases of the soul. Instances of this view are abundantly furnished by the history of every religion of which any record is preserved. Take Budhism for instance, whose fundamental idea is the perfect unreality of carnal life and all its occupations, and the attainment of peace beyond all worldly solicitations. Or take Christianity which means the reconciliation of will with the Supreme Will, and the extension of charity among all men. Or take Mahomedanism which fundamentally declares the unity, and obsolute power of God. Or among the multiform creeds of Hinduism, take the faith of the Vaishnava whose all-absorbing idea of Supreme Love has brought inspiration into so many hearts, or take the sublime faith of Shiva who practices his difficult principles of Yoga in the desert cave, and amid scenes of death and terror,—view it how you may, religion presents a primal all-pervading idea, embodied in various doctrines and orders of worship.

But there is another view. Religion is a Plan. The ideas, doctrines, relations, devotions, which surge in the soul, to last and do any real good must come into practice. Our lives must bear testimony to our faith. Our candle must be placed upon the candle-stick. What is the benefit if the Budhist, who holds the absolute unreality of all earthly occupations and pleasures, should live in the midst of the world and enjoy it as others do? If the Mahomedan becomes an idolator, and the Christian loses his charity retaining all other things, what is the gain? So religion prescribes rules of life, sets down disciplines, tries to govern the individual and corporate actions of its followers, establishes routines and forms, appoints fast days and feast-days, encourages church building, church-going, alms-giving, tending the sick, and the making of vows. Of such disciplines the history of every religion is as full as it is full of doctrines. A well-known necessity of human nature reduces doctrines and daily actions into a common order. As doctrines confine ideas within stated words and formulas, so disciplines confine doctrines within distinct forms of life and action. The one is as indispensable as the other, if men want to bind themselves into a Church and a Community, and want to make progress by mutual aid and example. Disciplines and rules of life may be differently modified, may exist in more or less rigorous form, but they cannot be dispensed with entirely.

With this two fold signification of religion in view, it remains for Brahmos to see how far their own church and faith answer thereto.

WHAT A MINISTER REQUIRED OF HIS DISCIPLES.

SEEK not honor; but let honor seek thee.

Short prayers for the sake of saving time, and long prayers for the sake of appearing devout before God and man—thou shalt avoid both these extremes.

Thou shalt treat little insects and reptiles with the tenderest regard, even to the extent of taking care that thy feet may not recklessly trample them to death.

Be content with simple food and raiment, and do not trouble thy neighbour by asking for good things to eat.

Offend not thy friend by refusing his gifts, but having thankfully accepted them, give them away where they are needed, so shalt thou harmonize asceticism and charity.

Do not strive to look handsome, nor shalt thou seek to appear a devotee by putting on an appearance of humility, gravity, and self-forgetfulness. Let thy looks be decent and natural, without affectation.

As thy face so must thy voice be, unaffected and natural. Let both be such as shall not hide, but reveal thy true self.

Before every good woman bow in thy heart. For every bad woman pray unto God.

Be not rich, for it is easy to be rich; be not poor, for it is easy to be poor. But cherish poverty amid abundance.

Be not grave, for gravity is artifical; be not gay, for gaiety is harmful. But be always cheerful and serene.

Remember that the true type of the human face is that wherein the lips smile, while the forehead shows seriousness.

Avoid as far as possible outward singularity.

Telegraphic Intelligence

Reuter's Telegrams.

LONDON, NOVEMBER 2.

Sir Charles Ellice succeeds General Sir Richard Airy as Adjutant-General of the forces. The Porte has accepted the Russian ultimatum, and the armistice has been signed with the concurrence of Servia.

Devotional

YOGA philosophy taught me, O God, that on the shores of the ocean of eternity there is a house where the weary traveller finds peace and forgets sorrow. I thank thee, thy merciful guidance has at last enabled me to find that house in my inmost soul. It is so quiet; its solemn stillness makes communion with thee quite natural, easy and sweet, while its extremely favorable situation, being contiguous to eternity, draws the heart away from this world, and prepares it for the next. Help me Unseen Spirit, to dwell with thee there, for thou art a Secret God, and lovest solitude.

Is it true that even spiritual friendship is dissolved after a time, and that the best of friends in thy house part! Lord, is this possible! How can I cease to love and esteem him whom I have once accepted for better and worse as my friend and companion for eternity! My Father, I cannot. Those whom thou hast united nothing can separate. In earlier days I met in the path of life one whom I loved warmly and passionately. He was next to my heart always. Now he is far away. Yet is he near, my God. The mysteries of true love who can comprehend! Teach me Everlasting God, to be faithful and affectionate in my heart, to all those whom thou hast brought to me and linked to my soul as friends and co-workers in thy kingdom.

I AM sadly deficient, O my God, in the knowledge of the geography of the soul, and I beseech thee to enlighten me. Thy wise and devoted children are enabled with the light of such knowledge to travel through the various countries within, seeing and enjoying all interesting places and gathering treasures here and there. Teach me Lord, where are those hills of faith, valleys of communion, gardens of love, oceans of peace of which seers and prophets have spoken so eloquently. Tell me also, kind Teacher, where, hid in deep places, lie those inexhaustible mines of spiritual wealth which have made so many of thy devotees truly rich. O God, teach me the geography of the inner regions, and vouchsafe unto me a complete knowledge of the heights and depths of the soul.

GOD of India, my educated countrymen are aspiring to high places in the service of the State, and their agitation in this matter shows how very earnest and eager they are. But how few alas! among them covet high places in the kingdom of Heaven! Lord, teach them to seek spiritual elevation, and grant that they may hunger and thirst for such honors as perish not. Let us all feel how poor we are in spirit, and, discontent with our present low position and resources, let us seek compensation and better prospects in heaven.

The Brahmo Somaj

THE following paragraph about Mr. Voysey's movement occurs in the *Times*:—"Upwards of five years have elapsed since the Rev. Charles Voysey, B.A., was deprived of his living, in consequence of his having expressed opinions at variance with the formularies of the Church of England. In July 1871 a number of his sympathizers formed themselves into a committee for establishing him in a church of his own in London, so that he might propagate his own religious views, and St. George's Hall, Langham-place, was hired, where, on the 1st of October, 1871, an inaugural service was held, and services were regularly conducted there until the congregation removed to Langham Hall. Yesterday being the fifth anniversary of their existence, Mr. Voysey made a statement respecting the progress of the movement. They might congratulate themselves, he said, on having falsified the predictions of their foes, and on having been able to raise for five years in succession little less than £1,200 a year, and to present pretty much the same balance sheet at the close of each year. Nearly £900 had been contributed towards the Building or Permanent Fund. Their position was peculiar. Sunday by Sunday there were present from 50 to 100 persons who might never be seen there again, as they came from curiosity or interest on their way through London from all quarters on the globe. The rest of the congregation were of two kinds, viz., habitual attendants, of whom several came from long distances; and those who always came when they could. He calculated that, if the whole of these could be present at once, they could fill a building three times the size of St. George's-hall. He found the number of secret sympathizers beyond all expectation. Even clergymen were communicating with him what steps they should take in consequence of their renunciation of orthodoxy. There was hardly a congregation anywhere not full of heresy, and beneath the exterior pretensions of conformity there lurked a rebellion against popular Christianity, only waiting for the right moment to burst into a flame. He suggested the establishment of a succession of suburban missions, and offered his own services during the ensuing winter if the rest of the necessary machinery could be acquired. Similar missions might subsequently be held in some of the provincial towns where there was not even a pretence to heresy. While all other denominations were more or less corporate, the Theists were without any representative assembly, which was the chief reason of the limitation of their works and their comparative obscurity. Their first principles must, of course, be rigidly maintained—the perfect right of every man to think and speak as he believed in matters of religion; that no one should ever dictate to another on such a question; that they were at open war with orthodox creeds, and with the assumption of what was popularly called Divine revelation; that they believed all the good of God they possibly could consistently with the dictates of reason, the moral sense, and their highest affections, with due regard to the facts of nature and humanity. Theists were now to be found in every section of Christendom and among the Jews. What they greatly needed was a simple standard round which all these Theists might rally."

THE subject of sermon preached in the Mandir on Sunday last, was, "The life is thy greatest Scripture." There in the life of every man, are to be found the clearest revelations of God's purposes about himself. A man is only to study with faith and reverence the various dispensations of God vouchsafed to him for his moral and spiritual well-being, and from such a study of the history of his own life he is sure to receive fresh light which will enable him to see clearly what is the will of God in regard to his special destiny in the spirit-world. In fact, there is no other book but that of one's own life in which the Wise and Benevolent Deity has written with His own Finger, His special intentions about even individual man. There are deep and indelible impressions of God's hand in every chapter of his past life. There are events in his life wherein he has felt the existence of a vastly Superior Will to his own. There are occasions when he evidently perceives the heavy touch of God upon his conscience. There are times when he is severely rebuked by a deeper Voice within which exorts him to eschew sin and aspire after holiness. There are sacred moments in his life when he understands the intimations of an Infinitely pure Nature to surrender his own self to the leadings of the Holy Spirit. There in the saddest hours of his existence when he sees nothing but dismal darkness both within and around himself, he receives direct comforts and consolations from the merciful Author of his being. Thus in the life of every truly religious man are revealed the ways how to get himself out of sin, despair, and misery, and how to advance in the eternal principles of holiness, hope, and joy. And in order to understand them thoroughly, and to obtain a clear knowledge of God's dispensations concerning himself, it is essentially required that a man should regard his own life as his highest gospel, and make it an important duty to study it every day faithfully and reverently.

Babu Keshub Chunder Sen has proceeded to Jubbulpore from Allahabad, where, we believe, he is to make a week's stay. He has received invitations from various places, but from what we hear, we expect he will return home by the third week of the present month.

Gleanings

What is it puts an end to peace and joy?
What is it overthrows all self-possession?
What is it, like a poisonous root,
Destroys all virtue of the heart and life?
To which Buddha replied;
"Destroy anger and there will be Rest,
Destroy anger and there will be Peace;
Anger is poisonous root which overthrows the
[growth of virtue.

As the butterfly alights on the flower
And destroys not it form or its sweetness,
But taking a sip, forth-with departs.
So the mendicant follower of Buddha
Takes not nor hurts another's possession,
Observes not another man's actions or omis-
[sions,
Looks only to his own behaviour and conduct.

Literary

A lecture on the "Native Press" will shortly be delivered in Bombay in connection with the Bombay Branch of the East India Association by a Parsi Editor of a Guzerati weekly.

Mr. Routledge (formerly of the *Friend of India*) is writing a book showing the progress of the freedom of the Press.

Latest News

—Sir Stephen Hill, late Governor of Newfoundland, is mentioned as the probable successor of Sir W. Gregory as Governor of Ceylon.

—The ex-Empress Eugenie has instituted legal proceedings against the Radical journal, *Les Droits del' Homme*, for the publication of an alleged document stating that she was not of legitimate birth.

—The Guickwar leaves Baroda for Delhi on the 7th December, and there is a rumour about that the Guickwar and Jumnabai on their return journey will visit several sacred Hindu shrines and places of note. There will also be an alms-giving on a grand scale.

—Mr. Luxmiputi Naidu, a Madrasi Barrister-at-law, has received special permission from the British Resident at Hyderabad to practice in the Courts of the Commissioner and Judicial Commissioner in the Berars.

—Throughout India during last year, 1875, there were 334,481 deaths registered from cholera alone. This fact is recorded in the last report of the Sanitary Commissioner with the Government of India.

—Lady Davies intends giving a Ball at Lahore on the 27th instant to their Excellencies Lord and Lady Lytton.

—It is rumoured that the Amir of Cabul will soon liberate Mohamud Yakub Khan, for all the inmates of the royal harem together with the mother of Abdulla Jan, have asked for his liberation, and the Amir has promised to liberate him on the condition of his admitting Abdulla Jan as the future successor to the throne of Cabul and putting his seal on the document of succession.

—Lord Lytton, it is said by an English paper, has to spend the next hot season in the Neilgherries.

—Mr. Haji Ismail Haji Hubib, the well-known merchant and head of the Memon community, of Bombay has been invited by His Excellency the Governor of Bombay to the Delhi Assemblage.

—There is a report that Colonel Duncan, the Resident at Mandalay who was created a C. S. I. the other day, is about to resign his appointment.

—We believe the object of the visit of the Lieutenant-Governor of Bengal to Noakhally, is connected with a representation made to the Viceroy by the inhabitants of Pergunnah Nazampore, in the District of Chittagong, against the Resolution of the Bengal Government, transferring to the District of Noakhally the revenue, civil and criminal jurisdictions of so much of Pergunnah Nazampore as lies to the north of the village of Kamuldah.

—The Native community of Allahabad presented Sir William Muir with an address before his departure to Bombay, *en route* to England. The address was read by Babu Dwarkanath Bannerji, Government Pleader, High Court, N. W. P. Sir William replied in suitable terms.

Dr. Lynn has been giving performance at Benares.

Calcutta.

No alteration has been made this week by the Bank of Bengal in its rates of interest and discount.

We are surprised to see that Henry Hearne who was, we believe, discharged from the Police Force sometime ago after the celebrated Hare School case, has been taken into the Force again, and appointed a Special Inspector, under the Indian Contagious Diseases' Act.

We notice that Mr. J. Hector, Deputy Secretary to the Bank of Bengal, has resigned the Bank's services and has proceeded home, we think, for good.

Dr. Thomas will arrive in Calcutta on the 19th instant.

We really do not see any necessity for Mr. Muir White's picture of the Imperial Assemblage, when the India Office is going to send Mr. Val Prinsep to paint it at a cost of a lac of rupees. Mr. Muir White should desist from his attempt.

The total number of deaths in Calcutta during the week ending the 28th ultimo, was rather large, *viz.* 245. That during the previous week was 225.

Mr. Soutter, the Superintendent of the Municipal Entally Workshops, has furnished an interesting report on the subject of apprentice mechanics. Mr. Kimber, the Engineer to the Calcutta Municipality, thinks the matter is of great importance and well worthy of consideration by the Municipality. He is of opinion, however, if the principle be adopted, that it should not be limited to the European or Eurasian community, but that Natives also should be admitted to its benefits in such proportion as may be deemed fit by the Commissioners. We hope Mr. Kimber's suggestion will be acted upon. Many young Natives will be glad to be apprentice mechanics.

DOMESTIC OCCURRENCE.

BIRTH.

Sirkar.—At Dhubri, Assam, on Monday, the 30th October 1876, Krishna Kanti, the wife of Babu Troylokhya Nath Sirkar, of a son.

Selection.

THE ARCHBISHOP OF CANTERBURY ON THEISM.

TO THE EDITOR OF THE *Times*.

Sir,—Whenever an injustice has been done, wilfully or otherwise, you are the first to help to remedy it; on any subject where ignorance prevails you are always ready to throw fresh light upon it.

In the interests of the public at large, who are always injured by misunderstandings, and in the interest of a number of persons occupying an influential position, I crave at your hands permission to make a few calm and respectful observations on that portion of the Primate's Charge which was reported in the *Mail* of yesterday.

You may trust me to say nothing which could lead to a theological controversy in your columns, not a word to wound the susceptibilities of your orthodox readers, or to give pain to the Archbishop of Canterbury.

Like the majority of orthodox Christians, His Grace has no true idea of what we Theists believe and teach, and therefore has, without the least intention to misrepresent us, done to us and to our precious faith a grievous wrong. Remembering his great kindness to myself when a curate in London, and his most patient endeavour to understand me thoroughly when he was my judge, I can testify that the Primate is the last man who would wilfully misrepresent an opponent. The passage in your report of His Grace's Charge of which I complain is the following:—

"There were a great number of persons who would altogether repudiate the name of Atheist, but who took the name of *Deist* or of Theist; and gladly did he welcome the declaration in any quarter of a belief in the existence of a God, provided the belief were real. What was a Deist? A man who believed in God. Did he believe that there was a Creator, a Governor, an ever-present and loving Father? Did he believe that He was a hearer of prayer? If so, there was good hope for him, for the logical consequence of a real devotional Deism would be to welcome the truths which were revealed to us in Jesus Christ. The Jews, to be sure, were such Deists as he had been speaking of; but they were prevented from welcoming the truths of the Christian doctrine by insuperable prejudices. If, however a man had made this amount of progress, and really believed in a Universal Father of the human race, and considered that he must have access to Him if his soul were to live, the natural and logical conclusion from this must be that he would welcome the manifestation of God in Christ and prize the doctrines which the Son of God had revealed. He was afraid, however, that there was very little chance of such Deism as this in the world. Among those who in this country or in other lands, had adopted some system of Deism, very little was said of a Creator, a Providential Guardianship, or of life eternal. Such persons rather entertained some notions of the laws of nature, which made it impossible even for the Almighty to interfere with their working—some idea that this life was, on the whole, so good that it might be the only sphere in which human souls had to display their energy. Where was the God which such a Deism recognized? Was this a return to the old philosophy of Epicurus, which led men to suppose that the gods, far away were enjoying themselves in contemplation, and could not be troubled with the concerns of this lower life; or was it that the Deity was altogether sublimated from the system, and that the practical anomaly was actually established that men who termed themselves Deists had ceased to believe in a God?"

First I will notice that the Archbishop uses the terms "Deist or Theist" as if they were synonymous. As a matter of etymology they are so, no doubt; but custom has made them now distinctive terms. We have adopted the term Theist on purpose that our faith should not be confounded with that of the Diests of the last century. Most of them did approach to the Epicurean philosophy, and some of them d…

figured their writings by a tone of ribaldry never to be found in the writings of modern Theism. The gravest injustice, however, is done to us when the Archbishop says:—

"Among those who in this country or in other lands had adopted some system of Deism, very little was said of a Creator, a Providential Guardianship, or of life eternal." Why, our whole *raison d'être* consists in our firm and vivid belief in God as the source of all things, as the unitiring and watchful Providence which overrules every event for good, and as the anchor of all our hopes for immortality. It is true we are more diffident than we once were in attempting to define the relations between the visible world and God as its Creator, but we never waver for one instant in regarding Him as the Great First Cause, and in resting upon that primary belief as the assurance of God's perpetual control and the promise of final and everlasting good to all mankind.

The Archbishop asks, as if certain of an answer in the negative, "Does the Deist believe that there is a Creator, a Governor, an ever-present and loving Father?" Of course we do, and we pride ourselves, if I may use such a term, on heartily believing it and realizing it; while others only say they believe, or else add so much more to their faith as to overcould and neutralize it altogether. Our renunciation of other doctrines has brought the Heavenly Father of the human race nearer to us than ever.

The Archbishop asks, "Does the Deist believe that God is a hearer of prayer?" Let His Grace examine our Prayer-book or witness our worship, and he will need no other answer. It is true, we do not believe in man's power to alter the Divine Will by his prayers, but we do believe in the value and privilege of earnest prayer and thanksgiving, and in the Archbishop's own words, we "must have access to God that our souls may live."

We, too, accept and give welcome to some of the doctrines taught by Jesus Christ. We accept His form of prayer and adhere to the model so rigidly as not to add to it intercessory petitions. We regard the parables of the Lost Sheep and the Prodigal Son as the best representations of the inexhaustible mercy and love of God. We regard Jesus Christ as one of the greatest Theistic teachers of ancient time, though we do not share His belief in evil spirits, nor can we admit that "many shall seek to enter into the Kingdom of Heaven and shall not be able." We believe that all men shall be made happy at the last only and solely by being made good and "redeemed," not from all punishment but "from all iniquity."

I have no right to ask for more space to explain to the Archbishop the reasons why we cannot become, in his definition of the word, Christians.' I trust I have said enough, to show that we Theists are true believers in the Loving Father of us all, and that we can live and die in the most perfect peace and in hope of a glorious immortality because He is the Father and Friend of mankind.

One word in reference to the Theists in "other lands." Theodore Parker has left behind him in America a vast body of followers. In India the members of the Brahmo Somaj are also Theists, and their organ, the *Indian Mirror*, alludes to myself as "the avowed representative of their cause in England." Of these Indian Theists Professor Max-Muller said, in Westminister Abbey, on the 3rd of December, 1873. "These Indian Puritans are with us and we with them for all the highest purposes of life, even though they may not repeat our Creeds and sign our Articles. I beg to enclose for your perusal the Prayer-book we use, a lecture recently given on "Our Faith and its Foundations," and my last three discourses on Divine Providence, two of which were occupied in the endeavour to vindicate the righteous Government of God in the face of the cruelties which abound in the earth.

I shall be sorry if I have trespassed on your space, and will promise not to trouble you with our affairs unless forced to do so in the public interests.

I am, Sir, your obedient servant,

October 5. CHARLES VOYSEY

Advertisements

LIGHT! LIGHT!! LIGHT!!!

PATENT PORTABLE AIR GAS MAKING APPARATUS,

SUITABLE FOR

Churches, Chapels, Schools, Country Mansions, Private Houses, Railway Stations, Barracks, Manufactories, Collieries, Mills, Offices, &c., &c.

THIS *simple* and *effective* Gas-making Apparatus supplies a want long felt of having Gas at places where no Gas Works exist. It may be introduced without any more trouble than the simply affixing of any ordinary Gas meter, and is about the same size for the same number of lights. The *piping* and *fitting* arrangements are in every respect the same as for the use of ordinary Gas. The *cost* of the Gas produced is about the same as is charged for ordinary Coal Gas, and the light produced is *more brilliant* and of *a greater illuminating power*; it is also *free from the impurities of Coal Gas*. The Gas, if used with the Patent Burner, is of great heating power, and hence suitable for cooking and heating purposes, or in manufactories for soldering, &c. The apparatus is PORTABLE; there is NO DANGER WHATEVER (ordinary care being used when filling it); the Gas is **PRODUCED IN AN INSTANT WITHOUT ANY FIRE OR OTHER ARTIFICIAL HEAT.**

Further particulars may be obtained from **MESSRS. EDWARD THOMSON & CO.**, Contractors for Drainage Water and Gas, who are appointed Sole Agents for the above apparatus, which can be seen working any week day between the hours of 6 A.M., and 6 P.M., at their place of business.

39, *BENTINCK STREET*, CALCUTTA.

India General Steam Navigation Company, Ld.

SCHOENE KILBURN & Co.—*Managing Agents*

ASSAM LINE.
NOTICE

Steamers leave Calcutta for Assam every Tuesday, **Goalundo every** Thursday and leave Debroo-ghur downward every Saturday.

THE Str. "CHUNAR" will leave Calcutta for Assam, on Tuesday, the 7th instant.

Cargo will be received at the Company's Godowns, Nimtollah Ghat, up till noon of Monday, the 6th.

THE Str. "RAJMEHAL" will leave Goalundo for Assam on Thursday, the 9th instant.

Cargo will be received at the Company's Godowns, No. 4, Fairlie Place, up till noon of Tuesday the 7th.

Goods forwarded to Goalundo for this vessel will be chargeable with Railway Freight from Calcutta to Goalundo, in addition to the regular Freight of this Company.

Passengers should leave for Goalundo by Train of Wednesday, the 8th.

CACHAR LINE NOTICE
REGULAR FORTNIGHTLY SERVICE.

Steamers **leave Calcutta** for Cachar and Intermediate Stations every alternate Friday, and leave Cachar downward every alternate Sunday.

THE Str. "COLGONG" will leave Calcutta for Cachar on Friday, the 17th instant.

Cargo will be received at the Company's Godowns, Nimtollah Ghat, up till noon of Thursday the 16th.

For further information regarding rates of Freight or passage-money, apply to

4, FAIRLIE PLACE, Calcutta, 2nd November, 1876. } G. J. SCOTT, *Secretary.*

DAY & COUSIN.

STATIONERS.
ENGRAVERS, PRINTERS
AND
PICTURE FRAMERS.
9, *Hasting's Street, Calcutta.*

SHIB CHURN DUTT & CO.,
GENERAL STORE KEEPERS
AND
IMPORTERS OF PHOTOGRAPHIC MATERIALS
7, *Council House Street.*

Rivers Steam Navigation Co. Limited.

The Steamer "OUDE" left Goalundo for Assam on 1st instant.

The Steamer "BENGAL" left Calcutta for Assam on 31st October and will leave Goalundo for Assam on 7th November.

The Steamer "BURMAH" will leave Calcutta for Assam on 14th current and Goalundo on 21st current.

For rates of Freight **and Passage**, apply to

No. 1, LYONS RANGE, 1st November, 1876. } MACNEILL & Co., Agents.

SEWING MACHINES.

BRADBURY & Co.'s celebrated Prize Medal, Domestic and Manufacturing Treadle and Hand.

PEARSON'S Wax-thread Harness Machine.

Sole Agents in India—MULLER & Co.

☞ Sub-Agents wanted.

KNITTING AND DARNING MACHINES, COTTONS, SILKS, LINEN THREAD,

And all Machine requisites, and extras.

Price lists free on application.

Ulcerations of all kinds.

There is no medicinal preparation which may be so thoroughly relied upon in the treatments of the above ailments as Hollways Ointment. Nothing can be more simple and safe than the manner in which it is applied, nothing more salutary than its action on the body, both locally and constitutionally. The Ointment rubbed round the part affected enters the pores as salt penetrates meat. It quickly penetrates to the core of the evil and drive it from the system.

ESTABLISHED 1863.

H. C. GANGOOLY & CO.

STATIONERS, DIE-SINKERS, ENGRAVERS PRINTERS, LITHOGRAPHERS &c.
24, *Mangoe Lane, Calcutta.*
Cash prices of the following :—

	Rs.	As.		Rs.
Whatman's Drawing paper double elephant sizes (40×27) each ...	0	7		9
Mathematical Instrument Boxes	2	8	to	16
Color Boxes	0	4	...	3

Drawing Pencils, Drawing and Mapping Steel pens and various other requisites in Stationery.

CHUNDER & BROTHERS.

25½ & 112, RADHA BAZAR,

STATIONERY in all its varieties.
PRINTING PRESSES, Inks & Materials.
LITHOGRAPHIC PRESS & Materials.
BOOK BINDING Materials &c.

HAROLD & CO.,

3, DALHOUSIE SQUARE, CALCUTTA

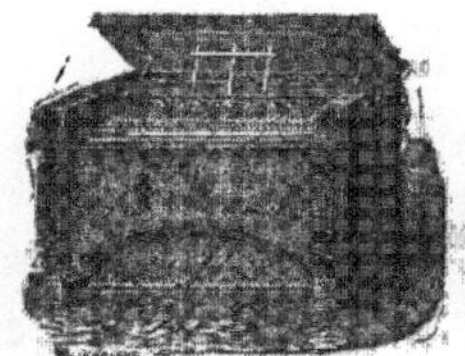

HARMONIUMS.

Harold and Co., call attention to their unequalled stock of rich-toned Harmoniums made especially for India.

FROM RS. 90 TO RS. 900 EACH.

All kinds of Musical Instruments of the best description are always kept in Stock.

SMITH, STANISTREET & CO.

Pharmaceutical Chemists & Druggists
BY APPOINTMENT
To His Excellency the Right Hon'ble
LORD LYTTON, G.M.S.I.
Governor-General of India,
&c., &c.

SYRUP OF LACTATE OF IRON

Prepared from the original recipe. Lactate of Iron, in various forms of preparation, have been in use in France, and generally through the continent of Europe, for some years past, and is highly esteemed as one of the most valuable Chalybeate Tonic remedies yet introduced. The Syrup, being the most agreeable as well as convenient form of administration is in most general use. It is a most valuable remedy in the following diseases:—Chlorosis or Green Sickness, Leucorrhœa, Neuralgia, Enlargement of the Spleen, &c. In combination with quinine, it has also been very successfully used in the cure of Fever, while to persons of delicate constitution, enfeebled by disease it is invaluable. In bottles. Rs. 2 each.

SYRUP OF THE PHOSPHATE OF IRON Rs. 2 per bottle.

SYRUP OF PHOSPHATE OF IRON AND STRYCHNINE, Rs. 2 per bottle.

SYRUP OF PHOSPHATE OF IRON AND QUININE. Price Rs. 2-8 per bottle.

SYRUP OF PHOSPHATE OF IRON, QUININE AND STRYCHNINE.(DR. ATKIN'S TRIPLE TONIC SYRUP,) Rs. 2-8 per bottle.

Smith, Stanistreet & Co.

Invite special attention to the following rates the quality guaranteed as the best procurable:—

Pure Ærated Waters.

Made from Pure Water, obtained by the new process through the Patent Charcoal Filters.

				Rs	As.
Ærated plain (Treble-Ærated), per doz.				0	15
Soda Water	ditto	„	...	0	12
Gingerade	ditto	„	...	1	4
Lemonade	ditto	„	...	1	4
Tonic (Quinine)	ditto	„	...	1	4

The *Cash* must be sent with the order to obtain advantage of the above rates.

THEISTIC BOOKS.

FOR SALE.

URDU.

Rahut Hakiki	Rs.	0	3	0
Nizam Komi	...	0	3	0
Kasufal Ilham	...	0	2	0
Kholasa, ol, Asool Brahm Dharm	...	0	1	6

HINDI.

Upasana Pudhati	Rs.	0	1	6
Benai Putrika or Hymn book	...	0	1	0
Tut Bodh	...	0	8	0
Upanashid Sar	...	0	8	0
Dhurm Dipika	...	0	0	6

ENGLISH.

Claims of so called Revealed Religion	Rs.	0	3	0
New Life	...	0	0	6
Living God	...	0	1	0
Higher and Lower Virtue ...	...	0	1	0

Apply to the Secretary,
BRAHMO SOMAJ OF THE PUNJAB,
Lahore.

MAKHON LOLL GHOSE.

No. 91, Radha Bazar, Calcutta.

BEGS to invite the attention of the public to several consignments of commercial and fancy stationery of all sorts, including account books of all sizes, made of handmade and machine-made paper, by steamers recently arrived, and which he is disposing of at moderate prices. He has been long in the trade, and presumes he has always afforded every satisfaction to the numerous merchants here who have constantly favored him with orders. Mofussil orders accompanied with remittances shall be promptly attended to.

CALCUTTA
The 18th August 1876.

BURAL BROTHERS

[ESTABLISHED IN 1870 A.D.]

JEWELLERS, GOLD AND SILVER-SMITHS AND WATCH-MAKERS,
BURAL BROTHERS,
10, HARE STREET.

BABU BASANTA KUMARA DATTA,

HOMŒOPATHIC PRACTITIONER
No. 20, Sonker Halder's Lane, Ahiritolah.
LONDON AGENT
MRS. HENRY TURNER & CO.

HOMŒOPATHIC

FRESH INDENT OF
Medicines and other Requisites.
Arrives every month from England.
Medicines, Boxes, Books, Pamphlets;
Absolute Alcohol ; Cholera-spirit Camphor.
SPECIAL REMEDIES.

For Supposed, Laborious and Difficult menses Leucorrhœa ; Hysteria.

For Spermatorrhœa ; Dysentery ; Diarrhœa ; Cholera.

For Asthma ; Pile ; Pain ; Sore and Diseases of the Children.

Ice, Lemonade, Soda and Tonic water always.

To be had at
DATTA'S HOMŒOPATHIC LABORATORY
No. 312, CHITPORE ROAD, BURTOLA, CALCUTTA.
TERMS—CASH.
☞ Price List can be had free on application.

DENONAUTH DEY AND SONS,

No. 80, CLIVE STREET.

Godown, No. 24, Machoa Bazaar Street.

IMPORTERS OF METALS, IRONMONGERY, HARDWARE, TEA GARDEN TOOLS,

Chubbs' Locks and Safes, Rodger's Cutlery Carpenters', Blacksmiths', Coopers', Engineers, Builders' and Planters' Tools.

SADDLERY, STEAM GAS & WATER-FITTINGS,

PAINTS, OILS, MARINE STORES &c., &c.

Priced Catalogues supplied on application, at Rs. 2. each.

Printed and published by M. M. RUKHIT, at the INDIAN MIRROR PRESS, No. 6, College Square, for the Proprietors.

The Indian Mirror.

SUNDAY EDITION.

VOL. XV.] CALCUTTA, SUNDAY, NOVEMBER, 12, 1876. {Registered at the General Post Office.} [No. 268

CONTENTS.

NOTICE.

All letters and communications relating to the literary department of the Paper should be addressed to the Editor. All other letters should be addressed to the Manager, to whom all remittances should be made payable.

Subscribers will be good enough to bring to the notice of the Manager any delay or irregularity in the delivery of the Paper.

Editorial Notes

THE gloomy signal of distress raised in the two presidencies on the approach of an extensive famine, is followed in Bengal by the terrible ravages of a destructive hurricane, which has perhaps done, in the course of a single night, much more towards the destruction of human life, than the famine can do in the course of many months. In Chittagong, Noakhaly, and Burrisal, the loss of life and property is simply incalculable. Whole islands have been swept into the sea, whole tracts of country have been swallowed by the deluge together with all men and cattle that lived there; large boats with cargoes of rice have been swamped, and no end of ships have been disabled, dismasted, and drowned. There is some fear of a famine in Bengal now, and the prices of rice in town have gone up wonderfully during the last two or three days. Disease and starvation have commenced to reign among the poor people who have survived the destructive fury of the cylone in the Eastern Bengal. Zemindars in Calcutta have been obliged to send large sums of money to save their tenants from the effects of the disaster. It is altogether a bad lookout, and seems to be an inauspicious season.

IT is foolish to talk of postponing the Delhi Assemblage. Matters have gone too far for that. But it is uncertain what shape the calamities which have broken out in the three presidencies will assume at the time of the proposed festivies, and what demands will have to he made both upon the public exchequer, and the private funds of the assembled noblemen to relieve the extensive popular sufferings on all sides. May we venture to suggest, therefore, that the days and occasions of festivity be curtailed and minimized as far as possible; that needless expenditures on races and ball &c., for which considerable pressure is said to be privately put upon the liberality of Native Princes and others, be disallowed and discouraged; that Princes and noblemen who feel, or are likely to feel it inconvenient to spend the amount of money requisite to maintain their dignity at the Assemblage, but have not the moral courage to decline the Government invitation, or acquaint the Government with their circumstances, be excused from attending. His Excellency the Viceroy and his advisers must realize the awkwardness of their position in committing themselves to the celebration of festivities on an unprecedentedly magnificent scale to express the joy of the country, when death, disease, disaster and starvation heavily darken the face of that country, and the population shares not in the ill-timed delight of their rulers. The utmost moderation has therefore to be observed that this "mirth in funeral" may not exceed its indispensable limits.

CURIOUSLY enough the sympathies of the Pope, as well as the Pope himself are said to be against the Servians in the terrible conflicts now raging between the Turks and Christians. His Holiness is said to "prefer the savagery and lust of Turkish barbarism to the bigotry of the rude Christian Slavs," because the Mahomedans interpose fewer obstacles to the free celebration of Roman Catholic worship than the members of the Greek Church do. The Catholics of Ireland however, ignore this strange reversion, of sympathy, and have called meetings to denounce the late "atrocities."

WE must speak in high praise of the *Christian Life*, the weekly paper, edited by Mr. Robert Spears, late Secretary to the British and Foreign Unitarian Association. It is a weekly journal, devoted to the spread of liberal Christian principles, and contains within a small compass a wonderful amount of information on all manner of subjects mostly religious. The articles are short, vigorous, clear, and healthful. The printing is excellent. The price is only twopence. Mr. Spears, whose energy and power of organization are even for an Englishman unusual, has evidently put his whole soul into the paper. We would wish to see it largely subscribed for in this country, for considering the nature of subjects treated, the paper would be quite interesting to Brahmos.

SINGING in church, though so often lightly and carelessly practised, is a very solemn thing. We are glad to find that the solemnity is being recognized in Christian churches. We are told by a contemporary that an interesting ceremony took place in the Church of St. James,' Gravesend, lately. It consisted of the formal induction of the whole of the new surpliced choir, numbering about 30 men and boys. The choir entered the church in procession, singing hymn 164, from "Hymns, Ancient and Modern." After a short but impressive service, the vicar delivered to each chorister, kneeling at the alter-rail, a card, in token of membership, saying at the same time, "A. B., thou art admitted into the choir of our church: what thou singest with thy mouth believe in thy heart, and what thou believest in thy heart, perform in thy life. And may the Lord receive thee as a singer of the sanctuary in this world, and in the world to come, through Jesus Christ our Lord, Amen." An address was then given by Rev. R. H. Atherton, assistant priest, and a hymn closed the service.

Is it possible that the clever and philosophical editors of the *Spectator* have been, or are soon to be converted into advocates of spiritualism and table-turning? We find a long article on the subject in a late issue of that paper, the tendency of which is suspicious. Not that the writer commits himself to any definite views on the side of belief, but the remarks he makes on Dr. Carpenter's opinion in the late British Association controversy on Professor Barrett's paper, and the remarks also on the exposure made by Dr. Lankester in the notorious Slade case, point to a somewhat distinct inclination to believe the phenomena of spiritualism. The question is what sort of mental attitude are we to maintain towards these phenomena? Must we reject them wholesale on *a priori* grounds because they are apparently opposed to certain known laws, and processes of Nature? Must we even refuse to investigate and inquire? We know some would say so. Some would think that the highest wisdom lies in assuming an air of perfect incredulity towards everything that is not within the dream of their little philosophy. We do not profess to know or account for a tithe of the marvels which Nature closely studied, and interrogated would place before us in every sphere. The nervous susceptibility of man for instance is all but a perfectly unexplored field of inquiry yet. And the phenomena of so called spiritualism which clearly relate to that sphere, certainly deserve study and analysis in the hands of scientific men. We do not deny the phenomena, we do not pretend to predicate imposture about their origin in every case, but we must be excused if we refuse to believe under present circumstances that the agency of disembodied souls has anything to do towards producing them.

SELF-ABASEMENT

MEN speak of processes for the attainment of scientific truth. Without these processes neither truths nor laws are attainable. Are their not processes also for the attainment of spiritual truth? Like the truths, the processes also are divinely appointed. And unless we submit to them we have no access to the wealth of the spiritual world. Of these processes one of the chiefest is self-abasement. The proud are repelled in their approach to the throne of grace, it is only the humble and the contrite in heart who are in a fit mood to receive and perceive the secrets of the heavenly kingdom. We often flatter ourselves with the belief that we have no pride because we are not conscious of the hard feeling of self-exultation every moment of our lives. Pride in most cases is not so much a feeling as a state. It is the natural attitude of certain minds towards God and man. As such, we are often unconscious of the hostility of our relation to those towards whom a continual attitude of humility is due. Like pride, self-abasement also is not a feeling, but a state. It is a continued lowliness of the heart, produced by circumstances, and a consciousness of relationship to heaven and earth. It is a perpetual posture of spiritual supplication for grace and help from above. It is supposed by some that self-abasement means passivity and weakness. This is a mistake. It is an activity of the very strongest kind that holds in utter subjection the dominant and violent propensities of the heart, and creates a profound calmness and equanimity which no provocation can break. It is a powerful faculty of endurance upon which the wrath and wrongs of the world break in vain. The man of self-abasement stands with dignity and firmness where others, who have been apt to boast of their so called active virtues, lose self-prossession, and rave in the madness of passion. Others again are prone to think that self-abasement must always bring pain and gloom with it. This is another grave mistake. The man who has committed his case to Heaven, and has no need of any anxiety or nervousness to defend a position in the world; the man who would resist no evil, and expect no high thing, who is ready to retire that others may have the places of honor; that man has no restlessness, but sleeps in peace, while others are troubled with a multiplication of cares. Nay we doubt whether in the religious world there can be any happiness but in a perfect immunity from care to keep up one's place and prospects. Above all self-abasement is a light. It is the light by which superior truths and superior natures are discernible. The single eye full of light that penetrates into everything whereupon it is cast, and discovers soul of truth everywhere is the eye of meekness. By driving away self into the back-ground it makes much room in the heart for the light and glory of Heaven to enter, and shine with brightness. Neither God, nor holy men would consent to abide with those whose haughty and contending spirits would question and cavil always, and whose predominant self would obstract and intercept the mediums through which truth and light can come. Experience brings at lucid moments the pure blessedness of those states of the soul wherein by some secret inworking force as it were, we recognized our place to be the lowest place in God's family, and meekly occupying that, we sat at the feet of others to learn, and practise, and pray in utter self-abasement.

Correspondence.

THE PHILOSOPHER AND THE THEISTS.

To the Editor of the *Indian Mirror.*

SIR,—"A Being presides over this universe." This is the voice that comes into the human consciousness. The vulgar believe it, but the philosopher starts up and begins at once to examine it by his tedious and careful analysis of the facts of consciousness collected from observation made up on the minds of the present as well as past generations, he finds that it is not an acquired but a universal and original idea taught by human instinct. He, therefore, acknowledges the idea as constitutional, and as such he hesitates not to accept it as the truth coming direct from the author of our mental constitution. Thus he is satisfied, but the scientist steps in—he would not believe the philosopher, he must judge for himself by his experiments. So he musters up all his physical sciences, and with their aid he unveils one by one the mysteries of the material world. He first comes across different kinds of forces working in this world, and proceeding on he finds that these different forces are regulated by one *mighty central force.* Proceeding still further he observes that this mighty Central Force is intelligent or what the philosopher calls Will, and the vulgar call, Person or Being. Thus the simple, vulgar, the thoughtful philosopher and the enlightened scientist meet together on the same platform.

But the work of investigation does not end, the world has yet to discover the nature of this Great and Mysterious Being and His relation to man. The labor of the philosopher and of the scientific man is over, but the labor of the Theist only begins, it is given to him, and him only to make glorious discoveries the like of which the humanity never saw before.

Yours Faithfully,
R. M. B.

Devotional

PHYSICIAN heal the maladies of my soul. I have tried the doctors and all the patent medicines of the world, but have found no benefit in them. Thou alone canst heal me, and thy medicines alone can bring me relief. The evils in my outward life thou hast already remedied in a great measure. But as in my blood and deep in my bones the seeds of corruption are lodged, administer the remedies of heaven there, O God, and make me altogether clean and healthy. I have often heard thee say, thou Healer of the soul, that I must go out of this world for a few weeks for a change if I desire a complete renowal of health. Be it so, Lord. Grant that I may breathe the purer air of heaven for some time in the regions of the saints above, and then return with renovated health.

IT is no longer a river; the sea, the open sea I behold all around, O God. The onward course of my life has brought my frail bark here, and I now feel more than I ever did before, the necessity of entire dependance upon thee. For who can navigate the sea? Its length and breadth and depth are appalling to me. The tremendous storm, the roaring waves I dare not face. And then I know not which is the east and which the west. All is dark, dismal, and fearful. O Captain, in thy hand must I leave the helm entirely amid all these dangers; and that heavy load, I carry with me, my own understanding, which may cause me to sink at any moment, I will throw overboard. Guide me, O guide me Heavenly Captain, into the haven of joy and blessedness.

WHAT is that land I see at a distance, half hid in mists, yet bright enough to attract my heart? Is that the land of joy and salvation which thou hast, O my God, promised to weary pilgrims. Then glory, glory, glory to thy hallowed name! Lord, hasten my movements and make me run, that I may soon finish my journey. Thou whisperest, O God, the home is yet very far, and it will take fifty thousand years yet to reach it. Only fifty thousand, dear Lord! That is nothing if I am sure of reaching that sweet home.

ON the first day of the New Year our Queen, O God, will be proclaimed Empress of Hindusthan, and that day will be observed as a day of general rejoicing. When will that day come, Father, when thou, King of kings and Lord of lords, shalt be declared the Sovereign of India, and the kingdom of heaven established in this land? That will indeed be a blessed day for all of us, when the tyranny of passions will cease, and the reign of ignorance, superstition, and sin will come to an end. Lord hasten that day!

The Brahmo Somaj

DURING his stay at Ghazipore our minister was treated with great kindness and hospitality by the local Brahmos and the Native community generally. We are assured there was no lack of service or love when his health was delicate. When we desired him to come back to Calcutta we never meant that there was fear of any inattention being shown to him, but that we naturally wanted to see him home, when we apprehended the change might not do the expected amount of good.

THE Brahmo friends at Lucknow and other places who invited Babu Keshub Chunder Sen, must have suffered some disappointment when they found that owing to his present state of health could not pay them the visit for which they had been looking out for sometime. We are sorry for this, and feel assured no one regrets this incapacity more than the minister himself. Let us hope at some future time he will be able to be present at these places.

ALLAHABAD.

[FROM OUR OWN CORRESPONDENT.]

BABU KESHUB CHUNDER SEN conducted the service in the local Brahmo Somaj yesterday evening. There were few outsiders present besides the members of the Somaj. The service from the beginning to the end was impressive, and his invocation, sermons and prayers were just like those of a true devotee. The sermon was on "True *Byragya*." It was as touching as it was sweet and instructive. I shall try to give you a substance of it though I know I shall not be able to do full justice to it. The minister commenced, where shall you go—within or without. There are two means by which the devoted children of God, restless with the pangs of their heart, filled with sin and sorrow, try to find peace, but struggle from the one to the other. When the house catches fire and there is no means to stop its fury, the inmate, to save his life, flies from it and takes shelter outside. In the same way when one meets with any danger outside and nothing can prevent it, he does not remain there for a moment's time but makes himself off and takes shelter in the house. Such is also the state of the minds of the devotees. When there is no rest within, the devotee goes without, and when there is no peace without the devotee comes within—his aim is how to find the peace and rest of a true *Byragya*. There is the Sanyasi with ashes and earth on his body who has left his family and home and travels from one country to another. There is the *Urdhabahu*, who keeps his hands raised whole day and night and has sacrificed all the pleasures and comforts of his life. There is the silent hermit, away from the bustle and difficulties of the world, who sits all day below the tree, and passes his life in deep meditation. Don't laugh at them—these devoted children of God, there is nothing in them to be laughed at. Their aim is the same as yours. Their minds are in fire according to their own notions, though the notions are not quite correct. But the question is which means is the best—which is the true *Byragya*? Where shall you go—*within* or *without*? Surely we shall have to come *within*. There is no peace *without*. True *Byragya* must be *within* not *without*. If you at all go *without*, that should be to bring things from *without* and store them up *within*. If you see the *Sanyasi* bring that *Sanyasi* within you. Wherefore do you work in the office and undergo so much trouble and inconvenience? It is only to take home salary and enjoy the comforts of this world. If you, therefore, wish to be a true *Byragi* leave without and come within. Of what avail will it be to apply ashes and earth to your body, what benefit will you derive by wearing the *gerua* colored cloth, what is the use of giving trouble to the body and other parts of it, unless you can apply to your mind the same ashes and earth, unless you can make your mind wear that cloth, unless your mind undergoes those sacrifices? It is becoming no *Sanyasi* if your mind is not *Sanyasi*, it is becoming no *Urdhabahu* if your mind is not *Urdhabahu*, it is becoming no hermit if your mind is not hermit. There is no *Kashi* Benares (if there) is not *Kashi* in your mind. There is no pilgrimage at all if there is no pilgrimage in your mind. Therefore the minister said true *Byragya* cannot be attained by outward means. It is the concern of the depth of our mind. If you want to be an outward *Byragya*, you can be such within a day—nay within an hour. The world will respect you, unthinking men will worship you, in fact you will be known as a pious and devoted man. But of what effect is such *Byragya*? Can you be satisfied with it, unless you can be such within your mind. Let your body remain as it is, let the outward world remain what it is. But adopt that which will make your mind a *Sanyasi*. If you have wealth, there is no necessity of leaving it, if you have family and home there is no need of seperating yourself from them. You can be a true *Byragi* without doing this. The minister then concluded the sermon with a prayer for the mercy of God in teaching us true *Byragya*.

THEOLOGICAL CLASS.

Sunday, September 10, 1876.

(NOTES.)

THE enumeration given above of the elementary facts of the human consciousness, upon which religion establishes a reasonable basis, relates principally to one side of human nature viz., to its cognitive side. All the facts that may be pointed out as having their seat within the depths of man's being, have not been distinguished. There is for instance, in the department of our physical existence, in its purely animal and as well as its intellectual relations, a very profound and irresistible sense of dependence upon unknown agencies that control the circumstances of our life and death. We are aware that we are not self-created, that we are not the masters of our own destiny, that we have very little direction over the circumstances that immediately or very remotely surround us, that there is a vague mystery always hanging before us, that stretches from the very next moment of our future life to a far and undiscovered lapse of time, that, as the prophet says, we live in the midst of death, and to-day we are and to-morrow we are cut away like grass, and thrown into the oven! This undoubted and universal dependence of human life upon a Superintending Destiny, "which shapes our actions, rough hew them as we will," most significantly suggests the existence of a Power feared by some, worshipped by others and set at defiance by a few.

Again in the emotional sphere of man's life there is the undoubted feeling of reverence and wonder which, though often excited and responded to by human actions, is by no means satisfied by the highest conditions of humanity. Man's heart must find its object of adoration, and the deeper the reverence which that adoration embodies, the greater is the depth of the feeling discovered to lie under it. It is an unalterable attitude of man's being when presented face to face as it were, with the mystery of life that overhangs creation. Modified in a thousand ways, often distorted, often exaggerated and strained, the feeling is found to pervade human life in all its phases and conditions. So much so is this the case that one of the advanced materialistic thinkers of the age, Professor Tyndall, would establish all religion on the basis of emotion only.

Coming so far, the subject necessarily leads us to the often disputed problem of the Idea of the Infinite. Very carefully avoiding the labyrinth of discussion which has for so many decades involved this question, we cannot but allude to the idea of the Infinite as a necessary condition of realizing the various modes of existence in space and time. Mr. Herbert Spencer, to whom belongs the chief merit of rearing up the philosophy of the Unknowable, is not so unceding as to deny the position that the Absolute and the Infinite of which we know absolutely nothing, limit the knowledge of all phenomena wherewith rational philosophy is concerned. How Mr. Herbert Spencer knew so much of the Infinite of which nothing he says, is knowable, is most difficult to find out. We may say with Professor Martineau that—Mr. Spencer takes a peep into the Infinite, gathers as much knowledge of it as will substantiate his own philosophy, then shuts the door to any further knowledge, and leaves mankind in utter darkness with his dogma about the Unknowable God.

Lastly the human mind is furnished with a distinctively spiritual faculty as apart from all other faculties as knowledge is from emotion. Faith, or in other words, the spiritual faculty in man constitutes its own world, a separate department of his being altogether, having its adaptations and counterpart in the outer creation as well as in the inner life of intelligent beings. And to this faith the facts of Divine existence, and some elements of the Divine attributes are presented in the course of life, and the faculty of religion in man spontaneously responds to the objects which concern it, and are cognizable by it.

Literary

THE *Edinburgh Review* contains an article condemning Mr. Gladstone's opposition to the Government, and speaking of Lord Hartington and Mr. Forster as the two future leaders of the Liberal party.

WE see in the *Times* that the first Indian paper at the late International Congress of Orientalists at St. Petersburg was "A Comparative Vocabulary and Grammar of the Languages between Cabul, Badakhshan and Cashmere" by Dr. G. W. Leitner, and that it was made over to the Publication Committee.

MR. J. MUIR D. C. L. of Edinburgh, has just published his "Additional Maxims and Sentiments from the Mahabharata," freely rendered into English Verse, a copy of which he has kindly sent us.

Scientific

IN the course of the Orientalist Congress at Marseilles, M. Lesseps (who has now arrived at Brussels and is the guest of the King) mentioned that his son, in concert with some officers of the Russian Staff, has gone to make the preparatory studies for a railway which should unite the Russian railway system with the English railways in India. He added that the Russian Emperor was warmly interested in this project. M. Lesseps also spoke on the project of flooding the Sahara, which he thinks a plan easily to be realized. It would improve rather than hurt the climate of Europe, while it would fertilise North Africa, and would allow the French to extend their Algerian possessions beyond the southern mountains, which at present cost more to watch than they are worth.

A SINGULAR phenomenon is recorded in the German journal, *Der Naturforscher*, as having happened in an orchard near the village of Brodelheim. A large fire occurred in the village in the beginning of September, and four weeks after it numerous trees in the orchard that had been singed by the fire began to vegetate anew, putting forth tender green leaves and blossoms, often by the side of fruits which the fire had spared. On examining the wood with a microscope, it was found that the contents of the cells were transformed into a pulpy mass. Sugar was found to be present both in the singed and unsinged trees.

Latest News.

—MR. VAL PRINSEP who is about to come to India to paint a picture on the subject of the forthcoming Imperial Proclamation at Delhi, will receive, the *Home News* says, £5,000 for his work, and £1,000 for travelling expenses.

—NAWAB SIR FYAZ ALLY KHAN has returned from Simla to Jeypore. It is said he does not go back to Kotah.

—THE Maharajah of Jeypore will, it is stated, give a banquet to the Viceroy at Delhi.

—THE *Pioneer* contradicts the report that the Delhi Assemblage will cost 50 lacs of rupees. It is in a position to state "with confidence" that it will not cost more than ten lacs of rupees.

—THE following gentlemen from Surat have been invited, through the Bombay Government, by Lord Lytton to be present at the Viceregal Durbar, in January next:—Mir Zulfukar Ali, son of the late Nawab of Surat; Mir Gulam Babakon, his brother-in-law; Dr. Dossabhoy Pestonji, and Mr. Manockji Cowasji Boti, the Full-Power Magistrate.

—THE last Mail steamer *Nepaul*, which arrived at Bombay on Tuesday last, brought an unusually large number of passengers, among whom we notice the following:—Mr. Bernard, the Thakore of Limri, Professor Monier Williams and his two sons, Miss Turkhud (daughter of Dr. Atmaram Pandurung) the Hon'ble Mr. Justice Jackson, Mr. M. Pestonji, Mr. Rustomji, the new Parsi Civilian, and the Hon'ble Mr. Justice White, the successor to Mr. Justice Phear.

—CARDINAL ANTONELLI is dead.

—LOYAL Madras observed the 9th instant as a close holiday, on account of the Prince of Wales' birth-day.

—ACCOUNTS from Bombay are most distressing. On the 5th instant, 25 persons died at Sholapore of starvation and cholera. More than 2 lacs of people have deserted the villages, a large number of them having gone to the Nizam's Dominions.

—THE Nizam will leave Hyderabad for Delhi on the 8th proximo.

—SIR PHILIP WODEHOUSE will return to Bombay on the 17th instant.

—MAHARAJAH HOLKAR is going to establish another Cotton Mill at Indore, the other one having proved a success.

—THE report increases in strength, says a Lucknow telegram to the *Statesman*, that Sir George Couper goes to the Punjab, and Mr. Inglis to the North-West, and that Oudh will be annexed to the North-West in January.

—LORD AND LADY LYTTON reached Dhurrumsala on Friday last.

—A TELEGRAM from Simla to the *Indian Daily News* says:—"Domestic bulletins are daily received by the Viceregal children of their parents' progress. The children, who are under Dr. Barnett's care, will leave Simla for Delhi on the 8th proximo."

—THE Amir of Cabul is laid up with gout, his old complaint.

—A CORRESPONDENT of a contemporary says:—"Everything in Dowlutkhan and some neighbouring places has disappeared as if nothing existed there." Besides the total destruction of the cutcheries, court records, &c., the Zemindars will suffer heavy loss in rents. They do not know how to pay the Government revenue. The country is strewn with corpses. The tanks are reported full of dead bodies, and drinking water is scarcely procurable. The Munsiff, the Sub-Registrar, the Doctor, the Excise Officer &c., of Dowlutkhan have been all killed. His Honor the Lieutenant-Governor has visited the devastated districts, and initiated action to relieve the prevailing distress.

—THE Duke of Buckingham's Camp at the Imperial Assemblage, will be the most gorgeous of all. The Duke's Aide-de-Camp, Captain Gordon, has been at Delhi for a month making preparations.

—TANKS are being built at convenient distances apart at Delhi, the roads are being re-metalled and new roads are being constructed. The demand for flowers and shrubs for the Camp is said to be enormous.

—AN official report, just received from the Bengal Government, informs us that more than ten thousand human lives and fifty thousand head of cattle have perished by drowning in Dukhin Shabazpore and the adjacent islands of Manpura and Hatia. The entire population of Dowlutkhan was either drowned on the spot, or carried away by the rush of waters. There is scarcely any vestige left of a house or building in Dowlutkhan.

—THE cyclone was experienced as far as Orissa.

Calcutta.

THERE was a special meeting of the Municipal Commissioners yesterday when the following matters (among others,) were discussed:—The extension of the drainage works and the doubling of the water-supply of the Town.

AFTER considerable discussion, the Committee of the Eurasian Association in Calcutta, have recommended the adoption of the name "Eurasian Association." The first act of the Association will be to present an address from the Eurasian community to the Queen on Her Majesty being proclaimed Empress of India.

CAPTAIN FRITH, the Extra Aide-de-Camp to the Lieutenant-Governor of Bengal, has gone to Delhi to make preparations for His Honor's Camp.

SIR HENRY NORMAN left Simla for Calcutta yesterday.

MR. BROUGHTON, the Administrator-General of Bengal, will return to Calcutta from furlough by the end of next month.

A YOUNG Bengali, Chandi Paramanick, is said by the *Statesman* to have attempted to murder his step-mother and step-brother, at Hugulkuriah, on Tuesday last.

WE hear that Mr. Horace Cockerell will shortly take the place of either Mr. Schalch or Mr. Money at the Board of Revenue.

THE *Pioneer* says:—"A handsome testimonial is to be presented, we understand, by the branch agents and junior officers of the Bank of Bengal to Mr. J. Hector, whose retirement from the office of Deputy Secretary was recently announced. The very highest opinion of, and the warmest regard for, Mr. Hector, seem to be generally entertained by his colleagues, and outsiders are not unnaturally surprised that he should be leaving India—and an institution always in need of such men—in the prime of life."

THE following is the list overland Mail Passengers, who arrived at Bombay, on Tuesday last, per P. & O. S. S. *Nepaul*:—

From Southampton—Mr. and Mrs. F. A. Gillet, Mrs. Battye, Two Misses Battye, Mr. W. D. Willcock, Mr. Dane, Mrs. R. Brown, Mr. and Mrs. E. C. Bernard and infant, Mr. and Mrs. C. McNaughten, The Thakore of Limri and followers, Col. and Mrs. Berkley, child and infant, Miss Price, Mrs. Wiskle John, Mr. and Mrs. G. Greig, Miss Greig, Miss Borne, Mrs. Jackson, Miss Jackson, Mr. E. H. Moscardie, Mrs. Higgins and infant, Mr. E. B. Armstrong, Mr. W. Sullivan, Mrs. Anderson, Mr. H. S. Cox, Miss Cox, Mr. W. McAllan, Mr. G. McAllan, Professor Monier Williams, Mr. S. Williams, Mr. C. R. Williams, Mrs. Losack, Miss M. Kemp, Mr. and Mrs. Glover, child and infant, Miss Merrick, Miss Hobson, Mrs. Malcolmson, Mrs. Finch, Mrs. K. Way, Miss Turkhud, Mrs. Hawkins child and infant, Mrs. Berry, two children and infant, Mr. J. Dalzell, Mrs. Veitch, Mr. J. G. Watson, Mr. A. Sullivan, Mr. F. W. Dod, Mr. R. W. Roberts, Mr. J. D. Burton, Mr. W. H. Cole, Mr. H. E. Haddon Mr. E. Leycester, Mr. E. Baker, Mr. G. Baker, Mr. A. T. Mullaly, Mr. W. C. Stevis, Mr. E. H. Clementson, Mr. T. Smith, Mr. and Mrs. Cooper, M. L. Pearson, Miss Walton, Mr. Rohde, Mrs. McCausland, Mr. Kennedy, Mrs. Austin, child and infant, Mrs. W. Philipps, two children and two infants, Mr. Collins, Mrs. Staines, Mr. Marriott, Col Chavier, Mrs. Kuke, Mrs. Gallither, Mr. Smethurst, Dr. E. J. Lawder, Mr. J. Edwards, Mrs. Walsh, Mr. Walsh, Mr. G. Brown, Miss Thacker, Mr. Beale, Mr. Bairy, infant and child, Mr. J. Baillie, Mr. M. Pestonji, Mr. R. Harding R. N., Col and Mrs. Reid.

From Venice.—Capt Reeves, Mr. Snow, Capt & Mrs. Cowan, Mrs. Salmon, Mr. & Mrs. Ferguson, & infant, Mr. Bag Shawe, Lieute. Co. & Mrs. Bouus, Hon. Mr. Justice Jackson, Mr. Brereton, Mr. Anderson, Mr. W. Payne, Mr. Koebel, Mr. Spooner, Mr. Alexander, Mr. Collingridge, Mr. Andrew, Mr. Mallett, Mr. Leitnitz, Major Schmidt.

From Brindisi.—Mr. E. L. Durant, Mr. and Mrs. McIver, child and infant, Dr. Duka, Mr. Rustomjee, Mr. Elliot, Mr. Eisenlohr, Mr. Gulics, Miss Gulies, Capt A. Murray, Mr. McEwan, Capt, Borrie, Mr. Molesworth, Mrs. Chapman, Mr. J. Roor, Mr. E. Rutteau, Mr. Sturrock, Hon'ble Mr. Justice White, Sir Gordon Cumming, Mr. D'Eroofe.

From Suez.—Mr. Deifenback, Mr. Ritchie, Mr. Baker.

From Aden—22 Natives.

MR. WHITE who succeeds Mr. Phear on the Bench of the Calcutta High Court has arrived in India. He is now at Bombay, and is expected here in a day or two. Mr. McEwan of the Small Cause Court has also arrived.

DOMESTIC OCCURRENCES.

BIRTH.

DAS.—On the night of Friday, the 3rd of November 1876, corresponding to 19th Kartic 1283, the wife of Babu Durga Mohun Das, of a still-born daughter, prematurely.

DEATH.

DAS.—On the morning of Monday, the 6th November 1876, corresponding to 22nd Kartic 1283, at her residence, No. 1, Lower Circular Road, Brahmamoyi Das, the beloved wife of Babu Durga Mohun Das, deeply mourned by her husband and children and a large circle of friends.

Selection.

PHILOSOPHERS AND SPIRITUALISM.

THE correspondence in the *Times* on the subject of "Dr. Slade" and his doings, was kept up all last week, but on Saturday it gave unmistakable signs of coming to a natural termination. Various members of the British Association had their say about the way in which Mr. Barrett's paper on the Mesmerism and Spiritualism was introduced to the notice of that august body; but this is a question in which the public do not take the least interest. They do not regard the cause of science as being committed to the keeping of the British Association, and they can calmly allow professors and other persons to fight out amongst themselves differences with respect to the formalities and technicalities of their committees. So far as the correspondence relates to the explanation of the way in which Slade performs his trick, or fulfils his task as a "spiritualist," general readers have probably followed the observations made in the newspapers of the day, with the attention which usually excited by matters affecting personal character, and with the zest which attaches to events alleged with at least some colorable pretence, to belong to that border-land of physical or psychical experience, of which we confessedly know very little. Slade himself closed the correspondence of the week with a letter. He corrects Mr. Barrett for stating that he (Slade) had failed "to produce writing on a slate enclosed in a sealed box, and in other ways ren lered inaccessible to ordinary manipulation." Slade's account is that he did not fail, but that he "declined using" these slates at all. He further states that after fifteen years' experience as a medium he claims to know something of the conditions under which these phenomena can occur, and that he objects to "using locks, boxes, or seals," because, as he says, rather inconsequently, "I claim to be as honest and earnest in this matter as those who call upon me for the purpose of investigation." "Therefore," he adds, again, with a kind of logic which we fail to follow, "I shall continue to object to all such worthless appliances whenever they are proposed. He announces, with what will appear to some an amusing simplicity and to others an audacious effrontery, that he will be happy to unite "in the further pursuit of these experiments" when the investigator comes to him "in the sprit of a seeker for truth instead of trying to prove him an impostor. Well, we should have thought honesty and earnestness" in these experiments would have led the performer readily to try various conditions, especially for the sake of satisfying such "a seeker for truth" as Mr. Barrett appears to be. In fact, Slade's letter considerably damages his case. We can understand it on the supposition that it is the production of a man who knows that he is performing a clever trick, and that he can only perform it under certain conditions; but we cannot understand it as a production of an earnest "seeker for truth," who believes the writing to be done by spirits and does not comprehend the process. "Spirits" who persist in using slates held in a somewhat peculiar position by two persons, who object strongly to sealing-wax and locks, and who, when they write at all, write very trivial "messages" in a scrawl often almost illegible, are suspicious characters, to say the least of it, and ought to be found out. Certainly this correspondence must have been a very valuable advertisement to "Dr. Slade," who, as we understand, admits two persons to a seance for the respectable fee of one guinea. But the golden s ower promises to be but brief, for we observe that a summons has been issued under the Vagrant Act against Slade and his assistant at the Bow-street Police-court. for "conspiracy to defraud." We surmise that this step has been taken at the instigation of one of those wrathful sons of science, who have shown so much warm temper in this discussion, and so much lofty contempt for all who would not instantly accept their dictum and dismiss the subject. The forms of the court would, we presume, allow Dr. Slade to produce some of his mysterious writing on the slate for the purpose of convincing the Magistrate who hears the case on Monday next, and surely if, as Dr. Slade professes to believe, these messages are written by the spirit of his late wife, this would be a most suitable opportunity for the exercise of her special gift and the manifestation of her sympathy. We shall look with interest to the proceedings of Monday, unless, indeed, they should be prudently forestalled by the departure of Slade and his companion to their native land. But even if Slade can be shown ever so conclusively to be an impostor, we shall still object to the disposition, manifested by persons of some authority in scientific matters, to pooh-pooh and knock on the head all careful inquiry into those subjects of which Mr. Barrett took note in his paper before the British Association. Because spiritualists have committed themselves to many absurdities, that is no reason why the phenomena to which they appeal should be scouted as unworthy of examination. They may be mesmeric, or clairvoyant, or something else. But let our wise men tell us what they are, and not snub us, as ignorant people too often snub inquiring youth, by the easy but unsatisfactory apothegm, "Little children should not ask questions."—*Christian World.*

Advertisements

LIGHT! LIGHT!! LIGHT!!!

PATENT PORTABLE AIR GAS MAKING APPARATUS,

SUITABLE FOR

Churches, Chapels, Schools, Country Mansions, Private Houses, Railway Stations, Barracks, Manufactories, Collieries, Mills, Offices, &c., &c.

THIS *simple* and *effective* Gas-making Apparatus supplies a want long felt of having Gas at places where no Gas Works exist. It may be introduced without any more trouble than the simply affixing of any ordinary Gas meter, and is about the same size for the same number of lights. The *piping* and *fitting* arrangements are in every respect the same as for the use of ordinary Gas. The *cost* of the Gas produced is about the same as is charged for ordinary Coal Gas, and the light produced is *more brilliant* and of *a greater illuminating power*; it is also *free from the impurities of Coal Gas.* The Gas, if used with the Patent Burner, is of great heating power, and hence suitable for cooking and heating purposes, or in manufactories for soldering, &c. The apparatus is PORTABLE; there is NO DANGER WHATEVER (ordinary care being used when filling it); the Gas is PRODUCED IN AN INSTANT WITHOUT ANY FIRE OR OTHER ARTIFICIAL HEAT.

Further particulars may be obtained from MESSRS. EDWARD THOMSON & CO, Contractors for Drainage Water and Gas, who are appointed Sole Agents for the above apparatus, which can be seen working any week day between the hours of 6 A.M., and 6 P.M., at their place of business.

39, BENTINCK STREET, CALCUTTA.

India General Steam Navigation Company, Ld.

SCHOENE KILBURN & Co.—*Managing Agents.*

ASSAM LINE.

NOTICE.

Steamers leave Calcutta for Assam every Tuesday. Goalundo every Friday and leave Debrooghur downward every Saturday.

THE Str. "MIRZAPORE," will leave Calcutta for Assam, on Tuesday, the 14th instant.

Cargo will be received at the Company's Godowns, Nimtollah Ghat, up till noon of Monday, the 13th.

THE Str. "CHUNAAR" will leave Goalundo for Assam on Friday, the 17th instant.

Cargo will be received at the Company's Godowns, No. 4, Fairlie Place, up till noon of Wednesday the 15th.

Goods forwarded to Goalundo for this vessel will be chargeable with Railway Freight from Calcutta to Goalundo in addition to the regular Freight of this Company.

Passengers should leave for Goalundo by Train of Thursday, the 16th.

CACHAR LINE NOTICE

REGULAR FORTNIGHTLY SERVICE.

Steamers leave Calcutta for Cachar and Intermediate Stations every alternate Friday, and leave Cachar downward every alternate Sunday.

THE Str. "CODGONG" will leave Calcutta for Cachar on Friday, the 27th instant.

Cargo will be received at the Company's Godowns, Nimtollah Ghat, up till noon of Thursday the 16th.

For further information regarding rates of Freight or passage-money, apply to,

4, FAIRLIE PLACE, Calcutta, 9th November, 1876. G. J. SCOTT *Secretary*

Rivers Steam Navigation Co. Limited.

The Steamer "OUDE" left Goalundo for Assam on 1st instant.

The Steamer "BENGAL" left Calcutta for Assam on 31st October and left Goalundo for Assam on 7th November.

The Steamer "BURMAH" will leave Calcutta for Assam on [illegible] [illegible] and Goalundo on 21st current. Freight and Passage, apply to [illegible]

For [illegible] of No. 1, LYONS [illegible] 1st November 1876. MACNEILL & Co., *Agents.*

P. W. FLEURY'S HALL OF ILLUSIONS,

LAST NIGHT OF THE GHOST SCENES!! LAST NIGHT OF THE GHOST SCENES!!

NO. 62 WELLESLEY STREET.

The exciting and interesting Melo-drama "THE KNIGHT WATCHING HIS ARMOUR," and the laughable Farce.

"TWO HEADS BETTER THAN ONE" will be represented, Ghosts and Spirits will be made to mingle with the actors, and to vanish in the most mysterious and unaccountable manner, the Hall, the whole while, being brilliantly illuminated.

WONDERFUL APPARITION OF SPIRIT HANDS!

SPIRIT VOICES !!

SPIRIT FORMS.

Tambourins propelled in mid air, and Bells ringing by invisible agency, from empty cabinets.

The most wonderful transformations are effected with the aid of mysterious agents. A Gentleman will walk into the cabinet which has room only for one person, and a Lady will walk out of it, almost simultaneously.

GRAND EXHIBITION of magnificent Views including scenes during the Indian tour of

H. R. H. THE PRINCE OF WALES.

The most pleasing and artistic effect of change from night to day and *vice versa* are produced

THE TAJ BY DAY AND NIGHT.

MOUNT VESUVIOUS,

ST. PETER'S CHURCH,

and other magnificent views, will be shown during the exhibition.

Performances on Wednesday, Friday and Saturday, at 8-30 P. M.

PRICES OF ADMISSION.

Reserved chairs ...	... Rs. 2
Unreserved Chairs ...	... Re. 1

Children and Students half price.

A reduction made for Family tickets.

HAROLD & CO.,

3, DALHOUSIE SQUARE, CALCUTTA

HARMONIUMS.

Harold and Co., call attention to their unequalled stock of rich-toned Harmoniums made especially for India.

FROM RS. 90 TO RS. 900 EACH.

All kinds of Musical Instruments of the best description are always kept in Stock.

SMITH, STANISTREET & CO.

Pharmaceutical Chemists & Druggists

BY APPOINTMENT

To His Excellency the Right Hon'ble

LORD LYTTON, G.M.S.I.

Governor-General of India,

&c., &c.

SYRUP OF LACTATE OF IRON

Prepared from the original recipe. Lactate of Iron, in various forms of preparation, have been in use in France, and generally through the continent of Europe, for some years past, and is highly esteemed as one of the most valuable Chalybeate Tonic remedies yet introduced. The Syrup, being the most agreeable as well as convenient form of administration is in most general use. It is a most valuable remedy in the following diseases :—Chlorosis or Green Sickness, Leucorrhœa, Neuralgia, Enlargement of the Spleen, &c. In combination with quinine, it has also been very successfully used in the cure of Fever, while to persons of delicate constitution, enfeebled by disease it is invaluable. In bottles. Rs. 2 each.

SYRUP OF THE PHOSPHATE OF IRON Rs. 2 per bottle.

SYRUP OF PHOSPHATE OF IRON AND STRYCHNINE, Rs. 2 per bottle.

SYRUP OF PHOSPHATE OF IRON AND QUININE. Price Rs. 2-8 per bottle.

SYRUP OF PHOSPHATE OF IRON, QUININE AND STRYCHNINE.(DR. ATKIN'S TRIPLE TONIC SYRUP,) Rs. 2-8 per bottle.

Smith, Stanistreet & Co.

Invite special attention to the following rates the quality guaranteed as the best procurable :—

Pure Ærated Waters.

Made from Pure Water, obtained by the new process through the Patent Charcoal Filters.

				Rs	As.
Ærated plain (Treble Ærated), per doz.				0	12
Soda Water	ditto	„	...	0	12
Gingerade	ditto	„	...	1	4
Lemonade	ditto	„	...	1	4
Tonic (Quinine)	ditto	„	...	1	4

The *Cash* must be sent with the order to obtain advantage of the above rates.

BABU BASANTA KUMARA DATTA,

HOMŒOPATHIC PRACTITIONER

No. 20, Sunker Halder's Lane, Ahiritolah.

LONDON AGENT

MRS. HENRY TURNER & CO.

HOMŒOPATHIC

FRESH INDENT OF

Medicines and other Requisites.
Arrives every month from England.
Medicines, Boxes, Books, Pamphlets;
Absolute Alcohol ; Cholera-spirit Camphor.

SPECIAL REMEDIES.

For Supposed, Laborious and Difficult menses Leucorrhœa ; Hysteria.

For Spermatorrhœa ; Dysentery ; Diarrhœa ; Cholera.

For Asthma ; Pile ; Pain ; Sore and Diseases of the Children.

Ice, Lemonade, Soda and Tonic water always.

To be had at

DATTA'S HOMŒOPATHIC LABORATORY

No. 312, CHITPORE ROAD, BURTOLA, CALCUTTA.

TERMS—CASH.

☞ Price List can be had free on application.

ESTABLISHED 1833

H. C. GANGOOLY & CO.

STATIONERS, DIE-SINKERS, ENGRAVERS PRINTERS, LITHOGRAPHERS &c.

24, Mangoe Lane, Calcutta.

Cash prices of the following :—

	Rs.	As.		Rs.
Whatman's Drawing paper double elephant sizes (40×27) each ...	0	7		0
Mathematical Instrument Boxes	2	8	to	16
Color Boxes	0	4	„	5

Drawing Pencils, Drawing and Mapping Steel pens and various other requisites in Stationery.

DAY & COUSIN.

STATIONERS,

ENGRAVERS, PRINTERS

AND

PCITURE FRAMERS.

9, Hasting's Street, Calcutta.

THEISTIC BOOKS.

FOR SALE.

URDU..

Rahut Hakiki	Rs.	0	3	0
Nizam Komi		0	2	0
Kasufal Ilham		0	2	0
Kholasa, ol, Asool Brahm Dharm ...		0	1	0

HINDI.

Upasana Pudhati	Rs.	0	1	0
Benai Putrika or Hymn book ...		0	1	0
Tut Bodh		0	8	0
Upanashid Sar		0	8	0
Dhurm Dipika		0	0	6

ENGLISH.

Claims of so called Revealed Religion	Rs.	0	3	0
New Life		0	0	6
Living God		0	1	0
Higher and Lower Virtue		0	1	0

Apply to the Secretary,

BRAHMO SOMAJ OF THE PUNJAB,

Lahore.

MAKHON LOLL GHOSE.

No. 91, Radha Bazar, Calcutta.

BEGS to invite the attention of the public to several consignments of commercial and fancy stationery of all sorts, including account books of all sizes, made of handmade and machine-made paper, by steamers recently arrived, and which he is disposing of at moderate prices. He has been long in the trade, and presumes he has always afforded every satisfaction to the numerous merchants here who have constantly favored him with orders. Mofussil orders accompanied with remittances shall be promptly attended to.

CALCUTTA }
The 18th August 1876. }

CHUNDER & BROTHERS.

25½ & 112, RADHA BAZAR,

STATIONERY in all its varieties.
PRINTING PRESSES, Inks & Materials.
LITHOGRAPHIC PRESS & Materials.
BOOK BINDING Materials &c.

CALCUTTA

106, Bowbazar Street.

DR. H. C. SARMA'S

MEDICINE FOR DEBILITY

[NERVOUS]

HAIR PRESERVER.

Copy of Letter received from Raja Chundernath Roy Bahadoor of Nattore.

Wellesley Street, No. 18, Molt's Lane, 29th March 1874.

MY DEAR HURRISH BABU,—

I shall thank you to send me another phial of your *"Excellent Hair Restorer."* In fact it has done me a great benefit and I should like to have more of it. It has disabused me (young as I am) of old age.

Your's Sincerely

C. N. of *Nattore*

MEDICINE FOR BALDNESS.

Will certainly cure baldness if applied on the bald portion, night & morning, according to directions given in the adjoining direction paper.

Price per two ounce phial ...	Re.	1 0 0
Postage &c.	„	0 6 0

HEEM-SAGAR OIL.

The best remedy for Headache arising from overstudy, intellectual occupation, overthinking, mental anxiety and weakness, as well as heat of head from living in hot places.

It cools the head and produces very agreeable sensation. Removes dandriff as well as all other impurities from the head. Promotes the strength and growth of the hair and prevents its premature falling-off.

Price per 4 ounce phial ...	Re.	1 0 0
Postage &c.	„	0 10 0

MEDICINE FOR LEPROSY.

Price with Postage &c. ...	Rs.	5 0 0

OIL FOR LEPROSY.

And Inveterate Skin Diseases.

Price per 8 ounce phial ...	Rs.	2 0 0
Postage &c.	„	0 12 0

NOTICE.

A special General Meeting of the Commissioners of the Town of Calcutta will be held at the Town Hall, on Monday, at 3-o'clock P. M.

ROBERT TURNBULL,
Secretary to the Corporation.

Cachar Native Joint Stock Co. Ld.

Having spued out 50 acres in tea on a garden of 700 acres, do hereby give notice that this Company has been duly registered under Act X of 1866 and is now prepared to sell Share at 25 each untill 31st December next. Tea manufactured to date 20 maunds. Further particulars can be had from the undersigned.

BYKUNTA CHUNDER GUPTA,
Secretary

S. C. GUPTA'S

DIARRHŒA PILLS

SEVERAL years of experience in private practice have proved these pills to be most efficacious in obstinate cases of Non-Inflammatory, Infantile, Choloric, Chronic and all sorts of Diarrhœa, and in all cases of Indigestion, Dyspepsia, Flatulence caused by disturbance of the digestive function.

Sold in Boxes containing 12 pills with full directions for use :—

Price ... ... Re. 1 0 per box
„ with postage ... „ 1 4 „

To be had of DURGA DASS GUPTA, care of the Manager, Indian Mirror, Calcutta.

PRIZE MEDALLISTS

For Excellency of Workmanship.

J. M. EDMOND & CO.,

27—28, BENTINCK STREET,

ESTABLISHED 1833.

Cabinet Makers, Upholsterers,

AND

Billiard Table Manufacturers.

Houses completely furnished. Furniture designed and made to order.

ESTIMATES given for all kinds of Carpentering, Painting, Polishing, Gilding and General Repairs; Marble Polished, Moulded, and Cleaned; Picture Frames made.

J. M. EDMOND & CO. in soliciting a continuance of public patronage beg to say they have ready for sale specimens of Ebonized and Gold Oxford style of Fancy Chairs, and are prepared to execute orders for other Furniture in the same style.

J. M. EDMOND & Co.'s New Show-Room is now replete with New Heraldic Style of Dining-room Chairs, and Rustic Chairs, Telescopic Dining **Tables, with Patent** Table Expanders, and a variety of finished Furniture.—Orders solicited.

BURN & CO.

RANEEGUNGE **Fire** bricks **are the best Fire** Bricks known ;—superior to Ramsay's.

8 Rs. per 100.

Fire clay, 40 Rs. per Ton.

Glazed Stone ware, Drainage pipes of all sizes

BURN & Co.,
7, Hastings Street, Calcutta.

ARLINGTON & CO.,

3 B. DALHOUSIE SQUARE, CALCUTTA.

THE 'PATENT PERPETUAL FOUNTAIN,'

TABLE EPERGNE OR CENTRE PIECE,

FOR SCENT OR FOR PUREWATER WATER.

In Richly Electro-Silvered Ware. [*One of the Greatest Novelties of the day.*]

Cash Price Rs. 175.

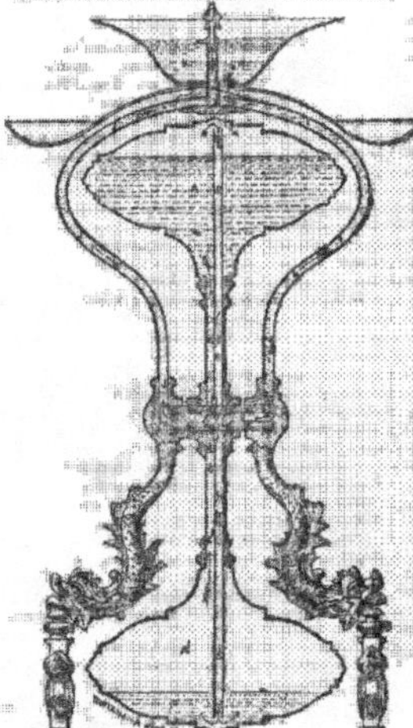

N. B.—The annexed drawing is not a correct representation of the Plated Table Fountains which A. & Co. have for sale. The drawing is only given to shew the internal arrangements of the Apparatus, and attention is invited to the following description :—

OBSERVE.—A, A1, are two cisterns or reservoirs, which are connected together by pipes or tubes B, B1, C, C1, mounted on a hollow axis of motion D, surrounding a fixed conical plug E, having suitable passages F, G, H, therein communicating with the pipes or tubes B, B1, C, C1, and I, and with the jet pipe J.

To put the fountain in operation water is poured into the dish or basin K until the lower reservoir is filled and the opening II is covered. The cisterns or reservoirs A, A1, are then turned on their axis of motion, so as to place the filled cistern or reservoir A at the top, when the water therefrom will flow to a level in the jet pipe J, and the water in the basin or dish K by passing down the pipes or tubes I and B1 into the lower cistern or reservoir A1, rises in such lower cistern or reservoir A1 and forces the air out therefrom through the pipe or tube C1, passage F, and tube B, into the upper part of the cistern or reservoir A, where it presses upon the surface of the water therein and forces it out therefrom through the tube C, passage H, and jet pipe J, until all the water in the upper cistern or reservoir A has passed through the jet pipe J and into the lower cistern or reservoir A1 by the pipe I, passage G, and pipe B1, when by turning the cistern or reservoirs A, A1, on their axis of motion until the cistern or reservoir A1 is at the top, the action of the fountain will be continued; the pipes or tubes B, C1, which had previously been air passages now becoming water passages, and the pipes or tubes B1, C, now becoming air passages which had previously served for the passage of water. By these improvements the necessity for alternately filling and emptying the cisterns or reservoirs A, A1, is obviated.

Printed and published by M. M. BOKHIT, at the INDIAN MIRROR PRESS, No. 6, College Square, for the Proprietors.

The Indian Mirror.

SUNDAY EDITION.

VOL. XVI] CALCUTTA, SUNDAY, NOVEMBER 19, 1876. {REGISTERED AT THE GENERAL POST OFFICE.} [NO. 274

CONTENTS.

NOTICE.

All letters and communications relating to the literary department of the Paper should be addressed to the Editor. All other letters should be addressed to the Manager, to whom all remittances should be made payable.

Subscribers will be good enough to bring to the notice of the Manager any delay or irregularity in the delivery of the Paper.

Editorial Notes

SO cast-prejudices even in Madras are getting slackend. There has been a meeting held to readmit into his caste Mr. Ruthnavalu Chetty, the young Madrasi gentleman who has reecently entered the Civil Service. Shastris have been consulted, and the Guru has been visited, and we hear that there is every likelihood of young Mr. Chetty, after his return from iconoclastic England, being received back into the bosom of his caste. We hope he cares for that privilege, and will enjoy it.

DR. SLADE, the spiritualistic medium, was being tried before the Bow Street Police Court, when the last mails left England. He has been summoned firstly on the charge of "unlawfully using certain subtle crafts and devices, to deceive and impose upon certain of Her Majesty's subjects, and secondly of "conspiring and combining to deceive the same persons, and to defraud them of their money." So far as the depositions went the case looked any thing but favorable to Dr. Slade's reputation. We await the result with curiosity.

WE read the other day that the Bishop of Bombay had agreed to open an orphanage for the children of the famine-stricken, but only on the condition that these children submitted to the ceremony of baptism. Mr. Narain Sheshadri the head of the Native Christian community in Bombay, has written a letter to the same effect in the *Bombay Guardian*. Now supposing that the victims of the famine refused to accept Christianity, would the Bishop of Bombay, and Mr. Narain refuse them the help they are competent and prepared to give? Perhaps they would. We need be suprised at the condition thus imoosed. This has been for a long time the policy of Indian proselytism. When the poor labourers find their harvests failing them, it is then that these Missionaries reap *their* harvests plentifully. Is this not a strange mockery of religious conversion?

THE most terrible accounts of death, devastation, and suffering continue to pour in from thecylone-stricken districts of East Bengal. Nobody can estimate the loss of human life. This is somewhat surprising. With the Lieutenant-Governor on the spot, aided by high local officers, why should not an approximate calculation of the loss of life and property be arrived at? Not much doubt that about a hundred thousand human beings have perished, and tens of thonsand are suffering terribly from disease, and from want of food and accommodation. Government relief as yet is on a meagre scale, and no efficient steps seem to have been taken to meet the terrible necessities of the case. If Sir Richard Temple displays half the energy and spends a quarter of the amount of money lavished to remove the apprehended famine in Behar, the country will bless him and his rule. But the cyclone does not seem to have yet attracted the attention of the highest officials, and though the suffering is horrible, sympathy is inadequate. Why will not the public bodies of move in the matter?

THE situation in Europe has become critical. Everyone thinks that war is almost acertainty. It cannot be confidently asserted whether England would at once take part in it, but the public feeling against Mahomedan atrocities in the Christian provinces of Turkey, is as strong as the feeling against Russian manœuvres to excite the Servians to continued revolt and successful resistance with a view to the long-looked-for possession of Constantinople. The two feelings are pretty nearly balanced, and though the *Times* says that "the Government must be perfectly well aware that neither Parliament nor the Country, would ever hear for a moment of our going to war on behalf of Turkey," yet there are mighty preparations of war, the import of which is unmistakable. We, who have deplored the blood-shed and violence taking place for the last few months, and especially the inhumanities perpetrated by some of the Turkish regiments upon Christians, feel yet more depressed at the prospect of a universal war. It is said that the French will not join the fight; Austria will very likely act in consert with Russia, Germany and Italy will stand remain neutral. So if there is any European war at all, it will be between England and Turkey on the one hand, and Russia on the other. Feeling in England is strongly divided on the subject, and it remains to be seen how Lord Beconsfield's Government will act in emergency. All these circumstances only increase the ominousness of the times, and intensify the awkwardness of the situation at the Delhi Assemblage.

IN reviewing Mr. Slater's book on "God Revealed," the *Friend of India*, discusses a very important question, namely how Christanity ought to be preached in India. He justly denounces the dogmatism in which well-meaning Evangelicals indulge without stint or measure, and compares it to "break-fasting on gravel." He agrees with Mr. Slater warmly when the latter observes that Christianity should be planted on Indian soil, not as a "system of conventional ideas" but, as "an eternal and manifested life," giving freedom and play to "true religious feeling round great spiritual facts and hopes." We are glad our contempory says this, and still more so that Mr. Slater, a member of the London Missionary Society, Madras, expresses such views most clearly in his book. Only the question is how is the feeling of sympathy with great spiritual facts and hopes such as rational and genuine Christianity sets forth, to be evoked in the Indian heart? In religious emotion the Hindu religion is not deficient, some of its moral precepts are most exalting. There are great spiritual facts and hopes also in some of the schools, and notably in the Vaishnava school of Hindu religion. Now if these various elements of real religious life in the land be added up, ordinary Christians will not find it very easy to put anything very new before the really advanced and spiritual Hindu. But still in the spirit of ttue Christianity there is a great deal that is not in Hinduism. And inorder to bring it home to the Hindu heart the greatest degree of sympathy will have to be shown towards the Hindu insticts and processes of religious development, and a willingness manifessed *to learn* as well as to teach. If the Christian Missionary is prepared to adopt what is good and true in Hindu principles, he will find the Hindu ready also to accept what is acceptable in Christianity. But if he comes as a *teacher* only, too wise and good to learn anything from those among whom he has come, he will find the really noble types of Hindu character will keep aloof from him for ever.

THE *Spectator* has a good article on *Zeal* of the good and bad discription. Zeal of the wrong kind, or rather zealotry, which actuates proselytizers and sensational meeting-holders, is not at all "the ardour with which his own convictions fill him," but "the ardour for absolutely ruling other minds and hearts." The zealot is angry, indiscriminate impatient of contradiction, he is fierce, perfunctory, hectoring, wants to frighten people, is nervous lest he be defeated, and tries to feel in all things that "order reigns."

With regard to zeal of the finer and nobler kind, we blieve that it is not only compatible with a very high sifting and discriminating power, but that the highest sifting and discriminating power cannot exist at all without it. It is a mistake to suppose that cold, calm minds are the best fitted to discriminate truth, just as it is a mistake to suppose that cold, calm minds are the best fitted to discriminate beauty, and for exactly the same reason. Cold, calm minds unquestionably judge better on what they have before them, than eager and impulsive minds which have precisely the same materials before them. But then they so seldom have the same materials before them. The liability to passion or affection is a power as well as a source of weakness; it brings new materials within the scope of the judgement, and new materials of the most important kind. The commonplace man does not *see* the same sights as the painter whose mind is filled with the love of beauty. The calm, critical intellect does not behold the same vision as the mystic whose heart is full of the love of God. Zeal in the highest sense,—the zeal which comes of true vision and the love of that vision,—is quite as much a discerning power as a motive power Zeal of the best sort has a fine discrimination of its own, but it often mistakes greatly the limits of that discrimination, and trusts to it in spheres with which it has really no competence to deal. Still we are fully persuaded of this,—that zeal as distinguished from zealotry,—the passion which the vision of truth itself inspires, has a human pliancy, an intellectual adaptability of its own which is a very great safeguard against bigotry of any kind. Undoubtedly, however, zeal of this sort is very much rarer than zealotry,—very much rarer than impatience of contradiction in that special sphere of prejudice which has got on it the conventional mark of "sacredness." We fear Bishop Temple is right that it is the latter zeal which chiefly fills Church Congresses and Denominational gatherings of all sorts, and that it is a sort of zeal generally much more dangerous than beneficial. Perhaps, however, even that is better than complete indifference to which zeal is often much more closely allied than the sometimes diametrically opposite external results which zealotry and indifference produce, would give any idea of. For occasionally we have an opportunity of seeing how cruel indifference can be,—as cruel as the zeal of the zealot, though it seems much less gloomy, and has much less excuse.

RIGHT INTERPRETATION.

REVELATION is one, interpretations are many. The greatest enemy perhaps that truth has next to falsehood is misinterpretation. And it has been well said that a whole falsehood is better than half the truth. The channel of truth ought to be as pure as truth itself. To be able to communicate the light of truth faithfully is a gift of which few are ambitious. Truth is divine, but the power of interpreting truth is by most considered to be human. This mistake lies at the bottom of all denominational religion. Commentaries and discourses can not explain revelation. If we want truth-speaking prophets who neyver fail, do we not also truth-speaking disciples—interpreters who truly represent? Let it be known that the duty of right interpretation is as difficult to discharge on the part of those upon whom it falls, as the duty of conceiving original truth in the first instance, and bringing it into light. The prophet and the apostle must go hand in hand. The faculty of rightly interpreting the ideas and principles of great minds, is developed under certain conditions, of which we purpose to take notice just now. In the first place, the mind of the interpreter must be free from every ambition except that of setting forth the light which enlightens his heart. Every form of personal advancement acts as an intercepting medium which is sure to distort, discolor, and hide the original illumination. The mind must be perfectly unoccupied and untampered with the counsels of private motives. The disciple that longs to be the faithful interpreter of his master's thoughts, must say with Hamlet :—

Yea, from the table of my memory
I'll wipe away all trivial fond records,
All saws of books, all forms, all pressures past,
That youth and observation copied there;
And thy commandment alone shall live
Within the book and volume of my brain,
Unmixed with baser matter.

In the second place there must be no secret passion for any anything that is foreign to the purposes and aims of the preceptor whose life and principles it is attempted to represent. A strong feeling, that is quite excusable under other circumstances of life, would not only be an obstruction, but a positive sin, if indulged in with the consciousness that it stands in the way of a full elucidation of the views and doctrines of those whose inward ideas have to be expressed, and laid before the world. Nothing is so inimical to thesmoothness and effectiveness of a medium of truth as a violent passion of any kind which warps all the faculties, and unfits the mind for the due reception of divine light. In the third place another, and a very delicate matter has to be touched. The intellect is an indispensable power, and there is no condition of life in which it does not operate, sometimes in subordination to, and in harmony with other things, and sometimes independent of them. The intellect when it has any real power, has, it must be admitted, the tendency to be imperious, and to sit in judgment over all matters. Now there are occasions and objects where this is legitimate, and the intellect must arbitrate for the guidance of the remaining part of our nature. But there are matters also over which the intellect has no jurisdiction. And the interpretation of truths which men greater than ourselves discover, and entrust to our hands to propagate, is exactly such a matter. Of course, these truths take a tinge from the mental constitution of the individuals through whom they have to pass, and the intellect as well as the feelings give that tinge. But in interpreting revelation, the intellect is but little help, and must not be permitted to take a prominent position. It is the simple childlike spirit which reflects best the light of truth poured from above. These are the negative conditions, but there are some positive ones also. We spoke on the subject of self-abasement in our last issue. And what is there like the putting back of Self which can successfully communicate to the world the sentiments and principles which emanate from natures superior to our own. Let the sphere of self be kept quite separate, and not mixed at all with the concerns that are higher and holier than anything it contains. Another thing which greatly helps the work of right interpretation is the strong personal love to the individual, or individuals whose innerlife will have to be interprefed. Nothing is so watchful as affection; nothing so closely marks and detects the peculiarities of life, tendency, example, and precept. Elaborate processes of moral and emotional interpretation, aided by the powerful action of the intellectual power, fail and become insignificant while the quickness of the eye of personal attachment easily interprets the secret meaning of the master whose heart can only be reached by heart. And when to this is added the fire of enthusiasm for truth, the fire dissolves so many hard obstructions that the disciple becomes at one with his prophet, the current of electric sympathy is complete, and the work of interpretation is really successful.

Correspondence.

THE CHITTAGONG CYCLONE RELIEF FUND.

WE the undersigned natives of Chittagong implore the charitable public in Calcutta to assist with their generous donations a few of our friends in Chittagong, who are relieving some of the most distressed sufferers from the late terrible cyclone and the storm-wave, which have devastated several districts in East Bengal. The donors will kindly send their subscriptions to the Editor of the *Indian Mirror* 11 Old Post Office Street, Calcutta.

Nobin Chunder Das, M. A.
Purna Chunder Dutta, B. A.
Raj Kumar Dutta.
Raj Kumar Sen.
Mohender Kumar Ray.

BRAHMOISM AT BANGALORE &C.

To the Editor of the *Indian Mirror*.

On the Steamer *Mongolia*
Coming up the Hughly,
November 12, 1876.

Home again, after a busy round about in Southern India. Calcutta to Madras by sea 800 miles; to Salem 200 miles further, by rail, to Coonoor upon the Nilgiri plateau, 150 miles further south and west; thence to Ootacamund, the navel of the Nilgiris; back again to Salem, where are some staunch Brahmos, few but undismayed; then by an elbow, round to Bangalore, where are two good Somajes, one in the town or Pettah and the other in Cantonments, a Sepoy Somaj; then after four days in Bangalore, full of cheer, down to the sea again; a week there, at Madras, where I hear of but one little Somaj determined to hope on, hope ever,—with a half audible murmur against the twenty Calcutta Somajes for not sending a missionary to Madras;—and so by a five days' sea-trip, cool, sweet, delightful and smooth as a lake, up the Bay of Bengal and back again to Calcutta. Brahmoism, however vital and deathless in its principles, cannot live and grow as a church visible and militant, without missionary aid and intercommunion. Brethren must go with apostolic faith, self-denial and trust in the Omnipresent,—go from city to city preaching the word, in season and out of season. If they do not, forms of faith, less true than "the pure theism of Jesus" will out-grow and over-grow and kill Brahmoism. Brahmoism will soon die in itself if it will not live and die for others. Its warmth must soon go down to zero, if it decline to spend and be spent for not only such as welcome it, but for them that hate and revile it. Would we had more such men as the Acharyya of the Town Somaj of Bangalore; and I may well add the Secretary of the Cantonment Somaj, who is the Subadar Major of the Native Infantry stationed there. The minister of the Town Somaj,—(and who has been so for five years, so a visitor at my room in the Cubbon Hotel, Bangalore, informed me,—(was once a Sunnyasi ! I speak not now of the Secretary, Mr. Ramasawmy Charty,—but of the preacher Mr Chunder Siker,—or as they have it here, Chandera Siker Aiyer. This man, as a Hindu devotee, left his home, years ago, in the Mahratha country, and, casting himself upon divine providence and human charity, wandered far and wide through Southern India. Thus, for several years, studying life and nature, he lived upon alms. His Native town is Gokurum. I am told that his hearers average about fifty,—and this could hardly be the case if he were not thoroughly in earnest. So far as my observation extends, very few of the Brahmo Somajes in the Madras Presidency that once had as many as fifty members, now have a regular attendance of more than ten or twelve. Such is the case with the Salem Somaj. Here the natural and healthful division into Conservatives and Progressives soon split the church in halves. But the good wit of the able leader of the Progressives, Narasimulu Naidu, soon united all parties not in the Prayer Meeting, but in a successful Reading Room. Here from day to day, and evening to evening, Native friends of truth are welcome—all who can afford to pay four annas a month or three rupees a year. A good many do afford it, and the Salem Reading Room, well lighted, to nine or ten o'clock at night, is much resorted to for study thought, and conversation. They have no Mandir, and no attractive or well-adapted place of meeting for the Salem Brahmo Samaj, but will meet in their rented room in the Bazaar, until some day when they can do better. In connection with the apparent stagnation of Theism in parts of the Madras Presidency, it is well to remember that Theism, with its bond of fraternity, and its freedom of inquiry, is showing itself, in Madras, Bangalore, Salem and elsewhere—in ways not less truly, if less apparently religious. Vencata Swamy Naidu, Parry & Co's best known Dubash, a young man of wealth and culture,—who visited England less than two years ago, and died soon after his return,—was, if not a Brahmo a man in full sympathy with Brahmoism. He often attended the meetings of a People's Association in Madras, which drew together, at stated intervals, men of all opinions, who were sufficiently emancipated from Hindu prejudices of caste &c., to clasp hands as fellow-men and dine together. And who shall say there is not true religion in this open communion of men, previously strangers, who dared to confess their brotherhood in actions that "speak louder than words" A somewhat similar association, I mean similarly theistic and liberalizing in its tendencies, is the "Bangalore Literary Union," which, they tell me, brings together a goodly number (some 50 or 60) to the support of its Library and Reading Room. In the Hall of this "Union" which I have good reason to remember, I gave, to crowded audiences (of 120 or more) of English-speaking gentlemen of Hindu birth, one lecture, presided over by a Native Barrister educated in England, C. Menacshiah Esq., on "The Progress and Prospects of Brahmoism in India," and another on "Theism in England and America" with the Hony. Secy. of the "Union" as Chairman, *i. e.*, Mr. T. Ananda Rao, son of Sir T. Madhava Rao, (of Baroda,) K.C.S.I. More cordial gatherings of inquiring men it has seldom been my privilege to address, and it would be unfair to them not to add that a good number of them including the efficient Librarian, Munuswamy Nagalinga, and others attended me to the station with wreaths of flowers and baskets of fruit for my journey—with a hearty call to come again. Amrita Babu was most kindly enquired after, and many would be glad to see him again.

Yours &c.
DALL.

Devotional

LORD! I thank thee for the sweetness of thy presence which Thou hast many times revealed even unto this sinner. I thank thee for the many consolations and deeply soothing glances of thy loving eyes on my soul in the midst of my great troubles; I thank thee for the deep joy of the sense of holy poverty, asceticism, and purity which Thou hast previleged me at times to enjoy. I dare not undervalue them. But, my God, what hast Thou done to my state, what shall I profit with these, however excellent they may be, if my inner self remains as unclean as before? Was I not told, my God, that in spite of thy many indulgences, and my sensible but momentary devotions, thy holiness will not spare a least speck on my soul in the day of reckoning? Thou knowest how restlessly I ponder over my state day and night. Have, therefore, a pitying glance on me, and see how miserable I am on account of my sins. I implore thy saving grace now to break asunder like a potter's vessel, my pride, selfishness, lust, envy and all that is amiss in my soul, make me white as snow, and create a new spirit in me. May the old monster entirely die away, and may I be born anew in thy holiness and peace—a new creature.

I VERILY perceive, my God, that Thou hast persued and attacked me, else why so much violence used towards me. Art Thou deaf to the idle and wicked pleadings of my perverted soul to enjoy a little more peace and a little more rest? Then accept me as I am, and do with me what seemeth good in thy sight. I did not know, my God, that Thou dost so forcibly lead sinners to thy path. I thought that Thou keepest thyself aloof from unwilling sinners, and only savest those that by their own free-will come and ask salvation from thee. I now see Lord, the doctrine of free-will as I understand it, turns out unsound.

SUPREME Directing Power, guide aright the good cause which thou hast placed in our hands. Help and enlighten those to whom important work is entrusted. From vain imaginations, unworthy dispositions, and obstructive selfishness set us free. Lord, let thy Spirit rule over our church, and all its details, over the purposes and plans of our leaders, over the actions and inclinations of our men and women. Our places of knowledge and instruction fill with the light of thy sober wisdom; our houses of worship make thy holy abode; our places of dwelling sanctify with the sweetness of thy love and service. O Lord, bless and prosper our movement according to thy will.

The Brahmo Somaj

THE subject of the sermon preached in the Mandir on Sunday, the 5th November, was: "God is the origin of all the *forces* which create and sustain the universe." In the course of the sermon it was affirmed that there could not be two supreme powers. There is in fact one Supreme Energy which produces the infinite variety of natural phenomena. From this immanent, all-pervading and indwelling Energy are derived the myriads of forces which we observe in the world.

BABU DEBENDER NATH TAGORE is in Calcutta just now. Yesterday he presided at a meeting for the improvement of the Bengali language and literature in the Theatre of the Hindu School. This morning, we believe, he conducts the monthly service of the Calcutta Brahmo Somaj at Jorasanko.

WE ought to have noticed in our last issue the lamented death of a distinguished Brahmica lady who has been for a long course of years connected with our church, and done a great deal of good in her quite unostentatious way. Mrs. D. M. Doss died on the 8th instant in her residence at South Circular Road, at the prime of life, leaving a large family, and many friends to regret her loss most sincerely. Many widows and orphans have been tended and protected by her and her good husband, many acts of female reform have been aided and encouraged by her, and many Brahmo families bear warm and vivid remembrances of her virtue and goodness. We pay a sorrowing tribute to her memory, and trust and pray that she may have rest and joy in heaven.

OUR Missionary, Babu Denonath Mozumdar, has visited Bankipore, Arrah and Dumraon. At Arrah a prayer meeting was held at the residence of Babu Bhoggobutty Churn Mitter, the Munsiff, and was respectably attended. The Deputy Magistrate, Babu Jadunath Bose, B.A., the Government Pleader, Babu Koylash Chunder Banerji M.A.B.L., and others were, present on the occasion.

Gleanings

THE GOLDEN A. B. C.

THIS is the Golden A. B. C., which the pious man set the Doctor to learn for the amending of his life, and which doubtless it were very profitable and needful for us all to repeat many times and oft, and amend our lives thereafter.

After a manly and not a childish sort, ye shall, with thorough earnestness, begin a new life.

Bad ways ye shall eschew, and practise all goodness with diligence and full purpose of mind.

Carefully endeavour to keep the middle path in all things, with seemliness and moderation.

Demean yourself humbly in word and work, from the inward holiness of your heart.

Entirely give up your own will evermore, cleave earnestly to God and forsake Him not.

Forward and ready shall ye be in all good works, without murmuring, whatever be commanded you.

Give heed to exercise yourself in all godly works of mercy toward the body or the spirit.

Have no backward glances after the world, or the creatures, or their doings.

Inwardly in your heart ponder over your past life with honesty, sincere repentence in the bitterness of your heart, and tears in your eyes.

Knightly and resolutely withstand the assaults of the Devil, the Flesh, and the world.

Learn to conquer long-cherished sloth with vigor together with all effeminacy of the body, and subservience to the Devil.

Make your abode in God, with fervent love, in certian hope, with strong faith, and be towards your neighbour as towards yourself.

No other man's good things shall ye desire, be they what they may, corporal or spiritual. Order all things so that you make the best and not the worst of them.

Penance, that is suffering for your sin, you shall take willingly, whether it comes from God or the creatures.

Quittance, remission, and absolution, you shall give to all who have ever done you wrong in thought, word, and deed.

Receive all things that befal you with meekness, and draw improvement from them.

Soul and body, estate and reputation, keep undefiled with all care and diligence.

Truthful and upright shall ye be towards all without guile or cunning.

Wantonness and excess, of whatsoever kind it may be, ye shall learn to lay aside, and turn from it with all your heart.

Christ, our Blessed Lord's life and death shall ye follow, and wholly conform yourself thereunto with all your might.

Ye shall evermore without ceasing, beseech our blessed Lady that she help you to learn this one lesson well.

Zealously keep a rein over your will and your senses that they may be at peace with all that God doth and also with all His creatures.

All this lesson must be learnt of a free heart and will without cavilling.

Tauler's Life.

Literary

MR. CARR STEPHEN'S "Archæology and Monumental Remains of Delhi," is just out.

MR. R. B. SHAW'S new linguistic works—his *Ghalchah Languages (Wakhi and Sarikoli)* and his grammar of the *Eastern Turki* language, are also out.

IT is stated that the defunct *Rangoon Mail* is shortly to be resuscitated, but under another name.

ON the last of January next, the *Statesman* and *Friend of India* will become one journal, under the title of *The Friend of India and Statesman*, the rate of subscription being raised. It is a pity that such an old paper as the *Friend of India*, should have no separate existence of its own, and the time-hallowed associations surrounding that journal, and its traditional fame as a weekly, should die away.

THERE seems to be some mystery hanging over the sudden disappearance of the *Behar Herald* of Bankipore. It is whispered it has fallen a prey to the present system of Government espionage in connection with the Press.

Latest News.

—THE *Straits Times* is in a position to state that the house of Mr. Lehmann, a planter at Soengei Diski, in the District of Deli, was attacked on the 17th ultimo by a party of Mahomedan Battaks, who brutally murdered Mrs. Lehmann and two children and seriously wounded Mr. Lehmann and his assistant, Mr. Reveneng. Thirty people have been arrested on suspicion, and have been taken to Labuan. There is no political motive attributed to the deed.

—NEWS of an extraordinary character has reached Paris from New Caledonia. A captain of marines, named Malret, sent out to quell a disturbance amongst the native tribes, has been captured and eaten by a warrior chief named Poindi Patchoussi.

—THE commercial treaty with the King of Burmah expires next year.

—IT is said that on the return of the Maharajah of Cashmere from Delhi there will be a general illumination and great rejoicings at Jummu in honor of the assumption by Her Majesty the Queen of the Title of Empress of India.

—THE *Golos* on the 15th ultimo published an article violently attacking Earl Beaconsfield. The semi-official *Journal de St. Petersburgh* on the following day, referring to the subject, expresses regret at the unseemly language used by the writer.

—THE heir apparent of Cashmere converses fluently in English. He greatly assists the Maharajah in transacting the affairs of the State.

—DAWAN ANANT RAM, the new Prime Minister of Cashmere, is a highly polished gentleman, who has received an excellent English education and promises to be a worthy successor to his late father, Dewan Kirpa Ram.

—THE China papers report that Sir Thomas Wade will leave China for England shortly, and that the Chinese Envoy will accompany him.

—A TYPE-WRITING machine has been in use for some time in the Examiner's Office of the Public Works Department at Madras, and it has proved such a success that the machine will, probably, be introduced into all the public offices.

—THE *Englishman* hears that Nawab Abdul Gunni Miah, C. S. I. and his son, Khajah Ahsanulla, although likely to be heavy losers by the damage done to their zemindaries during the late cyclone, no sooner heard of the distress in the division than they placed their steamers at the disposal of Government, and contributed large stocks of rice and salt for the sufferers. It is probable that, owing to the anxiety caused by the late storm, they will not attend the Delhi Assemblage.

—SIR RICHARD TEMPLE, according to the *Englishman*, who has just returned from the desolated districts in the Eastern Division of Bengal, "walked for miles and miles through the ruined villages and ascertained the exact losses of life from house to house, using these ascertained examples to test all estimates and reports. Many dreadful and sickening sights are reported to have been seen. The result of His Honor's enquiries as to the destruction is quite as unfavorable as anything which has been reported in the public prints; even worse, perhaps. But the condition of the survivors was ascertained to be not so bad as might have been feared. In every village the people were found drying their wet grain in the sun. They must have been much famished for the first two or three days, but their prospects are, apparently, improving every day. Great part of the ripening crops have been lost. No epidemic sickness has as yet broken out, though this is much feared. Relief centres are being established everywhere, not only to give relief wherever it is necessary to save life, but also to preserve order, and to give confidence to the people; so that business of all sorts may speedily revive."

—SPECIAL leave will be granted to military officers wishing to attend the Delhi Assemblage, between the 15th of December and the 15th of January, in all cases where their services can be spared.

—A FEARFUL murrain has broken out amongst the Egyptian horses. Three thousand horses have died in Cairo alone; even the Khedive's stables have been smitten.

—THE arrangements for the proposed Egyptian Expedition by the English are now confined to pen-and-ink preparations only.

—THE presence of the Bangalore Volunteers at the Imperial Assemblage, has been dispensed with.

—THE cyclone in Bengal was caused by the conflict of opposing parallel winds blowing from widely extended regions of high pressure to the north and south.

—THE loss of cattle in Dukhin Shabaspore, according to a correspondent of the *Indian Daily News*, has been immense—bullocks, cows, and buffaloes, scarcely any are left. All along the eastern side of the island of Tozimuddi is not to be seen a house standing, the people are all living in the open air, or in temporary booths. They live chiefly on damaged rice, scraped from the ruins of their houses and open cocoanuts and the edible parts of the plantain tree. Salt is the one thing they are most troubled about just now.

—THE Begum of Bhopal has rented the Delhi and London Bank premises at Delhi for Rs. 18,000.

—THE Delhi Municipality asked to be permitted to present an address to His Excellency the Governor-General; but His Lordship refused.

—EVERY train to Delhi is bringing in large quantities of theatrical appliances, and the station, it is said, will be flooded with theatrical talent.

Calcutta.

THE Government paper market is as low as ever. Four and Four-and-a-half per cents. are selling at 98-8 and Five and-a-half at 101-4.

THE Insolvent Court will sit on Tuesday next.

THE Governor-General's Council will be held in Calcutta on Wednesday next, General Sir Henry Norman presiding.

THE next Criminal Sessions of the High Court will be held to-morrow, Mr. Justice White presiding. Among other cases, that of Sir Stuart Hogg against Mr. James Wilson will be tried. It is fixed for hearing to-morrow.

THE following Chiefs from Bengal have been invited to the Delhi Assemblage :—The Rajah of Cuch Behar ; Maharajah Luchmessur Singh Bahadur, of Durbhanga ; Maharajah Moheshur Bux Singh of Dumraon ; Maharajah Krishna Pertap Sahi Bahadur of Hatwa ; Maharajah Sir Jey Mangal Singh Bahadur K.C.S.I. ; Rajah Harballub Narain Singh of Sonbansa ; the Maharajah of Burdwan ; Babu Degumber Mitter C.S.I. ; and Rajah Harendra Krishna Bahadur ; Rajah Narendra Krishna ; Rajah Jotendro Mohun Tagore Bahadur ; Nawab Abdul Gunny C.S.I. ; Nawab Synd Ashgur Ali Khan Bahadur C.S.I. ; Nawab Synd Muhammed Amir Ali Khan Bahadur ; Eldest son of King of Oudh ; Eldest son of Nawab Nazim ; and the Head of Mysore Family.

THE *Indian Church Gazette* writes as follows about the new Metropolitan :—"The new Bishop is expected to arrive in Calcutta some time about the middle of January. We hear that he is unmarried, about forty-eight years of age, and that he is held in high regard by all who know him, and has been much valued by the Bishops in whose diocese his work has chiefly lain. A retired Bengal Chaplain, who has had some opportunity for forming an opinion, writes that the Bishop-designate appears to him, so far as a short acquaintance enables him to judge, admirably fitted to meet the difficulties and requirements of the diocese."

ANOTHER new political association, to be called the Bengal Association, is to be started in this city. The object of the Association "shall be to interpret the views of Government to the people, to cement union between the Europeans and Natives, as well as to represent to Government the wants and wishes of the people. The proceedings of the Association shall not be conducted in the English, but in the vernacular language, and just in the style debates amongst villagemen, when they have any important object to carry out, are held—that is to say, there will be less of speeches, and more of action. None blinded by race feeling or prejudice shall be admitted a member of the Association. All communications to Government shall be made in Bengali, with translations attached to them."

THE East Indian Railway will issue Monthly Return Tickets to Delhi during the month of December next, which will be available for return on or before the 31st January 1877.

WE are requested announce that a public meeting of the Shambazar Gyandipica Library will be held to-day at 4 P. M., precisely, at the premises of the Shambazar Government Aided Vernacular School, No. 128, Shambazar Street, to appoint Trustees for the said Literary.

THE total number of deaths in Calcutta during the week ending the 11th instant, was unusually large, *viz*, 303.

Public Engagement

Monday, the 20th Nov.—A general meeting of the members of the Indian Association in the Association Rooms, 12, College Square N., for the puqpose of considering the rules that have been framed by the Committee, and for such other business as may be submitted.

Advertisements

LIGHT! LIGHT!! LIGHT!!!

PATENT PORTABLE AIR GAS MAKING APPARATUS,

SUITABLE FOR

Churches, Chapels, Schools, Country Mansions, Private Houses, Railway Stations, Barracks, Manufactories, Collieries, Mills, Offices, &c., &c.

THIS *simple* and *effective* Gas-making Apparatus supplies a want long felt of having Gas at places where no Gas Works exist. It may be introduced without any more trouble than the simply affixing of any ordinary Gas meter, and is about the same size for the same number of lights. The *piping* and *fitting* arrangements are in every respect the same as for the use of ordinary Gas. The *cost* of the Gas produced is about the same as is charged for ordinary Coal Gas, and the light produced is *more brilliant* and of *a greater illuminating power*; it is also *free from the impurities of Coal Gas.* The Gas, if used with the Patent Burner, is of great heating power, and hence suitable for cooking and heating purposes, or in manufactories for soldering, &c. The apparatus is PORTABLE; there is NO DANGER WHATEVER (ordinary care being used when filling it); the Gas is PRODUCED IN AN INSTANT WITHOUT ANY FIRE OR OTHER ARTIFICIAL HEAT.

Further particulars may be obtained from MESSRS. EDWARD THOMSON & CO., Contractors for Drainage Water and Gas, who are appointed Sole Agents for the above apparatus, which can be seen working any week day between the hours of 6 A.M., and 6 P.M., at their place of business.

39, BENTINCK STREET, CALCUTTA.

P. W. FLEURY & CO.,

BUILDERS, ENGINEERS,

AND

SCIENTIFIC INSTRUMENT MAKERS.

No. 44, Free School Street.

WE beg to intimate that we have been engaged in the above line of business for the past 20 years, and trust that our Constituents will continue to favor us with their work, which will meet with prompt attention on our part.

In connection with buildings, we undertake the erection and repairing of machinery at moderate charges; as also execute all descriptions of Iron and Brass work.

We can assure the Public that we undertake the repair and erection of Houses and the laying of Water-supply Pipes on moderate terms, and guarantee to keep all the water-pipes and brass fittings supplied by us in good working order for three years, free of extra charge. We also guarantee to keep dwelling-houses' roofs water-tight for three years, free of extra charge, for such houses as we have repaired.

For purposes of illumination, we prepare our patent Chromatic Transparencies representing Coat-of-Arms, Landscapes, Scenery, &c., at prices, ranging from Rs. 80 to 300 each, according to size and design.

FOR SALE.

Light! Light!! Light!!!

Electric Light Apparatus complete, worked with a battery of 50 large cells, on Bunsen's principle	500	0
Ditto ditto, with 40 cells, smaller size ...	400	0
Ditto ditto, with a powerful 44-cell Cast-iron Battery, on Callan's principle ...	300	0
Lime-Light Apparatus, complete, with Iron Gas-holder, and Copper Retort ...	150	0
Oxy-Hydrogen Light Apparatus, with safety Jets, 2 Iron Gas-holders, and Retorts, complete	200	0
Hink's Patent Duplex Wall Lamps, with chimney	5	8
Ditto Duplex Lamp, with chimney and globe	7	8

Patent Leblanche Battery

For constancy, durability, and cleanliness, this battery is unequalled; price for each cell, with chemicals	3
Bunsen's Galvanic Battery, 9 inches, by 4 inches	7
Magneto-Electric Machine, with single magnet	14
Prismatic Compass, 3-inch, in a lid leather case, by Eibot, *second hand*	25
Ditto 4-inch, by Simmons, *second hand* ...	36

P. W. FLEURY & Co

No. 44, FREE SCHOOL STREET.

R. K. GHOSH'S

HOMŒOPATHIC DISPENSARY.

No. 1, *Gour Mohun Mukerjee's Street, Simla.*

CALCUTTA.

HOMŒOPATHIC Medicine; Medicine chests of sizes, containing medicine in tube phials; Homœopathic Books, tracts and pamphlets (English and Bengali); Dr. Rubini's "Saturated spirits of Camphor,"—(the best preventive and cure for cholera where medical aid is not available); and other Homœopathic requisites are sold here at a moderate price. Terms cash. Mofussil orders are promptly executed.

R. K. GHOSH,

Homœopathic Practitioner,

Manager.

Ulcerations of all kinds.

There is no medicinal preparation which may be so thoroughly relied upon in the treatments of the above ailments as Hollways Ointment. Nothing can be more simple and safe than the manner in which it is applied, nothing more salutary than its action on the body, both locally and constitutionally. The Ointment rubbed round the part affected enters the pores as salt penetrates meat. It quickly penetrates to the core of the evil and drive it from the system.

CALCUTTA.

106, Bowbazar Street.

DR. H. C. SARMA'S

MEDICINE FOR DEBILITY

(NERVOUS.)

HAIR PRESERVER.

Copy of Letter received from Raja Chundernath Roy Bahadoor of Nattore.

Wellesley Street, No. 18, Mott's Lane, 29th March 1874.

MY DEAR HURRISH BABU,—

I shall thank you to send me another phial of your "*Excellent Hair Restorer.*" In fact it has done me a great benefit and I should like to have more of it. It has disabused me (young as I am) of old age.

Your's Sincerely

C. N. of *Nattore*

MEDICINE FOR BALDNESS.

Will certainly cure baldness if applied on the bald portion, night & morning, according to directions given in the adjoining direction paper.

Price per two ounce phial ...	Rs.	1	0	0
Postage &c.	"	0	6	0

HEEM-SAGAR OIL.

The best remedy for Headache arising from overstudy, intellectual occupation, overthinking, mental anxiety and weakness, as well as heat of head from living in hot places.

It cools the head and produces very agreeable sensation. Removes dandriff as well as all other impurities from the head. Promotes the strength and growth of the hair and prevents its premature falling-off.

Price per 4 ounce phial ...	Rs.	1	0	0
Postage &c.	"	0	10	0

MEDICINE FOR LEPROSY.

Price with Postage &c. ...	Rs.	5	0	0

OIL FOR LEPROSY.

And Inveterate Skin Diseases.

Price per 8 ounce phial ...	Rs.	2	0	0
Postage &c.	"	0	12	0

S. C. GUPTA'S

DIARRHŒA PILLS

SEVERAL years of experience in private practice **have proved these pills to be** most efficacious **in obstinate** cases **of Non-inflammatory**, Infantile, Choleric, Chronic **and all sorts** of Diarrhœa, and in all cases **of Indigestion,** Dyspepsia, Flatulence caused **by disturbance of** the digestive function.

Sold in Boxes **containing 12 pills** with full directions for use :—

Price	Rs.	1	0	per box
" with postage ...	"	1	4	"

To be had of DURGA DASS GUPTA, care of the Manager, Indian Mirror, Calcutta.

MAKHON LOLL GHOSE.

No. 91, Radha Bazar, Calcutta.

BEGS to invite the attention of the public to several consignments of commercial and fancy stationery of all sorts, including account books of all sizes, made of handmade and machine-made paper, by steamers recently arrived, and which he is disposing of at moderate prices. He has been long in the trade, and presumes he has always afforded every satisfaction to the numerous merchants here who have constantly favored him with orders. Mofussil orders accompanied with remittances shall be promptly attended to.

CALCUTTA }
The 18th August 1876. }

PRIZE MEDALLISTS

For Excellency of Workmanship.

J. M. EDMOND & CO.,

27—28, BENTINCK STREET,

ESTABLISHED 1833.

Cabinet Makers. Upholsterers,

AND

Billiard Table Manufacturers.

Houses completely furnished. Furniture designed and made to order.

ESTIMATES given for all kinds of Carpentering, Painting, Polishing, Gilding, and General Repairs; Marble Polished, Moulded, and Cleaned; Picture Frames made.

J. M. EDMOND & Co., in soliciting a continuance of public patronage, beg to say they have ready for sale specimens of Ebonized and Gold Oxford style of Fancy Chairs, and are prepared to execute orders for other Furniture in the same style.

J. M. EDMOND & Co.'s New Show-Room is now replete with New Heraldic Style of Dining-room Chairs, and Rustic Chairs, Telescopic Dining Tables, with Patent Table Expanders, and a variety of finished Furniture.—Orders solicited.

BURN & CO.

RANEEGUNGE Fire bricks are the best Fire Bricks known;—superior to Ramsay's.

9 Rs. per 100.

Fire clay, 40 Rs. per Ton.

Glazed Stone ware, Drainage pipes of all sizes

BURN & Co.,

7, Hastings Street, Calcutta.

ARLINGTON & CO.,

3 B. DALHOUSIE SQUARE, CALCUTTA.

THE 'PATENT PERPETUAL FOUNTAIN,'

TABLE EPERGNE OR CENTRE PIECE

FOR SCENT OR FOR PUREWATER WATER.

In Richly Electro-Silvered Ware. [*One of the Greatest Novelties of the day.*]

Cash Price Rs. 175.

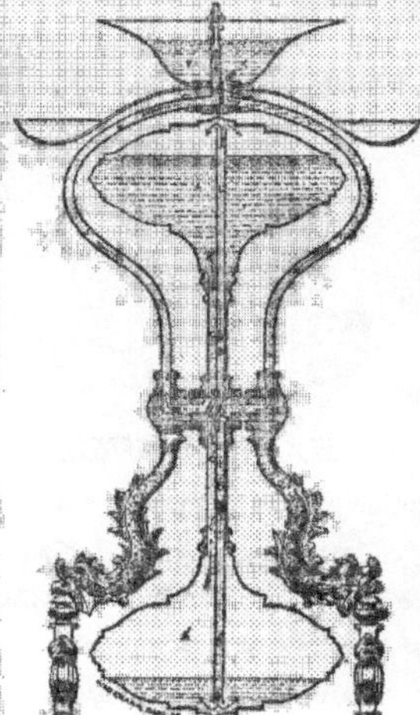

N. B.—**The annexed drawing is** not a correct representation **of the Plated Table** Fountains which A. & **Co. have for** sale. **The** drawing is only given **to show the** internal arrangements **of** the Apparatus, **and attention** is invited to the following description:—

OBSERVE—A, A1, **are** two cisterns or reservoirs, which are connected together by pipes or tubes B, **B1, C, C1,** mounted on a hollow axis of motion D, surrounding a fixed conical plug E, having suitable passages F, G, H, therein communicating with the pipes or tubes B, B1, C, C1, and I, and with the jet pipe J.

To put the Fountain in operation water is poured into the dish or basin K until the lower reservoir is filled and the opening K1 is covered. The cisterns or reservoirs A, A1, are then turned on their axis of motion, so as to place the filled cistern or reservoir A at the top, when the water therefrom will flow to a level in the jet pipe J, and the water in the basin or dish K by passing down the pipes or tubes I and [illegible] into the lower cistern or reservoir A1, rises in such lower cistern or reservoir A1 and forces the air out therefrom through the pipe or tube C1, passage F, and tube [illegible] into the upper parts of the cistern or reservoir A, where it presses upon the surface of the water therein and forces it out therefrom through the tube C, passage H, and jet **pipe J**, until all the water in the upper cistern **or** reservoir A has passed through the jet pipe J and into the lower cistern or reservoir A1 **by** the **pipe** I, passage **G, and** pipe **B1,** when by turning **the** cistern **or** reserviors **A, A1,** on their axis **of** motion until the **cistern or** reservoir A1 **is at the top, the action of** the fountain **will be continued; the pipes or** tubes B, C1, **which had** previously **been air** passages now becoming water passages, **and** the pipes or tubes B1, C, now becoming air passages which had previously served for the passage of water. By these improvements the necessity for alternately **filling** and emptying the cisterns or reservoirs **A, A1,** is obviated.

Printed and published by M. M. RUKHIT, at the INDIAN MIRROR PRESS, No. 6, College Square, for the Proprietors.

The Indian Mirror.

SUNDAY EDITION.

VOL. XV.] CALCUTTA, SUNDAY, NOVEMBER 26, 1876. { REGISTERED AT THE GENERAL POST OFFICE. } [No 280

CONTENTS.

NOTICE.

All letters and communications relating to the literary department of the Paper should be addressed to the Editor. All other letters should be addressed to the Manager, to whom all remittances should be made payable.

Subscribers will be good enough to bring to the notice of the Manager any delay or irregularity in the delivery of the Paper.

Editorial Notes.

WE are requested to announce that Babu Nobin Chunder Roy, the Honorary Secretary to the Asylum for Widows and Orphans, established at Allahabad sometime ago, is prepared to take charge of about fifty orphans. We understand he has already requested Mr. Mahadeo Govind Ranade to take charge temporarily on behalf of the Asylum of any orphans who may be found in the famine-striken districts of Bombay.

CALAMITIES and misfortunes have encompassed this ill-fated land, and there are wailings on all sides which indicate deep and wide-spread misery. Famine in the south and west, epidemic fever in the Punjab, and a terrible cyclone in Bengal bringing in its train destitution, disease and death,—such is the gloomy picture of India's present distress. May all the benevolence and philanthropy in the land run to the rescue of the afflicted!

WILL the Education Department account for the sum of Rs. 500, contributed, some two years ago, by Maharajah Holkar to the Calcutta Medical College, to be given away in the shape of a Prize to the student who would write the best essay on the Laws of Health? Surely the money must be lying idle somewhere, and somebody is responsible, no doubt, for the remissness. The present Director of Public Instruction and the able Principal of the Medical College are both new to their offices, but they should at least inquire and ascertain what has become of the money.

THE *Gazette of India* publishes a most graphic account of the effects of the late cyclone by Sir Richard Temple. A resolution of the Government of India on the minute of the Lieutenant-Governor is also published. The details are most harrowing. Sir Richard Temple estimates that in an area of 3,000 square miles, out of a population of about a million, some two lacs and fifteen thousand human beings have perished! The Queen soon after the occurrence of the calamity was telegraphed, and Her Majesty was graciously pleased to signify her deep concern at the terrible calamity which has thus overwhelmed a large body of Her Majesty's subjects.

IN speaking of the late cyclone and storm-wave in East Bengal the *Lucknow Witness* indulges in these natural remarks:—

Neither does God shew by their universal allotment how small a thing it is to suffer in these temporary ways. He does not think it worth His while to guard His children from such things. From all real evil He defends and delivers them without fail. Against physical pain and loss He gives them no guarantee. On the evil and the good fall of the refreshing shower and the devastating tornado. It is in other ways and in things of deeper import He makes His accurate distinctions, and with unerring justice gives or withholds. At the final balance we are perfectly sure that all will be exactly right. Then, too, we shall comprehend it fully; now we walk by faith.

PROFESSOR LIVINGSTONE of Dacca speaking at a meeting, called in honor of Dr. Ray in that city, made some very original observations on the subject of the study of the Physical Sciences. He said that too much study of Chemistry tends "to produce political revolutions. England in 1688 and France 1792 owed their bloody revolutions very largely to the intemperate way in which Chemistry and material Science had been studied." If Mr. Livingstone is rightly reported then our Government in encouraging the study of the Physical Sciences, is sowing the wind and may reap the whirlwind as soon as our young men learn the use of the lime and magnesium lights!

AFTER Vyasa had written the voluminous epic, the *Mahabharata*, he repented, so the legends inform us, for the work brought him no joy. With a distressed heart he referred to that devout Rishi Narada for advice and consolation. In reply he was enjoined by the sage to go and preach the doctrine of God's love, so he did, and the result was that precious book, *Srimatbagabat*. In Christianity, Old Testament-morality had to be supplemented by the gospel of love taught by Christ. So the dry and ponderous ethics of the *Mahabharata* had to be quickened and sweetened by the charming precepts on love in the *Srimatbhagbat* for the benefit of the Hidu community. Verily it is love that redeems and saves, not mere dry morality.

IT appears that there is more Theism among the European community in India than is generally believed. We do not mean to say that there is a considerable number of professed Theists among them, but there are hundreds who sympathize with the Theistic movement, and are ready to encourage it by all means in their power. A fact has just been brought to our knowledge, which goes far to illustrate what we mean. When Mr. Charles Voysey's intended visit to India was announced by some of his friends in a circular it was responded to, we are told, by "hundreds and hundreds!" "Christians, officers in both services holding the highest appointments under the Crown, enlisted themselves in promoting the scheme and they brought others, and gave money in abundance." This would have astonished many, a decade or two ago, but now Theism is slowly but surely leavening all classes of the community, and secretly influencing many a heart, apparently belonging to other folds.

WE are glad to make a note of the marriage of the daughter of Babu Woomesh Chunder Dutt, late Vice-Chairman of the Calcutta Municipality. He is a Christian, belonging to the well-known Dutt family of this city, almost all the members of which have been converted to Christianity. We notice the marriage because the ceremonies though partly European, were adapted to a certian extent to our national ideas. All the proceedings were in Bengali, and Mr. Bomwetch who is a sort of family priest to the Dutts, officiated on the occasion, reading long course of advice to the couple written in Bengali. The bridegroom is Babu Prandhone Bose, a young medical student. The bride, we are sorry to find is only thirteen years old. We wish that the marriage instead of being celebrated in St. John's Old Church, had been celebrated in the family house of Babu Woomesh Chunder. This gentleman however, in using the national language and partly national customs on this occasion, has shown moral courage, and set an example to those Native Christians who glory in the wholesale adoption of European usages in all their domestic and social observances.

IN spite of the conflicting telegrams and reports that confuse speculation, and depress the money market, we are still inclined to believe and hope that there will be no European war. We do think that the protestations of the Czar before Lord Loftus were in a great measure sincere, and the feeling of the British public is decidedly to stand by, and not mix in the fray. The arming and mobilizing that goes on appears more for the purpose of producing an effect and impression of earnestness upon the outside world than a determination to shed blood in and against the rotten cause of the Ottoman Empire. We do not mean to say that Lord Beaconsfield's Government is incapable of much worse things even than war; but in the bravery, love of truth, and righteousness of the British nation we have very great trust. Oppression and injustice in the Turkish provinces must cease. If their independence is necessary for that object, independence they shall have, no matter who is strengthened, and who is weakened thereby. But if on the other hand, Turkey will be reasonable enough to avert her dismemberment by acceding to sound and effective conditions for the protection of her Christian subjects, no one will more heartily congratulate that event than ourselves.

IT is really wonderful that the sinful custom trafficking in slave girls, still continues in East Bengal. This evil has often been pointed out, and condemned by the press, but, it secretly obtains still, and when cases of unusual outrage and brutality occur we come to see that our protests have been useless, and the executive authorities have indulged in negligence and supineness so far that the suppression of the evil custom is delayed indefinitely. The *Pioneer* publishes the following case:—

One evening after a sub-divisional officer had done, as he thought, with his official labors for the day, and was quietly smoking in front of his *bungalow*, a rather pretty girl of eighteen was brought before him with her neck closely bandaged up, and charged with having attempted to commit suicide by cutting her throat. The incident was alleged to have occurred about a week before in the *zenana* of a Mahomedan Zemindar, residing not five miles from the Magistrate's Court. The woman at once confessed her guilt, stating that she was a *chukri* or slave-girl of the Zemindar, and that she had rashly attempted to take her own life, because of the ill-treatment to which she had been subjected. This she said, consisted of excessive task work, tank digging and *surki* pounding, insufficient food, and repeated beating with a rattan. It also appeared that the attempted suicide had been concealed by the Zemindar till two other slave-girls had succeeded in escaping by night from the *zenana* enclosure. These in recounting their own woes at the Police station, mentioned the fact of the woman lying wounded in the Zemindar's female apartments. One of these two latter women was found by the sub-divisional officer to bear on her person evident stripes of a cane said to be inflicted by the Zemindar's wife.

SIR JOHN BYLES, late one of the Judges of His Majesty's Court of Common Pleas at Westminister, has written a book on rational Theism. He calls it *Foundations of Religion in the Mind and Heart of Man.* "He deals with the great and primary truths of religion only," says the *Literary Churchman*, "and does not attempt to go beyond these." The book being written by a trained lawyer of long experience, has been reasoned out in conformity with the severest rules of evidence, and is said to be "as difficult as Butler's great work." The conclusions of Sir John Byles are indicated in these words:—"The Divine Existence, His power, wisdom, and benevolence, are doctrines of all sound philosophy, demonstrable and clear beyond any reasonable doubt. They are also among the doctrines of all pure religion. Religion affirms a future life. Philosophy does not deny it. Religion believes; philosophy, at least, hopes and practically enjoins a man to regulate his life on the affirmative hypothesis. Religion teaches the duty and efficacy of Divine Worship. Philosophy does not deny either. Philosophy, on some points, may have its doubts; but whatever they may amount to, true practical Philosophy, nevertheless acts on the affirmative and in Christian countries generally, worships with the multitude, considering the substance to be of the last importance, but the form to be comparatively immaterial." These are just the conclusions of Theism.

A CHRISTIAN mission has been now established amidst the scene of Livingstone's labors in Central Africa. The Nyanza Church Mission party started from Zanzibar for the interior a few months ago, and vigorously pushed their way accompanied by Mr Holmwood, the Vice-Consul, who speaks the vernacular, and will thus be of use to the mission. At Bagamoyo they met with the hospitality of the Roman Catholic Mission. In the good work that has been thus commenced the difference of creed has been nobly set aside. We heartily wish the mission success, and hope it will elevate and instruct our benighted fellow-brethren of Central Africa. But unfortunately while attempts are thus being made to extend religion and humanity among the savage people of Nyanza, there is side by side another attempt to extend the evils of civilization in that neighborhood. Mr. Stanley, the enterprizing American gentleman who discovered Dr. Livingstone, is introducing the knowledge of dynamite and explosive bullets, we believe, together with their usual accessory—the inevitable "rum." Sir Welfrid Lawson's statement to the effect that England has begun the career of civilizing the world with rum and gunpowder, thus turns out to be literally correct. Mr. Stanley, we know, is not an English subject, but nevertheless to all practical intents and purpose he is an Englishman. Lord Derby, the British Foreign Minister, has, we are told, expressed disapproval of Mr. Stanley's proceedings in Central Africa, and a communication is to be made to Mr. Stanley "that he has no authority to hoist the English flag."

ON the occasion of the unveiling of the bust of Canon Kingsley, at Westminister Abbey, Canon Duckworth delivered the following interesting address:—"If the grand reverential soul which almost beams upon us from those sculptured features could find voice, would it not be to deprecate the least transfer to himself of the glory which belongs to God alone? I cannot but remember now what he himself has said of the illustrious company gathered here in what he has called 'England's Pantheon of beneficent and healthy manhood.' 'All wise words which they have spoken, all noble deeds which they have done, have come, must have come, from the one eternal source of wisdom, of nobleness, of every form of good—even from the Holy Spirit of God.' This is the thought which he would bespeak at this moment, when the joy of perpetuating his honored name and almost his very presence within these storied walls, mingles with a regret too deep for words. So let us recognise that by the grace of God he was what he was, the fearless champion of purity and truth, the tenderest and the manliest of men. Memories cluster around him at this spot worthy to be entwined with his. There is Maurice, to whose saintly soul his own was knit in bonds of such sympathy as only those can know who love God and man with an intensity like theirs. Yonder is Wordsworth, the poet of nature, whose marvels he delighted to explore and expound. There stands Keble, the sweet singer of that Church which never had a more loyal and devoted son. And the light which streams upon him passes fitly through the blazoned figures of Herbert and Cowper—offerings from the great kindred people which claims its part and lot in the worthies of England, and treasures the name of Charles Kingsley with an affection equal to our own. And now we leave this precious memorial, not only to attract for many a day the loving gaze of surviving disciples and friends, but to take its place among the permanent glories of the Abbey, and to be the heirloom of generations to come. Let us look at him once more, and judge his right to be here by the noble words in which he himself tested the right of others to commemoration in this shrine: 'What was your work? Did we admire you for it? Did we love you for it? And why? Because you made us, in some way or other, better men. Because you helped us somewhat toward whatsoever things are pure, true, just, honorable, of good report. Because, if there was any virtue—that is true valour and manhood; if there was any praise—that is, just honor in the sight of man, and, therefore, surely in the sight of the Son of Man, who died for men—you helped us to think on such things. You, in one word, helped to make us better men.'"

TRUE ECLECTICISM.

DID it ever strike Theistic believers that true eclecticism is only an adjustment of the soul in its right place amid the various spiritual forces pulling it in different directions? Liberalism is either theological or religious. In its theological aspect it is at best a mechanical and dry species of Latitudinarianism, which delights in a strange compound of creeds, and affects to patronise all prophets and scriptures. Of such a system we are neither admirers nor advocates. It is not the cold eclecticism of the intellect, but the warm eclecticism of the heart that we advocate. The one is thoroughly dogmatic and intellectual, and indicates only a nodding of the head to whatsoever is rational and correct in each creed. Whereas the other is a living and mighty force created and sustained by the interaction of different systems of faith. All creeds, all prophets, all scriptures represent specific ideas, and are so many spiritual forces, which act differently yet potently on the believer's soul. He stands, as it were, in the centre, and is pulled in all directions by these contending forces. If he is faithful and loyal to truth, and loves sincerely everything and every person that is good, his soul is held in equilibrium, and he becomes an eclectic. He is liberal not because he chooses to recognize all the good things in the various theologies of the world, but because he is forcibly driven to accept them by their own attractions. He is an eclectic, not by choice, but by necessity. It is not true that he may or may not recognize what is good in this or that religion; he *must*. His recognition of truth has all the irresistible impulsiveness of enthusiastic love. Because he loves God he is constrained to love whatsoever is of God. He is forcibly attracted towards every form of truth and goodness. Judaism, Christianity, Hinduism, Zoroastrianism, Budhism, Mahomedanism standing round him, attract his heart by the precious truths which constitute the essence of each, and he naturally succumbs to them all. So Jesus and Socrates, Moses and Paul, Confucius and Zoroaster, Gautama and Mahomed, Chaitanya and Nanak, Luther and Knox ply his heart ever and anon with the fascinations of their words and lives, and so overpower him by their heavenly charms that he is readily drawn as a captive towards the feet of each. They are so many mighty forces of attraction that hold him continually in a state of enchained but loving vassalage, and he cannot draw himself out of their grasp. They misunderstand and mis-represent the Theistic Eclectic, who hold that he may or may not love this prophet or honor that creed. We repeat, he has no choice in the matter. He is attracted by saints, by prophets, by contemplative Rishis, by ascetic Fathers, by dancing devotees, by self-sacrificing martyrs and by philanthrophists, and he cannot resist the attraction. He is forced into the central and many-sided position of an impartial eclectic, loving all things, honoring all things for God's sake, for truth's sake.

THE SUFFERERS IN EAST BENGAL.

WE are pained at the position which Government has taken up in regard to the miserable sufferers from the late cylone. We praise the Lieutenant-Governor's minute but cannot approve of his measures on the subject. The relief which the authorities give, is not only scarce and scanty; but there is practical a deep want of sympathy with the poor and bereaved. The letter published in the *Pioneer*, manifestly written by one of the Lieutenant-Governor's party describing the results of the calamity, is so full of cold indifference to the sufferings of the people who surrounded His Honor on his late visit to the scenes of distress, pouring forth their piteous appeals for commiseration and aid, and there are scattered throughout that letter such uncharitable insinuations, that we fear its publication will, among certain classes, prevent an adequate appreciation of the horrors which the storm has left behind it, and any sympathy with those who have survived it. There is no doubt now that more than two hundreds of thousand of all classes have perished, and a calamity which could cause such destruction of life, cannot but have left terrible sufferings behind for those who did not die. The sufferers who are poor, ignorant men, have been ruined and well nigh distracted by their helpless misery. But the gentleman of the Lieutenant-Governor's party, and there is little doubt he is a high official, of some kind because none but officials accompanied His Honor in the *Rhotas*, describes them thus:—"Their requests were certainly not deficient in boldness; but when asked if they had tried to do anything for themselves, they admitted they had not, but kept reiterating that they were starving and helpless—a statement not altogether borne out by their healthy and rotund appearance." Then again we are told that "the Natives no doubt thought it a splendid occasion to obtain the maximum amount relief for the minimum amount of suffering." We ask if such sentiments are worthy on such a terrible occasion of death, sadness, and want. We are not aware how far the Lieutenant-Governor himself sanctions such views and feelings; and whether as a sort of contradiction to the popular reports of horror and misery in almost all the newspapers of the country, he wished this letter should appear in the *Pioneer*, most plainly written by a Government official in a Government organ. Let us hope there was no participation between the chief and his party in this ill-timed and unworthy representation. But we must see whether the conduct of His Honor shows greater sympathy with the sufferers. In the sentiments set forth for in the minutely Sir Richard Temple, we believe it is distinctly said that the administration of relief is to be avoided as much possible, except in cases of proved necessity to save life. How is such necessity to be *proved* may we ask? How was it proved in Tirhoot in 1874, where boatfulls, and cartfulls of rice poured in, whether there was necesssity or no, to rot in the rain and sun?' How is it being settled in the Deccan at the present moment?' How can it be proved in any case but by the general aspect of the people, their dwelling-places, and their sufferings, pourtrayed by impartial and disinterested men? And have there not been heart-rending accounts of all this by the local correspondents of every newspaper except perhaps the aristocratic official who has written in the *Pioneer*? While such is the policy of the Government itself, Sir Richard Temple, we find, has instructed that the Zemindars, Talukdars, and other landholders be kept personally engaged in succouring their ryots. They should not only *send* assistance, but go in person This is doubtless humane, but for aught we know the Zemindars may just take a glance at the instructions which His Honor says he has issued for the guidance of the local authorities, and reasonably retort that far from *personally going* to give assistance, they too must *avoid* giving relief after the example of the Government as much as possible, except "in case of proved necessity to save life." Is this not one reason why the Zemindars in Calcutta have done nothing yet through their Association to organize any system of relief for the myriads of their starving ryots? We naturally wish that the Zemindars should at least remit a part of their revenue in the distressed tracts, and we trust several landholders are ready to do so; But what sort of example is it that Government is setting before them when His Honor gives the clear order—"do not listen to any applications for remission of land revenue." The provision which His Honor makes for the protection of the survivors of the storm-wave, is in some parts characteristic. Of course when so many men have died, there must be large numbers of women deserted and houseless. Taking pity upon them the Lieutenant-Governor opens his heart to his subordinates, and says that "if widows are found deserted, get them advantageously married"! How the Commissioner of a district for instance should in the midst of so many engagements, and the dignities of his office, fined time to make "advantageous" matches for deserted widows we fail to realize. There is a sort of grim irony in the junction which pains and humiliates us. Where a rupee or two would suffice to find protection and relief for a poor woman in the midst of the misery of her situation, she is to be led before the marriage altar!

Under these circumstances we are justified to think that much sympathy with the sufferers cannot be expected from the Government, and the Zemindars following the advice and example of their rulers, are not likely to do much. Will the generous public take into consideration the case of the poor sufferers, and be more energetic in their sympathy to afford help and relief.

Provincial

GAZIPORE.

[FROM OUR OWN CORRESPONDENT.]

The 21st, Nov. 1876.

As a sequel to my letter of the 18th November, I beg to send the following concerning the removal of our local Brahmo Somaj.

Early in the morning of the 5th of Agrahayan the local Brahmos full of joy and enthusiasm, went to the old Somaj-house. Babu Subhaswar Chatterji read his report showing the transactions of the past four years. When it was read he uttered a short prayer in Hindi. We then all repaired to the new Somaj which was neatly and tastefully decorated on all sides with leaves and flowers. No sooner were the words *sa yam ga ... omunu ...* uttered by Babu Dino Nath Mozumdar, than the whole congregation became wrapt in devotion; as if by a certain mysterious process a new light was poured into it to enliven its heart and soul. With a short prayer in Bengali and a few chosen hymns which were chanted in chorus terminated the proceedings of the morning service.

Towards the close of the day from 4½ to 6 P.M. we had *sankirtan*. Then commenced the evening service which was also conducted by Dino Babu. The Hall was fairly crowded with persons of all communities. The minister said in his prayer: "In endeavouring to obtain great objects and inculcate high principles, I have failed in little things. Perhaps, I was ambitious, O God; and my ambition has ruined me. I went about in quest of the Kingdom of Heaven, taught others how to live as a holy family, and always talked eloquently of regenerating heavenly life and such things. But my pride, O Lord, thou hast confounded. For I feel that even the smaller virtues, such as veracity, honesty, kindness to the poor, are far from me. Teach me, not to neglect these simple duties, and keep me, King God, from the baser forms of iniquity."

The sermon preached by the minister was very eloquent and attractive. Thus ended the celebration of the opening of the new Brahmo Somaj of Ghazipore.

The question now suggests itself who is the author of this mighty movement. A mighty movement, indeed, we find it to be when we consider the bitter animosity which the Natives of this place bore, only a few months ago, towards the Brahmo Somaj and the Brahmo community. The Brahmo Mandir used to be branded with the nicknames of Musjids and Girjahs. But now what a change! The bazaar people have become wise enough to substitute the word "Devalaya" in the stead of those nicknames. On the night of the opening of the new Brahmo Somaj, Hindus and Musulmans flocked together and found to their immense relief that their Narayan and Allah were one and the same. Our most reverened minister Babu Keshub Chunder Sen came here to recruit his health. His flying visit, therefore, instilled more of melancholy than of cheerful thoughts into our hearts. But this visit has wrought deeds whose fruits will for many a day to come, cheer the spirits of the Ghazipore people. Apart from all religious consideration the Europeans have begun to think more favourably of the Bengalis.

The exertions of Babu Dinonath Mozumdar and the other missionaries cannot be too fairly estimated. Honor, all honour to them.

Correspondence.

THE THEIST.

To the Editor of the *Indian Mirror.*

SIR,—In our last we have tried to show that the scientist and the philosopher, following each a distinct course, at last come to the knowledge which the simple vulgar obtains through intuition, *viz.*, the knowledge of a Being who is at the root of all the phenomena of this world. But this is not the ultimate limit of their knowledge, they can discover further that this Being is not only active but is wise, unchangeable, absolute, infinite and good generally. Thus far and no further they can go. They can see the God of mankind generally who works by fixed and general laws for the general good of His creatures, without being mindful of the particular or special wants of every individual creature. They can discover "our God" but not "my God." Here ends their work, and begins the work of the faithful or Bhakta worshipper. It is for him to discover the relations which God bears to every individual creature; it is for him to realize the teaching God, the guiding God, the answering God, the helping God, the rebuking God, the watchful God and the loving God. It is for him alone to realize all the sweet relations which God bears to man individually. As no philosopher or a scientist should accept a truth without investigation or experiment, so no worshipper should accept the testimonies or teachings of his elders or fellow-worshippers without experiencing the same in his own life. Hear-say will never do. One must see for himself. I do not, however, mean to say that we should disbelieve our teachers. No. We must believe them and give their sayings all possible trials that we may realize them for ourselves. But how could this be achieved? No resources of ourselves will do. The philosopher and the scientist must cast aside his academical costume of honor, and adopt the garb of Bhakta which consists of simplicity, total helplessness, a thorough distrust to oneself and absolute dependence and trust on God. This is the costume which passes a man to the regions of faith, where weakness not strength, ignorance not our knowledge and dependence not self-help avail.

Yours &c.,
R. M. B.

Devotional.

MERCIFUL God, thou hast made all other spiritual gifts hard of attainment, but the great blessing of hope in thy kingdom is easily available. Holiness, faith, and love are difficult to acquire but thou feedest the hungry soul with hope always. The high aspirations of the Brahmo's religious life may yet be very remote to realize, the great destiny which thou hast set forth before us may fail to obtain the sympathy of the world, but fill us with strong hope and lead us on, our Heavenly Captain, to our goal cheering us with righteous and real hope, and we shall be content to live and die before thee in peace.

TEACH us, O Lord, to understand the doctrine of communion with good men. Teach us to appreciate the inestimable good of being with them, and learn of thee in and from them. Make us worthy to sit with them, and benefit our souls by their example and conversation.

SUPREME Ruler, God of might and mercy, have compassion, we pray thee, upon the souls of the hundreds of thousand who have perished by the late cyclone in our country. Unaware, and unprepared they were hurled into sudden death, and we hear of them, their sufferings, and their terrible passing away, like a strange doom that is related! The mystery of thy dealings with the world is past our comprehension, we wonder, and we are struck with awe, and humble ourselves to the dust before thee. While we, unworthy as we are of life, are spared by thee in health and happiness, and everything is cheerful around us, so many of our brethren and sisters are torn away untimely from all that they prized. Our common Father, how can we forbear to ask thy gracious blessing on them in the other world. And while we pray for them we cannot forget the survivors and sufferers left behind amongst us by the wind and the flood. Lord rouse in our hearts the feelings of compassion, and the sense of duty. Give the rulers of the country to understand their responsibilities at the present moment of sadness and suffering. Incline the landlords and the rich to come forward to help the poor and unsheltered. Out of our energy and substance may we in the name of sacred duty spend for thy afflicted children, and do what we can to make them happy.

The Brahmo Somaj

BABU KESHUB CHUNDER SEN returned to Calcutta on Sunday last.

THE old Sangat, lately revived, is once more an attraction to earnest-minded Brahmos in Calcutta. The meetings are held every Wednesday at the Mission premises. Let not the debate prove unprofitable talk, but let it lead to earnest action.

WE think Babu Raj Narain Bose did injustice to Babu Akhai Kumar Dutta in his recent lecture on the "Bengali Language" at the Hindu School Theatre, when he said that the latter's style owed its elegance and vigor to Babu Debendro Nath Tagore's corrections.

ON Monday last the 13th instant, a Brahmo intermarriage under Act III of 1872, was celebrated here with great *eclat*. The Bridegroom was our friend Babu Kailash Chunder Nundy a young man of respectable parentage, of liberal education, of firmness and strength of character, a severe and zealous Brahmo, and the bride Bogala Sundari, one of the best pupils of our Adult Female School. The arrangements were befitting the occasion. The courtyard was filled and at last crowded to suffocation. Many of our worthy townsmen, independent gentlemen, Government officers and members of the Bar graced the assembly with their presence. We noticed with great pleasure the presence of a few European ladies and gentlemen. Mr. and Mrs. Archibald, Mr. and Mrs. Johnson, Dr. Robson, Messrs Ewbank, Stack, Mckenna, Livingstone, and Hussey were among the number. We notice this with pleasure, for the lively interest and the very kindly feeling with which they joined the rest in wishing the happy couple, peace and prosperity deserves our hearty pleasure. It is to an intercourse of this nature, to a like exchange of social civilities that we look for to bring on a happy union between us and Europeans, an early realization of which is at the present time most desirable. When all took their seats the bridegroom followed by his friends made his appearance and took his seat on the right side of the *vedi*. The bride richly dressed and ornamented, followed soon after and took her seat on the left. All preliminary arrangements having been ready Babu Bunge Chunder Ray mounted the *vedi* and commenced the usual service which was gone through with due reverence and solemnity. Reading of appropriate texts from the Hindu Shastras formed also a part of the service, which over, the brother of the bride presented her with expressions fraught with feeling and affection, after which the usual vows were exchanged, the bride's hand was placed on that of the bridegroom, a garland of flowers wound round their hands and the nuptial knot which was to bind them for life was tied at last. The ceremonial was conducted by Babu Gour Govinda Ray, a Missionary of the Brahmo Somaj of India, who was helped by Babu Ishan Chundra Sen. The minister then reminded the married couple of the new duties and responsibilities which devolved them on their entering a new life. A beautiful song composed by a friend for the occasion, was then sung by the precentors of the Brahmo Somaj. A prayer of benediction closed the ceremonies of the evening. Some of the European ladies and gentlemen even stayed behind for the supper, a sumptuous one having been provided beforehand. Khajeh Ahsanullah Khan Bahadur very kindly lent his music-band which added its power to cheer and enliven the assembly. Many of the guests lingered till midnight after which the courtyard was cleared. We heartily wish the bride and the bridegroom a long life of love, virtue, peace, happiness and prosperity. —*East.*

TRUE worship is nothing but the right posture of the soul in relation to God, so said the minister last Sunday, at the Brahmo Mandir. Prayer, meditation and adoration represent only that attitude of the soul in which it turns towards the Great Source of Light and gathers the rays of truth and love. The soul that sits properly at the feet of the Lord, in an humble, reverent and child-like posture, has realized all the conditions of prayer, it drinks in Divine light as naturally as his outward eyes catch the light of the Sun by simply turning towards it. Blessed are they who know how to sit

THE minister conducted divine service yesterday morning, at the anniversary of the Sindurispatty Family Brahmo Somaj. He pointed out the necessity of developing both manhood and womanhood in the individual and in society, as in this lies salvation and the perfection of humanity. The harmonious family circle represents heaven. Evening service was conducted by the venerable minister of the conservative Somaj.

VERY little was done towards the improvement of the Ghazipur Brahmo Somaj during our minister's stay there. We are glad, however, to hear that better success has attended the efforts of Babus Prosunno Cumar Sen, and Dino Nath Mozumdar. A house has been rented and numbers are said to flock to attend service.

BABU GOUR GOVIND ROY has gone to Commillah from Dacca. Babu Aughore Nath Gupta is at Deradun.

Literary

AMONGST the list of new books to be shortly published by Mr. Stanford in London is "The Northern Barrier of India," by Mr. F. Drew, author of the "Jummu and Cashmere Territories."

THE late *Calicut Observer* press was recently put up to auction at Calicut and purchased by the proprietor of the *Minerva Press* who, it appears, intends to issue a new paper under the designation of the *Calicut Observer* from next January.

Latest News

—THE Viceroy reached Attock on the 21st instant, where he met the Chief and General Roberts. His Excellency came on to Peshawar the next day, lunching with the 11th Bengal Cavalry at Nowshera. He entered the city at 3-15 under a Royal Salute. The garrison lined the road from the city to the Commissioner's house. The entry went off well; there was no contretemps of any kind. There was to be a levee on the 23rd and a review yesterday.

—THE Queen has telegraphed to the Government of India an expression of her deep concern at the appalling loss of life, caused by the recent storm-wave on the Bengal coast.

—THE Governor-General of Goa has determined to be present at the Imperial Assemblage.

—THE Khan of Khelat, says the *Pioneer*, not only accepted, but accepted with *empressement*, the invitation to meet the Viceroy which was taken to him by Colonel Colley. He left Khelat on the 3rd for Gundava, where Major Sandeman was to join him.

—OUR Native friends (says the *Bombay Gazette*) are going ahead. A correspondent sends us the following invitation, issued by a Native subordinate in the districts:—"Mr. ——(here name of rank) feel highly obliged if Mr. —— will give him the honor of his attendance (*sic*) to witness a Nautch and to partake of *pan supari*, &c."

—THE London *Academy* has been told that Mr. Val Prinsep's picture of the Imperial Proclamation will be presented to Her Majesty. People who may hope to get an engraving of the picture need not fear any disappointment; engravings of pictures in the possession of Her Majesty the Queen are well-known, and often for their excellence.

—DR. Ross, has been appointed the principal sanitary officer at Delhi during the Assemblage.

—CAPTAIN WYLIE with an escort of Jacobabad troops, 200 men and two mountain guns are with the Khan of Khelat and were on their way, when last heard of, to Gundava and Jacobabad.

—Two Parsi graduates in medicine, Messrs. S. H. Dantra and K. A. Dalal, having attained the rank of Surgeon in the army, have arrived in the troopship *Jumna*.

—THE *Rast Goftar* announces that Mr. Shantaram Narrayen, the well-known Vakeel of the High Court, has undertaken the framing of a memorial to the authorities, praying for a removal of the restrictions which prevent widow re-marriage, and make those who overleap them, objects of social dislike and persecution.

Calcutta.

MR. LINDSAY NEILL has already received charge of the office of Under-Secretary to the Government of India in the Home Department from Mr. T. J. Chichele Plowden.

THE Half-yearly General Meeting of Subscribers to the Bengal Civil Fund, will be held at the Town Hall on the 31st January next, at 3½ P.M., when, among other things, the following proposed addition to Art 25 of the Rules, will be brought forward for consideration:—"Provided that a declaration on oath by not less than two eye-witnesses will be considered sufficient proof of marriage in the cases of Messrs. Romesh Chunder Dutt and Behari Lal Gupta."

Advertisements

LIGHT! LIGHT!! LIGHT!!!

PATENT PORTABLE AIR GAS MAKING APPARATUS,

SUITABLE FOR

Churches, Chapels, Schools, Country Mansions, Private Houses, Railway Stations, Barracks, Manufactories, Collieries, Mills, Offices, &c., &c.

THIS *simple* and *effective* Gas-making Apparatus supplies a want long felt of having Gas at places where no Gas Works exist. It may be introduced without any more trouble than the simply affixing of any ordinary Gas meter, and is about the same size for the same number of lights. The *piping* and *fitting* arrangements are in every respect the same as for the use of ordinary Gas. The *cost* of the Gas produced is about the same as is charged for ordinary Coal Gas, and the light produced is *more brilliant* and of *a greater illuminating power;* it is also *free from the impurities of Coal Gas.* The Gas, if used with the Patent Burner, is of great heating power, and hence suitable for cooking and heating purposes, or in manufactories for soldering, &c. The apparatus is PORTABLE; there is NO DANGER WHATEVER (ordinary care being used when filling it); the Gas is PRODUCED IN AN INSTANT WITHOUT ANY FIRE OR OTHER ARTIFICIAL HEAT.

Further particulars may be obtained from MESSRS. EDWARD THOMSON & CO., Contractors for Drainage Water and Gas, who are appointed Sole Agents for the above apparatus, which can be seen working any week day between the hours of 6 A.M. and 6 P.M., at their place of business.

39, *BENTINCK STREET, CALCUTTA.*

P. W. FLEURY & CO.,

BUILDERS, ENGINEERS,

AND

SCIENTIFIC INSTRUMENT MAKERS.

No. 44, Free School Street.

WE beg to intimate that we have been engaged in the above line of business for the past 20 years, and trust that our Constituents will continue to favor us with their work, which will meet with prompt attention on our part.

In connection with buildings, we undertake the erection and repairing of machinery at moderate charges; as also execute all descriptions of Iron and Brass work.

We can assure the Public that we undertake the repair and erection of Houses, and the laying of Water-supply Pipes on moderate terms, and guarantee to keep all the water-pipes and brass fittings supplied by us in good working order for three years, free of extra charge. We also guarantee to keep dwelling-houses' roofs water-tight for three years, free of extra charge, for such houses as we have repaired.

For purposes of illumination, we prepare our patent Chromatic Transparencies representing Coat-of-Arms, Landscapes, Scenery, &c., at prices, ranging from Rs. 80 to 360 each, according to size and design.

FOR SALE.

Light! Light!! Light!!!

Electric Light Apparatus complete, worked with a battery of 50 large cells, on Bunsen's principle	500	0
Ditto ditto, with 40 cells, smaller size ...	400	
Ditto ditto, with a powerful 44-cell Cast-iron Battery, on Callan's principle ...	300	0
Lime Light Apparatus, complete, with Iron Gas-holder, and Copper Retort ...	150	0
Oxy-hydrogen Light Apparatus with safety Jets, 2 iron Gas-holders, and Retorts, complete	200	0
Hink's Patent Duplex Wall Lamps, with chimney	5	8
Ditto Duplex Lamp, with chimney and globe	7	8

Patent Leblanche Battery

For constancy, durability, and cleanliness, this battery is unequalled; price for each cell, with chemicals	3
Bunsen's Galvanic Battery, 9 inches, by 4 inches	7
Magneto-Electric Machine, with single magnet	14
Prismatic Compass, 3-inch in a-lid leather case, by Elbot, *second hand*	25
Ditto 4-inch, by Simmons, *second hand* ...	30

P. W. FLEURY & Co

No. 44, FREE SCHOOL STREET.

BABU BASANTA KUMAR DATTA,

HOMŒOPATHIC PRACTITIONER

No. 20, Sunker Halder's Lane, Ahiritolah.

LONDON AGENT

MRS. HENRY TURNER & CO.

HOMŒOPATHIC

FRESH INDENT OF

Medicines and other Requisites.

Arrives every month from England.

Medicines, Boxes, Books, Pamphlets;

Absolute Alcohol; Cholera-spirit Camphor.

SPECIAL REMEDIES.

For Suppressed, Laborious and Difficult menses-Leucorrhœa; Hysteria.

For Spermatorrhœa; Dysentery; Diarrhœa Cholera.

For Asthma; Pile; Pain; Sore and Diseases of the Children.

Ice, Lemonade, Soda and Tonic water always.

To be had at

DATTA'S HOMŒOPATHIC LABORATORY

No. 312, CHITPORE ROAD, BURTOLA, CALCUTTA.

TERMS—CASH.

☞ Price List can be had free on application.

R. K. GHOSH'S

HOMŒOPATHIC DISPENSARY.

No. 1, *Gour Mohun Mukerjee's Street, Simla.*

CALCUTTA.

HOMŒOPATHIC Medicine; Medicine chests of sizes,—containing medicine in tube phials; Homœopathic Books, tracts and pamphlets (English and Bengali); Dr. Rubin's "Saturated spirits of Camphor,"—(the best preventive and cure for cholera where medical aid is not available); and other Homœopathic requisites are sold here at a moderate price. Terms cash. Mofussil orders are promptly executed.

R. K. GHOSH,

Homœopathic Practitioner,

Manager.

HAROLD & CO.,

3, DALHOUSIE SQUARE, CALCUTTA

HARMONIUMS.

Harold and Co., call attention to their unequalled stock of rich-toned Harmoniums made especially for India.

FROM RS. 90 TO RS. 900 EACH.

All kinds of Musical Instruments of the best description are always kept in Stock.

SMITH, STANISTREET & CO.

Pharmaceutical Chemists & Druggists

BY APPOINTMENT

To His Excellency the Right Hon'ble

LORD LYTTON, G.M.S.I.

Governor-General of India,

&c., &c.

SYRUP OF LACTATE OF IRON

Prepared from the original recipe. Lactate of Iron, in various forms of preparation, have been in use in France, and generally through the continent of Europe, for some years past, and is highly esteemed as one of the most valuable Chalybeate Tonic remedies yet introduced. The Syrup, being the most agreeable as well as convenient form of administration is in most general use. It is a most valuable remedy in the following diseases:—Chlorosis or Green Sickness, Leucorrhœa, Neuralgia, Enlargement of the Spleen, &c. In combination with quinine, it has also been very successfully used in the cure of Fever, while to persons of delicate constitution, enfeebled by disease it is invaluable. In bottles. Rs. 2 each.

SYRUP OF THE PHOSPHATE OF IRON Rs. 2 per bottle.

SYRUP OF PHOSPHATE OF IRON AND STRYCHNINE. Rs. 2 per bottle.

SYRUP OF PHOSPHATE OF IRON AND QUININE. Price Rs. 2-8 per bottle.

SYRUP OF PHOSPHATE OF IRON, QUININE AND STRYCHNINE. (DR. ATKIN'S TRIPLE TONIC SYRUP,) Rs. 2-8 per bottle.

Smith, Stanistreet & Co.

Invite special attention to the following rates the quality guaranteed as the best procurable :—

Pure Ærated Waters.

Made from Pure Water, obtained by the new process through the Patent Charcoal Filters.

				Rs	As.
Ærated plain (Treble Ærated), per doz.				0	15
Soda Water	ditto	„	..	0	12
Gingerade	ditto	„	...	1	4
Lemonade	ditto	„	...	1	4
Tonic (Quinine)	ditto	„	...	1	4

The *Cash* must be sent with the order to obtain advantage of the above rates.

Rivers Steam Navigation Co. "Limited."

The Steamer "OUDE" left Goalundo for Assam on 1st instant.

The Steamer "BENGAL" left Goalundo for Assam on 7th November.

The Steamer "BURMAH" left Calcutta for Assam on the 14th current, and left Goalundo on 23rd current.

For rates of Freight and Passage, apply to

No. 1, Lyon's Range, } Macneill & Co.,
14th November, 1876. } Agents.

India General Steam Navigation Company, Ld.

Schoene Kilburn & Co.—*Managing Agents*

ASSAM LINE.

NOTICE.

Steamers leave Calcutta for Assam every Tuesday, Goalundo every Friday and leave Debrooghur downward every Saturday.

THE Str. "SIMLA" will leave Calcutta for Assam, on Tuesday, the 28th instant.

Cargo will be received at the Company's Godowns, Nimtollah Ghat, up till noon of Monday, the 27th.

THE Str. "AGRA" will leave Goalundo for Assam on Friday, the 1st December.

Cargo will be received at the Company's Godowns, No. 4, Fairlie Place, up till noon of Wednesday the 29th.

Goods forwarded to Goalundo for this vessel will be chargeable with Railway Freight from Calcutta to Goalundo in addition to the regular Freight of this Company.

Passengers should leave for Goalundo by Train of Thursday, the 30th.

CACHAR LINE NOTICE

REGULAR FORTNIGHTLY SERVICE

Steamers leave Calcutta for Cachar and Intermediate Stations every alternate Friday, and leave Cachar downward every alternate Sunday.

THE Str "SUCCESS" will leave Calcutta for Cachar on Friday, the 1st December.

Cargo will be received at the Company's Godowns, Nimtollah Ghat, up till noon of Thursday the 30th instant.

For further information regarding rates of Freight or passagemoney, apply to,

4, Fairlie Place, } G. J. SCOTT
Calcutta, 23rd November, 1876. } *Secretary.*

MAKHON LOLL GHOSE.

No. 91, Radha Bazar, Calcutta.

BEGS to invite the attention of the public to several consignments of commercial and fancy stationery of all sorts, including account books of all sizes, made of handmade and machine-made paper, by steamers recently arrived, and which he is disposing of at moderate prices. He has been long in the trade, and presumes he has always afforded every satisfaction to the numerous merchants here who have constantly favored him with orders. Mofussil orders accompanied with remittances shall be promptly attended to.

CALCUTTA }
The 18th August 1876. }

NOTICE.

Infallible Specifics for Asthma, Consumption, Colic, Gonorrhea, Spermatorrhea and Dysentery.

Used in all cases of Asthma, preceded by headache or sleepiness, or by various digestive or other disturbances, or without any warning.

Sold in boxes containing 7 pills (for one week only) with full directions for use :—

Price per box	...	...	Rs. 2	0
„ with postage ditto	...	...	2	4

For further particulars, Apply to

WOOPENDRA NATH PAL,

Care of the Manager, *Indian Mirror.*

CALCUTTA.

CHUNDER & BROTHERS.

25½ & 112, RADHA BAZAR,

STATIONERY in all its varieties.

PRINTING PRESSES, Inks & Materials.

LITHOGRAPHIC PRESS & Materials.

BOOK BINDING Materials &c.

Printed and published by M. M. RUKHIT, at the INDIAN MIRROR PRESS, No. 6, College Square, for the Proprietors.

The Indian Mirror.

SUNDAY EDITION.

VOL XV.] CALCUTTA, SUNDAY, DECEMBER 3, 1876. { REGISTERED AT THE GENERAL POST OFFICE. } [No. 286

CONTENTS.

NOTICE.

All letters and communications relating to the literary department of the Paper should be addressed to the Editor. All other letters should be addressed to the Manager, to whom all remittances should be made payable.

Subscribers will be good enough to bring to the notice of the Manager any delay or irregularity in the delivery of the Paper.

Editorial Notes.

WITH the return of winter the season for lectures has just commenced. It is to be hoped that Brahmo leaders will not be idle, but will organise a series of lectures, such at least as we had last year. Smaller meetings may also be held at intervals for debate and conversation.

IT is a pleasure to read Hafiz with the venerable minister, Babu Debendro Nath Tagore, as he reads and expounds verse after verse of that wonderful and sweet book of rapturous devotion, he grows really enthusiastic, and with passionate fervour follows each word of that wild poet into the depths of its hidden meaning. It would be a great thing if he could be induced to undertake a translation of Hafiz.

THE spiritualistic medium Dr. Slade, against whom proceedings were instituted at the Bow Street Police Court, at the instance of Professors Lankester and Donkin for cheating and vagrancy, has been sentenced, we believe, to three months imprisonment. This is a great blow to the cause of spiritualism in England at least. The advocates of spiritualism are raising funds to meet the expenses of appeal from the Magistrates Court.

MR. THOBURN's new church erected at Dhurumtolla is to be called the Tabernacle in imitation of Mr. Spurgeon. It is said this will be the largest place of Christian worship in Calcutta seating 1,500 persons. Many gifts of money, characteristic of the spirit of self denial in the givers, are recorded in connection with this church. But the amount of more than forty thousand rupees is still wanted to complete the building. considering the earnestness, and sincere piety of the Weslyans in every country, we have little doubt the required amount of money will be soon raised.

WHATEVER may be the merits or demerits of Mr. Gladstone's pamphlet, one great result it has unquestionably produced, it has prevented England from going to war on behalf of Turkey. It may be true that Russian intrigue has long been rife among the Christian provinces of Turkey, it may be true that the autonomy of these provinces will prove of immense political advantage to the Muscovite, but for all that Russia has identified herself with the cause of humanity and justice in the present instance. And if England in spite of political disadvantages and traditional jealousies takes up the same side for a wholesome regard of right against might, the national character of the Briton will have redeemed itself from the charges of selfishness and callousness so often preferred against it.

AN Irishman has turned a through *Byragi.* He calls himself Haridas, and puts on a *Kaupin.* The name Hari is always on his lips. This Irish Hindu devotee is now in Calcutta, having just come from Indore, and is on his way to Pooree. The history of his conversion, as it has been related to us, is brief. While holding the appointment of Police Inspector somewhere in Central India, he one day went out shooting. Overcome by hunger and quite exhausted he took shelter in a Yogi's Asrum. This Yogi on hearing of his adventures most strongly protested against the wickedness of shooting dumb animals, and gave him such lessons as gradually shook his faith and at last brought him into the Vaishnava fold.

WE in this country plead guilty to the charge of not valuing knowledge for its own sake, but merely as a means of acquiring an income. It is somewhat surprising to be told that in England too the cause of the poverty of educational institutions is the indifference of English society to "true knowledge." The Rev. Mark Pattison, Rector of Lincoln College, in his address on Education before the Social Science Association at Liverpool, the address that is much admired for its ability and brilliancy, in effect said that "if a father could be convinced that by spending £2000 on his daughters, education he could ensure her earning five per cent on the outlay, he would be glad to spend that sum. He looked on the whole question, as purely one of a profitable investment. If five per cent was not forthcoming, the education could be done without."

WE are very glad that our fellow subjects of the Eurasian community have now formed a definite programme of operations for their society which they call the Eurasian Association. The objects of the society will be to promote education among the Eurasian community by opening primary and middle class schools; to establish means for acquiring a knowledge of trades and professions, by opening training shops, by apprenticing young men to work-shops, &c; by enabling them to attain the highest university honors, and to proceed to England with a view to qualify themselves for Government service, and join a learned profesion; to aid members by opening a Provident Fund, and by affording temporary relief when members are in distress, and generally to further the interests of the community. These objects are very good no doubt, but we are afraid they are too expensive to be carried out all at once. The resources of the Association will be the amount of subscription realized from intending members. The subscription is 10 Rs. and 5 Rs. respectively, and a donation of 200 Rs. will entitle one to a life-membership. There will be no interference with the religious views of members, but we believe the majority of them will be Roman Catholics.

THE excesses to which religious bigotry can proceed in its belief and in its vindictiveness would be really an interesting study if any one could collect them. Our readers may have heard of the prayers which the theological opponents of Theodore Parker offered up in order that the mouth of the arch-heretic might be stopped. Among those who instituted these prayers was the revivalist President Finney. Now in a book which has recently appeared on the life of Finney the Revivalist, the following passage occurs :—"It was the late President Finney who caused the death of Theodore Parker—who caused the immediate causes of that death, and which promptly put a stop to the music hall abominations. It appears from the recently published life of President Finney, that while conducting a revival in Boston, he was hindered by the heretical and non-evangelical preaching of the Cromwell of radicalism. He therefore called upon Mr. Parker to persuade him to a cessation of his labours. But Mr. Parker refused even to see the Revivalist. It then occurred to Mr. Finney that Parker should be prayed down and out, and his mouth closed. Prayer meetings of the evangelical clergy were held for a purpose which would have been inhuman had it not been divine. The prayers were successful. Parker became hopelessly ill, was unable longer to speak in public, or even to write in private. He was forced to leave Boston, and, dying, his work perished with him! This, we take it, is chief among the laurels of the great Revivalist.' We scarcely know whether to laugh or moan at such a story published in the name of religion.

—

MISSIONARY journals like the *Bombay Guardian* and *Indian Evangelical Review* take advantage of the present conflicts between Mahomedans and Christians in Europe to level foul aspersions against the life and character of Mahomed which it has long been the usage of a certain school of Christianity to invent with the object of degrading the founders of those systems of faith which show any rivalry to their own. The prophet of Arabia is not only an imposter, but other crimes of a deeper dye are laid to his charge. A certain Mr. Nairne, who is a member of the Bombay Civil Service, writes an article in the October number of the *Evangelical Review*, the spirit of which is as narrow and uncharitable as the facts are distorted. Of course the *Bombay Guardian* makes capital of that article to speak in the most offensive manner possible of the religious pretensions of Mahomed. It was only the other day that a most disgraceful scene of bloodshed and lawlessness took place in Bombay on account of expressions much less hurtful to Mossulman feeling than the words now used in these missionary organs. And in the face of such facts a member of the Indian Civil Service joins with these indiscreet preachers of what they call the Christian religion, to foment the angriest feelings of hatred in the hearts of millions of Her Majesty's Indian subjects. Is the doctrime of peace and good will among mankind likely to be established in India by such conduct, or the harmony between the rulers and ruled promoted? The generous spirits among the Christian population should protest against such sentiments at the present time.

WARNINGS.

PHYSICAL infirmities and maladies may, and do often affect one's temper and shake his faith. Let healthy Brahmos hold themselves ready to meet trying diseases.

Youthful and newborn Zeal is not strong enough to ovetcome the temptation and cares of worldly life. Let youug Brahmos beware that they do not sink as soon as they enter the world and settle in business.

The powers of remedying social evils and disavowing idolatry and caste in the face of the strongest opposition may not, and often does not avail to promote inward sanctification and communion. Let Brahmo reformers take care that after winning laurels in the field of reformation they do not succumb to carnality and prayerlessness.

Poverty is a great stumbling-block. Let those who have practised religion successfully amid affluence and among helping friends be always prepared to retain the sweetness of prayer and the purity of character albeit poor and friendless.

THE DOCTRINE OF REPETANCE ONCE MORE.

FORMERLY the Brahmos used to talk very often on the subject of repentance, and attached a great deal of importance to the doctrine. They used to say that repentance is the only means of atoning for their sins, because Divine grace comes through it. Are we to think that they have given up this doctrine? This can not be. Or must we think that all their sins have left them, and there is no more occasion for repentance? This is still more absurd. For if some sins have grown weak in the Brahmo character, other sins have not, and perhaps owing to change of circumstance, and advance on years, some new faults have begun to appear. For the removal of the sinfulness which is thus found to cleave to the heart, various means are prescribed. We are taught to commence with the spirit of God as frequently as we can; we are advised to subject our lives to a strict religious discipline; we are directed to keep the company of holy men, and various other means are recommended. Now without at all underrating the importance of these instructions, we must ask what is to be the impulse which will lead us to their adoption. Means and disciplines are for those only who find it their necessity to adopt them. And how should we find them? We know there are some who willingly accept forms of religious life with the object of adding to their stock of piety. Some few there may also be to whom the appearance of a high order of religiousness in outward conduct has considerable attraction. These amateurs of religion congratulate themselves on such progress as they think they have made, and live unmolested within their imagined arena of sanctity. But there is another class of men somewhat different from them. To them the pursuit of religion is no honorary occupation to be prosecuted and given up as occasions and inclinations may tend. It is a deep necessity of removing the ineradicable sense of sinfulness within the heart. They are confused, ashamed, and intensely mortified to see the miserable condition of their spiritual nature. They find on reflection that in their past life, and in their present life also there are more sins within them than than they can think of, or picture in imagination, or time to act out in their daily avocations. "What should such fellows as I do crawling between earth and heaven?" They ask. Now such feelings are generally experienced by us as the results of grievously vile deeds done at a moment of rashness or passion. The rebound of a gross sin is an involuntary and terrible remorse, the full agony of which gives a sort of relief to the surcharged conscience. Brahmos in early times used to think this to be the natural state of repentence. But our standpoint has considerably changed of late. A man may not be guilty of grievious sins, his life may be outwardly very correct, nay to us all he may appear to be saintly and very pure, and on self-examination he may not be able to confess that he deliberately indulges in any form of positive sinfulness, but still within his mind there may be a load of guilt which he can neither throw off, nor bear. All the wickedness of past life would sometimes return with a vividness of remembrance that bows him down very low, and proves beyond mistake that there are patches and spots in the soul, too many to number, that still demand a washing away. And compared to the lofty standard of holiness to be attained in our life time, the present condition of he heart is so miserably deficient, that the grief caused thereby is very heavy at times. Such grief is occasional with some, habitual with a few. It is not the impetuous misery of remorse, not the consequence of dilliberate wrong doing, and violence to the moral nature. It is a saintly godly sorrow, a perpetual sense of unworthiness that is secret and reserved, but very effective nevertheless. This is the beginning of genuine repentance. It is the impulse which leads to the earnest and effectual adoption of the various means of grace and goodness. It consumes away slowly the remnants of secret sins, and guards against the advent of new forms of vice. It always burns as a sacred fire within, and the smoke of the sacrifice of the whole heart ascends to heaven day and night as a good, and acceptable offering.

Provincial

DEHRA DUN.

[FROM OUR OWN CORRESPONDENT.]

THE [illegible] anniversary of the Dhera Dun Brahmo Somaj came off on the 11th

November The service was conducted by our beloved Missionary, Babu Aghore Nath Gupta. The sermons preached both in the morning and evening, were on "High Communion in its Various Phases." There was nothing of the fervidness of eloquence in the Babu's preaching, but it was always very sweet, simple, touching and emotional. A service in Hindi was also held for the benefit of the Hindustanis. Several gentlemen were present among whom were some Christians. Articles of food as well as copper pieces were distributed among the poor. Upwards of a hundred and fifty persons gathered, and thankfully received the humble gifts which the Brahmos had prepared for the occasion.

Our anniversaries are pleasant oases in the great desert of our worldly life. Many on these occasions become what they ought to be. Woe to the wandering child who seizes not these most precious opportunities to return to the Father's house, and receive from Him those eternal blessings which he is ever ready to shower upon us. But alas, the effects of our anniversaries, though highly beneficial and lasting in some, are in too many instances proverbially transient. An evaporation succeeds, and our hearts are left as parched as ever. Utter neglect of spiritual exercises has with us become chronic and can only be cured by sustained efforts to conquer carnality and the steady development of our spiritual faculties. May the grace of God awaken us to a sense of our duties and responsibilities, and give us strength enough to enable us to sustain well the high relation, which we as Brahmos bear to heaven and earth.

Correspondence.

THE TRUTH.

(Continued.)

To the Editor of the *Indian Mirror*.

SIR,—Witness the sad difference amongst Christians arising from a mere question of the nature of God, leaving the substance they grasp at the shadow. The faith in Him which God requires of His creatures, has nothing to do with the composition of the Supreme Essence, but only with His existence and His attributes. What religion or what system of theology can undertake to analyze the constitution of the Incomprehensible? If it is really true what some Christians assert about the Godhead, then the Great Incomprehensible must admittedly be, if not wholly at least partly, *comprehensible*. Oh no. Let not man in his finite wisdom set bounds to the make of his mysterious maker. Where will the presumption of mankind? It is only the foolish that are presumptuous. Yes, faith in God as God, is quite distinct from the question about His constitution, and is nothing that can affect the salvation of man. Sufficient for faith is a belief in the existence of the Invisible in his goodness and might. Therefore, faith in the Trinity or Unity of God, is not faith in God as God, but is quite a different thing which God might let us better understand hereafter. If a subject has faith in the government, it is not necessary for him to have faith also in the fact that the government is constituted of several members of council. Some might say after seeing the above that the writer cannot, if he holds such views, believe in the divinity of Christ. I answer that it suffices for me to know and hopefully believe that Christ is my Redeemer, and that He is the Intercessor for the transgressions of the whole world. Enough is this for me. I do not think it necessary to enter into a discussion about His nature. Up to the time of Christ, God's chosen people said there is one God. Up to the crucifixion it could have been proved from Holy writ and teaching that God had two Persons, the Father and the Son. When afterwards Christ mentioned the Comforter, Christians concluded there must be three Persons. But as God is incomprehensible, and the Bible does not expressly declare that the Comforter was the last Person of the Godhead, it is quite as possible there being other Persons besides. But I do not wish to enter into a long argument. As I said, the nature of the Supreme Being it has pleased the Almighty to keep a mystery, and therefore let not foolish and presumptuous ecclesiastics pronounce condemnation against those who do not believe implicitly in a doubtful question which they, most presumptuous men, and not God and His prophets and apostles, have made into an article of faith, in a creed drawn up by them, proud mortals, worms of the dust that dare presume to define the nature of the Incomprehensible. Thus every creed has its pet dogmas and definitions of the Great Spirit. Each looks at the great question of life and immortality in the peculiar waste of its own lens,—a lens owing its origin to the inventions of priestcraft. Can I prevail upon any to view God and the mighty question in the light of Nature and proved Revelation? I say proved Revelation. Can I persuade any to put faith in such Revelation? Search the Holy Testaments of God and study His Evidences revealed from time to time in the suspension of the operations of Nature. A pure unmixed faith in Him, a service of love unshackled by the anathemas of creeds and eternal gratitude for the balms and consolations of Divine Revelation, will be the result. Oh, why did God permit the light of "The truth" to be obscured by the inventions of the human mind! Alas! no, why alas? If God permits sin, who am I that I should be so presumptuous as to thus express my pity for His mysterious workings. Let us pray that all will end well with all, and be content to abide by His own good pleasure.

The above is just a clue to the views I entertain as a Christain, and I think it will do to explain why I evinced no unwillingness to be present at the Anniversary celebration in the Brahmo Mandil here. So I went and was present, and the description of what I saw and heard, will form the concluding portion of this letter, for the length of which, Mr Editor, I ask for your indulgence.

HYDERABAD, SIND } Yours &c.
The 10*th Oct.* 1876. } NOT A BRAHMO

The Brahmo Somaj

SOME of the followers of the Thakoor of Morvee, a Native State between Cutch and Kettywar, attended divine service in the Brahmo Mandir on last Sunday. Two were Parsi gentlemen and one a Nagar Brahmin gentleman. We are glad to find that they sympathize with the principles of the Brahmo Somaj most sincerely. One of the Parsi gentleman had been tutor to the late Maharajah of Kolhapur, and was present when the unfortunate prince died at Florence.

WE are glad to be told that some of the Bramica ladies connected with the Sindurippatty Brahmo Somaj have made a regular organization for female education and improvement. A house has been purchased with this object, a girls' school is going on regularly, and fortnightly meeting of ladies takes place, where papers are read, and discussed. We should have much pleasure to know more of their movement, and encourage it.

FOR the last two Sundays the minister of the Brahmo Mandir has been giving sermons on the right place of the worshipper in regard to the Divine Spirit and in regard to the dispensation wherewith he is connected.

WE are glad to find that under the auspices of Babu Nobin Chunder Roy the Agra Brahmo Somaj has been resuscitated. The Hindustanis we are told are more enthusiastic about the new movement than Bengalis. At the weekly Service which is conducted in Hindi, about forty Hindustanis are present, and not more than four or five Bengalis. This is as it should be.

THEOLOGICAL CLASS.

Sunday, September 17, 1876.

To solve satisfactorily the problem of the existence of what is called *evil* in creation, it is necessary in the first place to determine its relations, if it has any, with the undeniable existence of the facts of imperfection and suffering in nature. Is imperfection an evil necessarily? That imperfections are not always pleasant or helpful to the development of our moral faculties, we must admit. But must we not also admit at the same time that such imperfections, whether they exist amidst physical conditions, or in the higher relations of life, gradually tend to correct themselves under the law of human progress? Conceding the capability, and the accomplishment, however partial, of that progress on the part of man, it is tacitly conceded that the imperfections complained of, involve within themselves their own remedy, and that such remedy, discovered by the independent exercise of the highest powers wherewith man is gifted, serves the purpose of moral harmony and moral strength much more effectively than if it had been found by the unconscious and instinctive action of the laws of nature and mind of man. The somewhat frivolous objection, therefore, that Mr. Mill so repeatedly and so seriously urges against Divine omnipotence and Divine benevolence at the same moment, is amply answered by the adjustment of unhappiness and imperfection to the elasticity and progressiveness discovered in the various conditions of being, in the midst of which man's life is continually passed in the world. In the second place *suffering* is a much more serious matter than mere imperfection and it is related much more closely to our moral nature than the other is. Imperfection is tolerated by many, ignored by not a few, while *suffering* is equally realized and detested by all. So much so is this the case that in nine cases out of every ten, *suffering* and *evil* are held synonymous. Now *physical suffering*, what the majority of us so strongly complain against, is not a very difficult problem to solve. John Stuart Mill himself acknowledge that "physical pains and pleasures are equally conservative," pleasure attracting us towards the obedience of natural laws, pain warning us against the consequences of violating them. If man were a physical being only, and his entire moral nature could be proved to merge in his nervous system, bodily pain would have been really more difficult to deal with. But when the deepest experiences and genuine welfare of our moral nature have often to be acquired at the cost of sensual enjoyments, any shock to the senses, and any disorder to the system where the senses are, can not only not establish the existence of any universal evil, but establishes on the other hand the fact that moral happiness and physical happiness are often in inverse ratio. To begin with, therefore, we must disconnect the fact of pain from the fact of evil, and we must maintain that physical evil in not a few instances, results in unquestionable moral harmony. Again, is moral harmony to be considered as a fact that exists beyond man's being, or is it subjective to him alone? Are the actions, the emotions, the desires and the sufferings which he condemns as evil in his case, equally evil in the rest of the sentient and material creation? Or does he detect evil in himself, and imputes it to other objects whenever he finds the latter in the midst of those circumstances where in the difficulty first emerged in his own consciousness? The whole question of *evil* in the shape of suffering resolves itself to certain feelings and judgments peculiar and exclusive to the moral nature of man, and it must be discussed within these narrow limits. The unpleasantness, the darkness, the profound deformity of such sufferings have in all ages opened the deepest insights into the higher relations of human life. The world has been taught saving truths by nothing so much as by pain. And if the fact of pain were eliminated the deep and noble life which underlies that pain, would remain unfelt. The philanthropy, the self-sacrifice, the unselfish love, nay the greatest efforts that man has made to glorify human nature, owe their existence to the presence of suffering in the world, and though this suffering in the case of such as have labored under it, was justly merited, it evoked from mankind at large those glorious impulses which have been embodied in the noblest institutions we see around us. *Suffering*, therefore, as it exists beyond the pale of human life, is often most wonderfully misconceived and misinterpreted, and *suffering* as it exists in human life generally tends to the highest good. In certain cases it is admittedly inapplicable, but we must be candid enough to acknowledge that we do not profess ourselves to be able to solve all the problems of pleasure and pain in the world.

Literary

A NEW edition of Mr. H. G. Keene's *Delhi Handbook* is on the eve of publication.

RANGOON will have a daily paper from the 1st January next, to be called the *Rangoon Daily News*.

Scientific

A FRENCH doctor has excited much attention in Paris by his declaration, that the best means to preserve health and cure diseases, is by scientific gymnastics. From the results of years of observations at the military gymnasium of Paris, he finds the soldiers' strength increased by 23 to 38 per cent., and their pulmonary capacity, by one-sixth.

COLONEL GORDON is now on his way to the Victoria Nyanza, and takes with him the parts of the small steamer *Khedive*, which he hopes to launch on the lake.

Latest News

—LORD SALISBURY has arrived at Rome. He had an interview with King Victor and the Minister for foreign affairs on Thursday last.

—THE Principal Queen of Burmah died on the 13th instant. She was half-sister to the King, as it is in accordance with ancient Burmese customs for the King of Burmah to marry one of his half-sisters, and to elevate her to the position of Principal Queen.

—IT is said that the King of Burmah will send an Embassy to England next year.

—WHY is not British Burmah made a part of Bengal? For all officers for Burmah are recruited from Bengal. It is stated that an Assistant Surgeon of the Bengal establishment is to be appointed Resident Medical Officer of the Rangoon dispensary.

—THREE Companies of the Q. O. Madras Sappers and Miners at Bangalore are to be held in readiness for service in Egypt.

—THE last *Gazette of India* publishes the report of the Commissioners appointed under the Nawab Nazim's Debts Act, 1873. It is a most interesting document, and makes some startling disclosures.

—LORD LYTTON in proposing the Maharajah of Cashmere's health at Madhopore, said:—"Ladies and Gentlemen,—I propose the health of our illustrious and distinguished host, the Maharajah of Cashmere. When I came to India, I had two desires next to my heart. The first was to see the most beautiful country in the world, the second, to make the acquaintance of its illustrious ruler. Providence has denied me the first, but I am highly gratified that I have been able to meet the Maharajah here and make his acquaintance. My object has not been to see the mountains, the lakes and the rivers, but to see the faithful and loyal ally of Her Majesty the Queen. His Highness' kind consideration for the comfort of myself, my staff, and Lady Lytton I will never forget. I am very glad to tell you, as it is written in history as well as in the hearts of all Englishmen, H. H. is ready to follow the footsteps of his illustrious father, the late Golab Sing."

—THE following is a summary of the reports on the state of the season and prospects of the crops for the week ending the 30th ultimo:—

"In Madras partial rain is reported from Madura, but it has been insufficient to benefit the standing crops; a little has also fallen at Tanjore elsewhere there has been none, and prospects are unchanged. No rain has fallen in Mysore, and relief works are being largely extended. In Bombay reports are favorable from Sind and Guzerat; elsewhere no rain has fallen, and the condition of things is unchanged. In the Central Provinces rain is in some districts, required for the *rabi*, but prospects are on the whole fair. In Berar rain is in many places much needed for the *rabi*. Reports from Central India and Rajputana are favorable. In Bengal there have been some slight showers in the central and eastern districts; the condition of the crops is excellent. A little rain has fallen in Assam, and also throughout Burmah; reports are good. No rain fell during the week in North-West Provinces or Oudh, where prospects are satisfactory. In the Punjab rain is reported from the northern and western districts; the crops promise well."

—THE calamity in Bombay seems, by common consent, to have attained the dimensions of a famine.

—THE Viceroy was to leave Lahore for Multan on Friday last.

—RUMOUR says that Babu Sattyendranath Tagore C. S. is to be removed from Ahmedabad to Surat.

—PROFESSOR MONIER WILLIAMS, his brother and nephew, are at Ahmedabad, staying in the house of the Judge, Babu Sattyendranath Tagore.

—COLONEL HUTCHINSON, Resident at Gwalior, on his return from Delhi, goes on twelve months' furlough, and Major Impey, who arrived by last mail, is to succeed him.

Calcutta,

ON Friday last, a monster meeting was held at the Mosque of Hadji Zachariah Mahomed for the purpose of signing the Memorial to Her Imperial Majesty, which was adopted by the Turkish Relief Committee, on the 22nd November last, at a general meeting held in the house of Nawab Amir Ali Khan Bahadur. The proceedings commenced after the usual *namaz*, with prayers for the Sultan Abdul Hamid, after which the Memorial to the Queen was read out, unanimously adopted, and signed by more than 6,000 members of the Mahomedan community who were present.

THE rate of conversion of Indian into sterling money for Overland Money Orders, has been changed to 1*s*. 9½*d*. per rupee.

MR. A. W. CROFT, M.A., has been appointed to officiate as Registrar of the University, *vice* Mr. Sutcliffe, who has resigned.

THE commencement of the Examinations for the Degrees of B.A. and B.L., has been postponed from Tuesday, the 2nd January, to Tuesday, the 9th January 1877.

RAJAH SOURINDRO MOHUN TAGORE combines in himself not musical abilities only, but a strong feeling of loyalty, and the outcome of this happy combination is the composition of the following books which are expected to be out at the time of the Delhi Durbar:—

I. Victoria Samrajyam, or a description, in Sanskrit verses, of all the British possessions and dependencies, set to the national music of the respective countries.

II. England and India, in two volumes, bound in one—represents that both the countries are *bound* together with a common bond of sympathy and are governed by the same sovereign. It is a history of England and India, in Bengali verses, and set to Bengali music.

III. Certain pieces of *Owen Meredith's* lyrics, set to Hindu Music. This book is dedicated, by permission, to the author of the lyrics, (the Viceroy,) who, we understand, has presented to Dr. Tagore, a brother-worker in the field of the muses, a copy of his "Fables in Songs."

A CHRISTIAN born of European parents, has embraced Hinduism, and is now living as a *fakir* somewhere near the Hughly Bridge. A correspondent of the *Indian Daily News* gives the following particulars:—"Who would have conceived half a century ago that a Christian, born of European parents, would embrace the Hindu religion? And yet we have, at the present moment, amongst us a Christian who abjures his own religion and embraces Hinduism. This personage was seen in our quarters yesterday. He was born, as he said, on the 11th December 1835, at Cawnpore, of European parents. Once, when he was on a hunting excursion, he met a *jogi* with three or four disciples living in a hut situated in the midst of a jungle generally believed to be the abode of ferocious animals. He became impressed with the utter regardlessness shown by the *jogi* of the pleasures of life; and was much startled to find him living among wild and ferocious animals. He had a talk with him, perhaps, on subjects of religion, and from that moment became his follower. At present he lives at the river-side. His clothes are those of a *fakir*. The pantaloon, the shirt, the waistcoat, the coat, the trousers, and the hat have no charm in his eyes. A coarse blanket and a piece of rough cloth is all that he likes. He lives the life of a *fakir*, but does not like them beg his bread from door to door. He asks no one for a morsel of bread or a glass of water, but eats what is given him from good will. Like a staunch Hindu, he does not eat anything which comes from the hand of a Mahomedan, a low caste *sudra*, or a Christian. He is always seen telling the beads. We are informed by a reliable source that several Eurasians, who frequent the Hughly Bridge, always step into the lonely abode of this man, and advise him to resume his former life. On being asked by us why he forsook Christianity he replied calmly that in it he found no rest for his soul, while in the Hindu religion he found it. Staunch Hindus will, perhaps, rejoice to hear of it."

THE question of providing refreshments to Native passengers on the East Indian Railway, has received the attention of the Agent and Chief Engineer during his recent inspection of the line, and his conclusions on the subject are thus expressed:—

"I made personal enquiry into this matter during my recent inspection, and it appeared to me that Native though travellers at present, get their wants sufficiently met by hawkers of refreshments on the station platforms. It is true that no special accommodation is provided for passengers wishing to halt at the larger stations; but the fact appears to be that the habits and customs of Native travellers are not such as to render any elaborate special provision for ministering to the wants of the upper class passengers as regards refreshments a paying speculation. Until they emancipate themselves to a certain extent from caste prejudices, and their peculiar notions about the seclusion of women, it would be premature to provide hotels, baths, &c., for Natives at the principal stations. Babu Nilcomal Mitter, the former contractor for Native refreshments, professed to supply the want of hotel accommodation in his serais that he built contiguous to some of the stations, but after a fair trial it was found that the system of monopoly did not answer, and had to be abandoned. The existing arrangements for refreshments include the provision for all classes of Native passengers wherever the trains halt for any time. The Native bunkers deposit fixed sums as security for good behavior. Fixed tariffs are carried out by them as far as possible, and traffic officers are always looking after them to ensure that they sell good articles at fair rates and behave properly. I trust that the Government will consider the present arrangements for the supply of food, &c., to Native passengers satisfactorily, and will concur with me in thinking that it is scarcely the business of the Company to furnish special hotel accommodation, apart from the bazaars and Government serais, at some of the larger stations. I am, however, of opinion that Native hotel accommodation, if really required, could best be supplied by private enterprise; and if any respectable Native contractors will come forward and make specific proposals, I shall have no objection to assist by granting convenient sites on the Company's premises, at a moderate rental, for hotels to be built on an approved plan, and of course to be subject to such regulations, sanitary rules, &c., as might be considered necessary. Special attention is always given to such matters as the opening of offices, avoidance of rough usage, the early release of passengers from the carriages at stations, the proper lighting of carriages, and supply of water and provisions."—*Indian Daily News.*

THE Government Paper market still continues low.

THE Pennah case in which Mr. H. Bell, the Legal Remembrancer, obtained a rule calling upon Messrs. Webster and McDonald to show cause why the fines that had been inflicted upon them by the lower Court, namely Rs. 500 and Rs. 100, should not be enhanced, came on for hearing on Friday last before the Hon'ble Mr. Justice Markby, the Hon'ble Mr. Justice Ainslie and the Hon'ble Mr. Justice Morris. Mr. Evans appeared for Mr. Webster to show cause against the rule, and Mr. J. D. Bell represented Mr. McDonald. Mr. H. Bell, the Legal Remembrancer, said that before his learned friends addressed their Lordships with their arguments on this rule, he would ask the permission of their Lordships to make a few remarks on one or two points as to everything he had said, and everything he had done, when he applied for this rule. He thought it necessary to do so as the matter had been so grossly and so grievously misrepresented. The Court, however, took no notice of what appeared in the papers. The other case in which some of the ryots are charged with perjury was heard in part yesterday, and is not yet over.

THE new Bishop of Calcutta, the Venerable Ralph Johnson, was consecrated, on Thursday last at St. Paul's Cathedral by the Archbishop of Canterbury.

A VESSEL in the river caught fire yesterday.

WE have received a copy of the programme of the Eurasian Association established in Calcutta:—

Membership will be acquired by payment of a subscription at one or the other of the following rates, at the option of members: Rs. 10 or Rs. 5 per annum in advance, or one Rupee or eight Annas if paid monthly. Payment of Rs. 200 will constitute life membership. The objects the Association proposes to carry out are:—(1.) Education. (2.) The acquiring of trades and professions. (3.) Aid to members. (4.) And generally to further the interests of the community. The carrying out of these objects will be effected by the following means:—Education will be promoted (1.) By opening new, or aiding existing primary schools. (2.) By establishing one or more middle class schools if considered necessary, giving a technical, as well as a general education. (3.) By educating unprovided orphans of members; by aiding members to educate their children when unable; and by extending the aid also to children wholly dependent on members unable to educate them. The acquiring of trades and professions will be promoted (1.) By opening training shops to initiate lads. (2) By apprenticing sons of members to workshops, trades, &c., and by extending the same advantages to children wholly dependent on members. (3.) By enabling young men (sons of, or wholly dependent on, members) attaining the highest University honors to proceed to England and qualify for Government service, or join a learned profession. Aid to members will be given (1.) By opening a Provident Fund to promote thrift and providence. (2.) By affording temporary relief, when in distress, to members and their families when they have been subscribers to the Provident Fund. The Association also proposes, at a suitable time, the establishment of a Provident Dispensary for the benefit of members, entitling them and their families to medical attendance and medicine by the payment of a small percentage on their incomes.

Miscellaneous.

FAITHFULNESS IN LITTLE THINGS.

WE doubt if with God there are any little things, as we speak of them. A drop of water is crowded with living creatures, fashioned and fed by his hand. A silken hair from our heads reveals, under the microscope, three distinct parts or shafts, one within another, the outer one made up of layers, and these clad on finely wrought plates, like the armor of the old warrior, and on some of the lower animals these plates display the most ornate sculpture. The same beauty and wonder are discoverable in all the material universe, in the minutest portions thereof. What, then, shall we say of the master's interest in the little things performed by or that relate to his intelligent creatures who are to endure when the mountains have vanished and the heavens are rolled away!

If the great Architect fashions the eye of a fly, or the atom of clay with as much care as he shapes a continent, how can frail man say of anything that comes to his hands to be done, "It is only a trifle, and can be slighted."

It is the carefulness in little things that makes *faithful* men, and builds up characters that stand when great trial and temptation come. If there be any one thing the young men of to-day need to resolve upon, it is that *whatever they do they will do it well.* Men who have formed that habit are always in demand. The best places are open to them; and in the end comes the crowning reward at the hand of the Great King, "Be thou *Faithful* unto death and I will give thee a crown of life."—*From the Lucknow Witness.*

Advertisements

LIGHT! LIGHT!! LIGHT!!!

PATENT PORTABLE AIR GAS MAKING APPARATUS,

SUITABLE FOR

Churches, Chapels, Schools, Country Mansions, Private Houses, Railway Stations, Barracks, Manufactories, Collieries, Mills, Offices, &c., &c.

THIS *simple* and *effective* Gas-making Apparatus supplies a want long felt of having Gas at places where no Gas Works exist. It may be introduced without any more trouble than the simply affixing of any ordinary Gas meter, and is about the same size for the same number of lights. The *piping* and *fitting* arrangements are in every respect the same as for the use of ordinary Gas. The *cost* of the Gas produced is about the same as is charged for ordinary Coal Gas, and the light produced is *more brilliant* and of *a greater illuminating power*; it is also *free from the impurities of Coal Gas*. The Gas, if used with the Patent Burner, is of great heating power, and hence suitable for cooking and heating purposes, or in manufactories for soldering, &c. The apparatus is PORTABLE; there is NO DANGER WHATEVER (ordinary care being used when filling it); the Gas is PRODUCED IN AN INSTANT WITHOUT ANY FIRE OR OTHER ARTIFICIAL HEAT.

Further particulars may be obtained from MESSRS. EDWARD THOMSON & CO., Contractors for Drainage, Water and Gas, who are appointed Sole Agents for the above apparatus, which can be seen working any week day between the hours of 6 A.M., and 6 P.M., at their place of business.

99, BENTINCK STREET, CALCUTTA.

P. W. FLEURY & CO.,

BUILDERS, ENGINEERS,

AND

SCIENTIFIC INSTRUMENT MAKERS.

No. 44, Free School Street.

We beg to intimate that we have been engaged in the above line of business for the past 20 years, and trust that our Constituents will continue to favor us with their work, which will meet with prompt attention on our part.

In connection with buildings, we undertake the erection and repairing of machinery at moderate charges; we also execute all descriptions of Iron and Brass work.

We can assure the Public that we undertake the repair and erection of Houses, and the laying of Water-supply Pipes on moderate terms, and guarantee to keep all the water-pipes and brass fittings supplied by us in good working order for three years, free of extra charge. We also guarantee to keep dwelling-houses' roofs water-tight for three years, free of extra charge, for such houses as we have repaired.

For purposes of illumination, we prepare our patent Chromatic Transparencies representing Coat-of-Arms, Landscapes, Scenery, &c., at prices, ranging from Rs. 80 to 300 each, according to size and design.

FOR SALE.

Light! Light!! Light!!!

Electric Light Apparatus, complete, worked with a battery of 50 large cells, on Bunsen's principle 500 0

Ditto ditto, with 40 cells, smaller size ... 400

Ditto ditto, with a powerful 15-cell Cast-iron Battery, on Callan's principle ... 300 0

Lime Light Apparatus, complete, with Iron Gas-holder, and Copper Retort ... 150 0

Oxy-Hydrogen Light Apparatus with safety Jets, Iron Gas-holders, and Retorts, complete 200 0

Hink's Patent Duplex Wall Lamps, with chimney 5 8

Ditto Duplex Lamp, with chimney and globe 7 8

Patent Leblanche Battery

For constancy, durability, and cleanliness, this battery is unequalled; price for each cell, with chemicals 3

Bunsen's Galvanic Battery, 8 inches, by 4 inches 7

Magneto-Electric Machine, with single magnet 14

Prismatic Compass, 3-inch, in solid leather case; by Elliot, *second hand* 22

Ditto, 4-inch, by Simmons, *second hand* ... 30

P. W. FLEURY & Co

No. 44, FREE SCHOOL STREET.

MAKHON LOLL GHOSE.

No. 91, Radha Bazar, Calcutta.

BEGS to invite the attention of the public to several consignments of commercial and fancy stationery of all sorts, including account books of all sizes, made of handmade and machine-made paper, by steamers recently arrived, and which he is disposing of at moderate prices. He has been long in the trade, and presumes he has always afforded every satisfaction to the numerous merchants here who have constantly favored him with orders. Mofussil orders accompanied with remittances shall be promptly attended to.

CALCUTTA }
The 18th August 1876. }

THEISTIC BOOKS,

FOR SALE.

URDU.

Rahm Hakiki	Rs.	0	3	0
Nizam Kamil	...	0	3	0
Kusaful Ilhan	...	0	8	0
Kholasa, al Asool Brahma Dharm ...	...	0	1	0
Daily Upasana	...	0	1	0
Dharm Anosandhan	...	0	4	0

HINDI.

Upasana Puddhati	Rs.	0	1	0
Bonal Putrika or Hymn book	...	0	1	0
Tut Bodh	...	0	8	0
Upanashid Sar	...	0	8	0
Dhurm Dipika	...	0	0	6
Vedant Sar	...	1	0	0
Prosonno ottor	...	0	8	0

(BRAUM DHARM)

Bojan Bichar	...	0	4	0

ENGLISH.

Claims of so called Revealed Religion	Rs.	0	3	0
New Life	...	0	0	6
Higher and Lower Virtue ...	...	0	1	0

Apply to the Secretary,
BRAHMO SOMAJ OF THE PUNJAB,
Lahore.

CALCUTTA

106, Bowbazar Street.

DR. H. C. SARMA'S

MEDICINE FOR DEBILITY

(NERVOUS.)

HAIR PRESERVER.

Copy of Letter received from Raja Chundernath Roy Bahadoor of Nattore:

Wellesley Street, No. 18, Mott's Lane. 29th March 1874.

MY DEAR HURRISH BABU,—I shall thank you to send me another phial of your *"Excellent Hair Restorer."* In fact it has done me a great benefit and I should like to have more of it. It has disabused me (young as I am) of old age.

Your's Sincerely
C. N. of *Nattore*

MEDICINE FOR BALDNESS.

Will certainly cure baldness if applied on the bald portion, night & morning, according to directions given in the adjoining direction paper.

Price per two ounce phial ...	Rs.	1 0 0
Postage &c.	„	0 6 0

HEEM-SAGAR OIL.

The best remedy for Headache arising from overstudy, intellectual occupation, overthinking, mental anxiety and weakness, as well as heat of head from living in hot places.

It cools the head and produces very agreeable sensation. Removes dandriff as well as all other impurities from the head. Promotes the strength and growth of the hair and prevents its premature falling-off.

Price per 4 ounce phial ...	Rs.	1 0 0
Postage &c.	„	0 10 0

MEDICINE FOR LEPROSY.

Price with Postage &c. ...	Rs.	5 0 0

OIL FOR LEPROSY.

And Inveterate Skin Diseases.

Price per 8 ounce phial ...	Rs.	2 0 0
Postage &c.	„	0 12 0

S. C. GUPTA'S

DIARRHEA PILLS.

SEVERAL years of experience in private practice have proved these pills to be most efficacious in obstinate cases of Non-inflammatory, Infantile, Choleric, Chronic and all sorts of Diarrhea and in all cases of Indigestion, Dyspepsia, Flatulence caused by disturbance of the digestive function.

Sold in Boxes containing 12 pills with full directions for use :—

Price ... ... Rs. 1 0 per box
„ with postage ... „ 1 4 „

To be had of DURGA DASS GUPTA, care of the Manager, Indian Mirror, Calcutta.

R. K. GHOSH'S

HOMŒOPATHIC DISPENSARY,

No. 1, *Gour Mohun Mukerjee's Street, Simla.*

CALCUTTA.

HOMŒOPATHIC Medicine; Medicine chests of sizes,—containing medicine in tube phials; Homœopathic Books, tracts and pamphlets (English and Bengali); Dr. Rubini's "Saturated spirits of Camphor,"—(the best preventive and cure for cholera where medical aid is not available); and other Homœopathic requisites are sold here at a moderate price. Terms cash. Mofussil orders are promptly executed.

R. K. GHOSH,
Homœopathic Practitioner,
Manager.

CHUNDER & BROTHERS.

25½ & 112, RADHA BAZAR,

STATIONERY in all its varieties.
PRINTING PRESSES, Inks & Materials.
LITHOGRAPHIC PRESS & Materials.
BOOK BINDING Materials &c.

PRIZE MEDALLISTS

For Excellency of Workmanship.

J. M. EDMOND & CO.,

27—28, BENTINCK STREET,

ESTABLISHED 1833.

Cabinet Makers, Upholsterers,

AND

Billiard Table Manufacturers.

Houses completely furnished. Furniture designed and made to order.

ESTIMATES given for all kinds of Carpentering, Painting, Polishing, Gilding, and General Repairs; Marble Polished, Moulded, and Cleaned; Picture Frames made.

J. M. EDMOND & Co., in soliciting a continuance of public patronage, beg to say they have ready for sale specimens of Ebonized and Gold Oxford style of Fancy Chairs, and are prepared to execute orders for other Furniture in the same style.

J. M. EDMOND & Co.'s New Show-Room is now replete with New Heraldic Style of Dining-room Chairs, and Rustic Chairs, Telescopic Dining Tables, with Patent Table Expanders, and a variety of finished Furniture.—Orders solicited.

BURN & CO.

RANEEGUNGE Fire bricks are the best Fire Bricks known;—superior to Ramsay's,
9 Rs. per 100.
Fire clay, 30 Rs. per Ton.
Glazed Stone ware, Drainage pipes of all sizes.

BURN & Co.,
7, Hastings Street, Calcutta.

ARLINGTON & CO.,

3 B. DALHOUSIE SQUARE, CALCUTTA.

THE 'PATENT PERPETUAL FOUNTAIN,'

TABLE EPERGNE OR CENTRE PIECE,

FOR SCENT OR FOR PUREWATER.

In Richly Electro-Silvered Ware. [*One of the Greatest Novelties of the day.*]

Cash Price Rs. 175.

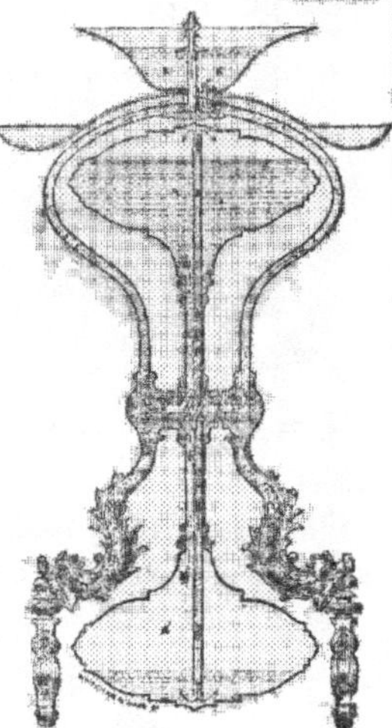

N. B.—The annexed drawing is not a correct representation of the Plated Table Fountains which A. & Co. have for sale. The drawing is only given to show the internal arrangements of the Apparatus, and attention is invited to the following description :—

OBSERVE.—A, A1, are two cisterns or reservoirs, which are connected together by pipes or tubes B, B1, C, C1, mounted on a hollow axis of motion D, surrounding a fixed conical plug E, having suitable passages F, G, H, therein communicating with the pipes or tubes B, B1, C, C1, and I, and with the jet pipe J.

To put the fountain in operation water is poured into the dish or basin K until the lower reservoir is filled and the opening 1 is covered. The cisterns or reservoirs A, A1, are then turned on their axis of motion, so as to place the filled cistern or reservoir A at the top, when the water therefrom will flow to a level in the jet pipe J, and the water in the basin or dish K by passing down the pipes or tubes I and B1 into the lower cistern or reservoir A1, rises in such lower cistern or reservoir A1 and forces the air out therefrom through the pipe or tube C1, passage F, and tube B, into the upper parts of the cistern or reservoir A, where it presses upon the surface of the water therein and forces it out therefrom through the tube C, passage H, and jet pipe J, until all the water in the upper cistern or reservoir A has passed through the jet pipe J and into the lower cistern or reservoir A1 by the pipe I, passage G, and pipe B1, when by turning the cistern or reservoirs A, A1, on their axis of motion until the cistern or reservoir A1 is at the top, the action of the fountain will be continued; the pipes or tubes B, C1, which had previously been air passages now becoming water passages, and the pipes or tubes B1, C, now becoming air passages which had previously served for the passage of water. By these improvements the necessity for alternately filling and emptying the cisterns or reservoirs A, A1, is obviated.

Printed and published by M. M. BUKSHI, at the INDIAN MIRROR PRESS, No. 6, College Square, for the Proprietors.

The Indian Mirror.

SUNDAY EDITION.

VOL. XV.] CALCUTTA, SUNDAY, DECEMBER 10, 1876. { REGISTERED AT THE GENERAL POST OFFICE. } [NO. 292

CONTENTS.

NOTICE.

All letters and communications relating to the literary department of the Paper should be addressed to the Editor. All other letters should be addressed to the Manager, to whom all remittances should be made payable.

Subscribers will be good enough to bring to the notice of the Manager any delay or irregularity in the delivery of the Paper.

Editorial Notes.

WE are glad to inform our Brahmo readers that Babu Jadu Money Ghose, a young Zemindar of Orissa, has presented the sum of Rs. 18,500 to the Brahmo Mission Fund, to be held as trust for the benefit of our Missionaries. The conditions of the trust are to be determined by a Committee to be appointed by the doner.

THE Brahma Mandir has not undergone repairs for a long time, and must soon go into the hands of the engineer. About a thousand rupees will, we believe, be needed to complete the necessary repairs. It is to be hoped that the amount required will be realized in time, so that the Mandir may be ready before the next anniversary, which comes off on the 23rd proximo.

IT is seriously stated that the Budhists of Japan are going to send a Missionary expedition to England for the purpose of opposing Christianity. Well, if the Missionaries going to be sent, are educated men, and really earnest, we can promise they will not be without success. The spirit of Budhism which means the absolute negation of worldliness in every form, appears to be much needed among a "highly civilized," ease-loving, and shop-keeping population like the English of the present day.

WE have great pleasure in publishing the letter of a friend who is studying at Leipzig on the subject of the progress of Brahmo Somaj movement in Germany. He is a young Bengali gentleman of considerable promise, and has been connected with the Brahmo Somaj sufficiently long to be able to represent its spirit and principles. He was one of the party of Hindu gentlemen who with our missionary, visited parts of Germany in 1874 and attended some meetings of the Protestanten Varien in Wiesbaden.

THERE does not seem to be much religious rivalry in South Australia at any rate. In Adelaide, we are told by the *Christian Life*, there are many churches, and handsome structures they are, all the different sects are on an equal footing, there being no Established Church, but all self-supporting. There seems to be very little dissatisfaction or jealousy among them. They all use the same cemetry, and seem to agree to differ in questions of doctrine. The Unitarian Church uses the hymn-book compiled by Drs. Martineau, and Sadler. It is attended by some of the heads of Government."

NOBODY will rejoice so heartily as the true Brahmo at the success of the enactment of the Dramatic Performance's Bill. The growing obscenity of our dramatic literature and the consequent deterioration of public morals among our gay youths, demanded an effective check, and we are glad the Legislature by imposing the needful check, has proved a faithful guardian of Native society, and saved unthinking young Bengal, men and—we may add, women!—from the pernicious influence of demoralizing exhibitions. Posterity will doubtless honor the names of Lord Northbrook and Mr. Hobhouse.

THE cold weather has set in, and is advancing. There may be people who from want of sufficient clothing may suffer from those diseases which weak chests, and vigorless systems often catch in the midst of night dews, and cold draughts. To them the following lines from the first volume of the Reminiscences of Mr. Macready may prove of great value:—

> Lord Gwydir recommended me a defence against cold, to which through my long life I have been constantly indebted, and by which, under east winds or in cold weather, I never fail even now to protect myself. This is simply two or three sheets of paper across the chest, buttoned under the waistcoat, forming a cuirass impenetrable by Boreas, Eurus, or any of the malignant gales that drive cough and too often consumption into the lungs of the unwary. This simple breastplate will, on the coldest day without extra upper clothing, diffuse under exercise warmth through the whole frame, and has proved to me one of the most valuable recibes.

A CHRISTIAN Parish lately advertised for a Minister. The qualifications demanded are of an extraordinary nature, though if found, would make the minister a model man:—

> He must possess all the Christian graces, and a few worldly ones; must have such tact and disposition as will enable him to side with all parties in the parish on all points, giving offense to none; should possess a will of his own, but agree with all; must be socially inclined and of dignified manners; affable to all, neither running after the wealthy nor turning his back upon the poor; a man of High-Low Church tendencies preferred; must be willing to preach first-class sermons and do first-class work at second-class compensation, salary should not be so much an object as he desire to be a zealous laborer in the vineyard; should be able to convince all that they are miserable sinners without giving offence; each sermon must be short and complete in itself—full of old-fashioned theology in modern dress—deep, but popular, and free from the eloquence peculiar to newly graduated theologians; should be young enough to be enthusiastic, but possess the judgment of one of ripe years and experience. He only who possesses the above qualifications, need apply.

IN the interests of morality and civilization may we ask those of our townsmen who have waxed so unnecessarily warm in the cause of that man Nobin, to beware how they encourage his example by lavishing money and sympathy upon him when he has received more than his due. It must not be forgotten that he murdered his unfortunate wife, and thus committed a grave and cowardly crime. There was provocation for it no doubt, but we think more sympathy is felt for that miserable girl than for her violent husband. And now that she is dead that sympathy is diverted from her to him. The strong indignation felt against the Mohunt of Tarakessur, has also operated to intensify that sympathy. It has spent itself in bringing back Nobin from the Andamans, and if certain newspapers agitate still to procure him with funds and make a professional beggar of him, they will not only do him incalculated harm but degrade the social and moral sympathies of the community at large.

WE are inclined to question the wisdom of the reluctance which both our rulers and our leading men have evinced to hold a public meeting on behalf of the sufferers by the cyclone in East Bengal. The necessity of large public subscriptions has already become apparent, as is proved not only by the urgent appeals that have come from the afflicted districts, but also by the fact that Maharani Sarnamayi, Nawab Abdul Gunny and others have been asked by the authorities to contribute. Money is urgently needed. The formality of a public meeting and the pomp of speechifying may well be avoided; but we beg the leaders of the Native community will promptly open a subscription list, headed by those who have already so generously contributed, and invite public subscriptions. This at least ought to be done, and quickly too. The Indian Reform Association have already sent a small quantity of medicines to Chittagong for the relief of cholera patients. Many might be saved if enough money were forthcoming. We would gladly undertake to send money or medicine to the proper quarter, if required.

A WIDE difference of views in the ministers in certain liberal churches in England, does not indicate a corresponding difference in the views of the congregations that attend those churches. Now for instance, what can be wider than the difference of views between Mr. Martineau and Mr. Moncure Conway? The latter is a Theist of the most radical type, and the former is a Unitarian of somewhat conservative tendencies. And still we hear that since Mr. Martineau's retirement from his Church many of his congregation have left the Portland-street chapel and joined Mr. Conway's congregation at Finsbury. Among those who have left, we find the name of the Professor Tyndal. Remembering the somewhat severe conflicts which Mr. Martineau has had with the celebrated scientist on his Belfast oration, we wonder that Professor Tyndal has been a regular attendant at the Portland-street Unitarian Church. Professor Tyndal, we believe, married Lord Cland Hamilton's daughter at one of the Established Churches. So the learned Professor is the member of a Unitarian congregation, attends a Theistic Service, has married according to High Church rites and believes in the religious doctrines of not one among the three.

IF the intensity of sympathy felt for Turkey under existing circumstances in different parts of India by the Mahomedan community, be estimated by its money value, Hyderabad, which contributes Rs. 50,000 to the Turkish funds, is much more devoted to the Sultan than the rest of the country. Next to that is the devotedness of the Punjab which contributes Rs. 32,000. Bombay ranks third giving two thousand less. In Calcutta not more than Rs. 13,000 could be raised, and Madras is even much worse giving 8000 Rs. only. The fact of such a large sum of money being collected in the Punjab, which is by no means very rich and seldom contributes anything worth mention on other occasions, shows how very strong and eager the element of real orthodox Mahomedanism is in that important province. The money which Bombay gives, is not so significant, as in the first place Bombay is liberal whenever she has to give to any cause, and secondly because there are wealthy Mahomedan foreigners constantly living in that city. The slender contribution of Calcutta, demonstrates the lip-loyalty in which some of our Mahomedan fellow-townsmen think it fit to indulge. Mahomedanism is not a social and political *reality* in our city. In the Punjab, and partly in Bombay also, it is not only a reality, but one of a somewhat formidable kind on occasions.

THE IMPERIAL ASSEMBLAGE, —A PARALLEL.

IT will interest the promoters of the Imperial Assemblage at Delhi to learn that three thousand years ago a similar Assemblage for a similar purpose was held in the neighbourhood of that city. The British Government is only trying to reproduce in a modern and European form what took place in ancient India in a purely Oriental style. The parallelism is most striking. The pious king Yudhisthira, so says the Mahabharata, the mightiest and holiest of kings, conceived the project of attaining the rank and wielding the sceptre of an Emperor over all India, and of solemnizing his installation at an Imperial Assembly of feudatory princes. With the aid of his valiant brothers, especially the redoubtable Bhima, Rajah Yudhisthira established his power and sovereignty, after vanquishing their most formidable foe Jarasandha. North, south, east and west his supremacy was acknowledged, and kings and princes were reduced to the position of tributary chiefs, paying tribute to the paramount power. The whole country being thus subdued, and his victorious brothers having returned, Rajah Yudhisthira made fitting preparations for the Rajsuya Yagna. Letters of invitation were issued and emissaries sent to all the princes and nobles, requesting their presence at the grand Assemblage which was to take place at Indraprastha. Among the illustrious guests were the Maharajah of Cashmere, the Chief of Sind, the King of Ceylon, several hill chiefs, the kings of the Malabar Coast, the Ruler of Burmah with 'Mletcha' retinue, the King of Bengal and the chiefs of Central and Southern India. To each chief was allotted a garden-house, "with tanks, trees and creepers," well-furnished and handsomely decorated, as his residence, in which there were abundant supplies of suitable provisions, "costly vestments, embroidered carpets and various fragrant scents." These palatial garden-houses enhanced the beauty of the central pavilion, which measured ten thousand cubits square, and was most splendidly decorated, so as to surpass in grandeur even the Devasabha in heaven. Able councillors and efficient officers were placed in charge of the different departments, and entrusted with distinct duties and responsibilities. There was Aswathama who had to look after the Brahmins; Sanjay attended to the wants of the kings and chiefs; Vishma and Dronacharjya as general directors, saw that everything was done in "due time and proper style;" Kripacharjya had charge of gold and jewels; the pious Bidur controlled the department of expenditure; Duryodhan was told off to receive Nazars; while the department of daily supply of refreshments was entrusted to Dushasan. All the guests were received with becoming honor by Yudisthira himself, and on the appointed day, in the presence of the assembled kings and nobles, the Rishis performed the installation ceremony according to the injunctions of the Vedas; and after the prescribed ablutions King Yudhisthira was proclaimed EMPEROR. Of this grand Imperial Assemblage the great author of the Mahabharata says:—"It is beyond the power of man to tell how many attended. Who can estimate the amount of treasure given away? Suffice it to say such Yagna was never before performed on earth." There is only one more point connected with this Assemblage which deserves notice. After advising the Emperor Yudhisthira to perform the Rajsuya Yagna, Devarshi Narada warned him that the measure was, according to popular tradition, fraught with danger. The least impropriety was known to cause the most disastrous revolutions on earth, and at the very commencement of the ceremony the warrior races were often found to kindle the flame of war.

INCONSISTENT PIETY.

IT is a blessed thing to hear a good man pray. When that prayer is warm, and tender, and deep, and real, the blessedness is correspondingly great. The precepts and prayers of pious men are so attractive that hundreds come from the distance of many miles to hear them, and profit by them. When they hear, they go away. There may be one or two who want to do something more than merely to listen. They want to know, and be instructed by the life of the minister. Good prayer makes an impression, but life models life. But how few have lives to show! There are not many who can offer true and heart-stirring prayers, but there are very few indeed who can model and change our lives by the example of what they do in every sphere of duty. Like learning, like power, piety also is often inconsistent. Let us all be fully assured that men may possess some very high rare spiritual gifts, and secure thereby the affection and admiration of their fellow-beings, but there may still lie within the depths of their character certain ingrained and constitutional vices uneradicated, and really difficult to root out. One may be careless of speech, another hasty in judgment, a third inactive and idle in habits, a fourth incorrect and impure in thoughts and magiaations, a fifth may be unsympathetic and somewhat selfish, a sixth may be avaricious, and full of secret conceit. These vices may not often come out to the surface of existence, so as to be easily noticeable; but there are nevertheless at the bottom of character influencing motives, creating difficulties and vexations, and arresting the genuine progress of the soul. A pious man, who is at the same time faultless in every department of his private life, is most difficult to find out. The world is content if in cojunction with devout precepts and prayers there is found a number of marketable virtues which bear the impress of local and conventional approbation. The people who come to hear, do not, and care not to look deeper. If Brahmo ministers and missionaries desire to be satisfied with this conventional standard, they may congratulate themselves on their present progress. But if they fear the eye of God and the accusing voice of conscience, they must be guided by other rules. We must secure as much as possible the uniformity of progress in religious life, and make our piety consistent with all we do, and all we think. A trained and disciplined religious man will display much less of these incoherencies than one who is only led by wild and unregulated impulses both good and bad. Natural impulses of piety are very beneficial and healthy no doubt, but they almost invariably co-exist with natural inclinations towards evil personal as well as heriditary, social as well as circumstancial. To root these out has been the endeavour of every religious soul, because unless they are rooted out we are not safe, and may any day bring disgrace upon our faith. Should we not with this view make a table as it were of our private and accustomed sins, such as have run parallel to our life in all stages of our moral and spiritual development, and take steady measures with the help of good men to cure them altogether? We talked of repentance last week, and how will such inward sorrow be possible unless we are clearly convinced, and stand self-condemned for our misdeeds?" There are pious men in our midst, as in the midst of every religious sect, but the number of those who possess consistent and all-sided piety, is exceedingly small. That we may have a larger number of consistently pious men, and thus secure a real basis of strength and progress for all, let our sins be found out, tabulated, and daily corrected with the help and grace of Heaven, and then with the help and affection of godly men.

THE BRAHMO SOMAJ IN GERMANY.

LEIPZIG NOV., 6TH 1876.

SIR,—It is doubtless known to most of your readears that in spite of the formidable hinderauce of language, the Brahmo Somaj movement in India has not failed to create a warm interest in Germany. If I have rightly watched the signs of the times, it appears to me that notwithstanding the fashionable atheism and materialism of the day, religious questions were never watched with greater interest, or discussed with more genuine enthusiasm than at present. The verdict of scientific discoveries and rational criticism—the conclusions of the leaders of science and speculative philosophy on "the problem of problems" as Huxley characterises religious questions, are seized with an amount of avidity equal, if not greater than that exhibited by the generation immediately preceding Martin Luther. Side by side with the church of traditional dogmas and antiquated superstitutions, there is already a growing class of dogmatic atheists and materialists who, unlike the true men of science who are so modest and reticent, hope to bring about the salvation of mankind by their crude hypotheses and half-formed theories. But there is another class who feel the need of real religiou so greatly—who, perfectly prepared to alter the *objective shadow* which Science and Philosophy might dissipate, nevertheless find the *subjective reality* so deeply grounded in themselves, that they lend their support neither to the one nor to the other. Hence their attitude is solitary. Hence they are misunderstood. Hence they cry as it were in the wilderness. Yet they, too, are preparing the way of the Lord. They, too, are anticipating the New Gospel that shall gladden the hearts of, and bring salvation to, mankind. I have been favored with the personal acquaintance of a few such men and the intense interest they express in every thing concerning the Brahmo Somaj, inclines me to think that they probably find in the same at least a partial approach to that harmony which they so eagerly long for. I have been repeatedly asked to give an account of the past history and the present movements of the Brahmo Somaj, and I have told them all that I know. But owing to the unfortunate circumstanse of having left most of my Brahmic books behind when I left for Europe, I have not been able to satisfy them as I could desire. It pained me to know how very little they knew of Ram Mohan Roy, and Devendra Nath Tagore, not to say of Akhaya Kumar Datta, and Raj Narain Bose—men to whom we owe much, and who could consequently never be passed over in silence without base ingratitude. I have given them all the Brahmic books I have had in my possession, among others a copy of the "True Faith" which was very kindly lent me by a Brahmo friend then in England. The "True Faith" has appeared in a German dress in the "Protestantesche Kerchenzeitung"—and I subjoin a translation of the short preface with which the translator—Dr. Caro of Chemintz—announced his theme on the 17th June last:—

"The remarkable movement of the Brahmo Somaj deserves to be kept before the eyes of the readers of this 'Kirchenzeitung.' It might, therefore, be of interest to read the following tract. It has been characterised to me as originating from Keshub Chunder Sen, and as containing the germ of the Brahmo or theistic faith by Nisi Kanta Chattopadhya (Chatterji)—an enthusiastic young representative of the Brahmo Somaj, at present studying in Leipzig, and to whom I am indebted for its communication. I have endeavoured to make this translation by sticking as faithfully as possible to the original which is written in English, in which certain hardness of expressions could not be avoided, if the characteristic peculiarities were not to be obliterated.

Chemintz. Caro.'

Further, in a leader in the "Protestantenblatt" of Schleswick on "Sabbath-Christians & Workday-Chritians" Dr. Caro spoke of the Brahmo Somaj in the following way. I ought to have subjoined this to the other, for the following appeared a fortnight before, that is to say on June 3rd:—

"Although endeavors to produce this unity between Christanity & Humanity are not, thank God, wanting in these days, yet the grand and remarkable phenomenon in this sphere—characteristic enough—confronts us not on the old Christian soil, but in circles originally outside the pales of Christianity. With this I do not hesitate to count the movement of the Brahmo Somaj of India, which, according to the judgment of Max Muller,—the great scholar on India as well as the celebrated teacher of the Comparative Science of Religion, is the greatest religious event in our eventful century. Established in 1830 by the great Brahman Ram Mohun Roy, at present under the leadership of both highly remarkable personages, Babu Keshub Chunder Sen and Babu Protap Chunder Mozumdar, this "Association of God" strives after a religious and moral regeneration of the Hindu people on the ground of a deep inward faith in one God—the Father of all mankind. It desires to be a revival of the old genuine Hindu religion—a purification of the same from every idolatory, but the ideas of this associatien are no other than the constitutional ideas of Christianity—the ideas of a filial relation between God and Man, and of charity, based on the brotherhood of men amongst one another. The adherents of the Brahmo Somaj do not call themselves Christians, perhaps less out of any dread of offence they might thereby give to their countrymen—since martyrdom at any rate they do not flee from—than chiefly for this reason that they cannot make up their minds to accept the dogmas of the old Christian faith. Christ they think very highly of, and they acknowledge candidly and with joy what they owe unto him, and the Bible plays with them a very conspicuous part. Side by side with the holy Scriptures of their own people, as well as those of the Parsis and Mahomedans of those sects in whom they announce the pure faith in one living God. the Bible is the chief fountain of their worship. In the sphere of morality, they work with great zeal and results—all those spheres which we are accustomed to comprehend under the name of "inner mission;" Temperance, popular education, female education &c.; but they have also commenced an assault on theology; they fight against the system of caste, and have already with the help of Englishmen, by the abolition of widow-burning and similar heathen atrocities, by the elevation of matrimonial and family relations (monogamy) and others of the kind, have brought remarkable things to pass. Of special importance it is that all these reformatory movements repose on a solid *religious* foundation, and flow out of the living fountain of *piety*. Whoever takes into consideration all circumstances—the earnest and vigorous moral strivings, the purity of religious conceptions, the inwardness of religious life which announces itself in the Brahmo Somaj, he must confess. Here is genuine Christianity, whose want of the Christian name and the undogmatic work-day dress, certainly do not tend to its prejudice, as long as it preserves itself in a living connection with the original Christianity—and that this will happen, can be expected with certainty. Only a short time ago has the Brahmo Somaj placed itself again in connection with strivings of spiritual relationship on the Christian soil, and through the despatch of three of their representatives (amongst them to wit: Mr. Mozumdar) on the Protestant-Day in Wiesbaden, has afforded us the opportunity of seeing it in person and countenance. The original freshness and childlikeness, the deep religious seriousness, the noble modest behaviour, the warm interest in philosophical questions possessed by these brown sons of Asia affect us quite beneficially, and a contact with them strongly invigorates the hope that the great World-Whitsuntide shall nevertheless once dawn, when the Father of our Lord Jesus Christ shall be worshipped in all tongues. Then, however, there shall be no Sabbath-Christians but simple work-day Christians who in the worship of God in spirit and in truth, shall celebrate the eternal Sabbath of pure Humanity."

The above will give a partial idea of the interest which the Brahmo Somaj has created and the expectations that are cherished about it by its German friends. How shall we keep up the former and realize the latter? No doubt, by opening our ears to all that Science and Philosophy have to say, while laying the utmost importance on the cultivation of a deep spiritual life. Religion is *living* and *knowing*. For my part, the materialism I am most afraid of, is not the so-called *materialism of philosophy* but the *materialisation of life* which is the foe that the Brahmo Somaj must swear to annihilate. I have sometimes met with men who call themselves materialists but who were nevertheless highly spiritual in all their longings and aspirations, while "pious" men on the other hand who were gross materialists in life. While the latter were chuckling over their secure booty of a whole stock of absolute truths on religion and morality, more than sufficient to ensure their temporary as well as eternal blessedness, and consequently needing no further effort of the brain to know more Truth or more Justice, the former on the other hand were constantly doubting and perhaps sometimes despairing, yet never ceasing to know more—to inquire more in order that they might perchance at last find a resting place for their souls. We have nothing to be afraid of in Science and Philosophy. They shall only serve to make us more spiritual—more religious.

Devotional

By seeing Thee thy true devotees have become pure. We have seen Thee, but we have not yet become pure. That vivid perception of Thy Holy face which instantly cleanseth the heart and induceth holiness do Thou vouchsafe unto me, Kind God. In the sweetness of Thy benign countenance I have found hope and comfort. Now in the light of Thy holy countenance may I find purity and righteousness.

God, at thy feet I lie prostrate as a debtor, encumbered with liabilities altogether beyond my power to redeem. Thou hast showered on me mercies untold and undeserved, and I feel with all my sins and iniquities that I can never make a return for such unceasing favors. Enchain me then as the hopeless debtor deserves to be enchained for having failed to meet his debts, and hold me a captive in the fetters of Thy love.

The Brahmo Somaj

With very sincere regret we have to announce the death of our Brahmo brother Arasappa of Mangalore who may be said in one manner to be the source of our missionary expedition to that remote part of the country in 1865, and our subsequent missionary operations there. He was a remarkable man in his way. Commencing life as the member of the despised Billawar community of South Canara, uneducated, and unassisted, he rose steadily by his singular energy and intelligence both in means and influence. He outgrew the strange superstitions and practices of his fellow-Billawars, wanted to exalt, and enlighten them, and remove the ban of social disability under which they were placed by the Brahmins. He invited our missionaries to Mangalore, and treated them in a spirit of brotherliness and goodness truly noble. He imbibed most readily the instructions he received, gave up time-honored usages in his family, established daily worship in his household, and, we are told, gave up the toddy-contract of the Abkari Department whereby he made his fortune. The Brahmo Somaj at Mangalore uniformly received his support, and was upheld by his liberality, and now that he is removed, will meet with unexpected trials. As we have received the intelligence of his death by telegram, we are yet unable to give the exact date of his death, and the nature of his disease. But he has passed away, and may his spirit find rest and joy.

Babu Durga Mohun Dass of this city made many charitable gifts on the occasion of the Shradh ceremony of his late wife.

Babu Durga Das Roy, a Professor of the Dacca Medical School, whose wife recently died, has endowed 200 Rs., the interest of which is to be spent on account of the Brahmo Mission Fund of Dacca and Calcutta.

A Brahmo marriage was celebrated last night in a village, called Dhakuria near Ballygunge. The bridegroom, Koylash Chunder Bannerji, is a young apothecary of Dacca, and the bride Proo Bala Chowdry, is a pupil of the Native Ladies' Normal School. We wish every happiness and prosperity to the pair. The bridegroom is about twenty-four years old, and the bride about fifteen.

Latest News

—Sir Bartle Frere addressed the Glasgow Chamber of Commerce in support of an International Society for the Exploration of Africa; and a Committee was subsequently formed to assist in carrying out the project.

—The Austrian Government is stated to intend making some additional military preparations.

—Prince Bismarck is still absent from Berlin, but he is actively engaged in public affairs. The various officials connected with the Ministry, have been enjoined to observe the strictest secrecy upon public affairs.

—The Duke of Edinburgh is about to return to Malta, to be present at the expected *accouchement* of the Duchess.

—Mr. H. S. Northcote will act as Private Secretary to the Marquis of Salisbury at Constantinople.

—Public feeling in Hungary is strongly excited against the Russians

—The German newspapers, especially the Liberal portion of the press, regard the action of Russia with suspicion, but support the view of the Government, that unless German interests are directly assailed there is no necessity for interference on its part.

—The Nizam's Government is doing its best to alleviate the present distress in Hyderabad.

—There is a rumour in Mian Mir that the 10th Bengal Lancers have been warned for duty. It is also rumoured that a large force will be concentrated in Cabul in order to give Russia an idea that we are not altogether asleep, and that we too have Servians whom we can influence.

—The brother of the Nawab of Maler Kotla has been added to the Punjab Secretariat as an Attaché, and he contemplates a visit to England in order to complete his education.

—About 20 tents have been taken up at Delhi for the Khan of Khelat and the brother of the Imam of Muscat.

—The Delhi Durbar and the divisional Durbars, says the Lahore paper, are driving the *quasi-Rajahs* to the tender mercies of the money-lenders. Bonds are being written for a *mere consideration*, exorbitant interests are being charged to make up for the unavoidable risk, and the seeds of small causes are being sown broadcast.

—There is a rumour that Sir Henry Davies, the Lieutenant-Governor of the Punjab, after his retirement from the office, intends to pay a visit to Persia.

—On the Municipal Hall at Multan, the following motto shone out: "Right Shall Prevail."

—THERE can be little doubt (says the *Indian Public Opinion)* that Lord Lytton has made up his mind that, there shall be a British Agent in Cabul. Sir Lewis Pelly has been mentioned as sure of the post. If necessary, armed force will be sent to support him.

—RUSSIAN emissaries, it is stated, visit Cabul every year.

—OUR Lahore contemporary re-asserts that he was correct in stating that three secret interviews took place between the Russian Agent and the Amir of Cabul.

—THE Kohat Affridis are reported to be turbulent and manifest hostile demonstrations.

—A BRANCH railway is to be constructed forthwith to Khelat.

—APPLICATIONS for visitors' tents at Delhi have been very numerous, and people wishing to go to Delhi, should lose no time in securing ground for their tents, for every available site is being rapidly taken up.

—BABU ISHAN CHUNDER BASU is appointed Assistant to the Accountant-General, Punjab.

—MAJOR E. C. IMPEY is posted as Political Agent, Meywar.

Calcutta.

CAPTAIN LIDDELL, Adie-de-Camp to the Viceroy, comes down from Delhi to Calcutta on the 13th instant, to receive His Grace the Duke of Buckingham on his arrival from Madras, and to attend on him during his journey to Delhi.

The Honorable the President in Council is pleased to notify that, upon condition that arrangements are made for the transaction of all urgent business, the Public Offices in Calcutta under the Government of India, shall be closed for public business from Monday, the 25th day of December 1876, to Thursday, the 4th day of January 1877, both days inclusive, on account of the Christmas Holidays, New Year's Day and in honor of the assumption by Her Most Gracious Majesty the Queen of the title of Empress of India.

THE Honorable Romesh Chunder Mitter, B. L., Acting Judge of the High Court, has obtained privilege leave for two months, with effect from the first instant.

THE Bank of Bengal and Public Debt Office will be closed on Monday, Tuesday, Wednesday, and Saturday, the 25th, 26th, 27th, and 30th December, and on Monday and Tuesday, the 1st and 2nd January next. The Calcutta Currency Office will be also closed for as many days.

MR. T. T. COOPER is to be an Attache in the Foreign Department, as a temporary arrangement, from the date on which he may report his arrival at Delhi.

MR. J. F. OGILVY, of the firm of Messrs. Gillanders, Arbuthnot and Company, is appointed Sheriff of Calcutta for the next year. He is an excellent gentleman.

MR. MARSHALL WOOD, the sculptor, has arrived in Calcutta *en route* to the Delhi Assemblage.

At the Chester Diocesan Synod the Bishop of the diocese presented a valedictory address from the clergy of the Archdeaconry of Chester to the Ven. Archdeacon Johnson, Bishop-designate of Calcutta. The *Bishop* said the loss of Archdeacon Johnson would be deeply felt all over the diocese, in the work of which he had been most active. He (the Bishop) knew the great aid which Archdeacon Johnson had rendered to the cause of religious education, his invaluable assistance to all the diocesan institutions, and the valuable help he had rendered to all who had asked his advice. While, however, the diocese sustained a great loss, India would experience a great gain. (Cheers.) A place more important could hardly be imagined in the Church of Christ. (Cheers.)

Archdeacon Johnson, who spoke with deep feeling, said he could not sufficiently thank the Bishop for the generous remarks he had made, or his reverned brethren for the kindness they had shown him since, some sixteen years ago, he came into the diocese. The present was a most anxious time, not only for himself, but for the part of the Church of Christ to which he was going. The present appointment must be looked upon as an experiment, and it was his earnest prayer that he might not hinder the advancement of Christ's kingdom upon earth. The prospects of work in India were most encouraging. On the death of his predecessor, it seemed as if the heart of India had risen to the determination that no other Bishop who should be appointed, should ever again be sacrificed in the attempt to perform work which it was absolutely impossible for one man to accomplish; and he thought it should be known that Lord Northbrook, Lord Lawrence, Sir Bartle Frere, and our Indian Secretary, Lord Salisbury, supported that determination, and had given him an assurance that he should not leave England without a good hope, that the burden should be lightened from his shoulders. (Cheers).

Miscellaneous.

AJUDHIA.

THE full moon of November brings tens of thousands of enthusiastic Hindus to "Ajudhia the blessed" a city lying "on pleasant Sarju's fertile side," whose praises were rapturously sung by Valmiki ages ago. The city, situated on the very bank of the historic river which rivals the Ganges in its width and shifting channel, the birthplace of Ram Chandra crowded with temples and rich in ruins, draws hosts of people every *mela* time from eastern Oudh and the adjoining districts of the North-West Provinces.

Ajudhia is crowded with temples. There are 200 separate sacred places in and about it, chiefly temples. At Lacshman Ghat where the river makes a graceful curve and where the soil seems very firm and unyielding, there are long rows of monasteries and temples reminding one as he walks between them of some crowded corners of London or New York where business blocks rise thick and t ll. Here are temples built by the Rajahs of Balrampore, Gonda, Busti, Rewah, by various Ranis, and by Pundits and wealthy Hindus of Fyzabad, Gorackpore, Jounpore, Lucknow, Bundelkund, and other places. Among the notable places are the "Janam Asthan" (where Ram Chandra is said to have been born), upon which the Emperor Baber built the mosque which still bears his name, A. D. 1528; and where in 1855 a fierce battle took place between the Hindus and Mahomedans in which the former were victorious and 75 of the latter were slain; the "Sargadwar" (the gate through which Ram Chandra passed into paradise, the people say—possibly the spot where his body was burned) over which Aurangzebe about 1658 built a mosque, is now in ruins;

WE hear that Dean Stanley's sermon on "Spiritual Religion" is about to be reprinted for large circulation. The text was "God is Spirit." The following is a summary:—"Any worship, even the plainest becomes unspiritual of which we have lost the meaning, and which does not tend to make us better and wiser—any worship, even the most elaborate, is spiritual if it help us to do our duty, to be more loving to man and more devoted to God. Keep your minds open as wide as you can, said a French nobleman to his children, 'but I entreat you keep your hearts open also.' 'Be as broad as the charity of Almighty God,' was the last speech of Norman Macleod, 'but be as narrow as His righteousness.' That is true religion of the spirit. And this value of the spiritual aspect of religion is yet more visible in proportion as we apply it to the history of the human race—of the human being. It is sometimes the custom to draw out schemes of various schools, or churches, or parties, and maintain that these exhaust all ages and tendencies of Christianity. But there is one element which in all such schemes or schools is often omitted and often despised, which nevertheless is the most important of all. It is the school which you can find in all the schools, the tendency which you can find happily running across all tendencies, those who believe in the religion of the Spirit and who are, as the German poet sang, true knights and soldiers of the Holy Ghost. There has never failed altogether a succession of those good men who have seen the spirit beneath the letter, the meaning beneath the form, the sense beneath the nonsense, the moral beyond the material; and these though little regarded in the strife of tongues, have been the true backbone of Christendom, the true soul of the Church and its doctrines."

Advertisements

CALCUTTA

106, Bowbazar Street.

DR. H. C. SARMA'S

MEDICINE FOR DEBILITY

(NERVOUS.)

HAIR PRESERVER.

Copy of Letter received from Rajah Chundernath Roy Bahadur of Nattore.

Wellesley Street, No. 18, Mott's Lane, 29th March 1874.

MY DEAR HURRISH BABU,—

I shall thank you to send me another phial of your "*Excellent Hair Restorer.*" In fact it has done me a great benefit, and I should like to have more of it. It has disabused me (young as I am) of old age.

Yours Sincerely

C. N. of *Nattore*

MEDICINE FOR BALDNESS.

Will certainly cure baldness if applied on the bald portion, night & morning, according to directions given in the adjoining direction paper.

Price per two ounce phial Re. 1 0 0
Postage &c. ... ... „ 0 6 0

HEEM-SAGAR OIL.

The best remedy for Headache arising from overstuday, intellectual occupation, over-thinking, mental anxiety and weakness, as well as heat of head from living in hot places.

It cools the head and produces very agreeable sensation. Removes dandruff as well as all other impurities from the head. Promotes the strength and growth of the hair and prevents its premature falling-off.

Price per 4 ounce phial Re. 1 0 0
Postage &c. ... ... „ 0 10 0

MEDICINE FOR LEPROSY.

Price with Postage &c ... Rs. 5 0 0

OIL FOR LEPROSY.

And Inveterate Skin Diseases.

Price per 8 ounce phial Rs. 2 0 0
Postage &c. ... ... „ 0 12 0

FOR SALE.

VALUABLE LANDED PROPERTY.

THE desirable Premises No. 101, Taltala Lane, Calcutta. Price Rs. 5,000.

AND

A very elegant Family Residence, with 15 BIGAH *Lukhiraj* Gardens, bordering River Hooghly, Situate in JUGGUDDUL, lying directly *East* of CHANDERNAGORE, and being approachable by *boat* or *road* from *Shamnuggur* Station, EASTERN BENGAL RAILWAY. Price Rs. 3,000.

Apply to BABU RADHA GOBIND CHATTERJEE at the above places.

NOTICE.

Infallible Specifics for Asthma, Consumption, Colic, Gonorrhea, Spermatorrhea and Dysentery.

Used in all cases of Asthma, preceded by headache or sleepiness, or by various digestive or other disturbances, or without any warning.

Sold in boxes containing 7 pills (for one week only) with full directions for use :—

Price per box ... ... Rs. 2 0
„ with postage ditto 2 4

For further particulars, Apply to

WOOPENDRA NATH PAL,
Care of the Manager, *Indian Mirror*.
CALCUTTA.

BURN & CO.

RANEEGUNGE Fire bricks are the best Fire Bricks known ;—superior to Ramsay's.

9 Rs. per 100.

Fire clay, 40 Rs. per Ton.

Glazed Stone ware, Drainage pipes of all sizes.

BURN & Co.,
7, Hastings Street, Calcutta.

PRIZE MEDALLISTS

For Excellency of Workmanship.

J. M. EDMOND & CO.,

97—98, BENTINCK STREET,

ESTABLISHED 1823.

Cabinet Makers, Upholsterers,

AND

Billiard Table Manufacturers,

Houses completely furnished. Furniture designed and made to order.

ESTIMATES given for all kinds of Carpentering, Painting, Polishing, Gilding and General Repairs; Marble Polished, Moulded, and Cleaned; Picture Frames made.

J. M. EDMOND & Co., in soliciting a continuance of public patronage, beg to say they have ready for sale specimens of Ebonized and Gold Oxford style of Fancy Chairs, and are prepared to execute orders for other Furniture in the same style.

J. M. EDMOND & Co.'s New Show-Room is now replete with New Heraldic Style of Dining-room Chairs, and Rustic Chairs, Telescopic Dining Tables, with Patent Table Expanders, and a variety of finished Furniture.—Orders solicited.

ESTABLISHED 1833

H. C. GANGOOLY & CO.

STATIONERS, DIESINKERS, ENGRAVERS PRINTERS, LITHOGRAPHERS &c.

24, Mangoe Lane, Calcutta.

Cash prices of the following :—

	Rs.	As.	Rs.
Whatman's Drawing paper double elephant sizes (40×27) each ...	0	7	0
Mathematical Instrument Boxes	2	8 to	16
Color Boxes	0	4 „	5

Drawing Pencils Drawing and Mapping Steel pens and various other requisites in Stationery,

---

ARLINGTON & CO.,

3 B. DALHOUSIE SQUARE, CALCUTTA.

THE 'PATENT PERPETUAL FOUNTAIN,'

TABLE EPERGNE OR CENTRE PIECE,

FOR SCENT OR FOR PUREWATER.

In Richly Electro-Silvered Ware. [*One of the Greatest Novelties of the day.*]

Cash Price Rs. 175.

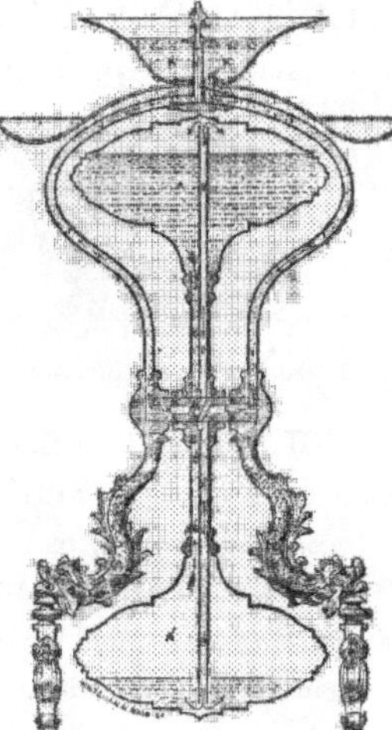

N. B.—The annexed drawing is not a correct representation of the Plated Table Fountains which A. & Co. have for sale. The drawing is only given to show the internal arrangements of the Apparatus, and attention is invited to the following description :—

OBSERVE—A, A1, are two cisterns or reservoirs, which are connected together by pipes or tubes B, B1, C, C1, mounted on a hollow axis of motion D, surrounding a fixed conical plug G, having suitable passages F, G, H, therein communicating with the pipes or tubes B, B1, C, C1, and I, and with the jet pipe J.

To put the fountain in operation water is poured into the dish or basin K until the lower reservoir is filled and the opening II is covered. The cisterns or reservoirs A, A1, are then turned on their axis of motion, so as to place the filled cistern or reservoir A at the top, when the water therefrom will flow to a level with the jet pipe J, and the water in the basin or dish K by passing down the pipes or tubes I and B1 into the lower cistern or reservoir A1, rises in such lower cistern or reservoir A1 and forces the air out therefrom through the pipe or tube C1, passage F, and tube B, into the upper part of the cistern or reservoir A, where it presses upon the surface of the water therein and forces it out therefrom through the tube C, passage H, and jet pipe J, until all the water in the upper cistern or reservoir A has passed through the jet pipe J and into the lower cistern or reservoir A1 by the pipe I, passage G, and pipe B1, when by turning the cistern or reservoirs A, A1, on their axis of motion until the cistern or reservoir A1 is at the top, the action of the fountain will be continued; the pipes or tubes B, C1, which had previously been air passages now becoming water passages, and the pipes or tubes B1, C, now becoming air passages which had previously served for the passage of water. By these improvements the necessity for alternately filling and emptying the cisterns or reservoirs A, A1, is obviated.

Printed and published by M. M. BOSE, at the INDIAN MIRROR PRESS, No. 6 College square, for the Proprietors.

The Indian Mirror.

SUNDAY EDITION.

VOL. XV.] CALCUTTA, SUNDAY, DECEMBER 17, 1876. { REGISTERED AT THE GENERAL POST OFFICE. } [No. 298

CONTENTS.

NOTICE.

All letters and communications relating to the literary department of the Paper should be addressed to the Editor. All other letters should be addressed to the Manager, to whom all remittances should be made payable.

Subscribers will be good enough to bring to the notice of the Manager any delay or irregularity in the delivery of the Paper.

Editorial Note.

JARUSALEM may in a manner be said to be the emporium of religious nationalities. There are about 5,000 Mahomedans, 4,000 Christians, 7,000 Jews. There are 2,000 members of the Greek Church, 900 Roman Catholics, 350 Armenians, besides Syrians, Abyssinians, Copts, and Protestants. It is good to think that in the city where the Prophet of Nazareth preached his world-embracing principles of love, truth, and salvation, so many nations still live and worship in peace, and we hope in good will also.

MR. BRADLAUGH in reviewing the progress of atheism and secularism, for Secularism has a regular propaganda, makes this remark:—"We succeed more with Church people than with others. For in every Dissenter there is some vitality." This is evidence from an unexpected quarter. It matters little to us theologically whether a man is "Church," or Dissenter, and matters equally little, we believe, to Mr. Bradlaugh, but religious vitality makes the whole difference between one man and another And when an enemy to all religion like Mr. Bradlaugh bears favorable testimony on behalf of the Dissenter, let us all agree that he deserves the compliment indeed.

WHEN Christian Missionaries in Calcutta, all of them of the orthodox Trinitarian type, cannot agree in the midst of themselves even in such a matter as a united religious service, it is too much to expect that they should extend the right hand of fellowship to us who are so far apart from them in theological position. Some of the Calcutta missionaries of different denominations determined upon a united religious service at the present season for the benefit of the public. The arrangements, we believe, were made, when at the eleventh hour the ministers of a certain church received an inhibition to join this organization of heretics. Proceedings like these are not calculated to produce much respect in the public mind.

THE Pope has generously, graciously, and in the genuine spirit of the religion he professes, has performed a requiem mass, or divine service for the repose of the souls " of all his enemies who, while living, were the most instrumental in afflicting him and bringing about his spoliation." Among these there are many Protestants and Italian statesmen who have acted in a determined and hostile manner to destroy the influence and sovereignty of the Church of Rome in Italy. Now for outsiders who do not believe in the Mass, or in prayers for the dead, who have suffered little or no real injury at the hands of their enemies, this may be no great matter. But in Roman Catholics who believe the enemies of the Church to be damned, or at least in Purgatory, who believe in the supernatural efficaciousness of their services, especially when solemnized by his holiness the Pope himself, who have suffered a dreadful deminution of power and position in these times, this is really most noble and charitable. We wish Roman Catholics in general to imitate the spirit of the Pope, and write and speak more charitably of such men as Garibaldi, and Prince Bismarck. If they are mercifully inclined towards the dead, why should they show charity and forgiveness to the living ?

PUNDUA must be a wonderful place, and the Mahomedan population there still more wonderful. How the latter could, in the face of the toleration and religious neutrality of the British Government, so long disallow the celebration of Hindu *Pujahs* and festivals, when the Hindus of Pundua are almost as numerous, and somewhat more influential than the Mahomedans, we cannot conjecture. Now when the Hindus have mustered courage enough to have their strange religious disabilities removed by the Magistrate, the Mussulman inhabitants have the effrontery to memorialize the Bengal Government to set aside the orders of the Magistrate in the matter. Of course the memorial could produce only one effect, and Sir Richard Temple rather curtly tells the zealous followers of the Prophet at Pundua that they must be good enough to let the Hindus of that place be religious in their own way, and not object to their festivals and processions. It is striking how in the midst of their loss of influence and position the Mahomedans still continue to retain their religious rigour and intolerance. And we may by this very well form some idea of the peculiar point of view from which the dominant Islamites of Turkey must regard their Christian populations lying powerless and prostrate at their feet. The moral consequences of Mahomedanism are not difficult to draw anywhere.

Is it no part of Lord Lytton's or at least his Councillors' duty to inquire why of all Presidencies and provinces Bengal should be so poorly represented at the Delhi Assemblage ? If there is no deliberate insult involved in the matter, grave injustice has surely been done to the foremost Presidency in India, foremost in intelligence, in loyalty and in public spirit. It cannot be Her Majesty the Queen's intention to draw into the Assemblage only Maharajahs and Rajahs, and make a display of crowned heads and jewellery, on the occasion of her assumption of the title of Empress of India, completely ignoring and throwing into the shade India's true leaders, educated and representative men who really influence the masses and govern Native society by their superior intelligence and patriotic spirit. The head of the Bengali community, Rajah Romanath Tagore, has not been invited. Rajah Jotendro Mohun Tagore and the Hon'ble Kristodas Paul have declined to go, for reasons which demand inquiry. Such scholars and patriots as Dr. Rajendralala Mitra, the Rev. Dr. Bannerji, Pundit Iswara Chandra Vidyasagar and Pundit Taranath Tarka Panchanan ought to have been invited to the Great Rajsuya Yagna of modern times.

A CEREMONY of the Roman Catholic Church is full of the profound sym.

bolism of spiritual life. How much of spiritual life there may yet be in the ceremonies it is difficult for us to say; but the symbolism, when witnessed, cannot fail to awaken in the mind an intense appreciation of the glorious genius which underlies the faith and practices of the Roman Catholic religion. Last week we witnessed a Reception service, at St. Thomas' Church, Middleton Row, with a number of Brahmica ladies. A young lady took the white veil of the novitiate, and the service was performed by His Grace Arch-Bishop Steins. In the precepts uttered on the occasion the principles of conventual life in relation to the freedom of will and deliberation allowed to those who adopt it were clearly explained, and the vows of Poverty, Purity, and Obedience were set forth and elucidated in a very effective manner. The young applicant for religious life seemed to understand her position very well. In fact so far as these principles go, we have little to find fault with, it is their application to life that first creates the difficulty. We believe the time will come when the extremes of religious freedom and faith, obedience and independence, purity and domesticity, poverty and simple enjoyment of life, in a word, when Theism and Roman Catholicism will unite.

THE *Indian Christian Herald* wants to know why we are against the ill-considered movement for raising funds for the pecuniary assistance of that man "Nobin." Our contemporary devotes nearly four of his leading columns to advocate Nobin's claims. Well, we were for Nobin's release because considering the provocation under which he committed the murder, a shorter and more lenient sentence would have quite served the ends of justice. Now that his pardon has been mercifully granted by Government, we think he has received all the consideration due to him. Any additional sympathy would be wrong and sinful. Undeserved sympathy for any man is wrong, for a criminal it is positively degrading. It is one thing to move for the mitigation of a severe sentence which a criminal has received in disproportion to his crime, it is another thing, when that sentence is *already* mitigated, to present him with a purse at the expense of the public, to indite sentimental and laudatory pieces of composition in his favor, and make a popular hero of him. Does not the *Herald* see there is much difference between these two things? The first attempts to promote justice and social purity; the second whitewashes crime, and puts a premium upon its commission.

POWER IN WEAKNESS.

REPENTANCE is an expression of weakness, because it expresses the sense of inward sin. Sin, according to the belief of the Brahmo Somaj, is but a stage of weakness. A confession of that weakness, continued sorrow for it, and an earnest endeavour to get out of it, constitute repentance. Repentance, in whomsoever found, evidences weakness. There is One only who cannot repent, the Almighty and Perfect Being. The highest, holiest, strongest, and wisest of mankind have repented; and the meanest, unholiest, poorest, weakest of mankind have repented. Sorrow seems to be the heritage of the sons of men, because there is weakness in them all. Yet this sorrow is of two kinds. There is the sorrow that heals, and there is the sorrow that weakens and kills. It is exactly the same thing as in the case of suffering. Suffering comes to injure, to weaken, and at last to kill. Suffering means the absence of health, deviation from the normal conditions of life. But again suffering is applied to remedy suffering. The treatment of disease is oftentimes as painful as the disease itself, and sometimes even more painful than the complaint it is meant to cure. In like manner there is a sense of sin and attendant sorrow, which, by constant repetition, tend to prostrate the soul, paralyze its powers of self-reformation, poison its joy, its health, and threaten its utter ruin. The unnatural confessions, thoughts, and sufferings of morbid sinfulness, prey upon the whole health and virtue of the soul diseased, and that which is really not bad in it appears and tends to appear bad; hope is undermined; things which ought to gladden, produce no perceptible influence upon the darkened and desolate spirit, nothing improves, nothing exalts, there is bitterness within and without. Thus from him that hath not is taken away even that which he hath. And we need not be surprised at it. Light cannot be extracted out of darkness, strength cannot come out of weakness. A man who hath committed a foul deed, cannot, by knowing that he hath committed it, get out of the effects of his vileness. On the contrary his vileness multiplies itself.

But there is another kind of sorrow which heals. It is the effect of grace, the gentle air of heaven that blows upon, and thaws the hard coldness of the sinful heart. It is the wound that God's mercy makes upon the soul whose salvation is not far. It is the fire of righteousness burning and purging away the inborn long-gathered impurities within. It is a perpetual striving after a higher plane of existence, not reaching which the soul mourns and is exceedingly cast down. It is the long laborsome struggle of the child to stand and walk, and the repeated failures, and downfalls, and pain that accompany that struggle. Yet this evidence of apparent weakness indicates the sure growth of a secret strength; the pain that exercises and tries the limbs, develops them and stores within them a deep source of future enjoyment and usefulness. The fire that burns in the heart cleanses and enobles the atmosphere within it. The weakness is human, the strength is divine. The pain is the voice of outraged nature that tends to preserve itself through remedial, deterrent, wholesome suffering; the joy is the benediction and reward of Heaven that fills up the vacancy which sacrificed selfishness and worldliness have left behind them. The power that is felt in the midst of weakness then, is the power of faith in the realized and all-sufficient grace of a beneficent Father who is ever near and ready to answer penitent prayer with His own peace, and with His own strength. Let, therefore, the Brahmo give up the mourning that does not bring strength and tranquility with it. Let all unavailing, weakening, deadening sorrow be forsaken. Let all cant phrases of false repentance be eschewed for ever, and yet let each word of confessed sin and sorrow bind up the soul in adamantine resolution and everlasting grace that guards against future fall and cures, and strengthens in the same time.

THE HOGG *CUM* WILSON CASE.

ANY comments on the case just decided between Sir Stuart Hogg and Mr. James Wilson, may not seem to come within the province of the Sunday edition of the *Indian Mirror*. But considering the important questions of public morals and journalistic duty which this interesting case involves, we feel bound to speak on behalf of the Brahmo community. Well, we must in the first place personally congratulate Mr. Wilson on his successful escape from the consequences of the statements for which he was prosecuted by Sir Stuart Hogg, or in other words by the Government of Bengal. And we must congratulate him also on the courage and presence of mind he manifested in conducting his own case, and in fighting it out with the well-trained and well-chosen Counsel for the prosecution. In the second place we must express our regret at the somewhat loose and careless arrangements which characterized the late municipal elections. That some amount of looseness and confusion was inevitable at the first experiment of the kind ever tried in this town, and would be equally inevitable under the same circumstances anywhere else in the world, we are ready to admit. But reflecting on the unhappy influence it exercised upon the minds of the Jury at the late trial, we cannot but regret the confusion. This done, we must distinctly and strongly condemn the verdict as unjust, and unwarrantable under the evidence. Either the charges were defamatory and false, or they were not. If they contained any truth, the "strong disapprobation" of the articles expressed by the Jury was perfectly out of place and order. If they *were* defamatory and false, the motive of Mr. Wilson was not far to seek. He had systematically maligned Sir Stuart

Hogg, and made occasional exhibitions of his bad feeling which, as on the arrival of the Prince of Wales, incurred the condemnation of the whole public, and made his conduct a scandal. He often wrote under the pique of private and personal dissatisfaction, and nowhere was this more prominent, than at his rejection, however regretable, at the late election. Though we highly respect Mr. Wilson's ability and independence, it must be admitted by every impartial newspaper reader that the disposition to insult and injure Sir Stuart Hogg has been manifest in the *Indian Daily News* for a long time. And if this disposition does not count as the absence of good faith, we do not know what does. Under circumstances such as these, Mr. Wilson goes out of the court rejoicing over the wrong and unjust statements he made on the character of a retiring public servant whose career, however high-handed and unpopular at times, has been signalized by unusual energy and success. And Sir Stuart Hogg leaves these shores under the undeserved stigma of unfairness and injustice cast upon him by those who are not worthy of a moment's comparison with him in integrity and worth. There has been a failure of strict justice in this case. Perhaps a defeat now and then may be wholesome to Government, and to officials at large. But a victory like that which Mr. Wilson has gained, is neither conducive to public welfare, nor to public morals. And further more such private animosities and personal motives in the conduct of the Press, will only make it obnoxious to every man of honor, and positively useless to influence the councels of Government.

Provincial

MULTAN.

[FROM OUR OWN CORRESPONDENT.]

MR. NELSON held a special meeting in the Mison School to address the "English speaking Natives." His subject was—"What ye think of the Lord Jesus Christ" "Can there be any doubt about the divinity of Jesus." To enable the audience to arrive at the right conclusion the Revd. gentleman said, "let us examine the witnesses *against* and *for* Jesus, and sum up the case with a view to pass our verdict what we think of Jesus Christ." He said he would bring on each side (*Seven*) witnesses, as this number 7 has been very "prominently mentioned in the Bible." "For instance, God created the world in six days and on the 7th day he ceased." What an idea of God. Whatever may be the worth of such stories to a Hindu mind, they appear to have been concocted on very wrong notions of the Most High. But instead of citing this illustration, which should appear irrational to any mind possessing common sense, it would have been more to the point, had he said that it is said somewhere in the Bible that true magnanimity of soul consists in forgiving one's enemies, not only *seven* times but *seventy* times *seven*. But alas! our instruction and education are so imperfect, and we are so much imposed upon, that when young, our innocent and trusting minds contract a habit of believing in and doing things, which if we were to analyse and ponder upon, would appear revolting to common sense and reason. Whatever may be the worth of some of the stories related in the Bible, and in what light soever they may be regarded by the rational public, to the lay mind, they possess a peculiar charm. But this is a digression. I now return to the "hallowed" number 7. The witness were then called in, in the following order:

Against Jesus.	*For Jesus:*
1 The Pharasis & Scribes of Jerusalem	1 John the Baptist
2 Judas Iscariot	2 } Two disciples of Jesus
3 Pontius Pilate	3 }
4 His (Pilate's) wife	4 Paul
5 Evil Spirits	5 Angels
6 Centurions	6 ———
7 Satan	7 The Almighty God.

and all that is said in the Bible by every one of the above witnesses, was, of course, minutely gone into, and in summing up he asked the audience "what ye think of Jesus." Abruptly the "curtain fell" as it were, and the audience was not allowed time to say "what they thought of Jesus." The reason probably was, that Mr. Nelson had to keep up another appointment in the Cantonments. However, he promised to hold another meeting the next day, which he did. On both the evenings Mr. Nelson entertained the audience with a few choice hymns on the organ.

The Brahmo Somaj

BABU GOUR GOVIND ROY has left Mymensing for Calcutta.

SELECT passages from Hafiz have been translated by our missionary Babu Grish Chunder Sen.

IT is proposed to publish in a collected form a number of striking passages, in the shape of aphorisms, from the sermons preached in the Mandir.

THE anniversary of the Northern India Brahmo Somaj takes place to-day, at Allahabad. Babu Aghore Nath Gupta will conduct service on the occasion. He is shortly expected back in Calcutta.

THE fifth anniversary of the Ahmedabad Prarthana Samaj is to be celebrated to-day in the Somaj Mandir. There is to be service in the morning and in the evening. There is to be a discourse by Babu Satyendra Nath Tagore, besides sermon, hymns, and Arti. This last is a peculiar form of service only in use in the Ahmedabad Prarthana Samaj. The whole congregation rise, and in a beautifully melodious chant recite the goodness of God, and express the soul's relation to Him. The Secretary will read the annual report.

WE are glad to find the weekly religious conversational meeting held at the Mission premises on Wednesday evenings, seems to be growing in interest. If the Brahmos who are present at these meetings mean to be useful to one another, they should earnestly and faithfully try to carry out the resolutions which they arrive at. May not more Brahmos attend than at present.

A GOOD number of our missionaries may now be expected in town as the anniversary is fast approaching. Is it not high time to be up and doing in preparation of that festival? Attempts should begin early that the Brahmo public may realize the importance of the occasion, and make themselves morally and spiritually fit for it.

WE have received the annual report of the Punjab Brahmo Somaj. We think it will be published in the next number of the Theistic Annual.

IT is contemplated to introduce articles and other matter in Bengali into the next Annual. Will Brahmo missionaries, and the public at large help the editor with contributions?

Literary

THE *Statesman* hears that Lord Lytton will during Christmas week, give a special dinner to the gentlemen of the Press, at which His Excellency will make an important speech regarding the relations of the Indian Press with the Government of the country.

Latest News

—IT is reported, according to the *Indian Tribune*, that His Highness the Maharana of Odeypur has refused to attend the Imperial Assemblage on the ground that he was never required by the Mogul Emperors to be present at their Durbars. We understand that His Highness is now staying at Ajmere.

—THE Viceroy decided at Peshawar not to send an expedition against the blockaded Afridis. The blockade continues.

—A SILVER throne was placed at the Durbar at Nattore with a stately umbrella attached to it, for the reception of Sir Richard Temple.

—SIR JOHN STRACHEY arrived at Bombay, on Thursday last, and will wait there to meet the Viceroy, coming up eventually with him to Delhi. Lady Strachey will come on at once to Allahabad, and accompany Sir George and Lady Couper to the Assemblage.

—MR. KIPLING, Principal of the Lahore School of Art, who has been put on special duty to design the heraldic devices for the throne and amphitheatre at Delhi, and also those for the Chiefs' banners, has arrived at Delhi, and is residing in the Political Camp. Mr. Griffiths, of the Bombay School of Art, also goes to Delhi to assist Mr. Kipling.

—MAJOR BADFORD has given over charge of the Press and Consul camp at Delhi to Baron Bentinck.

—AMONG the miscellaneous Camps at Delhi are the following:—Attaches, Consuls and European Press, Native Press, Police, Camp Bazaar and Telegraph and Post Offices.

—IT is rumoured at Delhi that a defalcation of Rs. 7,000 has been found out in the expenditure, in connection with the great spacious proclamation Shamianah, and a few of the employes have been suspended.

—THE *Statesman* has received the following telegram from Delhi:—"It is notified that at 12 o'clock on Thursday next there will be a rehearsal of the Viceroy's processional entry, Captain Badcock marshalling elephants. On the Viceroy's arrival, probably to save time occupied, some Native Chiefs have offered to line the road instead of joining. The Viceroy has provided Balrampore and two other chiefs accommodation in his own camp. Although cholera is reported to have disappeared, the Madras Body-guard are likely to go into quarantine on arrival here."

—H. E. SAYEED SAID, the Sultan of Oman's representative to the Delhi Assemblage, is shortly expected at Bombay

—COLONEL COLLEY is daily expected at Delhi to settle the details of the Viceroy's entrance into Delhi, in communication with Major-General Roberts and the Assemblage Committee. It has, we believe, been finally decided to meet the Chiefs, by provinces, on elephants at different points on the route along which His Excellency will proceed.

—THE Governor of Bombay has informed Mr. Morarji Goculdas that the Viceroy has been pleased to signify his wish to subscribe Rs. 2,000 towards the relief of the distressed inhabitants of the Presidency. The Chief Justice of Bombay has also subscribed Rs. 1,000.

—A SHARP earthquake was felt at Dacca, on the morning of Wednesday last.

—A CONCERT will be given in the Bombay Town Hall in aid of the Famine Relief Fund.

—HIS EXCELLENCY Dhir Shumshere Jung, Bahadur, the Nepalese Ambassador, will be at Patna on the 16th instant, at Benares on the 17th, at Allahabad on the 18th, at Cawnpore on the 20th, and will arrive at Delhi on the 21st instant.

Calcutta.

THE *Indian Daily News* understands that orders have been issued to remit to Delhi immediately the sum of one lac of the new Silver Rupees, with the inscription of "Victoria Empress," which have lately been struck off at the Calcutta Mint, by two instalments of Rs. 50,000 each. Our contemporary also been informed that a correspondence is now going on between the authorities concerned, on the subject of coining a few thousand gold mohurs with the new Royal title inscribed on them, to commemorate that auspicious event on the 1st of January, and thereby to utilize a portion of the gold bullion now in store.

THE reporter of the *Indian Daily News* says that immediately on the delivery of the verdict by the Jury in the case Sir Stuart Hogg vs. Mr. J. Wilson, "the prosecutor retired amidst some which were very like hisses from the spectators, though some people say they were cries of 'hush' for "silence."

A FEW days ago the Faculty of Arts of the Calcutta University met to consider whether the curriculum of studies, prescribed for the Entrance, First Arts and B. A. examinations, was to continue as heretofore or to be revised.

AT a public meeting held at the Town Hall, yesterday afternoon, under the presidency of Mr. Buckland, it was decided that suitable arrangements should be made for the proclamation on New Year's Day of the assumption by the Queen of the title of Empress of India. A Committee was appointed to carry out the details of the arrangements, consisting of the following gentlemen:—The Hon'ble Mr. Schalch Rajah Romanath Tagore, Babu Digumber Mitter, Dr. D. B. Smith, Mr. Croft, Mr. Wilson, Rajah Jotendro Mohun Tagore, the Hon'ble Kristodas Pal, Babu Keshub Chunder Sen and a few others.

THE Rev. Dr. Thoburn will deliver an address to Native gentlemen on "The Divine Guide" this day at 6 P. M., at the Free Church Institution, Nimtollah Street.

WE beg thankfully to acknowledge the following donations towards the Chittagong Cyclone Relief Fund.

Babu Ankhil Chunder Sen, M. A., Pleader, High Court.	Rs.	50	0	0
Navalrai, S. Advani Esq. Hyderabad, Sind.	„	25	0	0
Babu Bhuban Mohun Roy Lucknow	„	25	0	0
Indian Reform Association	„	10	0	0
Colootolah Brahmo Somaj	„	4	0	0
Babu Guru Churn Mahalanabis	„	3	12	0
„ Hari Churn Das	„	2	0	0
„ Gopal Chunder Bose	„	2	0	0
„ Kedar Nath Mukerji	„	1	0	0
„ Srinath Datta	„	1	0	0
„ Rajanikant Neogi	„	1	0	0
„ N. C. Das	„	2	0	0
Friends and sympathisers	„	6	0	0
A Native of Chittagong	„	5	0	0
Total	„	137	12	0

EURASIAN AND ANGLO-INDIAN ASSOCIATION.

A LARGE and influential meeting was held yesterday at the Town Hall for the inauguration of the above Association, Sir Richard Temple, Lieutenant-Governor of Bengal, presiding.

His Honor opened the proceedings by addressing the meeting at some length. He generally approved of the objects of the Association, especially those relating to the establishment of industrial schools. He then congratulated the meeting on the present movement, and hoped that the labors of the Association would be successful. The following resolutions were then passed:

I. "That an Association be established upon the basis of the programme framed by the Provisional Committee of the proposed Eurasian and Anglo-Indian Association in the Presidency of Fort William in Bengal." This resolution was proposed by His Grace Archbishop Steins, seconded by Dr Chambers, and supported by the Rev. Messrs. Dall and Williams, each of them addressing the meeting at some length.

II. "That the Association be called 'The Eurasian and Anglo-Indian Association,' and that it be composed of Europeans residing in India." This resolution was proposed by the Ven'ble Archdeacon Baly, and seconded by the Rev. Dr. Madlycott.

III. "That a Temporary Committee of Management be appointed for the purpose of framing rules for the working of the Association registering the names of subscribers, receiving subscriptions and donations, and taking the votes of all members registered up to the 31st January 1877, for the election of a Board of Direction consisting of a President, two or more Vice-Presidents, and twenty-four Members of the Association, who shall have power to appoint an Executive Committee and Sub-Committees out of their number." This resolution was proposed by Mr. H. Andrews, and seconded by Mr. L. W. D'Cruz.

IV. "That the following gentlemen be appointed a Committee of Management to carry out the objects of the third resolution, with power to incur all necessary expenditure, pending the election of the Board of Direction above refered to:—Mr. H. Andrews, Mr. C. T. Davis, Mr. C. Ross, Rev Dr. E. A. Medlycott, Dr. E. W. Chambers, Mr. J. H. Belchambers, Mr. H. F. Fink, Mr. R. Kerr, Mr. H. Haysham, Mr. L. A. Smith, Mr. L. W. D'Cruz, Mr. W. H. Kirkpatrick, Mr. D. Gautzer, Mr. L.C. Fleury, Mr. T.S. Smith, Mr. C.N. Manuel, Dr. E. Reilly, Mr. C. Frederick, Dr. C. F. Vonhinzgy, Mr. F. W. D'Monte, Mr. E. A. Baboneau, Mr. S. P. D'Rozario, and Mr. J. F. Hiss." This resolution was proposed by Mr. A. S. Phillips, and seconded by Mr. C. N. Manuel.

V. "That the Address of Congratulation to the Queen, which has been prepared by the Provisional Committee, be adopted and forwarded by the Committee of Management in the name and on behalf of the Association, through His Honor the Lieutenant-Governor of Bengal and His Excellency the Viceroy and Governor-General of India. This resolution was proposed by Mr. H. R. Fink, and seconded by Mr. C. Ross. The following is the Address of Congratulation adopted:—

"TO HER MOST GRACIOUS MAJESTY VICTORIA BY THE GRACE OF THE UNITED KINGDOM OF GREAT BRITAIN AND IRELAND, QUEEN, DEFENDER OF THE FAITH AND EMPRESS OF INDIA.

"May it please Your Majesty,

"We the members of the Eurasian and Anglo-Indian Association, who belong to a large section of your Majesty's subjects in India, comprising persons of European mixed descent, and Europeans settled in this country, beg leave humbly to approach your Majesty on behalf of our community with our sincere and hearty congratulations on the auspicious occasion of the assumption by your Most Gracious Majesty of the Imperial Title.

"We humbly take this opportunity on behalf of our community which has considerably increased throughout these vast dominions, to tender our heartfelt devotion and loyalty to your Imperial Majesty—a loyalty which in England's struggles in this country has ever found us faithful to your Majesty's standard. And we beg most respectfully to express our confidence that the benign intentions and liberal principles enunciated in your Majesty's Gracious Proclamation, on the transfer of the Government of India to the Crown, will be carried out with a due regard to the peculiar position, claims and necessities of our community.

"The visit of His Royal Highness the Prince of Wales to this country, undertaken with your Majesty's permission, has, we trust and believe, already been instrumental in drawing together in amity and union the numerous Princes, Chiefs, Nobles, and peoples of India around that fountain of Power and Justice—England's Throne; while the additional guarantee of your Gracious interest in the welfare of this country, given this day amidst Universal Rejoicings, will, we trust, draw still more closely the bonds which unite in one common allegiance the various nationalities inhabiting the vast territories of India.

"We deplore the present disturbed state of Eastern Europe, and earnestly pray that it may please God to be with your Majesty's Advisers and Councillors, and that the calm and dignified action of your Majesty's Cabinet may prevail for the ends of peace, the claim of humanity, and the furtherance of civilization and good government.

"With an earnest prayer that the Almighty may be pleased to grant your Majesty continued happiness, and to your Majesty's vast and mighty Empire uninterrupted prosperity and peace, we subscribe ourselves with the greatest respect, your Majesty's humble, loyal, and devoted servants."

After the passing of the third resolution, Sir Richard Temple, who had calculated that the meeting would be over at about one o'clock, and had accordingly fixed an engagement for that hour, asked permission to leave. Before he did so he asked that his name might be put down for a donation of Rs. 500 and also for a monthly subscription of Rs. 50, so long as he remained in Bengal. The announcement was received with great cheers. His Grace Archbishop Steins presided during the remainder of the proceedings.

Law

HIGH COURT, ORIGINAL SIDE.

PEREMPTORY CAUSE BOARD

FOR

Monday, the 18th December 1876.

BEFORE

The Hon'ble Mr. Justice Pontifex.

UNDEFENDED CASES.

Radhakissen Kapoor v. Gopal Chunder Mookerjee—Pittar.

Sett Sooltan Chand Bhunsale and another v. Norendro Chunder Roy—Pittar.

Koonjobehary Dhur v. Norendro Chunder Roy—Pittar.

S. M. Chundermoney Dossee v. S. M. Unnopoornah Dabee—Moses.

Ruttonloll v. Jogendrolell Byssack—Pittar.

Bepin Chunder Mitter v. Gogun Chunder Ghosal—Ghose & Bose.

Tariny Churn Bose v. A. B. Miller—W. C. Bonnerjee.

Sooltan Chand and anr. v. Koylas Chunder Bose—Pittar.

Sooltan Chand and anr. v. Juggobundoo Chatterjee and anr.—Pittar.

(SUIT UNDER THE INDIAN REGISTRATION ACT 1871.)

Dwarkanath Mitter v. Bhooban Mohun Bonnerjee & ors.—P. C. Mookerjee.

DEFENDED CASES.

(Settlement of Issues.)

S. M. Sowdamoney Dossee v. Joges Chunder Dutt and anr.—Ghose & Bose—P. C. Mookerjee.

S. M. Burnomoye Dossee v. Sotish Chunder Dutt and anr.—Gillanders—Kally N. Mitter, Mitter and Bhuje.

(Final Disposal.)

Sushodbur Shaw v. Suttolall Shaw & ors.—Gray & **Co.—Swinhoe** & Co., Carruthers.

Mocoondemoorey Shaw v. Suttolall Shaw & ors. (*To be heard together*)—Carruthers—Pittar, Gray & Co., Swinhoe & Co.

Mocoondamoorary Shaw v. Suttolall Shaw & ors. (*To be heard together*)—Carruthers—Swinhoe & Co., Pittar, Gray & Co.

E. S. Gubboy v. Ameena Bibee and others—Dutt and Mitter—Gillanders, Moses.

Nundolall Bhur v. Wooday Chund Day and others—Shumeldhone Dutt—Watson.

Sreenath Bose v. Amertonauth Jhaa—F. C. Mookerji—Francies.

Oday Chund Mundle and anr. v. Mohendronauth Day and ors.—Dhur and Mitter—Pittar.

Sani M. Lungshide v. Cadar Joseph Abdar—Gregory—Leslie.

Heriperaah Apcar v. A. A. Apcar—Carapiet—Gregory.

Buikisen Gree v. J. C. Charles—Gregory—Sanderson.

Dwarknauth Mudduck v. Koylas Chunder Doss & ors.—Pearson—Verlanaes & Doss—Dwarka N. Dutt.

Miscellaneous

UNITARIANS IN AMERICA.

In the first place it is true that 160 years ago there was not a Unitarian congregation in the United States; about thirty years ago the following may be relied on:—Number of Unitarian congregations in the United States of America: Unitarian, so-called 190; Universalists, 500; Quaker Unitarian, 450, members 60,000; Christians, Unitarian, 1,000; total 2140. This is some progress, in seventy years, of our views.

In Boston there were then nineteen congregations Unitarians; there are now, we believe, thirty-one, and the increase of societies has been from 190 to about 360 distinctly called Unitarian. The Universalists in this time have nearly doubled the number of their congregations, now over 900. The Quaker Unitarians have not increased; may be they are less in number; we are not sure. The Christian Connection has largely increased, and another section closely akin to the Christians, believing in the unity of God, numbering some 2500 churches, may be added to the numerical Unitarian force of the United States. We refer to the Christian Disciples. In addition to these, one or two other sections have adopted the Unitarian view of God, and now repudiate the doctrine of the Trinity. We refer to the Church of God, and a large section of the Adventists; making in all, we have heard from more than one authority, between five and six thousand churches in America, anti-trinitarian, where the worship and the views of our Heavenly Father are at one with ours. Therefore, while it is true, the so-called Unitarian churches have made no progress to boast of, the Unitarian doctrine, which will outlive all sectarian names, has made great progress.

ENGLISH SUPERSTITION A HUNDRED YEARS AGO.

In spite of the progress that Ritualism is now making on all sides, there is really ground for believing that our great grandfathers were much more superstitious than we are. In a letter of Mrs. Elizabeth Carter's in 1748, she thus describes the terror, which the approach of an eclipse was producing, even in London:—"You can have no idea of the uproar occasioned here by the eclipse, and the strange frights under which people labor. One is stunned all day with the bawling of lamentable prophecies, and a form of prayer. Some run away from London, and others, deeming it the safest place, come to it, and really such as one would imagine, should have more sense. The beggars in the streets actually insult folks who refuse to give them small beer, by clapping their hands, and threatening them that the day of judgment will be next Thursday. Others, as I find by a dialogue I overheard in a neighbouring court, are of opinion that all the women in the world only, are to die. Such are our apprehensions in the city. And I lately heard in St. James' Place, that a lady on receiving an invitation for a rout, excused herself, by thinking it really not decent to play cards on that day, so perhaps she thinks it more decent to put it off till Sunday." And two years afterwards a panic at least as great seems to have been caused by earthquakes. On Feb. 8th, 1750, London was shaken by an earthquake; and on March 8th, just four weeks afterwards, a second followed. Whereupon a crazy soldier prophesied that at the end of the next four weeks there would follow a third earthquake that would swallow up London and Westminster. His predictions were hawked about the streets, and threw the whole town into terror and confusion. Two days before the predicted day (April 5th) a correspondent in London writes to Mrs. Carter: "Young and old, happy and wretched, are all hurrying out of town on the dreadful expectation. The gloom that hangs over the town, and will hang over it for some time, induced me to return hither, that my mother might not be left to sleep after it alone. 'Tis surely an idle gloom; but disbelieve it as much as one will, a more than usual degree of seriousness will sit upon one's mind. All Sunday they were crying the Bishop of London's prayer, proper for all Christian families against the earthquake that is to be on Thursday morning." And again April 5 itself. "Yesterday the whole town was in hourly expectation of destruction. The churches were full all the morning, but at night the streets and open places were crowded. Thousands spent the night in Hyde Park and Lincoln's Inn-fields. Those who did the least, sat up half the night except some very few. 'Tis grievous to think of the scenes of distress among good though weak people, which last night was witness to. The King and Prince have done all they could to check this wildness of fear."

NOTICE.

Calcutta Society for the Prevention of Cruelty to Animals.

A general meeting of the above Society will be held at the Metcalfe Hall on Tuesday afternoon, the 19th instant, at 5 o'clock for the submission of a Report, the election of President, Vice-Presidents and Committee, and transaction of such other business as may be brought forward.

The attendance of all friendly to the Society is earnestly solicited.

By order,
C. GRANT,
Hony. Secretary.

LIGHT! LIGHT!! LIGHT!!!

PATENT PORTABLE AIR GAS MAKING APPARATUS,

SUITABLE FOR

Churches, Chapels, Schools, Country Mansions, Private Houses, Railway Stations, Barracks, Manufactories, Collieries, Mills, Offices, &c., &c.

THIS *simple* and *effective* Gas-making Apparatus supplies a want long felt of having Gas at places where no Gas Works exist. It may be introduced without any more trouble than the simply affixing of any ordinary Gas meter, and is about the same size for the same number of lights. The *piping* and *fitting* arrangements are in every respect the same as for the use of ordinary Gas. The *cost* of the Gas produced is about the same as is charged for ordinary Coal Gas, and the light produced is *more brilliant* and of *a greater illuminating power*; it is also *free from the impurities of Coal Gas*. The Gas, if used with the Patent Burner, is of great heating power, and hence suitable for cooking and heating purposes, or in manufactories for soldering, &c. The apparatus is PORTABLE; there is NO DANGER WHATEVER (ordinary care being used when filling it); the Gas is PRODUCED IN AN INSTANT WITHOUT ANY FIRE OR OTHER ARTIFICIAL HEAT.

Further particulars may be obtained from MESSRS. EDWARD THOMSON & CO., Contractors for Drainage, Water and Gas, who are appointed Sole Agents for the above apparatus, which can be seen working any week day between the hours of 6 A.M. and 6 P.M. at their place of business.

39, BENTINCK STREET, CALCUTTA.

P. W. FLEURY & CO.,

BUILDERS, ENGINEERS,

AND

SCIENTIFIC INSTRUMENT MAKERS.

No. 44, Free School Street.

WE beg to intimate that we have been engaged in the above line of business for the past 20 years, and trust that our Constituents will continue to favour us with their work, which will meet with prompt attention on our part.

In connection with buildings, we undertake the erection and repairing of machinery at moderate charges; as also execute all descriptions of Iron and Brass work.

We can assure the Public that we undertake the repair and erection of Houses and the laying of Water-supply Pipes on moderate terms, and guarantee to keep all the water pipes and brass fittings supplied by us in good working order for three years, free of extra charge. We also guarantee to keep dwelling-houses' roofs water-tight for three years, free of extra charge, for such houses as we have repaired.

For purposes of illumination, we prepare our patent Chromatic Transparencies representing Coat-of-Arms, Landscapes, Scenery, &c., at prices, ranging from Rs. 50 to 300 each, according to size and design.

FOR SALE.

Light! Light!! Light!!!

Electric Light apparatus complete, worked with a battery of 50 large cells, on Bunsen's principle	500	0
Ditto ditto, with 40 cells, smaller size ...	400	
Ditto ditto, with a powerful 44-cell Cast-iron Battery, on Callan's principle ...	300	0
Lime Light Apparatus, complete, with Iron Gas-holder, and Copper Retort ...	150	0
Oxy-Hydrogen Light Apparatus with safety Jets, 2 Iron Gas-holders, and Retorts, complete	200	
Hink's Patent Duplex Wall Lamps, with chimney	5	8
Ditto Duplex Lamp, with chimney and globe	7	8

Patent Leblanche Battery

For constancy, durability, and cleanliness, this battery is unequalled; price for each cell, with chemicals	3
Bunsen's Galvanic Battery, 9 inches, by 4 inches	7
Magneto-Electric Machine, with single magnet	14
Prismatic Compass 3-inch in a lid leather case, by Elliot, *second hand*	25
Ditto 4-inch by Simmons, *second hand* ...	30

P. W. FLEURY & Co.

No. 44, FREE SCHOOL STREET.

BABU BASANTA KUMARA DATTA,

HOMŒOPATHIC PRACTITIONER.

No. 20, Sunker Hulder's Lane, Ahiritolah.

LONDON AGENT

MESSRS. HENRY TURNER & CO.

HOMŒOPATHIC

FRESH

Medicines and other Requisites.
Arrives every month from England.
Medicines, Boxes, Books, Pamphlets;
Absolute Alcohol; Cholera-spirit Camphor.

SPECIAL REMEDIES.

For Suppressed, Laborious and Difficult menses; Leucorrhœa; Hysteria.

For Spermatorrhœa; Dysentery; Diarrhea; Cholera.

For Asthma; Piles; Pain; Sore and Diseases of the Children.

Lemonade, Soda and Tonic water always.

To be had at

DATTA'S HOMŒOPATHIC LABORATORY

No. 312, CHITPORE ROAD, BURTOLA, CALCUTTA.

TERMS—CASH.

☞ Price List can be had free on application

R. K. GHOSH'S

HOMŒOPATHIC DISPENSARY.

No. 1, *Gour Mohun Mukerjee's Street, Simla.*

CALCUTTA.

HOMŒOPATHIC Medicine; Medicine chests of sizes,—containing medicine in tube phials; Homœopathic Books, tracts and pamphlets (English and Bengali); Dr. Rubin's "Saturated spirits of Camphor,"—(the best preventive and cure for cholera where medical aid is not available); and other Homœopathic requisites are sold here at a moderate price. Terms cash. Mofussil orders are promptly executed.

R. K. GHOSH,

Homœopathic Practitioner,

Manager.

PRIZE MEDALLISTS
For Excellency of Workmanship.
J. M. EDMOND & CO.,
27—28, BENTINCK STREET,
ESTABLISHED 1833.
Cabinet Makers, Upholsterers,
AND
Billiard Table Manufacturers.

Houses completely furnished. Furniture designed and made to order.

ESTIMATES given for all kinds of Carpentering, Painting, Polishing, Gilding, and General Repairs; Marble Polished, Moulded, and Cleaned; Picture Frames made.

J. M. EDMOND & Co., in soliciting a continuance of public patronage, beg to say they have ready for sale specimens of Ebonized and Gold Oxford style of Fancy Chairs, and are prepared to execute orders for other Furniture in the same style.

J. M. EDMOND & Co.'s New Show-Room is now replete with New Heraldic Style of Dining-room Chairs, and Rustic Chairs, Telescopic Dining Tables, with Patent Table Expanders, and a variety of finished Furniture. Orders solicited.

NOTICE.

Infallible Specifics for Asthma, Consumption, Colic, Gonorrhœa, Spermatorrhœa and Dysentery.

Used in all cases of Asthma, preceded by headache or sleepiness, or by various digestive or other disturbances, or without any warning.

Sold in boxes containing 7 pills (for one week only) with full directions for use:—

Price per box ...	Rs. 2	0
" with postage ditto ...	2	4

For further particulars, Apply to
WOOPENDRA NATH PAL,
Care of the Manager, *Indian Mirror*.
CALCUTTA.

FOR SALE.

VALUABLE LANDED PROPERTY.

THE desirable Premises No. 101, Taltala Lane, Calcutta. Price Rs. 5,000.

AND

A very elegant Family Residence, with 15 BIGAS *Lakhiraj* Gardens, bordering River Hooghly, Situate in JUGGUDDUL, lying directly *East* of CHANDERNAGORE, and being approachable by *boat* or *road* from *Shamnuggur* Station, EASTERN BENGAL RAILWAY. Price Rs. 3,000.

Apply to BABU RADHA GOBIND CHATTERJEE at the above places.

Cachar Native Joint Stock Co. Ld.

Having opened out 50 acres in tea on a garden of 700 acres, do hereby give notice that this Company has been duly registered under Act X of 1866 and is now prepared to sell Shares at Rs. 25 each until the 31st instant. Tea manufactured to date, 20 maunds. Further particulars can be had from the undersigned.

BYKUNTA CHUNDERA GUPTA,
Secretary.

BURN & CO.

RANEEGUNGE Fire bricks are the best Fire Bricks known;—superior to Ramsay's.
9 Rs. per 100.
Fire clay, 40 Rs. per Ton.
Glazed Stone ware, Drainage pipes of all sizes.

BURN & Co.,
7, *Hastings Street, Calcutta.*

ARLINGTON & CO.,
3 B DALHOUSIE SQUARE, CALCUTTA.
THE 'PATENT PERPETUAL FOUNTAIN,'
TABLE EPERGNE OR CENTRE PIECE,
FOR SCENT OR FOR PUREWATER.
In Richly Electro-Silvered Ware, [*One of the Greatest Novelties of the day.*]
Cash Price Rs. 175.

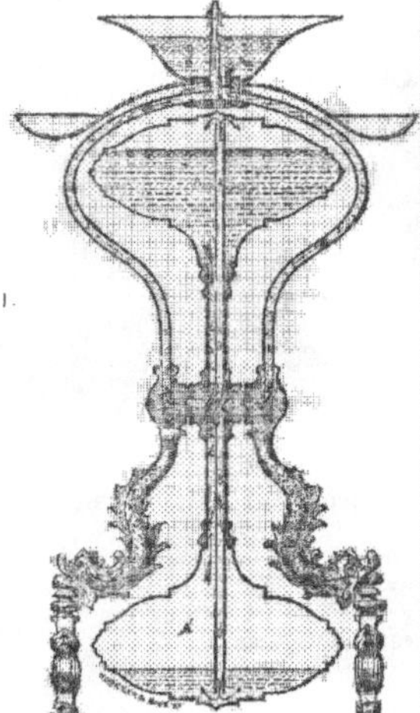

N. B.—The annexed drawing is not a correct representation of the Plated Table Fountains which A. & Co. have for sale. The drawing is only given to show the internal arrangements of the Apparatus, and attention is invited to the following description:—

OBSERVE.—A, A1, are two cisterns or reservoirs which are connected together by pipes or tubes B, B1, C, C1, mounted on a hollow axis of motion D, surrounding a fixed conical plug E, having suitable passages F, G, H, therein communicating with the pipes or tubes B, B1, C, C1, and I, and with the jet pipe J.

To put the fountain in operation water is poured into the dish or basin K until the lower reservoir is filled and the opening I1 is covered. The cisterns or reservoirs A, A1, are then turned on their axis of motion, so as to place the filled cistern or reservoir A at the top, when the water therefrom will flow to a level in the jet pipe J, and the water in the basin or dish K by passing down the pipes or tubes I and B1 into the lower cistern or reservoir A1, rises in such lower cistern or reservoir A1 and forces the air out therefrom through the pipe or tube C1, passage F, and tube B into the upper parts of the cistern or reservoir A, where it presses upon the surface of the water therein and forces it out therefrom through the tube C, passage H, and jet pipe J, until all the water in the upper cistern or reservoir A has passed through the jet pipe J and into the lower cistern or reservoir A1 by the pipe I, passage G, and pipe B1, when by turning the cistern or reserviors A, A1, on their axis of motion until the cistern or reservoir A1 is at the top, the action of the fountain will be continued; the pipes or tubes B, C1, which had previously been air passages now becoming water passages, and the pipes or tubes B1, C, now becoming air passages which had previously served for the passage of water. By these improvements the necessity for alternately filling and emptying the cisterns or reservoirs A, A1, is obviated.

CALCUTTA

106, Bowbazar Street.

DR. H. C. SARMA'S

MEDICINE FOR DEBILITY

(NERVOUS.)

HAIR PRESERVER.

Copy of Letter received from Rajah Chundernath Roy Bahadur of Nattore.

Wellesley Street, No. 38, Moti's Lane, 20th March 1874.

MY DEAR HURKISH BABU,—

I shall thank you to send me another phial of your "*Excellent Hair Restorer*." In fact it has done me a great benefit, and I should like to have more of it. It has disabused me (young as I am) of old age.

Yours Sincerely
C. N. of *Nattore*

MEDICINE FOR BALDNESS.

Will certainly cure baldness if applied on the bald portion, night & morning, according to directions given in the adjoining direction paper.

Price per two ounce phial Re.	1	0	0
Postage &c. ... ... "	0	6	0

HEEM-SAGAR OIL.

The best remedy for Headache arising from overstudy, intellectual occupation, over-thinking, mental anxiety and weakness, as well as heat of head from living in hot places.

It cools the head and produces very agreeable sensation. Removes dandriff as well as all other impurities from the head. Promotes the strength and growth of the hair and prevents its premature falling-off.

Price per 4 ounce phial Re.	1	0	0
Postage &c. ... ... "	0	10	0

MEDICINE FOR LEPROSY.

Price with Postage &c ... Rs. 5 0 0

OIL FOR LEPROSY.

And Inveterate Skin Diseases.

Price per 8 ounce phial Rs.	2	0	0
Postage &c. ... ... "	0	12	0

Printed and published by M. M. RUKHIT, at the INDIAN MIRROR PRESS, No. 6 College Square, for the Proprietors.

The Indian Mirror.

SUNDAY EDITION.

VOL. XV.] CALCUTTA, SUNDAY, DECEMBER 24, 1876. {REGISTERED AT THE GENERAL POST OFFICE.} [NO. 304

CONTENTS.

NOTICE.

All letters and communications relating to the literary department of the Paper should be addressed to the Editor. All other letters should be addressed to the Manager, to whom all remittances should be made payable.

Subscribers will be good enough to bring to the notice of the Manager any delay or irregularity in the delivery of the Paper.

Editorial Notes.

WHAT has become of the *Sanatan Dharma Rukhshini Sava* we wonder. Some of the wealthiest and most influential members of the Hindu community of our city, started this Society for the preservation of the orthodox religion of the land, and perhaps also opposing the spread of the principles of social and religious enlightenment. For sometime the Sava went on very well, and created a stir in the town. But latterly it has slowly died out, and its adherents have silently fallen off. This is a pity. We regret the absence of religious vitality among those of our countrymen who still profess belief in the ancestral religion from which so many of us have thought it our duty to part. The attempt to keep up an agitation on the subject of religion among our orthodox countrymen will at any rate prove morally useful amongst those who seeing the apathy, and religious decline of general society hasten to break loose from every manner of moral and social restraint.

THERE is not the least doubt but that among the Vaishnavas of Bengal, decayed and degraded as that sect is, there is considerably more warmth and earnestness than among the general order of Hindus. If the *Sanatan Dharma Rukhshini* has collapsed, the *Hari Savas*, established in different parts of the town and the suburbs are some of them flourishing very well. They get out processions at times, and we are told there are services of hymns and speeches made. Now both these societies were originally started to counteract the operations of the Brahmo Somaj. How far they have been able to do this we do not know. Brahmos have been so long very indifferent to them. But why should they be indifferent? Why not encourage them, and co-operate with them as far as Brahmos can conscientiously do so? We can enjoy and benefit by the Sunkirtan services held at the *Hari Sava*, and we can heartily and most profitably join in the researches and discussions on the Shasters which have sometimes characterized the proceedings of the *Sanatan Dharma Rukhshini*. Should the latter society resume its operations, we hope the leader Rajah Komul Krisna will invite our preceptors and *Pracharaks* to aid him. Of course our divergence will always be very great, however little we may like to show it, but that is no reason why we should not sympathize where enlightened and patriotic sympathy is possible.

WE are informed that the memorial which the Mahomedans of Bengal have forwarded to Her Majesty on the Eastern question, praying that England might interfere on behalf of Turkey, is signed by 9,000 men.

THE Akhund of Swat is a wonderful man. He was reported to be dying yesterday, and to-day he breathes fire and vengeance, preaching a *Jehad* at the Musid immediately after the Friday Namaz against the Feringee. If Roum fell into the Feringee's hands, the hopes of Islamism would be over. He could, he said, induce the Amir of Cabul to join in the *Jehad* against the Feringee. What Feringee is here meant? Is it the Russian or the Englishman? We suppose the Amir's friendliness to both is about the same.

OUR Mahomedan contemporary the *Urdu Gazette* is bristling with energetic and warlike paragraphs all on behalf of Islam, the Caliphate, and the Sultanate. Though we can not agree with him in many of the views he sets forth, we appreciate and esteem the evident earnestness and sincerity with which he writes. We think Sir George Campbell was mistaken in his estimate of the apathy and indifference with which he said the Indian Mahomedans would regard the affairs in Turkey.

IT is said that the conduct of the Bishops of Colombo and Bombay in opposing their clergy and introducing high-handed practices will considerably advance the cause of the disestablishment of the Anglican Church in this country. While, we know, a house divided against itself cannot stand, we know also that it will still be long before the British Government have learnt to be just enough to Hindus and Mahomedans not to pay a highly expensive ecclesiastical establishment out of their pockets.

IT is proposed to have special prayers in the course of the usual Service, on Sunday the 31st instant, at all the Brahmo Somajes in India, in connection with the assumption by Her Majesty the Queen of the title of Empress of India. We earnestly hope our Brahmo brethren, with whom our loyalty to the sovereign means faith in Providence, will with one heart invoke Divine blessings on the Queen and her subjects, and pray that the mutual relations between the rulers and the ruled may be conducive to their moral advancement.

EMPEROR Yudishthira's Imperial Assemblage, three thousand years ago, led to two unpleasant consequences. Its unsurpassed grandeur and dazzling splendour excited the jealousy of Duryodhan, and gave rise to the celebrated war of the Kuru Pandavas. Secondly, on the question of precedence being raised at the Assemblage, opinion was divided as to who should be honored first. The altercation rose to such a pitch that Sisupal, who indignantly and offensively opposed the proposal of investing Krisna with the highest honors, was forthwith murdered by him on the spot. It is to be hoped that the Assemblage at Delhi will pass off quietly, and that neither Native chiefs nor foreign powers will find in it any cause of irritation.

"WE have often been struck," says the *Friend of India*, "with the reticence of Native converts as to any heart-experience they may have had of the goodness of God towards themselves; especially as to their conversion from image worship. * * No *parading* is asked for or needed; but a devout and modest statement, whenever it may reasonably appear convenient, of the *consciousness* of change in their own hearts and characters would surely be of value, dispelling the doubts of many of their countrymen." Native Christians have been eminent as educationists, as literary men, as controversialists, but is it not singular that not one among them has distinguished himself by recording anything like spiritual experience as has such Christian conversion a made wonderful change in most thoer parts of the world. We do not say this in depreciation of Native Christian, but only to draw their attention to a deficiency which seems to be patent to every one else except themselves.

SPIRITUALISTIC mediums are positively on the discount in England. It was only the other day that Mr. Slade was sentenced to imprisonment, and straightway we hear of another "medium" who has got into a scrape. An English "medium," says the *Spectator*, a certain Rev. Francis Ward Monck, "formerly a minister at Bristol, who was asserted by his counsel to be a man of independent means, keeping his carriage and yacht at Bristol, was also charged yesterday week at the Huddersfield Police-court, under the Vagrant Act; and in his case it appears to be asserted that a number of false hands, musical boxes, and other properties of the trade were found in his possession. If that is so, it will probably go hard with him; and if it be true that he is really a man of considerable property, the case will be a very remarkable one in the history of morbid psychology. Dr. Monck is, we believe, the "medium" who was asserted by the Spiritualistic papers sometime ago to have travelled, spirit-borne, through the air, like the witches of old,—from Bristol to Stroud, if we remember rightly,—a kind of pretension the validity of which must have been somewhat rudely tested by the bars and locks of the Huddersfield police-officer."

CARDINAL Antonelli, the Pope's Secretary of state, is dead. He was a man of great talent and experience, and the Papal court at the present time of its misfortunes owes to him a great deal. Many rumours are afloat about him, about his great wealth, his character, his diplomacy, and personal habits. One of the Cardinal's apologists thus puts the position of the Roman Catholic Church. "The Church has a political and social attitude towards Governments and people as such, and therefore she employs in her diplomacy and state craft, so to call it, men trained for that career, and rewards such with her very highest dignities including the cardinalate." But in spite of all favorable representations it is evident the cardinal was a ven worldly man. A personal description of him is thus given by the *Times'* correspondent:—

"What may have been the exact value of Cardinal Antonelli's individual strength as the political bulwark of the Vatican, must be left for future historians to ascertain. But he formed a prominent feature in the social as well as in the political life of Pontifical Rome. Ten years ago, when receptions and ball commenced early, that the members of the Sacred College might take their part in society and retire before dancing began, the Cardinal was often to be met in English as well as Roman drawing rooms. There are many who will remember his slight compact figure, his strangely attractive face, which all thought ugly, and the majority ended by admiring his three tufts of raven hair, olive complexion, piercing eyes, full of innate intellect, slightly aquiline nose, and certain tyrannical lines about the mouth, contradicting an expression of the most perfect courtesy and gentleness. Upon women he seemed to exercise a peculiar influence. They were fascinated by his ugliness, and, without a single exception, they pronounced him charming. He seldom or never sat down, and it was noticed that he appeared to have a dislike to people standing behind him. At such times he would move and move until he had quietly brought all in front. His dress was, of course, the same worn by all Cardinals—a long black coat with red edges, and buttoned down the front with an infinity of small red buttons; but the way it sat upon him, the perfect fit of his scarlet stockings and knittiest of buckled shoes, distinguished him personally as much as his little brougham and fast bays distinguished his equipage from the lumbering double bodied carriages and funeral blacks of the other *Porporati*.

THAT noble piece of mechanism, the English character, examined by the light of recent events, divides itself into two parts one of which is broad humanity, and the other is exclusive self-interest. The former includes sympathy as well as co-operation, under all conditions of life, with those who struggle and suffer for freedom, or for right. This constitutes the Englishman the universal critic and final judge of all questions of disputed interests and international law. The latter includes the wonderful tenacity with which Englishmen are known to hold certain notions, principles, and insticts which in their essence, and in their practice, constitute the huckster and the bully. There are certain Englishmen who represent as living and close an embodiment of the former phase of character as possible; and there are certain others again in whom the shop-keeping and rowdyish intuitions prevail over everything else. In the great majority and mass of Englishmen the susceptibilities tend both ways alike, and are swayed and educated by the influences that are most paramount at the moment. Take for instance the vexed question of the English relation with Turkey and Russia, or take the question of the relation of the Government of British India with the vast population of this country. Do we not find the parallel operations of the two principles of character noted above? There are the humanitarians who hold that India is to be held in trust by England for the Indians only, and there are also those highly national Britons who maintain that the people of India in being conquered have lost all social and political rights. A great number believe that Turkey can do no wrong because she is subservient to British interests, and even if she massacred and outraged a few hundred thousand Christian men and women in her provinces, Russia must not be permitted to check her atrocities, because the advance of Russia it is imagined might one day interfere with the traffic on the Suez Canal. The two divisions of character could not be better incarnated than in the two political geniuses who rule the existence of the English nation. Mr. Gladstone represents the manliness of English humanity, and Lord Beaconsfield the exclusiveness of English shop-rivalry.

WORDS GOOD AND BAD.

WHO was the prophet that prayed that the Lord might rule his tongue, and keep the gates of his mouth? We all feel inclined at times to pray the same prayer. Few things in social or in religious circles cause so much mischief as words ill-chosen, unwise, and untimely. And on the other hand we know not of any means so easy, so costless, yet so powerful to produce the highest results as a few words spoken at the right moment, and with the right feeling. Men have been known who could govern their passions, bring their habits into moral subjection, discipline their body and all its wants, but who could not check the lawlessness of their tongue. Nay the more they improved in personal excellence, the more free and heedless they were with their tongue. Men have been known who could bear persecution in silence, could stand the physical and moral outrages of enemies, could suffer the pangs of disease and poverty without shrinking, but who lost all balance and peace of mind when subjected to the ordeal of hard and evil words. Good words are at the bottom of half the amenities of life; bad words cause more than the half the bitterness and misery under which so many households and communities lie. Words good and gentle produce by a secret reaction perhaps even more peace, grace, and joy in the mind of the speaker than in the mind of the person spoken to; and cruel bitter words similarly shed greater venom and unhappiness in the heart which is its source than outside. By a strange law of our mind a single word or look of kindness is remembered through long dark years in the midst of which a thousand events of greater importance are sunk in oblivion; and a single expression of cruel scorn outlives and rankles in the heart when worthier things are perfectly forgotten. Some great moral triumphs have been won by wise and seasonable words, and in the ordinary engagements of men and nations words of the right sort are known to have the utmost value. A kingdom is sometimes lost or gained, a fortune is sometimes made or forfeited, a man is sometimes made friend or enemy for ever by a word. Great wrath can be pacified, great enmity disarmed, great suffering relieved, great quarrels decided by a good and loving word. Have therefore a kind word for every one. Let your friends delight in and remember the sweetness of your speech. Let your servants love you and praise for the gentleness of your address. Let the stranger be comforted by what you can tell him. And it is best you should dismiss your enemy with a benediction.

It is better to talk little than to talk much. The least said, says the proverb, is soonest mended. This is specially true in the case of those persons who have not much control over their feelings. It is the feelings that lie at the bottom of good or bad words. When one is sure of his feeling, sure of his principle, let him speak. But even then in numberless cases silence is gold, and speech silver. A man of taciturn habits will, when he speaks at the right time, produce twenty times more effect by his good and well-chosen words, than a man whose advice is cheap, and who wears his opinions on his sleeves. In regulating our words therefore the regulation of the feelings must be first considered. Because even if a man be taciturn, but his feelings bad, though he but speak rarely, yet when he opens his mouth he will surely offend some one. Thus talkative and quarrelsome men by remaining quiet, gather more rage and venom, which they let off, with a vengeance when the provocation is too much for them to remain silent any longer Talking by itself ought to be a matter of severe and careful discipline. While practising it we must perseveringly avoid everything that can give offence or pain. We must take the utmost labor to say what is good, sweet, and courteous. But it is impossible, to say nothing of its artificialness, to do this when there are wrong, unamiable, and bitter feelings within. Because out of the fulness of the heart the mouth speaketh. The sweetness and peacefulness of the feelings must be first sought after. When the heart is full of blessedness and good will, of godly love, and heavenly grace, words, with but a moderate amount of care, will distil goodness and benediction. Nor is this all. We can not, we must not pledge ourselves to speak sweet and pleasant words always. There are times when sweet words are poison, and silence is death; when harsh piercing cutting words carry truth and healing on their wings. They must be spoken, because they are good words and gracious. Who has the right of speaking them? He whose feelings are irreproachable and whose heart is sweet. The thunders and storms of heaven make the atmosphere pure and sweet and clothe the earth with beauty and fruitfulness; and the gentle dews and showers give increase, brightness, and Joy. Let our hearts be filled with the loving benificence that pervades nature, and what we speak and what we withhold, whether it be outwardly harsh or agreeable, it will spread health, gladness and peace around.

HINDUS IN HIGH SERVICE.

IT is not only a political, but also a very important social and moral experiment that the Government of India is trying to introduce by the nomination of two Native gentlemen to really exalted posts in the Civil Service. No one, who has any regard for the interests of his country and countrymen, can fail to honor, and feel deeply thankful for the high-minded policy, which Lord Lytton, and Lord Salisbury, and our worthy Lieutenant-Governor withal have seen fit to pursue in convincing the whole population, that the British rule in Hindustan does really mean to benefit and elevate the Hindu. And the assumption of the Imperial title by Her Majesty will serve a good opportunity to celebrate the practical commencement of this righteous policy. We believe the intended recipients of the high offices will be formally installed into their new duties at Delhi. This is really very good, and our warm congratulations are due to those who give, as well as those who receive the honor. But let us view the subject from another point. It is not to be doubted that the somewhat unexpected bestowal of the honor, however agreeable to us and those upon whom it is bestowed, has awakened the jealousy and apprehension, and feelings not very amiable in their nature, in the hearts of a great many members of the Civil Service, both junior and senior, and of those who sympathize with them. The note of alarm which these gentlemen have raised does not seem to possess a sound and true ring. We are disposed to be rather sceptical as to the impending fate of the Civil Service, and see no indication of the panic which it is said, will spread among English universities and English households directly. Rajah Harendra Krishna is appointed as the Collector of Hughly. We believe all thoughtful men in the service generally and the English youth at home specially, will hear the misfortune with considerable equanimity and the Service will get on very much as usual. But there is one danger. The nomination may not prove successful in its results. And then the jealousy and watchfulness that are concentrated upon the objects with whom the experiment has begun, will not only get a handle to urge the future exclusion of Hindus from the Service altogether, but to denounce the social and moral capabilities of the whole race for real power and responsibility of any kind. Already this has been hinted in an unmistakable way and the objection will gather force with every fresh manifestation of deficiency and weakness. Because to speak the truth we do not believe that the nomination is unexceptionable. For many reasons the magistrateship of a district is much more important even than a High Court Judgeship, and a man who fills that high post for the first time is naturally understood to represent the whole talent and character of his countrymen. If he fails in intellect, or in aptitude, or in firmness, the whole community fails morally and intellectually through him. And the European members of the Civil Service will in that case find ample justification for what they urge individually against the present objects of the nomination, as well as against the whole policy of Government. Rajah Harendra Krishna may be very amiable and good, but if the votes of his countrymen had been taken we have grave doubts whether his nomination would have been the result. So long as the power of nomination will lie with patrons, and men in office similar results will follow. We recommend the elevation of real merit, of those who represent all that is best and highest in their people; and if they fail we are content to take their failure as our own, and abide by the consequences. Otherwise we may be personally glad at the good fortune of a friend or a fellow-countryman, but can not hold ourselves or our community responsible for the results of the nomination.

THE COMING DARBAR.

IT is difficult to look below the surface of things when all above is idle pageant and gorgeous trappings. Public mind seems to be taken up with the the approaching sight at Delhi. Every body seems to think that he is somehow interested in the great event that is to come. And it appears that the Government of this country is determined to make the auspicious day striking and important in all respects. The humblest peasant will thus be made to realize the momentous nature of the transactions that will happen on the 1st of January next. The sober mind dealing in the luxuries of its own thought, shrinks from this outside pomp and asks—what is the good of all this? Have our rulers devoted a s are thoughts or two to this side of the matter? Is external pomp and internal selfishness to be the *alpha* and *omega* of the event? Is not the assumption of the Imperial title intended to produce a moral effect also upon the people of this country? Captious minds may and, indeed, do detect flaws in the motives that have led to the inauguration of what we think will be a new regime. With them we have nothing to do. Nor do we much care for those who, setting aside the moral considerations of the case, delight to dwell upon the immense political effect which the event would produce upon the chiefs of India. This political effect, which means nothing more than so much intimidation, is urely to be deprecated, if it is not superseded by higher considerations and motive. What will be the good of the gathering? Will the princes of India be bullied in the same right royal fashion as hitherto? Will political functionaries learn nothing of the habit of tact and politeness in their dealings with the feudatories? Will the landlords relax nothing of their vigor in persecuting and oppressing the down-trodden ryot? Will the poor cottager that groans under the manifold evils of existence, receive no ray of comfort from the benignant smile of the Empress? Will the governors and the governed continue to be at daggers drawn with each other, and fight and struggle, rave and rant over their privileges and liberties? Will the spectre of race antagonism still drive away our hopes of peace and brotherly amity? Will there still be one law for the white and another for the black? Will the Natives remain for ever shut from higher employments and privileges? Will Victoria the Empress be the same personage as Victoria the Queen? Let all these questions be answered; and if our rulers are unable to return satisfactory replies to these questions, the event will, we submit, be a solemn mockery. If the object be merely to make the already humbled Princes of India to bend their knees more closely to the ground and bring their heads more closely in contact with the feet of British royalty, then we earnestly wish the pageant were done away with. What we want is a new regime, with fresh zeal for our welfare, and with better charity. Let each man and woman in India perceive and realize the change. Let the incessant booming of guns that would welcome the news of the inauguration of the Empire, thrill and excite every heart with renewed loyalty. Is it too much to expect such boons at the hands of our Government? Let our rulers answer.

Review

INDIAN SCHOOL BOOKS.*

EVERY well-wisher of Indian Education will congratulate Macmillan & Co., on the excellent series of Text books that are coming out from their press in rapid abundance for the benefit of our school students. We have now lying before us three of such works which for the special purpose for which they have been intended are decidedly the best works of their kind which have been issued from the Indian Press for some years. The names of the writers themselves are a virtual guarantee that their books will answer all the present purposes of Indian students. In Mr. C. B. Clarke, we have an able Inspector of schools who knows all the minutiæ connected with the education department, and in whom more than an ordinary amount of faith may be placed for the accuracy and skill of the work. The Geographical Primer is an excellent hand book for students. It is written in an easy style not much disfigured by pedantry, and its information is always reliable. We venture to anticipate that in a few months Mr. Clake's book will be read in all the schools of Bengal and Upper India which teach up to the matriculation standard of the Calcutta University. The next book on our table is Mr. Smith's Arithmetic for Indian Schools—a work which deserves still greater praise and recommendation, from the public. Mr. Smith is an experienced writer of school books and his name is almost a household word throughout Bengal. His Arithmetic and Algebra have hitherto been the favorites of all schoolmasters; and we dare say that the Indian edition of his Arithmetic will find a still readier acceptance in this country. One of the greatest recommendation of this book is that it has been specially prepared for the immediate use and wants of the Natives in India. To take an instance, the weights and measures in all existing books of Arithmetic are exclusively English, whereas for Indian students they ought to have been Indian as well. This point would of itself suffice to show the great weakness of the present system of education. Our students, we are assured by school masters, find the greatest facility in repeating from memory the English cloth measure or the English weight measure or the English table of money, but ask them to reduce so many sovereigns to rupees or so many pounds to maunds or so many miles to cros, their helplessness and surprise would manifest themselves immediately. We are glad that in the present work this want will be specially met. The questions for exercises are mostly such as an Indian would have to deal with in his every day life, while the arrangement of the chapters and the principles of definition and classification adopted by the author are beyond all praise. The last, book Mr. Todhunter's Mensuration is only a reprint of the easier portions of his English edition with the section on Surveying and an Appendix on practical surveying superadded.

* A Geographical Reader and Companion to the Atlas. By C. B. Clarke, M. A., F. L. S., F. G. S., Late fellow of Queen's College, Cambrige. London; Macmillan & Co. 1876.

Arithmetic for Indian schools. By Barnards Smith, M. A. London: Macmillan & Co. 1876.

Mensuration and Surveying for beginners by J. Todhunter, M. A., F. R. S. London: Macmillan & Co.

Social

THE Dramatic Performances Act received the assent of the Viceroy on the 16th instant, and even the most fastidious critic will not deny that by passing this measure the Government of India has not immensely exalted itself in the estimation both of the public and of itself. That the Government has struck at a growing evil, that it has, true to its traditions, recognised its duty once more of acting as the guardian of public morality, is a cheering fact for which we all ought to be grateful. We are glad to say that the fuss raised by certain sections of the community has been effectually silenced, and that there is now a very good prospect of the Native Drama thriving under circumstances both auspicious and beneficial. There are, it is true one or two features in the act which are opened to objection—the clause relating to *Jatras* and private performances especially being capable of being abused. But we hope for the best and trust, in the words of the Lieutenant-Governor that the forbearance of the legislature will not be abused and that it will never be necessary for the local Government to ask the council for farther powers in the respect of these private performances. It is the duty of the public to watch carefully the working of this act, and we have sufficient hope that the really guilty and evil disposed among us will not be able to escape the penalties of the law; and as for those gentlemen who have been beguiled or honestly persuaded to oppose the measure, we dare say they will be benefitted by the sage instructions given them by Mr. Hobhouse and the Lieutenant Governor in council. It mortifies us a little to learn that the result of so much education has been to make so many of our countrymen zealous advocates of the license, and not the liberty as they represent it, of the Press and the stage.

FEMALE education seems to be looking up in the sister Presidency of Bombay. The local university proposed some months ago to allow Native ladies to compete for the matriculation examination, and wrote to our own university asking if the latter were able to offer any suggestions or had any such scheme at heart. The reply was as disappointing as the action of the Bombay University was generous and well-meaning. It curtly stated that the Calcutta University was not in a position to co-operate the sister body in the matter. Should not the subject, we venture to ask, have received a more patient and careful consideration? None can maintain that if the old Hindu College had existed at the present day and no competitive system of examination had been allowed to come into play these nineteen years, the cause of education would have thriven so famously as it is doing now. The Calcutta University with its three thousand candidates every year, has become a glorious institution, solely because it has invited competition and maintained and fostered it by rewards, direct and indirect. We dare say that if female education be taken up by that examining body with the same ardour and vigour with which it has taken up male education, the results will be not only cheering but marvellous. Nay more. We may say that at the end of another two decades every B. A., will probably have a girl who is a degree holder, for his wife!

DR. JARDINE, the well-known Principal of the General Assembly's Institution Calcutta, has published his Psychology of Cognitions with the ostensible object of having it included as a text book for the B. A. examination. At least we learn this from a letter he addressed to the Syndicate of the Calcutta University. The text book already used is Sir William Hamilton's Lectures, and it was perfectly natural that the syndicate declined to comply with Dr. Jardine's request. As this gentleman is now a member of the governing body of the University, we fear that there is some chance of his influencing the counsels of colleagues in favor of his own book. We have nothing however to do with any decision that may be come to on the subject. All that we need say is, that Dr. Jardin has been a little too bold in his proposal. It is only a giant that would venture to supplant a giant; and Dr. Jardin has given no evidents of preternateral strength of this kind in his book.

Devotional

POUR Thy choicest blessings Almighty God, upon our sovereign, Fill her heart with Thy Holy Spirit when she assumes the title of Empress of India. Grant that she may feel that the title cometh from Thee, and bringeth with it a heavy trust and stupendous responsibilities. May not the Proclamation on New year's day prove an empty pageant but may thy daughter and servant Victoria, and may all her Councillors, and her representatives here all see in that ceremony Thy right hand placing the Empress' Crown on her head! May Victoria's reign be in future more and more conformable to Thy law of justice and charity. Gather Thou all the tribes and races of India with their rulers in Thy blessed fold that they may all be subject to Thy benignant sway for ever.

TRUE poverty I have yet to learn, my God. Sackcloth and ashes are not poverty, falling at the feet of others is not poverty, cooking one's own meal is not poverty, self-mortification is not poverty. Nor are they who weep incessantly to be accounted poor. Father, in lowliness of spirit is true poverty. May I not be as an arrogant prince in rags! Teach me to be poor in spirit. Teach me contentment, simplicity, meekness, forbearance, humility, and self-abnegation.

The Brahmo Somaj

WHY the conservative Somaj has renewed its attacks upon the marriages under the New Marriage Act is more than we can comprehend. The only cause to which such renewed antagonism rather late in the day, is attributable, is the striking evidence which a good number of Brahmo marriages, lately solemnized have furnished of the success of the Act. The warning administered evidently in a spirit of despair and helplessness by the *Tatwa Bodhinee Patrika* is not likely to be heeded in these days of progress. Our contemporary argues,—"We have lost our political liberty. Shall we sell our social liberty also?" Evidently it is not liberty but license that he advocates. Not to marry under the Act practically means with our friends of the other school the license to contract premature marriages. If men voluntarily and deliberately impose upon themselves the fetters of an Act created at their instance, binding themselves to eschew early marriage and bigamy and to promote intermarriages, they give proof not of cowardice and base subjection but of a high order of moral liberty and heroism.

THE NEW Year's Brahmo Diary is in the press, and will be shortly published.

THE Mission fund is at present, inadequate to meet the wants of our missionaries. There is, we are told, a monthly deficit of more than a hundred rupees. Certain arrangements are in contemplation with a view to rectify the defect of the present system.

THE donation of about nineteen thousand rupees we lately announced has not been, for obvious reason, accepted by the minister as an unconditional grant. The donor will have to reconsider the matter seriously and appoint his own men as directors or trustees, and frame proper rules for the efficient management of the fund.

Literary

MR. HEWLETT, the Superintendent of the London Missionary Society's Press at Mirzapur has published an Urdu translation of the Confessions of St. Augustine. Mr. Hewlett, we are told, "has exhibited in this instance an example of the somewhat rare combination of translator, printer, and publisher." Of the thirteen chapters into which the original work is divided, only the first ten contain the *Confessions*, properly so-called; the remaining three contain some discriminating and subtle dissertations of St. Augustine's on the subject of creation. The translator's work has ended here (at the tenth chapter) for the present; he promises, however, to add a translation of the remaining portion—the *Meditations*—if a second edition of the present work be required. The nature and intrinsic value of the *Confessions* are well described in the translator's preface.

THE *Friend of India*, at one time the ablest and most influential of Indian newspapers appeared for the last time yesterday. From the first of the next month, it is to be incorporated with the *Indian Statesman*, with the disappearance of the *Friend of India* there remains not a single weekly journal in this country conducted by Englishmen, that is worthy of educating and leading public opinion on important matters. Our contemporary thus strikes his own death note:—

The change which this journal is now about to undergo has not been suddenly resolved upon. It is the consequence of mature deliberation, and a clear conviction that it will be advantageous to the public, as well as to the Proprietors. A weekly *Newspaper* is becoming too slow for the times; a weekly *Review* is still premature in India. * * *
We shall not trouble our readers with a statement of all the reasons that have determined us to substitute one first class daily paper with a weekly edition for two distinct journals—a daily and a weekly. Suffice it to say, that we believe both papers will be improved by the change. All the power that has been divided between the two, will now be concentrated on the daily *Friend of India and Statesman*, and for those who still prefer a weekly paper the Overland Edition will be more valuable, both as a summary of news, and as a literary journal, than it has been possible to make the *Friend of India* hitherto: while it will contain the cream of the literary matter published daily, it will not be a mere reproduction of the daily paper. It will contain an original summary—not merely of the week's news, but also of the subjects of thought and speculation of general interest, that have been uppermost during the week. It will also contain the best information on financial subjects. Of the daily paper we need only say that all that the present Editor of the *Statesman*, and all that the present Editor of the *Friend of India* can do, with the assistance of an able staff of contributors on special subjects, will be done to give excellence to the Editorial columns, while a staff of reliable correspondents in different parts of India will, we believe, enable us to make the new journal unequalled as a newspaper.

The policy of the paper will be unchanged.

Scientific

AN allied topic is the blowing up of the dangerous reef of rocks which has for ages encumbered the channel between New York and Long Island, and with so much furious tidal commotion, that the first settlers named it Hell Gate. The mass of rock to be removed to make a clear channel twenty six feet deep was about seventy thousand cubic yards. Miners have been at work upon it for seven years; fifty thousand pounds of dynamite were packed in the borings and excavations; and on Sunday, September 24, the whole was fired. Beyond a slight tremor and a gush of water and smoke, nothing was seen or heard. Some of our readers may perhaps remember that Hell Gate and its neighbourhood was the scene of one of Washington Irving's early stories.

ARTILLERISTS and military engineers have something to talk about in the eighty-one ton gun which has been transported from Woolwich to Shoeburyness, where it throws its ponderous shot to a distance of five miles, and could double that distance if required, and with less noise than is made by guns not half the size. When four such guns are mounted in the turrets of the huge ironclad destined to receive them, she will be a formidable vessel either for attack or defence; able to batter an enemy's fortress from a distance of three miles. But already this monster gun has a rival, for guns weighing a hundred tons each has been constructed at Elswick on the Tyne for the Italian Government; and as they have been shipped to Italy, we shall so n hear of their acheivements.

Athenium and Daily News.

Incidents

"ACCORDING to the legend, King Edward was on his way to Westminster when he was met by a beggar, who implored him in the name of St. John—the Apostle peculiarly venerated by the monarch—to grant him assistance. The charitable King had exhausted his readymoney in alms-giving, but drew from his finger a ring, 'large, beautiful and royal which he gave to the beggar, who thereupon disappeared. Shortly afterwards, two English pilgrims in the Holy Land found themselves benighted and in the great distress, when suddenly the path before them was lighted up, and an old man, white and hoary, preceded by two tapers, accosted them. Upon [their] telling him to what country they belonged, the old man, 'joyously like to a clerk,' guided them to a hostelry, and announced that he was John the Evangilist, the special patron of King Edward, and gave them a ring to carry back to the monarch, with the warning that in six months' time the King would be with him in Paradise. The pilgrims returned, and found the King at his palace, called from this incident Havering-atte-Bower.' He recognised the ring, and prepared for his end accordingly. On the death of the Confessor, according to custom he was attired in his royal robes, the crown on his head, a crucifix and gold chain round his neck, and the Pilgrim's Ring' on his finger. The body was laid before the high altar at Westminster Abbey (A.D. 1066). On the translation of the remains of Henry II., the ring of St. John is said to have been withdrawn, and deposited as a relic among the crown jewels. During the reign of Henry III. some repairs were made at the Tower, and orders were given for drawing in the chapel of St. John two figures of St. Edward holding out a ring and delivering it to St. John the Evangelist."—*Fingh Ring Lore.*

WE COME AND GO.

If you or I,
To day should die,
The birds would sing as sweet to-morrow;
The vernal spring
Her flowers would bring,
And few would think of us with sorrow.

Yes, he is dead,
Would then be said;
The corn would flow, the grass yield hay,
The cattle low,
And summer go,
And few would heed us pass away.

How soon we pass!
How few, alas!
Remember those who turn to mould!
Whose faces fade
With autumn shade,
Beneath the sodded churchyard cold.

Yes, it is so;
We come, we go—
They hail our birth, they mourn us dead,
A day or more,
The winter o'er,
Another takes our place instead.

Latest News

—MR. HENRY succeeds Mr. Girdlestone as Resident at Nepaul.

—LORD BEACONSFIELD is unwell.

—ARCHBISHOP STEINS will attend the Imperial Assemblage, and be a guest of the Lieutenant-Governor of Bengal.

—THE Hon'ble Ashley Eden has been appointed an Additional Member of the Council of the Governor General for purpose of making Laws and Regulations.

—THE Hon'ble Mr. Inglis will be made a K. C. S. I. at the Imperial Assemblage.

Selections.

THE DRAMATIC PERFORMANCES ACT.

THE following Act of the Governor General of India in Council received the assent of His Excellency the Governor-General on the 16th December 1876, and is hereby promulgated for general information:—

WHEREAS it is expedient to empower the Government to prohibit public dramatic performances, which are scandalous, defamatory, seditious or obscene; It is hereby enacted as follows:—

1. This Act may be called "The Dramatic Performances Act, 1876."

It extends to the whole of British India;

And it shall come into force at once.

2. In this Act "Magistrate" means in the Presidency Towns a Magistrate of Police and elsewhere the Magistrate of the District.

3. Whenever the Local Government is of opinion that any play, pantomime, or other drama performed or about to be performed in a public place is—

(a) of a scandalous or defamatory nature, or

(b) likely to excite feelings of disaffection to the Government established by law in British India, or

(c) likely to deprave and corrupt persons present at the performance,

the Local Government, or outside the Presidency Towns and Rangoon, the Local Government or such Magistrate as it may empower in this behalf, may by order prohibit the performance,

Explanation.—Any building or enclosure to which the public are admitted to witness a performance on payment of money, shall be deemed a "public place" within the meaning of this section.

4. A copy of any such order may be served on any person about to take part in the performance so prohibited, or on the owner or occupier of any house, room or place in which such performance is intended to take place; and any person on whom such copy is served, and who does or willingly permits any act in disobedience to such order shall be published on conviction before a Magistrate with imprisonment for a term which may extend to three months, or with fine, or with both.

5. Any such order may be notified by proclamation and a written or printed notice thereof may be stuck up at any place or places adapted for giving information of the order to the persons intending to take part in or to witness the performance so prohibited.

6. Whoever, after the notification of any such order,—

(a) takes part in the performance prohibited thereby or in any performance substantially the same as the performance so prohibited or

(b) in any manner assists in conducting any such performance, or

(c) is in wilful disobedience to such order present as a spectator. during the whole or any part of any such performace, or

(d) being the owner or occupier, or having the use of, any house, room or place, opens, keeps or uses the same for any such performance, or permits the same to be opened, kept or used for any such performance,

shall be punishable on conviction before a Magistrate with imprisonment for a term which may extend to three months, or with fine, or with both.

7. For the purpose of ascertaining the character of any intended public dramatic performance, the Local Government or such officer as it may specially empower in this behalf, may apply to the author, proprietor or printer of the drama about to be performed or to the owner or occupier of the place in which it is intended to be performed, for such information as the Local Government or such officer thinks necessary.

Every person so applied to shall be bound to furnish the same to the best of his ability, and whoever contravenes this section shall be deemed to have committed an offence under section 176 of the Indian Penal Code.

8. If any Magistrate has reason to believe that any house, room or place is used, or is about to be used, for any performance prohibited under this Act, he may, by his warrant, authorize any officer of police to enter with such assistance as may be requisite, by night or by day, and by force if necessary, any such house, room or place, and to take into custody all persons whom he finds therein, and to seize all scenery, dresses and other articles found therein and reasonably suspected to have been used, or to be intended to be used, for the purpose of such performance.

9. No conviction under this Act shall bar a prosecution under section 124A or section 294 of the Indian Penal Code.

10. Whenever it appears to the Local Government that the provisions of this section are required in any local area, it may, with the sanction of the Governor General in Council, declare, by notification in the local official Gazette, that such provisions are applied to such area from a day to be fixed in the notification.

On and after that day, the Local Government may order that no dramatic performance shall take place in any place of public entertainment within such area, except under a license to be granted by such Local Government or such officer as it may specially empower in this behalf.

The Local Government may also order that no dramatic performance shall take place in any place of public entertainment within such area, unless a copy of the piece if and so far as it is written, or some sufficient account of its purport, if and so far as it is in pantomime, has been furnished, not less than three days before the performance, to the Local Government, or to such or to such officer as it may appoint in this behalf.

A copy of any order under this section may be served on any keeper of a place of public entertainment, and if thereafter he does, or willingly permits, any act in disobedience to such order, he shall be punishable on conviction before a Magistrate with imprisonment for a term which may extend to three months, or with fine. or with both.

11. The powers conferred by this Act on the Local Government may be exercised also by the Governor-General in Council.

12. Nothing in this Act applies to any *jatras* or performances of a like kind at religious festivals.

WHITLEY STOKES,
Sec. to the Govt. of India.

THE EMPRESS EUGENIE IN ENGLAND.

THE snow is thick upon the ground at Chiselhurst the sky is a level slate overhead, and an east wind is blowing. There is no cab at the damp little station, muddy with the thawings from travellers' shoes, and nothing for it but a walk up the hill in the teeth of the wind, charged with snow-powder that makes the face a denumbed mask. Across the common, floundering in the ruts and holes the snow has filled, to yonder gilded gates, where a policeman is crouching by the lodge away from the bitter breeze. The lodge is firmly closed as though no visitors could be expected this dismal January day; and while the keeper's wife is getting out of her comfortable quarters to answer the gate-bell, there is time to survey the sombre avenue of damp trees that leads to the house, the front of which is just visible. In this avenue, on a winter's day, the sometime master of the destinies of Europe took his last walk four years ago.

Sometimes the Empress receives in her boudoir—a most dainty *cabinet de travail* on the first floor, adjoining her Majesty's and the Prince's bed and dressing-rooms, with a well-loaded desk in a corner near and the window—which commands the avenue leading to the great gates—at which her Majesty spends many afternoons over her correspondence. One of the gentlemen in waiting taps at the boudoir door; a gentle voice from within cries, 'Entrez!' and the Empress turns from her writing to receive us. The same sad sweet smile, the same kindly grace, rounded with an impressive native dignity under the spell of which it has already been our privilege to speak of great events to one of the illustrious authors of them. Still draped and gloved in black, with that severe simplicity which French widows (who never show the least sign of coquetry in mourning, at any rate, and in this are an example to their British sisters) invariably observe, and the golden hair gathered close, the Empress Eugenie derives a new and a softer beauty from her sorrows. These have chastened—they could not break—her intrepid spirit. 'Her conduct after Sedan was heroic. It is impossible to conceive a nobler courage than she showed on the 4th of September,' an ex-Minister of the Empire said to us a few days ago. When the Empress speaks of the Empire or the Emperor, it is always with regret that the aims of Imperial institutions have been misrepresented and that the Emperor has been misunderstood. A zealous reader of the English papers, her Majesty watches the shiftings of our opinions on French affairs. On one occasion she observed that English journalists would not understand the democratic basis of the Empire. 'The Empire wanted and wants to give a direct voice to all Frenchmen in the Government; whereas other *regimes* would give a monopoly of power to the *bourgeois*, and make the people pay the taxes, and remain voiceless. If turbulent Frenchmen had only the calm in political matters of the English public!' It was at this interview that her Majesty observed, smiling, that she had a *dette de procès*. 'Monsieur Guizot pretends that he will force me to receive back the money the Emperor gave his son.' With great energy and flashing eyes the wife added, 'The Emperor was not in the habit of lending, but of giving.'—*World.*

RITUALISTS SUBDIVIDED.

SOCIALLY, the sacerdotal Ritualists are divided into three. There is the Ritualist who spends most of his time in his church, and the rest of it in confessing women, and in reading and inditing letters to the *Church Times* and similar publications. With parish work he does not trouble himself, leaving it for the most part to his more industrious brethren and to lay sisterhoods. He has usually a taste for music and a good library, and preaches controversial sermons. Then there is the Ritualist who devotes all his energies to his church and his parishioners, and who spares no pains to turn the hearts of the disobedient to his own way of thinking.

He is a very Jesuit in propagating his ideas and will not hesitate to canvass for and enlist recruits from the Evangelical, the Roman Catholic, or the Dissenting ranks, nor to rebuke insubordination with the infallibility of a Pope and the fire of a Knox. He is a stern, hard-working man, devoting his life to his labours; and if we may not agree with the narrow lines which he has laid down, we cannot but admire the earnestness of his belief and the consistency of his mode of living. He is the life and soul of Ritualism, being both recruiting-sergeant and rank and file, and withal content to leave the chief commands to others of the persuasion. He is no dandy in dress, though particular as to the cut of his clothes, and his "Noah's Ark coat" must assuredly most resemble that of him who was told off to do the dirty work of the floating menagerie. If a bachelor, as is generally the case, he is like the deaf adder, and refuses to hear the voice of any fair charmer, while showers of slippers, hymn-books, and tea-cosies slide off his heart like water from a duck's back. If he be married, he forms his wife into a kind of lady-help or an unordained and inferior curate believing her to be an estimable woman and a valuable coadjutor in his mission on earth. To his children he is rigorously kind correcting their sins with a strong hand and never failing to impress upon them the advantages which they possess in his rule and guidance. But in matters of pocket-money and clothes, he is (and often of necessity) not liberal. The third and last kind of Ritualist yields to none in the forms and customs of his party. He is vehement in his sermons, scrupulous in his symbolic gestures, resplendant in his vestments. But this work is strictly confined to limits of his church. Outside it he becomes a man of the world, and will shoot, play croquet, lawn tennis, and cricket, and even sing secular songs of an amatory nature. He is generally a popular personage, being all things to all men and women. He does not hesitate to play billiards or whist, and has even been known to indulge (very privately) in loo, *vingt-et-un*, and pokor. He does not often dance, but will at a pinch "make up" a quadrille on the carpet, whilst his evening attire is of itself a compromise, being composed of the ordinary, swallow tail-coat and an M. B. waistcoat, Unblievers, indeed, assert that he effects Ritualism because he believes it "to be the fashion;" but this is probably calumny. He is very particular, however, as to his local reputation; so much so that we have known him eschew ball on a Friday in his own neighbourhood, while having no objection to attend similar entertainments on the same day when away from home. He never goes to a burlesque theatre, but enjoys a ballet at the opera, or a farce at a melodramatic house. If you ask him to dinner he will devoutly cross himself before the soup, and yet tell you some very amusing stories over the wine and walnuts, and afterwards in the smoking-room will put you on a "good thing" for the Darby, which he himself has backed on, or rather through commission. Abroad he has no insular prejudices, and we remember some years ago passing a very pleasant Sunday afternoon with him and sundry bottles of *Asti spumante* in a cafe at Como. Yet he had an aversion, in common with his brethren, to Guy Fawkes, "William the Dutchman," Spurgeon, and Geneva gowns, and this is probably why an Evangelical fellow-traveller confided to us that he would not trust a Ritualist "farther than he could swing a bull by the tail."—*Vanity Fair.*

Advertisements

Wonderful Cure!!!

SOORJEE COOMAR SEN'S

Oil and Oxide for the Cure of Leprosy

PRICE Rs. 2-8

To be had at No. 16, College Street,

SOORJEE COOMAR SEN,

Manager of Ayurveda Dispensary.

ESTABLISHED 1833

H. C. GANGOOLY & CO.

STATIONERS, DIE-SINKERS, ENGRAVERS PRINTERS, LITHOGRAPHERS &c.

24, Mangoe Lane, Calcutta.

Cash prices of the following :—

	Rs.	As.	Rs.
Whatman's Drawing paper double elephant sizes (40×27) each ...	0	7	0
Mathematical Instrument Boxes	2	8 to	16
Color Boxes	0	4 „	5

Drawing Pencils, Drawing and Mapping Steel pens and various other requisites in Stationery.

MAKHON LOLL GHOSE.

No. 91, Radha Bazar,

CALCUTTA.

BEGS to invite the attention of the public to several consignments of commercial and fancy stationery of all sorts, including account books of all sizes, made of handmade and machine-made paper, by steamers recently arrived, and which he is disposing of at moderate prices.

Useful to Merchants and Bankers

JUST ARRIVED

LETTS'S DIARY FOR 1877

OF

VARIOUS SIZES AND SORTS

AND

AT MODERATE PRICES.

N. B.—None to be without a Copy of this Diary.

ESTABLISHED IN 1820.

C. LAZARUS & CO.

(INCORPORATED WITH SHEARWOOD & CO.)

CABINET MAKER, UPHOLSTERER

BILLIARD AND BAGATELLE TABLE MANUFACTURERS.

BY APPOINTMENT.

TO HIS EXCELLENCY

The Viceroy and Governor-General of India

AND

TO HIS ROYAL HIGHNESS

THE

DUKE OF EDINBURGH.

Billiard Tables

C. LAZARUS & Co., as manufacturers would invite particular attention to their large stock of full-sized Billiard Tables. One of the chief desiderata in a Billiard Table is to secure such an arrangement as will admit of a Ball being struck so as to attain the highest speed without its jumping. This, it need scarcely be said, depends entirely upon the arrangement of the cushions. C. L. & Co. mentioning this fact would state that the subject has largely occupied their attention and after repeated experiments and close consideration they have discovered a principle in the manufacture of cushions which answers admirably the end desired. Since the manufacture of their cushion on this new principle, C. L. & Co. have received testimonials from some of the first clubs in India speaking to the merits of the same. To secure *truth* with *speed*, that is to say, the maximum of speed compatible with preventing the Ball jumping, is the object which C. L. & Co. have had in view and which at length they have successfully attained. At the same time the cushions, it should be stated, are quite as durable or even more durable under the new principle of making up that under the old. With a view to the maintenance of the high character of their workmanship C. L. & Co. have secured for this branch of their business epecially, the services of a gentleman who for many years was foreman to the eminent makers, Messrs. Burroughes and Wates, whose experience is a guarantee of the highest possible excellence in the manufacture of Billiard Tables and of everything connected with that department of their business.

FRENCH MEDICINES

PREPARED BY

GRIMAULT & CO.,

PHARMACEUTICAL CHEMISTS,

8, RUE VIVIENNE, PARIS.

OF all the MEDICINES offered to the PUBLIC for many years past, none have met with such favorable reception, or been so generally approved by the Medical Profession, as those prepared by Messrs. Grimault and Co.

The model laboratories of this firm, situated at Neuilly-sur-Seine, and managed by Dr. Leconte, Professor in the Faculty of Medicine, ex-Pharmacist of the Hospitals of Paris, and formerly Assistant to Dr Claude Bernard, Professor of Physiology at the College of France, offer guarantees to be found in no other establishment.

NURSING, PREGNANCY, EXHAUSTION

DUSART'S

LACTOPHOSPHATE OF LIME PREPARATION.

The preparations having Lactophosphate of Lime at their base, known as DUSART'S WINE, SYRUP SOLUTION, are prime order reconstituents.

They promote the formation and the nutrition of tissues, render nurse's milk more rich and plentiful, and aid the formation of the infant during pregnancy.

They stimulate energetically the appetite, agree with feeble persons, convalescents, old people, and especially with children to counteract the invation of richets.

GRIMAULT & CO.'S

Syrup of Hypophosphite of Lime,

An excellent remedy for all affections of the chest; it relieves coughs, effectually prevents nocturnal perspiration, and restores the patient's strength. This syrup is the only one which, ever since 1857, has invariably been attended with satisfactory results—a fact due to the purity of the hypophosphite employed. Be sure to observe that it bears the signature Grimault and Co. on bottles of an oval shape, the Syrup being always of a rose colour.

GRIMAULT AND CO.'S

MATICO,

INJECTION AND CAPSULES.

Composed of the essence extracted from the plant so called, they have been constantly employed with the most brilliant success in a certain class of contagious diseases.

They combine extraordinary efficacy with the advantage of never causing nausea, eructations or pains in the stomach, as do the gelatinous capsules which contain Balsam of Copahu in a liquid state; or the structures that result from the use of injections having a metallic basis.

ASTHMA, ASTHMA.

GRIMAULT AND CO.'S

INDIAN-CIGARETTES-OF-CANNABIS-INDICA.

All the means hitherto employed to relieve Asthma have been only palliatives in varied forms, based on belladonna, stramonium, nicotiana, or opium. Recent experiments made in the Paris Hospitals have proved that our Cigarettes made of the extract of Indian Hemp possess remarkable virtues against this complaint, as well as against nervous coughs, chronic laryngitis, hoarseness, loss of voice, facial neuralgia and insomnia.

GRIMAULT AND CO.'S

GUARANA.

A single powder of this vegetable production is sufficient to cure instantly the most violent sick headache. It is the most valuable remedy against diarrhœa, dysentery, and all disorders proceeding from derangement of the stomach or bowels. This powder is indispensable for all families, and far more efficacious than opium or sub-nitrate of bismuth.

GRIMAULT AND CO.'S

SYRUP AND WINE OF PERUVIAN BARK AND IRON.

This medicine presents, in an agreeable form, the active principles of Peruvian Bark, the best of tonics, combined with iron, one of the principal bases of the Blood.

It rapidly removes the distressing stomach complaints, caused by anæmia, weakness, and other complaints to which ladies are liable, and is also excellent for pale, lymphatic and scrofulous children. Lastly, it excites the appetite, promotes digestion, and is extremely beneficial to all persons whose blood has been impoverished by illness or long and difficult convalescences.

AGENTS :

BATHGATE & Co..................	Calcutta.
CORFIELD & Co..................	Do.
SMITH STANISTREET & Co...	Do.
BARRIE & Co..................	Madras.
TREACHER & Co..................	Bombay.

NOTIFICATION.

Assumption by Her Most Gracious Majesty the Queen of the Title of Empress of India.

1. Under the authority of His Excellency the Viceroy of India and His Honor the Lieutenant-Governor of Bengal, the Proclamation of the assumption of the Title of Empress of India by Her Majesty Queen Victoria will be read in a Durbar, to be held on the Calcutta Maidan, on the 1st January 1877, at noon precisely.

2. Her Majesty's troops at the Presidency, with the Calcutta Volunteers, will parade under the command of Brigadier-General Ross, C. B., Commanding the Presidency Division.

3. Tents will be pitched on the Maidan, and the Proclamation will be read in English and the vernacular from a central dais.

4. Seats will be provided on and around the Dais for all Ladies and Gentlemen, European and Native, who may attend the Assemblage. A separate Notification is published to-day regarding the issue of Invitations and cards for admission to the Assemblage.

5. Precisely at noon, the Proclamation will be read in English, Bengali and Hindustani. The troops will then fire a *feu de joie*, and present arms and give three Cheers for Her Majesty the Queen and Empress of India. A salute of 101 guns will be fired by the Batteries of Royal Artillery on the ground.

6. An address in the English language will be delivered by the Presiding Officer, and a native gentleman of high rank will deliver a similar address in the vernacular language.

7. Honorary certificates will be presented to the Gentlemen who have been selected by Government to receive this distinction.

8. The troops will march past, and the ceremony will conclude.

By order,
C. T. BUCKLAND,
President of the Proclamation Durbar and Commissioner of the Presidency Division.

NOTIFICATION.

Assumption by Her Most Gracious Majesty the Queen of the Title of Empress of India.

At a Meeting of the Sub-Committee for the regulation of Invitations, and admission to the Proclamation Durbar on the 1st January 1877, it was decided, that lists of the Invitations to be issued should be prepared on behalf of the several sections of the Community by the Gentlemen who have kindly undertaken to act as the Representatives of the section of the Community to which they respectively belong. Seats will be available for rather than 3,000 persons, and Invitations will be issued upon lists drawn up by the Representative of each Section in numbers, roughly proportionate to the numbers likely to attend from that Section. Applications to be entered on the Invitation list may be made to the Gentlemen representing the section of the Community to which the applicant belongs.

When the total list of Invitation is complete, cards for admission will be issued indicating the block of seats in which a place is assigned to the person invited.

For the Hindoo community.—Baboo Degumber Mitter, C. S. I.

For the Mahomedan community—Moulvie Ahmed.

For the Jewish community.—Mr. Gubboy.

For the Parsee community.—Mr. C. M. Rustomjee.

For the Eurasian community—Dr. Chambers

For the Mercantile community—Mr. H. W. I. Wood.

For the Trades and Volunteers—Mr. Gordon Robb.

For the Military community—Brigadier-General Ross, C. B.

For the Marine community—Captain Warden.

For the Ladies and Gentlemen on the Government House List—Mr. Turnbull.

Native Residents of the 24-Pergunnahs—The Magistrate and Collector of the 24-Pergunnahs

C. T. BUCKLAND,
President of the Durbar Committee and Commissioner of the Presidency Division.

LIGHT! LIGHT!! LIGHT!!!

PATENT PORTABLE AIR GAS MAKING APPARATUS,

SUITABLE FOR

Churches, Chapels, Schools, Country Mansions, Private Houses, Railway Stations, Barracks, Manufactories, Collieries, Mills, Offices, &c., &c.

THIS *simple* and *effective* Gas-making Apparatus supplies a want long felt of having Gas at places where no Gas Works exist. It may be introduced without any more trouble than the simply affixing of any ordinary Gas meter, and is about the same size for the same number of lights. The *piping* and *fitting* arrangements are in every respect the same as for the use of ordinary Gas. The *cost* of the Gas produced is about the same as is charged for ordinary Coal Gas, and the light produced is *more brilliant* and of *a greater illuminating power*; it is also *free from the impurities of Coal Gas*. The Gas, if used with the Patent Burner, is of great heating power, and hence suitable for cooking and heating purposes, or in manufactories for soldering, &c. The apparatus is PORTABLE; there is NO DANGER WHATEVER (ordinary care being used when filling it); the Gas is PRODUCED IN AN INSTANT WITHOUT ANY FIRE OR OTHER ARTIFICIAL HEAT.

Further particulars may be obtained from MESSRS. EDWARD THOMSON & CO., Contractors for Drainage, Water and Gas, who are appointed Sole Agents for the above apparatus, which can be seen working any week day between the hours of 6 A.M., and 6 P.M., at their place of business.

39, *BENTINCK STREET, CALCUTTA.*

P. W. FLEURY & CO.,

BUILDERS, ENGINEERS,

AND

SCIENTIFIC INSTRUMENT MAKERS.

No. 44, Free School Street.

We beg to intimate that we have been engaged in the above line of business for the past 25 years, and trust that our Constituents will continue to favor us with their work, which will meet with prompt attention on our part.

In connection with buildings, we undertake the erection and repairing of machinery at moderate charges; as also execute all descriptions of Iron and Brass work.

We can assure the Public that we undertake the repair and erection of Houses, and the laying of Water-supply Pipes on moderate terms and guarantee to keep all the water-pipes and brass fittings supplied by us in good working order for three years, free of extra charge. We also guarantee to keep dwelling-houses' roofs water-tight for three years, free of extra charge, for such houses as are repaired.

For purposes of illumination, we prepare our patent Chromatic Transparencies representing Coat-of-Arms, Landscapes, Scenery, &c., at prices, ranging from Rs. 50 to 500 each, according to size and design.

FOR SALE.

Light! Light!! Light!!!

Electric Light Apparatus complete, worked with a battery of 60 large cells, on Bunsen's principle ...	500	0
Ditto ditto, with 40 cells, smaller size ...	400	
Ditto ditto, with a powerful 45-cell Cast-iron Battery, on Callan's principle ...	300	0
Lime Light Apparatus, complete, with Iron Gas-holder, and Copper Retort ...	150	0
Oxy-Hydrogen Light Apparatus, with safety Jets, 2 iron Gas-holders, and Retorts, complete	200	0
Hink's Patent Duplex Wall Lamps, with chimney	5	8
Ditto Duplex Lamp, with chimney and globe	7	8

Patent Leblanche Battery

For constancy, durability, and cleanliness, this battery is unequalled; price for each cell, with chemicals	3
Bunsen's Galvanic Battery, 9 inches, by 6 inches	7
Magneto-Electric Machine, with single magnet	14
Prismatic Compass, 3-inch, in solid leather case, by Elliot, second hand	32
Ditto, 4-inch, by Simmons, *second hand* ...	30

F. W. FLEURY & Co

No. 44, FREE SCHOOL STREET.

BABU BASANTA KUMAR DATTA,
HOMŒOPATHIC PRACTITIONER
No. 20, Sunker Halder's Lane, Ahiritolah.
LONDON AGENT
MESSRS. HENRY TURNER & CO.

HOMŒOPATHIC

FRESH
Medicines and other Requisites,
Arrives every month from England.
Medicines, Boxes, Books, Pamphlets;
Absolute Alcohol; Cholera-spirit Camphor.

SPECIAL REMEDIES.

For Supposed, Laborious and Difficult menses-Leucorrhœa; Hysteria.

For Spermatorrhœa; Dysentery; Diarrhea; Cholera.

For Asthma; Pile; Pain; Sore and Diseases of the Children.

Lemonade, Soda and Tonic water always.
To be had at
DATTA'S HOMŒOPATHIC LABORATORY
No. 312, CHITPORE ROAD, BURTOLA, CALCUTTA.
TERMS—CASH.
☞ Price List can be had free on application

R. K. GHOSH'S
HOMŒOPATHIC DISPENSARY,
No. 1, *Gour Mohun Mukerjee's Street, Simla.*
CALCUTTA.

HOMŒOPATHIC Medicine; Medicine chests of sizes,—containing medicine in tube phials; Homœopathic Books, tracts and pamphlets (English and Bengali); Dr. Rubini's "Saturated spirits of Camphor,"—(the best preventive and cure for cholera where medical aid is not available); and other Homœopathic requisites are sold here at a moderate price. Terms cash. Mofussil orders are promptly executed.

R. K. GHOSH,
Homœopathic Practitioner,
Manager.

SMITH STANISTREET & CO

Pharmaceutical Chemists & Druggists
BY APPOINTMENT
To His Excellency the Right Hon'ble
LORD LYTTON, G.M.S.I.
Governor-General of India,
&c., &c.

SYRUP OF LACTATE OF IRON

Prepared from the original receipe. Lactate of Iron, in various forms of preparation, have been in use in France, and generally through the continent of Europe, for some years past, and is highly esteemed as one of the most valuable Chalybeate Tonic remedies yet introduced. The Syrup, being the most agreeable as well as convenient form of administration is in most general use. It is a most valuable remedy in the following diseases :—Chlorosis or Green Sickness, Leucorrhœa, Neuralgia, Enlargement of the Spleen, &c. In combination with quinine, it has also been very successfully used in the cure of Fever, while to persons of delicate constitution, enfeebled by disease it is invaluable. In bottles. Rs. 2 each.

SYRUP OF THE PHOSPHATE OF IRON Rs. 2 per bottle.

SYRUP OF PHOSPHATE OF IRON AND STRYCHNINE, Rs. 2 per bottle.

SYRUP OF PHOSPHATE OF IRON AND QUININE. Price Rs. 2-8 per bottle.

SYRUP OF PHOSPHATE OF IRON, QUININE AND STRYCHNINE.(DR. ATKIN'S TRIPLE TONIC SYRUP), Rs. 2-8 per bottle.

Smith. Stanistreet & Co.

Invite special attention to the following rates the quality guaranteed as the best procurable :—

Pure Ærated Waters.

Made from Pure Water, obtained by the new process through the Patent Charcoal Filters.

				Rs	As.
Ærated plain (Treble Ærated), per doz.				0	12
Soda Water	ditto	„	...	0	12
Gingerade	ditto	„	...	1	4
Lemonade	ditto	„	...	1	4
Tonic (Quinine)	ditto	„	...	1	4

The *Cash* must be sent with the order to obtain advantage of the above rates.

Rivers Steam Navigation Co. "Limited."

The Steamer "BENGAL" will leave Calcutta for Assam on 2nd January.

The Steamer "NEPAUL" left Goalundo for Assam on the 21st instant.

The Steamer "OUDE" left Calcutta for Assam on the 22nd instant, and will leave Goalundo on 29th current.

For Rates of Freight and Passage, apply to

No 1, LYON'S RANGE, 22nd December, 1876. } MACNEILL & Co., Agents.

India General Steam Navigation Company, Ld.

SCHOENE KILBURN & Co.—*Managing Agents*

ASSAM LINE.
NOTICE.

Steamers leave Calcutta for Assam every Tuesday, Goalundo every Friday and leave Debroo-ghur downward every Saturday.

THE Str. "LUCKNOW" will leave Calcutta for Assam, on Tuesday, the 26th instant.

Cargo will be received at the Company's Godowns, Nimtollah Ghat, up till noon of Monday, the 25th.

THE Str. "ASSAM" will leave Goalundo for Assam on Friday, the 29th instant.

Cargo will be received at the Company's Godowns, No. 4, Fairlie Place, up till noon of Wednesday the 27th.

Goods forwarded to Goalundo for this vessel will be chargeable with Railway Freight from Calcutta to Goalundo in addition to the regular Freight of this Company.

Passengers should leave for Goalundo by Train of Thursday, the 28th.

CACHAR LINE NOTICE
REGULAR FORTNIGHTLY SERVICE.

Steamers leave Calcutta for Cachar and Intermediate Stations every alternate Friday, and leave Cachar downward every alternate Sunday.

THE Str. "COLGONG" will leave Calcutta for Cachar on Friday, the 29th instant.

Cargo will be received at the Company's Godowns, Nimtollah Ghat, up till noon of Thursday the 28th.

For further information regarding rates of Freights or passagemoney, apply to,

4, FAIRLIE PLACE, Calcutta, 21st December, 1876. } G. J. SCOTT *Secretary*.

SEWING MACHINES.

BRADBURY & Co.'s celebrated Prize Medal, PEARSON'S Wax-thread Harness Machine.

KNITTING AND DARNING MACHINES, COTTONS, SILKS, LINEN THREAD,
And all Machine requisites, and extras.
Price lists free on application.

MULLER CO.,
Engineers & General Agents,
5, HARE STREET, CALCUTTA.

CHUNDER & BROTHERS.

25½ & 112, RADHA BAZAR,

STATIONERY in all its varieties.
PRINTING PRESSES, Inks & Materials.
LITHOGRAPHIC PRESS & Materials.
BOOK BINDING Materials &c.

HAROLD & CO.,

3, DALHOUSIE SQUARE, CALCUTTA

HARMONIUMS.

Harold and Co., call attention to their unequalled stock of rich-toned Harmoniums made especially for India.

FROM RS. 90 TO RS. 900 EACH.

All kinds of Musical Instruments of the best description are always kept in Stock.

CALCUTTA

106, Bowbazar Street.

DR. H. C. SARMA'S

MEDICINE FOR DEBILITY

(NERVOUS)

HAIR PRESERVER.

Copy of Letter received from Rajah Chundernath Roy Bahadur of Nattore.

Wellesley Street, No. 18, Moti's Lane, 20th March 1874.

MY DEAR HURRISH BABU,—

I shall thank you to send me another phial of your "*Excellent Hair Restorer.*" In fact it has done me a great benefit, and I should like to have more of it. It has disabused me (young as I am) of old age.

Yours Sincerely

C. N. of *Nattore*

MEDICINE FOR BALDNESS.

Will certainly cure baldness if applied on the bald portion, night & morning, according to directions given in the adjoining direction paper.

Price per two ounce phial Re. 1 0 0
Postage &c. ... ... „ 0 6 0

HEEM-SAGAR OIL.

The best remedy for Headache arising from overstuday, intellectual occupation, over-thinking, mental anxiety and weakness, as well as heat of head from living in hot places.

It cools the head and produces very agreeable sensation. Removes dandriff as well as all other impurities from the head. Promotes the strength and growth of the hair and prevents its premature falling-off.

Price per 4 ounce phial Re. 1 0 0
Postage &c. ... ... „ 0 10 0

MEDICINE FOR LEPROSY.

Price with Postage &c ... Rs. 5 0 0

OIL FOR LEPROSY.

And Inveterate Skin Diseases.

Price per 8 ounce phial Rs. 2 0 0
Postage &c. ... ... „ 0 12 0

No More Pains!!!

THE

INFALLIBLE PAIN-CURER.

WARRANTED to cure pains of every description, arising from whatever cause, on any part of the human frame. A certain cure for Pains in the Back, Lumbago, Pains in the Chest, Sore Throats, Coughs, Colds, Tightness of the Chest, Colics, Rheumatism, Paralysis, Pains in the Groins, Contracted Joints, Gout, Swellings, Old sores, Piles, Ringworm, and Eruptions on the Skin.

Pains of every description have been cured by the outward application only of this medicine when all the skill of the medical art have been tried without effect.

Per bottle, First size ... ... Rs. 1
„ Second size ... ... Rs. 2
„ Third size 3

Postage and packing ans 8, ans 12, Re 1.

Remittance in half anna postage stamps need not be registered, but one anna should be more on every rupee for discounting the stamps.

DARLINGTON & Co.,
49, Dhurrumtollah Street, Calcutta.

FOR SALE.

VALUABLE LANDED PROPERTY.

THE desirable Premises No. 101, Taltala Lane, Calcutta. Price Rs. 5,000.

AND

A very elegant Family Residence, with 15 BIGAS *Lakhiraj* Gardens, bordering River Hooghly, Situate in Jeegomoy, lying directly *East* of CHANDERNAGORE, and being approachable by *boat* or *road* from *Shamnuggur* Station, EASTERN BENGAL RAILWAY. Price Rs. 3,000.

Apply to BABU RADHA GOBIND CHATTERJEE at the above places.

PRIZE MEDALLISTS

For Excellency of Workmanship.

J. M. EDMOND & CO.,

27—28, BENTINCK STREET,

ESTABLISHED 1832.

Cabinet Makers, Upholsterers,

AND

Billiard Table Manufacturers.

Houses completely furnished. Furniture designed and made to order.

ESTIMATES given for all kinds of Carpentering, Painting, Polishing, Gilding, and General Repairs; Marble Polished, Moulded, and Cleaned; Picture Frames made.

J. M. EDMOND & Co., in soliciting a continuance of public patronage, beg to say they have ready for sale specimens of Ebonized and Gold Oxford style of Fancy Chairs, and are prepared to execute orders for other Furniture in the same style.

J. M. EDMOND & Co.'s New Show-Room is now replete with New Heraldic Style of Dining-room Chairs, and Rustic Chairs, Telescope Dining Tables, with Patent Table Expanders, and a variety of finished Furniture.—Orders solicited.

BURN & CO.

RANEEGUNGE Fire-bricks are the best Fire Bricks known;—superior to Ramsay's. 9 Rs. per 100.

Fire clay, 40 Rs. per Ton.

Glazed Stone ware, Drainage pipes of all sizes.

BURN & Co.,
7, *Hastings Street, Calcutta.*

ARLINGTON & CO.,

3 B DALHOUSIE SQUARE, CALCUTTA.

THE 'PATENT PERPETUAL FOUNTAIN,'

TABLE EPERGNE OR CENTRE PIECE,

FOR SCENT OR FOR PUREWATER.

In Richly Electro-Silvered Ware. [*One of the Greatest Novelties of the day.*]

Cash Price Rs. 175.

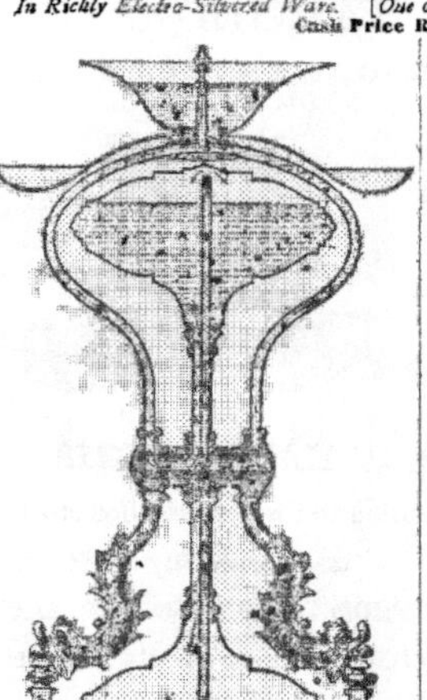

N. B.—The annexed drawing is not a correct representation of the Plated Table Fountains which A. & Co. have for sale. The drawing is only given to show the internal arrangements of the Apparatus, and attention is invited to the following description:—

OBSERVE.—A, A1, are two cisterns or reservoirs which are connected together by pipes or tubes B, B1, C, C1, mounted on a hollow axis of motion D, surrounding a fixed conical plug E, having suitable passages F, G, H, therein communicating with the pipes or tubes B, B1, C, C1, and I, and with the jet pipe J.

To put the fountain in operation water is poured into the dish or basin K until the lower reservoir is filled and the opening I1 is covered. The cisterns or reservoirs A, A1, are then turned on their axis of motion, so as to place the filled cistern or reservoir A at the top, when the water therefrom will flow to a level in the jet pipe J, and the water in the basin or dish K by passing down the pipes or tubes I and B1 into the lower cistern or reservoir A1, rises in such lower cistern or reservoir A1 and forces the air out therefrom through the pipe or tube C1, passage F, and tube B, into the upper parts of the cistern or reservoir A, where it presses upon the surface of the water therein and forces it out therefrom through the tube C, passage H, and jet pipe J, until all the water in the upper cistern or reservoir A has passed through the jet pipe J and into the lower cistern or reservoir A1 by the pipe I, passage G, and pipe B1, when by turning the cistern or reservoirs A, A1, on their axis of motion until the cistern or reservoir A1 is at the top, the action of the fountain will be continued; the pipes or tubes B, C1, which had previously been air passages now becoming water passages, and the pipes or tubes B1, C, now becoming air passages which had previously served for the passage of water. By these improvements the necessity for alternately filling and emptying the cisterns or reservoirs A, A1, is obviated.

Printed and published by M. M. BENERJI, at the INDIAN MIRROR PRESS, No. 6 College Square, for the Proprietors.

The Indian Mirror.

SUNDAY EDITION.

VOL. XV.] CALCUTTA, SUNDAY, DECEMBER 31, 1876. {REGISTERED AT THE GENERAL POST OFFICE.} [NO.

CONTENTS.

NOTICE.

All letters and communications relating to the literary department of the Paper should be addressed to the Editor. All other letters should be addressed to the Manager, to whom all remittances should be made payable.

Subscribers will be good enough to bring to the notice of the Manager any delay or irregularity in the delivery of the Paper.

Editorial Notes.

By the side of to the inhibition of a couple of clergymen to preach at a religious service held by the representatives of a number of Christian sects, the invitation recently held out by Dean Stanley to Dr. Duff to preah in Westminister Abbey on behalf of missions on Sir Andrew's day, presents a strange contrast. It is not a new remark to make that bigotry in every sect is in [inverse ratio to intelligence and true piety,

WE are exceedingly glad that Babu Keshub Chunder Sen has formed the plan of having a special service at Delhi to-day in honor of the auspicious occasion that is being celebrated in that ancient city. The sermon is to be on Loyalty. Both the service and sermon are to be in English we believe. No doubt a large number of those assembled at Delhi both among the Native and European gentry, will avail themselves of the present opportunity to hear what the leader of the Brahmo Somaj has to say to express the sympathy of his countrymen with the assumption of the Imperial title by Her Gracious Majesty. The sentiment of loyalty is a very strong feeling in the Hindu mind, and our countrymen will do well to foster in their hearts this national sentiment as much as possible. We publish elsewhere a number of Hindu texts from Menu and ancient Hindu writers bearing on this subject. These texts are to be recited by our minister in the course of the service.

THE condition of Chittagong is painful just now. As hinted in the Minute of His Honor the Lieutenant-Governor, disease has followed in the wake of the late cyclone and storm-wave, and almost as many are dying from cholera as died from the horrible catastrophe of the 31st October. Cholera has broken out nearly in every part of the district which was submerged, and how the epedemic can be stayed no one has been able to find out. We beg to draw the attention of our readers to an interesting statement on the relation between fever and cholera made by Dr. U. C. Kastogiri of Chittagong, who we may inform his friends, arrived only the other day in Calcutta. The frightful prevalence of cholera in Chittagong does indeed bear some testimony to the truth of his theory that cholera and fever in this country spring from the same source. Professor Tyndall's speculations on the subject of fermentation tend to bear out the same conclusion. We shall be glad to hear from our scientific correspondents on the matter.

SPIRITUALISTS, says the *Inquirer*, can no longer complain that men of science take no interest in their proceedings, and probably wish by this time that they had been less eager to court investigation by masters of the "observational method." It is not likely, however, that having once condescended to notice the matter the *savants* will release the wriggling "subjects" now under the microscope until they have rifled every secret of their pitiful organisms, and it bodes them no good that in his opening lecture the Professor of Moral Philosophy at the University of Edinburgh took the trouble to expose some of the most obvious weaknesses of the spiritualistic theory. Having drawn attention to the fact that a medium is always required for the evocation of spirits, that the behaviour of the spirits is puerile in the extreme, and that they betray a most suspicious want of conversational power, the Professor related what had happened at a *seance* he had attended. "He had," he stated, "been so far favored by the spirits that he was asked to call any one he pleased, and naturally wishing to speak with one whose thoughts he would understand, he had asked for Dugald Stewart, adding that he should like to hear this spirit's ideas on the philosophy with which he was connected. After this spirit had conversed with him for some time, during which he wrote down what was said, he desired it to stop, finding that what was being spoken was rubbish—was merely the haphazard answering of a man who did not know much about the subject." It seems to be about time that Professors, like the lower animals "except insects," should be classed as non-conductors, ineligible at a well-managed *seance*.

MISS Collet's year Book of which we made mention sometime ago, has appeared in England. We expect copies here before long. Miss Collet describes her publication thus :

The Brahmo Year-Book for 1876. Brief Records of Work and Life in the Theistic Churches of India. Edited by *Sophia Dobson Collet.*

Contents.

Glossary.
Preface.
Introduction.
1. From 1830 to 1866.
2. Ideals of Brahmoism.
3. Organization of Brahmoism.

General Survey of the Brahmo Somajes and their Work.
1. List of the Brahmo Somajes in 1876.
2. The Metropolitan Somajes.
3. Environs of Calcutta.
4. Eastern Bengal.
5. Western Bengal.
6. The Punjab.
7. Western India.
8. Southern India.
1. General Principles.
2. Improvement of Women.
3. Suppression of Intemperance.

There is a table of errata. The book is advertized to appear early in December. William and Norgate of 14 Henrietta Street, Covent Garden, are the publishers, and the price is one shilling a copy.

IT is somewhat striking that the principle, or rather the absence of principle which has characterized Government invitations in Calcutta to the Delhi Durbar, has drawn attention even in Bombay. They want to know why men like Rajah Romanath Tagore, and Babu Keshub Chunder Sen have not been invited, and they place the same erroneous construction that we were at first inclined to put on the inability of Rajah Jotendro Mohun, and Babu Kristo Dass Paul to proceed to Delhi. Of course they will be disabused as soon as they see the real reasons stated in our columns the other day. An esteemed correspondent of Bombay tells us that many Parsees have been invited, though their community, compared to the Hindus both here and in Western India, is so small. We congratulate our Parsee countrymen on the special favor with which they are regarded by Government, but we cannot understand why Hindus both in Bengal and the Mahratta country should not be esteemed equally well. Really the distinction is invidious.

THE distinction which a writer in last month's *Fraser*, makes between the Semitic and the Greek mind is exactly applicable to the distinction between the Hindu and European nature. "The Semitic mind," it has been alleged, "is destitute of the scientific instinct, looks upon man—every man—as standing in direct relation to God, who has not ceased his communications with His creatures, still speaking to them at times in dreams and visions, and at other times by the ordinary events of life. Nature is regarded as inanimate; her powers proceed from and are moved by the will of God. 'Pantheism in the Greek sense is utterly unkown to the Semites.' By its very nature the Semitic mind will ever throw itself confidently upon those primal intuitions which, if they do not admit of scientific or logical proof, are yet superior to scientific or logical disproof. Its inquiries, in spite of Tyndallism or Darwinism, will never go beyond the simple truth that, 'In the beginning God created the heaven and the earth.' The government of the world offers to the Semite an infinite problem which man can never solve, and hence the greatest aim of man should be the cultivation of those qualities in which he may most resemble God. Development among them was not in material, but in moral and intellectual forms. Hence while the Greek or Indo-European paid more attention to physical than to moral excellence, to the Semite the spirit, the mind of man, was the great object of development and culture—the inward character, rather than the outward form. The Mahomedan religion an offshoot from the Semitic mind, disregarding all adventitious circumstances, seeks for the real man, neglects the accidental for the essential, the adventitious for the integral. Hence it extinguishes all distinctions founded upon race, colour, or nationality. 'I admonish you to fear God' said Mahomed to his followers, 'and yield obedience to my successor although he may be a black slave."

THE PARTING YEAR.

THE New Year commences to-morrow! The old and well-approved custom is to give thanks for the many good things we have all enjoyed during the past twelve months to the Giver of all good; and to greet our friends, brethren, and supporters with the good wishes peculiar to the season. We have not enough space here to review all the important events through which we have passed and shall content ourselves with a brief reference to such factsas come more directly within our province on Sunday. The good people of our city, and to a great extent the country at large, were occupied on the opening day of the last year with the celebration of joy, felt for the presence in our midst of the Queen's eldest son, the future hope and ruler of this fair land. And the New Year opens to-morrow upon this vast Empire with renewed and heartier demonstrations of joy, because the august mother of that Prince has been graciously pleased to assume an imperial dignity as much in accordance with her power and position here, as with the history and traditions of ancient, medieval, as well as modern India. The visit of His Royal Highness and the loylty shown to him have a good deal to do with the wonderful political and social phenomenon now taking place at Delhi. Those, therefore, who averred at the time that the royal advent into this country would be barren of results, were very much mistaken. The moral and social advantages, to speak nothing of the political union and good feeling caused by what happened then and is happening now, are numerous; they will be more evident as the flurry and excitement incident upon all great events have subsided. One or two of these we shall try to point out. The relations between the ruling and governed races have been for a long time most unsatisfactory. The personal demeanour of Europeans towards the people of this country, has been a subject of standing complaint. A typical instance of such misdemeanour was furnished by what is known as the Fuller case of Agra, in which the Governor-General had to record his strong sentiments of disapprobation of the light sentence passed by the Allahabad High Court upon Mr. Fuller for assaulting his syce with a violence which caused the man's death. The Home Government strongly backed up the Viceroy inspite of the loud clamour which Anglo-Indians raised against His Excellency; and relying upon the testimony which the Prince and his party bore from their personal experience on the subject, some of the most influential papers and persons in England condemned the high-handedness and haughteur of their countrymen here. Though it is too much to hope that the personal bearing of such officials as Mr. Kirkwood of Chittagong will meet from Government with the reprobation they deserve, we may still reasonably think that assaults and outrages upon the people on the part of lawless Europeans will now cease gradually. The friendly feeling towards Native gentlemen of high rank shown by the Government, is also an effect of the same cause. Native society feels elevated at the elevation of Hindu gentlemen to positions of high honor and responsibility, and the cordiality shown to the Chiefs and Princes for their invariable loyalty. Professor Monier williams' project to found an Indian Institute at Oxford to afford facilities and protection to Hindu young men who proceed to England for the prosecution of their studies and advancement of their prospects, encouraged by the leading members of both the English and Indian society, is also a noteworthy fact of the last year. If the plan becomes succesful, it will very materially aid in forming the character and furthering the welfare of the persons on whose behalf it is started. Public morality in the countryhas been greatly advanced by the measures which the late Viceroy not long before his retirement, and Mr. Hobhouse, took to arrest the progress of indescent theatrical performances and exhibitions in and out of Calcutta. These measures have now been consolidated by the Dramatic Performances Bill which has been recently passed by the Imperial Council. The inauguration of the Albert Hall for the social intermingling of different races and clasess of the communities in Calcutta, and the encouragement and help given by the Government of Bengal towards that object, are also facts which deserves great prominence. It remains for us to hope that the Hall will always be well-filled and well-used by those for whom it is instituted. The opening of Dr. Sircar's Science Association also must be noted as a significant event of the last year Dr. Sircar who has been for years trying to establish a society for the scientific culture of his countrymen, cannot but congratulate himself as we congratuable him on the completion of his labors so far. And may the future of the Association realize the hopes of the past.

In the Brahmo Somaj the last year has been one of considerable importance. The austere and ascetic discipline of the previous year developed itself into what has been called the classification of devotees. The principles of this innovation were explained in a lecture about the commencement of the year by the leader of the Progressive Brahmos. Four definite departments of religious culture were laid down namely, *Yoga*, or contemplative communion with the Divine Spirit; *Bhakti*, the intense and ecstatic love of God; *Gyan*, or research, study, and the exercise of intelligent thought on the sacred writings of this and other countries; *Saba*, or training of the will in serving and promoting the welfare of fellow-men. Three Brahmo missionaries were initiated in the first three braches of the classification, and a lady volunteered to take up the fourth. Some of the teachings on these subjects have been translated in these columns. There has been much criticism on the principles of such classification, but it may be said to have ended in a sort of mutual understanding. Brahmo missionaries have gone forth into different parts of the country, and our mission operations have during the past twelvemonth mainly embraced the Punjab, parts of the N. W. Provinces, almost the whole of Behar, and parts of East Bengal. The Mission Fund, we are sorry to observe, has not been very well managed, and some of the branches of our work have been a good deal neglected. There have been more Brahmo marriages during the last year than in any previous year that we remember. There has been, we believe, one marriage to each month on the average. A number of prominent Brahmos have suffered domestic bereavements also. And this thought brings back to our mind the dreadful calamities which have recently befallen portions of this country. Famine is stalking forth in two of the sister presidencies, and an unprecedented catastrophe in the shape of storm and flood has swept away more than two hundred thousand lives from the eastern districts of Bengal. Amidst the widespread fear and mourning which these misfortunes have caused, we cannot but trust in the wisdom and mercy of Providence to guide the future of the country. May the assumption of imperial dignity on the part of our beloved Queen be auspicious and fruitful of good. May peace and justice and righteousness reign from one end of the country to the other in the coming year.

FOLLOW-DISCIPLESHIP.

THERE are many ready to speak on the benefit of self-abasement, but few are ready to give unto others the honor that is due to them. Many will bow before their friends and superiors as custom prescribes, but will be slow to recognize the real merit of those whom they thus salute. Many will choose to speak in their own dispraise, but will seldom discover any one whom they can praise more than they can praise themselves. Follow-discipleship is impossible under these conditions. Fellow-discipleship means fellowship in spirit. And such fellowship levels and equalizes all differences. Superiorities and inferiorities these must be; authority and obedience there must be; higher and lower positions there must be. But where these things appear in prominence, or become a matter of dispute and settlement, there is an end to all fellowship. Is there a subject of common interest to all; a master for whose worth there is felt a common admiration and love in many; is there a system of truth and harmony for the success and completion of which there is a common anxiety, and for which all are ready alike to labor and suffer? Where these conditions exist, fellow-discipleship becomes possible and practicable. If some grave wants are felt in common; some real feelings of sympathy arise in the heart for a common sorrow and difficulty; if men feel naturally inclined and bound to repose their confidence in each other and find their suspicions and fears allayed; if they feel no harm can accrue to themselves for trusting and resting on each other, and that the ground of mutual union is safe and strong, fellow-discipleship becomes a fact, quite within reach, if not already achieved. Where co-operation is not a duty but a delight, not a discipline but a matter of course; where men feel that common work is sure benefit, and common trials a sure source of strength; where name and fame and power if not altogether absent, are but secondary and quite subordinate and if obtained, become a matter for congratulation for each and all alike, the thing is perfectly possible. In the ordinary relations of life a man feels elevated and proud of the position, wealth, or acquirements of his friends though he himself be poor and small. How much more must religious men feel privileged and glad for being known as the fellow-disciples of saints and holy men! Who among us would not wish that he was a contemporary and companion of the prophets and martyrs? Yet what were the prophets and martyrs themselves but men under teaching and discipline who had as much need of the ordinary virtues of the heart and the mind as we have ourselves? But the very best of men have quarrelled and differed in spirit, instead of showing the exemplary relation of fellow-disciples. A man's best friends and worst enemies are of his own household. But unfortunately the friendship is much less common than the enmity. Devotion to masters many have shown; loyalty to genius is a sort of natural and universal homage, though so many demur to give it at the present day; but loyalty and devotion to those who are slightly superior or inferior to us, is a virtue yet to be embodied in human character. Where the superiority is very great, and the inferiority is unquestionable men can afford to be considerate to each other; but on ground where the question of precedence is not raised at all, they will not consent to stand or work very long. The Brahmo Somaj is composed of men who are very much of the same age and acquirements, and whose career and influence in the institution are nearly and concurrent; many prominent Brahmos live together, work at the same place, and are supported out of a common stock, and we believe their admiration and enlightenment also refer to a common centre, why should there not be the bond of fellow-discipleship in their midst, and why should they not leave behind them the example of preferring in honor and love their brethren before themselves?

THE IMPERIAL ASSEMBLAGE AT DELHI—II.

DELHI, *the 25th December* 1876.

YESTERDAY being Sunday, there was no State ceremonial, but Divine Service in the Camp. In the Viceroy's Camp there are the Lord Bishop of Madras and the Ven'ble Archdeacon J. Baly, M. A., to take care of the spiritual interests of the Christian inhabitants of this canvas city. Bishop Andrew of America is also here at this moment. Among the other ecclesiastics are to be found the Rev. F. Gell, the Rev. W. W. Elmes M. A., the Domestic Chaplain to the Bishop of Madras, the Rev. Father Lewis, the ev. Father Patrick, the Rev. Tarachand, the Rev. D. Rose, the Rev. Mr. Fordyce, Bishop Andrew, and the last two named gentlemen are putting up in the Camp of Mr. Inglis, the Chief Commissioner of Oudh.

The different Camps are so distant from each other that without a carriage and a pair, and a geographical guide in hand, it is far from convenient to travel from one to the other. The "Imperial Assemblage Directory" just issued will, therefore, prove most useful at this moment. Its compilers are Captain J. Robertson and Mr. L. A. Smith of the Office of the Quarter Master General in India, and it is printed at the "Pioneer" Press. It contains among other things, a map showing the positions of the several Camps. The publication bears internal evidence of having been hurried through the Press, for not a few typographical inaccuracies are to be found in its pages. For instance, the name of Mr. Manockji Rustomji, the Persian Consul in Calcutta who is here in the Consuls' Camp, is spelt "Ananckjee Ruthmajee." Sukharam Shahib, the consort of the Princess of Tanjore, is spelt "Luchoram Sahib." Barring these small errors, the book is of considerable value for the time being. Already several thousands of copies have been sold, the demand being so great for the book.

The only Native gentlemen who have got their tents in the Viceroy's Camp are the following:—The Maharajah of Benares, the Maharajah of Bulrampore and Rajah Nurendra-Krishna, additional members of the Viceroy's Council. The following distinguished visitors from England, have also got their tents in the Viceroy's Camp:—Mr. T. Cartwright M. P., Lord and Lady Dourne, Viscount Brooke, Lord Kilmaine, Sir Robert Abarcromby. Sir Richard Garth is also in the Viceroy's Camp. Portions of the Home Office, the Foreign Office, the Military Secretary's Office, the Private Secretary's Office, the Military Department, the Toshakhana and the Munshikhana are also located in the Camp.

Next to the Viceroy's Camp comes the Camp of the Governor of Madras, under the head of "Imperial Camps." Camp No. 3 Imperial—is that of the Governor of Bombay. No less than three Puisne Judges of the Bombay

High Court are to be found in this Camp. No other Puisne Judges have come from any other Presidency. The fourth Imperial Camp is that of Sir Richard Temple, the Lieutenant-Governor of Bengal. The following is the list of inmates of this Camp:—Sir Richard, Lady and Miss Temple, Mr. and Mrs. Lindsay, Colonel and Mrs. J. A. Steel; Miss Judge; Mr. R. L. Maugies, Mr. T. W. Grible, Mr. C. Sanderson, Government Solicitor; Mr. A Money, Lord Ulick Browne, Colonel J. E. T. Nicolls, Major R. J. Money; Major J. G. Lindsay, the Hon'ble H. Bell, Mr. J. H. Rivett-Carnac, Dr. T. E. Charles, Major General C. A. Barwell, Sir Stuart Hogg, Mr. C. T. Metcalfe, Colonel F. T. Haig, Mr. J. C. Murray, Mr. C. E. Buckland, Lieut. P. A. Buckland, Lieut. D. C. Dean Pitt, Captain J. S. Frith and Lieut. W. H. Firth. So Sir Richard, it appears, has got as many of his relatives as he possibly could. We are glad to find that he has got a non-official European gentleman of Calcutta in the person of Mr. J. C. Murray, Prsident of the Bengal Chamber of Comerce. The Hon'ble J. Bullen Smith's name appears in the Camp, occupied by the Hon'ble Mr. Inglis, the Chief Commissioner of Oudh. The other Imperial Camps are as follows:—Camp of the Lieutenant-Governor of the N. W. P., Camp of the Lieutenant-Governor of the Punjab, Camps of their Excellencies the Commander-in-Chief in India and the Commander-in-Chief of the Bombay Army (the Commander-in-Chief of the Madras Army has been unable to come, but he is being represented by the Adjutant General of the Madras Army). Camp of the Chief Commissioner of Oudh, Camp of the ChiefCommissioner of the Central Provinces, Camp of the Chief Commissioner of Barmah, Camp of the Chief Commissioner of Assam, Camp of the ChiefCommissioner of Mysore, Camp of the Resident at Hyderabad, Camp of Agent to Governor-General for Central India, Camp of Agent to Governor-General for Rajputana and Camp of Agent to Governor-General for Baroda. The only two Native gentlemen who are in the Camps of Agent to Governor-General for Central India and Agent to Governor-General for Rajputana respectively, are Shahibzada Mahomed Wahed-u-dind and Nur Mahomed Khan, Attaches. Among the Native Officers in the Camp of the Commander-in-Chief in India, we find Hon. Major Shaik Hedayut Ally Khan Bahadur, Sirdar Bahadur and Nawab Gholam Hossain Khan, Alazai Khan Bahadur C. S. I. In the Camp of the Lieutenant-Governor of the Punjab there are among other persons, Mr. Justice Boulnois, Mr Justice Campbell, and Kunwar and Kunwari Harman Sing. Mr. C. R. Bernard is in the Camp of the Chief Commissioner of the Central Provinces, and three Cossyah Chiefs are to be found in that of the Chief Commissioner of Assam. Beides these Camps there are several Military Camps containing the Troops, which are divided as follows:—The Escort of the Viceroy, the Cavalry Division, the Royal Artillery Division, the 1st Infantry Division and the 2nd Infantry Division. The Troops belong to Bengal, Madras Bombay and the Punjab respectively.

The Miscellaneous Camps consist of Post Offices, Barrack Departments, Imperial Camp Bazar, Commissariat, Government Telegraph Office, Field Telegraph Office, E. I. Railway Traffic and Telegraph Office, Attaches' Camp, Consuls' Camp, European Press Camp, Native Press Camp, European General Hospital, General Hospital for Natives, Punjab Civil Camp, Visitors' Camps, Police Head Quarters, Police Stations and Dak Works Camp.

The Attache for Bengal is Colonel H. M. Boddam. He is taking care of all gentlemen from Bengal who have been invited to the Assemblage by the great LocalGovernment. The tent of the great historian to the Assemblage, Mr. Talboys Wheeler, who is an Attache of the Foreign Office, is also in the Attaches' Camp. Among the Attaches are also to be found Captain E. Molloy, the Attache of the Yarkand Envoy; Major R. G. Sandeman, the Attache for Khelat; Captain Talbot of the Siamese Camp and Dr. Scully, the Attache for Nepal.

In the Consuls' Camp, we meet with the tents of Mr. R. Macallister, the Consul-General for the United States of America and Mr. Manickji Rostomji, the Consul for Persia. There are also the Consuls-General and Consuls for the German Empire, for Italy, for the Netherlands, for Spain, for France, for Denmark, for Belgium and Siam.

The European Press Camp represents only the following papers:—The *Friend of India*, the *Pioneer*, the *Englishman*, the *Indian Daily News*, the *Statesman*, the *Indian Public Opinion*, Reuter's Agent, the *Madras Athenaeum*, the *Bombay Gazette*, the *Times of India*, the *Madras Times*, the *Madras Mail*, the *Delhi Gazette*, the *Civil and Military Gazette*, the *Himalya Chronicle* and the *Graphic* of London.

The Native Press Camp consists of the representatives of the following papers:—The *Hindu Patriot*, the *Indian Mirror*, the *Sadharani*, Chinsurah; the *Dacca Prakach*, Dacca; the *Jam Jehannama*, Calcutta; the *Urdu Guide*, the *Amrita Bazar Patrika*, the *Bhaugulpore Gazette*, the *Koh-i-Noor*, Lahore; the *Punjab Akhbar*, Lahore; the *Oudh Akhbar*, Lucknow; the *Akhbar-i-Anjuman*, Lahore; the *Agra Akhbar*, Agra; the *Nur-ul-Absar*, Allahabad; the *Prabhakar*, Bombay; the *Native Opinion*, Bombay; the *Rast Goftar*, Bombay, the *Indu Prakash*, Bombay; the *Jam-i-Jamshed*, Bombay; the *Bombay Samachar*, Bombay, the *Krishful Akhbar*, the *Lawrence Gazette*, Mirut; the *Kasi Patrika*, Benares, and the *Berar Samachar*, Hyderabad.

In the Visitors' tents, are to be found Mr. Bradford Leslie, Agent, E. I. Railway; several members of the Civil and Military Services, Colonel E. C. S. Williams, Director of State Railways; Mr. Madhava Rao, Photographer; Mr. Bannerji and others.

The Special Native Camps consist of the Nizam of Hyderabad, the Gaekwar of Baroda, the Maharajah of Mysore, the Khan of Khelat, the Siam Deputation, the Nepal Deputation, His Highness Syud Turki, the Imaum of Muscat and His Highness Sayyed Said, the representative of the Sultan of Oman. The Nizam occupies Sir T. Metcalfe's house and four other new buildings on this estate.

The Camps of the Central India Chiefs include the Maharajah of Gwalior, the Maharajah of Indore, the Begum of Bhopal, the Maharajah of Rewah, the Maharajah of Orcha, the Maharajah of Duttia, the Rajah of Dhar, the Rajah of Dewas, the Rajah of Sumpthar, the Nawab of Jowrah, the Rajah of Rutlam, the Maharajah of Punna, the Maharajah of Chirkari, the Maharajah of Ajeyghur, the Rajah of Bejawur, the Rajah of Chutterpore, the Rajah of Beronda, the Rao of Tori, the Rao of Jigni, the Jagheredar of Alipore, the Jagheredar of Paldea and the Thakur of Piploda.

The Rajputana Chiefs are the following:—The Rana of Dholepore, the Maharajah of Kerowli, the Rajah of Bhurtpore, the Maharao Rajah of Bundi, the Maharajah of Kisheughur, the Nawab of Tonk, the Maharao Rajah of Ulwar, the Maharajah of Jodhpore, the Maharana of Oodeypore, the Maharaj Rana of Jhalawar and the Maharajah of Jeypore. There are also about fourteen nobles from Rajputana.

THE IMEPRIAL ASSEMBLAGE AT DELHI.—III.

Delhi, the 26th December.

THE Bombay Chiefs present here, are only six in number, *viz*, the Khan of Khyrpore, the Nawab of Junaghur, the Jam of Nowanugger, Thakur of Bhownugger, the Rajah of Rajpipla and the Thakur of Morvi. The number of Bombay Native gentlemen who are here, is a pretty large one. They are as follows:—The Hon'ble Rao Sahib Wishwanath Narayan Mandlik, Hon'ble Nacoda Mahomed Aly Ragay, Sir Jamsetji Jejibhoy, Bart, C. S. I., Haji Ismal, Haji Habib, Mr. Byramji Jijibhoy C. S. I., Mr. Shantaram Narayan, Mr. Rughunath Narayan Khote, Sir Munguldass Nathubhy, Knight, C. S. I., Mr Murarji Goculdas, the Honble Rao Bahadur, Becherdas Ambaidas, C. S. I., Rao Bahadur Gopal Rao Huri, Khanderao Saheb Raste, Mir Syed Alum Khan Saheb, Nawab of Behte, Jugjivandass Khusaldass, Mir Gulam Baba Veridas Ajubhai *alias* Bapu Saheb, and Rai Bahadur Shumbupersad. Only four of the Madras Chiefs have come, *viz*, the Prince of Arcot, the Princess of Tanjore, the Zemindar of Pittapore and the Zemindar of Kiliapurum. The Native gentlemen from Madras are only four, the Hon'ble Bujjupatti Rao, the Hon'ble Ramyangar, the Hon'ble Humayoon Jah Bahadur and Mr. Mustuswamy Iyer.

The Punjab Chiefs include the Maharajah of Cashmere, the Nawab of Bhawulpore, the Rajah of Jhind, the Rajah of Nabha, the Envoy from Yarkand, the Rajah of Mundi, the Rajah of Nahun, the Nawab of Malerkotta, the Rajah of Faridkote, the Rajah of Bilaspore, the Rajah of Chumba, the Rajah of Suket, the Nawab of Pataodi, the Nawab of Loharu, Nawab of Dojana and the Rajah of Gulevia. The Punjab Nobles are no less than 55 in number.

The Nawab of Rampore, the Rajah of Tehri and the Maharajah of Benares are the only three Chiefs, who come from the N. W. P., while there are thirty-three Nobles from those Provinces, including Rajah Sir Dinker Rao, Rajah Shiva Prasad, C.S.I., Sheoraj Singh, C.S.I., the Rajah of Kashipore, who was once a member of the Viceregal Legislative Council, and Rajah Jaikissen Dass, C.S.I.

The Central Provinces have sent twenty-three Chiefs and Nobles.

Bengal has sent no Chiefs, but only some Nobles and Native gentlemen. They are the Maharajah Krisnna Purtab Sahi Bahadur of Huttwah, Nawab Amir Aly Khan Bahadur, Maharajah Sir Jeymungal Singh Bahadur, K.C.S.I., of Bhaugulpore; Nawab Syud Ashgar Ally Khan Bahadur Diler Jung, C.S.I., Maharajah Maheshur Buksh Singh Bahadur of Dumraon, Rajah Nirpindar Narain Bhup of Cuch Behar, Rajah Hurbullub Narain Singh Bahadur of Somburash, Maharajah Sukh Messir Singh Bahadur of Durbhanga, Rajah Narendrakrishna Bahadur, Rajah Harendrakrishna Bahadur, Babu Jaggadanand Mukerji, Moulvie Abdul Lutif Khan Bahudur, Nawab Hussen Aly Khan Bahadur, and Nawab Anwar Shah, eldest son of the ex King of Oudh.

The Oudh Camp consists of three members of the ex-Royal family, and of about thirty Talukdars.

About six Burmese gentlemen have come from Burmah, and are in the Camp of the Chief Commissioner of Burmah.

The exhibition of jewellery and other articles of Indian manufacture and special excellence will be held in the District Court-houses. In the first building will be exhibited shawls, silks, embroidered fabrics, and "Kincobs" from Cashmere, Benares and other parts of India. Six more buildings will be occupied by artificers in brass, steel and glass from Kurnal and elsewhere. The three large rooms in the main building, will be devoted to a display of jewellery from all parts of India. On the ground floor, one large room will also be devoted to gold and silver work, the other being principally devoted to Indian brass work together with other articles of Indian manufacture having a special interest. There will be also a shed in which a shawl loom from Umritsur will be seen in actual operation.

The races will take place on the 4th and 6th proximo, commencing at about 3 P. M. each day. The Stewards of Races are the Honble Sir A. J. Arbuthnot, Major General Sir Henry Daly, K. C. B., Major General Sir Samuel Browne C. B., V. C., the Hon'ble R. A. Dalyell, Lord Ulick Browne and two others.

The following tradespeople have arrived from Calcutta :—Messrs M T. Martin and Co., Messrs Cooke and Kelvey, Messrs Bourne and Shepherd, Messrs Cooke and Co., Messrs Baker and Catliff and Messrs Hamilton and Co.

Poor Captain Clayten, Extra Aide-de-Camp to His Excellency the Viceroy, who took part in the procession the other day, died last night from the effects of the injury received by him by a fall from his house, while playing at a polo match.

SPECIAL TELEGRAMS FOR THE *INDIAN MIRROR*,

THE IMPERIAL CAMP.

Delhi, 29th December 1876.

Several petty Chiefs received by Viceroy to-day, have been created Rajahs, Raos and Rao Bahadurs. Khan of Khelat has received large presents. Cuch Behar was received as representative of Bengal Chiefs. A banner and medal given him. Cashmere appointed General in the Army and Nizam Imperial Grand Chamberlain.

Delhi 30th December 1876.

Three more Imperial Councillors are Jhind, Rampore, and Travancore. Increase of salutes, Oodeypore's from nineteen to twenty one guns, Rampore's for life from thirteen to fifteen guns. Bhownugger, Drangadra, Junaghur and Nowanugger's from eleven to fifteen guns. Life salute of eleven guns, to Tehree and Morvi and nine guns to other Kattywar Chiefs. Governors and Lieutenant-Governors have received banners and medals and Viceroy also. Other officials medals only.

All Native Nobles and gentlemen invited, have been presented with silver medals. Titles of Rajah, Rai Bahadur, Khan Bahadur and Rao Saheb have been conferred on some. Several Punjab Chiefs created Honorary Assistant Commissioners. Rajah Narendrakrishna, Rajah Harendrakrisha, Nawab Amir Ally, Babu Juggadanund, Moulvie Abdul Lutif and Rais Luchmiput and Dhun Putt, have all received silver medals. Sir Dinkar Rao has got the title of Rajah Mushir Khas Bahadur. Imperial Assemblage takes place on Monday noon. Proclamation will be read by Chief Herald. Viceroy will address the Assemblage. Sir Richard Temple holds another Durbar on Wednesday.

The Brahmo Somaj

AT the urgent and repeated invitation of His Highness the Holkar, Babu Keshub Chunder Sen has proceeded to Delhi. He may be expected back in Calcutta in about a fortnight more.

A BRAHMO marriage was celebrated in our neighbourhood on last Wednesday evening. The bridegroom Babu Parbati Charan Gupta is a Pleader of Purnea. He is a widower, and performed the first Brahmo intermarriage in 1864 which caused so much agitation, and produced such important consequences at the time. The bride Srimati Saradamoyi Bandopadhaya is a widow, and lost her first husband when she was not older than ten or eleven years. The marriage service was conducted by Babu Gourgovind Roy.

WE are glad that Dr. Prosonno Kumar Ray has consented to give a public lecture on Science and Theology. The lecture is to take place on Wednesday evening next at the Albert Hall. We expect a good gathering, and also that those who take interest in the promotion of Science, will be good enough to be present on the occasion. We believe Dr. Ray intends to deliver two lectures on the subject, and this is the first of the two.

AN appeal is made to the Brahmo public for the collection of funds with the object of executing necessary repairs upon the Brahmo Mandir which has suffered some damage during the last nine years since the erection of the edifice. The organ also which was presented by English friends, has suffered some damage, and requires to be repaired. The whole will cost about seven hundred rupees, and the repairs must be finished before the coming anniversary. Besides, the outstanding debts of the Mandir will amount to five hundred rupees. It is expected that the Brahmo public will charitably subscribe these twelve hundred rupees, and improve the appearance of their place of worship, and deliver it from old debts.

BABU DURGAMOHUN DASS has presented 250 copies of the life of his late wife to the Brahmo Samaj of India. The little book which is well printed and well bound, sells for three annas a copy.

WE are requested to state that the Brahmo Pocket Diary and Almanack for 1877 will be published tomorrow Price 8 annas per copy.

WE have the pleasure to give below an English translation of the Sanskrit texts that are to be read at the special service which our leader will hold at Delhi in honor of the assumption by Her Majesty of the Imperial title.

O SON, did not the king protect us, great oppression would afflict us and we could not practice religion with so much ease and comfort.—*Mahabharat Adiparba.* XLI.

PROTECTED by the virtuous kings, we happily conform to the various laws of religion and therefore a share of the fruits of our practised virtues belongs to them.—*Ibid.*

MANY forms of evil distress a country where anarchy prevails. The king governs with his rod those who are lawless. They exceedingly dread the rod and hence peace is established by it.—*Ibid.*

No religious rite and no great work can be well performed in confusion and misrule. And hence religion is established by the king, and by religion heaven comes down upon earth.—*Ibid.*

WHEN there was no king in this world, men through fear, wandered here and there,

For their protection God created king.—*Manu Chap.* VII.

No one should disregard the King even if he be a boy. He is a god disguised in human form.—*Ibid.*

FIRE only burns the person who carelessly approaches it, but the ire of king consumes not only its object, but also the whole progeny, the property and the cows and horses &c., that belong to it.—*Ibid.*

CONSIDERING the place, time and the powers at his command and the work to be done, the King exercises his various powers at different times to accomplish his virtuous ends.—*Ibid.*

He is indeed a most brilliant power in whose hand is property, in whose power is victory and in whose wrath is death.

THE destruction of that person is inevitable who rebels blindly against his king, for the king compasses his ruin.

No one should therefore infringe any of the civil or penal laws which are established by the king.

AN ERA or *Yuga* is formed by the reign of a king. And it is called *Satya, Treta, Dwaper* or *Kali* according to the character of the reigning monarch.—*Manu Chap.* IX.

WHEN the King is inactive or in other words, through idleness and want of intelligence he puts forth no efforts to govern his subjects well, his reign is called *Kali*. That period is styled *Dwapur* when the king possesses intelligence; but he does not act according to its promptings. That epoch is named *Treta* when the King wishes to put forth various efforts. And that is *Satya Yuga* when the king is *fully* active and looks after the well being of his subjects directly and personally.—*Ibid.*

Devotional

AT the early dawn of day, O my God, fill my soul with the presence of thy Spirit. I invoke thy light and love to enter into me, and inspire me with right feelings towards all men, and right motives under all circumstances of my daily life. In the blessedness of thy communion, and in the honorable occupation of working in thy field may the whole day pass.

"All hallowed be our walk this day,
May meekness form our early ray,
And faithfull love our noontide light,
And hope our sunset calm and bright;
May grace each idle thought control,
And sanctify our wayward soul;
May guile depart and malice cease,
And all within be joy and peace."

TEACH me sober wisdom, O Lord of Truth, and let me see things not according to my imagination, but in the light which fills thine eye. Let my relations to my circumstances and surroundings be regulated in the manner that appears best in thy sight.

How sweet and infinite is the motherliness of thy nature, O thou Holy Spirit, combining unspeakable beauty with unspeakable love. The most intense affection of this world is but the faint shadow of thy tenderness. Why should I not be enchanted with thy motherly love to me, I who am motherless and fatherless alike. Wash my wearied and friendless heart with the refreshing showers of thy tender grace, charm me with the celestial handsomeness of thy glorious presence, and draw me unto thee as a mother draweth her child.

OFTEN have I said I would lay my flesh unto the dust of this world, and fly to thy holy mansions above, O my Father. How often have I said I would crucify and renounce for ever all that is carnal in me. But O my Saviour, I am still a poor worm of this earth, grovelling in the midst of what is vile and carnal. When wilt thou give me rest, and put into my hand the cup of sanctity, which he who drinks becomes pure for ever. O Lord I long to be meek and holy as thy faithful children are.

Social

IT is not perhaps generally known that a Bengali Christian lady, named Chundramukhi Bose, of the Dehra Mission Girl School, appeared this year at the Calcutta University Entrance Examination, and would our readers believe it!—has passed most creditably in the second division. Of course, her name is not to be seen in the list of successful candidates issued from this office day before yesterday, the fact being that the Syndicate of the University wished to try the experiment of admiting ladies into its examinations. From what has come to our notice the experiment has been fairly successful. The lady alluded to, had to take up four such difficult subjects as English, Persian, History and Geography, Arithmetic, Euclid and Algebra. In the first three subjects she passed most creditably, and in Mathematics there was visible a slight difficiency for which the examiners justly made a reasonable allowance. The University, it is known, is not empowered by its charter to admit females to its examinations; and if only more candidates appear in the future, we are sure it will gladly apply to Government to have its charter modified in that respect.

THE fact noticed above leads to an exceedingly interesting question. It is perhaps the *Open Sesame* to the whole future of female education in India. A sad despondency seems to have caught the minds of the ruling authorities in respect of the prospects of that education generally. It does not seem to have entered into their heads that if only the University could be brought to lead in the matter, the whole amount of hindrances and obstacles that at present exist, would vanish in a moment. It need be only remembered, that in England the initiation of all large movements, such as the education of ladies and of the masses begins with the Universities. India ought to be no exception to the rule. The only doubt seems to be in the mixing together of the education of both sexes. Should girls and boys be educated and examined on the same model and according to the same plan? There are people and learned people too who do not believe that there is sex in the intellect. We for our part do not side with them. We believe that if female education is to be commenced at all, it must be placed on a different basis altogether from that of male education. The Calcutta University has, we think, made a great mistake in not recognising this great principle. There is nevertheless time enough for agitation and reflection. We certainly think there are some, if not many, Native ladies who are willing to compete for any examination that the University might institute. The late lamented Mr. Woodrow believed that some of the pupils of the Native Ladies' Normal School were perfectly fit to appear at the University Examinations. We would gladly welcome any change which would facilitate the education of our women. Only let such education be essentially female, and not such as would have the tendency of unsexing the other sex.

Literary

PROFESSOR Morely in an eloquent lecture lays down a beautiful process of making our knowledge our own "You know as I or any one can tell you, that knowledge is worth little or nothing until you have made it so perfectly your own, as to be capable of reproducing it in precise and definite form. Nobody can be sure that he has got clear ideas on a subject unless he has tried to put them down on a piece of paper in independent words of his own. It is an excellent plan, too, when you have read a good book, to sit down and write a short abstract of what you can remember of it. It is a still better plan, if you can make up your minds to a slight extra labor, to do what Lord Strafford, and Gibbon, and Daniel Webster did, after glancing over the title, subject, or design of a book, these eminent men would take a pen and write roughly what questions they expected to find answered in it, what difficulties solved, what kind of information imparted. Such practices keep us from reading with the eye only gliding vaguely over the page, and they help us to *place* our new acquisitions in relation with what we knew before. All this takes trouble, no doubt, but then it will not do to deal with ideas that we find in books or else where as a certain bird does with its eggs—leave them in the sand for the sun to hatch and chance to rear. People who follows this plan possess nothing better than ideas half-hatched, and convictions reared by accident."

A HOLIDAY EXCURSION.*

WHILE spending our holidays at Krishnaghur we heard about a pleasure garden called *Sriban*, which belongs to the Maha-Rajah of Krishnaghur, and is about four miles from the station. We were very anxious to see it. So one fine day, after our noontide meal, we started off in that direction. The gentlemen were in a buggy, and we in a *gari* drawn by a pair of Krishnaghur ponies. I think it nearly took an hour and half to reach the place. On both sides of the road there are rows of large shady trees, and beyond them beautiful green fields entirely covered with ripening paddy. We might have arrived sooner but for the delay which took place on the way. When we were nearing the garden, that part of the road (it was more a track than a road) being very muddy, because it was raining hard for the last two days, all the wheels of our carriage sunk and settled in the mud. So there we were, stuck fast, and the poor horses were unable to move the vehicle though they were cruelly whipped, and struggled ever so desperately. We had some real trouble in getting out. After a great deal of fear and annoyance, we stepped on a large bundle of dry sticks and thorns, which the people brought from somewhere to provide us with a dry and safe landing. So helped out of our difficulty we walked through the mud and water, and at last reached *Sriban*. O! what was our disappointment when we saw before us a desolate unclean looking place with hardly any trees, and positively no flowers or plants of any kind, instead of a beautiful, well-kept garden, where the kings and queens of Krishnaghur took their royal rest! There is a large fourstoried building, it is true, but a building is not a garden. We want to see the house. It is in a miserable state. No-

* This has been composed by a young lady belonging to the Native Ladies' Normal School, and revised by the Editor.

one takes any interest in this deserted palace, once carefully kept, perhaps, and certainly costly. The former Rajah is no more, and his favorite palace is now no longer looked after. This house must have been at one time clean and well furnished, and the ground beautifully planted. But now the rooms of the house are dark, dingy, damp, and full of dust, rats and cockroaches, and the walls oily and dirty. No rows of trees or sweet-cented flower plants outside. The aspect is not at all pleasant, it is more like a den of robbers and cobras, than the abode of royalty. *Sriban* itself is no longer a place where any one would care to go. But from the terrace of the house the distant views around were worth seeing. There is a pretty rippling river flowing along the house. On other sides far as our eyes could go, were magnificent green fields. We could just catch a glimpse of the trees which were beyond them. Over and above our heads the clear blue sky extended far towards the eastern and western horizon and looked as if it touched the ground on all sides, and pure white masses of clouds were floating under it. The scenery was very pleasant around us. We forgot our disappointment about the garden when we saw the scenery beyond. We then descended, and came to the river-side where a boat was ready to take us to a place where there is an immensely big, wonderful *Simul* tree. We were anxious to see it as well as to have the pleasure of rowing over the river. It was all very pleasant to us. The river is called the *Anjana*. On both its banks there were clumps of bamboo and other trees, the branches of some of which stooped down to the water as if to drink. The river is clear but overgrown with waterplants and flowers of all sorts and darkened by the shadows cast by the overhanging trees. One can see through it far below. Our boat glided along. One of the gentlemen sang the song "glide along our bonny bonny boat." There were plenty of water-lilies both white and red. They looked really pretty as they were rocked to and fro by the passing breeze. We gathered many of these as well as a kind of water fruit which grows below the surface of the river. There were some other kinds of white little flowers very pretty too. Little fishes frightened at the splash of the oars, began to spring swarm after swarm out of the water, and swim away as fast as they could, their silvery scales glistening under the bright sun. They looked like bright pieces of silver coin newly issued out of the mint.

The white-winged heron and other kinds of water-fowls which live near the river, were seen flying close over the stream and then suddenly high up in the air with their finny prey struggling in their talons.

At different places groups of village-women were seen standing by the river side or in the water and in shady places, looking at us with great astonishment, for people like ourselves are very uncommon to be met with in those out of the way places. The scenery around us was picturesque. One who has been there once will never forget it. At last we reached the place from which we had to walk a long and tedious distance through large wet fields to arrive at the spot where the famous *Simul* tree stands, and we were very much tired by the walking. The *Simul* tree is, indeed, a wonderful sight. Its trunk has grown immensely big, forming on three sides high and huge walls occupying such an amount of space as to form three compartments, two large and one small. Through one of these walls there is a large aparture which acts like a window to two of those rooms Some village women informed us that there is a large well inside the tree, and they also related how sometime back people used to hear the sacred sounds of bell and gong coming from this mysterious well. We could not see the well, nor I am sure that there is really a well within the bosom of this extraordinary tree. I suppose it is only a story.

We returned to our boat bringing with us some bright red fruits which we plucked from a tree on our way, and once more we were on the river, our boat floating away gently.

The day began to close now. The sun on the western horizon, shone with a mellowed splendour. Every thing was now serene and beautiful. The golden glory of the setting sun lighted up the tops of the trees and the face of the river. The soft breeze played with the water producing gentle ripples and passing through the leaves of the trees with a murmuring music. Nature smiled around us, for the sinless smile of the Holy Mother was reflected upon every thing. Gradually the bright golden light was dimmed, darkness began to fall upon the face of creation. The stars appeared one by one. And by the dim star-light the scene was obscurely visible. A solemn calmness reigned around us. The loving wings of the Mother of all creation covered every one giving rest and peace to all hearts.

We reached home at about 7 in the evening.

Scientific

THE RELATION BETWEEN CHOLERA AND FEVER.

(Exemplified by the present condition of Chittagong.)

THE following is my view of the close relation between cholera and fever in this country:—That both have their origin in vegetable organic germs which Professor Tyndall* has described to be minuter than the most powerful of microscopes has yet been able to disclose.

2. That these germs develop in damp humid soils under the influence of solar heat.

3. Hence soils favorable to the generation of *Malaria* or fever-producing germs, are also favorable to the generation of the germs of cholera. But when one species of these germs are being generated from a soil, the generation of the other is either restricted or altogether in abeyance. Hence at a place where cholera breaks out, there is then generally fever less prevalent; and *vice versa.*

4. The growth of vegetation visible to the naked eye, also prevents the *development* of fever, and cholera poisons. Hence in damp and water-logged soil or one with imperfect drainage, and in soil periodically submerged by the tides in tidal tracts, the growth of vegetation is a sanitary provision of nature, and cutting down trees and clearing jungles from such places is dangerous and suicidal as a measure of sanitation, and ought to be condemned and prohibited in all Mofussil Municipalities where such a thing is still considered as one of the principal means of improving their healthiness.

* Professor Tyndall argues with great force, from the ascertained phenomena of fermentation, that "reproductive parasitic life is at the root of epidemic disease."—ED. *I. M.*

5. The principal objection to cholera and malarious fever being brought under one catigary, is that while the choleraic discharge is popularly known to be contageous, the other is not so. But this objection has been removed by certain experiments recently performed by Doctors Cunningham and Lewis with cholera discharges and normal discharges from the alimentary canal of man, when introduced into the circulation the result being that in both sets of cases, there were only slight differences in the percentages of deaths and recoveries.

6. The condition of the soil detailed before, serves as the exciting cause of both the diseases; their predisposing causes may be different. For instance in the case of cholera bad and indigestible articles of food, intemperance in eating and drinking, new vegetable carries of the said season, drinking water excessively and repeatedly in the hot weather when the system is over heated, &c., &c., all these things serve as predisposing causes of the disease.

7. The panic, or violent fear of getting cholera, also acts as a strong predisposing cause of the disease in nervous persons. Nay, in certain places which are dry and otherwise healthy, and not favorable to the production of fever and cholera poison *de novo*, the outbreak of the disease is explained by panic alone, which, acting through the mind, exerts a paralysing effect on the network of nerves distributed within the stomach and intestines, and produces results, (*viz.*, vomiting, and purging) similar to what is takes place when the *mesenteric* nerve is divided in experiments on lower animals.

8. That cholera is not contagious, has been definitely proved by various facts the principal of which is, that Hospital attendants who continually attend cholera cases, and thereby become strengthened in their minds, are generally proof against attacks of the disease.

9. That cholera may be propagated by fright, acting from mind to mind, is proved by the facts that letters by Dak or messages by the wire conveying the intelligence of the death of a dear relation or a friend, by cholera, has often given occasion to attacks of the disease in persons of nervous temperament, in places far distant from that where the disease originally broke out from the defective condition of the soil.

10. The close relation of fever and cholera is also to be observed from the fact that the medicines (cinchona bark and arsenic) which are effectual in curing fever are also equally effectual in arresting cholera provided the medicines are used before collapse has set in, and in mild doses.

11. It is also seen very frequently that a case of fever may end in choleraic purging and vomiting or a case of cholera in fever.

12. In an ordinary case of cholera, the cold stage of fever can be traced to the vomiting and purging, and the hot stage, to the typhoid fever, which follows, or the reaction setting in often the stage of collapse.

13. The fearful outbreak of cholera now in Chittagong, is confined to those tracts which were submerged by the storm-wave, that accompanied the cyclone of the night of the 31st October last; and this supports the view I have taken of the origin of cholera. My theory, therefore, is that the source both of fever and cholera is common, located in organic germs of disease-producing poison which developes in humid soils when acted upon by the solar heat, the humidity in the

case of Chittagong being caused by the salt waterflood.

U. C. KASTOGIRI.

Review of the Week

NOT even the visit of the Prince of Wales so thoroughly succeeded in rousing the traditional lethargy of the Indian as the string of sensational events that are happening at this moment in the metropolis of the Great Mogul. Not that the assumption of the new title by the Queen has given birth to any new phase of loyalty in the people, or produced a change in their attitude towards the Sovereign. The Delhi Durbar proceeds on a different way, and seeks to influence the masses through their natural leaders. Viewed in this aspect the political significance of the Assemblage cannot be over-rated. For the first time have definite relations been established between the Government and its feudatories; and whatever the treaty rights may be, it is clear that the Native Princes have bent their heads in fealty to before the Imperial Crown.

THE change in the relations between the British power and its Feudatories has been produced in this manner. The Government is really making them its vassals and honorary of its bounties. It has given away more titles than was ever dreamt of, given more salutes than was perhaps conducive to economy, and recognised a larger number of services, real or imaginary, than was convenient. So rapidly did the wheel of fortune revolve within the past week that it would be difficult to remember distinctly its numerous changes. We shall, however, try to remember.

SINDIA and Cashmere have been made Generals of the British army. Certainly no finer complement could be given to the marshal instincts and propencities of the great Mahratta Chief. Holkar, Scindia, Cashmere, Jeypore and Bundi have been appointed Imperial Concillors, whatever that many mean. Bhurutpore has been created a G. C. S. I., a fitting return, we think, for a splendid Ball he lately gave at Simla, and for the readiness with which he has sacrificed his custom dues. The table of salutes has been altogether changed. Scindia, Holkar and Oodeypore and Cashmere will get in future 21 guns having been placed on the same level with the the Nizam and the Guekwar. Jodhpur will get 19 guns, and will be now equal in rank to Jeypore, as he formerly was. Towering above all these is the appointment of the Nizam as the Imperial Grand Chamberlain. What those offices really mean we don't know. We dare say they will be defined in some future act. That they are high sounding is clear. We hope they will be as real.

THERE is now every probability of war being averted, thanks to the firmness of Russia the vacillations of the English Ministary and the agitation set afloat by Mr. Gladstone. That Lord Baconsfield's distrust of Russia was unfounded in this instance, is confirmed by Lord Salisbury's decisive attitude towards the Sublime Porte. The Powers represented at the Conference proposed the appointment of Christian governors, and of an international Commission to be protected by a corps of foreign gendarmes to supervise the execution of reforms. Of course, Turkey would not submit. But on receiving clear intimation from Lord salisbury that the foreign ambassadors would withdraw if their proposals were not agreed to, she has shewn hesitation and will probably come to a compromise. The action o the E[illegible] Ministry has been spirited and reasonable. They have clearly profited by the utterances of Mr. Gladstone.

Local

A FIREMAN on board the Steam Tug *Alexandra*, met with a serious accident on board the vessel last Thursday. It appears that the steamer was steaming down to Saugor on the morning in question, and when off the Government Dock-yard, her engines connecting bolts flew off, causing the cylinder cap to fall on the fireman, who was engaged in firing immediately in front of the boilers. The man was knocked down insensible, and on his regaining consciousness was at once removed to the Howrah General Hospital.

A *lascar* named Nur Mahomed, while carrying an iron tank on board the *Enterprise* in the Government Dock-yard, received such injuries to his left hand by the jamming of it between the tank and the ship's side as to necessitate his removal to the General Hospital.

Public Engagement

WEDNESDAY, 3 January 1877 —at 7½ P. M. At the Albert Hall, under the auspices of the Society of Theistic Friend Dr. Prosonna Kumar Roy, D.S.C. Lond. and Edint., will deliver a lecture on Philosophy and Theology.

Selection.

ST. AUGUSTINE.

FROM the time of his conversion to Christianity his personal humility was such that he could not endure that anything should be said in his presence in depreciation of persons who were not present to speak in their own defence; accordingly, he had engraven on his dining-table a couplet to the following effect:—'Whoever finds pleasure in speaking in depreciation of absent persons, let him understand that he is forbidden to approach this table!' Nor did he stop at mere prohibition: he sought by instruction also to prevent his guests from falling into the evil habit referred to. Accordingly Posidius, the author of his history, relates that when, on one occasion, St. Augustine, with a number of his special friends was seated at his table, certain of them, in course of conversation, transgressed the rule. Thereupon the courageous host flying into a state of exasperation, exclaimed—'I must either obliterate these lines or else leave off eating and retire to my chamber'!

Advertisements

NOTICE.

A FREE enquiry after Truth. To be had of the Author Kisori Lal Ray, at Bogra, in Bengal. Price with postage Rs. 1-2.

☞ The work has given us great pleasure indeed. *Indian Mirror.*

BABU BASANTA KUMARA DATTA,

HOMŒOPATHIC PRACTITIONER

No. 20, Sunker Halder's Lane, Ahiritolah.

LONDON AGENT

MESSRS. HENRY TURNER & CO.

FRESH

Medicines and other Requisites.
Arrives every month from England.
Medicines, Boxes, Books, Pamphlets;
Absolute Alcohol; Cholera spirit Camphor.

SPECIAL REMEDIES.

For Suppressed, Laborious and Difficult menses-Leucorrhœa; Hysteria.

For Spermatorrhœa; Dysentery; Diarrhea; Cholera.

For Asthma; Pile; Pain; Sore and Diseases of the Children.

Lemonade, Soda and Tonic water always.
To be had at

DATTA'S HOMŒOPATHIC LABORATORY

No. 312, CHITPORE ROAD, BURTOLA, CALCUTTA.

TERMS—CASH.

☞ Price List can be had free on application.

ESTABLISHED 1833.

H. C. GANGOOLY & CO.

STATIONERS, DIESINKERS, ENGRAVERS PRINTERS, LITHOGRAPHERS &c.

24, Mangoe Lane, Calcutta.

Cash prices of the following :—

	Rs.	As.	Rs.
Whatman's Drawing paper double elephant sizes (40×27) each ...	0	7	0
Mathematical Instrument Boxes	2	8 to	16
Color Boxes	0	4 ,,	5

Drawing Pencils, Drawing and Mapping Steel pens and various other requisites in Stationery.

Cachar Native Joint Stock Co. Ld.

Having opened out 50 acres in tea on a garden of 100 acres, do hereby give notice that this Company has been duly registered under Act X of 1866 and is now prepared to sell Shares at Rs. 20 each until the 31st instant. Tea manufactured to date, 20 maunds. Further particulars can be had from the undersigned.

BYKUNTA CHUNDERA GUPTA,
Secretary.

THE GREAT INDIAN REMEDY
OF ALL
BILIOUS COMPLAINTS.

Indian Fevers, Indigestion, Spleen, Ague Jaundice, Piles, Costiveness, General Weakness, and every disorder depending on Functional Derangement of the Liver is

DR. E. J. LAZARUS'S

ESSENCE OF CHIRETTA

Prepared only by Messrs. E. J. Lazarus & Co., Medical Hall, Benares, from the original receipe of E. J. Lazarus, M. D., and sold by all Medicine Vendors at Rs. 1-8. 2-8, and , per bottle.

☞ **None other is genuine.** ☜

... indubitable proof of the great value of ... remedy is the various testi...

How to Enjoy Life

Is only known when the blood is pure, its circulation perfect, and the nerves in good order. The only safe and certain method of expelling all impurities is to take Holloway's Pills, which have the power of cleansing the blood from all noxious matters, expelling all humours which taint or impoverish it, thereby purify and invigorate and give general tone to the system. Young or old robust or delicate, may alike experience their beneficent effects. Myriads affirmed that these Pills possess marvellous power in securing these great secrets of health by purifying and regulating the fluids and strengthening the solids.

NOTICE

Gentlemen invited by the Magistrate of the 24-Pergunnahs to attend the Durbar to be held on the first of January, will receive tickets in exchange for their letters of invitation in presenting the latter at the Office of the Commissioner of the Presidency Division, between the hours of 11 and 4 on Saturday and Sunday next.

REV. WILSON
Magistrate 24-Perghs.

28th December 1876.

THE MOST ECONOMICAL
AND
EQUITABLE LIFE ASSURANCE COMPANY
IN THE WORLD!

Oriental Government Security Life Assurance Company, Ld.

CONSULTING ACTUARY.

J. Hill Williams, Esq.,—President Institute of Actuaries of Great Britain and Ireland.

NEW AND IMPORTANT ADVANTAGES.
POLICY-HOLDERS CAN VOTE AT MEETINGS.
AMALGAMATION OR TRANSFER OF BUSINESS PROHIBITED AND IMPOSSIBLE.

These essential features are not granted by any other Company, and they establish the existence of complete security to those Assured in the "Oriental."

No Entire Forfeiture of Policies.

Lapsed Policies Revived without Fine.

Promissory Notes issued.

Native Lives Assured at European Rates.

Entire Direction in India.

Funds Invested in Government Securities only, and remain in India.

Eighty per cent. of the Premiums are invested trust for Policy-holders.

A fixed and liberal Surrender Value after one year of 25 per cent. of the Tabular Premiums paid.

Economical Management [without this the best of systems cannot succeed]. Preliminary Expenses Rs. 970-15-0.

The ratio of expenses in 2 years, is less than English Companies of 10 years' standing.

The increase in the accumulated fund during the year is about 100 per cent.

New System for the self Assurance of European and Native Lives at English Rates, which are on an average 30 per cent. lower than Indian.

Annual Report, Prospectuses, and Forms of Proposal for effecting Assurances, Applications for Shares, and Agencies may be obtained from any of the Agents or from

D. McLAUCHLAN SLATER, F. I. A.,
Manager and Actuary.

8 Elphinstone Circle, Bombay.

R. K. GHOSH'S

HOMŒOPATHIC DISPENSARY.

No. 1, *Gour Mohun Mukerjee's Street, Simla.*

CALCUTTA.

HOMŒOPATHIC Medicine; Medicine chests of sizes,—containing medicine in tube phials; Homœopathic Books, tracts and pamphlets (English and Bengali); Dr. Rubin's "Saturated spirits of Camphor,"—(the best preventive and cure for cholera where medical aid is not available); and other Homœopathic requisites are sold here at a moderate price. Terms cash. Mofussil orders are promptly executed.

R. K. GHOSH,
Homœopathic Practitioner,
Manager.

SOLOMONS AND CO.

OPTICIANS,

7, Govt. Place, Calcutta.

Their R. H. the Prince and Princess of Wales beautifully photographed, and colored in gilt frames.

H. R. H. the Prince of Wales' Portrait chromolithographs Prince of Wales' pattern pocket Aneroid.

Steam Locomotive, Horizontal Beam and Vertical Engines;

Steam Phœnix Boats; Excelsior Boats; Paddle Steamers;

Screw Steamers; Sailing Schooners; Yachts; Cutters &c.;

Steam Nigger Dancers, and Fire Brigade Engines;

Clock work Paddle Boats, Nigger Dancers and moveable figures; Shell boxes of various kinds and sizes; beautifully arranged in design —Containing bottles of Scent, soap tablet with mottoes; suitable for birthday presents, or new year's gifts;

Surveying Instruments; Dumpy Levels Theodolites;

Prismatic Compasses; Bengali Surveying Compasses;

Magic Lanterns; Chromatropes and Slides. Carriage Clocks; and Time Pieces.

Spectacles of every description.

BY APPOINTMENT
TO
His Excellency the Viceroy and Governor-General of India.

THE CALCUTTA MUSICAL ESTABLISHMENT.

9, CHOWRINGHEE.

Late BURKINYOUNG & CO.

FOUNDED A.D. 1814.

Proprietor, CHARLES GOULD.

N. B.—Catalogue, with prices of Music and every Description of Musical Instruments for the Drawing-room or Military Band, may be obtained on application.

Kasipore (Kosipore)

Late Barranagore and Buckinsore Chemical Works.

NEAR CALCUTTA.

ACIDS, Ethers, and other Chemical preparations used in Medicine, Photograph and the Arts, made at these Works and supplied to wholesale purchasers.

Sulphuric Acid and other requisites for the manufacture of Aerated Water supplied.

Ether and Ammonia for Ice-machines.

Spirit of Wine, pure, Methylated and Caoutchouced.

Carbolic Acid, Chlorid...

...est description

are always kept in Stock.

LIGHT! LIGHT!! LIGHT!!!

PATENT PORTABLE AIR GAS MAKING APPARATUS,

SUITABLE FOR

Churches, Chapels, Schools, Country Mansions, Private Houses, Railway Stations, Barracks, Manufactories, Collieries, Mills, Offices, &c., &c.

THIS *simple* and *effective* Gas-making Apparatus supplies a want long felt of having Gas at places where no Gas Works exist. It may be introduced without any more trouble than the simply affixing of any ordinary Gas meter, and is about the same size for the same number of lights. The *piping* and *fitting* arrangements are in every respect the same as for the use of ordinary Gas. The *cost* of the Gas produced is about the same as is charged for ordinary Coal Gas, and the light produced is ***more brilliant*** and of ***a greater illuminating power***; it is also *free from the impurities of Coal Gas*. The Gas, if used with the Patent Burner, is of great heating power, and hence suitable for cooking and heating purposes, or in manufactories for soldering, &c. The apparatus is PORTABLE; there is NO DANGER WHATEVER (ordinary care being used when filling it); the Gas is PRODUCED IN AN INSTANT WITHOUT ANY FIRE OR OTHER ARTIFICIAL HEAT.

Further particulars may be obtained from MESSRS. EDWARD THOMSON & CO., Contractors for Drainage, Water and Gas, who are appointed Sole Agents for the above apparatus, which can be seen working any week day between the hours of 6 A.M., and 6 P.M., at their place of business.

39, *BENTINCK STREET, CALCUTTA.*

P. W. FLEURY & CO.,

BUILDERS, ENGINEERS,

AND

SCIENTIFIC INSTRUMENT MAKERS.

No. 44, Free School Street.

WE beg to intimate that we have been engaged in the above line of business for the past 20 years, and trust that our Constituents will continue to favor us with their work, which will meet with prompt attention on our part.

In connection with buildings, we undertake the erection and repairing of machinery at moderate charges, as also execute all descriptions of Iron and Brass work.

We can assure the Public that we undertake the repair and erection of Houses, and the laying of Water-supply Pipes on moderate terms, and guarantee to keep all the water-pipes and brass fittings supplied by us in good working order for three years, free of extra charge. We also guarantee to keep dwelling-houses' roofs water-tight for three years, free of extra charge, for such houses as we have repaired.

For purposes of illumination, we prepare our patent Chromatic Transparencies representing Coat-of-Arms, Landscapes, Scenery, &c., at prices, ranging from Rs. 80 to 300 each, according to size and design.

FOR SALE.

Ditto ditto, with 40 cells, smaller size ...	400	0
Ditto ditto, with a powerful 44-cell Cast iron Battery, on Callan's principle ...	500	0
Lime Light Apparatus, complete, with Iron Gas-holder, and Copper Retort ...	150	0
Oxy-Hydrogen Light Apparatus, with safety Jets, 2 iron Gas-holders, and Retorts, complete	200	0
Hink's Patent Duplex Wall Lamps, with chimney	5	8
Ditto Duplex Lamp, with chimney and globe	7	8

Patent Leblanche Battery

For constancy, durability, and cleanliness, this battery is unequalled; price for each cell, with chemicals	3
Bunsen's Galvanic Battery, 9 inches, by 4 inches	7
Magneto-Electric Machine, with single magnet	14
Prismatic Compass, 3-inch. in solid leather case, by Elbot, *second hand*	22
Ditto. 4-inch, by Simmons, *second hand* ...	38

For P. W. FLEURY & Co
WOOPENDICK'S STREET,
Care of the Manager, *Indian Mirror*.
CALCTTUA.

the -
of Christian governors, ... Light!! Light!!!
al Commission to be protected by a corps
of foreign gendarmes to supervise the
execution of reforms. Of course, Turkey
would not submit. But on receiving clear

THEISTIC BOOKS.

FOR SALE.

URDU.

Rahut Hakiki	Rs.	0	3	0
Nizam Komi	...	0	2	0
Kasufal Ilham	...	0	2	0
Khoolasa, of, Asool Brahm Dharm	...	0	1	0
Daily Upasana ...	...	0	1	0
Dhurm Anoosandhan ...	...	0	4	0
HINDI.				
Upasana Pudhati	Rs.	0	1	0
Benai Putrika or Hymn book	...	0	1	0
Tut Bodh	...	0	8	0
Upnushid Sar	...	0	8	0
Dhurm Dipika	...	0	0	6
Vedant Sar	...	1	0	0
Prosonno uttor	...	0	8	0
(BRAHM DHARM)				
Bojan Bichar	...	0	4	0
ENGLISH.				
Claims of so called Revealed Religion	Rs.	0	3	0
New Life	...	0	0	6
Higher and Lower Virtue ...	...	0	1	0

Apply to the Secretary.
BRAHMO SOMAJ OF THE PUNJAB.
Lahore.

MAKHON LOLL GHOSE.

No. 91, Radha Bazar,
CALCUTTA.

BEGS to invite the attention of the public to several consignments of commercial and fancy stationery of all sorts, including account books of all sizes, made of handmade and machine-made paper by steamers recently arrived, and which he is disposing of at moderate prices.

Useful to Merchants and Bankers

JUST ARRIVED

LETTS'S DIARY FOR 1877

OF

VARIOUS SIZES AND SORTS

AND

AT MODERATE PRICES.

N. B.—None to be without a Copy of ...

...eers.

REGISTERED No. 97.

CALCUTTA

106, Bowbazar Street.

DR. H. C. SARMA'S

MEDICINE FOR DEBILITY

(NERVOUS)

HAIR PRESERVER.

Copy of Letter received from Rajah Chundernath Roy Bahadur of Nattore.

Wellesley Street, No. 18, Mott's Lane, 29th March 1874.

MY DEAR HURRISH BABU,—

I shall thank you to send me another phial of your "*Excellent Hair Restorer.*" In fact it has done me a great benefit, and I should like to have more of it. It has disabused me (young as I am) of old age.

Yours Sincerely

C. N. of *Nattore*

—

MEDICINE FOR BALDNESS.

Will certainly cure baldness if applied on the bald portion, night & morning, according to directions given in the adjoining direction paper.

Price per two ounce phial Rc. 1 0 0
Postage &c. ... ... „ 0 6 0

—

HEEM-SAGAR OIL.

The best remedy for Headache arising from overstudy, intellectual occupation, over-thinking, mental anxiety and weakness, as well as heat of head from living in hot places.

It cools the head and produces very agreeable sensation. Removes dandriff as well as all other impurities from the head. Promotes the strength and growth of the hair and prevents its premature falling-off.

Price per 4 ounce phial Re. 1 0 0
Postage &c. ... ... „ 0 10 0

—

MEDICINE FOR LEPROSY.

Price with Postage &c ... Rs. 5 0 0

—

OIL FOR LEPROSY.

And Inveterate Skin Diseases.

Price per 8 ounce phial Rs. 2 0 0
Postage &c. ... ... „ 0 12 0

No More Pains !!!

THE

INFALLIBLE PAIN-CURER

WARRANTED to cure pains of every description, arising from whatever cause, on any part of the human frame. A certain cure for Pains in the Back, Lumbago, Pains in the Chest, Sore Throats, Coughs, Colds, Tightness of the Chest, Colics, Rheumatism, Paralysis, Pains in the Groins, Contracted Joints, Gout, Swellings, Old sores, Piles, Ringworm, and Eruptions on the Skin.

Pains of every description have been cured by the outward application only of this medicine when all the skill of the medical art have been tried without effect.

Per bottle, Re. 1 Postage and packing ans 8.

Remittance in half anna postage stamps need not be registered, but one anna should be more on every rupee for discounting the stamps.

DARLINGTON & Co.,

49, Dhurrumtollah Street, Calcutta.

FOR SALE.

VALUABLE LANDED PROPERTY.

THE desirable Premises No. 101, Taltala Lane, Calcutta. Price Rs. 5,000.

AND

A very elegant Family Residence, with 15 BIGAS *Lakhiraj* Gardens, bordering River Hooghly, Situate in JUGGODDUL, lying directly *East* of CHANDERNAGORE, and being approachable by *boat* or *road* from *Shamnuggur* Station, EASTERN BENGAL RAILWAY. Price Rs. 3,000.

Apply to BABU RADHA GOBIND CHATTERJEE at the above places.

PRIZE MEDALLISTS

For Excellency of Workmanship,

J. M. EDMOND & CO.,

27—28, BENTINCK STREET

ESTABLISHED 1833.

Cabinet Makers, Upholsterers,

AND

Billiard Table Manufacturers.

HOUSES completely furnished. Furniture designed and made to order.

ESTIMATES given for all kinds of Carpentering, Painting, Polishing, Gilding, and General Repairing; Marble Polished, Moulded, and Cleaned; Picture Frames made.

J. M. EDMOND & Co., in soliciting a continuance of public patronage, beg to say they have ready for sale specimens of Ebonized and Gold Oxford style of Fancy Chairs, and are prepared to execute orders for other Furniture in the same style.

J. M. EDMOND & Co.'s New Show-Room is now replete with New Heraldic Style of Dining-room Chairs, and Rustic Chairs, Telescopic Dining Tables, with Patent Table Expanders, and a variety of finished Furniture.—Orders solicited.

BURN & CO.

RANEEGUNGE Fire bricks are the best Fire Bricks known;—superior to Ramsay's.

9 Rs. per 100.

Fire clay, 40 Rs. per Ton.

Glazed Stone ware, Drainage pipes of all sizes.

BURN & Co.,

7, *Hastings Street, Calcutta.*

ARLINGTON & CO.,

3 B. DALHOUSIE SQUARE, CALCUTTA.

THE 'PATENT PERPETUAL FOUNTAIN,'

TABLE EPERGNE OR CENTRE PIECE

FOR SCENT OR FOR PUREWATER.

In Richly Electro-Silvered Ware, [*One of the Greatest Novelties of the day.*]

Cash Price Rs. 175.

N. B.—The annexed drawing is not a correct representation of the Plated Table Fountains which A. & Co. have for sale. The drawing is only given to show the internal arrangements of the Apparatus, and attention is invited to the following description:—

OBSERVE.—A, A1, are two cisterns or reservoirs, which are connected together by pipes or tubes B, B1, C, C1, mounted on a hollow axis of motion D, surrounding a fixed conical plug E, having suitable passages F, G, H, therein communicating with the pipes or tubes B, B1, C, C1, and I, and with the jet pipe J.

To put the fountain in operation water is poured into the dish or basin K until the lower reservoir is filled and the opening H is covered. The cisterns or reservoirs A, A1, are then turned on their axis of motion, so as to place the filled cistern or reservoir A at the top, when the water therefrom will flow to a level in the jet pipe J, and the water in the basin or dish K by passing down the pipes or tubes I and B1 into the lower cistern or reservoir A1, rises in such lower cistern or reservoir A1 and forces the air out therefrom through the pipe or tube C1, passage F, and tube B, into the upper parts of the cistern or reservoir A, where it presses upon the surface of the water therein and forces it out therefrom through the tube C, passage H, and jet pipe J, until all the water in the upper cistern or reservoir A has passed through the jet pipe J and into the lower cistern or reservoir A1 by the pipe I, passage G, and pipe B1, when by turning the cistern or reservoirs A, A1 on their axis of motion until the cistern or reservoir A1 is at the top, the action of the fountain will be continued; the pipes or tubes B, C1, which had previously been air passages now becoming water passages, and the pipes or tubes B1, C, now becoming air passages which had previously served for the passage of water. By these improvements the necessity for alternately filling and emptying the cisterns or reservoirs A, A1, is obviated.

www.ingramcontent.com/pod-product-compliance
Lightning Source LLC
Chambersburg PA
CBHW032312280326
41932CB00009B/792

* 9 7 8 3 7 4 2 8 2 2 0 9 3 *